COMMON SYMBOLS AND NOTATION

A	market value of assets, premerger total value of acquirer
APR	annual percentage rate
B	risk-free investment in the replicating portfolio
C	cash flow, call option price
$Corr(R_i, R_j)$	correlation between returns of i and j
$Cov(R_i, R_j)$	covariance between returns of i and j
CPN	coupon payment
D	market value of debt
d	debt-to-value ratio
Div_t	dividends paid in year t
dis	discount from face value
E	market value of equity
EAR	effective annual rate
EBIT	earnings before interest and taxes
EBITDA	earnings before interest, taxes, depreciation, and amortization
EPS_t	earnings per share on date t
$E[R_i]$	expected return of security i
F, F_T	one-year and T-year forward exchange rate
FCF_t	free cash flow at date t
FV	future value, face value of a bond
g	growth rate
I	initial investment or initial capital committed to the project
Int_t	interest expense interest expense on date t
IRR	internal rate of return
K	strike price
k	interest coverage ratio, compounding periods per year
L	lease payment, market value of liabilities
ln	natural logarithm
MV_i	total market capitalization of security i
N	number of cash flows, terminal date, notational principal of a swap contract
N_i	number of shares outstanding of security i
NPER	annuity spreadsheet notation for the number of periods or dates of the last cash flow
NPV	net present value
P	price, initial principal or deposit, or equivalent present value, put option price

P_i	price of security i
P/E	price-earnings ratio
PMT	annuity spreadsheet notation for cash flow
PV	present value; annuity spreadsheet notation for the initial amount
q	dividend yield
p	risk-neutral probability
r	interest rate, discount rate of cost of capital
R_i	return of security i
R_{mkt}	return of of the market portfolio
R_P	return on portfolio P
RATE	annuity spreadsheet notation for interest rate
r_E, r_D	equity and debt costs of capital
r_f	risk-free interest rate
r_i	required return or cost of capital of security i
r_U	unlevered cost of capital
r_{wacc}	weighted average cost of capital
S	stock price, spot exchange rate, value of all synergies
$SD(R_i)$	standard deviation (volatility) of return of security i
T	option expiration date, maturity date, market value of target
U	market value of unlevered equity
V_t	enterprise value on date t
$Var(R)$	variance of return R
x_i	portfolio weight of investment in i
YTC	yield to call on a callable bond
YTM	yield to maturity
α_i	alpha of security i
β_D, β_E	beta of debt or equity
β_i	beta of security i with respect to the market portfolio
β_s^P	beta of security i with respect to portfolio P
β_U	beta of unlevered firm
Δ	shares of stock in the replicating portfolio; sensitivity of option price to stock price
σ	volatility
τ	tax rate
τ_c	marginal corporate tax rate

CORPORATE FINANCE

The Addison-Wesley Series in Finance

Berk/DeMarzo
Corporate Finance

Copeland/Weston/Shastri
*Financial Theory
and Corporate Policy*

Dufey/Giddy
Cases in International Finance

Eakins
*Finance: Investments,
Institutions, and Management*

Eiteman/Stonehill/Moffett
Multinational Business Finance

Gitman
Principles of Managerial Finance

Gitman
*Principles of Managerial Finance—
Brief Edition*

Gitman/Joehnk
Fundamentals of Investing

Gitman/Madura
Introduction to Finance

Hughes/MacDonald
*International Banking:
Text and Cases*

Madura
Personal Finance

Marthinsen
*Risk Takers: Uses and Abuses
of Financial Derivatives*

McDonald
Derivatives Markets

Megginson
Corporate Finance Theory

Melvin
International Money and Finance

Mishkin/Eakins
Financial Markets and Institutions

Moffett
Cases in International Finance

Moffett/Stonehill/Eiteman
*Fundamentals of
Multinational Finance*

Rejda
*Principles of Risk Management
and Insurance*

Solnik/McLeavey
International Investments

CORPORATE FINANCE

JONATHAN BERK
UNIVERSITY OF CALIFORNIA, BERKELEY

PETER DEMARZO
STANFORD UNIVERSITY

PEARSON

Addison
Wesley

Boston San Francisco New York
London Toronto Sydney Tokyo Singapore Madrid
Mexico City Munich Paris Cape Town Hong Kong Montreal

Publisher: Greg Tobin
Editor in Chief: Denise Clinton
Senior Acquisitions Editor: Donna Battista
Director of Development: Kay Ueno
Development Editor: Rebecca Ferris-Caruso
Market Development Manager: Dona Kenly
Assistant Editors: Allison Stendardi, Sarah Bartlett
Managing Editor: Nancy Fenton
Senior Production Supervisor: Meredith Gertz
Cover Designer: Charles Spaulding
Supplements Editor: Jason Miranda
Supplements Coordinator: Heather McNally
Director of Media: Michelle Neil
Media Producer: Bridget Page
Software Project Manager: Susan Schoenberg
Content Lead, MyFinanceLab: Michael Griffin
Senior Marketing Manager: Roxanne Hoch
Marketing Assistant: Kate MacLean
Senior Prepress Supervisor: Caroline Fell
Senior Author Support/Technology Specialist: Joe Vetere
Rights and Permissions Advisors: Dana Weightman, Shannon Barbe
Senior Manufacturing Buyer: Carol Melville
Production Coordination, Composition, Illustrations, and Text Design: Thompson Steele Inc.
Cover Image: © Getty Images, David McNew

ISBN: 0-321-41680-5

1 2 3 4 5 6 7 8 9 10—QWT—10 09 08 07 06

Brief Contents

PART I
Introduction

Chapter 1	The Corporation	3
Chapter 2	Introduction to Financial Statement Analysis	19
Chapter 3	Arbitrage and Financial Decision Making	47

PART II
Tools

Chapter 4	The Time Value of Money	83
Chapter 5	Interest Rates	125
Chapter 6	Investment Decision Rules	149

PART III
Basic Valuation

Chapter 7	Fundamentals of Capital Budgeting	177
Chapter 8	Valuing Bonds	211
Chapter 9	Valuing Stocks	245

PART IV
Risk and Return

Chapter 10	Capital Markets and the Pricing of Risk	283
Chapter 11	Optimal Portfolio Choice	323
Chapter 12	The Capital Asset Pricing Model	363
Chapter 13	Alternative Models of Systematic Risk	401

PART V
Capital Structure

Chapter 14	Capital Structure in a Perfect Market	427
Chapter 15	Debt and Taxes	459
Chapter 16	Financial Distress, Managerial Incentives, and Information	491
Chapter 17	Payout Policy	531

PART VI
Valuation

| Chapter 18 | Capital Budgeting and Valuation with Leverage | 575 |
| Chapter 19 | Valuation and Financial Modeling: A Case Study | 623 |

PART VII
Options

Chapter 20	Financial Options	655
Chapter 21	Option Valuation	685
Chapter 22	Real Options	717

PART VIII
Long-Term Financing

Chapter 23	The Mechanics of Raising Equity Capital	751
Chapter 24	Debt Financing	779
Chapter 25	Leasing	801

PART IX
Short-Term Financing

| Chapter 26 | Working Capital Management | 829 |
| Chapter 27 | Short-Term Financial Planning | 851 |

PART X
Special Topics

Chapter 28	Mergers and Acquisitions	873
Chapter 29	Corporate Governance	903
Chapter 30	Risk Management	925
Chapter 31	International Corporate Finance	969

Contents

PART I INTRODUCTION 1

Chapter 1 The Corporation 3

1.1 **The Four Types of Firms 4**

Sole Proprietorships 4
Partnerships 5
▦ Interview with David Viniar 6
Limited Liability Companies 7
Corporations 7
Tax Implications for Corporate Entities 8

1.2 **Ownership Versus Control
of Corporations 9**

The Corporate Management Team 10
Ownership and Control
of Corporations 10
▦ Shareholder Activism
and Voting Rights 12

1.3 **The Stock Market 12**

The Largest Stock Markets 13
NYSE 13
Nasdaq 13

Summary 15 • Key Terms 15 •
Further Reading 16 • Problems 16

**Chapter 2 Introduction to Financial
Statement Analysis 19**

2.1 **The Disclosure of
Financial Information 20**

Preparation of Financial Statements 20
▦ International Financial
Reporting Standards 20
Types of Financial Statements 21

2.2 **The Balance Sheet 21**

Assets 21
Liabilities 23
Stockholders' Equity 24
Balance Sheet Analysis 25

2.3 **The Income Statement 27**

Earnings Calculations 27

Income Statement Analysis 29
▦ Common Mistake:
Mismatched Ratios 30

2.4 **The Statement of Cash Flows 32**

Operating Activity 32
Investment Activity 33
Financing Activity 33

2.5 **Other Financial
Statement Information 34**

▦ Interview with Sue Frieden 35
Management Discussion and Analysis 36
Statement of Stockholders' Equity 36
Notes to the Financial Statements 36

2.6 **Accounting Manipulation 37**

Enron 37
WorldCom 38
Sarbanes-Oxley Act 38

Summary 38 • Key Terms 40 •
Further Reading 40 • Problems 41
Data Case 45

**Chapter 3 Arbitrage and Financial
Decision Making 47**

3.1 **Valuing Costs and Benefits 48**

Using Market Prices to
Determine Cash Values 48
When Competitive Market Prices
Are Not Available 50

3.2 **Interest Rates and the
Time Value of Money 51**

The Time Value of Money 51
The Interest Rate:
An Exchange Rate Across Time 51

3.3 **Present Value and
the NPV Decision Rule 54**

Net Present Value 54
The NPV Decision Rule 55
NPV and Individual Preferences 57

3.4 Arbitrage and the Law of One Price 59

■ An Old Joke 60
Arbitrage 60
Law of One Price 60

3.5 No-Arbitrage and Security Prices 61

Valuing a Security 61
Determining the No-Arbitrage Price 62
■ Nasdaq SOES Bandits 63
Determining the Interest Rate from Bond Prices 64
The NPV of Trading Securities 64
Valuing a Portfolio 66
■ Stock Index Arbitrage 66

3.6 The Price of Risk 67

Risky Versus Risk-Free Cash Flows 68
Risk Aversion and the Risk Premium 68
The No-Arbitrage Price of a Risky Security 69
Risk Premiums Depend on Risk 70
Risk Is Relative to the Overall Market 70
Risk, Return, and Market Prices 72

3.7 Arbitrage with Transactions Costs 73

Summary 75 • Key Terms 76 •
Further Reading 76 • Problems 76

PART II TOOLS 81

Chapter 4 The Time Value of Money 83

4.1 The Timeline 84

4.2 The Three Rules of Time Travel 85

Comparing and Combining Values 85
Moving Cash Flows Forward in Time 86
Moving Cash Flows Back in Time 87
Applying the Rules of Time Travel 88

4.3 The Power of Compounding: An Application 90

4.4 Valuing a Stream of Cash Flows 91

4.5 The Net Present Value of a Stream of Cash Flows 94

4.6 Perpetuities, Annuities, and Other Special Cases 95

Perpetuities 95
■ Historical Examples of Perpetuities 97
■ Common Mistake: Discounting One Too Many Times 98
Annuities 98
Growing Cash Flows 101

4.7 Solving Problems with a Spreadsheet Program 106

4.8 Solving for Variables Other Than Present Value or Future Value 108

Solving for the Cash Flows 109
Internal Rate of Return 111
Solving for the Number of Periods 114
■ Common Mistake: Excel's NPV and IRR Functions 115
■ Rule of 72 116

Summary 117 • Key Terms 118 •
Further Reading 118 • Problems 119
Data Case 123

Chapter 5 Interest Rates 125

5.1 Interest Rate Quotes and Adjustments 126

The Effective Annual Rate 126
Adjusting the Discount Rate to Different Time Periods 126
Annual Percentage Rates 127
Application: Discount Rates and Loans 130

5.2 The Determinants of Interest Rates 131

Inflation and Real Versus Nominal Rates 131
Investment and Interest Rate Policy 132
The Yield Curve and Discount Rates 133
■ Common Mistake: Using the Annuity Formula When Discount Rates Vary 135
The Yield Curve and the Economy 136

5.3 Risk and Taxes 138

Risk and Interest Rates 138
After-Tax Interest Rates 139

**5.4 The Opportunity
Cost of Capital 140**

Summary 141 • Key Terms 142 •
Further Reading 142 • Problems 143
Chapter 5 Appendix:
Continuous Rate and Cash Flows 147

Chapter 6   Investment Decision Rules   149

**6.1 NPV and Stand-Alone
Projects 150**
NPV Rule 150
Measuring Sensitivity with IRR 150
Alternative Rules Versus NPV Rule 150

6.2 Alternative Decision Rules 151
The Payback Rule 151
The Internal Rate of Return Rule 152
Economic Profit or EVA 156
▩ Interview with Joel M. Stern 157
▩ Why Do Rules Other Than
the NPV Rule Persist? 160

**6.3 Mutually Exclusive Investment
Opportunities 161**
Differences in Scale 161
Timing of the Cash Flows 164
Incremental IRR Rule 164

**6.4 Project Selection with
Resource Constraints 166**
Evaluation of Projects with
Different Resource Requirements 166
Profitability Index 167
Shortcomings of the
Profitability Index 168

Summary 168 • Key Terms 169 •
Further Reading 169 • Problems 170
Data Case 173

PART III   BASIC VALUATION   175

**Chapter 7   Fundamentals of
Capital Budgeting   177**

7.1 Forecasting Earnings 178
Revenue and Cost Estimates 178
▩ Interview with Dick Grannis 179
Incremental Earnings Forecast 180

Indirect Effects on
Incremental Earnings 182
▩ Common Mistake: The Opportunity
Cost of an Idle Asset 183
Sunk Costs and Incremental Earnings 184
Real-World Complexities 184
▩ The Sunk Cost Fallacy 185

**7.2 Determining Free Cash
Flow and NPV 186**
Calculating the Free Cash
Flow from Earnings 186
Calculating Free Cash Flow Directly 188
Calculating the NPV 189
Choosing Among Alternatives 190
Further Adjustments to
Free Cash Flow 191

7.3 Analyzing the Project 196
Break-Even Analysis 196
Sensitivity Analysis 197
Scenario Analysis 198

Summary 200 • Key Terms 201 •
Further Reading 201 • Problems 201
Data Case 207
Chapter 7 Appendix:
MACRS Depreciation 209

Chapter 8   Valuing Bonds   211

**8.1 Bond Cash Flows,
Prices, and Yields 212**
Bond Terminology 212
Zero-Coupon Bonds 212
Coupon Bonds 214

**8.2 Dynamic Behavior
of Bond Prices 217**
Discounts and Premiums 217
Time and Bond Prices 218
▩ Clean and Dirty Prices
for Coupon Bonds 221
Interest Rate Changes
and Bond Prices 221

**8.3 The Yield Curve
and Bond Arbitrage 224**
Replicating a Coupon Bond 224
Valuing a Coupon Bond
Using Zero-Coupon Yields 225

Coupon Bond Yields   226
Treasury Yield Curves   227

8.4   Corporate Bonds   228

Corporate Bond Yields   228
◼ Interview with Lisa Black   230
Bond Ratings   231
Corporate Yield Curves   231

Summary 233 • Key Terms 235 •
Further Reading 235 • Problems 235
Data Case   239
Chapter 8 Appendix:
Forward Interest Rates   241

Chapter 9   Valuing Stocks   245

**9.1   Stock Prices, Returns,
and the Investment Horizon   246**

A One-Year Investor   246
Dividend Yields, Capital Gains,
and Total Returns   247
A Multiyear Investor   248

9.2   The Dividend-Discount Model   249

Constant Dividend Growth   249
Dividends Versus Investment
and Growth   250
Changing Growth Rates   252
◼ Interview with Marilyn Fedak   253
Limitations of the
Dividend-Discount Model   255
◼ John Burr Williams' *Theory
of Investment Value*   255

**9.3   Total Payout and Free Cash
Flow Valuation Models   256**

Share Repurchases and
the Total Payout Model   256
The Discounted Free
Cash Flow Model   258

**9.4   Valuation Based on
Comparable Firms   261**

Valuation Multiples   262
Limitations of Multiples   264
Comparison with Discounted
Cash Flow Methods   264
Stock Valuation Techniques:
The Final Word   265

**9.5   Information, Competition,
and Stock Prices   266**

Information in Stock Prices   266
Competition and Efficient Markets   268
Lessons for Investors
and Corporate Managers   271
The Efficient Markets
Hypothesis Versus No Arbitrage   271

Summary 272 • Key Terms 274 •
Further Reading 274 • Problems 275
Data Case   279

PART IV   RISK AND RETURN   281

**Chapter 10   Capital Markets and
the Pricing of Risk   283**

**10.1   A First Look at Risk
and Return   284**

**10.2   Common Measures
of Risk and Return   286**

Probability Distributions   286
Expected Return   286
Variance and Standard Deviation   287

**10.3   Historical Returns
of Stocks and Bonds   289**

Computing Historical Returns   289
Average Annual Returns   292
The Variance and Volatility
of Returns   293
Using Past Returns to Predict
the Future: Estimation Error   294
◼ Arithmetic Average Returns Versus
Compound Annual Returns   296

**10.4   The Historical Tradeoff
Between Risk and Return   297**

The Returns of Large Portfolios   297
The Returns of Individual Stocks   298

**10.5   Common Versus
Independent Risk   299**

**10.6   Diversification in
Stock Portfolios   303**

Firm-Specific Versus
Systematic Risk   303

No Arbitrage and the Risk Premium 305
- Common Mistake: A Fallacy
  of Long-Run Diversification 306

**10.7 Estimating the
Expected Return 307**

Measuring Systematic Risk 308
Estimating the Risk Premium 310

10.8 Risk and the Cost of Capital 311

10.9 Capital Market Efficiency 313

Notions of Efficiency 313
Empirical Evidence on Capital Market
Competition 313
- Interview with Randall Lert 314

Summary 315 • Key Terms 317 •
Further Reading 317 • Problems 318
Data Case 321

Chapter 11 Optimal Portfolio Choice 323

**11.1 The Expected Return
of a Portfolio 324**

**11.2 The Volatility of a
Two-Stock Portfolio 325**

Combining Risks 326
Determining Covariance
and Correlation 326
- Computing the Variance,
  Covariance and Correlation
  in Microsoft Excel 330
Computing a Portfolio's
Variance and Volatility 330

**11.3 The Volatility of a
Large Portfolio 332**

Diversification with an Equally
Weighted Portfolio of Many Stocks 332
Diversification with
General Portfolios 334

**11.4 Risk Versus Return: Choosing
an Efficient Portfolio 335**

Efficient Portfolios with Two Stocks 335
The Effect of Correlation 338
Short Sales 339
- The Mechanics of a Short Sale 340
Risk Versus Return: Many Stocks 341

**11.5 Risk-Free Saving
and Borrowing 345**

Investing in Risk-Free Securities 345
Borrowing and Buying
Stocks on Margin 346
Identifying the Tangent Portfolio 347

**11.6 The Efficient Portfolio
and the Cost of Capital 349**

How to Improve a Portfolio:
Beta and the Required Return 349
Expected Returns and the
Efficient Portfolio 351
Cost of Capital 352
- Nobel Prizes: Harry Markowitz
  and James Tobin 353
- Interview with
  Jonathan Clements 354

Summary 355 • Key Terms 357 •
Further Reading 358 • Problems 358
Data Case 361

**Chapter 12 The Capital Asset
Pricing Model 363**

**12.1 The Efficiency of
the Market Portfolio 364**

The CAPM Assumptions 364
Security Demand
Must Equal Supply 365
Optimal Investing:
The Capital Market Line 366

**12.2 Determining the
Risk Premium 368**

Market Risk and Beta 368
The Security Market Line 370
Alpha 373
Summary of the Capital
Asset Pricing Model 374

12.3 The Market Portfolio 375

Value-Weighted Portfolios 375
Common Stock Market Indexes 377
- Interview With John Bogle 378

12.4 Determining Beta 380

Estimating Beta from
Historical Returns 380

■ Why Not Estimate
   Expected Returns Directly?   382
Using Linear Regression   382

12.5   Extending the CAPM   383
Saving Versus Borrowing Rates   384
Investor Information and
Rational Expectations   386

12.6   The CAPM in Practice   388
Forecasting Beta   388
The Security Market Line   390
Evidence Regarding the CAPM   392
The Bottom Line on the CAPM   394
■ Nobel Prize: William Sharpe
   on the CAPM   395

Summary   396 • Key Terms   397 •
Further Reading   397 • Problems   398
Data Case   400

Chapter 13   Alternative Models
             of Systematic Risk   401

13.1   The Efficiency of
       the Market Portfolio   402
The Size Effect   402
Past Returns   406

13.2   Implication of Positive Alphas   406
Proxy Error   407
Non-tradeable Wealth   407
■ Common Mistake: Investing
   in Own Company Stock   408

13.3   Multifactor Models of Risk   409
Using Factor Portfolios   409
Building a Multifactor Model   411
Selecting the Portfolios   411
■ Interview with
   Rex A. Sinquefield   412
Calculating the Cost of Capital
Using the Fama-French-Carhart
Factor Specification   413

13.4   Characteristic Variable
       Models of Expected Returns   415

13.5   Methods Used in Practice   419

Summary   421 • Key Terms   422 •
Further Reading   422 • Problems   423

PART V   CAPITAL STRUCTURE   425

Chapter 14   Capital Structure
             in a Perfect Market   427

14.1   Equity Versus Debt Financing   428
Financing a Firm with Equity   428
Financing a Firm with
Debt and Equity   429
The Effect of Leverage on Risk
and Return   430

14.2   Modigliani-Miller I: Leverage,
       Arbitrage, and Firm Value   432
MM and the Law of One Price   432
■ MM and the Real World   433
Homemade Leverage   433
The Market Value Balance Sheet   435
Application: A Leveraged
Recapitalization   436

14.3   Modifliani-Miller II: Leverage,
       Risk, and the Cost of Capital   437
Leverage and the Equity
Cost of Capital   437
Capital Budgeting and the
Weighted Average Cost of Capital   439
■ Common Mistake: Is Debt
   Better Than Equity?   441
Computing the WACC
with Multiple Securities   442
Levered and Unlevered Betas   442
Cash and Net Debt   444
■ Microsoft's Dividend,
   Cash, and Beta   444

14.4   Capital Structure Fallacies   445
Leverage and Earnings per Share   445
Equity, Issuances, and Dilution   448

14.5   MM: Beyond the Propositions   449
■ Nobel Prize: Franco Modigliani
   and Merton Miller   450

Summary   451 • Key Terms   452 •
Further Reading   452 • Problems   453
Data Case   456

Chapter 15   Debt and Taxes   459

15.1   The Interest Tax Deduction   460

15.2 Valuing the Interest Tax Shield   462

The Interest Tax Shield
and Firm Value   462

The Interest Tax Shield
with Permanent Debt   463

▦ Pizza and Taxes   464

The Weighted Average Cost
of Capital with Taxes   465

The Interest Tax Shield
with a Target Debt-Equity Ratio   466

15.3 Recapitalizing to Capture the Tax Shield   468

The Tax Benefit   468

The Share Repurchase   468

No Arbitrage Pricing   469

Analyzing the Recap:
The Market Value Balance Sheet   470

15.4 Personal Taxes   471

Including Personal Taxes
in the Interest Tax Shield   471

Valuing the Interest Tax Shield
with Personal Taxes   474

Determining the Actual Tax
Advantage of Debt   475

▦ Cutting the Dividend Tax Rate   475

15.5 Optimal Capital Structure with Taxes   476

Do Firms Prefer Debt?   476

Limits to the Tax Benefit of Debt   478

Growth and Debt   481

Other Tax Shields   481

The Low Leverage Puzzle   481

▦ Employee Stock Options   482

▦ Interview with Andrew Balson   484

Summary   485 • Key Terms   485 •
Further Reading   486 • Problems   486
Data Case   490

Chapter 16 Financial Distress, Managerial Incentives, and Information   491

16.1 Default and Bankruptcy in a Perfect Market   492

Armin Industries: Leverage
and the Risk of Default   492

Bankruptcy and Capital Structure   493

16.2 The Cost of Bankruptcy and Financial Distress   494

The Bankruptcy Code   494

Direct Costs of Bankruptcy   495

Indirect Costs of Financial Distress   496

16.3 Financial Distress Costs and Firm Value   498

Armin Industries: The Impact
of Financial Distress Costs   499

Who Pays for Financial
Distress Costs?   500

16.4 Optimal Capital Structure: The Tradeoff Theory   501

Determinants of the Present
Value of Financial Distress Costs   501

Optimal Leverage   501

16.5 Exploiting Debt Holders: The Agency Costs of Leverage   503

Over-investment   503

Under-investment   504

Cashing Out   505

Agency Costs and the Value
of Leverage   505

Debt Maturity and Covenants   506

16.6 Motivating Managers: The Agency Benefits of Leverage   507

Concentration of Ownership   507

Reduction of Wasteful Investment   508

▦ Excessive Perks and
Corporate Scandals   509

Leverage and Commitment   510

16.7 Agency Costs and the Tradeoff Theory   511

The Optimal Debt Level   511

Debt Levels in Practice   512

16.8 Asymmetric Information and Capital Structure   512

Leverage as a Credible Signal   513

Issuing Equity and
Adverse Selection   514

▦ Nobel Prize: The 2001 Nobel Prize
in Economics   515

Implications for Equity Issuance   517

Implications for Capital Structure   517

16.9 Capital Structure:
      The Bottom Line   520

      Summary 521 • Key Terms 523 •
      Further Reading 523 • Problems 523

Chapter 17 Payout Policy   531

17.1 Distributions to Shareholders   532
      Dividends   532
      Share Repurchases   534

17.2 Comparison of Dividends
      and Share Repurchases   535
      Alternative Policy 1:
      Pay Dividend with Excess Cash   535
      Alternative Policy 2:
      Share Repurchase (No Dividend)   537
      ▓ Common Mistake: Repurchases
         and the Supply of Shares   538
      Alternative Policy 3:
      High Dividend (Equity Issue)   538
      Modigliani–Miller and the Dividend
      Policy Irrelevance   539
      ▓ Common Mistake:
         The Bird in Hand Fallacy   540
      Dividend Policy with Perfect
      Capital Markets   541

17.3 The Tax Disadvantage
      of Dividends   541
      Taxes on Dividends
      and Capital Gains   541
      Optimal Dividend Policy with Taxes   542

17.4 Dividend Capture and
      Tax Clienteles   545
      The Effective Dividend Tax Rate   545
      Tax Differences Across Investors   546
      Clientele Effects   547

17.5 Payout Versus Retention
      of Cash   549
      Retaining Cash with
      Perfect Capital Markets   549
      Taxes and Cash Retention   550
      Adjusting for Investor Taxes   552
      Issuance and Distress Costs   553
      Agency Costs of Retaining Cash   553

17.6 Signaling with Payout Policy   555
      Dividend Smoothing   555
      Dividend Signaling   556

      ▓ Royal & SunAlliance's
         Dividend Cut   557
      Signaling and Share Repurchases   558

17.7 Stock Dividends, Splits,
      and Spin-offs   560
      Stock Dividends and Splits   560
      ▓ Berkshire Hathaway's
         A & B Shares   561
      ▓ Interview with John Connors   562
      Spin-offs   563

      Summary 565 • Key Terms 566 •
      Further Reading 566 • Problems 567
      Data Case   570

PART VI VALUATION   573

**Chapter 18 Capital Budgeting and
            Valuation with Leverage   575**

18.1 Overview   576

18.2 The Weighted Average
      Cost of Capital Method   577
      Using the WACC to Value a Project   577
      Summary of the WACC Method   579
      Implementing a Constant
      Debt-Equity Ratio   580

18.3 The Adjusted Present
      Value Method   581
      The Unlevered Value of the Project   582
      Valuing the Interest Tax Shield   583
      Summary of the APV Method   584

18.4 The Flow-to-Equity Method   585
      Calculating the Free Cash
      Flow to Equity   586
      Valuing Equity Cash Flows   587
      Summary of the
      Flow-to-Equity Method   588
      ▓ What Counts as "Debt"?   589

18.5 Project-Based Costs
      of Capital   589
      Estimating the Unlevered
      Cost of Capital   589
      Project Leverage and the
      Equity Cost of Capital   590
      Determining the Incremental
      Leverage of a Project   591

■ Common Mistake:
Re-levering the WACC   592

18.6 **APV with Other
Leverage Policies   593**

Constant Interest Coverage Ratio   594
Predetermined Debt Levels   595
A Comparison of Methods   596

18.7 **Other Effects of Financing   597**

Issuance and Other Financing Costs   597
■ Airline Loan Guarantees after
September 11, 2001   598
Security Mispricing   598
Financial Distress and Agency Costs   599

18.8 **Advanced Topics
in Capital Budgeting   600**

Periodically Adjusted Debt   601
Leverage and the Cost of Capital   603
The WACC or FTE Method
with Changing Leverage   605
Personal Taxes   606

Summary 609 • Key Terms 610 •
Further Reading 610 • Problems 611
Data Case   617
Chapter 18 Appendix:
Foundations and Further Details   619

**Chapter 19 Valuation and Financial
Modeling: A Case Study   623**

19.1 **Valuation Using Comparables   624**

19.2 **The Business Plan   626**

Operational Improvements   626
Capital Expenditures:
A Needed Expansion   627
Working Capital Management   628
Capital Structure Changes:
Levering Up   628

19.3 **Building the Financial Model   629**

Forecasting Earnings   629
Working Capital Requirements   631
Forecasting Free Cash Flow   633
The Balance Sheet and Statement
of Cash Flows (Optional)   634

19.4 **Estimating the Cost of Capital   636**

CAPM-Based Estimation   636
Unlevering Beta   637

Ideko's Unlevered Cost of Capital   638

19.5 **Valuing the Investment   639**

The Multiples Approach
to Continuation Value   639
The Discounted Cash Flow Approach
to Continuation Value   640
■ Common Mistake: Continuation
Values and Long-Run Growth   643
APV Valuation of Ideko Equity   643
A Reality Check   644
■ Common Mistake:
Missing Assets or Liabilities   644
IRR and Cash Multiples   645
■ Interview with Joseph L. Rice, III   646

19.6 **Sensitivity Analysis   647**

Summary 648 • Key Terms 649 •
Further Reading 649 • Problems 649
Chapter 19 Appendix:
Compensating Management   652

PART VII   OPTIONS   653

Chapter 20   Financial Options   655

20.1 **Option Basics   656**

Understanding Option Contracts   656
Interpreting Stock Option
Quotations   656
Options on Other
Financial Securities   658

20.2 **Options Payoffs at Expiration   659**

Long Position in an Option Contract   659
Short Position in
an Option Contract   660
Profits for Holding
an Option to Expiration   662
Returns for Holding
an Option to Expiration   663
Combinations of Options   664

20.3 **Put-Call Parity   668**

20.4 **Factors Affecting
Option Prices   669**

Strike Price and Stock Price   670
Arbitrage Bounds on Option Prices   670
Option Prices and
the Exercise Date   670
Option Prices and Volatility   671

20.5 Exercising Options Early   671

Non-Dividend-Paying Stocks   672
Dividend-Paying Stocks   674

**20.6 Options and
Corporate Finance   676**

Equity as a Call Option   676
Debt as an Option Portfolio   677

Summary 680 • Key Terms 681 •
Further Reading 681 • Problems 681
Data Case   684

Chapter 21 Option Valuation   685

**21.1 The Binomial Option
Pricing Model   686**

A Two-State Single-Period Model   686
The Binomial Pricing Formula   688
A Multiperiod Model   690
Making the Model Realistic   693

**21.2 The Black-Scholes Option
Pricing Model   694**

The Black-Scholes Formula   694
■ Common Mistake: Valuing
Employee Stock Options   699
Implied Volatility   701
The Replicating Portfolio   702

21.3 Risk-Neutral Probabilities   704

A Risk-Neutral Two-State Model   704
Implications of the
Risk-Neutral World   705
Risk-Neutral Probabilities
and Option Pricing   706

21.4 Risk and Return of an Option   707

21.5 Beta of Risky Debt   710

■ Nobel Prize: The 1997 Nobel Prize
in Economics   712

Summary 713 • Key Terms 714 •
Further Reading 714 • Problems 715

Chapter 22 Real Options   717

22.1 Real Versus Financial Options   718

22.2 Decision Tree Analysis   718

Mapping Uncertainties
on a Decision Tree   719
Real Options   720

**22.3 The Option to Delay
an Investment Opportunity   721**

Investment as a Call Opton   721
Factors Affecting the
Timing of Investment   723
■ Why Are There Empty Lots
in Built-up Areas of Big Cities?   725

22.4 Growth Options   726

Valuing the Growth
Potential of a Firm   726
Staged Investment:
The Option to Expand   729
■ Interview with Scott Mathews   730

22.5 Abandonment Options   731

The Option to Shutdown   731
The Option to Prepay   733

**22.6 Application: Deciding Between
Mutually Exclusive Investments
of Different Lengths   734**

NPV of Each Design   735
NPV if Costs Rise   735
NPV if Future Costs Are Uncertain   735
Equivalent Annual Benefit Method   736

22.7 Rules of Thumb   737

The Profitability Index Rule   737
The Hurdle Rate Rule   738
Applying Hurdle Rates and the
Profitability Index Simultaneously   740

Summary 740 • Key Terms 741 •
Further Reading 741 • Problems 742
Chapter 22 Appendix: Calculating Mortgage
Interest Rates   747

PART VIII LONG-TERM FINANCING   749

**Chapter 23 The Mechanics of
Raising Equity Capital   751**

**23.1 Equity Financing for
Private Companies   752**

Sources of Funding   752
Outside Investors   755
Exiting an Investment
in a Private Company   756

23.2 The Initial Public Offering   757

Advantages and Disadvantages
of Going Public   757

Types of Offerings   758
■ Google's IPO   760
The Mechanics of an IPO   760
IPO Puzzles   765
Cyclicality   767
Cost of Issuing an IPO   769
Long-Run Underperformance   770

23.3 The Seasoned Equity Offering   770
The Mechanics of an SEO   770
Price Reaction   772
Costs   774
Summary 774 • Key Terms 775 •
Further Reading 775 • Problems 776

Chapter 24 Debt Financing   779

24.1 Corporate Debt   780
Public Debt   780
Private Debt   785

24.2 Other Types of Debt   786
Sovereign Debt   786
Agency Securities   788
Municipal Bonds   788

24.3 Bond Covenants   789

24.4 Repayment Provisions   789
Call Provisions   790
■ New York City Calls
Its Municipal Bonds   790
Sinking Funds   793
Convertible Provisions   794
Summary 796 • Key Terms 797 •
Further Reading 797 • Problems 798
Data Case   799

Chapter 25 Leasing   801

25.1 The Basics of Leasing   802
Examples of Lease Transactions   802
Lease Payments
and Residual Values   803
Leases Versus Loans   804
End-of-Term Lease Options   805
■ Calculating Auto Lease
Payments   806
Other Lease Provisions   807

**25.2 Accounting, Tax, and Legal
Consequences of Leasing   808**

Lease Accounting   808
■ Operating Leases at
Alaska Air Group   808
The Tax Treatment of Leases   810
Leases and Bankruptcy   811
■ Synthetic Leases   812

25.3 The Leasing Decision   813
Cash Flows for a True Tax Lease   813
Lease Versus Buy
(An Unfair Comparison)   814
Lease Versus Borrow
(The Right Comparison)   815
Evaluating a True Tax Lease   817
Evaluating a Non-tax Lease   818

25.4 Reasons for Leasing   819
Valid Arguments for Leasing   819
Suspect Arguments for Leasing   822
Summary 822 • Key Terms 823 •
Further Reading 824 • Problems 824

PART IX SHORT-TERM FINANCING   827

**Chapter 26 Working Capital
Management   829**

26.1 Overview of Working Capital   830
The Cash Cycle   830
Firm Value and Working Capital   832

26.2 Trade Credit   832
Trade Credit Terms   833
Trade Credit and Market Frictions   833
Managing Float   834

26.3 Receivables Management   835
Determining the Credit Policy   836
Monitoring Accounts Receivable   836

26.4 Payables Management   838
Determining Accounts Payable
Days Outstanding   839
Stretching Accounts Payable   839

26.5 Inventory Management   840
Benefits of Holding Inventory   840
Costs of Holding Inventory   841

26.6 Cash Management   841
Motivation for Holding Cash   842
Alternative Investments   842

■ Cash Balances   844

Summary 844 • Key Terms 845 •
Further Reading 845 • Problems 846
Data Case   849

**Chapter 27   Short-Term
Financial Planning   851**

27.1   **Forecasting Short-Term
Financing Needs   852**
Seasonalities   852
Negative Cash Flow Shocks   854
Positive Cash Flow Shocks   855

27.2   **The Matching Principle   857**
Permanent Working Capital   857
Temporary Working Capital   857
Financing Policy Choices   858

27.3   **Short-Term Financing
with Bank Loans   859**
Single, End-of-Period Payment Loan   859
Line of Credit   859
Bridge Loan   860
Common Loan
Stipulations and Fees   860

27.4   **Short-Term Financing
with Commercial Paper   862**

27.5   **Short-Term Financing
with Secured Financing   863**
Accounts Receivable as Collateral   863
■ A Seventeenth-Century
Financing Solution   864
Inventory as Collateral   864

Summary 866 • Key Terms 867 •
Further Reading 867 • Problems 868

PART X   SPECIAL TOPICS   871

Chapter 28   Mergers and Acquisitions   873

28.1   **Background and
Historical Trends   874**

28.2   **Market Reaction
to a Takeover   875**

28.3   **Reasons to Acquire   877**
Economies of Scale and Scope   877

Vertical Integration   877
Expertise   878
Monopoly Gains   878
Efficiency Gains   879
Operating Losses   879
Diversification   880
Earnings Growth   881

28.4   **The Takeover Process   883**
Valuation   883
The Offer   884
Merger "Arbitrage"   885
Tax and Accounting Issues   887
Board and Shareholder Approval   887

28.5   **Takeover Defenses   888**
Poison Pills   888
Staggered Boards   890
White Knights   890
Golden Parachutes   890
Recapitalization   890
Other Defensive Strategies   891
Regulatory Approval   891
■ Weyerhaeuser's Hostile Bid
for Willamette Industries   892

28.6   **Who Gets the Value Added
from a Takeover?   892**
The Free Rider Problem   893
Toeholds   893
The Leveraged Buyout   894
■ The Leveraged Buyout
of RJR-Nabisco by KKR   895
The Freezeout Merger   896
Competition   897

Summary 898 • Key Terms 899 •
Further Reading 899 • Problems 899
Data Case   901

Chapter 29   Corporate Governance   903

29.1   **Corporate Governance
and Agency Costs   904**

29.2   **Monitoring by the Board
of Directors   904**
Types of Directors   905
Board Independence   905
Board Size and Performance   906

29.3 Compensation Policies 906

Stock and Options 906
Pay and Performance Sensitivity 907

29.4 Managing Agency Conflict 908

Direct Action by Shareholders 909
■ Shareholder Activism
  at Blockbuster 910
Management Entrenchment 910
The Threat of Takeover 911

29.5 Regulation 911

The Sarbanes-Oxley Act 912
■ Interview with Lawrence E. Harris 913
The Cadbury Commission 914
■ Martha Stewart and ImClone 915
Insider Trading 915

**29.6 Corporate Governance
Around the World 916**

Protection of Shareholder Rights 916
Controlling Owners and Pyramids 916
The Stakeholder Model 919
Cross-holdings 919

**29.7 The Tradeoff of
Corporate Governance 921**

Summary 921 • Key Terms 922 •
Further Reading 923 • Problems 923

Chapter 30 Risk Management 925

30.1 Insurance 926

The Role of Insurance: An Example 926
Insurance Pricing in a Perfect Market 927
The Value of Insurance 928
The Costs of Insurance 930
The Insurance Decision 932

30.2 Commodity Price Risk 933

Hedging with Vertical
Integration and Storage 933
Hedging with Long-Term Contracts 934
Hedging with Futures Contracts 935
■ Common Mistake: Hedging Risk 938
Deciding to Hedge
Commodity Price Risk 938
■ Differing Hedging Strategies 939

30.3 Exchange Rate Risk 939

Exchange Rate Fluctuations 939
Hedging with Forward Contracts 941
Cash-and-Carry and the
Pricing of Currency Forwards 943
Hedging with Options 946

30.4 Interest Rate Risk 950

Interest Rate Risk
Measurement: Duration 950
Duration-Based Hedging 952
■ The Savings and Loan Crisis 954
Swap-Based Hedging 956

Summary 960 • Key Terms 962 •
Further Reading 962 • Problems 963

**Chapter 31 International
Corporate Finance 969**

**31.1 Internationally Integrated
Capital Markets 970**

**31.2 Valuation of Foreign
Currency Cash Flows 971**

WACC Valuation Method
in Domestic Currency 972
Application: Ityesi, Inc. 972
Using the Law of One Price
as a Robustness Check 974

**31.3 Valuation and
International Taxation 976**

Single Foreign Project with
Immediate Repatriation of Earnings 976
Multiple Foreign Projects and
Deferral of Earnings Repatriation 976

**31.4 Internationally Segmented
Capital Markets 977**

Differential Access to Markets 977
Macro-Level Distortions 978
Implications 979

**31.5 Capital Budgeting
with Exchange Risk 981**

Summary 983 • Key Terms 984 •
Further Reading 984 • Problems 984
Data Case 987

About the Authors

Jonathan Berk is a Professor of Finance in the Haas School of Business at the University of California, Berkeley and is a Research Associate at the National Bureau of Economic Research. He currently teaches the introductory Corporate Finance course for first-year MBA students at Berkeley. Before getting his Ph.D., he worked as an Associate at Goldman Sachs, where his education in finance really began.

Professor Berk is an Associate Editor of the *Journal of Finance*. His research interests in finance include corporate valuation, capital structure, mutual funds, asset pricing, experimental economics, and labor economics. His work has won a number of research awards including the TIAA-CREF Paul A. Samuelson Award, the Smith Breeden Prize, Best Paper of the Year in *The Review of Financial Studies*, and the FAME Research Prize. His paper, "A Critique of Size Related Anomalies," was recently selected as one of the two best papers ever published in *The Review of Financial Studies*. In recognition of his influence on the practice of finance he has received the Bernstein-Fabozzi/Jacobs Levy Award, the Graham and Dodd Award of Excellence, and the Roger F. Murray Prize.

Peter DeMarzo and Jonathan Berk

Born in Johannesburg, South Africa, Professor Berk is married, with two daughters aged 10 and 14, and is an avid skier and biker.

Peter DeMarzo is the Mizuho Financial Group Professor of Finance at the Stanford Graduate School of Business and is a Research Associate at the National Bureau of Economic Research. He currently teaches the "turbo" core finance course for Stanford's first-year MBA students. In addition to his experience at the Stanford Graduate School of Business, Professor DeMarzo has taught at the Haas School of Business and the Kellogg Graduate School of Management, and he was a National Fellow at the Hoover Institution.

Professor DeMarzo received the Sloan Teaching Excellence Award at Stanford in 2004 and 2006, and the Earl F. Cheit Outstanding Teaching Award at U.C. Berkeley in 1998. Professor DeMarzo has served as an Associate Editor for *The Review of Financial Studies, Financial Management*, and the *B.E. Journals in Economic Analysis and Policy*, as well as a Director of the Western Finance Association. Professor DeMarzo's research is in the area of corporate finance, asset securitization, and contracting, as well as market structure and regulation. His recent work has examined issues of the optimal design of securities, the regulation of insider trading and broker-dealers, and the influence of information asymmetries on corporate investment. He has received numerous awards including the Western Finance Association Corporate Finance Award and the Barclays Global Investors/Michael Brennan best-paper award from *The Review of Financial Studies*.

Professor DeMarzo was born in Whitestone, New York and is married with three boys. He and his family enjoy hiking, biking, and skiing.

Preface

When we told our friends and colleagues that we had decided to write a corporate finance textbook, most of them had the same response: *Why now?* There are three main reasons.

Pedagogy

As any student of the subject will attest to, corporate finance is challenging. Consequently, as the popularity of corporate finance has grown, textbook authors have attempted to make the subject more accessible by de-emphasizing the core theoretical ideas and instead concentrating on the results. In our over 30 years of combined teaching experience, we have found that leaving out core material deemed "too hard" actually makes the subject matter less accessible. The core concepts in finance are simple and intuitive. What makes the subject challenging is that it is often difficult for a novice to distinguish between these core ideas and other intuitively appealing approaches that, if used in financial decision making, will lead to incorrect decisions. De-emphasizing the core concepts that underlie finance strips students of the essential intellectual tools they need to differentiate between good and bad decision making. Therefore, our primary motivation for writing this book was to equip students with a solid grounding in the core financial concepts and tools needed to make good decisions.

In our experience, students learn best when the material in a course is presented as one unified whole rather than a series of separate ideas. As such, this book presents corporate finance as an application of a subset of simple, powerful ideas. At the heart of this core is the principal of the absence of arbitrage opportunities, or Law of One Price. We use the Law of One Price as a compass; it keeps financial decision makers on the right track.

Perspective

The past 30 years have witnessed an evolution in both the sophistication of the students taking the course and the field itself. Today's students arrive with first-hand knowledge of financial markets, either through their participation in stock markets or in their interaction with widely available financial products. Many students encounter financial concepts in their entry-level jobs out of college; they often have experience implementing financial decisions for the firms they work for, some receive stock and options as part of their compensation, and almost all have the option to make retirement plan contributions. We capitalize on the background that students bring to the classroom in our choice of terminology and examples, our use of real data, and by relating methodology to practice.

Much of the empirical evidence in financial economics amassed in the last 30 years supports the existing theory and strengthens the importance of understanding and applying corporate finance principles. However, in a number of applications, the evidence has not supported the theory. Although puzzles have emerged, none of them has invalidated the core principles of corporate finance that this book is built on. So rather than state theory as fact, we carefully evaluate the evidence and build on the sophistication students bring with them on the first day of class. By clearly communicating these subtleties to the student, we expose them to the dynamism of the field and avoid giving them false impressions that contradict their own experience.

Technology

Even though the Internet is now commonplace, we do not feel that it has been properly exploited in the field of education. The technology breakthrough in this book has the potential to fundamentally change the way students learn. MyFinanceLab is as much a part of the learning experience as classroom lectures and the textbook itself.

This product fundamentally changes how students learn finance. In the traditional approach, students learn by working end-of-chapter problems, yet the time lag between when the problem is worked and when feedback is received marginalizes the benefit of the feedback. MyFinanceLab completely removes this inefficiency by providing students with immediate feedback at the very point that they are most receptive to the knowledge.

These reasons motivated us to write a textbook that we hope will shape the way students learn corporate finance for years to come.

Corporate Finance's Innovative Approach

Corporate Finance carefully balances the latest advancements in research and practice with thorough coverage of core finance topics. Several key themes and innovations distinguish this textbook.

1. Using the Law of One Price as the Unifying Principle of Valuation

This book presents corporate finance as an application of a small set of simple core ideas. Modern finance theory and practice is grounded in the idea of the absence of arbitrage (or the Law of One Price) as the unifying concept in valuation. Chapter 3, "Arbitrage and Financial Decision Making," explicitly introduces the Law of One Price concept as the basis for NPV, the time value of money, and the evaluation of risk. The rest of the book relates major concepts to the Law of One Price, creating a framework to ground the student reader. Each part of the textbook begins by highlighting the Law of One Price connection. This methodology directly connects theory to practice and presents a unified approach to what might appear to students as disparate ideas.

2. Improving on the Basics: Timelines and Interest Rates

We introduce timelines in Chapter 4, "The Time Value of Money," and stress the importance of creating timelines for every problem that involves cash flows. Each subsequent example involving cash flows includes a timeline as the critical first step.

In Chapter 5, "Interest Rates," we explicitly walk students through the mechanics of adjusting discount rates for different time periods and explain how to interpret interest rate quotes. Separating the mechanics of how to compute the discount rate from the time value of money concept allows us to more effectively communicate these basic tools.

3. Emphasizing Capital Budgeting and Valuation

The capital budgeting decision is one of the most important decisions in finance and as such is the focus of many instructors' courses. We present capital budgeting and valuation in two stages.

The first stage comes early and focuses on identifying cash flows. Chapter 7, "Fundamentals of Capital Budgeting," examines the valuation of projects within a firm and provides a clear and systematic presentation of the difference between earnings and free cash flow. These concepts are then applied to stocks in Chapter 9, providing a unifying treatment of projects within the firm and the valuation of the firm as a whole. This early introduction into capital budgeting allows us to conceptually present the idea of the cost of capital, which we then use to motivate the risk and return coverage. In this way, we relate the cost of capital to risk and return, an otherwise challenging connection for new students of finance.

The second stage follows the discussion of the pricing of risk and capital structure. Chapter 18, "Capital Budgeting and Valuation with Leverage," presents the three main methods for capital budgeting with leverage and market imperfections: the weighted average cost of capital (WACC) method, the adjusted present value (APV) method, and the flow-to-equity (FTE) method. We communicate these traditionally difficult but important ideas by emphasizing the underlying assumptions and core principles behind them. This approach allows us to present these concepts in the context of progressively more complex financing policies for the firm, which allows students and professors to delve as deeply into these techniques as is appropriate for their needs. Next, Chapter 19, "Valuation and Financial Modeling: A Case Study" serves as a capstone chapter for the first six parts of the book and applies the financial tools developed thus far to build a valuation model for a case study, Ideko Corp. This chapter walks future financial managers through the process of building a financial valuation model using Excel.

4. Rethinking the Teaching of Risk and Return

Chapter 3 briefly introduces the concept of risk and return. Using the no-arbitrage concept alone, we explain conceptually one of the core principles of finance: that risk must be evaluated relative to a benchmark. Later, the flexible structure of Part IV allows professors to tailor coverage of risk and return to fit their course.

For those looking for a brief introduction to risk and return before moving directly to corporate finance topics, Chapter 10, "Capital Markets and the Pricing of Risk," provides the key intuition and motivation for the relation between risk and return. The chapter also explains the distinction between diversifiable and systematic risk, and introduces the CAPM in the way it is used in practice, as a means of identifying systematic risk and determining risk premia. This comprehensive yet succinct treatment allows instructors to skip subsequent risk and return chapters without sacrificing continuity.

Those opting for in-depth coverage of risk and return can include the following chapters:

- Chapter 11, "Optimal Portfolio Choice," develops the details of mean-variance portfolio optimization separately from the CAPM as they are of independent usefulness.

- Chapter 12, "The Capital Asset Pricing Model," presents the equilibrium argument for the CAPM, emphasizing that the CAPM is simply a means of identifying the market portfolio as an efficient portfolio, and discusses a number of practical issues that arise when implementing the CAPM.

- Chapter 13, "Alternative Models of Systematic Risk," moves beyond the CAPM, examining the relative strengths and weaknesses of other models, including multi-factor models and characteristic variable models. Because we have separated the discussion of mean-variance optimization from the CAPM in Chapters 11 and 12, this chapter is able to clearly differentiate the core concept that remains valid from the applications called into question by the empirical evidence. That is, the expected return of a stock is still given by its beta with an efficient portfolio but that portfolio might not be the standard proxies used for the market portfolio.

5. Stressing the Capital Structure Decision

We place heavy emphasis on the firm's capital structure in Chapters 14–17, but also allow instructors to tailor the coverage as suits them by presenting Modigliani and Miller in a perfect world at the outset and then layering on frictions in subsequent chapters. We tie the classic Modigliani and Miller results to the Law of One Price and maintain that central theme throughout our discussion of capital structure. Our full-chapter treatment of this foundational material highlights its importance to students and sets the stage for the remainder of this part of the text. Our in-depth look at the role of taxation, financial distress, and agency costs fully prepares the financial manager to account for real-world market imperfections in the capital budgeting process.

Organization

Corporate Finance offers coverage of the major topical areas for introductory-level MBA students as well as the depth required in a reference textbook for upper-division courses. Our focus is on financial decision-making related to the corporation's choice of which investments to make or how to raise the capital required to fund an investment.

Part-by-Part Overview

Parts I and II lay the foundation for our study of corporate finance. In Chapter 1, we introduce the corporation and other business forms. We examine how stock markets facilitate trading among investors, the role of the financial manager, and conflicts surrounding ownership and control of corporations. Chapter 2 reviews basic corporate accounting principles and the financial statements on which the financial manager relies. Chapter 3, "Arbitrage and Financial Decision Making," introduces the core ideas on which finance is built—the Law of One Price, net present value, and risk—that are the basis of the unifying framework that will guide the student throughout the course. This brief introduction to risk is an important innovation that allows us to discuss risk in the early chapters, in particular in the context of the early introduction to capital budgeting.

Part II presents the basic tools that are the cornerstones of corporate finance. Chapter 4 introduces the time value of money and describes methods for estimating the timing of cash flows and computing the net present value of various types of cash flow patterns. Chapter 5, "Interest Rates," provides an extensive overview of issues that arise in estimating the appropriate discount rate. In Chapter 6, "Investment Decision Rules," we present and critique alternatives to net present value for evaluating projects.

Part III applies these newly learned valuation principles for discounting cash flows developed from Part II to both real and financial assets. We explain the basics of valuation for capital projects (Chapter 7), bonds (Chapter 8), and stocks (Chapter 9). In Chapter 9 we also discuss the issue of market efficiency and implications for financial managers.

In Part IV, we look at the critical concept of risk and return. Chapter 10, "Capital Markets and the Pricing of Risk," introduces the relation between risk and return. Some professors may choose to cover only this one-chapter treatment of risk and return before proceeding directly to the capital structure unit. In Chapter 11, "Optimal Portfolio Choice," we introduce mean-variance optimization. In Chapter 12, we derive the Capital Asset Pricing Model. Chapter 13 examines the strengths and weaknesses of alternative models of risk and return.

Part V addresses how a firm should raise the funds it needs to undertake its investments and the firm's resulting capital structure. We focus on examining how the choice of capital structure affects the value of the firm in the perfect world in Chapter 14 and with frictions such as taxes and agency issues in Chapters 15 and 16. Payout policy is the focus of Chapter 17.

In Part VI, we return to the capital budgeting decision with the complexities of the real world. Chapter 18, "Capital Budgeting and Valuation with Leverage," introduces the three main methods for capital budgeting with leverage and market imperfections: the weighted average cost of capital (WACC) method, the adjusted present value (APV) method, and the flow-to-equity (FTE) method. Chapter 19, "Valuation and Financial Modeling: A Case Study," presents a capstone case that applies the techniques developed up to this point to build a valuation model for a firm.

Part VII focuses on options and the role they play in investing and financing decisions. Chapter 20 introduces the financial options, and Chapter 21 presents commonly used techniques for pricing options, including the Black-Scholes Option Pricing Model and Binomial Option Pricing Model. Chapter 22 highlights the role of real options in capital budgeting.

In Part VIII, we explain the institutional details associated with alternative long-term financing sources. Chapter 23, "The Mechanics of Raising Equity Capital," describes the process a company goes through when it raises equity capital. In Chapter 24, we review how firms can use the debt markets to raise capital. Chapter 25 introduces an alternative to long-term debt financing, leasing.

In Part IX, we turn to the details of running the financial side of a corporation on a day-to-day basis. In Chapter 26 we discuss how firms manage their working capital. In Chapter 27, we explain how firms manage their short-term cash needs.

Part X addresses special topics in corporate financial management. Chapter 28 discusses mergers and acquisitions, and Chapter 29 provides an overview of corporate governance. In Chapter 30, "Risk Management," we consider corporations' use of insurance and financial derivatives to manage risk. Chapter 31, "International Corporate Finance," introduces the issues a firm faces when making a foreign investment and addresses the valuation of foreign projects.

Customize Your Approach

In reviewing hundreds of syllabi in planning for this textbook, we came to appreciate that few professors work through a textbook linearly from start to finish. The vast majority of professors customize their classes by selecting a subset of chapters reflecting the subject matter they consider most important. We therefore designed the book from the outset with this need for flexibility in mind. Instructors are free to emphasize the topics they find most interesting.

We consider Parts II through VI as the core chapters in the book. We envision that most MBA programs will cover this material in the courses they teach. However, even within these core chapters instructors can pick and choose. Universities that teach corporate finance in a single quarter will likely cover Chapters 3–15. If time allows, or if students enter the course already familiar with the time value of money concepts, Chapters 16–19 can be added. In a semester-long course, other topics such as options, risk management, and international finance can be added at the instructor's choosing. The later chapters in the book can also be used in an advanced corporate finance course. Finally, the book allows for a stripped-down treatment of finance essentials for programs that only have a single mini-semester core finance course. In this case, we suggest covering Chapters 3–10, 14, and perhaps 15 if time allows.

A Complete Instructor and Student Support Package

MyFinanceLab

MyFinanceLab is a critical component of the text. This resource, a premium product that is available for packaging, will give all students the practice and tutorial help they need to learn finance efficiently. For more details, see pages xxxvi–xxxvii.

Solutions Manual

This essential companion to the text provides detailed, accuracy-verified solutions to every chapter problem. All the solutions, like the problems themselves, were written by the textbook authors, class tested by 10 MBA finance classes over the course of a semester, and scrutinized by Mark Simonson, Arizona State University, to guarantee unparalleled quality.

Study Guide

Written by Mark Simonson, Arizona State University, the Study Guide provides the learning tools students need to cement their understanding of the central concepts. Corresponding to each chapter, students will find a chapter synopsis that overviews the contents and a review of selected concepts and key terms to focus study time on the most critical topics. A handful of worked examples in each chapter with step-by-step solutions walk students through the thought process for arriving at each solution, instilling in them the intuition they need to tackle problems successfully on their own. A section of 5–10 questions and problems per chapter test students' grasp of the main concepts and ability to apply them to solve problems.

Instructor's Manual

The Instructor's Manual was written by Janet Payne and William Chittenden of Texas State University. Corresponding to each chapter, these authors provide: chapter overview and outline correlated to the PowerPoint Lecture Notes; learning objectives; guide to fresh worked examples in the PowerPoint Lecture Notes; and listing of end-of-chapter problems with an Excel icon (EXCEL) for which Spreadsheets are available via the online Instructor Resource Center and Instructor's Resource CD-ROM.

Test Bank

Prepared by James Nelson, East Carolina University, the Test Bank provides a wealth of accuracy-verified testing material. Each chapter offers a wide selection of multiple-choice, short-answer, and essay questions. Questions are qualified by difficulty level and skill type and correlated to the chapter topics. Numerical-based problems include step-by-step solutions.

Instructor's Resource Disk with PowerPoint Lecture Presentations

Compatible with Windows and Macintosh computers, this CD-ROM provides numerous resources for students and professors alike.

We offer PowerPoint Lecture Presentations, authored by Janet Payne and William Chittenden of Texas State University, tailored to both instructors and students. The instructor version offers outlines of each chapter with graphs, tables, key terms, and concepts from each chapter. To enliven classroom presentations, selected figures, tables, and timelines are incorporated. Fresh worked examples provide detailed, step-by-step solutions for students in the same format as the boxed examples from the text. New examples are correlated to the parallel examples from the textbook and include calculator keystrokes and Spreadsheet Solutions as appropriate. The student version of the presentation contains selected deletions and fill-in-the blanks to encourage active student listening and participation in the lectures.

For added convenience, the CD-ROM also includes Microsoft Word files for the entire contents of the Instructor's Manual and computerized Test Bank files. The easy-to-use testing software (TestGen with QuizMaster for Windows and Macintosh) is a valuable text preparation tool that allows professors to view, edit, and add questions.

Resources Available for Packaging with This Text

The following supplementary materials are available to aid and enhance students' mastery of concepts:

Wall Street Journal Edition

When packaged with this text, Addison-Wesley offers students a reduced-cost, 10- or 15-week subscription to the *Wall Street Journal* print edition and the *Wall Street Journal* Interactive Edition.

The Financial Times Edition

Featuring international news and analysis from journalists in more than 50 countries, *The Financial Times* will provide your students with insights and perspectives on economic developments around the world. For a small charge, a 15-week subscription to *The Financial Times* can be included with each new textbook.

Acknowledgments

Now that we have explained why we chose to write the text and how to use it, we can turn to thanking the people that made it happen. As any textbook writer will tell you, you cannot write a textbook of this scope without a substantial amount of help. First and foremost we thank Donna Battista, whose leadership, talent, and market savvy are imprinted on all aspects of the project and central to its success; Denise Clinton, a friend and a leader in fact not just in name, whose experience and knowledge are indispensable; Rebecca Ferris-Caruso, for her unparalleled expertise in managing the complex writing, reviewing, and editing processes and patience in keeping us on track; Dona Kenly, for spearheading the market development work; Michelle Neil, for embracing our vision for MyFinanceLab; and Kay Ueno, for her tireless efforts during the last leg of the textbook marathon. We were blessed to be approached by the best publisher in the business and we are both truly thankful for the indispensable help provided by these and other professionals, including Nancy Fenton, Nancy Freihofer, Meredith Gertz, Marianne Groth, Roxanne Hoch, Christine Lyons, Heather McNally, Jason Miranda, Bridget Page, Margaret Monahan-Pashall, Susan Schoenberg, Charles Spaulding, Allison Stendardi, and Sally Steele.

Without Jennifer Koski's help, we would have been unable to realize our vision for this textbook. Like us, she took on much more than she bargained for, but we will be forever grateful for her willingness to stick with us and provide her critical insights and knowledge that ultimately moved the book through the second and third drafts. Her belief in this project, tireless effort, and commitment ensured that it met her very high standards. Without her, there would not have been a book.

Many of the later, non-core chapters required specific detailed knowledge. Nigel Barradale, Reid Click, Jarrad Harford, and Marianne Plunkert ensured that this knowledge was effectively communicated. Joseph Vu and Vance P. Lesseig contributed their talents to the Concept Check questions and Data Cases, respectively.

Thomas Gilbert and Miguel Palacios worked every example and end-of-chapter problem in this book. In addition, they provided numerous insights that have greatly improved the exposition. They were both indispensable, and we are very grateful for their help. Creating a truly error-free text is a challenge we could not have lived up to it without our team of expert error checkers. Anand Goel and Mark Simonson each subjected the text to their exacting standards throughout the manuscript and production processes. Ting-Heng Chu, Robert James, Siddarth Tenneti, and Joseph Vu also contributed their sharp eyes.

The development of MyFinanceLab was an enormous undertaking, sometimes rivaling the book itself. Mike Griffin managed the whole process; without his financial experience and his attention to detail, MyFinanceLab would still be simply a nice idea. In addition, Shannon Donovan and Arline Savage provided invaluable support and we are very grateful to both of them.

A corporate finance textbook is the product of the talents and hard work of many talented colleagues. We are especially gratified with the work of those who developed an impressive array of print supplements to accompany the book: Mark Simonson, for the Solutions Manual and Study Guide; Janet Payne and William Chittenden, for the Instructor's Manual and PowerPoint; and James Nelson, for the Test Bank.

We're also appreciative Marlene Bellamy's work conducting the lively interviews that provide a critically important perspective, and to the interviewees who graciously provided their time and insights, including Andrew Balson, Lisa Black, John Bogle, Jonathan Clements, John Connors, Marilyn G. Fedak, Sue Frieden, Richard Grannis, Lawrence E. Harris, Randall P. Lert, Scott Mathews, Joseph L. Rice III, Joel Stern, Rex Sinquefield, and David Viniar.

As a colleague of both of us, Mark Rubinstein inspired us with his passion to get the history of finance right by correctly attributing the important ideas to the people who first enunciated them. Inspiration is one thing; actually undertaking the task is another. His book, *A History of the Theory of Investments: My Annotated Bibliography*, was indispensable—it provided the only available reference of the history of finance. As will be obvious to any reader, we have used it extensively in this text and we, as well as the profession as a whole, owe him a debt of gratitude for taking the time to write it all down.

We could not have written this text if we were not once ourselves students of finance. As any student knows, the key to success is having a great teacher. In our case we are lucky to have been taught and advised by the people who helped create modern finance: Ken Arrow, Darrell Duffie, Mordecai Kurz, Stephen Ross, and Richard Roll. It was from them that we learned the importance of the core principles of finance, including the Law of One Price, on which this book is based. The learning process does not end at graduation and like most people we have had especially influential colleagues and mentors from which we learned a great deal during our careers and we would like to recognize them explicitly here: Mike Fishman, Richard Green, Vasant Naik, Art Raviv, Mark Rubinstein, Joe Williams, and Jeff Zwiebel. We continue to learn from all of our colleagues and we are grateful to all of them. Finally, we would like to thank those with whom we have taught finance classes over the years: Anat Admati, Ming Huang, Robert Korajczyk, Paul Pfleiderer, Sergio Rebelo, Richard Stanton, and Raman Uppal. Their ideas and teaching strategies have without a doubt influenced our own sense of pedagogy and found their way into this text.

Finally, and most importantly, we owe our biggest debt of gratitude to our spouses, Rebecca Schwartz and Kaui Chun DeMarzo. Little did we (or they) know how much this project would impact our lives, and without their continued love and support—and especially their patience and understanding—this text could not have been completed. We owe a special thanks to Kaui DeMarzo, for her inspiration and support at the start of this project, and for her willingness to be our in-house editor, contributor, advisor, and overall sounding-board throughout each stage of its development.

Jonathan Berk
Peter DeMarzo

Contributors

We are truly thankful to have had so many manuscript reviewers, class testers, and focus group participants. We list all of these contributors below, but Gordon Bodnar, James Conover, Anand Goel, James Linck, Evgeny Lyandres, Marianne Plunkert, Mark Simonson, and Andy Terry went so far beyond the call of duty that we would like to single them out. We strived to incorporate every contributor's input and are truly grateful for the time each individual took to provide comments and suggestions. The book has benefited enormously from this input.

Reviewers

Ashok B. Abbott, *West Virginia University*
Michael Adams, *Jacksonville University*
Ibrahim Affaneh, *Indiana University of Pennsylvania*
Kevin Ahlgrim, *Illinois State University*
Confidence Amadi, *Florida A&M University*
Christopher Anderson, *University of Kansas*
Tom Arnold, *University of Richmond*
Nigel Barradale, *University of California, Berkeley*
Peter Basciano, *Augusta State University*
Thomas Bates, *University of Arizona*
Paul Bayes, *East Tennessee State University*
Gordon Bodnar, *Johns Hopkins University*

Waldo Born, *Eastern Illinois University*
Alex Boulatov, *Bauer College of Business, University of Houston*
George Chang, *Bradley University*
Ting-Heng Chu, *East Tennessee State University*
John H. Cochrane, *University of Chicago*
James Conover, *University of North Texas*
Henrik Cronqvist, *Ohio State University*
Maddur Daggar, *Citigroup*
Hazem Daouk, *Cornell University*
Daniel Deli, *Arizona State University*
Andrea DeMaskey, *Villanova University*
B. Espen Eckbo, *Dartmouth College*
Larry Eisenberg, *University of Southern Mississippi*

T. Hanan Eytan, *Baruch College*
Michael Gallmeyer, *Texas A&M University*
Diego Garcia, *University of North Carolina*
Tom Geurts, *Marist College*
Frank Ghannadian, *Mercer University*
Thomas Gilbert, *University of California, Berkeley*
Marc Goergen, *University of Sheffield*
David Goldenberg, *Rensselaer Polytechnic Institute*
Milton Harris, *University of Chicago*
Christopher Hennessy, *University of California, Los Angeles*
Vanessa Holmes, *Xavier University*
Wenli Huang, *Boston University School of Management*
Mark Hutchinson, *University College Cork*
Stuart Hyde, *University of Manchester*
Robert James, *Babson College*
Keith Johnson, *University of Kentucky*
Ayla Kayhan, *Louisiana State University*
Doseong Kim, *University of Akron*
Kenneth Kim, *State University of New York–Buffalo*
Halil Kiymaz, *Rollins College*
Brian Kluger, *University of Cincinnati*
John Knopf, *Seton Hall University*
George Kutner, *Marquette University*
Vance P. Lesseig, *Texas State University*
Martin Lettau, *New York University*
James Linck, *University of Georgia*
David Lins, *University of Illinois at Urbana–Champaign*
Michelle Lowry, *Pennsylvania State University*
Deborah Lucas, *Northwestern University*
Peng Lui, *University of California, Berkeley*
Evgeny Lyandres, *Rice University*
Balasundram Maniam, *Sam Houston State University*
Suren Mansinghka, *University of California, Irvine*
Daniel McConaughy, *California State University, Northridge*
Robert McDonald, *Northwestern University*
Mark McNabb, *University of Cincinnati*
Ilhan Meric, *Rider University*
Timothy Michael, *James Madison University*
Dag Michalsen, *Norwegian School of Management*
James Miles, *Penn State University*
Arjen Mulder, *RSM Erasmus University*
Michael Muoghalu, *Pittsburg State University*
Jeryl Nelson, *Wayne State College*
Tom Nelson, *University of Colorado*
Chee Ng, *Fairleigh Dickinson University*
Ben Nunnally, *University of North Carolina, Charlotte*
Frank O'Hara, *University of San Francisco*
Henry Oppenheimer, *University of Rhode Island*
Miguel Palacios, *University of California, Berkeley*
Mitchell Petersen, *Northwestern University*

Marianne Plunkert, *University of Colorado at Denver*
Michael Provitera, *Barry University*
Brian Prucyk, *Marquette University*
P. Raghavendra Rau, *Purdue University*
Charu Raheja, *Vanderbilt University*
Latha Ramchand, *University of Houston*
William A. Reese, Jr., *Tulane University*
Ali Reza, *San Jose State University*
Steven P. Rich, *Baylor University*
Antonio Rodriguez, *Texas A&M International University*
Bruce Rubin, *Old Dominion University*
Mark Rubinstein, *University of California, Berkeley*
Harley E. Ryan, Jr., *Georgia State University*
Jacob A. Sagi, *University of California, Berkeley*
Harikumar Sankaran, *New Mexico State University*
Frederik Schlingemann, *University of Pittsburgh*
Mark Seasholes, *University of California, Berkeley*
Eduardo Schwartz, *University of California, Los Angeles*
Mark Shackleton, *Lancaster University*
Jay Shanken, *Emory University*
Dennis Sheehan, *Penn State University*
Anand Shetty, *Iona College*
Mark Simonson, *Arizona State University*
Rajeev Singhal, *Oakland University*
Erik Stafford, *Harvard Business School*
David Stangeland, *University of British Columbia*
Richard H. Stanton, *University of California, Berkeley*
Mark Hoven Stohs, *California State University, Fullerton*
Ilya A. Strebulaev, *Stanford University*
Ryan Stever, *Bank for International Settlements*
John Strong, *College of William and Mary*
Diane Suhler, *Columbia College*
Lawrence Tai, *Loyola Marymount University*
Mark Taranto, *University of Pennsylvania*
Amir Tavakkol, *Kansas State University*
Andy Terry, *University of Arkansas at Little Rock*
John Thornton, *Kent State University*
Alex Triantis, *University of Maryland*
Sorin Tuluca, *Fairleigh Dickinson University*
Joe Walker, *University of Alabama at Birmingham*
Edward Waller, *University of Houston, Clear Lake*
Peihwang Wei, *University of New Orleans*
Peter Went, *Bucknell University*
John White, *Georgia Southern University*
Michael Williams, *University of Denver*
Annie Wong, *Western Connecticut State University*
K. Matthew Wong, *St. John's University*
Bob Wood, Jr., *Tennessee Tech University*
Lifan Wu, *California State University, Los Angeles*
Tzyy-Jeng Wu, *Pace University*
Jamie Zender, *University of Colorado*
Jeffrey H. Zwiebel, *Stanford University*

Chapter Class Testers

Jack Aber, *Boston University*
John Adams, *University of South Florida*
James Conover, *University of North Texas*
Lou Gingerella, *Rensselaer Polytechnic Institute*
Tom Geurts, *Marist College*
Mark Hoven Stohs, *California State University, Fullerton*
Keith Johnson, *University of Kentucky*
Gautum Kaul, *University of Michigan*
Doseong Kim, *University of Akron*
Jennifer Koski, *University of Washington*
George Kutner, *Marquette University*
Larry Lynch, *Roanoke College*
Vasil Mihov, *Texas Christina University*
Jeryl Nelson, *Wayne State College*
Chee Ng, *Fairleigh Dickinson University*
Ben Nunnally, *University of North Carolina, Charlotte*
Michael Proviteria, *Barry University*
Charu G. Raheja, *Vanderbilt University*
Bruce Rubin, *Old Dominion University*
Mark Seasholes, *University of California, Berkeley*
Dennis Sheehan, *Pennsylvania State University*
Ravi Shukla, *Syracuse University*
Andy Terry, *University of Arkansas*
Sorin Tuluca, *Fairleigh Dickinson University*
Joe Ucng, *University of Saint Thomas*
Bob Wood, *Tennessee Technological University*

End-of-Chapter Problems Class Testers

James Angel, *Georgetown University*
Ting-Heng Chu, *East Tennessee State University*
Robert Kravchuk, *Indiana University*
George Kutner, *Marquette University*
James Nelson, *East Carolina University*
Don Panton, *University of Texas at Arlington*
P. Raghavendra Rau, *University of California, Los Angeles*
Carolyn Reichert, *University of Texas at Dallas*
Mark Simonson, *Arizona State University*
Diane Suhler, *Columbia College*

Focus Group Participants

Christopher Anderson, *University of Kansas*
Chenchu Bathala, *Cleveland State University*
Matthew T. Billett, *University of Iowa*
Andrea DeMaskey, *Villanova University*
Anand Desai, *Kansas State University*
Ako Doffou, *Sacred Heart University*
Shannon Donovan, *Bridgewater State University*
Ibrahim Elsaify, *Goldey-Beacom College*
Mark Holder, *Kent State University*
Steve Isberg, *University of Baltimore*

Arun Khanna, *Butler University*
Brian Kluger, *University of Cincinnati*
Greg LaBlanc, *University of California, Berkeley*
Dima Leshchinskii, *Rensselaer Polytechnic University*
James S. Linck, *University of Georgia*
Larry Lynch, *Roanoke College*
David C. Mauer, *Southern Methodist University*
Alfred Mettler, *Georgia State University*
Stuart Michelson, *Stetson University*
Vassil Mihov, *Texas Christian University*
Jeryl Nelson, *Wayne State College*
Chee Ng, *Fairleigh Dickinson University*
Ben Nunnally, *University of North Carolina at Charlotte*
Sunny Onyiri, *Campbellsville University*
Janet Payne, *Texas State University*
Michael Provitera, *Barry University*
Avri Ravid, *Rutgers University*
William A. Reese, Jr., *Tulane University*
Mario Reyes, *University of Idaho*
Hong Rim, *Shippensburg University*
Robert Ritchey, *Texas Tech University*
Antonio Rodriquez, *Texas A&M International University*
Dan Rogers, *Portland State University*
Harley E. Ryan, Jr., *Georgia State University*
Harikumar Sankaran, *New Mexico State University*
Sorin Sorescu, *Texas A&M University*
David Stangeland, *University of Manitoba*
Jonathan Stewart, *Abilene Christian University*
Mark Hoven Stohs, *California State University, Fullerton*
Tim Sullivan, *Bentley College*
Olie Thorp, *Babson College*
Harry Turtle, *Washington State University*
Joseph Vu, *DePaul University*
Joe Walker, *University of Alabama at Birmingham*
Jill Wetmore, *Saginaw Valley State University*
Jack Wolf, *Clemson University*
Bob Wood, Jr., *Tennessee Tech University*
Donald H. Wort, *California State University, East Bay*
Scott Wright, *Ohio University*
Tong Yao, *University of Arizona*

BRIDGING THEORY AND PRACTICE

PART

I

Introduction

Chapter 1
The Corporation

Chapter 2
Introduction to
Financial Statement
Analysis

Chapter 3
Arbitrage and Financial
Decision Making

The Law of One Price Connection. Why study Corporate Finance? No matter what your role in a corporation, an understanding of why and how financial decisions are made is essential. The focus of this book is how to make optimal corporate financial decisions. In this part of the book we lay the foundation for our study of corporate finance. We begin, in Chapter 1, by introducing the corporation and related business forms. We then examine the role of financial managers and outside investors in decision making for the firm. To make optimal decisions, a decision maker needs information. As a result, in Chapter 2 we review an important source of information for corporate decision making—the firm's accounting statements. Then, in Chapter 3 we introduce the most important idea in this book, the concept of the *absence of arbitrage* ...... Price. The Law of One Price states th......

The Law of One Price as the Unifying Valuation Framework

The Law of One Price framework reflects the modern idea that the absence of arbitrage is the unifying concept of valuation. This critical insight is introduced in Chapter 3, revisited in each Part Opener, and integrated throughout the text—motivating all major concepts and connecting theory to practice.

Study Aids with a Practical Focus

To be successful, students need to master the core concepts and learn to identify and solve problems that today's practitioners face.

- **Common Mistakes** boxes alert students to frequently made mistakes stemming from misunderstanding core concepts and calculations, as well as mistakes made in practice.

COMMON MISTAKE | **Discounting One Too Many Times**

The perpetuity formula assumes that the first payment occurs at the end of the first period (at date 1). Sometimes perpetuities have cash flows that start later in the future. In this case, we can adapt the perpetuity formula to compute the present value, but we need to do so carefully to avoid a common mistake.

To illustrate, consider the MBA graduation party described in Example 4.6. Rather than starting immediately, suppose that the first party will be held two years from today (for the current entering class). How would this delay change the amount of the donation required?

Now the timeline looks like this:

We need to determine the present value of these cash flows, as it tells us the amount of money in the bank needed today to finance the future parties. We cannot apply the perpetuity formula directly, however, because these cash flows are not *exactly* a perpetuity as we defined it. Specifically, the cash flow in the first period is "missing." But consider the situation on date 1—at that point, the

first party is one period away and then the cash flows are periodic. From the perspective of date 1, this *is* a perpetuity, and we can apply the formula. From the preceding calculation, we know we need $375,000 on date 1 to have enough to start the parties on date 2. We rewrite the timeline as follows:

Our goal can now be restated more simply: How much do we need to invest today to have $375,000 in one year? This is a simple present value calculation:

$$PV = \$375,000 / 1.08 = \$347,222 \text{ today}$$

A common mistake is to discount the $375,000 twice because the first party is in two periods. Remember—*the present value formula for the perpetuity already discounts the cash flows to one period prior to the first cash flow.* Keep in mind that this common mistake may be made with perpetuities, annuities, and all of the other special cases discussed in this section. All of these formulas discount the cash flows to one period prior to the first cash flow.

- **Worked Examples** accompany every important concept using a step-by-step procedure that illustrates both Problem and Solution. Clear labels make them easy to find for help with homework or studying. Many include an Excel spreadsheet calculator.

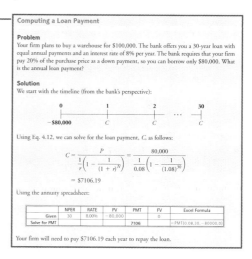

Computing a Loan Payment

Problem
Your firm plans to buy a warehouse for $100,000. The bank offers you a 30-year loan with equal annual payments and an interest rate of 8% per year. The bank requires that your firm pay 20% of the purchase price as a down payment, so you can borrow only $80,000. What is the annual loan payment?

Solution
We start with the timeline (from the bank's perspective):

Using Eq. 4.12, we can solve for the loan payment, C, as follows:

$$C = \frac{P}{\frac{1}{r}\left(1 - \frac{1}{(1+r)^N}\right)} = \frac{80,000}{\frac{1}{0.08}\left(1 - \frac{1}{(1.08)^{30}}\right)}$$

$$= \$7106.19$$

Using the annuity spreadsheet:

	NPER	RATE	PV	PMT	FV	Excel Formula
Given	30	8.00%	−80,000		0	
Solve for PMT				7106		=PMT(0.08,30,−80000,0)

Your firm will need to pay $7106.19 each year to repay the loan.

INTERVIEW WITH
Lawrence E. Harris

A Chief Economist of the U.S. Securities and Exchange Commission from 2002 to 2004, Dr. Lawrence E. Harris was the primary advisor to the SEC on all economic issues. He participated extensively in the development of Sarbanes-Oxley (SOX) regulations. Currently Dr. Harris holds the Fred V. Keenan Chair in Finance at the University of Southern California's Marshall School of Business.

QUESTION: *Why is legislation such as Sarbanes-Oxley necessary to protect shareholders?*

ANSWER: Public investors will supply capital to entrepreneurs seeking to fund new business ventures only if they believe it will be used wisely. Regrettably, history has shown that management too often has violated that trust.

The interests of managers and shareholders often conflict. To solve this agency problem, shareholders rely upon information produced by corporate accounting systems. Sarbanes-Oxley mandated accounting and audit standards to improve the quality of corporate financial disclosure.

Opponents of governance regulation believe that shareholders can—and should—take care of themselves. Unfortunately, shareholders often cannot exercise the control necessary to solve agency problems that they could not have anticipated when the firm was first ....d. The firm's governance structure, which may ....

What many people perceive as costs of SOX are really expenditures that weak firms avoided. All well-managed firms must ensure the integrity of their accounting. SOX merely requires that people adopt *existing best practice*. Many companies were already fully compliant with SOX in most essential respects.

Critics claim that SOX made going public more difficult for small firms by increasing the cost of being a public firm. But a public firm must have secure control mechanisms to protect shareholders. SOX may decrease the number of firms that go public, but it will also decrease the losses suffered by public investors.

SOX established the Public Corporation Auditing Oversight Board to regulate auditors. Previous efforts at self-regulation failed because accountants would not discipline their peers. Following numerous notable failures, Congress stepped in and created the PCAOB.

QUESTION: *Is SOX a good law?*

ANSWER: Regulators are blamed for failing to regulate when crises occur, but they are often unaware of their regulations. This asymmetry often causes them to under-estimate the costs of their actions and ......

Applications That Reflect Real Practice

Corporate Finance features actual companies and leaders in the field.

- Real-company examples open each chapter

- Interviews with notable practitioners are featured in many chapters

- General Interest boxes highlight timely material from financial publications that shed light on business problems and real-company practices

TEACHING STUDENTS TO THINK FINANCE

With a consistency in presentation and an innovative set of learning aids, *Corporate Finance* simultaneously meets the needs of both future financial managers and non-financial managers. This textbook truly shows every student how to "think finance."

Simplified Presentation of Mathematics

One of the hardest parts of learning finance is mastering the jargon, math, and non-standardized notation. *Corporate Finance* systematically uses:

notation	
NPV	net present value
r_f	risk-free interest rate
PV	present value
r_s	discount rate for security *s*

- **Notation Boxes:** Each chapter begins with a Notation box that defines the variables and the acronyms used in the chapter and serves as 'legend' for students' reference.
- **Numbered and Labeled Equations:** The first time a full equation is given in notation form it is numbered. Key equations are titled and revisited in the summary and in end papers.

Future Value of an Annuity

$$FV(\text{annuity}) = PV \times (1 + r)^N$$
$$= \frac{C}{r}\left(1 - \frac{1}{(1 + r)^N}\right) \times (1 + r)^N$$
$$= C \times \frac{1}{r}((1 + r)^N - 1) \tag{4.8}$$

- **Spreadsheet Tables:** Select tables are available on the textbook Web site as Excel files, enabling students to change inputs and manipulate the underlying calculations.

Practice Finance to Learn Finance

Working problems is the proven way to cement and demonstrate an understanding of finance.

- **Concept Check questions** at the end of each section enable students to test their understanding and target areas in which they need further review.

- **End-of-chapter problems written personally by Jonathan Berk and Peter DeMarzo** offer instructors the opportunity to assign first-rate materials to students for homework and practice with the confidence that the problems are consistent with the chapter content. Both the problems and solutions, which were also written by the authors, have been class-tested and accuracy checked to ensure quality.

End-of-Chapter Materials Reinforce Learning

Testing understanding of central concepts is crucial to learning finance.

- **Chapter Summaries and Key Terms lists** are vital aids for studying and review.
- **Data Cases** present in-depth scenarios in a business setting with questions designed to guide students' analysis. Many questions involve the use of Internet resources.
- **Further Readings** direct the student reader to seminal studies and late-breaking research to encourage independent study.

Because practice with homework problems is crucial to learning finance, each copy of *Corporate Finance* is available with MyFinanceLab, a fully integrated homework and tutorial system.

MyFinanceLab revolutionizes homework and practice with a unique hint and partial credit system written and developed by Jonathan Berk and Peter DeMarzo.

Online Assessment Using End-of-Chapter Problems

The seamless integration among the textbook, assessment materials, and online resources sets a new standard in corporate finance education.

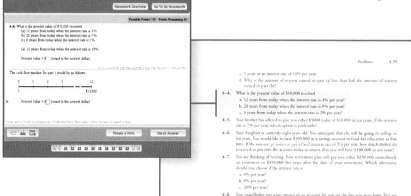

- **End-of-chapter problems** appear online. The values in the problems are algorithmically generated, giving students many opportunities for practice and mastery. Problems can be assigned by professors and completed online by students.

- **Helpful tutorial tools**, along with the same pedagogical aids from the text, support students as they study. Links to the eText direct students right to the material they most need to review.

Revolutionary Hint and Partial Credit System

MyFinanceLab provides 'hints' that coach students through difficult problems. Rather than scoring an entire problem right or wrong, the partial credit system rewards students for their efforts.

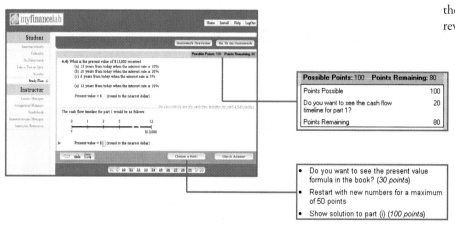

To learn more about MyFinanceLab, contact your local Addison-Wesley representative or go online to www.myfinancelab.com

HANDS-ON PRACTICE, HANDS-OFF GRADING.

Hands-on, Targeted Practice

Students can take pre-loaded Practice Tests for each chapter, and their test results will generate an individualized Study Plan. With the Study Plan, students learn to focus their energies on the topics they need to be successful in class, on exams, and, ultimately, in their future careers.

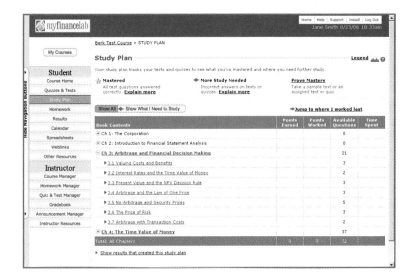

Powerful Instructor Tools

MyFinanceLab provides flexible tools that enable instructors to easily customize the online course materials to suit their needs.

- **Easy-to-Use Homework Manager.** Instructors can easily create and assign tests, quizzes, or graded homework assignments. In addition to pre-loaded MyFinanceLab questions, the Test Bank is also available so that instructors have ample material with which to create assignments.

- **Flexible Gradebook.** MyFinanceLab saves time by automatically grading students' work and tracking results in an online Gradebook.

- **Downloadable Classroom Resources.** Instructors also have access to online versions of each instructor supplement, including the Instructor's Manual, PowerPoint Lecture Notes, and Test Bank.

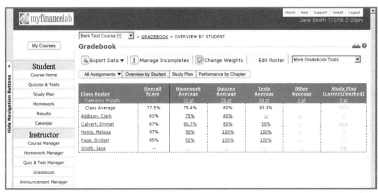

PART

I

Chapter 1
The Corporation

Chapter 2
Introduction to Financial Statement Analysis

Chapter 3
Arbitrage and Financial Decision Making

Introduction

The Law of One Price Connection. Why study Corporate Finance? No matter what your role in a corporation, an understanding of why and how financial decisions are made is essential. The focus of this book is how to make optimal corporate financial decisions. In this part of the book we lay the foundation for our study of corporate finance. We begin, in Chapter 1, by introducing the corporation and related business forms. We then examine the role of financial managers and outside investors in decision making for the firm. To make optimal decisions, a decision maker needs information. As a result, in Chapter 2 we review an important source of information for corporate decision making—the firm's accounting statements. Then, in Chapter 3 we introduce the most important idea in this book, the concept of *the absence of arbitrage* or *Law of One Price.* The Law of One Price states that we can use market prices to determine the value of an investment opportunity to the firm.

We will demonstrate that the Law of One Price is the one unifying principle that underlies all of financial economics and links all of the ideas throughout this book. We will return to this theme throughout our study of Corporate Finance.

1

The Corporation

The modern U.S. corporation was born in a courtroom in Washington, D.C., on February 2, 1819. On that day the U.S. Supreme Court established the legal precedent that the property of a corporation, like that of a person, is private and entitled to protection under the U.S. Constitution. Today, it is hard to entertain the possibility that a corporation's private property would not be protected by the Constitution. However, before the 1819 Supreme Court ruling, the owners of a corporation were exposed to the possibility that the state could take their business. This concern was real enough to stop most businesses from incorporating and, indeed, in 1816 that concern was realized: The state seized Dartmouth College.

Dartmouth College was incorporated in 1769 as a private educational institution governed by a self-perpetuating board of trustees. By 1816, this board of trustees was largely made up of Federalists (the political party most closely associated with George Washington), but the state government of New Hampshire was dominated by Republicans (the political party of Thomas Jefferson, later to become the modern Democratic Party). Unhappy with the political leanings of the college, the state legislature effectively took control of Dartmouth by passing legislation that established a governor-appointed board of overseers to run the school. The legislation had the effect of turning a private university under private control into a state university under state control. If such an act were constitutional, it implied that any state (or the federal government) could, at will, nationalize any corporation.

Dartmouth sued for its independence and the case made it to the Supreme Court in 1818. The chief justice at the time, John Marshall, delayed rendering a decision until 1819 to allow time to garner a nearly unanimous 5–1 ruling. He realized the importance of this decision and wanted the court to speak with a single voice. The court first ruled that a corporation was a "contract." Then, under Article 1 of the Constitution, the court noted that, "the state legislatures were forbidden to pass any law impairing the obligation of contracts" and struck down the New Hampshire law.[1] The precedent was clear: An owner of businesses could incorporate and thereby enjoy the protection of private property, as well as protection from seizure, both guaranteed by the U.S. Constitution. The modern business corporation was born.

The effect of this decision was dramatic. In 1800, the number of corporations that produced goods in the whole of the United States stood at eight. By 1830, more than 1400 corporations were involved in commerce and production in New England alone. In 1890, the number of U.S. chartered business corporations had risen to 50,000. Today the corporate structure is ubiquitous, not only in the United States (where they are responsible for 85% of business revenue), but all over the world.

This book is about how corporations make financial decisions. The purpose of this chapter is to introduce the corporation, as well as explain alternative business organizational forms. A key factor in the success of corporations is the ability to easily trade ownership shares, and so we will also explain the role of stock markets in facilitating trading among investors in a corporation and the implications that has for the ownership and control of corporations.

1.1 The Four Types of Firms

We begin by introducing the four major types of firms: sole proprietorships, partnerships, limited liability companies, and corporations. We explain each organizational form in turn, but our primary focus is on the most important form—the corporation. In addition to describing what a corporation is, we also provide an overview of why corporations are so successful.

Sole Proprietorships

A **sole proprietorship** is a business owned and run by one person. Sole proprietorships are usually very small with few, if any, employees. Although they do not account for much sales revenue in the economy, they are the most common type of firm in the world, as shown in Figure 1.1. Statistics indicate that 72% of businesses in the United States are sole proprietorships, although they generate only 5% of the revenue.[2] Contrast this with corporations which make up only 20% of firms but are responsible for 85% of U.S. revenue. Other organizational forms such as partnerships and limited liability companies make up the remaining 8% of firms and are responsible for 10% of U.S. revenue.

The advantage of a sole proprietorship is that it is straightforward to set up. Consequently, many new businesses use this organizational form. The principal limitation of a sole proprietorship is that there is no separation between the firm and the owner—the

---

1. The full text of John Marshall's decision can be found at http://www.constitution.org/dwebster/dartmouth_decision.htm.

2. This information, as well as other small business statistics, can be found at www.bizstats.com/businesses.htm. See their on-site disclosures page for a description of their methodology.

Types of U.S. Firms
There are four different types of firms in the United States. As (a) and (b) show, although the majority of U.S. firms are sole proprietorships, they generate only a small fraction of total revenue, in contrast to corporations.
Source: www.bizstats.com

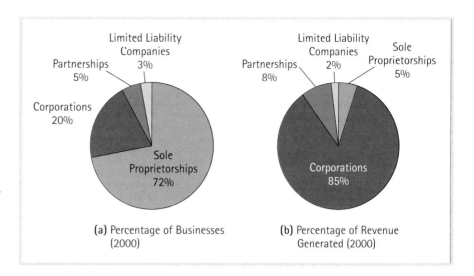

(a) Percentage of Businesses (2000)

(b) Percentage of Revenue Generated (2000)

firm can have only one owner. If there are other investors, they cannot hold an ownership stake in the firm. The owner has unlimited personal liability for any of the firm's debts. That is, if the firm defaults on any debt payment, the lender can (and will) require the owner to repay the loan from personal assets. If the owner cannot afford to repay the loan, he or she must declare personal bankruptcy. In addition, the life of a sole proprietorship is limited to the life of the owner. It is also difficult to transfer ownership of a sole proprietorship.

For most businesses, the disadvantages of a sole proprietorship outweigh the advantages. As soon as the firm reaches the point at which it can borrow without the owner agreeing to be personally liable, the owners typically convert the business into a form that limits the owner's liability.

Partnerships

A **partnership** is like a sole proprietorship but with more than one owner. In a partnership, *all* partners are liable for the firm's debt. That is, a lender can require *any* partner to repay all the firm's outstanding debts. The partnership ends on the death or withdrawal of any single partner. However, partners can avoid liquidation if the partnership agreement provides for alternatives such as a buyout of a deceased or withdrawn partner.

Some old and established businesses remain partnerships or sole proprietorships. Often these firms are the types of businesses in which the owners' personal reputations are the basis for the businesses. For example, law firms, groups of doctors, and accounting firms are often organized as partnerships. For such enterprises, the partners' personal liability increases the confidence of the firm's clients that the partners will continue to work to maintain their reputation.

A **limited partnership** is a partnership with two kinds of owners, general partners and limited partners. General partners have the same rights and privileges as partners in a (general) partnership—they are personally liable for the firm's debt obligations. Limited partners, however, have **limited liability**—that is, their liability is limited to their investment. Their private property cannot be seized to pay off the firm's outstanding debts. Furthermore, the death or withdrawal of a limited partner does not dissolve the

David Viniar

David Viniar is Chief Financial Officer and head of the Operations, Technology and Finance Division at Goldman Sachs—the last major investment bank to convert from a partnership to a corporation. He joined the firm in 1980 and worked in Investment Banking, Treasury, and Controllers. In his role as the firm's CFO he played a leading role in the firm's conversion to a corporation in 1999.

QUESTION: *What are the advantages of partnerships and corporations?*

ANSWER: We debated this question at length when we were deciding whether to go public or stay a private partnership in the mid-1990s. There were good arguments on both sides, and smart people were taking strong positions for and against.

Those in favor of going public argued we needed greater financial and strategic flexibility to achieve our aggressive growth and market leadership goals. As a public corporation, we would have a more stable equity base to support growth and disperse risk; increased access to large public debt markets; publicly traded securities with which to undertake acquisitions and reward and motivate our employees; and a simpler and more transparent structure with which to increase scale and global reach.

Those against going public argued our private partnership structure worked well and would enable us to achieve our financial and strategic goals. As a private partnership, we could generate enough capital internally and in the private placement markets to fund growth; take a longer-term view of returns on our investments with less focus on earnings volatility, which is not valued in public companies; and retain voting control and alignment of the partners and the firm.

A big perceived advantage of our private partnership was its sense of distinctiveness and mystique, which reinforced our culture of teamwork and excellence and helped differentiate us from our competitors. Many questioned whether the special qualities of our culture would survive if the firm went public.

QUESTION: *What was the driving force behind the conversion?*

ANSWER: We ultimately decided to go public for three main reasons: to secure permanent capital to grow; to be able to use publicly traded securities to finance strategic acquisitions; and to enhance the culture of ownership and gain compensation flexibility.

QUESTION: *Did the conversion achieve its goals?*

ANSWER: Yes. As a public company, we have a simpler, bigger and more permanent capital base, including enhanced long-term borrowing capacity in the public debt markets. We have drawn on substantial capital resources to serve clients, take advantage of new business opportunities, and better control our own destiny though changing economic and business conditions. We have been able to use stock to finance key acquisitions and support large strategic and financial investments. Given how the stakes in our industry changed, how the capital demands grew, going public when we did fortunately positioned us to compete effectively through the cycle.

Our distinctive culture of teamwork and excellence has thrived in public form, and our equity compensation programs turned out better than we could have hoped. Making everyone at Goldman Sachs an owner, rather than just 221 partners, energized all our employees. The growing size and scope of our business—not the change to public form—has presented the greatest challenges to the positive aspects of our culture.

QUESTION: *Goldman Sachs was the last of the major banks to convert. Why was that and in retrospect, should it have converted sooner?*

ANSWER: We were very successful as a private partnership, and it took time to reach a consensus among the partners that an IPO would permit us to achieve even greater success. We looked at going public many times in the years leading up to our conversion—and believe we chose the right moment for the IPO in view of our business, financial and strategic needs.

partnership, and a limited partner's interest is transferable. However, a limited partner has no management authority and cannot legally be involved in the managerial decision making for the business.

Limited Liability Companies

A **limited liability company** (LLC) is a limited partnership without a general partner. That is, all the owners have limited liability, but unlike limited partners, they can also run the business.

The LLC is a relatively new phenomenon in the United States. The first state to pass a statute allowing the creation of an LLC was Wyoming in 1977; the last was Hawaii in 1997. Internationally, companies with limited liability are much older and established. LLCs rose to prominence first in Germany over 100 years ago as a *Gesellschaft mit beschränkter Haftung* (GmbH) and then in other European and Latin American countries. An LLC is known in France as a Société à responsabilité limitée (SAR), and by similar names in Italy (SRL) and Spain (SL).

Corporations

The distinguishing feature of a **corporation** is that it is a legally defined, artificial being (a judicial person or legal entity), separate from its owners. As such, it has many of the legal powers that people have. It can enter into contracts, acquire assets, incur obligations, and, as we have already established, it enjoys protection under the U.S. Constitution against the seizure of its property. Because a corporation is a legal entity separate and distinct from its owners, it is solely responsible for its own obligations. Consequently, the owners of a corporation (or its employees, customers, etc.) are not liable for any obligations the corporation enters into. Similarly, the corporation is not liable for any personal obligations of its owners.

Formation of a Corporation. Corporations must be legally formed, which means that the state in which it is incorporated must formally give its consent to the incorporation by chartering it. Setting up a corporation is therefore considerably more costly than setting up a sole proprietorship. The state of Delaware has a particularly attractive legal environment for corporations, so many corporations choose to incorporate there. For jurisdictional purposes, a corporation is a citizen of the state in which it is incorporated. Most firms hire lawyers to create a corporate charter that includes formal articles of incorporation and a set of bylaws. The corporate charter specifies the initial rules that govern how the corporation is run.

Ownership of a Corporation. There is no limit on the number of owners a corporation can have. Because most corporations have many owners, each owner owns only a fraction of the corporation. The entire ownership stake of a corporation is divided into shares known as **stock**. The collection of all the outstanding shares of a corporation is known as the **equity** of the corporation. An owner of a share of stock in the corporation is known as a **shareholder**, **stockholder**, or **equity holder** and is entitled to **dividend payments**, that is, payments made at the discretion of the corporation to its equity holders. Shareholders usually receive a share of the dividend payments that is proportional to the amount of stock they own. For example, a shareholder who owns 25% of the firm's shares will be entitled to 25% of the total dividend payment.

A unique feature of a corporation is that there is no limitation on who can own its stock. That is, an owner of a corporation need not have any special expertise or qualification. This feature allows free trade in the shares of the corporation and provides one of the most important advantages of organizing a firm as a corporation rather than as sole proprietorship, partnership, or LLC. Corporations can raise substantial amounts of capital because they can sell ownership shares to anonymous outside investors.

The availability of outside funding has enabled corporations to dominate the economy (see Figure 1.1b). Let's take one of the world's largest firms, Microsoft Corporation, as an example. Microsoft reported annual revenue of $39.8 billion over the 12 months from July 2004 through June 2005. The total value of the company (the wealth in the company the owners collectively owned) as of September 2005 was $284.7 billion. It employed 61,000 people. Let's put these numbers into perspective. The $39.8 billion in gross domestic product (GDP) in 2004 would rank Microsoft (with Kazakhstan) as the 59th richest *country* (out of more than 200).[3] Kazakhstan has almost 15 million people, about 250 times as many people as employees at Microsoft. Indeed, if the number of employees were used as the "population" of Microsoft, Microsoft would rank with the Marshall Islands as the tenth least populous country on earth!

Tax Implications for Corporate Entities

An important difference between the types of organizational forms is the way they are taxed. Because a corporation is a separate legal entity, a corporation's profits are subject to taxation separate from its owners' tax obligations. In effect, shareholders of a corporation pay taxes twice. First, the corporation pays tax on its profits, and then when the remaining profits are distributed to the shareholders, the shareholders pay their own personal income tax on this income. This system is sometimes referred to as double taxation.

Taxation of Corporate Earnings

Problem

You are a shareholder in a corporation. The corporation earns $5 per share before taxes. After it has paid taxes, it will distribute the rest of its earnings to you as a dividend. The dividend is income to you, so you will then pay taxes on these earnings. The corporate tax rate is 40% and your tax rate on dividend income is 15%. How much of the earnings remains after all taxes are paid?

Solution

First, the corporation pays taxes. It earned $5 per share, but must pay $0.40 \times \$5 = \$2$ to the government in corporate taxes. That leaves $3 to distribute. However, you must pay $0.15 \times \$3 = 45$ cents in income taxes on this amount, leaving $\$3 - \$0.45 = \$2.55$ per share after all taxes are paid. As a shareholder you only end up with $2.55 of the original $5 in earnings; the remaining $\$2 + \$0.45 = \$2.45$ is paid as taxes. Thus, your total effective tax rate is $2.45 / 5 = 49\%$.

---

3. World Development Indicators database, July 15, 2005. For quick reference tables on GDP, go to http://www.worldbank.org/data/quickreference.html.

In most countries, there is some relief from double taxation. Thirty countries make up the Organization for Economic Co-operation and Development (OECD), and of these countries, only Ireland and Switzerland offer no relief from double taxation. The United States offers some relief by having a lower tax rate on dividend income than on other sources of income. As of 2005, dividend income is taxed at 15%, which, for most investors, is significantly below their personal income tax rate. A few countries, including Australia, Finland, Mexico, New Zealand, and Norway, offer complete relief by effectively not taxing dividend income.

The corporate organizational structure is the only organizational structure subject to double taxation. In addition, the U.S. Internal Revenue Code allows an exemption from double taxation for certain corporations. These corporations are called **"S" corporations** because they elect subchapter S tax treatment. Under these tax regulations, the firm's profits (and losses) are not subject to corporate taxes, but instead are allocated directly to shareholders based on their ownership share. The shareholders must include these profits as income on their individual tax returns (even if no money is distributed to them). However, after the shareholders have paid income taxes on these profits, no further tax is due.

EXAMPLE 1.2

Taxation of S Corporation Earnings

Problem

Rework Example 1.1 assuming the corporation in that example has elected subchapter S treatment and your tax rate on non-dividend income is 30%.

Solution

In this case, the corporation pays no taxes. It earned $5 per share. Whether or not the corporation chooses to distribute or retain this cash, you must pay $0.30 \times \$5 = \$1.50$ in income taxes, which is substantially lower than the $2.45 you paid in Example 1.1.

The government places strict limitations on the qualifications for subchapter S tax treatment. In particular, the shareholders of such corporations must be individuals who are U.S. citizens or residents, and there can be no more than 75 of them. Because most corporations have no restrictions on who owns their shares or the number of shareholders, they cannot qualify for subchapter S treatment. Thus most corporations are **"C" corporations**, which are corporations subject to corporate taxes.

CONCEPT CHECK

1. What are the advantages and disadvantages of organizing a business as a corporation?

2. What is a limited liability company (LLC)? How does it differ from a limited partnership?

1.2 Ownership Versus Control of Corporations

Unlike the owner of a sole proprietorship, which has direct control of the firm, it is often not feasible for the owners of a corporation to have direct control of the firm because there are many owners of a corporation, each of whom can freely trade their stock. That is, in a corporation, direct control and ownership are often separate. Rather than the owners the *board of directors* and *chief executive officer* possess direct control of the corporation. In this section, we explain how the responsibilities for the corporation are divided between these two entities.

The Corporate Management Team

The shareholders of a corporation exercise their control by electing a **board of directors**, a group of people who have the ultimate decision-making authority in the corporation. In most corporations, each share of stock gives a shareholder one vote in the election of the board of directors, so investors with more shares have more influence. When one or two shareholders own a very large proportion of the outstanding stock, these shareholders might either themselves be on the board of directors, or they may have the right to appoint a number of directors.

The board of directors makes rules on how the corporation should be run (including how the top managers in the corporation are compensated), sets policy, and monitors the performance of the company. The board of directors delegates most decisions that involve day-to-day running of the corporation to its management, which is headed by the **chief executive officer (or CEO)**. This person is charged with running the corporation by instituting the rules and policies set by the board of directors. The size of the rest of the management team varies from corporation to corporation. The separation of powers within corporations is not always distinct. In fact, it is not uncommon for the CEO also to be the chairman of the board of directors.

Ownership and Control of Corporations

In theory, the goal of a firm should be determined by the firm's owners. A sole proprietorship has a single owner who runs the firm, so the goals of a sole proprietorship are the same as the owner's goals. But in organizational forms with multiple owners, the goal of the firm is not as clear.

Many corporations have thousands of owners (shareholders). Each owner is likely to have different interests and priorities. Whose interests and priorities determine the goals of the firm? Later in the book, we examine this question in more detail. However, you might be surprised to learn that the interests of shareholders are aligned for many, if not most, important decisions. For example, if the decision is whether to develop a new product that will be a profitable investment for the corporation, all shareholders will very likely agree that developing this product is a good idea.

Even when all the owners of a corporation agree on the goals of the corporation, these goals must be implemented. In a simple organizational form like a sole proprietorship, the owner, who runs the firm, can ensure that the firm's goals match his own. But a corporation is run by a management team, separate from its owners. How can the owners of a corporation ensure that the management team will implement their goals?

Principal-Agent Problem.   Many people claim that because of the separation of ownership and control in a corporation, managers have little incentive to work in the interests of the shareholders when this means working against their own self-interest. Economists call this a **principal-agent problem**. The most common way the principal-agent problem is addressed in practice is by minimizing the number of decisions managers make that require putting their self-interest against the interests of the shareholders. For example, managers' compensation contracts are designed to ensure that most decisions in the shareholders' interest are also in the managers' interests; shareholders often tie the compensation of top managers to the corporation's profits or perhaps to its stock price. There is, however, a limitation to this strategy. By tying compensation too closely to performance, the shareholders might be asking managers to take on more risk than they are comfortable taking and so the managers may not make decisions that the shareholders want them to, or it might be hard to find talented managers willing to accept the job.

The CEO's Performance.   Another way shareholders can encourage managers to work in the interests of shareholders is to discipline them if they don't. If shareholders are unhappy with a CEO's performance, they could, in principle, pressure the board to oust the CEO. However, directors and top executives are very rarely replaced through a grass-roots shareholder uprising. Instead, dissatisfied investors often choose to sell their shares. Of course, somebody must be willing to buy the shares from the dissatisfied shareholders. If enough shareholders are dissatisfied, the only way to entice investors to buy (or hold) the shares is to offer them a low price. Similarly, investors who see a well-managed corporation will want to purchase shares, which drives the stock price up. Thus, the stock price of the corporation is a barometer for corporate leaders that continuously gives them feedback on their shareholders' opinion of their performance.

When the stock performs poorly, the board of directors might react by replacing the CEO. In some corporations, however, the senior executives are entrenched because boards of directors do not have the will to replace them. Often the reluctance to fire results because the board is comprised of people who are close friends of the CEO and lack objectivity. In corporations in which the CEO is entrenched and doing a poor job, the expectation of continued poor performance will cause the stock price to be low. Low stock prices create a profit opportunity. In a **hostile takeover**, an individual or organization— sometimes known as a corporate raider—can purchase a large fraction of the stock and in doing so get enough votes to replace the board of directors and the CEO. With a new superior management team, the stock is a much more attractive investment, which would likely result in a price rise and a profit for the corporate raider and the other shareholders. Although the words "hostile" and "raider" have negative connotations, corporate raiders themselves provide an important service to shareholders. The mere threat of being removed as a result of a hostile takeover is often enough to discipline bad managers and motivate boards of directors to make difficult decisions. Consequently, the fact that a corporation's shares can be publicly traded creates a "market for corporate control" that encourages managers and boards of directors to act in the interests of their shareholders.

Corporate Bankruptcy.   Because a corporation is a separate legal entity, when it fails to repay its debts, the people who lent to the firm, the debt holders, are entitled to seize the assets of the corporation in compensation for the default. To prevent such a seizure, the firm may attempt to renegotiate with the debt holders, or file for bankruptcy protection in a federal court. We describe the details of the bankruptcy process and its implications for corporate decisions in much more detail in Part V of the text, but because of its importance in corporate decision making, it is useful to understand some of the main aspects of default and corporate bankruptcy even at this early stage.

In bankruptcy, management is given the opportunity to reorganize the firm and renegotiate with debt holders. If this process fails, control of the corporation generally passes to the debt holders. In most cases, the original equity holders are left with little or no stake in the firm. Thus, when a firm fails to repay its debts, the end result is often a change in ownership of the firm, with control passing from equity holders to debt holders. Importantly, bankruptcy need not result in a **liquidation** of the firm, which involves shutting down the business and selling off its assets. Even if control of the firm passes to the debt holders, it is in the debt holders' interest to run the firm in the most profitable way

Shareholder Activism and Voting Rights

In reaction to poor stock market performance and several accounting scandals, the number of *shareholder initiatives* (when shareholders request that a specific firm policy or decision be put to a direct vote of all shareholders) has increased dramatically in recent years. According to the Investor Responsibility Research Center, the number of shareholder proposals increased from about 800 during 2002 to over 1100 during 2004. Shareholder initiatives have covered a range of topics, including shareholder voting rights, takeovers and anti-takeover provisions, election of members of the board of directors, and changes in the time or location of shareholder meetings.

One of the recent trends in shareholder activism is to withhold voting support for nominees to the board of directors. In March 2004, shareholders withheld support for Michael Eisner (the Disney CEO) as chairman of the board. As a result, he lost the Disney chairmanship but retained his position as CEO. The California Public Employees' Retirement System (Calpers), the world's largest pension fund, has withheld votes for at least one of the directors in 90% of the 2700 companies in which it invests.

Source: Adapted from John Goff, "Who's the Boss?" *CFO Magazine,* September 1, 2004, pp. 56–66.

possible. Doing so often means keeping the business operating. For example, in 1990, Federated Department Stores declared bankruptcy. One of its best known assets at the time was Bloomingdale's, a nationally known department store. Because Bloomingdale's was a profitable business, neither equity holders nor debt holders had any desire to shut it down, and it continued to operate in bankruptcy. In 1992, when Federated Department Stores was reorganized and emerged from bankruptcy, Federated's original equity holders had lost their stake in Bloomingdale's, but this flagship chain continued to perform well for its new owners, and its value as a business was not adversely affected by the bankruptcy.

Thus, a useful way to understand corporations is to think of there being two sets of investors with claims to its cash flows—debt holders and equity holders. As long as the corporation can satisfy the claims of the debt holders, ownership remains in the hands of the equity holders. If the corporation fails to satisfy debt holders' claims, debt holders may take control of the firm. Thus a corporate bankruptcy is best thought of as a *change in ownership* of the corporation, and not necessarily as a failure of the underlying business.

CONCEPT CHECK

1. What is a principal-agent problem that may exist in a corporation?

2. How does the board of directors control a corporation?

3. How may a corporate bankruptcy filing affect the ownership of a corporation?

1.3 The Stock Market

From an outside investors' point of view, an important feature of an investment in the equity of a corporation is its *liquidity*. An investment is said to be **liquid** if it is possible to easily sell it for close to the price you can contemporaneously buy it for. The shares of many corporations are liquid because they trade on organized markets, called **stock markets (or stock exchanges)**. These kinds of corporations are known as **public companies**.

An investor in a public company can easily and quickly turn his investment into cash by simply selling his shares on one of these markets. However, not all corporations are public companies. Some corporations known as **private companies** do not allow trading or limit trading to privately brokered transactions among investors.

The Largest Stock Markets

The best known U.S. stock market and the largest stock market in the world is the New York Stock Exchange (NYSE). Billions of dollars of stock are exchanged every day on the NYSE. Other U.S. stock markets include the American Stock Exchange (AMEX), Nasdaq (which stands for the National Association of Security Dealers Automated Quotation), and regional exchanges such as the Midwest Stock Exchange. Most other countries have at least one stock market. Outside the United States, the biggest stock markets are the London Stock Exchange (LSE) and the Tokyo Stock Exchange (TSE).

Figure 1.2 ranks the world's largest stock markets by two of the most common measures: the total value of all domestic corporations listed on the exchange and the total annual volume of shares traded on the exchange.

NYSE

The NYSE is a physical place. On the floor of the NYSE, **market makers** (known on the NYSE as **specialists**) match buyers and sellers. They post two prices for every stock they make a market in: the price they stand willing to buy the stock at (the **bid price**) and a price they stand willing to sell the stock for (the **ask price**). If a customer comes to them wanting to make a trade at these prices, they will honor the price (up to a limited number of shares) and make the trade even if they do not have another customer willing to take the other side of the trade. In this way, they ensure that the market is liquid because customers can always be assured they can trade at the posted prices. The exchange has rules that attempt to ensure that bid and ask prices do not get too far apart and that large price changes take place through a series of small changes, rather than one big jump.

Ask prices exceed bid prices. This difference is called the **bid-ask spread**. Because customers always buy at the ask (the higher price) and sell at the bid (the lower price), the bid-ask spread is a **transaction cost** investors have to pay in order to trade. Because specialists in a physical market like the NYSE take the other side of the trade from their customers, this cost accrues to them as a profit. It is the compensation they demand for providing a liquid market by standing ready to honor any quoted price. Investors also pay other forms of transactions costs like commissions.

Nasdaq

In today's economy, a stock market does not need to have a physical location. Stock transactions can be made (perhaps more efficiently) over the phone or by computer network. Consequently, some stock markets are a collection of dealers or market makers connected by computer network and telephone. The most famous example of such a market is Nasdaq. An important difference between the NYSE and Nasdaq is that on the NYSE, each stock has only one market maker. On Nasdaq, stocks can and do have multiple market makers who compete with each other. Each market maker must post bid and ask prices in the Nasdaq network where they can be viewed by all participants. The Nasdaq system posts the best prices first and fills orders accordingly. This process guarantees investors the best possible price at the moment, whether they are buying or selling.

FIGURE 1.2

Worldwide Stock Markets Ranked by Two Common Measures

The 10 biggest stock markets in the world ranked (a) by total value of all domestic corporations listed on the exchange at year-end 2004 and (b) by total volume of shares traded on exchange in 2004.

Source: www.world-exchanges.org

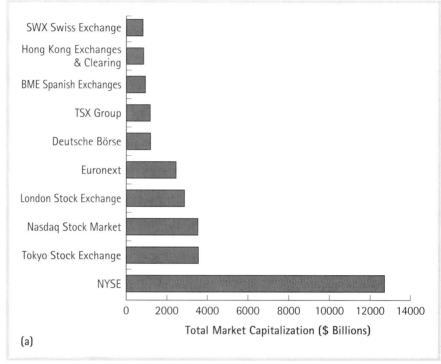

(a)

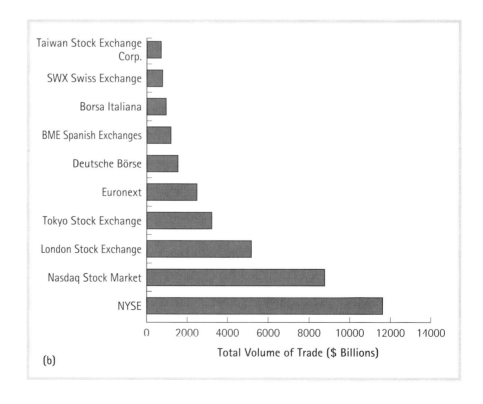

(b)

CONCEPT CHECK   **1.** What is the New York Stock Exchange (NYSE)?

2. What advantage does a stock market provide to corporate investors?

Summary

1. There are four types of firms in the United States: sole proprietorships, partnerships, limited liability companies, and corporations.

2. Firms with unlimited personal liability include sole proprietorships and partnerships.

3. Firms with limited liability include limited partnerships, limited liability companies, and corporations.

4. A corporation is a legally defined artificial being (a judicial person or legal entity) that has many of the legal powers people have. It can enter into contracts, acquire assets, incur obligations, and, as we have already established, it enjoys the protection under the U.S. Constitution against the seizure of its property.

5. The shareholders in a C corporation effectively must pay tax twice. The corporation pays tax once and then investors must pay personal tax on any funds that are distributed.

6. S corporations are exempt from the corporate income tax.

7. The ownership of a corporation is divided into shares of stock collectively known as equity. Investors in these shares are called shareholders, stockholders, or equity holders.

8. The ownership and control of a corporation are separated. Shareholders exercise their control indirectly through the board of directors.

9. Corporate bankruptcy can be thought of as a change in ownership and control of the corporation. The equity holders give up their ownership and control to the debt holders.

10. The shares of public corporations are traded on stock markets. The shares of private corporations do not trade on a stock market.

Key Terms

ask price *p. 13*
bid price *p. 13*
bid-ask spread *p. 13*
board of directors *p. 10*
"C" corporations *p. 9*
chief executive officer (or CEO) *p. 10*
corporation *p. 7*
dividend payments *p. 7*
equity *p. 7*
equity holder *p. 7*
hostile takeover *p. 11*
limited liability *p. 5*
limited liability company *p. 7*
limited partnership *p. 5*
liquid *p. 12*

liquidation *p. 11*
market makers *p. 13*
partnership *p. 5*
principal-agent problem *p. 10*
private companies *p. 13*
public companies *p. 12*
"S" corporations *p. 9*
shareholder *p. 7*
sole proprietorship *p. 4*
specialists *p. 13*
stock *p. 7*
stockholder *p. 7*
stock markets (or stock exchanges) *p. 12*
transaction cost *p. 13*

Further Reading

Readers interested in John Marshall's decision in the Dartmouth College case can find a more detailed description of the decision in J. E. Smith, *John Marshall: Definer of a Nation* (New York: Henry Holt, 1996), pp. 433–38.

An informative discussion that describes the objective of a corporation can be found in M. Jensen, "Value Maximization, Stakeholder Theory, and the Corporate Objective Function," *Journal of Applied Corporate Finance* (Fall 2001): 8–21.

Readers interested in what determines the goals of corporate managers and how they differ from shareholder's goals can either wait until we discuss these issues in more detail or can read M. C. Jensen and W. Meckling, "Theory of the Firm: Managerial Behavior, Agency Costs and Ownership Structure," *Journal of Financial Economics* 3(4), (1976): 305–60; J. E. Core, W. R. Guay, and D. F. Larker, "Executive Equity Compensation and Incentives: A Survey," *Federal Reserve Bank of New York Economic Policy Review* 9 (April 2003): 27–50.

The following papers explain corporate governance and ownership around the world: F. Barca and M. Becht, *The Control of Corporate Europe* (Oxford University Press, 2001); D. K. Denis and J. S. McConnel, "International Corporate Governance," *Journal of Financial Quantitative Analysis* 38 (March 2003); R. La Porta, F. Lopez-De-Silanes, and A. Shleifer, "Corporate Ownership Around the World," *Journal of Finance* 54(2) (1999): 471–517. Readers interested in a more detailed discussion of how taxes affect incorporation can consult J. K. Mackie-Mason and R. H. Gordon, "How Much Do Taxes Discourage Incorporation?" *Journal of Finance* 52(2) (1997): 477–505.

Problems

A blue box (■) indicates problems available in MyFinanceLab.

The Four Types of Firms

1. What is the most important difference between a corporation and *all* other organization forms?

2. What does the phrase *limited liability* mean in a corporate context?

3. Which organizational forms give their owners limited liability?

4. What are the main advantages and disadvantages of organizing a firm as a corporation?

5. Explain the difference between an S and a C corporation.

6. You are a shareholder in a C corporation. The corporation earns $2 per share before taxes. Once it has paid taxes it will distribute the rest of its earnings to you as a dividend. The corporate tax rate is 40% and the personal tax rate on (both dividend and non-dividend) income is 30%. How much is left for you after all taxes are paid?

7. Repeat Problem 6 assuming the corporation is an S corporation.

Ownership Versus Control of Corporations

8. Corporate managers work for the owners of the corporation. Consequently, they should make decisions that are in the interests of the owners, rather than their own. What strategies are available to shareholders to help ensure that managers are motivated to act this way?

9. What is the difference between a public and private corporation?

10. Explain why the bid-ask spread is a transaction cost.

11. The following quote on Yahoo! stock appeared on August 30, 2004, on Yahoo! Finance:

YAHOO! INC (NasdaqNM: YHOO) Quote data by Reuters				Edit
Last Trade:	**28.69**	Day's Range:	28.35 − 29.07	YHOO 30-Aug @ 11:45am (C)Yahoo!
Trade Time:	11:42AM ET	52wk Range:	16.56 − 36.51	
Change:	⬇ 0.61 (2.08%)	Volume:	7,374,448	
Prev Close:	29.30	Avg Vol (3m)	20,232,318	
Open:	29.04	Market Cap:	39.03B	1d 5d 3m 6m 1y 2y 5y max
Bid:	28.69 × 1000	P/E (ttm):	112.51	Annual Report for YHOO
Ask:	28.70 × 5800	EPS (ttm):	0.255	
1y Target Est:	36.53	Div & Yield·	N/A (N/A)	

If you wanted to buy Yahoo!, what price would you pay? How much would you receive if you wanted to sell Yahoo!?

Introduction to Financial Statement Analysis

As we discussed in Chapter 1, one of the great advantages of the corporate organizational form is that it places no restriction on who can own shares in the corporation. Anyone with money to invest is a potential investor. As a result, corporations are often widely held, with investors ranging from individuals who hold 100 shares to mutual funds and institutional investors who own millions of shares. For example, in 2004, International Business Machines Corporation (IBM) had over 1.6 billion shares outstanding held by over 670,000 stockholders. Although the corporate organizational structure greatly facilitates the firm's access to investment capital, it also means that stock ownership is most investors' sole tie to the company. How, then, do investors learn enough about a company to know whether or not they should invest in it? How can financial managers assess the success of their own firm and compare it to competitors? One way firms evaluate their performance and communicate this information to investors is through their *financial statements*.

Firms issue financial statements regularly to communicate financial information to the investment community. A detailed description of the preparation and analysis of these statements is sufficiently complicated that to do it justice would require an entire book. Here we briefly review the subject, emphasizing only the material that investors and corporate financial managers need in order to make the corporate-finance decisions we discuss in the text.

We review the four main types of financial statements, present examples of these statements for a firm, and discuss where an investor or manager might find various types of information about the company. We also discuss some of the financial ratios that investors and analysts use to assess a firm's performance and value. We close the chapter with a look at highly publicized financial reporting abuses at Enron and WorldCom.

2.1   The Disclosure of Financial Information

Financial statements are firm-issued accounting reports with past performance information that a firm issues periodically (usually quarterly and annually). U.S. public companies are required to file their financial statements with the U.S. Securities and Exchange Commission (SEC) on a quarterly basis on form **10-Q** and annually on form **10-K**. They must also send an **annual report** with their financial statements to their shareholders each year. Private companies often also prepare financial statements, but they usually do not have to disclose these reports to the public. Financial statements are important tools through which investors, financial analysts, and other interested outside parties (such as creditors) obtain information about a corporation. They are also useful for managers within the firm as a source of information for corporate financial decisions. In this section, we examine the guidelines for preparing financial statements and the types of financial statements.

Preparation of Financial Statements

Reports about a company's performance must be understandable and accurate. **Generally Accepted Accounting Principles (GAAP)** provide a common set of rules and a standard format for public companies to use when they prepare their reports. This standardization also makes it easier to compare the financial results of different firms.

International Financial Reporting Standards

Because Generally Accepted Accounting Principles (GAAP) differ among countries, companies face tremendous accounting complexities when they operate internationally. Investors also face difficulty interpreting financial statements of foreign companies, which is often considered a major barrier to international capital mobility. As companies and capital markets become more global, however, interest in harmonization of accounting standards across countries has increased.

The most important harmonization project began in 1973 when representatives of ten countries (including the United States) established the International Accounting Standards Committee. This effort led to the creation of the International Accounting Standards Board (IASB) in 2001, with headquarters in London. Now the IASB has issued a set of International Financial Reporting Standards (IFRS).

The IFRS are taking root throughout the world. The European Union (EU) approved an accounting regulation in 2002 requiring all publicly traded EU companies to follow IFRS in their consolidated financial statements starting in 2005. Many other countries have adopted IFRS for all listed companies, including Australia and several countries in Latin America and Africa. Indeed all

major stock exchanges around the world accept IFRS except the United States and Japan, which maintain their local GAAP.

The main conceptual difference between U.S. GAAP and IFRS is that U.S. GAAP are based primarily on accounting rules with specific guidance in applying them, whereas IFRS are based more on principles requiring professional judgment by accountants, and specific guidance in application is limited. In implementation, the main difference is how assets and liabilities are valued. Whereas U.S. GAAP is based primarily on historical cost accounting, IFRS places more emphasis on "fair value" of assets and liabilities, or estimates of market values.

Effort to achieve convergence between U.S. GAAP and IFRS was spurred by the Sarbanes-Oxley Act of 2002 in the United States. It included a provision that U.S. accounting standards move toward international convergence on high-quality accounting standards. Currently SEC regulations require companies using IFRS to reconcile to U.S. GAAP in order to list in U.S. financial markets, but in 2005, the U.S. SEC and the EU reached an agreement to eliminate this requirement, possibly by 2007, but no later than 2009.

Investors also need some assurance that the financial statements are prepared accurately. Corporations are required to hire a neutral third party, known as an **auditor**, to check the annual financial statements, ensure they are prepared according to GAAP, and verify that the information is reliable.

Types of Financial Statements

Every public company is required to produce four financial statements: the *balance sheet,* the *income statement,* the *statement of cash flows,* and the *statement of stockholders' equity.* These financial statements provide investors and creditors with an overview of the firm's financial performance. In the sections that follow, we take close look at the content of these financial statements.

CONCEPT CHECK   1. What are the four financial statements that all public companies must produce?

2. What is the role of an auditor?

2.2   The Balance Sheet

The **balance sheet** lists the firm's *assets* and *liabilities,* providing a snapshot of the firm's financial position at a given point in time. Table 2.1 shows the balance sheet for a fictitious company, Global Conglomerate Corporation. Notice that the balance sheet is divided into two parts ("sides"): the assets on the left side and the liabilities on the right. The **assets** list the cash, inventory, property, plant and equipment, and other investments the company has made; the **liabilities** show the firm's obligations to creditors. Also shown with liabilities on the right side of the balance sheet is the *stockholders' equity.* **Stockholders' equity**, the difference between the firm's assets and liabilities, is an accounting measure of the firm's net worth.

The assets on the left side show how the firm uses its capital (its investments), and the right side summarizes the sources of capital, or how a firm raises the money it needs. Because of the way stockholder's equity is calculated, the left and right sides must balance:

The Balance Sheet Identity

$$\text{Assets} = \text{Liabilities} + \text{Stockholders' Equity} \qquad (2.1)$$

In Table 2.1, total assets for 2005 ($177.7 million) are equal to total liabilities ($155.5 million) plus stockholders' equity ($22.2 million).

We now examine the assets, liabilities, and stockholders' equity in more detail. Finally, we evaluate the firm's financial standing by analyzing the information contained in the balance sheet.

Assets

In Table 2.1, Global's assets are divided into current and long-term assets. We discuss each in turn.

Current Assets.   **Current assets** are either cash or assets that could be converted into cash within one year. This category includes:

1. Cash and other **marketable securities**, which are short-term, low-risk investments that can be easily sold and converted to cash (such as money market investments like government debt that matures within a year);

TABLE 2.1	Global Conglomerate Corporation Balance Sheet for 2005 and 2004

GLOBAL CONGLOMERATE CORPORATION
Consolidated Balance Sheet
Year ended December 31 (in $ millions)

Assets	2005	2004	Liabilities and Stockholders' Equity	2005	2004
Current Assets			Current Liabilities		
Cash	21.2	19.5	Accounts payable	29.2	24.5
Accounts receivable	18.5	13.2	Notes payable / short-term debt	3.5	3.2
Inventories	15.3	14.3	Current maturities of long-term debt	13.3	12.3
Other current assets	2.0	1.0	Other current liabilities	2.0	4.0
Total current assets	57.0	48.0	Total current liabilities	48.0	44.0
Long-Term Assets			Long-Term Liabilities		
Land	22.2	20.7	Long-term debt	99.9	56.3
Buildings	36.5	30.5	Capital lease obligations	—	—
Equipment	39.7	33.2	Total debt	99.9	56.3
Less accumulated depreciation	(18.7)	(17.5)	Deferred taxes	7.6	7.4
Net property, plant, and equipment	79.7	66.9	Other long-term liabilities	—	—
Goodwill	20.0	—	Total long-term liabilities	107.5	63.7
Other long-term assets	21.0	14.0	**Total Liabilities**	**155.5**	**107.7**
Total long-term assets	120.7	80.9	**Stockholders' Equity**	**22.2**	**21.2**
Total Assets	**177.7**	**128.9**	**Total Liabilities and Stockholders' Equity**	**177.7**	**128.9**

2. **Accounts receivable**, which are amounts owed to the firm by customers who have purchased goods or services on credit;

3. **Inventories**, which are composed of raw materials as well as work-in-progress and finished goods;

4. Other current assets, which is a catch-all category that includes items such as prepaid expenses (expenses, such as rent or insurance, that have been paid in advance).

Long-Term Assets.   The first category of long-term assets is net property, plant, and equipment. These include assets such as real estate or machinery that produce tangible benefits for more than one year. If Global spends $2 million on new equipment, this $2 million will be included with property, plant, and equipment on the balance sheet. Because equipment tends to wear out or become obsolete over time, Global will reduce the value recorded for this equipment each year by deducting an amount called **depreciation**. The firm reduces the value of fixed assets (other than land) over time according to a depreciation schedule that depends on the asset's life span. Depreciation is not an actual cash expense that the firm pays; it is a way of recognizing that buildings and equipment wear out and thus become less valuable the older they get. The **book value** of an asset is equal to its acquisition cost less accumulated depreciation. Net property, plant, and equipment shows the total book value of these assets.

When a firm acquires another company, it will acquire a set of assets that will then be listed on its balance sheet. In many cases, however, the firm may pay more for the company than the total book value of the assets it acquires. In this case, the difference between the price paid for the company and the book value assigned to its assets is recorded as **goodwill**. For example, Global paid $25 million in 2005 for a firm whose assets had a book value of $5 million. Thus, $20 million is recorded as goodwill in Table 2.1. Goodwill captures the value of other "intangibles" that the firm acquired through the acquisition. If the value of these intangible assets declines over time, the amount of goodwill listed on the balance sheet will be reduced by an **amortization** charge that captures the change in value of the acquired assets. Like depreciation, amortization is not an actual cash expense.

Other long-term assets can include such items as property not used in business operations, start-up costs in connection with a new business, trademarks and patents, and property held for sale. The sum of all the firms' assets is the total assets at the bottom of the left side of the balance sheet in Table 2.1.

Liabilities

We now examine the liabilities shown on the right side of the balance sheet, which are divided into *current* and *long-term liabilities.*

Current Liabilities.   Liabilities that will be satisfied within one year are known as **current liabilities**. They include:

1. **Accounts payable**, the amounts owed to suppliers for products or services purchased with credit;

2. Notes payable, short-term debt, and current maturities of long-term debt, which are all repayments of debt that will occur within the next year;

3. Items such as salary or taxes that are owed but have not yet been paid, and deferred or unearned revenue, which is revenue that has been received for products that have not yet been delivered.

The difference between current assets and current liabilities is the firm's **net working capital**, the capital available in the short term to run the business. For example, in 2005, Global's net working capital totaled $9.0 million ($57.0 million in current assets − $48.0 million in current liabilities). Firms with low (or negative) net working capital may face a shortage of funds.

Long-term Liabilities.   Long-term liabilities are liabilities that extend beyond one year. We describe the main types below.

1. **Long-term debt** is any loan or debt obligation with a maturity of more than a year. When a firm needs to raise funds to purchase an asset or make an investment, it may borrow those funds through a long-term loan.

2. **Capital leases** are long-term lease contracts that obligate the firm to make regular lease payments in exchange for use of an asset.[1] They allow a firm to gain use of an asset by leasing it from the asset's owner. For example, a firm may lease a building to serve as its corporate headquarters.

---

1. See Chapter 25 for a precise definition of a capital lease.

3. **Deferred taxes** are taxes that are owed but have not yet been paid. Firms generally keep two sets of financial statements: one for financial reporting and one for tax purposes. Occasionally, the rules for the two types of statements differ. Deferred tax liabilities generally arise when the firm's financial income exceeds its income for tax purposes. Because deferred taxes will eventually be paid, they appear as a liability on the balance sheet.[2]

Stockholders' Equity

The sum of the current liabilities and long-term liabilities is total liabilities. The difference between the firm's assets and liabilities is the stockholders' equity; it is also called the **book value of equity**. As we stated earlier, it represents the net worth of the firm from an accounting perspective.

Ideally, the balance sheet would provide us with an accurate assessment of the true value of the firm's equity. Unfortunately, this is unlikely to be the case. First, many of the assets listed on the balance sheet are valued based on their historical cost rather than their true value today. For example, an office building is listed on the balance sheet according to its historical cost net of depreciation. But the actual value of the office building today may be very different than this amount, and it may be much *more* than the amount the firm paid for it years ago. The same is true for other property, plant, and equipment, as well as goodwill: The true value today of an asset may be very different from, and even exceed, its book value. A second, and probably more important, problem is that *many of the firm's valuable assets are not captured on the balance sheet.* For example, the expertise of the firm's employees, the firm's reputation in the marketplace, the relationships with customers and suppliers, and the quality of the management team are all assets that add to the value of the firm that do not appear on the balance sheet.

For these reasons, the book value of equity is an inaccurate assessment of the actual value of the firm's equity. Thus, it is not surprising that it will often differ substantially from the amount investors are willing to pay for the equity. The total market value of a firm's equity equals the market price per share times the number of shares, referred to as the company's **market capitalization**. The market value of a stock does not depend on the historical cost of the firm's assets; instead, it depends on what investors expect those assets to produce in the future.

Market Versus Book Value

Problem
If Global has 3.6 million shares outstanding, and these shares are trading for a price of $14 per share, what is Global's market capitalization? How does the market capitalization compare to Global's book value of equity?

Solution
Global's market capitalization is (3.6 million shares) × ($14 / share) = $50.4 million. This market capitalization is significantly higher than Global's book value of equity of $22.2 million. In fact, the ratio of its market value to its book value is 50.4 / 22.2 = 2.27, meaning that investors are willing to pay more than twice the amount Global's shares are "worth" according to their book value.

---

2. A firm may also have deferred tax assets related to tax credits it has earned that it will receive in the future.

Finally, we note that the book value of equity can be negative (liabilities exceed assets), and that a negative book value of equity is not necessarily an indication of poor performance. Successful firms are often able to borrow in excess of the book value of their assets because creditors recognize that the market value of the assets is far higher. For example, in June 2005, Amazon.com had total liabilities of $2.6 billion and a book value of equity of −$64 million. At the same time, the market value of its equity was over $15 billion. Clearly, investors recognized that Amazon's assets were worth far more than their book value.

Balance Sheet Analysis

What can we learn from analyzing a firm's balance sheet? Although the book value of a firm's equity is not a good estimate of its true value as an ongoing firm, it is sometimes used as an estimate of the **liquidation value** of the firm, the value that would be left if its assets were sold and liabilities paid. We can also learn a great deal of useful information from a firm's balance sheet that goes beyond the book value of the firm's equity. We now discuss analyzing the balance sheet to assess the firm's value, its leverage, and its short-term cash needs.

Market-to-Book Ratio.   In Example 2.1, we computed the **market-to-book ratio** (also called the **price-to-book [P/B] ratio**) for Global, which is the ratio of its market capitalization to the book value of stockholders' equity.

$$\text{Market-to-Book Ratio} = \frac{\text{Market Value of Equity}}{\text{Book Value of Equity}} \qquad (2.2)$$

It is one of many financial ratios used by analysts to evaluate a firm. The market-to-book ratio for most successful firms substantially exceeds 1, indicating that the value of the firm's assets when put to use exceeds their historical cost (or liquidation value). Variations in this ratio reflect differences in fundamental firm characteristics as well as the value added by management.

In early 2006, General Motors Corporation (GM) had a market-to-book ratio of 0.5, a reflection of investors' assessment that many of GM's plants and other assets were unlikely to be profitable and were worth less than their book value. At the same time, the average market-to-book ratio for the auto industry was about 1.5, and for large U.S. firms it was close to 4.0. In contrast, consider that Google (GOOG) had a market-to-book ratio of over 15, and the average for technology firms was about 6.0. Analysts often classify firms with low market-to-book ratios as **value stocks**, and those with high market-to-book ratios as **growth stocks**.

Debt-Equity Ratio.   Another important piece of information that we can learn from a firm's balance sheet is the firm's **leverage**, or the extent to which it relies on debt as a source of financing. The **debt-equity ratio** is a common ratio used to assess a firm's leverage. We calculate this ratio by dividing the total amount of short- and long-term debt (including current maturities) by the total stockholders' equity:

$$\text{Debt-Equity Ratio} = \frac{\text{Total Debt}}{\text{Total Equity}} \qquad (2.3)$$

We can calculate this ratio using either book or market values for equity and debt. From Table 2.1, note Global's debt in 2005 includes notes payable ($3.5 million), current maturities of long-term debt ($13.3 million), and long-term debt ($99.9 million), for a total of $116.7 million. Therefore, its *book* debt-equity ratio is 116.7 / 22.2 = 5.3, using the book value of equity. Note the large increase from 2004, when the book debt-equity ratio was only (3.2 + 12.3 + 56.3) / 21.2 = 3.4.

Because of the difficulty interpreting the book value of equity, the book debt-equity ratio is not especially useful. It is more informative to compare the firm's debt to the market value of its equity. Global's debt-equity ratio in 2005 using the market value of equity (from Example 2.1) is 116.7 / 50.4 = 2.3, which means Global's debt is a bit more than double the market value of its equity.[3] As we see later in the text, a firm's *market* debt-equity ratio has important consequences for the risk and return of its stock.

Enterprise Value.   A firm's market capitalization measures the market value of the firm's equity, or the value that remains after the firm has paid its debts. But what is the value of the business itself? The **enterprise value** of a firm assesses the value of the underlying business assets, unencumbered by debt and separate from any cash and marketable securities. We compute it as follows:

$$\text{Enterprise Value} = \text{Market Value of Equity} + \text{Debt} - \text{Cash} \qquad (2.4)$$

For example, given its market capitalization from Example 2.1, Global's enterprise value in 2005 is 50.4 + 116.7 − 21.2 = $145.9 million. The enterprise value can be interpreted as the cost to take over the business. That is, it would cost 50.4 + 116.7 = $167.1 million to buy all of Global's equity and pay off its debts, but because we would acquire Global's $21.2 million in cash, the net cost is only 167.1 − 21.2 = $145.9 million.

EXAMPLE 2.2

Computing Enterprise Value

Problem

In April 2005, H.J. Heinz Co. (HNZ) had a share price of $36.87, 347.6 million shares outstanding, a market-to-book ratio of 4.93, a book debt-equity ratio of 1.80, and cash of $1.08 billion. What was Heinz's market capitalization? What was its enterprise value?

Solution

Heinz had a market capitalization of $36.87 × 347.6 million shares = $12.82 billion. We divide the market value of equity by Heinz's market-to-book ratio to calculate Heinz's book value of equity as 12.82 / 4.93 = $2.60 billion. Given a book debt-equity ratio of 1.80, Heinz had total debt of 1.80 × 2.60 = $4.68 billion. Thus, Heinz's enterprise value was 12.82 + 4.68 − 1.08 = $16.42 billion.

Other Balance Sheet Information.   Creditors often compare a firm's current assets and current liabilities to assess whether the firm has sufficient working capital to meet its short-term needs. This comparison is sometimes summarized in the firm's **current ratio**, the ratio of current assets to current liabilities, or its **quick ratio**, the ratio of current assets other than inventory to current liabilities. A higher current or quick ratio implies less risk of the firm experiencing a cash shortfall in the near future.

---

3. In this calculation, we have compared the market value of equity to the book value of debt. Strictly speaking, it would be best to use the market value of debt. But because the market value of debt is generally not very different from its book value, this distinction is often ignored in practice.

Analysts also use the information on the balance sheet to watch for trends that could provide information regarding the firm's future performance. For example, an unusual increase in inventory could be an indicator that the firm is having difficulty selling its products.

CONCEPT CHECK

1. The book value of a company's assets usually does not equal the market value of those assets. What are some reasons for this difference?

2. What is a firm's enterprise value?

2.3 The Income Statement

When you want somebody to get to the point, you might ask them for the "bottom line." This expression comes from the *income statement*. The **income statement** lists the firm's revenues and expenses over a period of time. The last or "bottom" line of the income statement shows the firm's **net income**, which is a measure of its profitability during the period. The income statement is sometimes called a profit and loss, or "P&L," statement, and the net income is also referred to as the firm's **earnings**. In this section, we examine the components of the income statement in detail and introduce ratios we can use to analyze this data.

Earnings Calculations

Whereas the balance sheet shows the firm's assets and liabilities at a given point in time, the income statement shows the flow of revenues and expenses generated by those assets and liabilities between two dates. Table 2.2 shows Global's income statement for 2005. We examine each category on the statement.

Gross Profit.   The first two lines of the income statement list the revenues from sales of products and the costs incurred to make and sell the products. The third line is **gross profit**, the difference between sales revenues and the costs.

Operating Expenses.   The next group of items is operating expenses. These are expenses from the ordinary course of running the business that are not directly related to producing the goods or services being sold. They include administrative expenses and overhead, salaries, marketing costs, and research and development expenses. The third type of operating expense, depreciation and amortization, is not an actual cash expense but represents an estimate of the costs that arise from wear and tear or obsolescence of the firm's assets.[4] The firm's gross profit net of operating expenses is called **operating income**.

Earnings Before Interest and Taxes.   We next include other sources of income or expenses that arise from activities that are not the central part of a company's business. Cash flows from the firm's financial investments are one example of other income that would be listed here. After we have adjusted for other sources of income or expenses, we have the firm's earnings before interest and taxes, or **EBIT**.

---

4. Only certain types of amortization are deductible as a pretax expense (e.g., amortization of the cost of an acquired patent). Amortization of goodwill is not a pretax expense and is generally included as an extraordinary item after taxes are deducted.

TABLE 2.2	Global Conglomerate Corporation Income Statement Sheet for 2005 and 2004

GLOBAL CONGLOMERATE CORPORATION
Income Statement
Year ended December 31 (in $ millions)

	2005	2004
Total sales	186.7	176.1
Cost of sales	(153.4)	(147.3)
Gross Profit	33.3	28.8
Selling, general, and administrative expenses	(13.5)	(13.0)
Research and development	(8.2)	(7.6)
Depreciation and amortization	(1.2)	(1.1)
Operating Income	10.4	7.1
Other income	—	—
Earnings before interest and taxes (EBIT)	10.4	7.1
Interest income (expense)	(7.7)	(4.6)
Pretax income	2.7	2.5
Taxes	(0.7)	(0.6)
Net Income	2.0	1.9
Earnings per share:	$0.556	$0.528
Diluted earnings per share:	$0.526	$0.500

Pretax and Net Income.   From EBIT, we deduct the interest paid on outstanding debt to compute Global's pretax income, and then we deduct corporate taxes to determine the firm's net income.

Net income represents the total earnings of the firm's equity holders. It is often reported on a per-share basis as the firm's **earnings per share (EPS)**. We compute EPS by dividing net income by the total number of shares outstanding:

$$\text{EPS} = \frac{\text{Net Income}}{\text{Shares Outstanding}} = \frac{\$2.0 \text{ million}}{3.6 \text{ million shares}} = \$0.556 \text{ per share} \qquad (2.5)$$

Although Global has only 3.6 million shares outstanding as of the end of 2005, the number of shares outstanding may grow if Global compensates its employees or executives with **stock options** that give the holder the right to buy a certain number of shares by a specific date at a specific price. If the options are "exercised," the company issues new stock and the number of shares outstanding will grow. The number of shares may also grow if the firm issues **convertible bonds**, a form of debt that can be converted to shares. Because there will be more total shares to divide the same earnings, this growth in the number of shares is referred to as **dilution**. Firms disclose the potential for dilution from options they have awarded by reporting **diluted EPS**, which shows the earnings per share the company would have if the stock options were exercised. For example, if Global has awarded 200,000 stock options to its key executives, its diluted EPS is $2.0 million / 3.8 million shares = $0.526.

Income Statement Analysis

The income statement provides very useful information regarding the profitability of a firm's business and how it relates to the value of the firm's shares. We now discuss several ratios that are often used to evaluate a firm's performance and value.

Profitability Ratios.   The **operating margin** of a firm is the ratio of operating income to revenues:

$$\text{Operating Margin} = \frac{\text{Operating Income}}{\text{Total Sales}} \tag{2.6}$$

The operating margin reveals how much a company earns before interest and taxes from each dollar of sales. Global's operating margin in 2005 was 10.4 / 186.7 = 5.57%, an increase from its 2004 operating margin of 7.1 / 176.1 = 4.03%. By comparing operating margins across firms within an industry, we can assess the relative efficiency of firms' operations. For example, in 2004, American Airlines (AMR) had an operating margin of −0.77% (i.e., they lost 0.77 cents for each dollar in revenues). However, competitor Southwest Airlines (LUV) had an operating margin of 8.48%.

Differences in operating margins can also result from differences in strategy. For example, in 2004, high-end retailer Neiman Marcus had an operating margin of 9.8%; Wal Mart Stores had an operating margin of only 5.9%. In this case, Wal-Mart's lower operating margin is not a result of its inefficiency but is part of its strategy of offering lower prices to sell common products in high volume. Indeed, Wal-Mart's sales were more than 80 times higher than those of Neiman Marcus.

A firm's **net profit margin** is the ratio of net income to revenues:

$$\text{Net Profit Margin} = \frac{\text{Net Income}}{\text{Total Sales}} \tag{2.7}$$

The net profit margin shows the fraction of each dollar in revenues that is available to equity holders after the firm pays interest and taxes. Global's net profit margin in 2005 was 2.0 / 186.7 = 1.07%. Differences in net profit margins can be due to differences in efficiency, but they can also result from differences in leverage, which determines the amount of interest payments.

Working Capital Days.   We can use the combined information in the firm's income statement and balance sheet to gauge how efficiently the firm is utilizing its net working capital. For example, we can express the firm's accounts receivable in terms of the number of days' worth of sales that it represents, called the **accounts receivable days**:[5]

$$\text{Accounts Receivable Days} = \frac{\text{Accounts Receivable}}{\text{Average Daily Sales}} \tag{2.8}$$

Given average daily sales of $186.7 million / 365 = $0.51 million in 2005, Global's receivables of $18.5 million represent 18.5 / 0.51 = 36 days' worth of sales. In other words, Global takes a little over one month to collect payment from its customers, on average. In 2004, Global's accounts receivable represented only 27 days worth of sales. Although the number of receivable days can fluctuate seasonally, a significant unexplained

---

5. Accounts Receivable Days can also be calculated based on the average accounts receivable at the end of current and prior year.

increase could be a cause for concern (perhaps indicating the firm is doing a poor job collecting from its customers or is trying to boost sales by offering generous credit terms). Accounts payable can also be expressed in terms of the number of days' worth of cost of goods sold, as can inventory.

EBITDA. Financial analysts often compute a firm's earnings before interest, taxes, depreciation, and amortization, or **EBITDA**. Because depreciation and amortization are not cash expenses for the firm, EBITDA reflects the cash a firm has earned from its operations. Global's EBITDA in 2005 was $10.4 + 1.2 = \$11.6$ million.

Leverage Ratios. Lenders often assess a firm's leverage by computing an **interest coverage ratio**. Common ratios consider operating income, EBIT, or EBITDA as a multiple of the firm's interest expenses. When this ratio is high, it indicates that the firm is earning much more than is necessary to meet its required interest payments.

Investment Returns. Analysts often evaluate the firm's return on investment by comparing its income to its investment using ratios such as the firm's **return on equity (ROE)**:[6]

$$\text{Return on Equity} = \frac{\text{Net Income}}{\text{Book Value of Equity}} \qquad (2.9)$$

Global's ROE in 2005 was $2.0 / 22.2 = 9.0\%$. The ROE provides a measure of the return that firm has earned on its past investments. A high ROE may indicate the firm is able to find investment opportunities that are very profitable. Of course, one weakness of this measure is the difficulty in interpreting the book value of equity. Another common measure is the **return on assets (ROA)**, which is net income divided by the total assets.

Valuation Ratios. Analysts use a number of ratios to gauge the market value of the firm. The most important is the firm's **price-earnings ratio (P/E)**:

$$\text{P / E Ratio} = \frac{\text{Market Capitalization}}{\text{Net Income}} = \frac{\text{Share Price}}{\text{Earnings per Share}} \qquad (2.10)$$

COMMON MISTAKE   **Mismatched Ratios**

When considering valuation (and other) ratios, be sure that the items you are comparing both represent amounts related to the entire firm or that both represent amounts related solely to equity holders. For example, a firm's share price and market capitalization are values associated with the firm's equity. Thus, it makes sense to compare them to the firm's earnings per share or net income, which are amounts to equity holders after interest has been paid to debt holders. We must be careful, however, if we compare a firm's market capitalization to its revenues, operating income, or EBITDA because these amounts are related to the whole firm, and both debt and equity holders have a claim to them. Thus, it is better to compare revenues, operating income, or EBITDA to the enterprise value of the firm, which includes both debt and equity.

---

6. Because net income is measured over the year, the ROE can also be calculated based on the average book value of equity at the end of the current and prior year.

That is, the P/E ratio is the ratio of the value of equity to the firm's earnings, either on a total basis or on a per-share basis. For example, Global's P/E ratio in 2005 was 50.4 / 2.0 − 14 / 0.56 = 25.2. The P/E ratio is a simple measure that is used to assess whether a stock is over- or under-valued based on the idea that the value of a stock should be proportional to the level of earnings it can generate for its shareholders. P/E ratios can vary widely across industries and tend to be higher for industries with high growth rates. For example, in 2005, the average large U.S. firm had a P/E ratio of about 21. But biotechnology firms, which have low current earnings but the promise of high future earnings if they develop successful drugs, had an average P/E ratio of 48.

The P/E ratio considers the value of the firm's equity and so depends on its leverage. To assess the market value of the underlying business, it is common to consider valuation ratios based on the firm's enterprise value. Common ratios include the ratio of enterprise value to revenue, or enterprise value to operating income or EBITDA. These ratios compare the value of the business to its sales, operating profits, or cash flow. Like the P/E ratio, these ratios are used to make intra-industry comparisons of how firms are priced in the market.

The P/E ratio is not useful when the firm's earnings are negative. In this case, it is common to look at the firm's enterprise value relative to sales. The risk in doing so, however, is that earnings might be negative because the firm's underlying business model is fundamentally flawed, as was the case for many Internet firms in the late 1990s.

EXAMPLE 2.3

Computing Profitability and Valuation Ratios

Problem

Consider the following data from 2004 for Wal-Mart Stores and Target Corporation ($ billions):

	Wal-Mart Stores (WMT)	Target Corporation (TGT)
Sales	288	47
Operating Income	17	3.6
Net Income	10	1.9
Market Capitalization	228	45
Cash	5	1
Debt	32	9

Compare Wal-Mart and Target's operating margin, net profit margin, P/E ratio, and the ratio of enterprise value to operating income and sales.

Solution

Wal-Mart had an operating margin of 17 / 288 = 5.9%, a net profit margin of 10 / 288 = 3.5%, and a P/E ratio of 228 / 10 = 22.8. Its enterprise value was 228 + 32 − 5 = $255 billion, which has a ratio of 255 / 17 = 15.0 to operating income and 255 / 288 = 0.89 to sales.

Target had an operating margin of 3.6 / 47 = 7.7%, a net profit margin of 1.9 / 47 = 4.0%, and a P/E ratio of 45 / 1.9 = 23.7. Its enterprise value was 45 + 9 − 1 = $53 billion, which has a ratio of 53 / 3.6 = 14.7 to operating income and 53 / 47 = 1.13 to sales.

Note that despite their large difference in size, Target and Wal-Mart's P/E and enterprise value to operating income ratios were very similar. Target's profitability was somewhat higher than Wal-Mart's, however, explaining the difference in the ratio of enterprise value to sales.

1. What is the diluted earnings per share?

2. How do you use the price-earnings (P/E) ratio to gauge the market value of a firm?

2.4 The Statement of Cash Flows

The income statement provides a measure of the firm's profit over a given time period. However, it does not indicate the amount of *cash* the firm has earned. There are two reasons that net income does not correspond to cash earned. First, there are non-cash entries on the income statement, such as depreciation and amortization. Second, certain uses of cash, such as the purchase of a building or expenditures on inventory, are not reported on the income statement. The firm's **statement of cash flows** utilizes the information from the income statement and balance sheet to determine how much cash the firm has generated, and how that cash has been allocated, during a set period. As we will see, from the perspective of an investor attempting to value the firm, the statement of cash flows provides what may be the most important information of the four financial statements.

The statement of cash flows is divided into three sections: operating activities, investment activities, and financing activities. The first section, operating activity, starts with net income from the income statement. It then adjusts this number by adding back all non-cash entries related to the firm's operating activities. The next section, investment activity, lists the cash used for investment. The third section, financing activity, shows the flow of cash between the firm and its investors. Global Conglomerate's statement of cash flows is shown in Table 2.3. In this section, we take a close look at each component of the statement of cash flows.

Operating Activity

The first section of Global's statement of cash flows adjusts net income by all non-cash items related to operating activity. For instance, depreciation is deducted when computing net income, but it is not an actual cash expense. Thus, we add it back to net income when determining the amount of cash the firm has generated. Similarly, we add back any other non-cash expenses (for example, deferred taxes).

Next, we adjust for changes to net working capital that arise from changes to accounts receivable, accounts payable, or inventory. When a firm sells a product, it records the revenue as income even though it may not receive the cash from that sale immediately. Instead, it may grant the customer credit and let the customer pay in the future. The customer's obligation adds to the firm's accounts receivable. Because this sale was recorded as part of net income, but the cash has not yet been received from the customer, we must adjust the cash flows by *deducting* the increases in accounts receivable. This increase represents additional lending by the firm to its customers, and it reduces the cash available to the firm. Similarly, we *add* increases in accounts payable. Accounts payable represents borrowing by the firm from its suppliers. This borrowing increases the cash available to the firm. Finally, we *deduct* increases to inventory. Increases to inventory are not recorded as an expense and do not contribute to net income (the cost of the goods are only included in net income when the goods are actually sold). However, the cost of increasing inventory is a cash expense for the firm and must be deducted.

The changes in these working capital items can be found from the balance sheet. For example, from Table 2.1, Global's accounts receivable increased from $13.2 million in 2004 to $18.5 million in 2005. We deduct the increase of 18.5 − 13.2 = $5.3 million on the statement of cash flows. Note that although Global showed positive net income on

TABLE 2.3	**Global Conglomerate Corporation Statement of Cash Flows for 2005 and 2004**

GLOBAL CONGLOMERATE CORPORATION
Statement of Cash Flows
Year ended December 31 (in $ millions)

	2005	2004
Operating activities		
Net Income	2.0	1.9
Depreciation and amortization	1.2	1.1
Other non-cash items	(2.8)	(1.0)
Cash effect of changes in		
Accounts receivable	(5.3)	(0.3)
Accounts payable	4.7	(0.5)
Inventory	(1.0)	(1.0)
Cash from operating activities	(1.2)	0.2
Investment activities		
Capital expenditures	(14.0)	(4.0)
Acquisitions and other investing activity	(27.0)	(2.0)
Cash from investing activities	(41.0)	(6.0)
Financing activities		
Dividends paid	(1.0)	(1.0)
Sale or purchase of stock	—	—
Increase in short-term borrowing	1.3	3.0
Increase in long-term borrowing	43.6	2.5
Cash from financing activities	43.9	4.5
Change in Cash and Cash Equivalents	1.7	(1.3)

the income statement, it actually had a negative $1.2 million cash flow from operating activity, in large part because of the increase in accounts receivable.

Investment Activity

The next section of the statement of cash flows shows the cash required for investment activities. Purchases of new property, plant, and equipment are referred to as **capital expenditures**. Recall that capital expenditures do not appear immediately as expenses on the income statement. Instead, the firm depreciates these assets and deducts depreciation expenses over time. To determine the firm's cash flow, we already added back depreciation because it is not an actual cash expense. Now, we subtract the actual capital expenditure that the firm made. Similarly, we also deduct other assets purchased or investments made by the firm, such as acquisitions. In Table 2.3, we see that in 2005, Global spent $41 million in cash on investing activities.

Financing Activity

The last section of the statement of cash flows shows the cash flows from financing activities. Dividends paid to shareholders are a cash outflow. Global paid $1 million to its shareholders as dividends in 2005. The difference between a firm's net income and the amount it spends on dividends is referred to as the firm's **retained earnings** for that year:

$$\text{Retained Earnings} = \text{Net Income} - \text{Dividends} \qquad (2.11)$$

Global retained $2 million − $1 million = $1 million, or 50% of its earnings in 2005.

Also listed under financing activity is any cash the company received from the sale of its own stock, or cash spent buying (repurchasing) its own stock. Global did not issue or repurchase stock during this period.

The last items to include in this section result from changes to Global's short-term and long-term borrowing. Global raised money by issuing debt, so the increases in short-term and long-term borrowing represent cash inflows. The last line of the statement of cash flows combines the cash flows from these three activities to calculate the overall change in the firm's cash balance over the period of the statement. In this case, Global had cash inflows of $1.7 million. By looking at the statement in Table 2.3 as a whole, we can determine that Global chose to borrow (mainly in the form of long-term debt) to cover the cost of its investment and operating activities. Although the firm's cash balance has increased, Global's negative operating cash flows and relatively high expenditures on investment activities might give investors some reasons for concern. If that pattern continues, Global will need to continue to borrow to remain in business.

The Impact of Depreciation on Cash Flow

Problem

Suppose Global had an additional $1 million depreciation expense in 2005. If Global's tax rate on pretax income is 26%, what would be the impact of this expense on Global's earnings? How would it impact Global's cash at the end of the year?

Solution

Depreciation is an operating expense, so Global's operating income, EBIT, and pretax income would fall by $1 million. This decrease in pretax income would reduce Global's tax bill by 26% × $1 million = $0.26 million. Therefore, net income would fall by 1 − 0.26 = $0.74 million.

On the statement of cash flows, net income would fall by $0.74 million, but we would add back the additional depreciation of $1 million because it is not a cash expense. Thus, cash from operating activities would rise by −0.74 + 1 = $0.26 million. Thus, Global's cash balance at the end of the year would increase by $0.26 million, the amount of the tax savings that resulted from the additional depreciation deduction.

CONCEPT CHECK   1. Why does a firm's net income not correspond to cash earned?

2. What are the components of the statement of cash flows?

2.5 Other Financial Statement Information

The most important elements of a firm's financial statements are the balance sheet, income statement, and the statement of cash flows, which we have already discussed. Several other pieces of information contained in the financial statements warrant brief mention: the management discussion and analysis, the statement of stockholders' equity, and notes to the financial statement.

INTERVIEW WITH
Sue Frieden

*S*ue Frieden is Ernst & Young's *Global Managing Partner, Quality & Risk Management. A member of the Global Executive board, she is responsible for every aspect of quality and risk management—employees, services, procedures, and clients.*

QUESTION: ***Do today's financial statements give the investing public what they need?***

ANSWER: Globally, we are seeing an effort to provide more forward-looking information to investors. But fundamental questions remain, such as how fully do investors understand financial statements and how fully do they read them? Research shows that most individual investors don't rely on financial statements much at all. We need to determine how the financial statement and related reporting models can be improved. To do that we will need a dialogue involving investors, regulators, analysts, auditors, stock exchanges, academics and others to ensure that financial statements and other reporting models are as relevant as they can be.

QUESTION: ***Ernst & Young is a global organization. How do accounting standards in the U.S. compare to those elsewhere?***

ANSWER: In January of 2005, 100 countries outside the U.S. began the process of adopting new accounting standards (International Financial Reporting Standards) that would in large measure be based on principles rather than rules. As global markets become more complex, it is clear that we all need to be playing by the same set of rules, but as a first step we need to have consistency from country to country. There are definite challenges to overcome in reconciling principle-based and rules-based systems, but we are optimistic that these challenges will inevitably get resolved. At the same time, there are efforts underway to ensure that auditing standards are globally consistent. Ultimately, financial statements prepared under global standards and audited under consistent global auditing standards will better serve investors.

QUESTION: ***What role does the audit firm play in our financial markets, and how has that changed since the collapse of Arthur Anderson?***

ANSWER: All of us—the entire business community—have gone through a pivotal, historic moment. And certainly the accounting profession has seen unprecedented change in the past few years as well. The passage of Sarbanes-Oxley and other changes are helping to restore public trust. Things are certainly very different from what we've known before. We're now engaging on a regular basis with a wider range of stakeholders—companies, boards, policymakers, opinion leaders, investors and academia. And we've had the chance to step back and ask ourselves why we do what we do as accounting professionals, and why it matters. In terms of the services we offer, much of what we do helps companies comply with regulations, guard against undue risks, and implement sound transactions. And part of the value in what we do is providing the basis to all stakeholders to understand whether companies are playing by the rules—whether it is accounting rules, financial reporting rules, or tax rules. We help create confidence in financial data. The public may not fully understand precisely what auditors do or how we do it, but they care that we exist because it provides them the confidence they so badly need and want.

QUESTION: ***How does a global accounting firm such as Ernst & Young ensure that each of its partners adheres to the appropriate standards?***

ANSWER: People often tell me, as the global leader for quality and risk management, how hard my job is and how much is on my shoulders. The truth is, doing the right thing—adhering and often exceeding the standards expected of us as independent public auditors—rests on the shoulders of everyone in the organization. All of our more than 107,000 people around the world know it is their responsibility to make this happen. What's more, they know it is their responsibility to raise questions when they have concerns. Perhaps most importantly, all of our people know that no client is too big to walk away from if we sense the company's management is not committed to doing the right thing.

Management Discussion and Analysis

The **management discussion and analysis (MD&A)** is a preface to the financial statements in which the company's management discusses the recent year (or quarter), providing a background on the company and any significant events that may have occurred. Management may also discuss the coming year, and outline goals and new projects.

Management should also discuss any important risks that the firm faces or issues that may affect the firm's liquidity or resources. Management is also required to disclose any **off-balance sheet transactions**, which are transactions or arrangements that can have a material impact on the firm's future performance yet do not appear on the balance sheet. For example, if a firm has made guarantees that it will compensate a buyer for losses related to an asset purchased from the firm, these guarantees represent a potential future liability for the firm that must be disclosed as part of the MD&A.

Statement of Stockholders' Equity

The **statement of stockholders' equity** breaks down the stockholders' equity computed on the balance sheet into the amount that came from issuing new shares versus retained earnings. Because the book value of stockholders' equity is not a useful assessment of value for financial purposes, the information contained in the statement of stockholders' equity is also not particularly insightful.

Notes to the Financial Statements

In addition to the four financial statements, companies provide extensive notes with further details on the information provided in the statements. For example, the notes document important accounting assumptions that were used in preparing the statements. They often provide information specific to a firm's subsidiaries or its separate product lines. They show the details of the firm's stock-based compensation plans for employees and the different types of debt the firm has outstanding. Details of acquisitions, spin-offs, leases, taxes, and risk management activities are also given. The information provided in the notes is often very important to interpret fully the firm's financial statements.

Sales by Product Category

Problem

In the notes to its financial statements, H. J. Heinz (HNZ) reported the following sales revenues by product category ($ thousands):

	2005	2004
Ketchup, condiments, and sauces	$3,234,229	$3,047,662
Frozen foods	2,209,586	1,947,777
Convenience meals	2,005,468	1,874,272
Infant foods	855,558	908,469
Other	607,456	636,358

Which category showed the highest percentage growth? If Heinz has the same percentage growth by category from 2005 to 2006, what will its total revenues be in 2006?

Solution

The percentage growth in ketchup and condiment sales was $(3,234,229 - 3,047,662) / 3,047,662 = 6.1\%$. Similarly, growth in frozen foods was 13.4% and in convenience meals was 7.0%. However, sales of infant foods fell by 5.8% and other sales fell by 4.5%. Thus, frozen foods showed the highest growth.

If these growth rates continue for another year, ketchup and condiment sales will be $3,234,229 \times 1.061 = \$3.43$ billion, and the other categories will be $2.51 billion, $2.15 billion, $0.81 billion, and $0.58 billion, respectively, for total revenues of $9.48 billion.

CONCEPT CHECK

1. Where do off-balance sheet transactions appear in a firm's financial statements?

2. What information do the notes to financial statements provide?

2.6 Accounting Manipulation

The various financial statements we have examined are of critical importance to investors and financial managers alike. Even with safeguards such as GAAP and auditors, though, financial reporting abuses unfortunately do take place. We now review two of the most infamous recent examples.

Enron

Enron was the most well known of the accounting scandals of the early 2000s. Enron started as an operator of natural-gas pipelines but evolved into a global trader dealing in a range of products including gas, oil, electricity, and even broadband Internet capacity. A series of events unfolded that led Enron to file the largest bankruptcy filing in U.S. history in December 2001. By the end of 2001, the market value of Enron's shares had fallen by over $60 billion.

Interestingly, throughout the 1990s and up to late 2001, Enron was touted as one of the most successful and profitable companies in America. *Fortune* rated Enron "The Most Innovative Company in America" for six straight years, from 1995 to 2000. But while many aspects of Enron's business were successful, subsequent investigations suggest that Enron executives had been manipulating Enron's financial statements to mislead investors and artificially inflate the price of Enron's stock and maintain its credit rating. In 2000, for example, 96% of Enron's reported earnings were the result of accounting manipulation.[7]

Although the accounting manipulations that Enron used were quite sophisticated, the essence of most of the deceptive transactions was surprisingly simple. Enron sold assets at inflated prices to other firms (or, in many cases, business entities that Enron's CFO Andrew Fastow had created), together with a promise to buy back those assets at an even higher future price. Thus, Enron was effectively borrowing money, receiving cash today in exchange for a promise to pay more cash in the future. But Enron recorded the incoming cash as revenue and then hid the promises to buy them back in a variety of ways.[8] In the end, much of their revenue growth and profits in the late 1990s were the result of this type of manipulation.

---

7. John R. Kroger, "Enron, Fraud and Securities Reform: An Enron Prosecutor's Perspective," *University of Colorado Law Review* (December 2005): pp. 57–138.

8. In some cases, these promises were called "price risk management liabilities" and hidden with other trading activities; in other cases they were off-balance sheet transactions that were not fully disclosed.

WorldCom

On July 21, 2002, WorldCom entered the largest bankruptcy of all time. At its peak, WorldCom had a market capitalization of $120 billion. Again, a series of accounting manipulations beginning in 1998 hid the firm's financial problems from investors.

In WorldCom's case, the fraud was to reclassify $3.85 billion in operating expenses as long-term investment. The immediate impact of this change was to boost WorldCom's reported earnings: Operating expenses are deducted from earnings immediately, whereas long-term investments are depreciated slowly over time. Of course, this manipulation would not boost WorldCom's cash flows, because long-term investments must be deducted on the cash flow statement at the time they are made.

Some investors were concerned by WorldCom's excessive investment compared to the rest of the industry. As one investment advisor commented, "Red flags [were] things like big deviations between reported earnings and excess cash flow . . . [and] excessive capital expenditures for a long period of time. That was what got us out of WorldCom in 1999."[9]

Sarbanes-Oxley Act

Enron and WorldCom highlight the importance to investors of accurate and up-to-date financial statements for firms they choose to invest in. In 2002, Congress passed the Sarbanes-Oxley Act that requires, among other things, that CEOs and CFOs certify the accuracy and appropriateness of their firm's financial statements and increases the penalties against them if the financial statements later prove to be fraudulent.[10]

CONCEPT CHECK

1. Describe the transactions Enron used to increase its reported earnings.

2. What is the Sarbanes-Oxley Act?

Summary

1. Financial statements are accounting reports that a firm issues periodically to describe its past performance.

2. Investors, financial analysts, managers, and other interested parties such as creditors rely on financial statements to obtain reliable information about a corporation

3. The main types of financial statements are the balance sheet, the income statement, and the statement of cash flows.

4. The balance sheet shows the current financial position (assets, liabilities, and stockholders' equity) of the firm at a single point in time.

5. The two sides of the balance sheet must balance:

$$\text{Assets} = \text{Liabilities} + \text{Stockholder's Equity} \tag{2.1}$$

6. Stockholder's equity is the book value of the firm's equity. It differs from market value of the firm's equity, its market capitalization, because of the way assets and liabilities are recorded for accounting purposes. A successful firm's market-to-book ratio typically exceeds 1.

---

9. Robert Olstein, as reported in the *Wall Street Journal*, August 23, 2002.

10. We discuss these and other related corporate governance issues further in Chapter 29.

7. A common ratio used to assess a firm's leverage is

$$\text{Debt Equity Ratio} = \frac{\text{Total Debt}}{\text{Total Equity}} \tag{2.3}$$

This ratio is most informative when computed using the market value of equity. It indicates the degree of leverage of the firm.

8. The enterprise value of a firm is the total value of its underlying business operations:

$$\text{Enterprise Value} = \text{Market Capitalization} + \text{Debt} - \text{Cash} \tag{2.4}$$

9. The income statement reports the firm's revenues and expenses, and it computes the firm's bottom line of net income, or earnings.

10. Net income is often reported on a per-share basis as the firms earnings per share:

$$\text{Earnings per share (EPS)} = \text{Net Income} / \text{Shares Outstanding} \tag{2.5}$$

We compute diluted EPS by adding to the number of shares outstanding the possible increase in the number of shares from the exercise of stock options the firm has awarded.

11. Profitability ratios show the firm's operating or net income as a fraction of sales, and they are an indication of a firm's efficiency and its pricing strategy.

12. Working capital ratios express the firm's working capital as a number of days of sales (for receivables) or cost of sales (for inventory or payables).

13. Interest coverage ratios indicate the ratio of the firm's income or cash flows to its interest expenses, and they are a measure of financial strength.

14. Return on investment ratios such as ROE or ROA express the firm's net income as a return on the book value of its equity or total assets.

15. Valuation ratios compute market capitalization or enterprise value of the firm relative to its earnings or operating income.

16. The P/E ratio computes the value of a share of stock relative to the firm's EPS. P/E ratios tend to be high for fast-growing firms.

17. When comparing valuation ratios, it is important to be sure both numerator and denominator match in terms of whether they include debt.

18. The statement of cash flows reports the sources and uses of the firm's cash. It shows the adjustments to net income for non-cash expenses and changes to net working capital, as well as the cash used (or provided) from investing and financing activities.

19. The management discussion and analysis section of the financial statements contains management's overview of the firm's performance, as well as disclosure of risks the firm faces, including those from off-balance sheet transactions.

20. The statement of stockholders' equity breaks down the stockholders' equity computed on the balance sheet into the amount that came from issuing new shares versus retained earnings. It is not particularly useful for financial valuation purposes.

21. The notes to a firm's financial statements generally contain important details regarding the numbers used in the main statements.

22. Recent accounting scandals have drawn attention to the importance of financial statements. New legislation has increased the penalties for fraud, and tightened the procedures firms must use to assure that statements are accurate.

Key Terms

accounts payable *p. 23*

accounts receivable *p. 22*

accounts receivable days *p. 29*

amortization *p. 23*

annual report *p. 20*

assets *p. 21*

auditor *p. 21*

balance sheet *p. 21*

book value *p. 22*

book value of equity *p. 24*

capital expenditures *p. 33*

capital leases *p. 23*

convertible bonds *p. 28*

current assets *p. 21*

current liabilities *p. 23*

current ratio *p. 26*

debt-equity ratio *p. 25*

deferred taxes *p. 24*

depreciation *p. 22*

diluted EPS *p. 28*

dilution *p. 28*

earnings per share (EPS) *p. 28*

EBIT *p. 27*

EBITDA *p. 30*

enterprise value *p. 26*

financial statements *p. 20*

Generally Accepted Accounting
    Principles (GAAP) *p. 20*

goodwill *p. 23*

gross profit *p. 27*

growth stocks *p. 25*

income statement *p. 27*

interest coverage ratio *p. 30*

inventories *p. 22*

leverage *p. 25*

liabilities *p. 21*

liquidation value *p. 25*

long-term debt *p. 23*

management discussion
    and analysis (MD&A) *p. 36*

market capitalization *p. 24*

marketable securities *p. 21*

market-to-book ratio
    (price-to-book [P/B] ratio) *p. 25*

net income or earnings *p. 27*

net profit margin *p. 29*

net working capital *p. 23*

off-balance sheet transactions *p. 36*

operating income *p. 27*

operating margin *p. 29*

price-earnings ratio (P/E) *p. 30*

quick ratio *p. 26*

retained earnings *p. 34*

return on assets (ROA) *p. 30*

return on equity (ROE) *p. 30*

statement of cash flows *p. 32*

statement of stockholders' equity *p. 36*

stockholders' equity *p. 21*

stock options *p. 28*

10-K *p. 20*

10-Q *p. 20*

value stocks *p. 25*

working capital days *p. 29*

Further Reading

For a basic primer on financial statements, see T. R. Ittelson, *Financial Statements: A Step-By-Step Guide to Understanding and Creating Financial Reports*, 1st ed. (Career Press, 1998).

For additional information on financial accounting, there are many introductory, MBA-level financial accounting textbooks. Two examples are J. Pratt, *Financial Accounting in an Economic Context*, 5th ed. (John Wiley & Sons, 2003); and C. Stickney and R. Weil, *Financial Accounting*, 10th ed. (Thomson/South-Western, 2003).

For more on financial statement analysis, see K. G. Palepu, P. M. Healy, V. L. Bernard, *Business Analysis and Valuation: Using Financial Statements* (South-Western College Pub, 2003); and L. Revsine, D. W. Collins, W. B. Johnson, *Financial Reporting & Analysis* (Prentice Hall, 1999).

A great deal of public information is available regarding the alleged accounting abuses at Enron Corporation. A useful starting point is a report produced by a committee established by Enron's own board of directors: Report of the Special Investigative Committee of the Board of Directors of Enron (Powers Report), released February 2, 2002 (available online).

Problems

A blue box (■) indicates problems available in MyFinanceLab. An asterisk (*) indicates problems with a higher level of difficulty.

The Disclosure of
Financial Information

1. What four financial statements can be found in a firm's 10-K filing? What checks are there on the accuracy of these statements?

2. Who reads financial statements? List at least three different categories of people. For each category, provide an example of the type of information they might be interested in and discuss why.

3. Find the most recent financial statements for Starbuck's corporation (SBUX) using the following sources:

   a. From the company's Web page www.starbucks.com (*Hint:* Search for "investor relations.")

   b. From the SEC Web site www.sec.gov. (*Hint:* Search for company filings in the EDGAR database.)

   c. From the Yahoo finance Web site finance.yahoo.com.

   d. From at least one other source. (*Hint:* Enter "SBUX 10K" at www.google.com.)

The Balance Sheet

4. Consider the following potential events that might have occurred to Global Conglomerate on December 30, 2005. For each one, indicate which line items in Global's balance sheet would be affected and by how much. Also indicate the change to Global's book value of equity.

   a. Global used $20 million of its available cash to repay $20 million of its long-term debt.

   b. A warehouse fire destroyed $5 million worth of uninsured inventory.

   c. Global used $5 million in cash and $5 million in new long-term debt to purchase a $10 million building.

   d. A large customer owing $3 million for products it already received declared bankruptcy, leaving no possibility that Global would ever receive payment.

   e. Global's engineers discover a new manufacturing process that will cut the cost of its flagship product by over 50%.

   f. A key competitor announces a radical new pricing policy that will drastically undercut Global's prices.

5. What was the change in Global Conglomerate's book value of equity from 2004 to 2005 according to Table 2.1? Does this imply that the market price of Global's shares increased in 2005? Explain.

6. In March 2005, General Electric (GE) had a book value of equity of $113 billion, 10.6 billion shares outstanding, and a market price of $36 per share. GE also had cash of $13 billion, and total debt of $370 billion.

   a. What was GE's market capitalization? What was GE's market-to-book ratio?

   b. What was GE's book debt-equity ratio? What was GE's market debt-equity ratio?

   c. What was GE's enterprise value?

7. Find online the annual 10-K report for Peet's Coffee and Tea (PEET) filed in March 2005. Answer the following questions from their balance sheet:

   a. How much cash did Peet's have at the start of 2005?

   b. What was Peet's total assets?

   c. What was Peet's total liabilities? How much debt did Peet's have?

   d. What was the book value of Peet's equity?

The Income Statement

8. Find online the annual 10-K report for Peet's Coffee and Tea (PEET) filed in March 2005. Answer the following questions from the income statement:

a. What were Peet's revenues for 2004? By what percentage did revenues grow from 2003?

b. What was Peet's operating and net profit margin in 2004? How do they compare with its margins in 2003?

c. What was Peet's diluted earnings per share in 2004? What number of shares is this EPS based on?

EXCEL 9. Suppose that in 2006, Global launched an aggressive marketing campaign that boosts sales by 15%. However, their operating margin fell from 5.57% to 4.50%. Suppose that they have no other income, interest expenses are unchanged, and taxes are the same percentage of pretax income as in 2005.

a. What is Global's EBIT in 2006?

b. What is Global's income in 2006?

c. If Global's P/E ratio and number of shares outstanding remains unchanged, what is Global's share price in 2006?

EXCEL 10. Suppose a firm's tax rate is 35%.

a. What effect would a $10 million operating expense have on this year's earnings? What effect would it have on next year's earnings?

b. What effect would a $10 million capital expense have on this year's earnings, if the capital is depreciated at a rate of $2 million per year for 5 years? What effect would it have on next year's earnings?

*11. Quisco Systems has 6.5 billion shares outstanding and a share price of $18. Quisco is considering developing a new networking product in house at a cost of $500 million. Alternatively, Quisco can acquire a firm that already has the technology for $900 million worth (at the current price) of Quisco stock. Suppose that absent the expense of the new technology, Quisco will have EPS of $0.80.

a. Suppose Quisco develops the product in house. What impact would the development cost have on Quisco's EPS? Assume all costs are incurred this year and are treated as an R&D expense, Quisco's tax rate is 35%, and the number of shares outstanding is unchanged.

b. Suppose Quisco does not develop the product in house but instead acquires the technology. What effect would the acquisition have on Quisco's EPS this year? (Note that acquisition expenses do not appear directly on the income statement. Assume the acquired firm has no revenues or expenses of its own, so that the only effect on EPS is due to the change in the number of shares outstanding.)

c. Which method of acquiring the technology has a smaller impact on earnings? Is this method cheaper? Explain.

12. In July 2005, American Airlines (AMR) had a market capitalization of $2.3 billion, debt of $14.3 billion, and cash of $3.1 billion. American Airlines had revenues of $18.9 billion. British Airways (BAB) had a market capitalization of $5.2 billion, debt of $8.0 billion, cash of $2.9 billion, and revenues of $13.6 billion.

a. Compare the market capitalization-to-revenue ratio (also called the price-to-sales ratio) for American Airlines and British Airways.

b. Compare the enterprise value-to-revenue ratio for American Airlines and British Airways.

c. Which of these comparisons is more meaningful? Explain.

13. Find online the annual 10-K report for Peet's Coffee and Tea (PEET) filed in March 2005. Answer the following questions from their cash flow statement:

   a. How much cash did Peet's generate from operating activities in 2004?

   b. What was Peet's depreciation expense in 2004?

   c. How much cash was invested in new property and equipment (net of any sales) in 2004?

   d. How much did Peet's raise from the sale of shares of its stock (net of any purchases) in 2004?

14. Can a firm with positive net income run out of cash? Explain.

15. See the cash flow statement here for H.J. Heinz (HNZ) (in $ thousands):

Statement of Cash Flows:	27-Apr-05	26-Jan-05	27-Oct-04	28-Jul-04
Net Income	206,487	152,411	198,965	194,836
Operating Activities, Cash Flows Provided by or Used In				
Depreciation	67,752	65,388	60,229	59,083
Adjustments to net income	150,588	12,616	−43,557	62,140
Changes in accounts receivables	−84,612	55,787	−55,303	129,979
Changes in liabilities	135,732	−206,876	223,953	−202,123
Changes in inventories	140,434	51,280	−210,093	−6,936
Changes in other operating activities	38,266	−4,022	47,384	−50,799
Total Cash Flow From Operating Activities	654,647	126,584	221,578	186,180
Investing Activities, Cash Flows Provided by or Used In				
Capital expenditures	−109,647	−48,404	−44,180	−38,440
Investments	40,000	—	−19,179	19,179
Other cash flows from investing activities	−69,275	−24,197	45,296	−15,207
Total Cash Flows From Investing Activities	−138,922	−72,601	−18,063	−34,468
Financing Activities, Cash Flows Provided by or Used In				
Dividends paid	−99,617	−99,730	−99,552	−99,970
Sale purchase of stock	−102,286	20,903	−63,357	−67,225
Net borrowings	−11,409	−440,029	1,955	−4,520
Other cash flows from financing activities	2,629	—	—	11,323
Total Cash Flows from Financing Activities	−210,683	−518,856	−160,954	−160,392
Effect of exchange rate changes	−16,098	31,984	51,496	2,278
Change in Cash and Cash Equivalents	$288,944	($432,889)	$94,057	($6,402)

   a. What was Heinz's cumulative earnings over these four quarters? What was its cumulative cash flows from operating activities?

   b. What fraction of the cash from operating activities was used for investment over the four quarters?

   c. What fraction of the cash from operating activities was used for financing activities over the four quarters?

16. Suppose your firm receives a $5 million order on the last day of the year. You fill the order with $2 million worth of inventory. The customer picks up the products the same day, pays $1 million now, and will pay the remaining balance in 30 days. Suppose your firm's tax rate is 0% (i.e., ignore taxes). Determine the consequences of this transaction for each of the following:

a. Revenues

b. Earnings

c. Receivables

d. Inventory

e. Cash

17. Nokela Industries purchases a $40 million cyclo-converter. The cyclo-converter will be depreciated by $10 million per year over four years, starting this year. Suppose Nokela's tax rate is 40%.

a. What impact will the cost of the purchase have on earnings for each of the next four years?

b. What impact will the cost of the purchase have on the firm's cash flow for the next four years?

Other Financial Statement Information

18. The balance sheet information for Clorox Co. (CLX) in 2004–2005 is shown here, with data in $ thousands:

Balance Sheet:	31-Mar-05	31-Dec-04	30-Sep-04	30-Jun-04
Assets				
Current Assets				
Cash and cash equivalents	293,000	300,000	255,000	232,000
Net receivables	401,000	362,000	385,000	460,000
Inventory	374,000	342,000	437,000	306,000
Other current assets	60,000	43,000	53,000	45,000
Total Current Assets	**1,128,000**	**1,047,000**	**1,130,000**	**1,043,000**
Long term investments	128,000	97,000	—	200,000
Property, plant, and equipment	979,000	991,000	995,000	1,052,000
Goodwill	744,000	748,000	736,000	742,000
Other assets	777,000	827,000	911,000	797,000
Total Assets	**3,756,000**	**3,710,000**	**3,772,000**	**3,834,000**
Liabilities				
Current Liabilities				
Accounts payable	876,000	1,467,000	922,000	980,000
Short/current long-term debt	410,000	2,000	173,000	288,000
Other current liabilities	—	—	—	—
Total Current Liabilities	**1,286,000**	**1,469,000**	**1,095,000**	**1,268,000**
Long-term debt	2,381,000	2,124,000	474,000	475,000
Other liabilities	435,000	574,000	559,000	551,000
Total Liabilities	**4,102,000**	**4,167,000**	**2,128,000**	**2,294,000**
Total Stockholder Equity	**−346,000**	**−457,000**	**1,644,000**	**1,540,000**
Total Liabilities & Stockholder Equity	**$3,756,000**	**$3,710,000**	**$3,772,000**	**$3,834,000**

  a. What change in the book value of Clorox's equity took place at the end of 2004?

  b. Is Clorox's market-to-book ratio meaningful? Is its book debt-equity ratio meaningful? Explain.

  c. Find online Clorox's other financial statements from that time. What was the cause of the change to Clorox's book value of equity at the end of 2004?

  d. Does Clorox's book value of equity in 2005 imply that the firm is unprofitable? Explain.

19. Find online the annual 10-K report for Peet's Coffee and Tea (PEET) filed in March 2005. Answer the following questions from the notes to their financial statements:

  a. Under stock-based compensation, what was Peet's net income in 2004 after deducting the fair value of options granted to employees?

  b. What was Peet's inventory of raw materials at the end of 2004?

  c. What was the fair value of Peet's holdings of marketable government securities at the end of 2004?

  d. What property does Peet's lease? What are the minimum lease payments due in 2005?

  e. How many stock options did Peet's grant in 2004?

  f. What fraction of Peet's 2004 sales came from coffee beans and tea products? What fraction came from beverages and pastries?

Accounting Manipulation

20. Find online the annual 10-K report for Peet's Coffee and Tea (PEET) filed in March 2005.

  a. Which auditing firm certified these financial statements?

  b. Which officers of Peet's certified the financial statements?

21. WorldCom reclassified $3.85 billion of operating expenses as capital expenditures. Explain the effect this reclassification would have on WorldCom's cash flows. (*Hint:* Consider taxes.) WorldCom's actions were illegal and clearly designed to deceive investors. But if a firm could legitimately choose how to classify an expense for tax purposes, which choice is truly better for the firm's investors?

Data Case

This is your second interview with a prestigious brokerage firm for a job as an equity analyst. You survived the morning interviews with the department manager and the Vice President of Equity. Everything has gone so well that they want to test your ability as an analyst. You are seated in a room with a computer and a list with the names of two companies—Ford (F) and Microsoft (MSFT). You have 90 minutes to complete the following tasks:

1. Download the annual income statements, balance sheets, and cash flow statements for the last four fiscal years from MarketWatch (www.marketwatch.com). Enter each company's stock symbol and then go to "financials." Export the statements to Excel by right-clicking while the cursor is inside each statement.

2. Find historical stock prices for each firm from Yahoo! Finance (http://finance.yahoo.com). Enter your stock symbol, click on "Historical Prices" in the left column, and enter the proper date range to cover the last day of the month corresponding to the date of each financial statement. Use the closing stock prices (not the adjusted close). To calculate the firm's market capitalization at each date, we multiply the number of shares outstanding (see "Basic Weighted Shares Outstanding" on the income statement) by the firm's historic stock price.

3. For each of the four years of statements, compute the following ratios for each firm:

   Valuation Ratios

   Price-Earnings Ratio (for EPS use Diluted EPS Total)

   Market-to-Book Ratio

   Enterprise Value-to-EBITDA

   (For debt, include long-term and short-term debt; for cash, include marketable securities.)

   Profitability Ratios

   Operating Margin (Use Operating Income after Depreciation)

   Net Profit Margin

   Return on Equity

   Financial Strength Ratios

   Current Ratio

   Book Debt–Equity Ratio

   Market Debt–Equity Ratio

   Interest Coverage Ratio (EBIT ÷ Interest Expense)

4. Obtain industry averages for each firm from Reuters.com (http://today.reuters.com/investing/default.aspx).[11] Enter the stock symbol on top of the homepage and then click on "Ratios" in the left column.

   a. Compare each firm's ratios to the available industry ratios for the most recent year. (Ignore the "Company" column as your calculations will be different.)

   b. Analyze the performance of each firm versus the industry and comment on any trends in each individual firm's performance. Identify any strengths or weaknesses you find in each firm.

5. Examine the Market-to-Book ratios you calculated for each firm. Which, if any, of the two firms can be considered "growth firms" and which, if any, can be considered "value firms"?

6. Compare the valuation ratios across the two firms. How do you interpret the difference between them?

7. Consider the enterprise value of each firm for each of the four years. How have the values of each firm changed over the time period?

---

11. Reuters requires free registration for access to the site. Professors may want to set up an account with a class e-mail and password.

3

Arbitrage and Financial Decision Making

In July 2005, Jeff Fettig, CEO of appliance maker Whirlpool, offered to buy rival Maytag Corporation for $1.43 billion in cash and stock. The same month, Hewlett-Packard CEO Mark Hurd announced that HP would cut 14,500 jobs, or 10% of its full-time staff, over the next 18 months in order to reduce costs. And Tom Gahan, CEO of Deutsche Bank Securities, authorized the firm's traders to buy and sell over $600 billion worth of the largest U.S. stocks in a strategy referred to as stock index arbitrage. How did these CEOs decide that these decisions were good for their firms?

Every decision has future consequences, and these consequences can be either beneficial or costly. For example, after raising its offer, Whirlpool ultimately succeeded in its attempt to acquire Maytag. In addition to the upfront cost of $1.73 billion for the acquisition, Whirlpool will also incur the ongoing costs of paying Maytag employees, developing and producing new Maytag products, and so on. The benefits of the acquisition include the future sales revenues that Maytag's products will generate and the possible increase in Whirlpool's sales as a result of reduced competition. Purchasing Maytag was a good decision if the future benefits justify the upfront and future costs. If the benefits exceed the costs, the decision will increase the value of the firm and therefore the wealth of its investors.

Comparing costs and benefits is complicated because they often occur at different points in time, may be in different currencies, or may have different risks associated with them. To make a valid comparison, we must use the tools of finance to express all costs and benefits in common terms. In particular, the tools we develop will allow us to take costs and benefits that occur at different times, in different currencies, or with different risks, and express them in terms of cash today. We will then be able to evaluate a decision by answering this question: *Does the cash value today of its benefits exceed the cash value today of its costs?* In addition, we will see that the difference between the cash value of the benefits and costs indicates the net amount by which the decision will increase wealth.

In this chapter, we introduce the concept of *net present value (NPV)* as a way to compare the costs and benefits of a project in terms of a common unit—namely, dollars today. We use these same tools to determine the prices of investment opportunities that trade in the market. More fundamentally, in deriving these tools we discuss strategies called *arbitrage* that allow us to exploit situations in which the prices of publicly available investment opportunities do not conform to the values that we will determine. Because investors trade rapidly to take advantage of arbitrage opportunities, we argue that equivalent investment opportunities trading simultaneously in competitive markets must have the same price. This *Law of One Price* is the unifying theme of valuation that we use throughout this text.

3.1 Valuing Costs and Benefits

The first step in evaluating a project is to identify its costs and benefits. Suppose your firm is an importer of frozen seafood, and you find the following opportunity: You can buy $1000 of frozen shrimp today and immediately resell it to a customer for $1500 today. If you were certain about these costs and benefits, the right decision would be obvious: You should seize this opportunity because the firm will gain $1500 − $1000 = $500. Thus taking this opportunity contributes $500 to the value of the firm, in the form of cash that can be paid out immediately to the firm's investors.

Of course, real-world opportunities are usually much more complex than in this example, and the costs and benefits are more difficult to quantify. The analysis will often involve skills from other management disciplines, as in the following examples:

Marketing: to determine the increase in revenues resulting from an advertising campaign

Economics: to determine the increase in demand from lowering the price of a product

Organizational Behavior: to determine the effect of changes in management structure on productivity

Strategy: to determine a competitor's response to a price increase

Operations: to determine production costs after the modernization of a manufacturing plant

For the remainder of this text, we assume that the analysis of these other disciplines has been completed to quantify the costs and benefits associated with a decision. Once that task is done, the financial manager must compare the costs and benefits and determine whether the opportunity is worthwhile. In this section, we focus on the use of market prices to determine the current cash value of different costs and benefits.

Using Market Prices to Determine Cash Values

For our shrimp trader, both costs and benefits were expressed in terms of cash today: $1000 invested and $1500 received today. In practice, benefits and costs are often expressed in different terms, and we must convert them to an equivalent cash value.

Suppose a jewelry manufacturer has the opportunity to trade 10 ounces of platinum and receive 20 ounces of gold today. Because an ounce of gold differs in value from an ounce of platinum, it is incorrect to compare 20 ounces to 10 ounces and conclude that the larger quantity is better. Instead, to compare the costs and benefits, we first need to convert them to a common unit.

Consider the gold. What is its cash value today? Suppose gold can be bought and sold for a current market price of $250 per ounce. Then the 20 ounces of gold we receive has a cash value of[1]

(20 ounces of gold today) $\times$ ($250 today / ounce of gold today) = $5000 today

Similarly, if the current market price for platinum is $550 per ounce, then the 10 ounces of platinum we give up has a cash value of

(10 ounces of platinum today) $\times$ ($550 today / ounce of platinum today)

= $5500 today

Therefore, the jeweler's opportunity has a benefit of $5000 today and a cost of $5500 today. Because the benefits and costs are in the same units, they are comparable. In this case, the net value of the project is $5000 − $5500 = −$500 today. Because it is negative, the costs exceed the benefits and the jeweler should reject the trade. If he were to take it, it would be the same as giving up $500 today.

Note that for both gold and platinum, we used the current market price to convert from ounces of the metal to dollars. We did not concern ourselves with whether the jeweler thought that the price was fair or whether the jeweler would use the gold or platinum. Do such considerations matter? Suppose, for example, that the jeweler does not need the gold, or he thinks the current price of gold is too high. Would he value the gold at less than $5000? The answer is no—he can always sell the gold at the current market price and receive $5000 right now. Similarly, even if he really needs the gold or thinks the price of gold is too low, he can always buy 20 ounces of gold for $5000 and so should not value it at more than that amount.

Because the jeweler can both buy and sell gold at its current market price, his personal preferences or use for the gold and his opinion of the fair price are irrelevant in evaluating the value of this opportunity. In general, whenever a good trades in a **competitive market**—by which we mean a market in which it can be bought *and* sold at the same price—that price determines the cash value of the good. This extremely powerful and general idea is one of the foundations of all finance.

EXAMPLE

3.1

Competitive Market Prices Determine Value

Problem
Suppose the jeweler can produce $10,000 worth of jewelry from 20 ounces of gold but only $6000 worth of jewelry from 10 ounces of platinum. Should he trade 10 ounces of platinum for 20 ounces of gold?

---

1. You might worry about commissions or other transactions costs that are incurred when buying or selling gold, in addition to the market price. For now, we will ignore transactions costs, and discuss their effect in Section 3.7.

Solution

Given the value of the jewelry he can produce, the jeweler should exchange his platinum for gold. However, rather than accept the trading opportunity, he can do better by using the market to trade. At current market prices the jeweler could exchange his platinum for $5500. He could then use this money to purchase $5500 ÷ ($250 / ounce of gold) = 22 ounces of gold. This amount is more than the 20 ounces he would receive if he engaged in the direct trade. As we emphasized earlier, whether this trade is attractive depends on its net cash value using market prices. Because this value is negative, the trade is not appealing no matter what the jeweler can produce from the materials.

Because competitive markets exist for most commodities and financial assets, we can use them to determine cash values and evaluate decisions in most situations. Let's consider another example.

Calculating Cash Values Using Market Prices

Problem

You are offered the following investment opportunity: In exchange for $20,000 today, you will receive 200 shares of stock in the Coca-Cola Company today and 11,000 euros today. The current market price is $40 per share for Coca-Cola stock and the current exchange rate is 0.80 euro per dollar. Should you take this opportunity? How valuable is it? Would your decision change if you believed the value of the euro would plummet over the next month?

Solution

We need to convert the costs and benefits to their cash values. Assuming the market prices are competitive, we have

$$(200 \text{ shares}) \times (\$40 / \text{share today}) = \$8000 \text{ today}$$

$$(€11,000) \div (0.80€ / \$ \text{ today}) = \$13,750 \text{ today}$$

The net value of the opportunity is $8000 + $13,750 − $20,000 = $1750 today. Because the net value is positive, we should take it. This value depends only on the current market prices for Coca-Cola stock and the euro. Even if we thought the value of the euro were about to plummet, because we can sell euros immediately at the current exchange rate of 0.80€ / $, the value of this investment is unchanged. Our own personal opinion about the future prospects of the euro and Coca-Cola Company does not alter the value of the decision today.

When Competitive Market Prices Are Not Available

Competitive market prices allow us to calculate the value of a decision without worrying about the tastes or opinions of the decision maker. When competitive prices are not available, we can no longer do this. Prices at retail stores, for example, are one sided: You can buy at the posted price, but you cannot sell the good to the store at that same price. We cannot use these one-sided prices to determine an exact cash value. They determine the maximum value of the good (since it can always be purchased at that price), but an individual may value it for much less depending on his or her preferences for the good.

When Value Depends on Preferences

Problem

The local Lexus dealer hires you as an extra in a commercial. As part of your compensation, the dealer offers to sell you today a new Lexus for $33,000. The best available retail price for the Lexus is $40,000, and the price you could sell it for in the used car market is $35,000. How would you value this compensation?

Solution

If you plan to buy a Lexus anyway, then the value to you of the Lexus is $40,000, the price you would otherwise pay for it. In this case, the value of the dealer's offer is $40,000 − $33,000 = $7000. But suppose you do not want or need a Lexus. If you were to buy it from the dealer and then sell it, the value of taking the deal would be $35,000 − $33,000 = $2000. Thus, depending on your desire to own a new Lexus, the dealer's offer is worth somewhere between $2000 (you don't want a Lexus) and $7000 (you definitely want one). Because the price of the Lexus is not competitive (you cannot buy and sell at the same price), the value of the offer is ambiguous and depends on your preferences.

CONCEPT CHECK   1. If crude oil trades in a competitive market, would an oil refiner that has a use for the oil value it differently than another investor?

3.2 Interest Rates and the Time Value of Money

For most financial decisions, unlike in the examples presented so far, costs and benefits occur at different points in time. For example, typical investment projects incur costs upfront and provide benefits in the future. In this section, we show how to account for this time difference when evaluating a project.

The Time Value of Money

Consider an investment opportunity with the following certain cash flows:

Cost: $100,000 today

Benefit: $105,000 in one year

Because both are expressed in dollar terms, it might appear that the cost and benefit are directly comparable so that the project's net value is $105,000 − $100,000 = $5000. But this calculation ignores the timing of the costs and benefits, and it treats money today as equivalent to money in one year.

In general, a dollar today is worth more than a dollar in one year. If you have $1 today, you can invest it. For example, if you deposit it in a bank account paying 7% interest, you will have $1.07 at the end of one year. We call the difference in value between money today and money in the future the **time value of money**.

The Interest Rate: An Exchange Rate Across Time

By depositing money into a savings account, we can convert money today into money in the future with no risk. Similarly, by borrowing money from the bank, we can exchange money in the future for money today. The rate at which we can exchange money today for money in the future is determined by the current interest rate. In the same way that an exchange rate allows us to convert money from one currency to another, the interest rate allows us to convert money from one point in time to another. In essence, an interest rate is like an exchange rate across time. It tells us the market price today of money in the future.

Suppose the current annual interest rate is 7%. By investing or borrowing at this rate, we can exchange $1.07 in one year for each $1 today. More generally, we define the **risk-free interest rate**, r_f, for a given period as the interest rate at which money can be borrowed or lent without risk over that period. We can exchange $(1 + r_f)$ dollars in the future per dollar today, and vice versa, without risk. We refer to $(1 + r_f)$ as the **interest rate factor** for risk-free cash flows; it defines the exchange rate across time, and has units of "$ in one year / $ today."

As with other market prices, the risk-free interest rate depends on supply and demand. In particular, at the risk-free interest rate the supply of savings equals the demand for borrowing. After we know the risk-free interest rate, we can use it to evaluate other decisions in which costs and benefits are separated in time without knowing the investor's preferences.

Let's reevaluate the investment we considered earlier, this time taking into account the time value of money. If the interest rate is 7%, then we can express our costs as

$$\text{Cost} = (\$100,000 \text{ today}) \times (1.07 \text{ $ in one year / $ today})$$

$$= \$107,000 \text{ in one year}$$

Think of this amount as the opportunity cost of spending $100,000 today: We give up the $107,000 we would have had in one year if we had left the money in the bank. Alternatively, if we were to borrow the $100,000, we would owe $107,000 in one year.

Both costs and benefits are now in terms of "dollars in one year," so we can compare them and compute the investment's net value:

$$\$105,000 - \$107,000 = -\$2000 \text{ in one year}$$

In other words, we could earn $2000 more in one year by putting our $100,000 in the bank rather than making this investment. We should reject the investment: If we took it, we would be $2000 poorer in one year than if we didn't.

The previous calculation expressed the value of the costs and benefits in terms of dollars in one year. Alternatively, we can use the interest rate factor to convert to dollars today. Consider the benefit of $105,000 in one year. What is the equivalent amount in terms of dollars today? That is, how much would we need to have in the bank today so that we would end up with $105,000 in the bank in one year? We find this amount by dividing by the interest rate factor:

$$\text{Benefit} = (\$105,000 \text{ in one year}) \div (1.07 \text{ $ in one year / $ today})$$

$$= \$98,130.84 \text{ today}$$

This is also the amount the bank would lend to us today if we promised to repay $105,000 in one year.[2] Thus, it is the competitive market price at which we can "buy" or "sell" $105,000 in one year.

Now we are ready to compute the net value of the investment:

$$\$98,130.84 - \$100,000 = -\$1869.16 \text{ today}$$

---

2. We are assuming the bank will both borrow and lend at the risk-free interest rate. We discuss the case when these rates differ in Section 3.7.

Once again, the negative result indicates that we should reject the investment. Taking the investment would make us $1869.16 poorer today because we have given up $100,000 for something worth only $98,130.84.

Thus, our decision is the same whether we express the value of the investment in terms of dollars in one year or dollars today: We should reject the investment. Indeed, if we convert from dollars today to dollars in one year,

$$(-\$1869.16 \text{ today}) \times (1.07 \, \$ \text{ in one year} / \$ \text{ today}) = -\$2000 \text{ in one year}$$

we see that the two results are equivalent, but expressed as values at different points in time.

In the preceding calculation, we can interpret

$$\frac{1}{1+r} = \frac{1}{1.07} = 0.93458$$

as the *price* today of $1 in one year. Note that the value is less than $1—money in the future is worth less today, and so its price reflects a discount. Because it provides the discount at which we can purchase money in the future, the amount $\frac{1}{1+r}$ is called the one-year **discount factor**. The risk-free interest rate is also referred to as the **discount rate** for a risk-free investment.

EXAMPLE

3.4

Comparing Costs at Different Points in Time

Problem
The cost of rebuilding the San Francisco Bay Bridge to make it earthquake-safe was approximately $3 billion in 2004. At the time, engineers estimated that if the project were delayed to 2005, the cost would rise by 10%. If the interest rate was 2%, what was the cost of a delay in terms of dollars in 2004?

Solution
If the project were delayed, it would cost $3 billion × (1.10) = $3.3 billion in 2005. To compare this amount to the cost of $3 billion in 2004, we must convert it using the interest rate of 2%:

$$\$3.3 \text{ billion in 2005} \div (\$1.02 \text{ in 2005} / \$ \text{ in 2004}) = \$3.235 \text{ billion in 2004}$$

Therefore, the cost of a delay of one year was

$$\$3.235 \text{ billion} - \$3 \text{ billion} = \$235 \text{ million in 2004}$$

That is, delaying the project for one year was equivalent to giving up $235 million in cash.

We can use the risk-free interest rate to determine values in the same way we used competitive market prices. Figure 3.1 illustrates how we use competitive market prices, exchange rates, and interest rates to convert between dollars today and other goods, currencies, or dollars in the future.

CONCEPT CHECK

1. Is the value today of money to be received in one year higher or lower when interest rates are high than when interest rates are low?

2. How do you compare costs at different points in time?

Converting Between Dollars Today and Gold, Euros, or Dollars in the Future

We can convert dollars today to different goods, currencies, or points in time by using the competitive market price, exchange rate, or interest rate.

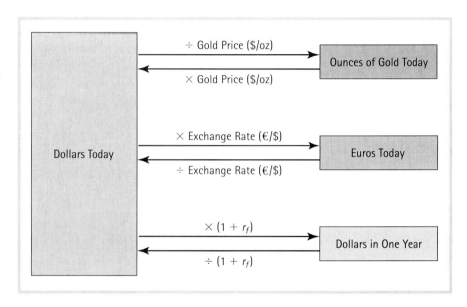

3.3 Present Value and the NPV Decision Rule

In Section 3.2, we converted between cash today and cash in the future using the risk-free interest rate. As long as we convert costs and benefits to the same point in time, we can compare them to make a decision. As a matter of practice, however, most corporations prefer to measure values in terms of cash today using *net present value*, the focus of this section.

Net Present Value

When the value of a cost or benefit is computed in terms of cash today, we refer to it as the **present value (PV)**. Similarly, we define the **net present value (NPV)** of a project or investment as the difference between the present value of its benefits and the present value of its costs:

Net Present Value

$$NPV = PV(\text{Benefits}) - PV(\text{Costs}) \tag{3.1}$$

If we use positive cash flows to represent benefits and negative cash flows to represent costs, and calculate the present value of multiple cash flows as the sum of present values for individual cash flows, we can write this definition as

$$NPV = PV(\text{All project cash flows}) \tag{3.2}$$

That is, the NPV is the total of the present values of all project cash flows.

Let's consider a simple example. Suppose you are offered the following investment opportunity: In exchange for $500 today, you will receive $550 in one year with certainty. If the risk-free interest rate is 8% per year then

$$PV(\text{Benefit}) = (\$550 \text{ in one year}) \div (1.08 \text{ \$ in one year} / \text{\$ today})$$
$$= \$509.26 \text{ today}$$

This PV is the amount we would need to put in the bank today to generate $550 in one year ($509.26 × 1.08 = $550). In other words, *the present value is the cash cost today of "doing it yourself"—it is the amount you need to invest at the current interest rate to recreate the cash flow.*

Once the costs and benefits are in present value terms, we can compute the investment's NPV:

$$NPV = \$509.26 - \$500 = \$9.26 \text{ today}$$

But what if you don't have the $500 needed to cover the initial cost of the project? Does the project still have the same value? Because we computed the value using competitive market prices, it should not depend on your tastes or the amount of cash you have in the bank. If you don't have the $500, suppose you borrow $509.26 from the bank at the 8% interest rate and then take the project. What are your cash flows in this case?

Today: $509.26 (loan) − $500 (invested in the project) = $9.26

In one year: $550 (from project) − $509.26 × 1.08 (loan balance) = $0

This transaction leaves you with exactly $9.26 extra cash in your pocket today and no future net obligations. So taking the project is like having an extra $9.26 in cash up front. Thus, the NPV expresses the value of an investment decision as an amount of cash received today.

The NPV Decision Rule

The NPV represents the value of the project in terms of cash today. Therefore, good projects are those with a positive NPV—they make the investor wealthier. Projects with negative NPVs have costs that exceed their benefits, and accepting them is equivalent to losing money today.

Because NPV is expressed in terms of cash today, it simplifies decision making. Decisions that increase wealth are superior to those that decrease wealth. Note that we don't need to know anything about the investor's preferences to reach this conclusion: As long as we have correctly captured all of the cash flows of a project, being wealthier increases our options[3] and makes us better off whatever our preferences are. We capture this logic in the **NPV Decision Rule**:

When making an investment decision, take the alternative with the highest NPV. Choosing this alternative is equivalent to receiving its NPV in cash today.

Accepting or Rejecting a Project.   A common financial decision is whether to accept or reject a project. Because rejecting the project generally has *NPV* = 0 (there are no new costs or benefits from not doing the project), the NPV decision rule implies that we should

- Accept those projects with positive NPV because accepting them is equivalent to receiving their NPV in cash today, and

- Reject those projects with negative NPV; accepting them would reduce the wealth of investors, whereas not doing them has no cost (NPV = 0).

---

3. Including giving the extra wealth away, if one should so desire.

EXAMPLE

3.5

The NPV Is Equivalent to Cash Today

Problem

You are offered an investment opportunity in which you will receive $9500 today in exchange for paying $10,000 in one year. Suppose the risk-free interest rate is 7% per year. Is this investment a good deal? Show that its NPV represents cash in your pocket.

Solution

The benefit of $9500 today is already in PV terms. The cost, however, is in terms of dollars in one year. We therefore convert it at the risk-free interest rate:

$$PV(\text{Cost}) = (\$10,000 \text{ in one year}) \div (1.07 \, \$ \text{ in one year} / \$ \text{ today}) = \$9345.79 \text{ today}$$

The NPV is the difference between the benefits and the costs:

$$NPV = \$9500 - \$9345.79 = \$154.21 \text{ today}$$

The NPV is positive, so the investment is a good deal. In fact, undertaking this investment is like having an extra $154.21 in your pocket today. Suppose you undertake the investment and save $9345.79 of it in a bank paying 7% interest. Then your net cash flows are as follows:

	Date 0	Date 1
Investment	+$ 9500.00	−$ 10,000
Savings	−$ 9345.79	+$ 10,000
Net Cash Flow	$ 154.21	$ 0

Therefore, this investment is equivalent to receiving $154.21 today, without any future net obligations.

Choosing Among Projects.   We can also use the NPV decision rule to choose among projects. Suppose we must choose only one of three projects that have the risk-free cash flows depicted in Table 3.1. If the risk-free interest rate is 20%, which project is the best choice?

TABLE 3.1	Cash Flows of Three Possible Projects	
Project	**Cash Flow Today ($)**	**Cash Flow in One Year ($)**
A	42	42
B	−20	144
C	−100	225

We can find the best project by comparing the NPV of each. See the calculations in Table 3.2. All three projects have positive NPV, and we would accept all three if possible. But if we must choose only one project, Project B has the highest NPV of $100 and therefore is the best choice. It is equivalent to receiving $100 in cash today.

| TABLE 3.2 | | Computing the NPV of Each Project | |

Project	Cash Flow Today ($)	PV of Cash Flow in One Year ($)	NPV ($ Today)
A	42	$42 \div 1.20 = 35$	$42 + 35 = 77$
B	-20	$144 \div 1.20 = 120$	$-20 + 120 = 100$
C	-100	$225 \div 1.20 = 187.5$	$-100 + 187.5 = 87.5$

NPV and Individual Preferences

When we compare projects with different patterns of present and future cash flows, we may have preferences regarding when to receive the cash. Some may need cash today; others may prefer to save for the future. Although Project B has the highest NPV in the last example, it does require a $20 cash outlay. Suppose we would prefer to avoid the negative cash flow today. Would Project A be a better choice in that case? Alternatively, if we would prefer to save for the future, would Project C be a better choice? In other words, should our individual preferences about present versus future cash flows affect our choice of projects?

As was true for the jeweler considering trading platinum for gold in Section 3.1, the answer is again no. As long as we are able to borrow and lend at the risk-free interest rate, Project B is superior whatever our preferences regarding the timing of the cash flows. To see why, suppose we invest in Project B and borrow $62 at the risk-free rate of 20%. Our total cash flows are shown in Table 3.3. Compare these cash flows to those for Project A. This combination generates the same initial cash flow as Project A, but with a higher final cash flow ($69.60 versus $42). Thus we are better off by investing in Project B and borrowing $62 today than we would be by accepting Project A.

| TABLE 3.3 | | Cash Flows from Combining Project B with Borrowing | |

	Cash Flow Today ($)	Cash Flow in One Year ($)
Project B	-20	144
Borrow	62	$-62 \times (1.20) = -74.4$
Total	42	69.6

Similarly, we can combine Project B with saving $80 at the risk-free rate of 20% (see Table 3.4). This combination has the same initial cash flow as Project C (see Table 3.2), but again has a higher final cash flow.

TABLE 3.4	Cash Flows from Combining Project B with Saving	
	Cash Flow Today ($)	Cash Flow in One Year ($)
Project B	−20	144
Save	−80	$80 \times (1.20) = 96$
Total	−100	240

Thus, no matter what pattern of cash flows we prefer, Project B is the superior choice. This example illustrates the following general principle:

Regardless of our preferences for cash today versus cash in the future, we should always maximize NPV first. We can then borrow or lend to shift cash flows through time and find our most preferred pattern of cash flows.

We illustrate this result in Figure 3.2. In the figure, the three projects are plotted such that the horizontal axis represents cash today and the vertical axis represents cash in one

FIGURE 3.2

Comparing Projects A, B, and C

The line through each project represents the combination of cash flows today and in one year that can be achieved by combining the project with borrowing or saving. By saving, we decrease today's cash flows and increase our cash flows in one year. By borrowing, we increase today's cash flows and decrease our cash flows in one year. The NPV of the project is the value of the project expressed solely in terms of cash today. The combinations attainable with the highest NPV project exceed all others.

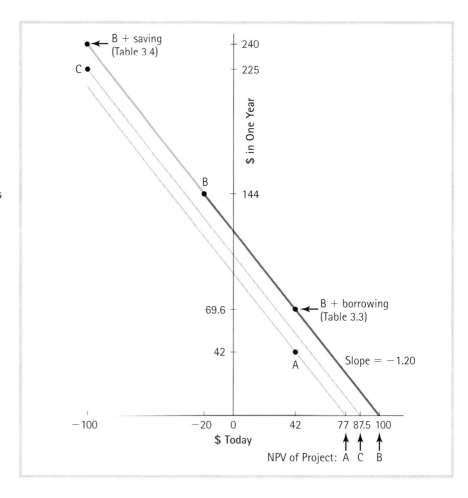

year. We determine the NPV of each project by converting the cash flows in one year to cash flows today at the risk-free rate of 20%, represented in Figure 3.2 by a line with slope −1.20, which corresponds to the conversion rate of ($1.20 in one year / $1 today). Project B has cash flows of −$20 today and +$144 in one year. If we follow the line with slope −1.20 from Project B down to the horizontal axis, we see the value of Project B expressed in today's dollars, an NPV of $100.

Notice that all points on this line are achievable by combining Project B with an appropriate amount of borrowing or lending. Similarly, all points on the line through Project A are achievable by combining Project A with either borrowing or lending, and all points on the line through Project C represent combinations of Project C with either borrowing or lending at the 20% interest rate. The project with the highest NPV, Project B, is on the highest line in Figure 3.2 and so provides the best alternatives whatever pattern of cash flows we prefer.

CONCEPT CHECK   1. What is the NPV decision rule?

2. Why doesn't the NPV decision rule depend on the investor's preferences?

3.4 Arbitrage and the Law of One Price

So far, we have emphasized the importance of using competitive market prices to compute the NPV. But is there always only one such price? What if the same good trades for different prices in different markets? Consider gold. Gold trades in many different markets, with the largest markets in New York and London. To value an ounce of gold we could look up the competitive price in either of these markets. But suppose gold is trading for $250 per ounce in New York and $300 per ounce in London. Which price should we use?

Fortunately, such situations do not arise, and it is easy to see why. Recall that these are competitive market prices, at which you can both buy *and* sell. Thus, you can make money in this situation simply by buying gold for $250 per ounce in New York and then immediately selling it for $300 per ounce in London.[4] You will make $300 − $250 = $50 per ounce for each ounce you buy and sell. Trading 1 million ounces at these prices, you would make $50 million with no risk or investment! This is a case where that old adage, "Buy low, sell high," can be followed perfectly.

Of course, you will not be the only one making these trades. Everyone who sees these prices will want to trade as many ounces as possible. Within seconds, the market in New York would be flooded with buy orders, and the market in London would be flooded with sell orders. Although a few ounces (traded by the lucky individuals who spotted this opportunity first) might be exchanged at these prices, the price of gold in New York would quickly rise in response to all the orders, and the price in London would rapidly fall.[5] Prices would continue to change until they were equalized somewhere in the middle, such as $275 per ounce. This example illustrates an *arbitrage opportunity*, the focus of this section.

---

4. There is no need to transport the gold from New York to London because investors in these markets trade ownership rights to gold that is stored securely elsewhere.

5. As economists would say, supply would not equal demand in these markets. In New York, demand would be infinite because everyone would want to buy. For equilibrium to be restored so that supply equals demand, the price in New York would have to rise. Similarly, in London there would be infinite supply until the price there fell.

An Old Joke

There is an old joke that many finance professors enjoy telling their students. It goes like this:

A finance professor and a student are walking down a street. The student notices a $100 bill lying on the pavement and leans down to pick it up. The finance professor immediately intervenes and says, "Don't bother; there is no free lunch. If that were a real $100 bill lying there, somebody would already have picked it up!"

This joke invariably generates much laughter because it makes fun of the principle of no arbitrage in competitive markets. But once the laughter dies down, the pro-

fessor then asks whether anyone has ever *actually* found a real $100 bill lying on the pavement. The ensuing silence is the real lesson behind the joke.

This joke sums up the point of focusing on markets in which no arbitrage opportunities exist. Free $100 bills lying on the pavement, like arbitrage opportunities, are extremely rare for two reasons: (1) Because $100 is a large amount of money, people are especially careful not to lose it, and (2) in the rare event when someone does inadvertently drop $100, the likelihood of your finding it before someone else does is extremely small.

Arbitrage

The practice of buying and selling equivalent goods in different markets to take advantage of a price difference is known as **arbitrage**. More generally, we refer to any situation in which it is possible to make a profit without taking any risk or making any investment as an **arbitrage opportunity**. Because an arbitrage opportunity has positive NPV, whenever an arbitrage opportunity appears in financial markets, investors will race to take advantage of it. Those investors who spot the opportunity first and who can trade quickly will have the ability to exploit it. Once they place their trades, prices will respond, causing the arbitrage opportunity to evaporate.

Arbitrage opportunities are like money lying in the street; once spotted, they will quickly disappear. Thus the normal state of affairs in markets should be that no arbitrage opportunities exist. We call a competitive market in which there are no arbitrage opportunities a **normal market**.[6]

Law of One Price

In a normal market, the price of gold at any point in time will be the same in London and New York. The same logic applies more generally whenever equivalent investment opportunities trade in two different competitive markets. If the prices in the two markets differ, investors will profit immediately by buying in the market where it is cheap and selling in the market where it is expensive. In doing so, they will equalize the prices. As a result, prices will not differ (at least not for long). This important property is the **Law of One Price**:

If equivalent investment opportunities trade simultaneously in different competitive markets, then they must trade for the same price in both markets.

---

6. The term *efficient market* is also sometimes used to describe a market that, along with other properties, is without arbitrage opportunities. We avoid the term because it is often vaguely (and inconsistently) defined.

One useful consequence of the Law of One Price is that when evaluating costs and benefits to compute a net present value, we can use any competitive price to determine a cash value, without checking the price in all possible markets.

CONCEPT CHECK

1. If the Law of One Price were violated, how could investors profit?

2. When investors exploit an arbitrage opportunity, how do their actions affect prices?

3.5 No-Arbitrage and Security Prices

An investment opportunity that trades in a financial market is known as a **financial security** (or, more simply, a **security**). The notions of arbitrage and the Law of One Price have important implications for security prices.

Valuing a Security

Consider a simple security that promises a one-time payment to its owner of $1000 in one year's time. Suppose there is no risk that the payment will not be made. One example of this type of security is a **bond**, a security sold by governments and corporations to raise money from investors today in exchange for the promised future payment. If the risk-free interest rate is 5%, what can we conclude about the price of this bond in a normal market?

To answer this question, consider an alternative investment that would generate the same cash flow as this bond. Suppose we invest money at the bank at the risk-free interest rate. How much do we need to invest today to receive $1000 in one year? As we saw in Section 3.3, the cost today of recreating a future cash flow on our own is its present value:

$$PV(\$1000 \text{ in one year}) = (\$1000 \text{ in one year}) \div (1.05 \text{ \$ in one year} / \text{ \$ today})$$

$$= \$952.38 \text{ today}$$

If we invest $952.38 today at the 5% risk-free interest rate, we will have $1000 in one year's time with no risk.

We now have two ways to receive the same cash flow: (1) buy the bond or (2) invest $952.38 at the 5% risk-free interest rate. Because these transactions produce equivalent cash flows, the Law of One Price implies that in a normal market, they must have the same price (or cost). Therefore,

$$\text{Price(Bond)} = \$952.38$$

Recall that the Law of One Price is based on the possibility of arbitrage: If the bond had a different price, there would be an arbitrage opportunity. For example, suppose the bond traded for a price of $940. How could we profit in this situation?

In this case, we can buy the bond for $940 and at the same time borrow $952.38 from the bank. Given the 5% interest rate, we will owe the bank $952.38 × 1.05 = $1000 in one year. Our overall cash flows from this pair of transactions are as shown in Table 3.5. Using this strategy we can earn $12.38 in cash today for each bond that we buy, without taking any risk or paying any of our own money in the future. Of course, as we—and others who see the opportunity—start buying the bond, its price will quickly rise until it reaches $952.38 and the arbitrage opportunity disappears.

TABLE 3.5	Net Cash Flows from Buying the Bond and Borrowing	
	Today ($)	**In One Year ($)**
Buy the bond	−940.00	+1000.00
Borrow from the bank	+952.38	−1000.00
Net cash flow	+12.38	0.00

A similar arbitrage opportunity arises if the bond price is higher than $952.38. For example, suppose the bond is trading for $960. In that case, we should sell the bond and invest $952.38 at the bank. As shown in Table 3.6, we then earn $7.62 in cash today, yet keep our future cash flows unchanged by replacing the $1000 we would have received from the bond with the $1000 we will receive from the bank. Once again, as people begin selling the bond to exploit this opportunity, the price will fall until it reaches $952.38 and the arbitrage opportunity disappears.

TABLE 3.6	Net Cash Flows from Selling the Bond and Investing	
	Today ($)	**In One Year ($)**
Sell the bond	+960.00	−1000.00
Invest at the bank	−952.38	+1000.00
Net cash flow	+7.62	0.00

When the bond is overpriced, the arbitrage strategy involves selling the bond and investing some of the proceeds. But if the strategy involves selling the bond, does this mean that only the current owners of the bond can exploit it? The answer is no; in financial markets it is possible to sell a security you do not own by doing a *short sale.* In a **short sale**, the person who intends to sell the security first borrows it from someone who already owns it. Later, that person must either return the security by buying it back or pay the owner the cash flows he or she would have received. For example, we could short sell the bond in the example by promising to repay the current owner $1000 in one year. By executing a short sale, it is possible to exploit the arbitrage opportunity when the bond is overpriced even if you do not own it.

Determining the No-Arbitrage Price

We have shown that at any price other than $952.38, an arbitrage opportunity exists for our bond. Thus, in a normal market, the price of this bond must be $952.38. We call this price the **no-arbitrage price** for the bond.

We can apply the argument we used for the simple bond described earlier to price other securities. First, we identify the cash flows that will be paid by the security. Then, we determine the cost of replicating those cash flows on our own. This "do-it-yourself"

Nasdaq SOES Bandits

The Nasdaq stock market differs from other markets such as the NYSE in that it includes multiple dealers who all trade the same stock. For example, on a given day, as many as ten or more dealers may post prices at which they are willing to trade Apple Computer stock (AAPL). The Nasdaq also has a Small Order Execution System (SOES) that allows individual investors to execute trades of up to 1000 shares instantly through an electronic system.

A type of trader sometimes referred to as a "SOES bandit" exploits the ability to execute trades instantly. These traders watch the quotes of different dealers, waiting for arbitrage opportunities to arise. If one dealer is offering to sell AAPL at $20.25 and another is willing to buy at $20.30, the SOES bandit can profit by instantly buying 1000 shares at $20.25 from the first dealer and selling 1000 shares at $20.30 to the second dealer. Such a trade yields an arbitrage profit of $1000 \times \$0.05 = \$50$.

In the past, by making trades like this one many times per day, these traders could make a reasonable amount of money. Before long, the activity of these traders forced dealers to monitor their own quotes much more actively so as to avoid being "picked off" by these bandits. Today, this sort of arbitrage opportunity rarely appears.*

*SOES bandits can still profit by trading on information before dealers have updated their quotes. See J. Harris and P. Schultz, "The Trading Profits of SOES Bandits," *Journal of Financial Economics* 50 (2) (October 1998): 39–62.

cost is the present value of the security's cash flows. Unless the price of the security equals this present value, an arbitrage opportunity will appear. Thus, the general formula is

No Arbitrage Price of a Security

$$\text{Price(Security)} = PV(\text{All cash flows paid by the security}) \tag{3.3}$$

Computing the No-Arbitrage Price

Problem

Consider a security that pays its owner $100 today and $100 in one year, without any risk. Suppose the risk-free interest rate is 10%. What is the no-arbitrage price of the security today (before the first $100 is paid)? If the security is trading for $195, what arbitrage opportunity is available?

Solution

We need to compute the present value of the security's cash flows. In this case there are two cash flows: $100 today, which is already in present value terms, and $100 in one year. The present value of the second cash flow is

$$\$100 \text{ in one year} \div (1.10 \ \$ \text{ in one year} / \$ \text{ today}) = \$90.91 \text{ today}$$

Therefore, the total present value of the cash flows is $100 + $90.91 = $190.91 today, which is the no-arbitrage price of the security.

If the security is trading for $195, we can exploit its overpricing by selling it for $195. We can then use $100 of the sale proceeds to replace the $100 we would have received from the security today and invest $90.91 of the sale proceeds at 10% to replace the $100 we would have received in one year. The remaining $195 − $100 − $90.91 = $4.09 is an arbitrage profit.

Determining the Interest Rate from Bond Prices

Given the risk-free interest rate, the no-arbitrage price of a risk-free bond is determined by Eq. 3.3. The reverse is also true: If we know the price of a risk-free bond, we can use Eq. 3.3 to determine what the risk-free interest rate must be if there are no arbitrage opportunities.

For example, suppose a risk-free bond that pays $1000 in one year is currently trading with a competitive market price of $929.80 today. From Eq. 3.3, we know that the bond's price equals the present value of the $1000 cash flow it will pay:

$$\$929.80 \text{ today} = (\$1000 \text{ in one year}) \div (1 + r_f \ \$ \text{ in one year} / \$ \text{ today})$$

We can rearrange this equation to determine the risk-free interest rate:

$$1 + r_f = \frac{\$1000 \text{ in one year}}{\$929.80 \text{ today}} = 1.0755 \ \$ \text{ in one year} / \$ \text{ today}$$

That is, if there are no arbitrage opportunities, the risk-free interest rate must be 7.55%.

In practice, this method is the way interest rates are actually calculated. When financial news services report current interest rates, they have derived these rates based on the current prices of risk-free government bonds trading in the market.

Note that the risk-free interest rate equals the percentage gain that you earn from investing in the bond, which is called the bond's **return**:

$$\text{Return} = \frac{\text{Gain at end of year}}{\text{Initial Cost}}$$

$$= \frac{1000 - 929.80}{929.80} = \frac{1000}{929.80} - 1 = 7.55\% \tag{3.4}$$

Thus, if there is no arbitrage, the risk-free interest rate is equal to the return from investing in a risk-free bond. If the bond offered a higher return, then investors would earn a profit by borrowing at the risk-free interest rate and investing in the bond. If the bond had a lower return, investors would sell the bond and invest the proceeds at risk-free interest rate. No arbitrage is therefore equivalent to the idea that *all risk-free investments should offer investors the same return.*

The NPV of Trading Securities

When securities trade at no-arbitrage prices, what can we conclude about the value of trading them? We can think of buying a security as an investment decision. The cost of the decision is the price we pay for the security, and the benefit is the cash flows that we will receive from owning the security. From Eq. 3.3, these two are equal in a normal market and so the NPV of buying a security is zero:

$$NPV(\text{Buy security}) = PV(\text{All cash flows paid by the security}) - \text{Price}(\text{Security})$$
$$= 0$$

Similarly, if we sell a security, the price we receive is the benefit and the cost is the cash flows we give up. Again the NPV is zero:

$$NPV(\text{Sell security}) = \text{Price}(\text{Security}) - PV(\text{All cash flows paid by the security})$$
$$= 0$$

Thus, the NPV of trading a security in a normal market is zero. This result is not surprising. If the NPV of buying a security were positive, then buying the security would be equivalent to receiving cash today—that is, it would present an arbitrage opportunity. Because arbitrage opportunities do not exist in normal markets, the NPV of all security trades must be zero.

Another way to understand this result is to remember that every trade has both a buyer and a seller. If the trade offered a positive NPV to one, it must give a negative NPV to the other. But then one of the two parties would not agree to the trade. Because all trades are voluntary, they must occur at prices at which neither party is losing value, and therefore for which the trade is zero NPV.

In normal markets trading securities neither creates nor destroys value. Value is created by the real investment projects in which the firm engages, such as developing new products, opening new stores, or creating more efficient production methods. Financial transactions are not sources of value but merely serve to adjust the timing and risk of the cash flows to best suit the needs of the firm or its investors.

An important consequence of this result is the idea that we can evaluate a decision by focusing on its real components, rather than its financial ones. That is, we can separate the firm's investment decision from its financing choice. We refer to this concept as the **Separation Principle**:

Security transactions in a normal market neither create nor destroy value on their own. Therefore, we can evaluate the NPV of an investment decision separately from the decision the firm makes regarding how to finance the investment or any other security transactions the firm is considering.

EXAMPLE 3.7

Separating Investment and Financing

Problem

Your firm is considering a project that will require an upfront investment of $10 million today and will produce $12 million in cash flow for the firm in one year without risk. Rather than pay for the $10 million investment entirely using its own cash, the firm is considering raising additional funds by issuing a security that will pay investors $5.5 million in one year. Suppose the risk-free interest rate is 10%. Is pursuing this project a good decision without issuing the new security? Is it a good decision with the new security?

Solution

Without the new security, the cost of the project is $10 million today and the benefit is $12 million in one year. Converting the benefit to a present value

$12 million in one year ÷ (1.10 $ in one year / $ today) = $10.91 million today

we see that the project has $NPV = \$10.91$ million $- \$10$ million $= \$0.91$ million today.

Now suppose the firm issues the new security. In a normal market, the price of this security will be the present value of its future cash flow:

Price(Security) = $5.5 million ÷ 1.10 = $5 million today

Thus, after it raises $5 million by issuing the new security, the firm will only need to invest an additional $5 million to take the project.

To compute the project's NPV in this case, note that in one year the firm will receive the $12 million payout of the project, but owe $5.5 million to the investors in the new security, leaving $6.5 million for the firm. This amount has a present value of

$6.5 million in one year ÷ (1.10 \$ in one year / \$ today) = $5.91 million today

Thus, the project has $NPV =$ $5.91 million − $5 million = $0.91 million today, as before.

In either case, we get the same result for the NPV. The separation principle indicates that we will get the same result for any choice of financing for the firm that occurs in a normal market. We can therefore evaluate the project without explicitly considering the different financing possibilities the firm might choose.

Valuing a Portfolio

So far, we have discussed the no-arbitrage price for individual securities. The Law of One Price also has implications for packages of securities. Consider two securities, A and B. Suppose a third security, C, has the same cash flows as A and B combined. In this case, security C is equivalent to a **portfolio** or combination, of the securities A and B. What can we conclude about the price of security C as compared to the prices of A and B?

Because security C is equivalent to the portfolio of A and B, by the Law of One Price, they must have the same price. This idea leads to the relationship known as **value additivity**; that is, the price of C must equal the price of the portfolio, which is the combined price of A and B.

Value Additivity

$$\text{Price(C)} = \text{Price(A + B)} = \text{Price(A)} + \text{Price(B)} \tag{3.5}$$

Because security C has cash flows equal to the sum of A and B, its value or price must be the sum of the values of A and B. Otherwise, an obvious arbitrage opportunity would exist. For example, if the total price of A and B were lower than the price of C, then we could make a profit buying A and B and selling C. This arbitrage activity would quickly push prices until the price of security C equals the total price of A and B.

Stock Index Arbitrage

Value additivity is the principle behind a type of trading activity known as stock index arbitrage. Common stock indices (such as the Dow Jones Industrial Average and the Standard and Poor's 500) represent portfolios of individual stocks. It is possible to trade the individual stocks in an index on the New York Stock Exchange and NASDAQ. It is also possible to trade the entire index (as a single security) on the futures exchanges in Chicago. When the price of the index in Chicago is below the total price of the individual stocks, traders buy the index and sell the stocks to capture the price differ-ence. Similarly, when the price of the index in Chicago is above the total price of the individual stocks, traders sell the index and buy the individual stocks. The investment banks that engage in stock index arbitrage automate the process by tracking the prices and submitting the orders via computer; as a result, this activity is also referred as "program trading." It is not uncommon for 5% to 10% of the daily volume of trade on the NYSE to be due to index arbitrage activity. The actions of these arbitrageurs ensure that the index prices in Chicago and the individual stock prices track each other very closely.

More generally, value additivity implies that the value of a portfolio is equal to the sum of the values of its parts. That is, the "à la carte" price and the package price must coincide. This feature of financial markets does not hold in many other, noncompetitive markets.[7]

Valuing an Asset in a Portfolio

Problem
Holbrook Holdings is a publicly traded company with only two assets: It owns 60% of Harry's Hotcakes restaurant chain and an ice hockey team. Suppose the market value of Holbrook Holdings is $160 million, and the market value of the entire Harry's Hotcakes chain (which is also publicly traded) is $120 million. What is the market value of the hockey team?

Solution
We can think of Holbrook as a portfolio consisting of a 60% stake in Harry's Hotcakes and the hockey team. By value additivity, the sum of the value of the stake in Harry's Hotcakes and the hockey team must equal the $160 million market value of Holbrook. Because the 60% stake in Harry's Hotcakes is worth 60% × $120 million = $72 million, the hockey team has a value of $160 million − $72 million = $88 million.

Value additivity has an important consequence for the value of an entire firm. The cash flows of the firm are equal to the total cash flows of all projects and investments within the firm. Therefore, by value additivity, the price or value of the entire firm is equal to the sum of the values of all projects and investments within it. In other words, our NPV decision rule coincides with maximizing the value of the entire firm:

To maximize the value of the entire firm, managers should make decisions that maximize NPV. The NPV of the decision represents its contribution to the overall value of the firm.

CONCEPT CHECK

1. If a firm makes an investment that has a positive NPV, how does the value of the firm change?

2. What is the separation principle?

3.6 The Price of Risk

Thus far we have considered only cash flows that have no risk. But in many settings, cash flows are risky. In this section, we examine how to determine the present value of a risky cash flow.

---

7. For example, a round-trip airline ticket often costs much less than two separate one-way tickets. Of course, airline tickets are not sold in a competitive market—you cannot buy *and* sell the tickets at the listed prices. Only airlines can sell tickets, and they have strict rules against reselling tickets. Otherwise, you could make money buying round-trip tickets and selling them to people who need one-way tickets.

Risky Versus Risk-free Cash Flows

Suppose the risk-free interest rate is 4% and that over the next year the economy is equally likely to strengthen or weaken. Consider an investment in a risk-free bond, and one in the stock market index (a portfolio of all stocks in the market). The risk-free bond has no risk and will pay $1100 whatever the state of the economy. The cash flow from an investment in the market index, however, depends on the strength of the economy. Let's assume that the market index will be worth $1400 if the economy is strong but only $800 if the economy is weak. Table 3.7 summarizes these payoffs.

TABLE 3.7	Cash Flows and Market Prices (in $) of a Risk-Free Bond and an Investment in the Market Portfolio		

Security	Market Price Today	Cash Flow in One Year	
		Weak Economy	**Strong Economy**
Risk-free bond	1058	1100	1100
Market index	1000	800	1400

In Section 3.5 we saw that the no-arbitrage price of a security is equal to the present value of its cash flows. For example, the price of the risk-free bond corresponds to the 4% risk-free interest rate:

$$\text{Price(Risk-free Bond)} = \text{PV(Cash Flows)}$$
$$= (\$1100 \text{ in one year}) \div (1.04 \text{ \$ in one year / \$ today})$$
$$= \$1058 \text{ today}$$

Now consider the market index. An investor who buys it today can sell it in one year for a cash flow of either $800 or $1400, with an average payoff of $\frac{1}{2}$ ($800) + $\frac{1}{2}$ ($1400) = $1100. Although this average payoff is the same as the risk-free bond, the market index has a lower price today. It pays $1100 *on average*, but its actual cash flow is risky, so investors are only willing to pay $1000 for it today rather than $1058. What accounts for this lower price?

Risk Aversion and the Risk Premium

Intuitively, investors pay less to receive $1100 on average than to receive $1100 with certainty because they don't like risk. That is, *the personal cost of losing a dollar in bad times is greater than the benefit of an extra dollar in good times.* Thus, the benefit from receiving an extra $300 ($1400 versus $1100) when the economy is strong is less important than the loss of $300 ($800 versus $1100) when the economy is weak. As a result, investors prefer to receive $1100 with certainty.

The notion that investors prefer to have a safe income rather than a risky one of the same average amount is called **risk aversion**. It is an aspect of an investor's preferences, and different investors may have different degrees of risk aversion. The more risk averse investors are, the lower the current price of the market index will be compared to a risk-free bond with the same average payoff.

Because investors care about risk, we cannot use the risk-free interest rate to compute the present value of a risky future cash flow. When investing in a risky project, investors will expect a return that appropriately compensates them for the risk. For example, investors who buy the market index for its current price of $1000 receive $1100 on average at the end of the year, which is an average gain of $100, or a 10% return on their initial investment. When we compute the return of a security based on the payoff we expect to receive on average, we call it the **expected return**:

$$\text{Expected return of a risky investment} = \frac{\text{Expected Gain at end of year}}{\text{Initial Cost}} \quad (3.6)$$

Of course, although the expected return of the market index is 10%, its *actual* return will be higher or lower. If the economy is strong, the market index will rise to 1400, which represents a return of

$$\text{Market return if economy is strong} = (1400 - 1000) / 1000 = 40\%$$

If the economy is weak, the index will drop to 800, for a return of

$$\text{Market return if economy is weak} = (800 - 1000) / 1000 = -20\%$$

We can also calculate the 10% expected return by computing the average of these actual returns: $\frac{1}{2}(40\%) + \frac{1}{2}(-20\%) = 10\%$.

Thus, investors in the market index earn an expected return of 10% rather than the risk-free interest rate of 4% on their investment. The difference of 6% between these returns is called the market index's **risk premium**. The risk premium of a security represents the additional return that investors expect to earn to compensate them for the security's risk. Because investors are risk averse, the price of a risky security cannot be calculated by simply discounting its expected cash flow at the risk-free interest rate. Rather,

When a cash flow is risky, to compute its present value we must discount the cash flow we expect on average at a rate that equals the risk-free interest rate plus an appropriate risk premium.

The No-Arbitrage Price of a Risky Security

Just as the risk-free interest rate is determined by investors' preferences to save versus consume, the risk premium of the market index is determined by investors' preferences toward risk. The risk premium is just large enough so that the demand to invest in the market index equals the supply that is available.

In the same way we used the risk-free interest rate to determine the no-arbitrage price of other risk-free securities, we can use the risk premium of the market index to value other risky securities. For example, suppose security A will pay investors $600 if the economy is strong and nothing if it is weak. Let's see how we can determine the market price of security A using the Law of One Price.

As shown in Table 3.8, if we combine security A with a risk-free bond that pays $800 in one year, the cash flows of the portfolio in one year are identical to the cash flows of the market index. By the Law of One Price, the total market value of the bond and security A must equal $1000, the value of the market index. Given a risk-free interest rate of 4%, the market price of the bond is

$$(\$800 \text{ in one year}) \div (1.04 \text{ \$ in one year} / \text{\$ today}) = \$769 \text{ today}$$

Therefore, the initial market price of security A is $1000 - 769 = \$231$. If the price of security were higher or lower than $231, then the value of the portfolio of the bond and

| TABLE 3.8 | Determining the Market Price of Security A (cash flows in $) |

Security	Market Price Today	Cash Flow in One Year	
		Weak Economy	Strong Economy
Risk-free bond	769	800	800
Security A	?	0	600
Market index	1000	800	1400

security A would differ from the value of the market index, violating the Law of One Price and creating an arbitrage opportunity.

Risk Premiums Depend on Risk

Given an initial price of $231 and an expected payoff of $\frac{1}{2}(0) + \frac{1}{2}(600) = 300$, security A has an expected return of

$$\text{Expected return of security A} = \frac{300 - 231}{231} = 30\%$$

Note that this expected return exceeds the 10% expected return of the market portfolio. Investors in security A earn a risk premium of $30\% - 4\% = 26\%$ over the risk-free interest rate, compared to a 6% risk premium for the market portfolio. Why are the risk premiums so different?

The reason for the difference becomes clear if we compare the actual returns for the two securities. When the economy is weak, investors in security A lose everything, for a return of -100%, and when the economy is strong, they earn a return of $(600 - 231) / 231 = 160\%$. In contrast, the market index loses 20% in a weak economy and gains 40% in a strong economy. Given its much more variable returns, it is not surprising that security A must pay investors a higher risk premium.

Risk Is Relative to the Overall Market

The example of security A suggests that the risk premium of a security will depend on how variable its returns are. But before drawing any conclusions, it is worth considering one further example.

EXAMPLE 3.9

A Negative Risk Premium

Problem
Suppose security B pays $600 if the economy is weak and $0 if the economy is strong. What is its no-arbitrage price, expected return, and risk premium?

Solution
If we combine the market index and security B together in a portfolio, we earn the same payoff as a risk-free bond that pays $1400, as shown here (cash flows in $):

| | | Cash Flow in One Year | |
Security	Market Price Today	Weak Economy	Strong Economy
Market index	1000	800	1400
Security B	?	600	0
Risk-free bond	1346	1400	1400

Because the market price of the risk-free bond is $1400 ÷ 1.04 = $1346 today, we can conclude from the Law of One Price that security B must have a market price of $1346 − 1000 = $346 today.

If the economy is weak, security B pays a return of (600 − 346) / 346 = 73.4%. If the economy is strong, security B pays nothing, for a return of −100%. The expected return of security B is therefore $\frac{1}{2}(73.4\%) + \frac{1}{2}(-100\%) = -13.3\%$. Its risk premium is −13.3% − 4% = −17.3%; that is, security B pays investors 17.3% *less* on average than the risk-free interest rate.

The results for security B are quite striking. Looking at securities A and B in isolation, they seem very similar—both are equally likely to pay $600 or $0. Yet security A has a much lower market price than security B ($231 vs. $346). In terms of returns, security A pays investors an expected return of 30%; security B pays −13.3%. Why are their prices and expected returns so different? And why would risk-averse investors be willing to buy a risky security with an expected return below the risk-free interest rate?

To understand this result, note that security A pays $600 when the economy is strong, and B pays $600 when the economy is weak. Recall that our definition of risk aversion is that investors value an extra dollar of income more in bad times than in good times. Thus, because security B pays $600 when the economy is weak and the market index performs poorly, it pays off when investors' wealth is low and they value money the most. In fact, security B is not really "risky" from an investor's point of view; rather, security B is an insurance policy against an economic decline. By holding security B together with the market index, we can eliminate our risk from market fluctuations. Risk-averse investors are willing to pay for this insurance by accepting a return below the risk-free interest rate.

This result illustrates an extremely important principle. The risk of a security cannot be evaluated in isolation. Even when a security's returns are quite variable, if the returns vary in a way that offsets other risks investors are holding, the security will reduce rather than increase investors' risk. As a result, risk can only be assessed relative to the other risks that investors face; that is,

The risk of a security must be evaluated in relation to the fluctuations of other investments in the economy. A security's risk premium will be higher the more its returns tend to vary with the overall economy and the market index. If the security's returns vary in the opposite direction of the market index, it offers insurance and will have a negative risk premium.

Table 3.9 compares the risk and risk premiums for the different securities we have considered thus far. For each security we compute the difference in its return when the economy is strong versus weak. Note that the risk premium for each security is proportional to this difference, and the risk premium is negative when the returns vary in the opposite direction of the market.

TABLE 3.9   **Risk and Risk Premiums for Different Securities**

Security	Returns		Difference in Returns	Risk Premium
	Weak Economy	**Strong Economy**		
Risk-free bond	4%	4%	0%	0%
Market index	−20%	40%	60%	6%
Security A	−100%	160%	260%	26%
Security B	73%	−100%	−173%	−17.3%

Risk, Return, and Market Prices

We have shown that when cash flows are risky, we can use the Law of One Price to compute present values by constructing a portfolio that produces cash flows with identical risk. As shown in Figure 3.3, computing prices in this way is equivalent to converting between cash flows today and the *expected* cash flows received in the future using a discount rate r_s that includes a risk premium appropriate for the investment's risk:

$$r_s = r_f + \text{(risk premium for investment } s) \qquad (3.7)$$

For the simple setting considered here with only a single source of risk (the strength of the economy), we have seen that the risk premium of an investment depends on how its returns vary with the overall economy. In Part IV of the text we show that this result holds for more general settings with many sources of risk and more than two possible states of the economy.

Using the Risk Premium to Compute a Price

Problem
Consider a risky bond with a cash flow of $1100 when the economy is strong and $1000 when the economy is weak. Suppose a 1% risk premium is appropriate for this bond. If the risk-free interest rate is 4%, what is the price of the bond today?

Solution
From Eq. 3.7, the appropriate discount rate for the bond is

$$r_b = r_f + \text{(Risk Premium for the Bond)} = 4\% + 1\% = 5\%$$

The expected cash flow of the bond is $\frac{1}{2}(\$1100) + \frac{1}{2}(\$1000) = \$1050$ in one year. Thus, the price of the bond today is

$$\text{Bond Price} = \text{(Average cash flow in one year)} \div (1 + r_b \text{ \$ in one year / \$ today})$$

$$= (\$1050 \text{ in one year}) \div (1.05 \text{ \$ in one year / \$ today})$$

$$= \$1000 \text{ today}$$

Given this price, the bond's return is 10% when the economy is strong, and 0% when the economy is weak. (Note that the difference in the returns is 10%, which is 1/6 as variable as the market index; see Table 3.9. Correspondingly, the risk premium of the bond is 1/6 that of the market index as well.)

FIGURE 3.3

Converting Between Dollars Today and Dollars in One Year with Risk

When cash flows are risky, Eq. (3.7) determines the expected return, r_s, that we can use to convert between prices or present values today and the expected cash flow in the future.

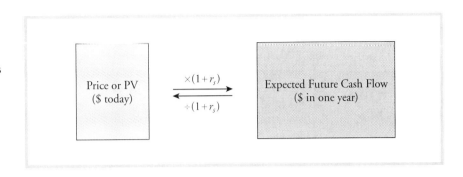

CONCEPT CHECK

1. Why does the expected return of a risky security generally differ from the risk-free interest rate? What determines the size of its risk premium?

2. Explain why the risk of a security should not be evaluated in isolation.

3.7 Arbitrage with Transactions Costs

In our examples up to this point, we have ignored the costs of buying and selling goods or securities. In most markets, you must pay **transactions costs** to trade securities. As discussed in Chapter 1, when you trade securities in markets such as the NYSE and Nasdaq, you must pay two types of transactions costs. First, you must pay your broker a commission on the trade. Second, because you will generally pay a slightly higher price when you buy a security (the ask price) than you receive when you sell (the bid price), you will also pay the bid-ask spread. For example, a share of Dell Inc. stock (ticker symbol DELL) might be quoted as follows:

Bid: $40.50   Ask: $40.70

We can interpret these quotes as if the competitive price for DELL is $40.60, but there is a transaction cost of $0.10 per share when buying or selling.[8]

What consequence do these transaction costs have for no-arbitrage prices and the Law of One Price? Earlier we stated that the price of gold in New York and London must be identical in competitive markets. Suppose, however, that total transactions costs of $5 per ounce are associated with buying gold in one market and selling it in the other. Then if the price of gold is $250 per ounce in New York and $252 per ounce in London, the "Buy low, sell high" strategy no longer works:

Cost: $250 per ounce (buy gold in New York) + $5(transactions costs)

Benefit: $252 per ounce (sell gold in London)

NPV: $252 − $250 − $5 = −$3 per ounce

Indeed, there is no arbitrage opportunity in this case until the prices diverge by more than $5, the amount of the transactions costs.

---

8. Any price in between the bid price and the ask price could be the competitive price, with differing transaction costs for buying and selling.

In general, we need to modify our previous conclusions about no arbitrage prices by appending the phrase "up to transactions costs." In this example, there is only one competitive price for gold—up to a discrepancy of the $5 transactions cost.

The other conclusions of this chapter have the same qualifier. The package price should equal the à la carte price, up to the transaction costs associated with packaging and unpackaging. The price of a security should equal the present value of its cash flows, up to the transaction costs of trading the security and the cash flows.

Fortunately, for most financial markets, these costs are small. For example, in January 2005, typical bid-ask spreads for large NYSE stocks were between 2 and 5 cents per share. As a first approximation we can ignore these spreads in our analysis. Only in situations in which the NPV is small (relative to the transactions costs) will any discrepancy matter. In that case, we will need to carefully account for all transaction costs to decide whether the NPV is positive or negative.

EXAMPLE 3.11

The No-Arbitrage Price Range

Problem

Consider a bond that pays $1000 at the end of the year. Suppose the market interest rate for deposits is 6%, but the market interest rate for borrowing is 6.5%. What is the no-arbitrage price *range* for the bond? That is, what is the highest and lowest price the bond could trade for without creating an arbitrage opportunity?

Solution

The no-arbitrage price for the bond equals the present value of the cash flows. In this case, we can use either of two interest rates to compute the present value, depending on whether we are borrowing or lending. For example, the amount we would need to put in the bank today to receive $1000 in one year is

$$(\$1000 \text{ in one year}) \div (1.06 \text{ \$ in one year / \$ today}) = \$943.40 \text{ today}$$

where we have used the 6% interest rate that we will earn on our deposit. The amount that we can borrow today if we plan to repay $1000 in one year is

$$(\$1000 \text{ in one year}) \div (1.065 \text{ \$ in one year / \$ today}) = \$938.97 \text{ today}$$

where we have used the higher 6.5% rate that we will have to pay if we borrow.

Suppose the bond price P exceeded $943.40. Then you could profit by selling the bond at its current price and investing $943.40 of the proceeds at the 6% interest rate. You would still receive $1000 at the end of the year, but you would get to keep the difference $(P - 943.40)$ today. This arbitrage opportunity will keep the price of the bond from going higher than $943.40.

Alternatively, suppose the bond price P were less than $938.97. Then you could borrow $938.97 at 6.5% and use P of it to buy the bond. This would leave you with $(938.97 - P)$ today, and no obligation in the future because you can use the $1000 bond payoff to repay the loan. This arbitrage opportunity will keep the price of the bond from falling below $938.97.

If the bond price P is between $938.97 and $943.40, then both of the preceding strategies will lose money, and there is no arbitrage opportunity. Thus no arbitrage implies a narrow range of possible prices for the bond ($938.97 to $943.40), rather than an exact price.

To summarize, when there are transactions costs, arbitrage keeps prices of equivalent goods and securities close to each other. Prices can deviate, but not by more than the transactions cost of the arbitrage.

CONCEPT CHECK
1. In the presence of transactions costs, why might different investors disagree about the value of an investment opportunity?
2. By how much could this value differ?

Summary

1. To evaluate a decision, we must value the incremental costs and benefits associated with that decision. A good decision is one for which the value of the benefits exceeds the value of the costs.

2. To compare costs and benefits that occur at different points in time, in different currencies, or with different risks, we must put all costs and benefits in common terms. Typically, we convert costs and benefits into cash today.

3. A competitive market is one in which a good can be bought and sold at the same price. We use prices from competitive markets to determine the cash value of a good.

4. The time value of money is the difference in value between money today and money in the future. The rate at which we can exchange money today for money in the future by borrowing or investing is the current market interest rate. The risk-free interest rate, r_f, is the rate at which money can be borrowed or lent without risk.

5. The present value (PV) of a cash flow is its value in terms of cash today.

6. The net present value (NPV) of a project is

$$PV(\text{Benefits}) - PV(\text{Costs}) \tag{3.1}$$

7. A good project is one with a positive net present value. The NPV Decision Rule states that when choosing from among a set of alternatives, choose the one with the highest NPV. The NPV of a project is equivalent to the cash value today of the project.

8. Regardless of our preferences for cash today versus cash in the future, we should always first maximize NPV. We can then borrow or lend to shift cash flows through time and find our most preferred pattern of cash flows.

9. Arbitrage is the process of trading to take advantage of equivalent goods that have different prices in different competitive markets.

10. A normal market is a competitive market with no arbitrage opportunities.

11. The Law of One Price states that if equivalent goods or securities trade simultaneously in different competitive markets, they will trade for the same price in each market. This law is equivalent to saying that no arbitrage opportunities should exist.

12. The No-Arbitrage Price of a Security is

$$PV(\text{All cash flows paid by security}) \tag{3.3}$$

13. Value additivity implies that the value of a portfolio is equal to the sum of the values of its parts.

14. To maximize the value of the entire firm, managers should make decisions that maximize the NPV. The NPV of the decision represents its contribution to the overall value of the firm.

15. The Separation Principle states that security transactions in a normal market neither create nor destroy value on their own. As a consequence, we can evaluate the NPV of an investment decision separately from the security transactions the firm is considering.

16. When cash flows are risky, we cannot use the risk-free interest rate to compute present values. Instead, we can determine the present value by constructing a portfolio that produces cash flows with identical risk, and then applying the Law of One Price.

17. The risk of a security must be evaluated in relation to the fluctuations of other investments in the economy. A security's risk premium will be higher the more its returns tend to vary with the overall economy and the market index. If the security's returns vary in the opposite direction of the market index, it offers insurance and will have a negative risk premium.

18. When there are transactions costs, the prices of equivalent securities can deviate from each other, but not by more than the transactions costs of the arbitrage.

Key Terms

arbitrage *p. 60*
arbitrage opportunity *p. 60*
bond *p. 61*
competitive market *p. 49*
discount factor *p. 53*
discount rate *p. 53*
expected return *p. 69*
financial security *p. 61*
interest rate factor *p. 52*
Law of One Price *p. 60*
net present value (NPV) *p. 54*
no-arbitrage price *p. 62*
normal market *p. 60*

NPV Decision Rule *p. 55*
portfolio *p. 66*
present value (PV) *p. 54*
return *p. 64*
risk aversion *p. 68*
risk-free interest rate *p. 52*
risk premium *p. 69*
Separation Principle *p. 65*
short sale *p. 62*
time value of money *p. 51*
transactions costs *p. 73*
value additivity *p. 66*

Further Reading

Many of the fundamental principles of this chapter were developed in the classic text by I. Fisher, *The Theory of Interest: As Determined by Impatience to Spend Income and Opportunity to Invest It* (New York: Macmillan, 1930); reprinted (New York: Augustus M. Kelley, 1955).

To learn more about the principle of no arbitrage and its importance as the foundation for modern finance theory, see S. A. Ross, *Neoclassical Finance* (Princeton, NJ: Princeton University Press, 2004).

For a discussion of arbitrage and rational trading and their role in determining market prices, see M. Rubinstein, "Rational Markets: Yes or No? The Affirmative Case," *Financial Analysts Journal* (May/June 2001): 15–29.

For a discussion of some of the limitations to arbitrage that may arise in practice, see Shleifer and Vishny, "Limits of Arbitrage," *Journal of Finance*, 52 (1997): 35–55.

Problems

All problems in this chapter are available in MyFinanceLab. An asterisk (*) indicates problems with a higher level of difficulty.

Valuing Costs
and Benefits

1. Honda Motor Company is considering offering a $2000 rebate on its minivan, lowering the vehicle's price from $30,000 to $28,000. The marketing group estimates that this rebate will increase sales over the next year from 40,000 to 55,000 vehicles. Suppose Honda's profit margin with the rebate is $6000 per vehicle. If the change in sales is the only consequence of this decision, what are its costs and benefits? Is it a good idea?

2. You are an international shrimp trader. A food producer in the Czech Republic offers to pay you 2 million Czech koruna today in exchange for a year's supply of frozen shrimp. Your Thai supplier will provide you with the same supply for 3 million Thai baht today. If the current competitive market exchange rates are 25.50 koruna per dollar and 41.25 baht per dollar, what is the value of this deal?

3. Suppose your employer offers you a choice between a $5000 bonus and 100 shares of the company stock. Whichever one you choose will be awarded today. The stock is currently trading for $63 per share.

    a. Suppose that if you receive the stock bonus, you are free to trade it. Which form of the bonus should you choose? What is its value?

    b. Suppose that if you receive the stock bonus, you are required to hold it for at least one year. What can you say about the value of the stock bonus now? What will your decision depend on?

Interest Rates and the
Time Value of Money

4. Suppose the risk-free interest rate is 4%.

    a. Having $200 today is equivalent to having what amount in one year?

    b. Having $200 in one year is equivalent to having what amount today?

    c. Which would you prefer, $200 today or $200 in one year? Does your answer depend on when you need the money? Why or why not?

5. You have an investment opportunity in Japan. It requires an investment of $1 million today and will produce a cash flow of ¥114 million in one year with no risk. Suppose the risk-free interest rate in the United States is 4%, the risk-free interest rate in Japan is 2%, and the current competitive exchange rate is ¥110 per $1. What is the NPV of this investment? Is it a good opportunity?

Present Value and the
NPV Decision Rule

6. You run a construction firm. You have just won a contract to build a government office building. Building it will require an investment of $10 million today and $5 million in one year. The government will pay you $20 million in one year upon the building's completion. Suppose the cash flows and their times of payment are certain, and the risk-free interest rate is 10%.

    a. What is the NPV of this opportunity?

    b. How can your firm turn this NPV into cash today?

7. Your firm has identified three potential investment projects. The projects and their cash flows are shown here:

Project	Cash Flow Today ($)	Cash Flow in One Year ($)
A	−10	20
B	5	5
C	20	−10

Suppose all cash flows are certain and the risk-free interest rate is 10%.

    a. What is the NPV of each project?

    b. If the firm can choose only one of these projects, which should it choose?

    c. If the firm can choose any two of these projects, which should it choose?

8. Your computer manufacturing firm must purchase 10,000 keyboards from a supplier. One supplier demands a payment of $100,000 today plus $10 per keyboard payable in one year. Another supplier will charge $21 per keyboard, also payable in one year. The risk-free interest rate is 6%.

    a. What is the difference in their offers in terms of dollars today? Which offer should your firm take?

    b. Suppose your firm does not want to spend cash today. How can it take the first offer and not spend $100,000 of its own cash today?

Arbitrage and the Law
of One Price

9. Suppose Bank One offers a risk-free interest rate of 5.5% on both savings and loans, and Bank Enn offers a risk-free interest rate of 6% on both savings and loans.

    a. What arbitrage opportunity is available?

    b. Which bank would experience a surge in the demand for loans? Which bank would receive a surge in deposits?

    c. What would you expect to happen to the interest rates the two banks are offering?

10. Throughout the 1990s, interest rates in Japan were lower than interest rates in the United States. As a result, many Japanese investors were tempted to borrow in Japan and invest the proceeds in the United States. Explain why this strategy does not represent an arbitrage opportunity.

11. An American Depositary Receipt (**ADR**) is security issued by a U.S. bank and traded on a U.S. stock exchange that represents a specific number of shares of a foreign stock. For example, Nokia Corporation trades as an ADR with symbol NOK on the NYSE. Each ADR represents one share of Nokia Corporation stock, which trades with symbol NOK1V on the Helsinki stock exchange. If the U.S. ADR for Nokia is trading for $17.96 per share, and Nokia stock is trading on the Helsinki exchange for 14.78 € per share, use the Law of One Price to determine the current $/€ exchange rate.

No-Arbitrage and
Security Prices

  12. The promised cash flows of three securities are listed here. If the cash flows are risk-free, and the risk-free interest rate is 5%, determine the no-arbitrage price of each security before the first cash flow is paid.

Security	Cash Flow Today ($)	Cash Flow in One Year ($)
A	500	500
B	0	1000
C	1000	0

13. An Exchange-Traded Fund (ETF) is a security that represents a portfolio of individual stocks. Consider an ETF for which each share represents a portfolio of two shares of Hewlett-Packard (HP), one share of Sears, Roebuck (S), and three shares of Ford Motor (F). Suppose the current stock prices of each individual stock are as shown here:

Stock	Current Market Price
HP	$28
S	$40
F	$14

   a. What is the price per share of the ETF in a normal market?

   b. If the ETF currently trades for $120, what arbitrage opportunity is available? What trades would you make?

   c. If the ETF currently trades for $150, what arbitrage opportunity is available? What trades would you make?

EXCEL   14.   Consider two securities that pay risk-free cash flows over the next two years and that have the current market prices shown here:

Security	Price Today ($)	Cash Flow in One Year ($)	Cash Flow in Two Years ($)
B1	94	100	0
B2	85	0	100

   a. What is the no-arbitrage price of a security that pays cash flows of $100 in one year and $100 in two years?

   b. What is the no-arbitrage price of a security that pays cash flows of $100 in one year and $500 in two years?

   c. Suppose a security with cash flows of $50 in one year and $100 in two years is trading for a price of $130. What arbitrage opportunity is available?

   15.   Suppose a security with a risk-free cash flow of $150 in one year trades for $140 today. If there are no arbitrage opportunities, what is the current risk-free interest rate?

EXCEL   16.   Xia Corporation is a company whose sole assets are $100,000 in cash and three projects that it will undertake. The projects are risk-free and have the following cash flows:

Project	Cash Flow Today ($)	Cash Flow in One Year ($)
A	−20,000	30,000
B	−10,000	25,000
C	−60,000	80,000

   Xia plans to invest any unused cash today at the risk-free interest rate of 10%. In one year, all cash will be paid to investors and the company will be shut down.

   a. What is the NPV of each project? Which projects should Xia undertake and how much cash should it retain?

   b. What is the total value of Xia's assets (projects and cash) today?

   c. What cash flows will the investors in Xia receive? Based on these cash flows, what is the value of Xia today?

   d. Suppose Xia pays any unused cash to investors today, rather than investing it. What are the cash flows to the investors in this case? What is the value of Xia now?

   e. Explain the relationship in your answers to parts (b), (c), and (d).

The Price of Risk

   17.   The table here shows the no-arbitrage prices of securities A and B that we calculated in Section 3.6.

Security	Market Price Today	Cash Flow in One Year	
		Weak Economy	Strong Economy
Security A	230.77	0	600
Security B	346.77	600	0

a. What are the payoffs of a portfolio of one share of security A and one share of security B?

b. What is the market price of this portfolio? What expected return will you earn from holding this portfolio?

18. Suppose security C has a payoff of $600 when the economy is weak and $1800 when the economy is strong. The risk-free interest rate is 4%.

a. Security C has the same payoffs as what portfolio of the securities A and B in problem 17?

b. What is the no-arbitrage price of security C?

c. What is the expected return of security C if both states are equally likely? What is its risk premium?

d. What is the difference between the return of security C when the economy is strong and when it is weak?

e. If security C had a risk premium of 10%, what arbitrage opportunity would be available?

*19. Suppose a risky security pays an expected cash flow of $80 in one year. The risk-free rate is 4%, and the expected return on the market index is 10%.

a. If the returns of this security are high when the economy is strong and low when the economy is weak, but the returns vary by only half as much as the market index, what risk premium is appropriate for this security?

b. What is the security's market price?

Arbitrage with Transactions Costs

20. Suppose Hewlett-Packard (HP) stock is currently trading on the NYSE with a bid price of $28.00 and an ask price of $28.10. At the same time, a NASDAQ dealer posts a bid price for HP of $27.85 and an ask price of $27.95.

a. Is there an arbitrage opportunity in this case? If so, how would you exploit it?

b. Suppose the NASDAQ dealer revises his quotes to a bid price of $27.95 and an ask price of $28.05. Is there an arbitrage opportunity now? If so, how would you exploit it?

c. What must be true of the highest bid price and the lowest ask price for no arbitrage opportunity to exist?

*21. Consider a portfolio of two securities: one share of Citigroup stock and a bond that pays $100 in one year. Suppose this portfolio is currently trading with a bid price of $131.65 and an ask price of $132.25, and the bond is trading with a bid price of $91.75 and an ask price of $91.95. In this case, what is the no-arbitrage price range for Citigroup stock?

PART

II

Chapter 4
The Time Value of Money

Chapter 5
Interest Rates

Chapter 6
Investment Decision Rules

Tools

The Law of One Price Connection. In this part of the text, we introduce the basic tools for making financial decisions. For a financial manager, evaluating financial decisions involves computing the net present value of a project's future cash flows. In Chapter 4 we use the Law of One Price to derive a central concept in financial economics—the *time value of money*. We explain how to value a stream of future cash flows and derive a few useful shortcuts for computing the net present value of various types of cash flow patterns. Chapter 5 considers how to use market interest rates to determine the appropriate discount rate for a set of cash flows. We apply the Law of One Price to demonstrate that the discount rate will depend on the rate of return of investments with maturity and risk similar to the cash flows being valued. This observation leads to the important concept of the *cost of capital* of an investment decision. In Chapter 6, we compare the net present value rule to other investment rules firms sometimes use and explain why the net present value rule is superior.

4

The Time Value of Money

notation

r	interest rate
C	cash flow
FV_n	future value on date n
PV	present value; annuity spreadsheet notation for the initial amount
C_n	cash flow at date n
N	date of the last cash flow in a stream of cash flows
NPV	net present value
P	initial principal or deposit, or equivalent present value
FV	future value; annuity spreadsheet notation for the extra final payment
g	growth rate
$NPER$	annuity spreadsheet notation for the number of periods or dates of the last cash flow
$RATE$	annuity spreadsheet notation for interest rate
PMT	annuity spreadsheet notation for cash flow
IRR	internal rate of return
PV_n	present value on date n

As discussed in Chapter 3, to evaluate a project a financial manager must compare its costs and benefits. In most cases, the cash flows in financial investments involve more than one future period. For example, early in 2003, the Boeing Company announced that it was developing the 7E7, a highly efficient, long-range airplane able to seat 200 to 250 passengers. Boeing's project involves revenues and expenses that will occur many years or even decades into the future. How can financial managers evaluate a project such as the 7E7 airplane?

As we learned in Chapter 3, Boeing should make the investment in the 7E7 if the NPV is positive. Calculating the NPV requires tools to evaluate cash flows lasting several periods. We develop these tools in this chapter. The first tool is a visual method for representing a stream of cash flows: the *timeline*. After constructing a timeline, we establish three important rules for moving cash flows to different points in time. Using these rules, we show how to compute the present and future values of the costs and benefits of a general stream of cash flows, and how to compute the NPV. Although these techniques can be used to value any type of asset, certain types of assets have cash flows that follow a regular pattern. We develop shortcuts for *annuities*, *perpetuities*, and other special cases of assets with cash flows that follow regular patterns.

4.1   The Timeline

We begin our look at valuing cash flows lasting several periods with some basic vocabulary and tools. We refer to a series of cash flows lasting several periods as a **stream of cash flows**. We can represent a stream of cash flows on a **timeline**, a linear representation of the timing of the expected cash flows. Timelines are an important first step in organizing and then solving a financial problem. We use them throughout this text.

To illustrate how to construct a timeline, assume that a friend owes you money. He has agreed to repay the loan by making two payments of $10,000 at the end of each of the next two years. We represent this information on a timeline as follows:

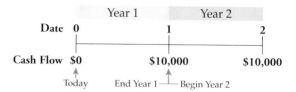

Date 0 represents the present. Date 1 is one year later and represents the end of the first year. The $10,000 cash flow below date 1 is the payment you will receive at the end of the first year. Date 2 is two years from now; it represents the end of the second year. The $10,000 cash flow below date 2 is the payment you will receive at the end of the second year.

You will find the timeline most useful in tracking cash flows if you interpret each point on the timeline as a specific date. The space between date 0 and date 1 then represents the time period between these dates—in this case, the first year of the loan. Date 0 is the beginning of the first year, and date 1 is the end of the first year. Similarly, date 1 is the beginning of the second year, and date 2 is the end of the second year. By denoting time in this way, date 1 signifies *both* the end of year 1 and the beginning of year 2, which makes sense since those dates are effectively the same point in time.[1]

In this example, both cash flows are inflows. In many cases, however, a financial decision will involve both inflows and outflows. To differentiate between the two types of cash flows, we assign a different sign to each: Inflows are positive cash flows, whereas outflows are negative cash flows.

To illustrate, suppose you're still feeling generous and have agreed to lend your brother $10,000 today. Your brother has agreed to repay this loan in two installments of $6000 at the end of each of the next two years. The timeline is:

Notice that the first cash flow at date 0 (today) is represented as −$10,000 because it is an outflow. The subsequent cash flows of $6000 are positive because they are inflows.

So far, we have used timelines to show the cash flows that occur at the end of each year. Actually, timelines can represent cash flows that take place at the end of any time period.

---

1. That is, there is no real time difference between a cash flow paid at 11:59 P.M. on December 31 and one paid at 12:01 A.M. on January 1, although there may be some other differences such as taxation that we overlook for now.

For example, if you pay rent each month, you could use a timeline like the one in our first example to represent two rental payments, but you would replace the "year" label with "month."

Many of the timelines included in this chapter are very simple. Consequently, you may feel that it is not worth the time or trouble to construct them. As you progress to more difficult problems, however, you will find that timelines identify events in a transaction or investment that are easy to overlook. If you fail to recognize these cash flows, you will make flawed financial decisions. Therefore, we recommend that you approach *every* problem by drawing the timeline as we do in this chapter.

Constructing a Timeline

Problem
Suppose you must pay tuition of $10,000 per year for the next two years. Your tuition payments must be made in equal installments at the start of each semester. What is the timeline of your tuition payments?

Solution
Assuming today is the start of the first semester, your first payment occurs at date 0 (today). The remaining payments occur at semester intervals. Using one semester as the period length, we can construct a timeline as follows:

Date (Semesters)	0	1	2	3	4
Cash Flow	−$5000	−$5000	−$5000	−$5000	$0

CONCEPT CHECK

1. What are the key elements of a timeline?

2. How can you distinguish cash inflows from outflows on a timeline?

4.2 The Three Rules of Time Travel

Financial decisions often require comparing or combining cash flows that occur at different points in time. In this section, we introduce three important rules central to financial decision making that allow us to compare or combine values.

Comparing and Combining Values

Our first rule is that it is only possible to compare or combine values at the same point in time. This rule restates a conclusion introduced in Chapter 3: Only cash flows in the same units can be compared or combined. *A dollar today* and *a dollar in one year* are not equivalent. Having money now is more valuable than having money in the future; if you have the money today you can earn interest on it.

To compare or combine cash flows that occur at different points in time, you first need to convert the cash flows into the same units or *move* them to the same point in time. The next two rules show how to move the cash flows on the timeline.

Moving Cash Flows Forward in Time

Suppose we have $1000 today, and we wish to determine the equivalent amount in one year's time. If the current market interest rate is 10%, we can use that rate as an exchange rate to move the cash flow forward in time. That is,

$$(\$1000 \text{ today}) \times (1.10 \text{ \$ in one year} / \text{\$ today}) = \$1100 \text{ in one year}$$

In general, if the market interest rate for the year is r, then we multiply by the interest rate factor, $(1 + r)$, to move the cash flow from the beginning to the end of the year. This process of moving a value or cash flow forward in time is known as **compounding**. *Our second rule stipulates that to move a cash flow forward in time, you must compound it.*

We can apply this rule repeatedly. Suppose we want to know how much the $1000 is worth in two years' time. If the interest rate for year 2 is also 10%, then we convert as we just did:

$$(\$1100 \text{ in one year}) \times (1.10 \text{ \$ in two years} / \text{\$ in one year}) = \$1210 \text{ in two years}$$

Let's represent this calculation on a timeline:

Given a 10% interest rate, all of the cash flows—$1000 at date 0, $1100 at date 1, and $1210 at date 2—are equivalent. They have the same value but are expressed in different units (different points in time). An arrow that points to the right indicates that the value is being moved forward in time—that is, compounded.

The value of a cash flow that is moved forward in time is known as its **future value**. In the preceding example, $1210 is the future value of $1000 two years from today. Note that the value grows as we move the cash flow further in the future. The equivalent value of two cash flows at two different points in time is sometimes referred to as the **time value of money**. By having money sooner, you can invest it and end up with more money later. Note also that the equivalent value grows by $100 the first year, but by $110 the second year. In the second year we earn interest on our original $1000, plus we earn interest on the $100 interest we received in the first year. This effect of earning "interest on interest" is known as **compound interest**.

How does the future value change if we move the cash flow three years? Continuing to use the same approach, we compound the cash flow a third time. Assuming the competitive market interest rate is fixed at 10%, we get

$$\$1000 \times (1.10) \times (1.10) \times (1.10) = \$1000 \times (1.10)^3 = \$1331$$

In general, to take a cash flow C forward n periods into the future, we must compound it by the n intervening interest rate factors. If the interest rate r is constant, this calculation yields

Future Value of a Cash Flow

$$FV_n = C \times \underbrace{(1 + r) \times (1 + r) \times \cdots \times (1 + r)}_{n \text{ times}} = C \times (1 + r)^n \quad (4.1)$$

Moving Cash Flows Back in Time

The third rule describes how to move cash flows backward in time. Suppose you would like to compute the value today of $1000 you anticipate receiving in one year. If the current market interest rate is 10%, you can compute this value by converting units as we did in Chapter 3:

$$(\$1000 \text{ in one year}) \div (1.10 \ \$ \text{ in one year} / \$ \text{ today}) = \$909.09 \text{ today}$$

That is, to move the cash flow backward in time, we divide it by the interest rate factor, $(1 + r)$, where r is the interest rate. This process of moving a value or cash flow backward in time—finding the equivalent value today of a future cash flow—is known as **discounting**. *Our third rule stipulates that to move a cash flow back in time, we must discount it.*

To illustrate, suppose that you anticipate receiving the $1000 two years from today rather than in one year. If the interest rate for both years is 10%, we can prepare the following timeline:

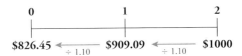

When the interest rate is 10%, all of the cash flows—$826.45 at date 0, $909.09 at date 1, and $1000 at date 2—are equivalent. They represent the same value in different units (different points in time). The arrow points to the left to indicate that the value is being moved backward in time or discounted. Note that the value decreases as we move the cash flow further back.

The value of a future cash flow at an earlier point on the timeline is its present value at the earlier point in time. That is, $826.45 is the present value at date 0 of $1000 in two years. Recall from Chapter 3 that the present value is the "do-it-yourself" price to produce a future cash flow. Thus, if we invested $826.45 today for two years at 10% interest, we would have a future value of $1000, using the second rule of time travel:

Suppose the $1000 were three years away and you wanted to compute the present value. Again, if the interest rate is 10%, we have

That is, the present value today of a cash flow of $1000 in three years is given by

$$\$1000 \div (1.10) \div (1.10) \div (1.10) = \$1000 \div (1.10)^3 = \$751.31$$

In general, to move a cash flow C backward n periods, we must discount it by the n intervening interest rate factors. If the interest rate r is constant, this yields

Present Value of a Cash Flow

$$PV = C \div (1 + r)^n = \frac{C}{(1 + r)^n} \tag{4.2}$$

Present Value of a Single Future Cash Flow

Problem

You are considering investing in a savings bond that will pay $15,000 in ten years. If the competitive market interest rate is fixed at 6% per year, what is the bond worth today?

Solution

The cash flows for this bond are represented by the following timeline:

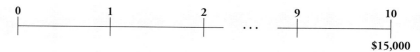

Thus, the bond is worth $15,000 in ten years. To determine the value today, we compute the present value:

$$PV = \frac{15,000}{1.06^{10}} = \$8375.92 \text{ today}$$

The bond is worth much less today than its final payoff because of the time value of money.

Applying the Rules of Time Travel

The rules of time travel allow us to compare and combine cash flows that occur at different points in time. Suppose we plan to save $1000 today, and $1000 at the end of each of the next two years. If we earn a fixed 10% interest rate on our savings, how much will we have three years from today?

Again, we start with a timeline:

The timeline shows the three deposits we plan to make. We need to compute their value at the end of three years.

We can use the rules of time travel in a number of ways to solve this problem. First, we can take the deposit at date 0 and move it forward to date 1. Because it is then in the same time period as the date 1 deposit, we can combine the two amounts to find out the total in the bank on date 1:

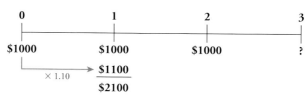

Using the first two rules of time travel, we find that our total savings on date 1 will be $2100. Continuing in this fashion, we can solve the problem as follows:

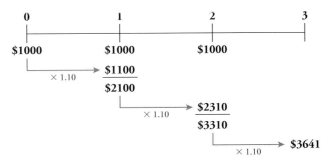

The total amount we will have in the bank at the end of three years is $3641. This amount is the future value of our $1000 savings deposits.

Another approach to the problem is to compute the future value in year 3 of each cash flow separately. Once all three amounts are in year 3 dollars, we can then combine them.

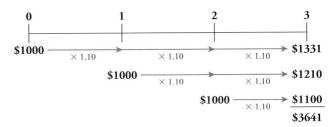

Both calculations give the same future value. As long as we follow the rules, we get the same result. The order in which we apply the rules does not matter. The calculation we choose depends on which is more convenient for the problem at hand. Table 4.1 summarizes the three rules of time travel and their associated formulas.

TABLE 4.1	The Three Rules of Time Travel	
Rule 1	Only values at the same point in time can be compared or combined.	
Rule 2	To move a cash flow forward in time, you must compound it.	Future Value of a Cash Flow $FV_n = C \times (1 + r)^n$
Rule 3	To move a cash flow backward in time, you must discount it.	Present Value of a Cash Flow $PV = C \div (1 + r)^n = \dfrac{C}{(1 + r)^n}$

EXAMPLE 4.3

Computing the Future Value

Problem

Let's revisit the savings plan we considered earlier: We plan to save $1000 today and at the end of each of the next two years. At a fixed 10% interest rate, how much will we have in the bank three years from today?

Solution

Let's solve this problem in a different way than we did in the text. First compute the present value of the cash flows. There are several ways to perform this calculation. Here we treat each cash flow separately and then combine the present values.

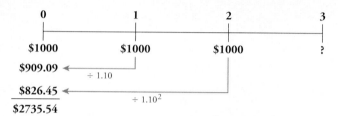

Saving $2735.54 today is equivalent to saving $1000 per year for three years. Now let's compute its future value in year 3:

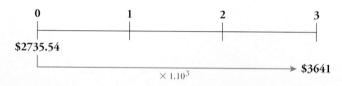

This answer of $3641 is precisely the same result we found earlier. As long as we apply the three rules of time travel, we will always get the correct answer.

<table>
<tr><td>CONCEPT CHECK</td><td>1. Can you compare or combine cash flows at different times?</td></tr>
<tr><td></td><td>2. How do you move a cash flow backward and forward in time?</td></tr>
</table>

4.3 The Power of Compounding: An Application

When you put money into a savings account and choose to leave the earned interest in the account, you will earn interest on the past interest payments. Although initially this "interest on interest" is small, it can eventually become very large. Consider putting $1000 into a bank account that earns a fixed 10% per year. At the end of the first year, you will receive $100 in interest, so your balance will grow to $1100. In the second year, the interest paid is $110, so the "interest on interest" amounts to an extra $10. What about in the twentieth year?

Using the formula for the future value, we see that after 20 years the money will have grown to

$$\$1000 \times 1.10^{20} = \$6727.50$$

The interest paid in the twenty-first year will be 10% of $6727.50, or $672.75. Of that amount, $100 corresponds to interest on the initial $1000 principal, and $572.75 is

FIGURE 4.1

The Power of Compounding

The graph illustrates the future value of $1000 invested at a 10% interest rate. Because interest is paid on past interest, the future value grows exponentially—after 50 years the money grows 117-fold and in 75 years (only 25 years later), it is 1272 times larger than the value today.

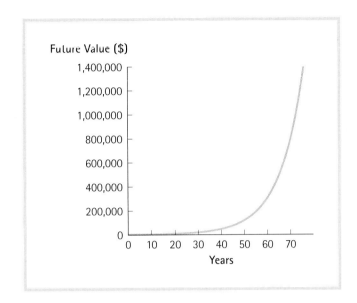

interest on accumulated interest. Note also that in 20 years the money has grown more than sixfold. What will happen over the next 20 years? You may be tempted to guess a 12-fold increase. In fact, in 40 years the amount will have grown to

$$\$1000 \times 1.10^{40} = \$1000 \times 1.10^{20} \times 1.10^{20} = \$45,259.26$$

Rather than doubling, the value of each dollar invested for 40 years is the square of the value after 20 years ($6.7^2 \approx 45$). This kind of growth is called geometric growth. Figure 4.1 shows how impressive this growth can be. After 75 years, $1000 would have grown to more than $1 million. Imagine if one of your grandparents had bequeathed $1000 to you 75 years ago, and it had grown in this way!

CONCEPT CHECK

1. What is compound interest?

2. Why does the future value of an investment grow faster in later years as shown in Figure 4.1?

4.4 Valuing a Stream of Cash Flows

Most investment opportunities have multiple cash flows that occur at different points in time. In Section 4.2, we applied the rules of time travel to value such cash flows. Now we formalize this approach by deriving a general formula for valuing a stream of cash flows.

Consider a stream of cash flows: C_0 at date 0, C_1 at date 1, and so on, up to C_N at date N. We represent this cash flow stream on a timeline as follows:

Using the time travel techniques, we compute the present value of this cash flow stream in two steps. First, we compute the present value of each individual cash flow. Then, once the cash flows are in common units of dollars today, we can combine them.

For a given interest rate r, we represent this process on the timeline as follows:

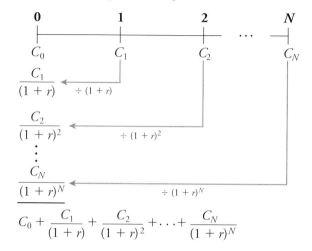

This timeline provides the general formula for the present value of a cash flow stream:

$$PV = C_0 + \frac{C_1}{(1 + r)} + \frac{C_2}{(1 + r)^2} + \cdots + \frac{C_N}{(1 + r)^N}$$

We can also write this formula as a summation:

Present Value of a Cash Flow Stream

$$PV = \sum_{n=0}^{N} PV(C_n) = \sum_{n=0}^{N} \frac{C_n}{(1 + r)^n} \qquad (4.3)$$

The summation sign, Σ, means "sum the individual elements for each date n from 0 to N." Note that $(1 + r)^0 = 1$, so this shorthand matches precisely the previous equation. That is, the present value of the cash flow stream is the sum of the present values of each cash flow. Recall from Chapter 3 how we defined the present value as the dollar amount you would need to invest today to produce the single cash flow in the future. The same idea holds in this context. The present value is the amount you need to invest today to generate the cash flows stream $C_0, C_1, \ldots, C_N$. That is, receiving those cash flows is equivalent to having their present value in the bank today.

EXAMPLE
4.4

Present Value of a Stream of Cash Flows

Problem

You have just graduated and need money to buy a new car. Your rich Uncle Henry will lend you the money so long as you agree to pay him back within four years, and you offer to pay him the rate of interest that he would otherwise get by putting his money in a savings account. Based on your earnings and living expenses, you think you will be able to pay him $5000 in one year, and then $8000 each year for the next three years. If Uncle Henry would otherwise earn 6% per year on his savings, how much can you borrow from him?

Solution

The cash flows you can promise Uncle Henry are as follows:

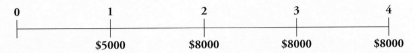

How much money should Uncle Henry be willing to give you today in return for your promise of these payments? He should be willing to give you an amount that is equivalent to these payments in present value terms. This is the amount of money that it would take him to produce these same cash flows, which we calculate as follows:

$$PV = \frac{5000}{1.06} + \frac{8000}{1.06^2} + \frac{8000}{1.06^3} + \frac{8000}{1.06^4}$$

$$= 4716.98 + 7119.97 + 6716.95 + 6336.75$$

$$= 24{,}890.65$$

Thus, Uncle Henry should be willing to lend you $24,890.65 in exchange for your promised payments. This amount is less than the total you will pay him ($5000 + $8000 + $8000 + $8000 = $29,000) due to the time value of money.

Let's verify our answer. If your uncle kept his $24,890.65 in the bank today earning 6% interest, in four years he would have

$$FV = \$24{,}890.65 \times (1.06)^4 = \$31{,}423.87 \text{ in 4 years}$$

Now suppose that Uncle Henry gives you the money, and then deposits your payments to him in the bank each year. How much will he have four years from now?

We need to compute the future value of the annual deposits. One way to do so is to compute the bank balance each year:

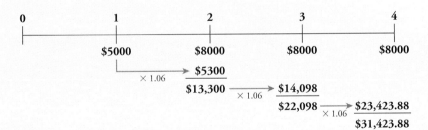

We get the same answer both ways (within a penny, which is because of rounding).

The last section of Example 4.4 illustrates a general point. If you want to compute the future value of a stream of cash flows, you can do it directly (the second approach used in Example 4.4), or you can first compute the present value and then move it to the future (the first approach). Because we obey the laws of time travel in both cases, we get the same result. This principle can be applied more generally to write the following formula for the future value in year n in terms of the present value of a set of cash flows:

Future Value of a Cash Flow Stream with a Present Value of PV

$$FV_n = PV \times (1 + r)^n \tag{4.4}$$

1. How do you calculate the present value of a cash flow stream?

2. How do you calculate the future value of a cash flow stream?

4.5 The Net Present Value of a Stream of Cash Flows

Now that we have established the rules of time travel, and determined how to compute present and future values, we are ready to address our central goal: calculating the NPV of future cash flows to evaluate an investment decision. Recall from Chapter 3 that we defined the net present value (NPV) of an investment decision as follows:

$$NPV = PV(\text{benefits}) - PV(\text{costs})$$

In this context, the benefits are the cash inflows and the costs are the cash outflows. We can represent any investment decision on a timeline as a cash flow stream where the cash outflows (investments) are negative cash flows and the inflows are positive cash flows. Thus, the NPV of an investment opportunity is also the *present value* of the stream of cash flows of the opportunity:

$$NPV = PV(\text{benefits}) - PV(\text{costs}) = PV(\text{benefits} - \text{costs})$$

Net Present Value of an Investment Opportunity

Problem
You have been offered the following investment opportunity: If you invest $1000 today, you will receive $500 at the end of each of the next three years. If you could otherwise earn 10% per year on your money, should you undertake the investment opportunity?

Solution
As always, start with a timeline. We denote the upfront investment as a negative cash flow (because it is money we need to spend) and the money we receive as a positive cash flow.

To decide whether we should accept this opportunity, we compute the NPV by computing the present value of the stream:

$$NPV = -1000 + \frac{500}{1.10} + \frac{500}{1.10^2} + \frac{500}{1.10^3} = \$243.43$$

Because the NPV is positive, the benefits exceed the costs and we should make the investment. Indeed, the NPV tells us that taking this opportunity is like getting an extra $243.43 that you can spend today. To illustrate, suppose you borrow $1000 to invest in the opportunity and an extra $243.43 to spend today. How much would you owe on the $1243.43 loan in three years? At 10% interest, the amount you would owe would be

$$FV = (\$1000 + \$243.43) \times (1.10)^3 = \$1655 \text{ in 3 years}$$

At the same time, the investment opportunity generates cash flows. If you put these cash flows into a bank account, how much will you have saved three years from now? The future value of the savings is

$$FV = (\$500 \times 1.10^2) + (\$500 \times 1.10) + \$500 = \$1655 \text{ in 3 years}$$

As you see, you can use your bank savings to repay the loan. Taking the opportunity therefore allows you to spend $243.43 today at no extra cost.

In principle, we have explained how to answer the question we posed at the beginning of the chapter: How should financial managers evaluate a project such as undertaking the development of the 7E7 airplane? We have shown how to compute the NPV of an investment opportunity such as the 7E7 airplane that lasts more than one period. In practice, when the number of cash flows exceeds four or five (as it most likely will), the calculations can become tedious. Fortunately, a number of special cases do not require us to treat each cash flow separately. We derive these shortcuts in the next section.

CONCEPT CHECK

1. How do you calculate the net present value of a cash flow stream?

2. What benefit does a firm receive when it accepts a project with a positive *NPV*?

4.6 Perpetuities, Annuities, and Other Special Cases

The formulas we have developed so far allow us to compute the present or future value of any cash flow stream. In this section we consider two types of assets, *perpetuities* and *annuities*, and learn shortcuts for valuing them. These shortcuts are possible because the cash flows follow a regular pattern.

Perpetuities

A **perpetuity** is a stream of equal cash flows that occur at regular intervals and last forever. One example is the British government bond called a **consol** (or perpetual bond). Consol bonds promise the owner a fixed cash flow every year, forever.

Here is the timeline for a perpetuity:

Note from the timeline that the first cash flow does not occur immediately; *it arrives at the end of the first period.* This timing is sometimes referred to as payment *in arrears* and is a standard convention that we adopt throughout this text.

Using the formula for the present value, the present value of a perpetuity with payment *C* and interest rate *r* is given by

$$PV = \frac{C}{(1 + r)} + \frac{C}{(1 + r)^2} + \frac{C}{(1 + r)^3} + \cdots = \sum_{n=1}^{\infty} \frac{C}{(1 + r)^n}$$

Notice that $C_n = C$ in the present value formula because the cash flow for a perpetuity is constant. Also, because the first cash flow is in one period, $C_0 = 0$.

To find the value of a perpetuity one cash flow at a time would take forever—literally! You might wonder how, even with a shortcut, the sum of an infinite number of positive terms could be finite. The answer is that the cash flows in the future are discounted for an ever increasing number of periods, so their contribution to the sum eventually becomes negligible.[2]

To derive the shortcut, we calculate the value of a perpetuity by creating our own perpetuity. We can then calculate the present value of the perpetuity because, by the Law of One Price, the value of the perpetuity must be the same as the cost we incurred to create our own perpetuity. To illustrate, suppose you could invest $100 in a bank account paying 5% interest per year forever. At the end of one year, you will have $105 in the bank— your original $100 plus $5 in interest. Suppose you withdraw the $5 interest and reinvest the $100 for a second year. Again you will have $105 after one year, and you can withdraw $5 and reinvest $100 for another year. By doing this year after year, you can withdraw $5 every year in perpetuity:

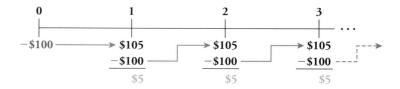

By investing $100 in the bank today, you can, in effect, create a perpetuity paying $5 per year. Recall from Chapter 3 that the Law of One Price tells us that the same good must have the same price in every market. Because the bank will "sell" us (allow us to create) the perpetuity for $100, the present value of the $5 per year in perpetuity is this "do-it-yourself" cost of $100.

Now let's generalize this argument. Suppose we invest an amount P in the bank. Every year we can withdraw the interest we have earned, $C = r \times P$, leaving the principal, P, in the bank. The present value of receiving C in perpetuity is therefore the upfront cost $P = C / r$. Therefore,

Present Value of a Perpetuity

$$PV(C \text{ in perpetuity}) = \frac{C}{r} \tag{4.5}$$

By depositing the amount $\frac{C}{r}$ today, we can withdraw interest of $\frac{C}{r} \times r = C$ each period in perpetuity.

Note the logic of our argument. To determine the present value of a cash flow stream, we computed the "do-it-yourself" cost of creating those same cash flows at the bank. This is an extremely useful and powerful approach—and is much simpler and faster than summing those infinite terms![3]

---

2. In mathematical terms, this is a geometric series, so it converges if $r > 0$.

3. Another mathematical derivation of this result exists (see the online appendix), but it is less intuitive. This case is a good example of how the Law of One Price can be used to derive useful results.

Historical Examples of Perpetuities

Companies sometimes issue bonds that they call perpetuities, but in fact are not really perpetuities. For example, according to *Dow Jones International News* (February 26, 2004), in 2004 Korea First Bank sold $300 million of debt in "the form of a so-called 'perpetual bond' that has no fixed maturity date." Although the bond has no fixed maturity date, Korea First Bank has the right to pay it back after 10 years, in 2014. Korea First Bank also has the right to extend the maturity of the bond for another 30 years after 2014. Thus, although the bond does not have a fixed maturity date, it will eventually mature—in either 10 or 40 years. The bond is not really a perpetuity because it does not pay interest forever.

Perpetual bonds were some of the first bonds ever issued. The oldest perpetuities that are still making interest payments were issued by the *Hoogheemraadschap Lekdijk Bovendams*, a seventeenth-century Dutch water board responsible for upkeep of the local dikes. The oldest bond dates from 1624. Two finance professors at Yale University, William Goetzmann and Geert Rouwenhorst, personally verified that these bonds continue to pay interest. On behalf of Yale, they purchased one of these bonds on July 1, 2003, and collected 26 years of back interest. On its issue date in 1648, this bond originally paid interest in Carolus guilders. Over the next 355 years, the currency of payment changed to Flemish pounds, Dutch guilders, and most recently euros. Currently, the bond pays interest of €11.34 annually.

Although the Dutch bonds are the oldest perpetuities still in existence, the first perpetuities date from much earlier times. For example, *cencus agreements* and *rentes*, which were forms of perpetuities and annuities, were issued in the twelfth century in Italy, France, and Spain. They were initially designed to circumvent the usury laws of the Catholic Church: Because they did not require the repayment of principal, in the eyes of the church they were not considered loans.

EXAMPLE 4.6

Endowing a Perpetuity

Problem
You want to endow an annual MBA graduation party at your alma mater. You want the event to be a memorable one, so you budget $30,000 per year forever for the party. If the university earns 8% per year on its investments, and if the first party is in one year's time, how much will you need to donate to endow the party?

Solution
The timeline of the cash flows you want to provide is

This is a standard perpetuity of $30,000 per year. The funding you would need to give the university in perpetuity is the present value of this cash flow stream. From the formula,

$$PV = C/r = \$30,000 / 0.08 = \$375,000 \text{ today}$$

If you donate $375,000 today, and if the university invests it at 8% per year forever, then the MBAs will have $30,000 every year for their graduation party.

COMMON MISTAKE   **Discounting One Too Many Times**

The perpetuity formula assumes that the first payment occurs at the end of the first period (at date 1). Sometimes perpetuities have cash flows that start later in the future. In this case, we can adapt the perpetuity formula to compute the present value, but we need to do so carefully to avoid a common mistake.

To illustrate, consider the MBA graduation party described in Example 4.6. Rather than starting immediately, suppose that the first party will be held two years from today (for the current entering class). How would this delay change the amount of the donation required?

Now the timeline looks like this:

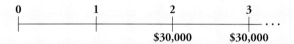

We need to determine the present value of these cash flows, as it tells us the amount of money in the bank needed today to finance the future parties. We cannot apply the perpetuity formula directly, however, because these cash flows are not *exactly* a perpetuity as we defined it. Specifically, the cash flow in the first period is "missing." But consider the situation on date 1—at that point, the

first party is one period away and then the cash flows are periodic. From the perspective of date 1, this *is* a perpetuity, and we can apply the formula. From the preceding calculation, we know we need $375,000 on date 1 to have enough to start the parties on date 2. We rewrite the timeline as follows:

Our goal can now be restated more simply: How much do we need to invest today to have $375,000 in one year? This is a simple present value calculation:

$$PV = \$375,000 / 1.08 = \$347,222 \text{ today}$$

A common mistake is to discount the $375,000 twice because the first party is in two periods. *Remember—the present value formula for the perpetuity already discounts the cash flows to one period prior to the first cash flow.* Keep in mind that this common mistake may be made with perpetuities, annuities, and all of the other special cases discussed in this section. All of these formulas discount the cash flows to one period prior to the first cash flow.

Annuities

An **annuity** is a stream of N equal cash flows paid at regular intervals. The difference between an annuity and a perpetuity is that an annuity ends after some fixed number of payments. Most car loans, mortgages, and some bonds are annuities. We represent the cash flows of an annuity on a timeline as follows.

Note that just as with the perpetuity, we adopt the convention that the first payment takes place at date 1, one period from today. The present value of an N-period annuity with payment C and interest rate r is

$$PV = \frac{C}{(1 + r)} + \frac{C}{(1 + r)^2} + \frac{C}{(1 + r)^3} + \cdots + \frac{C}{(1 + r)^N} = \sum_{n=1}^{N} \frac{C}{(1 + r)^n}$$

To find a simpler formula, we use the same approach we followed with the perpetuity: find a way to create an annuity. To illustrate, suppose you invest $100 in a bank account paying 5% interest. At the end of one year, you will have $105 in the bank—your original $100 plus $5 in interest. Using the same strategy as for a perpetuity, suppose you withdraw the $5 interest and reinvest the $100 for a second year. Once again you will have $105 after one year, and you can repeat the process, withdrawing $5 and reinvesting $100, every year. For a perpetuity, you left the principal in forever. Alternatively, you might decide after 20 years to close the account and withdraw the principal. In that case, your cash flows will look like this:

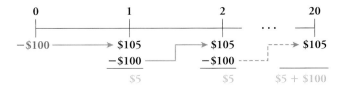

With your initial $100 investment, you have created a 20-year annuity of $5 per year, plus you will receive an extra $100 at the end of 20 years. By the Law of One Price, because it took an initial investment of $100 to create the cash flows on the timeline, the present value of these cash flows is $100, or

$$\$100 = PV(\text{20-year annuity of \$5 per year}) + PV(\$100 \text{ in 20 years})$$

Rearranging terms gives

$$PV(\text{20-year annuity of \$5 per year}) = \$100 - PV(\$100 \text{ in 20 years})$$

$$= 100 - \frac{100}{(1.05)^{20}} = \$62.31$$

So the present value of $5 for 20 years is $62.31. Intuitively, the value of the annuity is the initial investment in the bank account minus the present value of the principal that will be left in the account after 20 years.

We can use the same idea to derive the general formula. First, we invest P in the bank, and withdraw only the interest $C = r \times P$ each period. After N periods, we close the account. Thus, for an initial investment of P, we will receive an N-period annuity of C per period, *plus* we will get back our original P at the end. P is the total present value of the two sets of cash flows,[4] or

$$P = PV(\text{annuity of } C \text{ for } N \text{ periods}) + PV(P \text{ in period } N)$$

By rearranging terms, we compute the present value of the annuity:

$$PV(\text{annuity of } C \text{ for } N \text{ periods}) = P - PV(P \text{ in period } N)$$

$$= P - \frac{P}{(1 + r)^N} = P\left(1 - \frac{1}{(1 + r)^N}\right) \quad (4.6)$$

Recall that the periodic payment C is the interest earned every period; that is, $C = r \times P$ or, equivalently, solving for P provides the upfront cost in terms of C,

$$P = C / r$$

Making this substitution for P, in Eq. 4.6, provides the formula for the present value of an annuity of C for N periods.

---

4. Here we are using value additivity (see Chapter 3) to separate the present value of the cash flows into separate pieces.

Present Value of an Annuity[5]

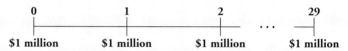

$$PV(\text{annuity of } C \text{ for } N \text{ periods with interest rate } r) = C \times \frac{1}{r}\left(1 - \frac{1}{(1+r)^N}\right) \quad (4.7)$$

EXAMPLE 4.7

Present Value of a Lottery Prize Annuity

Problem

You are the lucky winner of the $30 million state lottery. You can take your prize money either as (a) 30 payments of $1 million per year (starting today), or (b) $15 million paid today. If the interest rate is 8%, which option should you take?

Solution

Option (a) provides $30 million in prize money but paid over time. To evaluate it correctly, we must convert it to a present value. Here is the timeline:

0	1	2		29
$1 million	$1 million	$1 million	⋯	$1 million

Because the first payment starts today, the last payment will occur in 29 years (for a total of 30 payments).[6] The $1 million at date 0 is already stated in present value terms, but we need to compute the present value of the remaining payments. Fortunately, this case looks like a 29-year annuity of $1 million per year, so we can use the annuity formula:

$$PV(\text{29-year annuity of $1 million}) = \$1 \text{ million} \times \frac{1}{0.08}\left(1 - \frac{1}{1.08^{29}}\right)$$

$$= \$1 \text{ million} \times 11.16$$

$$= \$11.16 \text{ million today}$$

Thus, the total present value of the cash flows is $1 million + $11.16 million = $12.16 million. In timeline form:

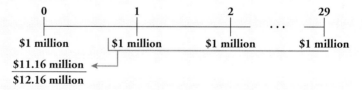

Option (b), $15 million upfront, is more valuable—even though the total amount of money paid is half that of option (a). The reason for the difference is the time value of money. If you have the $15 million today, you can use $1 million immediately and invest the remaining $14 million at an 8% interest rate. This strategy will give you $14 million × 8% = $1.12 million per year in perpetuity! Alternatively, you can spend $15 million − $11.16 million = $3.84 million today, and invest the remaining $11.16 million, which will still allow you to withdraw $1 million each year for the next 29 years before your account is depleted.

---

5. An early derivation of this formula is attributed to the astonomer Edmond Halley ("Of Compound Interest," published after Halley's death by Henry Sherwin, Sherwin's Mathematical Tables, London: W. and J. Mount, T. Page and Son, 1761).

6. An annuity in which the first payment occurs immediately is sometimes called an *annuity due*. Throughout this text, we always use the term "annuity" to mean one that is paid in arrears.

Now that we have derived a simple formula for the present value of an annuity, it is easy to find a simple formula for the future value. If we want to know the value N years in the future, we move the present value N periods forward on the timeline; that is, we compound the present value for N periods at interest rate r:

Future Value of an Annuity

$$FV(\text{annuity}) = PV \times (1 + r)^N$$

$$= \frac{C}{r}\left(1 - \frac{1}{(1 + r)^N}\right) \times (1 + r)^N$$

$$= C \times \frac{1}{r}\left((1 + r)^N - 1\right) \tag{4.8}$$

This formula is useful if we want to know how a savings account will grow over time.

Retirement Savings Plan Annuity

Problem

Ellen is 35 years old, and she has decided it is time to plan seriously for her retirement. At the end of each year until she is 65, she will save $10,000 in a retirement account. If the account earns 10% per year, how much will Ellen have saved at age 65?

Solution

As always, we begin with a timeline. In this case, it is helpful to keep track of both the dates and Ellen's age:

Ellen's savings plan looks like an annuity of $10,000 per year for 30 years. (*Hint:* It is easy to become confused when you just look at age, rather than at both dates and age. A common error is to think there are only $65 - 36 = 29$ payments. Writing down both dates and age avoids this problem.)

To determine the amount Ellen will have in the bank at age 65, we compute the future value of this annuity:

$$FV = \$10,000 \times \frac{1}{0.10}(1.10^{30} - 1)$$

$$= \$10,000 \times 164.49$$

$$= \$1.645 \text{ million at age 65}$$

Growing Cash Flows

So far, we have considered only cash flow streams that have the same cash flow every period. If instead the cash flows are expected to grow at a constant rate in each period, we can also derive a simple formula for the present value of the future stream.

Growing Perpetuity.   A **growing perpetuity** is a stream of cash flows that occur at regular intervals and grow at a constant rate forever. For example, a growing perpetuity with a first payment of $100 that grows at a rate of 3% has the following timeline:

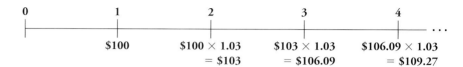

In general, a growing perpetuity with a first payment C and a growth rate g will have the following series of cash flows:

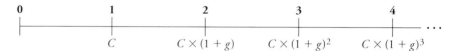

As with perpetuities with equal cash flows, we adopt the convention that the first payment occurs at date 1. Note a second important convention: *The first payment does not grow.* That is, the first payment is C, even though it is one period away. Similarly, the cash flow in period n undergoes only $n - 1$ periods of growth. Substituting the cash flows from the preceding timeline into the general formula for the present value of a cash flow stream gives

$$PV = \frac{C}{(1 + r)} + \frac{C(1 + g)}{(1 + r)^2} + \frac{C(1 + g)^2}{(1 + r)^3} + \cdots = \sum_{n=1}^{\infty} \frac{C(1 + g)^{n-1}}{(1 + r)^n}$$

Suppose $g \geq r$. Then the cash flows grow even faster than they are discounted; each term in the sum gets larger, rather than smaller. In this case, the sum is infinite! What does an infinite present value mean? Remember that the present value is the "do-it-yourself" cost of creating the cash flows. An infinite present value means that no matter how much money you start with, it is *impossible* to reproduce those cash flows on your own. Growing perpetuities of this sort cannot exist in practice because no one would be willing to offer one at any finite price. A promise to pay an amount that forever grew faster than the interest rate is also unlikely to be kept (or believed by any savvy buyer).

The only viable growing perpetuities are those where the growth rate is less than the interest rate, so that each successive term in the sum is less than the previous term and the overall sum is finite. Consequently, we assume that $g < r$ for a growing perpetuity.

To derive the formula for the present value of a growing perpetuity, we follow the same logic used for a regular perpetuity: Compute the amount you would need to deposit today to create the perpetuity yourself. In the case of a regular perpetuity, we created a constant payment forever by withdrawing the interest earned each year and reinvesting the principal. To increase the amount we can withdraw each year, the principal that we reinvest each year must grow. We can accomplish this by withdrawing less than the full amount of interest earned each period, using the remaining interest to increase our principal.

Let's consider a specific case. Suppose you want to create a perpetuity growing at 2%, so you invest $100 in a bank account that pays 5% interest. At the end of one year, you will have $105 in the bank—your original $100 plus $5 in interest. If you withdraw only $3, you will have $102 to reinvest—2% more than the amount you had initially. This amount will then grow to $102 \times 1.05 = 107.10 in the following year, and you can withdraw $3 \times 1.02 = \$3.06$, which will leave you with principal of $107.10 − $3.06 = $104.04. Note that $102 \times 1.02 = \$104.04$. That is, both the amount you withdraw and the principal you reinvest grow by 2% each year. On a timeline, these cash flows look like this:

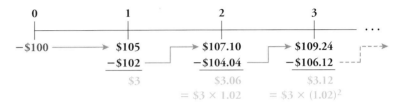

By following this strategy, you have created a growing perpetuity that starts at $3 and grows 2% per year. This growing perpetuity must have a present value equal to the cost of $100.

We can generalize this argument. In the case of an equal-payment perpetuity, we deposited an amount P in the bank and withdrew the interest each year. Because we always left the principal P in the bank, we could maintain this pattern forever. If we want to increase the amount we withdraw from the bank each year by g, then the principal in the bank will have to grow by the same factor g. That is, instead of reinvesting P in the second year, we should reinvest $P(1 + g) = P + gP$. In order to increase our principal by gP, we can only withdraw $C = rP − gP = P(r − g)$.

$$
\begin{array}{c|cccc}
0 & 1 & 2 & 3 \\
\hline
-P & P(1 + r) & P(1 + g)(1 + r) & P(1 + g)^2(1 + r) & \cdots \\
 & -P(1 + g) & -P(1 + g)(1 + g) & -P(1 + g)^2(1 + g) \\
 & P(r - g) & P(1 + g)(r - g) & P(1 + g)^2(r - g) \\
 & = C & = C(1 + g) & = C(1 + g)^2 \\
\end{array}
$$

From the timeline, we see that after one period we can withdraw $C = P(r − g)$ and keep our account balance and cash flow growing at a rate of g forever. Solving this equation for P gives

$$P = \frac{C}{r - g}$$

The present value of the growing perpetuity with initial cash flow C is P, the initial amount deposited in the bank account:

Present Value of a Growing Perpetuity

$$PV(\text{growing perpetuity}) = \frac{C}{r - g} \tag{4.9}$$

To understand the formula for a growing perpetuity intuitively, start with the formula for a perpetuity. In the earlier case, you had to put enough money in the bank to ensure that the interest earned matched the cash flows of the regular perpetuity. In the case of a growing perpetuity, you need to put more than that amount in the bank because you have to finance the growth in the cash flows. How much more? If the bank pays interest at a rate of 10%, then all that is left to take out if you want to make sure the principal grows

3% per year is the difference: 10% − 3% = 7%. So instead of the present value of the perpetuity being the first cash flow divided by the interest rate, it is now the first cash flow divided by the *difference* between the interest rate and the growth rate.

Endowing a Growing Perpetuity

Problem

In Example 4.6, you planned to donate money to your alma mater to fund an annual $30,000 MBA graduation party. Given an interest rate of 8% per year, the required donation was the present value of

$$PV = \$30,000 \,/\, 0.08 = \$375,000 \text{ today}$$

Before accepting the money, however, the MBA student association has asked that you increase the donation to account for the effect of inflation on the cost of the party in future years. Although $30,000 is adequate for next year's party, the students estimate that the party's cost will rise by 4% per year thereafter. To satisfy their request, how much do you need to donate now?

Solution

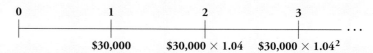

The cost of the party next year is $30,000, and the cost then increases 4% per year forever. From the timeline, we recognize the form of a growing perpetuity. To finance the growing cost, you need to provide the present value today of

$$PV = \$30,000 \,/\, (0.08 - 0.04) = \$750,000 \text{ today}$$

You need to double the size of your gift!

Growing Annuity.   A **growing annuity** is a stream of N growing cash flows, paid at regular intervals. It is a growing perpetuity that eventually comes to an end. The following timeline shows a growing annuity with initial cash flow C, growing at rate g every period until period N:

The conventions used earlier still apply: (1) The first cash flow arrives at the end of the first period, and (2) the first cash flow does not grow. The last cash flow therefore reflects only $N - 1$ periods of growth.

The present value of an N-period growing annuity with initial cash flow C, growth rate g, and interest rate r is given by

Present Value of a Growing Annuity

$$PV = C \times \frac{1}{r - g}\left(1 - \left(\frac{1 + g}{1 + r}\right)^{N}\right) \tag{4.10}$$

Because the annuity has only a finite number of terms, Eq. 4.10 also works when $g > r$.[7] The process of deriving this simple expression for the present value of a growing annuity is the same as for a regular annuity. Interested readers may consult the online appendix for details.

Retirement Savings with a Growing Annuity

Problem

In Example 4.8, Ellen considered saving $10,000 per year for her retirement. Although $10,000 is the most she can save in the first year, she expects her salary to increase each year so that she will be able to increase her savings by 5% per year. With this plan, if she earns 10% per year on her savings, how much will Ellen have saved at age 65?

Solution

Her new savings plan is represented by the following timeline:

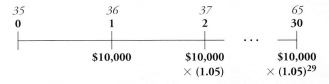

This example involves a 30-year growing annuity, with a growth rate of 5%, and an initial cash flow of $10,000. The present value of this growing annuity is given by

$$PV = \$10,000 \times \frac{1}{0.10 - 0.05}\left(1 - \left(\frac{1.05}{1.10}\right)^{30}\right)$$

$$= \$10,000 \times 15.0463$$

$$= \$150,463 \text{ today}$$

Ellen's proposed savings plan is equivalent to having $150,463 in the bank *today*. To determine the amount she will have at age 65, we need to move this amount forward 30 years:

$$FV = \$150,463 \times 1.10^{30}$$

$$= \$2.625 \text{ million in 30 years}$$

Ellen will have saved $2.625 million at age 65 using the new savings plan. This sum is almost $1 million more than she had without the additional annual increases in savings.

The formula for the growing annuity is a general solution. In fact, we can deduce all of the other formulas in this section from the expression for a growing annuity. To see how to derive the other formulas from this one, first consider a growing perpetuity. It is a growing annuity with $N = \infty$. If $g < r$, then

$$\frac{1 + g}{1 + r} < 1$$

---

7. Eq. 4.10 does not work for $g = r$. But in that case, growth and discounting cancel out, and the present value is simply $PV = C \times N$.

and so

$$\left(\frac{1 + g}{1 + r}\right)^{N} \rightarrow 0 \text{ as } N \rightarrow \infty$$

The formula for a growing annuity when $N = \infty$ therefore becomes

$$PV = \frac{C}{r - g}\left(1 - \left(\frac{1 + g}{1 + r}\right)^{N}\right) = \frac{C}{r - g}(1 - 0) = \frac{C}{r - g}$$

which is the formula for a growing perpetuity. The formulas for a regular annuity and perpetuity also follow from the formula if we let the growth rate $g = 0$.

CONCEPT CHECK

1. How do you calculate the present value of a
   a. Perpetuity?
   b. Annuity?
   c. Growing perpetuity?
   d. Growing annuity?

2. How are the formulas for the present value of a perpetuity, annuity, growing perpetuity, and growing annuity related?

4.7 Solving Problems with a Spreadsheet Program

In the previous section, we derived formulas that were shortcuts for computing the present values of cash flows that have special patterns. Two other kinds of shortcuts simplify the calculation of present values—the use of spreadsheets and financial calculators. In this section we focus on spreadsheets.

Spreadsheet programs such as Excel have a set of functions that perform the calculations that finance professionals do most often. In Excel, the functions are called NPER, RATE, PV, PMT, and FV. The functions are all based on the timeline of an annuity:

together with an interest rate, denoted by *RATE*. Thus, there are a total of five variables: *NPER, RATE, PV, PMT,* and *FV.* Each function takes four of these variables as inputs and returns the value of the fifth one that ensures that the NPV of the cash flows is zero. That is, the functions all solve the problem

$$NPV = PV + PMT \times \frac{1}{RATE}\left(1 - \frac{1}{(1 + RATE)^{NPER}}\right) + \frac{FV}{(1 + RATE)^{NPER}} = 0 \quad (4.11)$$

In words, the present value of the annuity payments *PMT,* plus the present value of the final payment *FV,* plus the initial amount *PV,* has a net present value of zero. Let's tackle a few examples.

Computing the Future Value In Excel

Problem

Suppose you plan to invest $20,000 in an account paying 8% interest. How much will you have in the account in 15 years?

Solution

We represent this problem with the following timeline:

0	1	2	$NPER = \mathbf{15}$
$PV = -\$20{,}000$	$PMT = \$0$	$\$0$	$FV = ?$

To compute the solution, we enter the four variables we know ($NPER = 15$, $RATE = 8\%$, $PV = -20{,}000$, $PMT = 0$) and solve for the one we want to determine (FV) using the Excel function FV (RATE, NPER, PMT, PV). The spreadsheet here calculates a future value of $63,443.

	NPER	RATE	PV	PMT	FV	Excel Formula
Given	15	8.00%	−20,000	0		
Solve for FV					63,443	=FV(0.08,15,0,−20000)

Note that we entered PV as a negative number (the amount we are putting *into* the bank), and FV is shown as a positive number (the amount we can take *out* of the bank). It is important to use signs correctly to indicate the direction in which the money is flowing when using the spreadsheet functions.

To check the result, we can solve this problem directly:

$$FV = \$20{,}000 \times 1.08^{15} = \$63{,}443$$

This Excel spreadsheet in Example 4.11 is available at the text Web site and is set up to allow you to compute any one of the five variables. We refer to this spreadsheet as the **annuity spreadsheet**. You simply enter the four input variables on the top line and leave the variable you want to compute blank. The spreadsheet computes the fifth variable and displays the answer on the bottom line. The spreadsheet also displays the Excel function that is used to get the answers. Let's work through a more complicated example that illustrates the convenience of the annuity spreadsheet.

Using the Annuity Spreadsheet

Problem

Suppose that you invest $20,000 in an account paying 8% interest. You plan to withdraw $2000 at the end of each year for 15 years. How much money will be left in the account after 15 years?

Solution

Again, we start with the timeline:

The timeline indicates that the withdrawals are an annuity payment that we receive from the bank account. Note that PV is negative (money *into* the bank), while PMT is positive (money *out* of the bank). We solve for the final balance in the account, FV, using the annuity spreadsheet:

	NPER	RATE	PV	PMT	FV	Excel Formula
Given	15	8.00%	−20,000	2000		
Solve for FV					9139	=FV(0.08,15,2000,−20000)

We will have $9139 left in the bank after 15 years.

We can also compute this solution directly. One approach is to think of the deposit and the withdrawals as being separate accounts. In the account with the $20,000 deposit, our savings will grow to $63,443 in 15 years, as we computed in Example 4.11. Using the formula for the future value of an annuity, if we borrow $2000 per year for 15 years at 8%, at the end our debt will have grown to

$$\$2000 \times \frac{1}{0.08}(1.08^{15} - 1) = \$54,304$$

After paying off our debt, we will have $63,443 − $54,304 = $9139 remaining after 15 years.

You can also use a handheld financial calculator to do the same calculations. The calculators work in much the same way as the annuity spreadsheet. You enter any four of the five variables, and the calculator calculates the fifth variable.

CONCEPT CHECK

1. What are the two shortcuts that you can use to simplify the calculation of present values?

2. How do you use a spreadsheet to simplify financial calculations?

4.8 Solving for Variables Other Than Present Value or Future Value

So far, we have calculated the present value or future value of a stream of cash flows. Sometimes, however, we know the present value or future value but do not know one of the variables we have previously been given as an input. For example, when you take out a loan, you may know the amount you would like to borrow, but may not know the loan payments that will be required to repay it. Or, if you make a deposit into a bank account, you may want to calculate how long it will take before your balance reaches a certain level. In such situations, we use the present and/or future values as inputs, and solve for the variable we are interested in. We examine several special cases in this section.

Solving for the Cash Flows

Let's consider an example where we know the present value of an investment, but do not know the cash flows. The best example is a loan—you know how much you want to borrow (the present value) and you know the interest rate, but you do not know how much you need to repay each year. Suppose you are opening a business that requires an initial investment of $100,000. Your bank manager has agreed to lend you this money. The terms of the loan state that you will make equal annual payments for the next ten years and will pay an interest rate of 8% with the first payment due one year from today. What is your annual payment?

From the bank's perspective, the timeline looks like this:

The bank will give you $100,000 today in exchange for ten equal payments over the next decade. You need to determine the size of the payment C that the bank will require. For the bank to be willing to lend you $100,000, the loan cash flows must have a present value of $100,000 when evaluated at the bank's interest rate of 8%. That is,

$$100{,}000 = PV(\text{10-year annuity of } C \text{ per year, evaluated at the loan rate})$$

Using the formula for the present value of an annuity,

$$100{,}000 = C \times \frac{1}{0.08}\left(1 - \frac{1}{1.08^{10}}\right) = C \times 6.71$$

Solving this equation for C gives

$$C = \frac{100{,}000}{6.71} = \$14{,}903$$

You will be required to make ten annual payments of $14,903 in exchange for $100,000 today.

We can also solve this problem with the annuity spreadsheet:

	NPER	RATE	PV	PMT	FV	Excel Formula
Given	10	8.00%	100,000		0	
Solve for PMT				−14,903		=PMT(0.08,10,100000,0)

In general, when solving for a loan payment, think of the amount borrowed (the loan principal) as the present value of the payments. If the payments of the loan are an annuity, we can solve for the payment of the loan by inverting the annuity formula. Writing this procedure formally, we begin with the timeline (from the bank's perspective) for a loan with principal P, requiring N periodic payments of C and interest rate r:

Setting the present value of the payments equal to the principal,

$$P = PV(\text{annuity of } C \text{ for } N \text{ periods}) = C \times \frac{1}{r}\left(1 - \frac{1}{(1 + r)^N}\right)$$

Solving this equation for C gives the general formula for the loan payment in terms of the outstanding principal (amount borrowed), P; interest rate, r; and number of payments, N:

Loan Payment

$$C = \frac{P}{\dfrac{1}{r}\left(1 - \dfrac{1}{(1 + r)^N}\right)} \tag{4.12}$$

Computing a Loan Payment

Problem

Your firm plans to buy a warehouse for $100,000. The bank offers you a 30-year loan with equal annual payments and an interest rate of 8% per year. The bank requires that your firm pay 20% of the purchase price as a down payment, so you can borrow only $80,000. What is the annual loan payment?

Solution

We start with the timeline (from the bank's perspective):

Using Eq. 4.12, we can solve for the loan payment, C, as follows:

$$C = \frac{P}{\dfrac{1}{r}\left(1 - \dfrac{1}{(1 + r)^N}\right)} = \frac{80,000}{\dfrac{1}{0.08}\left(1 - \dfrac{1}{(1.08)^{30}}\right)}$$

$$= \$7106.19$$

Using the annuity spreadsheet:

	NPER	RATE	PV	PMT	FV	Excel Formula
Given	30	8.00%	−80,000		0	
Solve for PMT				7106		=PMT(0.08,30,−80000,0)

Your firm will need to pay $7106.19 each year to repay the loan.

We can use this same idea to solve for the cash flows when we know the future value rather than the present value. As an example, suppose you have just had a child. You decide to be prudent and start saving this year for her college education. You would like to have $60,000 saved by the time your daughter is 18 years old. If you can earn 7% per year on your savings, how much do you need to save each year to meet your goal?

The timeline for this example is

That is, you plan to save some amount C per year, and then withdraw $60,000 from the bank in 18 years. Therefore, we need to find the annuity payment that has a future value of $60,000 in 18 years. Using the formula for the future value of an annuity from Eq. 4.8,

$$60,000 = FV(\text{annuity}) = C \times \frac{1}{0.07}(1.07^{18} - 1) = C \times 34$$

Therefore, $C = \frac{60,000}{34} = \$1765$. So you need to save $1765 per year. If you do, then at a 7% interest rate your savings will grow to $60,000 by the time your child is 18 years old.

Now let's solve this problem with the annuity spreadsheet:

	NPER	RATE	PV	PMT	FV	Excel Formula
Given	18	7.00%	0		60,000	
Solve for PMT				−1765		=PMT(0.07,18,0,60000)

Once again, we find that we need to save $1765 for 18 years to accumulate $60,000.

Internal Rate of Return

In some situations, you know the present value and cash flows of an investment opportunity but you do not know the interest rate that equates them. This interest rate is called the **internal rate of return (IRR)**, defined as the interest rate that sets the net present value of the cash flows equal to zero.

For example, suppose that you have an investment opportunity that requires a $1000 investment today and will have a $2000 payoff in six years. On a timeline,

One way to analyze this investment is to ask the question: What interest rate, r, would you need so that the NPV of this investment is zero?

$$NPV = -1000 + \frac{2000}{(1 + r)^6} = 0$$

Rearranging gives

$$1000 \times (1 + r)^6 = 2000$$

That is, r is the interest rate you would need to earn on your $1000 to have a future value of $2000 in six years. We can solve for r as follows:

$$1 + r = \left(\frac{2000}{1000}\right)^{1/6} = 1.1225$$

or $r = 12.25\%$. This rate is the IRR of this investment opportunity. Making this investment is like earning 12.25% per year on your money for six years.

When there are just two cash flows, as in the preceding example, it is easy to compute the IRR. Consider the general case in which you invest an amount P today, and receive FV in N years. Then

$$P \times (1 + \text{IRR})^N = FV$$
$$1 + \text{IRR} = (FV/P)^{1/N}$$

That is, we take the total return of the investment over N years, FV/P, and convert it to an equivalent one-year rate by raising it to the power $1/N$.

Now let's consider a more sophisticated example. Suppose your firm needs to purchase a new forklift. The dealer gives you two options: (1) a price for the forklift if you pay cash and (2) the annual payments if you take out a loan from the dealer. To evaluate the loan that the dealer is offering you, you will want to compare the rate on the loan with the rate that your bank is willing to offer you. Given the loan payment that the dealer quotes, how do you compute the interest rate charged by the dealer?

In this case, we need to compute the IRR of the dealer's loan. Suppose the cash price of the forklift is $40,000, and the dealer offers financing with no down payment and four annual payments of $15,000. This loan has the following timeline:

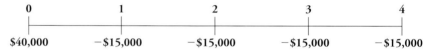

From the timeline it is clear that the loan is a four-year annuity with a payment of $15,000 per year and a present value of $40,000. Setting the NPV of the cash flows equal to zero requires that the present value of the payments equals the purchase price:

$$40,000 = 15,000 \times \frac{1}{r}\left(1 - \frac{1}{(1 + r)^4}\right)$$

The value of r that solves this equation, the IRR, is the interest rate charged on the loan. Unfortunately, in this case there is no simple way to solve for the interest rate r.[8] The only way to solve this equation is to guess values of r until you find the right one.

Start by guessing $r = 10\%$. In this case, the value of the annuity is

$$15,000 \times \frac{1}{0.10}\left(1 - \frac{1}{(1.10)^4}\right) = 47,548$$

The present value of the payments is too large. To lower it, we need to use a higher interest rate. We guess 20% this time:

$$15,000 \times \frac{1}{0.20}\left(1 - \frac{1}{(1.20)^4}\right) = 38,831$$

Now the present value of the payments is too low, so we must pick a rate between 10% and 20%. We continue to guess until we find the right rate. Let us try 18.45%:

---

8. With five or more periods and general cash flows, there is *no* general formula to solve for r; trial and error (by hand or computer) is the *only* way to compute the IRR.

$$15,000 \times \frac{1}{0.1845}\left(1 - \frac{1}{(1.1845)^4}\right) = 40,000$$

The interest rate charged by the dealer is 18.45%.

An easier solution than guessing the IRR and manually calculating values is to use a spreadsheet or calculator to automate the guessing process. When the cash flows are an annuity, as in this example, we can use the annuity spreadsheet in Excel to compute the IRR. Recall that the annuity spreadsheet solves Eq. 4.11. It ensures that the NPV of investing in the annuity is zero. When the unknown variable is the interest rate, it will solve for the interest rate that sets the NPV equal to zero—that is, the IRR. For this case,

	NPER	RATE	PV	PMT	FV	Excel Formula
Given	4		40,000	− 15,000	0	
Solve for Rate		18.45%				=RATE(4, − 15000,40000,0)

The annuity spreadsheet correctly computes an IRR of 18.45%.

Computing the Internal Rate of Return with the Annuity Spreadsheet in Excel

Problem
Jessica has just graduated with her MBA. Rather than take the job she was offered at a prestigious investment bank—Baker, Bellingham, and Botts—she has decided to go into business for herself. However, Baker, Bellingham, and Botts was so impressed with Jessica that it has decided to fund her business. In return for an initial investment of $1 million, Jessica has agreed to pay the bank $125,000 at the end of each year for the next 30 years. What is the internal rate of return on Baker, Bellingham, and Botts's investment in Jessica's company, assuming she fulfills her commitment?

Solution
Here is the timeline (from Baker, Bellingham, and Botts's perspective):

The timeline shows that the future cash flows are a 30-year annuity. Setting the NPV equal to zero requires

$$1,000,000 = \frac{125,000 \times 1}{r}\left(1 - \frac{1}{(1 + r)^{30}}\right)$$

Using the annuity spreadsheet to solve for r,

	NPER	RATE	PV	PMT	FV	Excel Formula
Given	30		−1,000,000	125,000	0	
Solve for Rate		12.09%				=RATE(30,125000, − 1000000,0)

The IRR on this investment is 12.09%.

In a few cases, it is possible to solve for the IRR directly. The next example demonstrates one such case.

Computing the Internal Rate of Return Directly

Problem
Baker, Bellingham, and Botts offers Jessica a second option for repayment of the loan. She can pay $100,000 the first year, increase the amount by 4% each year, and continue to make these payments forever, rather than for 30 years. What is the IRR in this case?

Solution
The timeline is

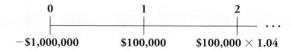

The timeline shows that the future cash flows are a growing perpetuity with a growth rate of 4%. Setting the NPV equal to zero requires

$$1,000,000 = \frac{100,000}{r - 0.04}$$

We can solve this equation for r

$$r = 0.04 + \frac{100,000}{1,000,000} = 0.14$$

The IRR on this investment is 14%.

Solving for the Number of Periods

In addition to solving for cash flows or the interest rate, we can solve for the amount of time it will take a sum of money to grow to a known value. In this case, the interest rate, present value, and future value are all known. We need to compute how long it will take for the present value to grow to the future value.

Suppose we invest $10,000 in an account paying 10% interest, and we want to know how long it will take for the amount to grow to $20,000.

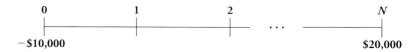

We want to determine N.

In terms of our formulas, we need to find N so that the future value of our investment equals $20,000:

$$FV = \$10,000 \times 1.10^N = \$20,000 \qquad (4.13)$$

One approach is to use trial and error to find N, as with the IRR. For example, with $N = 7$ years, $FV = \$19,487$, so it will take longer than 7 years. With $N = 8$ years, $FV = \$21,436$, so it will take between 7 and 8 years.

COMMON MISTAKE   **Excel's NPV and IRR Functions**

Although spreadsheets and financial calculators can simplify the process of solving problems, their designers have adopted specific conventions that you will need to be aware of to avoid making mistakes. In particular, before using any built-in financial function, always read the documentation for that function carefully to be aware of the correct format and any assumptions that are made by the software. Here we describe two functions in Excel, NPV and IRR, and some pitfalls to watch out for.

NPV

Excel's NPV function has the format, NPV(rate, value1, value2, ...) where "rate" is the interest rate per period used to discount the cash flows, and "value1", "value2", etc. ar the cash flows (or ranges of cash flows). The NPV function computes the present value of the cash flows *assuming the first cash flow occurs at date 1*. Therefore, if a project's first cash flow occurs at date 0, we cannot use the NPV function by itself to compute the NPV. We can use the NPV function to compute the present value of the cash flows from date 1 onwards, and then must add the date 0 cash flow to that result to calculate the NPV.

Another pitfall with the NPV function is that cash flows that are left blank are treated differently from cash flows that are equal to zero. If the cash flow is left blank, *both the cash flow and the period are ignored*. For example, the NPV function is used to evaluate the two equivalent

cash flow streams shown below. In the second case, the NPV function ignores the blank cell at date 2 and assumes the cash flow is 10 at date 1 and 110 at date 2, which is clearly not what is intended and is incorrect.

		Date	
NPV @ 10%	**1**	**2**	**3**
$91.74	10	0	110
$100.00	10		110

Because of these idiosyncrasies, we avoid using Excel's NPV function, and find it to be more reliable to compute the present value of each cash flow separately in Excel, and then sum them to determine the NPV.

IRR

Excel's IRR function has the format, IRR(values, guess), where "values" is the range containing the cash flows, and "guess" is an optional starting guess where Excel begins its search for an IRR. There are two things to note about the IRR function. First, the values given to the IRR function should include all of the cash flows of the project, including the one at date 0. In this sense, the IRR and NPV functions in Excel are inconsistent. Second, like the NPV function, the IRR ignores the period associated with any blank cells.

Alternatively, this problem can be solved on the annuity spreadsheet. In this case, we solve for N:

	NPER	RATE	PV	PMT	FV	Excel Formula
Given		10.00%	−10,000	0	20,000	
Solve for NPER	7.27					=NPER(0.10,0,−10000,20000)

It will take about 7.3 years for our savings to grow to $20,000.

Finally, this problem can be solved mathematically. Dividing both sides of Eq. 4.13 by $10,000, we have

$$1.10^N = 20{,}000\,/\,10{,}000 = 2$$

To solve for an exponent, we take the logarithm of both sides, and use the fact that $\ln(x^y) = y\ln(x)$:

$$N\ln(1.10) = \ln(2)$$

$$N = \ln(2)\,/\,\ln(1.10) = 0.6931\,/\,0.0953 \approx 7.3 \text{ years}$$

Solving for the Number of Periods in a Savings Plan

Problem

You are saving to make a down payment on a house. You have $10,050 saved already, and you can afford to save an additional $5000 per year at the end of each year. If you earn 7.25% per year on your savings, how long will it take you to save $60,000?

Solution

The timeline for this problem is

We need to find N so that the future value of our current savings plus the future value of our planned additional savings (which is an annuity) equals our desired amount:

$$10{,}050 \times 1.0725^N + 5000 \times \frac{1}{0.0725}(1.0725^N - 1) = 60{,}000$$

To solve mathematically, rearrange the equation to

$$1.0725^N = \frac{60{,}000 \times 0.0725 + 5000}{10{,}050 \times 0.0725 + 5000} = 1.632$$

We can then solve for N:

$$N = \frac{\ln(1.632)}{\ln(1.0725)} = 7 \text{ years}$$

It will take seven years to save the down payment. We can also solve this problem using the annuity spreadsheet:

	NPER	RATE	PV	PMT	FV	Excel Formula
Given		7.25%	−10,050	−5000	60,000	
Solve for N	7.00					=NPER(0.0725,−5000,−10050,60000)

Rule of 72

Another way to think about the effect of compounding and discounting is to consider how long it will take your money to double given different interest rates. Suppose we want to know how many years it will take for $1 to grow to a future value of $2. We want the number of years, N, to solve

$$FV = \$1 \times (1 + r)^N = \$2$$

If you solve this formula for different interest rates, you will find the following approximation:

Years to double $\approx 72 \div$ (interest rate in percent)

This simple "Rule of 72" is fairly accurate (i.e., within one year of the exact doubling time) for interest rates higher than 2%. For example, if the interest rate is 9%, the doubling time should be about $72 \div 9 = 8$ years. Indeed, $1.09^8 = 1.99$! So, given a 9% interest rate, your money will approximately double every 8 years.

CONCEPT CHECK   1. How do you calculate the cash flow of an annuity?

2. What is the internal rate of return, and how do you calculate it?

3. How do you solve for the number of periods to pay off an annuity?

Summary

1. Timelines are a critical first step in organizing the cash flows in a financial problem.

2. There are three rules of time travel:
   a. Only cash flows that occur at the same point in time can be compared or combined.
   b. To move a cash flow forward in time, you must compound it.
   c. To move a cash flow backward in time, you must discount it.

3. The future value in n years of a cash flow C today is

$$C \times (1 + r)^n \tag{4.1}$$

4. The present value today of a cash flow C received in n years is

$$C \div (1 + r)^n \tag{4.2}$$

5. The present value of a cash flow stream is

$$PV = \sum_{n=0}^{N} \frac{C_n}{(1 + r)^n} \tag{4.3}$$

6. The future value on date n of a cash flow stream with a present value of PV is

$$FV_n = PV \times (1 + r)^n \tag{4.4}$$

7. The NPV of an investment opportunity is PV(benefits − costs).

8. A perpetuity is a constant cash flow C paid every period, forever. The present value of a perpetuity is

$$\frac{C}{r} \tag{4.5}$$

9. An annuity is a constant cash flow C paid every period for N periods. The present value of an annuity is

$$C \times \frac{1}{r} \left(1 - \frac{1}{(1 + r)^N} \right) \tag{4.7}$$

The future value of an annuity at the end of the annuity is

$$C \times \frac{1}{r} \left((1 + r)^N - 1 \right) \tag{4.8}$$

10. In a growing perpetuity or annuity, the cash flows grow at a constant rate g each period. The present value of a growing perpetuity is

$$\frac{C}{r - g} \tag{4.9}$$

The present value of a growing annuity is

$$C \times \frac{1}{r-g}\left(1 - \left(\frac{1+g}{1+r}\right)^N\right) \tag{4.10}$$

11. The annuity and perpetuity formulas can be used to solve for the annuity payments when either the present value or the future value is known. The periodic payment on an N-period loan with principal P and interest rate r is

$$C = \frac{P}{\frac{1}{r}\left(1 - \frac{1}{(1+r)^N}\right)} \tag{4.12}$$

12. The internal rate of return (IRR) of an investment opportunity is the interest rate that sets the NPV of the investment opportunity equal to zero.

13. The annuity formulas can be used to solve for the number of periods it takes to save a fixed amount of money.

Key Terms

annuity *p. 98*

annuity spreadsheet *p. 107*

compounding *p. 86*

compound interest *p. 86*

consol *p. 95*

discounting *p. 87*

future value *p. 86*

growing annuity *p. 104*

growing perpetuity *p. 102*

internal rate of return (IRR) *p. 111*

perpetuity *p. 95*

stream of cash flows *p. 84*

timeline *p. 84*

time value of money *p. 86*

Further Reading

The earliest known published work that introduces the ideas in this chapter was in 1202 by the famous Italian mathematician Fibonacci (or Leonardo of Pisa) in Liber Abaci (recently translated into English by Laurence Sigler, *Fibonacci's Liber Abaci, A Translation into Modern English of Leonardo Pisano's Book of Calculation*, New York: Springer-Verlag, 2002). In this book, Fibonacci provides examples demonstrating the rules of time travel for cash flows.

Students who are interested in the early origins of finance and the historical development of the annuity formula will be interested in reading (1) M. Rubinstein, *A History of the Theory of Investments: My Annotated Bibliography* (Hoboken: John Wiley and Sons, 2006) and (2) W. N. Goetzmann and K. G. Rouwenhorst, eds., *Origins of Value: Innovations in the History of Finance* (New York: Oxford University Press, 2005).

The material in this chapter should provide the foundation you need to understand the time value of money. For assistance using Excel, other spreadsheet programs, or financial calculators to compute present values, consult available help files and user manuals for additional information and examples.

Students in the lucky position of having to decide how to receive lottery winnings may consult A. B. Atkins and E. A. Dyl, "The Lotto Jackpot: The Lump Sum versus the Annuity," *Financial Practice and Education* (Fall/Winter 1995): 107–11.

Problems

All problems in this chapter are available in MyFinanceLab. An asterisk (*) indicates problems with a higher level of difficulty.

The Timeline

1. You have just taken out a five-year loan from a bank to buy an engagement ring. The ring costs $5000. You plan to put down $1000 and borrow $4000. You will need to make annual payments of $1000 at the end of each year. Show the timeline of the loan from your perspective. How would the timeline differ if you created it from the bank's perspective?

2. You currently have a four-year-old mortgage outstanding on your house. You make monthly payments of $1500. You have just made a payment. The mortgage has 26 years to go (i.e., it had an original term of 30 years). Show the timeline from your perspective. How would the timeline differ if you created it from the bank's perspective?

The Three Rules of Time Travel

3. Calculate the future value of $2000 in
   a. 5 years at an interest rate of 5% per year.
   b. 10 years at an interest rate of 5% per year.
   c. 5 years at an interest rate of 10% per year.
   d. Why is the amount of interest earned in part (a) less than half the amount of interest earned in part (b)?

4. What is the present value of $10,000 received
   a. 12 years from today when the interest rate is 4% per year?
   b. 20 years from today when the interest rate is 8% per year?
   c. 6 years from today when the interest rate is 2% per year?

5. Your brother has offered to give you either $5000 today or $10,000 in ten years. If the interest rate is 7% per year, which option is preferable?

The Power of Compounding: An Application

6. Your daughter is currently 8 years old. You anticipate that she will be going to college in ten years. You would like to have $100,000 in a savings account to fund her education at that time. If the account promises to pay a fixed interest rate of 3% per year, how much money do you need to put into the account today to ensure that you will have $100,000 in ten years?

7. You are thinking of retiring. Your retirement plan will pay you either $250,000 immediately on retirement or $350,000 five years after the date of your retirement. Which alternative should you choose if the interest rate is
   a. 0% per year?
   b. 8% per year?
   c. 20% per year?

8. Your grandfather put some money in an account for you on the day you were born. You are now 18 years old and are allowed to withdraw the money for the first time. The account currently has $3996 in it and pays an 8% interest rate.
   a. How much money would be in the account if you left the money there until your 25th birthday?
   b. What if you left the money until your 65th birthday?
   c. How much money did your grandfather originally put in the account?

Valuing a Stream
of Cash Flows

 9. You have just received a windfall from an investment you made in a friend's business. He will be paying you $10,000 at the end of this year, $20,000 at the end of the following year, and $30,000 at the end of the year after that (three years from today). The interest rate is 3.5% per year.

    a. What is the present value of your windfall?

    b. What is the future value of your windfall in three years (on the date of the last payment)?

 10. You have a loan outstanding. It requires making three annual payments at the end of the next three years of $1000 each. Your bank has offered to allow you to skip making the next two payments in lieu of making one large payment at the end of the loan's term in three years. If the interest rate on the loan is 5%, what final payment will the bank require you to make so that it is indifferent between the two forms of payment?

The Net Present Value of a
Stream of Cash Flows

 11. You have been offered a unique investment opportunity. If you invest $10,000 today, you will receive $500 one year from now, $1500 two years from now, and $10,000 ten years from now.

    a. What is the NPV of the opportunity if the interest rate is 6% per year? Should you take the opportunity?

    b. What is the NPV of the opportunity if the interest rate is 2% per year? Should you take it now?

EXCEL 12. Marian Plunket owns her own business and is considering an investment. If she undertakes the investment, it will pay $4000 at the end of each of the next three years. The opportunity requires an initial investment of $1000 plus an additional investment at the end of the second year of $5000. What is the NPV of this opportunity if the interest rate is 2% per year? Should Marian take it?

Perpetuities, Annuities,
and Other Special Cases

13. Your buddy in mechanical engineering has invented a money machine. The main drawback of the machine is that it is slow. It takes one year to manufacture $100. However, once built, the machine will last forever and will require no maintenance. The machine can be built immediately, but it will cost $1000 to build. Your buddy wants to know if he should invest the money to construct it. If the interest rate is 9.5% per year, what should your buddy do?

14. How would your answer to Problem 4.13 change if the machine takes one year to build?

15. The British government has a consol bond outstanding paying £100 per year forever. Assume the current interest rate is 4% per year.

    a. What is the value of the bond immediately after a payment is made?

    b. What is the value of the bond immediately before a payment is made?

16. What is the present value of $1000 paid at the end of each of the next 100 years if the interest rate is 7% per year?

***17.** You are head of the Schwartz Family Endowment for the Arts. You have decided to fund an arts school in the San Francisco Bay area in perpetuity. Every five years, you will give the school $1 million. The first payment will occur five years from today. If the interest rate is 8% per year, what is the present value of your gift?

***18.** When you purchased your house, you took out a 30-year annual-payment mortgage with an interest rate of 6% per year. The annual payment on the mortgage is $1200. You have just made a payment and have now decided to pay the mortgage off by repaying the outstanding balance. What is the payoff amount if

a. You have lived in the house for 12 years (so there are 18 years left on the mortgage)?

b. You have lived in the house for 20 years (so there are 10 years left on the mortgage)?

c. You have lived in the house for 12 years (so there are 18 years left on the mortgage) and you decide to pay off the mortgage immediately *before* the twelfth payment is due?

EXCEL **19.** Your grandmother has been putting $1000 into a savings account on every birthday since your first (that is, when you turned 1). The account pays an interest rate of 3%. How much money will be in the account on your 18th birthday immediately after your grandmother makes the deposit on that birthday?

EXCEL **20.** A rich relative has bequeathed you a growing perpetuity. The first payment will occur in a year and will be $1000. Each year after that, you will receive a payment on the anniversary of the last payment that is 8% larger than the last payment. This pattern of payments will go on forever. If the interest rate is 12% per year,

a. What is today's value of the bequest?

b. What is the value of the bequest immediately after the first payment is made?

*21. You are thinking of building a new machine that will save you $1000 in the first year. The machine will then begin to wear out so that the savings *decline* at a rate of 2% per year forever. What is the present value of the savings if the interest rate is 5% per year?

22. You work for a pharmaceutical company that has developed a new drug. The patent on the drug will last 17 years. You expect that the drug's profits will be $2 million in its first year and that this amount will grow at a rate of 5% per year for the next 17 years. Once the patent expires, other pharmaceutical companies will be able to produce the same drug and competition will likely drive profits to zero. What is the present value of the new drug if the interest rate is 10% per year?

EXCEL **23.** Your oldest daughter is about to start kindergarten at a private school. Tuition is $10,000 per year, payable at the *beginning* of the school year. You expect to keep your daughter in private school through high school. You expect tuition to increase at a rate of 5% per year over the 13 years of her schooling. What is the present value of the tuition payments if the interest rate is 5% per year?

EXCEL **24.** A rich aunt has promised you $5000 one year from today. In addition, each year after that, she has promised you a payment (on the anniversary of the last payment) that is 5% larger than the last payment. She will continue to show this generosity for 20 years, giving a total of 20 payments. If the interest rate is 5%, what is her promise worth today?

EXCEL *25. You are running a hot Internet company. Analysts predict that its earnings will grow at 30% per year for the next five years. After that, as competition increases, earnings growth is expected to slow to 2% per year and continue at that level forever. Your company has just announced earnings of $1,000,000. What is the present value of all future earnings if the interest rate is 8%? (Assume all cash flows occur at the end of the year.)

Solving for Variables Other Than Present Value or Future Value

26. You have decided to buy a perpetuity. The bond makes one payment at the end of every year forever and has an interest rate of 5%. If you initially put $1000 into the bond, what is the payment every year?

EXCEL **27.** You are thinking of purchasing a house. The house costs $350,000. You have $50,000 in cash that you can use as a down payment on the house, but you need to borrow the rest of the purchase price. The bank is offering a 30-year mortgage that requires annual payments and has an interest rate of 7% per year. What will your annual payment be if you sign up for this mortgage?

*28. You are thinking about buying a piece of art that costs $50,000. The art dealer is proposing the following deal: He will lend you the money, and you will repay the loan by making the same payment every two years for the next 20 years (i.e., a total of 10 payments). If the interest rate is 4%, how much will you have to pay every two years?

EXCEL *29. You would like to buy the house and take the mortgage described in Problem 4.27. You can afford to pay only $23,500 per year. The bank agrees to allow you to pay this amount each year, yet still borrow $300,000. At the end of the mortgage (in 30 years), you must make a *balloon* payment; that is, you must repay the remaining balance on the mortgage. How much will this balloon payment be?

EXCEL 30. You are saving for retirement. To live comfortably, you decide you will need to save $2 million by the time you are 65. Today is your 30th birthday, and you decide, starting today and continuing on every birthday up to and including your 65th birthday, that you will put the same amount into a savings account. If the interest rate is 5%, how much must you set aside each year to make sure that you will have $2 million in the account on your 65th birthday?

EXCEL *31. You realize that the plan in Problem 4.30 has a flaw. Because your income will increase over your lifetime, it would be more realistic to save less now and more later. Instead of putting the same amount aside each year, you decide to let the amount that you set aside grow by 7% per year. Under this plan, how much will you put into the account today? (Recall that you are planning to make the first contribution to the account today.)

32. You have an investment opportunity that requires an initial investment of $5000 today and will pay $6000 in one year. What is the IRR of this opportunity?

33. You are shopping for a car and read the following advertisement in the newspaper: "Own a new Spitfire! No money down. Four annual payments of just $10,000." You have shopped around and know that you can buy a Spitfire for cash for $32,500. What is the interest rate the dealer is advertising (what is the IRR of the loan in the advertisement)? Assume that you must make the annual payments at the end of each year.

34. A local bank is running the following advertisement in the newspaper: "For just $1000 we will pay you $100 forever!" The fine print in the ad says that for a $1000 deposit, the bank will pay $100 every year in perpetuity, starting one year after the deposit is made. What interest rate is the bank advertising (what is the IRR of this investment)?

*35. The Tillamook County Creamery Association manufactures Tillamook Cheddar Cheese. It markets this cheese in four varieties: aged 2 months, 9 months, 15 months, and 2 years. At the shop in the dairy, it sells 2 pounds of each variety for the following prices: $7.95, $9.49, $10.95, and $11.95, respectively. Consider the cheese maker's decision whether to continue to age a particular 2-pound block of cheese. At 2 months, he can either sell the cheese immediately or let it age further. If he sells it now, he will receive $7.95 immediately. If he ages the cheese, he must give up the $7.95 today to receive a higher amount in the future. What is the IRR (expressed in percent per month) of the investment of giving up $79.50 today by choosing to store 20 pounds of cheese that is currently 2 months old and instead selling 10 pounds of this cheese when it has aged 9 months, 6 pounds when it has aged 15 months, and the remaining 4 pounds when it has aged 2 years?

*36. Your grandmother bought an annuity from Rock Solid Life Insurance Company for $200,000 when she retired. In exchange for the $200,000, Rock Solid will pay her $25,000 per year until she dies. The interest rate is 5%. How long must she live after the day she retired to come out ahead (that is, to get more in *value* than what she paid in)?

EXCEL *37. You are thinking of making an investment in a new plant. The plant will generate revenues of $1 million per year for as long as you maintain it. You expect that the maintenance cost will start at $50,000 per year and will increase 5% per year thereafter. Assume that all revenue and maintenance costs occur at the end of the year. You intend to run the plant as long as it continues to make a positive cash flow (as long as the cash generated by the plant exceeds the maintenance costs). The plant can be built and become operational immediately. If the plant costs $10 million to build, and the interest rate is 6% per year, should you invest in the plant?

EXCEL *38. You have just turned 30 years old, have just received your MBA, and have accepted your first job. Now you must decide how much money to put into your retirement plan. The plan works as follows: Every dollar in the plan earns 7% per year. You cannot make withdrawals until you retire on your sixty-fifth birthday. After that point, you can make withdrawals as you see fit. You decide that you will plan to live to 100 and work until you turn 65. You estimate that to live comfortably in retirement, you will need $100,000 per year starting at the end of the first year of retirement and ending on your one hundredth birthday. You will contribute the same amount to the plan at the end of every year that you work. How much do you need to contribute each year to fund your retirement?

EXCEL *39. Problem 4.38 is not very realistic because most retirement plans do not allow you to specify a fixed amount to contribute every year. Instead, you are required to specify a fixed percentage of your salary that you want to contribute. Assume that your starting salary is $75,000 per year and it will grow 2% per year until you retire. Assuming everything else stays the same as in Problem 4.38, what percentage of your income do you need to contribute to the plan every year to fund the same retirement income?

Data Case

Assume today is August 1, 2006. Natasha Kingery is 30 years old and has a Bachelor of Science degree in computer science. She is currently employed as a Tier 2 field service representative for a telephony corporation located in Seattle, Washington, and earns $38,000 a year that she anticipates will grow at 3% per year. Natasha hopes to retire at age 65 and has just begun to think about the future.

Natasha has $75,000 that she recently inherited from her aunt. She invested this money in 10-year Treasury Bonds. She is considering whether she should further her education and would use her inheritance to pay for it.[9]

She has investigated a couple of options and is asking for your help as a financial planning intern to determine the financial consequences associated with each option. Natasha has already been accepted to both of these programs, and could start either one soon.

One alternative that Natasha is considering is attaining a certification in network design. This certification would automatically promote her to a Tier 3 field service representative in her company. The base salary for a Tier 3 representative is $10,000 more than what she currently earns and she anticipates that this salary differential will grow at a rate of 3% a year as long as she keeps working. The certification program requires the completion of 20 Web-based courses and a score of 80% or better on an exam at the end of the course work. She has learned that the average amount of time necessary to finish the program is one year. The total cost of the program is $5,000, due when she enrolls in the program. Because she will do all the work for the certification on her own time, Natasha does not expect to lose any income during the certification.

Another option is going back to school for an MBA degree. With an MBA degree, Natasha expects to be promoted to a managerial position in her current firm. The managerial position

9. If Natasha lacked the cash to pay for her tuition up front, she could borrow the money. More intriguingly, she could sell a fraction of her future earnings, an idea that has received attention from researchers and entrepreneurs; see Miguel Palacios, *Investing in Human Capital: A Capital Markets Approach to Student Funding*, Cambridge University Press, 2004.

pays $20,000 a year more than her current position. She expects that this salary differential will also grow at a rate of 3% per year for as long as she keeps working. The evening program, which will take three years to complete, costs $25,000 per year, due at the beginning of each of her three years in school. Because she will attend classes in the evening, Natasha doesn't expect to lose any income while she is earning her MBA if she chooses to undertake the MBA.

1. Determine the interest rate she is currently earning on her inheritance by going to Yahoo! Finance (http://finance.yahoo.com) and clicking on the 10-year bond link in the market summary. Then go to "Historical Prices" and enter the appropriate date, August 1, 2006, to obtain the closing yield or interest rate that she is earning. Use this interest rate as the discount rate for the remainder of this problem.

2. Create a timeline in Excel for her current situation, as well as the certification program and MBA degree options, using the following assumptions:
   - Salaries for the year are paid only once, at the end of the year.
   - The salary increase becomes effective immediately upon graduating from the MBA program or being certified. That is, because the increases become effective immediately but salaries are paid at the end of the year, the first salary increase will be paid exactly one year after graduation or certification.

3. Calculate the present value of the salary differential for completing the certification program. Subtract the cost of the program to get the NPV of undertaking the certification program.

4. Calculate the present value of the salary differential for completing the MBA degree. Calculate the present value of the cost of the MBA program. Based on your calculations, determine the NPV of undertaking the MBA.

5. Based on your answers to Questions 3 and 4, what advice would you give to Natasha? What if the two programs are mutually exclusive?—if Natasha undetakes one of the programs there is no further benefit to undertaking the other program. Would your advice change?

CHAPTER

5

Interest Rates

notation

EAR	effective annual rate
r	interest rate or discount rate
PV	present value
FV	future value
C	cash flow
APR	annual percentage rate
k	number of compounding periods per year
r_r	real interest rate
i	rate of inflation
NPV	net present value
C_n	cash flow that arrives in period *n*
n	number of periods
r_n	interest rate or discount rate for an *n*-year term
τ	tax rate

In Chapter 4, we explored the mechanics of computing present values and future values given a market interest rate. But how do we determine that interest rate? In practice, interest is paid and interest rates are quoted in different ways. For example, in mid-2006, ING Direct offered savings accounts with an interest rate of 5.25% paid at the end of one year, while New Century Bank offered an interest rate of 5.12%, but with the interest paid on a daily basis. Interest rates can also differ depending on the investment horizon. In January 2004, investors earned only about 1% on one-year risk-free investments, but could earn more than 5% on fifteen-year risk-free investments. Interest rates can also vary due to risk or tax consequences. For example, the U.S. government is able to borrow at a much lower interest rate than General Motors Corporation.

In this chapter, we consider the factors that affect interest rates and discuss how to determine the appropriate discount rate for a set of cash flows. We begin by looking at the way interest is paid and interest rates are quoted, and we show how to calculate the effective interest paid in one year given different quoting conventions. We then consider some of the main determinants of interest rates—namely, inflation and government policy. Because interest rates tend to change over time, investors will demand different interest rates for different investment horizons based on their expectations. Finally, we examine the role of risk in determining interest rates and show how to adjust interest rates to determine the effective amount received (or paid) after accounting for taxes.

5.1　Interest Rate Quotes and Adjustments

To determine the appropriate discount rate from an interest rate, we need to understand the ways that interest rates are quoted. Also, because interest rates may be quoted for different time intervals, such as monthly, semiannual, or annual, it is often necessary to adjust the interest rate to a time period that matches that of our cash flows. We explore these mechanics of interest rates in this section.

The Effective Annual Rate

Interest rates are often stated as an **effective annual rate (EAR)**, which indicates the total amount of interest that will be earned at the end of one year.[1] This method of quoting the interest rate is the one we have used thus far in this textbook, and in Chapter 4 we used the EAR as the discount rate r in our time value of money calculations. For example, with an EAR of 5%, a $100,000 investment grows to

$$\$100,000 \times (1 + r) = \$100,000 \times (1.05) = \$105,000$$

in one year. After two years it will grow to

$$\$100,000 \times (1 + r)^2 = \$100,000 \times (1.05)^2 = \$110,250$$

Adjusting the Discount Rate to Different Time Periods

The preceding example shows that earning an effective annual rate of 5% for two years is equivalent to earning 10.25% in total interest over the entire period:

$$\$100,000 \times (1.05)^2 = \$100,000 \times 1.1025 = \$110,250$$

In general, by raising the interest rate factor $(1 + r)$ to the appropriate power, we can compute an equivalent interest rate for a longer time period.

We can use the same method to find the equivalent interest rate for periods shorter than one year. In this case, we raise the interest rate factor $(1 + r)$ to the appropriate fractional power. For example, earning 5% interest in one year is equivalent to receiving

$$(1 + r)^{0.5} = (1.05)^{0.5} = \$1.0247$$

for each $1 invested every six months. That is, a 5% effective annual rate is equivalent to an interest rate of approximately 2.47% earned every six months. We can verify this result by computing the interest we would earn in one year by investing for two six-month periods at this rate:

$$(1 + r)^2 = (1.0247)^2 = \$1.05$$

In general, we can convert a discount rate of r for one period to an equivalent discount rate for n periods using the following formula:

$$\text{Equivalent } n\text{-Period Discount Rate} = (1 + r)^n - 1 \qquad (5.1)$$

In this formula, n can be larger than 1 (to compute a rate over more than one period) or smaller than 1 (to compute a rate over a fraction of a period). When computing present

---

1. The effective annual rate is often referred to as the *effective annual yield* (EAY) or the *annual percentage yield* (APY).

or future values, it is convenient to adjust the discount rate to match the time period of the cash flows. This adjustment is *necessary* to apply the perpetuity or annuity formulas, as in the following example.

Valuing Monthly Cash Flows

Problem
Suppose your bank account pays interest monthly with an effective annual rate of 6%. What amount of interest will you earn each month? If you have no money in the bank today, how much will you need to save at the end of each month to accumulate $100,000 in 10 years?

Solution
From Eq. 5.1, a 6% EAR is equivalent to earning $(1.06)^{1/12} - 1 = 0.4868\%$ per month. To determine the amount to save each month to reach the goal of $100,000 in 10 years, we must determine the amount C of the monthly payment that will have a future value of $100,000 in 10 years, given an interest rate of 0.4868% per month. We can use the annuity formula from Chapter 4 to solve this problem if we write the timeline for our savings plan using *monthly* periods:

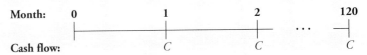

That is, we can view the savings plan as a monthly annuity with $10 \times 12 = 120$ monthly payments. From the future value of an annuity formula, Eq. 4.8:

$$FV(\text{annuity}) = C \times \tfrac{1}{r}[(1 + r)^n - 1]$$

We can solve for the payment C using the equivalent monthly interest rate $r = 0.4868\%$, and $n = 120$ months:

$$C = \frac{FV(\text{annuity})}{\tfrac{1}{r}[(1 + r)^n - 1]} = \frac{\$100,000}{\tfrac{1}{0.004868}[(1.004868)^{120} - 1]} = \$615.47 \text{ per month}$$

We can also compute this result using the annuity spreadsheet:

	NPER	RATE	PV	PMT	FV	Excel Formula
Given	120	0.4868%	0		100,000	
Solve for PMT				−615.47		=PMT(0.004868,120,0,100000)

Thus, if we save $615.47 per month and we earn interest monthly at an effective annual rate of 6%, we will have $100,000 in 10 years.

Annual Percentage Rates

Banks also quote interest rates in terms of an **annual percentage rate (APR)**, which indicates the amount of **simple interest** earned in one year, that is, the amount of interest earned *without* the effect of compounding. Because it does not include the effect of compounding, the APR quote is typically less than the actual amount of interest that you will earn. To compute the actual amount that you will earn in one year, the APR must first be converted to an effective annual rate.

For example, suppose Granite Bank advertises savings accounts with an interest rate of "6% APR with monthly compounding." In this case, you will earn 6% / 12 = 0.5% every month. So an APR with monthly compounding is actually a way of quoting a *monthly* interest rate, rather than an annual interest rate. Because the interest compounds each month, you will earn

$$\$1 \times (1.005)^{12} = \$1.061678$$

at the end of one year, for an effective annual rate of 6.1678%. The 6.1678% that you earn on your deposit is higher than the quoted 6% APR due to compounding: In later months, you earn interest on the interest paid in earlier months.

It is important to remember that because the APR does not reflect the true amount you will earn over one year, *the APR itself cannot be used as a discount rate.* Instead, the APR with k compounding periods is a way of quoting the actual interest earned each compounding period:

$$\text{Interest Rate per Compounding Period} = \frac{\text{APR}}{k \text{ periods / year}} \qquad (5.2)$$

Once we have computed the interest earned per compounding period from Eq. 5.2, we can compute the equivalent interest rate for any other time interval using Eq. 5.1. Thus the effective annual rate corresponding to an APR with k compounding periods per year is given by the following conversion formula:

Converting an APR to an EAR

$$1 + EAR = \left(1 + \frac{APR}{k}\right)^k \qquad (5.3)$$

Table 5.1 shows the effective annual rates that correspond to an APR of 6% with different compounding intervals. The EAR increases with the frequency of compounding because of the ability to earn interest on interest sooner. Investments can compound even more frequently than daily. In principle, the compounding interval could be hourly or every second. In the limit we approach the idea of **continuous compounding**, in which we compound the interest every instant.[2] As a practical matter, compounding more frequently than daily has a negligible impact on the effective annual rate and is rarely observed.

TABLE 5.1	Effective Annual Rates for a 6% APR with Different Compounding Periods
Compounding Interval	**Effective Annual Rate**
Annual	$(1 + 0.06 / 1)^1 - 1 = 6\%$
Semiannual	$(1 + 0.06 / 2)^2 - 1 = 6.09\%$
Monthly	$(1 + 0.06 / 12)^{12} - 1 = 6.1678\%$
Daily	$(1 + 0.06 / 365)^{365} - 1 = 6.1831\%$

---

2. A 6% APR with continuous compounding results in an EAR of approximately 6.1837%, which is almost the same as daily compounding. See the appendix for further discussion of continuous compounding.

When working with APRs, we must first convert the APR to a discount rate per compounding interval using Eq. 5.2, or to an EAR using Eq. 5.3, before evaluating the present or future value of a set of cash flows.

Converting the APR to a Discount Rate

Problem

Your firm is purchasing a new telephone system, which will last for four years. You can purchase the system for an upfront cost of $150,000, or you can lease the system from the manufacturer for $4000 paid at the end of each month.[3] Your firm can borrow at an interest rate of 5% APR with semiannual compounding. Should you purchase the system outright or pay $4000 per month?

Solution

The cost of leasing the system is a 48-month annuity of $4000 per month:

We can compute the present value of the lease cash flows using the annuity formula, but first we need to compute the discount rate that corresponds to a period length of one month. To do so, we convert the borrowing cost of 5% APR with semiannual compounding to a monthly discount rate. Using Eq. 5.2, the APR corresponds to a six-month discount rate of 5% / 2 = 2.5%. To convert a six-month discount rate into a one-month discount rate, we compound the six-month rate by 1/6 using Eq. 5.1:

$$(1.025)^{1/6} - 1 = 0.4124\% \text{ per month}$$

(Alternatively, we could first use Eq. 5.3 to convert the APR to an EAR: $1 + EAR = (1 + 0.05 / 2)^2 = 1.050625$. Then we can convert the EAR to a monthly rate using Eq. 5.1: $(1.050625)^{1/12} - 1 = 0.4124\%$ per month.)

Given this discount rate, we can use the annuity formula (Eq. 4.7) to compute the present value of the monthly payments:

$$PV = 4000 \times \frac{1}{0.004124}\left(1 - \frac{1}{1.004124^{48}}\right) = \$173,867$$

We can also use the annuity spreadsheet:

	NPER	RATE	PV	PMT	FV	Excel Formula
Given	48	0.4124%		−4,000	0	
Solve for PV			173,867			=PV(0.004124,48,−4000,0)

Thus paying $4000 per month for 48 months is equivalent to paying a present value of $173,867 today. This cost is $173,867 − $150,000 = $23,867 higher than the cost of purchasing the system, so it is better to pay $150,000 for the system rather than lease it. One way to interpret this result is as follows: At a 5% APR with semiannual compounding, by promising to repay $4000 per month your firm can borrow $173,867 today. With this loan it could purchase the phone system and have an additional $23,867 to use for other purposes.

---

3. In addition to these cash flows, there may be tax and accounting considerations when comparing a purchase with a lease. We ignore these complications in this example, and consider leases in detail in Chapter 25.

Application: Discount Rates and Loans

Now that we have explained how to compute the discount rate from an interest rate quote, let's apply the concept to solve two common financial problems: calculating a loan payment and calculating the remaining balance on a loan.

Computing Loan Payments. To calculate a loan payment, we first compute the discount rate from the quoted interest rate of the loan, and then equate the outstanding loan balance with the present value of the loan payments and solve for the loan payment.

Many loans, such as mortgages and car loans, have monthly payments and are quoted in terms of an APR with monthly compounding. These types of loans are **amortizing loans**, which means that each month you pay interest on the loan plus some part of the loan balance. Each monthly payment is the same, and the loan is fully repaid with the final payment. Typical terms for a new car loan might be "6.75% APR for 60 months." When the compounding interval for the APR is not stated explicitly, it is equal to the interval between the payments, or one month in this case. Thus this quote means that the loan will be repaid with 60 equal monthly payments, computed using a 6.75% APR with monthly compounding. Consider the timeline for a $30,000 car loan with these terms:

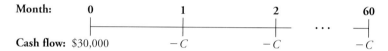

The payment, C, is set so that the present value of the cash flows, evaluated using the loan interest rate, equals the original principal amount of $30,000. In this case, the 6.75% APR with monthly compounding corresponds to a one-month discount rate of 6.75% / 12 = 0.5625%. Because the loan payments are an annuity, we can use Eq. 4.12 to find C:

$$C = \frac{P}{\frac{1}{r}\left(1 - \frac{1}{(1+r)^N}\right)} = \frac{30,000}{\frac{1}{0.005625}\left(1 - \frac{1}{(1 + 0.005625)^{60}}\right)} = \$590.50$$

Alternatively, we can solve for the payment C using the annuity spreadsheet:

	NPER	RATE	PV	PMT	FV	Excel Formula
Given	60	0.5625%	30,000		0	
Solve for PMT				−590.50		=PMT(0.005625,60,30000,0)

Computing the Outstanding Loan Balance. The outstanding balance on a loan, also called the outstanding principal, is equal to the present value of the remaining future loan payments, again evaluated using the loan interest rate. We calculate the outstanding loan balance by determining the present value of the remaining loan payments using the loan rate as the discount rate.

Computing the Outstanding Loan Balance

Problem

Ten years ago your firm borrowed $3 million to purchase an office building using a loan with a 7.80% APR and monthly payments for 30 years. How much do you owe on the loan today? How much interest was paid on the loan in the past year?

Solution

The first step is to solve for the monthly loan payment. Here is the timeline (in months):

An APR of 7.80% with monthly compounding is equivalent to 7.80% / 12 = 0.65% per month. The monthly payment is then

$$C = \frac{P}{\frac{1}{r}\left(1 - \frac{1}{(1+r)^N}\right)} = \frac{3{,}000{,}000}{\frac{1}{0.0065}\left(1 - \frac{1}{(1.0065)^{360}}\right)} = \$21{,}596$$

The remaining balance on the loan is the present value of the remaining 20 years, or 240 months, of payments:

$$\text{Balance after 10 years} = \$21{,}596 \times \frac{1}{0.0065}\left(1 - \frac{1}{1.0065^{240}}\right) = \$2{,}620{,}759$$

Thus, after 10 years, you owe $2,620,759 on the loan.

During the past year, your firm made total payments of $21,596 × 12 = $259,152 on the loan. To determine how much of that amount was interest, it is easiest to first determine the amount that was used to repay the principal. Your loan balance one year ago, with 21 years (252 months) remaining, was

$$\text{Balance after 9 years} = \$21{,}596 \times \frac{1}{0.0065}\left(1 - \frac{1}{1.0065^{252}}\right) = \$2{,}673{,}248$$

Therefore, the balance declined by $2,673,248 − $2,620,759 = $52,489 in the past year. Of the total payments made, $52,489 was used to repay the principal and the remaining $259,152 − $52,489 = $206,663 was used to pay interest.

CONCEPT CHECK
1. What is the difference between an EAR and an APR quote?
2. Why can't the APR be used as a discount rate?

5.2 The Determinants of Interest Rates

How are interest rates determined? Fundamentally, interest rates are determined in the market based on individuals' willingness to borrow and lend. In this section, we look at some of the factors that may influence interest rates, such as inflation, government policy, and expectations of future growth.

Inflation and Real Versus Nominal Rates

The interest rates that are quoted by banks and other financial institutions, and that we have used for discounting cash flows, are **nominal interest rates**, which indicate the rate at which your money will grow if invested for a certain period. Of course, if prices in the economy are also growing due to inflation, the nominal interest rate does not represent the increase in purchasing power that will result from investing. The rate of growth of your purchasing power, after adjusting for inflation, is determined by the **real interest rate**, which we denote by r_r. If r is the nominal interest rate and i is the rate of inflation, we can calculate the rate of growth of purchasing power as follows:

$$\text{Growth in Purchasing Power} = 1 + r_r = \frac{1 + r}{1 + i} = \frac{\text{Growth of Money}}{\text{Growth of Prices}} \quad (5.4)$$

We can rearrange Eq. 5.4 to find the following formula for the real interest rate, together with a convenient approximation for the real interest rate when inflation rates are low:

The Real Interest Rate

$$r_r = \frac{r - i}{1 + i} \approx r - i \quad (5.5)$$

That is, the real interest rate is approximately equal to the nominal interest rate less the rate of inflation.[4]

EXAMPLE 5.4

Calculating the Real Interest Rate

Problem

In the year 2000, short-term U.S. government bond rates were about 5.8% and the rate of inflation was about 3.4%. In 2003, interest rates were about 1% and inflation was about 1.9%. What was the real interest rate in 2000 and 2003?

Solution

Using Eq. 5.5, the real interest rate in 2000 was (5.8% − 3.4%) / (1.034) = 2.32% (which is approximately equal to the difference between the nominal rate and inflation: 5.8% − 3.4% = 2.4%). In 2003, the real interest rate was (1% − 1.9%) / (1.019) = −0.88%. Note that the real interest rate was negative in 2003, indicating that interest rates were insufficient to keep up with inflation: Investors in U.S. government bonds were able to buy less at the end of the year than they could have purchased at the start of the year.

Figure 5.1 shows the history of nominal interest rates and inflation rates in the United States since 1955. Note that the nominal interest rate tends to move with inflation. Intuitively, individuals' willingness to save will depend on the growth in purchasing power they can expect (given by the real interest rate). Thus, when the inflation rate is high, a higher nominal interest rate is needed to induce individuals to save.

Investment and Interest Rate Policy

Interest rates affect not only individuals' propensity to save, but also firms' incentive to raise capital and invest. Consider a risk-free investment opportunity that requires an upfront investment of $10 million and generates a cash flow of $3 million per year for four years. If the risk-free interest rate is 5%, this investment has an NPV of

$$NPV = -10 + \frac{3}{1.05} + \frac{3}{1.05^2} + \frac{3}{1.05^3} + \frac{3}{1.05^4} = \$0.638 \text{ million}$$

---

4. The real interest rate should not be used as a discount rate for future cash flows. It can be used as a discount rate only if the cash flows are not the expected cash flows that will be paid, but are the equivalent cash flows before adjusting them for growth due to inflation (in that case, we say the cash flows are in *real terms*). This approach is error prone, however, so throughout this book we will always forecast cash flows including any growth due to inflation, and discount using nominal interest rates.

FIGURE 5.1

U.S. Interest Rates and Inflation Rates, 1955–2005

Interest rates are average three-month Treasury bill rates and inflation rates are based on annual increases in the U.S. Bureau of Labor Statistics' consumer price index. Note that interest rates tend to be high when inflation is high.

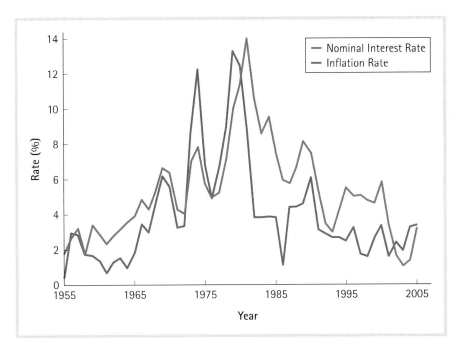

If the interest rate is 9%, the NPV falls to

$$NPV = -10 + \frac{3}{1.09} + \frac{3}{1.09^2} + \frac{3}{1.09^3} + \frac{3}{1.09^4} = -\$0.281 \text{ million}$$

and the investment is no longer profitable. The reason, of course, is that we are discounting the positive cash flows at a higher rate, which reduces their present value. The cost of $10 million occurs today, however, so its present value is independent of the discount rate.

More generally, when the costs of an investment precede the benefits, an increase in the interest rate will decrease the investment's NPV. All else equal, higher interest rates will therefore tend to shrink the set of positive-NPV investments available to firms. The Federal Reserve in the United States and central banks in other countries use this relationship between interest rates and investment incentives when trying to guide the economy. They can lower interest rates to stimulate investment if the economy is slowing, and they can raise interest rates to reduce investment if the economy is "overheating" and inflation is on the rise.

The Yield Curve and Discount Rates

You may have noticed that the interest rates that banks offer on investments or charge on loans depend on the horizon, or *term*, of the investment or loan. The relationship between the investment term and the interest rate is called the **term structure** of interest rates. We can plot this relationship on a graph called the **yield curve**. Figure 5.2 shows the term structure and corresponding yield curve of risk-free U.S. interest rates that was available to investors in January of 2004, 2005, and 2006. In each case, note that the interest rate depends on the horizon, and that the difference between short-term and long-term interest rates was especially pronounced in 2004.

FIGURE 5.2   **Term Structure of Risk-Free U.S. Interest Rates, January 2004, 2005, and 2006**

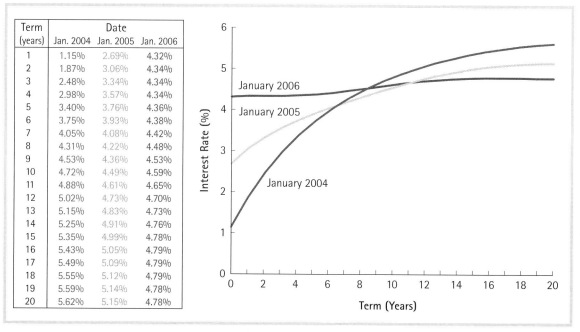

Term (years)	Date		
	Jan. 2004	Jan. 2005	Jan. 2006
1	1.15%	2.69%	4.32%
2	1.87%	3.06%	4.34%
3	2.48%	3.34%	4.34%
4	2.98%	3.57%	4.34%
5	3.40%	3.76%	4.36%
6	3.75%	3.93%	4.38%
7	4.05%	4.08%	4.42%
8	4.31%	4.22%	4.48%
9	4.53%	4.36%	4.53%
10	4.72%	4.49%	4.59%
11	4.88%	4.61%	4.65%
12	5.02%	4.73%	4.70%
13	5.15%	4.83%	4.73%
14	5.25%	4.91%	4.76%
15	5.35%	4.99%	4.78%
16	5.43%	5.05%	4.79%
17	5.49%	5.09%	4.79%
18	5.55%	5.12%	4.79%
19	5.59%	5.14%	4.78%
20	5.62%	5.15%	4.78%

The figure shows the interest rate available from investing in risk-free U.S. Treasury securities with different investment terms. In each case, the interest rates differ depending on the horizon. (Data from U.S. Treasury STRIPS.)

We can use the term structure to compute the present and future values of a risk-free cash flow over different investment horizons. For example, $100 invested for one year at the one-year interest rate in January 2004 would grow to a future value of

$$\$100 \times 1.0115 = \$101.15$$

at the end of one year, and $100 invested for ten years at the ten-year interest rate in January 2004 would grow to[5]

$$\$100 \times (1.0472)^{10} = \$158.60$$

The same logic can be applied when computing the present value of cash flows with different maturities. A risk-free cash flow received in two years should be discounted at the two-year interest rate, and a cash flow received in ten years should be discounted at the ten-year interest rate. In general, a risk-free cash flow of C_n received in n years has present value

$$PV = \frac{C_n}{(1 + r_n)^n} \tag{5.6}$$

where r_n is the risk-free interest rate for an n-year term. In other words, when computing a present value we must match the term of the cash flow and term of the discount rate.

---

5. We could also invest for ten years by investing at the one-year interest rate for ten years in a row. However, because we do not know what future interest rates will be, our ultimate payoff would not be risk free.

Combining Eq. 5.6 for cash flows in different years leads to the general formula for the present value of a cash flow stream:

Present Value of a Cash Flow Stream Using a Term Structure of Discount Rates

$$PV = \frac{C_1}{1 + r_1} + \frac{C_2}{(1 + r_2)^2} + \cdots + \frac{C_N}{(1 + r_N)^N} = \sum_{n=1}^{N} \frac{C_n}{(1 + r_n)^n} \tag{5.7}$$

Note the difference between Eq. 5.7 and Eq. 4.3. Here, we use a different discount rate for each cash flow, based on the rate from the yield curve with the same term. When the yield curve is relatively flat, as it was in January 2006, this distinction is relatively minor and is often ignored by discounting using a single "average" interest rate r. But when short-term and long-term interest rates vary widely, as they did in January 2004, Eq. 5.7 should be used.

Warning: All of our shortcuts for computing present values (annuity and perpetuity formulas, the annuity spreadsheet) are based on discounting all of the cash flows *at the same rate*. They *cannot* be used in situations in which cash flows need to be discounted at different rates.

EXAMPLE 5.5

Using the Term Structure to Compute Present Values

Problem

Compute the present value of a risk-free five-year annuity of $1000 per year, given the yield curve for January 2005 in Figure 5.2.

Solution

To compute the present value, we discount each cash flow by the corresponding interest rate:

$$PV = \frac{1000}{1.0269} + \frac{1000}{1.0306^2} + \frac{1000}{1.0334^3} + \frac{1000}{1.0357^4} + \frac{1000}{1.0376^5} = \$4522$$

Note that we cannot use the annuity formula here because the discount rates differ for each cash flow.

COMMON MISTAKE   **Using the Annuity Formula When Discount Rates Vary**

When computing the present value of an annuity, a common mistake is to use the annuity formula with a single interest rate even though interest rates vary with the investment horizon. For example, we *cannot* compute the present value of the five-year annuity in Example 5.5 using the five-year interest rate from January 2005:

$$PV \neq \$1000 \times \frac{1}{0.0376} \left(1 - \frac{1}{1.0376^5}\right) = \$4482$$

If we want to find the single interest rate that we could use to value the annuity, we must first compute the present value of the annuity using Eq. 5.7 and then solve for its IRR. For the annuity in Example 5.5, we use the annuity spreadsheet below to find its IRR of 3.45%. The IRR of the annuity is always between the highest and lowest discount rates used to calculate its present value, as is the case in this example.

	NPER	RATE	PV	PMT	FV	Excel Formula
Given	5		−4,522	1,000	0	
Solve for Rate		3.45%				=RATE(5,1000,−4522,0)

The Yield Curve and the Economy

As Figure 5.3 illustrates, the yield curve changes over time. Sometimes, short-term rates are close to long-term rates, and at other times they may be very different. What accounts for the changing shape of the yield curve?

The Federal Reserve determines very short-term interest rates through its influence on the **federal funds rate**, which is the rate at which banks can borrow cash reserves on an overnight basis. All other interest rates on the yield curve are set in the market and are adjusted until the supply of lending matches the demand for borrowing at each loan term. As we shall see in a moment, expectations of future interest rate changes have a major effect on investors' willingness to lend or borrow for longer terms and, therefore, on the shape of the yield curve.

Suppose short-term interest rates are equal to long-term interest rates. If interest rates are expected to rise in the future, investors would not want to make long-term investments. Instead, they could do better by investing on a short-term basis and then reinvesting after interest rates rose. Thus, if interest rates are expected to rise, long-term interest rates will tend to be higher than short-term rates to attract investors.

Similarly, if interest rates are expected to fall in the future, then borrowers would not wish to borrow at long-term rates that are equal to short-term rates. They would do better

| **FIGURE 5.3** | **Short-Term Versus Long-Term U.S. Interest Rates and Recessions** |

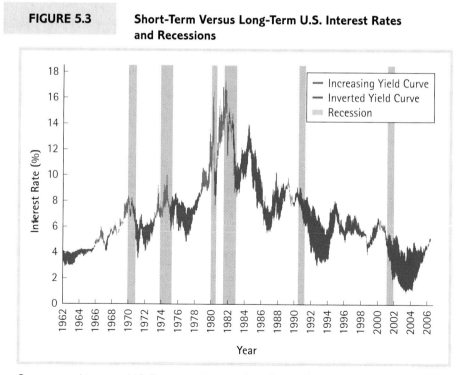

One-year and ten-year U.S. Treasury rates are plotted, with the spread between them shaded in blue if the shape of the yield curve is increasing (the one-year rate is below the ten-year rate) and in red if the yield curve is inverted (the one-year rate exceeds the ten-year rate). Gray bars show the dates of U.S. recessions. Note that inverted yield curves tend to precede recessions as determined by the National Bureau of Economic Research. In recessions, interest rates tend to fall, with short-term rates dropping further. As a result, the yield curve tends to be steep coming out of a recession.

by borrowing on a short-term basis, and then taking out a new loan after rates fall. So, if interest rates are expected to fall, long-term rates will tend to be lower than short-term rates to attract borrowers.

These arguments imply that the shape of the yield curve will be strongly influenced by interest rate expectations. A sharply increasing (*steep*) yield curve, with long-term rates much higher than short-term rates, generally indicates that interest rates are expected to rise in the future. A decreasing (*inverted*) yield curve, with long-term rates lower than short-term rates, generally signals an expected decline in future interest rates. Because interest rates tend to drop in response to a slowdown in the economy, an inverted yield curve is often interpreted as a negative forecast for economic growth. Indeed, as Figure 5.3 illustrates, each of the last six recessions in the United States was preceded by a period in which the yield curve was inverted. Conversely, the yield curve tends to be steep as the economy comes out of a recession and interest rates are expected to rise.[6]

Clearly, the yield curve provides extremely important information for a business manager. In addition to specifying the discount rates for risk-free cash flows that occur at different horizons, it is also a potential leading indicator of future economic growth.

Comparing Short- and Long-Term Interest Rates

Problem
Suppose the current one-year interest rate is 1%. If it is known with certainty that the one-year interest rate will be 2% next year and 4% the following year, what will the interest rates r_1, r_2, and r_3 of the yield curve be today? Is the yield curve flat, increasing, or inverted?

Solution
We are told already that the one-year rate $r_1 = 1\%$. To find the two-year rate, note that if we invest \$1 for one year at the current one-year rate and then reinvest next year at the new one-year rate, after two years we will earn

$$\$1 \times (1.01) \times (1.02) = \$1.0302$$

We should earn the same payoff if we invest for two years at the current two-year rate r_2:

$$\$1 \times (1 + r_2)^2 = \$1.0302$$

Otherwise, there would be an arbitrage opportunity: If investing at the two-year rate led to a higher payoff, investors could invest for two years and borrow at the one-year rate. If investing at the two-year rate led to a lower payoff, investors could invest at the one-year rate and borrow at the two-year rate.

Solving for r_2, we find that

$$r_2 = (1.0302)^{1/2} - 1 = 1.499\%$$

Similarly, investing for three years at the one-year rates should have the same payoff as investing at the current three-year rate:

$$(1.01) \times (1.02) \times (1.04) = 1.0714 = (1 + r_3)^3$$

We can solve for $r_3 = (1.0714)^{1/3} - 1 = 2.326\%$. Therefore, the current yield curve has $r_1 = 1\%$, $r_2 = 1.499\%$, and $r_3 = 2.326\%$. The yield curve is increasing as a result of the anticipated higher interest rates in the future.

---

6. Other factors besides interest rate expectations—most notably risk—can have an impact on the shape of the yield curve. See Chapter 8 for further discussion.

1. What is the difference between a nominal and real interest rate?

2. How are interest rates and the level of investment made by businesses related?

5.3   Risk and Taxes

In this section, we discuss two other factors that are important when evaluating interest rates: risk and taxes.

Risk and Interest Rates

We have already seen that interest rates vary with the investment horizon. Interest rates also vary based on the identity of the borrower. For example, Table 5.2 lists the interest rates paid by a number of different borrowers in mid-2006 for a five-year loan.

Why do these interest rates vary so widely? The lowest interest rate is the rate paid on U.S. Treasury notes. U.S. Treasury securities are widely regarded to be risk-free because there is virtually no chance the government will fail to pay the interest and default on these bonds. Thus, when we refer to the "risk-free interest rate," we mean the rate on U.S. Treasuries.

All other borrowers have some risk of default. For these loans, the stated interest rate is the *maximum* amount that investors will receive. Investors may receive less if the company has financial difficulties and is unable to fully repay the loan. To compensate for the risk that they will receive less if the firm defaults, investors demand a higher interest rate than the rate on U.S. Treasuries. The difference between the interest rate of the loan and the Treasury rate will depend on investors' assessment of the likelihood that the firm will default.

Later in the textbook we will develop tools to evaluate the risk of different investments and determine the interest rate or discount rate that appropriately compensates investors for the level of risk they are taking. For now, we should remember that when discounting future cash flows, it is important to use a discount rate that matches both the horizon and the risk of the cash flows. Specifically, *the right discount rate for a cash flow is the rate of return available in the market on other investments of comparable risk and term.*

TABLE 5.2	Interest Rates on Five-Year Loans for Various Borrowers, June 2006

Borrower	Interest Rate
U.S. government (Treasury Notes)	4.94%
J. P. Morgan Chase & Co.	5.44%
Abbott Laboratories	5.45%
Time Warner	5.86%
RadioShack Corp.	6.60%
General Motors Acceptance Corp.	8.22%
Goodyear Tire and Rubber Co.	8.50%

Discounting Risky Cash Flows

Problem

Suppose the U.S. government owes your firm $1000, to be paid in five years. Based on the interest rates in Table 5.2, what is the present value of this cash flow? Suppose instead Goodyear Tire and Rubber Company owes your firm $1000. Estimate the present value in this case.

Solution

Assuming we can regard the government's obligation as risk free (there is no chance you won't be paid), then we discount the cash flow using the risk-free interest rate of 4.94%:

$$PV = \$1000 \div (1.0494)^5 = \$785.77$$

The obligation from Goodyear is not risk-free. There is no guarantee that Goodyear will not have financial difficulties and fail to pay the $1000. Because the risk of this obligation is likely to be comparable to the five-year loan quoted in Table 5.2, the 8.50% interest rate of the loan is a more appropriate discount rate to use to compute the present value in this case:

$$PV = \$1000 \div (1.0850)^5 = \$665.05$$

Note the substantially lower present value in this case, due to the risk of default.

After-Tax Interest Rates

If the cash flows from an investment are taxed, the actual cash flow that the investor will get to keep will be reduced by the amount of the tax payments. We will discuss the taxation of corporate investments in detail in later chapters. Here, we consider the effect of taxes on the interest earned on savings (or paid on borrowing). Taxes reduce the amount of interest the investor can keep, and we refer to this reduced amount as the **after-tax interest rate**.

Consider an investment that pays 8% interest (EAR) for one year. If you invest $100 at the start of the year, you will earn 8% × $100 = $8 in interest at year-end. This interest may be taxable as income.[7] If you are in a 40% tax bracket, you will owe

$$(40\% \text{ income tax rate}) \times (\$8 \text{ interest}) = \$3.20 \text{ tax liability}$$

Thus you will receive only $8 − $3.20 = $4.80 after paying taxes. This amount is equivalent to earning 4.80% interest and not paying any taxes, so the after-tax interest rate is 4.80%.

In general, if the interest rate is r and the tax rate is τ, then for each $1 invested you will earn interest equal to r and owe tax of $\tau \times r$ on the interest. The equivalent after-tax interest rate is therefore

After-Tax Interest Rate

$$r - (\tau \times r) = r(1 - \tau) \tag{5.8}$$

Applying this formula to our previous example of an 8% interest rate and a 40% tax rate, we find the interest rate is 8% × (1 − 0.40) = 4.80% after taxes.

---

7. In the United States, interest income for individuals is taxable as income unless the investment is held in a tax-sheltered retirement account or the investment is from tax-exempt securities (such as municipal bonds). Interest from U.S. Treasury securities is exempt from state and local taxes. Interest income earned by a corporation is also taxed at the corporate tax rate.

10. Higher interest rates tend to reduce the NPV of typical investment projects. The U.S. Federal Reserve raises interest rates to moderate investment and combat inflation and lowers interest rates to stimulate investment and economic growth.

11. Interest rates differ with the investment horizon according to the term structure of interest rates. The graph plotting interest rates as a function of the horizon is called the yield curve.

12. Cash flows should be discounted using the discount rate that is appropriate for their horizon. Thus the PV of a cash flow stream is

$$PV = \frac{C_1}{1 + r_1} + \frac{C_2}{(1 + r_2)^2} + \cdots + \frac{C_N}{(1 + r_N)^N} = \sum_{n=1}^{N} \frac{C_n}{(1 + r_n)^n} \qquad (5.7)$$

13. Annuity and perpetuity formulas cannot be applied when discount rates vary with the horizon.

14. The shape of the yield curve tends to vary with investors' expectations of future economic growth and interest rates. It tends to be inverted prior to recessions and to be steep coming out of a recession.

15. U.S. government Treasury rates are regarded as risk-free interest rates. Because other borrowers may default, they will pay higher interest rates on their loans.

16. The correct discount rate for a cash flow is the expected return available in the market on other investments of comparable risk and term.

17. If the interest on an investment is taxed at rate τ, or if the interest on a loan is tax deductible, then the effective after-tax interest rate is

$$r(1 - \tau) \qquad (5.8)$$

Key Terms

after-tax interest rate *p. 139*	federal funds rate *p. 136*
amortizing loan *p. 130*	nominal interest rate *p. 131*
annual percentage rate (APR) *p. 127*	real interest rate *p. 131*
continuous compounding *p. 128*	simple interest *p. 127*
(opportunity) cost of capital *p. 141*	term structure *p. 133*
effective annual rate (EAR) *p. 126*	yield curve *p. 133*

Further Reading

An interesting account of the history of interest rates over the past four millennia is provided in S. Homer and R. Sylla, *A History of Interest Rates*, 4th ed. (New Jersey: John Wiley & Sons, Inc., 2005).

For a deeper understanding of interest rates, how they behave with changing market conditions, and how risk can be managed, see J. C. Van Horne, *Financial Market Rates and Flows*, 6th ed. (Prentice Hall, 2000).

For further insights into the relationship between interest rates, inflation, and economic growth, see a macroeconomics text such as A. Abel and B. Bernanke, *Macroeconomics*, 5th ed. (Boston: Pearson Addison Wesley, 2005).

For further analysis of the yield curve, and how it is measured and modeled, see M. Choudhry, *Analyzing and Interpreting the Yield Curve* (New Jersey, John Wiley & Sons, Inc., 2004).

Problems

All problems in this chapter are available in MyFinanceLab. An asterisk (*) indicates problems with a higher level of difficulty.

1. Your bank is offering you an account that will pay 20% interest in total for a two-year deposit. Determine the equivalent discount rate for a period length of
   a. Six months.
   b. One year.
   c. One month.

EXCEL 2. Which do you prefer: a bank account that pays 5% per year (EAR) for three years or
   a. An account that pays $2\frac{1}{2}$% every six months for three years?
   b. An account that pays $7\frac{1}{2}$% every 18 months for three years?
   c. An account that pays $\frac{1}{2}$% per month for three years?

EXCEL 3. Many academic institutions offer a sabbatical policy. Every seven years a professor is given a year free of teaching and other administrative responsibilities at full pay. For a professor earning $70,000 per year who works for a total of 42 years, what is the present value of the amount she will earn while on sabbatical if the interest rate is 6% (EAR)?

4. You have found three investment choices for a one-year deposit: 10% APR compounded monthly, 10% APR compounded annually, and 9% APR compounded daily. Compute the EAR for each investment choice. (Assume that there are 365 days in the year.)

5. Your bank account pays interest with an EAR of 5%. What is the APR quote for this account based on semiannual compounding? What is the APR with monthly compounding?

6. Suppose the interest rate is 8% APR with monthly compounding. What is the present value of an annuity that pays $100 every six months for five years?

EXCEL 7. Your son has been accepted into college. This college guarantees that your son's tuition will not increase for the four years he attends college. The first $10,000 tuition payment is due in six months. After that, the same payment is due every six months until you have made a total of eight payments. The college offers a bank account that allows you to withdraw money every six months and has a fixed APR of 4% (semiannual) guaranteed to remain the same over the next four years. How much money must you deposit today if you intend to make no further deposits and would like to make all the tuition payments from this account, leaving the account empty when the last payment is made?

8. You make monthly payments on your mortgage. It has a quoted APR of 5% (monthly compounding). What percentage of the outstanding principal do you pay in interest each month?

9. Capital One is advertising a 60-month, 5.99% APR motorcycle loan. If you need to borrow $8000 to purchase your dream Harley Davidson, what will your monthly payment be?

10. Oppenheimer Bank is offering a 30-year mortgage with an EAR of $5\frac{3}{8}$%. If you plan to borrow $150,000, what will your monthly payment be?

11. You have decided to refinance your mortgage. You plan to borrow whatever is outstanding on your current mortgage. The current monthly payment is $2356 and you have made every payment on time. The original term of the mortgage was 30 years, and the mortgage is exactly four years and eight months old. You have just made your monthly payment. The mortgage interest rate is $6\frac{3}{8}$% (APR). How much do you owe on the mortgage today?

12. You have just sold your house for $1,000,000 in cash. Your mortgage was originally a 30-year mortgage with monthly payments and an initial balance of $800,000. The mortgage is currently exactly $18\frac{1}{2}$ years old, and you have just made a payment. If the interest rate on the mortgage is 5.25% (APR), how much cash will you have from the sale once you pay off the mortgage?

13. You have just purchased a home and taken out a $500,000 mortgage. The mortgage has a 30-year term with monthly payments and an APR of 6%.

   a. How much will you pay in interest, and how much will you pay in principal, during the first year?

   b. How much will you pay in interest, and how much will you pay in principal, during the twentieth year (i.e., between 19 and 20 years from now)?

EXCEL ***14.** You have an outstanding student loan with required payments of $500 per month for the next four years. The interest rate on the loan is 9% APR (monthly). You are considering making an extra payment of $100 today (that is, you will pay an extra $100 that you are not required to pay). If you are required to continue to make payments of $500 per month until the loan is paid off, what is the amount of your final payment? What effective rate of return (expressed as an APR with monthly compounding) have you earned on the $100?

EXCEL ***15.** Consider again the setting of Problem 14. Now that you realize your best investment is to prepay your student loan, you decide to prepay as much as you can each month. Looking at your budget, you can afford to pay an extra $250 per month in addition to your required monthly payments of $500, or $750 in total each month. How long will it take you to pay off the loan?

*16. If you decide to take the mortgage in Problem 10, Oppenheimer Bank will offer you the following deal: Instead of making the monthly payment you computed in that problem every month, you can make half the payment every two weeks (so that you will make $52 / 2 = 26$ payments per year). How long will it take to pay off the mortgage if the EAR remains the same at $5\frac{3}{8}$%?

EXCEL ***17.** Your friend tells you he has a very simple trick for taking one-third off the time it takes to repay your mortgage: Use your Christmas bonus to make an extra payment on January 1 of each year (that is, pay your monthly payment due on that day twice). If you take out your mortgage on July 1, so your first monthly payment is due August 1, and you make an extra payment every January 1, how long will it take to pay off the mortgage? Assume that the mortgage has an original term of 30 years and an APR of 12%.

EXCEL **18.** You need a new car and the dealer has offered you a price of $20,000, with the following payment options: (a) pay cash and receive a $2000 rebate, or (b) pay a $5000 down payment and finance the rest with a 0% APR loan over 30 months. But having just quit your job and started an MBA program, you are in debt and you expect to be in debt for at least the next $2\frac{1}{2}$ years. You plan to use credit cards to pay your expenses; luckily you have one with a low (fixed) rate of 15% APR (monthly). Which payment option is best for you?

19. The mortgage on your house is 5 years old. It required monthly payments of $1402, had an original term of 30 years, and had an interest rate of 10% (APR). In the intervening 5 years, interest rates have fallen and so you have decided to refinance—that is, you will roll over the outstanding balance into a new mortgage. The new mortgage has a 30-year term, requires monthly payments, and has an interest rate of $6\frac{2}{8}$% (APR).

   a. What monthly repayments will be required with the new loan?

   b. If you still want to pay off the mortgage in 25 years, what monthly payment should you make after you refinance?

c. Suppose you are willing to continue making monthly payments of $1402. How long will it take you to pay off the mortgage after refinancing?

d. Suppose you are willing to continue making monthly payments of $1402, and want to pay off the mortgage in 25 years. How much additional cash can you borrow today as part of the refinancing?

20. You have credit card debt of $25,000 that has an APR (monthly compounding) of 15%. Each month you pay minimum monthly payment only. You are required to pay only the outstanding interest. You have received an offer in the mail for an otherwise identical credit card with an APR of 12%. After considering all your alternatives, you decide to switch cards, roll over the outstanding balance on the old card into the new card, and borrow additional money as well. How much can you borrow today on the new card without changing the minimum monthly payment you will be required to pay?

The Determinants of Interest Rates

21. In 1975, interest rates were 7.85% and the rate of inflation was 12.3% in the United States. What was the real interest rate in 1975? How would the purchasing power of your savings have changed over the year?

22. If the rate of inflation is 5%, what nominal interest rate is necessary for you to earn a 3% real interest rate on your investment?

23. Can the nominal interest rate available to an investor be negative? (*Hint:* Consider the interest rate earned from saving cash "under the mattress.") Can the real interest rate be negative? Explain.

24. Consider a project that requires an initial investment of $100,000 and will produce a single cash flow of $150,000 in five years.

a. What is the NPV of this project if the five-year interest rate is 5% (EAR)?

b. What is the NPV of this project if the five-year interest rate is 10% (EAR)?

c. What is the highest five-year interest rate such that this project is still profitable?

EXCEL 25. Suppose the term structure of risk-free interest rates is as shown below:

Term	1 year	2 years	3 years	5 years	7 years	10 years	20 years
Rate (EAR, %)	1.99	2.41	2.74	3.32	3.76	4.13	4.93

a. Calculate the present value of an investment that pays $1000 in two years and $2000 in five years for certain.

b. Calculate the present value of receiving $500 per year, with certainty, at the end of the next five years. To find the rates for the missing years in the table, linearly interpolate between the years for which you do know the rates. (For example, the rate in year 4 would be the average of the rate in year 3 and year 5.)

*c. Calculate the present value of receiving $2300 per year, with certainty, for the next 20 years. Infer rates for the missing years using linear interpolation. (*Hint:* Use a spreadsheet.)

EXCEL 26. Using the term structure in Problem 25, what is the present value of an investment that pays $100 at the end of each of years 1, 2, and 3? If you wanted to value this investment correctly using the annuity formula, which discount rate should you use?

EXCEL 27. What is the shape of the yield curve given the term structure in Problem 25? What expectations are investors likely to have about future interest rates?

EXCEL   28. Suppose the current one-year interest rate is 6%. One year from now, you believe the economy will start to slow and the one-year interest rate will fall to 5%. In two years, you expect the economy to be in the midst of a recession, causing the Federal Reserve to cut interest rates drastically and the one-year interest rate to fall to 2%. The one-year interest rate will then rise to 3% the following year, and continue to rise by 1% per year until it returns to 6%, where it will remain from then on.

   a. If you were certain regarding these future interest rate changes, what two-year interest rate would be consistent with these expectations?

   b. What current term structure of interest rates, for terms of 1 to 10 years, would be consistent with these expectations?

   c. Plot the yield curve in this case. How does the one-year interest rate compare to the ten-year interest rate?

Risk and Taxes

29. Based on the data in Table 5.2, which would you prefer: $500 from General Motors Acceptance Corporation paid today or a promise that the firm will pay you $700 in five years? Which would you choose if J. P. Morgan offered you the same alternatives?

30. Your best taxable investment opportunity has an EAR of 4%. You best tax-free investment opportunity has an EAR of 3%. If your tax rate is 30%, which opportunity provides the higher after-tax interest rate?

31. Your uncle Fred just purchased a new boat. He brags to you about the low 7% interest rate (APR, monthly compounding) he obtained from the dealer. The rate is even lower than the rate he could have obtained on his home equity loan (8% APR, monthly compounding). If his tax rate is 25% and the interest on the home equity loan is tax deductible, which loan is truly cheaper?

32. You are enrolling in an MBA program. To pay your tuition, you can either take out a standard student loan (so the interest payments are not tax deductible) that has an EAR of $5\frac{1}{2}$% or you can use a tax-deductible home equity loan with an APR (monthly) of 6%. You anticipate being in a very low tax bracket, so your tax rate will be only 15%. Which loan should you use?

33. Your best friend consults you for investment advice. You learn that his tax rate is 35%, and he has the following current investments and debts:

   • A car loan with an outstanding balance of $5000 and a 4.8% APR (monthly compounding)

   • Credit cards with an outstanding balance of $10,000 and a 14.9% APR (monthly compounding)

   • A regular savings account with a $30,000 balance, paying a 5.50% EAR

   • A money market savings account with a $100,000 balance, paying a 5.25% APR (daily compounding)

   • A tax-deductible home equity loan with an outstanding balance of $25,000 and a 5.0% APR (monthly compounding)

   a. Which savings account pays a higher after-tax interest rate?

   b. Should your friend use his savings to pay off any of his outstanding debts? Explain.

34. Suppose you have outstanding debt with an 8% interest rate that can be repaid anytime, and the interest rate on U.S. Treasuries is only 5%. You plan to repay your debt using any cash that you don't invest elsewhere. Until your debt is repaid, what cost of capital should you use when evaluating a new risk-free investment opportunity? Why?

notation

e 2.71828...

ln natural logarithm

r_{cc} continuously compounded discount rate

g_{cc} continuously compounded growth rate

$\overline{C}_1$ total cash flows received in first year

Continuous Rates and Cash Flows

In this appendix we consider how to discount cash flows when interest is paid, or cash flows are received, on a continuous basis.

Discount Rates for a Continuously Compounded APR

Some investments compound more frequently than daily. As we move from daily to hourly ($k = 24 \times 365$) to compounding every second ($k = 60 \times 60 \times 24 \times 365$), we approach the limit of continuous compounding, in which we compound every instant ($k = \infty$). Equation 5.3 on page 128 cannot be used to compute the discount rate from an APR quote based on continuous compounding. In this case, the discount rate for a period length of one year—that is, the EAR—is given by Eq. 5A.1:

The EAR for a Continuously Compounded APR

$$(1 + EAR) = e^{APR} \tag{5A.1}$$

where the mathematical constant[9] $e = 2.71828 \ldots$. Once you know the EAR, you can compute the discount rate for any compounding period length using Eq. 5.2.

Alternatively, if we know the EAR and want to find the corresponding continuously compounded APR, we can invert Eq. 5A.1 by taking the natural logarithm (ln) of both sides:[10]

The Continuously Compounded APR for an EAR

$$APR = \ln(1 + EAR) \tag{5A.2}$$

Continuously compounded rates are not often used in practice. Sometimes, banks offer them as a marketing gimmick, but there is little actual difference between daily and continuous compounding. For example, with a 6% APR, daily compounding provides an EAR of $(1 + 0.06/365)^{365} - 1 = 6.18313\%$, whereas with continuous compounding the EAR is $e^{0.06} - 1 = 6.18365\%$.

Continuously Arriving Cash Flows

How can we compute the present value of an investment whose cash flows arrive continuously? For example, consider the cash flows of an online book retailer. Suppose the firm forecasts cash flows of $10 million per year. The $10 million will be received throughout each year, not at year-end, that is, the $10 million is paid *continuously* throughout the year.

We can compute the present value of cash flows that arrive continuously using a version of the growing perpetuity formula. If cash flows arrive, starting immediately, at an initial rate of $C per year, and if the cash flows grow at rate g per year, then given a discount rate (expressed as an EAR) of r per year, the present value of the cash flows is

Present Value of a Continuously Growing Perpetuity[11]

$$PV = \frac{C}{r_{cc} - g_{cc}} \tag{5A.3}$$

where $r_{cc} = \ln(1 + r)$ and $g_{cc} = \ln(1 + g)$ are the discount and growth rates expressed as continuously compounded APRs, respectively.

---

9. The constant e raised to a power is also written as the function *exp*. That is, $e^{APR} = exp\,(APR)$. This function is built into most spreadsheets and calculators.

10. Recall that $\ln(e^x) = x$

11. Given the perpetuity formula, we can value an annuity as the difference between two perpetuities.

There is another, approximate method for dealing with continuously arriving cash flows. Let $\overline{C}_1$ be the total cash flows that arrive during the first year. Because the cash flows arrive throughout the year, we can think of them arriving "on average" in the middle of the year. In that case, we should discount the cash flows by $\frac{1}{2}$ year less:

$$\frac{C}{r_{cc} - g_{cc}} \approx \frac{\overline{C}_1}{r - g} \times (1 + r)^{1/2} \qquad (5A.4)$$

In practice, the approximation in Eq. 5A.4 works quite well. More generally, it implies that when cash flows arrive continuously, we can compute present values reasonably accurately by pretending that all of the cash flows for the year arrive in the middle of the year.

Valuing Projects with Continuous Cash Flows

Problem
Your firm is considering buying an oil rig. The rig will initially produce oil at a rate of 30 million barrels per year. You have a long-term contract that allows you to sell the oil at a profit of $1.25 per barrel. If the rate of oil production from the rig declines by 3% over the year and the discount rate is 10% per year (EAR), how much would you be willing to pay for the rig?

Solution
According to the estimates, the rig will generate profits at an initial rate of (30 million barrels per year) $\times$ ($1.25 / barrel) = $37.5 million per year. The 10% discount rate is equivalent to a continuously compounded APR of $r_{cc} = \ln(1 + 0.10) = 9.531\%$; similarly, the growth rate has an APR of $g_{cc} = \ln(1 - 0.03) = -3.046\%$. From Eq. 5A.3, the present value of the profits from the rig is

$PV(\text{profits}) = 37.5 / (r_{cc} - g_{cc}) = 37.5 / (0.09531 + 0.03046) = \$298.16$ million

Alternatively, we can closely approximate the present value as follows. The initial profit rate of the rig is $37.5 million per year. By the end of the year, the profit rate will have declined by 3% to $37.5 \times (1 - 0.03) = \$36.375$ million per year. Therefore, the average profit rate during the year is approximately $(37.5 + 36.375) / 2 = \$36.938$ million. Valuing the cash flows as though they occur at the middle of each year, we have

$$PV(\text{profits}) = [36.938 / (r - g)] \times (1 + r)^{1/2}$$
$$= [36.938 / (0.10 + 0.03)] \times (1.10)^{1/2} = \$298.01 \text{ million}$$

Note that both methods produce very similar results.

CHAPTER

6

Investment Decision Rules

notation

r discount rate

NPV net present value

IRR internal rate of return

PV present value

EVA_n Economic Value Added at date n

C_n cash flow that arrives at date n

I initial investment or initial capital committed to the project

I_n capital committed to the project at date n

When Cisco Systems decided whether to acquire the Linksys Group in 2003, it needed to consider both the costs and the benefits of the proposed acquisition. The costs included the initial purchase price and the ongoing costs of operating the business. Benefits would be future revenues from sales of the Linksys products. The right way for Cisco to evaluate this decision was to compare the cash value today of the costs to the cash value today of the benefits by computing the **NPV** of this acquisition; Cisco should have undertaken the acquisition only if it had a positive **NPV**.

Although the **NPV** investment rule maximizes the value of the firm, some firms nevertheless use other techniques to evaluate investments and decide which projects to pursue. In this chapter, we explain several commonly used techniques—namely, the *payback rule*, the *internal rate of return rule*, and the *economic profit* or *EVA® rule*. In each case, we define the decision rule and compare decisions based on this rule to decisions based on the NPV rule. We also illustrate the circumstances in which some of the alternative rules are likely to lead to bad investment decisions. After establishing these rules in the context of a single, stand-alone project, we broaden our perspective to include deciding among mutually exclusive investment opportunities. We conclude with a look at project selection when the firm faces resource constraints.

6.1   NPV and Stand-Alone Projects

We begin our discussion of investment decision rules by considering a take-it-or-leave-it decision involving a single, stand-alone project. By undertaking this project, the firm does not constrain its ability to take other projects. We initiate our analysis with the familiar NPV rule.

NPV Rule

Researchers at Fredrick Feed and Farm (FFF) have made a breakthrough. They believe that they can produce a new, environmentally friendly fertilizer at a substantial cost saving over the company's existing line of fertilizer. The fertilizer will require a new plant that can be built immediately at a cost of $250 million. Financial managers estimate that the benefits of the new fertilizer will be $35 million per year, starting at the end of the first year and lasting forever, as shown by the following timeline:

As we explained in Chapter 4, the NPV of this cash flow stream, given a discount rate *r*, is

$$\text{NPV} = -250 + \frac{35}{r}$$

Figure 6.1 plots the NPV as a function of the discount rate, *r*. Notice that the NPV is positive only for discount rates that are less than 14%, the internal rate of return (IRR). To decide whether to invest (using the NPV rule), we need to know the cost of capital. The financial managers responsible for this project estimate a cost of capital of 10% per year. Referring to Figure 6.1, we see that when the discount rate is 10%, the NPV is $100 million, which is positive. The NPV investment rule indicates that by making the investment, FFF will increase the value of the firm by $100 million, so FFF should undertake this project.

Measuring Sensitivity with IRR

If you are unsure of your cost of capital estimate, it is important to determine how sensitive your analysis is to errors in this estimate. The IRR can provide this information. For FFF, if the cost of capital estimate is more than the 14% IRR, the NPV will be negative (see Figure 6.1). In general, *the difference between the cost of capital and the IRR is the maximum amount of estimation error in the cost of capital estimate that can exist without altering the original decision.*

Alternative Rules Versus the NPV Rule

The NPV rule indicates that FFF should undertake the investment in fertilizer technology. As we evaluate alternative rules for project selection, keep in mind that sometimes other investment rules may give the same answer as the NPV rule, but at other times they may disagree. When the rules conflict, following the alternative rule means we are not taking a positive NPV project and thus we are not maximizing wealth. In these cases, the alternative rules lead to bad decisions.

FIGURE 6.1

NPV of FFF's New Project

The graph shows the NPV as a function of the discount rate. The NPV is positive only for discount rates that are less than 14%, the internal rate of return (IRR). Given the cost of capital of 10%, the project has a positive NPV of $100 million.

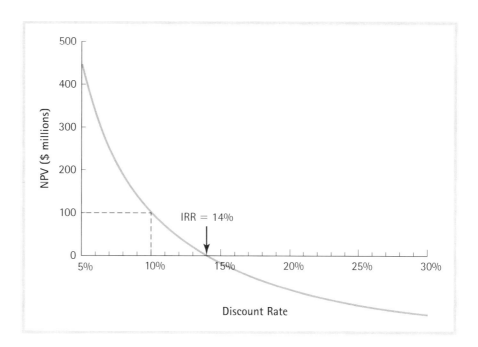

1. Explain the NPV rule for stand-alone projects.

2. How can you interpret the difference between the cost of capital and the IRR?

6.2 Alternative Decision Rules

In a 2001 study, Graham and Harvey[1] found that 74.9% of the firms they surveyed used the NPV rule for making investment decisions. This result is substantially different from that found in a similar study in 1977 by Gitman and Forrester,[2] who found that only 9.8% of firms used the NPV rule. MBA students in recent years have been listening to their finance professors! Even so, Graham and Harvey's study indicates that one fourth of U.S. corporations do not use the NPV rule. Exactly why other capital budgeting techniques are used in practice is not always clear. However, because you may encounter these techniques in the business world, you should know what they are, how they are used, and how they compare to NPV. In this section, we examine alternative decision rules for single, stand-alone projects within the firm. The focus here is on the *payback rule, IRR rule*, and *Economic Value Added*.

The Payback Rule

The simplest investment rule is the **payback investment rule**, which is based on the notion that an opportunity that pays back its initial investment quickly is a good idea. To apply the payback rule, you first calculate the amount of time it takes to pay back the

1. John Graham and Campbell Harvey, "The Theory and Practice of Corporate Finance: Evidence from the Field," *Journal of Financial Economics* 60 (2001): 187–243.

2. L. J. Gitman and J. R. Forrester, Jr., "A Survey of Capital Budgeting Techniques Used by Major U.S. Firms," *Financial Management* 6 (1977): 66–71.

initial investment, called the **payback period**. If the payback period is less than a prespecified length of time—usually a few years—you accept the project. Otherwise, you turn it down. For example, a firm might adopt any project with a payback period of less than two years.

Using the Payback Rule

Problem
Assume FFF requires all projects to have a payback period of five years or less. Would the firm undertake the fertilizer project under this rule?

Solution
The sum of the cash flows from year 1 to year 5 is $35 \times 5 = \$175$ million, which will not cover the initial investment of \$250 million. Because the payback period for this project exceeds 5 years, FFF will reject the project.

As a result of the payback rule analysis in Example 6.1, FFF rejected the project. However, as we saw earlier, with a cost of capital of 10%, the NPV is \$100 million. Following the payback rule would be a mistake because it would leave FFF worth \$100 million less.

The payback rule is not reliable because it ignores the time value of money and does not depend on the cost of capital. No rule that ignores the set of alternative investment opportunities can be optimal. Despite this failing, Graham and Harvey found that about 50% of the firms they surveyed reported using the payback rule for making decisions.

Why do some companies consider the payback rule? The answer probably relates to its simplicity. This rule is typically used for small investment decisions—for example, whether to purchase a new copy machine or to service the old one. In such cases, the cost of making an incorrect decision might not be large enough to justify the time required to calculate the NPV. The appeal of the payback rule is that it biases the decision toward short-term projects. Also, if the required payback period is short (1–2 years), then most projects that satisfy the payback rule will have a positive NPV. So firms might save effort by first applying the payback rule, and only if it fails take the time to compute NPV.

The Internal Rate of Return Rule

Like the payback rule, the **internal rate of return (IRR) investment rule** is based on an intuitive notion: If the return on the investment opportunity you are considering is greater than the return on other alternatives in the market with equivalent risk and maturity (i.e., the project's cost of capital), you should undertake the investment opportunity. We state the rule formally as follows:

IRR Investment Rule: *Take any investment opportunity where IRR exceeds the opportunity cost of capital. Turn down any opportunity whose IRR is less than the opportunity cost of capital.*

The IRR investment rule will give the correct answer (that is, the same answer as the NPV rule) in many—but not all—situations. For instance, it gives the correct answer for FFF's fertilizer opportunity. From Figure 6.1, whenever the cost of capital is below the IRR (14%), the project has a positive NPV and you should undertake the investment. In general, the IRR rule works for a stand-alone project if all of the project's negative cash flows precede its positive cash flows. But in other cases, the IRR rule may disagree with the NPV rule and thus be incorrect. Let's examine several situations in which the IRR fails.

Delayed Investments.   John Star, the founder of SuperTech, the most successful company in the last 20 years, has just retired as CEO. A major publisher has offered him a $1 million "how I did it" book deal. That is, the publisher will pay him $1 million upfront if Star agrees to write a book about his experiences. He estimates that it will take him three years to write the book. The time that he spends writing will cause him to forgo alternative sources of income amounting to $500,000 per year. Considering the risk of his alternative income sources and available investment opportunities, Star estimates his opportunity cost of capital to be 10%. The timeline of Star's investment opportunity is:

0	1	2	3
$1,000,000	$-$500,000	$-$500,000	$-$500,000

The NPV of Star's investment opportunity is

$$NPV = 1{,}000{,}000 - \frac{500{,}000}{1 + r} - \frac{500{,}000}{(1 + r)^2} - \frac{500{,}000}{(1 + r)^3}$$

By setting the NPV equal to zero and solving for r, we find the IRR. Using the annuity spreadsheet:

	NPER	RATE	PV	PMT	FV	Excel Formula
Given	3		1,000,000	$-$500,000	0	
Solve for I		23.38%				RATE(3, 500000, 1000000, 0)

The 23.38% IRR is larger than the 10% opportunity cost of capital. According to the IRR rule, Star should sign the deal. But what does the NPV rule say?

$$NPV = 1{,}000{,}000 - \frac{500{,}000}{1.1} - \frac{500{,}000}{1.1^2} - \frac{500{,}000}{1.1^3} = -\$243{,}426$$

At a 10% discount rate, the NPV is negative, so signing the deal would reduce Star's wealth. He should not sign the book deal.

Figure 6.2 plots the NPV of the investment opportunity. It shows that, no matter what the cost of capital is, the IRR rule and the NPV rule will give exactly opposite recommendations. That is, the NPV is positive only when the opportunity cost of capital is *above* 23.38% (the IRR). Star should accept the investment only when the opportunity cost of capital is greater than the IRR, the opposite of what the IRR rule recommends.

Figure 6.2 also illustrates the problem with using the IRR rule in this case. For most investment opportunities, expenses occur initially and cash is received later. In this case, Star gets cash *upfront* and incurs the costs of producing the book *later*. It is as if Star borrowed money, and when you borrow money you prefer as *low* a rate as possible. Star's optimal rule is to borrow money so long as the rate at which he borrows is *less* than the cost of capital.

Even though the IRR rule fails to give the correct answer in this case, the IRR itself still provides useful information *in conjunction* with the NPV rule. As mentioned earlier, the IRR provides information on how sensitive the investment decision is to uncertainty in the cost of capital estimate. In this case, the difference between the cost of capital and

FIGURE 6.2

NPV of Star's $1 million Book Deal

When the benefits of an investment occur before the costs, the NPV is an *increasing* function of the discount rate.

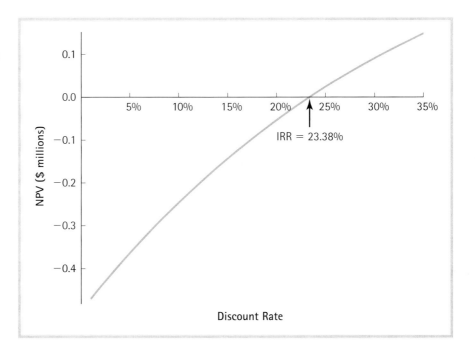

the IRR is large—13.38%. Star would have to have underestimated the cost of capital by 13.38% to make the the NPV positive.

Nonexistent IRR.   Luckily for John Star, he has other opportunities available to him. An agent has approached him and guaranteed $1 million in each of the next three years if he will agree to give four lectures per month over that period. Star estimates that preparing and delivering the lectures would take the same amount of time as writing the book—that is, the cost would be $500,000 per year. Therefore, his net cash flow will be $500,000 per year. What is the IRR of this opportunity? Here is the new timeline:

The NPV of Star's new investment opportunity is

$$NPV = \frac{500,000}{1 + r} + \frac{500,000}{(1 + r)^2} + \frac{500,000}{(1 + r)^3}$$

By setting the NPV equal to zero and solving for r, we find the IRR. In this case, however, there is *no* discount rate that will set the NPV equal to zero. As shown in Figure 6.3, the NPV of this opportunity is always positive, no matter what the cost of capital is. But do not be fooled into thinking that whenever the IRR does not exist the NPV will always be positive. It is quite possible for no IRR to exist when the NPV is always negative (see Problem 11).

In such situations, we cannot use the IRR rule because it provides no recommendation at all. Thus, our only choice is to rely on the NPV rule.

FIGURE 6.3

NPV of Lecture Contract

No IRR exists because the NPV is positive for all values of the discount rate. Thus the IRR rule cannot be used.

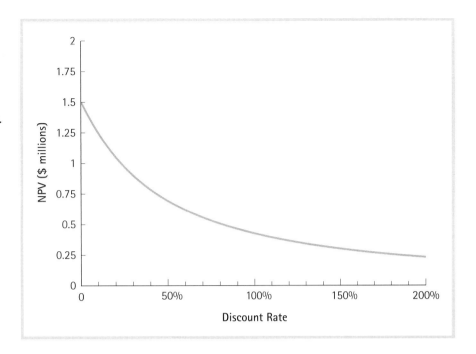

Multiple IRRs. Unfortunately, Star's lecture deal fell through. So Star has informed the publisher that it needs to sweeten the deal before he will accept it. In response, the publisher has agreed to make royalty payments. Star expects these payments to amount to $20,000 per year forever, starting once the book is published in three years. Should he accept or reject the new offer?

We begin with the new timeline:

0	1	2	3	4	5	
$1,000,000	$-$500,000	$-$500,000	$-$500,000	$20,000	$20,000	$\cdots$

Using the annuity and perpetuity formulas, the NPV of Star's new investment opportunity is

$$NPV = 1,000,000 - \frac{500,000}{1+r} - \frac{500,000}{(1+r)^2} - \frac{500,000}{(1+r)^3} + \frac{20,000}{(1+r)^4} + \frac{20,000}{(1+r)^5} + \cdots$$

$$= 1,000,000 - \frac{500,000}{r}\left(1 - \frac{1}{(1+r)^3}\right) + \frac{1}{(1+r)^3}\left(\frac{20,000}{r}\right)$$

By setting the NPV equal to zero and solving for r, we find the IRR. In this case, there are *two* IRRs—that is, there are two values of r that set the NPV equal to zero. You can verify this fact by substituting IRRs of 4.723% and 19.619% into the equation. Because there is more than one IRR, we cannot apply the IRR rule.

For guidance, let's turn to the NPV rule. Figure 6.4 plots the NPV of the opportunity. If the cost of capital is *either* below 4.723% or above 19.619%, Star should undertake the opportunity. Otherwise, he should turn it down. Notice that even though the IRR rule

FIGURE 6.4

NPV of Star's Book Deal with Royalties

In this case, there is more than one IRR, invalidating the IRR rule. If the opportunity cost of capital is *either* below 4.723% or above 19.619%, Star should make the investment.

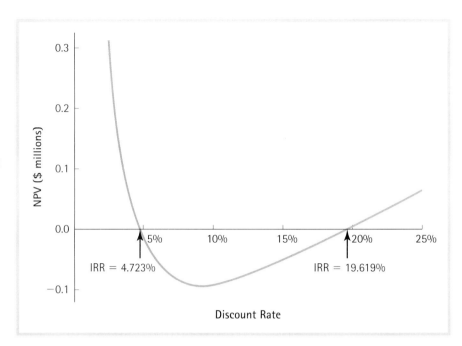

fails in this case, the two IRRs are still useful as bounds on the cost of capital. If the cost of capital estimate is wrong, and it is actually smaller than 4.723% or larger than 19.619%, the decision not to pursue the project will change. Because these bounds are far from the actual cost of capital of 10%, Star can have a high degree of confidence in his decision to reject the deal.

There is no easy fix for the IRR rule when there are multiple IRRs. Although the NPV is negative between the IRRs in this example, the reverse is also possible (see Problem 9). In this case, the project would have a positive NPV for discount rates between the IRRs rather than for discount rates lower or higher than the IRRs. Furthermore, there are situations in which more than two IRRs exist.[3] In such situations, our only choice is to rely on the NPV rule.

IRR Versus the IRR Rule.   Throughout this subsection, we have distinguished between the IRR itself and the IRR rule. While we have pointed out the shortcomings of using the IRR rule to make investment decisions, the IRR itself remains a very useful tool. Not only does the IRR measure the sensitivity of the NPV to estimation error in the cost of capital, but it also measures the average return of the investment.

Economic Profit or EVA

The concept of **economic profit** was originally suggested by Alfred Marshall more than 100 years ago. It has been popularized recently by a consulting firm, Stern Stewart, that specializes in increasing firms' efficiency. This firm renamed the concept **Economic Value Added** and even went so far as registering the acronym EVA as a trademark. EVA

---

3. In general, there can be as many IRRs as the number of times the project's cash flows change sign over time.

Joel M. Stern

Joel M. Stern has been the managing partner of Stern Stewart & Company since its founding in 1982. He is a pioneer and leading advocate of the concept of managing for shareholder value and, with Bennett Stewart, developed EVA.

QUESTION: *EVA has become a popular tool among successful companies to measure performance. How does EVA work, and how does it differ from traditional performance measures?*

ANSWER: There are two popular models used for the purpose of evaluation. The first is the PV of expected future free cash flow, which is operating profit minus new investment in working capital and plant. The second model adds the PV of expected future EVA to a firm's book value, but only after adjusting the book value to include all investments in intangible assets including goodwill, acquisitions, brand value, research and development, and the training development cost in human capital. The two models provide identical answers because NPV and EVA offer identical answers. The much more interesting question, then, is, Why bother with EVA? Under NPV, there is no way to keep score year by year to see whether the project is generating positive value in that year. Because we can measure EVA year by year and quite deep into an organization, it can be used to design incentive compensation plans at almost all levels of an organization.

Virtually all methods for measuring management and determining variable compensation are tied to accounting earnings. These numbers suffer from two principal shortcomings: There is no charge for equity capital on the P&L and intangible assets are expensed. Intangible assets represent an investment that builds long-term value and should be treated as such. EVA corrects these issues by taking into account all capital costs, assessing a charge for using that capital, and capitalizing intangible assets. Managers then care about managing assets as well as income.

EVA provides a single consistent financial measure that links all decision making to improving EVA. Plus EVA cascades the incentive structure down deep into

the organization. In an EVA system, people work harder and smarter. *All* employees have incentives to come up with ideas to improve the value of the firm. The first company to implement EVA throughout the organization, from the shop floor to the CEO, was Briggs and Stratton (they make lawnmower engines), and the effect was unbelievable. The U.S. Postal Service implemented EVA in 1996. After teaching more than 700,000 people to understand EVA and how the incentive program worked, the USPS eliminated more than $2.4 billion in annual losses and achieved improvements in operating efficiency.

QUESTION: *What is EVA's relevance as an investment rule* ex ante *as opposed to a performance measure* ex post?

ANSWER: NPV is a very cumbersome *measurement* process, ex post. You lay out a case today and expect cash flows in the future. How do you measure whether you've done well? You can determine this only by looking at cash outflows and inflows over the life of the project. Under NPV, there is no way to keep score year by year. EVA can be measured just as easily as NPV, but unlike NPV it allows boards of directors to design incentives that encourage wealth creation.

QUESTION: *What are the challenges to implementing EVA in a firm?*

ANSWER: To implement EVA, a firm must (1) measure EVA correctly, making adjustments to put intangibles on the balance sheet and apply a capital charge; (2) train employees about EVA and how to influence EVA and the firm's success by improving their own efficiencies; (3) set firm's priorities from greatest to least EVA opportunities, so the goal is improving EVA; (4) use EVA as the basis for incentive compensation as well as performance; and (5) communicate your EVA system and how you've designed it to the markets. All of this clearly requires a change in the management mindset and corporate culture, from "bigger is better" to "value is best."

was not originally invented as an investment rule, and even today it is not primarily used that way. Nevertheless, EVA is based on many of the same concepts underlying the NPV calculation. We will define an investment decision rule based on EVA and relate it to NPV.

EVA and Economic Profit.   Joel Stern, of Stern Stewart, realized that some companies were rewarding managers simply because they made money for the company, without taking into account the resources the manager used while making this money. The distinction between simply making money and creating value is the essence of the NPV calculation. For example, a manager could easily make $1 million per year for a company by simply putting $20 million into a bank account paying an interest rate of 5%. He has made money, but created no value: The NPV of putting $20 million into a bank account is zero. Whereas the NPV is a measure of wealth created over the life of the project, managers are rewarded annually. As a result, Stern turned to Marshall's concept of economic profit, which rewarded managers based on the NPV they created each year. The result, EVA, measures the annual value added by the manager over and above the cost to tie up and use the capital the project requires.

EVA When Invested Capital Is Constant.   Consider a project that requires an initial investment in capital with a cost of I dollars. Suppose that the capital lasts forever, and generates a cash flow of C_n at each future date n. The EVA in year n is the value added of the project over and above the opportunity cost of tying up the capital required to run the project. If the cost of capital is r, then the cost of tying up I in capital in the project rather than investing it elsewhere is $r \times I$ each period (this is the expected return we could have earned). We refer to the opportunity cost associated with the project's use of capital as the **capital charge**. The EVA in period n is the difference between the project's cash flow and the capital charge:

$$\text{EVA in Period } n \text{ (When Capital Lasts Forever)}$$

$$EVA_n = C_n - rI \tag{6.1}$$

The **EVA investment rule** can be stated as follows: Accept any investment opportunity in which the present value of all future EVAs is positive when we compute the present value using the project's cost of capital r.

How does the EVA investment rule compare with the NPV rule? Note that if we discount the capital charge of rI every period at rate r, the present value is simply $rI / r = I$. Thus, if we discount the project's EVA at the project's cost of capital r, then $PV(EVA_n) = PV(C_n) - PV(rI) = PV(C_n) - I = $ NPV. Thus, the EVA rule and the IRR rule will coincide.

EXAMPLE 6.2

Calculating EVA When Invested Capital Is Constant

Problem
Compute the EVA of FFF's fertilizer opportunity, which required an upfront investment of $250 million, and had a benefit of $35 million each year. Using this information, decide whether to make the investment.

Solution

The EVA in every year is

$$C_n - 250r = 35 - 250r$$

Using the perpetuity formula, the present value of these EVAs is

$$PV(EVA) = \sum_{n=1}^{\infty} \frac{35 - 250r}{(1 + r)^n} = \frac{35 - 250r}{r} = \frac{35}{r} - 250$$

This present value matches our earlier calculation of the project's NPV in Section 6.1, and so FFF should make the investment if the cost of capital is below 14%.

EVA When Invested Capital Changes.   Typically, the capital invested in a project will change over time. Existing capital will tend to become less valuable over time (e.g., machines wear out with use), and new investment may need to be made. Let I_{n-1} be the amount of capital allocated to the project at date $n-1$, which is the start of period n. Then the capital charge in period n should include the opportunity cost of tying up this capital, $r I_{n-1}$. It should also take into account the cost of the wear and tear from the use of the capital, which is the amount by which the value of the capital depreciates over the period. Thus,

EVA in Period n (When Capital Depreciates)

$$EVA_n = C_n - rI_{n-1} - (\text{Depreciation in Period } n) \tag{6.2}$$

With this definition of the EVA, the EVA and NPV rules again coincide.

EXAMPLE 6.3

Calculating EVA When Invested Capital Changes

Problem

You are considering installing new energy-efficient lighting in your firm's warehouse. The installation will cost $300,000, and you estimate total savings of $75,000 per year. The lights will depreciate evenly over the 5 years, at which point they must be replaced. The cost of capital is 7% per year. What do the NPV and EVA rules indicate about whether you should install the lights?

Solution

The timeline for the investment is (in $ thousands):

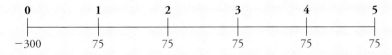

Therefore, the NPV is

$$NPV = -300 + \frac{75}{0.07}\left(1 - \frac{1}{(1.07)^5}\right) = \$7.51 \text{ thousand}$$

So, the lights should be installed. Let's see that we get the same result with EVA. If the lights depreciate by $300,000/5 = $60,000 each year, then the EVA is calculated as follows:

Year	0	1	2	3	4	5
Capital	300	240	180	120	60	0
Cash Flow		75.0	75.0	75.0	75.0	75.0
Capital Charge		(21.0)	(16.8)	(12.6)	(8.4)	(4.2)
Depreciation		(60.0)	(60.0)	(60.0)	(60.0)	(60.0)
EVA		−6.0	−1.8	2.4	6.6	10.8

For example, $EVA_1 = 75 - 7\%(300) - 60 = -6.0$, and $EVA_2 = 75 - 7\%(240) - 60 = -1.8$. The present value of the EVAs at the project's cost of capital of 7% is

$$PV(EVA) = -\frac{-6.0}{1.07} + \frac{-1.8}{1.07^2} + \frac{2.4}{1.07^3} + \frac{6.6}{1.07^4} + \frac{10.8}{1.07^5} = \$7.51 \text{ thousand}$$

Why Do Rules Other Than the NPV Rule Persist?

Professors Graham and Harvey found that a sizable minority of firms (25%) in their study do not use the NPV rule at all. In addition, about 50% of firms surveyed used the payback rule. Furthermore, it appears that most firms use *both* the NPV rule and the IRR rule. Why do firms use rules other than NPV if they can lead to erroneous decisions?

One possible explanation for this phenomenon is that Graham and Harvey's survey results might be misleading. CFOs who were using the IRR as a sensitivity measure in conjunction with the NPV rule might have checked both the IRR box and the NPV box on the survey. The question they were asked was, "How frequently does your firm use the following techniques when deciding which projects or acquisitions to pursue?" By computing the IRR and using it in conjunction with the NPV rule to estimate the sensitivity of their results, they might have felt they were using *both* techniques. Nevertheless, a significant minority of managers surveyed replied that they used only the IRR rule, so this explanation cannot be the whole story.

One common reason that managers give for using the IRR rule exclusively is that you do not need to know the opportunity cost of capital to calculate the IRR. On a superficial level, this is true: The IRR does not depend on the cost of capital. You may not need to know the cost of

capital to *calculate* the IRR, but you certainly need to know the cost of capital when you *apply* the IRR rule. Consequently, the opportunity cost is as important to the IRR rule as it is to the NPV rule.

In our opinion, some firms use the IRR rule exclusively because the IRR sums up the attractiveness of investment opportunity in a single number without requiring the person running the numbers to make an assumption about the cost of capital. However, if a CFO wants a brief summary of an investment opportunity but does not want her employee to make a cost of capital assumption, she can also request a plot of the NPV as a function of the discount rate. Neither this request nor a request for the IRR requires knowing the cost of capital, but the NPV graph has the distinct advantage of being much more informative and reliable.

If you are employed by a firm that uses the IRR rule exclusively, our advice is to always calculate the NPV. If the two rules agree, you can feel comfortable reporting the IRR rule recommendation. If they do not agree, you should investigate why the IRR rule failed by using the concepts in this section. Once you have identified the problem, you can alert your superiors to it and perhaps persuade them to adopt the NPV rule.

CONCEPT CHECK

1. When other investment rules do not give the same answer as the NPV rule, which rule should you follow? Why?

2. Explain the term *Economic Value Added* (EVA).

6.3 Mutually Exclusive Investment Opportunities

Thus far, we have considered only decisions where the choice is either to accept or to reject a single, stand-alone project. Sometimes, however, a firm must choose just one project from among several possible projects. For example, a manager may be evaluating alternative marketing campaigns for a single new-product launch.

When projects, like the market campaigns, are mutually exclusive, it is not enough to determine which projects have positive NPV. With **mutually exclusive projects**, the manager's goal is to rank the projects and choose the best one. In this situation, the NPV rule provides a straightforward answer: *Pick the project with the highest NPV.*

Because the IRR is a measure of the expected return of investing in the project, you might be tempted to extend the IRR investment rule to the case of mutually exclusive projects by picking the project with the highest IRR. Unfortunately, picking one project over another simply because it has a larger IRR can lead to mistakes. Problems arise when the mutually exclusive investments have differences in scale (require different initial investments) and when they have different cash flow patterns. We discuss each of these situations in this section.

Differences in Scale

If a project has a positive NPV, then if we can double its size, its NPV will double: By the Law of One Price, doubling the cash flows of an investment opportunity must make it worth twice as much. However, the IRR rule does not have this property—it is unaffected by the scale of the investment opportunity because the IRR measures the average return of the investment. Hence the IRR rule cannot be used to compare projects of different scales. Let's illustrate this concept in the context of an example.

Identical Scale. We begin by considering two mutually exclusive projects with the same scale. Don is evaluating two investment opportunities. If he went into business with his girlfriend, he would need to invest $1000 and the business would generate incremental cash flows of $1100 per year, declining at 10%, forever. Alternatively, he could start a single-machine laundromat. The washer and dryer cost a total of $1000 and will generate $400 per year, declining, because of maintenance costs, at 20% per year, forever. The opportunity cost of capital for both opportunities is 12% and both will require all his time, so Don must choose between them. Which one should he choose?

The timeline for the investment with his girlfriend is

The future cash flows are a perpetuity with a growth rate of -10%, so the NPV of the investment opportunity when $r = 12\%$ is

$$NPV = -1000 + \frac{1100}{r + 0.1} = -1000 + \frac{1100}{0.12 + 0.1} = \$4000$$

We can determine the IRR of this investment by setting the NPV equal to zero and solving for r:

$$1000 = \frac{1100}{r + 0.1} \quad \text{implies} \quad r = 100\%$$

Thus the IRR for Don's investment in his girlfriend's business is 100%.

The timeline for his investment in the laundromat is

Once again the future cash flows are a perpetuity, this time with a negative growth rate of -20%. The NPV of the investment opportunity is

$$NPV = -1000 + \frac{400}{r + 0.2} = -1000 + \frac{400}{0.12 + 0.2} = \$250$$

The $250 NPV of the laundromat is lower than the $4000 NPV for his girlfriend's business, so Don should join his girlfriend in business. Luckily, it appears that Don does not need to choose between his checkbook and his relationship!

If we compare IRRs, note that for the laundromat, setting the NPV equal to zero and solving for r gives an IRR of 20%. The laundromat has a lower IRR than the investment in his girlfriend's business. As Figure 6.5 shows, in this case the project with the higher IRR has the higher NPV.

FIGURE 6.5

NPV of Don's Investment Opportunities with the Single-Machine Laundromat

The NPV of his girlfriend's business is always larger than the NPV of the single-machine laundromat. The same is true for the IRR; the IRR of his girlfriend's business is 100%, while the IRR for the laundromat is 20%.

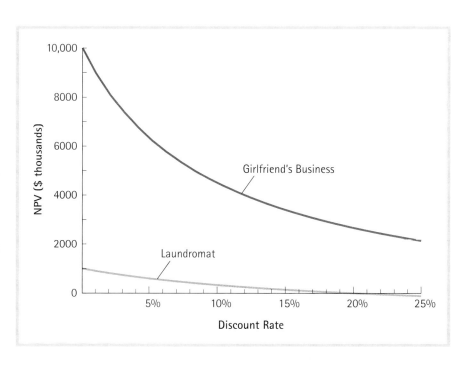

Change in Scale.   What happens if we change the scale of one of the projects? Don's finance professor points out that, given the space available in the facility, he could just as easily install 20 machines in the laundromat. What should Don do now?

Note that the IRR is unaffected by the scale. A 20-machine laundromat has exactly the same IRR as a single-machine Laundromat, so his girlfriend's business still has a higher IRR than the Laundromat. However, the NPV of the Laundromat does grow by the scale: It is 20 times larger.

$$NPV = 20\left(-1000 + \frac{400}{0.12 + 0.2}\right) = \$5000$$

Now Don should invest in the 20-machine laundromat. As Figure 6.6 shows, the NPV of the 20-machine laundromat exceeds the NPV of going into business with his girlfriend whenever the cost of capital is less than 13.9%. In this case, even though the IRR of going into business with his girlfriend exceeds the IRR of the laundromat, picking the investment opportunity with the higher IRR does not result in taking the opportunity with the higher NPV.

Percentage Return Versus Dollar Impact on Value.   This result might seem counterintuitive. Why would anyone turn down an investment opportunity with a 100% return (IRR) in favor of one with only a 20% return? The answer is that the latter opportunity makes more money. To demonstrate, consider this set of alternatives: Would you prefer a 200% return on $1 dollar or a 10% return on $1 million? The former investment certainly gives you great bragging rights, but at the end of the day you make only $2. The latter opportunity gives no bragging rights, but you make $100,000. The IRR is a measure

FIGURE 6.6

NPV of Don's Investment Opportunities with the 20-Machine Laundromat

As in Figure 6.5, the IRR of his girlfriend's business is 100%, while the IRR for the laundromat is 20%. But in this case, the NPV of his girlfriend's business is larger than the NPV of the 20-machine laundromat only for discount rates in excess of 13.9%.

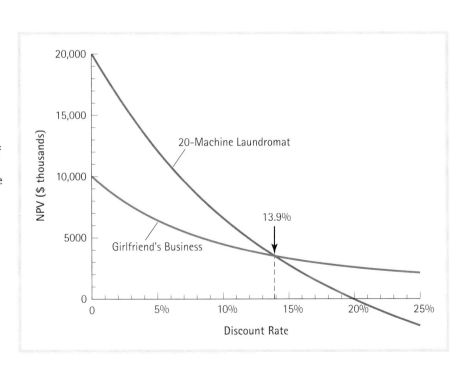

of the average return, which can be valuable information. When you are comparing mutually exclusive projects of different scale, however, you need to know the dollar impact on value, or the NPV.

Timing of the Cash Flows

Another failing of the IRR is that it can be altered by changing the timing of the cash flows, even when that change in timing does not affect the NPV. Therefore, it is possible to alter the ranking of projects' IRRs without changing their ranking in terms of NPV. Hence you cannot use the IRR to choose between mutually exclusive investments. To see this in the context of an example, let's return to Don's laundromat.

A salesman has offered Don a maintenance contract on his machines under which Don would pay $250 per year for maintenance on each machine. With this contract, Don would not have to pay for his own maintenance and so the cash flows from the machines would not decline. The expected cash flows would then be the cash flows from the machines minus the cost of the contract: $400 − $250 = $150 per year per machine, forever.

Don must now decide between two mutually exclusive investment opportunities: the laundromat with or without the contract. We begin with the timeline:

Notice that the maintenance contract does not change the NPV:

$$NPV = 20\left(-1000 + \frac{150}{r}\right) = \$5000 \tag{6.3}$$

As a consequence, Don is indifferent between taking the maintenance contract or not taking it. Setting the NPV equal to zero and solving for r gives an IRR of 15%. Recall that the IRR without the maintenance contract was 20%, so the maintenance contract has lowered the IRR by 5 percentage points. Figure 6.7 demonstrates that picking the alternative with the higher IRR always results in Don turning down the maintenance contract. However, the correct decision is to agree to the contract if the cost of capital is less than 12% and to decline the contract if the cost of capital exceeds 12%. With a 12% cost of capital, Don is indifferent.

As this example makes clear, picking the investment opportunity with the largest IRR can lead to a mistake. We now turn our attention to a "fix" aimed at addressing the IRR rule's deficiencies when comparing mutually exclusive projects.

The Incremental IRR Rule

The **incremental IRR investment rule** applies the IRR rule to the difference between the cash flows of the two mutually exclusive alternatives (the *increment* to the cash flows of one investment over the other). To illustrate, assume you are comparing two mutually exclusive opportunities, A and B, and the IRRs of both opportunities exceed the cost of capital. If you subtract the cash flows of opportunity B from the cash flows of opportunity A, then you should take opportunity A if the incremental IRR exceeds the cost of capital. Otherwise, you should take opportunity B.

FIGURE 6.7

NPV with and Without the Maintenance Contract

The NPV without the maintenance contract exceeds the NPV with the contract for discount rates that are in excess of 12%. However, the IRR without the maintenance contract (20%) is larger than the IRR with the maintenance contract (15%).

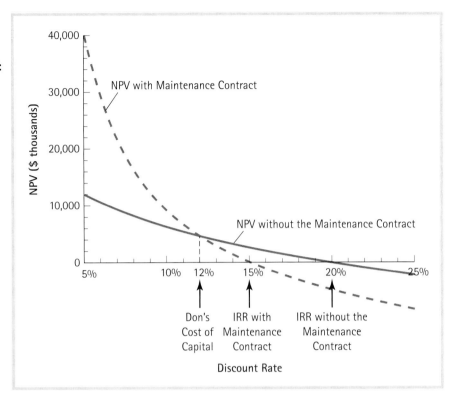

Incremental IRR Rule Application. Let's apply the incremental IRR rule to Don's dilemma. The following timeline illustrates the incremental cash flows of the maintenance contract laundromat over the laundromat without the contract:

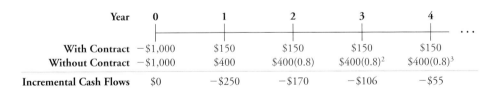

Year	0	1	2	3	4	
With Contract	−$1,000	$150	$150	$150	$150	⋯
Without Contract	−$1,000	$400	$400(0.8)	$400(0.8)²	$400(0.8)³	
Incremental Cash Flows	$0	−$250	−$170	−$106	−$55	

The NPV of the incremental cash flow is very difficult to calculate directly in this case, because it does not grow at a constant rate. We can compute it easily, though, as the difference of the NPV with and without the contract:

$$NPV = \frac{150}{r} - \frac{400}{r + 0.2}$$

Setting this equation equal to zero and solving for r gives an IRR of 12%. Applying the incremental IRR rule, Don should take the contract when the cost of capital is less than 12%. Because his cost of capital is 12%, he is indifferent. Recall that this finding concurs with the NPV rule, so in this case the incremental IRR rule gives the correct answer.

Shortcomings of the Incremental IRR Rule.   Although the incremental IRR rule resolves some problems with mutually exclusive investments, it still uses the IRR rule on the incremental cash flows. As a result, it shares several problems with the regular IRR rule:

- The fact that the IRR exceeds the cost of capital for both projects does not imply that both projects have positive NPV.

- The incremental IRR need not exist.

- Many incremental IRRs could exist. In fact, the likelihood of multiple IRRs is greater with the incremental IRR rule than with the regular IRR rule.

- You must keep track of which project is the incremental project and ensure that the incremental cash flows are initially negative and then become positive. Otherwise, the incremental IRR rule will have the negative initial investment problem and will give the wrong answer.

- The incremental IRR rule assumes that the riskiness of the two projects is the same. When the risks are different, the cost of capital of the incremental cash flows is not obvious, making it difficult to know whether the incremental IRR exceeds the cost of capital. In this case only the NPV rule, which allows each project to be discounted at its own cost of capital, will give a reliable answer.

In summary, although the incremental IRR rule can provide a reliable method for choosing among projects, it can be difficult to apply correctly. It is much simpler to use the NPV rule.

CONCEPT CHECK   1. What is the incremental IRR rule and what are its shortcomings?

2. For mutually exclusive projects, explain why picking one project over another because it has a larger IRR can lead to mistakes.

6.4   Project Selection with Resource Constraints

In the preceeding section, we considered the decision between two mutually exclusive investment opportunities. We implicitly assumed that both projects had *identical* resource needs—for example, that both the laundromat or his girlfriend's business demanded 100% of Don's time.

In some situations, different investment opportunities demand different amounts of a particular resource. If there is a fixed supply of the resource so that you cannot undertake all possible opportunities, simply picking the highest-NPV opportunity might not lead to the best decision.

Evaluation of Projects with Different Resource Requirements

Assume you are considering the three projects in Table 6.1, all of which require warehouse space. Table 6.1 shows the NPV of each project and the amount of available warehouse space that each project requires. Project A has the highest NPV but it uses up the entire resource (the warehouse); thus it would be a mistake to take this opportunity. Projects B and C can *both* be undertaken (together they use all the available space), and their combined NPV exceeds the NPV of project A; thus you should initiate them both. Together their NPV is $150 million, compared to just $100 million for project A alone.

TABLE 6.1		Possible Projects Requiring Warehouse Space	
Project	NPV ($ millions)	Fraction of Warehouse Required (%)	Profitability Index
A	100	100	1
B	75	60	1.25
C	75	40	1.875

Profitability Index

In this simple example, identifying the optimal combination of projects to undertake is straightforward. In actual situations replete with many projects and resources, finding the optimal combination can be difficult. Practitioners often use the **profitability index** to identify the optimal combination of projects to undertake in such situations:

Profitability Index

$$\text{Profitability Index} = \frac{\text{Value Created}}{\text{Resource Consumed}} = \frac{\text{NPV}}{\text{Resource Consumed}} \qquad (6.4)$$

The profitability index measures the "bang for your buck"—that is, the value created in terms of NPV per unit of resource consumed. After computing the profitability index, we can rank projects based on it. Starting with the project with the highest index, we move down the ranking, taking all projects until the resource is consumed. In Table 6.1, we have calculated the profitability index for each of the three projects. Note how the profitability index rule would select projects B and C.

Profitability Index with a Human Resource Constraint

Problem
Your division at NetIt, a large networking company, has put together a project proposal to develop a new home networking router. The expected NPV of the project is $17.7 million, and the project will require 50 software engineers. NetIt has a total of 190 engineers available, and the router project must compete with the following other projects for these engineers:

Project	NPV ($ millions)	Engineering Headcount
Router	17.7	50
Project A	22.7	47
Project B	8.1	44
Project C	14.0	40
Project D	11.5	61
Project E	20.6	58
Project F	12.9	32
Total	**107.5**	**332**

How should NetIt prioritize these projects?

Solution

The goal is to maximize the total NPV we can create with 190 employees (at most). We compute the profitability index for each project, using Engineering Headcount in the denominator, and then sort projects based on the index:

Project	NPV ($ millions)	Engineering Headcount (EHC)	Profitability Index (NPV per EHC)	Total EHC Required
Project A	22.7	47	0.483	47
Project F	12.9	32	0.403	79
Project E	20.6	58	0.355	137
Router	17.7	50	0.354	187
Project C	14.0	40	0.350	
Project D	11.5	61	0.189	
Project B	8.1	44	0.184	

We now assign the resource to the projects in descending order according to the profitability index. The final column shows the cumulative use of the resource as each project is taken on until the resource is used up. To maximize NPV within the constraint of 190 employees, NetIt should choose the first four projects on the list. The resource constraint forces NetIt to forgo three otherwise valuable projects.

Shortcomings of the Profitability Index

Although the profitability index is simple to compute and use, in some situations it does not give an accurate answer. For example, suppose in Example 6.4 that NetIt has an additional small project with a NPV of only $100,000 that requires 3 engineers. The profitability index in this case is 0.1/3 = 0.03, so this project would appear at the bottom of the ranking. However, notice that 3 of the 190 employees are not being used after the first four projects are selected. As a result, it would make sense to take on this project even though it would be ranked last.

A more serious problem occurs when multiple resource constraints apply. In this case, the profitability index can break down completely. The only surefire way to find the best combination of projects is to search through all of them. Although this process may sound exceedingly time-consuming, linear and integer programming techniques have been developed specifically to tackle this kind of problem. By using these techniques on a computer, the solution can usually be obtained almost instantaneously (see Further Reading for references).

CONCEPT CHECK

1. Explain why picking the project with the highest NPV might not be optimal when you evaluate mutually exclusive projects with different resource requirements.

2. Explain why practitioners often use the profitability index to identify the optimal combinations of projects to undertake.

Summary

1. If your objective is to maximize wealth, the NPV rule always gives the correct answer.

2. The difference between the cost of capital and the IRR is the maximum amount of estimation error that can exist in the cost of capital estimate without altering the original decision.

3. Payback investment rule: Calculate the amount of time it takes to pay back the initial investment (the payback period). If the payback period is less than a prespecified length of time, accept the project. Otherwise, turn it down.

4. IRR investment rule: Take any investment opportunity whose IRR exceeds the opportunity cost of capital. Turn down any opportunity whose IRR is less than the opportunity cost of capital.

5. The IRR rule may give the wrong answer if the cash flows have an upfront payment (negative investment). When there are multiple IRRs or the IRR does not exist, the IRR rule cannot be used.

6. The EVA in year n is the cash flow in that year minus the cost of tying up and using up the capital required to run the project—it is the value added in that year over the life of the project:

$$EVA_n = C_n - rI_{n-1} - \text{(Depreciation in Period } n) \qquad (6.2)$$

7. EVA investment rule: Accept any investment opportunity in which the present value, using the project's cost of capital r, of all future EVAs is positive.

8. When choosing among mutually exclusive investment opportunities, pick the opportunity with the highest NPV. Do not use IRR to choose among mutually exclusive investment opportunities.

9. Incremental IRR rule: Assume you are comparing two mutually exclusive opportunities, A and B, and the IRRs of both opportunities exceed the cost of capital. If you subtract the cash flows of opportunity B from the cash flows of opportunity A, then you should take opportunity A if the incremental IRR exceeds the cost of capital. Otherwise, take opportunity B.

10. When choosing among projects competing for the same resource, ranking the projects by their profitability indices and picking the set of projects with the highest profitability indices that can still be undertaken given the limited resource often produces the best result.

$$\text{Profitability Index} = \frac{\text{Value Created}}{\text{Resource Consumed}} = \frac{\text{NPV}}{\text{Resource Consumed}} \qquad (6.4)$$

Key Terms

capital charge *p. 158*
economic profit *p. 156*
Economic Value Added *p. 156*
EVA investment rule *p. 158*
incremental IRR investment
    rule *p. 164*

internal rate of return (IRR) investment
    rule *p. 152*
mutually exclusive projects *p. 161*
payback investment rule *p. 151*
payback period *p. 152*
profitability index *p. 167*

Further Reading

For readers who would like to learn more about economic profit (or EVA) and how it is used, see A. Ehrbar, *EVA: The Real Key to Creating Wealth.* (New York: John Wiley and Sons, 1998).

Readers who would like to know more about what managers actually do should consult J. Graham and C. Harvey, "How CFOs Make Capital Budgeting and Capital Structure

Decisions," *Journal of Applied Corporate Finance* 15(1) (2002): 8–23; S. H. Kim, T. Crick, and S. H. Kim, "Do Executives Practice What Academics Preach?" *Management Accounting* 68 (November 1986): 49–52; and P. Ryan and G. Ryan, "Capital Budgeting Practices of the Fortune 1000: How Have Things Changed?" *Journal of Business and Management* 8(4) (2002): 355–364.

For readers interested in how to select among projects competing for the same set of resources, the following references will be helpful: M. Vanhoucke, E. Demeulemeester, and W. Herroelen, "On Maximizing the Net Present Value of a Project Under Renewable Resource Constraints," *Management Science* 47(8) (2001): 1113–1121; and H. M. Weingartner, *Mathematical Programming and the Analysis of Capital Budgeting Problems.* (Englewood Cliffs, NJ: Prentice-Hall, 1963).

Problems

All problems in this chapter are available in MyFinanceLab. An asterisk (*) indicates problems with a higher level of difficulty.

NPV and Stand-Alone Projects

1. You are considering opening a new plant. The plant will cost $100 million upfront and will take one year to build. After that, it is expected to produce profits of $30 million at the end of every year of production. The cash flows are expected to last forever. Calculate the NPV of this investment opportunity if your cost of capital is 8%. Should you make the investment? Calculate the IRR and use it to determine the maximum deviation allowable in the cost of capital estimate to leave the decision unchanged.

EXCEL 2. Bill Clinton reportedly was paid $10 million to write his book *My Way*. The book took three years to write. In the time he spent writing, Clinton could have been paid to make speeches. Given his popularity, assume that he could earn $8 million per year (paid at the end of the year) speaking instead of writing. Assume his cost of capital is 10% per year.

   a. What is the NPV of agreeing to write the book (ignoring any royalty payments)?

   b. Assume that, once the book is finished, it is expected to generate royalties of $5 million in the first year (paid at the end of the year) and these royalties are expected to decrease at a rate of 30% per year in perpetuity. What is the NPV of the book with the royalty payments?

EXCEL *3. FastTrack Bikes, Inc., is thinking of developing a new composite road bike. Development will take six years and the cost is $200,000 per year. Once in production, the bike is expected to make $300,000 per year for 10 years.

   a. Assume the cost of capital is 10%.

      i. Calculate the NPV of this investment opportunity. Should the company make the investment?

      ii. Calculate the IRR and use it to determine the maximum deviation allowable in the cost of capital estimate to leave the decision unchanged.

      iii. How long must development last to change the decision?

   b. Assume the cost of capital is 14%.

      i. Calculate the NPV of this investment opportunity. Should the company make the investment?

      ii. How much must this cost of capital estimate deviate to change the decision?

      iii. How long must development last to change the decision?

4. You are a real estate agent thinking of placing a sign advertising your services at a local bus stop. The sign will cost $5000 and will be posted for one year. You expect that it will generate additional revenue of $500 per month. What is the payback period?

5. Does the IRR rule agree with the NPV rule in Problem 1?

EXCEL 6. How many IRRs are there in part (a) of Problem 2? Does the IRR rule give the right answer in this case?

EXCEL 7. How many IRRs are there in part (b) of Problem 2? Does the IRR rule work in this case?

8. Professor Wendy Smith has been offered the following deal: A law firm would like to retain her for an upfront payment of $50,000. In return, for the next year the firm would have access to 8 hours of her time every month. Smith's rate is $550 per hour and her opportunity cost of capital is 15% (EAR). What does the IRR rule advise regarding this opportunity? What about the NPV rule?

9. Innovation Company is thinking about marketing a new software product. Upfront costs to market and develop the product are $5 million. The product is expected to generate profits of $1 million per year for ten years. The company will have to provide product support expected to cost $100,000 per year in perpetuity. Assume all profits and expenses occur at the end of the year.

   a. What is the NPV of this investment if the cost of capital is 5.438761%? Should the firm undertake the project? Repeat the analysis for discount rates of 2.745784% and 10.879183%.

   b. What is the IRR of this investment opportunity?

   c. What does the IRR rule indicate about this investment?

10. You own a coal mining company and are considering opening a new mine. The mine itself will cost $120 million to open. If this money is spent immediately, the mine will generate $20 million for the next ten years. After that, the coal will run out and the site must be cleaned and maintained at environmental standards. The cleaning and maintenance are expected to cost $2 million per year in perpetuity. What does the IRR rule say about whether you should accept this opportunity? If the cost of capital is 8%, what does the NPV rule say?

EXCEL *11. You are considering investing in a new gold mine in South Africa. Gold in South Africa is buried very deep, so the mine will require an initial investment of $250 million. Once this investment is made, the mine is expected to produce revenues of $30 million per year for the next 20 years. It will cost $10 million per year to operate the mine. After 20 years, the gold will be depleted. The mine must then be stabilized on an ongoing basis, which will cost $5 million per year in perpetuity. Calculate the IRR of this investment. (*Hint:* Plot the NPV as a function of the discount rate.)

12. Calculate the present value of the EVAs in Problem 1 and determine whether the outcome with the EVA rule agrees with the outcome with the NPV rule.

EXCEL *13. You are considering constructing a new plant to manufacture a new product. You anticipate that the plant will take a year to build and cost $100 million upfront. Once built, it will generate cash flows of $15 million at the end of every year over the life of the plant. The plant will wear out 20 years after its completion. At that point you expect to get $10 million in salvage value for the plant. Using a cost of capital of 12%, calculate the present value of the EVAs and verify that they equal the NPV.

14. You are considering making a movie. The movie is expected to cost $10 million upfront and take a year to make. After that, it is expected to make $5 million in the year it is released and $2 million for the following four years. What is the payback period of this investment? If you

require a payback period of two years, will you make the movie? Does the movie have positive NPV if the cost of capital is 10%?

15. You work for a company that uses IRR exclusively. The reason is that the CEO does not like to read long memos. He is fond of saying, "I don't like two-handed economists!"[4] He likes to distill all decisions down to a single number like the IRR. Your boss has asked you to calculate the IRR of a project. He refuses to give you the cost of capital for the project, but you know that once you compute the IRR he will compare it to the cost of capital and use that information to make the investment decision. What should you do?

Mutually Exclusive Investment Opportunities

16. You are deciding between two mutually exclusive investment opportunities. Both require the same initial investment of $10 million. Investment A will generate $2 million per year (starting at the end of the first year) in perpetuity. Investment B will generate $1.5 million at the end of the first year and its revenues will grow at 2% per year for every year after that.

    a. Which investment has the higher IRR?

    b. Which investment has the higher NPV when the cost of capital is 7%?

    c. In this case, when does picking the higher IRR give the correct answer as to which investment is the best opportunity?

17. Use the incremental IRR rule to correctly choose between the investments in Problem 16 when the cost of capital is 7%.

18. You work for an outdoor play structure manufacturing company and are trying to decide between two projects:

Project	Year-End Cash Flows ($ thousands)			
	0	1	2	IRR
Playhouse	−30	15	20	10.4%
Fort	−80	39	52	8.6%

You can undertake only one project. If your cost of capital is 8%, use the incremental IRR rule to make the correct decision.

Project Selection with Resource Constraints

19. Kartman Corporation is evaluating four real estate investments. Management plans to buy the properties today and sell them three years from today. The annual discount rate for these investments is 15%. The following table summarizes the initial cost and the sale price in three years for each property.

	Cost Today	Sale Price in Year 3
Parkside Acres	$500,000	$ 900,000
Real Property Estates	800,000	1,400,000
Lost Lake Properties	650,000	1,050,000
Overlook	150,000	350,000

Kartman has a total capital budget of $800,000 to invest in properties. Which properties should it choose?

---

4. U.S. President Harry Truman is purported to have complained that the problem with all economists is that they always have two hands. When asked to give advice, they always said, "On the one hand . . . but on the other hand . . ."

20. Orchid Biotech Company is evaluating several development projects for experimental drugs. Although the cash flows are difficult to forecast, the company has come up with the following estimates of the initial capital requirements and NPVs for the projects. Given a wide variety of staffing needs, the company has also estimated the number of research scientists required for each development project (all cost values are given in millions of dollars).

Project Number	Initial Capital	Number of Research Scientists	NPV
I	$10	2	$10.1
II	15	3	19.0
III	15	4	22.0
IV	20	3	25.0
V	30	10	60.2

a. Suppose that Orchid has a total capital budget of $60 million. How should it prioritize these projects?

b. Suppose that Orchid currently has 12 research scientists and does not anticipate being able to hire any more in the near future. How should Orchid prioritize these projects?

Data Case

On October 6, 2004 Sirius Satellite Radio announced that it had reached an agreement with Howard Stern to broadcast his radio show exclusively on their system. As a result of this announcement, the Sirius stock price increased dramatically. You are currently working as a stock analyst for a large investment firm and XM Radio, also a satellite radio firm, is one of the firms you track. Your boss wants to be prepared if XM follows Sirius in trying to sign a major personality. Therefore, she wants you to estimate the net cash flows the market had anticipated from the signing of Stern. She advises that you treat the value anticipated by the market as the NPV of the signing, then work backward from the NPV to determine the annual cash flows necessary to generate that value. The potential deal had been rumored for some time prior to the announcement. As a result, the stock price for Sirius increased for several days before the announcement. Thus, your boss advises that the best way to capture all of the value is to take the change in stock price from September 28, 2004 through October 7, 2004. You nod your head in agreement, trying to look like you understand how to proceed. You are relatively new to the job and the term NPV is somewhat familiar to you.

1. To determine the change in stock price over this period, go to Yahoo! Finance (http://finance.yahoo.com) and enter the stock symbol for Sirius (SIRI). Then click on "Historical Prices" and enter the appropriate dates. Use the adjusted closing prices for the two dates.

2. To determine the change in value, multiply the change in stock price by the number of shares outstanding. The number of shares outstanding around those dates can be found by going to finance.google.com and typing "SIRI" into the "Search" window. Next, select the Income Statement link on the left side of the screen, and then select "Annual Data" in the upper right-hand corner. The "Diluted Weighted Average Shares" can be found for the 12/31/2004 income statement on that page.

3. Because the change in value represents the "expected" NPV of the project, you will have to find the annual net cash flows that would provide this NPV. For this analysis, you will need to estimate the cost of capital for the project. We show how to calculate the cost of capital

in subsequent chapters; for now, use the New York University (NYU) cost of capital Web site (http://pages.stern.nyu.edu/~adamodar/New_Home_Page/datafile/wacc.htm). Locate the cost of capital in the far-right column for the "Entertainment Tech" industry.

4. Use the cost of capital from the NYU Web site and the NPV you computed to calculate the constant annual cash flow that provides this NPV. Compute cash flows for 5-, 10-, and 15-year horizons.

5. Your boss mentioned that she believes that the Howard Stern signing by Sirius was actually good for XM because it signaled that the industry has valuable growth potential. To see if she appears to be correct, find the percentage stock price reaction to XM (XMSR) over this same period.

Basic Valuation

Chapter 7
Fundamentals of
Capital Budgeting

Chapter 8
Valuing Bonds

Chapter 9
Valuing Stocks

The Law of One Price Connection.   Now that the tools for financial decision making are in place, we can begin to apply them. One of the most important decisions facing a financial manager is the choice of which investments the corporation should make. The process of allocating the firm's capital for investment is known as capital budgeting and in Chapter 7 we outline the discounted cash flow method for making such decisions. Chapter 7 provides a practical demonstration of the power of the tools that were introduced in Part II.

Firms raise the capital they need to make investments by issuing securities such as stocks and bonds. In the next two chapters, we use these same tools to explain how to value bonds and stocks. In Chapter 8, Valuing Bonds, the Law of One Price allows us to link bond prices and their yields to the term structure of market interest rates. Similarly, in Chapter 9, Valuing Stocks, we show how the Law of One Price leads to several alternative methods for valuing a firm's equity by considering its future dividends, free cash flows, or how its value compares to that of similar, publicly traded companies.

7

Fundamentals of Capital Budgeting

In early 2004, Kellogg Company, the world's leading producer of cereal and other convenience foods, announced the introduction of its Low-Sugar Frosted Flakes and Froot Loops cereals. As described by Jeff Montie, Morning Foods Division North America President at Kellogg, "The Frosted Flakes and Froot Loops brand extensions represent a great new option for parents and their families. Consumer research indicates that parents value the fact that Kellogg was able to maintain great taste without adding artificial sweeteners. As a result, we're confident that we have two new products that parents and kids will enthusiastically agree on." The decision by Kellogg to introduce brand extensions of two of its most popular cereals represents a classic capital budgeting decision. How did Kellogg quantify the costs and benefits of this project, and decide to introduce its new cereals? We will develop the tools to evaluate projects such as this one in this chapter.

An important responsibility of corporate financial managers is determining which projects or investments a firm should undertake. *Capital budgeting* is the process of analyzing investment opportunities and deciding which ones to accept. It requires computing the NPV and accepting projects for which the NPV is positive. The first step in this process is estimating the project's expected cash flows by forecasting the project's revenues and costs. Using these cash flows, we can then compute the project's NPV—its contribution to shareholder value. Finally, because the cash flow forecasts almost always contain uncertainty, we demonstrate how to compute the sensitivity of the NPV to the uncertainty in the forecasts.

7.1   Forecasting Earnings

A **capital budget** lists the projects and investments that a company plans to undertake during the coming year. To determine this list, firms analyze alternate projects and decide which ones to accept through a process called **capital budgeting**. This process begins with forecasts of the project's future consequences for the firm. Some of these consequences will affect the firm's revenues; others will affect its costs. Our ultimate goal is to determine the effect of the decision on the firm's cash flows.

As we emphasized in Chapter 2, *earnings are not actual cash flows*. However, as a practical matter, to derive the forecasted cash flows of a project, financial managers often begin by forecasting earnings. Thus, we *begin* by determining the **incremental earnings** of a project—that is, the amount by which the firm's earnings are expected to change as a result of the investment decision. Then, in Section 7.2, we demonstrate how to use the incremental earnings to forecast the *cash flows* of the project.

Let's consider a hypothetical capital budgeting decision faced by managers of the Linksys division of Cisco Systems, a maker of consumer networking hardware. Linksys is considering the development of a wireless home networking appliance, called HomeNet, that will provide both the hardware and the software necessary to run an entire home from any Internet connection. In addition to connecting PCs and printers, HomeNet will control new Internet-capable stereos, digital video recorders, heating and air-conditioning units, major appliances, telephone and security systems, office equipment, and so on. Linksys has already conducted an intensive, $300,000 feasibility study to assess the attractiveness of the new product.

Revenue and Cost Estimates

We begin by reviewing the revenue and cost estimates for HomeNet. HomeNet's target market is upscale residential "smart" homes and home offices. Based on extensive marketing surveys, the sales forecast for HomeNet is 100,000 units per year. Given the pace of technological change, Linksys expects the product will have a four-year life. It will be sold through high-end stereo and electronics stores for a retail price of $375, with an expected wholesale price of $260.

Developing the new hardware will be relatively inexpensive, as existing technologies can be simply repackaged in a newly designed, home-friendly box. Industrial design teams will make the box and its packaging aesthetically pleasing to the residential market. Linksys expects total engineering and design costs to amount to $5 million. Once the design is finalized, actual production will be outsourced at a cost (including packaging) of $110 per unit.

In addition to the hardware requirements, Linksys must build a new software application to allow virtual control of the home from the Web. This software development project requires coordination with each of the Web appliance manufacturers and is expected to take a dedicated team of 50 software engineers a full year to complete. The cost of a software engineer (including benefits and related costs) is $200,000 per year. To verify the compatibility of new consumer Internet-ready appliances with the HomeNet system as they become available, Linksys must also build a new lab for testing purposes. This lab will occupy existing facilities but will require $7.5 million of new equipment.

The software and hardware design will be completed, and the lab will be operational, at the end of one year. At that time, HomeNet will be ready to ship. Linksys expects to spend $2.8 million per year on marketing and support for this product.

INTERVIEW WITH
Dick Grannis

Dick Grannis is Senior Vice President and Treasurer of QUALCOMM Incorporated, a world leader in digital wireless communications technology and semiconductors, headquartered in San Diego. He joined the company in 1991 and oversees the company's $10 billion cash investment portfolio. He works primarily on investment banking, capital structure, and international finance.

QUESTION: *QUALCOMM has a wide variety of products in different business lines. How does your capital budgeting process for new products work?*

ANSWER: QUALCOMM evaluates new projects (such as new products, equipment, technologies, research and development, acquisitions, and strategic investments) by using traditional financial measurements including DCF models, IRR levels, peak funding requirements, the time needed to reach cumulative positive cash flows, and the short-term impact of the investment on our reported net earnings. For strategic investments, we consider the possible value of financial, competitive, technology and/or market value enhancements to our core businesses—even if those benefits cannot be quantified. Overall, we make capital budgeting decisions based on a combination of objective analyses and our own business judgment.

We do not engage in capital budgeting and analysis if the project represents an immediate and necessary requirement for our business operations. One example is new software or production equipment to start a project that has already received approval.

We are also mindful of the opportunity costs of allocating our internal engineering resources on one project vs. another project. We view this as a constantly challenging but worthwhile exercise, because we have many attractive opportunities but limited resources to pursue them.

QUESTION: *How often does QUALCOMM evaluate its hurdle rates and what factors does it consider in setting them? How do you allocate capital across areas and regions and assess the risk of non-U.S. investments?*

ANSWER: QUALCOMM encourages its financial planners to utilize hurdle (or discount) rates that vary according to the risk of the particular project. We expect a rate of return commensurate with the project's risk. Our finance staff considers a wide range of discount rates and chooses one that fits the project's expected risk profile and time horizon. The range can be from 6.00% to 8.00% for relatively safe investments in the domestic market to 50% or more for equity investments in foreign markets that may be illiquid and difficult to predict. We re-evaluate our hurdle rates at least every year.

We analyze key factors including: (i) market adoption risk (whether or not customers will buy the new product or service at the price and volume we expect), (ii) technology development risk (whether or not we can develop and patent the new product or service as expected), (iii) execution risk (whether we can launch the new product or service cost effectively and on time), and (iv) dedicated asset risk (the amount of resources that must be consumed to complete the work).

QUESTION: *How are projects categorized and how are the hurdle rates for new projects determined? What would happen if QUALCOMM simply evaluated all new projects against the same hurdle rate?*

ANSWER: We primarily categorize projects by risk level, but we also categorize projects by the expected time horizon. We consider short-term and long-term projects to balance our needs and achieve our objectives. For example, immediate projects and opportunities may demand a great amount of attention, but we also stay focused on long-term projects because they often create greater long-term value for stockholders.

If we were to evaluate all new projects against the same hurdle rate, then our business planners would, by default, consistently choose to invest in the highest risk projects because those projects would appear to have the greatest expected returns in DCF models or IRR analyses. That approach would probably not work well for very long.

Incremental Earnings Forecast

Given the revenue and cost estimates, we can forecast HomeNet's incremental earnings, as shown in Table 7.1 Spreadsheet. After the product is developed in year 0, it will generate sales of 100,000 units × $260 / unit = $26 million each year for the next four years. The cost of producing these units is 100,000 units × $110 / unit = $11 million per year. Thus, HomeNet will produce a gross profit of $26 million − $11 million = $15 million per year, as shown in line 3 of the spreadsheet in Table 7.1.[1]

The project's operating expenses include $2.8 million per year in marketing and support costs, which are listed as selling, general, and administrative expenses. In year 0, Linksys will spend $5 million on design and engineering, together with 50 × $200,000 = $10 million on software, for a total of $15 million in research and development expenditures.

TABLE 7.1 SPREADSHEET	HomeNet's Incremental Earnings Forecast					

Year	0	1	2	3	4	5
Incremental Earnings Forecast ($000s)						
1 Sales	—	26,000	26,000	26,000	26,000	—
2 Cost of Goods Sold	—	(11,000)	(11,000)	(11,000)	(11,000)	—
3 **Gross Profit**	—	15,000	15,000	15,000	15,000	—
4 Selling, General, and Administrative	—	(2,800)	(2,800)	(2,800)	(2,800)	—
5 Research and Development	(15,000)	—	—	—	—	—
6 Depreciation	—	(1,500)	(1,500)	(1,500)	(1,500)	(1,500)
7 **EBIT**	(15,000)	10,700	10,700	10,700	10,700	(1,500)
8 Income Tax at 40%	6,000	(4,280)	(4,280)	(4,280)	(4,280)	600
9 **Unlevered Net Income**	(9,000)	6,420	6,420	6,420	6,420	(900)

Capital Expenditures and Depreciation.   HomeNet also requires $7.5 million in equipment for a new lab. Recall from Chapter 2 that while investments in plant, property, and equipment are a cash expense, they are not directly listed as expenses when calculating *earnings*. Instead, the firm deducts a fraction of the cost of these items each year as depreciation. Several different methods are used to compute depreciation. The simplest method is **straight line depreciation**, in which the asset's cost is divided equally over its life (we discuss other methods in Section 7.2). If we assume straight-line depreciation over a five-year life for the lab equipment, HomeNet's depreciation expense is $1.5 million per year. Deducting these depreciation expenses leads to the forecast for HomeNet's earnings before interest and taxes (EBIT) shown in line 7 of Table 7.1 Spreadsheet. This treatment of capital expenditures is one of the key reasons why earnings are not an accurate representation of cash flows.

Interest Expenses.   In Chapter 2, we saw that to compute a firm's net income, we must first deduct interest expenses from EBIT. When evaluating a capital budgeting decision like the HomeNet project, however, we generally *do not include interest expenses.* Any

---

1. While revenues and costs occur throughout the year, the standard convention, which we adopt here, is to list revenues and costs in the year in which they occur. Thus cash flows that occur at the end of one year will be listed in a different column than those that occur at the start of the next year, even though they may occur only weeks apart. When additional precision is required, cash flows are often estimated on a quarterly or monthly basis. (See also the Appendix to Chapter 5 for a method of converting continuously arriving cash flows to annual ones.)

incremental interest expenses will be related to the firm's decision regarding how to finance the project. Here we wish to evaluate the project on its own, separate from the financing decision.[2] Thus we evaluate the HomeNet project *as if* Cisco will not use any debt to finance it (whether or not that is actually the case), and we postpone the consideration of alternative financing choices until Part V of this book. For this reason, we refer to the net income we compute in the spreadsheet in Table 7.1 as the **unlevered net income** of the project, to indicate that it does not include any interest expenses associated with leverage.

Taxes.   The final expense we must account for is corporate taxes. The correct tax rate to use is the firm's **marginal corporate tax rate**, which is the tax rate it will pay on an *incremental* dollar of pre-tax income. In Table 7.1 Spreadsheet, we assume the marginal corporate tax rate for the HomeNet project is 40% each year. The incremental income tax expense is calculated in line 8 as

$$\text{Income Tax} = \text{EBIT} \times \tau_c \qquad (7.1)$$

where τ_c is the firm's marginal corporate tax rate.

In year 1, HomeNet will contribute an additional $10.7 million to Cisco's EBIT, which will result in an additional $10.7 million $\times$ 40% = $4.28 million in corporate tax that Cisco will owe. We deduct this amount to determine HomeNet's after-tax contribution to net income.

In year 0, however, HomeNet's EBIT is negative. Are taxes relevant in this case? Yes. HomeNet will reduce Cisco's taxable income in year 0 by $15 million. As long as Cisco earns taxable income elsewhere in year 0 against which it can offset HomeNet's losses, Cisco will owe $15 million $\times$ 40% = $6 million *less* in taxes in year 0. The firm should credit this tax savings to the HomeNet project. A similar credit applies in year 5, when the firm claims its final depreciation expense for the lab equipment.

Taxing Losses for Projects in Profitable Companies

Problem
Kellogg Company plans to launch a new line of high-fiber, zero-trans-fat breakfast pastries. The heavy advertising expenses associated with the new product launch will generate operating losses of $15 million next year for the product. Kellogg expects to earn pre-tax income of $460 million from operations other than the new pastries next year. If Kellogg pays a 40% tax rate on its pre-tax income, what will it owe in taxes next year without the new pastry product? What will it owe with the new pastries?

Solution
Without the new pastries, Kellogg will owe $460 million $\times$ 40% = $184 million in corporate taxes next year. With the new pastries, Kellogg's pre-tax income next year will be only $460 million $-$ $15 million = $445 million, and it will owe $445 million $\times$ 40% = $178 million in tax. Thus, launching the new product reduces Kellogg's taxes next year by $184 million $-$ $178 million = $6 million.

---

2. This approach is motivated by the Separation Principle from Chapter 3: When securities are fairly priced, the net present value of a fixed set of cash flows is independent of how those cash flows are financed. Later in the text we will consider cases in which financing may influence the project's value, and we will extend our capital budgeting techniques accordingly in Chapter 18.

TABLE 7.5 SPREADSHEET	**Computing HomeNet's NPV**						

Year	0	1	2	3	4	5
Net Present Value ($000s)							
1 Free Cash Flow		(16,500)	5,100	7,200	7,200	7,200	2,700
2 Project Cost of Capital	12%						
3 Discount Factor		1.000	0.893	0.797	0.712	0.636	0.567
4 PV of Free Cash Flow		(16,500)	4,554	5,740	5,125	4,576	1.532
5 NPV		5,027					

Based on our estimates, HomeNet's NPV is $5,027 million. While HomeNet's upfront cost is $16.5 million, the present value of the additional free cash flow that Cisco will receive from the project is $21.5 million. Thus, taking the HomeNet project is equivalent to Cisco having an extra $5 million in the bank today.

Choosing Among Alternatives

Thus far, we have considered the capital budgeting decision to launch the HomeNet product line. To analyze the decision, we computed the project's free cash flow and calculated the NPV. Because *not* launching HomeNet produces an additional NPV of zero for the firm, launching HomeNet is the best decision for the firm if its NPV is positive. In many situations, however, we must compare mutually exclusive alternatives, each of which has consequences for the firm's cash flows. As we explained in Chapter 6, in such cases we can make the best decision by first computing the free cash flow associated with each alternative and then choosing the alternative with the highest NPV.

Evaluating Manufacturing Alternatives.   Suppose Cisco is considering an alternative manufacturing plan for the HomeNet product. The current plan is to fully outsource production at a cost of $110 per unit. Alternatively, Cisco could assemble the product in-house at a cost of $95 per unit. However, the latter option will require $5 million in upfront operating expenses to reorganize the assembly facility, and Cisco will need to maintain inventory equal to one month's production.

To choose between these two alternatives, we compute the free cash flow associated with each choice and compare their NPVs to see which is most advantageous for the firm. When comparing alternatives, we need to compare only those cash flows that differ between them. We can ignore any cash flows that are the same under either scenario (e.g., HomeNet's revenues).

The spreadsheet in Table 7.6 compares the two assembly options, computing the NPV of the cash costs for each. The difference in EBIT results from the upfront cost of setting up the in-house facility in year 0, and the differing assembly costs: $110/unit × 100,000 units/yr = $11 million/yr outsourced, versus $95/unit × 100,000 units/yr = $9.5 million/yr in-house. Adjusting for taxes, we see the consequences for unlevered net income on lines 3 and 9.

Because the options do not differ in terms of capital expenditures (there are none associated with assembly), to compare the free cash flow for each, we only need to adjust for their different net working capital requirements. If assembly is outsourced, payables account for 15% of the cost of goods, or 15% × $11 million = $1.65 million. This amount is the credit Cisco will receive from its supplier in year 1 and will maintain until year 5. Because Cisco will borrow this amount from its supplier, net working capital *falls*

TABLE 7.6 SPREADSHEET	NPV Cost of Outsourced Versus In-House Assembly of HomeNet

	Year	0	1	2	3	4	5
Outsourced Assembly ($000s)							
1 EBIT		—	(11,000)	(11,000)	(11,000)	(11,000)	—
2 Income Tax at 40%		—	4,400	4,400	4,400	4,400	—
3 Unlevered Net Income		—	(6,600)	(6,600)	(6,600)	(6,600)	—
4 Less: Increases in NWC		—	1,650	—	—	—	(1,650)
5 Free Cash Flow		—	(4,950)	(6,600)	(6,600)	(6,600)	(1,650)
6 NPV at 12%		(19,510)					

	Year	0	1	2	3	4	5
In-House Assembly ($000s)							
1 EBIT		(5,000)	(9,500)	(9,500)	(9,500)	(9,500)	—
2 Income Tax at 40%		2,000	3,800	3,800	3,800	3,800	—
3 Unlevered Net Income		(3,000)	(5,700)	(5,700)	(5,700)	(5,700)	—
4 Less: Increases in NWC		—	633	—	—	—	(633)
5 Free Cash Flow		(3,000)	(5,067)	(5,700)	(5,700)	(5,700)	(633)
6 NPV at 12%		(20,107)					

by $1.65 million in year 1, adding to Cisco's free cash flow. In year 5, Cisco's net working capital will increase as Cisco pays its suppliers, and free cash flow will fall by an equal amount.

If assembly is done in-house, payables are 15% × $9.5 million = $1.425 million. However, Cisco will need to maintain inventory equal to one month's production, which has cost of $9.5 million ÷ 12 = $0.792 million. Thus Linksys's net working capital will decrease by $1.425 million − $0.792 million = $0.633 million in year 1 and will increase by the same amount in year 5.

Comparing Free Cash Flows for Cisco's Alternatives.   Adjusting for increases to net working capital, we compare the free cash flow of each alternative on lines 5 and 11 and compute their NPVs using the project's 12% cost of capital.[7] In each case, the NPV is negative, as we are evaluating only the costs of production. Outsourcing, however, is somewhat cheaper, with a present value cost of $19.5 million versus $20.1 million if the units are produced in-house.[8]

Further Adjustments to Free Cash Flow

Here we describe a number of complications that can arise when estimating a project's free cash flow.

Other Non-cash Items.   In general, other non-cash items that appear as part of incremental earnings should not be included in the project's free cash flow. The firm should

---

7. The risks of these options could potentially differ from the risk of the project overall and from the risks of each other, requiring a different cost of capital for each case. We ignore any such differences here.

8. It is also possible to compare these two cases in a single spreadsheet where we compute the difference in the free cash flows directly, rather than compute the free cash flows separately for each option. We prefer to do them separately, as it is clearer and generalizes to the case when there are more than two options.

include only actual cash revenues or expenses. For example, the firm adds back any amortization of intangible assets (such as patents) to unlevered net income when calculating free cash flow.

Timing of Cash Flows. For simplicity, we have treated the cash flows for HomeNet as if they occur at annual intervals. In reality, cash flows will be spread throughout the year. We can forecast free cash flow on a quarterly, monthly, or even continuous basis when greater accuracy is required.

Accelerated Depreciation. Because depreciation contributes positively to the firm's cash flow through the depreciation tax shield, it is in the firm's best interest to use the most accelerated method of depreciation that is allowable for tax purposes. By doing so, the firm will accelerate its tax savings and increase their present value. In the United States, the most accelerated depreciation method allowed by the IRS is MACRS (Modified Accelerated Cost Recovery System) depreciation. With **MACRS depreciation**, the firm first categorizes assets according to their recovery period. Based on the recovery period, MACRS depreciation tables assign a fraction of the purchase price that the firm can recover each year. We provide MACRS tables and recovery periods for common assets in the appendix.

Computing Accelerated Depreciation

Problem

What depreciation deduction would be allowed for the lab equipment using the MACRS method, assuming the lab equipment is designated to have a five-year recovery period?

Solution

Table 7A.1 in the appendix provides the percentage of the cost that can be depreciated each year. Based on the table, the allowable depreciation expense for the lab equipment is shown below (in thousands of dollars):

	Year	0	1	2	3	4	5
	MACRS Depreciation						
1	Lab Equipment Cost	(7,500)					
2	MACRS Depreciation Rate	20.00%	32.00%	19.20%	11.52%	11.52%	5.76%
3	Depreciation Expense	(1,500)	(2,400)	(1,440)	(864)	(864)	(432)

Compared with straight-line depreciation, the MACRS method allows for larger depreciation deductions earlier in the asset's life, which increases the present value of the depreciation tax shield and so will raise the project's NPV. In the case of HomeNet, computing the NPV using MACRS depreciation leads to an NPV of $5.34 million.

Liquidation or Salvage Value. Assets that are no longer needed often have a resale value, or some salvage value if the parts are sold for scrap. Some assets may have a negative liquidation value. For example, it may cost money to remove and dispose of the used equipment.

In the calculation of free cash flow, we include the liquidation value of any assets that are no longer needed and may be disposed of. When an asset is liquidated, any capital gain is taxed as income. We calculate the capital gain as the difference between the sale price and the book value of the asset:

$$\text{Capital Gain} = \text{Sale Price} - \text{Book Value} \tag{7.8}$$

The book value is equal to the asset's original cost less the amount it has already been depreciated for tax purposes:

$$\text{Book Value} = \text{Purchase Price} - \text{Accumulated Depreciation} \tag{7.9}$$

We must adjust the project's free cash flow to account for the after-tax cash flow that would result from an asset sale:

$$\text{After-Tax Cash Flow from Asset Sale} =$$
$$\text{Sale Price} - (\tau_c \times \text{Capital Gain}) \tag{7.10}$$

Adding Salvage Value to Free Cash Flow

Problem
Suppose that in addition to the $7.5 million in new equipment required for HomeNet's lab, equipment will be transferred to the lab from another Linksys facility. This equipment has a resale value of $2 million and a book value of $1 million. If the equipment is kept rather than sold, its remaining book value can be depreciated next year. When the lab is shut down in year 5, the equipment will have a salvage value of $800,000. What adjustments must we make to HomeNet's free cash flow in this case?

Solution
The existing equipment could have been sold for $2 million. The after-tax proceeds from this sale are an opportunity cost of using the equipment in the HomeNet lab. Thus we must reduce HomeNet's free cash flow in year 0 by $2 million − 40% × ($2 million − $1 million) = $1.6 million.

In year 1, the remaining $1 million book value of the equipment can be depreciated, creating a depreciation tax shield of 40% × $1 million = $400,000. In year 5, the firm will sell the equipment for a salvage value of $800,000. Because the equipment will be fully depreciated at that time, the entire amount will be taxable as a capital gain, so the after tax cash flow from the sale is $800,000 × (1 − 40%) = $480,000.

The spreadsheet below shows these adjustments to the free cash flow from Table 7.3 Spreadsheet and recalculates HomeNet's free cash flow and NPV in this case.

	Year	0	1	2	3	4	5
Free Cash Flow and NPV ($000s)							
1	Free Cash Flow w/o equipment	(16,500)	5,100	7,200	7,200	7,200	2,700
	Adjustments for use of existing equipment						
2	After-Tax Salvage Value	(1,600)	—	—	—	—	480
3	Depreciation Tax Shield	—	400	—	—	—	—
4	Free Cash Flow with equipment	(18,100)	5,500	7,200	7,200	7,200	3,180
5	NPV at 12%	4,055					

Terminal or Continuation Value.   Sometimes the firm explicitly forecasts free cash flow over a shorter horizon than the full horizon of the project or investment. This is necessarily true for investments with an indefinite life, such as an expansion of the firm. In this case, we estimate the value of the remaining free cash flow beyond the forecast horizon by including an additional, one-time cash flow at the end of the forecast horizon called the **terminal** or **continuation value** of the project. This amount represents the market value (as of the last forecast period) of the free cash flow from the project at all future dates.

Depending on the setting, we use different methods for estimating the continuation value of an investment. For example, when analyzing investments with long lives, it is common to explicitly calculate free cash flow over a short horizon, and then assume that cash flows grow at some constant rate beyond the forecast horizon.

Continuation Value with Perpetual Growth

Problem

Base Hardware is considering opening a set of new retail stores. The free cash flow projections for the new stores are shown below (in millions of dollars):

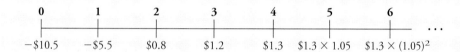

0	1	2	3	4	5	6	
−$10.5	−$5.5	$0.8	$1.2	$1.3	$1.3 × 1.05	$1.3 × (1.05)²	⋯

After year 4, Base Hardware expects free cash flow from the stores to increase at a rate of 5% per year. If the appropriate cost of capital for this investment is 10%, what continuation value in year 3 captures the value of future free cash flows in year 4 and beyond? What is the NPV of the new stores?

Solution

The expected free cash flow from the store in year 4 is $1.30 million, with future free cash flow beyond year 4 expected to grow at 5% per year. The continuation value in year 3 of the free cash flow in year 4 and beyond can therefore be calculated as a constant growth perpetuity:

$$\text{Continuation Value in Year 3} = \text{PV(FCF in Year 4 and Beyond)}$$

$$= \frac{FCF_4}{r - g} = \frac{\$1.30 \text{ million}}{0.10 - 0.05} = \$26 \text{ million}$$

We can restate the free cash flows of the investment as follows (in thousands of dollars):

Year	0	1	2	3
Free Cash Flow (Years 0–3)	(10,500)	(5,500)	800	1,200
Continuation Value				26,000
Free Cash Flow	(10,500)	(5,500)	800	27,200

The NPV of the investment in the new stores is

$$NPV = -10,500 - \frac{5500}{1.10} + \frac{800}{1.10^2} + \frac{27,200}{1.10^3} = \$5597$$

or $5.597 million.

Tax Carryforwards. A firm generally identifies its marginal tax rate by determining the tax bracket that it falls into based on its overall level of pre-tax income. Two additional features of the tax code, called **tax loss carryforwards and carrybacks**, allow corporations to take losses during a current year and offset them against gains in nearby years. Since 1997, companies can "carry back" losses for two years and "carry forward" losses for 20 years. This tax rule means that the firm can offset losses during one year against income for the last two years, or save the losses to be offset against income during the next 20 years. When a firm can carry back losses, it receives a refund for back taxes in the current year. Otherwise, the firm must carry forward the loss and use it to offset future taxable income. When a firm has tax loss carryforwards well in excess of its current pre-tax income, then additional income it earns today will simply increase the taxes it owes after it exhausts its carryforwards.

EXAMPLE 7.8

Tax Loss Carryforwards

Problem

Verian Industries has outstanding tax loss carryforwards of $100 million from losses over the past six years. If Verian earns $30 million per year in pre-tax income from now on, when will it first pay taxes? If Verian earns an extra $5 million this coming year, in which year will its taxes increase?

Solution

With pre-tax income of $30 million per year, Verian will be able to use its tax loss carryforwards to avoid paying taxes until year 4 (in millions of dollars):

Year	1	2	3	4	5
Pre-tax Income	30	30	30	30	30
Tax Loss Carryforward	−30	−30	−30	−10	
Taxable Income	0	0	0	20	30

If Verian earns an additional $5 million the first year, it will owe taxes on an extra $5 million in year 4:

Year	1	2	3	4	5
Pre-tax Income	35	30	30	30	30
Tax Loss Carryforward	−35	−30	−30	−5	
Taxable Income	0	0	0	25	30

Thus, when a firm has tax loss carryforwards, the tax impact of current earnings will be delayed until the carryforwards are exhausted. This delay reduces the present value of the tax impact, and firms sometimes approximate the effect of tax loss carryforwards by using a lower marginal tax rate.

CONCEPT CHECK

1. Explain why it is advantageous for a firm to use the most accelerated depreciation schedule possible for tax purposes.

2. What is the continuation or terminal value of a project?

7.3 Analyzing the Project

When evaluating a capital budgeting project, financial managers should make the decision that maximizes NPV. As we have discussed, to compute the NPV for a project, you need to estimate the incremental cash flows and choose a discount rate. Given these inputs, the NPV calculation is relatively straightforward. The most difficult part of capital budgeting is deciding how to estimate the cash flows and cost of capital. These estimates are often subject to significant uncertainty. In this section, we look at methods that assess the importance of this uncertainty and identify the drivers of value in the project.

Break-Even Analysis

When we are uncertain regarding the input to a capital budgeting decision, it is often useful to determine the **break-even** level of that input, which is the level for which the investment has an NPV of zero. One example that we have already considered is the calculation of the internal rate of return (IRR). Recall from Chapter 6 that the difference between the IRR of a project and the cost of capital tells you how much error in the cost of capital it would take to change the investment decision. Using the Excel function IRR, the spreadsheet in Table 7.7 calculates an IRR of 24.1% for the free cash flow of the HomeNet project.[9] Hence, the true cost of capital can be as high as 24.1% and the project will still have positive NPV.

TABLE 7.7 SPREADSHEET	**HomeNet IRR Calculation**

	Year	0	1	2	3	4	5
NPV ($000s) and IRR							
1 Free Cash Flow		(16,500)	5,100	7,200	7,200	7,200	2,700
2 NPV at 12%		5,027					
3 IRR		24.1%					

There is no reason to limit our attention to the uncertainty in the cost of capital estimate. In a **break-even analysis**, for each parameter, we calculate the value at which the NPV of the project is zero. Table 7.8 shows the break-even level for several key parameters.

TABLE 7.8	**Break-Even Levels for HomeNet**

Parameter	**Break-Even Level**
Units sold	79,759 units per year
Wholesale price	$232 per unit
Cost of goods	$138 per unit
Cost of capital	24.1%

---

9. The format in Excel is = IRR(FCF0:FCF5).

For example, based on the initial assumptions, the HomeNet project will break even with a sales level of just under 80,000 units per year. Alternatively, at a sales level of 100,000 units per year, the project will break even with a sales price of $232 per unit.

We have examined the break-even levels in terms of the project's NPV, which is the most useful perspective for decision making. Other accounting notions of break-even are sometimes considered, however. For example, we could compute the **EBIT break-even** for sales, which is the level of sales for which the project's EBIT is zero. While HomeNet's EBIT break-even level of sales is only about 32,000 units per year, given the large upfront investment required in HomeNet, its NPV is $-$11.8 million at that sales level.

Sensitivity Analysis

Another important capital budgeting tool is sensitivity analysis. **Sensitivity analysis** breaks the NPV calculation into its component assumptions and shows how the NPV varies as the underlying assumptions change. In this way, sensitivity analysis allows us to explore the effects of errors in our NPV estimates for the project. By conducting a sensitivity analysis, we learn which assumptions are the most important; we can then invest further resources and effort to refine these assumptions. Such an analysis also reveals which aspects of the project are most critical when we are actually managing the project.

To illustrate, consider the assumptions underlying the calculation of HomeNet's NPV. There is likely to be significant uncertainty surrounding each revenue and cost assumption. Table 7.9 shows the base-case assumptions, together with the best and worst cases, for several key aspects of the project.

| TABLE 7.9 | Best- and Worst-Case Parameter Assumptions for HomeNet |

Parameter	Initial Assumption	Worst Case	Best Case
Units sold (thousands)	100	70	130
Sale price ($/unit)	260	240	280
Cost of goods ($/unit)	110	120	100
NWC ($ thousands)	2100	3000	1600
Cannibalization	25%	40%	10%
Cost of capital	12%	15%	10%

To determine the importance of this uncertainty, we recalculate the NPV of the HomeNet project under the best- and worst-case assumptions for each parameter. For example, if the number of units sold is only 70,000 per year, the NPV of the project falls to $-$2.4 million. We repeat this calculation for each parameter. The result is shown in Figure 7.1, which reveals that the most important parameter assumptions are the number of units sold and the sale price per unit. These assumptions deserve the greatest scrutiny during the estimation process. In addition, as the most important drivers of the project's value, these factors deserve close attention when managing the project.

HomeNet's NPV Under Best- and Worst-Case Parameter Assumptions

Green bars show the change in NPV under the best-case assumption for each parameter; red bars show the change under the worst-case assumption. Also shown are the break-even levels for each parameter. Under the initial assumptions, HomeNet's NPV is $5.0 million.

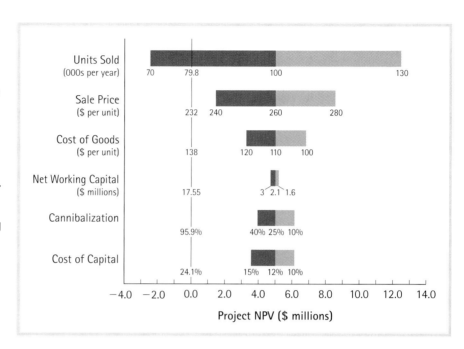

Sensitivity to Marketing and Support Costs

Problem

The current forecast for HomeNet's marketing and support costs is $3 million per year during years 1–4. Suppose the marketing and support costs may be as high as $4 million per year. What is HomeNet's NPV in this case?

Solution

We can answer this question by changing the selling, general, and administrative expense to $4 million in Table 7.3 Spreadsheet and computing the NPV of the resulting free cash flow. We can also calculate the impact of this change as follows: A $1 million increase in marketing and support costs will reduce EBIT by $1 million and will, therefore, decrease HomeNet's free cash flow by an after-tax amount of $1 million × (1 − 40%) = $0.6 million per year. The present value of this decrease is

$$PV = \frac{-0.6}{1.12} + \frac{-0.6}{1.12^2} + \frac{-0.6}{1.12^3} + \frac{-0.6}{1.12^4} = -\$1.8 \text{ million}$$

HomeNet's NPV would fall to $5.0 million − $1.8 million = $3.2 million.

Scenario Analysis

In the analysis thus far, we have considered the consequences of varying only one parameter at a time. In reality, certain factors may affect more than one parameter. **Scenario analysis** considers the effect on NPV of changing multiple project parameters. For example, lowering HomeNet's price may increase the number of units sold. We can use scenario

TABLE 7.10	**Scenario Analysis of Alternative Pricing Strategies**		
Strategy	**Sale Price ($/unit)**	**Expected Units Sold (thousands)**	**NPV ($ thousands)**
Current strategy	260	100	5027
Price reduction	245	110	4582
Price increase	275	90	4937

FIGURE 7.2

Price and Volume Combinations for HomeNet with Equivalent NPV

The graph shows alternative price per unit and annual volume combinations that lead to an NPV of $5.0 million. Pricing strategies with combinations above this line will lead to a higher NPV and are superior.

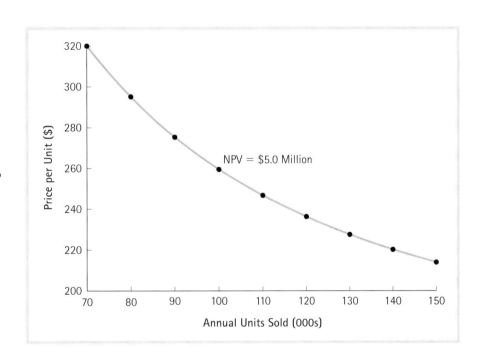

analysis to evaluate alternative pricing strategies for the HomeNet product in Table 7.10. In this case, the current strategy is optimal. Figure 7.2 shows the combinations of price and volume that lead to the same NPV of $5 million for HomeNet as the current strategy. Only strategies with price and volume combinations above the line will lead to a higher NPV.

CONCEPT CHECK   **1.** What is sensitivity analysis?

2. How does scenario analysis differ from sensitivity analysis?

Summary

1. Capital budgeting is the process of analyzing investment opportunities and deciding which ones to accept. A capital budget is a list of all projects that a company plans to undertake during the next period.

2. We use the NPV rule to evaluate capital budgeting decisions, making decisions that maximize NPV. When deciding to accept or reject a project, we accept projects with a positive NPV.

3. The incremental earnings of a project comprise the amount by which the project is expected to change the firm's earnings.

4. Incremental earnings should include all incremental revenues and costs associated with the project, including project externalities and opportunity costs, but excluding sunk costs and interest expenses.

   a. Project externalities are cash flows that occur when a project affects other areas of the company's business.

   b. An opportunity cost is the cost of using an existing asset.

   c. A sunk cost is an unrecoverable cost that has already been incurred.

   d. Interest and other financing-related expenses are excluded to determine the project's unlevered net income.

5. We estimate taxes using the marginal tax rate, based on the net income generated by the rest of the firm's operations, as well as any tax loss carrybacks or carryforwards.

6. We compute free cash flow from incremental earnings by eliminating all non-cash expenses and including all capital investment.

   a. Depreciation is not a cash expense, so it is added back.

   b. Actual capital expenditures are deducted.

   c. Increases in net working capital are deducted. Net working capital is defined as

   $$\text{Cash} + \text{Inventory} + \text{Receivables} - \text{Payables} \tag{7.3}$$

7. The basic calculation for free cash flow is

$$\text{Free Cash Flow} = \overbrace{(\text{Revenues} - \text{Costs} - \text{Depreciation}) \times (1 - \tau_c)}^{\text{Unlevered Net Income}}$$
$$+ \text{Depreciation} - \text{CapEx} - \Delta NWC \tag{7.5}$$

   Free cash flow should also include the (after-tax) liquidation or salvage value of any assets that are disposed of. It may also include a terminal (continuation) value if the project continues beyond the forecast horizon.

8. Depreciation expenses affect free cash flow only through the depreciation tax shield. The firm should use the most accelerated depreciation schedule possible.

9. The discount rate for a project is its cost of capital: The expected return of securities with comparable risk and horizon.

10. Break-even analysis computes the level of a parameter that makes the project's NPV equal zero.

11. Sensitivity analysis breaks the NPV calculation down into its component assumptions, showing how the NPV varies as the values of the underlying assumptions change.

12. Scenario analysis considers the effect of changing multiple parameters simultaneously.

Key Terms

break-even *p. 196*
break-even analysis *p. 196*
cannibalization *p. 183*
capital budget *p. 178*
capital budgeting *p. 178*
depreciation tax shield *p. 189*
EBIT break-even *p. 197*
free cash flow *p. 186*
incremental earnings *p. 178*
MACRS depreciation *p. 192*
marginal corporate tax rate *p. 181*

opportunity cost *p. 182*
overhead expenses *p. 184*
project externalities *p. 182*
scenario analysis *p. 198*
sensitivity analysis *p. 197*
straight-line depreciation *p. 180*
sunk cost *p. 184*
tax loss carryforwards and carrybacks *p. 195*
terminal (continuation value) *p. 194*
trade credit *p. 187*
unlevered net income *p. 181*

Further Reading

For an excellent overview of the history of the concept of present value and its use in capital budgeting, see M. Rubinstein, "Great Moments in Financial Economics: I. Present Value," *Journal of Investment Management* (First Quarter 2003).

Irving Fisher was one of the first to apply the Law of One Price to propose that any capital project should be evaluated in terms of its present value; see I. Fisher, *The Rate of Interest: Its Nature, Determination and Relation to Economic Phenomena* (New York: Macmillan, 1907). I. Fisher, *The Theory of Interest: As Determined by Impatience to Spend Income and Opportunity to Invest It* (New York: Macmillan, 1930); reprinted (New York: Augustus M. Kelley, 1955).

The use of this approach for capital budgeting was later popularized in the following book: J. Dean, *Capital Budgeting* (New York: Columbia University Press, 1951).

We will revisit the topics of this chapter in greater depth in Part VI of this book. Additional readings for more advanced topics will be provided there.

Problems

All problems in this chapter are available in MyFinanceLab. An asterisk (*) indicates problems with a higher level of difficulty.

Forecasting Earnings

1. Pisa Pizza, a seller of frozen pizza, is considering introducing a healthier version of its pizza that will be low in cholesterol and contain no trans fats. The firm expects that sales of the new pizza will be $20 million per year. While many of these sales will be to new customers, Pisa Pizza estimates that 40% will come from customers who switch to the new, healthier pizza instead of buying the original version.

    a. Assume customers will spend the same amount on either version. What level of incremental sales is associated with introducing the new pizza?

    b. Suppose that 50% of the customers who will switch from Pisa Pizza's original pizza to its healthier pizza will switch to another brand if Pisa Pizza does not introduce a healthier pizza. What level of incremental sales is associated with introducing the new pizza in this case?

2. Kokomochi is considering the launch of an advertising campaign for its latest dessert product, the Mini Mochi Munch. Kokomochi plans to spend $5 million on TV, radio, and print advertising this year for the campaign. The ads are expected to boost sales of the Mini Mochi Munch by $9 million this year and by $7 million next year. In addition, the company expects that new consumers who try the Mini Mochi Munch will be more likely to try Kokomochi's other products. As a result, sales of other products are expected to rise by $2 million each year.

   Kokomochi's gross profit margin for the Mini Mochi Munch is 35%, and its gross profit margin averages 25% for all other products. The company's marginal corporate tax rate is 35% both this year and next year. What are the incremental earnings associated with the advertising campaign?

3. Home Builder Supply, a retailer in the home improvement industry, currently operates seven retail outlets in Georgia and South Carolina. Management is contemplating building an eighth retail store across town from its most successful retail outlet. The company already owns the land for this store, which currently has an abandoned warehouse located on it. Last month, the marketing department spent $10,000 on market research to determine the extent of customer demand for the new store. Now Home Builder Supply must decide whether to build and open the new store.

   Which of the following should be included as part of the incremental earnings for the proposed new retail store?

   a. The cost of the land where the store will be located.

   b. The cost of demolishing the abandoned warehouse and clearing the lot.

   c. The loss of sales in the existing retail outlet, if customers who previously drove across town to shop at the existing outlet become customers of the new store instead.

   d. The $10,000 in market research spent to evaluate customer demand.

   e. Construction costs for the new store.

   f. The value of the land if sold.

   g. Interest expense on the debt borrowed to pay the construction costs.

4. Hyperion, Inc., currently sells its latest high-speed color printer, the Hyper 500, for $350. It plans to lower the price to $300 next year. Its cost of goods sold for the Hyper 500 is $200 per unit, and this year's sales are expected to be 20,000 units.

   a. Suppose that if Hyperion drops the price to $300 immediately, it can increase this year's sales by 25% to 25,000 units. What would be the incremental impact on this year's EBIT of such a price drop?

   b. Suppose that for each printer sold, Hyperion expects additional sales of $75 per year on ink cartridges for the next three years, and Hyperion has a gross profit margin of 70% on ink cartridges. What is the incremental impact on EBIT for the next three years of a price drop this year?

5. Castle View Games would like to invest in a division to develop software for video games. To evaluate this decision, the firm first attempts to project the working capital needs for this operation. Its chief financial officer has developed the following estimates (in millions of dollars):

	Year 1	Year 2	Year 3	Year 4	Year 5
Cash	6	12	15	15	15
Accounts receivable	21	22	24	24	24
Inventory	5	7	10	12	13
Accounts payable	18	22	24	25	30

Assuming that Castle View currently does not have any working capital invested in this division, calculate the cash flows associated with changes in working capital for the first five years of this investment.

6. Elmdale Enterprises is deciding whether to expand its production facilities. Although long-term cash flows are difficult to estimate, management has projected the following cash flows for the first two years (in millions of dollars):

	Year 1	Year 2
Revenues	125	160
Operating expenses (other than depreciation)	40	60
Depreciation	25	36
Increase in working capital	5	8
Capital expenditures	30	40
Marginal corporate tax rate	35%	35%

a. What are the incremental earnings for this project for years 1 and 2?

b. What are the free cash flows for this project for the first two years?

EXCEL 7. You are a manager at Percolated Fiber, which is considering expanding its operations in synthetic fiber manufacturing. Your boss comes into your office, drops a consultant's report on your desk, and complains, "We owe these consultants $1 million for this report, and I am not sure their analysis makes sense. Before we spend the $25 million on new equipment needed for this project, look it over and give me your opinion." You open the report and find the following estimates (in millions of dollars):

	Project Year				
	1	2	...	9	10
Sales revenue	30,000	30,000		30,000	30,000
− Cost of goods sold	18,000	18,000		18,000	18,000
= Gross profit	12,000	12,000		12,000	12,000
− General, sales, and administrative expenses	2,000	2,000		2,000	2,000
− Depreciation	2,500	2,500		2,500	2,500
= Net operating income	7,500	7,500		7,500	7,500
− Income tax	2,625	2,625		2,625	2,625
= Net income	4,875	4,875		4,875	4,875

All of the estimates in the report seem correct. You note that the consultants used straight-line depreciation for the new equipment that will be purchased today (year 0), which is what the accounting department recommended. The report concludes that because the project will increase earnings by $4.875 million per year for ten years, the project is worth $48.75 million. You think back to your halcyon days in finance class and realize there is more work to be done!

First, you note that the consultants have not factored in the fact that the project will require $10 million in working capital upfront (year 0), which will be fully recovered in year 10. Next, you see they have attributed $2 million of selling, general and administrative expenses to the project, but you know that $1 million of this amount is overhead that will be incurred even if the project is not accepted. Finally, you know that accounting earnings are not the right thing to focus on!

   a. Given the available information, what are the free cash flows in years 0 through 10 that should be used to evaluate the proposed project?

   b. If the cost of capital for this project is 14%, what is your estimate of the value of the new project?

8. Cellular Access, Inc., is a cellular telephone service provider that reported net income of $250 million for the most recent fiscal year. The firm had depreciation expenses of $100 million, capital expenditures of $200 million, and no interest expenses. Working capital increased by $10 million. Calculate the free cash flow for Cellular Access for the most recent fiscal year.

9. Markov Manufacturing recently spent $15 million to purchase some equipment used in the manufacture of disk drives. The firm expects that this equipment will have a useful life of five years, and its marginal corporate tax rate is 35%. The company plans to use straight-line depreciation.

   a. What is the annual depreciation expense associated with this equipment?

   b. What is the annual depreciation tax shield?

   c. Rather than straight-line depreciation, suppose Markov will use the MACRS depreciation method for five-year property. Calculate the depreciation tax shield each year for this equipment under this accelerated depreciation schedule.

   d. If Markov has a choice between straight-line and MACRS depreciation schedules, and its marginal corporate tax rate is expected to remain constant, which should it choose? Why?

   e. How might your answer to part (d) change if Markov anticipates that its marginal corporate tax rate will increase substantially over the next five years?

10. Bay Properties is considering starting a commercial real estate division. It has prepared the following four-year forecast of free cash flows for this division:

	Year 1	**Year 2**	**Year 3**	**Year 4**
Free cash flow	−$185,000	−$12,000	$99,000	$240,000

Assume cash flows after year 4 will grow at 3% per year, forever. If the cost of capital for this division is 14%, what is the continuation value in year 4 for cash flows after year 4? What is the value today of this division?

11. Your firm would like to evaluate a proposed new operating division. You have forecasted cash flows for this division for the next five years, and have estimated that the cost of capital is 12%. You would like to estimate a continuation value. You have made the following forecasts for the last year of your five-year forecasting horizon (in millions of dollars):

	Year 5
Revenues	1,200
Operating income	100
Net income	50
Free cash flows	110
Book value of equity	400

   a. You forecast that future free cash flows after year 5 will grow at 2% per year, forever. Estimate the continuation value in year 5, using the perpetuity with growth formula.

   b. You have identified several firms in the same industry as your operating division. The average P/E ratio for these firms is 30. Estimate the continuation value assuming the

P/E ratio for your division in year 5 will be the same as the average P/E ratio for the comparable firms today.

c. The average market/book ratio for the comparable firms is 4.0. Estimate the continuation value using the market/book ratio.

EXCEL **12.** One year ago, your company purchased a machine used in manufacturing for $110,000. You have learned that a new machine is available that offers many advantages; you can purchase it for $150,000 today. It will be depreciated on a straight-line basis over ten years and has no salvage value. You expect that the new machine will produce a gross margin (revenues minus operating expenses other than depreciation) of $40,000 per year for the next ten years. The current machine is expected to produce a gross margin of $20,000 per year. The current machine is being depreciated on a straight-line basis over a useful life of 11 years, and has no salvage value, so depreciation expense for the current machine is $10,000 per year. The market value today of the current machine is $50,000. Your company's tax rate is 45%, and the opportunity cost of capital for this type of equipment is 10%. Should your company replace its year-old machine?

EXCEL **13.** Beryl's Iced Tea currently rents a bottling machine for $50,000 per year, including all maintenance expenses. It is considering purchasing a machine instead, and is comparing two options:

a. Purchase the machine it is currently renting for $150,000. This machine will require $20,000 per year in ongoing maintenance expenses.

b. Purchase a new, more advanced machine for $250,000. This machine will require $15,000 per year in ongoing maintenance expenses and will lower bottling costs by $10,000 per year. Also, $35,000 will be spent upfront in training the new operators of the machine.

Suppose the appropriate discount rate is 8% per year and the machine is purchased today. Maintenance and bottling costs are paid at the end of each year, as is the rental of the machine. Assume also that the machines will be depreciated via the straight-line method over seven years and that they have a ten-year life with a negligible salvage value. The marginal corporate tax rate is 35%. Should Beryl's Iced Tea continue to rent, purchase its current machine, or purchase the advanced machine?

Analyzing the Project

14. Bauer Industries is an automobile manufacturer. Management is currently evaluating a proposal to build a plant that will manufacture lightweight trucks. Bauer plans to use a cost of capital of 12% to evaluate this project. Based on extensive research, it has prepared the following incremental free cash flow projections (in millions of dollars):

	Year 0	Years 1–9	Year 10
Revenues		100.0	100.0
− Manufacturing expenses (other than depreciation)		−35.0	−35.0
− Marketing expenses		−10.0	−10.0
− Depreciation		−15.0	−15.0
= EBIT		40.0	40.0
− Taxes (35%)		−14.0	−14.0
= Unlevered net income		26.0	26.0
+ Depreciation		+15.0	+15.0
− Additions to working capital		−5.0	−5.0
− Capital expenditures	−150.0		
+ Continuation value			+12.0
= Free cash flow	−150.0	36.0	48.0

As Figure 8.2 demonstrates, prior to maturity the bond is exposed to interest rate risk. If an investor chooses to sell and the bond's yield to maturity has decreased, then the investor will receive a high price and earn a high return. If the yield to maturity has increased, the bond price is low at the time of sale and the investor will earn a low return. In the appendix to this chapter, we discuss one way corporations manage this type of risk.

CONCEPT CHECK   1. If a bond's yield to maturity does not change, how does its cash price change between coupon payments?

2. What risk does an investor in a default-free bond face if she plans to sell the bond prior to maturity?

8.3   The Yield Curve and Bond Arbitrage

Thus far, we have focused on the relationship between the price of an individual bond and its yield to maturity. In this section, we explore the relationship between the prices and yields of different bonds. Using the Law of One Price, we show that given the spot interest rates, which are the yields of default-free zero-coupon bonds, we can determine the price and yield of any other default-free bond. As a result, the yield curve provides sufficient information to evaluate all such bonds.

Replicating a Coupon Bond

Because it is possible to replicate the cash flows of a coupon bond using zero-coupon bonds, we can use the Law of One price to compute the price of a coupon bond from the prices of zero-coupon bonds. For example, we can replicate a three-year, $1000 bond that pays 10% annual coupons using three zero-coupon bonds as follows:

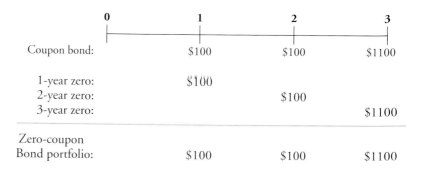

We match each coupon payment to a zero-coupon bond with a face value equal to the coupon payment and a term equal to the time remaining to the coupon date. Similarly, we match the final bond payment (final coupon plus return of face value) in three years to a three-year, zero-coupon bond with a corresponding face value of $1100. Because the coupon bond cash flows are identical to the cash flows of the portfolio of zero-coupon bonds, the Law of One Price states that the price of the portfolio of zero-coupon bonds must be the same as the price of the coupon bond.

TABLE 8.2	Yields and Prices (per $100 Face Value) for Zero-Coupon Bonds			
Maturity	**1 year**	**2 years**	**3 years**	**4 years**
YTM	3.50%	4.00%	4.50%	4.75%
Price	$96.62	$92.45	$87.63	$83.06

To illustrate, assume that current zero-coupon bond yields and prices are as shown in Table 8.2 (they are the same as in Example 8.1). We can calculate the cost of the zero-coupon bond portfolio that replicates the three-year coupon bond as follows:

Zero-Coupon Bond	Face Value Required	Cost
1 year	100	96.62
2 years	100	92.45
3 years	1100	$11 \times 87.63 = 963.93$
	Total Cost:	**$1153.00**

By the Law of One Price, the three-year coupon bond must trade for a price of $1153. If the price of the coupon bond were higher, you could earn an arbitrage profit by selling the coupon bond and buying the zero-coupon bond portfolio. If the price of the coupon bond were lower, you could earn an arbitrage profit by buying the coupon bond and short selling the zero-coupon bonds.

Valuing a Coupon Bond Using Zero-Coupon Yields

To this point, we have used the zero-coupon bond *prices* to derive the price of the coupon bond. Alternatively, we can use the zero-coupon bond *yields*. Recall that the yield to maturity of a zero-coupon bond is the competitive market interest rate for a risk-free investment with a term equal to the term of the zero-coupon bond. Therefore, the price of a coupon bond must equal the present value of its coupon payments and face value discounted at the competitive market interest rates (see Eq. 5.7 in Chapter 5):

Price of a Coupon Bond

$$P = PV(\text{Bond Cash Flows})$$

$$= \frac{CPN}{1 + YTM_1} + \frac{CPN}{(1 + YTM_2)^2} + \cdots + \frac{CPN + FV}{(1 + YTM_n)^n} \tag{8.6}$$

where CPN is the bond coupon payment, YTM_n is the yield to maturity of a *zero-coupon* bond that matures at the same time as the nth coupon payment, and FV is the face value of the bond. For the three-year, $1000 bond with 10% annual coupons considered earlier, we can use Eq. 8.6 to calculate its price using the zero-coupon yields in Table 8.2:

$$P = \frac{100}{1.035} + \frac{100}{1.04^2} + \frac{100 + 1000}{1.045^3} = \$1153$$

This price is identical to the price we computed earlier by replicating the bond. Thus we can determine the no-arbitrage price of a coupon bond by discounting its cash flows using the zero-coupon yields. In other words, the information in the zero-coupon yield curve is sufficient to price all other risk-free bonds.

Coupon Bond Yields

Given the yields for zero-coupon bonds, we can use Eq. 8.6 to price a coupon bond. In Section 8.1, we saw how to compute the yield to maturity of a coupon bond from its price. Combining these results, we can determine the relationship between the yields of zero-coupon bonds and coupon-paying bonds.

Consider again the three-year, $1000 bond with 10% annual coupons. Given the zero-coupon yields in Table 8.2, we calculate a price for this bond of $1153. From Eq. 8.5, the yield to maturity of this bond is the rate y that satisfies

$$P = 1153 = \frac{100}{(1 + y)} + \frac{100}{(1 + y)^2} + \frac{100 + 1000}{(1 + y)^3}$$

We can solve for the yield by using the annuity spreadsheet:

	NPER	RATE	PV	PMT	FV	Excel Formula
Given	3		−1,153	100	1,000	
Solve for Rate		4.44%				=RATE(3,100,−1153,1000)

Therefore, the yield to maturity of the bond is 4.44%. We can check this result directly as follows:

$$P = \frac{100}{1.0444} + \frac{100}{1.0444^2} + \frac{100 + 1000}{1.0444^3} = \$1153$$

Because the coupon bond provides cash flows at different points in time, the yield to maturity of a coupon bond is a weighted average of the yields of the zero-coupon bonds of equal and shorter maturities. The weights depend (in a complex way) on the magnitude of the cash flows each period. In this example, the zero-coupon bonds yields were 3.5%, 4.0%, and 4.5%. For this coupon bond, most of the value in the present value calculation comes from the present value of the third cash flow because it includes the principal, so the yield is closest to the three-year, zero-coupon yield of 4.5%.

EXAMPLE 8.8

Yields on Bonds with the Same Maturity

Problem

Given the following zero-coupon yields, compare the yield to maturity for a three-year, zero-coupon bond; a three-year, coupon bond with 4% annual coupons; and a three-year coupon bond with 10% annual coupons. All of these bonds are default free.

Maturity	1 year	2 years	3 years	4 years
Zero-coupon YTM	3.50%	4.00%	4.50%	4.75%

Solution

From the information provided, the yield to maturity of the three-year, zero-coupon bond is 4.50%. Also, because the yields match those in Table 8.2, we already calculated the yield to maturity for the 10% coupon bond as 4.44%. To compute the yield for the 4% coupon bond, we first need to calculate its price. Using Eq. 8.6, we have

$$P = \frac{40}{1.035} + \frac{40}{1.04^2} + \frac{40 + 1000}{1.045^3} = \$986.98$$

The price of the bond with a 4% coupon is $986.98. From Eq. 8.5, its yield to maturity solves the following equation:

$$\$986.98 = \frac{40}{(1 + y)} + \frac{40}{(1 + y)^2} + \frac{40 + 1000}{(1 + y)^3}$$

We can calculate the yield to maturity using the annuity spreadsheet:

	NPER	RATE	PV	PMT	FV	Excel Formula
Given	3		−986.98	40	1,000	
Solve for Rate		4.47%				= RATE(3, 40, −986.98, 1000)

To summarize, for the three-year bonds considered,

Coupon rate	0%	4%	10%
YTM	4.50%	4.47%	4.44%

Example 8.8 shows that coupon bonds with the same maturity can have different yields depending on their coupon rates. The yield to maturity of a coupon bond is a weighted average of the yields on the zero-coupon bonds. As the coupon increases, earlier cash flows become relatively more important than later cash flows in the calculation of the present value. If the yield curve is upward sloping (as it is for the yields in Example 8.8), the resulting yield to maturity decreases with the coupon rate of the bond. Alternatively, when the zero-coupon yield curve is downward sloping, the yield to maturity will increase with the coupon rate. When the yield curve is flat, all zero-coupon and coupon-paying bonds will have the same yield, independent of their maturities and coupon rates.

Treasury Yield Curves

As we have shown in this section, we can use the zero-coupon yield curve to determine the price and yield to maturity of other risk-free bonds. The plot of the yields of coupon bonds of different maturities is called the **coupon-paying yield curve**. When U.S. bond traders refer to "the yield curve," they are often referring to the coupon-paying Treasury yield curve. As we showed in Example 8.8, two coupon-paying bonds with the same maturity may have different yields. By convention, practitioners always plot the yield of the most recently issued bonds, termed the **on-the-run bonds**. Using similar methods to those employed in this section, we can apply the Law of One Price to determine the zero-coupon bond yields using the coupon-paying yield curve (see Problem 22). Thus either type of yield curve provides enough information to value all other risk-free bonds.

CONCEPT CHECK 1. Why does the zero-coupon yield curve for the default-free bonds provide sufficient information to value all other default-free bonds?

2. Explain why two coupon bonds with the same maturity may each have a different yield to maturity.

8.4 Corporate Bonds

So far in this chapter, we have focused on default-free bonds such as U.S. Treasury securities, for which the cash flows are known with certainty. For other bonds such as **corporate bonds** (bonds issued by corporations), the issuer may default—that is, it might not pay back the full amount promised in the bond prospectus. This risk of default, which is known as the **credit risk** of the bond, means that the bond's cash flows are not known with certainty.

Corporate Bond Yields

How does the credit risk of default affect bond prices and yields? Because the cash flows promised by the bond are the most that bondholders can hope to receive, the cash flows that a purchaser of a bond with credit risk *expects* to receive may be less than that amount. As a result, investors pay less for bonds with credit risk than they would for an otherwise identical default-free bond. Because the yield to maturity for a bond is calculated using the *promised* cash flows, the yield of bonds with credit risk will be higher than that of otherwise identical default-free bonds. Let's illustrate the effect of credit risk on bond yields and investor returns by comparing different cases.

No Default. Suppose that the one-year, zero-coupon Treasury bill has a yield to maturity of 4%. What are the price and yield of a one-year, $1000, zero-coupon bond issued by Avant Corporation? First, suppose that all investors agree that there is *no* possibility that Avant will default within the next year. In that case, investors will receive $1000 in one year for certain, as promised by the bond. Because this bond is risk free, the Law of One Price guarantees that it must have the same yield as the one-year, zero-coupon Treasury bill. The price of the bond will therefore be

$$P = \frac{1000}{1 + YTM_1} = \frac{1000}{1.04} = \$961.54$$

Certain Default. Now suppose that investors believe that Avant will default with certainty at the end of one year and will be able to pay only 90% of its outstanding obligations. Then, even though the bond promises $1000 at year-end, bondholders know they will receive only $900. Investors can predict this shortfall perfectly, so the $900 payment is risk free, and the bond is still a one-year risk-free investment. We therefore compute the price of the bond by discounting this cash flow using the risk-free interest rate as the cost of capital:

$$P = \frac{900}{1 + YTM_1} = \frac{900}{1.04} = \$865.38$$

The prospect of default lowers the cash flow investors expect to receive and hence the price they are willing to pay.

Given the bond's price, we can compute the bond's yield to maturity. When computing this yield, we use the *promised* rather than the *actual* cash flows. Thus

$$YTM = \frac{FV}{P} - 1 = \frac{1000}{865.38} - 1 = 15.56\%$$

The 15.56% yield to maturity of Avant's bond is much higher than the yield to maturity of the default-free Treasury bill. But this result does not mean that investors who buy the bond will earn a 15.56% return. Because Avant will default, the expected return of the bond equals its 4% cost of capital:

$$\frac{900}{865.38} = 1.04$$

Note that *the yield to maturity of a defaultable bond is not equal to the expected return of investing in the bond.* Because we calculate the yield to maturity using the promised cash flows rather than the expected cash flows, the yield will always be higher than the expected return of investing in the bond.

Risk of Default.   The two Avant examples were extreme cases, of course. In the first case, we assumed the probability of default was zero; in the second case, we assumed Avant would definitely default. In reality, the chance that Avant will default lies somewhere in between these two extremes (and for most firms, is probably much closer to zero).

To illustrate, again consider the one-year, $1000, zero-coupon bond issued by Avant. This time, assume that the bond payoffs are uncertain. In particular, there is a 50% chance that the bond will repay its face value in full and a 50% chance that the bond will default and you will receive $900. Thus, on average, you will receive $950.

To determine the price of this bond, we must discount this expected cash flow using a cost of capital equal to the expected return of other securities with equivalent risk. If Avant is more likely to default if the economy is weak than if the economy is strong, the results of Chapter 3 suggest that investors will demand a risk premium to invest in this bond. Thus Avant's debt cost of capital, which is the expected return Avant's debt holders will require to compensate them for the risk of the bond's cash flows, will be higher than the 4% risk-free interest rate.

Let's suppose investors demand a risk premium of 1.1% for this bond, so that the appropriate cost of capital is 5.1%. Then the present value of the bond's cash flow is

$$P = \frac{950}{1.051} = \$903.90$$

Consequently, in this case the bond's yield to maturity is 10.63%:

$$YTM = \frac{FV}{P} - 1 = \frac{1000}{903.90} - 1 = 1.1063$$

Of course, the 10.63% promised yield is the most investors will receive. If Avant defaults, they will receive only $900, for a return of $900 / 903.90 - 1 = -0.43\%$. The average return is $0.50(10.63\%) + 0.50(-0.43\%) = 5.1\%$, the bond's cost of capital.

*20. Prices of zero-coupon, default-free securities with face values of $1000 are summarized in the following table.

Maturity (years)	1	2	3
Price (per $1000 face value)	$970.87	$938.95	$904.56

Suppose you observe that a three-year, default-free security with an annual coupon rate of 10% and a face value of $1000 has a price today of $1183.50. Is there an arbitrage opportunity? If so, show specifically how you would take advantage of this opportunity. If not, why not?

*21. Assume there are four default-free bonds with the following prices and future cash flows:

Bond	Price Today	Cash Flows		
		Year 1	Year 2	Year 3
A	$ 934.58	1,000	0	0
B	881.66	0	1,000	0
C	1,118.21	100	100	1,100
D	839.62	0	0	1,000

Do these bonds present an arbitrage opportunity? If so, how would you take advantage of this opportunity? If not, why not?

EXCEL *22. Suppose you are given the following information about the default-free, coupon-paying yield curve:

Maturity (years)	1	2	3	4
Coupon rate (annual payments)	0.00%	10.00%	6.00%	12.00%
YTM	2.000%	3.908%	5.840%	5.783%

a. Use arbitrage to determine the yield to maturity of a two-year, zero-coupon bond.
b. What is the zero-coupon yield curve for years 1 through 4?

Corporate Bonds

23. Explain why the expected return of a corporate bond does not equal its yield to maturity.

24. The following table summarizes the yields to maturity on several one-year, zero-coupon securities:

Security	Yield (%)
Treasury	3.1
AAA corporate	3.2
BBB corporate	4.2
B corporate	4.9

a. What is the price (expressed as a percentage of the face value) of a one-year, zero-coupon corporate bond with a AAA rating?
b. What is the credit spread on AAA-rated corporate bonds?
c. What is the credit spread on B-rated corporate bonds?
d. How does the credit spread change with the bond rating? Why?

25. Andrew Industries is contemplating issuing a 30-year bond with a coupon rate of 7% (annual coupon payments) and a face value of $1000. Andrew believes it can get a rating of A from

Standard and Poor's. However, due to recent financial difficulties at the company, Standard and Poor's is warning that it may downgrade Andrew Industries bonds to BBB. Yields on A-rated, long-term bonds are currently 6.5%, and yields on BBB-rated bonds are 6.9%.

   a. What is the price of the bond if Andrew maintains the A rating for the bond issue?

   b. What will the price of the bond be if it is downgraded?

EXCEL   **26.** HMK Enterprises would like to raise $10 million to invest in capital expenditures. The company plans to issue five-year bonds with a face value of $1000 and a coupon rate of 6.5% (annual payments). The following table summarizes the yield to maturity for five-year (annual-pay) coupon corporate bonds of various ratings:

Rating	AAA	AA	A	BBB	BB
YTM	6.20%	6.30%	6.50%	6.90%	7.50%

   a. Assuming the bonds will be rated AA, what will the price of the bonds be?

   b. How much total principal amount of these bonds must HMK issue to raise $10 million today, assuming the bonds are AA rated? (Because HMK cannot issue a fraction of a bond, assume that all fractions are rounded to the nearest whole number.)

   c. What must the rating of the bonds be for them to sell at par?

   d. Suppose that when the bonds are issued, the price of each bond is $959.54. What is the likely rating of the bonds? Are they junk bonds?

   27. A BBB-rated corporate bond has a yield to maturity of 8.2%. A U.S. Treasury security has a yield to maturity of 6.5%. These yields are quoted as APRs with semiannual compounding. Both bonds pay semiannual coupons at a rate of 7% and have five years to maturity.

   a. What is the price (expressed as a percentage of the face value) of the Treasury bond?

   b. What is the price (expressed as a percentage of the face value) of the BBB-rated corporate bond?

   c. What is the credit spread on the BBB bonds?

Data Case

You are an intern with Sirius Satellite Radio in their corporate finance division. The firm is planning to issue $50 million of 12% annual coupon bonds with a ten-year maturity. The firm anticipates an increase in its bond rating. Your boss wants you to determine the gain in the proceeds of the new issue if the issue is rated above the firm's current bond rating. To prepare this information, you will have to determine Sirius' current debt rating and the yield curve for their particular rating. Strangely, no one at Sirius seems to have this information; apparently they are still busy trying to figure out who decided it was a good idea to hire Howard Stern.

   1. Begin by finding the current U.S. Treasury yield curve. At the Treasury Web site (www .treas.gov), search using the term "yield curve" and select "US Treasury—Daily Treasury Yield Curve." *Beware:* There will likely be two links with the same title. Look at the description below the link and select the one that does NOT say "Real Yield . . ." You want the nominal rates. The correct link is likely to be the first link on the page. Download that table into Excel by right clicking with the cursor in the table and selecting "Export to Microsoft Excel."

   2. Find the current yield spreads for the various bond ratings. Unfortunately, the current spreads are available only for a fee, so you will use old ones. Go to BondsOnline (www.bondsonline.com) and click on "Today's Market." Next click on "Corporate Bond

Spreads." Download this table to Excel and copy and paste it to the same file as the Treasury yields.

3. Find the current bond rating for Sirius. Go to Standard & Poor's Web site (www. standardandpoors.com). Select "Find a Rating" from the list at the left of the page, then select "Credit Ratings Search." At this point you will have to register (it's free) or enter the username and password provided by your instructor. Next you will be able to search by Organization Name—enter Sirius and select Sirius Satellite Radio. Use the credit rating for the organization, not the specific issue ratings.

4. Return to Excel and create a timeline with the cash flows and discount rates you will need to value the new bond issue.

   a. To create the required spot rates for Sirius' issue add the appropriate spread to the Treasury yield of the same maturity.

   b. The yield curve and spread rates you have found do not cover every year that you will need for the new bonds. Specifically, you do not have yields or spreads for four-, six-, eight-, and nine-year maturities. Fill these in by linearly interpolating the given yields and spreads. For example, the four-year spot rate and spread will be the average of the three- and five-year rates. The six-year rate and spread will be the average of the five- and seven-year rates. For years eight and nine you will have to spread the difference between years seven and ten across the two years.

   c. To compute the spot rates for Sirius' current debt rating, add the yield spread to the Treasury rate for each maturity. However, note that the spread is in basis points, which are 1/100th of a percentage point.

   d. Compute the cash flows that would be paid to bondholders each year and add them to the timeline.

5. Use the spot rates to calculate the present value of each cash flow paid to the bondholders.

6. Compute the issue price of the bond and its initial yield to maturity.

7. Repeat steps 4–6 based on the assumption that Sirius is able to raise its bond rating by one level. Compute the new yield based on the higher rating and the new bond price that would result.

8. Compute the additional cash proceeds that could be raised from the issue if the rating were improved.

notation

f_n one-year forward
rate for year n

Forward Interest Rates

Given the risk associated with interest rate changes, corporate managers require tools to help manage this risk. One of the most important is the interest rate forward contract. An **interest rate forward contract** (also called a **forward rate agreement**) is a contract today that fixes the interest rate for a loan or investment in the future. In this appendix, we explain how to derive forward interest rates from zero-coupon yields.

Computing Forward Rates

A **forward interest rate** (or **forward rate**) is an interest rate that we can guarantee today for a loan or investment that will occur in the future. Throughout this section, we will consider only interest rate forward contracts for investments of one year. For example, when we refer to the forward rate for year 5, we mean the rate available *today* on a one-year investment that begins four years from today and is repaid five years from today.

We can use the Law of One Price to calculate the forward rate from the zero-coupon yield curve. The forward rate for year 1 is the rate on an investment that starts today and is repaid in one year; it is equivalent to an investment in a one-year, zero-coupon bond. Therefore, by the Law of One Price, these rates must coincide:

$$f_1 = YTM_1 \tag{8A.1}$$

Now consider the two-year forward rate. Suppose the one-year, zero-coupon yield is 5.5% and the two-year, zero-coupon yield is 7.0%. There are two ways to invest money risk free for two years. First, we can invest in the two-year, zero-coupon bond at rate of 7.0% and earn $\$(1.07)^2$ after two years per dollar invested. Second, we can invest in the one-year bond at a rate of 5.5%, which will pay $1.055 at the end of one year, and simultaneously guarantee the interest rate we will earn by reinvesting the $1.055 for the second year by entering into an interest rate forward contract for year 2 at rate f_2. In that case, we will earn $\$(1.055)(1 + f_2)$ at the end of two years.

Because both strategies are risk free, by the Law of One Price, they must have the same return:

$$(1.07)^2 = (1.055)(1 + f_2)$$

Rearranging, we have

$$(1 + f_2) = \frac{1.07^2}{1.055} = 1.0852$$

Therefore, in this case the forward rate for year 2 is $f_2 = 8.52\%$.

In general, we can compute the forward rate for year n by comparing an investment in an n-year, zero-coupon bond to an investment in an $(n - 1)$ year, zero-coupon bond, with the interest rate earned in the nth year being guaranteed through an interest rate forward contract. Because both strategies are risk free, they must have the same payoff or else an arbitrage opportunity would be available. Comparing the payoffs of these strategies, we have

$$(1 + YTM_n)^n = (1 + YTM_{n-1})^{n-1}(1 + f_n)$$

We can rearrange this equation to find the general formula for the forward interest rate:

$$f_n = \frac{(1 + YTM_n)^n}{(1 + YTM_{n-1})^{n-1}} - 1 \tag{8A.2}$$

Computing Forward Rates

Problem

Calculate the forward rates for years 1 through 5 from the following zero-coupon yields:

Maturity	1	2	3	4
YTM	5.00%	6.00%	6.00%	5.75%

Solution

Using Eqs. 8A.1 and 8A.2:

$$f_1 = YTM_1 = 5.00\%$$

$$f_2 = \frac{(1 + YTM_2)^2}{(1 + YTM_1)} - 1 = \frac{1.06^2}{1.05} - 1 = 7.01\%$$

$$f_3 = \frac{(1 + YTM_3)^3}{(1 + YTM_2)^2} - 1 = \frac{1.06^3}{1.06^2} - 1 = 6.00\%$$

$$f_4 = \frac{(1 + YTM_4)^4}{(1 + YTM_3)^3} - 1 = \frac{1.0575^4}{1.06^3} - 1 = 5.00\%$$

Note that when the yield curve is increasing in year n (that is, when $YTM_n > YTM_{n-1}$), the forward rate is higher than the zero-coupon yield, $f_n > YTM_n$. Similarly, when the yield curve is decreasing, the forward rate is less than the zero-coupon yield. When the yield curve is flat, the forward rate equals the zero-coupon yield.

Computing Bond Yields from Forward Rates

Equation 8A.2 computes the forward interest rate using the zero-coupon yields. It is also possible to compute the zero-coupon yields from the forward interest rates. To see this, note that if we use interest rate forward contracts to lock in an interest rate for an investment in year 1, year 2, and so on through year n, we can create an n-year, risk-free investment. The return from this strategy must match the return from an n-year, zero-coupon bond. Therefore:

$$(1 + f_1) \times (1 + f_2) \times \cdots \times (1 + f_n) = (1 + YTM_n)^n \qquad (8A.3)$$

For example, using the forward rates from Example 8A.1, we can compute the four-year zero-coupon yield:

$$1 + YTM_4 = [(1 + f_1)(1 + f_2)(1 + f_3)(1 + f_4)]^{1/4}$$

$$= [(1.05)(1.0701)(1.06)(1.05)]^{1/4}$$

$$= 1.0575$$

Forward Rates and Future Interest Rates

A forward rate is the rate that you contract for today for an investment in the future. How does this rate compare to the interest rate that will actually prevail in the future? It is tempting to believe that the forward interest rate should be a good predictor of future interest rates. In reality, this will generally not be the case. Instead, it is a good predictor only when investors do not care about risk.

Forward Rates and Future Spot Rates

Problem

JoAnne Wilford is corporate treasurer for Wafer Thin Semiconductor. She must invest some of the cash on hand for two years in risk-free bonds. The current one-year, zero-coupon yield is 5%. The one-year forward rate is 6%. She is trying to decide between two possible strategies. The first strategy is risk free—she would invest the money for one year and guarantee the rate in the second year by entering into an interest rate forward contract. The second strategy is risky—she would invest in a risk-free asset for one year but would forgo the forward contract. Instead, she would take her chances and simply accept whatever one-year rate prevails in the market in one year. Under what conditions would she be better off following the risky strategy?

Solution

We first work out the future rate that would leave her indifferent. The risk-free strategy returns $(1.05)(1.06)$. The risky strategy returns $(1.05)(1 + r)$, where r is the one-year interest rate next year. If the future interest rate is 6%, then the two strategies will offer the same return. Thus Wafer Thin Semiconductor is better off with the risky strategy if the interest rate next year is greater than the forward rate—6%—and worse off if the interest rate is lower than 6%.

As Example 8A.2 makes clear, we can think of the forward rate as a break-even rate. If this rate actually prevails in the future, investors will be indifferent between investing in a two-year bond and investing in a one-year bond and rolling over the money in one year. If investors did not care about risk, then they would be indifferent between the two strategies whenever the expected one-year spot rate equals the current forward rate. However, investors *do* generally care about risk. If the expected returns of both strategies were the same, investors would prefer one strategy or the other depending on whether they want to be exposed to future interest rate risk fluctuations. In general, the expected future spot interest rate will reflect investors' preferences toward the risk of future interest rate fluctuations. Thus

$$\text{Expected Future Spot Interest Rate}$$
$$= \text{Forward Interest Rate} + \text{Risk Premium} \qquad (8A.4)$$

This risk premium can be either positive or negative depending on investors' preferences.[5] As a result, forward rates tend not be good predictors of future spot rates.

Key Terms

forward interest rate (forward rate) *p. 241*   interest rate forward contract *p. 241*
forward rate agreement *p. 241*

---

5. Empirical research suggests that the risk premium tends to be negative when the yield curve is upward sloping, and positive when it is downward sloping. See Eugene F. Fama and Robert R. Bliss, "The Information in Long-Maturity Forward Rates," *American Economic Review* 77(4) (1987): 680–692; and John Y. Campbell and Robert J. Shiller, "Yield Spreads and Interest Rate Movements: A Bird's Eye View," *Review of Economic Studies* 58(3) (1991): 495–514.

Problems

All problems in this Appendix are available in MyFinanceLab. An asterisk (*) indicates problems with a higher level of difficulty.

Problems A.1–A.4 refer to the following table:

Maturity (years)	1	2	3	4	5
Zero-coupon YTM	4.0%	5.5%	5.5%	5.0%	4.5%

A.1. What is the forward rate for year 2 (the forward rate quoted today for an investment that begins in one year and matures in two years)?

A.2. What is the forward rate for year 3 (the forward rate quoted today for an investment that begins in two years and matures in three years)? What can you conclude about forward rates when the yield curve is flat?

A.3. What is the forward rate for year 5 (the forward rate quoted today for an investment that begins in four years and matures in five years)?

*A.4.** Suppose you wanted to lock in an interest rate for an investment that begins in one year and matures in five years. What rate would you obtain if there are no arbitrage opportunities?

*A.5.** The yield on a one-year, zero-coupon bond is 5%. The forward rate for year 2 is 4%, and the forward rate for year 3 is 3%. What is the yield to maturity of a zero-coupon bond that matures in three years?

CHAPTER

9

Valuing Stocks

notation

P_t stock price at the end of year t

r_E equity cost of capital

N terminal date or forecast horizon

g expected dividend growth rate

Div_t dividends paid in year t

EPS_t earnings per share on date t

PV present value

$EBIT$ earnings before interest and taxes

FCF_t free cash flow on date t

V_t enterprise value on date t

τ_c corporate tax rate

r_{wacc} weighted average cost of capital

g_{FCF} expected free cash flow growth rate

$EBITDA$ earnings before interest, taxes, depreciation, and amortization

On January 16, 2006, footwear and apparel maker Kenneth Cole Productions, Inc., announced that its president, Paul Blum, had resigned to pursue "other opportunities." The price of the company's stock had already dropped more than 16% over the prior two years, and the firm was in the midst of a major undertaking to restructure its brand. News that its president, who had been with the company for more than 15 years, was now resigning was taken as a bad sign by many investors. The next day, Kenneth Cole's stock price dropped by more than 6% on the New York Stock Exchange to $26.75, with over 300,000 shares traded, more than twice its average daily volume. How might an investor decide whether to buy or sell a stock such as Kenneth Cole at this price? Why would the stock suddenly be worth 6% less on the announcement of this news? What actions can Kenneth Cole's managers take to increase the stock price?

To answer these questions, we turn to the Law of One Price. As we demonstrated in Chapter 3, the Law of One Price implies that the price of a security should equal the present value of the expected cash flows an investor will receive from owning it. In this chapter, we apply this idea to stocks. Thus, to value a stock, we need to know the expected cash flows an investor will receive and the appropriate cost of capital with which to discount those cash flows. Both of these quantities can be challenging to estimate, and many of the details needed to do so will be developed throughout the remainder of the text. In this chapter, we will begin our study of stock valuation by identifying the relevant cash flows and developing the main tools that practitioners use to evaluate them.

Our analysis begins with a consideration of the dividends and capital gains received by investors who hold the stock for different periods, from which we develop the dividend-discount model of stock valuation. Next, we apply Chapter 7's tools to value stocks based on the free cash flows generated by the firm. Having developed these stock valuation methods based on discounted cash flows, we then relate them to the practice of using valuation multiples based on comparable firms. **We conclude the chapter by discussing the role of competition in the information contained in stock prices and its implications for investors and corporate managers.**

9.1   Stock Prices, Returns, and the Investment Horizon

The Law of One Price implies that to value any security, we must determine the expected cash flows an investor will receive from owning it. Thus, we begin our analysis of stock valuation by considering the cash flows for an investor with a one-year investment horizon. In that case, we show how the stock's price and the investor's return from the investment are related. We then consider the perspective of investors with long investment horizons. Finally, we show that, if investors have the same beliefs, their valuation of the stock will not depend on their investment horizon.

A One-Year Investor

There are two potential sources of cash flows from owning a stock. First, the firm might pay out cash to its shareholders in the form of a dividend. Second, the investor might generate cash by choosing to sell the shares at some future date. The total amount received in dividends and from selling the stock will depend on the investor's investment horizon. Let's begin by considering the perspective of a one-year investor.

When an investor buys a stock, she will pay the current market price for a share, P_0. While she continues to hold the stock, she will be entitled to any dividends the stock pays. Let Div_1 be the total dividends paid per share of the stock during the year. At the end of the year, the investor will sell her share at the new market price, P_1. Assuming for simplicity that all dividends are paid at the end of the year, we have the following timeline for this investment:

Of course, the future dividend payment and stock price in the timeline above are not known with certainty; rather, these values are based on the investor's expectations at the time the stock is purchased. Given these expectations, the investor will be willing to pay a price today up to the point that this transaction has a zero NPV—that is, up to the point at which the current price equals the present value of the expected future dividend and sale price. Because these cash flows are risky, we cannot discount them using the risk-free interest rate. Instead, we must discount them based on the **equity cost of capital**, r_E, for the stock, which is the expected return of other investments available in the market with equivalent risk to the firm's shares. Doing so leads to the following equation for the stock price:

$$P_0 = \frac{Div_1 + P_1}{1 + r_E} \tag{9.1}$$

If the current stock price were less than this amount, it would be a positive-NPV investment. We would therefore expect investors to rush in and buy it, driving up the stock's price. If the stock price exceeded this amount, selling it would have a positive NPV and the stock price would quickly fall.

Dividend Yields, Capital Gains, and Total Returns

We can reinterpret Eq. 9.1 if we multiply by $(1 + r_E)$, divide by P_0, and subtract 1 from both sides:

Total Return

$$r_E = \frac{Div_1 + P_1}{P_0} - 1 = \underbrace{\frac{Div_1}{P_0}}_{\text{Dividend Yield}} + \underbrace{\frac{P_1 - P_0}{P_0}}_{\text{Capital Gain Rate}} \tag{9.2}$$

The first term on the right side of Eq. 9.2 is the stock's **dividend yield**, which is the expected annual dividend of the stock divided by its current price. The dividend yield is the percentage return the investor expects to earn from the dividend paid by the stock. The second term on the right side of Eq. 9.2 reflects the **capital gain** the investor will earn on the stock, which is the difference between the expected sale price and purchase price for the stock, $P_1 - P_0$. We divide the capital gain by the current stock price to express the capital gain as a percentage return, called the **capital gain rate**.

The sum of the dividend yield and the capital gain rate is called the **total return** of the stock. The total return is the expected return that the investor will earn for a one-year investment in the stock. Thus Eq. 9.2 states that the stock's total return should equal the equity cost of capital. In other words, *the expected total return of the stock should equal the expected return of other investments available in the market with equivalent risk.*

This result is what we should expect: The firm must pay its shareholders a return commensurate with the return they can earn elsewhere while taking the same risk. If the stock offered a higher return than other securities with the same risk, investors would sell those other investments and buy the stock instead. This activity would drive up the stock's current price, lowering its dividend yield and capital gain rate until Eq. 9.2 holds true. If the stock offered a lower expected return, investors would sell the stock and drive down its price until Eq. 9.2 was again satisfied.

Stock Prices and Returns

Problem

Suppose you expect Longs Drug Stores to pay dividends of $0.56 per share in the coming year and trade for $45.50 per share at the end of the year. If investments with equivalent risk to Longs' stock have an expected return of 6.80%, what is the most you would pay today for Longs' stock? What dividend yield and capital gain rate would you expect at this price?

Solution

Using Eq. 9.1, we have

$$P_0 = \frac{Div_1 + P_1}{1 + r_E} = \frac{0.56 + 45.50}{1.0680} = \$43.13$$

At this price, Longs' dividend yield is $Div_1 / P_0 = 0.56 / 43.13 = 1.30\%$. The expected capital gain is $\$45.50 - \$43.13 = \$2.37$ per share, for a capital gain rate of $2.37 / 43.13 = 5.50\%$. Therefore, at this price Long's expected total return is $1.30\% + 5.50\% = 6.80\%$, which is equal to its equity cost of capital.

A Multiyear Investor

Equation 9.1 depends upon the expected stock price in one year, P_1. But suppose we planned to hold the stock for two years. Then we would receive dividends in both year 1 and year 2 before selling the stock, as shown in the following timeline:

$$\begin{array}{c|c|c}
0 & 1 & 2 \\
\hline
-P_0 & Div_1 & Div_2 + P_2
\end{array}$$

Setting the stock price equal to the present value of the future cash flows in this case implies[1]

$$P_0 = \frac{Div_1}{1 + r_E} + \frac{Div_2 + P_2}{(1 + r_E)^2} \qquad (9.3)$$

Equations 9.1 and 9.3 are different: As a two-year investor we care about the dividend and stock price in year 2, but these terms do not appear in Eq. 9.1. Does this difference imply that a two-year investor will value the stock differently than a one-year investor?

The answer to this question is no. While a one-year investor does not care about the dividend and stock price in year 2 directly, she will care about them indirectly because they will affect the price for which she can sell the stock at the end of year 1. For example, suppose the investor sells the stock to another one-year investor with the same beliefs. The new investor will expect to receive the dividend and stock price at the end of year 2, so he will be willing to pay

$$P_1 = \frac{Div_2 + P_2}{1 + r_E}$$

for the stock. Substituting this expression for P_1 into Eq. 9.1, we get the same result as in Eq. 9.3:

$$P_0 = \frac{Div_1 + P_1}{1 + r_E} = \frac{Div_1}{1 + r_E} + \frac{1}{1 + r_E} \overbrace{\left(\frac{Div_2 + P_2}{1 + r_E} \right)}^{P_1}$$

$$- \frac{Div_1}{1 + r_E} + \frac{Div_2 + P_2}{(1 + r_E)^2}$$

Thus the formula for the stock price for a two-year investor is the same as the one for a sequence of two one-year investors.

We can continue this process for any number of years by replacing the final stock price with the value that the next holder of the stock would be willing to pay. Doing so leads to the general **dividend-discount model** for the stock price, where the horizon N is arbitrary:

Dividend-Discount Model

$$P_0 = \frac{Div_1}{1 + r_E} + \frac{Div_2}{(1 + r_E)^2} + \cdots + \frac{Div_N}{(1 + r_E)^N} + \frac{P_N}{(1 + r_E)^N} \qquad (9.4)$$

---

1. By using the same equity cost of capital for both periods, we are assuming that the equity cost of capital does not depend on the term of the cash flows. Otherwise, we would need to adjust for the term structure of the equity cost of capital (as we did with the yield curve for risk-free cash flows in Chapter 5). This step would complicate the analysis but would not change the results.

Equation 9.4 applies to a single N-year investor, who will collect dividends for N years and then sell the stock, or to a series of investors who hold the stock for shorter periods and then resell it. Note that Eq. 9.4 holds for *any* horizon N. Thus all investors (with the same beliefs) will attach the same value to the stock, independent of their investment horizons. How long they intend to hold the stock and whether they collect their return in the form of dividends or capital gains is irrelevant. For the special case in which the firm eventually pays dividends and is never acquired, it is possible to hold the shares forever. Consequently, we can let N go to infinity in Eq. 9.4 and write it as follows:

$$P_0 = \frac{Div_1}{1 + r_E} + \frac{Div_2}{(1 + r_E)^2} + \frac{Div_3}{(1 + r_E)^3} + \cdots = \sum_{n=1}^{\infty} \frac{Div_n}{(1 + r_E)^n} \qquad (9.5)$$

That is, *the price of the stock is equal to the present value of the expected future dividends it will pay.*

CONCEPT CHECK   1. How do you calculate the total return of a stock?

2. What discount rate do you use to discount the future cash flows of a stock?

9.2 The Dividend-Discount Model

Equation 9.5 expresses the value of the stock in terms of the expected future dividends the firm will pay. Of course, estimating these dividends—especially for the distant future—is difficult. A common approximation is to assume that in the long run, dividends will grow at a constant rate. In this section, we will consider the implications of this assumption for stock prices and explore the tradeoff between dividends and growth.

Constant Dividend Growth

The simplest forecast for the firm's future dividends states that they will grow at a constant rate, g, forever. That case yields the following timeline for the cash flows for an investor who buys the stock today and holds it:

Because the expected dividends are a constant growth perpetuity, we can use Eq. 4.9 to calculate their present value. We then obtain the following simple formula for the stock price:[2]

Constant Dividend Growth Model

$$P_0 = \frac{Div_1}{r_E - g} \qquad (9.6)$$

According to the **constant dividend growth model**, the value of the firm depends on the current dividend level, divided by the equity cost of capital adjusted by the growth rate.

---

2. As we discussed in Chapter 4, this formula requires that $g < r_E$. Otherwise, the present value of the growing perpetuity is infinite. The implication here is that it is impossible for a stock's dividends to grow at a rate $g > r_E$ *forever*. If the growth rate does exceed r_E, it must be temporary, and the constant growth model cannot be applied in such a case.

Valuing a Firm with Constant Dividend Growth

Problem

Consolidated Edison, Inc. (Con Edison), is a regulated utility company servicing the New York City area. Suppose Con Edison plans to pay $2.30 per share in dividends in the coming year. If its equity cost of capital is 7% and dividends are expected to grow by 2% per year in the future, estimate the value of Con Edison's stock.

Solution

If dividends are expected to grow perpetually at a rate of 2% per year, we can use Eq. 9.6 to calculate the price of a share of Con Edison stock:

$$P_0 = \frac{Div}{r_E - g} = \frac{\$2.30}{0.07 - 0.02} = \$46.00$$

For another interpretation of Eq. 9.6, note that we can rearrange it as follows:

$$r_E = \frac{Div_1}{P_0} + g \tag{9.7}$$

Comparing Eq. 9.7 with Eq. 9.2, we see that g equals the expected capital gain rate. In other words, with constant expected dividend growth, the expected growth rate of the share price matches the growth rate of dividends.

Dividends Versus Investment and Growth

In Eq. 9.6, the firm's share price increases with the current dividend level, Div_1, and the expected growth rate, g. To maximize its share price, a firm would like to increase both these quantities. Often, however, the firm faces a tradeoff: Increasing growth may require investment, and money spent on investment cannot be used to pay dividends. We can use the constant dividend growth model to gain insight into this tradeoff.

A Simple Model of Growth.   What determines the rate of growth of a firm's dividends? If we define a firm's **dividend payout rate** as the fraction of its earnings that the firm pays as dividends each year, then we can write the firm's dividend per share at date t as follows:

$$Div_t = \underbrace{\frac{\text{Earnings}_t}{\text{Shares Outstanding}_t}}_{EPS_t} \times \text{Dividend Payout Rate}_t \tag{9.8}$$

That is, the dividend each year is the firm's earnings per share (EPS) multiplied by its dividend payout rate. Thus the firm can increase its dividend in three ways: (1) by increasing its earnings (net income); (2) by increasing its dividend payout rate; or (3) by decreasing its shares outstanding. Let's suppose for now that the firm does not issue new shares (or buy back its existing shares), so that the number of shares outstanding is fixed, and explore the tradeoff between options 1 and 2.

A firm can do one of two things with its earnings: It can pay them out to investors, or it can retain and reinvest them. By investing cash today, a firm can increase its future dividends. For simplicity, let's assume that if no investment is made, the firm does not grow, so the current level of earnings generated by the firm remains constant. If all increases in future earnings result exclusively from new investment made with retained earnings, then

$$\text{Change in Earnings} = \text{New Investment} \times \text{Return on New Investment} \quad (9.9)$$

New investment equals earnings multiplied by the firm's **retention rate**, the fraction of current earnings that the firm retains:

$$\text{New Investment} = \text{Earnings} \times \text{Retention Rate} \quad (9.10)$$

Substituting Eq. 9.10 into Eq. 9.9 and dividing by earnings gives an expression for the growth rate of earnings:

$$\text{Earnings Growth Rate} = \frac{\text{Change in Earnings}}{\text{Earnings}}$$

$$= \text{Retention Rate} \times \text{Return on New Investment} \quad (9.11)$$

If the firm chooses to keep its dividend payout rate constant, then the growth in dividends will equal growth of earnings:

$$g = \text{Retention Rate} \times \text{Return on New Investment} \quad (9.12)$$

Profitable Growth.   Equation 9.12 shows that a firm can increase its growth rate by retaining more of its earnings. However, if the firm retains more earnings, it will be able to pay out less of those earnings, which from Eq. 9.8 means that the firm will have to reduce its dividend. If a firm wants to increase its share price, should it cut its dividend and invest more, or should it cut investment and increase its dividend? Not surprisingly, the answer will depend on the profitability of the firm's investments. Let's consider an example.

Cutting Dividends for Profitable Growth

Problem
Crane Sporting Goods expects to have earnings per share of $6 in the coming year. Rather than reinvest these earnings and grow, the firm plans to pay out all of its earnings as a dividend. With these expectations of no growth, Crane's current share price is $60.

   Suppose Crane could cut its dividend payout rate to 75% for the foreseeable future and use the retained earnings to open new stores. The return on its investment in these stores is expected to be 12%. Assuming its equity cost of capital is unchanged, what effect would this new policy have on Crane's stock price?

Solution
First, let's estimate Crane's equity cost of capital. Currently, Crane plans to pay a dividend equal to its earnings of $6 per share. Given a share price of $60, Crane's dividend yield is $6 / $60 = 10%. With no expected growth ($g = 0$), we can use Eq. 9.7 to estimate r_E:

$$r_E = \frac{Div_1}{P_0} + g = 10\% + 0\% = 10\%$$

In other words, to justify Crane's stock price under its current policy, the expected return of other stocks in the market with equivalent risk must be 10%.

Next, we consider the consequences of the new policy. If Crane reduces its dividend payout rate to 75%, then from Eq. 9.8 its dividend this coming year will fall to $Div_1 = EPS_1 \times 75\% = \$6 \times 75\% = \$4.50$. At the same time, because the firm will now retain 25% of its earnings to invest in new stores, from Eq. 9.12 its growth rate will increase to

$$g = \text{Retention Rate} \times \text{Return on New Investment} = 25\% \times 12\% = 3\%$$

Assuming Crane can continue to grow at this rate, we can compute its share price under the new policy using the constant dividend growth model of Eq. 9.6:

$$P_0 = \frac{Div_1}{r_E - g} = \frac{\$4.50}{0.10 - 0.03} = \$64.29$$

Thus Crane's share price should rise from $60 to $64.29 if it cuts its dividend to increase investment and growth, implying the investment has positive NPV.

In Example 9.3, cutting the firm's dividend in favor of growth raised the firm's stock price. But this is not always the case, as the next example demonstrates.

Unprofitable Growth

Problem
Suppose Crane Sporting Goods decides to cut its dividend payout rate to 75% to invest in new stores, as in Example 9.3. But now suppose that the return on these new investments is 8%, rather than 12%. Given its expected earnings per share this year of $6 and its equity cost of capital of 10%, what will happen to Crane's current share price in this case?

Solution
Just as in Example 9.3, Crane's dividend will fall to $\$6 \times 75\% = \$4.50$. Its growth rate under the new policy, given the lower return on new investment, will now be $g = 25\% \times 8\% = 2\%$. The new share price is therefore

$$P_0 = \frac{Div_1}{r_E - g} = \frac{\$4.50}{0.10 - 0.02} = \$56.25$$

Thus, even though Crane will grow under the new policy, the new investments have negative NPV and its share price will fall if it cuts its dividend to make new investments with a return of only 8%.

Comparing Example 9.3 with Example 9.4, we see that the effect of cutting the firm's dividend to grow crucially depends on the return on new investment. In Example 9.3, the return on new investment of 12% exceeds the firm's equity cost of capital of 10%, so the investment has positive NPV. In Example 9.4, the return on new investment is only 8%, so the new investment has negative NPV (even though it will lead to earnings growth). Thus *cutting the firm's dividend to increase investment will raise the stock price if, and only if, the new investments have a positive NPV.*

Changing Growth Rates

Successful young firms often have very high initial earnings growth rates. During this period of high growth, it is not unusual for these firms to retain 100% of their earnings to exploit profitable investment opportunities. As they mature, their growth slows to rates

INTERVIEW WITH
Marilyn Fedak

Marilyn G. Fedak is the Head of Global Value Equities at AllianceBernstein, a publicly-traded global asset management firm with approximately $618 billion in assets.

QUESTION: *What valuation methods do you use to identify buying opportunities?*

ANSWER: Since the early 1980s we have used the dividend discount model for U.S. large cap stocks. At its most basic level, the dividend discount model provides a way to evaluate how much we need to pay today for a company's future earnings. All things being equal, we are looking to buy as much earnings power as cheaply as we can.

It is a very reliable methodology, *if* you have the right forecasts for companies' future earnings. The key to success in using the dividend discount model is having deep fundamental research— a large team of analysts who use a consistent process for modeling earnings. We ask our analysts to provide us with 5-year forecasts for the companies they follow.

For non-U.S. stocks and for small caps, we use quantitative return models that are based upon companies' current characteristics rather than forecasts. The universes for these asset classes are too large to populate them with quality forecasts, even with our 50+ research team. The quant models encompass a variety of valuation measures, such as P/E and price-to-book ratios and selected success factors—for example, ROE and price momentum. We rank companies in their appropriate universes and focus on the stocks that rank the highest. Then the investment policy group meets with the analysts who follow these securities to determine whether the quant edge tool is correctly reflecting the likely financial future of each company.

QUESTION: *Are there drawbacks to the dividend discount model?*

ANSWER: Two things make the dividend discount model hard to use in practice. First, you need a huge research department to generate good forecasts for a large universe of stocks—in the large cap universe alone that means more than 650 companies. Since this is a relative valuation methodology, you need to have as much confidence in the forecast for the stock that ranks 450 as well as the one that ranks 15. Second, it is very hard to live by the results of the dividend discount model. At the peak of the bubble in 2000, for example, dividend discount models found tech stocks to be extremely overvalued. This was hard for most portfolio managers, because the pressure to override the model—to say it isn't working right—was enormous. That situation was extreme, but a dividend discount model almost always puts you in a contrarian position—a difficult position to constantly maintain.

QUESTION: *Why have you focused on value stocks?*

ANSWER: We don't assign labels to companies. Our valuation model is such that we will buy any company if it is selling cheaply relative to our vision of its long-term earnings. Today, for example, we own Microsoft, GE, TimeWarner—companies that were considered premier growth stocks just a few years ago. By using this consistent methodology and investing heavily in research, we have been able to produce strong investment results for our clients over long periods of time. And we believe that this process will continue to be successful in the future because it relies on enduring characteristics of human behavior (such as loss aversion) and the flows of capital in a free economic system.

more typical of established companies. At that point, their earnings exceed their investment needs and they begin to pay dividends.

We cannot use the constant dividend growth model to value the stock of such a firm, for several reasons. First, these firms often pay *no* dividends when they are young. Second, their growth rate continues to change over time until they mature. However, we can use the general form of the dividend-discount model to value such a firm by applying the constant growth model to calculate the future share price of the stock P_N once the firm matures and its expected growth rate stabilizes:

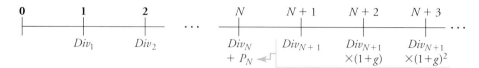

Specifically, if the firm is expected to grow at a long-term rate g after year $N + 1$, then from the constant dividend growth model:

$$P_N = \frac{Div_{N+1}}{r_E - g} \tag{9.13}$$

We can then use this estimate of P_N as a terminal (continuation) value in the dividend-discount model. Combining Eq. 9.4 with Eq. 9.13, we have

Dividend-Discount Model with Constant Long-Term Growth

$$P_0 = \frac{Div_1}{1 + r_E} + \frac{Div_2}{(1 + r_E)^2} + \cdots + \frac{Div_N}{(1 + r_E)^N} + \frac{1}{(1 + r_E)^N}\left(\frac{Div_{N+1}}{r_E - g}\right) \tag{9.14}$$

EXAMPLE 9.5

Valuing a Firm with Two Different Growth Rates

Problem
Small Fry, Inc., has just invented a potato chip that looks and tastes like a french fry. Given the phenomenal market response to this product Small Fry is reinvesting all of its earnings to expand its operations. Earnings were $2 per share this past year and are expected to grow at a rate of 20% per year until the end of year 4. At that point, other companies are likely to bring out competing products. Analysts project that at the end of year 4, Small Fry will cut investment and begin paying 60% of its earnings as dividends and its growth will slow to a long-run rate of 4%. If Small Fry's equity cost of capital is 8%, what is the value of a share today?

Solution
We can use Small Fry's projected earnings growth rate and payout rate to forecast its future earnings and dividends as shown in the following spreadsheet:

	Year	0	1	2	3	4	5	6
Earnings								
1	EPS Growth Rate (versus prior year)		20%	20%	20%	20%	4%	4%
2	EPS	$2.00	$2.40	$2.88	$3.46	$4.15	$4.31	$4.49
Dividends								
3	Dividend Payout Rate		0%	0%	0%	60%	60%	60%
4	Div	$ —	$ —	$ —		$2.49	$2.59	$2.69

Starting from $2.00 in year 0, EPS grows by 20% per year until year 4, after which growth slows to 4%. Small Fry's dividend payout rate is zero until year 4, when competition reduces its investment opportunities and its payout rate rises to 60%. Multiplying EPS by the dividend payout ratio, we project Small Fry's future dividends in line 4.

From year 4 onward, Small Fry's dividends will grow at the expected long-run rate of 4% per year. Thus we can use the constant dividend growth model to project Small Fry's share price at the end of year 3. Given its equity cost of capital of 8%,

$$P_3 = \frac{Div_4}{r_E - g} = \frac{\$2.49}{0.08 - 0.04} = \$62.25$$

We then apply the dividend-discount model (Eq. 9.4) with this terminal value:

$$P_0 = \frac{Div_1}{1 + r_E} + \frac{Div_2}{(1 + r_E)^2} + \frac{Div_3}{(1 + r_E)^3} + \frac{P_3}{(1 + r_E)^3} = \frac{\$62.25}{(1.08)^3} = \$49.42$$

Limitations of the Dividend-Discount Model

The dividend-discount model values the stock based on a forecast of the future dividends paid to shareholders. But unlike a Treasury bond, whose cash flows are known with virtual certainty, a tremendous amount of uncertainty is associated with any forecast of a firm's future dividends.

Let's consider the example of Kenneth Cole Productions (KCP), mentioned in the introduction to this chapter. In early 2006, KCP paid annual dividends of $0.72. With an equity cost of capital of 11% and expected dividend growth of 8%, the constant dividend growth model implies a share price for KCP of

$$P_0 = \frac{Div_1}{r_E - g} = \frac{\$0.72}{0.11 - 0.08} = \$24$$

John Burr Williams' *Theory of Investment Value*

The first formal derivation of the dividend-discount model appeared in the *Theory of Investment Value*, written by John Burr Williams in 1938.* The book was an important landmark in the history of corporate finance, because Williams demonstrated for the first time that corporate finance relied on certain principles that could be derived using formal analytical methods. As Williams wrote in the preface:

The truth is that the mathematical method is a new tool of great power whose use promises to lead to notable advances in Investment Analysis. Always it has been the rule in the history of science that the invention of new tools is the key to new discoveries, and we may expect the same rule to hold true in this branch of Economics as well.

By the time Williams died in 1989, the importance of the mathematical method in corporate finance was indis-putable and the discoveries that resulted from this "new" tool fundamentally changed the practice of corporate finance. Academics and practitioners alike now rely on principles developed in the intervening years whose origins can be traced to Williams' book and the mathematical method he brought to bear.

What happened to Williams himself? His book comprised his Ph.D. dissertation at Harvard University, which was accepted in 1940 (legend has it that his Ph.D. committee held a lively debate as to whether the work actually met the standard at Harvard, but in the end decided it did!). After earning his degree, Williams returned to the investment industry (in his own words, he "took time off to earn a Ph.D. in economics") and died a very wealthy man, presumably applying the principles and discoveries he helped initiate.

*This book contains many other ideas that are now central to modern finance (see Chapter 14 for a further reference).

which is reasonably close to the $26.75 share price the stock had at the time. With a 10% dividend growth rate, however, this estimate would rise to $72 per share; with a 5% dividend growth rate, the estimate falls to $12 per share. As we see, even small changes in the assumed dividend growth rate can lead to large changes in the estimated stock price.

Furthermore, it is difficult to know which estimate of the dividend growth rate is more reasonable. KCP more than doubled its dividend between 2003 and 2005, but earnings have remained relatively flat over the past few years. Consequently, this rate of increase is not sustainable. From Eq. 9.8, forecasting dividends requires forecasting the firm's earnings, dividend payout rate, and future share count. But future earnings will depend on interest expenses (which in turn depend on how much the firm borrows), and its share count and dividend payout rate will depend on whether the firm uses a portion of its earnings to repurchase shares. Because borrowing and repurchase decisions are at management's discretion, they can be more difficult to forecast reliably than other, more fundamental aspects of the firm's cash flows.[3] We look at two alternative methods that avoid some of these difficulties in the next section.

CONCEPT CHECK

1. In what three ways can a firm increase its future dividend per share?

2. Under what circumstances can a firm increase its share price by cutting its dividend and investing more?

9.3 Total Payout and Free Cash Flow Valuation Models

In this section, we outline two alternative approaches to valuing the firm's shares that avoid some of the difficulties of the dividend-discount model. First, we consider the total payout model, which allows us to ignore the firm's choice between dividends and share repurchases. Then we consider the discounted free cash flow model, which focuses on the cash flows to all of the firm's investors, both debt and equity holders, and allows us to avoid estimating the impact of the firm's borrowing decisions on earnings.

Share Repurchases and the Total Payout Model

In our discussion of the dividend-discount model, we implicitly assumed that any cash paid out by the firm to shareholders takes the form of a dividend. However, in recent years, an increasing number of firms have replaced dividend payouts with share repurchases. In a **share repurchase**, the firm uses excess cash to buy back its own stock. Share repurchases have two consequences for the dividend-discount model. First, the more cash the firm uses to repurchase shares, the less it has available to pay dividends. Second, by repurchasing shares, the firm decreases its share count, which increases its earning and dividends on a per-share basis.

In the dividend-discount model, we valued a share from the perspective of a single shareholder, discounting the dividends the shareholder will receive:

$$P_0 = PV(\text{Future Dividends per Share}) \tag{9.15}$$

An alternative method that may be more reliable when a firm repurchases shares is the **total payout model**, which values *all* of the firm's equity, rather than a single share. To do so, we discount the total payouts that the firm makes to shareholders, which is the total

3. We discuss management's decision to borrow funs or repurchase shares in Part V of the text.

amount spent on both dividends *and* share repurchases.[4] Then we divide by the current number of shares outstanding to determine the share price.

Total Payout Model

$$P_0 = \frac{PV(\text{Future Total Dividends and Repurchases})}{\text{Shares Outstanding}_0} \tag{9.16}$$

We can apply the same simplifications that we obtained by assuming constant growth in Section 9.2 to the total payout method. The only change is that *we discount total dividends and share repurchases and use the growth rate of earnings (rather than earnings per share) when forecasting the growth of the firm's total payouts.* This method can be more reliable and easier to apply when the firm uses share repurchases.

EXAMPLE 9.6

Valuation with Share Repurchases

Problem

Titan Industries has 217 million shares outstanding and expects earnings at the end of this year of $860 million. Titan plans to pay out 50% of its earnings in total, paying 30% as a dividend and using 20% to repurchase shares. If Titan's earnings are expected to grow by 7.5% per year and these payout rates remain constant, determine Titan's share price assuming an equity cost of capital of 10%.

Solution

Titan will have total payouts this year of 50% × $860 million = $430 million. Based on the equity cost of capital of 10% and an expected earnings growth rate of 7.5%, the present value of Titan's future payouts can be computed as a constant growth perpetuity:

$$PV(\text{Future Total Dividends and Repurchases}) = \frac{\$430 \text{ million}}{0.10 - 0.075} = \$17.2 \text{ billion}$$

This present value represents the total value of Titan's equity (i.e., its market capitalization). To compute the share price, we divide by the current number of shares outstanding:

$$P_0 = \frac{\$17.2 \text{ billion}}{217 \text{ million shares}} = \$79.26 \text{ per share}$$

Using the total payout method, we did not need to know the firm's split between dividends and share repurchases. To compare this method with the dividend-discount model, note that Titan will pay a dividend of 30% × $860 million / (217 million shares) = $1.19 per share, for a dividend yield of 1.19 / 79.26 = 1.50%. From Eq. 9.7, Titan's expected EPS, dividend, and share price growth rate is $g = r_E - Div_1 / P_0 = 8.50\%$. This growth rate exceeds the 7.50% growth rate of earnings because Titan's share count will decline over time due to share repurchases.[5]

---

4. You can think of the total payouts as the amount you would receive if you owned 100% of the firm's shares: You would receive all of the dividends, plus the proceeds from selling shares back to the firm in the share repurchase.

5. We can check that an 8.5% EPS growth rate is consistent with 7.5% earnings growth and Titan's repurchase plans as follows. Given an expected share price of $79.26 × 1.085 = $86.00 next year, Titan will repurchase 20% × $860 million ÷ ($86.00 per share) = 2 million shares next year. With the decline in the number of shares from 217 million to 215 million, EPS grows by a factor of 1.075 × (217 / 215) = 1.085 or 8.5%.

The Discounted Free Cash Flow Model

In the total payout model, we first value the firm's equity, rather than just a single share. The **discounted free cash flow model** goes one step further and begins by determining the total value of the firm to all investors—both equity *and* debt holders. That is, we begin by estimating the firm's enterprise value, which we defined in Chapter 2 as[6]

$$\text{Enterprise Value} = \text{Market Value of Equity} + \text{Debt} - \text{Cash} \qquad (9.17)$$

The enterprise value is the value of the firm's underlying business, unencumbered by debt and separate from any cash or marketable securities. We can interpret the enterprise value as the net cost of acquiring the firm's equity, taking its cash, paying off all debt, and thus owning the unlevered business. The advantage of the discounted free cash flow model is that it allows us to value a firm without explicitly forecasting its dividends, share repurchases, or its use of debt.

Valuing the Enterprise.   How can we estimate a firm's enterprise value? To estimate the value of the firm's equity, we computed the present value of the firm's total payouts to equity holders. Likewise, to estimate a firm's enterprise value, we compute the present value of the *free cash flow* (FCF) that the firm has available to pay all investors, both debt and equity holders. We saw how to compute the free cash flow for a project in Chapter 7; we now perform the same calculation for the entire firm:

$$\text{Free Cash Flow} = \overbrace{EBIT \times (1 - \tau_c)}^{\text{Unlevered Net Income}} + \text{Depreciation}$$
$$- \text{Capital Expenditures} - \text{Increases in Net Working Capital} \qquad (9.18)$$

Free cash flow measures the cash generated by the firm before any payments to debt or equity holders are considered.

Thus, just as we determine the value of a project by calculating the NPV of the project's free cash flow, we estimate a firm's current enterprise value V_0 by computing the present value of the firm's free cash flow:

Discounted Free Cash Flow Model

$$V_0 = PV(\text{Future Free Cash Flow of Firm}) \qquad (9.19)$$

Given the enterprise value, we can estimate the share price by using Eq. 9.17 to solve for the value of equity and then divide by the total number of shares outstanding:

$$P_0 = \frac{V_0 + \text{Cash}_0 - \text{Debt}_0}{\text{Shares Outstanding}_0} \qquad (9.20)$$

Intuitively, the difference between the discounted free cash flow model and the dividend-discount model is that in the dividend-discount model, the firm's cash and debt are included indirectly through the effect of interest income and expenses on earnings. In the discounted free cash flow model, we ignore interest income and expenses because free cash flow is based on EBIT, but then adjust for cash and debt directly in Eq. 9.20.

Implementing the Model.   A key difference between the discounted free cash flow model and the earlier models we have considered is the discount rate. In previous calcula-

---

6. To be precise, by cash we are referring to the firm's cash in excess of its working capital needs, which is the amount of cash it has invested at a competitive market interest rate.

tions we used the firm's equity cost of capital, r_E, because we were discounting the cash flows to equity holders. Here we are discounting the free cash flow that will be paid to both debt and equity holders. Thus we should use the firm's **weighted average cost of capital (WACC)**, denoted by r_{wacc}; it is the cost of capital that reflects the risk of the overall business, which is the combined risk of the firm's equity *and* debt. For now, we interpret r_{wacc} as the expected return the firm must pay to investors to compensate them for the risk of holding the firm's debt and equity together. If the firm has no debt, then $r_{wacc} = r_E$. We will develop methods to calculate the WACC explicitly in Parts IV and V of the text.[7]

Given the firm's weighted average cost of capital, we implement the discounted free cash flow model in much the same way as we did the dividend-discount model. That is, we forecast the firm's free cash flow up to some horizon, together with a terminal (continuation) value of the enterprise:

$$V_0 = \frac{FCF_1}{1 + r_{wacc}} + \frac{FCF_2}{(1 + r_{wacc})^2} + \cdots + \frac{FCF_N}{(1 + r_{wacc})^N} + \frac{V_N}{(1 + r_{wacc})^N} \quad (9.21)$$

Often, the terminal value is estimated by assuming a constant long-run growth rate g_{FCF} for free cash flows beyond year N, so that

$$V_N = \frac{FCF_{N+1}}{r_{wacc} - g_{FCF}} = \left(\frac{1 + g_{FCF}}{r_{wacc} - g_{FCF}}\right) \times FCF_N \quad (9.22)$$

The long-run growth rate g_{FCF} is typically based on the expected long-run growth rate of the firm's revenues.

EXAMPLE
9.7

Valuing Kenneth Cole Using Free Cash Flow

Problem
Kenneth Cole's (KCP) had sales of $518 million in 2005. Suppose you expect its sales to grow at a 9% rate in 2006, but that this growth rate will slow by 1% per year to a long-run growth rate for the apparel industry of 4% by 2011. Based on KCP's past profitability and investment needs, you expect EBIT to be 9% of sales, increases in net working capital requirements to be 10% of any increase in sales, and capital expenditures to equal depreciation expenses. If KCP has $100 million in cash, $3 million in debt, 21 million shares outstanding, a tax rate of 37%, and a weighted average cost of capital of 11%, what is your estimate of the value of KCP's stock in early 2006?

Solution
We can estimate KCP's future free cash flow based on the estimates above as follows:

	Year	2005	2006	2007	2008	2009	2010	2011
FCF Forecast ($ million)								
1	Sales	518.0	564.6	609.8	652.5	691.6	726.2	755.3
2	*Growth versus Prior Year*		9.0%	8.0%	7.0%	6.0%	5.0%	4.0%
3	EBIT (9% of sales)		50.8	54.9	58.7	62.2	65.4	68.0
4	Less: Income Tax (37%)		(18.8)	(20.3)	(21.7)	(23.0)	(24.2)	(25.1)
5	Plus: Depreciation		—	—	—	—	—	—
6	Less: Capital Expenditures		—	—	—	—	—	—
7	Less: Inc. in NWC (10% ΔSales)		(4.7)	(4.5)	(4.3)	(3.9)	(3.5)	(2.9)
8	**Free Cash Flow**		27.4	30.1	32.7	35.3	37.7	39.9

---

7. We can also interpret the firm's weighted average cost of capital as the average cost of capital associated with all of the firm's projects. In that sense, the WACC reflects the average risk of the firm's investments.

Note that because captial expenditures are expected to equal depreciation, lines 5 and 6 in the spreadsheet cancel out, and so we can set them both to zero rather than explicitly forecast them. Because we expect KCP's free cash flow to grow at a constant rate after 2011, we can use Eq. 9.22 to compute a terminal enterprise value:

$$V_{2011} = \left(\frac{1 + g_{FCF}}{r_{wacc} - g_{FCF}}\right) \times FCF_{2011} = \left(\frac{1.04}{0.11 - 0.04}\right) \times 39.9 = \$592.8 \text{ million}$$

From Eq. 9.21, KCP's current enterprise value is the present value of its free cash flows plus terminal value:

$$V_0 = \frac{27.4}{1.11} + \frac{30.1}{1.11^2} + \frac{32.7}{1.11^3} + \frac{35.3}{1.11^4} + \frac{37.7}{1.11^5} + \frac{39.9}{1.11^6} + \frac{592.8}{1.11^6} = \$456.9 \text{ million}$$

We can now estimate the value of a share of KCP's stock using Eq. 9.20:

$$P_0 = \frac{456.9 + 100 - 3}{21} = \$26.38$$

Connection to Capital Budgeting.   There is an important connection between the discounted free cash flow model and the NPV rule for capital budgeting that we developed in Chapter 7. Because the firm's free cash flow is equal to the sum of the free cash flows from the firm's current and future investments, we can interpret the firm's enterprise value as the total NPV that the firm will earn from continuing its existing projects and initiating new ones. Hence, the NPV of any individual project represents its contribution to the firm's enterprise value. To maximize the firm's share price, we should accept projects that have a positive NPV.

Recall also from Chapter 7 that many forecasts and estimates were necessary to estimate the free cash flows of a project. The same is true for the firm: We must forecast future sales, operating expenses, taxes, capital requirements, and other factors. On the one hand, estimating free cash flow in this way gives us flexibility to incorporate many specific details about the future prospects of the firm. On the other hand, some uncertainty inevitably surrounds each assumption. It is therefore important to conduct a sensitivity analysis, as we described in Chapter 7, to translate this uncertainty into a range of potential values for the stock.

EXAMPLE 9.8

Sensitivity Analysis for Stock Valuation

Problem

In Example 9.7, KCP's EBIT was assumed to be 9% of sales. If KCP can reduce its operating expenses and raise its EBIT to 10% of sales, how would your estimate of the stock's value change?

Solution

EBIT will increase by 1% of sales compared to Example 9.7. Thus, in year 1, EBIT will be 1% × $564.6 million = $5.6 million higher. After taxes, this increase will raise FCF in year 1 by (1 − 0.37) × $5.6 million = $3.5 million, to $30.9 million. Doing the same calculation for each year, we get the following revised FCF estimates:

Year	2006	2007	2008	2009	2010	2011
FCF	30.9	33.9	36.8	39.7	42.3	44.7

We can now reestimate the stock price as in the prior example. The terminal value is V_{2011} = $[1.04 / (0.11 - 0.04)] \times 44.7 = \$664.1$ million, so

$$V_0 = \frac{30.9}{1.11} + \frac{33.9}{1.11^2} + \frac{36.8}{1.11^3} + \frac{39.7}{1.11^4} + \frac{42.3}{1.11^5} + \frac{44.7}{1.11^6} + \frac{664.1}{1.11^6} = \$512.5 \text{ million}$$

The new estimate for the value of the stock is $P_0 = (512.5 + 100 - 3) / 21 = \$29.02$ per share, a difference of about 10% compared to the previous example.

Figure 9.1 summarizes the different valuation methods we have discussed thus far. The value of the stock is determined by the present value of its future dividends. We can estimate the total market capitalization of the firm's equity from the present value of the firm's total payouts, which includes dividends and share repurchases. Finally, the present value of the firm's free cash flow, which is the cash the firm has available to make payments to equity or debt holders, determines the firm's enterprise value.

FIGURE 9.1   **A Comparison of Discounted Cash Flow Models of Stock Valuation**

Present Value of ...	Determines the ...
Dividend Payments	Stock Price
Total Payouts (All Dividends and Repurchases)	Equity Value
Free Cash Flow (Cash available to pay all security holders)	Enterprise Value

By computing the present value of the firm's dividends, total payouts or free cash flows, we can estimate the value of the stock, the total value of the firm's equity, or the firm's enterprise value.

CONCEPT CHECK

1. How does the growth rate used in the total payout model differ from the growth rate used in the dividend-discount model?

2. Why do we ignore interest payments on the firm's debt in the discounted free cash flow model?

9.4 Valuation Based on Comparable Firms

Thus far, we have valued a firm or its stock by considering the expected future cash flows it will provide to its owner. The Law of One Price then tells us that its value is the present value of its future cash flows, because the present value is the amount we would need to invest elsewhere in the market to replicate the cash flows with the same risk.

Another application of the Law of One Price is the method of comparables. In the **method of comparables** (or "comps"), rather than value the firm's cash flows directly, we estimate the value of the firm based on the value of other, comparable firms or investments that we expect will generate very similar cash flows in the future. For example, consider the case of a new firm that is *identical* to an existing publicly traded company. If these firms will generate identical cash flows, the Law of One Price implies that we can use the value of the existing company to determine the value of the new firm.

Of course, identical companies do not exist. Even two firms in the same industry selling the same types of products, while similar in many respects, are likely to be of a different size or scale. In this section, we consider ways to adjust for scale differences to use comparables to value firms with similar business, and then discuss the strengths and weaknesses of this approach.

Valuation Multiples

We can adjust for differences in scale between firms by expressing their value in terms of a **valuation multiple**, which is a ratio of the value to some measure of the firm's scale. As an analogy, consider valuing an office building. A natural measure to consider would be the price per square foot for other buildings recently sold in the area. Multiplying the size of the office building under consideration by the average price per square foot would typically provide a reasonable estimate of the building's value. We can apply this same idea to stocks, replacing square footage with some more appropriate measure of the firm's scale.

The Price-Earnings Ratio.   The most common valuation multiple is the price-earnings (P/E) ratio, which we introduced in Chapter 2. A firm's P/E ratio is equal to the share price divided by its earnings per share. The intuition behind its use is that when you buy a stock, you are in a sense buying the rights to the firm's future earnings and differences in the scale of firms' earnings are likely to persist. Therefore, you should be willing to pay proportionally more for a stock with higher current earnings. Thus we can estimate the value of a firm's share by multiplying its current earnings per share by the average P/E ratio of comparable firms.

We can compute a firm's P/E ratio by using either **trailing earnings** (earnings over the prior 12 months) or **forward earnings** (expected earnings over the coming 12 months), with the resulting ratio called the **trailing P/E** or **forward P/E**, respectively. For valuation purposes, the forward P/E is generally preferred, as we are most concerned about future earnings.[8] We can interpret the forward P/E in terms of the dividend-discount model or total payout model that we introduced earlier. For example, in the case of constant dividend growth, dividing through Eq. 9.6 by EPS_1, we find that

$$\text{Forward P/E} = \frac{P_0}{EPS_1} = \frac{Div_1 \,/\, EPS_1}{r_E - g} = \frac{\text{Dividend Payout Rate}}{r_E - g} \qquad (9.23)$$

Equation 9.23 implies that if two stocks have the same payout and EPS growth rates, as well as equivalent risk (and therefore the same equity cost of capital), then they should

---

8. Because we are interested in the persistent components of the firm's earnings, it is also common practice to exclude extraordinary items that will not be repeated when calculating a P/E ratio for valuation purposes.

have the same P/E. It also shows that firms and industries with high growth rates, and which generate cash well in excess of their investment needs so that they can maintain high payout rates, should have high P/E multiples.

EXAMPLE 9.9

Valuation Using the Price-Earnings Ratio

Problem
Suppose furniture manufacturer Herman Miller, Inc., has earnings per share of $1.38. If the average P/E of comparable furniture stocks is 21.3, estimate a value for Herman Miller using the P/E as a valuation multiple. What are the assumptions underlying this estimate?

Solution
We estimate a share price for Herman Miller by multiplying its EPS by the P/E of comparable firms. Thus $P_0 = \$1.38 \times 21.3 = \$29.39$. This estimate assumes that Herman Miller will have similar future risk, payout rates, and growth rates to comparable firms in the industry.

Enterprise Value Multiples. It is also common practice to use valuation multiples based on the firm's enterprise value. As we discussed in Section 9.3, because it represents the total value of the firm's underlying business rather than just the value of equity, using the enterprise value is advantageous if we want to compare firms with different amounts of leverage.

Because the enterprise value represents the entire value of the firm before the firm pays its debt, to form an appropriate multiple, we divide it by a measure of earnings or cash flows before interest payments are made. Common multiples to consider are enterprise value to EBIT, EBITDA (earnings before interest, taxes, depreciation, and amortization), and free cash flow. However, because capital expenditures can vary substantially from period to period (e.g., a firm may need to add capacity and build a new plant one year, but then not need to expand further for many years), most practitioners rely on enterprise value to EBITDA multiples. From Eq. 9.22, if expected free cash flow growth is contant, then

$$\frac{V_0}{EBITDA_1} = \frac{FCF_1 \,/\, EBITDA_1}{r_{wacc} - g_{FCF}} \tag{9.24}$$

As with the P/E multiple, this valuation multiple is higher for firms with high growth rates and low capital requirements (so that free cash flow is high in proportion to EBITDA).

EXAMPLE 9.10

Valuation Using an Enterprise Value Multiple

Problem
Suppose Rocky Shoes and Boots (RCKY) has earnings per share of $2.30 and EBITDA of $30.7 million. RCKY also has 5.4 million shares outstanding and debt of $125 million (net of cash). You believe Deckers Outdoor Corporation is comparable to RCKY in terms of its underlying business, but Deckers has no debt. If Deckers has a P/E of 13.3 and an enterprise value to EBITDA multiple of 7.4, estimate the value of RCKY's shares using both multiples. Which estimate is likely to be more accurate?

Solution

Using Decker's P/E, we would estimate a share price for RCKY of $P_0 = \$2.30 \times 13.3 = \$30.59$. Using the enterprise value to EBITDA multiple, we would estimate RCKY's enterprise value to be $V_0 = \$30.7$ million $\times 7.4 = \$227.2$ million. We then subtract debt and divide by the number of shares to estimate RCKY's share price: $P_0 = (227.2 - 125) / 5.4 = \$18.93$. Because of the large difference in leverage between the firms, we would expect the second estimate, which is based on enterprise value, to be more reliable.

Other Multiples.   Many other valuation multiples are possible. Looking at enterprise value as a multiple of sales can be useful if it is reasonable to assume that the firms will maintain similar margins in the future. For firms with substantial tangible assets, the ratio of price to book value of equity per share is sometimes used. Some multiples are specific to an industry. In the cable TV industry, for example, it is natural to consider enterprise value per subscriber.

Limitations of Multiples

If comparables were identical, the firms' multiples would match precisely. Of course, firms are not identical. Thus the usefulness of a valuation multiple will depend on the nature of the differences between firms and the sensitivity of the multiples to these differences.

Table 9.1 lists several valuation multiples for firms in the footwear industry, as of January 2006. Also shown is the average for each multiple, together with the range around the average (in percentage terms). For all of the multiples, a fair amount of dispersion across the industry is apparent. While the enterprise value to EBITDA multiple shows the smallest variation, even with it we cannot expect to obtain a precise estimate of value.

The differences in these multiples are most likely due to differences in expected future growth rates, risk (and therefore costs of capital), and, in the case of Puma, differences in accounting conventions between the United States and Germany. Investors in the market understand that these differences exist, so the stocks are priced accordingly. But when valuing a firm using multiples, there is no clear guidance about how to adjust for these differences other than by narrowing the set of comparables used.

Another limitation of comparables is that they provide only information regarding the value of the firm *relative to* the other firms in the comparison set. Using multiples will not help us determine if an entire industry is overvalued, for example. This issue became especially important during the Internet boom of the late 1990s. Because many of these firms did not have positive cash flows or earnings, new multiples were created to value them (e.g., price to "page views"). While these multiples could justify the value of these firms in relation to one another, it was much more difficult to justify the stock prices of many of these firms using a realistic estimate of cash flows and the discounted free cash flow approach.

Comparison with Discounted Cash Flow Methods

Using a valuation multiple based on comparables is best viewed as a "shortcut" to the discounted cash flow methods of valuation. Rather than separately estimate the firm's cost of capital and future earnings or free cash flows, we rely on the market's assessment of the value of other firms with similar future prospects. In addition to its simplicity, the multiples approach has the advantage of being based on actual prices of real firms, rather than what may be unrealistic forecasts of future cash flows.

TABLE 9.1   **Stock Prices and Multiples for the Footwear Industry, January 2006**

Ticker	Name	Stock Price ($)	Market Capitalization ($ million)	Enterprise Value ($ million)	P/E	Price / Book	Enterprise Value / Sales	Enterprise Value / EBITDA
NKE	Nike	84.20	21,830	20,518	16.64	3.59	1.43	8.75
PMMAY	Puma AG	312.05	5,088	4,593	14.99	5.02	2.19	9.02
RBK	Reebok International	58.72	3,514	3,451	14.91	2.41	0.90	8.58
WWW	Wolverine World Wide	22.10	1,257	1,253	17.42	2.71	1.20	9.53
BWS	Brown Shoe Co.	43.36	800	1,019	22.62	1.91	0.47	9.09
SKX	Skechers U.S.A.	17.09	683	614	17.63	2.02	0.62	6.88
SRR	Stride Rite Corp.	13.70	497	524	20.72	1.87	0.89	9.28
DECK	Deckers Outdoor Corp.	30.05	373	367	13.32	2.29	1.48	7.44
WEYS	Weyco Group	19.90	230	226	11.97	1.75	1.06	6.66
RCKY	Rocky Shoes & Boots	19.96	106	232	8.66	1.12	0.92	7.55
DFZ	R.G. Barry Corp.	6.83	68	92	9.2	8.11	0.87	10.75
BOOT	LaCrosse Footwear	10.40	62	75	12.09	1.28	0.76	8.30
				Average	**15.01**	**2.84**	**1.06**	**8.49**
				Maximum	+51%	+186%	+106%	+27%
				Minimum	−42%	−61%	−56%	−22%

One shortcoming of the comparables approach is that it does not take into account the important differences among firms. The fact that a firm has an exceptional management team, has developed an efficient manufacturing process, or has just secured a patent on a new technology is ignored when we apply a valuation multiple. Discounted cash flows methods have the advantage that they allow us to incorporate specific information about the firm's cost of capital or future growth. Thus, because the true driver of value for any firm is its ability to generate cash flows for its investors, the discounted cash flow methods have the potential to be more accurate than the use of a valuation multiple.

Stock Valuation Techniques: The Final Word

In the end, no single technique provides a final answer regarding a stock's true value. All approaches require assumptions or forecasts that are too uncertain to provide a definitive assessment of the firm's value. Most real-world practitioners use a combination of these approaches and gain confidence if the results are consistent across a variety of methods.

Figure 9.2 compares the ranges of values for Kenneth Cole Productions using the different valuation methods that we have discussed in this chapter. Kenneth Cole's stock price of $26.75 in January 2006 is within the range estimated by all of these methods. Hence, based on this evidence alone we would not conclude that the stock is obviously under- or over-priced.

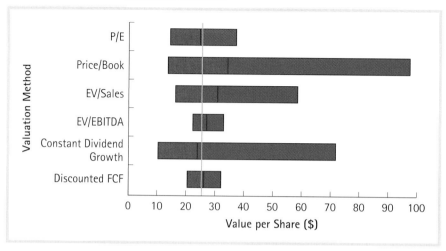

FIGURE 9.2   **Range of Valuations for KCP Stock Using Alternative Valuation Methods**

Valuations from multiples are based on the low, high, and average values of the comparable firms from Table 9.1 (see Problems 17 and 18). The constant dividend growth model is based on an 11% equity cost of capital and 5%, 8%, and 10% dividend growth rates, as discussed at the end of Section 9.2. The discounted free cash flow model is based on Example 9.7 with the range of parameters in Problem 16. (Midpoints are based on average multiples or base case assumptions. Red and blue regions show the variation between the lowest-multiple/worst-case scenario and the highest-multiple/best-case scenario. KCP's actual share price of $26.75 is indicated by the gray line.)

CONCEPT CHECK   1. What are some common valuation multiples?

2. What implicit assumptions are made when valuing a firm using multiples based on comparable firms?

9.5   Information, Competition, and Stock Prices

As shown in Figure 9.3, the models described in this chapter link the firm's expected future cash flows, its cost of capital (determined by its risk), and the value of its shares. But what conclusions should we draw if the actual market price of a stock doesn't appear to be consistent with our estimate of its value? Is it more likely that the stock is mispriced or that we are mistaken about its risk and future cash flows? We close this chapter with a consideration of this question and the implications for corporate managers.

Information in Stock Prices

Consider the following situation. You are a new junior analyst assigned to research Kenneth Cole Productions stock and assess its value. You scrutinize the company's recent financial statements, look at the trends in the industry, and forecast the firm's future earnings, dividends, and free cash flows. You carefully run the numbers and estimate the stock's value at $30 per share. On your way to present your analysis to your boss, you run

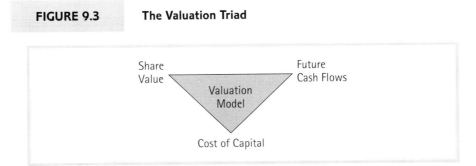

FIGURE 9.3   **The Valuation Triad**

Valuation models determine the relationship among the firm's future cash flows, its cost of capital, and the value of its shares. The stock's expected cash flows and cost of capital can be used to assess its market price. Conversely, the market price can be used to assess the firm's future cash flows or cost of capital.

into a slightly more experienced colleague in the elevator. It turns out your colleague has been researching the same stock. But according to her analysis, the value of the stock is only $20 per share. What would you do?

Although you could just assume your colleague is wrong, most of us in this situation would reconsider our own analysis. The fact that someone else who has carefully studied the stock has come to a very different conclusion is powerful evidence that we might be mistaken. In the face of this information from our colleague, we would probably adjust our assessment of the stock's value downward. Of course, our colleague might also revise her opinion based on our assessment. After sharing our analyses, we would likely end up with a consensus estimate somewhere between $20 and $30 per share.

This type of encounter happens millions of times every day in the stock market. When a buyer seeks to buy a stock, the willingness of other parties to sell the same stock suggests that they value the stock differently. This information should lead buyers and sellers to revise their valuations. Ultimately, investors trade until they reach a consensus regarding the value of the stock. In this way, stock markets aggregate the information and views of many different investors.

Thus, if your valuation model suggests a stock is worth $30 per share when it is trading for $20 per share in the market, the discrepancy is equivalent to knowing that thousands of investors—many of them professionals who have access to the best information—disagree with your assessment. This knowledge should make you reconsider your original analysis. You would need a very compelling reason to trust your own estimate in the face of such contrary opinions.

What conclusion can we draw from this discussion? Recall Figure 9.3, in which a valuation model links the firm's future cash flows, its cost of capital, and its share price. In other words, given accurate information about any two of these variables, a valuation model allows us to make inferences about the third variable. Thus the way we use a valuation model will depend on the quality of our information: The model will tell us the most about the variable for which our prior information is the least reliable.

For a publicly traded firm, its market price should already provide very accurate information, aggregated from a multitude of investors, regarding the true value of its shares. Therefore, in most situations, a valuation model is best applied to tell us something about the firm's future cash flows or cost of capital, based on its current stock price. Only in the relatively rare case in which we have some superior information that other investors lack regarding the firm's cash flows and cost of capital would it make sense to second-guess the stock price.

EXAMPLE
9.11

Using the Information in Market Prices

Problem

Suppose Tecnor Industries will pay a dividend this year of $5 per share. Its equity cost of capital is 10%, and you expect its dividends to grow at a rate of about 4% per year, though you are somewhat unsure of the precise growth rate. If Tecnor's stock is currently trading for $76.92 per share, how would you update your beliefs about its dividend growth rate?

Solution

If we apply the constant dividend growth model based on a 4% growth rate, we would estimate a stock price of $P_0 = 5 / (0.10 - 0.04) = \$83.33$ per share. The market price of $76.92, however, implies that most investors expect dividends to grow at a somewhat slower rate. If we continue to assume a constant growth rate, we can solve for the growth rate consistent with the current market price using Eq. 9.7:

$$g = r_E - Div_1 / P_0 = 10\% - 5 / 76.92 = 3.5\%$$

Thus, given this market price for the stock, we should lower our expectations for the dividend growth rate unless we have very strong reasons to trust our own estimate.

Competition and Efficient Markets

The idea that markets aggregate the information of many investors, and that this information is reflected in security prices, is a natural consequence of investor competition. If information were available that indicated that buying a stock had a positive NPV, investors with that information would choose to buy the stock; their attempts to purchase it would then drive up the stock's price. By a similar logic, investors with information that selling a stock had a positive NPV would sell it and the stock's price would fall.

The idea that competition among investors works to eliminate *all* positive-NPV trading opportunities is referred to as the **efficient markets hypothesis**. It implies that securities will be fairly priced, based on their future cash flows, given all information that is available to investors.

The underlying rationale for the efficient markets hypothesis is the presence of competition. What if new information becomes available that affects the firm's value? The degree of competition, and therefore the accuracy of the efficient markets hypothesis, will depend on the number of investors who possess this information. Let's consider two important cases.

Public, Easily Interpretable Information. Information that is available to all investors includes information in news reports, financials statements, corporate press releases, or in other public data sources. If the impact of this information on the firm's future cash flows can be readily ascertained, then all investors can determine the effect of this information on the firm's value.

In this situation, we expect competition between investors to be fierce and the stock price to react nearly instantaneously to such news. A few lucky investors might be able to trade a small quantity of shares before the price fully adjusted. Most investors, however, would find that the stock price already reflected the new information before they were able to trade on it. In other words, we expect the efficient markets hypothesis to hold very well with respect to this type of information.

Stock Price Reactions to Public Information

Problem
Myox Labs announces that due to potential side effects, it is pulling one of its leading drugs from the market. As a result, its future expected free cash flow will decline by $85 million per year for the next ten years. Myox has 50 million shares outstanding, no debt, and an equity cost of capital of 8%. If this news came as a complete surprise to investors, what should happen to Myox's stock price upon the announcement?

Solution
In this case, we can use the discounted free cash flow method. With no debt, $r_{wacc} = r_E = 8\%$. Using the annuity formula, the decline in expected free cash flow will reduce Myox's enterprise value by

$$\$85 \text{ million} \times \frac{1}{0.08}\left(1 - \frac{1}{1.08^{10}}\right) = \$570 \text{ million}$$

Thus the share price should fall by $570 / 50 = $11.40 per share. Because this news is public and its effect on the firm's expected free cash flow is clear, we would expect the stock price to drop by this amount nearly instantaneously.

Private or Difficult-to-Interpret Information. Some information is not publicly available. For example, an analyst might spend time and effort gathering information from a firm's employees, competitors, suppliers, or customers that is relevant to the firm's future cash flows. This information is not available to other investors who have not devoted a similar effort to gathering it.

Even when information is publicly available, it may be difficult to interpret. Non-experts in the field may find it difficult to evaluate research reports on new technologies, for example. It may take a great deal of legal and accounting expertise and effort to understand the full consequences of a highly complicated business transaction. Certain consulting experts may have greater insight into consumer tastes and the likelihood of a product's acceptance. In these cases, while the fundamental information may be public, the interpretation of how that information will affect the firm's future cash flows is itself private information.

When private information is relegated to the hands of a relatively small number of investors, these investors may be able to profit by trading on their information.[9] In this case, the efficient markets hypothesis will not hold in the strict sense. However, as these informed traders begin to trade, they will tend to move prices, so over time prices will begin to reflect their information as well.

---

9. Even with private information, informed investors may find it difficult to profit from that information, because they must find others who are willing to trade with them; that is, the market for the stock must be sufficiently *liquid*. A liquid market requires that other investors in the market have alternative motives to trade (e.g., selling shares of a stock to purchase a house) and so be willing to trade even when facing the risk that other traders may be better informed.

19. In an efficient market, investors will not find positive-NPV trading opportunities without some source of competitive advantage. By contrast, the average investor will earn a fair return on his or her investment.

20. In an efficient market, to raise the stock price corporate managers should focus on maximizing the present value of the free cash flow from the firm's investments, rather than accounting consequences or financial policy.

Key Terms

capital gain *p. 247*
capital gain rate *p. 247*
constant dividend growth model *p. 249*
discounted free cash flow model *p. 258*
dividend-discount model *p. 248*
dividend payout rate *p. 250*
dividend yield *p. 247*
efficient markets hypothesis *p. 268*
equity cost of capital *p. 246*
forward earnings *p. 262*
forward P/E *p. 262*

method of comparables *p. 262*
retention rate *p. 251*
share repurchase *p. 256*
total payout model *p. 256*
total return *p. 247*
trailing earnings *p. 262*
trailing P/E *p. 262*
valuation multiple *p. 262*
weighted average cost of capital
    (WACC) *p. 259*

Further Reading

For a more thorough discussion of different stock valuation methods, see T. Copeland, T. Koller, and J. Murrin, *Valuation: Measuring and Managing the Value of Companies*, 3rd ed. (Hoboken: NJ: John Wiley & Sons, 2001).

For a comparison of the discounted free cash flow model and the method of comparables for a sample of 51 highly leveraged transactions, see S. N. Kaplan and R. S. Ruback "The Valuation of Cash Flow Forecasts: An Empirical Analysis," *Journal of Finance* 50 (1995): 1059–1093.

An entertaining introduction to efficient markets can be found in B. Malkiel's popular book, *A Random Walk Down Wall Street: Completely Revised and Updated Eighth Edition* (New York: W. W. Norton, 2003).

For a classic discussion of market efficiency, the arguments that support it, and important empirical tests, see E. F. Fama, "Efficient Capital Markets: A Review of Theory and Empirical Work," *Journal of Finance* 25 (1970): 383–417, and "Efficient Capital Markets: II," *The Journal of Finance* 46(5) (1991):1575–1617. Another review of the literature and apparent anomalies can be found in R. Ball, "The Development, Accomplishments and Limitations of the Theory of Stock Market Efficiency," *Managerial Finance* 20(2,3) (1994): 3–48.

For two sides of the debate of whether the price of Internet companies in the late 1990s could be justified by a valuation model, see: L. Pástor and P. Veronesi, "Was There a Nasdaq Bubble in the Late 1990s?" *Journal of Financial Economics* 2006 (in press); M. Richardson and E. Ofek, "DotCom Mania: The Rise and Fall of Internet Stock Prices," *Journal of Finance* 58 (2003): 1113–1138.

Problems

All problems in this chapter are available in MyFinanceLab. An asterisk (*) indicates problems with a higher level of difficulty.

Stock Price, Returns, and the Investment Horizon

1. Suppose Acap Corporation will pay a dividend of $2.80 per share at the end of this year and $3.00 per share next year. You expect Acap's stock price to be $52.00 in two years. If Acap's equity cost of capital is 10%:

   a. What price would you be willing to pay for a share of Acap stock today, if you planned to hold the stock for two years?

   b. Suppose instead you plan to hold the stock for one year. What price would you expect to be able to sell a share of Acap stock for in one year?

   c. Given your answer in part (b), what price would you be willing to pay for a share of Acap stock today, if you planned to hold the stock for one year? How does this compare to your answer in part (a)?

2. Krell Industries has a share price of $22.00 today. If Krell is expected to pay a dividend of $0.88 this year, and its stock price is expected to grow to $23.54 at the end of the year, what is Krell's dividend yield and equity cost of capital?

The Dividend-Discount Model

3. NoGrowth Corporation currently pays a dividend of $0.50 per quarter, and it will continue to pay this dividend forever. What is the price per share if its equity cost of capital is 15%?

4. Summit Systems will pay a dividend of $1.50 this year. If you expect Summit's dividend to grow by 6% per year, what is its price per share if its equity cost of capital is 11%?

5. Dorpac Corporation has a dividend yield of 1.5%. Dorpac's equity cost of capital is 8%, and its dividends are expected to grow at a constant rate.

   a. What is the expected growth rate of Dorpac's dividends?

   b. What is the expected growth rate of Dorpac's share price?

6. DFB, Inc., expects earnings this year of $5 per share, and it plans to pay a $3 dividend to shareholders. DFB will retain $2 per share of its earnings to reinvest in new projects with an expected return of 15% per year. Suppose DFB will maintain the same dividend payout rate, retention rate, and return on new investments in the future and will not change its number of outstanding shares.

   a. What growth rate of earnings would you forecast for DFB?

   b. If DFB's equity cost of capital is 12%, what price would you estimate for DFB stock?

   c. Suppose DFB instead paid a dividend of $4 per share this year and retained only $1 per share in earnings. If DFB maintains this higher payout rate in the future, what stock price would you estimate now? Should DFB raise its dividend?

7. Cooperton Mining just announced it will cut its dividend from $4 to $2.50 per share and use the extra funds to expand. Prior to the announcement, Cooperton's dividends were expected to grow at a 3% rate, and its share price was $50. With the new expansion, Cooperton's dividends are expected to grow at a 5% rate. What share price would you expect after the announcement? (Assume Cooperton's risk is unchanged by the new expansion.) Is the expansion a positive NPV investment?

8. Gillette Corporation will pay an annual dividend of $0.65 one year from now. Analysts expect this dividend to grow at 12% per year thereafter until the fifth year. After then, growth will level off at 2% per year. According to the dividend-discount model, what is the value of a share of Gillette stock if the firm's equity cost of capital is 8%?

9. Colgate-Palmolive Company has just paid an annual dividend of $0.96. Analysts are predicting an 11% per year growth rate in earnings over the next five years. After then, Colgate's earnings are expected to grow at the current industry average of 5.2% per year. If Colgate's equity cost of capital is 8.5% per year and its dividend payout ratio remains constant, what price does the dividend-discount model predict Colgate stock should sell for?

10. What is the value of a firm with initial dividend Div, growing for n years (i.e., until year $n + 1$) at rate g_1 and after that at rate g_2 forever, when the equity cost of capital is r?

11. Halliford Corporation expects to have earnings this coming year of $3 per share. Halliford plans to retain all of its earnings for the next two years. For the subsequent two years, the firm will retain 50% of its earnings. It will then retain 20% of its earnings from that point onward. Each year, retained earnings will be invested in new projects with an expected return of 25% per year. Any earnings that are not retained will be paid out as dividends. Assume Halliford's share count remains constant and all earnings growth comes from the investment of retained earnings. If Halliford's equity cost of capital is 10%, what price would you estimate for Halliford stock?

The Total Payout and Free Cash Flow Valuation Models

12. Suppose Cisco Systems pays no dividends but spent $5 billion on share repurchases last year. If Cisco's equity cost of capital is 12%, and if the amount spent on repurchases is expected to grow by 8% per year, estimate Cisco's market capitalization. If Cisco has 6 billion shares outstanding, what stock price does this correspond to?

13. Maynard Steel plans to pay a dividend of $3 this year. The company has an expected earnings growth rate of 4% per year and an equity cost of capital of 10%.

    a. Assuming Maynard's dividend payout rate and expected growth rate remains constant, and Maynard does not issue or repurchase shares, estimate Maynard's share price.

    b. Suppose Maynard decides to pay a dividend of $1 this year and use the remaining $2 per share to repurchase shares. If Maynard's total payout rate remains constant, estimate Maynard's share price.

    c. If Maynard maintains the dividend and total payout rate given in part (b), at what rate are Maynard's dividends and earnings per share expected to grow?

EXCEL 14. Heavy Metal Corporation is expected to generate the following free cash flows over the next five years:

Year	1	2	3	4	5
FCF ($ million)	53	68	78	75	82

After then, the free cash flows are expected to grow at the industry average of 4% per year. Using the discounted free cash flow model and a weighted average cost of capital of 14%:

    a. Estimate the enterprise value of Heavy Metal.

    b. If Heavy Metal has no excess cash, debt of $300 million, and 40 million shares outstanding, estimate its share price.

15. Sora Industries has 60 million outstanding shares, $120 million in debt, $40 million in cash, and the following projected free cash flow for the next four years:

	Year	0	1	2	3	4
	Earnings and FCF Forecast ($ million)					
1	Sales	433.0	468.0	516.0	547.0	574.3
2	*Growth versus Prior Year*		*8.1%*	*10.3%*	*6.0%*	*5.0%*
3	Cost of Goods Sold		(313.6)	(345.7)	(366.5)	(384.8)
4	**Gross Profit**		154.4	170.3	180.5	189.5
5	Selling, General, and Administrative		(93.6)	(103.2)	(109.4)	(114.9)
6	Depreciation		(7.0)	(7.5)	(9.0)	(9.5)
7	**EBIT**		53.8	59.6	62.1	65.2
8	Less: Income Tax at 40%		(21.5)	(23.8)	(24.8)	(26.1)
9	Plus: Depreciation		7.0	7.5	9.0	9.5
10	Less: Capital Expenditures		(7.7)	(10.0)	(9.9)	(10.4)
11	Less: Increase in NWC		(6.3)	(8.6)	(5.6)	(4.9)
12	**Free Cash Flow**		25.3	24.6	30.8	33.3

a. Suppose Sora's revenue and free cash flow are expected to grow at a 5% rate beyond year 4. If Sora's weighted average cost of capital is 10%, what is the value of Sora's stock based on this information?

b. Sora's cost of goods sold was assumed to be 67% of sales. If its cost of goods sold is actually 70% of sales, how would the estimate of the stock's value change?

c. Let's return to the assumptions of part (a) and suppose Sora can maintain its cost of goods sold at 67% of sales. However, now suppose Sora reduces its selling, general, and administrative expenses from 20% of sales to 16% of sales. What stock price would you estimate now? (Assume no other expenses, except taxes, are affected.)

*d. Sora's net working capital needs were estimated to be 18% of sales (which is their current level in year 0). If Sora can reduce this requirement to 12% of sales starting in year 1, but all other assumptions remain as in part (a), what stock price do you estimate for Sora? (*Hint:* This change will have the largest impact on Sora's free cash flow in year 1.)

 16. Consider the valuation of Kenneth Cole Productions in Example 9.7.

a. Suppose you believe KCP's initial revenue growth rate will be between 7% and 11%. What range of share prices for KCP is consistent with these forecasts?

b. Suppose you believe KCP's initial revenue EBIT margin will be between 8% and 10% of sales. What range of share prices for KCP is consistent with these forecasts?

c. Suppose you believe KCP's weighted average cost of capital is between 10.5% and 12%. What range of share prices for KCP is consistent with these forecasts?

d. What range of share prices is consistent if you vary the estimates as in parts (a), (b), and (c) simultaneously?

Valuation Based on Comparable Firms

 17. Suppose that in January 2006, Kenneth Cole Productions had EPS of $1.65 and a book value of equity of $12.05 per share.

a. Using the average P/E multiple in Table 9.1, estimate KCP's share price.

b. What range of share prices do you estimate based on the highest and lowest P/E multiples in Table 9.1?

c. Using the average price to book value multiple in Table 9.1, estimate KCP's share price.

d. What range of share prices do you estimate based on the highest and lowest price to book value multiples in Table 9.1?

EXCEL   **18.**   Suppose that in January 2006, Kenneth Cole Productions had sales of $518 million, EBITDA of $55.6 million, excess cash of $100 million, $3 million of debt, and 21 million shares outstanding.

a. Using the average enterprise value to sales multiple in Table 9.1, estimate KCP's share price.

b. What range of share prices do you estimate based on the highest and lowest enterprise value to sales multiples in Table 9.1?

c. Using the average enterprise value to EBITDA multiple in Table 9.1, estimate KCP's share price.

d. What range of share prices do you estimate based on the highest and lowest enterprise value to EBITDA multiples in Table 9.1?

EXCEL   **19.**   In addition to footwear, Kenneth Cole Productions designs and sells handbags, apparel, and other accessories. You decide, therefore, to consider comparables for KCP outside the footwear industry.

a. Suppose that Fossil, Inc., has an enterprise value to EBITDA multiple of 9.73 and a P/E multiple of 18.4. What share price would you estimate for KCP using each of these multiples, based on the data for KCP in Problems 17 and 18?

b. Suppose that Tommy Hilfiger Corporation has an enterprise value to EBITDA multiple of 7.19 and a P/E multiple of 17.2. What share price would you estimate for KCP using each of these multiples, based on the data for KCP in Problems 17 and 18?

EXCEL   **20.**   Consider the following data for the auto industry in mid-2006 (EV = enterprise value, BV = book value, NM = not meaningful because divisor is negative). Discuss the usefulness of using multiples to value an auto company.

Company Name	Market Cap	EV	EV/Sales	EV/EBITDA	EV/EBIT	P/E	P/BV
Honda Motor Co. Ltd.	55,694.1	77,212.4	0.9×	8.2×	10.8×	10.9×	1.6×
DaimlerChrysler AG	47,462.2	136,069.6	0.7×	6.6×	28.7×	13.2×	1.2×
Nissan Motor Co. Ltd.	44,463.2	93,138.3	1.2×	7.3×	11.8×	NM	NM
Volkswagen AG	25,215.6	84,922.0	0.7×	5.7×	22.3×	14.5×	1.2×
General Motors Corp.	15,077.9	274,336.9	1.4×	44.3×	NM	NM	1.1×
PSA Peugeot Citroen	13,506.7	44,015.1	0.6×	7.2×	18.6×	10.6×	1.3×
Ford Motor Co.	11,931.1	145,009.1	0.8×	11.9×	NM	490.8×	2.0×
Mitsubishi Motors Corp.	7,919.4	9,633.3	0.6×	207.2×	NM	NM	3.9×
Daihatsu Motor Co. Ltd.	3,666.3	6,913.8	0.6×	7.9×	17.7×	15.9×	1.6×

Source: Capital IQ.

Information, Competition, and Stock Prices

21.   In mid-2006, Coca-Cola Company had a share price of $43. Its dividend was $1.24, and you expect Coca-Cola to raise this dividend by approximately 7% per year in perpetuity.

a. If Coca-Cola's equity cost of capital is 8%, what share price would you expect based on your estimate of the dividend growth rate?

b. Given Coca-Cola's share price, what would you conclude about your assessment of Coca-Cola's future dividend growth?

22. Roybus, Inc., a manufacturer of flash memory, just reported that its main production facility in Taiwan was destroyed in a fire. While the plant was fully insured, the loss of production will decrease Roybus's free cash flow by $180 million at the end of this year and by $60 million at the end of next year.

   a. If Roybus has 35 million shares outstanding and a weighted average cost of capital of 13%, what change in Roybus's stock price would you expect upon this announcement? (Assume the value of Roybus' debt is not affected by the event.)

   b. Would you expect to be able to sell Roybus's stock on hearing this announcement and make a profit? Explain.

23. Apnex, Inc., is a biotechnology firm that is about to announce the results of its clinical trials of a potential new cancer drug. If the trials were successful, Apnex stock will be worth $70 per share. If the trials were unsuccessful, Apnex stock will be worth $18 per share. Suppose that the morning before the announcement is scheduled, Apnex shares are trading for $55 per share.

   a. Based on the current share price, what sort of expectations do investors seem to have about the success of the trials?

   b. Suppose hedge fund manager Paul Kliner has hired several prominent research scientists to examine the public data on the drug and make their own assessment of the drug's promise. Would Kliner's fund be likely to profit by trading the stock in the hours prior to the announcement?

   c. What would limit the fund's ability to profit on its information?

Data Case

A new analyst for a large brokerage firm, you are anxious to demonstrate the skills you learned in your MBA program and prove that you are worth your attractive salary. Your first assignment is to analyze the stock of the General Electric Corporation. Your boss recommends determining prices based on both the dividend-discount model and discounted free cash flow valuation methods. GE uses a cost of equity of 10.5% and an after-tax weighted average cost of capital of 7.5%. The expected return on new investments is 12%. However, you are a little concerned because your finance professor has told you that these two methods can result in widely differing estimates when applied to real data. You are really hoping that the two methods will reach similar prices. Good luck with that!

1. Go to Yahoo! Finance (http://finance.yahoo.com) and enter the symbol for General Electric (GE). From the main page for GE gather the following information and enter it onto a spreadsheet:

   a. The current stock price (last trade) at the top of the page.

   b. The current dividend amount, which is in the bottom-right cell in the same box as the stock price.

2. Next click on "Key Statistics" from the left side of the page. From the Key Statistics page gather the following information and enter it on the same spreadsheet:

   a. The number of shares of stock outstanding.

   b. The Payout ratio.

3. Next click on "Analyst Estimates" from the left side of the page. From the Analyst Estimates page find the expected growth rate for the next 5 years and enter it onto your spreadsheet. It will be near the very bottom of the page.

4. Next click on "Income Statement" near the bottom of the menu on the left. Place the cursor in the middle of the income statements and right-click. Select "Export to Microsoft Excel." Copy and paste the entire three years of income statements into a new worksheet in your existing Excel file. Repeat this process for both the balance sheet and cash flow statement for General Electric. Keep all the different statements in the same Excel worksheet.

5. To determine the stock value based on the dividend-discount model:

    a. Create a timeline in Excel for five years.

    b. Use the dividend obtained from Yahoo! Finance as the current dividend to forecast the next 5 annual dividends based on the five-year growth rate.

    c. Determine the long-term growth rate based on GE's payout ratio (which is one minus the retention ratio) using Eq. 9.12.

    d. Use the long-term growth rate to determine the stock price for year five using Eq. 9.13.

    e. Determine the current stock price using Eq. 9.14.

6. To determine the stock value based on the discounted free cash flow method:

    a. Forecast the free cash flows using the historic data from the financial statements downloaded from Yahoo! to compute the three-year average of the following ratios:

        i. EBIT/Sales

        ii. Tax Rate (Income Tax Expense/Income Before Tax)

        iii. Property Plant and Equipment/Sales

        iv. Depreciation/Property Plant and Equipment

        v. Net Working Capital/Sales

    b. Create a timeline for the next seven years.

    c. Forecast future sales based on the most recent year's total revenue growing at the five-year growth rate from Yahoo! for the first five years and the long-term growth rate for years six and seven.

    d. Use the average ratios computed in part (a) to forecast EBIT, property, plant and equipment, depreciation, and net working capital for the next seven years.

    e. Forecast the free cash flow for the next seven years using Eq. 9.18.

    f. Determine the horizon enterprise value for year 5 using Eq. 9.22.

    g. Determine the enterprise value of the firm as the present value of the free cash flows

    h. Determine the stock price using Eq. 9.20.

7. Compare the stock prices from the two methods to the actual stock price. What recommendations can you make as to whether clients should buy or sell General Electric's stock based on your price estimates?

8. Explain to your boss why the estimates from the two valuation methods differ. Specifically address the assumptions implicit in the models themselves as well as those you made in preparing your analysis. Why do these estimates differ from the actual stock price of GE?

Risk and Return

Chapter 10
**Capital Markets and
the Pricing of Risk**

Chapter 11
Optimal Portfolio Choice

Chapter 12
**The Capital Asset
Pricing Model**

Chapter 13
**Alternative Models
of Systematic Risk**

The Law of One Price Connection. To apply the Law of One Price correctly requires comparing investment opportunities of equivalent risk. The objective in this part of the book is to explain how to measure and compare risks across investment opportunities. Chapter 10 introduces the key insight that investors only demand a risk premium for risk they cannot remove themselves without cost by diversifying their portfolios. Hence, only non-diversifiable risk will matter when comparing investment opportunities. In Chapter 11, we quantify this idea and thereby derive investors' optimal investment portfolio choices. In Chapter 12 we consider the implications of assuming all investors choose their portfolio of investments optimally. This assumption leads to the Capital Asset Pricing Model (CAPM), the central model in financial economics that quantifies what an equivalent risk is and thereby provides the relation between risk and return. Chapter 13 examines the strengths and weaknesses of alternative models of risk and return.

Capital Markets and the Pricing of Risk

notation

p_R probability of return R

$Var(R)$ variance of return R

$SD(R)$ standard deviation of return R

$E[R]$ expectation of return R

Div_t dividend paid on date t

P_t price on date t

R_t realized or total return of a security from date $t - 1$ to t

$\overline{R}$ average return

β_s beta of security s

r Cost of capital of an investment opportunity

Over the four-year period 2001 through 2004, investors in Anheuser-Busch Companies, Inc., earned an average return of 4.4% per year. Within this period there was some variation, with the annual return ranging from almost 11% in 2003 to −2% in 2004. Over the same period, investors in Yahoo! Inc. earned an average return of 25.8%. These investors, however, lost 41% in 2001 and gained 175% in 2003. Finally, investors in three-month U.S. Treasury bills earned an average return of 1.8% during the period, with a high return of 3.3% in 2001 and a low return of 1.0% in 2003. Clearly, these three investments offered returns that were very different in terms of their average level and their variability. What accounts for these differences?

In this chapter, we will explain why these differences exist. Our goal is to develop a theory that explains the relationship between average returns and the variability of returns and thereby derive the risk premium that investors require to hold different securities and investments. We then use this theory to explain how to determine the cost of capital for an investment opportunity.

We begin our investigation of the relationship between risk and return by examining historical data for publicly traded securities. We will see, for example, that while stocks are riskier investments than bonds, they have also earned higher average returns. We can interpret the higher average return on stocks as compensation to investors for the greater risk they are taking.

But we will also find that not all risk needs to be compensated. By holding a portfolio containing many different investments, investors can eliminate risks that are specific to individual securities. It is only those risks that cannot be eliminated by holding a large portfolio that determine the risk premium required by investors. These observations will allow us to refine our definition of what risk is, how it can be measured, and how the cost of capital is determined.

10.1 A First Look at Risk and Return

Suppose your great-grandparents invested $100 on your behalf at the end of 1925. They instructed their broker to reinvest any dividends or interest earned in the account until the beginning of 2005. How would that $100 have grown if it were placed in one of the following investments?

1. Standard & Poor's 500 (S&P 500): A portfolio, constructed by Standard and Poor's, of 500 U.S. stocks. The firms represented are leaders in their respective industries and are among the largest firms, in terms of market value, traded on U.S. markets.

2. Small Stocks: A portfolio of stocks of U.S. firms whose market values are in the bottom 10% of all stocks traded on the NYSE. (As stocks' market values change, this portfolio is updated so it always consists of the smallest 10% of stocks.)

3. World Portfolio: A portfolio of international stocks from all of the world's major stock markets in North America, Europe, and Asia.[1]

4. Corporate Bonds: A portfolio of long-term, AAA-rated U.S. corporate bonds. These bonds have a maturity of approximately 20 years.

5. Treasury Bills: An investment in three-month U.S. Treasury bills.

Figure 10.1 shows the result, through 2005, of investing $100 at the end of 1925 in each of these five investment portfolios, ignoring transactions costs. The graph is striking—had your great-grandparents invested $100 in the small stock portfolio, the investment would be worth more than $8 million in 2005! By contrast, if they had invested in Treasury bills, the investment would be worth only about $2000.

For comparison, we also show how prices changed during the same period using the consumer price index (CPI). During this period in the United States, small stocks experienced the highest long-term return, followed by the large stocks in the S&P 500, the international stocks in the world portfolio, corporate bonds, and finally Treasury bills. All of the investments grew faster than inflation (as measured by the CPI).

A second pattern is also evident in Figure 10.1. While the small stock portfolio performed the best in the long run, its value also experienced the largest fluctuations. For example, investors in small stocks had the largest loss during the Depression era of the 1930s: Had your great-grandparents put the $100 in a small stock portfolio intended for their own retirement 15 years later in 1940, they would have had only $175 to retire on, compared with $217 from the same investment in corporate bonds. Moreover, during the 15-year period, they would have seen the value of their investment drop as low as $33. On the other hand, if they had invested in Treasury bills, they would not have experienced any losses during the period, but rather would have enjoyed steady—albeit modest—gains each year. Indeed, if we were to rank the investments by the size of their increases and decreases in value, we would obtain the same ranking as before: Small stocks had the most variable returns, followed by the S&P 500, the world portfolio, corporate bonds, and finally Treasury bills.

In Chapter 3, we explained why investors are averse to fluctuations in the value of their investments and why riskier investments have higher expected returns. Investors do not

---

1. This index is based on the Morgan Stanley Capital International World Index from 1970–2005. Prior to 1970, the index is constructed by Global Financial data, with approximate initial weights of 44% North America, 44% Europe, and 12% Asia, Africa, and Australia.

FIGURE 10.1

Value of $100 Invested at the End of 1925 in U.S. Large Stocks (S&P 500), Small Stocks, World Stocks, Corporate Bonds, and Treasury Bills

These returns assume all dividends and interest are reinvested and exclude transactions costs. Also shown is the change in the consumer price index (CPI).

Source: Chicago Center for Research in Security Prices (CRSP) for U.S. stocks and CPI, Global Finance Data for the World Index, Treasury bills and corporate bonds.

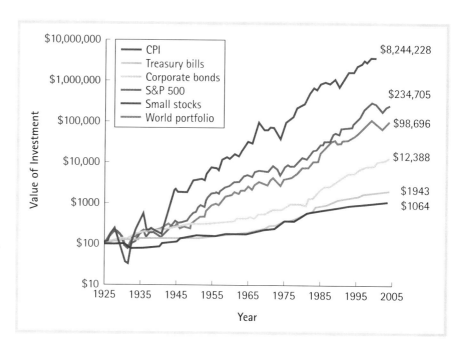

like to be hit when they are already down—when times are bad, they do not like to have their problems further compounded by experiencing losses on their investments. In fact, even if your great-grandparents had actually put the $100 into a small stock portfolio in 1925, it is unlikely you would have seen any of it. More likely, in the depths of the Great Depression your great-grandparents would have turned to their investment to get them through the bad times. Unfortunately, the small stock portfolio would not have helped much in this regard—in 1932, their original $100 investment would have been worth only $33. With the benefit of 80 years of hindsight the small stock portfolio looks like a great investment, but in 1932 it would have seemed like a huge mistake. Perhaps this is the reason your great-grandparents did not actually invest money for you in small stocks. The pleasure of knowing that your great-grandchild might one day be a millionaire may not make up for the pain of the investment going bust at precisely the time when the money is needed for other things.

Although we understand the general principle explaining why investors do not like risk and demand a risk premium to bear it, our goal in this chapter is to quantify this relationship. We would like to explain *how much* investors demand (in terms of a higher expected return) to bear a given level of risk. To quantify the relationship, we must first develop tools that will allow us to measure risk and return. That is the objective of the next section.

CONCEPT CHECK

1. From 1926 to 2005, which of the following investments had the highest return: Standard & Poor's 500, small stocks, world portfolio, corporate bonds, or Treasury bills?

2. From 1926 to 2005, which investment grew in value in every year? Which investment had the greatest variability?

10.2

That is, as we discussed in Chapter 9, the realized return, R_{t+1}, is the total return we earn from dividends and capital gains, expressed as a percentage of the initial stock price.[4]

If you hold the stock beyond the date of the first dividend, then to compute your return you must specify how you invest any dividends you receive in the interim. To focus on the returns of a single security, let's assume that *all dividends are immediately reinvested and used to purchase additional shares of the same stock or security.* In this case, we can use Eq. 10.4 to compute the stock's return between dividend payments, and then compound the returns from each dividend interval to compute the return over a longer horizon. For example, if a stock pays dividends at the end of each quarter, with realized returns $R_{Q1}, \ldots, R_{Q4}$ each quarter, then its annual realized return, R_{annual}, is computed as

$$1 + R_{annual} = (1 + R_{Q1})(1 + R_{Q2})(1 + R_{Q3})(1 + R_{Q4}) \tag{10.5}$$

EXAMPLE

10.2

Realized Returns for GM Stock

Problem
What were the realized annual returns for GM stock in 1999 and in 2004?

Solution
First we look up GM stock price data at the start and end of the year, as well as at any dividend dates (see the book's Web site for online sources of stock price and dividend data). From these data we can construct the following table:

Date	Price ($)	Dividend ($)	Return	Date	Price ($)	Dividend ($)	Return
12/31/98	71.56			12/31/03	53.40		
2/2/99	89.44	0.50	25.68%	2/11/04	49.80	0.50	−5.81%
5/11/99	85.75	0.50	−3.57%	5/12/04	44.48	0.50	−9.68%
5/28/99[5]	69.00	13.72	−3.53%	8/11/04	41.74	0.50	−5.04%
8/10/99	60.81	0.50	−11.14%	11/4/04	39.50	0.50	−4.17%
11/8/99	69.06	0.50	14.39%	12/31/04	40.06		1.42%
12/31/99	72.69		5.26%				

We compute each period's return using Eq. 10.4. For example, the return from December 31, 1998, until February 2, 1999, is equal to

$$\frac{0.50 + 89.44}{71.56} - 1 = 25.68\%$$

---

4. We can compute the realized return for any security in the same way, by replacing the dividend payments with any cash flows paid by the security (for example, with a bond, coupon payments would replace dividends).

5. This large dividend was a special dividend related to GM's spinoff of auto parts maker Delphi Automotive Systems. For each share of GM stock owned, each GM shareholder received 0.69893 share of Delphi common stock, which had a value of $13.72 based on Delphi's closing stock price of $19.625. When we compute GM's annual return, we assume these shares of Delphi were sold and the proceeds were immediately reinvested in GM. In that way the returns reflect GM's performance exclusively.

We then determine the annual returns using Eq. 10.5:

$$R_{1999} = (1.2568)(0.9643)(0.9647)(0.8886)(1.1439)(1.0526) - 1 = 25.09\%$$
$$R_{2004} = (0.9419)(0.9032)(0.9496)(0.9583)(1.0142) - 1 = -21.48\%$$

Example 10.2 illustrates two features of the returns from holding a stock like GM. First, both dividends and capital gains contribute to the total realized return—ignoring either one would give a very misleading impression of GM's performance. Second, the returns are risky. In years like 1999 the returns are quite high, but in other years like 2004 they are negative, meaning GM's shareholders lost money over the year.

We can compute realized returns in this same way for any investment. We can also compute the realized returns for an entire portfolio, by keeping track of the interest and dividend payments paid by the portfolio during the year, as well as the change in the market value of the portfolio. For example, the realized returns for the S&P 500 index are shown in Table 10.2, which for comparison purposes also lists the returns for GM and for three-month Treasury bills.

Once we have calculated the realized annual returns, we can compare them to see which investments performed better in a given year. From Table 10.2, we can see that GM stock outperformed the S&P 500 in 1999 and 2001 through 2003. Also, in 2000 through 2002, Treasury bills performed better than both GM stock and the S&P 500. Note the overall tendency for GM's return to move in the same direction as the S&P 500.

TABLE 10.2	Realized Return for the S&P 500, GM, and Treasury Bills, 1996–2004				
Year End	S&P 500 Index	Dividends Paid*	S&P 500 Realized Return	GM Realized Return	3-Month T-Bill Return
1995	615.93				
1996	740.74	16.61	23.0%	8.6%	5.1%
1997	970.43	17.2	33.4%	19.6%	5.2%
1998	1229.23	18.5	28.6%	21.3%	4.9%
1999	1469.25	18.1	21.0%	25.1%	4.8%
2000	1320.28	15.7	−9.1%	−27.8%	6.0%
2001	1148.08	15.2	−11.9%	−1.0%	3.3%
2002	879.82	14.53	−22.1%	−20.8%	1.6%
2003	1111.92	20.8	28.7%	52.9%	1.0%
2004	1211.92	20.98	10.9%	−21.5%	1.4%

*Total dividends paid by the 500 stocks in the portfolio, based on the number of shares of each stock in the index, adjusted until the end of the year, assuming they were reinvested when paid.

Source: Standard & Poor's, GM, and Global Financial Data.

Over any particular period we observe only one draw from the probability distribution of returns. If the realized return in each period is drawn from the same probability distribution, however, we can observe multiple draws by observing the realized return over multiple periods. By counting the number of times the realized return falls within a particular range, we can estimate the underlying probability distribution. Let's illustrate this process with the data in Figure 10.1.

Figure 10.4 plots the annual returns for each U.S. investment in Figure 10.1 in a histogram. The height of each bar represents the number of years that the annual returns were in each range indicated on the x-axis. When we plot the probability distribution in this way using historical data, we refer to it as the **empirical distribution** of the returns.

Average Annual Returns

The **average annual return** of an investment during some historical period is simply the average of the realized returns for each year. That is, if R_t is the realized return of a security in year t, then the average annual return for years 1 through T is

Average Annual Return of a Security

$$\bar{R} = \frac{1}{T}(R_1 + R_2 + \cdots + R_T) = \frac{1}{T}\sum_{t=1}^{T} R_t \qquad (10.6)$$

Notice that the average annual return is the balancing point of the empirical distribution—in this case, the probability of a return occurring in a particular range is measured by the number of times the realized return falls in that range. Therefore, if the probability distribution of the returns is the same over time, the average return provides an estimate of the expected return.

FIGURE 10.4

The Empirical Distribution of Annual Returns for U.S. Large Stocks (S&P 500), Small Stocks, Corporate Bonds, and Treasury Bills, 1926–2004.

The height of each bar represents the number of years that the annual returns were in each 5% range. Note the greater variability of stock returns (especially small stocks) compared to the returns of corporate bonds or Treasury bills.

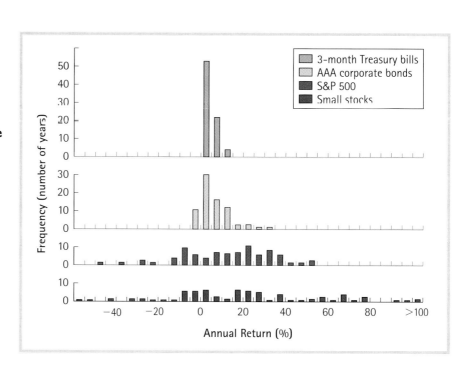

TABLE 10.3	Average Annual Returns for U.S. Small Stocks, Large Stocks (S&P 500), Corporate Bonds, and Treasury Bills, 1926–2004

Investment	Average Annual Return
Small stocks	22.11%
S&P 500	12.32%
Corporate bonds	6.52%
Treasury bills	3.87%

For example, using the data from Table 10.2, the average return for S&P 500 for the years 1996–2004 is

$$\bar{R} = \frac{1}{9}(0.230 + 0.334 + 0.286 + 0.210 - 0.091 \\ - 0.119 - 0.221 + 0.287 + 0.109) = 11.4\%$$

The average Treasury bill return from 1996–2004 was 3.7%. Therefore, investors earned 11.4% − 3.7% = 7.7% more on average holding the S&P 500 than investing in Treasury bills during this period. Table 10.3 provides the average returns for different U.S. investments from 1926–2004.

The Variance and Volatility of Returns

Looking at Figure 10.4, we can see that the variability of the returns is very different for each investment. The distribution of small stocks' returns shows the widest spread. The large stocks of the S&P 500 have returns that vary less than those of small stocks, but much more than the returns of corporate bonds or Treasury bills.

To quantify this difference in variability, we can estimate the standard deviation of the probability distribution. As before, we will use the empirical distribution to derive this estimate. Using the same logic as we did with the mean, we estimate the variance by computing the average squared deviation from the mean. The only complication is that we do not actually know the mean, so instead we use the best estimate of the mean—the average realized return.[6]

Variance Estimate Using Realized Returns

$$Var(R) = \frac{1}{T-1} \sum_{t=1}^{T} (R_t - \bar{R})^2 \tag{10.7}$$

We estimate the standard deviation or volatility as the square root of the variance.[7]

6. You may wonder why we divide by $T-1$ rather than by T here. It is because we are not computing deviations from the true expected return; instead, we are computing deviations from the estimated average return $\bar{R}$. Because the average return is derived from the same data, we lose a degree of freedom (in essence, we use up one of the data points), so that when computing the variance we really have only $T-1$ additional data points to base it on.

7. If the returns used in Eq. 10.7 are not annual returns, the variance is typically converted to annual terms by multiplying the number of periods per year. For example, when using monthly returns, we multiply the variance by 12 and, equivalently, the standard deviation by $\sqrt{12}$.

Computing a Historical Volatility

Problem

Using the data from Table 10.2, what are the variance and volatility of the S&P 500's returns for the years 1996–2004?

Solution

Earlier we calculated the average annual return of the S&P 500 during this period to be 11.4%. Therefore,

$$Var(R) = \frac{1}{T-1} \sum_t (R_t - \bar{R})^2$$

$$= \frac{1}{9-1} [(0.230 - 0.114)^2 + (0.334 - 0.114)^2 + \cdots + (0.109 - 0.114)^2]$$

$$= 0.0424$$

The volatility or standard deviation is therefore $SD(R) = \sqrt{Var(R)} = \sqrt{0.0424} = 20.6\%$.

We can compute the standard deviation of the returns to quantify the differences in the variability of the distributions that we observed in Figure 10.4. These results are shown in Table 10.4.

TABLE 10.4   **Volatility of U.S. Small Stocks, Large Stocks (S&P 500), Corporate Bonds, and Treasury Bills, 1926–2004**

Investment	Return Volatility (Standard Deviation)
Small stocks	42.75%
S&P 500	20.36%
Corporate bonds	7.17%
Treasury bills	3.18%

Comparing the volatilities in Table 10.4 we see that, as expected, small stocks have had the most variable historical returns, followed by large stocks. The returns of corporate bonds and Treasury bills are much less variable than stocks, with Treasury bills being the least volatile investment category.

Using Past Returns to Predict the Future: Estimation Error

To estimate the cost of capital for an investment, we need to determine the expected return that investors will require to compensate them for that investment's risk. If we assume that the distribution of past returns and the distribution of future returns are the same, one approach we could take is to look at the return investors expected to earn in the past on the same or similar investments, and assume they will require the same return in the future.

Two difficulties arise with this approach. The first difficulty is that we do not know what investors expected in the past; we can only observe the actual returns that were realized. In 2002, for example, investors lost more than 22% investing in the S&P 500, which is surely not what they expected at the beginning of the year (or they would have invested in Treasury bills instead!). If we believe that investors are neither overly optimistic nor overly pessimistic on average, however, then over time the average realized return should match investors' expected return.

Armed with this assumption, we can use a security's historical average return to estimate its actual expected return. But here we encounter the second difficulty—the average return is just an estimate of the expected return. As with all statistics, an estimation error will occur. Given the volatility of stock returns, this estimation error will be large even when we have many years of data.

We measure the degree of estimation error statistically through the standard error of the estimate. The **standard error** is the standard deviation of the estimated value of the mean of the actual distribution around its true value; that is, it is the standard deviation of the average return. The standard error provides an indication of how far the sample average might deviate from the expected return. If we assume that the distribution of a stock's return is identical each year, and that each year's return is independent of prior years' returns,[8] then the standard error of the estimate of the expected return can be found from the following formula:

Standard Error of the Estimate of the Expected Return

$$SD(\text{Average of Independent, Identical Risks}) = \frac{SD(\text{Individual Risk})}{\sqrt{\text{Number of Observations}}} \quad (10.8)$$

Because the average return will be within two standard errors of the true expected return approximately 95% of the time,[9] the standard error can be used to determine a reasonable range for the true expected value. The **95% confidence interval** for the expected return is defined as

$$\text{Historical Average Return} \pm (2 \times \text{Standard Error}) \quad (10.9)$$

For example, from 1926 to 2004 the average return of the S&P 500 was 12.3% with a volatility of 20.36%. Assuming its returns are drawn from an independent and identical distribution (IID) each year, the 95% confidence interval for the expected return of the S&P 500 during this period is

$$12.3\% \pm 2\left(\frac{20.36\%}{\sqrt{79}}\right) = 12.3\% \pm 4.6\%$$

or a range from 7.7% to 16.9%. Thus, even with 79 years of data, we cannot estimate the expected return of the S&P 500 very accurately. If we believe the distribution may have

---

8. The assumption that the returns of a security are independent and identically distributed (IID) means that the likelihood that this year's return has a given outcome is the same as in prior years and does not depend on past returns, in the same way that the odds of a coin coming up heads do not depend on past flips. It turns out to be a reasonable first approximation for stock returns.

9. If returns are independent and from a normal distribution, then the estimated mean will be within two standard errors of the true mean 95.44% of the time. Even if returns are not normally distributed, this formula is approximately correct with a sufficient number of independent observations.

Arithmetic Average Returns Versus Compound Annual Returns

We compute average annual returns by calculating an *arithmetic* average. An alternative is the compound annual return (also called the compound annual growth rate, or CAGR), which is computed as the *geometric* average of the annual returns $R_1, \ldots, R_T$:

Compound Annual Return =
$$[(1 + R_1) \times (1 + R_2) \times \cdots \times (1 + R_T)]^{1/T} - 1$$

In other words, we compute the return from year 1 through T by compounding the annual returns, and then convert the result to an annual yield by taking it to the power $1/T$.

For the S&P 500, the compound annual return for 1926–2004 was 10.32%. That is, $1 invested at 10.32% for the 79 years from 1926 to 2004 would grow to

$$\$100 \times (1.1032)^{79} = \$234,253$$

This is equivalent (up to rounding error) to the growth in the S&P 500 during the same period. Similarly, the compound annual return for small stocks is 15.41%, for corporate bonds is 6.29%, and for Treasury bills is 3.83%.

In each case, the compound annual return is below the average annual return shown in Table 10.3. This difference reflects the fact that returns are volatile. To see the effect of volatility, suppose an investment has annual returns of +20% one year and −20% the next year. The average annual return is $\frac{1}{2}(20\% - 20\%) = 0\%$. But the value of $1 invested after two years is

$$\$1 \times (1.20) \times (0.80) = \$0.96$$

That is, an investor would have lost money. Why? Because the 20% gain happens on a $1 investment, whereas the 20% loss happens on a larger investment of $1.20. In this case, the compound annual return is

$$(0.96)^{1/2} - 1 = -2.02\%$$

This logic implies that the compound annual return will always be below the average return, and the difference grows with the volatility of the annual returns. (Typically, the difference is about half of the variance of the returns.)

Which is a better description of an investment's return? The compound annual return is a better description of the long-run *historical* performance of an investment. It describes the equivalent risk-free return that would be required to duplicate the investment's performance over the same time period. The ranking of the long-run performance of different investments coincides with the ranking of their compound annual returns. Thus the compound annual return is the return that is most often used for comparison purposes. For example, mutual funds generally report their compound annual returns over the last five or ten years.

Conversely, we should use the average annual return when we are trying to estimate an investment's *expected* return over a *future* horizon based on its past performance. If we view past annual returns as independent draws from the same distribution, then we know from statistics that the arithmetic average provides the best estimate of the true mean. If the investment mentioned above is equally likely to have annual returns of +20% and −20% in the future, then the payoff from a $1 investment after two years is equally likely to be

$$\$1 \times (1.20) \times (1.20) = \$1.44$$
$$\$1 \times (1.20) \times (0.80) = \$0.96$$
$$\$1 \times (0.80) \times (1.20) = \$0.96$$
$$\$1 \times (0.80) \times (0.80) = \$0.64$$

This implies an expected payoff of 25%(1.44) + 50%(0.96) + 25%(0.64) − $1, consistent with the arithmetic average return of 0%.

changed over time and we can use only more recent data to estimate the expected return, then the estimate will be even less accurate.

Individual stocks tend to be even more volatile than large portfolios, and many have been in existence for only a few years, providing little data with which to estimate returns. Because of the relatively large estimation error in such cases, the average return investors earned in the past is not a reliable estimate of a security's expected return. Instead, we need to derive an alternative method to estimate the expected return—one that relies on more reliable statistical estimates. In the remainder of this chapter, the strategy we will follow is to first consider how to measure a security's risk, and then use the relationship between risk and return—which we must still determine—to estimate its expected return.

The Accuracy of Expected Return Estimates

Problem

Using the returns for the S&P 500 from 1996–2004 only (see Table 10.2), what is the 95% confidence interval for our estimate of the S&P 500's expected return?

Solution

Earlier, we calculated the average return for the S&P 500 during this period to be 11.4%, with a volatility of 20.6% (see Example 10.3). The standard error of our estimate of the expected return is $20.6\% / \sqrt{9} = 6.9\%$, and the 95% confidence interval is $11.4\% \pm (2 \times 6.9\%)$, or from -2.4% to 25.2%. As this example shows, with only a few years of data, we cannot reliably estimate expected returns for stocks.

CONCEPT CHECK

1. How do we estimate the average annual return of an investment?

2. We have 79 years of data on the S&P 500 returns, yet we cannot estimate the expected return of the S&P 500 very accurately. Why?

10.4 The Historical Tradeoff Between Risk and Return

In Chapter 3, we discussed the idea that investors are risk averse: The benefit they receive from an increase in income is smaller than the personal cost of an equivalent decrease in income. This idea suggests that investors would not choose to hold a portfolio that is more volatile unless they expected to earn a higher return. In this section, we quantify the historical relationship between volatility and average returns.

The Returns of Large Portfolios

In Tables 10.3 and 10.4, we computed the historical average returns and volatilities for several different types of investments. We combine those data in Table 10.5, which lists the volatility and excess return for each investment. The **excess return** is the difference between the average return for the investment and the average return for Treasury bills, a risk-free investment.

TABLE 10.5   **Volatility Versus Excess Return of U.S. Small Stocks, Large Stocks (S&P 500), Corporate Bonds, and Treasury Bills, 1926–2004**

Investment	Return Volatility (Standard Deviation)	Excess Return (Average Return in Excess of Treasury Bills)
Small stocks	42.75%	18.24%
S&P 500	20.36%	8.45%
Corporate bonds	7.17%	2.65%
Treasury bills	3.18%	0.00%

FIGURE 10.5

The Historical Tradeoff Between Risk and Return in Large Portfolios, 1926–2004

Also included are a mid-cap portfolio composed of the 10% of U.S. stocks whose size is just below the median of all U.S. stocks, and a world portfolio of large stocks from North America, Europe, and Asia. Note the general increasing relationship between historical volatility and average return for these large portfolios.

Source: CRSP, Morgan Stanley Capital International and Global Financial Data.

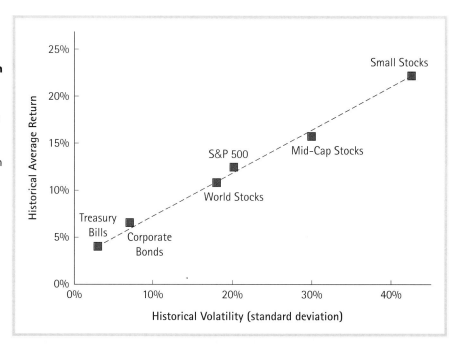

In Figure 10.5, we plot the average return versus the volatility of each type of investment given in Table 10.5. We also include data for a large portfolio of mid-cap stocks, or stocks of median size in the U.S. market, as well as a world index of the largest stocks traded in stock markets in North America, Europe, and Asia. Note the positive relationship: The investments with higher volatility have rewarded investors with higher average returns. Figure 10.5 is consistent with our view that investors are risk averse. Riskier investments must offer investors higher average returns to compensate them for the extra risk they are taking on.

The Returns of Individual Stocks

Figure 10.5 suggests the following simple model of the risk premium: Investments with higher volatility should have a higher risk premium and therefore higher returns. Indeed, looking at Figure 10.5 it is tempting to draw a line through the portfolios and conclude that all investments should lie on or near this line—that is, expected return should rise proportionately with volatility. This conclusion appears to be approximately true for the large portfolios we have looked at so far. Is it correct? Does it apply to individual stocks?

Unfortunately, the answer to both questions is no. Figure 10.6 shows that, if we look at the volatility and return of individual stocks, we do not see any clear relationship between them. Each point represents the returns from 1926 to 2004 of investing in the Nth largest stock traded in the United States (updated quarterly) for $N = 1$ to 500.

We can make several important observations from these data. First, there is a relationship between size and risk: Larger stocks have lower volatility overall. In addition, even the largest stocks are typically more volatile than a portfolio of large stocks, the S&P 500. Finally, there is no clear relationship between volatility and return. While the smallest

FIGURE 10.6

Historical Volatility and Return for 500 Individual Stocks, by Size, Updated Quarterly, 1926–2004

Unlike the case for large portfolios, there is no precise relationship between volatility and average return for individual stocks. Individual stocks have higher volatility and lower average returns than the relationship shown for large portfolios.

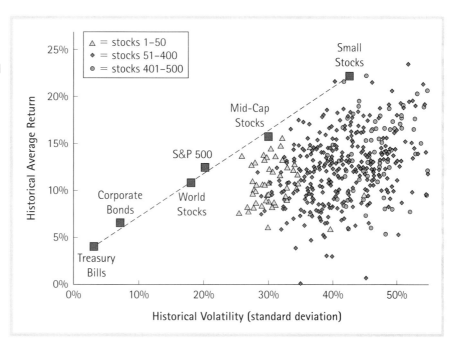

stocks have a slightly higher average return, many stocks have higher volatility and lower average returns than other stocks. And all stocks seem to have higher risk and lower returns than we would have predicted from a simple extrapolation of our data from large portfolios.

Thus, while volatility seems be a reasonable measure of risk when evaluating a large portfolio, it is not adequate to explain the returns of individual securities. What are we to make of this fact? Why wouldn't investors demand a higher return from stocks with a higher volatility? And how is it that the S&P 500—a portfolio of the 500 largest stocks— is so much less risky than all of the 500 stocks individually? To answer these questions, we need to think more carefully about how to measure risk for an investor.

CONCEPT CHECK

1. What is the excess return?

2. Is it true that expected returns for individual stocks increase proportionately with volatility?

10.5 Common Versus Independent Risk

In this section we explain why the risk of an individual security differs from the risk of a portfolio composed of similar securities. We begin with an example from the insurance industry. Consider two types of home insurance: theft insurance and earthquake insurance. Let us assume, for the purpose of illustration, that the risk of each of these two hazards is similar for a given home in the San Francisco area. Each year there is about a 1% chance that the home will be robbed and a 1% chance that the home will be damaged by an earthquake.

FIGURE 10.7

Likelihood of Different Numbers of Annual Claims for a Portfolio of 100,000 Theft Insurance Policies

The distribution assumes that there is a 1% chance of theft for an individual home, and that the incidence of theft is independent across homes. The number of claims is generally very close to 1000, or 1% of the policies written. The number of claims will almost always be between 875 and 1125 (0.875% and 1.125% of the number of policies written).

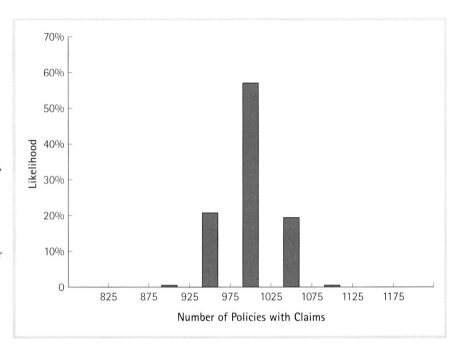

In this case, the chance the insurance company will pay a claim for a single home is the same for both types of insurance policies. Suppose an insurance company writes 100,000 policies of each type for homeowners in San Francisco. We know that the risks of the individual policies are similar, but are the risks of the portfolios of policies similar?

First consider theft insurance. Because the chance of a theft for any given home is 1%, we would expect about 1% of the 100,000 homes to experience a robbery. Thus the number of theft claims will be about 1000 per year. The actual number of claims may be a bit higher or lower each year, but not by much. Indeed, Figure 10.7 shows the likelihood that the insurance company will receive different numbers of claims, assuming that instances of theft are independent of one another (that is, the fact that one house is robbed does not change the odds of other houses being robbed). Figure 10.7 shows that the number of claims will almost always be between 875 and 1125 (0.875% and 1.125% of the number of policies written). In this case, if the insurance company holds reserves sufficient to cover 1200 claims, it will almost certainly have enough to meet its obligations on its theft insurance policies.

Now consider earthquake insurance. There is a 99% chance that an earthquake will not occur. All of the homes are in the same city, so if an earthquake does occur, all homes are likely to be affected and the insurance company can expect 100,000 claims. As a result, the insurance company will have to hold reserves sufficient to cover claims on all 100,000 policies it wrote to meet its obligations if an earthquake occurs.

Thus earthquake and theft insurance lead to portfolios with very different risk characteristics. For earthquake insurance, the number of claims is very risky. It will most likely be zero, but there is a 1% chance that the insurance company will have to pay claims on *all* the policies it wrote. In this case, the risk of the portfolio of insurance policies is no different from the risk of any single policy—it is still all or nothing. Conversely, for theft insurance the number of claims in a given year is quite predictable. Year in and year out, it will be very close to 1% of the total number of policies, or 1000 claims. The portfolio of theft insurance policies has almost no risk![10]

Why are the portfolios of insurance policies so different when the individual policies themselves are quite similar? Intuitively, the key difference between them is that an earthquake affects all houses simultaneously, so the risk is perfectly correlated across homes. We call risk that is perfectly correlated **common risk**. In contrast, we assume that thefts in different houses are not related to each other, so the risk of theft is uncorrelated and independent across homes. We call this type of risk **independent risk**. When risks are independent, some individual homeowners are unlucky and others are lucky, but overall the number of claims is quite predictable. The averaging out of independent risks in a large portfolio is called **diversification**.[11]

We can quantify this difference in terms of the standard deviation of the percentage of claims. First consider the standard deviation for an individual homeowner. At the beginning of the year, the homeowner expects a 1% chance of placing a claim for either type of insurance. But at the end of the year, the homeowner will have filed a claim (100%) or not (0%). Using Eq. 10.2 the standard deviation is

$$SD(\text{Claim}) = \sqrt{Var(\text{Claim})}$$
$$= \sqrt{0.99 \times (0 - 0.01)^2 + 0.01 \times (1 - 0.01)^2} = 9.95\%$$

For the homeowner, this standard deviation is the same for a loss from earthquake or theft.

Now consider the standard deviation of the percentage of claims for the insurance company. In the case of earthquake insurance, because the risk is common, the percentage of claims is either 100% or 0%, just as it was for the homeowner. Thus the percentage of claims received by the earthquake insurer is also 1% on average, with a 9.95% standard deviation.

While the theft insurer also receives 1% of claims on average, because the risk of theft is independent across households, the portfolio is much less risky. To quantify this difference, let's calculate the standard deviation of the average claim using Eq. 10.8. Recall that when risks are independent and identical, the standard deviation of the average is known as the standard error, which declines with the square root of the number of observations. Therefore,

$$SD(\text{Percentage Theft Claims}) = \frac{SD(\text{Individual Claim})}{\sqrt{\text{Number of Observations}}}$$
$$= \frac{9.95\%}{\sqrt{100,000}} = 0.03\%$$

Thus there is almost *no* risk for the theft insurer.

---

10. In the case of insurance, this difference in risk—and therefore in required reserves—can lead to a significant difference in the cost of the insurance. Indeed, earthquake insurance is generally thought to be more expensive to purchase, even though the risk to an individual household may be similar to other risks, such as theft or fire.

11. Harry Markowitz was the first to formalize the role of diversification in forming an optimal stock market portfolio. See H. M. Markowitz, "Portfolio Selection," *Journal of Finance* 7 (1952): 77–91.

The principle of diversification is used routinely in the insurance industry. In addition to theft insurance, many other forms of insurance (life, health, auto) rely on the fact that the number of claims is relatively predictable in a large portfolio. Even in the case of earthquake insurance, insurers can achieve some diversification by selling policies in different geographical regions or by combining different types of policies. Diversification is used to reduce risk in many other settings. For example, many systems are designed with redundancy to decrease the risk of a disruption: Firms often add redundancy to critical parts of the manufacturing process, NASA puts more than one antenna on its space probes, automobiles contain spare tires, and so forth.

Diversification and Gambling

Problem
Roulette wheels are typically marked with the numbers 1 through 36 plus 0 and 00. Each of these outcomes is equally likely every time the wheel is spun. If you place a bet on any one number and are correct, the payoff is 35 : 1; that is, if you bet $1, you will receive $36 if you win ($35 plus your original $1) and nothing if you lose. Suppose you place a $1 bet on your favorite number. What is the casino's expected profit? What is the standard deviation of this profit for a single bet? Suppose 9 million similar bets are placed throughout the casino in a typical month. What is the standard deviation of the casino's average revenues per dollar bet each month?

Solution
Because there are 38 numbers on the wheel, the odds of winning are 1 / 38. The casino loses $35 if you win, and makes $1 if you lose. Therefore, using Eq. 10.1, the casino's expected profit is

$$E[\text{Payoff}] = (1 / 38) \times (-\$35) + (37 / 38) \times (\$1) = \$0.0526$$

That is, for each dollar bet, the casino earns 5.26 cents on average. For a single bet, we calculate the standard deviation of this profit using Eq. 10.2 as

$$SD(\text{Payoff}) = \sqrt{(1 / 38) \times (-35 - 0.0526)^2 + (37 / 38) \times (1 - 0.0526)^2} = \$5.76$$

This standard deviation is quite large relative to the magnitude of the profits. But if many such bets are placed, the risk will be diversified. Using Eq. 10.8, the standard deviation of the casino's average revenues per dollar bet is only

$$SD(\text{Average Payoff}) = \frac{\$5.76}{\sqrt{9,000,000}} = \$0.0019$$

In other words, the 95% confidence interval for the casino's profits per dollar bet is $0.0526 $\pm$ (2 × 0.0019) = $0.0488 to $0.0564. Given $9 million in bets placed, the casino's monthly profits will almost always be between $439,000 and $508,000, which is very little risk. The key assumption, of course, is that the outcome of each bet is independent of each other. If the $9 million were placed in a single bet, the casino's risk would be large—losing 35 × $9 million = $315 million if the bet wins. For this reason, casinos often impose limits on the amount of any individual bet.

CONCEPT CHECK   1. What is the difference between common risk and independent risk?

2. Under what circumstances will risk be diversified in a large portfolio of insurance contracts?

10.6 Diversification in Stock Portfolios

As the insurance example indicates, the risk of a portfolio of insurance contracts depends on whether the individual risks within it are common or independent. Independent risks are diversified in a large portfolio, whereas common risks are not. Let's consider the implication of this distinction for the risk of stock portfolios.

Firm-Specific Versus Systematic Risk

Over any given time period, the risk of holding a stock is that the dividends plus the final stock price will be higher or lower than expected, which makes the realized return risky. What causes dividends or stock prices, and therefore returns, to be higher or lower than we expect? Usually, stock prices and dividends fluctuate due to two types of news:

1. *Firm-specific news* is good or bad news about the company itself. For example, a firm might announce that it has been successful in gaining market share within its industry.

2. *Market-wide news* is news about the economy as a whole and therefore affects all stocks. For instance, the Federal Reserve might announce that it will lower interest rates to boost the economy.

Fluctuations of a stock's return that are due to firm-specific news are independent risks. Like theft across homes, these risks are unrelated across stocks. This type of risk is also referred to as **firm-specific, idiosyncratic, unsystematic, unique,** or **diversifiable risk**.

Fluctuations of a stock's return that are due to market-wide news represent common risk. As with earthquakes, all stocks are affected simultaneously by the news. This type of risk is also called **systematic, undiversifiable,** or **market risk**.

When we combine many stocks in a large portfolio, the firm-specific risks for each stock will average out and be diversified. Good news will affect some stocks, and bad news will affect others, but the amount of good or bad news overall will be relatively constant. The systematic risk, however, will affect all firms—and therefore the entire portfolio—and will not be diversified.

Let's consider an example. Suppose type S firms are affected *only* by the strength of the economy, a systematic risk which has a 50–50 chance of being either strong or weak. If the economy is strong, type S stocks will earn a return of 40%; if the economy is weak, their return will be −20%. Because these firms face systematic risk (the strength of the economy), holding a large portfolio of type S firms will not diversify the risk. When the economy is strong, the portfolio will have the same return of 40% as each type S firm; when the economy is weak, the portfolio will also have a return of −20%.

Now consider type I firms, which are affected only by idiosyncratic, firm-specific risks. Their returns are equally likely to be 35% or −25%, based on factors specific to each firm's local market. Because these risks are firm specific, if we hold a portfolio of the stocks of many type I firms, the risk is diversified. About half of the firms will have returns of 35%, and half will have returns of −25%, so that the return of the portfolio will be the average return of 50% (0.35) + 50% (−0.25) = 5%.

Figure 10.8 illustrates how volatility declines with the size of the portfolio for type S and I firms. Type S firms have only systematic risk. As with earthquake insurance, the volatility of the portfolio does not change as the number of firms increases. Type I firms have only idiosyncratic risk. As with theft insurance, the risk is diversified as the number of firms increases, and volatility declines. As is evident from Figure 10.8, with a large number of firms, the risk is essentially eliminated.

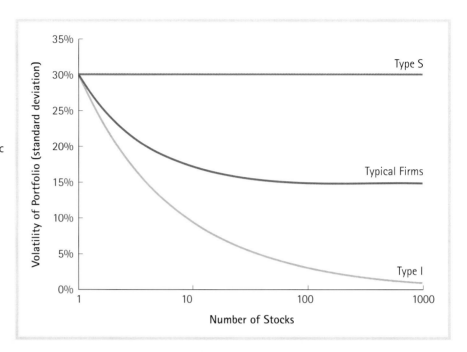

Of course, actual firms are not like type S or I firms. Firms are affected by both systematic, market-wide risks and firm-specific risks. Figure 10.8 also shows how the volatility changes with the size of a portfolio containing the stocks of typical firms. When firms carry both types of risk, only the firm-specific risk will be diversified when we combine many firm's stocks into a portfolio. The volatility will therefore decline until only the systematic risk, which affects all firms, remains.

This example explains one of the puzzles in Figure 10.6. There we saw that the S&P 500 had much lower volatility than any of the individual stocks. Now we can see why: The individual stocks each contain firm-specific risk, which is eliminated when we combine them into a large portfolio. Thus the portfolio as a whole can have lower volatility than each of the stocks within it.

EXAMPLE
10.6

Portfolio Volatility

Problem
What is the volatility of the average return of ten type S firms? What is the volatility of the average return of ten type I firms?

Solution
Type S firms have equally likely returns of 40% or −20%. Their expected return is $\frac{1}{2}(40\%) + \frac{1}{2}(-20\%) = 10\%$, so

$$SD(R_S) = \sqrt{\tfrac{1}{2}(0.40 - 0.10)^2 + \tfrac{1}{2}(-0.20 - 0.10)^2} = 30\%$$

Because all type S firms have high or low returns at the same time, the average return of ten type S firms is also 40% or −20%. Thus it has the same volatility of 30%, as shown in Figure 10.8.

Type I firms have equally likely returns of 35% or -25%. Their expected return is $\frac{1}{2}(35\%) + \frac{1}{2}(-25\%) = 5\%$, so

$$SD(R_I) = \sqrt{\frac{1}{2}(0.35 - 0.05)^2 + \frac{1}{2}(-0.25 - 0.05)^2} = 30\%$$

Because the returns of type I firms are independent, using Eq. 10.8, the average return of ten type I firms has volatility of $30\% / \sqrt{10} = 9.5\%$, as shown in Figure 10.8.

No Arbitrage and the Risk Premium

Consider again type I firms, which are affected only by firm-specific risk. Because each individual type I firm is risky, should investors expect to earn a risk premium when investing in type I firms?

In a competitive market, the answer is no. To see why, suppose the expected return of type I firms exceeds the risk-free interest rate. Then by holding a large portfolio of many type I firms, investors could diversify the firm-specific risk of these firms and earn a return above the risk-free interest rate without taking on any significant risk.

The situation just described is very close to an arbitrage opportunity, which investors would find very attractive. They would borrow money at the risk-free interest rate and invest it in a large portfolio of type I firms, which offers a higher return with only a tiny amount of risk.[12] As more investors take advantage of this situation and purchase shares of type I firms, the current share prices for type I firms would rise, lowering their expected return—recall that the current share price P_t is the denominator when computing the stock's return as in Eq. 10.4. This trading would stop only after the return of type I firms equaled the risk-free interest rate. Competition between investors drives the return of type I firms down to the risk-free return.

The preceding argument is essentially an application of the Law of One Price: Because a large portfolio of type I firms has no risk, it must earn the risk-free interest rate. This no-arbitrage argument suggests the following more general principle:

The risk premium for diversifiable risk is zero, so investors are not compensated for holding firm-specific risk.

This principle can be applied not just to type I firms, but to all stocks and securities. It implies that the risk premium of a stock is not affected by its diversifiable, firm-specific risk. If the diversifiable risk of stocks were compensated with an additional risk premium, then investors could buy the stocks, earn the additional premium, and simultaneously diversify and eliminate the risk. By doing so, investors could earn an additional premium without taking on additional risk. This opportunity to earn something for nothing would quickly be exploited and eliminated.[13]

Because investors can eliminate firm-specific risk "for free" by diversifying their portfolios, they will not require a reward or risk premium for holding it. However, diversification does not reduce systematic risk: Even holding a large portfolio, an investor will be exposed to risks that affect the entire economy and therefore affect all securities. Because investors are risk averse, they will demand a risk premium to hold systematic risk; otherwise

---

12. If investors could actually hold a large enough portfolio and completely diversify all the risk, then this would be a true arbitrage opportunity.

13. The main thrust of this argument can be found in S. Ross, "The Arbitrage Theory of Capital Asset Pricing," *Journal of Economic Theory* 13 (December 1976): 341–360.

they would be better off selling their stocks and investing in risk-free bonds. Because idio-syncratic risk can be eliminated for free by diversifying, whereas systematic risk can be elim-inated only by sacrificing expected returns, it is a security's systematic risk that determines the risk premium investors require to hold it. This fact leads to a second key principle:

The risk premium of a security is determined by its systematic risk and does not depend on its diversifiable risk.

This principle implies that a stock's volatility, which is a measure of total risk (that is, systematic risk plus diversifiable risk), is not especially useful in determining the risk pre-mium that investors will earn. For example, consider again type S and I firms. As calcu-lated in Example 10.6, the volatility of a single type S or I firm is 30%. Although both types of firms have the same volatility, type S firms have an expected return of 10% and type I firms have an expected return of 5%. The difference in expected returns derives from the difference in the kind of risk each firm bears. Type I firms have only firm-specific risk, which does not require a risk premium, so the expected return of 5% for type I firms equals the risk-free interest rate. Type S firms have only systematic risk. Because investors will require compensation for taking on this risk, the expected return of 10% for type S firms provides investors with a 5% risk premium above the risk-free interest rate.

COMMON MISTAKE   A Fallacy of Long-Run Diversification

We have seen that investors can greatly reduce their risk by dividing their investment dollars over many different investments, eliminating the diversifiable risk in their portfolios. It is sometimes argued that the same logic applies over time: By investing for many years, we can also diversify the risk we face during any particular year. Is this correct? In the long run, does risk still matter?

Equation 10.8 tells us that if returns each year are independent, the volatility of the average annual return declines with the number of years that we invest. Of course, as long-term investors, we don't care about the volatility of our *average* return; instead, we care about the volatility of our *cumulative* return over the period. This volatility grows with the investment horizon, as illustrated in the following example.

In 1925, large U.S. stocks increased in value by about 30%. In fact, a $77 investment at the start of 1925 would have grown to $77 × 1.30 = $100 by the end of the year. We see from Figure 10.1 that if that $100 were invested in the S&P 500 from 1926 onward, it would have grown to about $234,000 by the start of 2005. But suppose that mining and transportation strikes had caused stocks to drop by 35% in 1925. Then the initial $77 invested would be worth only $77 × (1 − 35%) = $50 at the beginning of 1926. If returns from then on were unchanged, the investment would be worth half as much in 2005, or $117,000.

Thus, if future returns are not affected by today's return, then an increase or a decline in the value of our portfolio today will translate into the same percentage increase or decrease in the value of our portfolio in the future, so there is no diversification over time. The only way the length of the time horizon can reduce risk is if a below-average return this year implies that returns are more likely to be above average in the future (and vice versa), a phenomenon sometimes referred to as *mean reversion*. Mean reversion implies that past low returns can be used to predict future high returns in the stock market.

For short horizons of a few years, there is no evidence of mean reversion in the stock market. For longer hori-zons, there is some evidence of mean reversion historically, but it is not clear how reliable this evidence is (there are not enough decades of accurate stock market data avail-able) or whether the pattern will continue. Even if there is long-run mean reversion in stock returns, a buy-and-hold diversification strategy is still not optimal: Because mean reversion implies that past returns can be used to predict future returns, one should invest more in stocks when returns are predicted to be high, and invest less when they are predicted to be low. This strategy is very different from the diversification we achieve by holding many stocks, where we cannot predict which stocks will have good or bad firm-specific shocks.

We now have an explanation for the second puzzle of Figure 10.6. While volatility might be a reasonable measure of risk for a large portfolio, it is not an appropriate metric for an individual security. Thus, there should be no clear relationship between volatility and average returns for individual securities. Consequently, to estimate a security's expected return, we need to find a measure of a security's systematic risk.

In Chapter 3, we used a simple example to show that an investment's risk premium depends on how its returns move in relation to the overall economy. In particular, risk-averse investors will demand a premium to invest in securities that will do poorly in bad times (recall, for example, the performance of small stocks in Figure 10.1 during the Great Depression). This idea coincides with the notion of systematic risk we have defined in this chapter. Economy-wide risk—that is, the risk of recessions and booms—is systematic risk that cannot be diversified. Therefore an asset that moves with the economy contains systematic risk and so requires a risk premium.

EXAMPLE 10.7

Diversifiable Versus Systematic Risk

Problem
Which of the following risks of a stock are likely to be firm-specific, diversifiable risks, and which are likely to be systematic risks? Which risks will affect the risk premium that investors will demand?
  a. The risk that the founder and CEO retires
  b. The risk that oil prices rise, increasing production costs
  c. The risk that a product design is faulty and the product must be recalled
  d. The risk that the economy slows, reducing demand for the firm's products

Solution
Because oil prices and the health of the economy affect all stocks, risks (b) and (d) are systematic risks. These risks are not diversified in a large portfolio, and so will affect the risk premium that investors require to invest in a stock. Risks (a) and (c) are firm-specific risks, and so are diversifiable. While these risks should be considered when estimating a firm's future cash flows, they will not affect the risk premium that investors will require and, therefore, will not affect a firm's cost of capital.

CONCEPT CHECK

1. Explain why the risk premium of diversifiable risk is zero.

2. Why is the risk premium of a security determined only by its systematic risk?

10.7 Estimating the Expected Return

When evaluating the risk of an investment, an investor will care about its systematic risk, which cannot be eliminated through diversification. In exchange for bearing systematic risk, investors want to be compensated by earning a higher return. So, to determine the expected return investors will require to undertake an investment, we must take two steps:

1. Measure the investment's systematic risk.

2. Determine the risk premium required to compensate for that amount of systematic risk.

Once we have completed steps (1) and (2), we can estimate the expected return of the investment. In this section, we outline the main method used in practice.

Measuring Systematic Risk

To measure the systematic risk of a stock, we must determine how much of the variability of its return is due to systematic, market-wide risks versus diversifiable, firm-specific risks. That is, we would like to know how sensitive the stock is to systematic shocks that affect the economy as a whole.

If we wanted to determine how sensitive a stock's return is to interest rate changes, for example, we would look at how much the return tends to change on average for each 1% change in interest rates. Similarly, if we want to determine how sensitive a stock's return is to oil prices, we would examine the average change in the return for each 1% change in oil prices. In the same way, if we wanted to determine how sensitive a stock is to systematic risk, we can look at the average change in the return for each 1% change in the return of *a portfolio that fluctuates solely due to systematic risk.*

Thus the key step to measuring systematic risk is finding a portfolio that contains *only* systematic risk. Then changes in the price of this portfolio will correspond to systematic shocks to the economy. We call such a portfolio an **efficient portfolio**. An efficient portfolio cannot be diversified further—that is, there is no way to reduce the risk of the portfolio without lowering its expected return.

As we will see over the next few chapters, the best way to identify an efficient portfolio is one of the key questions in modern finance. Because diversification improves with the number of stocks held in a portfolio, an efficient portfolio should be a large portfolio containing many different stocks. Thus it is reasonable to consider a portfolio that contains all shares of all stocks and securities in the market. We call this portfolio the **market portfolio**. Because it is difficult to find data for the returns of many bonds and small stocks, it is common in practice to use the S&P 500 portfolio as an approximation for the market portfolio, under the assumption that the S&P 500 is large enough to be essentially fully diversified.

If we assume that the market portfolio (or the S&P 500) is efficient, then changes in the value of the market portfolio represent systematic shocks to the economy. Knowing this, we can measure the systematic risk of a security's return by its beta. The **beta (β)** of a security is the sensitivity of the security's return to the return of the overall market. More precisely,

The beta is the expected percent change in the excess return of a security for a 1% change in the excess return of the market portfolio.

EXAMPLE 10.8

Estimating Beta

Problem

Suppose the market portfolio excess return tends to increase by 47% when the economy is strong and decline by 25% when the economy is weak. What is the beta of a type S firm whose excess return is 40% on average when the economy is strong and -20% when the economy is weak? What is the beta of a type I firm that bears only idiosyncratic, firm-specific risk?

Solution

The systematic risk of the strength of the economy produces a $47\% - (-25\%) = 72\%$ change in the return of the market portfolio. The type S firm's return changes by $40\% - (-20\%) = 60\%$ on average. Thus the firm's beta is $\beta_S = 60\% / 72\% = 0.833$. That is, each 1% change in the return of the market portfolio leads to a 0.833% change in the type S firm's return on average.

The return of a type I firm that has only firm-specific risk, however, is not affected by the strength of the economy. Its return is affected only by factors that are specific to the firm. Whether the economy is strong or weak, it will have the same expected return, and thus $\beta_I = 0\% / 72\% = 0$.

We will look at statistical techniques for estimating beta from historical data in Chapter 12. It is important to note that we can estimate beta reasonably accurately using just a few years of data (which was not the case for expected returns, as we saw in Example 10.4). Using the S&P 500 to represent the market's return, Table 10.6 shows the betas of several stocks, as well as the average betas for stocks within their industry, during 2000–2005. As shown in the table, each 1% change in the excess return of the market during this period led, on average, to a 2.17% change in the excess return for Intel, but only a 0.50% change in the excess return for Coca-Cola.

TABLE 10.6 **Betas With Respect to the S&P 500 for Individual Stocks and Average Betas for Stocks in Their Industries (based on monthly data for 2000–2005)**

Industry	Beta	Ticker	Firm	Beta
Gold and Silver	−0.04	NEM	Newmont Mining Corporation	0.02
Beverages (Alcoholic)	0.23	BUD	Anheuser-Busch Companies, Inc.	0.10
Personal and Household Prods.	0.25	PG	The Procter & Gamble Company	0.19
Food Processing	0.34	HNZ	H. J. Heinz Company	0.37
		HSY	The Hershey Company	−0.10
Beverages (Nonalcoholic)	0.43	KO	The Coca-Cola Company	0.50
Electric Utilities	0.48	EIX	Edison International	0.50
Major Drugs	0.48	PFE	Pfizer Inc.	0.54
Restaurants	0.69	SBUX	Starbucks Corporation	0.60
Retail (Grocery)	0.74	SWY	Safeway Inc.	0.67
Conglomerates	0.84	GE	General Electric Company	0.85
Forestry and Wood Products	0.95	WY	Weyerhaeuser Company	0.96
Recreational Products	1.00	HDI	Harley-Davidson, Inc.	1.14
Apparel/Accessories	1.12	LIZ	Liz Claiborne, Inc.	0.90
Retail (Home Improvement)	1.22	HD	Home Depot, Inc.	1.43
Auto and Truck Manufacturers	1.44	GM	General Motors Corporation	1.20
Computer Hardware	1.60	AAPL	Apple Computer, Inc.	1.35
Software and Programming	1.74	ADBE	Adobe Systems, Inc.	1.84
		MSFT	Microsoft Corporation	1.12
Computer Services	1.77	YHOO	Yahoo! Inc.	2.80
Communications Equipment	2.20	CSCO	Cisco Systems, Inc.	2.28
Semiconductors	2.59	AMD	Advanced Micro Devices, Inc.	3.23
		INTC	Intel Corporation	2.17

Beta measures the sensitivity of a security to market-wide risk factors. For a stock, this value is related to how sensitive its underlying revenues and cash flows are to general economic conditions. Stocks in cyclical industries, in which revenues tend to vary greatly over the business cycle, are likely to be more sensitive to systematic risk and have higher betas than stocks in less sensitive industries.

For example, notice the relatively low betas of Edison International (a utility company), Anheuser-Busch (a beer-brewing company), and H. J. Heinz (a ketchup manufacturer). Utilities tend to be stable and highly regulated, and thus are insensitive to fluctuations in the overall market. Brewing and food companies are also very insensitive—the demand for their products appears to be unrelated to the booms and busts of the economy as a whole.

At the other extreme, technology stocks tend to have the highest betas; the average for the industry is close to 2, with the betas of Internet stocks (such as Yahoo!) being even higher. Shocks in the economy have an amplified impact on these stocks: When the market as a whole is up, Intel tends to rise almost twice as much; but when the market stumbles, Intel tends to fall almost twice as far.

Recall that beta differs from volatility. Volatility measures total risk—that is, both market and firm-specific risks—so that there is no necessary relationship between volatility and beta. Consider that Pfizer (a drug company) and Intel may have similar volatilities. Pfizer, however, has a much lower beta. While drug companies face a great deal of risk related to the development and approval of new drugs, this risk is unrelated to the rest of the economy. And though health care expenditures do vary a little with the state of the economy, they vary much less than expenditures on technology.

Estimating the Risk Premium

An investment opportunity with a beta of 2 carries twice as much systematic risk as an investment in the S&P 500. That is, for each dollar we invest in the opportunity, we could invest twice that amount in the S&P 500 and be exposed to the same amount of systematic risk. In general, the beta of an investment opportunity measures its amplification of systematic risk compared to the market as a whole, and investors will require a commensurate risk premium to make such an investment.

The risk premium investors can earn by holding the market portfolio is the difference between the market portfolio's expected return and the risk-free interest rate:

$$\text{Market Risk Premium} = E[R_{Mkt}] - r_f$$

The market risk premium is the reward investors expect to earn for holding a portfolio with a beta of 1. Because the systematic risk of any traded security is proportional to its beta, its risk premium will be proportional to beta. Therefore, to compensate investors for the time value of their money as well as the systematic risk they are taking by investing in security s, the expected return of the traded security should satisfy the following formula:

Estimating a Traded Security's Expected Return from Its Beta

$$E[R] = \text{Risk-Free Interest Rate} + \text{Risk Premium}$$
$$= r_f + \beta \times (E[R_{Mkt}] - r_f) \tag{10.10}$$

As an example, suppose the market risk premium is 6% and the risk-free interest rate is 5%. According to Eq. 10.10, investors' expected return for Yahoo! and Anheuser-Busch stocks is

$$E[R_{YHOO}] = 5\% + 2.80 \times 6\% = 21.8\%$$
$$E[R_{BUD}] = 5\% + 0.10 \times 6\% = 5.6\%$$

Thus, the difference in the average returns of these two stocks reported in the introduction of this chapter is not so surprising. Investors in Yahoo! expect a much higher return on average to compensate them for Yahoo!'s much higher systematic risk.

EXAMPLE 10.9

Expected Returns and Beta

Problem
Suppose the risk-free rate is 5% and the economy is equally likely to be strong or weak. Verify that Eq. 10.10 holds for the type S firms considered in Example 10.8.

Solution
If the economy is equally likely to be strong or weak, the expected return of the market is $E[R_{Mkt}] = 50\%(0.47) + 50\%(-0.25) = 11\%$, and the market risk premium is $E[R_{Mkt}] - r_f = 11\% - 5\% = 6\%$. Given the beta of 0.833 for type S firms that we calculated in Example 10.8, the estimate of the expected return for type S firms from Eq. 10.10 is

$$E[R] = r_f + \beta \times (E[R_{Mkt}] - r_f) = 5\% + 0.833 \times (11\% - 5\%) = 10\%$$

This matches their expected return: $50\%(0.4) + 50\%(-0.2) = 10\%$.

What happens if a stock has a negative beta? According to Eq. 10.10, such a stock would have a negative risk premium—it would have an expected return below the risk-free rate. While this might seem unreasonable at first, note that stock with a negative beta will tend to do well when times are bad, so owning it will provide insurance against the systematic risk of other stocks in the portfolio. (We saw an example of such a security in Example 3.10 in Chapter 3.) Risk-averse investors are willing to pay for this insurance by accepting a return below the risk-free interest rate.

CONCEPT CHECK

1. What is the market portfolio?
2. Define the beta of a security.

10.8 Risk and the Cost of Capital

Now that we have a means to measure systematic risk and determine the expected return of a traded security, we can turn to the final goal of this chapter: explaining how to calculate the cost of capital for an investment.

Recall that a firm's cost of capital for an investment or project is the expected return that its investors could earn on other securities with the same risk and maturity. Because the risk that determines expected returns is systematic risk, which is measured by beta, the cost of capital for an investment is the expected return available on securities with the same beta. Equation 10.10 gives the expected return for investing in such a traded security, so it also is the cost of capital for investing in the project. Hence, the cost of capital, r, for investing in a project with a beta, β, is

Cost of Capital of a Project

$$r = r_f + \beta \times (E[R_{Mkt}] - r_f) \tag{10.11}$$

INTERVIEW WITH
Randall Lert

Randall P. Lert is the chief portfolio strategist for Russell Investment Group, the creators of the Russell 2000® Index. Randy is involved in the formation and implementation of investment policy for the firm, which manages more than $170 billion in assets (as of June 30, 2006) and advises clients who represent more than $2.4 trillion.

QUESTION: *How does diversification affect portfolio strategy and the risk-return tradeoff?*

ANSWER: Holding a large, strategically allocated portfolio across many asset classes maximizes your return for a given level of risk, because different markets are not perfectly correlated to each other. The *number* of stocks per se does not drive diversification; *weighting* does. A 1,000-stock portfolio with very divergent weightings from the market index will have more idiosyncratic risk than a 100-stock portfolio whose weights approximate the index. If I hold 100 stocks but underweight the 50 largest, which constitute half the market capitalization of the index, my portfolio will diverge more from the benchmark than a 100 stock portfolio holding the top 50 relatively close to market weight but scattering the other 50 stocks.

QUESTION: *In the U.S., history shows a relatively large reward for taking systematic equity risk versus holding bonds. What is your firm's view of this risk—reward tradeoff going forward?*

ANSWER: We believe that the reward for holding equity risk will be smaller in the future. The economic environment is less volatile, given the current-day regulatory climate and more stable central bank policy worldwide. For strategic asset allocation modeling purposes, we define the equity risk premium as the expected return for holding a well-diversified equity portfolio minus the risk free rate. We assume there is a premium for longer maturity bonds and fixed income securities with credit risk—currently we, and others in the industry, believe that risk premium is about 3 percent relative to cash, and the risk premium of stocks relative to long-term bonds is another 3 percent, for about 6 percent equity risk premium.

QUESTION: *Historical evidence suggests that it is difficult for active fund managers to "beat the market." Why is this the case?*

ANSWER: Active management—trying to generate performance in excess of the market index—is a zero sum game, because "the market" is nothing more than the collection of investors participating in that asset class. Before transactions costs, the average investor's return must equal the market return. When measured against a correctly specified index, about half of all managers should outperform and half should under-perform. However, active managers have much higher transaction costs than an unmanaged index, so the number of underperforming managers is often higher. However, in a world where everybody indexed, there would be no market activity forcing securities to their current valuation levels. This process of active management, then, serves as the primary price discovery mechanism in modern capital markets.

QUESTION: *Given these challenges, how do you manage the risk of the portfolio yet still maximize performance?*

ANSWER: Active portfolio managers focus on idiosyncratic risk, which is normally measured as the standard deviation of a portfolio's return relative to the benchmark index. Most establish a *risk budget* that sets targets for this risk and then seek to generate the highest returns possible within that band of risk. Managers take that risk in two ways. They can bet on industry or economic sectors—for example, the airline industry—and overweight their portfolio to that industry. Or they can take a broader view and hold most economic sectors at roughly market weights, picking specific stocks in sectors that they think will outperform—say, Southwest Airlines. Generally, a larger number of small bets is better than a few large bets. If you bet on two sectors and they are the wrong ones, you are out of luck. Spreading the bet over many sectors gives you a greater chance of some working and balancing out the ones that don't. It diversifies your active management risk.

into account the fees that are charged by these funds, the empirical evidence indeed shows that active portfolio managers appear to have no ability to provide returns to their investors that outperform the market portfolio.[17]

The inability of portfolio managers to outperform the market is likely driven by competition. Investors flock to invest with mutual funds that have done well in the past. As a result, active portfolio managers who do well experience an inflow of new capital.[18] This inflow of capital, however, reduces the fund's returns: Now managers are forced to make larger trades (that have a greater impact on prices) or spread their trades over more (and potentially less attractive) stocks. In practice, successful funds do not continue to outperform other active funds, as competition among investors drives down their future returns.[19]

These arguments and results suggest that capital markets are competitive and so the market portfolio should be approximately efficient. As a result, for a corporate manager who is not a skilled portfolio manager, the assumption that the market portfolio is efficient is a reasonable first approximation.

CONCEPT CHECK

1. What is an efficient capital market?

2. How is the CAPM a stronger hypothesis than an efficient capital market?

Summary

1. A probability distribution summarizes information about possible different returns and their likelihood of occurring.

    a. The expected, or mean, return is the return we expect to earn on average:

    $$\text{Expected Return} = E[R] = \sum_R p_R \times R \tag{10.1}$$

    b. The variance or standard deviation measures the variability of the returns:

    $$Var(R) = E[(R - E[R])^2] = \sum_R p_R \times (R - E[R])^2$$

    $$SD(R) = \sqrt{Var(R)} \tag{10.2}$$

    c. The standard deviation of a return is also called its volatility.

---

17. This widely supported result was first documented by I Friend, F. E. Brown, E. S. Herman and D. Vickers, "A Study of Mutual Funds: Investment Policy and Investment Company Performance," Report No. 2274, 87th Congress, Second Session (August 28, 1962) and I. Horowitz, "The Varying Quality of Investment Trust Management," *Journal of the American Statistical Association* 58 (1963):1011–1032.

18. See M. J. Gruber, "Another Puzzle: The Growth in Actively Managed Mutual Funds," *Journal of Finance* 51 (1996): 783–810; E. R. Sirri and P. Tufano, "Costly Search and Mutual Fund Flows," *Journal of Finance* 53 (1998): 1589–1622; J. Chevalier and G. Ellison, "Risk Taking by Mutual Funds as a Response to Incentives," *Journal of Political Economy* 105 (1997): 1167–1200. For a theoretical model that considers the equilibrium impact of these fund flows, see J. B. Berk and R. C. Green, "Mutual Fund Flows and Performance in Rational Markets," *Journal of Political Economy* 112 (2004): 1269–1295.

19. See M. Carhart, "On Persistence in Mutual Fund Performance," *Journal of Finance* 52 (1997): 57–82.

Solution

In Figure 11.3, we can see that Sally can invest up to 40% in Intel stock without increasing her volatility. Because Intel stock has a higher expected return than Coca-Cola stock, she will earn higher expected returns by putting more money in Intel stock. Therefore, you should recommend that Sally put 40% of her money in Intel stock, leaving 60% in Coca-Cola stock. This portfolio has the same volatility of 25%, but an expected return of 14% rather than the 6% she has now.

The Effect of Correlation

In Figure 11.3, we assumed that the returns of Intel and Coca-Cola stocks are uncorrelated. Let's consider how the risk and return combinations in the figure would change if the correlations were different.

Correlation has no effect on the expected return of a portfolio. For example, a 40–60 portfolio will still have an expected return of 14%. However, the volatility of the portfolio will differ depending on the correlation, as we saw in Section 11.2. In particular, the lower the correlation, the lower the volatility we can obtain. In terms of Figure 11.3, as we lower the correlation and therefore the volatility of the portfolios, the curve showing the portfolios will bend to the left to a greater degree. This effect is illustrated in Figure 11.4.

When the stocks are perfectly positively correlated, the set of portfolios is identified by the straight line between them. In this extreme case (the red line in Figure 11.4), the volatility of the portfolio is equal to the weighted average volatility of the two stocks—

FIGURE 11.4

Effect on Volatility and Expected Return of Changing the Correlation between Intel and Coca-Cola Stock

This figure illustrates correlations of 1, 0.5, 0, −0.5, and −1. The lower the correlation, the lower the risk of the portfolios.

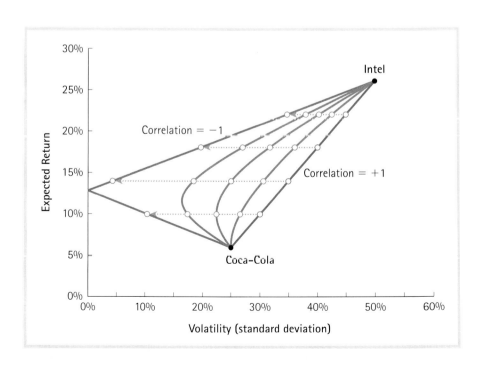

there is no diversification. When the correlation is less than 1, however, the volatility of the portfolios is reduced due to diversification, and the curve bends to the left. The reduction in risk (and the bending of the curve) becomes greater as the correlation decreases. At the other extreme of perfect negative correlation (blue line), the line again becomes straight, this time reflecting off the vertical axis. In particular, when the two stocks are perfectly negatively correlated, it becomes possible to hold a portfolio that bears absolutely no risk.

Short Sales

Thus far we have considered only portfolios in which we invest a positive amount in each stock. A positive investment in a security can be referred to as a **long position** in the security. But it is also possible to invest a *negative* amount in a stock, called a **short position**, by engaging in a **short sale**, a transaction in which you sell a stock that you do not own and then buy that stock back in the future.

Short selling is an advantageous strategy if, for example, you expect a stock price to decline in the future. In that case, you receive more upfront for the shares than you need to pay to replace them in the future. But as Example 11.10 shows, short selling can also be advantageous even if the stock price rises, as long as the portfolio is long another stock with a higher realized return.

Returns from a Short Sale

Problem

Suppose you have $20,000 in cash to invest. You decide to short sell $10,000 worth of Coca-Cola stock and invest the proceeds from your short sale, plus your $20,000, in Intel. At the end of the year, you decide to liquidate your portfolio. If the two stocks have the following realized returns, what is the return on your portfolio?

	P_0	$Div_1 + P_1$	Return
Intel	25.00	31.50	26%
Coca-Cola	40.00	42.40	6%

Solution

You short sold $10,000 or $10,000 / $40 = 250 shares of Coca-Cola stock and invested the $10,000, plus your $20,000, in Intel. That is, you purchased $30,000 or $30,000 / $25 = 1200 shares of Intel stock.

At year-end, your 1200 shares of Intel stock are worth 1200 × $31.50 = $37,800. However, you need to close your short sale by purchasing the 250 Coca-Cola shares that you sold, which costs 250 × $42.40 = $10,600. Thus your final proceeds are $37,800 − $10,600 = $27,200. Given your initial out-of-pocket expense of $20,000, you have earned a return of $7200 / $20,000 = 36%, a higher return than the return of either stock.

What are the portfolio weights corresponding to a short sale? We interpret a short sale as a negative investment in the corresponding stock. For instance, in Example 11.10, our initial investment is −$10,000 in Coca-Cola stock, and +$30,000 in Intel stock, for a

The Mechanics of a Short Sale

In mid-October 2004, Delta Air Lines stood on the verge of bankruptcy. Its only hope of avoiding bankruptcy in the near future was to reach an agreement with the pilots union to cut pilots' salaries by one-third. In the face of this crisis, the stock price had fallen by more than

any dividends that Delta would have paid him had you not borrowed his shares.*

The chart illustrates the cash flows from a short sell. First you receive the current price of the stock. Then you must pay any dividends. Finally you pay the future stock

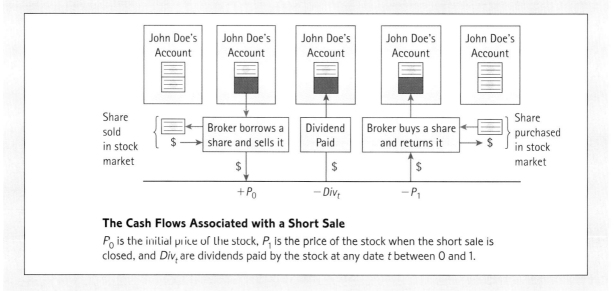

The Cash Flows Associated with a Short Sale

P_0 is the initial price of the stock, P_1 is the price of the stock when the short sale is closed, and Div_t are dividends paid by the stock at any date t between 0 and 1.

70% in the prior year. And many investors apparently felt the stock would fall further—the **short interest** (number of shares sold short) in Delta exceeded 65 million, representing more than 50% of Delta's outstanding shares.

How do you sell Delta stock if you do not own it? To short sell a stock, you must contact your broker. Your broker will try to borrow the stock from someone who currently owns it. Suppose John Doe currently holds Delta stock in a brokerage account. Your broker can lend you shares from John Doe's account so that you can sell them in the market at the current stock price. Of course, at some point you must close the short sale and return the shares to John Doe. So, you will buy the shares in the market, and your broker will replace them in John Doe's account. In the meantime, you must also pay John Doe

price. This is exactly the reverse of the cash flows you receive from buying a stock:

	Date 0	Date t	Date 1
Cash flows from buying a stock	$-P_0$	$+Div_t$	$+P_1$
Cash flows from short selling a stock	$+P_0$	$-Div_t$	$-P_1$

Because the cash flows are reversed, if you short sell a stock, rather than receiving its return, you must *pay* its return to the person you borrowed the stock from. In this way, short selling is like borrowing money at an interest rate equal to the return on the stock (which is unknown until the transaction is completed).[†] Investors who believed Delta stock would have a low or negative return might therefore decide to short sell the stock.

---

*In practice, John Doe may not even know his shares of the stock have been borrowed. He continues to receive dividends as before and, should he need the shares for any reason, the broker will replace them either by (1) borrowing shares from someone else or (2) forcing the short-seller to close his position and buy the shares in the market.

[†]Typically, the broker will charge a fee for finding the shares to borrow, and require the short-seller to deposit collateral guaranteeing the short-seller's ability to buy the stock later. The fees and the opportunity cost of depositing collateral tend to be small, so we ignore them in our analysis.

total net investment of $\$30,000 - \$10,000 = \$20,000$ cash. The corresponding portfolio weights are

$$x_I = \frac{\text{Value of investment in Intel}}{\text{Total value of portfolio}} = \frac{30,000}{20,000} = 150\%$$

$$x_C = \frac{\text{Value of investment in Coca-Cola}}{\text{Total value of portfolio}} = \frac{-10,000}{20,000} = -50\%$$

Note that the portfolio weights still add up to 100%. Using these portfolio weights, we can calculate the return of the portfolio using Eq. 11.2:

$$R_P = \sum_i x_i R_i = (150\%)(26\%) + (-50\%)(6\%) = 36\%$$

All of the equations in this chapter continue to hold if we interpret short sales in this fashion. In general, we say a portfolio is short those stocks that have negative portfolio weights, and long those stocks that have positive portfolio weights.

EXAMPLE
11.11

Volatility with Short Sales

Problem

Suppose Intel stock has a volatility of 50%, Coca-Cola stock has a volatility of 25%, and the stocks are uncorrelated. What is the volatility of a portfolio that is short $10,000 of Coca-Cola and long $30,000 of Intel?

Solution

We can compute the volatility from Eq. 11.8, using portfolio weights $x_I = 150\%$ and $x_C = -50\%$. The volatility of the portfolio is

$$SD(R_P) = \sqrt{Var(R_P)} = \sqrt{x_I^2 Var(R_I) + x_C^2 Var(R_C) + 2x_I x_C Cov(R_I, R_C)}$$

$$= \sqrt{1.5^2 \times 0.50^2 + (-0.5)^2 \times 0.25^2 + 2(1.5)(-0.5)(0)} = 76.0\%$$

Note that when we allow for short sales, the volatility of the portfolio can exceed the volatility of the stocks within it.

In Figure 11.5, we show the effect on the investor's choice set when we allow for short sales. Short selling Intel to invest in Coca-Cola is not efficient (blue dashed curve)—other portfolios exist that have a higher expected return *and* a lower volatility. However, short selling Coca-Cola to invest in Intel is efficient in this case. While such a strategy leads to a higher volatility, it also provides the investor with a higher expected return. This strategy could be attractive to an aggressive investor. In general, short selling leads to higher expected returns if the stocks that are shorted are expected to have lower returns than the stocks in which the portfolio is long.

Risk Versus Return: Many Stocks

Recall from Section 11.3 that adding more stocks to a portfolio reduces risk through diversification. Let's consider the effect of adding a third stock to our portfolio, Bore Industries,

FIGURE 11.5

Portfolios of Intel and Coca-Cola Allowing for Short Sales

Labels indicate portfolio weights (x_I, x_C) for Intel and Coca-Cola stocks. Red indicates efficient portfolios, blue indicates inefficient portfolios. The dashed curves indicate positions that require shorting either Coca-Cola (red) or Intel (blue). Shorting Intel to invest in Coca-Cola is inefficient. Shorting Coca-Cola to invest in Intel is efficient and might be attractive to an aggressive investor who is seeking high expected returns.

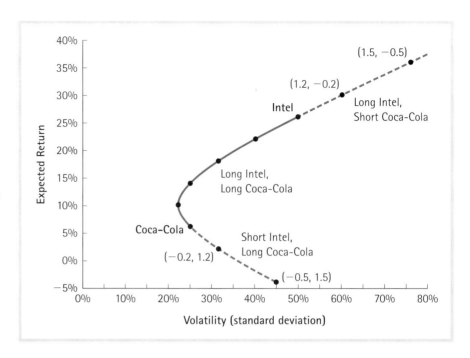

which is uncorrelated with Intel and Coca-Cola but is expected to have a very low return of 2%:

Stock	Expected Return	Volatility	Correlation with		
			Intel	Coca-Cola	Bore Ind.
Intel	26%	50%	1.0	0.0	0.0
Coca-Cola	6%	25%	0.0	1.0	0.0
Bore Industries	2%	25%	0.0	0.0	1.0

Figure 11.6 illustrates the portfolios that we can construct using these three stocks.

Because Bore stock is inferior to Coca-Cola stock—it has the same volatility but a lower return—you might guess that no investor would want to hold a long position in Bore. However, that conclusion ignores the diversification opportunities that Bore provides. Figure 11.6 shows the results of combining Bore with Coca-Cola or with Intel (light blue curves), or combining Bore with a 50–50 portfolio of Coca-Cola and Intel (dark blue curve).[7] We can see from the figure that some of the portfolios we obtained by combining only Intel and Coca-Cola (black curve) are inferior to these new possibilities.

When we combine Bore stock with every portfolio of Intel and Coca-Cola, and allow for short sales as well, we get an entire region of risk and return possibilities rather than just a single curve. This region is depicted as the shaded area in Figure 11.7. But note that

---

7. When a portfolio includes another portfolio, we can compute the weight of each stock by multiplying the portfolio weights. For example, a portfolio with 30% in Bore stock and 70% in the *portfolio* of (50% Intel, 50% Coca-Cola) has 30% in Bore stock, 70% × 50% = 35% in Intel stock, and 70% × 50% = 35% in Coca-Cola stock.

FIGURE 11.6

Expected Return and Volatility for Selected Portfolios of Intel, Coca-Cola, and Bore Industries Stocks

By combining Bore (B) with Intel (I), Coca-Cola (C), and portfolios of Intel and Coca-Cola, we introduce new risk and return possibilities. We can also do better than with just Coca-Cola and Intel alone (the black curve). Portfolios of Bore and Coca-Cola (B + C) and Bore and Intel (B + I) are shown in light blue in the figure. The dark blue curve is a combination of Bore with a portfolio of Intel and Coca-Cola.

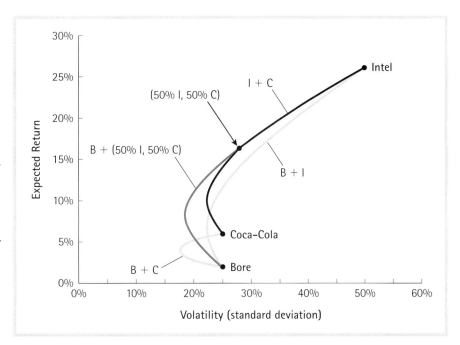

FIGURE 11.7

The Volatility and Expected Return for All Portfolios of Intel, Coca-Cola, and Bore Stock

Portfolios of all three stocks are shown, with the dark blue area showing portfolios without short sales, and the light blue area showing portfolios that include short sales. The best risk–return combinations are on the efficient frontier (red curve). The efficient frontier improves (has a higher return for each level of risk) when we move from two to three stocks.

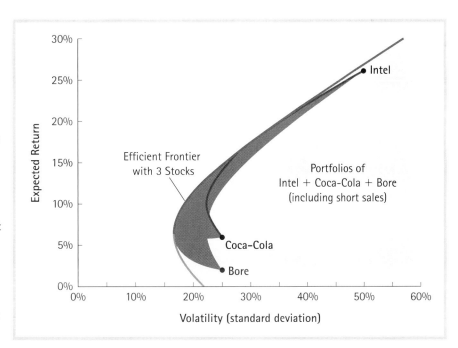

most of these portfolios are inefficient. The efficient portfolios—those offering the highest possible expected return for a given level of volatility—are those on the northwest edge of the shaded region, which we call the **efficient frontier** for these three stocks. In this case none of the stocks, on its own, is on the efficient frontier, so it would not be efficient to put all our money in a single stock.

When the set of investment opportunities increases from two to three stocks, the efficient frontier improves. Visually, the old frontier with any two stocks is located inside the new frontier. In general, adding new investment opportunities allows for greater diversification and improves the efficient frontier. Figure 11.8 uses historical data to show the effect of increasing the set from three stocks (Exxon Mobil, GE, and IBM) to ten stocks. Even though the added stocks appear to offer inferior risk–return combinations on their own, because they allow for additional diversification, the efficient frontier improves with their inclusion. Thus, to arrive at the best possible set of risk and return opportunities, we should keep adding stocks until all investment opportunities are represented. Ultimately, based on our estimates of returns, volatilities, and correlations, we can construct the efficient frontier for *all* available risky investments showing the best possible risk and return combinations that can be obtained by optimal diversification.

CONCEPT CHECK

1. How does the correlation between two stocks affect the risk and return of portfolios that combine them?

2. What is the efficient frontier, and how does it change when more stocks are used to construct portfolios?

FIGURE 11.8

Efficient Frontier with Ten Stocks Versus Three Stocks

The efficient frontier expands as new investments are added. (Based on monthly returns, 1996–2004.)

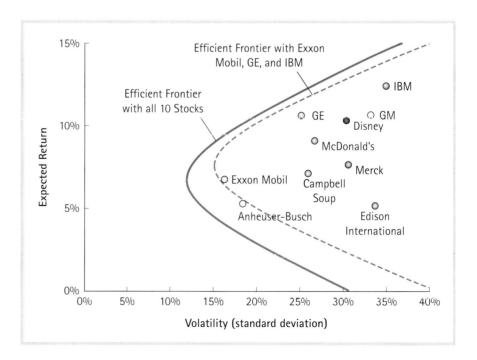

11.5 Risk-Free Saving and Borrowing

Thus far, we have considered the risk and return possibilities that result from combining risky investments into portfolios. By including all risky investments in the construction of the efficient frontier, we achieve maximum diversification.

There is another way besides diversification to reduce risk that we have not yet considered: We can keep some of our money in a safe, no-risk investment like Treasury bills. Of course, doing so will likely reduce our expected return. Conversely, if we are an aggressive investor who is seeking high expected returns, we might decide to borrow money to invest even more in the stock market. In this section we will see that the ability to choose the amount to invest in risky versus riskless securities allows us to determine the *optimal portfolio* of risky securities for an investor.

Investing in Risk-Free Securities

Consider an arbitrary risky portfolio with returns R_P. Let's look at the effect on risk and return of putting a fraction x of our money in the portfolio, while leaving the remaining fraction $(1 - x)$ in risk-free Treasury bills with a yield of r_f.

Using Eq. 11.3 and Eq. 11.8, we calculate the expected return and variance of this portfolio, whose return we will denote by R_{xP}. First, the expected return is

$$
\begin{aligned}
E[R_{xP}] &= (1 - x)r_f + xE[R_P] \\
&= r_f + x(E[R_P] - r_f)
\end{aligned}
\tag{11.15}
$$

The first equation simply states that the expected return is the weighted average of the expected returns of Treasury bills and the portfolio. (Because we know upfront the current interest rate paid on Treasury bills, we do not need to compute an expected return for them.) The second equation rearranges the first to give a useful interpretation. Starting with an investment solely in Treasury bills, we can interpret x as the fraction of Treasury bills we have replaced with portfolio P, gaining the expected difference in their returns. This difference, $(E[R_P] - r_f)$, is the portfolio's risk premium or excess return. In summary, our expected return is equal to the risk-free rate plus a fraction of the risk premium of the portfolio based on the amount we invest in it.

Next let's compute the volatility. The volatility of the risk-free investment is zero; the risk-free rate r_f is known when we make our investment. Because our return on the risk-free investment is fixed and does not move with (or against) our portfolio, the covariance between the risk-free investment and the portfolio is also zero. Thus,

$$
\begin{aligned}
SD(R_{xP}) &= \sqrt{(1 - x)^2 Var(r_f) + x^2 Var(R_P) + 2(1 - x)x\, Cov(r_f, R_P)} \\
&= \sqrt{x^2 Var(R_P)} \\
&= x\, SD(R_P)
\end{aligned}
\tag{11.16}
$$

That is, the volatility is only a fraction of the volatility of the portfolio, based on the amount we invest in it.

The blue line in Figure 11.9 illustrates combinations of volatility and expected return for different choices of x. Looking at Eq. 11.15 and Eq. 11.16, as we increase the fraction x invested in P, we increase both our risk and our risk premium proportionally. Hence the line is *straight* from the risk-free investment through P.

FIGURE 11.9

The Risk–Return Combinations from Combining a Risk-Free Investment and a Risky Portfolio

Given a risk-free rate of 5%, the risk-free investment is represented in the graph by the point with 0% volatility and an expected return of 5%. The blue line shows the portfolios obtained by investing x in portfolio P and $(1 - x)$ in the risk-free investment. Investments with weight $x > 100\%$ in portfolio P require borrowing at the risk-free interest rate.

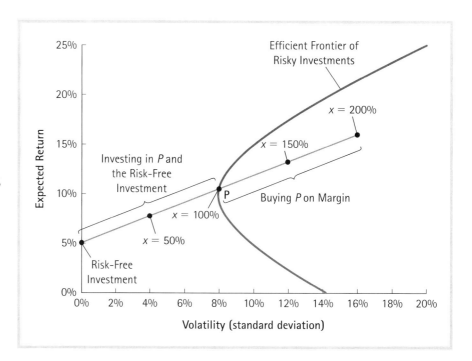

Borrowing and Buying Stocks on Margin

As we increase the fraction x invested in the portfolio P from 0 to 100%, we move along the line in Figure 11.9 from the risk-free investment to P. If we increase x beyond 100%, we get points beyond P in the graph. In this case, we are short selling the risk-free investment, so we must pay the risk-free return. That is, short selling the risk-free investment is equivalent to borrowing money at the risk-free interest rate through a standard loan.

Borrowing money to invest in stocks is referred to as **buying stocks on margin** or using leverage. A portfolio that consists of a short position in the risk-free investment is known as a *levered* portfolio. As you might expect, margin investing is a risky investment strategy. Note that the region of the blue line in Figure 11.9 with $x > 100\%$ has higher risk than the portfolio P itself. At the same time, margin investing can provide higher expected returns than investing in P using only the funds we have available.

EXAMPLE 11.12

Margin Investing

Problem

Suppose you have $10,000 in cash, and you decide to borrow another $10,000 at a 5% interest rate to invest in the stock market. You invest the entire $20,000 in portfolio Q with a 10% expected return and a 20% volatility. What is the expected return and volatility of your investment? What is your realized return if Q goes up 30% over the course of the year? What return do you realize if Q falls by 10% over the course of the year?

Solution

You have doubled your investment in Q by buying stocks on margin, so $x = 200\%$. Using Eq. 11.15 and Eq. 11.16,

$$E[R_{xQ}] = r_f + x(E[R_Q] - r_f) = 5\% + 2 \times (10\% - 5\%) = 15\%$$
$$SD(R_{xQ}) = x\,SD(R_Q) = 2 \times (20\%) = 40\%$$

You have increased both your expected return and your risk relative to the portfolio Q.

If Q goes up 30%, your investment will be worth $26,000 at year-end. However, you will owe $10,000 \times 1.05 = \$10,500$ on your loan. After repaying your loan, you will have $26,000 - \$10,500 = \$15,500$. Because you initially invested $10,000 of your own money, this is a 55% return.

If Q drops by 10%, you are left with $18,000 - \$10,500 = \$7500$, and your return is -25%.

Note that your returns are more extreme than those of the portfolio: 55% and -25% versus 30% and -10%, respectively. In fact, the range is doubled to $55\% - (-25\%) = 80\%$ from $30\% - (-10\%) = 40\%$. This doubling corresponds to the doubling of the volatility of the portfolio.

Identifying the Tangent Portfolio

Looking back at Figure 11.9, we can see that portfolio P is not the best portfolio to combine with the risk-free investment. By forming a portfolio out of the risk-free asset and a portfolio somewhat higher on the efficient frontier than portfolio P, we will get a line that is steeper than the line through P. If the line is steeper, then for any level of volatility, we will earn a higher expected return.

To earn the highest possible expected return for any level of volatility we must find the portfolio that generates the steepest possible line when combined with the risk-free investment. The slope of the line through a given portfolio P is often referred to as the **Sharpe ratio** of the portfolio:

$$\text{Sharpe Ratio} = \frac{\text{Portfolio Excess Return}}{\text{Portfolio Volatility}} = \frac{E[R_P] - r_f}{SD(R_P)} \qquad (11.17)$$

The Sharpe ratio measures the ratio of reward-to-volatility provided by a portfolio.[8] The optimal portfolio to combine with the risk-free asset will be the one with the highest Sharpe ratio, as it will lead to the steepest possible line. The portfolio with the highest Sharpe ratio is the portfolio where the line with the risk-free investment just touches, and so is tangent to, the efficient frontier of risky investments, as shown in Figure 11.10. The portfolio that generates this tangent line is known as the **tangent portfolio**. All other portfolios of risky assets lie below this line. Because the tangent portfolio has the highest Sharpe ratio of any portfolio in the economy, the tangent portfolio provides the biggest reward per unit of volatility of any portfolio available.[9]

---

8. The Sharpe ratio was first introduced by William Sharpe as a measure to compare the performance of mutual funds. See William Sharpe, "Mutual Fund Performance," *Journal of Business* (January 1966): 119–138.

9. In addition to the steepness of the line in Figure 11.10, there is another interpretation to the Sharpe ratio: It is the number of standard deviations the portfolio's return would have to fall to underperform the risk-free investment. Thus, if returns are normally distributed, the portfolio with the highest Sharpe ratio can be interpreted as the portfolio with the greatest chance of earning a return above the risk-free rate.

FIGURE 11.10

The Tangent or Efficient Portfolio

The tangent portfolio is the portfolio with the highest Sharpe ratio. Investments on the green line connecting the risk-free investment and the tangent portfolio provide the best risk and return tradeoff available to an investor. As a result, the tangent portfolio is also referred to as the efficient portfolio.

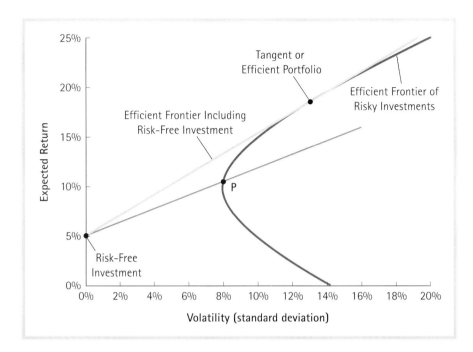

As is evident from Figure 11.10, combinations of the risk-free asset and the tangent portfolio provide the best risk and return tradeoff available to an investor. This observation has a striking consequence. It means that the tangent portfolio is efficient and that, once we include the risk-free investment, all efficient portfolios are combinations of the risk-free investment and the tangent portfolio. That is, no other portfolio that consists of only risky assets is efficient. Therefore, the optimal portfolio of *risky* investments no longer depends on how conservative or aggressive the investor is; every investor should invest in the tangent portfolio *independent of his or her taste for risk*. The investor's preferences will determine only *how much* to invest in the tangent portfolio versus the risk-free investment. Conservative investors will invest a small amount, choosing a portfolio on the line near the risk-free investment. Aggressive investors will invest more, choosing a portfolio that is near the tangent portfolio or even beyond it by buying stocks on margin. Both types of investors will choose to hold the *same* portfolio of risky assets, the tangent portfolio.

EXAMPLE 11.13

Optimal Portfolio Choice

Problem

Your uncle calls and asks for investment advice. Currently, he has $100,000 invested in portfolio *P* as graphed in Figure 11.10. This portfolio has an expected return of 10.5% and a volatility of 8%. Suppose the risk-free rate is 5%, and the tangent portfolio has an expected return of 18.5% and a volatility of 13%. To maximize your uncle's expected return without increasing his volatility, which portfolio would you recommend? If your uncle prefers to keep his expected return the same but minimize his risk, which portfolio would you recommend?

Solution

In either case the best portfolios are combinations of the risk-free investment and the tangent portfolio. If we invest an amount x in the tangent portfolio T, using Eq. 11.15 and Eq. 11.16 the expected return and volatility are

$$E[R_{xT}] = r_f + x(E[R_T] - r_f) = 5\% + x(18.5\% - 5\%)$$

$$SD(R_{xT}) = x\,SD(R_T) = x(13\%)$$

So, to maintain the volatility at 8%, $x = 8\% / 13\% = 61.5\%$. In this case, your uncle should invest 61.5% of his money ($61,500) in the tangent portfolio, and the remaining 38.5% ($38,500) in the risk-free investment. His expected return will then be 5% + (61.5%)(13.5%) = 13.3%, the highest possible given his level of risk.

Alternatively, to keep the expected return equal to the current value of 10.5%, x must satisfy 5% + x(13.5%) = 10.5%, so x = 40.7%. Now your uncle should invest $40,700 in the tangent portfolio and $59,300 in the risk-free investment, lowering his volatility level to (40.7%)(13%) = 5.29%, the lowest possible given his expected return.

We have achieved one of the primary goals of this chapter and explained how to identify the efficient portfolio of risky assets. The **efficient portfolio** is the tangent portfolio, the portfolio with the highest Sharpe ratio in the economy. By combining it with the risk-free investment, an investor will earn the highest possible expected return for any level of volatility he or she is willing to bear.

CONCEPT CHECK
1. Explain the concept of buying stocks on margin.
2. What is the Sharpe ratio of a portfolio?
3. What do we know about the Sharpe ratio of the efficient portfolio?

11.6 The Efficient Portfolio and the Cost of Capital

Now that we have identified the efficient portfolio, let's see how we can use it to determine the cost of capital for an investment.

How to Improve a Portfolio: Beta and the Required Return

Consider a portfolio of risky securities, P. If we invest more in this portfolio and less in the risk-free investment, our expected return and volatility will change. The Sharpe ratio of the portfolio tells us how much our expected return will increase for a given increase in volatility. The portfolio P is efficient if it has the highest possible Sharpe ratio; that is, it is efficient if it provides the largest increase in expected return possible for a given increase in volatility.

To determine whether P has the highest possible Sharpe ratio, let's consider whether we could raise its Sharpe ratio by adding more of some investment i to the portfolio. From Eq. 11.13, the contribution of investment i to the volatility of the portfolio depends on the risk that i has in common with the portfolio, which is measured by i's volatility multiplied by its correlation with P. If we purchase more of investment i by borrowing, we will earn the expected return of i minus the risk-free return. Thus adding i to the portfolio P will improve our Sharpe ratio if [10]

$$\underbrace{E[R_i] - r_f}_{\substack{\text{Additional return} \\ \text{from investment } i}} > \underbrace{SD(R_i) \times Corr(R_i, R_p)}_{\substack{\text{Incremental volatility} \\ \text{from investment } i}} \times \underbrace{\frac{E[R_p] - r_f}{SD(R_p)}}_{\substack{\text{Return per unit of volatilty} \\ \text{available from portfolio } P}} \quad (11.18)$$

To provide a further interpretation for this condition, we define the beta of an investment i with portfolio P:

Beta of Portfolio i with Portfolio P

$$\beta_i^P \equiv \frac{SD(R_i) \times Corr(R_i, R_p)}{SD(R_p)} = \frac{Cov(R_i, R_p)}{Var(R_p)} \quad (11.19)$$

where the second equation follows from the definition of the correlation in terms of the covariance. β_i^P measures the sensitivity of the investment i to the fluctuations of the portfolio P. That is, for each 1% change in the portfolio's excess return, the investment's excess return is expected to change by β_i^P percent due to risks that i has in common with P. With this definition, we can restate Eq. 11.18 as follows:

$$E[R_i] > r_f + \beta_i^P \times (E[R_p] - r_f)$$

Therefore increasing the amount invested in i will increase the Sharpe ratio of portfolio P if its expected return $E[R_i]$ exceeds the required return r_i, which is given by

Required Return for Investment i Given Current Portfolio P

$$r_i = r_f + \beta_i^P \times (E[R_p] - r_f) \quad (11.20)$$

The **required return** is the expected return that is necessary to compensate for the risk investment i will contribute to the portfolio. The required return for an investment i is equal to the risk-free interest rate plus a risk premium that is equal to the risk premium of the investor's current portfolio, P, scaled by β_i^P. If i's expected return exceeds this required return, then adding more of it will improve the performance of the portfolio.

The Required Return of a New Investment

Problem

You are currently invested in the Omega Fund, a broad-based fund that invests in stocks and other securities with an expected return of 15% and a volatility of 20%, as well as in risk-free Treasuries paying 3%. Your broker suggests that you add a real estate fund to your current portfolio. The real estate fund has an expected return of 9%, a volatility of 35%, and a correlation of 0.10 with the Omega Fund. Will adding the real estate fund improve your portfolio?

---

10. If $Corr(R_p, R_p)$ is positive, we can write Eq. 11.18 more intuitively as a comparison of the ratio of the gain in expected return to the incremental volatility from security i with the Sharpe ratio of the portfolio:

$$\frac{E[R_i] - r_f}{SD(R_i) \times Corr(R_i, R_p)} > \frac{E[R_p] - r_f}{SD(R_p)}$$

Solution

Let R_{re} be the return of the real estate fund and R_O be the return of the Omega Fund. From Eq. 11.19, the beta of the real estate fund with the Omega Fund is

$$\beta_{re}^O = \frac{SD(R_{re})\,Corr(R_{re},R_O)}{SD(R_O)} = \frac{35\% \times 0.10}{20\%} = 0.175$$

We can then use Eq. 11.20 to determine the required return that makes the real estate fund an attractive addition to our portfolio:

$$r_{re} = r_f + \beta_{re}^O(E[R_O] - r_f) = 3\% + 0.175 \times (15\% - 3\%) = 5.1\%$$

The real estate fund has an expected return of 9% that exceeds the required return of 5.1%. Therefore, we can improve the performance of our current portfolio by investing some amount in the real estate fund.

Expected Returns and the Efficient Portfolio

If a security's expected return exceeds its required return given our current portfolio, then we can improve the performance of our portfolio by adding more of the security. But how much more should we add? As we buy shares of security i, its correlation with our portfolio will increase, ultimately raising its required return until $E[R_i] = r_i$. At this point our holdings of security i are optimal.

Similarly, if security i's expected return is less than the required return r_i, we should reduce our holdings of i. As we do so the correlation and the required return r_i will fall until $E[R_i] = r_i$.

Thus, if we have no restrictions on our ability to buy or sell securities that are traded in the market, we will continue to trade until the expected return of each security equals its required return—that is, until $E[R_i] = r_i$ holds for all i. At this point, no trade can possibly improve the risk–reward ratio of the portfolio, and our portfolio is the optimal, efficient portfolio. That is,

A portfolio is efficient if and only if the expected return of every available security equals its required return.

From Eq. 11.20, this result implies the following relationship between the expected return of any security and its beta with the efficient portfolio:

Expected Return of a Security

$$E[R_i] = r_i \equiv r_f + \beta_i^{eff} \times (E[R_{eff}] - r_f) \tag{11.21}$$

where R_{eff} is the return of the efficient portfolio, the portfolio with the highest Sharpe ratio of any portfolio in the economy.

Identifying the Efficient Portfolio

Problem

Consider the Omega Fund and real estate fund of Example 11.14. Suppose you have $100 million invested in the Omega Fund. In addition to this position, how much should you invest in the real estate fund to form an efficient portfolio of these two funds?

Solution

Suppose that for each \$1 invested in the Omega Fund, we borrow x_{re} dollars (or sell x_{re} worth of Treasury bill) to invest in the real estate fund. Then our portfolio has a return of $R_P = R_O + x_{re}(R_{re} - r_f)$, where R_O is the return of the Omega Fund and R_{re} is the return of the real estate fund. Table 11.5 shows the change to the expected return and volatility of our portfolio as we increase the investment x_{re} in the real estate fund, using the formulas

$$E[R_P] = E[R_O] + x_{re}(E[R_{re}] - r_f)$$

$$Var(R_P) = Var[R_O + x_{re}(R_{re} - r_f)] = Var(R_O) + x_{re}^2 Var(R_{re}) + 2x_{re}Cov(R_{re},R_O)$$

Adding the real estate fund initially improves the Sharpe ratio of the portfolio, as defined by Eq. 11.17. As we add more of the real estate fund, however, its correlation with our portfolio rises, computed as

$$Corr(R_{re},R_P) = \frac{Cov(R_{re},R_P)}{SD(R_{re})SD(R_P)} = \frac{Cov(R_{re},R_O + x_{re}(R_{re} - r_f))}{SD(R_{re})SD(R_P)}$$

$$= \frac{x_{re}Var(R_{re}) + Cov(R_{re},R_O)}{SD(R_{re})SD(R_P)}$$

The beta of the real estate fund—computed from Eq. 11.19—also rises, increasing the required return. The required return equals the 9% expected return of the real estate fund at about $x_{re} = 11\%$, which is the same level of investment that maximizes the Sharpe ratio. Thus the efficient portfolio of these two funds includes \$0.11 in the real estate fund per \$1 invested in the Omega Fund.

| TABLE 11.5 | | Sharpe Ratio and Required Return for Different Investments in the Real Estate Fund | | | | |

x_{re}	$E[R_P]$	$SD(R_P)$	Sharpe Ratio	$Corr(R_{re}, R_P)$	β_{re}^P	Required Return r_{re}
0%	15.00%	20.00%	0.6000	10.0%	0.18	5.10%
4%	15.24%	20.19%	0.6063	16.8%	0.29	6.57%
8%	15.48%	20.47%	0.6097	23.4%	0.40	8.00%
10%	15.60%	20.65%	0.6103	26.6%	0.45	8.69%
11%	15.66%	20.74%	0.6104	28.2%	0.48	9.03%
12%	15.72%	20.84%	0.6103	29.7%	0.50	9.35%
16%	15.96%	21.30%	0.6084	35.7%	0.59	10.60%

Cost of Capital

In this chapter, we have focused on the optimal portfolio choice decision faced by an individual investor. The results of this section provide the link between the optimal portfolio choice and an investment's cost of capital. Intuitively, for an investor to benefit from a new investment, its expected return should exceed its required return as calculated in Eq. 11.20. The required return depends on the risk that the investment has in common

Nobel Prizes   Harry Markowitz and James Tobin

The techniques of mean-variance portfolio optimization, which allow an investor to find the portfolio with the highest expected return for any level of variance (or volatility), were developed in an article, "Portfolio Selection," published in the *Journal of Finance* in 1952 by Harry Markowitz. Markowitz's approach has evolved into one of the main methods of portfolio optimization used on Wall Street. In recognition for his contribution to the field, Markowitz was awarded the Nobel Prize for economics in 1990. The same ideas were developed concurrently by Andrew Roy in "Safety First and the Holding of Assets," published in *Econometrica* in the same year in which Markowitz's article appeared. In 1999, after winning the Nobel Prize, Markowitz wrote "I am often called the father of modern portfolio theory, but Roy can claim an equal share of this honor."[*] Ironically Mark Rubinstein[†] appears to have discovered another article that develops these ideas published twelve years earlier in 1940

by Bruno de Finetti in the Italian journal *Giornale dell'Instituto Italiano degli Attuari*. It has remained in obscurity perhaps because it was first translated into English in only 2004 (by Luca Barone).[**]

James Tobin furthered this theory with the important insight that by combining risky securities with a risk-free investment, an optimal tangent portfolio could be found that does not depend on an investor's tolerance for risk. In his article "Liquidity Preference as Behavior Toward Risk" published in the *Review of Economic Studies* in 1958, Tobin proved a "Separation Theorem," which showed that Markowitz's techniques could be applied to find the tangent portfolio, and then investors could choose their exposure to risk by varying their investments in the tangent portfolio and the risk-free investment. Tobin was awarded the Nobel Prize for economics in 1981 for his contributions to finance and economics.

---

[*]H. M. Markowitz, "The Early History of Portfolio Theory: 1600–1960," *Financial Analysts Journal* 55 (1999): 5–16.

[†]M. Rubinstein, "A History of the Theory of Investments," (New Jersey: John Wiley and Sons, 2006): p. 349.

[**]English translation forthcoming in *Journal of Investment Management*, Third Quarter, 2006.

---

with investor's current portfolio. Because the investor will optimally hold an efficient portfolio, *the appropriate risk premium for an investment can be determined from its beta with the efficient portfolio:*

Cost of Capital for Investment *i*

$$r_i = r_f + \beta_i^{eff} \times (E[R_{eff}] - r_f) \qquad (11.22)$$

We can interpret Eq. 11.22 as follows: From Figure 11.10, the best investments available to an investor in the market are combinations of the risk-free asset and the efficient portfolio. We can construct a portfolio with the same systematic risk as the investment opportunity by investing the fraction $x = \beta_i^{eff}$ in the efficient portfolio and the fraction $(1 - x)$ in the risk-free asset. From Eq. 11.15, this portfolio has the expected return given in Eq. 11.22. Therefore, *the cost of capital of investment i is equal to the expected return of the best available portfolio in the market with the same sensitivity to systematic risk, given by Eq. 11.22.*

We derived the same expression for the cost of capital in Chapter 10. Now, however, we have a more precise definition for the efficient portfolio: It is the tangent portfolio, or the portfolio that has the highest Sharpe ratio of any portfolio in the economy. This portfolio provides the benchmark that identifies the systematic risk present in the economy. Because all other risk is diversifiable, it is an investment's beta with respect to the efficient portfolio that measures its sensitivity to systematic risk, and therefore determines its cost of capital.

Jonathan Clements is the personal-finance columnist for The Wall Street Journal. *His "Getting Going" column, launched in October 1994, now appears every Wednesday in the Journal and most Sundays in over 80 U.S. newspapers.*

QUESTION: *You have written for years on personal finance. How has academic theory influenced investor behavior?*

ANSWER: When I started writing about mutual funds in the late 1980s, investors would ask, "What are your favorite funds?" Today, they are more likely to say, "I'm looking to add a foreign-stock fund to my portfolio. Which funds in that category do you like? Or should I just index?"

We have clearly gotten away from the blind pursuit of market-beating returns, and there is more focus on portfolio construction and a growing willingness to consider indexing. That reflects the impact of academic research.

What has really influenced investors has been the academic "grunt work" of the past four decades, which has given us a decent grasp of what historical market returns look like. Thanks to that research, many ordinary investors have a better understanding of how stocks have performed relative to bonds. They realize that most actively managed stock mutual funds don't beat the market, and thus there is a case for indexing. They appreciate that different market sectors perform well at different times, so there is a real value in diversifying.

QUESTION: *Academics talk about efficient frontiers and optimal portfolios. How does that translate into advice for someone looking to build a portfolio?*

ANSWER: While academic research has influenced ordinary investors, we shouldn't overstate the case. To some extent, the research has merely codified what investors already knew intuitively. For instance, investors have always thought about risk as well as return, and they have always been inclined to diversify. The academic research may have made investors a little more rigorous in their thinking, but it didn't radically change their behavior.

Moreover, to the extent that the research doesn't fit with investors' intuition, they have clearly rejected it. Investors still behave in ways that academics would consider suboptimal. They don't build well-diversified portfolios—and then focus on the risk and return of the overall portfolio. Instead, they build moderately diversified portfolios—and then pay a lot of attention to the risk and reward of each investment they own.

QUESTION: *How does risk tolerance affect the type of portfolio a person should build?*

ANSWER: In theory, investors should hold the globally diversified all-asset "market portfolio" and then, depending on their risk tolerance, either add risk-free assets to reduce volatility or use leverage to boost returns. But almost nobody invests that way. In fact, I once tried to find out what the market portfolio looks like—and discovered that nobody knows for sure.

Among the vast majority of ordinary investors, the idea of using leverage to buy investments is an anathema. In practice, of course, many are doing just that. They hold a portfolio of assets, including stocks, bonds and real estate, and they have a heap of debt, including their mortgage, auto loans and credit-card balances. But the implication—that they effectively have a leveraged stock-market bet—would horrify most investors. Mental accounting still dominates.

While nobody seems to know what the market portfolio looks like, investors have become willing to consider a broader array of assets. In recent years, ordinary U.S. investors have increased their investment in foreign stocks, real-estate investment trusts and commodities. While there is an element of performance chasing in all this, I think the trend will continue, as people come to realize that they can lower a portfolio's risk level by adding apparently risky investments.

EXAMPLE
11.16

Computing the Cost of Capital for a Project

Problem

Alphatec is seeking to raise capital from a large group of investors to expand its operations. Suppose the S&P 500 portfolio is the efficient portfolio of risky securities (so that these investors have holdings in this portfolio). The S&P 500 portfolio has a volatility of 15% and an expected return of 10%. The investment is expected to have a volatility of 40% and a 50% correlation with the S&P 500. If the risk-free interest rate is 4%, what is the appropriate cost of capital for Alphatec's expansion?

Solution

First we determine the beta of the investment relative to the S&P 500 (the efficient portfolio):

$$\beta_A^{SP} = \frac{SD(R_A) \times Corr(R_A, R_{Sp})}{SD(R_{SP})} = 0.50 \times \frac{40\%}{15\%} = 1.33$$

Then we use Eq. 11.20 to determine the required return that makes the investment an attractive addition to the investors' portfolio:

$$r_A = r_f + \beta_A^{SP} \times (E[R_{SP}] - r_f) = 4\% + 1.33 \times (10\% - 4\%) = 12\%$$

Because Alphatec's investors will require this return, this return is the appropriate cost of capital for the expansion.

CONCEPT CHECK   1. Define the required return for an investment.

2. What determines the cost of capital for an investment?

Summary

1. The portfolio weight is the initial fraction x_i of an investor's money invested in each asset. Portfolio weights add up to 1.

$$x_i = \frac{\text{Value of investment } i}{\text{Total value of portfolio}} \qquad (11.1)$$

2. The expected return of a portfolio is the weighted average of the expected returns of the investments within it, using the portfolio weights.

$$E[R_p] = \sum_i x_i E[R_i]$$

3. To find the risk of a portfolio, we need to know the degree to which stock returns move together. Covariance and correlation measure the co-movement of returns.

   a. The covariance between returns R_i and R_j is defined by

$$Cov(R_i, R_j) = E[(R_i - E[R_i])(R_j - E[R_j])] \qquad (11.4)$$

   and is estimated from historical data using

$$Cov(R_i, R_j) = \frac{1}{T-1}\sum_t (R_{i,t} - \bar{R}_i)(R_{j,t} - \bar{R}_j) \qquad (11.5)$$

b. The correlation is defined as the covariance of the returns divided by the standard deviation of each return. The correlation is always between -1 and $+1$. It represents the fraction of the volatility due to risk that is common to the securities.

$$Corr(R_i,R_j) = \frac{Cov(R_i,R_j)}{SD(R_i)\,SD(R_j)} \tag{11.6}$$

4. The variance of a portfolio depends on the covariance of the stocks within it.

   a. For a portfolio with two stocks, the portfolio variance is

   $$Var(R_P) = x_1^2 Var(R_1) + x_2^2 Var(R_2) + 2x_1 x_2 Cov(R_1,R_2) \tag{11.8}$$

   b. If the portfolio weights are positive, as we lower the covariance between the two stocks in a portfolio, we lower the portfolio variance.

5. The variance of an equally weighted portfolio is

$$Var(R_P) = \frac{1}{n}(\text{Average Variance of the Individual Stocks})$$

$$+ \left(1 - \frac{1}{n}\right)(\text{Average Covariance between the Stocks}) \tag{11.12}$$

6. Diversification eliminates independent risks. The volatility of a large portfolio results from the common risk between the stocks in the portfolio.

7. Each security contributes to the volatility of the portfolio according to its total risk scaled by its correlation with the portfolio, which adjusts for the fraction of the total risk that is common to the portfolio.

$$SD(R_P) = \sum_i x_i \times SD(R_i) \times Corr(R_i,R_P) \tag{11.13}$$

8. Efficient portfolios offer investors the highest possible expected return for a given level of risk. The set of efficient portfolios is called the efficient frontier. As investors add stocks to a portfolio, the efficient portfolio improves.

   a. An investor seeking high expected returns and low volatility should invest only in efficient portfolios.

   b. Investors will choose from the set of efficient portfolios based on their own preferences for return versus risk.

9. Investors may use short sales in their portfolios. A portfolio is short those stocks with negative portfolio weights. Short selling extends the set of possible portfolios.

10. Portfolios can be formed by combining the risk-free asset with a portfolio of risky assets.

   a. The expected return for this type of portfolio is

   $$E[R_{xP}] = r_f + x(E[R_P] - r_f) \tag{11.15}$$

   b. Volatility for this type of portfolio is

   $$SD(R_{xP}) = x\,SD(R_P) \tag{11.16}$$

   c. The risk–return combinations of the risk-free investment and a risky portfolio lie on a straight line connecting the two investments.

11. The goal of an investor who is seeking to earn the highest possible expected return for any level of volatility is to find the portfolio that generates the steepest possible line when combined with the risk-free investment. The slope of this line is called the Sharpe ratio of the portfolio.

$$\text{Sharpe Ratio} = \frac{\text{Portfolio Excess Return}}{\text{Portfolio Volatility}} = \frac{E[R_P] - r_f}{SD(R_P)} \tag{11.17}$$

12. The risky portfolio with the highest Sharpe ratio is called the efficient portfolio. The efficient portfolio is the optimal combination of risky investments independent of the investor's appetite for risk. An investor can select a desired degree of risk by choosing the amount to invest in the efficient portfolio relative to the risk-free investment.

13. The beta of an investment with a portfolio is

$$\beta_i^P \equiv \frac{SD(R_i) \times Corr(R_i, R_P)}{SD(R_P)} = \frac{Cov(R_i, R_P)}{Var(R_P)} \tag{11.19}$$

Beta indicates the sensitivity of the investment's return to fluctuations in the portfolio's return.

14. Buying shares of security i improves the performance of a portfolio if its expected return exceeds the required return:

$$r_i = r_f + \beta_i^P \times (E[R_P] - r_f) \tag{11.20}$$

15. A portfolio is efficient when $E[R_i] = r_i$ for all securities. The following relationship therefore holds between beta and expected returns for traded securities:

$$E[R_i] = r_i \equiv r_f + \beta_i^{eff} \times (E[R_{eff}] - r_f) \tag{11.21}$$

16. Because the investor will optimally hold an efficient portfolio, the risk premium for an investment can be determined from its beta with the efficient portfolio:

$$r_i = r_f + \beta_i^{eff} \times (E[R_{eff}] - r_f) \tag{11.22}$$

This cost of capital of investment i is equal to the expected return of the best available portfolio in the market with the same sensitivity to systematic risk.

Key Terms

buying stocks on margin *p. 346*
correlation *p. 327*
covariance *p. 327*
efficient frontier *p. 344*
efficient portfolio *p. 349*
equally weighted portfolio *p. 332*
inefficient portfolio *p. 337*
long position *p. 339*

portfolio weights *p. 324*
required return *p. 350*
Sharpe ratio *p. 347*
short interest *p. 340*
short position *p. 339*
short sale *p. 339*
tangent portfolio *p. 347*

Further Reading

The following text presents in more depth optimal portfolio choice: W. F. Sharpe, *Investments* (Upper Saddle River, NJ: Prentice Hall, 1999).

Two seminal papers on optimal portfolio choice are: H. M. Markowitz, "Portfolio Selection," *Journal of Finance* 7 (March 1952): 77–91; and J. Tobin, "Liquidity Preference as Behavior Toward Risk," *Review of Economic Studies* 25 (February 1958): 65–86.

The insight that the expected return of a security is given by its beta with an efficient portfolio was first derived in the following paper: R. Roll, "A Critique of the Asset Pricing Theory's Tests," *Journal of Financial Economics* 4 (1977): 129–176.

The following paper provides a historical account of how researchers recognized the impact that short-sales constraints may have in the expected returns of assets: M. Rubinstein, "Great Moments in Financial Economics: III. Short-Sales and Stock Prices," *Journal of Investment Management* 2(1) (First Quarter 2004): 16–31.

Problems

All problems in this chapter are available in MyFinanceLab. An asterisk (*) indicates problems with a higher level of difficulty.

The Expected Return of a Portfolio

1. You are considering how to invest part of your retirement savings. You have decided to put $200,000 into three stocks: 50% of the money in GoldFinger (currently $25 / share), 25% of the money in Moosehead (currently $80 / share), and the remainder in Venture Associates (currently $2 / share). If GoldFinger stock goes up to $30 / share, Moosehead stock drops to $60 / share, and Venture Associates stock rises to $3 per share,

    a. What is the new value of the portfolio?

    b. What return did the portfolio earn?

    c. If you don't buy or sell shares after the price change, what are your new portfolio weights?

2. There are two ways to calculate the expected return of a portfolio: either calculate the expected return using the value and dividend stream of the portfolio as a whole, or calculate the weighted average of the expected returns of the individual stocks that make up the portfolio. Which return is higher?

The Volatility of a Two Stock Portfolio

3. If the return of two stocks has a correlation of 1, what does this imply about the relative movements in the stock prices?

EXCEL 4. Using the data in the following table, estimate (a) the average return and volatility for each stock, (b) the covariance between the stocks, and (c) the correlation between these two stocks.

Year	Realized Returns	
	Stock A	Stock B
1998	−10%	21%
1999	20%	30%
2000	5%	7%
2001	−5%	−3%
2002	2%	−8%
2003	9%	25%

EXCEL
5. The following spreadsheet contains monthly returns for Coca-Cola (Ticker: KO) and Exxon Mobil (Ticker: XOM) for 1990. Using these data, estimate (a) the average monthly return and volatility for each stock, (b) the covariance between the stocks, and (c) the correlation between these two stocks.

Date	KO	XOM
19900131	−10.84%	−6.00%
19900228	2.36%	1.28%
19900330	6.60%	−1.86%
19900430	2.01%	−1.90%
19900531	18.36%	7.40%
19900629	−1.22%	−0.26%
19900731	2.25%	8.36%
19900831	−6.89%	−2.46%
19900928	−6.04%	−2.00%
19901031	13.61%	0.00%
19901130	3.51%	4.68%
19901231	0.54%	2.22%

EXCEL
6. Using the data from Table 11.3, what is the covariance between the stocks of American Air Lines and Delta Air Lines?

EXCEL
7. Using your estimates from Problem 4, calculate the volatility (standard deviation) of a portfolio that is 70% invested in stock A and 30% invested in stock B.

EXCEL
8. Using the spreadsheet from Problem 5, calculate the volatility (standard deviation) of a portfolio that is 55% invested in Coca-Cola stock and 45% invested in Exxon Mobil stock. Calculate the volatility by (a) using Eq. 11.8, (b) using Eq. 11.9, and (c) calculating the monthly returns of the portfolio and computing its volatility directly. How do your results compare?

EXCEL
*9. Plot the volatility (standard deviation) of a portfolio of Coca-Cola and Exxon Mobil stocks as a function of the fraction invested in Coca-Cola. Use the spreadsheet from Problem 5. Base any statistical estimates that you need on the data in the spreadsheet.

The Volatility of a
Large Portfolio

10. How would you calculate the volatility (standard deviation) of a portfolio containing many stocks?

11. What is the volatility (standard deviation) of a very large portfolio of equally weighted stocks within an industry in which the stocks have a volatility of 50% and a correlation of 40%?

Risk Versus Return:
Choosing an Efficient
Portfolio

12. Using the data in Table 11.4 but assuming that Coca-Cola and Intel stocks are perfectly negatively correlated (their correlation coefficient is −1),
   a. Calculate the portfolio weights that remove all risk.
   b. What is the risk-free rate of interest in this economy?

For problems 13–15, suppose Johnson & Johnson and the Walgreen Company have expected returns and volatilities shown below, with a correlation of 22%.

	E[R]	SD[R]
Johnson & Johnson	7%	16%
Walgreen Company	10%	20%

13. Calculate (a) the expected return and (b) the volatility (standard deviation) of a portfolio that is equally invested in Johnson & Johnson's and Walgreen's stock.

14. Calculate (a) the expected return and (b) the volatility (standard deviation) of a portfolio that consists of a long position of $10,000 in Johnson & Johnson and a short position of $2000 in Walgreen's.

*15. Using the same data as for Problems 13 and 14, calculate the expected return and the volatility (standard deviation) of a portfolio consisting of Johnson & Johnson's and Walgreen's stocks using a wide range of portfolio weights. Plot the expected return as a function of the portfolio volatility. Using your graph, identify the range of Johnson & Johnson's portfolio weights that yield efficient combinations of the two stocks, rounded to the nearest percentage point.

Risk-Free Saving and Borrowing

*16. Suppose you have $100,000 in cash, and you decide to borrow another $15,000 at a 4% interest rate to invest in the stock market. You invest the entire $115,000 in a portfolio J with a 15% expected return and a 25% volatility.

  a. What is the expected return and volatility (standard deviation) of your investment?

  b. What is your realized return if J goes up 25% over the year?

  c. What return do you realize if J falls by 20% over the year?

17. Assume all investors want to hold a portfolio that, for a given level of volatility, has the maximum possible expected return. Explain why, when a risk-free asset exists, all investors will choose to hold the same portfolio of risky stocks.

Calculating the Beta of a Traded Security

18. You are currently invested in the Farrallon Fund, a broad-based fund of stocks and other securities with an expected return of 12% and a volatility of 25%. Currently, the risk-free rate of interest is 4%. Your broker suggests that you add a venture capital fund to your current portfolio. The venture capital fund has an expected return of 20%, a volatility of 80%, and a correlation of 0.2 with the Farrallon Fund. Calculate the required return and use it to decide whether you should add the venture capital fund to your portfolio.

19. You have noticed a market investment opportunity that, given your current portfolio, has an expected return that exceeds your required return. What can you conclude about your current portfolio?

20. Kaui Surf Boards is seeking to raise capital from a large group of investors to expand its operations. Suppose these investors currently hold the S&P 500 portfolio, which has a volatility of 15% and an expected return of 10%. The investment is expected to have a volatility of 30% and a 15% correlation with the S&P 500. If the risk-free interest rate is 4%, what is the appropriate cost of capital for Kaui Surf Boards' expansion?

Data Case

Your manager was so impressed with your work analyzing the return and standard deviations of the twelve stocks from Chapter 10 that he would like you to continue your analysis. Specifically, he wants you to update the stock portfolio by:

- Rebalancing the portfolio with the optimum weights that will provide the best risk and return combinations for the new 12-stock portfolio.

- Determining the improvement in the return and risk that would result from these optimum weights compared to the current method of equally weighting the stocks in the portfolio.

Use the Solver function in Excel to perform this analysis (the time-consuming alternative is to find the optimum weights by trial-and-error).

1. Begin with the equally weighted portfolio analyzed in Chapter 10. Establish the portfolio returns for the stocks in the portfolio using a formula that depends on the portfolio weights. Initially, these weights will all equal 1/12. You would like to allow the portfolio weights to vary, so you will need to list the weights for each stock in separate cells and establish another cell that sums the weights of the stocks. The portfolio returns for each month MUST reference these weights for Excel solver to be of any use.

2. Compute the values for the monthly mean return and standard deviation of the portfolio. Convert these values to annual numbers (as you did in Chapter 10) for easier interpretation.

3. Compute the efficient frontier when short sales are not allowed. To activate the Solver function in Excel, click the "Tools," select "Add-Ins . . .", check "Solver Add-in" in the pop-up dialog box, and then click "OK". (*Note:* You may have to install the Solver function using the Microsoft Office Disk 1 for the installation.) To set the Solver parameters:

    a. Set the target cell as the cell of interest, making it the cell that computes the (annual) portfolio standard deviation. Minimize this value.

    b. Establish the "By Changing Cells" by holding the control key and clicking in each of the 12 cells containing the weights of each stock.

    c. Add constraints by clicking on the add button next to the "Subject to the Constraints" box. One set of constraints will be the weight of each stock that is greater than or equal to zero. Calculate the constraints individually. A second constraint is that the weights will sum to one.

    d. Compute the portfolio with the lowest standard deviation for a given expected return. Start by finding this portfolio with an expected return of 5%. To do this, add a constraint that the (annual) portfolio return equals 0.05.

    e. If the parameters are set correctly, you should get a solution when you click "Solve." If there is an error, you will need to double-check the parameters, especially the constraints.

4. Record the resulting standard deviation for the "optimally weighted" portfolio with a return of 0.05 in a separate cell on the spreadsheet. Repeat step 3 to solve for the portfolio with the lowest standard deviation for several different choices of expected return: 0.1, 0.2, 0.3, and 0.4. Record these values. Plot the efficient frontier with the constraint of no short sales. To do this, create an XY Scatter Plot (similar to what you did in Chapter 10), with portfolio standard deviation on the *x*-axis and the return on the *y*-axis.

between risk and return. For his contributions to the theory, William Sharpe was awarded the Nobel Prize in economics in 1990.

12.1 The Efficiency of the Market Portfolio

To evaluate the NPV of an investment, we must determine the appropriate discount rate, or cost of capital, for that investment. The results we derived at the conclusion of Chapter 11 provide a link between investors' optimal portfolio choice and the cost of capital for a firm's investment project. There we showed that the expected return of any traded security is determined by its beta with the efficient portfolio:

$$E[R_i] = r_i = r_f + \beta_i^{eff} \times (E[R_{eff}] - r_f) \tag{12.1}$$

Moreover, if investors hold the efficient portfolio, then the cost of capital for any investment project is equal to its required return r_i from Eq. 12.1, again based on its beta with the efficient portfolio.

While Eq. 12.1 provides a way to calculate an investment's cost of capital, when using it we face an important challenge: How do we identify the efficient portfolio? As we saw in Chapter 11, to identify the efficient portfolio (of risky assets) we must know the expected returns, volatilities, and correlations between investments. These quantities are difficult to forecast. Furthermore, investors' beliefs may differ, and are not necessarily known by the firm. Under these circumstances, how can we determine the efficient portfolio?

To answer this question we develop the Capital Asset Pricing Model (CAPM). This model allows corporate executives to identify the efficient portfolio (of risky assets) without having any knowledge of the expected return of each security. Instead, the CAPM uses the actions of investors themselves as input. With this insight, the model identifies the efficient portfolio as the **market portfolio**—the portfolio of all stocks and securities in the market. To obtain this remarkable result, we make three assumptions regarding the behavior of investors.

The CAPM Assumptions

There are three main assumptions that underlie the CAPM. The first is a familiar one that we have adopted since Chapter 3:

Investors can buy and sell all securities at competitive market prices (without incurring taxes or transactions costs) and can borrow and lend at the risk-free interest rate.

The second assumption is that investors choose a portfolio of traded securities that offers the highest possible expected return given the level of volatility they are willing to accept:

Investors hold only efficient portfolios of traded securities—portfolios that yield the maximum expected return for a given level of volatility.

In Chapter 11, we looked at the consequences that these first two assumptions have for portfolio choice. We found that given an investor's estimates of volatilities, correlations, and expected returns, there is a unique combination of risky securities, called the efficient portfolio. By combining the efficient portfolio with risk-free borrowing or lending, the investor can obtain the highest possible expected return for whichever level of volatility the investor is prepared to accept.

Of course, there are many investors in the world, and each may have his or her own estimates of the volatilities, correlations, and expected returns of the available securities. But investors don't come up with these estimates arbitrarily; they base them on historical patterns and other information (including market prices) that is widely available to the public. If all investors use publicly available information sources, then their estimates are likely to be similar. Consequently, it is not unreasonable to consider a special case in which all investors have the same estimates concerning future investments and returns, called **homogeneous expectations**. Although investors' expectations are not completely identical in reality, assuming homogeneous expectations should be a reasonable approximation in many markets, and represents the third simplifying assumption of the CAPM:

Investors have homogeneous expectations regarding the volatilities, correlations, and expected returns of securities.

Security Demand Must Equal Supply

If investors have homogeneous expectations, then each investor will identify the same portfolio as having the highest Sharpe ratio in the economy. Thus all investors will demand the *same* efficient portfolio of risky securities, adjusting only their investment in risk-free securities to suit their particular appetite for risk. That means that each investor will hold the different risky securities in the same proportions. Without any further information, can we determine the composition this portfolio?

The answer is yes. To see why, consider what happens if we combine the portfolios held by different investors. Because all investors are holding the risky securities in the same proportions as the efficient portfolio, their combined portfolios will also reflect the same proportions as the efficient portfolio. For example, if investors have twice as much invested in stock A as in stock B, together they also have twice as much invested in A as in B. By the same logic, the combined portfolio of risky securities of *all* investors must equal the efficient portfolio.

Furthermore, because every security is owned by someone, the sum of all investors' portfolios must equal the portfolio of all risky securities available in the market, which we defined in Chapter 10 as the market portfolio. Therefore, the efficient portfolio (the portfolio that all investors hold) must be the same portfolio as the market portfolio of all risky securities.

The insight that the market portfolio is efficient is really just the statement that *demand must equal supply.* All investors demand the efficient portfolio, and the supply of securities is the market portfolio; hence the two must coincide. If some security were not part of the efficient portfolio, then no investor would want to own it, and demand for this security would not equal its supply. This security's price would fall, causing its expected return to rise until it became an attractive investment. In this way, prices in the market will adjust so that the efficient portfolio and the market portfolio coincide, and demand equals supply.

The Market Portfolio with Two Stocks

Problem

Suppose it is the year 2525 and there has been a great wave of mergers that has left only two large stocks remaining for investors to invest in: Western Wares and Eastern Enterprises. Western Wares and Eastern Enterprises each have 100 shares outstanding. Under the CAPM assumptions, what is the composition of the efficient portfolio?

Solution

Under the CAPM assumptions, all investors have carefully researched the stocks and are holding the efficient portfolio. At the same time, investors must be holding 100 shares of each stock in total, because these are the shares outstanding in the market. Thus, the efficient portfolio is the market portfolio, which contains 100 shares of Western Wares and 100 shares of Eastern Enterprises.

Optimal Investing: The Capital Market Line

When the CAPM assumptions hold, choosing an optimal portfolio is relatively straightforward: It is a combination of the risk-free investment and the market portfolio. We illustrate this result in Figure 12.1. As we pointed out in Chapter 11, the tangent line graphs the highest possible expected return that can be achieved for any level of volatility. When the tangent line goes through the market portfolio, it is called the **capital market line (CML)**.

Consider a portfolio on the CML, with a fraction x invested in the market portfolio and the remaining $(1 - x)$ invested in the risk-free investment. Using Eqs. 11.15 and 11.16 from Chapter 11 for combining a portfolio with risk-free borrowing and lending, the expected return and volatility of this capital market line portfolio are as follows:

$$E[R_{xCML}] = (1 - x)r_f + xE[R_{Mkt}] = r_f + x(E[R_{Mkt}] - r_f) \qquad (12.2)$$

$$SD(R_{xCML}) = x\,SD(R_{Mkt}) \qquad (12.3)$$

FIGURE 12.1

The Capital Market Line

When investors have homogeneous expectations, the market portfolio and the efficient portfolio coincide. Therefore the capital market line (CML), which is the line from the risk-free investment through the market portfolio, represents the highest expected return available for any level of volatility. (Also shown are individual stocks from Figure 11.8.)

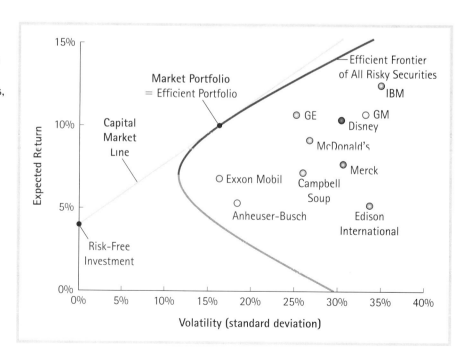

That is, the portfolio's risk premium and volatility are determined by the fraction x that is invested in the market. Recall that when x is larger than 1, the investor borrows money to increase the investment in the market. That is, the investor uses a margin loan to purchase the market portfolio.

Choosing a CML Portfolio

Problem

Your brother-in-law's investment portfolio consists solely of $10,000 invested in McDonald's stock. Suppose the risk-free rate is 4%, McDonald's stock has an expected return of 9% and a volatility of 27%, and the market portfolio has an expected return of 10% and a volatility of 16%. Under the CAPM assumptions, which portfolio has the lowest possible volatility while having the same expected return as McDonald's stock? Which portfolio has the highest possible expected return while having the same volatility as McDonald's stock?

Solution

The CAPM assumptions imply that the best possible risk–return combinations are combinations of the risk-free investment and the market portfolio—portfolios on the capital market line. First let's find the CML portfolio that has an expected return of 9%, equal to the McDonald's return. From Eq. 12.2, we need to determine the amount x to invest in the market so that

$$9\% = E[R_{xCML}] = r_f + x(E[R_{Mkt}] - r_f) = 4\% + x(10\% - 4\%)$$

Solving for x, we get $x = 0.8333$. That is, your brother-in-law should sell his McDonald's stock and invest $8333 in the market portfolio and the remaining $1667 in the risk-free investment. Using Eq. 12.3, this portfolio has a volatility of only

$$SD(R_{xCML}) = 0.8333(16\%) = 13.3\%$$

This volatility is much lower than the volatility of McDonald's stock, and is the lowest possible volatility given an expected return of 9%.

Alternatively, we can choose the CML portfolio that matches McDonald's volatility of 27%. To do so, we use Eq. 12.3 to find x such that

$$27\% = SD(R_{xCML}) = x(16\%)$$

In this case $x = 1.6875$, so the expected return is

$$E[R_{xCML}] = 4\% + 1.6875(10\% - 4\%) = 14.1\%$$

This expected return is much higher than the expected return of McDonald's stock, and the highest possible return we can earn without increasing the volatility. To achieve this portfolio, your brother-in-law needs to sell his McDonald's stock, add (or borrow) an additional $6875, and invest $16,875 in the market portfolio.

Figure 12.2 illustrates the two alternatives to investing in McDonald's stock. Any portfolio on the capital market line between these two portfolios (that is, investing between $8333 and $16,875 in the market) will have both a higher expected return and a lower volatility than investing in McDonald's stock alone.

A Value-Weighted Portfolio

Problem

Suppose we have $100,000 to invest in the following stocks: Microsoft (MSFT), IBM, Wal-Mart (WMT), and Southwest Airlines (LUV). If the stock prices and number of shares outstanding are as shown in the table, what number of shares of each should we buy to construct a value-weighted portfolio?

Stock	Shares Outstanding (billions)	Stock Price ($)
MSFT	10.70	24.92
IBM	1.69	79.00
WMT	4.41	47.30
LUV	0.775	13.02

Solution

First we compute the market capitalization for each stock by multiplying the number of shares outstanding by the current price per share. For example, Microsoft has a market capitalization of 10.70 billion × $24.92 = $267 billion. Next we compute the total market capitalization for the four stocks and determine the percentage represented by each.

Stock	Market Cap ($ billions)	Percent of Total	Initial Investment	Shares Purchased	Ownership
MSFT	$267	43.1%	$43,100	1730	0.000016%
IBM	134	21.6%	21,600	273	0.000016%
WMT	209	33.7%	33,700	712	0.000016%
LUV	10	1.6%	1,600	123	0.000016%
Total	$620	100.0%	$100,000		

Based on the value weights, we can then determine the dollar amount to invest in each stock. For example, because Microsoft's market capitalization is about 43.1% of the total, we invest 43.1% × $100,000 = $43,100 in Microsoft stock. Given Microsoft's stock price of $24.92, investing $43,100 corresponds to purchasing $43,100/$24.92 = 1730 shares of Microsoft stock. We compute the number of shares for each of the other stocks similarly.

In the last column of the table, we also compute the fraction of the total number of shares outstanding that we will purchase. For Microsoft, we are buying 1730 of 10.70 billion shares, or 0.000016% of the total outstanding. Note that the percentage is the same for each stock.

In Example 12.7, we computed the number of shares purchased as a percentage of the total number of shares outstanding for each stock. Note that when buying a value-weighted portfolio, we end up purchasing the same percentage of shares of each firm. That is, a value-weighted portfolio is an **equal-ownership portfolio**: We hold an equal fraction of the total number of shares outstanding of each security in the portfolio.

This last observation is useful because it implies that to maintain a value-weighted portfolio, we do not need to trade securities and rebalance the portfolio unless the number of shares outstanding of some security changes. If the number of shares does not change, but only prices change, the portfolio will remain value weighted. Because very little trading is required to maintain it, a value-weighted portfolio is called a **passive portfolio**.

- *The market portfolio is the efficient portfolio.* Therefore, the best expected return–volatility combinations are portfolios on the capital market line described by Eqs. 12.2 and 12.3.

- *The risk premium for any security is proportional to its beta with the market.* Therefore, the relationship between risk and the required return is given by the security market line described by Eqs. 12.4 and 12.5.

Of course, the CAPM model is only an approximation based on rather strong assumptions. And some of its conclusions not completely accurate—it is certainly not the case that every investor holds the market portfolio, for instance. We will explore why in more detail in Chapter 13, where we also consider extensions that have been proposed to the CAPM. Nevertheless, financial economists find the qualitative intuition underlying the CAPM compelling, so it is still the most commonly used model of risk.

Many practitioners believe it sensible to *use* the CAPM and the security market line as a practical means to estimate a stock's required return and therefore a firm's equity cost of capital. In the rest of this chapter, we will explain how to implement this model. We will look more closely at the construction of the market portfolio and develop a means to estimate betas.

CONCEPT CHECK   1. What is the security market line?

2. What is a stock's alpha?

12.3 The Market Portfolio

To estimate the equity cost of capital using the CAPM, the first thing we need to do is identify the market portfolio. We have defined the market portfolio as the portfolio of *all* risky investments. But in what proportions? If you are an investor in the U.S. stock market, for example, how many shares of each security should you buy?

The answer is simple: Because the market portfolio is defined as the total supply of securities, the proportions should correspond exactly to the proportion of the total market that each security represents. Thus the market portfolio contains more of the largest stocks and less of the smallest stocks. Specifically, the investment in each security i is proportional to its **market capitalization**, which is the total market value of its outstanding shares:

$$MV_i = (\text{Number of Shares of } i \text{ Outstanding}) \times (\text{Price of } i \text{ per Share})$$
$$= N_i \times P_i \tag{12.7}$$

Value-Weighted Portfolios

A portfolio like the market portfolio, in which each security is held in proportion to its market capitalization, is called a **value-weighted portfolio**. In such a portfolio, the portfolio weights are determined as follows:

$$x_i = \frac{\text{Market Value of } i}{\text{Total Market Value of All Securities}} = \frac{MV_i}{\sum_j MV_j}$$

That is, the fraction of money invested in security i corresponds to its share of the total market value of all securities in the portfolio.

A Value-Weighted Portfolio

Problem

Suppose we have $100,000 to invest in the following stocks: Microsoft (MSFT), IBM, Wal-Mart (WMT), and Southwest Airlines (LUV). If the stock prices and number of shares outstanding are as shown in the table, what number of shares of each should we buy to construct a value-weighted portfolio?

Stock	Shares Outstanding (billions)	Stock Price ($)
MSFT	10.70	24.92
IBM	1.69	79.00
WMT	4.41	47.30
LUV	0.775	13.02

Solution

First we compute the market capitalization for each stock by multiplying the number of shares outstanding by the current price per share. For example, Microsoft has a market capitalization of 10.70 billion × $24.92 = $267 billion. Next we compute the total market capitalization for the four stocks and determine the percentage represented by each.

Stock	Market Cap ($ billions)	Percent of Total	Initial Investment	Shares Purchased	Ownership
MSFT	$267	43.1%	$43,100	1730	0.000016%
IBM	134	21.6%	21,600	273	0.000016%
WMT	209	33.7%	33,700	712	0.000016%
LUV	10	1.6%	1,600	123	0.000016%
Total	$620	100.0%	$100,000		

Based on the value weights, we can then determine the dollar amount to invest in each stock. For example, because Microsoft's market capitalization is about 43.1% of the total, we invest 43.1% × $100,000 = $43,100 in Microsoft stock. Given Microsoft's stock price of $24.92, investing $43,100 corresponds to purchasing $43,100/$24.92 = 1730 shares of Microsoft stock. We compute the number of shares for each of the other stocks similarly.

In the last column of the table, we also compute the fraction of the total number of shares outstanding that we will purchase. For Microsoft, we are buying 1730 of 10.70 billion shares, or 0.000016% of the total outstanding. Note that the percentage is the same for each stock.

In Example 12.7, we computed the number of shares purchased as a percentage of the total number of shares outstanding for each stock. Note that when buying a value-weighted portfolio, we end up purchasing the same percentage of shares of each firm. That is, a value-weighted portfolio is an **equal-ownership portfolio**: We hold an equal fraction of the total number of shares outstanding of each security in the portfolio.

This last observation is useful because it implies that to maintain a value-weighted portfolio, we do not need to trade securities and rebalance the portfolio unless the number of shares outstanding of some security changes. If the number of shares does not change, but only prices change, the portfolio will remain value weighted. Because very little trading is required to maintain it, a value-weighted portfolio is called a **passive portfolio**.

Maintaining a Value-Weighted Portfolio

Problem

Starting with the portfolio in Example 12.7, suppose that the price of Microsoft stock drops to $21 per share and Southwest Airlines' stock price rises to $26 per share. What trades are necessary to keep the portfolio value weighted?

Solution

Let's compute the value of each of the holdings:

Stock	Stock Price ($)	Shares Held	Value of Shares ($)	Percent of Portfolio
MSFT	21.00	1730	$36,330	38.3%
IBM	79.00	273	21,567	22.8%
WMT	47.30	712	33,678	35.5%
LUV	26.00	123	3,198	3.4%
		Total	$94,773	100.0%

The total value of the portfolio has dropped from $100,000 to $94,773, and each of the portfolio weights has changed. But compare the portfolio weights to the market value weights:

Stock	Shares Outstanding (billions)	Stock Price ($)	Market Cap ($ billions)	Percent of Total
MSFT	10.70	21.00	$225	38.3%
IBM	1.69	79.00	134	22.8%
WMT	4.41	47.30	209	35.5%
LUV	0.775	26.00	20	3.4%
		Total	$588	100.0%

The portfolio weights remain consistent with the market value weights. Therefore, no trades are necessary to keep the portfolio value weighted.

Common Stock Market Indexes

The CAPM says that individual investors should hold the market portfolio, a value-weighted portfolio of all risky securities in the market. What does this portfolio correspond to in practice? Is there a way to trade the market portfolio directly?

If we focus our attention on U.S. stocks, we find that several popular market indexes try to represent the performance of the U.S. stock market. A **market index** reports the value of a particular portfolio of securities. The most familiar stock index in the United States is the Dow Jones Industrial Average (DJIA), which consists of a portfolio of 30 large industrial stocks. While these stocks are chosen to be representative of different sectors of the economy, they clearly do not represent the entire market. Also, the DJIA is a price-weighted (rather than value-weighted) portfolio. A **price-weighted portfolio** holds an equal number of shares of each stock, independent of their size. Despite being non-representative of the entire market, the DJIA remains widely cited because it is one of the oldest stock market indexes (first published in 1884).

INTERVIEW WITH

John Bogle

*J*ohn C. Bogle founded The Vanguard Group in 1974 and created the first index mutual fund, the Vanguard 500 Index Fund, in 1975. He served as Vanguard's Chairman and Chief Executive Officer until 1996 and Senior Chairman until 2000. He is currently President of the Bogle Financial Markets Research Center.

QUESTION: *Vanguard is known for its index funds. Why is indexing as popular as it is?*

ANSWER: Indexing is popular because it works. The average mutual fund manager cannot beat the market. All fund managers like to say they will beat the market; over a decade, almost 80 percent are wrong. It's the triumph of hope over experience. Over the last 20 years, the average annual return of the S&P 500 was about 13.2%. The average equity mutual fund returned several percentage points less because of expenses, turnover costs, and initial sales charges.

To make matters worse, many fund investors also incur timing and selection penalties. They invest very little when the market's low and a lot when it is high. They buy the wrong funds—telecommunications funds, technology funds, new economy funds—at the market's high. History has shown that after costs and penalties, most mutual fund investors earned returns considerably below returns earned by the average fund. An index fund has no sales charges and an all-in cost of 0.15%, versus an all-in cost of about 3% for active equity funds. Indexing wins, only because it can't lose.

QUESTION: *As a pioneer of indexing, can you explain how theory and evidence came together in the 1970s to suggest that indexing was a smart investment strategy?*

ANSWER: The seed was planted in the 1950s when I was writing my senior thesis at Princeton on mutual funds and did studies showing that funds couldn't outperform market averages. Opportunity and motive came together when I started Vanguard in 1974. We had a company to run, and the only way to beat the market was to remove costs from the equation. I told Vanguard's directors that

I wanted to start an index fund as a way to put Vanguard on the map. Paul Samuelson recently described that creation as the equivalent of the alphabet and the wheel.

We can argue about efficient markets forever. I would say they are strongly efficient, but not perfectly so. Indexing is a smart investment strategy because it's based on the "Cost Matters Hypothesis": gross return − costs = net return to investors. We took the costs out of the equation. Beating the market is a zero sum game on average. Subtract intermediation costs, and it becomes a losing game. Indexing is not magic. It's infinite diversification, infinitely small costs, tiny portfolio turnover, and therefore high tax efficiency. But it took a long while for people to accept this idea.

QUESTION: *Exchange Traded Funds (ETFs) are growing rapidly. What are the tradeoffs between an ETF and a traditional index fund?*

ANSWER: The two are essentially the same. ETFs come in two distinct types. One is all-stock-market ETFs, like VIPERS and SPDRs (based on the S&P 500), and the others are others are sector funds—European, Asian, technology, energy sectors. I don't believe in sectors. I believe in owning the whole market. We pay selection and timing penalties when we buy sectors. ETFs also charge commissions, so the costs mount up if you want to invest a small amount each month or trade them.

There is nothing wrong with buying a SPDR or VIPER, or buying a Vanguard S&P Index fund or total stock market index fund, and holding it forever. However, people tend to hold their index funds for a long time and use ETFs largely as trading vehicles. Long-term investing and short-term speculation are opposite sides of the same coin. I believe in ETFs for buying and holding purposes—which they are rarely used for—and I don't believe in them for speculative and trading purposes.

A better representation of the entire U.S. stock market is the S&P 500, a value-weighted portfolio of 500 of the largest U.S. stocks.[4] The S&P 500 was the first widely publicized value-weighted index (S&P began publishing its index in 1923, though it was based on a smaller number of stocks at that time), and it has become a benchmark for professional investors. This index is the most commonly cited index when evaluating the overall performance of the U.S. stock market. It is also the standard portfolio used to represent "the market" when using the CAPM in practice. Even though the S&P 500 includes only 500 of the more than 7000 individual U.S. stocks in existence, because the S&P 500 includes the largest stocks, it represents more than 70% of the U.S. stock market in terms of market capitalization.

More recently created indexes, such as the Wilshire 5000, provide a value-weighted index of *all* U.S. stocks listed on the major stock exchanges.[5] While more complete than the S&P 500, and therefore more representative of the overall market, these indexes do not share the popularity of the S&P 500. This lack of popularity may in part stem from the fact that the S&P 500 and the Wilshire 5000 have very similar returns; during the 1990s, the correlation between their daily returns exceeded 98%. Given this similarity, may investors view the S&P 500 as an adequate measure of overall U.S. stock market performance.

The S&P 500 and the Wilshire 5000 indexes are both well-diversified indexes that roughly correspond to the market of U.S. stocks (with the Wilshire 5000 being somewhat more representative). Not only are these indexes widely reported, but they are also easy to invest in. Many mutual fund companies offer funds, called **index funds**, that invest in either of these portfolios. In addition, there are exchange-traded funds that represent these portfolios. An **exchange-traded fund (ETF)** is a security that trades directly on an exchange, like a stock, but represents ownership in a portfolio of stocks. For example, Standard and Poor's Depository Receipts (SPDR, nicknamed "spiders") trade on the American Stock Exchange (symbol SPY) and represent ownership in the S&P 500. Vanguard's Total Stock Market ETF (symbol VTI, nicknamed "viper") is based on the Wilshire 5000 index. By investing in an index or an exchange-traded fund, an individual investor with only a small amount to invest can easily achieve the benefits of broad diversification.

Although practitioners commonly use the S&P 500 as the market portfolio in the CAPM, no one does so because of a belief that this index is actually the market portfolio. Instead they view the index as a **market proxy**—a portfolio whose return they believe closely tracks the true market portfolio. Of course, how well the model works will depend on how closely the market proxy actually tracks the true market portfolio. We will return to this issue in Chapter 13.

CONCEPT CHECK

1. How is the weight of a stock in the market portfolio determined?

2. What is an exchange-traded fund (ETF)?

---

4. Standard and Poor's periodically replaces stocks in the index (on average about seven or eight stocks per year). While size is one criterion, Standard and Poor's also tries to maintain appropriate representation of different segments of the economy and chooses firms that are leaders in their industries. Also, from 2005, the value weights in the index are based on the number of shares available for public trading.

5. The Wilshire 5000 began with approximately 5000 stocks when it was first published in 1974. While the name has not changed, the number of stocks in the index has grown with U.S. equity markets.

12.4 Determining Beta

Having identified the S&P 500 as a market proxy, the next step in calculating the risk premium for a security is to determine the security's beta, which was defined in Eq. 12.5 as

$$\beta_i = \frac{SD(R_i)\,Corr(R_i, R_{Mkt})}{SD(R_{Mkt})} = \frac{Cov(R_i, R_{Mkt})}{Var(R_{Mkt})}$$

Beta measures the market risk of a security, as opposed to its diversifiable risk, and is the appropriate measure of the risk of a security for an investor holding the market portfolio.

One difficulty when trying to estimate beta for a security is that beta depends on the correlation and volatility of the security's and market's returns *in the future*. That is, it is based on investors' expectations. However, it is common practice to estimate beta based on the historical correlation and volatilities. This approach makes sense if a stock's beta remains relatively stable over time.

Many data sources provide estimates of beta based on historical data. Typically, these data sources estimate correlations and volatilities from two to five years of weekly or monthly returns and use the S&P 500 as the market portfolio. Table 10.6 on page 309 shows estimated betas for a number of large firms and their industries.

As we discussed in Chapter 10, the differences in betas by industry reflect the sensitivity of each industry's profits to the general health of the economy. For example, Intel and other technology stocks have high betas (near 2.0) because demand for their products usually varies with the business cycle: Companies tend to expand and upgrade their information technology infrastructure when times are good, but they cut back on these expenditures when the economy slows. In contrast, the demand for personal and household products has very little relation to the state of the economy. Firms producing these types of goods, such as Procter & Gamble, tend to have very low betas (below 0.50).

Estimating Beta from Historical Returns

In Chapter 10, we interpreted beta as the sensitivity of a security's excess return (the difference between the security's return and the risk free rate) to the overall market. Specifically,

Beta is the expected percent change in the excess return of the security for a 1% change in the excess return of the market portfolio.

That is, beta represents the amount by which risks that affect the overall market are amplified for a given stock or investment. Securities whose returns tend to move in tandem with the market on average have a beta of 1. Securities that tend to move more than the market have higher betas, while those that move less than the market have lower betas.

Let's look at Cisco Systems stock as an example. Figure 12.6 shows the monthly returns for Cisco and the monthly returns for the S&P 500 from the beginning of 1996 to 2005. Note the overall tendency for Cisco to have a high return when the market is up and a low return when the market is down. Indeed, Cisco tends to move in the same direction as the market, but with greater amplitude. The pattern suggests that Cisco's beta is larger than 1.

Rather than plot the returns over time, we can see Cisco's sensitivity to the market even more clearly by plotting Cisco's return as a function of the S&P 500 return, as shown in Figure 12.7. Each point in this figure represents the return of Cisco and the S&P 500 from one of the months in Figure 12.6. For example, in November 2002, Cisco was up

FIGURE 12.6

Monthly Returns for Cisco Stock and for the S&P 500, 1996–2005

Cisco's returns tend to move in the same direction, but with greater amplitude, than those of the S&P 500.

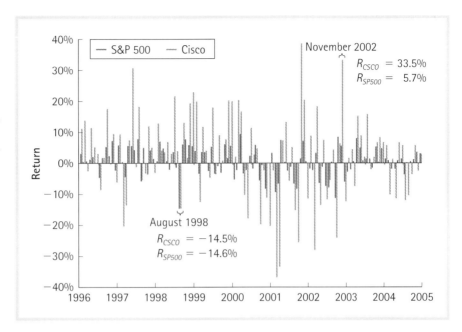

FIGURE 12.7

Scatterplot of Monthly Excess Returns for Cisco Versus the S&P 500, 1996–2005

Beta corresponds to the slope of the best-fitting line. Beta measures the expected change in Cisco's excess return per 1% change in the market's excess return. Deviations from the best-fitting line correspond to diversifiable, non-market-related risk.

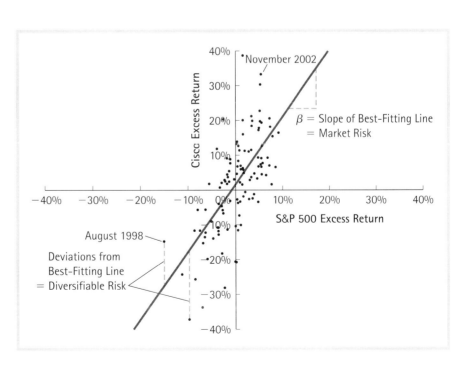

Why Not Estimate Expected Returns Directly?

If the CAPM requires us to use historical data to estimate beta and determine a security's expected return (or an investment's cost of capital), why not just use the security's historical average return as an estimate for its expected return instead? This method would certainly be simpler and more direct.

As we saw in Chapter 10, however, it is extremely difficult to infer the average return of individual stocks from historical data. For a stock with a volatility of 30%, even with 100 years of data the standard error of our estimate would be $30\% / \sqrt{100} = 3\%$ leading to 95% confidence

bounds of $\pm 6\%$. Even worse, few firms have existed for 100 years, and those that have probably bear little resemblance today to what the firms were like 100 years ago. If we use 9 years of data, the confidence bounds would be $\pm 20\%$.

At the same time, as our Cisco example shows, beta can be inferred from historical data reasonably accurately with just a few years of data. In theory at least, the CAPM can provide much more accurate estimates of expected returns for stocks than we could obtain from their historical average return.

33.5% and the S&P 500 was up 5.7%. Note the best-fitting line drawn through these points.[6]

As the scatterplot makes clear, Cisco's returns have a positive covariance with the market: Cisco tends to be up when the market is up, and vice versa. Moreover, from the best-fitting line, we can see that a 10% change in the market's return corresponds to about a 20% change in Cisco's return. That is, Cisco's return moves about two for one with the overall market, so Cisco's beta is about 2. More generally,

Beta corresponds to the slope of the best-fitting line in the plot of the security's excess returns versus the market excess return.

To fully understand this result, recall that beta measures the market risk of a security. The best-fitting line in Figure 12.7 captures the components of a security's return that can be explained by market risk factors. In any individual month, the security's returns will be higher or lower than the best-fitting line. Such deviations from the best-fitting line result from risk that is not related to the market as a whole. These deviations are zero on average in the graph, as the points above the line balance out the points below the line. This firm-specific risk is diversifiable risk that averages out in a large portfolio.

Using Linear Regression

The statistical technique that identifies the best-fitting line through a set of points is called **linear regression**. In Figure 12.7, linear regression corresponds to writing the excess return of a security as the sum of three components:

$$(R_i - r_f) = \alpha_i + \beta_i(R_{Mkt} - r_f) + \varepsilon_i \tag{12.8}$$

The first term, α_i, is the constant or intercept term of the regression. The second term, $\beta_i(R_{Mkt} - r_f)$, represents the sensitivity of the stock to market risk. For example, if the market excess return is 1% higher, there is a $\beta_i\%$ increase in the security's return. We refer to the last term, ε_i, as the **error term**: It represents the deviation from the best-fitting

---

6. By "best fitting," we mean the line that minimizes the sum of the squared deviations from the line.

line and is zero on average. (If the average error were not zero in the sample, you could improve the fit by increasing α_i.) In the CAPM, this error term corresponds to the diversifiable risk of the stock, which is unrelated to the market.

If we take expectations of both sides of Eq. 12.8, because the regression line is calculated so that average error is zero (that is, $E[\varepsilon_i] = 0$), we get

$$E[R_i] = \underbrace{r_f + \beta_i(E[R_{Mkt}] - r_f)}_{\text{Expected return for } i \text{ from the SML}} + \underbrace{\alpha_i}_{\text{Distance above / below the SML}}$$

Thus α_i measures the historical performance of the security relative to the expected return predicted by the SML. The constant term α_i is the distance the stock's average return is above or below the SML. If α_i is positive, the stock has performed better than predicted by the CAPM—its historical return is above the security market line. If α_i is negative, the stock's historical return is below the SML. Thus α_i represents a risk-adjusted performance measure for the historical returns. According to the CAPM, α_i should not be significantly different from zero.[7]

Given data for r_f, R_i, and R_{Mkt}, statistical packages for linear regression (available in most spreadsheet programs) can estimate β_i. The formula for β_i that these programs use corresponds to Eq. 12.5, where the covariance and variance are estimated from the data. If we perform this regression for Cisco using the monthly returns for 1996–2004, the estimated beta is 1.94, indicating that Cisco's returns tended to move about twice as much as the market's returns during this period. The 95% confidence interval for the estimate of beta estimate is 1.52 to 2.36. Assuming Cisco's beta remain stable over time, we would expect Cisco's beta to be in this range in the near future.

The estimate of Cisco's alpha from the regression is 1.2%. In other words, given its beta, Cisco's average monthly return was 1.2% higher than required by the security market line. The standard error of the alpha estimate is 1%, however, so that statistically the estimate is not significantly different from zero. Alphas, like expected returns, are difficult to estimate with much accuracy without a very long data series. Moreover, the alphas for individual stocks have very little persistence. Thus, although Cisco's return has exceeded its required return in the past, it may not necessarily continue to do so.

CONCEPT CHECK
1. How can a stock's beta be estimated from historical returns?
2. How is a stock's alpha defined, and what is its interpretation?

12.5 Extending the CAPM

In building the CAPM, we made no distinction between the interest rate on saving and borrowing, and we assumed that all investors had the same information about a security's risk and return. In the real world, borrowers pay higher interest rates than savers receive, and investors have different information about securities. In this section, we demonstrate that the CAPM still holds (with some qualifications) even under these considerations.

---

7. When used in this way, α_i is often referred to as Jensen's alpha. Using this regression as a test of the CAPM was introduced by F. Black, M. Jensen, and M. Scholes in "The Capital Asset Pricing Model: Some Empirical Tests." In M. Jensen, ed., *Studies in the Theory of Capital Markets.* (New York: Praeger, 1972.)

Saving Versus Borrowing Rates

In Chapter 11, we assumed that investors faced the same risk-free interest rate whether they were saving or borrowing. In practice, investors receive a lower rate when they save than they must pay when they borrow. For example, short-term margin loans from a broker are often 1% to 2% higher than the rates paid on short-term Treasury securities. Banks, pension funds, and other investors with large amounts of collateral can borrow at rates that are generally within 1% of the rate on risk-free securities, but there is still a difference. Do these differences in interest rates affect the conclusions of the CAPM?

The Efficient Frontier with Differing Saving and Borrowing Rates.   Figure 12.8 plots the risk and return possibilities when the saving and borrowing rates differ. In this graph, $r_S = 3\%$ is the rate earned on risk-free savings or lending, and $r_B = 6\%$ is the rate paid on borrowing. Each rate is associated with a different tangent portfolio, labeled T_S and T_B, respectively. A conservative investor who desires a low-risk portfolio can combine the portfolio T_S with saving at rate r_S to achieve risk and return combinations along the lower green line. An aggressive investor who desires high expected returns can invest in the portfolio T_B, using some amount of borrowed funds at rate r_B. By adjusting the amount of borrowing, the investor can achieve risk and return combinations on the upper green line. The combinations on the upper line are not as desirable as the combinations that would result if the investor could borrow at rate r_S, but the investor is unable to borrow at the lower rate. Finally, investors with intermediate preferences may choose portfolios on the red curve between T_S and T_B, which do not involve borrowing or lending.

If borrowing and lending rates differ, then, investors with different preferences will choose different portfolios of risky securities. Some will choose T_S combined with saving,

FIGURE 12.8

Tangent Portfolios with Different Saving and Borrowing Rates

Investors who save at rate r_S will invest in portfolio T_S, and investors who borrow at rate r_B will invest in portfolio T_B. Some investors may neither save nor borrow and invest in a portfolio on the efficient frontier between T_S and T_B.

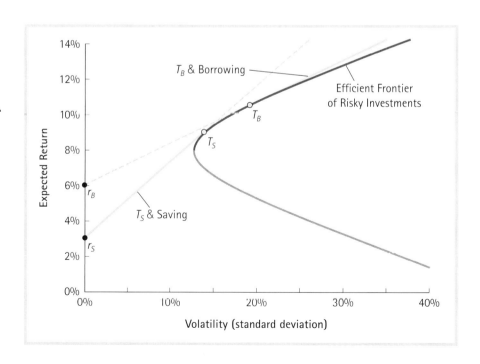

some will choose T_B combined with borrowing, and some will choose portfolios on the curve between T_S and T_B. So, the first conclusion of the CAPM—that the market portfolio is the unique efficient portfolio of risky investments—is no longer valid.

The Security Market Line with Differing Interest Rates.   The more important conclusion of the CAPM for corporate finance is the security market line, which relates the risk of an investment to its required return. It turns out that the SML is still valid when interest rates differ. To see why, we make use of the following result:

A combination of portfolios on the efficient frontier of risky investments is also on the efficient frontier of risky investments.[8]

Because all investors hold portfolios on the efficient frontier between T_S and T_B, and because all investors collectively hold the market portfolio, the market portfolio must lie on the frontier between T_S and T_B. As a result, the market portfolio will be tangent for some risk-free interest rate r^* between r_S and r_B, as illustrated in Figure 12.9. Because our determination of the security market line depends only on the market portfolio being tangent for some interest rate, the SML still holds in the following form:

$$E[R_i] = r^* + \beta_i(E[R_{Mkt}] - r^*) \tag{12.9}$$

FIGURE 12.9

Market Portfolio and Determination of r^* When Saving and Borrowing Rates Differ

Because all investors choose portfolios on the efficient frontier from T_S to T_B, the market portfolio is on the efficient frontier between them. The tangent line through the market portfolio determines the interest rate r^* that can be used in the SML.

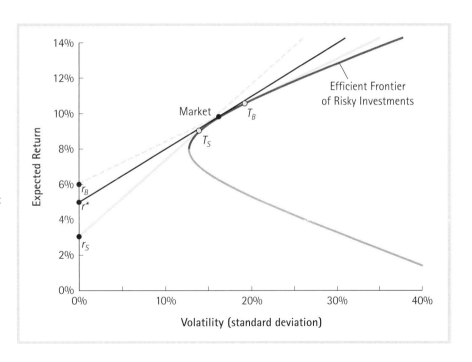

8. To understand this result intuitively, note that portfolios on the efficient frontier contain no diversifiable risk (otherwise we could reduce risk further without lowering the expected return). But a combination of portfolios that contain no diversifiable risk also contains no diversifiable risk, so it is also efficient.

That is, the SML holds with some rate r^* between r_S and r_B in place of r_f. The rate r^* depends on the proportion of savers and borrowers in the economy. But even without knowing those proportions, because saving and borrowing rates tend to be close to each other, r^* must be in a narrow range and we can use Eq. 12.9 to provide reasonable estimates of expected returns.[9]

We can make a similar argument regarding the choice of which risk-free rate to use. As discussed in Chapter 8, the risk-free rate varies with the investment horizon according to the yield curve. When an investor chooses her optimal portfolio, she will do so by finding the tangent line using the risk-free rate that corresponds to her investment horizon. If all investors have the same horizon, then the risk-free rate corresponding to that horizon will determine the SML. If investors have different horizons (but still have homogeneous expectations), then the SML (Eq. 12.9) will hold for some r^* on the current yield curve, with the rate depending on the proportion of investors with each investment horizon.[10]

Investor Information and Rational Expectations

We introduced the CAPM by stating its assumptions that all investors were equally sophisticated and had the same information regarding a security's expected returns, volatilities, and correlations (that is, they have homogeneous expectations). We adopted this strategy so we could focus attention on the important implications of the model, not because we believed that it is an accurate description of the world. In reality, investors have different information and spend varying amounts of effort on research for assorted stocks. Even so, there are reasons to believe that if investors do not have homogeneous expectations, the CAPM will be valid.

An important conclusion of the CAPM is that investors should hold the market portfolio combined with risk-free investments. Note that this investment advice *does not depend on the quality of an investor's information.* Even naive investors with no information can follow this investment advice. But what about sophisticated investors? As we described in Section 12.2, if the market portfolio is not efficient, savvy investors who recognize that the market portfolio is not optimal will push prices and expected returns back into balance. For example, if an investor who is researching eBay stock concludes that its expected return is above the SML and tries to buy shares of eBay, his purchase will drive up the price and lower eBay's expected return back toward the SML. If he is alone in making these trades, the investor's actions are unlikely to drive the return back toward the SML. But it is unlikely that he will be alone. If such opportunities exist, other investors will be looking out for them, too. The ones who discover this opportunity will compete with one another to capitalize on it, and together their actions will drive the price of eBay stock back to the SML. Thus, even though different investors may research different stocks, as we discussed in Chapter 9 their information will ultimately be shared through its influence on prices. Eventually, all investors will want to hold the market portfolio.

9. This result was shown by M. Brennan, "Capital Market Equilibrium with Divergent Borrowing and Lending Rates," *Journal of Financial and Quantitative Analysis* 6 (1971): 1197–1205.

10. The arguments in this section can be generalized further to settings in which there is no risk-free asset; see Fischer Black, "Capital Market Equilibrium with Restricted Borrowing," *Journal of Business* 45 (1972): 444–455, and Mark Rubinstein, "The Fundamental Theorem of Parameter-Preference Security Valuation," *Journal of Financial and Quantitative Analysis* 1 (1973): 61–69.

As we see, the CAPM does not require making the strong assumption of homogeneous expectations. A more plausible notion is the idea of **rational expectations**, which stipulates that

Investors may have different information regarding expected returns, correlations, and volatilities, but they correctly interpret that information and the information contained in market prices and adjust their estimates of expected returns in a rational way.

Investors may learn different information through their own research and observations. As long as they understand these differences in information and learn from other investors by observing prices, the CAPM conclusions—that the market portfolio is the efficient portfolio and that beta determines expected returns—are still true.[11] The intuition for this result is explained in Example 12.9.

EXAMPLE 12.9

How to Avoid Being Outsmarted in Financial Markets

Problem

Suppose you are an investor without access to any information regarding stocks. You know that all other investors in the market possess a great deal of information and are actively using that information to select an efficient portfolio by finding the portfolio that has the highest expected return given the level of volatility they are comfortable with. You are concerned that because of your informational disadvantage, your portfolio will underperform the portfolios of these informed investors. How can you prevent that outcome and guarantee that your portfolio will do as well as that of the average informed investor?

Solution

You can guarantee yourself the same return as the average informed investor simply by holding the market portfolio. Because the average of all investors' portfolios must equal the market portfolio (that is, demand must equal supply), if you hold the market portfolio then so must the average informed investor. To see why, suppose that the informed investors held *more* Google stock than its share of the market portfolio. For supply to equal demand, you must be holding *less* Google stock than its share of the market portfolio. But this cannot be true if you are holding the market portfolio.

Conversely, if you do not hold the market portfolio, then whatever stocks you hold more of, the informed investors hold less of, and vice versa. Because the informed investors have chosen their portfolios based on their superior information, their portfolios must be better than the market—that is, their portfolios have a positive alpha. But because your portfolio deviates from the market in precisely the opposite way, your portfolio must have a negative alpha.

Example 12.9 is very powerful. It implies that every investor, regardless of how much information he has access to, can guarantee himself an alpha of zero by holding the market portfolio (which is always on the security market line). Thus no investor should choose a portfolio with a negative alpha. However, because the average portfolio of all investors is

---

11. See, for example, P. DeMarzo and C. Skiadas, "Aggregation, Determinacy, and Informational Efficiency for a Class of Economies with Asymmetric Information," *Journal of Economic Theory* 80 (1998): 123–152.

the market portfolio, the average alpha of all investors is zero. If no investor earns a negative alpha, then no investor can earn a positive alpha, and the market portfolio must be efficient.

The only way it can be possible to earn a positive alpha and beat the market is if some investors are holding portfolios with negative alphas. Because these investors could have earned a zero alpha by holding the market portfolio, we reach the following important conclusion:

The market portfolio can be inefficient only if a significant number of investors either

1. *Misinterpret information and believe they are earning a positive alpha when they are actually earning a negative alpha, or*

2. *Care about aspects of their portfolios other than expected return and volatility, and so are willing to hold inefficient portfolios of securities.*

CONCEPT CHECK
1. Is the market portfolio the unique efficient portfolio of risky investments when saving and borrowing rates are different?

2. Under what conditions will it be possible to earn a positive alpha and beat the market?

12.6 The CAPM in Practice

The CAPM is a significant and elegant theory of the relationship between risk and return. As with all theories, we must make a number of practical choices when using the CAPM. In this section, we discuss some key considerations that arise when using the CAPM to estimate a firm's cost of capital.

Forecasting Beta

We estimate stock betas in practice by regressing past stock returns on returns of the market portfolio. Important choices in estimating beta include (1) the time horizon used, (2) the index used as the market portfolio, and (3) the method used to extrapolate from past betas to future betas.

Time Horizon.   When estimating beta by using past returns, there is a tradeoff regarding which time horizon to use to measure returns. If we use too short a time horizon, our estimate of beta will be unreliable. If we use very old data, they may be unrepresentative of the current market risk of the security. For stocks, common practice is to use at least two years of weekly return data or five years of monthly return data.[12]

The Market Proxy.   The CAPM predicts that a security's expected return depends on its beta with regard to the market portfolio of *all* risky investments available to investors.

---

12. While daily returns would provide even more sample points, we generally do not use them due to the concern—especially for smaller, less liquid stocks—that short-term factors might influence daily returns that are not representative of the longer-term risks affecting the security. Ideally, we should use a return interval equal to our investment horizon. The need for sufficient data, however, makes monthly returns the longest practical choice.

As mentioned earlier, in practice the S&P 500 is used as the market proxy. Other proxies, such as the NYSE Composite Index (a value-weighted index of all NYSE stocks), the Wilshire 5000 index of all U.S. stocks, or an even broader market index that includes both equities and fixed-income securities, are sometimes used as well. When evaluating international stocks, it is common practice to use a country or international market index.

Beta Extrapolation.   When using historical data, there is always the possibility of estimation error. Thus we should be suspicious of estimates that are extreme relative to industry norms; in fact, many practitioners prefer to use average industry betas rather than individual stock betas. In addition, evidence suggests that betas tend to regress toward the average beta of 1.0 over time.[13] For both of these reasons, many practitioners use **adjusted betas**, which are calculated by averaging the estimated beta with 1.0. For example, Bloomberg computes adjusted betas using the following formula:

$$\text{Adjusted Beta of Security } i = \tfrac{2}{3}\beta_i + \tfrac{1}{3}(1.0) \tag{12.10}$$

The estimation methodologies of three data providers appear in Table 12.1. Each employs a unique methodology, which leads to differences in the reported betas.

TABLE 12.1	Estimation Methodologies Used by Selected Data Providers		
	Value Line	**Reuters**	**Bloomberg**
Returns	Weekly	Monthly	Weekly
Horizon	5 years	5 years	2 years
Market Index	NYSE Composite	S&P 500	S&P 500
Adjusted	Yes	No	Yes

Outliers.   The beta estimates we obtain from linear regression can be very sensitive to outliers, which are returns of unusually large magnitude. As an example, Figure 12.10 shows a scatterplot of Genentech's monthly returns versus the S&P 500 for 2002–2004. Based on these returns, we estimate a beta of 1.21 for Genentech. Looking closely at the monthly returns, however, we find two data points with unusually large returns: In April 2002, Genentech's stock price fell by almost 30%, and in May 2003, Genentech's stock price rose by almost 65%. In each case the extreme moves were a reaction to Genentech's announcement of news related to new drug development. In April 2002, Genentech reported a setback in the development of psoriasis drug Raptiva. In May 2003, the company reported the successful clinical trial of its anticancer drug Avastin. These two returns more likely represent firm-specific rather than market-wide risk. But because these large returns happened to occur during months when the market also moved in the same direction, they bias the estimate of beta that results from a standard regression. If we redo the regression replacing Genentech's returns during these two months with the average return of similar biotechnology firms during the same months, we obtain a much lower estimate

---

13. See M. Blume, "Betas and Their Regression Tendencies," *Journal of Finance* 30 (1975): 785–795.

FIGURE 12.10

Beta Estimation with and without Outliers for Genentech Using Monthly Returns for 2002–2004

Genentech's returns in April 2002 and May 2003 are largely due to firm-specific news. By replacing those returns (blue points) with industry average returns (red points), we obtain a more accurate assessment of Genentech's market risk during this period.

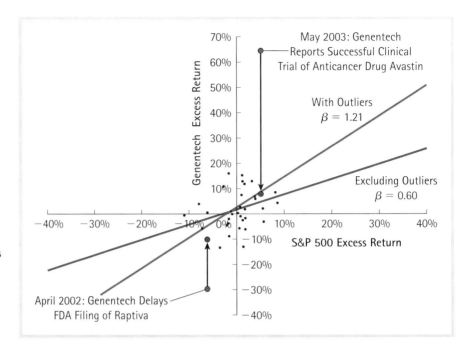

of 0.60 for Genentech's beta, as shown in Figure 12.10. This latter estimate is probably a much more accurate assessment of Genentech's market risk during this period.

There may be other reasons to exclude certain historical data as anomalous when estimating beta. For example, some practitioners advocate ignoring data from 1998–2000 to avoid distortions related to the technology, media, and telecommunications speculative bubble.[14]

Other Considerations.   When using historical returns to forecast future betas, we must be mindful of changes in the environment that might cause the future to differ from the past. For example, if a firm were to change industries, using its historical beta would be inferior to using the beta of other firms in the new industry. Also bear in mind that many practitioners analyze other information in addition to past returns, such as industry characteristics, firm size, and other financial characteristics of a firm, when they forecast betas. In the end, forecasting betas, like most types of forecasting, is as much art as science, and the best estimates require a thorough knowledge of the particulars of a firm and its industry.

The Security Market Line

In addition to beta, estimating the cost of capital from the security market line requires a risk-free interest rate and a risk-premium for the market index. We discuss next some of the considerations that determine these inputs.

---

14. For example, see A. Annema and M. H. Goedhart, "Better Betas," *McKinsey on Finance* (Winter 2003): 10–13.

The Risk-Free Interest Rate.   The risk-free interest rate is generally determined using the yields of U.S. Treasury securities, which are free from default risk. However, even U.S. Treasuries are subject to interest rate risk unless we select a maturity equal to our investment horizon. Which horizon should we choose?

As we discussed in Section 12.5, the CAPM states that we should use the risk-free interest corresponding to the investment horizon of the firm's investors. It may also be appropriate to use a rate that exceeds the rate on government bonds to account for the cost of borrowing. When surveyed, the vast majority of large firms and financial analysts report using the yields of long-term (10- to 30-year) bonds to determine the risk-free rate.[15]

The Market Risk Premium.   To determine the risk premium for a stock using the security market line, we need an estimate of the market risk premium, $E[R_{Mkt}] - r_f$. To estimate the expected return of the market, we can use a variety of approaches. For example, we can look at the historical average excess return of the market over the risk-free interest rate.[16] With this approach, it is important to use historical returns for the same market index used to calculate beta, and to compare the return over the same time horizon as that used for the risk-free interest rate.

Because we are interested in the *future* market risk premium, we again face a tradeoff in terms of the amount of data we use. As we noted in Chapter 10, it takes many years of data to produce even moderately accurate estimates of expected returns. Yet data that are very old may have little relevance for investors' expectations of the market risk premium today.

Table 12.2 reports excess returns of the S&P 500 versus one-year and ten-year Treasury rates. Since 1926, the S&P 500 has had an average return of 8.0% above the rate for one-year Treasuries. However, some evidence indicates that the market risk premium has declined over time. Since 1955, the S&P 500 has shown an excess return of only 5.7% over the rate for one-year Treasuries. Compared with ten-year Treasuries, the S&P 500 had an average excess return of only 4.5% (due primarily to the fact that ten-year Treasury bond rates tend to be higher than one-year rates). One reasonable explanation for

TABLE 12.2	**Historical Excess Returns of the S&P 500 Compared to One-Year Treasury Bills and Ten-Year Treasury Notes**	
Risk-free Security	**Period**	**S&P 500 Excess Return**
One-year Treasury	1926–2005	8.0%
	1955–2005	5.7%
Ten-year Treasury*	1955–2005	4.5%

*Based on a comparison of compounded returns over a ten-year holding period.

---

15. See Robert Bruner, et al., "Best Practices in Estimating the Cost of Capital: Survey and Synthesis," *Financial Practice and Education* 8 (1998): 13–28.

16. Because we are interested in the expected return, the correct average to use is the arithmetic average. See Chapter 10.

this decline is that as more investors have begun to participate in the stock market and the costs of constructing a diversified portfolio have declined, investors tend to hold less risky portfolios, so the return they require as compensation for taking on that risk has diminished. In addition, the overall volatility of the market has declined over time. Some researchers believe that the future expected returns for the market are likely to be even lower than these historical numbers, in a range of about 3–5% over Treasury bills.[17]

Using historical data to estimate the market risk premium suffers from two drawbacks. First, despite using 50 years (or more) of data, the standard errors of the estimates are large. (For example, even using data from 1926, the standard error of the excess return over one-year Treasury bills is 2.3%, implying a 95% confidence interval of $\pm 4.6\%$.) Second, they are backward looking, so we cannot be sure they are representative of current expectations.

As an alternative, we can take a fundamental approach toward estimating the market risk premium. Given an assessment of firms' future cash flows, we can estimate the expected return of the market by solving for the discount rate that is consistent with the current level of the index. For example, if we use the constant expected growth model presented in Chapter 9, the expected market return is equal to

$$r_{mkt} = \frac{Div_1}{P_0} + g = \text{Dividend Yield} + \text{Expected Dividend Growth Rate} \quad (12.11)$$

While this model is highly inaccurate for an individual firm, the assumption of constant expected growth is more reasonable when considering the overall market. If, for instance, the S&P 500 has a current dividend yield of 2%, and we assume that both earnings and dividends are expected to grow 6% per year, this model would estimate the expected return of the S&P 500 as 8%. Following such methods, researchers generally report estimates in the 3–5% range for the future equity risk premium.[18]

Evidence Regarding the CAPM

Researchers have conducted numerous studies to evaluate the performance of the CAPM. Two of the earliest and most important studies were done by Black, Jensen, and Scholes (1972) and by Fama and MacBeth (1973).[19] They compared actual average returns with those predicted by the security market line. They concluded that expected returns were related to betas, as predicted by the CAPM, rather than to other measures of risk such as the security's volatility. However, they did find some deviation from the security market line. In particular, the empirically estimated security market line is somewhat flatter than that predicted by the CAPM, as shown in Figure 12.11. That is, low-beta stocks have

---

17. See Ivo Welch, "The Equity Premium Consensus Forecast Revisited," Cowles Foundation Discussion Paper 1325 (2001), and John Graham and Campbell Harvey, "The Long-Run Equity Risk Premium," SSRN working paper (2005).

18. See, for example, Eugene Fama and Kenneth French, "The Equity Premium," *Journal of Finance* 57 (2002): 637–659; Ravi Jagannathan, Ellen McGrattan, and Anna Scherbina, "The Declining US Equity Premium," NBER working paper 8172 (2001); and Jeremy Siegel, "The Long-Run Equity Risk Premium," CFA Institute Conference proceedings *Points of Inflection: New Directions for Portfolio Management* (2004).

19. Eugene F. Fama and James MacBeth, "Risk, Return and Equilibrium: Some Empirical Tests," *Journal of Political Economy* 8 (1973): 607–636.

FIGURE 12.11

Empirical SML Versus SML Predicted by CAPM (Black, Jensen, and Scholes, 1972)

Low-beta stocks tend to be somewhat above the SML, and high-beta stocks tend to be somewhat below the SML.

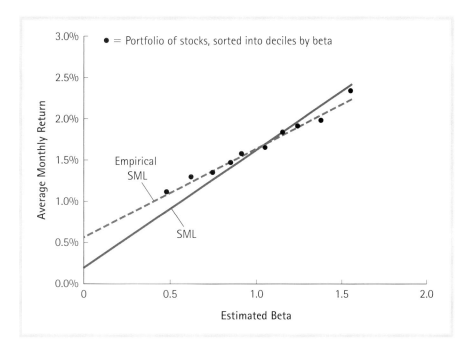

tended to perform somewhat better than the CAPM predicts, while the highest-beta stocks do worse.

While they may identify some flaws, these studies do support the qualitative conclusions of the CAPM. More recent research, however, has questioned the performance of the CAPM. A series of influential papers published in 1992 and 1993 by Eugene Fama and Kenneth French[20] argue that, based on more current data and taking other characteristics of securities into account, beta is not helpful in explaining average returns. An ongoing debate among researchers focuses on the use of more refined techniques to determine whether beta is an adequate measure of risk. (We discuss this debate further in Chapter 13, where we also describe proposed modifications to the CAPM.) Despite more than a decade of research, however, no consensus has been reached regarding the best way to improve upon the CAPM. A number of difficulties arise in resolving this debate:

- *Betas are not observed.* If betas change over time, simple historical estimates of beta are not likely to be accurate. Evidence against the CAPM may be the result of mismeasuring betas.

- *Expected returns are not observed.* Even if beta is a perfect measure of risk, average returns need not match expected returns. It takes many years of data to obtain even moderately accurate measures of the true mean of returns. Moreover, the realized average return need not match investors' expectations; for example, investors may be concerned about risks that do not come to pass.

---

20. Eugene Fama and Kenneth French, "The Cross-Section of Expected Stock Returns," *Journal of Finance* 47 (1992): 427–465; and "Common Risk Factors in the Returns on Stocks and Bonds," *Journal of Financial Economics* 33 (1993): 3–56.

FIGURE 12.12

Relative Weights of International Stock Markets by Market Capitalization, June 2004

The true market portfolio includes both domestic and international investments.

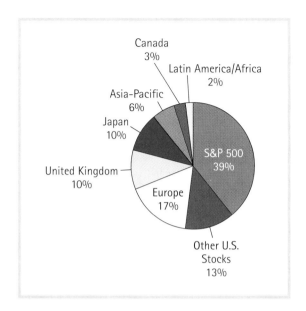

- *The market proxy is not correct.* While the S&P 500 is routinely used, it is not the true market portfolio. Although it is a reasonable proxy for the U.S. stock market, investors hold many other assets. The stock market captures less than 50% of the securities traded within the United States once government bonds, corporate bonds, and mortgage-related securities are taken into account. In addition, we should include privately held firms and real estate investments. Finally, the U.S. stock market represents only about 50% of world equity markets, as shown in Figure 12.12. Thus any failure of the CAPM may simply be the result of our failure to find a good measure of the market portfolio.[21]

Better statistical methods that attempt to address these issues, as well as allowing betas and expected returns to vary over time, may ultimately provide more conclusive evidence regarding the accuracy of the CAPM and the best ways to improve upon it.

The Bottom Line on the CAPM

While the CAPM many not be perfect, it is unlikely that a truly perfect model will be found in the foreseeable future. Furthermore, the imperfections of the CAPM may not be critical in the context of capital budgeting and corporate finance, where errors in estimating project cash flows are likely to be far more important than small discrepancies in

---

21. This observation was originally pointed out in an influential paper written by Richard Roll ["A Critique of the Asset Pricing Theory's Tests," *Journal of Financial Economics* 4 (1977): 129–176], in which he showed that because we can never know how close the portfolio we are using is to the true market portfolio, it is *impossible* to verify empirically whether the market portfolio is efficient.

Nobel Prize   William Sharpe on the CAPM

William Sharpe received the Nobel Prize in 1990 for his development of the Capital Asset Pricing Model. Here are his comments on the CAPM from a 1998 interview with Jonathan Burton:[*]

Portfolio theory focused on the actions of a single investor with an optimal portfolio. I said, What if everyone was optimizing? They've all got their copies of Markowitz and they're doing what he says. Then some people decide they want to hold more IBM, but there aren't enough shares to satisfy demand. So they put price pressure on IBM and up it goes, at which point they have to change their estimates of risk and return, because now they're paying more for the stock. That process of upward and downward pressure on prices continues until prices reach an equilibrium and everyone collectively wants to hold what's available. At that point, what can you say about the relationship between risk and return? The answer is that expected return is proportionate to beta relative to the market portfolio.

The CAPM was and is a theory of equilibrium. Why should anyone expect to earn more by investing in one security as opposed to another? You need to be compensated for doing badly when times are bad. The security that is going to do badly just when you need money when

times are bad is a security you have to hate, and there had better be some redeeming virtue or else who will hold it? That redeeming virtue has to be that in normal times you expect to do better. The key insight of the Capital Asset Pricing Model is that higher expected returns go with the greater risk of doing badly in bad times. Beta is a measure of that. Securities or asset classes with high betas tend to do worse in bad times than those with low betas.

The CAPM was a very simple, very strong set of assumptions that got a nice, clean, pretty result. And then almost immediately, we all said, Let's bring more complexity into it to try to get closer to the real world. People went on—myself and others—to what I call "extended" Capital Asset Pricing Models, in which expected return is a function of beta, taxes, liquidity, dividend yield, and other things people might care about.

Did the CAPM evolve? Of course. But the fundamental idea remains that there's no reason to expect reward just for bearing risk. Otherwise, you'd make a lot of money in Las Vegas. If there's reward for risk, it's got to be special. There's got to be some economics behind it or else the world is a very crazy place. I don't think differently about those basic ideas at all.

*Jonathan Burton, "Revisiting the Capital Asset Pricing Model," *Dow Jones Asset Manager* (May/June 1998): 20–28.

the cost of capital. In that sense, the CAPM may be good enough, especially relative to the effort required to implement a more sophisticated model. The CAPM remains the predominant model used in practice to determine the equity cost of capital.

Even if the CAPM is not completely correct, the security market line still provides the required return for any investment for an investor who currently holds the market index and who cares about expected return and volatility. Given the large number of investors who follow an indexing strategy, this constituency is likely to be an important one for the firm. Furthermore, the average investor must hold the market index, because the sum of all investor portfolios equals the total supply of all securities. Thus, despite its potential flaws, there are very good reasons to use the CAPM as a basis for calculating the cost of capital.

CONCEPT CHECK   1. For stocks, why do we use weekly or monthly return data to estimate beta?

2. If the CAPM is not perfect, why do we continue to use it in corporate finance?

Summary

1. Three main assumptions underlie the Capital Asset Pricing Model (CAPM):

   a. Investors trade securities at competitive market prices (without incurring taxes or transaction costs) and can borrow and lend at the risk-free rate.

   b. Investors choose efficient portfolios.

   c. Investors have homogeneous expectations regarding the volatilities, correlations, and expected returns of securities.

2. Because the supply of securities must equal the demand for securities, the CAPM implies that the market portfolio of all risky securities is the efficient portfolio.

3. The capital market line (CML) is the set of portfolios with the highest possible expected return for any level of volatility.

   a. Under the CAPM assumptions, the CML is the line through the risk-free security and the market portfolio.

   b. The expected return and volatility of a portfolio on the CML with fraction x invested in the market portfolio and the remainder invested in the risk-free asset are calculated as follows:

$$E[R_{xCML}] = (1 - x)r_f + xE[R_{Mkt}] = r_f + x(E[R_{Mkt}] - r_f) \qquad (12.2)$$

$$SD(R_{xCML}) = x\,SD(R_{Mkt}) \qquad (12.3)$$

4. Under the CAPM assumptions, the risk premium of any security is equal to the market risk premium multiplied by the beta of the security. This relationship is called the security market line (SML), and it determines the required return for an investment:

$$E[R_i] = r_i = r_f + \underbrace{\beta_i^{Mkt}(E[R_{Mkt}] - r_f)}_{\text{Risk premium for security } i} \qquad (12.4)$$

5. The beta of a security measures the amount of the security's risk that is common to the market portfolio or market risk.

   a. Beta is defined as follows:

$$\beta_i^{Mkt} \equiv \beta_i = \frac{\overbrace{SD(R_i) \times Corr(R_i, R_{Mkt})}^{\text{Volatility of } i \text{ that is common with the market}}}{SD(R_{Mkt})} = \frac{Cov(R_i, R_{Mkt})}{Var(R_{Mkt})} \qquad (12.5)$$

   b. The beta of a portfolio is the weighted-average beta of the securities in the portfolio.

6. The difference between a security's expected return and its required return from the security market line is the security's alpha. According to the CAPM:

   a. All stocks and securities should be on the security market line and have an alpha of zero.

   b. If some securities have a nonzero alpha, the market portfolio is not efficient, and its performance can be improved upon by buying securities with positive alphas and selling those with negative alphas.

7. To estimate a security's return using the CAPM, we must estimate the model's parameters.

   a. The market portfolio in theory is a value-weighted index of all risky investments. In practice, we often use a stock market index such as the S&P 500 to represent the market.

b. To estimate beta, we often use historical returns and assume that historical values are reasonable estimates of future returns. Most data sources use five years of monthly returns to estimate beta.

c. Beta corresponds to the slope of the best-fitting line in the plot of a security's returns versus the market's returns. We use a linear regression to find the best-fitting line.

8. If we regress a stock's excess returns against the market's excess returns, the intercept is referred to as the stock's alpha. It measures how the stock has performed historically relative to the security market line.

9. While betas tend to be stable over time, alphas do not seem to be persistent.

10. While the historical excess return of the S&P 500 has been about 8.4% more than Treasury bills since 1926, the appropriate market risk premium to use in the security market line is likely to be lower. Since 1955, the average excess return of the S&P 500 has been 5.7%, and research suggests that future excess returns are likely to be even lower.

11. When we relax some of the CAPM assumptions, most of the main results still hold.

a. If investors borrow and lend at different rates, the SML holds in the following form:

$$r_i = r^* + \beta_i(E[R_{Mkt}] - r^*)$$

The rate r^* is between the borrowing and lending rates, and depends on the proportion of savers and borrowers in the economy.

b. If investors have rational expectations (rather than homogeneous expectations), the market portfolio is efficient and the CAPM holds.

c. For the market portfolio to be inefficient, a significant fraction of investors must be willing to hold negative-alpha portfolios.

12. Recent research questions the reliability of beta in explaining average returns. There are some difficulties in trying to resolve this debate, but the CAPM remains the most important method for estimating the equity cost of capital.

Key Terms

adjusted betas *p. 389*
alpha *p. 373*
capital market line (CML) *p. 366*
equal-ownership portfolio *p. 376*
error term *p. 382*
exchange-traded fund *p. 379*
homogeneous expectations *p. 365*
index funds *p. 379*
linear regression *p. 382*

market capitalization *p. 375*
market index *p. 377*
market portfolio *p. 364*
market proxy *p. 379*
passive portfolio *p. 376*
price-weighted portfolio *p. 377*
rational expectations *p. 387*
security market line (SML) *p. 370*
value-weighted portfolio *p. 375*

Further Reading

The following classic papers developed the CAPM: J. Lintner, "The Valuation of Risk Assets and the Selection of Risky Investments in Stock Portfolios and Capital Budgets," *Review of Economics and Statistics* 47 (February 1965): 13–37; J. Mossin, "Equilibrium in a Capital Asset Market," *Econometrica* 34 (1966): 768–783; W. F. Sharpe, "Capital Asset Prices: A Theory of Market Equilibrium under Conditions of Risk," *Journal of Finance* 19 (September 1964): 425–442; and J. Treynor, "Toward a Theory of the Market Value of Risky Assets," unpublished manuscript (1961).

The following articles provide some additional insights on the CAPM: F. Black, "Beta and Return," *Journal of Portfolio Management* 20 (Fall 1993): 8–18; and B. Rosenberg and J. Guy, "Beta and Investment Fundamentals," *Financial Analysts Journal* (May–June 1976): 60–72.

Although not a focus of this chapter, there is an extensive body of literature on testing the CAPM. Besides the articles mentioned in the text, here are a few others that an interested reader might want to consult: W. E. Ferson and C. R. Harvey "The Variation of Economic Risk Premiums," *Journal of Political Economy* 99 (1991): 385–415; M. R. Gibbons, S. A. Ross, and J. Shanken, "A Test of the Efficiency of a Given Portfolio," *Econometrica* 57 (1989): 1121–1152; S. P. Kothari, Jay Shanken, and Richard G. Sloan, "Another Look at the Cross-Section of Expected Stock Returns," *Journal of Finance* 50 (March 1995): 185–224; and R. A. Levy, "On the Short-Term Stationarity of Beta Coefficients," *Financial Analysts Journal* (November–December 1971): 55–62.

Problems

All problems in this chapter are available in MyFinanceLab. An asterisk (*) indicates problems with a higher level of difficulty.

The Efficiency of the Market Portfolio

1. When the CAPM correctly prices risk, the market portfolio is an efficient portfolio. Explain why.

2. Your investment portfolio consists of $15,000 invested in only one stock—Microsoft. Suppose the risk-free rate is 5%, Microsoft stock has an expected return of 12% and a volatility of 40%, and the market portfolio has an expected return of 10% and a volatility of 18%. Under the CAPM assumptions,
   a. What alternative investment has the lowest possible volatility while having the same expected return as Microsoft?
   b. What investment has the highest possible expected return while having the same volatility as Microsoft?

3. What is the volatility of the portfolio in part (a) of Problem 2?

4. What is the expected return of the portfolio in part (b) of Problem 2?

5. Plot the capital market line from the data in Problem 2 and mark the set of portfolios that dominates investing all your money in Microsoft stock—that is, the set of portfolios that has both a higher expected return and a lower volatility than investing in Microsoft stock alone.

Determining the Risk Premium

6. Suppose the risk-free return is 4% and the market portfolio has an expected return of 10% and a volatility of 16%. Johnson and Johnson Corporation (Ticker: JNJ) stock has a 20% volatility and a correlation with the market of 0.06.
   a. What is Johnson and Johnson's beta with respect to the market?
   b. Under the CAPM assumptions, what is its expected return?

7. What is the sign of the risk premium of a negative-beta stock? Explain. (Assume the risk premium of the market portfolio is positive.)

8. Suppose Intel stock has a beta of 2.16, whereas Boeing stock has a beta of 0.69. If the risk-free interest rate is 4% and the expected return of the market portfolio is 10%, what is the expected return of a portfolio that consists of 60% Intel stock and 40% Boeing stock, according to the CAPM?

*9.   What is the risk premium of a zero-beta stock? Does this mean you can lower the volatility of a portfolio without changing the expected return by substituting out any zero-beta stock in a portfolio and replacing it with the risk-free asset?

The Market Portfolio

    10.   Suppose all possible investment opportunities in the world are limited to the five stocks listed in the table below. What does the market portfolio consist of?

Stock	Price/Share ($)	Number of Shares Outstanding (millions)
A	10	10
B	20	12
C	8	3
D	50	1
E	45	20

EXCEL   11.   Given $100,000 to invest, construct a value-weighted portfolio of the four stocks listed below.

Stock	Price/Share ($)	Number of Shares Outstanding (millions)
Golden Seas	13	1000
Jacobs and Jacobs	22	1.25
MAG	43	30
PDJB	5	10

12.   If one stock in a value-weighted portfolio goes up in price and all other stock prices remain the same, what trades are necessary to keep the portfolio value weighted?

Determining Beta

    *13.   Go to Chapter Resources on MyFinanceLab and use the data in the spreadsheet provided to estimate the beta of Nike stock using linear regression.

    *14.   Using the same data as in Problem 13,
    a. Estimate the alpha of Nike stock over the period covered by the data.
    b. Calculate the 95% confidence interval. Is alpha significantly different from zero?

Extending the CAPM

15.   Assume that all the assumptions underlying the CAPM hold, but investors have to borrow and lend at different rates. Will all investors hold a combination of the market portfolio and risk-free borrowing or lending?

16.   Assume that all the assumptions underlying the CAPM hold, but investors have to borrow and lend at different rates. Will the market portfolio be efficient?

*17.   List all the conditions under which the market portfolio may not be efficient.

The CAPM in Practice

18.   Describe two methods to estimate the market risk premium.

*19.   Assume the CAPM is correct. Give a reason why an empirical test of the CAPM might indicate that the model does not work—that is, that stocks have alphas that are statistically significantly different from zero.

Data Case

You are still working for the budget-strapped financial planning firm. Your boss has been so impressed with your work in the Data Cases in Chapters 10 and 11 related to the stocks in the client's portfolio that he has one more request: Use the CAPM to compute expected returns for all twelve stocks in the portfolio from Chapter 10. Specifically, he would like you to calculate betas for each stock using five years of monthly data and an expected return using the historical risk premium of 4.5%. He would like you to calculate the betas using excess returns as in Eq. 12.5 with the S&P 500 as the market index and the one-month Eurodollar rate as the risk-free rate.[22] Additionally, he wants you to compute the expected return for the 12-stock portfolio beta using the equally weighted portfolio, and using one of the efficient portfolios derived from Chapter 11. In particular, you should consider the efficient portfolio from Chapter 11 with an expected return of 10%, when short selling is allowed. In preparing your analysis, you'll need to draw on your Excel data from Chapters 10 and 11.

1. Gather the monthly returns from the Chapter 10 Data Case.

2. Get the returns for the S&P 500 from Yahoo! Finance (http://finance.yahoo.com). Click on S&P 500 in the Market Summary box on the left side of the main page. Then click on "Historical Prices" on the left side of the page. Again use May 24, 2001 as the start date and May 1, 2006 as the end date to obtain the prices and remember to click "monthly". Then download those prices and add the adjusted closing prices to your spreadsheet.

3. Get the one-month Eurodollar rate from the Federal Reserve Web site (http://www.federalreserve.gov/releases/h15/data.htm). Click on Data Download. Go to Select and choose: 1.) Series type–selected interest rates 2.) Instrument–ED Eurodollar deposits (London) 3.) Maturity–1 month 4.) Frequency–monthly. Go to Format, Select Dates–From 2001 May to 2006 May, File Type–Excel. Go to download, open, and then save these rates to an Excel file.

4. Create monthly returns for the S&P 500 following the procedure you used for individual stocks. For the Eurodollar rate, convert to a monthly rate, take the yield and divide it by 100 to convert it to a decimal. Then divide the decimal by 12. The resulting rate will be the risk-free rate used in the CAPM.

5. Create separate return columns that compute the excess returns for each stock and the S&P 500. Recall that the excess return is the actual monthly return minus the risk-free rate.

6. Compute the beta of each stock using Eq. 12.5 from this chapter. Recall that Excel computes covariance as the population covariance, so you will have to compute the correlation first and then use the standard deviations of the stock and market index.

7. Using the current Eurodollar rate and the historical market risk premium, determine the expected return of each stock.

8. Determine the expected returns and portfolio betas for the equally weighted portfolio and for the efficient portfolio from Chapter 11 with an expected return of 10% when short selling is allowed.

   a. Is either portfolio "better" in terms of risk and return than the other is? Why or why not?

   b. What do the portfolio results indicate about the investment decision using the SML relative to using standard deviation?

---

22. This rate is the rate London banks charge on loans to one another. It is reflective of the institutional borrowing/lending rate, and is used as the risk-free rate in some financial applications such as derivatives pricing.

13

Alternative Models of Systematic Risk

notation

x_i portfolio weight of investment in i

R_s return of stock s

r_f risk-free rate of interest

α_s alpha of stock s

β_s^i beta of stock s with portfolio i

ε_s residual risk of stock s

w_s^i standardized weight of the ith characteristic for firm s

For the ten-year period from 1995 through 2004, the average annual return of the market portfolio of U.S. stock was 12.5%. During the same period, the smallest 10% of U.S. stocks had an annual return of almost 20%. And while the small stock portfolio was much more volatile than the market portfolio, its beta during this time period was slightly less than one. Thus, according to the CAPM, small stocks should not have outperformed the market. What accounts for this discrepancy? Was the positive alpha of small U.S. stock during this period a random occurrence, or was it indicative of potential systematic inaccuracies inherent in the CAPM? And if the CAPM is inaccurate, what alternative methods can be used to estimate a security's expected return and the cost of capital for an investment?

This chapter addresses these questions. We begin by describing several firm characteristics that seem to be related to returns. When criteria such as firm size, the book-to-market ratio, and past returns are used to form portfolios, these portfolios appear to have positive alphas—that is, they plot above the security market line. This evidence indicates that the market portfolio may not be efficient. In light of this evidence, we explain how to calculate the cost of capital if the market portfolio is not efficient. We derive an alternative model of risk—the multifactor asset pricing model. Finally, we introduce an alternative approach to estimating the cost of capital—the characteristic model of expected returns.

13.1 The Efficiency of the Market Portfolio

Let's begin by reviewing the results of empirical studies that have examined whether the market portfolio is efficient. As we saw in Chapter 12, the market portfolio is efficient if expected returns are related to betas according to the security market line. That is, if the market portfolio is efficient, securities should not have alphas that are significantly different from zero.

It is not difficult to find individual stocks that, *in the past*, have not plotted on the SML. For example, during the period 1996–2005, Cisco's stock had a positive alpha of 1.2% per month, but the standard error was 1%, indicating a confidence interval between −0.8% per month to 3.2% per month. The uncertainty in Cisco's alpha estimate is not exceptional. For most stocks the standard errors of the alpha estimates are large, so it is impossible to conclude that the alphas are statistically different from zero.

If the market portfolio is efficient, then all securities and portfolios must plot on the SML, not just individual stocks. Because the expected returns of large, well-diversified, portfolios can be estimated with a greater degree of accuracy, one way to construct a more powerful test of the CAPM is to see whether portfolios of stocks plot on the SML. Hence, instead of testing whether individual stocks plot on the SML, researchers have studied whether portfolios of stocks plot on this line.

To make the test of the CAPM as powerful as possible, researchers have searched for portfolios that would be most likely to have nonzero alphas. Researchers had already identified a number of characteristics that can be used to pick stocks that produce high average returns, so they used the same criteria to form their portfolios for testing purposes. Let's begin with the most widely used characteristic, market capitalization.

The Size Effect

Small stocks (those with lower market capitalizations) have higher average returns. This empirical result is called the **size effect**. Researchers have analyzed the size effect by considering the performance of portfolios based on stocks' market capitalizations. For example, Eugene Fama and Kenneth French[1] measured the excess returns of ten portfolios formed each year by collecting the smallest 10% (decile) of stocks into the first portfolio, the next 10% into the second portfolio, on up to the biggest 10% of stocks, which they formed into the tenth portfolio. Fama and French then recorded the excess return of each portfolio in each month over the following year. They repeated this process for all years in their sample. Finally, they calculated the average excess return of each portfolio and the beta of the portfolio; Figure 13.1 shows the result. As you can see, although the portfolios with higher betas yield higher returns, most portfolios plot above the security market line—all except one portfolio had a positive alpha. The most extreme effect is seen in the smallest deciles.

As is evident from Figure 13.1, even these portfolios have large standard errors—none of the alpha estimates is individually significantly different from zero—all the confidence intervals include zero. However, nine of the ten portfolios plot above the SML. If the positive alphas were due purely to statistical error, we would expect as many portfolios to appear above the line as below it. Consequently, a test of whether the alphas of all ten portfolios are jointly all equal to zero can be statistically rejected.

---

1. See Eugene Fama and Kenneth French, "The Cross-Section of Stock Returns," *Journal of Finance* 47 (1992): 427–465.

| FIGURE 13.1 | Excess Return of Size Portfolios, 1926–2005 |

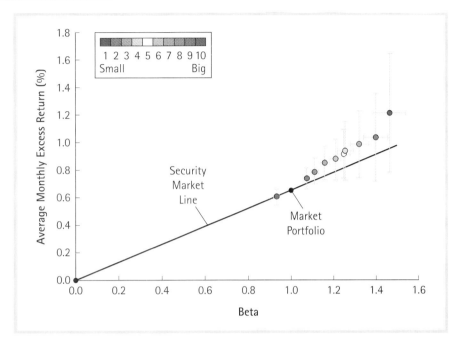

The plot shows the average excess return (the return minus the three-month risk-free rate) for ten portfolios formed in each month over 80 years using the firms' market capitalizations. The average excess return of each portfolio is plotted as a function of the portfolio's beta (estimated over the same time period). The black line is the security market line. If the market portfolio is efficient and there is no measurement error, all portfolios would plot along this line. The error bars mark the 95% confidence bands of the beta and expected excess return estimates.

Researchers have found similar results when they used the **book-to-market ratio**, the ratio of the book value of equity to the market value of equity, to form stocks into portfolios. Figure 13.2 demonstrates that eight out of the ten portfolios formed using the stocks' book-to-market ratios plot above the SML (i.e., have positive alphas). Once again, a joint test of whether all ten portfolios had an alpha of zero is rejected.

The size effect—the observation that small stocks (or stocks with a high book-to-market ratio) have positive alphas—was first discovered in 1981 by Rolf Banz.[2] At the time, researchers did not find the evidence to be convincing because financial economists had been *searching* the data, looking for stocks with positive alphas. As we have already pointed out, because of the existence of significant estimation error, it is always possible to find stocks with positive alphas; indeed, if we look hard enough, it is also always possible to find something these stocks have in common. As a consequence, many researchers

2. See R. Banz, "The Relationship between Return and Market Values of Common Stock," *Journal of Financial Economics* 9 (1981): 3–18. A similar relation between a stock's price (rather than its size) and its future return was documented earlier in M. E. Blume and F. Husic, "Price, Beta and Exchange Listing," *Journal of Finance* 28(2): 283–299.

FIGURE 13.2   **Excess Return of Book-to-Market Portfolios, 1926–2005**

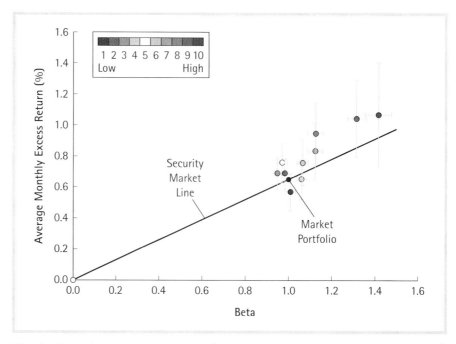

The plot shows the average excess return (the return minus the three-month risk-free rate) for ten portfolios formed in each month over 80 years using the stocks' book-to-market ratios. The average excess return of each portfolio is plotted as a function of the portfolio's beta (estimated over the same time period). The black line is the security market line. If the market portfolio is efficient and there is no measurement error, all portfolios would plot along this line. The error bars mark the 95% confidence bands of the beta and expected excess return estimates.

were inclined to view Banz's findings as due to a **data snooping bias**, which is the idea that given enough characteristics, it will always be possible to find some characteristic that by pure chance happens to be correlated with the estimation error of average returns.

After the publication of Banz's study, however, a theoretical reason emerged that explained the relationship between market capitalization and expected returns. Financial economists realized that when the market portfolio is not efficient, we should *expect* to observe the size effect.[3] To understand why, suppose that the market portfolio is not efficient. Some stocks will therefore plot above the SML, and some will plot below this line. Suppose we take a stock that plots above the line (i.e., has a positive alpha). All else equal, a positive alpha implies that the stock also has a relatively higher expected return. A higher expected return implies a lower price—the only way to offer a higher expected return is for investors to buy the stock's dividend stream at a lower price. A lower price means a lower market capitalization (and similarly a higher book-to-market ratio—market capitalization is in the *denominator* of the book-to-market ratio). Thus, when a financial econ-

3. See J. B. Berk, "A Critique of Size Related Anomalies," *Review of Financial Studies* 8 (1995): 275–286.

omist forms a portfolio of stocks with low market capitalizations (or high book-to-market ratios), that collection contains stocks that will likely have higher expected returns and, if the market portfolio is not efficient, positive alphas. Similarly, a stock that plots below the security market line will have a lower expected return and, therefore, a higher price, implying that it has a higher market capitalization and lower book-to-market ratio. Hence a portfolio of stocks with high market capitalizations or low book-to-market ratios will have negative alphas if the market portfolio is not efficient. Let's illustrate with a simple example.

Risk and the Market Value of Equity

Problem
Consider two firms, SM Industries and BiG Corporation, which are expected to pay the same dividend stream, $1 million per year in perpetuity. Of course, this dividend stream is expected, not guaranteed; actual dividends will depart from this number. SM's dividend stream is riskier, so its cost of capital is 14% per year. BiG's cost of capital is 10%. Which firm has the higher market value? Which firm has the higher expected return? Now assume both stocks have the same estimated beta, either because of estimation error, or because the market portfolio is not efficient. Based on this beta, the CAPM would assign an expected return of 12% to both stocks. Which firm has the higher alpha? How do the market values of the firms relate to their alphas?

Solution
The timeline of dividends is the same for both firms:

To calculate the market value of SM, we calculate the present value of its future expected dividends using the perpetuity formula and a cost of capital of 14%:

$$\text{Market Value of SM} = \frac{1}{0.14} = \$7.143 \text{ million}$$

Similarly, the market value of BiG is

$$\text{Market Value of BiG} = \frac{1}{0.10} = \$10 \text{ million}$$

SM has the lower market value, and a higher expected return (14% vs. 10%). It also has the higher alpha:

$$\alpha_{SM} = 0.14 - 0.12 = 2\%$$
$$\alpha_{BiG} = 0.10 - 0.12 = -2\%$$

Consequently, the firm with the lower market value has the higher alpha.

When the market portfolio is not efficient, theory predicts that stocks with low market capitalizations or high book-to-market ratios will have positive alphas. In light of this discovery, it became clear to most researchers that the evidence Banz uncovered was, indeed, evidence against the efficiency of the market portfolio.

Past Returns

A second criterion people have used to form portfolios with positive alphas are past stock returns. For example, for the years 1965 to 1989, Narishiman Jegadeesh and Sheridan Titman[4] ranked stocks each month by their realized returns over the prior six months. They found that the best performing stocks had positive alphas over the next six months. This is evidence against the CAPM: When the market portfolio is efficient, past returns should not predict alphas.

Over the years since the discovery of the CAPM, it has become increasingly clear to researchers and practitioners alike that by forming portfolios based on market capitalization, book-to-market ratios, and past returns, one can construct trading strategies that have a positive alpha. For example, one can buy stocks that have had past high returns and (short) sell stocks that have had past low returns. Many investors use such a **momentum strategy**. Researchers have found that this strategy is profitable. For example, Jegadeesh and Titman showed that over the period 1965–1989 it would have produced positive risk-adjusted returns of 12.83% per year.

CONCEPT CHECK   1. What is the size effect?

2. What is a momentum trading strategy?

13.2   Implication of Positive Alphas

What are the implications if trading strategies based on positive alphas really do exist? You might expect a few investors to be able to generate positive-alpha strategies because of informational advantages. But, *anyone* can implement a momentum trading strategy (it requires no special information, only knowledge of past returns) and, therefore, generate a positive alpha-investment opportunity. If the CAPM correctly computes the risk premium, an investment opportunity with a positive alpha is a positive-NPV investment opportunity, and investors should flock to invest in such strategies. In doing so they would drive down the return on these strategies; indeed, they would stop investing only when they expected the alpha of such a strategy to be zero.

The alpha of these trading strategies, however, does not appear to be zero when we examine real-world data. If, indeed, these alphas are positive, we are left to draw one of two conclusions:

1. Investors are systematically ignoring positive-NPV investment opportunities. That is, the CAPM correctly computes risk premiums, but investors are ignoring opportunities to earn extra returns without bearing any extra risk, either because they are unaware of them or because the costs to implement the strategies are larger than the NPV of undertaking them.

2. The positive-alpha trading strategies contain risk that investors are unwilling to bear but the CAPM does not capture. That is, a stock's beta with the market portfolio does not adequately measure a stock's systematic risk, and so the CAPM does not correctly compute the risk premium.

The only way a positive-NPV opportunity can exist in a market is if some barrier to entry restricts competition. In this case, it is very difficult to identify what these barriers might be. The existence of the momentum trading strategy has been widely known for at

---

4. See Narishiman Jegadeesh and Sheridan Titman, "Returns to Buying Winners and Selling Losers: Implications for Market Efficiency," *Journal of Finance* 48 (1993): 65–91.

least ten years. The fact that we are presenting this evidence in a corporate finance text-book implies that the possibility that people just don't realize that these opportunities exist is unlikely. Furthermore, the costs of implementing the strategy do not seem excessively high. Not only is the information required to form the portfolios readily available for free, but many mutual funds exist that follow both the momentum-based trading strategy and the market capitalization/book-to-market–based strategy. Hence, the first conclusion does not seem likely.

That leaves the second possibility: The market portfolio is not efficient, and therefore a stock's beta with the market is not an adequate measure of its systematic risk. Stated another way, the so-called profits (positive alphas) from the trading strategy are really returns for bearing risk that investors are averse to and the CAPM does not capture. There are two reasons why the market portfolio might not be efficient. First, we might be using the wrong proxy portfolio to calculate alphas; the true market portfolio of all invested wealth might be efficient, but the proxy portfolio might not track the actual market very well. Second, even the true market portfolio may not be efficient because a significant fraction of investors might care about aspects of their portfolios other than expected return and volatility, and so would be willing to hold inefficient investment portfolios. Let's examine each possibility in turn.

Proxy Error

The true market portfolio consists of all traded investment wealth in the economy. It therefore contains much more than just stocks—it includes bonds, real estate, art, precious metals, and any other investment vehicles available. Yet, we cannot include most of these investments in the market proxy because they do not trade in competitive markets. Instead, researchers use a proxy portfolio like the S&P 500 and assume that it will be highly correlated to the true market portfolio. But what if this assumption is false?

If the true market portfolio is efficient but the proxy portfolio is not highly correlated with the true market, then the proxy will not be efficient and stocks will have nonzero alphas.[5] In this case, the alphas merely indicate that the wrong proxy is being used; they do not indicate forgone positive-NPV investment opportunities.[6]

Non-tradeable Wealth

Another possibility is that the true market portfolio is inefficient—investors might care about characteristics other than the expected returns and volatility of their portfolios. Two conditions might cause investors to care about characteristics other than the expected return and volatility of their portfolios: They might care about other measures of uncertainty (e.g., the skewness of the distribution of returns), or they might have significant wealth invested in investments that are not tradeable. Consider an investor who trades off expected return and volatility and thus picks an efficient portfolio of *all* her investments,

---

5. Richard Roll and Stephen Ross have shown that when the true market portfolio is efficient, even a small difference between the proxy and true market portfolio can lead to an insignificant relation between beta and returns. See Richard Roll and Stephen A. Ross, "On the Cross-Sectional Relation between Expected Returns and Beta," *Journal of Finance* 49(1) (March 1994): 101–121.

6. If the market proxy *is* efficient, we cannot conclude that the *true* market portfolio is efficient. Because the test of the CAPM requires finding that the *true* market portfolio is efficient, the CAPM theory is untestable. This point was first made by Richard Roll, "A Critique of the Asset Pricing Theory's Tests," *Journal of Financial Economics* 4 (1977): 129–176. Of course, from a corporate manager's perspective, whether the CAPM is testable is irrelevant—as long as an efficient portfolio can be identified, he or she can use it to compute the cost of capital.

COMMON MISTAKE   Investing in Own Company Stock

When Enron Corporation filed for bankruptcy in December 2001, 62% of the assets held in the corporation's 401(k) retirement plan consisted of shares of Enron stock.* The value of these assets had declined greatly as Enron's shares, worth $80 per share one year earlier, traded for just $0.70 one month after the bankruptcy. Consequently, the collapse of Enron not only robbed many employees of their jobs, but also wiped out their retirement savings.

Why did the employees of Enron choose to hold inefficient portfolios, thereby significantly increasing their exposure to Enron's idiosyncratic risk? One explanation is that Enron made matching contributions to the plan in the form of Enron stock that it prohibited employees under the age of 50 from selling. However, according to the company, only 11% of the wealth invested in Enron stock can be traced to its matching contributions to the pension plan.

Enron was not the only company that encouraged its employees to invest their pension money in company stock. Shlomo Benartzi** found that about one third of the assets of large defined-contribution retirement plans are invested in company stock.

Such investment behavior is difficult to fathom. Employees, through their human capital, already have a significant fraction of their wealth tied to the fortunes of the company they work for. If anything, they should substantially underweight their investments in their own company stock. Why these employees choose to hold inefficient portfolios by further concentrating their wealth in their own company stock is a mystery. In any case, this evidence indicates that not all investors adequately diversify, and as a result hold inefficient portfolios.

---

*Congressional Research Service Report for Congress, March 11, 2002.

**"Excessive Extrapolation and the Allocation of 401(k) Accounts to Company Stock," *Journal of Finance* 56 (2001): 1747–1764.

---

whether tradeable or not. Although the entire portfolio is efficient, there is no reason why just the tradeable part of the portfolio should be efficient.

The most important example of a non-tradeable wealth is human capital.[7] People are naturally exposed to the risk in the industry in which they work. A banker working for Goldman Sachs is exposed to risk in the financial sector, while an electrical engineer working in Silicon Valley is exposed to risk in the high-tech sector. When an investor diversifies, he or she should take into account these inherent exposures. The investment banker is likely to underweight or perhaps hold a short position in financial services stocks; her job already exposes her to risk in the financial services sector. Similarly, the electrical engineer should not hold high-tech stocks. Thus, even if both investors hold efficient portfolios, their portfolios of *traded* securities need not be efficient and are unlikely to be the same. Furthermore, it is unlikely that either investor will choose to hold the market portfolio of traded securities.

If investors have a significant amount of non-tradeable wealth, this wealth will be an important part of their portfolios, but will not be part of the market portfolio of tradeable securities. In such a world, the market portfolio of tradeable securities will likely not be efficient. Indeed, researchers have found evidence that the presence of human capital can explain at least part of the reason for the inefficiency of the most commonly used market proxies.[8]

---

7. Although rare, there are innovative new markets that allow people to trade their human capital to finance their education, see Miguel Palacios, *Investing in Human Capital: A Capital Markets Approach to Student Funding*, Cambridge University Press, 2004.

8. See Ravi Jagannathan and Zhenu Wang, "The Conditional CAPM and the Cross-Sections of Expected Returns," *Journal of Finance* 51 (1996): 3–53; and Ignacio Palacios-Huerta, "The Robustness of the Conditional CAPM with Human Capital," *Journal of Financial Econometrics* 1 (2003): 272–289.

In light of the evidence against the efficiency of the market portfolio, researchers have developed alternative models of risk. In the next section we will derive the multifactor model of risk.

1. What does the existence of a positive alpha trading strategy imply?

2. If investors have a significant amount of non-tradeable (but risky) wealth, why might the market portfolio not be efficient?

13.3 Multifactor Models of Risk

In Chapter 11, we showed that the expected return of any marketable security can be written as a function of the expected return of the efficient portfolio:

$$E[R_s] = r_f + \beta_s^{eff} \times (E[R_{eff}] - r_f) \tag{13.1}$$

When the market portfolio is not efficient, we have to find a method to identify an efficient portfolio before we can use Eq. 13.1.

As a practical matter, it is extremely difficult to identify portfolios that are efficient because we cannot measure the expected return and the standard deviation of a portfolio with great accuracy. Although we might not be able to identify the efficient portfolio itself, we know some characteristics of the efficient portfolio. First, any efficient portfolio will be well diversified. Second, an efficient portfolio can be constructed from other diversified portfolios. This latter observation may seem trivial, but it is actually quite useful: It implies that so long as an efficient portfolio can be constructed from a collection of portfolios, the collection itself can be used to measure risk. *It is not actually necessary to identify the efficient portfolio itself.* All that is required is to identify a collection of portfolios from which the efficient portfolio can be constructed.

Using Factor Portfolios

Let's keep things simple. Assume that we have identified two portfolios that we know can be combined to form an efficient portfolio; we call these portfolios **factor portfolios** and denote their returns by R_{F1} and R_{F2}. The efficient portfolio consists of some (unknown) combination of these two factor portfolios, represented by portfolio weights x_1 and x_2:

$$R_{eff} = x_1 R_{F1} + x_2 R_{F2} \tag{13.2}$$

To see that we can use these factor portfolios to measure risk, consider regressing the excess returns of some stock s on the excess returns of *both* factors:

$$R_s - r_f = \alpha_s + \beta_s^{F1}(R_{F1} - r_f) + \beta_s^{F2}(R_{F2} - r_f) + \varepsilon_s \tag{13.3}$$

This statistical technique is known as a **multiple regression**—it is exactly the same as the linear regression technique described in Chapter 12, except now we have two regressors, $R_{F1} - r_f$ and $R_{F2} - r_f$, whereas in Chapter 12 we only had one regressor, the excess return of the market portfolio. Otherwise the interpretation is the same. The excess return of stock s is written as the sum of a constant, α_s, plus the variation in the stock that is related to each factor, and an error term ε_s that has an expectation of zero and is uncorrelated with either factor. The error term represents the risk of the stock that is unrelated to either factor.

If the two factor portfolios can be used to construct the efficient portfolio, as in Eq. 13.2, then the constant term α_s in Eq. 13.3 is zero (up to estimation error). To see why, consider a portfolio in which we buy stock s, then sell a fraction β_s^{F1} of the first factor portfolio and β_s^{F2} of the second factor portfolio, and invest the proceeds from these sales in the risk-free investment. This portfolio, which we call P, has return

$$R_P = R_s - \beta_s^{F1} R_{F1} - \beta_s^{F2} R_{F2} + (\beta_s^{F1} + \beta_s^{F2}) r_f$$
$$= R_s - \beta_s^{F1}(R_{F1} - r_f) - \beta_s^{F2}(R_{F2} - r_f) \tag{13.4}$$

Using Eq. 13.3 to replace R_s and simplifying, the return of this portfolio is

$$R_P = r_f + \alpha_s + \varepsilon_s \tag{13.5}$$

That is, portfolio P has a risk premium of α_s and risk given by ε_s. Now, because ε_s is uncorrelated with each factor, it must be uncorrelated with the efficient portfolio; that is,

$$Cov(R_{eff}, \varepsilon_s) = Cov(x_1 R_{F1} + x_2 R_{F2}, \varepsilon_s)$$
$$= x_1 Cov(R_{F1}, \varepsilon_s) + x_2 Cov(R_{F2}, \varepsilon_s)$$
$$= 0 \tag{13.6}$$

But recall from Chapter 11 that *risk that is uncorrelated with the efficient portfolio is diversifiable risk that does not command a risk premium.* Therefore, the expected return of portfolio P is r_f, which means α_s must be zero.[9]

Setting α_s equal to zero and taking expectations of both sides of Eq. 13.3, we get the following two-factor model of expected returns:

$$E[R_s] = r_f + \beta_s^{F1}(E[R_{F1}] - r_f) + \beta_s^{F2}(E[R_{F2}] - r_f) \tag{13.7}$$

Eq. 13.7 says that the risk premium of any marketable security can be written as the sum of the risk premium of each factor multiplied by the sensitivity of the stock with that factor—the **factor betas**. Neither portfolio itself must be efficient; we just need to be able to construct the efficient portfolio out of the two portfolios.

There is nothing inconsistent between Eq. 13.7, which gives the expected return in terms of two factors, and Eq. 13.1, which gives the expected return in terms of just the efficient portfolio. *Both* equations hold; the difference between them is simply the portfolios that we use. When we use an efficient portfolio, it alone will capture all systematic risk. Consequently, we often refer to this model as a **single-factor model**. If we use more than one portfolio as factors, then together these factors will capture all systematic risk, but note that each factor in Eq. 13.7 captures different components of the systematic risk. When we use more than one portfolio to capture risk, the model is known as a **multi-factor model**. The portfolios themselves can be thought of as either a risk factor itself or a portfolio of stocks correlated with an unobservable risk factor. This particular form of the multifactor model was originally developed by Stephen Ross, although Robert Merton had developed an alternative multifactor model earlier.[10] The model is also referred to as the **Arbitrage Pricing Theory (APT)**.

---

9. That is, Eq. 13.6 implies $\beta_P^{eff} = \frac{Cov(R_{eff}, \varepsilon_s)}{Var(R_{eff})} = 0$. Substituting this result into Eq. 13.1 gives $E[R_p] = r_f$. But from Eq. 13.5, $E[R_p] = r_f + \alpha_s$, and hence $\alpha_s = 0$.

10. See Stephen A. Ross, "The Arbitrage Theory of Capital Asset Pricing," *Journal of Economic Theory* 13 (1976): 341–360; and Robert C. Merton, "An Intertemporal Capital Asset Pricing Model," *Econometrica* 41 (1973): 867–887.

Building a Multifactor Model

Although we derived Eq. 13.7 using only two portfolios, the model is easily extended to any number of portfolios. Indeed, it often makes sense to use more than two portfolios because a larger number increases the probability that an efficient portfolio can be constructed out of the portfolios. If we use N factor portfolios with returns $R_{F1}, \ldots, R_{FN}$, the expected return of asset s is given by

Multifactor Model of Risk

$$E[R_s] = r_f + \beta_s^{F1}(E[R_{F1}] - r_f) + \beta_s^{F2}(E[R_{F2}] - r_f) + \cdots + \beta_s^{FN}(E[R_{FN}] - r_f)$$

$$= r_f + \sum_{n=1}^{N} \beta_s^{Fn}(E[R_{Fn}] - r_f) \tag{13.8}$$

Here $\beta_s^1, \ldots, \beta_s^N$ are the factor betas, one for each risk factor, and have the same interpretation as the beta in the CAPM. Each factor beta is the expected percent change in the excess return of a security for a 1% change in the excess return of the factor portfolio.

We can simplify Eq. 13.8 a bit further. We can think of the expected excess return of each factor, $E[R_{Fn}] - r_f$, as the expected return of a portfolio in which we borrow the funds at rate r_f to invest in the factor portfolio. Because this portfolio costs nothing to construct (we are borrowing the funds to invest), it is called a **self-financing portfolio**. We can also construct a self-financing portfolio by going long some stocks, and going short other stocks with equal market value. In general, a self-financing portfolio is any portfolio with portfolio weights that sum to zero rather than one. If we require that all factor portfolios are self-financing (either by borrowing funds or shorting stocks), then we can rewrite Eq. 13.8 as

Multifactor Model of Risk with Self-Financing Portfolios

$$E[R_s] = r_f + \beta_s^{F1}E[R_{F1}] + \beta_s^{F2}E[R_{F2}] + \cdots + \beta_s^{FN}E[R_{FN}]$$

$$= r_f + \sum_{n=1}^{N} \beta_s^{Fn}E[R_{Fn}] \tag{13.9}$$

To recap, we have shown that it is possible to calculate the cost of capital without actually identifying the efficient portfolio using a multifactor risk model. Rather than relying on the efficiency of a single portfolio (such as the market), multifactor models rely on the weaker condition that an efficient portfolio can be constructed from a collection of well-diversified portfolios or factors. We next explain how to select the factors.

Selecting the Portfolios

In this section, we explain the method most commonly used to identify a collection of portfolios that contain the efficient portfolio. The most obvious portfolio to use in the collection is the market portfolio itself. Historically, the market portfolio has commanded a large premium over short-term risk-free investments, such as Treasury Bills. Even if the market portfolio is not efficient, it still captures at least some components of systematic risk. As Figures 13.1 and 13.2 demonstrate, even when the model fails, portfolios with higher average returns *do* tend to have higher betas. Thus the first portfolio in the collection is the return of the market portfolio less the risk-free interest rate.

How do we go about picking the other portfolios? As we pointed out earlier, trading strategies based on market capitalization, book-to-market ratios, and momentum have

INTERVIEW WITH
Rex A. Sinquefield

Rex A. Sinquefield is a director, co-founder, and former co-chairman and chief investment officer of Dimensional Fund Advisors, Inc. One of the first money managers to successfully apply the findings of academic finance to money management, he formed many of the first index funds at American National Bank of Chicago in the early 1970s.

QUESTION: *In the last 25 years, researchers have uncovered several characteristics, such as size, book-to-market ratio, and momentum, that can extend the traditional CAPM pricing model. How has this research changed the ways practitioners think about risk?*

ANSWER: Most people now realize that there are three sources of risk: general market risk, the value/growth factor, and the size risk (the risk associated with small companies). Momentum is a real conundrum. It is more a case of falling stocks continuing to fall than rising stocks continuing to rise. It primarily occurs in the small stock universe, and it's not readily exploitable. So we can set it aside. One might take it into account in running portfolios.

QUESTION: *Do you think these characteristics represent real risk characteristics or do they reflect mispricings in the market?*

ANSWER: I think this is real risk. I don't buy the idea of mispricing, or the market would have learned by now. These patterns are too systematic. They have been going on for almost 80 years in the United States and 30 years around the world. We find the size effect and the value/growth effect in almost every developed country and in emerging markets. Dimensional's core belief is that the market doesn't misvalue securities. The prices are right.

If you believe in active management, you're saying that people can make valuation judgments that are superior to the market.

QUESTION: *How does Dimensional apply these alternative pricing models in building highly diversified portfolios structured around risk factors?*

ANSWER: In building portfolios, we actually don't use the risk factors directly but instead use characteristics such as a stock's book-to-market ratio and the company's market capitalization. We use this construction technique for all types of funds, both domestic and international. These funds, which hold hundreds or even thousands of securities, track a specific part of a market. They are passive—their holdings don't vary—so they stay true to what they are doing.

Once a portfolio is built and running, we can perform multiple regression analyses, using the return history of the portfolio, to look at how the return history relates to the three risk factors. Then we can evaluate a portfolio or compare it to another portfolio.

We don't believe that money managers can consistently beat markets by picking stocks or market timing—and many studies support this. The evidence is overwhelming that markets work very, very well. Dimensional uses risk factors first to set boundaries to identify the securities according to a characteristic such as size or book-to-market. Then we are prepared to buy nearly all the securities in that category. So we don't pick stocks in the conventional sense. Second, we find that the best way to get above-market returns is to add more value or size risk. Investors can then "tilt" their portfolio to achieve above-market returns by holding value and small cap funds in above-market proportions, while recognizing this requires taking more risk.

been developed that appear to have positive alphas. A positive alpha means that the portfolios that implement the trading strategy capture risk that is not captured by the market portfolio. Hence these portfolios are good candidates for the other portfolios in a multifactor model. We will construct three additional portfolios out of the trading strategies that have produced positive risk-adjusted returns historically. The first trading strategy selects stocks based on their market capitalization, the second uses the book-to-market ratio, and the third uses past returns. We begin with the strategy that uses market capitalization.

Each year, let's place firms into one of two portfolios based on their market value of equity: Firms with market values below the median of NYSE firms in that month form an equally weighted portfolio, S, and firms above the median market value form an equally weighted portfolio, B. A trading strategy that each year buys portfolio S (small stocks) and finances this position by short selling portfolio B (big stocks) has produced positive risk-adjusted returns historically. This self-financing portfolio is widely known as the **small-minus-big (SMB) portfolio**.

A second trading strategy that has produced positive risk-adjusted returns historically uses the book-to-market ratio to select stocks. Each year firms with book-to-market ratios less than the 30th percentile of NYSE firms form an equally weighted portfolio called the low portfolio, L. Firms with book-to-market ratios greater than the 70th percentile of NYSE firms form an equally weighted portfolio called the high portfolio, H. A trading strategy that each year takes a long position in portfolio H, which it finances with a short position in portfolio L, has produced positive risk-adjusted returns. We add this self-financing portfolio (high minus low book-to-market stocks) to our collection and call it the **high-minus-low (HML) portfolio**.

The third trading strategy is a momentum strategy. Each year stocks are ranked by their return over the last one year,[11] and a portfolio is constructed that goes long the top 30% of stocks and short the bottom 30%. This trading strategy requires holding this portfolio for a year; a new self-financing portfolio is then formed and held for another year. This process is repeated annually. The resulting self-financing portfolio is known as the **prior one-year momentum (PR1YR) portfolio**.

The collection of these four portfolios—the excess return of the market (Mkt − r_f), SMB, HML, and PR1YR—is currently the most popular choice for the multifactor model. Using this collection, the expected return of security s is given by Eq. 13.10:

Fama-French-Carhart Factor Specification

$$E[R_s] = r_f + \beta_s^{Mkt}(E[R_{Mkt}] - r_f) + \beta_s^{SMB}E[R_{SMB}]$$
$$+ \beta_s^{HML}E[R_{HML}] + \beta_s^{PR1\,YR}E[R_{PR1\,YR}] \qquad (13.10)$$

where $\beta_s^{Mkt}, \beta_s^{SMB}, \beta_s^{HML}$, and $\beta_s^{PR1\,YR}$ are the factor betas of stock s and measure the sensitivity of the stock to each portfolio. Because the four portfolios in Eq. 13.10 were identified by Eugene Fama, Kenneth French, and Mark Carhart, we will refer to this collection of portfolios as the **Fama-French-Carhart (FFC) factor specification**.

Calculating the Cost of Capital Using the Fama-French-Carhart Factor Specification

Multifactor models have a distinct advantage over single-factor models in that it is much easier to identify a collection of portfolios that captures systematic risk than just a single portfolio. They also have an important disadvantage, however: We must estimate the expected return of each portfolio. Because expected returns are not easy to estimate, each portfolio that is added to the collection increases the difficulty of implementing the model. What makes this task especially complex is that it is unclear *which* economic risk the portfolios capture, so we cannot hope to come up with a reasonable estimate of what

---

11. Because of short-term trading effects, the most recent month's return is often dropped, so actually an 11-month return is used.

the return should be (as we did with the CAPM) based on an economic argument. If we want to implement the model, we have little choice other than to use historical average returns on the portfolios.[12]

Because the returns on the FFC portfolios are so volatile, we use 80 years of data to estimate the expected return. Table 13.1 shows the monthly average return as well as the 95% confidence bands of the FFC portfolios (we use a value-weighted portfolio of all NYSE, AMEX, and NASDAQ stocks as the proxy for the market portfolio). Even with 80 years of data, however, all of the estimates of the expected returns are imprecise.

TABLE 13.1	FFC Portfolio Average Monthly Returns, 1926–2005	
Factor Portfolio	Average Monthly Return (%)	95% Confidence Band (%)
Mkt $- r_f$	0.64	±0.35
SMB	0.17	±0.21
HML	0.53	±0.23
PR1YR	0.76	±0.30

Data Source: Kenneth French.

EXAMPLE 13.2

Using the FFC Factor Specification to Calculate the Cost of Capital

Problem

You are considering making an investment in a project in the food and beverages industry. You determine that the project has the same level of non-diversifiable risk as investing in Coca-Cola stock. Determine the cost of capital by using the FFC factor specification.

Solution

You decide to use data over the past five years to estimate the factor betas of Coca-Cola stock (ticker: KO). You therefore regress the monthly excess return (the realized return in each month minus the risk-free rate) of your company's stock on the return of each portfolio. The coefficient estimates are the factor betas. Here are the estimates of the four factor betas based on data from years 2000 through 2004:

$$\beta_{KO}^{Mkt} = 0.158$$

$$\beta_{KO}^{SMB} = 0.302$$

$$\beta_{KO}^{HML} = 0.497$$

$$\beta_{KO}^{PR1YR} = -0.276$$

---

12. There is a second, more subtle disadvantage to most factor models. Because factor models are designed to price traded securities, there is no guarantee that they will accurately price risks that are not currently traded (e.g., the risk associated with a new technology). In practice, it is assumed that any non-traded risk is idiosyncratic, and therefore does not command a risk premium.

Using these estimates and the current risk-free monthly rate of 5%/12 = 0.42%, you calculate the monthly expected return of investing in Coca-Cola stock:

$$E[R_{KO}] = r_f + \beta_{KO}^{Mkt}(E[R_{Mkt}] - r_f) + \beta_{KO}^{SMB}E[R_{SMB}] + \beta_{KO}^{HML}E[R_{HML}] + \beta_{KO}^{PR1\ YR}E[R_{KO}]$$

$$= 0.42\% + 0.158 \times 0.64\% + 0.302 \times 0.17\% + 0.497 \times 0.53\% - 0.276 \times 0.76\%$$

$$= 0.626\%$$

The annual expected return is 0.626% × 12 = 7.512%. The annual cost of capital of the investment opportunity is about 7.5%.

The FFC factor specification was identified a little more than ten years ago. Although it is widely used in academic literature to measure risk, much debate persists about whether it really is a significant improvement over the CAPM.[13] The one area where researchers have found that the FFC factor specification does appear to do better than the CAPM is measuring the risk of actively managed mutual funds. Researchers have found that funds with high returns in the past have positive alphas under the CAPM.[14] When Mark Carhart repeated the same test using the FFC factor specification to compute alphas, he found no evidence that mutual funds with high past returns had future positive alphas.[15]

CONCEPT CHECK

1. What is the advantage of a multifactor model over a single factor model?

2. What is the Fama-French-Carhart factor specification?

13.4 Characteristic Variable Models of Expected Returns

Calculating the cost of capital using multifactor models like the FFC factor specification or the CAPM relies on accurate estimates of risk premiums and betas. Often, however, accurately estimating these quantities is difficult. Many years of data are required to estimate risk premiums, and both risk premiums and betas may not remain stable over time. Consider, for example, the CAPM beta estimates of General Electric, General Motors, IBM, and Procter & Gamble plotted in Figure 13.3. As the figure illustrates, the beta estimate may vary substantially depending on the time period during which the beta is estimated.

Why are the betas of firms like IBM and GM so variable? One reason is statistical error. Figure 13.3 plots beta estimates, and some of the variation likely reflects measurement error. However, there is also an economic reason why firm's betas might vary—the firm itself varies. When firms make new investments in new areas or shut down unprofitable projects in old areas their risk profiles change as well.[16] Thus an economist trying

---

13. See M. Cooper, R. Gutierrez, Jr., and B. Marcum, "On the Predictability of Stock Returns in Real Time," *Journal of Business* 78 (2005): 469–500.

14. See M. Grinblatt and S. Titman, "The Persistence of Mutual Fund Performance," *Journal of Finance* 47 (1992): 1977–1984; and D. J. Hendricks, J. Patel, and R. Zeckhauser, "Hot Hands in Mutual Funds: Short-Run Persistence of Performance 1974–1988," *Journal of Finance* 4 (1993): 93–130.

15. See M. Carhart, "On Persistence in Mutual Fund Performance," *Journal of Finance* 52 (1997): 57–82.

16. For a model of the dynamics of real investment and its effect on beta, see J. B. Berk, R. C. Green, and V. Naik, "Optimal Investment, Growth Options and Security Returns," *Journal of Finance* 54 (1999): 1553–1607.

Variation of CAPM Beta in Time

The plot shows the CAPM beta estimates of General Electric (GE), General Motors (GM), IBM, and Procter & Gamble (PG). The estimates are made over the previous five years using monthly data. We use a value-weighted portfolio of all NYSE, AMEX, and NASDAQ stocks as the proxy for the market portfolio.

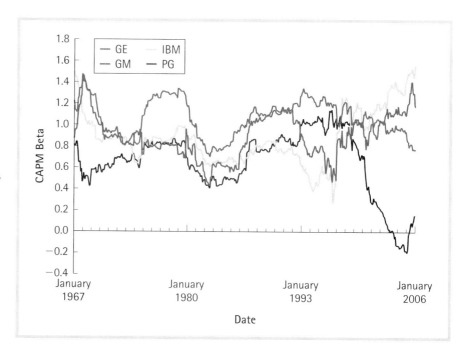

to measure a firm's beta faces an inevitable tradeoff. Using a long period of time to estimate beta reduces measurement error, but because firms evolve dynamically, old data might not reflect the current risk profile of the firm.

To address these concerns, some practitioners have developed a different approach to measuring risk, the **characteristic variable model** of returns. Rather than attempt to estimate the risk and expected return of the firm directly, this approach views firms as a portfolio of different measurable "characteristics" that together determine the firm's risk and return. If the relation between risk and these characteristics is stable over time, then a long time series can be used to estimate the risk and return associated with each characteristic. But even though the risk and return associated with each characteristic may remain stable, because the characteristics of a firm may change over time, so will the firm's risk and expected return. That is, if we view the firm as a portfolio of these characteristics, over time the portfolio weights change, and hence so does the risk of the firm.

As an example of this approach, Table 13.2 lists the characteristics that are used by one company that provides data for such an approach, MSCI Barra. The MSCI Barra model estimates risk and return based on 12 firm characteristics, together with 55 industry classifications. MSCI Barra standardizes the characteristic variables by measuring the characteristic of each firm as the number of standard deviations away the firm is from the average firm with respect to that characteristic. Table 13.3 lists these values for Coca-Cola and GE based on data from 2005. So, for example, both these firms were above average on the size characteristic, yet were below average with respect to growth. In addition to these generic characteristics Barra also includes characteristic variables that measure the weight of each firm in the sectors it produces in. For example Coca-Cola was classified as 100% in the food and beverage industry, whereas GE was classified as having 48% of its business in financial services, 29% in electrical equipment, 10% in media, 7% in medical products, and 6% in chemicals.

TABLE 13.2	Firm Characteristics Used by MSCI Barra

Characteristic	Description
Volatility	The stock's relative volatility using both long-term and short-term measures of the stock's historical beta and volatility
Momentum	The degree to which a stock has had positive excess returns in the recent past
Size	The log of the stock's market capitalization
Size non-linearity	The cube of the log of the stock's market capitalization (allows for a non-linear relationship between returns and the log of market capitalization)
Trading activity	The amount of trading in a stock based on its share turnover rate
Growth	The stock's expected future earnings growth, based on its historical growth and profitability measures
Earnings yield	Combines the stock's current, historical, and analyst-predicted earnings-to-price ratio
Value	The ratio of book value of equity to market capitalization
Earnings variability	The variability in earnings and cash flows using both historical measures and analyst predictions
Leverage	The financial leverage of a company
Currency sensitivity	The sensitivity of a company's stock return to the return on a basket of foreign currencies
Dividend yield	The stock's predicted dividend yield using the past history of dividends and the market price behavior of the stock

Once the characteristic variables have been identified and measured for each firm, the return of each characteristic can be inferred from the data. We do not observe the returns of the characteristic variables directly, but their returns in each period are estimated indirectly from firms' returns by regressing the return of all firms onto the value of the characteristic variables. Specifically, if w_s^i is the index (or weight) of stock s for characteristic or industry i, and if R_{ci} is the return associated with characteristic or industry i, then the return of stock s can be written as

The Characteristic Variable Model of Stock Returns

$$R_s = w_s^1 R_{c1} + w_s^2 R_{c2} + \cdots + w_s^N R_{cN} + \varepsilon_s \qquad (13.11)$$

There is an important difference between the characteristic variable model described by Eq. 13.11 and the multifactor models we considered earlier. In the multifactor models, the returns of the factor portfolios are observed, and we estimate the sensitivity of each stock to the different factors (the factor betas). In the characteristic variable model, the weight of each stock on each characteristic is observed, and then we estimate the return R_{cn} associated with each characteristic. Table 13.3 shows the average monthly return estimate for the MSCI Barra characteristics during 2000–2005.[17]

There are a number of ways that people use the estimated relation between the characteristic variables and returns. Perhaps the most straightforward approach is simply to use the relation to estimate each stock's expected return. That is, if you view a stock as

---

17. We thank MSCI Barra (in particular, Dan Stefek and John Taymuree) for providing these data.

MSCI Barra Characteristic Weights and Return Estimates

The characteristic weight of each firm is the number of standard deviations away the firm is from the average firm with respect to that characteristic. The characteristic returns are estimated as the coefficients R_{cn} in Eq. 13.11. Reported are the characteristic weights for 2005, and average characteristic returns for 2000–2005.

Characteristic	Characteristic Weight (standardized)		Characteristic Return
	Coca-Cola	GE	(% per month)
Volatility	−0.498	−0.355	0.117
Momentum	−1.212	−0.216	−0.333
Size	1.004	2.047	−0.481
Size non-linearity	0.210	0.210	0.214
Trading activity	−0.496	−0.577	−0.028
Growth	−0.625	−0.204	−0.026
Earnings yield	−0.223	−0.189	0.629
Value	−0.665	−0.414	0.058
Earnings variability	−0.444	−0.627	−0.057
Leverage	−0.462	−0.158	0.045
Currency sensitivity	−0.275	0.326	0.067
Dividend yield	0.403	0.481	0.004

portfolio of characteristic variables, then the stock's expected return is the sum over all the variables of the amount of each characteristic variable the stock contains times the expected return of that variable:[18]

$$E[R_s] = w_s^1 E[R_{c1}] + w_s^2 E[R_{c2}] + \cdots + w_s^N E[R_{cN}] \qquad (13.12)$$

Robert Haugen and Nardin Baker[19] evaluated the usefulness of the characteristic variable approach by ranking stocks based on their characteristics model; they formed stocks into 10 ranked portfolios based on their characteristics model's prediction of expected return. They then measured the return of each portfolio over the following month. If the characteristic model correctly differentiates stocks the ranking of the portfolios would be preserved by the returns—the top-ranked portfolio would have the highest return. This is exactly what Haugen and Baker found, as we illustrate in Figure 13.4.

Another approach is to use the estimated returns of the characteristic variables to estimate the covariance between pairs of stocks, or between a stock and the market index. The idea behind this approach is that if firms' characteristics change over time, the covariance between the characteristic returns may be more stable than the covariance between stocks themselves. In this case, the residual risk ε_s in Eq. 13.11 is generally assumed to be firm-specific risk, uncorrelated with the characteristic returns or the returns of other firms.

---

18. Equation 13.12 follows from Eq. 13.11 if we assume the residual risk ε_s, has mean zero.

19. R. A. Haugen and N. L. Baker, "Commonality in the Determinants of Expected Stock Returns," *Journal of Financial Economics* 41 (1996): 401–439.

FIGURE 13.4

Returns of Portfolios Ranked by the Characteristic Variable Model

The figure shows the subsequent returns of portfolios formed by ranking stocks based on the characteristic variable model of returns. The portfolio of stocks ranked low subsequently had low returns, and the portfolio of stocks ranked high subsequently had high returns.

Source: Adapted from Figure 5-1 p. 52 from R. A. Haugen, *The Inefficient Market*, 2nd ed.

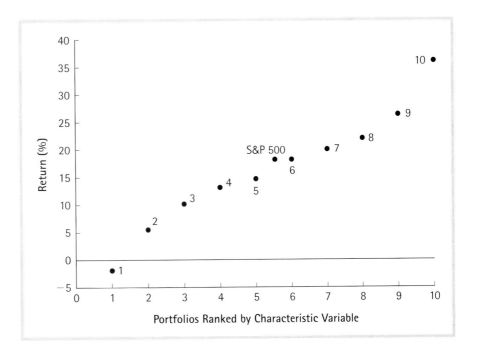

Then, by viewing each stock as a portfolio of characteristics, we can use the techniques of Chapter 11 to calculate the covariance between two different stocks i and j as

$$Cov(R_i, R_j) = \sum_{n=1}^{N} \sum_{m=1}^{N} w_i^n w_j^m Cov(R_{cn}, R_{cm}) \qquad (13.13)$$

Similarly, the beta of each stock can then be calculated from the beta of the characteristic variables in the same way a beta of a portfolio can be computed from the beta of its constituent securities: The beta of a stock is equal to the weighted-average of the characteristic variable betas where the weights are the amounts of each characteristic variable the stock contains. Because the amount of each characteristic variable a stock contains changes as the firm evolves in time, its beta will change accordingly to reflect its new level of risk.

CONCEPT CHECK
1. How does a characteristic variable model differ from a multifactor model of returns?
2. How are characteristic variable models used?

13.5 Methods Used in Practice

Surveying 392 CFOs, John Graham and Campbell Harvey found that 73.5% of the firms that they questioned use the CAPM to calculate the cost of capital, as indicated in Figure 13.5. They also found that larger firms were more likely to use the CAPM than were smaller firms.

FIGURE 13.5   **How Firms Calculate the Cost of Capital**

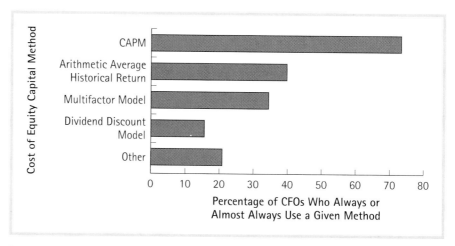

The figure shows the percentage of firms that use the CAPM, multifactor models, the historical average return, and the dividend discount model. Because practitioners often refer to characteristic variable models as factor models, the multifactor model characterization includes characteristic variable models. The dividend discount model is presented in Chapter 9.

Source: J. R. Graham and C. R. Harvey, "The Theory and Practice of Corporate Finance: Evidence from the Field," *Journal of Financial Economics* 60 (2001): 187–243.

What about the other techniques we covered in this chapter? Among the firms Graham and Harvey surveyed, only about one third reported using a multifactor model to calculate the cost of capital. Because practitioners often refer to the characteristic variable model as a factor model, this number likely includes both multifactor models and characteristic variable models.

Two other methods that some firms in the survey reported using are historical average returns (40%) and the dividend discount model (16%). By dividend discount model, practitioners mean Eq. 9.7 in Chapter 9: They estimate the firm's expected future growth rate and add the current dividend yield to determine the stock's expected total return.

In short, there is no clear answer to the question of which technique is used to measure risk in practice—it very much depends on the organization and the sector. It is not difficult to see why there is so little consensus in practice about which technique to use. *All the techniques we covered are imprecise.* Financial economics has not yet reached the point where we can provide a theory of expected returns that gives a precise estimate of the cost of capital. Consider, too, that all techniques are not equally simple to implement. Because the tradeoff between simplicity and precision varies across sectors, practitioners apply the techniques that best suit their particular circumstances.

When making a capital budgeting decision, the cost of capital is just one of several imprecise estimates that go into the NPV calculation. Indeed, in many cases the imprecision in the cost of capital estimate is less important than the imprecision in the estimate of future cash flows. Often the least complicated models to implement are used most often—the CAPM or even historical average returns.

CONCEPT CHECK   1. Which is the most popular method used by corporations to calculate the cost of capital?

2. What other techniques do corporations use to calculate the cost of capital?

Summary

1. The size effect refers to the observation that historically small stocks have had positive alphas compared to the predictions of the CAPM. The size effect is evidence that the market portfolio is not efficient, which suggests that the CAPM does not accurately model expected returns. Researchers find similar results using the book-to-market ratio instead of firm size.

2. A momentum trading strategy that goes long stocks with high past risk-adjusted returns and short stocks with low past returns also generates positive CAPM alphas, providing further evidence that the market portfolio is not efficient and that the CAPM does not accurately model expected returns.

3. Securities may have non-zero alphas if the market portfolio used is not a good proxy for the true market portfolio.

4. Two conditions might cause investors to care about characteristics other than the expected return and the volatility of their portfolios: They might care about other measures of uncertainty (e.g., the skewness of the distribution of returns), or they might have significant wealth invested in investments that are not tradeable.

5. When more than one portfolio is used to capture risk, the model is known as a multifactor model. This model is also sometimes called the Arbitrage Pricing Theory (APT). Using a collection of N well-diversified portfolios, the expected return of stock s is

$$E[R_s] = r_f + \beta_s^{F1}(E[R_{F1}] - r_f) + \beta_s^{F2}(E[R_{F2}] - r_f) + \cdots + \beta_s^{FN}(E[R_{FN}] - r_f)$$

$$= r_f + \sum_{n=1}^{N} \beta_s^{Fn}(E[R_{Fn}] - r_f) \tag{13.8}$$

6. A simpler way to write multifactor models is to express risk premiums as the expected return on a self-financing portfolio. A self-financing portfolio is a portfolio that costs nothing to construct. By using the expected returns of self-financing portfolios, the expected return of a stock can be expressed as

$$E[R_s] = r_f + \beta_s^{F1} E[R_{F1}] + \beta_s^{F2} E[R_{F2}] + \cdots + \beta_s^{FN} E[R_{FN}]$$

$$= r_f + \sum_{n=1}^{N} \beta_s^{Fn} E[R_{Fn}] \tag{13.9}$$

7. The portfolios that are most commonly used in a multifactor model are the market portfolio (Mkt), small-minus-big (SMB) portfolio, high-minus-low (HML) portfolio, and prior one-year momentum (PR1YR) portfolio. This model is known as the Fama-French-Carhart factor specification:

$$E[R_s] = r_f + \beta_s^{Mkt}(E[R_{Mkt}] - r_f) + \beta_s^{SMB} E[R_{SMB}]$$

$$+ \beta_s^{HML} E[R_{HML}] + \beta_s^{PR1YR} E[R_{PR1YR}] \tag{13.10}$$

8. Characteristic variable models of returns associate the risk and return of the firm with the returns attributable to measurable firm characteristics.

a. Given characteristic weights w_s^i for each stock s, the return associated with each characteristic are inferred from the regression:

$$R_s = w_s^1 R_{c1} + w_s^2 R_{c2} + \cdots + w_s^N R_{cN} + \varepsilon_s \tag{13.11}$$

b. The expected return and beta of the firm can be calculated by interpreting the firm as a portfolio of characteristics, and using estimated returns and covariances for the characteristics.

Key Terms

Arbitrage Pricing Theory (APT) *p. 410*
book-to-market ratio *p. 403*
characteristic variable models *p. 416*
data snooping bias *p. 404*
factor betas *p. 410*
factor portfolios *p. 409*
Fama-French-Carhart (FFC) factor
　specification *p. 413*
high-minus-low (HML) portfolio *p. 413*

momentum strategy *p. 406*
multifactor model *p. 410*
multiple regression *p. 409*
prior one-year momentum (PR1YR)
　portfolio *p. 413*
self-financing portfolio *p. 411*
single-factor model *p. 410*
size effect *p. 402*
small-minus-big (SMB) portfolio *p. 413*

Further Reading

More detail on the theoretical relation between firm size and returns can be found in J. B. Berk, "Does Size Really Matter?" *Financial Analysts Journal* (September/October 1997): 12–18.

A summary of the empirical evidence on the relationship between risk-adjusted return and market value can be found in the following article: E. F. Fama and K. R. French, "The Cross-Section of Expected Stock Returns," *Journal of Finance* 47 (June 1992): 427–465.

The evidence that momentum strategies produce positive risk-adjusted returns was first published in the following article: N. Jegadeesh and S. Titman, "Returns to Buying Winners and Selling Losers: Implications for Stock Market Efficiency," *Journal of Finance* 48 (March 1993): 65–91.

The following two articles provide details on the FFC factor specification: E. F. Fama and K. R. French, "Common Risk Factors in the Returns on Stocks and Bonds," *Journal of Financial Economics* 33 (1993): 3–56; and M. Carhart, "On Persistence in Mutual Fund Performance," *Journal of Finance* 52 (March 1997): 57–82.

The first evidence that characteristic variable models could be useful in predicting firm betas was shown by W. H. Beaver, P. Kettler, and M. Scholes, "The Association between Marker Determined and Accounting Determined Risk Measures," *Accounting Review* 45 (October 1970), 654–682. Readers interested in how money managers use the characteristic variable model should consult the following book: R. C. Grinold and R. N. Kahn, *Active Portfolio Management*, 2nd ed. (New York: McGraw-Hill, 1999).

Problems

A blue box (■) indicates problems available in MyFinanceLab. An asterisk (*) indicates problems with a higher level of difficulty.

1. Explain what the size effect is.

2. What is the implication of predictability in returns?

3. What are the implications of a trading strategy with a positive alpha?

4. Explain how to construct a positive-alpha trading strategy if stocks that have had relatively high returns in the past tend to have positive alphas and stocks that have had relatively low returns in the past tend to have negative alphas.

*5. If you can use past returns to construct a trading strategy that makes money (has a positive alpha), it is evidence that market portfolio is not efficient. Explain why.

*6. Assume all firms have the same expected dividends. If they have different expected returns, how will their market values and expected returns be related? What about the relation between their dividend yields and expected returns?

7. Each of the six firms in the table below is expected to pay the listed dividend payment every year in perpetuity.

Firm	Dividend ($ million)	Cost of Capital (%/Year)
S1	10	8
S2	10	12
S3	10	14
B1	100	8
B2	100	12
B3	100	14

  a. Using the cost of capital in the table, calculate the market value of each firm.

  b. Rank the three S firms by their market values and look at how their cost of capital is ordered. What would be the expected return for a self financing portfolio that went long on the firm with the largest market value and shorted the firm with the lowest market value? (The expected return of a self financing portfolio is the weighted average return of the consituent securities.) Repeat using the B firms.

  c. Rank all six firms by their market values. How does this ranking order the cost of capital? What would be the expected return for a self financing portfolio that went long on the firm with the largest market value and shorted the firm with the lowest market value?

  d. Repeat part (c) but rank the firms by the dividend yield instead of the market value. What can you conclude about the dividend yield ranking compared to the market value ranking?

8. Explain why you might expect stocks to have nonzero alphas if the proxy portfolio is not highly correlated with the true market portolio, even if the true market portfolio is efficient.

9. Explain why an employee who cares only about expected return and volatility will likely underweight the amount of money he invests in his own company's stock relative to an investor who does not work for his company.

10. Derive Eq. 13.8 using three portfolios from which the efficient portfolio can be constructed.

 11. Using the factor beta estimates in Table 13.4 below and the expected return estimates in Table 13.1, calculate the risk premium of General Electric stock (ticker: GE) using the FFC factor specification.

TABLE 13.4	Estimated Factor Betas		
Factor	MSFT	XOM	GE
MKT	1.068	0.243	0.747
SMB	−0.374	0.125	−0.478
HML	−0.814	0.144	−0.232
PR1YR	−0.226	−0.185	−0.147

 12. You are currently considering an investment in a project in the energy sector. The investment has the same riskiness as Exxon Mobil stock (ticker: XOM). Using the data in Table 13.1 and Table 13.4, calculate the cost of capital using the FFC factor specification if the current risk-free rate is 6% per year.

13. You work for Microsoft Corporation (ticker: MSFT), and you are considering whether to develop a new software product. The risk of the investment is the same as the risk of the company. Using the data in Table 13.1 and Table 13.4, calculate the cost of capital using the FFC factor specification if the current risk-free rate is 5.5% per year.

14. You have noticed that firm betas vary, that is, firms' risk vary in time. Explain how a characteristics-based model that assumes that the expected return associated with each characteristic does not vary (is constant in time) can capture this variation and correctly price risk.

15. What variables are taken as observable (that is, are not inferred from the data) in the characteristics model of expected returns? What about in a factor of expected returns?

V

Capital Structure

Chapter 14
Capital Structure
in a Perfect Market

Chapter 15
Debt and Taxes

Chapter 16
Financial Distress,
Managerial Incentives,
and Information

Chapter 17
Payout Policy

The Law of One Price Connection. One of the fundamental questions of corporate finance is how a firm should choose the set of securities it will issue to raise capital from investors. This decision determines the firm's capital structure, which is the total amount of debt, equity, and other securities that a firm has outstanding. Does the choice of capital structure affect the value of the firm? In Chapter 14 we consider this question in a perfect capital market. There we apply the Law of One Price to show that as long as the cash flows generated by the firm's assets are unchanged, then the value of the firm—which is the total value of its outstanding securities—does not depend on its capital structure. Therefore, if capital structure has a role in determining the firm's value, it must come from important market imperfections that we explore in subsequent chapters. In Chapter 15, we analyze the role of debt in reducing the taxes a firm or its investors will pay, while in Chapter 16 we consider the costs of financial distress and changes to managerial incentives that result from leverage. Finally, in Chapter 17, we consider the firm's choice of payout policy and ask: Which is the best method for the firm to return capital to its investors? Again, the Law of One Price implies that the firm's choice to pay dividends or repurchase its stock will not affect its value in a perfect capital market. We then examine how market imperfections affect this important insight and shape the firm's optimal payout policy.

CHAPTER

14

Capital Structure in a Perfect Market

notation

PV	present value
NPV	net present value
E	market value of levered equity
D	market value of debt
U	market value of unlevered equity
A	market value of firm assets
R_D	return on debt
R_E	return on levered equity
R_U	return on unlevered equity
r_D	expected return (cost of capital) of debt
r_E	expected return (cost of capital) of levered equity
r_U	expected return (cost of capital) of unlevered equity
r_A	expected return (cost of capital) of firm assets
r_{wacc}	weighted average cost of capital
β_E	beta of levered equity
β_U	beta of unlevered equity
β_D	beta of debt
EPS	earnings per share

When a firm needs to raise new funds to undertake its investments, it must decide which type of security it will issue to investors. Even absent a need for new funds, firms can issue new securities and use the funds to repay debt or repurchase shares. What considerations should guide these decisions?

Consider the case of Dan Harris, Chief Financial Officer of Electronic Business Services (EBS), who has been reviewing plans for a major expansion of the firm. To pursue the expansion, EBS plans to raise $50 million from outside investors. One possibility is to raise the funds by selling shares of EBS stock. Due to the firm's risk, Dan estimates that equity investors will require a 10% risk premium over the 5% risk-free interest rate. That is, the company's equity cost of capital is 15%.

Some senior executives at EBS, however, have argued that the firm should consider borrowing the $50 million instead. EBS has not borrowed previously and, given its strong balance sheet, it should be able to borrow at a 6% interest rate. Does the low interest rate of debt make borrowing a better choice of financing for EBS? If EBS does borrow, will this choice affect the NPV of the expansion, and therefore change the value of the firm and its share price?

We explore these questions in this chapter in a setting of *perfect capital markets*, in which all securities are fairly priced, there are no taxes or transaction costs, and the total cash flows of the firm's projects are not affected by how the firm finances them. Although in reality capital markets are not perfect, this setting provides an important benchmark. Perhaps surprisingly, with perfect capital markets, the Law of One Price implies that the choice of debt or equity financing will *not* affect the total value of a firm, its share price, or its cost of capital. Thus, in a perfect world, EBS will be indifferent regarding the choice of financing for its expansion.

14.1 Equity Versus Debt Financing

The relative proportions of debt, equity, and other securities that a firm has outstanding constitute its **capital structure**. When corporations raise funds from outside investors, they must choose which type of security to issue. The most common choices are financing through equity alone and financing through a combination of debt and equity. We begin our discussion by considering both of these options.

Financing a Firm with Equity

Consider an entrepreneur with the following investment opportunity. For an initial investment of $800 this year, a project will generate cash flows of either $1400 or $900 next year. The cash flows depend on whether the economy is strong or weak, respectively. Both scenarios are equally likely, and are shown in Table 14.1.

TABLE 14.1	The Project Cash Flows	
Date 0	**Date 1**	
	Strong Economy	**Weak Economy**
−$800	$1400	$900

Because the project cash flows depend on the overall economy, they contain market risk. As a result, suppose investors demand a risk premium over the current risk-free interest rate of 5% to invest in this project. Suppose that given the market risk of the investment, the appropriate risk premium is 10%.

What is the NPV of this investment opportunity? Given a risk-free interest rate of 5% and a risk premium of 10%, the cost of capital for this project is 15%. Because the expected cash flow in one year is $\frac{1}{2}(\$1400) + \frac{1}{2}(\$900) = \$1150$, we get

$$NPV = -\$800 + \frac{\$1150}{1.15} = -\$800 + \$1000$$
$$= \$200$$

Thus the investment has a positive NPV.

If this project is financed using equity alone, how much would investors be willing to pay for the firm's shares? Recall from Chapter 3 that, in the absence of arbitrage, the price of a security equals the present value of its cash flows. Because the firm has no other liabilities, equity holders will receive all of the cash flows generated by the project on date 1. Hence the market value of the firm's equity today will be

$$PV(\text{equity cash flows}) = \frac{\$1150}{1.15} = \$1000$$

So, the entrepreneur can raise $1000 by selling the equity in the firm. After paying the investment cost of $800, the entrepreneur can keep the remaining $200—the project NPV—as a profit. In other words, the project's NPV represents the value to the initial owners of the firm (in this case, the entrepreneur) created by the project.

TABLE 14.2	**Cash Flows and Returns for Unlevered Equity**

	Date 0	Date 1: Cash Flows		Date 1: Returns	
	Initial Value	**Strong Economy**	**Weak Economy**	**Strong Economy**	**Weak Economy**
Unlevered equity	$1000	$1400	$900	40%	−10%

What are the cash flows and returns for the shareholders who purchase the firm's equity? Equity in a firm with no debt is called **unlevered equity**. Because there is no debt, the date 1 cash flows of the unlevered equity are equal to those of the project. Given equity's initial value of $1000, shareholder's returns are either 40% or −10% as shown in Table 14.2.

The strong and weak economy outcomes are equally likely, so the expected return on the unlevered equity is $\frac{1}{2}(40\%) + \frac{1}{2}(-10\%) = 15\%$. Because the risk of unlevered equity equals the risk of the project, shareholders are earning an appropriate return for the risk they are taking.

Financing a Firm with Debt and Equity

Financing the firm exclusively with equity is not the entrepreneur's only option. She can also raise part of the initial capital using debt. Suppose she decides to borrow $500 initially, in addition to selling equity. Because the project's cash flow will always be enough to repay the debt, the debt is risk free. Thus the firm can borrow at the risk-free interest rate of 5%, and it will owe the debt holders $500 \times 1.05 = \$525$ in one year.

Equity in a firm that also has debt outstanding is called **levered equity**. Promised payments to debt holders must be made before any payments to equity holders are distributed. Given the firm's $525 debt obligation, the shareholders will receive only $1400 − $525 = $875 if the economy is strong and $900 − $525 = $375 if the economy is weak. Table 14.3 shows the cash flows of the debt, the levered equity, and the total cash flows of the firm.

What price E should the levered equity sell for, and which is the best capital structure choice for the entrepreneur? In an important paper, researchers Franco Modigliani and Merton Miller proposed an answer to this question that surprised researchers and

TABLE 14.3	**Values and Cash Flows for Debt and Equity of the Levered Firm**

	Date 0	Date 1: Cash Flows	
	Initial Value	**Strong Economy**	**Weak Economy**
Debt	$500	$525	$525
Levered equity	$E = ?$	$875	$375
Firm	$1000	$1400	$900

practitioners at the time.[1] They argued that with perfect capital markets, the total value of a firm should not depend on its capital structure. Their reasoning: The firm's total cash flows still equal the cash flows of the project, and therefore have the same present value of $1000 calculated earlier (see the last line in Table 14.3). Because the cash flows of the debt and equity sum to the cash flows of the project, by the Law of One Price the combined values of debt and equity must be $1000. Therefore, if the value of the debt is $500, the value of the levered equity must be $E = \$1000 - \$500 = \$500$.

Because the cash flows of levered equity are smaller than those of unlevered equity, levered equity will sell for a lower price ($500 versus $1000). However, the fact that the equity is less valuable with leverage does not mean that the entrepreneur is worse off. She will still raise a total of $1000 by issuing both debt and levered equity, just as she did with unlevered equity alone. As a consequence, she will be indifferent between these two choices for the firm's capital structure.

The Effect of Leverage on Risk and Return

Modigliani and Miller's conclusion went against the common view, which stated that even with perfect capital markets, leverage would affect a firm's value. In particular, it was thought that the value of the levered equity would exceed $500, because the present value of its expected cash flow at 15% is

$$\frac{\frac{1}{2}(\$875) + \frac{1}{2}(\$375)}{1.15} = \$543$$

The reason this is *not* correct is that leverage increases the risk of the equity of a firm. Therefore, it is inappropriate to discount the cash flows of levered equity at the same discount rate of 15% that we used for unlevered equity. Investors in levered equity require a higher expected return to compensate for its increased risk.

Table 14.4 compares the equity returns if the entrepreneur chooses unlevered equity financing with the case in which she borrows $500 and raises an additional $500 using levered equity. Note that the returns to equity holders are very different with and without leverage. Unlevered equity has a return of either 40% or −10%, for an expected return

TABLE 14.4	**Returns to Equity with and without Leverage**					
	Date 0	**Date 1: Cash Flows**		**Date 1: Returns**		
	Initial Value	**Strong Economy**	**Weak Economy**	**Strong Economy**	**Weak Economy**	**Expected Return**
Debt	$500	$525	$525	5%	5%	**5%**
Levered equity	$500	$875	$375	75%	−25%	**25%**
Unlevered equity	$1000	$1400	$900	40%	−10%	**15%**

1. F. Modigliani and M. Miller, "The Cost of Capital, Corporation Finance and the Theory of Investment," *American Economic Review* 48(3) (1958): 261–297.

of 15%. But levered equity has higher risk, with a return of either 75% or −25%. To compensate for this risk, levered equity holders receive a higher expected return of 25%.

We can evaluate the relationship between risk and return more formally by computing the sensitivity of each security's return to the systematic risk of the economy. (In our simple two-state example, this sensitivity determines the security's beta; recall also our discussion of risk in Chapter 3.) Table 14.5 shows the return sensitivity and the risk premium for each security. Because the debt's return bears no systematic risk, its risk premium is zero. In this particular case, however, levered equity has twice the systematic risk of unlevered equity. As a result, levered equity holders receive twice the risk premium.

TABLE 14.5 **Systematic Risk and Risk Premiums for Debt, Unlevered Equity, and Levered Equity**

	Return Sensitivity (Systematic Risk)	Risk Premium
	$\Delta R = R(\text{strong}) - R(\text{weak})$	$E[R] - r_f$
Debt	5% − 5% = 0%	5% − 5% = 0%
Unlevered equity	40% − (−10%) = 50%	15% − 5% = 10%
Levered equity	75% − (−25%) = 100%	25% − 5% = 20%

To summarize, in the case of perfect capital markets, if the firm is 100% equity financed, the equity holders will require a 15% expected return. If the firm is financed 50% with debt and 50% with equity, the debt holders will receive a lower return of 5%, while the levered equity holders will require a higher expected return of 25% because of their increased risk. As this example shows, *leverage increases the risk of equity even when there is no risk that the firm will default.* Thus, while debt may be cheaper when considered on its own, it raises the cost of capital for equity. Considering both sources of capital together, the firm's average cost of capital with leverage is $\frac{1}{2}(5\%) + \frac{1}{2}(25\%) = 15\%$, the same as for the unlevered firm.

Leverage and the Equity Cost of Capital

Problem

Suppose the entrepreneur borrows only $200 when financing the project. According to Modigliani and Miller, what should the value of the equity be? What is the expected return?

Solution

Because the value of the firm's total cash flows is still $1000, if the firm borrows $200, its equity will be worth $800. The firm will owe $200 × 1.05 = $210 in one year. Thus, if the economy is strong, equity holders will receive $1400 − $210 = $1190, for a return of $1190 / $800 − 1 = 48.75%. If the economy is weak, equity holders will receive $900 − $210 = $690, for a return of $690 / $800 − 1 = −13.75%. The equity has an expected return of $\frac{1}{2}(48.75\%) + \frac{1}{2}(-13.75\%) = 17.5\%$.

Nobel Prize   Franco Modigliani and Merton Miller

Franco Modigliani and Merton Miller, the authors of the Modigliani-Miller Propositions, have each won the Nobel Prize in economics for their work in financial economics, including their capital structure propositions. Modigliani won the Nobel Prize in 1985 for his work on personal savings and for his capital structure theorems with Miller. Miller earned his prize in 1990 for his analysis of portfolio theory and capital structure.

Miller once described the MM propositions in an interview this way:

People often ask: Can you summarize your theory quickly? Well, I say, you understand the M&M theorem if you know why this is a joke: The pizza delivery man comes to Yogi Berra after the game and says, "Yogi, how do you want this pizza cut, into quarters or eighths?" And Yogi says, "Cut it in eight pieces. I'm feeling hungry tonight."

Everyone recognizes that's a joke because obviously the number and shape of the pieces don't affect the size of the pizza. And similarly, the stocks, bonds, warrants, et cetera, issued don't affect the aggregate value of the firm. They just slice up the underlying earnings in different ways.*

Modigliani and Miller each won the Nobel Prize in large part for their observation that the value of a firm should be unaffected by its capital structure in perfect capital markets. While the intuition underlying the MM propositions may be as simple as slicing pizza, their implications for corporate finance are far-reaching. The propositions imply that the true role of a firm's financial policy is to deal with (and potentially exploit) financial market imperfections such as taxes and transaction costs. Modigliani and Miller's work began a long line of research into these market imperfections, which we look at over the next several chapters.

*Peter J. Tanous, *Investment Gurus* (New York: Institute of Finance, 1997).

issued to the company's owner. Furthermore no change in the investment value of the enterprise as a whole would result from a change in its capitalization. Bonds could be retired with stock issues, or two classes of junior securities could be combined into one, without changing the investment value of the company as a whole. Such constancy of investment value is analogous to the indestructibility of matter or energy: it leads us to speak of the Law of the Conservation of Investment Value, just as physicists speak of the Law of the Conservation of Matter, or the Law of the Conservation of Energy.

Thus, the results in this chapter can be interpreted more broadly as the **conservation of value principle** for financial markets: *With perfect capital markets, financial transactions neither add nor destroy value, but instead represent a repackaging of risk (and therefore return).*

The conservation of value principle extends far beyond questions of debt versus equity or even capital structure. It implies that any financial transaction that appears to be a good deal in terms of adding value either is too good to be true or is exploiting some type of market imperfection. To make sure the value is not illusory, it is important to identify the market imperfection that is the source of value. In the next several chapters we will examine different types of market imperfections and the potential sources of value that they introduce for the firm's capital structure choice and other financial transactions.

CONCEPT CHECK
1. Consider the questions facing Dan Harris, CFO of EBS, at the beginning of this chapter. What answers would you give based on the Modigliani-Miller Propositions? What considerations should the capital structure decision be based on?

2. State the conservation of value principle for financial markets.

Summary

1. The collection of securities a firm issues to raise capital from investors is called the firm's capital structure. Equity and debt are the securities most commonly used by firms. When equity is used without debt, the firm is said to be unlevered. Otherwise, the amount of debt determines the firm's leverage.

2. The owner of a firm should choose the capital structure that maximizes the total value of the securities issued.

3. Capital markets are said to be perfect if they satisfy three conditions:

   a. Investors and firms can trade the same set of securities at competitive market prices equal to the present value of their future cash flows.

   b. There are no taxes, transaction costs, or issuance costs associated with security trading.

   c. A firm's financing decisions do not change the cash flows generated by its investments, nor do they reveal new information about them.

4. According to MM Proposition I, with perfect capital markets the value of a firm is independent of its capital structure.

   a. With perfect capital markets, homemade leverage is a perfect substitute for firm leverage.

   b. If otherwise identical firms with different capital structures have different values, the Law of One Price would be violated and an arbitrage opportunity would exist.

5. The market value balance sheet shows that the total market value of a firm's assets equals the total market value of the firm's liabilities, including all securities issued to investors. Changing the capital structure therefore alters how the value of the assets is divided across securities, but not the firm's total value.

6. A firm can change its capital structure at any time by issuing new securities and using the funds to pay its existing investors. An example is a leveraged recapitalization in which the firm borrows money (issues debt) and repurchases shares (or pays a dividend). MM Proposition I implies that such transactions will not change the share price.

7. According to MM Proposition II, the cost of capital for levered equity is

$$r_E = r_U + \frac{D}{E}(r_U - r_D) \tag{14.5}$$

8. Debt is less risky than equity, so it has a lower cost of capital. Leverage increases the risk of equity, however, raising the equity cost of capital. The benefit of debt's lower cost of capital is offset by the higher equity cost of capital, leaving a firm's weighted average cost of capital (WACC) unchanged with perfect capital markets:

$$r_{wacc} = \frac{E}{E + D}r_E + \frac{D}{E + D}r_D = r_U = r_A \tag{14.7, 14.8}$$

9. The market risk of a firm's assets can be estimated by its unlevered beta:

$$\beta_U = \frac{E}{E + D}\beta_E + \frac{D}{E + D}\beta_D \tag{14.9}$$

10. Leverage increases the beta of a firm's equity:

$$\beta_E = \beta_U + \frac{D}{E}(\beta_U - \beta_D) \tag{14.10}$$

11. A firm's net debt is equal to its debt less its holdings of cash and other risk-free securities. We can compute the cost of capital and the beta of the firm's business assets, excluding cash, by using its net debt when calculating its WACC or unlevered beta.

12. Leverage can raise a firm's expected earnings per share, but it also increases the volatility of earnings per share. As a result, shareholders are not better off and the value of equity is unchanged.

13. As long as shares are sold to investors at a fair price, there is no cost of dilution associated with issuing equity. While the number of shares increases when equity is issued, the firm's assets also increase because of the cash raised, and the per-share value of equity remains unchanged.

14. With perfect capital markets, financial transactions are a zero-NPV activity that neither add nor destroy value on their own, but rather repackage the firm's risk and return. Capital structure—and financial transactions more generally—affect a firm's value only because of its impact on some type of market imperfection.

Key Terms

capital structure *p. 428*

conservation of value principle *p. 450*

debt-to-value ratio *p. 440*

dilution *p. 448*

homemade leverage *p. 433*

leveraged recapitalization *p. 436*

levered equity *p. 429*

market value balance sheet *p. 435*

net debt *p. 444*

perfect capital markets *p. 432*

unlevered beta *p. 443*

unlevered equity *p. 429*

weighted average cost of capital (WACC) *p. 439*

Further Reading

For further details on MM's argument, especially their use of the Law of One Price to derive their results, see MM's original paper: F. Modigliani and M. H. Miller, "The Cost of Capital, Corporation Finance and the Theory of Investment," *American Economic Review* 48(3) (1958): 261–297.

For a retrospective look at the work of Modigliani and Miller and its importance in corporate finance, see the collection of articles in Volume 2, Issue 4 of the *Journal of Economic Perspectives* (1988), which includes: "The Modigliani-Miller Propositions After Thirty Years," by M. Miller (pp. 99–120), "Comment on the Modigliani-Miller Propositions," by S. Ross (pp. 127–133), "Corporate Finance and the Legacy of Modigliani and Miller," by S. Bhattacharya (pp. 135–147), and "MM—Past, Present, Future," by F. Modigliani (pp. 149–158).

For an interesting interview with Merton Miller about his work, see: P. J. Tanous, *Investment Gurus* (New York: Prentice Hall Press, 1997).

For a more recent discussion of MM's contribution to the development of capital structure theory, see: R. Cookson, "A Survey of Corporate Finance ('The Party's Over' and 'Debt Is Good for You')," *The Economist* (January 27, 2001): 5–8.

A historical account of Miller-Modigliani's result is provided in these sources: P. L. Bernstein, *Capital Ideas: The Improbable Origins of Modern Wall Street* (Free Press, 1993); and M. Rubinstein, "Great Moments in Financial Economics: II. Modigliani-Miller Theorem," *Journal of Investment Management* 1(2) (2003).

Problems

All problems in this chapter are available in MyFinanceLab. An asterisk (*) indicates problems with a higher level of difficulty.

Equity Versus
Debt Financing

1. Consider a project with free cash flows in one year of $130,000 or $180,000, with each outcome being equally likely. The initial investment required for the project is $100,000, and the project's cost of capital is 20%. The risk-free interest rate is 10%.

    a. What is the NPV of this project?

    b. Suppose that to raise the funds for the initial investment, the project is sold to investors as an all-equity firm. The equity holders will receive the cash flows of the project in one year. How much money can be raised in this way—that is, what is the initial market value of the unlevered equity?

    c. Suppose the initial $100,000 is instead raised by borrowing at the risk-free interest rate. What are the cash flows of the levered equity, and what is its initial value according to MM?

2. You are an entrepreneur starting a biotechnology firm. If your research is successful, the technology can be sold for $30 million. If your research is unsuccessful, it will be worth nothing. To fund your research, you need to rasie $2 million. Investors are willing to provide you with $2 million in initial capital in exchange for 50% of the unlevered equity in the firm.

    a. What is the total market value of the firm without leverage?

    b. Suppose you borrow $1 million. According to MM, what fraction of the firm's equity will you need to sell to raise the additional $1 million you need?

    c. What is the value of your share of the firm's equity in cases (a) and (b)?

3. Acort Industries owns assets that will have an 80% probability of having a market value of $50 million in one year. There is a 20% chance that the assets will be worth only $20 million. The current risk-free rate is 5%, and Acort's assets have a cost of capital of 10%.

    a. If Acort is unlevered, what is the current market value of its equity?

    b. Suppose instead that Acort has debt with a face value of $20 million due in one year. According to MM, what is the value of Acort's equity in this case?

    c. What is the expected return of Acort's equity without leverage? What is the expected return of Acort's equity with leverage?

    d. What is the lowest possible realized return of Acort's equity with and without leverage?

Modigliani-Miller I:
Leverage, Arbitrage,
and Firm Value

4. Suppose there are no taxes. Firm ABC has no debt, and firm XYZ has debt of $5000 on which it pays interest of 10% each year. Both companies have identical projects that generate free cash flows of $800 or $1000 each year. After paying any interest on debt, both companies use all remaining free cash flows to pay dividends each year.

    a. Fill in the table below showing the payments debt and equity holders of each firm will receive given each of the two possible levels of free cash flows.

| | ABC | | XYZ | |
FCF	Debt Payments	Equity Dividends	Debt Payments	Equity Dividends
$ 800				
$1000				

b. Suppose you hold 10% of the equity of ABC. What is another portfolio you could hold that would provide the same cash flows?

c. Suppose you hold 10% of the equity of XYZ. If you can borrow at 10%, what is an alternative strategy that would provide the same cash flows?

5. Suppose Alpha Industries and Omega Technology have identical assets that generate identical cash flows. Alpha Industries is an all-equity firm, with 10 million shares outstanding that trade for a price of $22 per share. Omega Technology has 20 million shares outstanding as well as debt of $60 million.

a. According to MM Proposition 1, what is the stock price for Omega Technology?

b. Suppose Omega Technology stock currently trades for $11 per share. What arbitrage opportunity is available? What assumptions are necessary to exploit this opportunity?

6. Cisoft is a highly profitable technology firm that currently has $5 billion in cash. The firm has decided to use this cash to repurchase shares from investors, and it has already announced these plans to investors. Currently, Cisoft is an all-equity firm with 5 billion shares outstanding. These shares currently trade for $12 per share. Cisoft has issued no other securities except for stock options given to its employees. The current market value of these options is $8 billion.

a. What is the market value of Cisoft's non-cash assets?

b. With perfect capital markets, what is the market value of Cisoft's equity after the share repurchase? What is the value per share?

EXCEL 7. Zetatron is an all-equity firm with 100 million shares outstanding, which are currently trading for $7.50 per share. A month ago, Zetatron announced it will change its capital structure by borrowing $100 million in short-term debt, borrowing $100 million in long-term debt, and issuing $100 million of preferred stock. The $300 million raised by these issues, plus another $50 million in cash that Zetatron already has, will be used to repurchase existing shares of stock. The transaction is scheduled to occur today. Assume perfect capital markets.

a. What is the market value balance sheet for Zetatron

    i. Before this transaction?

    ii. After the new securities are issued but before the share repurchase?

    iii. After the share repurchase?

b. At the conclusion of this transaction, how many shares outstanding will Zetatron have, and what will the value of those shares be?

*Modigliani-Miller II:
Leverage, Risk, and
the Cost of Capital*

8. Explain what is wrong with the following argument: "If a firm issues debt that is risk free, because there is no possibility of default, the risk of the firm's equity does not change. Therefore, risk-free debt allows the firm to get the benefit of a low cost of capital of debt without raising its cost of capital of equity."

9. Consider the entrepreneur described in Section 14.3. Suppose she funds the project by borrowing $750 rather than $500.

a. According to MM Proposition I, what is the value of the equity? What are its cash flows if the economy is strong? What are its cash flows if the economy is weak?

b. What is the return of the equity in each case? What is its expected return?

c. What is the risk premium of equity in each case? What is the sensitivity of the levered equity return to systematic risk? How does its sensitivity compare to that of unlevered equity? How does its risk premium compare to that of unlevered equity?

      d. What is the debt-equity ratio of the firm in this case?

      e. What is the firm's WACC in this case?

10. Hardmon Enterprises is currently an all-equity firm with an expected return of 12%. It is considering a leveraged recapitalization in which it would borrow and repurchase existing shares.

      a. Suppose Hardmon borrows to the point that its debt-equity ratio is 0.50. With this amount of debt, the debt cost of capital is 6%. What will the expected return of equity be after this transaction?

      b. Suppose instead Hardmon borrows to the point that its debt-equity ratio is 1.50. With this amount of debt, Hardmon's debt will be much riskier. As a result, the debt cost of capital will be 8%. What will the expected return of equity be in this case?

      c. A senior manager argues that it is in the best interest of the shareholders to choose the capital structure that leads to the highest expected return for the stock. How would you respond to this argument?

11. Global Pistons (GP) has common stock with a market value of $200 million and debt with a value of $100 million. Investors expect a 15% return on the stock and a 6% return on the debt. Assume perfect capital markets.

      a. Suppose GP issues $100 million of new stock to buy back the debt. What is the expected return of the stock after this transaction?

      b. Suppose instead GP issues $50 million of new debt to repurchase stock.

        i. If the risk of the debt does not change, what is the expected return of the stock after this transaction?

        ii. If the risk of the debt increases, would the expected return of the stock be higher or lower than in part (i)?

12. Hubbard Industries is an all-equity firm whose shares have an expected return of 10%. Hubbard does a leveraged recapitalization, issuing debt and repurchasing stock, until its debt-equity ratio is 0.60. Due to the increased risk, shareholders now expect a return of 13%. Assuming there are no taxes and Hubbard's debt is risk free, what is the interest rate on the debt?

13. Hartford Mining has 50 million shares that are currently trading for $4 per share and $200 million worth of debt. The debt is risk free and has an interest rate of 5%, and the expected return of Hartford stock is 11%. Suppose a mining strike causes the price of Hartford stock to fall 25% to $3 per share. The value of the risk-free debt is unchanged. Assuming there are no taxes and the unlevered beta of Hartford's assets is unchanged, what happens to Hartford's equity cost of capital?

*14. Indell stock has a current market value of $120 million and a beta of 1.50. Indell currently has risk-free debt as well. The firm decides to change its capital structure by issuing $30 million in additional risk-free debt, and then using this $30 million plus another $10 million in cash to repurchase stock. With perfect capital markets, what will the beta of Indell stock be after this transaction?

Capital Structure Fallacies

15. Yerba Industries is an all-equity firm whose stock has a beta of 1.2 and an expected return of 12.5%. Suppose it issues new risk-free debt with a 5% yield and repurchases 40% of its stock. Assume perfect capital markets.

      a. What is the beta of Yerba stock after this transaction?

      b. What is the expected return of Yerba stock after this transaction?

Suppose that prior to this transaction, Yerba expected earnings per share this coming year of $1.50, with a forward P/E ratio (that is, the share price divided by the expected earnings for the coming year) of 14.

    c. What is Yerba's expected earnings per share after this transaction? Does this change benefit shareholders? Explain.

    d. What is Yerba's forward P/E ratio after this transaction? Is this change in the P/E ratio reasonable? Explain.

16. You are CEO of a high-growth technology firm. You plan to raise $180 million to fund an expansion by issuing either new shares or new debt. With the expansion, you expect earnings next year of $24 million. The firm currently has 10 million shares outstanding, with a price of $90 per share. Assume perfect capital markets.

    a. If you raise the $180 million by selling new shares, what will the forecast for next year's earnings per share be?

    b. If you raise the $180 million by issuing new debt with an interest rate of 5%, what will the forecast for next year's earnings per share be?

    c. What is the firm's forward P/E ratio (that is, the share price divided by the expected earnings for the coming year) if it issues equity? What is the firm's forward P/E ratio if it issues debt? How can you explain the difference?

17. Zelnor, Inc., is an all-equity firm with 100 million shares outstanding currently trading for $8.50 per share. Suppose Zelnor decides to grant a total of 10 million new shares to employees as part of a new compensation plan. The firm argues that this new compensation plan will motivate employees and is a better strategy than giving salary bonuses because it will not cost the firm anything.

    a. If the new compensation plan has no effect on the value of Zelnor's assets, what will the share price of the stock be once this plan is implemented?

    b. What is the cost of this plan for Zelnor's investors? Why is issuing equity costly in this case?

Data Case

You work in the corporate finance division of The Home Depot and your boss has asked you to review the firm's capital structure. Specifically, your boss is considering changing the firm's debt level. Your boss remembers something from his MBA program about capital structure being irrelevant, but isn't quite sure what that means. You know that capital structure is irrelevant under the conditions of perfect markets and will demonstrate this point for your boss by showing that the weighted average cost of capital remains constant under various levels of debt. So, for now, suppose that capital markets are perfect as you prepare responses for your boss.

You would like to analyze relatively modest changes to Home Depot's capital structure. You would like to consider two scenarios: the firm issues $1 billion in new debt to repurchase stock, and the firm issues $1 billion in new stock to repurchase debt. Use Excel to answer the following questions using Eq. 14.5 and Eq. 14.7 from this chapter, and assuming a cost of unlevered equity (r_U) of 12 percent.

1. Obtain the financial information you need for Home Depot.

    a. Go to Nasdaq.com (www.nasdaq.com), click on "Summary Quotes" on the left-hand side, and enter Home Depot's stock symbol (HD). Click on Go. From the Summary Quotes page, get the current stock price and number of shares outstanding.

    b. Click on "Company Financials" and the annual income statement should appear. Put the cursor in the middle of the statement, right-click your mouse, and select "Export to Microsoft Excel." (You will not need the income statement until Chapter 15, but collect all of the background data in one step.) Go back to the Nasdaq Web page and select the balance sheet. Export that to Excel as well and then cut and paste the balance sheet to the same worksheet as the income statement.

c. To get the cost of debt for Home Depot, go to NASD BondInfo (http://www .nasdbondinfo.com). Search by symbol and enter Home Depot's symbol. The next page will contain information for all of Home Depot's outstanding and recently matured bonds. Select the latest yield on an outstanding bond with the shortest remaining maturity (the maturity date is on the line describing each issue; sometimes the list also contains recently retired bonds, so make sure not to use one of those).

2. Compute the market D/E ratio for Home Depot. Approximate the market value of debt by the book value of net debt; include both Long-Term Debt and Short-Term Debt/ Current Portion of Long-Term Debt from the balance sheet and subtract any cash holdings. Use the stock price and number of shares outstanding to calculate the market value of equity.

3. Compute the cost of levered equity (r_E) for Home Depot using their current market debt-to-equity ratio and Eq. 14.5 from the chapter.

4. Compute the current weighted average cost of capital (WACC) for Home Depot using Eq. 14.7 and the existing yield on the outstanding bonds as r_D given their current debt-to-equity ratio.

5. Repeat steps 3 and 4 for the two scenarios you would like to analyze, issuing $1 billion in debt to repurchase stock, and issuing $1 billion in stock to repurchase debt. (Although you realize that the cost of debt capital (r_D) may change with changes in leverage, for these modestly small changes you decide to assume that r_D remains constant. We will explore the relation between changing leverage and changing r_D more fully in Chapter 16.) What is the market D/E ratio in each of these cases?

6. Prepare a written explanation for your boss explaining the relationship between capital structure and the cost of capital in this exercise.

7. What implicit assumptions in this exercise generate the results found in question 5? How might your results differ in the "real world"?

Debt and Taxes

Int	interest expense
PV	present value
r_f	risk-free interest rate
D	market value of debt
r_E	equity cost of capital
τ_c	marginal corporate tax rate
E	market value of equity
r_{wacc}	weighted average cost of capital
r_D	debt cost of capital
V^U	value of the unlevered firm
V^L	value of the firm with leverage
τ_i	marginal personal tax rate on income from debt
τ_e	marginal personal tax rate on income from equity
τ^*	effective tax advantage of debt
τ^*_{ex}	effective tax advantage on interest in excess of EBIT

In a perfect capital market, the Law of One Price implies that all financial transactions have an NPV of zero and neither create nor destroy value. Consequently, in the previous chapter we found that the choice of debt versus equity financing does not affect the value of a firm: The funds raised from issuing debt equal the present value of the future interest and principal payments the firm will make. While leverage increases the risk and cost of capital of the firm's equity, the firm's weighted average cost of capital (WACC), total value, and share price are unaltered by a change in leverage. That is, *in a perfect capital market, a firm's choice of capital structure is unimportant.*

This statement is at odds, however, with the observation that firms invest significant resources, both in terms of managerial time and effort and investment banking fees, in managing their capital structures. In many instances, the choice of leverage is of critical importance to a firm's value and future success. As we will show, there are large and systematic variations in the typical capital structures for different industries. For example, at year-end 2004, Amgen, a biotechnology and drug company, had debt of $5 billion and a market capitalization of more than $81 billion, giving the firm a debt-equity ratio of 0.06. In constrast, Navistar International, an auto and truck manufacturer, had a debt-equity ratio of 0.95. Truck manufacturers in general have higher debt ratios than biotechnology and drug companies. If capital structure is unimportant, why do we see such consistent differences in capital structures across firms and industries? Why do managers dedicate so much time, effort, and expense to the capital structure choice?

As Modigliani and Miller made clear in their original work, capital structure does not matter in *perfect* capital markets.[1] Recall from Chapter 14 that a perfect capital market exists under the following assumptions:

1. Investors and firms can trade the same set of securities at competitive market prices equal to the present value of their future cash flows.

2. There are no taxes, transaction costs, or issuance costs associated with security trading.

3. A firm's financing decisions do not change the cash flows generated by its investments, nor do they reveal new information about them.

Thus, if capital structure *does* matter, then it must stem from a market *imperfection*. In this chapter, we focus on one such imperfection—taxes. Corporations and investors must pay taxes on the income they earn from their investments. As we will see, a firm can enhance its value by using leverage to minimize the taxes it, and its investors, pay.

15.1   The Interest Tax Deduction

Corporations must pay taxes on the income that they earn. Because they pay taxes on their profits after interest payments are deducted, interest expenses reduce the amount of corporate tax firms must pay. This feature of the tax code creates an incentive to use debt.

Let's consider the impact of interest expenses on the taxes paid by Safeway, Inc., a grocery store chain. Safeway had earnings before interest and taxes of approximately $1.25 billion in 2005, and interest expenses of about $400 million. Given Safeway's marginal corporate tax rate of 35%,[2] the effect of leverage on Safeway's earnings is shown in Table 15.1.

TABLE 15.1	**Safeway's Income with and without Leverage, 2005 ($ million)**	
	With Leverage	**Without Leverage**
EBIT	$1,250	$1,250
Interest expense	−400	0
Income before tax	850	1,250
Taxes (35%)	−298	−438
Net income	$552	$812

---

1. See F. Modigliani and M. H. Miller, "The Cost of Capital, Corporation Finance and the Theory of Investment," *American Economic Review* 48 (June 1958): 261–297. In their 1963 paper, "Corporate Income Taxes and the Cost of Capital: A Correction," *American Economic Review* 53 (June 1963): 433–443, Modigliani and Miller adjusted their analysis to incorporate taxes.

2. Safeway paid an average tax rate of approximately 33.9% in 2004, after accounting for other credits and deferrals. Because we are interested in the impact of a change in leverage, Safeway's marginal tax rate—the tax rate that would apply to additional taxable income—is relevant to our discussion.

As we can see from Table 15.1, Safeway's net income in 2005 was lower with leverage than it would have been without leverage. Thus Safeway's debt obligations reduced the value of its equity. But more importantly, the *total* amount available to *all* investors was higher with leverage:

	With Leverage	Without Leverage
Interest paid to debt holders	400	0
Income available to equity holders	552	812
Total available to all investors	$952	$812

With leverage, Safeway was able to pay out $952 million in total to its investors, versus only $812 million without leverage, representing an increase of $140 million.

It might seem odd that a firm can be better off with leverage even though its earnings are lower. But recall from Chapter 14 that the value of a firm is the total amount it can raise from all investors, not just equity holders. So, if the firm can pay out more in total with leverage, it will be able to raise more total capital initially.

Where does the additional $140 million come from? Looking at Table 15.1, we can see that this gain is equal to the reduction in taxes with leverage: $438 million − $298 million = $140 million. Because Safeway does not owe taxes on the $400 million of earnings it used to make interest payments, this $400 million is *shielded* from the corporate tax, providing the tax savings of 35% × $400 million = $140 million.

In general, the gain to investors from the tax deductibility of interest payments is referred to as the **interest tax shield**. The interest tax shield is the additional amount that a firm would have paid in taxes if it did not have leverage. We can calculate the amount of the interest tax shield each year as follows:

$$\text{Interest Tax Shield} = \text{Corporate Tax Rate} \times \text{Interest Payments} \qquad (15.1)$$

Computing the Interest Tax Shield

Problem

Shown below is the income statement for D.F. Builders (DFB). Given its marginal corporate tax rate of 35%, what is the amount of the interest tax shield for DFB in years 2003 through 2006?

DFB Income Statement ($ million)	2003	2004	2005	2006
Total sales	$3,369	$3,706	$4,077	$4,432
Cost of sales	−2,359	−2,584	−2,867	−3,116
Selling, general, and administrative expense	−226	−248	−276	−299
Depreciation	−22	−25	−27	−29
Operating income	762	849	907	988
Other income	7	8	10	12
EBIT	769	857	917	1,000
Interest expense	−50	−80	−100	−100
Income before tax	719	777	817	900
Taxes (35%)	−252	−272	−286	−315
Net income	$467	$505	$531	$585

Solution

From Eq. 15.1, the interest tax shield is the tax rate of 35% multiplied by the interest payments in each year:

($ million)	2003	2004	2005	2006
Interest expense	−50	−80	−100	−100
Interest tax shield (35% × interest expense)	**17.5**	**28**	**35**	**35**

CONCEPT CHECK   1. With corporate income taxes, explain why a firm's value can be higher with leverage even though its earnings are lower.

2. What is the interest tax shield?

15.2 Valuing the Interest Tax Shield

When a firm uses debt, the interest tax shield provides a corporate tax benefit each year. To determine the benefit of leverage for the value of the firm, we must compute the present value of the stream of future interest tax shields the firm will receive.

The Interest Tax Shield and Firm Value

Each year a firm makes interest payments, the cash flows it pays to investors will be higher than they would be without leverage by the amount of the interest tax shield:

$$\left(\begin{array}{c} \text{Cash Flows to Investors} \\ \text{with Leverage} \end{array} \right) = \left(\begin{array}{c} \text{Cash Flows to Investors} \\ \text{without Leverage} \end{array} \right) + (\text{Interest Tax Shield})$$

Figure 15.1 illustrates this relationship. Here you can see how each dollar of pretax cash flows is divided. The firm uses some fraction to pay taxes, and it pays the rest to investors. By increasing the amount paid to debt holders through interest payments, the amount of the pretax cash flows that must be paid as taxes decreases. The gain in total cash flows to investors is the interest tax shield.

Because the cash flows of the levered firm are equal to the sum of the cash flows from the unlevered firm plus the interest tax shield, by the Law of One Price the same must be true for the present values of these cash flows. Thus, letting V^L and V^U represent the value of the firm with and without leverage, respectively, we have the following change to MM Proposition I in the presence of taxes:

The total value of the levered firm exceeds the value of the firm without leverage due to the present value of the tax savings from debt:

$$V^L = V^U + PV(\text{Interest Tax Shield}) \tag{15.2}$$

Clearly, there is an important tax advantage to the use of debt financing. But how large is this tax benefit? To compute the increase in the firm's total value associated with the interest tax shield, we need to forecast how a firm's debt—and therefore its interest payments—will vary over time. Given a forecast of future interest payments, we can determine the interest tax shield and compute its present value by discounting it at a rate that corresponds to its risk.

FIGURE 15.1

The Cash Flows of the Unlevered and Levered Firm

By increasing the cash flows paid to debt holders through interest payments, a firm reduces the amount paid in taxes. The increase in total cash flows paid to investors is the interest tax shield. (Figure assumes a 40% marginal corporate tax rate.)

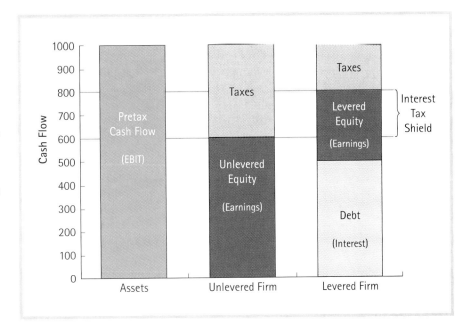

EXAMPLE 15.2

Valuing the Interest Tax Shield Without Risk

Problem

Suppose DFB plans to pay $100 million in interest each year for the next 10 years, and then repay the principal of $2 billion in year 10. These payments are risk free, and DFB's marginal tax rate will remain 35% throughout this period. If the risk-free interest rate is 5%, by how much does the interest tax shield increase the value of DFB?

Solution

In this case, the interest tax shield is 35% × $100 million = $35 million each year for the next 10 years. Therefore, we can value it as a 10-year annuity. Because the tax savings are known and not risky, we can discount them at the 5% risk-free rate:

$$PV(\text{Interest Tax Shield}) = \$35 \text{ million} \times \frac{1}{5\%}\left(1 - \frac{1}{1.05^{10}}\right)$$

$$= \$270 \text{ million}$$

The final repayment of principal in year 10 is not deductible, so it does not contribute to the tax shield.

The Interest Tax Shield with Permanent Debt

In Example 15.2 we know with certainty the firm's future tax savings. In practice, this case is rare. Typically, the level of future interest payments varies due to changes the firm makes in the amount of debt outstanding, changes in the interest rate on that debt, and the risk

Pizza and Taxes

In Chapter 14, we mentioned the pizza analogy that Merton Miller once used to describe the MM Propositions with perfect capital markets: No matter how you slice it, you still have the same amount of pizza.

We can extend this analogy to the setting with taxes, but the story is a bit different. In this case, every time the owner sells a slice of pizza to equity holders, he must give a slice to Uncle Sam as a tax payment. But if the owner sells a slice to debt holders, there is no tax. Thus, by selling more slices to debt holders than to equity holders, the revenues from a single pizza are increased. While the total amount of pizza does not change, the owner will give less away in taxes, leaving more pizza to sell to customers.

that the firm may default and fail to make an interest payment. In addition, the firm's marginal tax rate may fluctuate due to changes in the tax code and changes in the firm's income bracket.

Rather than attempting to account for all possibilities here, we will consider the special case in which the firm issues debt and plans to keep the dollar amount of debt constant forever.[3] For example, the firm might issue a perpetual consol bond, making only interest payments but never repaying the principal. More realistically, suppose the firm issues short-term debt, such as a five-year coupon bond. When the principal is due, the firm raises the money needed to pay it by issuing new debt. In this way, the firm never pays off the principal but simply refinances it whenever it comes due. In this situation, the debt is effectively permanent.

Many large firms have a policy of maintaining a certain amount of debt on their balance sheets. As old bonds and loans mature, new borrowing takes place. What is special here is that we are considering the value of the interest tax shield with a *fixed* dollar amount of outstanding debt, rather than an amount that changes with the size of the firm.

Suppose a firm borrows debt D and keeps the debt permanently. If the firm's marginal tax rate is τ_c, and if the debt is riskless with a risk-free interest rate r_f, then the interest tax shield each year is $\tau_c \times r_f \times D$, and we can value the tax shield as a perpetuity:

$$PV(\text{Interest Tax Shield}) = \frac{\tau_c \times \text{Interest}}{r_f} = \frac{\tau_c \times (r_f \times D)}{r_f}$$

$$= \tau_c \times D$$

This calculation assumes the debt is risk free and the risk-free interest rate is constant. These assumptions are not necessary, however. If the debt is fairly priced, no arbitrage implies that its market value must equal the present value of the future interest payments:[4]

$$\text{Market Value of Debt} = D = PV(\text{Future Interest Payments}) \tag{15.3}$$

---

3. We discuss how to value the interest tax shield with more complicated leverage policies, such as maintaining a constant debt-equity or interest coverage ratio, in Chapter 18.

4. Equation 15.3 holds even if interest rates fluctuate and the debt is risky, as long as any new debt is also fairly priced. It requires only that the firm never repay the principal on the debt (it either refinances or defaults on the principal). The result follows by the same argument that we used in Chapter 9 to show that the price of equity should equal the present value of the future dividends.

If the firm's marginal tax rate is constant,[5] then we have the following general formula:

Value of the Interest Tax Shield of Permanent Debt

$$PV(\text{Interest Tax Shield}) = PV(\tau_c \times \text{ Future Interest Payments})$$
$$= \tau_c \times PV(\text{Future Interest Payments})$$
$$= \tau_c \times D \qquad (15.4)$$

This formula shows the magnitude of the interest tax shield. Given a 35% corporate tax rate, it implies that for every $1 in new permanent debt that the firm issues, the value of the firm increases by $0.35.

The Weighted Average Cost of Capital with Taxes

The tax benefit of leverage can also be expressed in terms of the weighted average cost of capital. When a firm uses debt financing, the cost of the interest it must pay is offset to some extent by the tax savings from the interest tax shield. For example, suppose a firm with a 35% tax rate borrows $100,000 at 10% interest per year. Then its net cost at the end of the year is

		Year-End
Interest expense	$r \times \$100,000 =$	10,000
Tax savings	$-\tau_c \times r \times \$100,000 =$	$-3,500$
Effective after-tax cost of debt	$r \times (1 - \tau_c) \times \$100,000 =$	$6,500

The effective cost of the debt is only $6,500/$100,000 = 6.50% of the loan amount, rather than the full 10% interest. Thus, the tax deductibility of interest lowers the effective cost of debt financing for the firm. More generally,

With tax-deductible interest, the effective after-tax borrowing rate is $r(1 - \tau_c)$.[6]

In Chapter 14, we calculated the weighted average cost of capital, which is the average return that the firm must pay to its investors (equity holders and debt holders). The WACC represents the cost of capital for the free cash flow generated by the firm's assets. Because the firm's free cash flow is computed without considering the firm's leverage, we account for the benefit of the interest tax shield by calculating the WACC using the after-tax cost of debt:

Weighted Average Cost of Capital with Taxes[7]

$$r_{wacc} = \frac{E}{E + D} r_E + \frac{D}{E + D} r_D (1 - \tau_c) \qquad (15.5)$$

---

5. The tax rate may not be constant if the firm's taxable income fluctuates sufficiently to change the firm's tax bracket (we discuss this possibility further in Section 15.5). If the firm's taxable income were to fall into a lower tax bracket for an extended period, the value of the tax shield would be reduced.

6. We derived this same result in Chapter 5 when considering the implications of tax-deductible interest for individuals (for example, with a home mortgage).

7. Appendix 18A.1 of Chapter 18 contains a formal derivation of this formula. Equation 15.5 assumes the interest on debt and its expected return r_D are equal, which is a reasonable approximation if the debt has very low risk and is trading near par. If not, the more precise expression for the after-tax debt cost of capital is $(r_D - \tau_c \bar{r}_D)$, where $\bar{r}_D =$ (current interest expense)/(market value of debt).

If we set the tax rate to zero in Eq. 15.5, we have precisely the formula for the WACC without taxes that we defined in Chapter 14. Relative to that case, corporate taxes lower the effective cost of debt financing, which translates into a reduction in the weighted average cost of capital. In fact, Eq. 15.5 implies

$$r_{wacc} = \underbrace{\frac{E}{E + D}r_E + \frac{D}{E + D}r_D}_{\text{Pretax WACC}} - \underbrace{\frac{D}{E + D}r_D\tau_c}_{\substack{\text{Reduction Due} \\ \text{to Interest Tax Shield}}} \qquad (15.6)$$

Thus, the reduction in the WACC increases with the amount of debt financing. The higher the firm's leverage, the more the firm exploits the tax advantage of debt, and the lower its WACC. Figure 15.2 illustrates this decline in the WACC with leverage. The figure also shows the pretax WACC, the WACC computed without taxes.

The Interest Tax Shield with a Target Debt-Equity Ratio

The decline of the WACC with leverage is an alternative way to view the tax benefits associated with debt financing. As we discuss further in Chapter 18, when a firm adjusts its leverage to maintain a target debt-equity ratio rather than maintain a permanent level of debt, we can compute its value with leverage, V^L, by discounting its free cash flow using

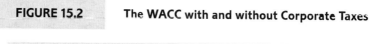

FIGURE 15.2   The WACC with and without Corporate Taxes

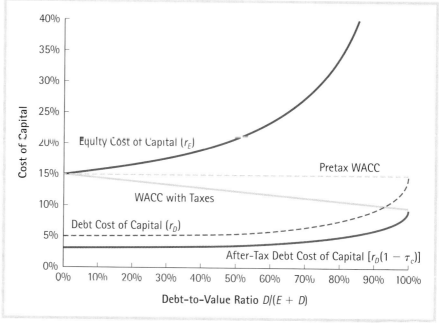

We compute the WACC as a function of leverage using Eq. 15.5. Without taxes the WACC is constant, as shown in Figure 14.1. With taxes, the WACC declines as the firm increases its reliance on debt financing and the interest tax shield grows. The figure assumes a marginal corporate income tax rate of $\tau_c = 35\%$.

the weighted average cost of capital. The value of the interest tax shield can be found by comparing V^L to the unlevered value, V^U, of the free cash flow discounted at the firm's unlevered cost of capital, the pretax WACC.[8]

EXAMPLE

15.3

Valuing the Interest Tax Shield with a Target Debt-Equity Ratio

Problem

Western Lumber Company expects to have free cash flow in the coming year of $4.25 million, and its free cash flow is expected to grow at a rate of 4% per year thereafter. Western Lumber has an equity cost of capital of 10% and a debt cost of capital of 6%, and it pays a corporate tax rate of 35%. If Western Lumber maintains a debt-equity ratio of 0.50, what is the value of its interest tax shield?

Solution

We can estimate the value of Western Lumber's interest tax shield by comparing its value with and without leverage. We compute its unlevered value by discounting its free cash flow at its pretax WACC:

$$\text{Pretax WACC} = \frac{E}{E+D}r_E + \frac{D}{E+D}r_D = \frac{1}{1+0.5}10\% + \frac{0.5}{1+0.5}6\% = 8.67\%$$

Because Western Lumber's free cash flow is expected to grow at a constant rate, we can value it as a constant growth perpetuity:

$$V^U = \frac{4.25}{8.67\% - 4\%} = \$91 \text{ million}$$

To compute Western Lumber's levered value, we calculate its WACC:

$$\text{WACC} = \frac{E}{E+D}r_E + \frac{D}{E+D}r_D(1 - \tau_c)$$

$$= \frac{1}{1+0.5}10\% + \frac{0.5}{1+0.5}6\%(1 - 0.35) = 7.97\%$$

Thus Western Lumber's value including the interest tax shield is

$$V^L = \frac{4.25}{7.97\% - 4\%} = \$107 \text{ million}$$

The value of the interest tax shield is therefore

$$PV(\text{Interest Tax Shield}) = V^L - V^U = 107 - 91 = \$16 \text{ million}$$

CONCEPT CHECK

1. With corporate taxes as the only market imperfection, how does the value of the firm with leverage differ from its value without leverage?

2. How does leverage affect a firm's weighted average cost of capital?

---

8. As we show in Chapter 18, if the firm adjusts its leverage to maintain a target debt-equity ratio or interest coverage ratio, then its pretax WACC remains constant and equal to its unlevered cost of capital. See Chapter 18 for a full discussion of the relationship between the firm's levered and unlevered costs of capital.

15.3 Recapitalizing to Capture the Tax Shield

When a firm makes a significant change to its capital structure, the transaction is called a recapitalization (or simply a "recap"). In Chapter 14, we introduced a leveraged recapitalization in which a firm issues a large amount of debt and uses the proceeds to pay a special dividend or to repurchase shares. Leveraged recaps were especially popular in the mid- to late-1980s, when many firms found that these transactions could reduce their tax payments.

Let's see how such a transaction might benefit current shareholders. Midco Industries has 20 million shares outstanding with a market price of $15 per share and no debt. Midco has had consistently stable earnings, and pays a 35% tax rate. Management plans to borrow $100 million on a permanent basis through a leveraged recap in which they would use the borrowed funds to repurchase outstanding shares. Their expectation is that the tax savings from this transaction will boost Midco's stock price and benefit shareholders. Let's see if this expectation is realistic.

The Tax Benefit

First, we examine the tax consequences of Midco's leveraged recap. Without leverage, Midco's total market value is the value of its unlevered equity. Assuming the current stock price is the fair price for the shares without leverage:

$$V^U = (20 \text{ million shares}) \times (\$15/\text{share}) = \$300 \text{ million}$$

With leverage, Midco will reduce its annual tax payments. If Midco borrows $100 million using permanent debt, the present value of the firm's future tax savings is

$$PV(\text{interest tax shield}) = \tau_c D = 35\% \times \$100 \text{ million} = \$35 \text{ million}$$

Thus the total value of the levered firm will be

$$V^L = V^U + \tau_c D = \$300 \text{ million} + \$35 \text{ million} = \$335 \text{ million}$$

This total value represents the combined value of the debt and the equity after the recapitalization. Because the value of the debt is $100 million, the value of the equity is

$$E = V^L - D = \$335 \text{ million} - \$100 \text{ million} = \$235 \text{ million}$$

While total firm value has increased, the value of equity dropped after the recap. How do shareholders benefit from this transaction?

Even though the value of the shares outstanding drops to $235 million, shareholders will also receive the $100 million that Midco will pay out through the share repurchase. In total, they will receive the full $335 million, a gain of $35 million over the value of their shares without leverage. Let's trace the details of the share repurchase and see how it leads to an increase in the stock price.

The Share Repurchase

Suppose Midco repurchases its shares at their current price of $15 per share. The firm will repurchase $100 million ÷ $15 per share = 6.67 million shares, and it will then have 20 − 6.67 = 13.33 million shares outstanding. Because the total value of equity is $235 million, the new share price is

$$\frac{\$235 \text{ million}}{13.33 \text{ million shares}} = \$17.625$$

The shareholders who keep their shares earn a capital gain of $17.625 − $15 = $2.625 per share, for a total gain of

$$\$2.625/\text{share} \times 13.33 \text{ million shares} = \$35 \text{ million}$$

In this case, the shareholders who remain after the recap receive the benefit of the tax shield. However, you may have noticed something odd in the previous calculations. We assumed that Midco was able to repurchase the shares at the initial price of $15 per share, and then demonstrated that the shares would be worth $17.625 after the transaction. Why would a shareholder agree to sell the shares for $15 when they are worth $17.625?

No Arbitrage Pricing

The previous scenario represents an arbitrage opportunity. Investors could *buy* shares for $15 immediately before the repurchase, and they could sell these shares immediately afterward at a higher price. But this activity would raise the share price above $15 even before the repurchase: Once investors know the recap will occur, the share price will rise immediately to a level that reflects the $35 million value of the interest tax shield that the firm will receive. That is, the value of the Midco's equity will rise *immediately* from $300 million to $335 million. With 20 million shares outstanding, the share price will rise to

$$\$335 \text{ million} \div 20 \text{ million shares} = \$16.75 \text{ per share}$$

Midco must offer at least this price to repurchase the shares.

With a repurchase price of $16.75, the shareholders who tender their shares and the shareholders who hold their shares both gain $16.75 − $15 = $1.75 per share as a result of the transaction. The benefit of the interest tax shield goes to all 20 million of the original shares outstanding for a total benefit of $1.75/share × 20 million shares = $35 million. In other words,

When securities are fairly priced, the original shareholders of a firm capture the full benefit of the interest tax shield from an increase in leverage.

EXAMPLE 15.4

Alternative Repurchase Prices

Problem
Suppose Midco announces a price at which it will repurchase $100 million worth of its shares. Show that $16.75 is the lowest price it could offer and expect shareholders to tender their shares. How will the benefits be divided if Midco offers more than $16.75 per share?

Solution
For each repurchase price, we can compute the number of shares Midco will repurchase, as well as the number of shares that will remain after the share repurchase. Dividing the $235 million total value of equity by the number of remaining shares gives Midco's new share price after the transaction. No shareholders will be willing to sell their shares unless the repurchase price is at least as high as the share price after the transaction; otherwise, they would be better off waiting to sell their shares. As the table shows, the repurchase price must be at least $16.75 for shareholders to be willing to sell rather than waiting to receive a higher price.

Repurchase Price ($/share)	Shares Repurchased (million)	Shares Remaining (million)	New Share Price ($/share)
P_R	$R = 100/P_R$	$N = 20 - R$	$P_N = 235/N$
15.00	6.67	13.33	$17.63
16.25	6.15	13.85	16.97
16.75	5.97	14.03	16.75
17.25	5.80	14.20	16.55
17.50	5.71	14.29	16.45

If Midco offers a price above $16.75, then all existing shareholders will be eager to sell their shares, because the shares will have a lower value after the transaction is completed. In this case, Midco's offer to repurchase shares will be oversubscribed and Midco will need to use a lottery or some other rationing mechanism to choose from whom it will repurchase shares. In that case, more of the benefits of the recap will go to the shareholders who are lucky enough to be selected for the repurchase.

Analyzing the Recap: The Market Value Balance Sheet

We can analyze the recapitalization using the market value balance sheet, a tool we developed in Chapter 14. It states that the total market value of a firm's securities must equal the total market value of the firm's assets. In the presence of corporate taxes, *we must include the interest tax shield as one of the firm's assets.*

We analyze the leveraged recap by breaking this transaction into steps, as shown in Table 15.2. First, the recap is announced. At this point, investors anticipate the future interest tax shield, raising the value of Midco's assets by $35 million. Next, Midco issues

TABLE 15.2   **Market Value Balance Sheet for the Steps in Midco's Leveraged Recapitalization**

Market Value Balance Sheet ($ million)	Initial	Step 1: Recap Announced	Step 2: Debt Issuance	Step 3: Share Repurchase
Assets				
Cash	0	0	100	0
Original assets (V^U)	300	300	300	300
Interest tax shield	0	35	35	35
Total assets	300	335	435	335
Liabilities				
Debt	0	0	100	100
Equity = Assets − Liabilities	300	335	335	235
Shares outstanding (million)	20	20	20	14.03
Price per share	$15.00	$16.75	$16.75	$16.75

$100 million in new debt, increasing both Midco's cash and liabilities by that amount. Finally, Midco uses the cash to repurchase shares at their market price of $16.75. In this step, Midco's cash declines, as does the number of shares outstanding.

Note that the share price rises at the announcement of the recap. This increase in the share price is due solely to the present value of the (anticipated) interest tax shield. Thus, even though leverage reduces the total value of equity, shareholders capture the benefits of the interest tax shield upfront.[9]

CONCEPT CHECK

1. How can shareholders benefit from a leveraged recap when it reduces the total value of equity?

2. How does the interest tax shield enter into the maket value balance sheet?

15.4 Personal Taxes

So far, we have looked at the benefits of leverage with regard to the taxes a corporation must pay. By reducing a firm's corporate tax liability, debt allows the firm to pay more of its cash flows to investors.

Unfortunately for investors, after they receive the cash flows, they are generally taxed again. For individuals, interest payments received from debt are taxed as income. Equity investors also must pay taxes on dividends and capital gains. What are the consequences to firm value of these additional taxes?

Including Personal Taxes in the Interest Tax Shield

The value of a firm is equal to the amount of money the firm can raise by issuing securities. The amount of money an investor will pay for a security ultimately depends on the benefits the investor will receive—namely, the cash flows the investor will receive *after all taxes have been paid.* Thus, just like corporate taxes, personal taxes reduce the cash flows to investors and diminish firm value. As a result, the actual interest tax shield depends on the reduction in the total taxes (both corporate and personal) that are paid.[10]

Personal taxes have the potential to offset some of the corporate tax benefits of leverage that we have described. In particular, in the United States and many other countries, interest income has historically been taxed more heavily than capital gains from equity. Table 15.3 shows recent top federal tax rates in the United States. The average rate on equity income listed in the table is an average of the top capital gains and dividend tax rates.

To determine the true tax benefit of leverage, we need to evaluate the combined effect of both corporate and personal taxes. Consider a firm with $1 of earnings before interest and taxes. The firm can either pay this $1 to debt holders as interest, or it can pay the $1 to equity holders directly, as a dividend, or indirectly, by retaining it so that shareholders receive the $1 through a capital gain. Figure 15.3 shows the tax consequences of each option.

---

9. We are ignoring other potential side effects of leverage, such as costs of future financial distress. We discuss such costs in Chapter 16.

10. This point was made most forcefully in yet another path-breaking article by Merton Miller, "Debt and Taxes," *Journal of Finance* 32 (1977): 261–275. See also Merton H. Miller and Myron S. Scholes, "Dividends and Taxes," *Journal of Financial Economics* (December 1978): 333–364.

TABLE 15.3   **Top Federal Tax Rates in the United States, 1971–2005**

| Year | Corporate Tax Rate[†] | Personal Tax Rates[*] | | | |
		Interest Income	Average Rate on Equity Income	Dividends	Capital Gains
1971–1978	48%	70%	53%	70%	35%
1979–1981	46%	70%	49%	70%	28%
1982–1986	46%	50%	35%	50%	20%
1987	40%	39%	33%	39%	28%
1988–1990	34%	28%	28%	28%	28%
1991–1992	34%	31%	30%	31%	28%
1993–1996	35%	40%	34%	40%	28%
1997–2000	35%	40%	30%	40%	20%
2001–2002	35%	39%	30%	39%	20%
2003–2005	35%	35%	15%	15%	15%

[*]Interest income is taxed as ordinary income. Until 2003, dividends were also taxed as ordinary income. The average tax rate on equity income is an average of dividend and capital gain tax rates (consistent with a 50% dividend payout ratio and annual realization of capital gains), where the capital gain tax rate is the long-term rate applicable to assets hold more than one year.

[†]The corporate rate shown is for C corporations with the highest level of income. Marginal rates can be higher for lower brackets. (For example, since 2000, the 35% tax rate applies to income levels above $18.3 million, while the tax rate for income levels between $100,000 and $335,000 is 39%.)

FIGURE 15.3

After-Tax Investor Cash Flows Resulting from $1 in EBIT

Interest income is taxed at rate τ_i for the investor. Dividend or capital gain income is taxed at rate τ_c for the corporation, and again at rate τ_e for the investor.

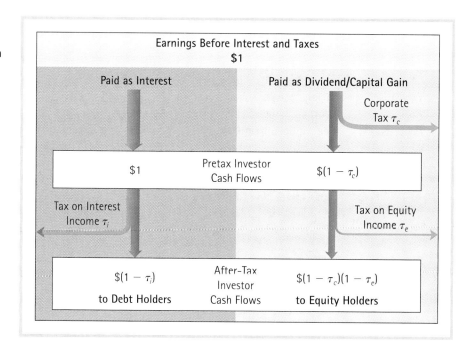

Using 2005 tax rates, debt offers a clear tax advantage with respect to corporate taxes: For every $1 in pretax cash flows that debt holders receive, equity holders receive $\tau_c = 35\%$ less under current tax rates. But at the personal level, the income tax rate on interest income is $\tau_i = 35\%$, whereas the tax rate on equity income is only $\tau_e = 15\%$. Combining corporate and personal rates leads to the following comparison:

	After-Tax Cash Flows	**Using Current Tax Rates**
To debt holders	$(1 - \tau_i)$	$(1 - 0.35) = 0.65$
To equity holders	$(1 - \tau_c)(1 - \tau_e)$	$(1 - 0.35)(1 - 0.15) = 0.5525$

While a tax advantage to debt remains, it is not as large as we calculated based on corporate taxes alone. To express the comparison in relative terms, note that equity holders receive

$$\tau^* = \frac{0.65 - 0.5525}{0.65} = 15\%$$

less after taxes than debt holders. In this case, personal taxes reduce the tax advantage of debt from 35% to 15%.

In general, every $1 received after taxes by debt holders from interest payments costs equity holders $\$(1 - \tau^*)$ on an after-tax basis, where

Effective Tax Advantage of Debt

$$\tau^* = \frac{(1 - \tau_i) - (1 - \tau_c)(1 - \tau_e)}{(1 - \tau_i)} = 1 - \frac{(1 - \tau_c)(1 - \tau_e)}{(1 - \tau_i)} \tag{15.7}$$

When there are no personal taxes, or when the personal tax rates on debt and equity income are the same $(\tau_i = \tau_e)$, this formula reduces to $\tau^* = \tau_c$. But when equity income is taxed less heavily $(\tau_i > \tau_e)$, then τ^* is less than τ_c.

EXAMPLE 15.5

Calculating the Effective Tax Advantage of Debt

Problem
What was the effective tax advantage of debt in 1980? In 1990?

Solution
Using Eq. 15.7 and the tax rates in Table 15.3, we can calculate

$$\tau^*_{1980} = 1 - \frac{(1 - 0.46)(1 - 0.49)}{(1 - 0.70)} = 8.2\%$$

$$\tau^*_{1990} = 1 - \frac{(1 - 0.34)(1 - 0.28)}{(1 - 0.28)} = 34\%$$

Given the tax rates at the time, the effective tax advantage of debt was much lower in 1980 than in 1990.

Figure 15.4 depicts the effective tax advantage of debt since 1971 in the United States. It has varied widely over time with changes in the tax code.

The Effective Tax Advantage of Debt with and without Personal Taxes, 1971–2005

After adjusting for personal taxes, the tax advantage of debt τ^* is generally below τ_c, but still positive. It has also varied widely with changes to the tax code.

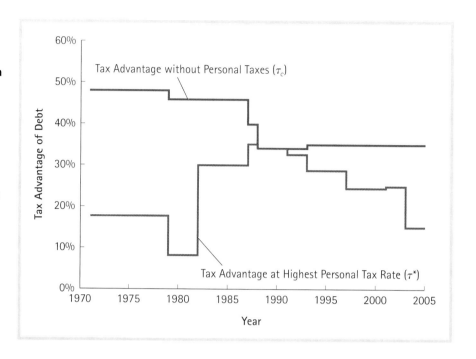

Valuing the Interest Tax Shield with Personal Taxes

How does the foregoing analysis of personal taxes affect our valuation of the debt tax shield? We postpone a detailed answer to this question until Chapter 18, and limit our discussion here to a few important observations. First, as long as $\tau^* > 0$, then despite any tax disadvantage of debt at the personal level, a net tax advantage for leverage remains. In the case of permanent debt, the value of the firm with leverage becomes

$$V^L = V^U + \tau^* D \tag{15.8}$$

Because the personal tax disadvantage of debt generally implies $\tau^* < \tau_c$, comparing Eq. 15.8 with Eq. 15.4 we see that the benefit of leverage is reduced.

Personal taxes have a similar, but indirect, effect on the firm's weighted average cost of capital. While we still compute the WACC using the corporate tax rate τ_c as in Eq. 15.5, with personal taxes the firm's equity and debt costs of capital will adjust to compensate investors for their respective tax burdens. The net result is that a personal tax disadvantage for debt causes the WACC to decline more slowly with leverage than it otherwise would.

Estimating the Interest Tax Shield with Personal Taxes

Problem
Estimate the value of Midco after its $100 million leveraged recap, accounting for personal taxes in 2005.

Solution

Given $\tau^* = 15\%$ in 2005, and given Midco's current value $V^U = \$300$ million, we estimate $V^L = V^U + \tau^* D = \$300$ million $+ 15\%(\$100$ million$) = \$315$ million. With 20 million original shares outstanding, the stock price would increase by $\$15$ million $\div$ 20 million shares $= \$0.75$ per share.

Determining the Actual Tax Advantage of Debt

In estimating the effective tax advantage of debt after taking personal taxes into account, we made several assumptions that may need adjustment when determining the actual tax benefit for a particular firm or investor.

First, with regard to the capital gains tax rate, we assumed that investors paid capital gains taxes every year. But unlike taxes on interest income or dividends, which are paid annually, capital gains taxes are paid only at the time the investor sells the stock and realizes the gain. Deferring the payment of capital gains taxes lowers the present value of the taxes, which can be interpreted as a lower *effective* capital gains tax rate. For example, given a capital gains tax rate of 15% and an interest rate of 6%, holding the asset for 10 more years lowers the effective tax rate this year to $(15\%)/1.06^{10} = 8.4\%$. Also, investors with accrued losses that they can use to offset gains face a zero effective capital gains tax rate. As a consequence, investors with longer holding periods or with accrued losses face a lower tax rate on equity income, decreasing the effective tax advantage of debt.

A second key assumption in our analysis is the computation of the tax rate on equity income τ_e. Using the average dividend and capital gains tax rate is reasonable for a firm that pays out 50% of its earnings as dividends, so that shareholder gains from additional earnings were evenly split between dividends and capital gains. For firms with much higher or much lower payout ratios, however, this average would not be accurate. For

Cutting the Dividend Tax Rate

In January 2003, President George W. Bush unveiled a proposal to boost the U.S. economy with a $674 billion tax cut plan, half of which would come from eliminating taxes on dividends. From the moment it was announced, this tax cut generated tremendous controversy.

Proponents argued that easing the tax bite on investors' dividend income would boost the stock market and stimulate the sluggish economy. Critics quickly denounced it as a tax cut for the rich. But one of the underlying motives of the plan, authored in large part by economist R. Glenn Hubbard, was to end the current distortion in tax laws that encourages companies to accumulate debt because interest is deductible but dividend payments are not.

Levying taxes both on corporate earnings and on the dividends or capital gains paid to investors is known as

double taxation. The lower rates on capital gains have provided some relief from double taxation. In 2002, however, dividends were still taxed at the same rate as ordinary income, leading to a combined tax rate in excess of 60% on dividends—one of the highest tax rates on dividends of any industrialized nation. As we have seen, this double taxation results in a tax advantage to debt financing.

Ultimately, policy makers agreed to a compromise that reduced the tax rate for individuals on both dividends (for stocks held for more than 60 days) and capital gains (for assets held for more than one year) to 15%. This compromise, set to expire in 2008, still gives a tax advantage to debt, but at a decreased level from prior years (see Figure 15.4).

example, for firms that do not pay dividends, the capital gains tax rate should be used as the tax rate on equity income.

Finally, we assumed the top marginal federal income tax rates for the investor. In reality, rates vary for individual investors, and many investors face lower rates. (We have also ignored state taxes, which vary widely by state and have an additional impact.) At lower rates, the effects of personal taxes are less substantial. Moreover, *many investors face no personal taxes*. Consider investments held in retirement savings accounts or pension funds that are not subject to taxes.[11] For these investors, the effective tax advantage of debt is $\tau^* = \tau_c$, the full corporate tax rate. This full tax advantage would also apply to securities dealers for whom interest, dividends, and capital gains are all taxed equivalently as income.

What is the bottom line? Calculating the effective tax advantage of debt accurately is extremely difficult, and this advantage will vary across firms (and from investor to investor). A firm must consider the tax bracket of its typical debt holders to estimate τ_i, and the tax bracket and holding period of its typical equity holders to determine τ_e. If, for instance, a firm's investors hold shares primarily through their retirement accounts, $\tau^* \approx \tau_c$. While τ^* is likely to be somewhat below τ_c for the typical firm, exactly how much lower is open to debate. Our calculation of τ^* in Figure 15.4 should be interpreted as a very rough guide at best.[12]

CONCEPT CHECK   1. Why is there a personal tax disadvantage of debt?

2. How does the personal tax disadvantage of debt change the value of leverage for the firm?

15.5 Optimal Capital Structure with Taxes

In Modigliani and Miller's setting of perfect capital markets, firms could use any combination of debt and equity to finance their investments without changing the value of the firm. In effect, any capital structure was optimal. In this chapter we have seen that taxes change that conclusion because interest payments create a valuable tax shield. Even after adjusting for personal taxes, the value of a firm with leverage exceeds the value of an unlevered firm, and there is a tax advantage to using debt financing.

Do Firms Prefer Debt?

Do firms show a preference for debt in practice? Figure 15.5 illustrates the net new issues of equity and debt by U.S. corporations. For equity, the figure shows the total amount of new equity issued, less the amount retired through share repurchases and acquisitions. For debt, it shows the total amount of new borrowing less the amount of loans repaid.

Figure 15.5 makes clear that when firms raise new capital from investors, they do so primarily by issuing debt. In fact, in most years aggregate equity issues are negative, meaning that firms are reducing the amount of equity outstanding by buying shares. (This

---

11. Evidence from the mid-1990s suggests that the growth in pension funds has lowered the average marginal tax rate for investors to about half the rates shown in Table 15.3. See James Poterba, "The Rate of Return to Corporate Capital and Factor Shares: New Estimates Using Revised National Income Accounts and Capital Stock Data," NBER working paper no. 6263 (1997).

12. For a discussion of methods of estimating τ^* and the need to include personal taxes, see John R. Graham, "Do Personal Taxes Affect Corporate Financing Decisions?" *Journal of Public Economics* 73 (August 1999): 147–185.

FIGURE 15.5

Net External Financing and Capital Expenditures by U.S. Corporations, 1975–2005

In aggregate, firms have raised external capital primarily by issuing debt. These funds have been used to retire equity and fund investment, but the vast majority of capital expenditures are internally funded.

Source: Federal Reserve, *Flow of Funds Accounts of the United States*, 2005.

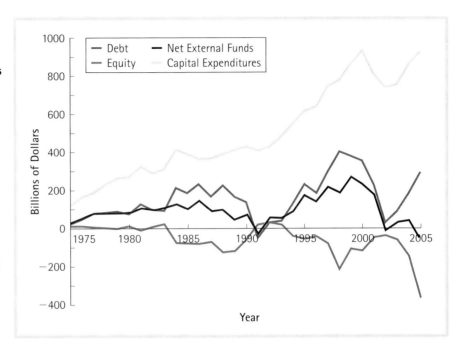

observation does not mean that *all* firms raised funds using debt. Many firms may have sold equity to raise funds. However, at the same time other firms were buying or repurchasing an equal amount so that, in aggregate, no new equity financing occurred.) The data show a clear preference for debt as a source of external financing for the total population of U.S. firms.

While firms seem to prefer debt when raising external funds, not all investment is externally funded. As Figure 15.5 also shows, capital expenditures greatly exceed firms' external financing, implying that most investment and growth is supported by internally generated funds, such as retained earnings. Thus, even though firms have not *issued* new equity, the market value of equity has risen over time as firms have grown. In fact, as shown in Figure 15.6, debt as a fraction of firm value has varied in a range from 30–45% for the average firm. The average debt-to-value ratio fell during the 1990s bull market, with the trend reversing only when the stock market and interest rates declined from 2000 through 2003.

While debt accounted for about 36% of the capital structure of the average firm in 2005, the use of debt also varied greatly by industry. Figure 15.7 shows debt as a fraction of firm value for a number of industries and the overall market. Clearly, there are large differences across industries. Firms in growth industries like biotechnology or high technology carry very little debt, whereas airlines, automakers, utilities, and financial firms have high leverage ratios. Thus the differences in the leverage ratios of Amgen and Navistar International noted in the introduction to this chapter are not unique to these firms, but rather are typical of their respective industries.

These data raise important questions. If debt provides a tax advantage that lowers a firm's weighted average cost of capital and increases firm value, why does debt make up less than half of the capital structure of most firms? And why does the leverage choice vary so much across industries? To begin to answer these questions, let's consider a bit more carefully what the optimal capital structure is from a tax perspective.

Debt-to-Value Ratio [$D/(E + D)$] of U.S. Firms, 1975–2005

Although firms have primarily issued debt rather than equity, the average proportion of debt in their capital structures has not increased due to the growth in value of existing equity.

Source: Compustat and Federal Reserve, *Flow of Funds Accounts of the United States*, 2005.

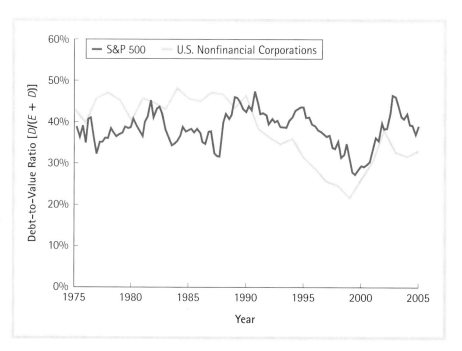

Limits to the Tax Benefit of Debt

To receive the full tax benefits of leverage, a firm need not use 100% debt financing. A firm receives a tax benefit only if it is paying taxes in the first place. That is, the firm must have taxable earnings. This constraint may limit the amount of debt needed as a tax shield.

To determine the optimal level of leverage, compare the three leverage choices shown in Table 15.4 for a firm with earnings before interest and taxes (EBIT) equal to $1000 and a corporate tax rate of $\tau_c = 35\%$. With no leverage, the firm owes tax of $350 on the full $1000 of EBIT. If the firm has high leverage with interest payments equal to $1000, then it can shield its earnings from taxes, thereby saving the $350 in taxes. Now consider a third case, in which the firm has excess leverage so that interest payments exceed EBIT. In this case, the firm has a net operating loss, but there is no increase in the tax savings. Because the firm is paying no taxes already, there is no immediate tax shield from the excess leverage.[13]

Thus no corporate tax benefit arises from incurring interest payments that regularly exceed EBIT. And, because interest payments constitute a tax disadvantage at the investor level as discussed in Section 15.4, investors will pay higher personal taxes with excess leverage, making them worse off.[14] We can quantify the tax disadvantage for excess interest

---

13. If the firm paid taxes during the prior two years, it could "carry back" the current year's net operating loss to apply for a refund of some of those taxes. Alternatively, the firm could "carry forward" the net operating loss up to 20 years to shield future income from taxes (although waiting to receive the credit reduces its present value). Thus there can be a tax benefit from interest in excess of EBIT if it does not occur on a regular basis. For simplicity, we ignore carrybacks and carryforwards in this discussion.

14. Of course, another problem can arise from having excess leverage: The firm may not be able to afford the excess interest and could be forced to default on the loan. We discuss financial distress (and its potential costs) in Chapter 16.

FIGURE 15.7

**Debt-to-Value Ratio
[D/(E + D)] for Select
Industries**

Debt levels are determined
by book values, and equity
by market values. The
average debt financing for
all U.S. stocks was about
36%, but note the large
differences by industry.

Source: Reuters, 2005.

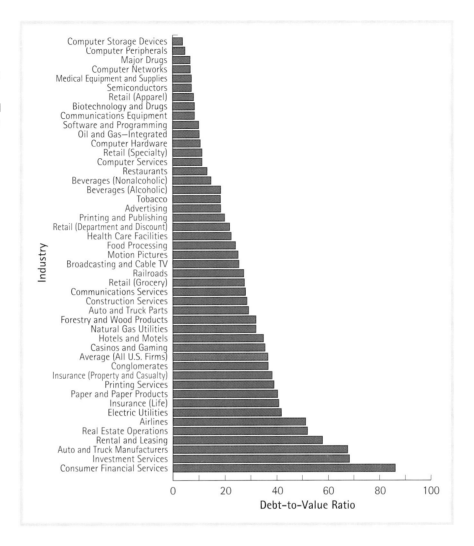

TABLE 15.4   **Tax Savings with Different Amounts of Leverage**

	No Leverage	High Leverage	Excess Leverage
EBIT	$1,000	$1,000	$1,000
Interest expense	0	−1,000	−1,100
Income before tax	1,000	0	0
Taxes (35%)	−350	0	0
Net income	650	0	−100
Tax savings from leverage	$0	$350	$350

payments by setting $\tau_c = 0$ (assuming there is no reduction in the corporate tax for excess interest payments) in Eq. 15.7 for τ^*:

$$\tau_{ex}^* = 1 - \frac{(1 - \tau_e)}{(1 - \tau_i)} = \frac{\tau_e - \tau_i}{(1 - \tau_i)} < 0 \qquad (15.9)$$

Note that τ_{ex}^* is negative because equity is taxed less heavily than interest for investors $(\tau_e < \tau_i)$. At 2005 tax rates, this disadvantage is

$$\tau_{ex}^* = \frac{15\% - 35\%}{(1 - 35\%)} = -30.8\%$$

Therefore, the optimal level of leverage from a tax saving perspective is the level such that interest equals EBIT. The firm shields all of its taxable income, and it does not have any tax-disadvantaged excess interest. Figure 15.8 shows the tax savings at different levels of interest payments when EBIT equals $1000 with certainty. In this case, an interest payment of $1000 maximizes the tax savings.

Of course, it is unlikely that a firm can predict its future EBIT precisely. If there is uncertainty regarding EBIT, then with a higher interest expense there is a greater risk that interest will exceed EBIT. As a result, the tax savings for high levels of interest falls, possibly reducing the optimal level of the interest payment, as shown in Figure 15.8.[15] In general, as a firm's interest expense approaches its expected taxable earnings, the marginal tax advantage of debt declines, limiting the amount of debt the firm should use.

FIGURE 15.8

Tax Savings for Different Levels of Interest

When EBIT is known with certainty, the tax savings is maximized if the interest expense is equal to EBIT. When EBIT is uncertain, the tax savings declines for high levels of interest because of the risk that the interest payment will be in excess of EBIT.

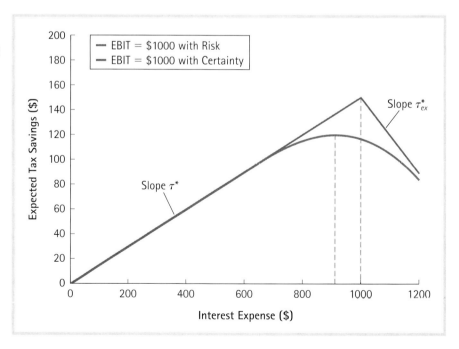

---

15. Details of how to compute the optimal level of debt when earnings are risky can be found in a paper by John Graham, "How Big Are the Tax Benefits of Debt?" *Journal of Finance* 55(5) (October 2000): 1901–1941.

Growth and Debt

In a tax-optimal capital structure, the level of interest payments depends on the level of EBIT. What does this conclusion tell us about the optimal fraction of debt in a firm's capital structure?

If we examine young technology or biotechnology firms, we often find that these firms do not have any taxable income. Their value comes mainly from the prospect that they will produce high future profits. A biotech firm might be developing drugs with tremendous potential, but it has yet to receive any revenue from these drugs. Such a firm will not have taxable earnings. In that case, a tax-optimal capital structure does not include debt. We would expect such a firm to finance its investments with equity alone. Only later, when the firm matures and becomes profitable, will it have taxable cash flows. At that time it should add debt to its capital structure.

Even for a firm with positive earnings, growth will affect the optimal leverage ratio. To avoid excess interest, this type of firm should have debt with interest payments that are below its expected taxable earnings:

$$\text{Interest} = r_D \times \text{Debt} \leq \text{EBIT} \quad \text{or} \quad \text{Debt} \leq EBIT / r_D$$

That is, from a tax perspective, the firm's optimal level of debt is proportional to its current earnings. However, the value of the firm's equity will depend on the growth rate of earnings: The higher the growth rate, the higher the value of equity (and equivalently, the higher the firm's price-earnings multiple). As a result, *the optimal proportion of debt in the firm's capital structure* $[D/(E + D)]$ *will be lower, the higher the firm's growth rate.*[16]

Other Tax Shields

Up to this point, we have assumed that interest is the only means by which firms can shield earnings from corporate taxes. But there are numerous other provisions in the tax laws for deductions and tax credits, such as depreciation, investment tax credits, carry-forwards of past operating losses, and the like. For example, many high-tech firms paid little or no taxes in the late 1990's because of tax deductions related to employee stock options (see box, next page). To the extent that a firm has other tax shields, its taxable earnings will be reduced and it will rely less heavily on the interest tax shield.[17]

The Low Leverage Puzzle

Do firms choose capital structures that fully exploit the tax advantages of debt? The results of this section imply that to evaluate this question, we should compare the level of firms' interest payments to their taxable income, rather than simply consider the fraction of debt in their capital structures. Figure 15.9 compares interest expenses and EBIT for firms in the S&P 500. It reveals two important patterns. First, firms have used debt to shield a greater percentage of their earnings from taxes in recent years than they did in the 1970s and early 1980s. This pattern mirrors the increase in the effective tax advantage of debt

---

16. This explanation for the low leverage of high growth firms is developed in a paper by J. L. Berens and C. J. Cuny, "The Capital Structure Puzzle Revisited," *Review of Financial Studies* 8(4) (Winter 1995): 1185–1208.

17. See H. DeAngelo and R. Masulis, "Optimal Capital Structure Under Corporate and Personal Taxation," *Journal of Financial Economics* 8 (March 1980): 3–27. For a discussion of methods to estimate a firm's marginal tax rate to account for these effects, see John R. Graham, "Proxies for the Corporate Marginal Tax Rate," *Journal of Financial Economics* 42 (April 1996): 187–221.

Employee Stock Options

Employee stock options can serve as an important tax shield for some firms. The typical employee stock option allows employees of a firm to buy the firm's stock at a discounted price (often, the price of the stock when they started employment). When an employee exercises a stock option, the firm is essentially selling shares to the employee at a discount. If the discount is large, the employee can exercise the option and earn a large profit.

The amount of the discount is a cost for the firm's equity holders because selling shares at a price below their market value dilutes the value of the firm's shares. To reflect this cost, the IRS allows firms to deduct the amount of the discount from their earnings for tax purposes. (The IRS taxes employees on the gain, so the tax burden does not go away, but moves from the firm to the employees.) Unlike the interest tax shield, the tax deduction from employee stock options does not add to the value of the firm. If the same amounts were paid to employees through salary rather than options, the firm would be able to deduct the extra salary from its taxable income as well. Until recently, however, employee stock options did not affect EBIT, so that EBIT overstated the taxable income of firms with option expenses.

During the stock market boom of the late 1990s, many technology firms and other firms that issued a large number of employee stock options were able to claim these deductions and lower their taxes relative to what one would naively have imputed from EBIT. In 2000, some of the most profitable companies in the United States (based on net income), such as Microsoft, Cisco Systems, Dell, and QUALCOMM, had *no* taxable income—using the stock option deduction, they were able to report a loss for tax purposes.[*] A recent study by J. R. Graham, M. H. Lang, and D. A. Shackelford[†] reported that in 2000, stock option deductions for the entire Nasdaq 100 exceeded aggregate pretax earnings. For these firms, there would have been no tax advantage associated with debt—which may help explain why they used little to no debt financing.

Under new accounting rules, firms are required to expense employee stock options. However, the rules for expensing the options are not the same as the tax deduction. As a consequence, even after this rule change, stock options may continue to result in a significant difference between firms' accounting income and their income for tax purposes.

---

[*]See M. Sullivan, "Stock Options Take $50 Billion Bite Out of Corporate Taxes," *Tax Notes* (March 18, 2002): 1396–1401.

[†]"Employee Stock Options, Corporate Taxes and Debt Policy," *Journal of Finance* 59 (2004): 1585–1618.

---

shown in Figure 15.4. Second, firms shield only about one-third of their earnings in this way. That is, firms have far less leverage than our analysis of the interest tax shield would predict.[18]

This low level of leverage is not unique to U.S. firms. Table 15.5 shows international leverage levels from a 1995 study by Raghuram Rajan and Luigi Zingales using 1990 data. Note that firms worldwide have similar low proportions of debt financing, with firms in the United Kingdom exhibiting especially low leverage. Also, with the exception of Italy and Canada, firms shield less than half of their taxable income using interest payments. The corporate tax codes are similar across all countries in terms of the tax advantage of debt. Personal tax rates vary more significantly, however, leading to greater variation in τ^*.

Why are firms under-leveraged? Either firms are content to pay more taxes than necessary rather than maximize shareholder value, or there is more to the capital structure story than we have uncovered so far. While some firms may deliberately choose a suboptimal capital structure, it is hard to accept that most firms are acting suboptimally. The

---

18. Additional evidence is provided by John Graham in "How Big Are the Tax Benefits of Debt?" *Journal of Finance* 55(5) (October 2000): 1901–1941, where he estimates that the typical firm exploits less than half of the potential tax benefits of debt.

FIGURE 15.9

Interest Payments as a Percentage of EBIT for S&P 500 Firms, 1975–2005

While firms have increased their use of the interest tax shield since the 1970s, they still shield less than 50% of their taxable income in this way.

Source: Compustat.

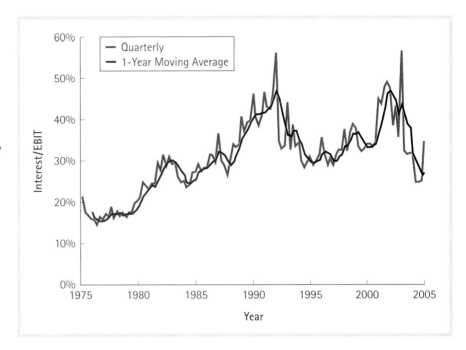

TABLE 15.5   **International Leverage and Tax Rates (1990)**

Country	$D/(E + D)$	Net of Cash $D/(E + D)$	Interest/EBIT	τ_c	τ^*
United States	28%	23%	41%	34.0%	34.0%
Japan	29%	17%	41%	37.5%	31.5%
Germany	23%	15%	31%	50.0%	3.3%
France	41%	28%	38%	37.0%	7.8%
Italy	46%	36%	55%	36.0%	18.6%
United Kingdom	19%	11%	21%	35.0%	24.2%
Canada	35%	32%	65%	38.0%	28.9%

Source: R. Rajan and L. Zingales, "What Do We Know About Capital Structure? Some Evidence from International Data," *Journal of Finance* 50(5) (December 1995): 1421–1460. Data is for median firms and top marginal tax rates.

consensus of so many managers in choosing low levels of leverage suggests that debt financing has other costs that prevent firms from using the interest tax shield fully.

Talk to financial managers and they will quickly point out a key cost of debt missing from our analysis: Increasing the level of debt increases the probability of bankruptcy. Aside from taxes, another important difference between debt and equity financing is that debt payments *must* be made to avoid bankruptcy, whereas firms have no similar obligation to pay dividends or realize capital gains. If bankruptcy is costly, these costs might offset the tax advantages of debt financing. We explore the role of financial bankruptcy costs and other market imperfections in Chapter 16.

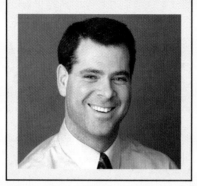

A ndrew Balson is a Managing Director of Bain Capital, a leading private investment firm with nearly $40 billion in assets under management. Prior to joining the firm in 1996, he was a consultant at Bain & Company. Bain Capital specializes in leveraged buyout (LBO) transactions, in which a firm is purchased and recapitalized with debt-to-value ratios often exceeding 70%. Bain Capital has invested in many well-known companies including Domino's Pizza, Burger King, Dunkin' Brands, Sealy Mattress Company, Michael's Stores, Toys 'R Us and many others. Bain Capital is a participant in the $33 billion proposed LBO of HCA Inc., the largest LBO in history.

QUESTION: *What is the role of private investment firms such as Bain Capital, and what types of firms make the best LBO candidates?*

ANSWER: Our business serves as an alternate capital market for companies that don't really belong as public companies, either during a transition period or permanently, and don't have a logical fit within another larger corporation. In that context, we've done buyouts for companies across many different industries and types. There really isn't one particular type that is best. We look for companies that are well-positioned in their industries, have advantages relative to their competitors, and provide real value to their customers. Some may be underperforming but change can enable them to turn around. Others may be performing well but could do even better. Perhaps the management team has not been given appropriate incentives, or the company has not been optimized or managed aggressively enough. Occasionally, we find a company we can buy at a low price compared to its inherent value. That was a big part of our business 10 years ago but is less so today. We pay relatively full valuations compared to the company's current earnings. What makes this work is our ability to improve current earnings or cash flow.

QUESTION: *How does leverage affect risk and return for investors?*

ANSWER: Based on my experience, if we've found interesting companies where we can change the profit trajectory, leverage will ultimately serve to magnify both the impact of the investments we make and the returns for our investors. Over the past 20 years, the Bain Capital portfolio has far outperformed any equity benchmarks. That performance comes from improved operating profits that are magnified by leverage. Growth is an important driver of our success, so we strive to create efficient capital structures that complement our strategy and enable us to invest in business opportunities. The line between too much and not enough is not distinct, however. We try to use as much debt as we can without changing how our management teams run our businesses.

QUESTION: *What are the potential tax advantages of debt, and can leverage decisions be strategic as well, affecting a firm's competitive position in the product market?*

ANSWER: In today's capital markets, we consider debt a cheaper form of capital than equity—even on a pretax basis. The tax deductibility of interest makes the net cost of debt even cheaper. While the amount of debt matters, so do the terms of the debt. Since the late 1980s, the terms of debt have changed to require less amortization and also fewer covenants, putting less financial pressure on companies. Thus we can create operating value with what traditional markets would consider relatively high leverage. Most of the high returns we earn are from improved profits, not financial engineering. A flexible debt structure enables us to invest in our businesses while at the same time enjoy the equity return benefits of leverage.

We view leverage differently from the public markets. We've run many companies successfully with high levels of leverage. When we take that company public, however, we are advised to pay off much of the debt first and run them on a relatively unlevered basis. Either we were wrong having that level of debt, or the public markets are wrong in valuing companies based on lower leverage. We believe that many public companies are miscapitalized. Our ability to use leverage in many instances makes our overall cost of capital lower than that of the public markets, even though our equity returns are higher.

CONCEPT CHECK **1.** How does the growth rate of a firm affect the optimal fraction of debt in the capital structure?

2. Do firms choose capital structures that fully exploit the tax advantages of debt?

Summary

1. Because interest expense is tax deductible, leverage increases the total amount of income available to all investors.

2. The gain to investors from the tax deductibility of interest payments is called the interest tax shield.

$$\text{Interest Tax Shield} = \text{Corporate Tax Rate} \times \text{Interest Payments} \qquad (15.1)$$

3. When we consider corporate taxes, the total value of a levered firm equals the value of an unlevered firm plus the present value of the interest tax shield.

$$V^L = V^U + PV(\text{Interest Tax Shield}) \qquad (15.2)$$

4. When a firm's marginal tax rate is constant, and there are no personal taxes, the present value of the interest tax shield from permanent debt equals the tax rate times the value of the debt, $\tau_c D$.

5. The weighted average cost of capital with corporate taxes is

$$r_{wacc} = \frac{E}{E+D} r_E + \frac{D}{E+D} r_D (1 - \tau_c) \qquad (15.5)$$

Absent other market imperfections, the WACC declines with a firm's leverage.

6. When securities are fairly priced, the original shareholders of a firm capture the full benefit of the interest tax shield from an increase in leverage.

7. Personal taxes offset some of the corporate tax benefits of leverage. Every $1 received after taxes by debt holders from interest payments costs equity holders $(1 - \tau^*)$ on an after tax basis, where

$$\tau^* = 1 - \frac{(1 - \tau_c)(1 - \tau_e)}{(1 - \tau_i)} \qquad (15.7)$$

8. The optimal level of leverage from a tax-saving perspective is the level such that interest equals EBIT. In this case, the firm takes full advantage of the corporate tax deduction of interest, but avoids the tax disadvantage of excess leverage at the personal level.

9. The optimal fraction of debt, as a proportion of a firm's capital structure, declines with the growth rate of the firm.

10. The interest expense of the average firm is well below its taxable income, implying that firms do not fully exploit the tax advantages of debt.

Key Terms

interest tax shield *p. 461*

Further Reading

These are classic works in how taxation affects the cost of capital and optimal capital structure: M. King, "Taxation and the Cost of Capital," *Review of Economic Studies* 41 (1974): 21–35; M. H. Miller, "Debt and Taxes," *Journal of Finance* 32(2) (1977): 261–275; M. H. Miller and M. S. Scholes, "Dividends and Taxes," *Journal of Financial Economics* 6 (December 1978): 333–364; F. Modigliani and M. H. Miller, "Corporate Income Taxes and the Cost of Capital: A Correction," *American Economic Review* 53 (June 1963): 433–443; and J. Stiglitz, "Taxation, Corporate Financial Policy, and the Cost of Capital," *Journal of Public Economics* 2 (1973): 1–34.

For an analysis of how firms respond to tax incentives, see J. MacKie-Mason, "Do Taxes Affect Corporate Financing Decisions?" *Journal of Finance* 45(5) (1990): 1471–1493.

For a recent review of the literature of taxes and corporate finance, see J. R. Graham, "Taxes and Corporate Finance: A Review," *Review of Financial Studies* 16(4) (2003): 1075–1129.

These articles analyze in depth several issues regarding taxation and optimal capital structure: M. Bradley, G. A. Jarrell, and E. H. Kim, "On the Existence of an Optimal Capital Structure: Theory and Evidence," *The Journal of Finance* 39(3) (1984): 857–878; M. J. Brennan and E. S. Schwartz, "Corporate Income Taxes, Valuation, and the Problem of Optimal Capital Structure*,*" *Journal of Business* 51(1) (1978): 103–114; H. DeAngelo and R. Masulis, "Optimal Capital Structure Under Corporate and Personal Taxation," *Journal of Financial Economics* 8 (March 1980): 3–29; and S. Titman and R. Wessels, "The Determinants of Capital Structure Choice," *Journal of Finance* 43(1) (1988): 1–19.

The following articles contain information on what managers say about their capital structure decisions: J. R. Graham and C. Harvey, "How Do CFOs Make Capital Budgeting and Capital Structure Decisions?" *Journal of Applied Corporate Finance* 15 (2002): 8–23; R. R. Kamath, "Long-Term Financing Decisions: Views and Practices of Financial Managers of NYSE Firms," *Financial Review* 32(2) (May 1997): 331–356; E. Norton, "Factors Affecting Capital Structure Decisions," *Financial Review* 26 (August 1991): 431–446; and J. M. Pinegar and L. Wilbricht, "What Managers Think of Capital Structure Theory: A Survey," *Financial Management* 18(4) (Winter 1989): 82–91.

For additional insight into capital structure decisions internationally, see also F. Bancel and U. R. Mittoo, "Cross-Country Determinants of Capital Structure Choice: A Survey of European Firms," *Financial Mangement* 33 (Winter 2004): 103–132; R. La Porta, F. Lopez-de-Silanes, A. Shleifer, and R. Vishny, "Legal Determinants of External Finance," *Journal of Finance* 52 (1997): 1131–1152; and L. Booth, V. Aivazian, A. Demirguq-Kunt, and V. Maksimovic, "Capital Structures in Developing Countries," *Journal of Finance* 56 (2001): 87–130.

Problems

All problems in this chapter are available in MyFinanceLab. An asterisk (*) indicates problems with a higher level of difficulty.

The Interest Tax Deduction

1. Pelamed Pharmaceuticals has EBIT of $325 million in 2006. In addition, Pelamed has interest expenses of $125 million and a corporate tax rate of 40%.

   a. What is Pelamed's 2006 net income?

   b. What is the total of Pelamed's 2006 net income and interest payments?

c. If Pelamed had no interest expenses, what would its 2006 net income be? How does it compare to your answer in part (b)?

d. What is the amount of Pelamed's interest tax shield in 2006?

2. Grommit Engineering expects to have net income next year of $20.75 million and free cash flow of $22.15 million. Grommit's marginal corporate tax rate is 35%.

a. If Grommit increases leverage so that its interest expense rises by $1 million, how will its net income change?

b. For the same increase in interest expense, how will free cash flow change?

3. Suppose the corporate tax rate is 40%. Consider a firm that earns $1000 before interest and taxes each year with no risk. The firm's capital expenditures equal its depreciation expenses each year, and it will have no changes to its net working capital. The risk-free interest rate is 5%.

a. Suppose the firm has no debt and pays out its net income as a dividend each year. What is the value of the firm's equity?

b. Suppose instead the firm makes interest payments of $500 per year. What is the value of equity? What is the value of debt?

c. What is the difference between the total value of the firm with leverage and without leverage?

d. The difference in part (c) is equal to what percentage of the value of the debt?

EXCEL 4. Braxton Enterprises currently has debt outstanding of $35 million and an interest rate of 8%. Braxton plans to reduce its debt by repaying $7 million in principal at the end of each year for the next five years. If Braxton's marginal corporate tax rate is 40%, what is the interest tax shield from Braxton's debt in each of the next five years?

Valuing the Interest Tax Shield

EXCEL 5. Your firm currently has $100 million in debt outstanding with a 10% interest rate. The terms of the loan require the firm to repay $25 million of the balance each year. Suppose that the marginal corporate tax rate is 40%, and that the interest tax shields have the same risk as the loan. What is the present value of the interest tax shields from this debt?

6. Arnell Industries has $10 million in debt outstanding. The firm will pay interest only on this debt. Arnell's marginal tax rate is expected to be 35% for the foreseeable future.

a. Suppose Arnell pays interest of 6% per year on its debt. What is its annual interest tax shield?

b. What is the present value of the interest tax shield, assuming its risk is the same as the loan?

c. Suppose instead that the interest rate on the debt is 5%. What is the present value of the interest tax shield in this case?

7. Bay Transport Systems (BTS) currently has $30 million in debt outstanding. In addition to 6.5% interest, it plans to repay 5% of the remaining balance each year. If BTS has a marginal corporate tax rate of 40%, and if the interest tax shields have the same risk as the loan, what is the present value of the interest tax shield from the debt?

8. Rumolt Motors has 30 million shares outstanding with a price of $15 per share. In addition, Rumolt has issued bonds with a total current market value of $150 million. Suppose Rumolt's equity cost of capital is 10%, and its debt cost of capital is 5%.

a. What is Rumolt's pretax weighted average cost of capital?

b. If Rumolt's corporate tax rate is 35%, what is its after-tax weighted average cost of capital?

9. Summit Builders has a market debt-equity ratio of 0.65 and a corporate tax rate of 40%, and it pays 7% interest on its debt. The interest tax shield from its debt lowers Summit's WACC by what amount?

10. Restex maintains a debt-equity ratio of 0.85, and has an equity cost of capital of 12% and a debt cost of capital of 7%. Restex's corporate tax rate is 40%, and its market capitalization is $220 million.

   a. If Restex's free cash flow is expected to be $10 million in one year, what constant expected future growth rate is consistent with the firm's current market value?

   b. Estimate the value of Restex's interest tax shield.

11. Acme Storage has a market capitalization of $100 million and debt outstanding of $40 million. Acme plans to maintain this same debt-equity ratio in the future. The firm pays an interest rate of 7.5% on its debt and has a corporate tax rate of 35%.

   a. If Acme's free cash flow is expected to be $7 million next year and is expected to grow at a rate of 3% per year, what is Acme's WACC?

   b. What is the value of Acme's interest tax shield?

Recapitalizing to Capture the Tax Shield

12. Milton Industries expects free cash flow of $5 million each year. Milton's corporate tax rate is 35%, and its unlevered cost of capital is 15%. The firm also has outstanding debt of $19.05 million, and it expects to maintain this level of debt permanently.

   a. What is the value of Milton Industries without leverage?

   b. What is the value of Milton Industries with leverage?

13. Kurz Manufacturing is currently an all-equity firm with 20 million shares outstanding and a stock price of $7.50 per share. Although investors currently expect Kurz to remain an all-equity firm, Kurz plans to announce that it will borrow $50 million and use the funds to repurchase shares. Kurz will pay interest only on this debt, and it has no further plans to increase or decrease the amount of debt. Kurz is subject to a 40% corporate tax rate.

   a. What is the market value of Kurz's existing assets before the announcement?

   b. What is the market value of Kurz's assets (including any tax shields) just after the debt is issued, but before the shares are repurchased?

   c. What is Kurz's share price just before the share repurchase? How many shares will Kurz repurchase?

   d. What are Kurz's market value balance sheet and share price after the share repurchase?

14. Rally, Inc., is an all-equity firm with assets worth $25 billion and 10 billion shares outstanding. Rally plans to borrow $10 billion and use these funds to repurchase shares. The firm's corporate tax rate is 35%, and Rally plans to keep its outstanding debt equal to $10 billion permanently.

   a. Without the increase in leverage, what would Rally's share price be?

   b. Suppose Rally offers $2.75 per share to repurchase its shares. Would shareholders sell for this price?

   c. Suppose Rally offers $3.00 per share, and shareholders tender their shares at this price. What will Rally's share price be after the repurchase?

   d. What is the lowest price Rally can offer and have shareholders tender their shares? What will its stock price be after the share repurchase in that case?

Personal Taxes

15. Suppose the corporate tax rate is 40%, and investors pay a tax rate of 15% on income from dividends or capital gains and a tax rate of 33.3% on interest income. Your firm decides to add debt so it will pay an additional $15 million in interest each year. It will pay this interest expense by cutting its dividend.

a. How much will debt holders receive after paying taxes on the interest they earn?

b. By how much will the firm need to cut its dividend each year to pay this interest expense?

c. By how much will this cut in the dividend reduce equity holders' annual after-tax income?

d. How much less will the government receive in total tax revenues each year?

e. What is the effective tax advantage of debt τ^*?

16. Markum Enterprises is considering permanently adding $100 million of debt to its capital structure. Markum's corporate tax rate is 35%.

    a. Absent personal taxes, what is the value of the interest tax shield from the new debt?

    b. If investors pay a tax rate of 40% on interest income, and a tax rate of 20% on income from dividends and capital gains, what is the value of the interest tax shield from the new debt?

*17. Garnet Corporation is considering issuing risk-free debt or risk-free preferred stock. The tax rate on interest income is 35%, and the tax rate on dividends or capital gains from preferred stock is 15%. However, the dividends on preferred stock are not deductible for corporate tax purposes, and the corporate tax rate is 40%.

    a. If the risk-free interest rate for debt is 6%, what is cost of capital for risk-free preferred stock?

    b. What is the after-tax debt cost of capital for the firm? Which security is cheaper for the firm?

    c. Show that the after-tax debt cost of capital is equal to the preferred stock cost of capital multiplied by $(1 - \tau^*)$.

*18. Suppose the tax rate on interest income is 35%, and the average tax rate on capital gains and dividend income is 10%. How high must the marginal corporate tax rate be for debt to offer a tax advantage?

Optimal Capital Structure
with Taxes

19. With its current leverage, Impi Corporation will have net income next year of $4.5 million. If Impi's corporate tax rate is 35% and it pays 8% interest on its debt, how much additional debt can Impi issue this year and still receive the benefit of the interest tax shield next year?

*20. Colt Systems will have EBIT this coming year of $15 million. It will also spend $6 million on total capital expenditures and increases in net working capital, and have $3 million in depreciation expenses. Colt is currently an all-equity firm with a corporate tax rate of 35% and a cost of capital of 10%.

    a. If Colt is expected to grow by 8.5% per year, what is the market value of its equity today?

    b. If the interest rate on its debt is 8%, how much can Colt borrow now and still have non-negative net income this coming year?

    c. Is there a tax incentive for Colt to choose a debt-to-value ratio that exceeds 50%? Explain.

EXCEL *21. PMF, Inc., is equally likely to have EBIT this coming year of $10 million, $15 million, or $20 million. Its corporate tax rate is 35%, and investors pay a 15% tax rate on income from equity and a 35% tax rate on interest income.

    a. What is the effective tax advantage of debt if PMF has interest expenses of $8 million this coming year?

    b. What is the effective tax advantage of debt for interest expenses in excess of $20 million? (Ignore carryforwards.)

    c. What is the expected effective tax advantage of debt for interest expenses between $10 million and $15 million? (Ignore carryforwards.)

    d. What level of interest expense provides PMF with the greatest tax benefit?

Data Case

Your boss was impressed with your presentation regarding the irrelevance of capital structure from the previous chapter but, as expected, has realized that market imperfections like taxes must be accounted for. You have now been asked to include taxes in your analysis. Your boss knows that interest is deductible and has decided that the stock price of Home Depot should increase if the firm increases its use of debt. Thus, your boss wants to propose a share repurchase program using the proceeds from a new debt issue and wants to present this plan to the CEO and perhaps to the Board of Directors.

Your boss would like you to examine the impact of two different scenarios, adding a modest level of debt and adding a higher level of debt. In particular, your boss would like to consider issuing $1 billion in new debt or $5 billion in new debt. In either case, Home Depot would use the proceeds to repurchase stock.

1. Using the financial statements for Home Depot that you downloaded in Chapter 14, determine the average corporate tax rate for Home Depot over the last four years by dividing Income Tax by Earnings before Tax for each of the last four years.

2. Begin by analyzing the scenario with $1 billion in new debt. Assuming the firm plans to keep this new debt outstanding forever, determine the present value of the tax shield of the new debt. What additional assumptions did you need to make for this calculation?

3. Determine the new stock price if the $1 billion in debt is used to repurchase stock.

   a. Use the current market value of Home Depot's equity that you calculated in Chapter 14.

   b. Determine the new market value of the equity if the repurchase occurs.

   c. Determine the new number of shares and the stock price after the repurchase is announced.

4. What will Home Depot's D/E ratio based on book values be after it issues new debt and repurchases stock? What will its market value D/E ratio be?

5. Repeat stesp 2–4 for the scenario in which Home Depot issues $5 billion in debt and repurchases stock.

6. Based on the stock price, does the debt increase and stock repurchase appear to be a good idea? Why or why not? What issues might the executives of Home Depot raise that aren't considered in your analysis?

16

Financial Distress, Managerial Incentives, and Information

notation

E	market value of equity
D	market value of debt
PV	present value
V^U	value of the unlevered firm
V^L	value of the firm with leverage
τ^*	effective tax advantage of debt

Modigliani and Miller demonstrated that capital structure does not matter in a perfect capital market. In Chapter 15, we found a tax benefit of leverage, at least up to the point that a firm's EBIT exceeds the interest payments on the debt. Yet we saw that the average U.S. firm shields only about one-third of its earnings in this way. Why don't firms use more debt?

We can gain some insight by looking at United Airlines (UAL Corporation). For the five-year period 1996 through 2000, UAL paid interest expenses of $1.7 billion, relative to EBIT of more than $6 billion. During this period, it reported a total provision for taxes on its income statement exceeding $2.2 billion. The company appeared to have a level of debt that did not fully exploit its tax shield. Even so, as a result of high fuel and labor costs, a decline in travel following the terrorist attacks of September 11, 2001, and increased competition from discount carriers, UAL filed for bankruptcy court protection in December 2002. As this case demonstrates, firms such as airlines whose future cash flows are unstable and highly sensitive to shocks in the economy run the risk of bankruptcy if they use too much leverage. The costs of bankruptcy may at least partially offset the benefits of the interest tax shield, prompting firms to use less leverage than if they were motivated by tax savings alone.

When a firm has trouble meeting its debt obligations we say the firm is in **financial distress**. In this chapter, we consider how a firm's choice of capital structure can, due to market imperfections, affect its costs of financial distress, alter managers' incentives, and signal information to investors. Each of these consequences of the capital structure decision can be significant, and each may offset the tax benefits of leverage when leverage is high. Thus these imperfections may help to explain the levels of debt that we generally observe. In addition, because their effects are likely to vary widely across different types of firms, they may help to explain the large discrepancies in leverage choices that exist across industries, as documented in the previous chapter in Figure 15.7.

16.1   Default and Bankruptcy in a Perfect Market

Debt financing puts an obligation on a firm. A firm that fails to make the required interest or principal payments on the debt is in **default**. After the firm defaults, debt holders are given certain rights to the assets of the firm. In the extreme case, the debt holders take legal ownership of the firm's assets through a process called bankruptcy. Recall that equity financing does not carry this risk. While equity holders hope to receive dividends, the firm is not legally obligated to pay them.

Thus it seems that an important consequence of leverage is the risk of bankruptcy. Does this risk represent a disadvantage to using debt? Not necessarily. As we pointed out in Chapter 14, Modigliani and Miller's results continue to hold in a perfect market even when debt is risky and the firm may default. Let's review that result by considering a hypothetical example.

Armin Industries: Leverage and the Risk of Default

Armin Industries faces an uncertain future in a challenging business environment. Due to increased competition from foreign imports, its revenues have fallen dramatically in the past year. Armin's managers hope that a new product in the company's pipeline will restore its fortunes. While the new product represents a significant advance over Armin's competitors' products, whether that product will be a hit with consumers remains uncertain. If it is a hit, revenues and profits will grow, and Armin will be worth $150 million at the end of the year. If it fails, Armin will be worth only $80 million.

Armin Industries may employ one of two alternative capital structures: (1) It can use all-equity financing or (2) it can use debt that matures at the end of the year with a total of $100 million due. Let's look at the consequences of these capital structure choices when the new product succeeds, and when it fails, in a setting of perfect capital markets.

Scenario 1: New Product Succeeds.

If the new product is successful, Armin is worth $150 million. Without leverage, equity holders own the full amount. With leverage, Armin must make the $100 million debt payment, and Armin's equity holders will own the remaining $50 million.

But what if Armin does not have $100 million in cash available at the end of the year? Even though its assets will be worth $150 million, much of that value may come from anticipated *future* profits from the new product, rather than cash in the bank. In that case, if Armin has debt, will it be forced to default?

With perfect capital markets, the answer is no. As long as the value of the firm's assets exceeds its liabilities, Armin will be able to repay the loan. Even if it does not have the cash immediately available, it can raise the cash by obtaining a new loan or by issuing new shares.

For example, suppose Armin currently has 10 million shares outstanding. Because the value of its equity is $50 million, these shares are worth $5 per share. At this price, Armin can raise $100 million by issuing 20 million new shares and use the proceeds to pay off the debt. After the debt is repaid, the firm's equity is worth $150 million. Because there is now a total of 30 million shares, the share price remains $5 per share.

This scenario shows that if a firm has access to capital markets and can issue new securities at a fair price, *then it need not default as long as the market value of its assets exceeds its liabilities.* That is, whether default occurs depends on the relative values of the firm's assets and liabilities, not on its cash flows. Many firms experience years of negative cash flows yet remain solvent.

Scenario 2: New Product Fails. If the new product fails, Armin is worth only $80 million. If the company has all-equity financing, equity holders will be unhappy but there is no immediate legal consequence for the firm. In contrast, if Armin has $100 million in debt due, it will experience financial distress. The firm will be unable to make its $100 million debt payment and will have no choice except to default. In bankruptcy, debt holders will receive legal ownership of the firm's assets, leaving Armin's shareholders with nothing. Because the assets the debt holders receive have a value of $80 million, they will suffer a loss of $20 million relative to the $100 million they were owed. Equity holders in a corporation have limited liability, so the debt holders cannot sue Armin's shareholders for this $20 million—they must accept the loss.

Comparing the Two Scenarios. Table 16.1 compares the outcome of each scenario without leverage and with leverage. Both debt and equity holders are worse off if the product fails rather than succeeds. Without leverage, if the product fails equity holders lose $150 million − $80 million = $70 million. With leverage, equity holders lose $50 million, and debt holders lose $20 million, *but the total loss is the same*—$70 million. Overall, *if the new product fails, Armin's investors are equally unhappy whether the firm is levered and declares bankruptcy or whether it is unlevered and the share price declines.*[1]

TABLE 16.1	Value of Debt and Equity with and without Leverage ($ million)			
	Without Leverage		**With Leverage**	
	Success	**Failure**	**Success**	**Failure**
Debt value	—	—	100	80
Equity value	150	80	50	0
Total to all investors	150	80	150	80

This point is an important one. When a firm declares bankruptcy, the news often makes headlines. Much attention is paid to the firm's poor results and the loss to investors. But the decline in value is not *caused* by bankruptcy: The decline is the same whether or not the firm has leverage. That is, if the new product fails, Armin will experience **economic distress**, which is a significant decline in the value of a firm's assets, whether or not it experiences financial distress due to leverage.

Bankruptcy and Capital Structure

With perfect capital markets, Modigliani-Miller (MM) Proposition I applies: The total value to all investors does not depend on the firm's capital structure. Investors as a group are *not* worse off because a firm has leverage. While it is true that bankruptcy results from a firm having leverage, bankruptcy alone does not lead to a greater reduction in the total value to investors. Thus there is no disadvantage to debt financing, and a firm will have the same total value and will be able to raise the same amount initially from investors with either choice of capital structure.

---

1. There is a temptation to look only at shareholders and to say they are worse off when Armin has leverage because their shares are worthless. In fact, shareholders are worse off $50 million relative to success when the firm is levered, versus $70 million without leverage. What really matters is the total value to all investors, which will determine the total amount of capital the firm can raise initially.

Bankruptcy Risk and Firm Value

Problem

Suppose the risk-free rate is 5%, and Armin's new product is equally likely to succeed or to fail. For simplicity, suppose that Armin's cash flows are unrelated to the state of the economy (i.e., the risk is diversifiable), so that the project has a beta of 0 and the cost of capital is the risk-free rate. Compute the value of Armin's securities at the beginning of the year with and without leverage, and show that MM Proposition I holds.

Solution

Without leverage, the equity is worth either $150 million or $80 million at year-end. Because the risk is diversifiable, no risk premium is necessary and we can discount the expected value of the firm at the risk-free rate to determine its value without leverage at the start of the year:[2]

$$\text{Equity (unlevered)} = V^U = \frac{\frac{1}{2}(150) + \frac{1}{2}(80)}{1.05} = \$109.52 \text{ million}$$

With leverage, equity holders receive $50 million or nothing, and debt holders receive $100 million or $80 million. Thus

$$\text{Equity (levered)} = \frac{\frac{1}{2}(50) + \frac{1}{2}(0)}{1.05} = \$23.81 \text{ million}$$

$$\text{Debt} = \frac{\frac{1}{2}(100) + \frac{1}{2}(80)}{1.05} = \$85.71 \text{ million}$$

Therefore, the value of the levered firm is $V^L = E + D = 23.81 + 85.71 = \$109.52$ million. With or without leverage, the total value of the securities is the same, verifying MM Proposition I. The firm is able to raise the same amount from investors using either capital structure.

CONCEPT CHECK

1. With perfect capital markets, under what conditions will a levered firm default?

2. Does the risk of default reduce the value of the firm?

16.2   The Costs of Bankruptcy and Financial Distress

With perfect capital markets, the *risk* of bankruptcy is not a disadvantage of debt—bankruptcy simply shifts the ownership of the firm from equity holders to debt holders without changing the total value available to all investors.

Is this description of bankruptcy realistic? No. Bankruptcy is rarely simple and straightforward—equity holders don't just "hand the keys" to debt holders the moment the firm defaults on a debt payment. Rather, bankruptcy is a long and complicated process that imposes both direct and indirect costs on the firm and its investors that the assumption of perfect capital markets ignores.

The Bankruptcy Code

We know that when a firm fails to make a required payment to debt holders, it is in default. Debt holders can then take legal action against the firm to collect payment by seizing the firm's assets. Because most firms have multiple creditors, without coordination

---

2. If the risk were not diversifiable and a risk premium were needed, the calculations here would become more complicated but the end result would not change.

it is difficult to guarantee that each creditor will be treated fairly. Moreover, because the assets of the firm might be more valuable if kept together, creditors seizing assets in a piecemeal fashion might destroy much of the remaining value of the firm.

The U.S. bankruptcy code was created to organize this process so that creditors are treated fairly and the value of the assets is not needlessly destroyed. According to the provisions of the 1978 Bankruptcy Reform Act, U.S. firms can file for two forms of bankruptcy protection: Chapter 7 or Chapter 11.

In **Chapter 7 liquidation**, a trustee is appointed to oversee the liquidation of the firm's assets through an auction. The proceeds from the liquidation are used to pay the firm's creditors, and the firm ceases to exist.

In the more common form of bankruptcy for large corporations, **Chapter 11 reorganization**, all pending collection attempts are automatically suspended, and the firm's existing management is given the opportunity to propose a reorganization plan. While developing the plan, management continues to operate the business. The reorganization plan specifies the treatment of each creditor of the firm. In addition to cash payment, creditors may receive new debt or equity securities of the firm. The value of cash and securities is generally less than the amount each creditor is owed, but more than the creditors would receive if the firm were shut down immediately and liquidated. The creditors must vote to accept the plan, and it must be approved by the bankruptcy court.[3] If an acceptable plan is not put forth, the court may ultimately force a Chapter 7 liquidation of the firm.

Direct Costs of Bankruptcy

The bankruptcy code is designed to provide an orderly process for settling a firm's debts. However, the process is still complex, time-consuming, and costly. When a corporation becomes financially distressed, outside professionals, such as legal and accounting experts, consultants, appraisers, auctioneers, and others with experience selling distressed assets, are generally hired. Investment bankers may also assist with a potential financial restructuring.

These outside experts are costly. At the time Enron entered Chapter 11 bankruptcy, it reportedly spent a record $30 million per month on legal and accounting fees, and the total cost ultimately exceeded $750 million. WorldCom paid its advisors $657 million as part of its reorganization to become MCI. Between 2003 and 2005, United Airlines paid a team of over 30 advisory firms an average of $8.6 million per month for legal and professional services related to its Chapter 11 reorganization.[4]

In addition to the money spent by the firm, the creditors may incur costs during the bankruptcy process. In the case of Chapter 11 reorganization, creditors must often wait several years for a reorganization plan to be approved and to receive payment. To ensure that their rights and interests are respected, and to assist in valuing their claims in a proposed reorganization, creditors may seek separate legal representation and professional advice.

---

3. Specifically, management holds the exclusive right to propose a reorganization plan for the first 120 days, and this period may be extended indefinitely by the bankruptcy court. Thereafter, any interested party may propose a plan. Creditors who will receive full payment or have their claims fully reinstated under the plan are deemed unimpaired, and do not vote on the reorganization plan. All impaired creditors are grouped according to the nature of their claims. If the plan is approved by creditors holding two-thirds of the claim amount in each group and a majority in the number of the claims in each group, the court will confirm the plan. Even if all groups do not approve the plan, the court may still impose the plan (in a process commonly known as a "cram down") if it deems the plan fair and equitable with respect to each group that objected.

4. Julie Johnsson, "UAL a Ch. 11 Fee Machine," *Crain's Chicago Business,* June 27, 2005.

Whether paid by the firm or its creditors, these direct costs of bankruptcy reduce the value of the assets that the firm's investors will ultimately receive. In the case of Enron, reorganization costs may approach 10% of the value of the assets. Studies typically report that the average direct costs of bankruptcy are approximately 3% to 4% of the pre-bankruptcy market value of total assets.[5] The costs are likely to be higher for firms with more complicated business operations and for firms with larger numbers of creditors, because it may be more difficult to reach agreement among many creditors regarding the final disposition of the firm's assets. Because many aspects of the bankruptcy process are independent of the size of the firm, the costs are typically higher, in percentage terms, for smaller firms. A study of Chapter 7 liquidations of small businesses found that the average direct costs of bankruptcy were 12% of the value of the firm's assets.[6]

Given the substantial legal and other direct costs of bankruptcy, firms in financial distress can avoid filing for bankruptcy by first negotiating directly with creditors. When a financially distressed firm is successful at reorganizing outside of bankruptcy; it is called a **workout**. Consequently, the direct costs of bankruptcy should not substantially exceed the cost of a workout. Another approach is a **prepackaged bankruptcy** (or "prepack"), in which a firm will *first* develop a reorganization plan with the agreement of its main creditors, and *then* file Chapter 11 to implement the plan (and pressure any creditors who attempt to hold out for better terms). With a prepack, the firm emerges from bankruptcy quickly and with minimal direct costs.[7]

Indirect Costs of Financial Distress

Aside from the direct legal and administrative costs of bankruptcy, many other *indirect* costs are associated with financial distress (whether or not the firm has formally filed for bankruptcy). While these costs are difficult to measure accurately, they are often much larger than the direct costs of bankruptcy.

Loss of Customers. Because bankruptcy may enable firms to walk away from future commitments to their customers, customers may be unwilling to purchase products whose value depends on future support or service from the firm. This problem affects many technology firms because customers may hesitate to commit to a hardware or software platform that may not be supported or upgraded in the future. Airlines face sim-

---

5. See Jerold Warner, "Bankruptcy Costs: Some Evidence," *Journal of Finance* 32 (1977): 337–347; Lawrence Weiss, "Bankruptcy Resolution: Direct Costs and Violation of Priority of Claims," *Journal of Financial Economics* 27 (1990): 285–314; Edward Altman, "A Further Empirical Investigation of the Bankruptcy Cost Question," *Journal of Finance* 39 (1984): 1067–1089; and Brian Betker, "The Administrative Costs of Debt Restructurings: Some Recent Evidence," *Financial Management* 26 (1997): 56–68. Lynn LoPucki and Joseph Doherty report that direct costs of bankruptcy may have fallen by more than 50% during the 1990s, due to a reduction in the length of time spent in bankruptcy; these authors estimate them at approximately 1.5% of firm value ("The Determinants of Professional Fees in Large Bankruptcy Reorganization Cases," *Journal of Empirical Legal Studies* 1 (2004): 111–141).

6. Robert Lawless and Stephen Ferris, "Professional Fees and Other Direct Costs in Chapter 7 Business Liquidations," *Washington University Law Quarterly* (Fall 1997): 1207–1236. For comparative international data, see K. Thorburn, "Bankruptcy Auctions: Costs, Debt Recovery and Firm Survival," *Journal of Financial Economics* 58 (2000): 337–368, and A. Raviv and S. Sundgren, "The Comparative Efficiency of Small-firm Bankruptcies: A Study of the U.S. and the Finnish Bankruptcy Codes," *Financial Management* 27 (1998): 28–40.

7. See E. Tashjian, R. C. Lease, and J. J. McConnell, "An Empirical Analysis of Prepackaged Bankruptcies," *Journal of Financial Economics* 40 (1996): 135–162.

ilar problems: Tickets are sold in advance, so customers will be reluctant to buy tickets if they believe the airline may cease operations or fail to honor their accumulated frequent-flier mileage. Manufacturers of durable goods may lose potential customers who are worried that warranties will not be honored or replacement parts will not be available. In contrast, the loss of customers is likely to be small for producers of raw materials (such as sugar or aluminum), as the value of these goods, once delivered, does not depend on the seller's continued success.[8]

Loss of Suppliers. Customers are not the only ones who retreat from a firm in financial distress. Suppliers may be unwilling to provide a firm with inventory if they fear they will not be paid. For example, Kmart Corporation filed for bankruptcy protection in January 2002 in part because the decline in its stock price scared suppliers, which then refused to ship goods. Similarly, Swiss Air was forced to shut down because its suppliers refused to fuel its planes. This type of disruption is an important financial distress cost for firms that rely heavily on trade credit.

Loss of Employees. Because firms in distress cannot offer job security with long-term employment contracts, they may have difficulty hiring new employees, and existing employees may quit or be hired away. Retaining key employees may be costly: Pacific Gas and Electric Corporation implemented a retention program costing over $80 million to retain 17 key employees while in bankruptcy.[9] This type of financial distress cost is likely to be high for firms whose value is derived largely from their human resources.

Loss of Receivables. Firms in financial distress tend to have difficulty collecting money that is owed to them. According to one of Enron's bankruptcy lawyers, "Many customers who owe smaller amounts are trying to hide from us. They must believe that Enron will never bother with them because the amounts are not particularly large in any individual case."[10] Knowing that the firm's resources are already spread thinly, debtors assume they may have an opportunity to avoid their obligations to the firm.

Fire Sales of Assets. Companies in distress may be forced to sell assets quickly to raise cash. Of course, selling assets quickly may not be optimal, which means accepting a lower price than the assets are actually worth. A study of airlines by Todd Pulvino shows that companies in bankruptcy or financial distress sell their aircraft at prices that are 15% to 40% below the prices received by financially healthy firms.[11] Discounts are also observed when distressed firms attempt to sell subsidiaries. The costs of selling assets below their value are greatest for firms with assets that lack competitive, liquid markets.

---

8. This argument was put forth by Sheridan Titman, "The Effect of Capital Structure on a Firm's Liquidation Decision," *Journal of Financial Economics* 13 (1984): 137–151. Timothy Opler and Sheridan Titman report 17.7% lower sales growth for highly leveraged firms compared to their less leveraged competitors in R&D-intensive industries during downturns ("Financial Distress and Corporate Performance," *Journal of Finance* 49 (1994): 1015–1040).

9. Rick Jurgens, "PG&E to Review Bonus Program," *Contra Costa Times,* December 13, 2003.

10. Kristen Hays, "Enron Asks Judge to Get Tough on Deadbeat Customers," *Associated Press,* August 19, 2003.

11. "Do Asset Fire-Sales Exist? An Empirical Investigation of Commercial Aircraft Transactions," *Journal of Finance* 53 (1998): 939–978, and "Effects of Bankrutpcy Court Protection on Asset Sales," *Journal of Financial Economics* 52 (1999): 151–186. For examples from other industries, see Timothy Kruse, "Asset Liquidity and the Determinants of Asset Sales by Poorly Performing Firms," *Financial Management* 31 (2002): 107–129.

Delayed Liquidation. Bankruptcy protection can be used by management to delay the liquidation of a firm that should be shut down. A study by Lawrence Weiss and Karen Wruck estimates that Eastern Airlines lost more than 50% of its value while in bankruptcy because management was allowed to continue making negative-NPV investments.[12]

Costs to Creditors. Aside from the direct legal costs that creditors may incur when a firm defaults, there may be other indirect costs to creditors. If the loan to the firm was a significant asset for the creditor, default of the firm may lead to costly financial distress *for the creditor.*[13] For example, in 1998 Russia's default on its bonds led to the collapse of Long Term Capital Management (LTCM), and fears arose that some of LTCM's creditors might become distressed as well.

Overall Impact of Indirect Costs.   In total, the indirect costs of financial distress may be substantial. When estimating them, however, we must remember two important points. First, we need to identify losses to total firm value (and not solely losses to equity holders or debt holders, or transfers between them). Second, we need to identify the incremental losses that are associated with financial distress, above and beyond any losses that would occur due to the firm's economic distress.[14] A study of highly levered firms by Gregor Andrade and Steven Kaplan estimated a potential loss due to financial distress of 10% to 20% of firm value.[15] We next consider the consequences of these potential costs of leverage for firm value.

CONCEPT CHECK

1. If a firm files for bankruptcy under Chapter 11 of the bankruptcy code, which party gets the first opportunity to propose a plan for the firm's reorganization?

2. Why are the losses of debt holders whose claims are not fully repaid not a cost of financial distress, whereas the loss of customers who fear the firm will stop honoring warranties is?

16.3 Financial Distress Costs and Firm Value

The costs of financial distress described in the previous section represent an important departure from Modigliani and Miller's assumption of perfect capital markets. MM assumed that the cash flows of a firm's assets do not depend on its choice of capital structure. As we have discussed, however, levered firms risk incurring financial distress costs that reduce the cash flows available to investors.

---

12. "Information Problems, Conflicts of Interest, and Asset Stripping: Ch. 11's Failure in the Case of Eastern Airlines," *Journal of Financial Economics* 48, 55–97.

13. While these costs are borne by the creditor and not by the firm, the creditor will consider these potential costs when setting the rate of the loan.

14. For an insightful discussion of this point, see Robert Haugen and Lemma Senbet, "Bankruptcy and Agency Costs: Their Significance to the Theory of Optimal Capital Structure," *Journal of Financial and Quantitative Analysis* 23 (1988): 27–38, where they also point out that the magnitude of financial distress costs can be no larger than the costs of restructuring the firm before the costs are incurred.

15. Gregor Andrade and Steven Kaplan, "How Costly Is Financial (Not Economic) Distress? Evidence from Highly Leveraged Transactions That Became Distressed," *Journal of Finance* 53 (1998): 1443–1493.

Armin Industries: The Impact of Financial Distress Costs

To illustrate how these financial distress costs affect firm value, consider again the example of Armin Industries. With all-equity financing, Armin's assets will be worth $150 million if its new product succeeds and $80 million if the new product fails. In contrast, with debt of $100 million, Armin will be forced into bankruptcy if the new product fails. In this case, some of the value of Armin's assets will be lost to bankruptcy and financial distress costs. As a result, debt holders will receive less than $80 million. We show the impact of these costs in Table 16.2, where we assume debt holders receive only $60 million after accounting for the costs of financial distress.

TABLE 16.2	**Value of Debt and Equity with and without Leverage ($ million)**			
	Without Leverage		**With Leverage**	
	Success	**Failure**	**Success**	**Failure**
Debt value	—	—	100	60
Equity value	150	80	50	0
Total to all investors	150	80	150	60

As Table 16.2 shows, the total value to all investors is now less with leverage than it is without leverage when the new product fails. The difference of $80 million − $60 million = $20 million is due to financial distress costs. These costs will lower the total value of the firm with leverage, and MM's Proposition I will no longer hold, as illustrated in Example 16.2.

Firm Value When Financial Distress Is Costly

Problem

Compare the current value of Armin Industries with and without leverage, given the data in Table 16.2. Assume that the risk-free rate is 5%, the new product is equally likely to succeed or fail, and the risk is diversifiable.

Solution

With and without leverage, the payments to equity holders are the same as in Example 16.1. There we computed the value of unlevered equity as $109.52 million and the value of levered equity as $23.81 million. But due to bankruptcy costs, the value of the debt is now

$$\text{Debt} = \frac{\frac{1}{2}(100) + \frac{1}{2}(60)}{1.05} = \$76.19 \text{ million}$$

The value of the levered firm is $V^L = E + D = 23.81 + 76.19 = \$100$ million, which is less than the value of the unlevered firm, $V^U = \$109.52$ million. Thus, due to bankruptcy costs, the value of the levered firm is $9.52 million less than its value without leverage. This loss equals the present value of the $20 million in financial distress costs the firm will pay if the product fails:

$$PV(\text{Financial Distress Costs}) = \frac{\frac{1}{2}(0) + \frac{1}{2}(20)}{1.05} = \$9.52 \text{ million}$$

Who Pays for Financial Distress Costs?

The financial distress costs in Table 16.2 reduce the payments to the debt holders when the new product has failed. In that case, the equity holders have already lost their investment and have no further interest in the firm. It might seem as though these costs are irrelevant from the shareholders' perspective. Why should equity holders care about costs borne by debt holders?

It is true that after a firm is in bankruptcy, equity holders care little about bankruptcy costs. But debt holders are not foolish—they recognize that when the firm defaults, they will not be able to get the full value of the assets. As a result, they will pay less for the debt initially. How much less? Precisely the amount they will ultimately give up—the present value of the bankruptcy costs.

But if the debt holders pay less for the debt, there is less money available for the firm to pay dividends, repurchase shares, and make investments. That is, this difference is money out of the equity holders' pockets. This logic leads to the following general result:

When securities are fairly priced, the original shareholders of a firm pay the present value of the costs associated with bankruptcy and financial distress.

<table>
<tr><td>

EXAMPLE 16.3

</td><td>

Financial Distress Costs and the Stock Price

Problem
Suppose that at the beginning of the year, Armin Industries has 10 million shares outstanding and no debt. Armin then announces plans to issue one-year debt with a face value of $100 million and to use the proceeds to repurchase shares. Given the data in Table 16.2, what will the new share price be? As in the previous examples, assume the risk-free rate is 5%, the new product is equally likely to succeed or fail, and this risk is diversifiable.

Solution
From Example 16.1, the value of the firm without leverage is $109.52 million. With 10 million shares outstanding, this value corresponds to an initial share price of $10.952 per share. In Example 16.2, we saw that with leverage, the total value of the firm is only $100 million. In anticipation of this decline in value, the price of the stock should fall to $100 million ÷ 10 million shares = $10.00 per share on announcement of the recapitalization.

Let's check this result. From Example 16.2, due to bankruptcy costs, the new debt is worth $76.19 million. Thus, at a price of $10 per share, Armin will repurchase 7.619 million shares, leaving 2.381 million shares outstanding. In Example 16.1, we computed the value of levered equity as $23.81 million. Dividing by the number of shares gives a share price after the transaction of

$$\$23.81 \text{ million} \div 2.381 \text{ million shares} = \$10.00 \text{ per share}$$

Thus the recapitalization will cost shareholders $0.952 per share or $9.52 million in total. This cost matches the present value of financial distress costs computed in Example 16.2. Thus, although debt holders bear these costs in the end, shareholders pay the present value of the costs of financial distress upfront.

</td></tr>
</table>

CONCEPT CHECK

1. In Examples 16.1 through 16.3, Armin incurred financial distress costs only in the event that the new product failed. Why might Armin incur financial distress costs even *before* the success or failure of the new product is known?

2. Why should shareholders be concerned about financial distress costs that will be borne by debt holders?

16.4 Optimal Capital Structure: The Tradeoff Theory

We can now combine our knowledge of the benefits of leverage from the interest tax shield (discussed in Chapter 15) with the costs of financial distress to determine the amount of debt that a firm should issue to maximize its value. The analysis presented in this section is called the **tradeoff theory** because it weighs the benefits of debt that result from shielding cash flows from taxes against the costs of financial distress associated with leverage.

According to this theory, *the total value of a levered firm equals the value of the firm without leverage plus the present value of the tax savings from debt, less the present value of financial distress costs:*

$$V^L = V^U + PV(\text{Interest Tax Shield}) - PV(\text{Financial Distress Costs}) \quad (16.1)$$

Equation 16.1 shows that leverage has costs as well as benefits. Firms have an incentive to increase leverage to exploit the tax benefits of debt. But with too much debt, they are more likely to risk default and incur financial distress costs.

Determinants of the Present Value of Financial Distress Costs

Aside from simple examples, calculating the precise present value of financial distress costs is quite complicated. Two key qualitative factors determine the present value of financial distress costs: (1) the probability of financial distress and (2) the magnitude of the costs after a firm is in distress. In Example 16.3, when Armin is levered, the present value of its financial distress costs depends on the probability that the new product will fail (50%) and the magnitude of the costs if it does fail ($20 million).

What determines each of these factors? The magnitude of the financial distress costs will depend on the relative importance of the sources of these costs discussed in Section 16.2 and is likely to vary by industry. For example, technology firms are likely to incur high costs when they are in financial distress, due to the potential for loss of customers and key personnel, as well as a lack of tangible assets that can be easily liquidated. In contrast, real estate firms are likely to have low costs of financial distress, as much of their value derives from assets that can be sold relatively easily.

The probability of financial distress depends on the likelihood that a firm will be unable to meet its debt commitments and therefore default. This probability increases with the amount of a firm's liabilities (relative to its assets). It also increases with the volatility of a firm's cash flows and asset values. Thus firms with steady, reliable cash flows, such as utility companies, are able to use high levels of debt and still have a very low probability of default. Firms whose value and cash flows are very volatile (for example, semiconductor firms) must have much lower levels of debt to avoid a significant risk of default.

Optimal Leverage

Figure 16.1 shows how the value of a levered firm, V^L, varies with the level of permanent debt, D, according to Eq. 16.1. With no debt, the value of the firm is V^U. For low levels of debt, the risk of default remains low and the main effect of an increase in leverage is an increase in the interest tax shield, which has present value $\tau^* D$, where τ^* is the effective tax advantage of debt calculated in Chapter 15. If there were no costs of financial distress, the value would continue to increase at this rate until the interest on the debt exceeds the firm's earnings before interest and taxes and the tax shield is exhausted.

FIGURE 16.1

Optimal Leverage with Taxes and Financial Distress Costs

As the level of debt, D, increases, the tax benefits of debt increase by τ^*D until the interest expense exceeds the firm's EBIT. The probability of default, and hence the present value of financial distress costs, also increase with D. The optimal level of debt, D^*, occurs when these effects balance out and V^L is maximized. D^* will be lower for firms with higher costs of financial distress.

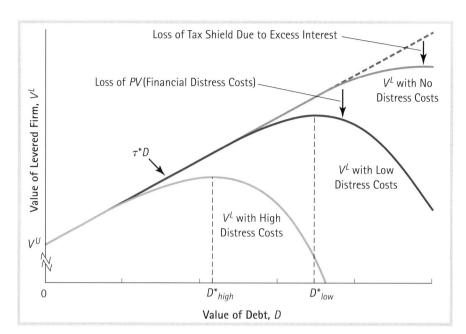

The costs of financial distress reduce the value of the levered firm, V^L. The amount of the reduction increases with the probability of default, which in turn increases with the level of the debt D. The tradeoff theory states that firms should increase their leverage until it reaches the level D^* for which V^L is maximized. At this point, the tax savings that result from increasing leverage are just offset by the increased probability of incurring the costs of financial distress.

Figure 16.1 also illustrates the optimal debt choices for two types of firms. The optimal debt choice for a firm with low costs of financial distress is indicated by D^*_{low}, and the optimal debt choice for a firm with high costs of financial distress is indicated by D^*_{high}. Not surprisingly, with higher costs of financial distress, it is optimal for the firm to choose lower leverage.

The tradeoff theory helps to resolve two puzzles regarding leverage that arose in Chapter 15. First, the presence of financial distress costs can explain why firms choose debt levels that are too low to fully exploit the interest tax shield. Second, differences in the magnitude of financial distress costs and the volatility of cash flows can explain the differences in the use of leverage across industries. Furthermore, the tradeoff theory can be easily extended to include other effects of leverage—which may be even more important than financial distress costs—that we discuss next.

EXAMPLE

16.4

Choosing an Optimal Debt Level

Problem

Greenleaf Industries is considering adding leverage to its capital structure. Greenleaf's managers believe they can add as much as $35 million in debt and exploit the benefits of the tax shield (for which they estimate $\tau^* = 15\%$). However, they also recognize that higher debt increases the risk of financial distress. Based on simulations of the firm's future cash flows, the CFO has made the following estimates (in millions of dollars):[16]

Debt	0	10	20	25	30	35
PV(Interest tax shield)	0.00	1.50	3.00	3.75	4.50	5.25
PV(Financial distress costs)	0.00	0.00	0.38	1.62	4.00	6.38

What is the optimal debt choice for Greenleaf?

Solution

From Eq. 16.1, the net benefit of debt is determined by subtracting PV(Financial distress costs) from PV(Interest tax shield). The net benefit for each level of debt is

Debt	0	10	20	25	30	35
Net benefit	0.00	1.50	2.62	2.13	0.50	−1.13

The level of debt that leads to the highest net benefit is $20 million. Greenleaf will gain $3 million due to tax shields, and lose $0.38 million due to the present value of distress costs, for a net gain of $2.62 million.

CONCEPT CHECK

1. Describe the tradeoff theory.

2. According to the tradeoff theory, all else being equal, which type of firm has a higher optimal level of debt: a firm with very volatile cash flows or a firm with very safe, predictable cash flows?

16.5 Exploiting Debt Holders: The Agency Costs of Leverage

In this section, we consider another way that capital structure can affect a firm's cash flows: It can alter managers' incentives and change their investment decisions. If these changes have a negative NPV, they will be costly for the firm.

The type of costs we describe in this section are examples of **agency costs**—costs that arise when there are conflicts of interest between stakeholders. Because top managers often hold shares in the firm and are hired and retained with the approval of the board of directors, which itself is elected by shareholders, managers will generally make decisions that increase the value of the firm's equity. When a firm has leverage, a conflict of interest exists if investment decisions have different consequences for the value of equity and the value of debt. Such a conflict is most likely to occur when the risk of financial distress is high. In some circumstances, managers may take actions that benefit shareholders but harm the firm's creditors and lower the total value of the firm.

We illustrate this possibility by considering a firm that is facing financial distress, Baxter Inc. Baxter has a loan of $1 million due at the end of the year. Without a change in its strategy, the market value of its assets will be only $900,000 at that time, and Baxter will default on its debt.

Over-investment

Baxter executives are considering a new strategy that seemed promising initially but appears risky after closer analysis. The new strategy requires no upfront investment, but it has only a 50% chance of success. If it succeeds, it will increase the value of the firm's assets

---

16. The PV of the interest tax shield is computed as $\tau^* D$. The PV of financial distress costs is difficult to estimate and requires option valuation techniques we introduce in Part VII of the text.

to $1.3 million. If it fails, the value of the firm's assets will fall to $300,000. Therefore, the expected value of the firm's assets under the new strategy is 50% × $1.3 million + 50% × $300,000 = $800,000, a decline of $100,000 from their value of $900,000 under the old strategy. Despite the negative expected payoff, some within the firm have suggested that Baxter should go ahead with the new strategy, in the interest of better serving its shareholders. How can shareholders benefit from this decision?

As Table 16.3 shows, if Baxter does nothing, it will ultimately default and equity holders will get nothing with certainty. Thus equity holders have nothing to lose if Baxter tries the risky strategy. If the strategy succeeds, equity holders will receive $300,000 after paying off the debt. Given a 50% chance of success, the equity holders' expected payoff is $150,000.

TABLE 16.3	Outcomes for Baxter's Debt and Equity Under Each Strategy ($ thousand)			
	Old Strategy	**New Risky Strategy**		
		Success	**Failure**	**Expected**
Value of assets	**900**	1300	300	**800**
Debt	**900**	1000	300	**650**
Equity	**0**	300	0	**150**

Clearly, equity holders gain from this strategy, even though it has a negative expected payoff. Who loses? The debt holders: If the strategy fails, they bear the loss. As shown in Table 16.3, if the project succeeds, debt holders are fully repaid and receive $1 million. If the project fails, they receive only $300,000. Overall, the debt holders' expected payoff is $650,000, a loss of $250,000 relative to the $900,000 they would have received under the old strategy. This loss corresponds to the $100,000 expected loss of the risky strategy and the $150,000 gain of the equity holders. Effectively, the equity holders are gambling with the debt holders' money.

This example illustrates a general point: *When a firm faces financial distress, shareholders can gain by making sufficiently risky investments, even if they have negative NPV.*[17] This result leads to an **over-investment problem**: Shareholders have an incentive to invest in risky negative-NPV projects. But a negative-NPV project destroys value for the firm overall. Anticipating this bad behavior, security holders will pay less for the firm initially. This cost is likely to be highest for firms that can easily increase the risk of their investments.

Under-investment

Suppose Baxter does not pursue the risky strategy. Instead, the firm's managers consider an attractive investment opportunity that requires an initial investment of $100,000 and will generate a risk-free return of 50%. That is, it has the following cash flows (in thousands of dollars):

---

17. This problem is also referred to as *asset substitution:* After issuing debt, equity holders have an incentive to substitute risky investments for safe ones. See Michael Jensen and William Meckling, "Theory of the Firm: Managerial Behavior, Agency Costs and Ownership Structure," *Journal of Financial Economics* 3 (1976): 305–360.

If the current risk-free rate is 5%, this investment clearly has a positive NPV. The only problem is that Baxter does not have the cash on hand to make the investment.

Could Baxter raise the $100,000 by issuing new equity? Unfortunately, it cannot. Suppose equity holders were to contribute the $100,000 in new capital required. Their payoff at the end of the year is shown in Table 16.4.

TABLE 16.4	Outcomes for Baxter's Debt and Equity with and without the New Project ($ thousand)	
	Without New Project	**With New Project**
Existing assets	900	900
New project		150
Total firm value	900	1050
Debt	900	1000
Equity	0	50

Thus, if equity holders contribute $100,000 to fund the project, they get back only $50,000. The other $100,000 from the project goes to the debt holders, whose payoff increases from $900,000 to $1 million. Because the debt holders receive most of the benefit, this project is a negative-NPV investment opportunity for equity holders, even though it offers a positive NPV for the firm.

This example illustrates another general point: *When a firm faces financial distress, it may choose not to finance new, positive-NPV projects.*[18] In this case, there is an **under-investment problem**: Shareholders choose to not invest in a positive-NPV project. This failure to invest is costly for debt holders and for the overall value of the firm, because it is giving up the NPV of the missed opportunities. The cost is highest for firms that are likely to have profitable future growth opportunities requiring large investments.

Cashing Out

When a firm faces financial distress, shareholders have an incentive not to invest and to withdraw money from the firm if possible. As an example, suppose Baxter has equipment it can sell for $25,000 at the beginning of the year. It will need this equipment to continue normal operations during the year; without it, Baxter will have to shut down some operations and the firm will be worth only $800,000 at year-end. Although selling the equipment reduces the value of the firm by $100,000, if it is likely that Baxter will default at year-end, this cost would be borne by the debt holders. So, equity holders gain if Baxter sells the equipment and uses the $25,000 to pay an immediate cash dividend. This incentive to liquidate assets at prices below their actual value is another form of under-investment that occurs when a firm faces financial distress.

Agency Costs and the Value of Leverage

These examples illustrate how leverage can encourage managers and shareholders to act in ways that reduce firm value. In each case, the equity holders benefit at the expense of the debt holders. But, as with financial distress costs, it is the shareholders of the firm who

---

18. This cost of debt, also referred to as *debt overhang*, was formalized by Stewart Myers, "Determinants of Corporate Borrowing," *Journal of Financial Economics* 5 (1977): 147–175.

ultimately bear these agency costs. When a firm initially chooses to add leverage to its capital structure, the decision has two effects on the share price. First, the share price benefits from equity holders' ability to exploit debt holders in times of distress. Second, the debt holders recognize this possibility and pay less for the debt when it is issued, reducing the amount the firm can distribute to shareholders. Because debt holders lose more than shareholders gain from these activities, the net effect is a reduction in the initial share price of the firm. The amount of this reduction will correspond to the negative NPV of the decisions.

These agency costs of debt can arise only if there is some chance the firm will default and impose losses on its debt holders. The magnitude of the agency costs increases with the risk, and therefore the amount, of the firm's debt. Agency costs, therefore, represent another cost of increasing the firm's leverage that will affect the firm's optimal capital structure choice.

EXAMPLE 16.5

Agency Costs and the Amount of Leverage

Problem
Would the agency costs described previously arise if Baxter had less leverage and owed $400,000 rather than $1 million?

Solution
If Baxter makes no new investments or changes to its strategy, the firm will be worth $900,000. Thus the firm will remain solvent and its equity will be worth $900,000 − $400,000 = $500,000.

If Baxter takes the risky strategy, its assets will be worth either $1.3 million or $300,000, so equity holders will receive $900,000 or $0. In this case, the equity holders' expected payoff with the risky project is only $450,000. Thus equity holders will reject the risky strategy.

What about under-investment? If Baxter raises $100,000 from equity holders to fund a new investment that increases the value of assets by $150,000, the equity will be worth

$$\$900,000 + \$150,000 - \$400,000 = \$650,000$$

This is a gain of $150,000 over the $500,000 equity holders would receive without the investment. Because their payoff has gone up by $150,000 for a $100,000 investment, they will be willing to invest in the new project.

Similarly, Baxter has no incentive to cash out and sell equipment to pay a dividend. If the firm pays the dividend, equity holders receive $25,000 today. But their future payoff declines to $800,000 − $400,000 = $400,000. Thus they give up $100,000 in one year for a $25,000 gain today. For any reasonable discount rate, this is a bad deal and stockholders will reject the dividend.

Debt Maturity and Covenants

Several things can be done to mitigate the agency costs of debt. First, note that the magnitude of agency costs likely depends on the maturity of debt. With long-term debt, equity holders have more opportunities to profit at the debt holders' expense before the debt matures. Thus agency costs are smallest for short-term debt.[19] For example, if Baxter's debt were due today, the firm would be forced to default or renegotiate with debt holders

---

19. See Shane Johnson, "Debt Maturity and the Effects of Growth Opportunities and Liquidity on Leverage," *Review of Financial Studies* 16 (March 2003): 209–236, for empirical evidence supporting this hypothesis.

before it could increase risk, fail to invest, or cash out. However, by relying on short-term debt the firm will be obligated to repay or refinance its debt more frequently. Short-term debt may also increase the firm's risk of financial distress and its associated costs.

Second, as a condition of making a loan, creditors often place restrictions on the actions that the firm can take. Such restrictions are referred to as **debt covenants**. Covenants may limit the firm's ability to pay large dividends or the types of investments that the firm can make. These covenants are often designed to prevent management from exploiting debt holders, so they may help to reduce agency costs. Conversely, because covenants hinder management flexibility, they have the potential to get in the way of positive NPV opportunities and so can have costs of their own.[20]

CONCEPT CHECK

1. What is the purpose of debt covenants in a bond contract?

2. Why would debt holders desire covenants that restrict the firm's ability to pay dividends, and why might shareholders also benefit from this restriction?

16.6 Motivating Managers: The Agency Benefits of Leverage

In Section 16.5, we took the view that managers act in the interests of the firm's equity holders, and we considered the potential conflicts of interest between debt holders and equity holders when a firm has leverage. Of course, managers also have their own personal interests, which may differ from those of both equity holders and debt holders. Although managers often do own shares of the firm, in most large corporations they own only a very small fraction of the outstanding shares. And while the shareholders, through the board of directors, have the power to fire managers, they rarely do so unless the firm's performance is exceptionally poor.[21]

This separation of ownership and control creates the possibility of **management entrenchment**; facing little threat of being fired and replaced, managers are free to run the firm in their own best interests. As a result, managers may make decisions that benefit themselves at investors' expense. In this section, we consider how leverage can provide incentives for managers to run the firm more efficiently and effectively. The benefits we describe in this section, in addition to the tax benefits of leverage, give the firm an incentive to use debt rather than equity financing.

Concentration of Ownership

One advantage of using leverage is that it allows the original owners of the firm to maintain their equity stake. As major shareholders, they will have a strong interest in doing what is best for the firm. Next we consider an example of such a situation.

Ross Jackson is the owner of a successful furniture store. He plans to expand by opening several new stores. Ross can either borrow the funds needed for expansion or raise the money by selling shares in the firm. If he issues equity, he will need to sell 40% of the firm to raise the necessary funds.

---

20. For an analysis of the costs and benefits of bond covenants, see C. W. Smith and J. B. Warner, "On Financial Contracting: An Analysis of Bond Covenants," *Journal of Financial Economics* (June 1979): 117–161.

21. See, for example, Jerold Warner, Ross Watts, and Karen Wruck, "Stock Prices and Top Management Changes," *Journal of Financial Economics* 20 (1988): 461–492.

If Ross uses debt, he retains ownership of 100% of the firm's equity. As long as the firm does not default, any decision Ross makes that increases the value of the firm by $1 increases the value of his own stake by $1. But if Ross issues equity, he retains only 60% of the equity. Thus Ross gains only $0.60 for every $1 increase in firm value.

The difference in Ross's ownership stake changes his incentives in running the firm. Suppose the value of the firm depends largely on Ross's personal effort. Ross is then likely to work harder, and the firm will be worth more, if he receives 100% of the gains rather than only 60%.

Another effect of issuing equity is Ross's temptation to enjoy corporate perks, such as a large office with fancy artwork, a corporate limo and driver, a corporate jet, or a large expense account. With leverage, Ross is the sole owner and will bear the full cost of these perks. But with equity, Ross bears only 60% of the cost; the other 40% will be paid for by the new equity holders. Thus, with equity financing, it is more likely that Ross will overspend on these luxuries.

The costs of reduced effort and excessive spending on perks are another form of agency cost. These agency costs arise in this case due to the dilution of ownership that occurs when equity financing is used. Who pays these agency costs? As always, if securities are fairly priced, the original owners of the firm pay the cost. In our example, Ross will find that if he chooses to issue equity, the new investors will discount the price they will pay to reflect Ross's lower effort and increased spending on perks. In this case, using leverage can benefit the firm by preserving ownership concentration and avoiding these agency costs.[22]

Reduction of Wasteful Investment

While ownership is often concentrated for small, young firms, ownership typically becomes diluted over time as a firm grows. First, the original owners of the firm may retire, and the new managers likely will not hold a large ownership stake. Second, firms often need to raise more capital for investment than can be sustained using debt alone (recall the discussion of debt capacity and growth in Chapter 15). Third, owners will often choose to sell off their stakes and invest in a well-diversified portfolio to reduce risk.[23] As a result, for large U.S. firms, most CEOs own less than 1% of their firms' shares.

With such low ownership stakes, the potential for conflict of interest between managers and equity holders is high. Appropriate monitoring and standards of accountability are required to prevent abuse. While most successful firms have implemented appropriate mechanisms to protect shareholders, each year scandals are revealed in which managers have acted against shareholders' interests.

While overspending on personal perks may be a problem for large firms, these costs are likely to be small relative to the overall value of the firm. A more serious concern for large corporations is that managers may make large, unprofitable investments: Bad investment

---

22. This potential benefit of leverage is discussed by Michael Jensen and William Meckling, "Theory of the Firm: Managerial Behavior, Agency Costs and Ownership Structure," *Journal of Financial Economics* 3 (1976): 305–360. Note also that because managers who own a large block of shares are more difficult to replace, increased ownership concentration may also lead to increased entrenchment and reduce incentives; see Randall Morck, Andrei Shleifer, and Robert W. Vishny, "Management Ownership and Market Valuation," *Journal of Financial Economics* 20 (1988): 293–315.

23. According to a recent study, original owners tend to reduce their stake by more than 50% within nine years after the firm becomes a public company (Branko Urošević, "Essays in Optimal Dynamic Risk Sharing in Equity and Debt Markets," Ph.D. thesis, 2002, University of California, Berkeley).

Excessive Perks and Corporate Scandals

While most CEOs and managers exercise proper restraint when spending shareholders' money, there have been some highly publicized exceptions in the corporate scandals that have come to light.

Former Enron CFO Andrew Fastow reportedly used complicated financial transactions to enrich himself with at least $30 million of shareholder money. Tyco Corporation's ex-CEO Dennis Kozlowski will be remembered for his $6000 shower curtain, $6300 sewing basket, and $17 million Fifth Avenue condo, all paid for with Tyco funds. In total, he and former CFO Mark Swartz were convicted of pilfering $600 million from company coffers.* Former WorldCom CEO Bernie Ebbers, who was convicted for his role in the firm's $11 billion accounting scandal, borrowed more than $400 million from the company at favorable terms from late 2000 to early 2002. Among other things, he used the money from these loans to give gifts to friends and family, as well as build a house.† John Rigas and his son Timothy, former CEO and CFO of Adelphia Communications, were convicted of stealing $100 million from the firm as well as hiding $2 billion in corporate debt.

But these are certainly exceptional cases. And they were not, in and of themselves, the cause of the firms' downfalls, but rather a symptom of a broader problem of a lack of oversight and accountability within these firms, together with an opportunistic attitude of the managers involved.

*Melanie Warner, "Exorcism at Tyco," *Fortune Magazine,* April 28, 2003, p. 106.

†Andrew Backover, "Report Slams Culture at WorldCom," *USA Today*, November 5, 2002, p. 1B.

---

decisions have destroyed many otherwise successful firms. But what would motivate managers to make negative-NPV investments?

Some financial economists explain a manager's willingness to engage in negative-NPV investments as *empire building*. According to this view, managers prefer to run large firms rather than small ones, so they will take on investments that increase the size—rather than the profitability—of the firm. One potential reason for this preference is that managers of large firms tend to earn higher salaries, and they may also have more prestige and garner greater publicity than managers of small firms. As a result, managers may expand (or fail to shut down) unprofitable divisions, pay too much for acquisitions, make unnecessary capital expenditures, or hire unnecessary employees.

Another reason that managers may over-invest is that they are overconfident. Even when managers attempt to act in shareholders' interests, they may make mistakes. Managers tend to be bullish on the firm's prospects and so may believe that new opportunities are better than they actually are. They may also become committed to investments the firm has already made and continue to invest in projects that should be cancelled.[24]

For managers to engage in wasteful investment, they must have the cash to invest. This observation is the basis of the **free cash flow hypothesis**, the view that wasteful spending is more likely to occur when firms have high levels of cash flow in excess of what is needed to make all positive-NPV investments and payments to debt holders.[25] Only

---

24. For evidence of the relationship between CEO overconfidence and investment distortions, see Ulrike Malmendier and Geoffrey Tate, "CEO Overconfidence and Corporate Investment," *Journal of Finance* 60 (2005): 2661–2700. See also J. B. Heaton "Managerial Optimism and Corporate Finance," *Financial Management* 31 (2002): 33–45; and Richard Roll, "The Hubris Hypothesis of Corporate Takeovers," *Journal of Business* 59 (1986): 197–216.

25. The hypothesis that excess cash flow induces empire building was put forth by M. Jensen, "Agency Costs of Free Cash Flow, Corporate Finance, and Takeovers," *American Economic Review* 76 (1986): 323–329.

when cash is tight will managers be motivated to run the firm as efficiently as possible. According to this hypothesis, leverage increases firm value because it commits the firm to making future interest payments, thereby reducing excess cash flows and wasteful investment by managers.[26]

A related idea is that leverage can reduce the degree of managerial entrenchment because managers are more likely to be fired when a firm faces financial distress. Managers who are less entrenched may be more concerned about their performance and less likely to engage in wasteful investment. In addition, when the firm is highly levered, creditors themselves will closely monitor the actions of managers, providing an additional layer of management oversight.[27]

Leverage and Commitment

Leverage may also tie managers' hands and commit them to pursue strategies with greater vigor than they would without the threat of financial distress. For example, when American Airlines was in labor negotiations with its unions in April 2003, the firm was able to win wage concessions by explaining that higher costs would push it into bankruptcy. (A similar situation enabled Delta Airlines to persuade its pilots to accept a 33% wage cut in November 2004.) Without the threat of financial distress, American's managers might not have reached agreement with the union as quickly or achieved the same wage concessions.[28]

A firm with greater leverage may also become a fiercer competitor and act more aggressively in protecting its markets because it cannot risk the possibility of bankruptcy. This commitment to aggressive behavior can scare off potential rivals. (This argument could work in reverse: A firm weakened by too much leverage might become so financially fragile that it crumbles in the face of competition, allowing other firms to erode its markets.)[29]

CONCEPT CHECK

1. In what ways might managers benefit by overspending on acquisitions?

2. How might shareholders use the firm's capital structure to prevent this problem?

---

26. Of course, if the firm did not generate sufficient free cash flow, managers could also raise new capital for wasteful investment. But new investors would be reluctant to contribute to such an endeavor and would offer unfavorable terms. In addition, raising external funds would likely attract greater scrutiny and public criticism regarding the investment.

27. See for example M. Harris and A. Raviv, "Capital Structure and the Informational Role of Debt," *Journal of Finance* 45 2 (1990): 321–349.

28. See E. C. Perotti and K. E. Spier, "Capital Structure as a Bargaining Tool: The Role of Leverage in Contract Renegotiation," *American Economic Review* (December 1993): 1131–1141. Debt can also affect a firm's bargaining power with its suppliers; see S. Dasgupta and K. Sengupta, "Sunk Investment, Bargaining and Choice of Capital Structure," *International Economic Review* (February 1993): 203–220; and O. H. Sarig, "The Effect of Leverage on Bargaining with a Corporation," *Financial Review* 33 (February 1998): 1–16. Debt may also enhance a target's bargaining power in a control contest; see M. Harris and A. Raviv, "Corporate Control Contests and Capital Structure," *Journal of Financial Economics* (March 1988): 55–86; and R. Israel, "Capital Structure and the Market for Corporate Control: The Defensive Role of Debt Financing," *Journal of Finance* (September 1991): 1391–1409.

29. This idea was formalized by James Brander and Tracy Lewis, "Oligopoly and Financial Structure: The Limited Liability Effect," *American Economic Review* 76 (1986): 956–970. In an empirical study, Judy Chevalier finds that leverage reduces the competitiveness of supermarket firms ["Capital Structure and Product-Market Competition: Empirical Evidence from the Supermarket Industry," *American Economic Review* 85 (1995): 415–435]. Patric Bolton and David Scharfstein discuss the effects of not having deep pockets in "A Theory of Predation Based on Agency Problems in Financial Contracting," *American Economic Review* 80 (1990): 93–106.

16.7 Agency Costs and the Tradeoff Theory

We can now adjust Eq. 16.1 for the value of the firm to include the costs and benefits of the incentives that arise when the firm has leverage. This more complete equation is shown below:

$$V^L = V^U + PV(\text{Interest Tax Shield}) - PV(\text{Financial Distress Costs})$$
$$- PV(\text{Agency Costs of Debt}) + PV(\text{Agency Benefits of Debt}) \quad (16.2)$$

The net effect of the costs and benefits of leverage on the value of a firm is illustrated in Figure 16.2. With no debt, the value of the firm is V^U. As the debt level increases, the firm benefits from the interest tax shield (which has present value $\tau^* D$). The firm also benefits from improved incentives for management, which reduce wasteful investment and perks. If the debt level is too large, however, firm value is reduced due to the loss of tax benefits (when interest exceeds EBIT), financial distress costs, and the agency costs of leverage. The optimal level of debt, D^*, balances the costs and benefits of leverage.

The Optimal Debt Level

It is important to note that the relative magnitudes of the different costs and benefits of debt vary with the characteristics of the firm. Likewise, the optimal level of debt varies. As an example, let's contrast the optimal capital structure choice for two types of firms.

R&D-Intensive Firms.   Firms with high R&D costs and future growth opportunities typically maintain low debt levels. These firms tend to have low current free cash flows, so they need little debt to provide a tax shield or to control managerial spending. In addition, they tend to have high human capital, so there will be large costs as a result of financial

FIGURE 16.2

Optimal Leverage with Taxes, Financial Distress, and Agency Costs

As the level of debt, D, increases, the value of the firm increases from the interest tax shield as well as improvements in managerial incentives. If leverage is too high, however, the present value of financial distress costs, as well as the agency costs from debt holder–equity holder conflicts, dominates and reduces firm value. The optimal level of debt, D^*, balances these benefits and costs of leverage.

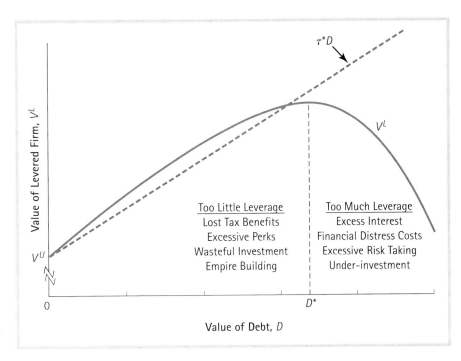

distress. Also, these firms may find it easy to increase the risk of their business strategy (by pursuing a riskier technology) and often need to raise additional capital to fund new investment opportunities. Thus their agency costs of debt are also high. Biotechnology and technology firms often maintain less than 10% leverage.

Low-Growth, Mature Firms. Mature, low-growth firms with stable cash flows and tangible assets often fall into the high-debt category. These firms tend to have high free cash flows with few good investment opportunities. Thus the tax shield and incentive benefits of leverage are likely to be high. With tangible assets, the financial distress costs of leverage are likely to be low, as the assets can be liquidated for close to their full value. Examples of low-growth industries in which firms typically maintain greater than 20% leverage include real estate, utilities, and supermarket chains.

Debt Levels in Practice

The tradeoff theory explains how firms *should* choose their capital structures to maximize value to current shareholders. However, these results need not coincide with what firms actually *do* in practice. Keep in mind that, like investment decisions, capital structure decisions are made by managers who have their own incentives. Proponents of the **management entrenchment theory** of capital structure believe that managers choose a capital structure to avoid the discipline of debt and maintain their own job security. Thus managers seek to *minimize* leverage to prevent the job loss that would accompany financial distress. Managers are constrained from using too little debt, however, to keep shareholders happy. If managers sacrifice too much firm value, disgruntled shareholders may try to replace them or sell the firm to an acquirer. Under this hypothesis, firms will have leverage that is less than the optimal level D^* in Figure 16.2, and increase it toward D^* only in response to a takeover threat or the threat of shareholder activism.[30]

CONCEPT CHECK   1. Describe how the management entrenchment can affect the value of the firm.

2. Coca-Cola Enterprises is almost 50% debt financed, while Amgen, a biotechnology firm, is less than 10% debt financed. Why might these firms choose such different capital structures?

16.8 Asymmetric Information and Capital Structure

Throughout this chapter, we have assumed that managers, stockholders, and creditors have the same information. We have also assumed that securities are fairly priced: The firm's shares and debt are priced according to their true underlying value. These assumptions may not always be accurate in practice. Managers' information about the firm and its future cash flows is likely to be superior to that of outside investors—there is **asymmetric information** between managers and investors. In this section, we consider how asymmetric information may motivate managers to alter a firm's capital structure.

---

30. See Jeffrey Zwiebel, "Dynamic Capital Structure Under Managerial Entrenchment," *American Economic Review* 86 (1996): 1197–1215; Luigi Zingales and Walter Novaes, "Capital Structure Choice When Managers are in Control: Entrenchment versus Efficiency," *Journal of Business* 76 (2002): 49–82; and Erwan Morellec, "Can Managerial Discretion Explain Observed Leverage Ratios," *Review of Financial Studies* 17 (2004): 257–294. Zechner "Human Capital, Bankruptcy and Capital Structure," working paper, 2006.

Leverage as a Credible Signal

Consider the plight of Kim Smith, CEO of Beltran International, who believes her company's stock is undervalued. Market analysts and investors are concerned that several of Beltran's key patents will expire soon, and that new competition will force Beltran to cut prices or lose customers. Smith believes that new product innovations and soon-to-be-introduced manufacturing improvements will keep Beltran ahead of its competitors and enable it to sustain its current profitability well into the future. She seeks to convince investors of Beltran's promising future and to increase Beltran's current stock price.

One potential strategy is to launch an investor relations campaign. Smith can issue press releases, describing the merits of the new innovations and the manufacturing improvements. But Smith knows that investors may be skeptical of these press releases if their claims cannot be verified. After all, managers, much like politicians, have an incentive to sound optimistic and confident about what they can achieve.

Because investors expect her to be biased, to convince the market Smith must take actions that give credible signals of her knowledge of the firm. That is, she must take actions that the market understands she would be unwilling to do unless her statements were true. This idea is more general than manager–investor communication; it is at the heart of much human interaction. We call it the **credibility principle**:

Claims in one's self-interest are credible only if they are supported by actions that would be too costly to take if the claims were untrue.

This principle is the essence behind the adage, "Actions speak louder than words."

One way a firm can credibly convey its strength to investors is by making statements about its future prospects that investors and analysts can ultimately verify. Because the penalties for intentionally deceiving investors are large,[31] investors will generally believe such statements.

For example, suppose Smith announces that pending long-term contracts from the U.S., British, and Japanese governments will increase revenues for Beltran by 30% next year. Because this statement can be verified after the fact, it would be costly to make it if untrue. For deliberate misrepresentation, the U.S. Securities and Exchange Commission (SEC) would likely fine the firm and file charges against Smith. The firm could also be sued by its investors. These large costs would likely outweigh any potential benefits to Smith and Beltran for temporarily misleading investors and boosting the share price. Thus investors will likely view the announcement as credible.

But what if Beltran cannot yet reveal specific details regarding its future prospects? Perhaps the contracts for the government orders have not yet been signed or cannot be disclosed for other reasons. How can Smith credibly communicate her positive information regarding the firm?

One strategy is to commit the firm to large future debt payments. If Smith is right, then Beltran will have no trouble making the debt payments. But if Smith is making false claims and the firm does not grow, Beltran will have trouble paying its creditors and will experience financial distress. This distress will be costly for the firm and also for Smith, who will likely lose her job. Thus Smith can use leverage as a way to convince investors that she does have information that the firm will grow, even if she cannot provide verifiable details about the sources of growth. Investors know that Beltran would be at risk of

---

31. The Sarbanes-Oxley Act of 2002 increased the penalties for securities fraud to include up to ten years of imprisonment.

defaulting without growth opportunities, so they will interpret the additional leverage as a credible signal of the CEO's confidence. The use of leverage as a way to signal good information to investors is known as the **signaling theory of debt**.[32]

Debt Signals Strength

Problem

Suppose that Beltran currently uses all-equity financing, and that Beltran's market value in one year's time will be either $100 million or $50 million depending on the success of the new strategy. Currently, investors view the outcomes as equally likely, but Smith has information that success is virtually certain. Will leverage of $25 million make Smith's claims credible? How about leverage of $55 million?

Solution

If leverage is substantially less than $50 million, Beltran will have no risk of financial distress regardless of the outcome. As a result, there is no cost of leverage even if Smith does not have positive information. Thus leverage of $25 million would not be a credible signal of strength to investors.

However, leverage of $55 million is likely to be a credible signal. If Smith has no positive information, there is a significant chance that Beltran will face bankruptcy under this burden of debt. Thus Smith would be unlikely to agree to this amount of leverage unless she is certain about the firm's prospects.

Issuing Equity and Adverse Selection

Suppose a used-car dealer tells you he is willing to sell you a nice-looking sports car for $5000 less than its typical price. Rather than feel lucky, perhaps your first reaction should be one of skepticism: If the dealer is willing to sell it for such a low price, there must be something wrong with the car—it is probably a "lemon."

The idea that buyers will be skeptical of a seller's motivation for selling was formalized by George Akerlof.[33] Akerlof showed that if the seller has private information about the quality of the car, then his *desire to sell* reveals the car is probably of low quality. Buyers are therefore reluctant to buy except at heavily discounted prices. Owners of high-quality cars are reluctant to sell because they know buyers will think they are selling a lemon and offer only a low price. Consequently, the quality and prices of cars sold in the used-car market are both low. This result is referred to as **adverse selection**: The selection of cars sold in the used-car market is worse than average.

Adverse selection extends beyond the used-car market. In fact, it applies in any setting in which the seller has more information than the buyer. Adverse selection leads to the **lemons principle**:

When a seller has private information about the value of a good, buyers will discount the price they are willing to pay due to adverse selection.

---

32. Such a theory is developed by Stephen Ross, "The Determination of Financial Structure: The Incentive-Signalling Approach," *Bell Journal of Economics* 8 (1977): 23–40.

33. "The Market for Lemons: Quality, Uncertainty, and the Market Mechanism," *Quarterly Journal of Economics* 84 (1970): 488–500.

Nobel Prize   The 2001 Nobel Prize in Economics

In 2001, George Akerlof, Michael Spence, and Joseph Stiglitz jointly received the Nobel Prize in economics for their analyses of markets with asymmetric information and adverse selection. In this chapter, we discuss the implications of their theory for firm capital structure. This theory, however, has much broader applications. As described on the Nobel Prize Web site (www.nobelprize.org):

Many markets are characterized by asymmetric information: Actors on one side of the market have much better information than those on the other. Borrowers know more

than lenders about their repayment prospects, managers and boards know more than shareholders about the firm's profitability, and prospective clients know more than insurance companies about their accident risk. During the 1970s, this year's Laureates laid the foundation for a general theory of markets with asymmetric information. Applications have been abundant, ranging from traditional agricultural markets to modern financial markets. The Laureates' contributions form the core of modern information economics.

© The Nobel Foundation

We can apply this principle to the market for equity.[34] Suppose the owner of a start-up company tells you that his firm is a wonderful investment opportunity—and then offers to sell you 70% of his stake in the firm. He states that he is selling *only* because he wants to diversify. Although you appreciate this desire, you also suspect the owner may be eager to sell such a large stake because he has negative information about the firm's future prospects. That is, he may be trying to cash out before the bad news becomes known.[35]

As with the used-car dealer, a firm owner's desire to sell equity may lead you to question how good an investment opportunity it really is. Based on the lemons principle, you therefore reduce the price you are willing to pay. This discount of the price due to adverse selection is a potential cost of issuing equity, and it may make owners with good information refrain from issuing equity.

Adverse Selection in Equity Markets

Problem

Zycor stock is worth either $100 per share, $80 per share, or $60 per share. Investors believe each case is equally likely, and the current share price is equal to the average value of $80.

Suppose the CEO of Zycor announces he will sell most of his holdings of the stock to diversify. Diversifying is worth 10% of the share price—that is, the CEO would be willing to receive 10% less than the shares are worth to achieve the benefits of diversification. If investors believe the CEO knows the true value, how will the share price change if he tries to sell? Will the CEO sell at the new share price?

---

34. This observation is due to Hayne Leland and David Pyle, "Information Asymmetries, Financial Structure and Financial Intermediation," *Journal of Finance* 32 (1977): 371–387.

35. Again, if the owner of the firm (or the car, in the earlier example) has very specific information that can be verified ex-post, there are potential legal consequences for not revealing that information to a buyer. Generally, however, there is a great deal of subtle information the seller might have that would be impossible to verify.

Solution

If the true value of the shares were $100, the CEO would not be willing to sell at the market price of $80 per share, which would be 20% below their true value. So, if the CEO tries to sell, shareholders can conclude the shares are worth either $80 or $60. In that case, share price should fall to the average value of $70. But again, if the true value were $80, the CEO would be willing to sell for $72, but not $70 per share. So, if he still tries to sell, investors will know the true value is $60 per share. Thus the CEO will sell only if the true value is the lowest possible price, $60 per share. If the CEO knows the firm's stock is worth $100 or $80 per share, he will not sell.

In explaining adverse selection, we considered an owner of a firm selling his or her *own* shares. What if a manager of the firm decides to sell securities on the *firm's* behalf? If the securities are sold at a price below their true value, the buyer's windfall represents a cost for the firm's current shareholders. Acting on behalf of the current shareholders, the manager may be unwilling to sell.[36]

Let's consider a simple example. Gentec is a biotech firm with no debt, and its 20 million shares are currently trading at $10 per share, for a total market value of $200 million. Based on the prospects for one of Gentec's new drugs, management believes the true value of the company is $300 million, or $15 per share. Management believes the share price will reflect this higher value after the clinical trials for the drug are concluded next year.

Gentec has already announced plans to raise $60 million from investors to build a new research lab. It can raise the funds today by issuing 6 million new shares at the current price of $10 per share. In that case, after the good news comes out, the value of the firm's assets will be $300 million (from the existing assets) plus $60 million (new lab), for a total value of $360 million. With 26 million shares outstanding, the new share price will be $360 million ÷ 26 million shares = $13.85 per share.

But suppose Gentec waits for the good news to come out and the share price to rise to $15 *before* issuing the new shares. At that time, the firm will be able to raise the $60 million by selling 4 million shares. The firm's assets will again be worth a total of $360 million, but Gentec will have only 24 million shares outstanding, which is consistent with the share price of $360 million ÷ 24 million shares = $15 per share.

Thus issuing new shares when management knows they are underpriced is costly for the original shareholders. Their shares will be worth only $13.85 rather than $15. As a result, if Gentec's managers care primarily about the firm's current shareholders, they will be reluctant to sell securities at a price that is below their true value. If they believe the shares are underpriced, managers will prefer to wait until after the share price rises to issue equity.

This preference not to issue equity that is underpriced leads us to the same lemons problem we had before: Managers who know securities have a high value will not sell, and those who know they have a low value will sell. Due to this adverse selection, investors will be willing to pay only a low price for the securities. The lemons problem creates a

---

36. Stewart Myers and Nicholas Majluf demonstrated this result, and a number of its implications for capital structure, in an influential paper, "Corporate Financing and Investment Decisions When Firms Have Information that Investors Do Not Have," *Journal of Financial Economics* 13 (1984): 187–221.

FIGURE 16.4

Aggregate Source
Funding for Capit
Expenditures,
U.S. Corporations

In aggregate, firms t
to repurchase equit
and issue debt. But
than 70% of capital
expenditures are fu
from retained earni

Source: Federal Reserv
of Funds.

cost for firms that need to raise capital from investors to fund new investments. If they try to issue equity, investors will discount the price they are willing to pay to reflect the possibility that managers are privy to bad news.

Implications for Equity Issuance

Adverse selection has a number of important implications for equity issuance. First and foremost, the lemons principle directly implies that

1. *The stock price declines on the announcement of an equity issue.*

When a firm issues equity, it signals to investors that its equity may be overpriced. As a result, investors are willing to pay less for the equity and the stock price declines. Numerous studies have confirmed this result, finding that the stock price falls about 3% on average on the announcement of an equity issue by a publicly traded firm in the United States.[37]

As was true for Gentec, managers issuing equity have an incentive to delay the issue until any news that might positively affect the stock price becomes public. In contrast, there is no incentive to delay the issue if managers expect negative news to come out. These incentives lead to the following pattern:

2. *The stock price tends to rise prior to the announcement of an equity issue.*

This result is also supported empirically, as illustrated in Figure 16.3 using data from a study by Deborah Lucas and Robert McDonald.[38] They found that stocks with equity issues outperformed the market by almost 50% in the year and a half prior to the announcement of the issue.

Managers may also try to avoid the price decline associated with adverse selection by issuing equity at times when they have the smallest informational advantage over investors. For example, because a great deal of information is released to investors at the time of earnings announcements, equity issues are often timed to occur immediately after these announcements. That is,

3. *Firms tend to issue equity when information asymmetries are minimized, such as immediately after earnings announcements.*[39]

Implications for Capital Structure

Because managers find it costly to issue equity that is underpriced, they may seek alternative forms of financing. While debt issues may also suffer from adverse selection, because the value of low-risk debt is not very sensitive to managers' private information about the firm (but is instead determined mainly by interest rates), the degree of underpricing

---

37. See, for example, Paul Asquith and David Mullins, "Equity Issues and Offering Dilution," *Journal of Financial Economics* 15 (1986): 61–89; Ronald Masulis and Ashok Korwar, "Seasoned Equity Offerings: An Empirical Investigation," *Journal of Financial Economics* 15 (1986): 91–118; and Wayne Mikkelson and Megan Partch, "Valuation Effects of Security Offerings and the Issuance Process," *Journal of Financial Economics* 15 (1986): 31–60.

38. "Equity Issues and Stock Price Dynamics," *Journal of Finance* 45 (1990): 1019–1043.

39. In a 1991 study, Robert Korajczyk, Deborah Lucas, and Robert McDonald confirmed this timing and reported that the negative stock price reaction is smallest immediately after earnings announcements, and becomes larger as the amount of time since the last earnings announcement increases ["The Effect of Information Releases on the Pricing and Timing of Equity Issues," *Review of Financial Studies* 4 (1991): 685–708].

$95 million, and $80 million. These outcomes are all equally likely, and this risk is diversifiable. Suppose the risk-free interest rate is 5% and assume perfect capital markets.

   a. What is the initial value of Gladstone's equity without leverage?

Now suppose Gladstone has zero-coupon debt with a $100 million face value due next year.

   b. What is the initial value of Gladstone's debt?

   c. What is the yield-to-maturity of the debt? What is its expected return?

   d. What is the initial value of Gladstone's equity? What is Gladstone's total value with leverage?

2.   Baruk Industries has no cash and a debt obligation of $36 million that is now due. The market value of Baruk's assets is $81 million, and the firm has no other liabilities. Assume perfect capital markets.

   a. Suppose Baruk has 10 million shares outstanding. What is Baruk's current share price?

   b. How many new shares must Baruk issue to raise the capital needed to pay its debt obligation?

   c. After repaying the debt, what will Baruk's share price be?

The Costs of Bankruptcy and Financial Distress

3.   When a firm defaults on its debt, debt holders often receive less than 50% of the amount they are owed. Is the difference between the amount debt holders are owed and the amount they receive a *cost* of bankruptcy?

4.   Which type of firm is more likely to experience a loss of customers in the event of financial distress:

   a. Campbell Soup Company or Intuit, Inc. (a maker of accounting software)?

   b. Allstate Corporation (an insurance company) or Reebok International (a footwear and clothing firm)?

5.   Which type of asset is more likely to be liquidated for close to its full market value in the event of financial distress:

   a. An office building or a brand name?

   b. Product inventory or raw materials?

   c. Patent rights or engineering "know-how"?

Financial Distress Costs and Firm Value

  6.   As in Problem 1, Gladstone Corporation is about to launch a new product. Depending on the success of the new product, Gladstone may have one of four values next year: $150 million, $135 million, $95 million, and $80 million. These outcomes are all equally likely, and this risk is diversifiable. Suppose the risk-free interest rate is 5% and that, in the event of default, 25% of the value of Gladstone's assets will be lost to bankruptcy costs. (Ignore all other market imperfections, such as taxes.)

   a. What is the initial value of Gladstone's equity without leverage?

Now suppose Gladstone has zero-coupon debt with a $100 million face value due next year.

   b. What is the initial value of Gladstone's debt?

   c. What is the yield-to-maturity of the debt? What is its expected return?

   d. What is the initial value of Gladstone's equity? What is Gladstone's total value with leverage?

Suppose Gladstone has 10 million shares outstanding and no debt at the start of the year.

   e. If Gladstone does not issue debt, what is its share price?

f. If Gladstone issues debt of $100 million due next year and uses the proceeds to repurchase shares, what will its share price be? Why does your answer differ from that in part (e)?

7. Kohwe Corporation plans to issue equity to raise $50 million to finance a new investment. After making the investment, Kohwe expects to earn free cash flows of $10 million each year. Kohwe currently has 5 million shares outstanding, and it has no other assets or opportunities. Suppose the appropriate discount rate for Kohwe's future free cash flows is 8%, and the only capital market imperfections are corporate taxes and financial distress costs.

   a. What is the NPV of Kohwe's investment?

   b. What is Kohwe's share price today?

   Suppose Kohwe borrows the $50 million instead. The firm will pay interest only on this loan each year, and it will maintain an outstanding balance of $50 million on the loan. Suppose that Kohwe's corporate tax rate is 40%, and expected free cash flows are still $10 million each year.

   c. What is Kohwe's share price today if the investment is financed with debt?

   Now suppose that with leverage, Kohwe's expected free cash flows will decline to $9 million per year due to reduced sales and other financial distress costs. Assume that the appropriate discount rate for Kohwe's future free cash flows is still 8%.

   d. What is Kohwe's share price today given the financial distress costs of leverage?

Optimal Capital Structure:
The Tradeoff Theory

8. Hawar International is a shipping firm with a current share price of $5.50 and 10 million shares outstanding. Suppose Hawar announces plans to lower its corporate taxes by borrowing $20 million and repurchasing shares.

   a. With perfect capital markets, what will the share price be after this announcement?

   Suppose that Hawar pays a corporate tax rate of 30%, and that shareholders expect the change in debt to be permanent.

   b. If the only imperfection is corporate taxes, what will the share price be after this announcement?

   c. Suppose the only imperfections are corporate taxes and financial distress costs. If the share price rises to $5.75 after this announcement, what is the PV of financial distress costs Hawar will incur as the result of this new debt?

9. Marpor Industries has no debt and expects to generate free cash flows of $16 million each year. Marpor believes that if it permanently increases its level of debt to $40 million, the risk of financial distress may cause it to lose some customers and receive less favorable terms from its suppliers. As a result, Marpor's expected free cash flows with debt will be only $15 million per year. Suppose Marpor's tax rate is 35%, the risk-free rate is 5%, the expected return of the market is 15%, and the beta of Marpor's free cash flows is 1.10 (with or without leverage).

   a. Estimate Marpor's value without leverage.

   b. Estimate Marpor's value with the new leverage.

10. Real estate purchases are often financed with at least 80% debt. Most corporations, however, have less than 50% debt financing. Provide an explanation for this difference using the trade-off theory.

Exploiting Debt Holders:
The Agency Costs
of Leverage

11. Dynron Corporation's primary business is natural gas transportation using its vast gas pipeline network. Dynron's assets currently have a market value of $150 million. The firm is exploring the possibility of raising $50 million by selling part of its pipeline network and investing the

$50 million in a fiber-optic network to generate revenues by selling high-speed network bandwidth. While this new investment is expected to increase profits, it will also substantially increase Dynron's risk. If Dynron is levered, would this investment be more or less attractive to equity holders than if Dynron had no debt?

12. Consider a firm whose only asset is a plot of vacant land, and whose only liability is debt of $15 million due in one year. If left vacant, the land will be worth $10 million in one year. Alternatively, the firm can develop the land at an upfront cost of $20 million. The developed land will be worth $35 million in one year. Suppose the risk-free interest rate is 10%, assume all cash flows are risk-free, and assume there are no taxes.

   a. If the firm chooses not to develop the land, what is the value of the firm's equity today? What is the value of the debt today?

   b. What is the NPV of developing the land?

   c. Suppose the firm raises $20 million from equity holders to develop the land. If the firm develops the land, what is the value of the firm's equity today? What is the value of the firm's debt today?

   d. Given your answer to part (c), would equity holders be willing to provide the $20 million needed to develop the land?

EXCEL 13. Zymase is a biotechnology start-up firm. Researchers at Zymase must choose one of three different research strategies. The payoffs (after-tax) and their likelihood for each strategy are shown below. The risk of each project is diversifiable.

Strategy	Probability	Payoff ($ million)
A	100%	75
B	50%	140
	50%	0
C	10%	300
	90%	40

   a. Which project has the highest expected payoff?

   b. Suppose Zymase has debt of $40 million due at the time of the project's payoff. Which project has the highest expected payoff for equity holders?

   c. Suppose Zymase has debt of $110 million due at the time of the project's payoff. Which project has the highest expected payoff for equity holders?

   d. If management chooses the strategy that maximizes the payoff to equity holders, what is the expected agency cost to the firm from having $40 million in debt due? What is the expected agency cost to the firm from having $110 million in debt due?

Motivating Managers:
The Agency Benefits
of Leverage

14. You own your own firm, and you want to raise $30 million to fund an expansion. Currently, you own 100% of the firm's equity, and the firm has no debt. To raise the $30 million solely through equity, you will need to sell two-thirds of the firm. However, you would prefer to maintain at least a 50% equity stake in the firm to retain control.

   a. If you borrow $20 million, what fraction of the equity will you need to sell to raise the remaining $10 million? (Assume perfect capital markets.)

   b. What is the smallest amount you can borrow to raise the $30 million without giving up control? (Assume perfect capital markets.)

15. Empire Industries forecasts net income this coming year as shown below (in thousands of dollars):

EBIT	$1,000
Interest expense	0
Income before tax	1,000
Taxes	−350
Net income	$650

Approximately $200,000 of Empire's earnings will be needed to make new, positive-NPV investments. Unfortunately, Empire's managers are expected to waste 10% of its net income on needless perks, pet projects, and other expenditures that do not contribute to the firm. All remaining income will be returned to shareholders through dividends and share repurchases.

a. What are the two benefits of debt financing for Empire?

b. By how much would each $1 of interest expense reduce Empire's dividend and share repurchases?

c. What is the increase in the *total* funds Empire will pay to investors for each $1 of interest expense?

EXCEL 16. Ralston Enterprises has assets that will have a market value in one year as shown below:

Probability	1%	6%	24%	38%	24%	6%	1%
Value ($ million)	70	80	90	100	110	120	130

That is, there is a 1% chance the assets will be worth $70 million, a 6% chance the assets will be worth $80 million, and so on. Suppose the CEO is contemplating a decision that will benefit her personally but will reduce the value of the firm's assets by $10 million. The CEO is likely to proceed with this decision unless it substantially increases the firm's risk of bankruptcy.

a. If Ralston has debt due of $75 million in one year, the CEO's decision will increase the probability of bankruptcy by what percentage?

b. What level of debt provides the CEO with the biggest incentive not to proceed with the decision?

Agency Costs and the
Tradeoff Theory

EXCEL 17. If it is managed efficiently, Remel Inc. will have assets with a market value of $50 million, $100 million, or $150 million next year, with each outcome being equally likely. However, managers may engage in wasteful empire building, which will reduce the firm's market value by $5 million in all cases. Managers may also increase the risk of the firm, changing the probability of each outcome to 50%, 10%, and 40%, respectively.

a. What is the expected value of Remel's assets if it is run efficiently?

Suppose managers will engage in empire building unless that behavior increases the likelihood of bankruptcy. They will choose the risk of the firm to maximize the expected payoff to equity holders.

b. Suppose Remel has debt due in one year as shown below. For each case, indicate whether managers will engage in empire building, and whether they will increase risk. What is the expected value of Remel's assets in each case?

    i. $44 million   iii. $90 million

    ii. $49 million   iv. $99 million

c. Suppose the tax savings from the debt, after including investor taxes, is equal to 10% of the expected payoff of the debt. The proceeds from the debt, as well as the value of any tax savings, will be paid out to shareholders immediately as a dividend when the debt is issued. Which debt level in part (b) is optimal for Remel?

18. Which of the following industries have low optimal debt levels according to the tradeoff theory? Which have high optimal levels of debt?

    a. Tobacco firms

    b. Accounting firms

    c. Mature restaurant chains

    d. Lumber companies

    e. Cell phone manufacturers

19. According to the managerial entrenchment theory, managers choose capital structure so as to preserve their control of the firm. On the one hand, debt is costly for managers because they risk losing control in the event of default. On the other hand, if they do not take advantage of the tax shield provided by debt, they risk losing control through a hostile takeover.

    Suppose a firm expects to generate free cash flows of $90 million per year, and the discount rate for these cash flows is 10%. The firm pays a tax rate of 40%. A raider is poised to take over the firm and finance it with $750 million in permanent debt. The raider will generate the same free cash flows, and the takeover attempt will be successful if the raider can offer a premium of 20% over the current value of the firm. What level of permanent debt will the firm choose, according to the managerial entrenchment hypothesis?

Asymmetric Information and Capital Structure

20. Info Systems Technology (IST) manufacturers microprocessor chips for use in appliances and other applications. IST has no debt and 100 million shares outstanding. The correct price for these shares is either $14.50 or $12.50 per share. Investors view both possibilities as equally likely, so the shares currently trade for $13.50.

    IST must raise $500 million to build a new production facility. Because the firm would suffer a large loss of both customers and engineering talent in the event of financial distress, managers believe that if IST borrows the $500 million, the present value of financial distress costs will exceed any tax benefits by $20 million. At the same time, because investors believe that managers know the correct share price, IST faces a lemons problem if it attempts to raise the $500 million by issuing equity.

    a. Suppose that if IST issues equity, the share price will remain $13.50. To maximize the long-term share price of the firm once its true value is known, would managers choose to issue equity or borrow the $500 million if

       i. They know the correct value of the shares is $12.50?

       ii. They know the correct value of the shares is $14.50?

    b. Given your answer to part (a), what should investors conclude if IST issues equity? What will happen to the share price?

    c. Given your answer to part (a), what should investors conclude if IST issues debt? What will happen to the share price in that case?

    d. How would your answers change if there were no distress costs, but only tax benefits of leverage?

21. During the internet boom of the late 1990's, the stock prices of many internet firms soared to extreme heights. As CEO of such a firm, if you believed your stock was significantly overvalued, would using your stock to acquire non-internet stocks be a wise idea, even if you had to pay a small premium over their fair market value to make the acquisition?

*22. "We R Toys" (WRT) is considering expanding into new geographic markets. The expansion will have the same business risk as WRT's existing assets. The expansion will require an initial investment of $50 million and is expected to generate perpetual EBIT of $20 million per year. After the initial investment, future capital expenditures are expected to equal depreciation, and no further additions to net working capital are anticipated.

WRT's existing capital structure is composed of $500 million in equity and $300 million in debt (market values), with 10 million equity shares outstanding. The unlevered cost of capital is 10%, and WRT's debt is risk free with an interest rate of 4%. The corporate tax rate is 35%, and there are no personal taxes.

a. WRT initially proposes to fund the expansion by issuing equity. If investors were not expecting this expansion, and if they share WRT's view of the expansion's profitability, what will the share price be once the firm announces the expansion plan?

b. Suppose investors think that the EBIT from WRT's expansion will be only $4 million. What will the share price be in this case? How many shares will the firm need to issue?

c. Suppose WRT issues equity as in part (b). Shortly after the issue, new information emerges that convinces investors that management was, in fact, correct regarding the cash flows from the expansion. What will the share price be now? Why does it differ from that found in part (a)?

d. Suppose WRT instead finances the expansion with a $50 million issue of permanent risk-free debt. If WRT undertakes the expansion using debt, what is its new share price once the new information comes out? Comparing your answer with that in part (c), what are the two advantages of debt financing in this case?

17

Payout Policy

notation

PV	present value
P_{cum}	cum-dividend stock price
P_{ex}	ex-dividend stock price
P_{rep}	stock price with share repurchase
τ_d	dividend tax rate
τ_g	capital gains tax rate
τ_d^*	effective dividend tax rate
τ_c	corporate tax rate
P_{retain}	stock price if excess cash is retained
τ_i	tax rate on interest income
τ_{retain}^*	effective tax rate on retained cash

For many years, Microsoft Corporation chose to distribute cash to investors primarily by repurchasing its own stock. During the five fiscal years ending June 2004, for example, Microsoft spent an average of $5.4 billion per year on share repurchases. Microsoft began paying dividends to investors in 2003, with what CFO John Connors called "a starter dividend" of $0.08 per share. Then, on July 20, 2004, Microsoft stunned financial markets by announcing plans to pay the largest single cash dividend payment in history, a one-time dividend of $32 billion, or $3 per share, to all shareholders of record on November 17, 2004. In addition to this dividend, Microsoft announced plans to repurchase up to $30 billion of its stock over the next four years and pay regular quarterly dividends at an annual rate of $0.32 per share.

When a firm's investments generate free cash flow, the firm must decide how to use that cash. If the firm has new positive-NPV investment opportunities, it can reinvest the cash and increase the value of the firm. Many young, rapidly growing firms reinvest 100% of their cash flows in this way. But mature, profitable firms such as Microsoft often find that they generate more cash than they need to fund all of their attractive investment opportunities. When a firm has excess cash, it can hold those funds as part of its cash reserves or pay the cash out to shareholders. If the firm decides to follow the latter approach, it has two choices: It can pay a dividend or it can repurchase shares from current owners. These decisions represent the firm's payout policy.

In this chapter, we show that, as with capital structure, a firm's payout policy is shaped by market imperfections, such as taxes, agency costs, transaction costs, and asymmetric information between managers and investors. We look at why some firms prefer to pay dividends, whereas others pay no dividends at all and rely exclusively on share repurchases. In addition, we explore why some firms retain cash and build up large reserves, while others tend to pay out their excess cash.

17.1   Distributions to Shareholders

Figure 17.1 illustrates the alternative uses of free cash flow.[1] The way a firm chooses between these alternatives is referred to as its **payout policy**. We begin our discussion of a firm's payout policy by considering the choice between paying dividends and repurchasing shares. In this section, we examine the details of these methods of paying cash to shareholders.

Dividends

A public company's board of directors determines the amount of the firm's dividend. The board sets the amount per share that will be paid and decides when the payment will occur. The date on which the board authorizes the dividend is the **declaration date**. After the board declares the dividend, the firm is legally obligated to make the payment.

The firm will pay the dividend to all shareholders of record on a specific date, set by the board, called the **record date**. Because it takes three business days for shares to be registered, only shareholders who purchase the stock at least three days prior to the record date receive the dividend. As a result, the date two business days prior to the record date is known as the **ex-dividend date**; anyone who purchases the stock on or after the ex-dividend date will not receive the dividend. Finally, on the **payable date** (or **distribution date**), which is generally about a month after the record date, the firm mails dividend checks to the registered shareholders. Figure 17.2 shows these dates for Microsoft's $3.00 dividend.

Most companies that pay dividends pay them at regular, quarterly intervals. Companies typically adjust the amount of their dividends gradually, with little variation in the amount of the dividend from quarter to quarter. Occasionally, a firm may pay a one-time, **special dividend** that is usually much larger than a regular dividend, as was Microsoft's

FIGURE 17.1

Uses of Free Cash Flow

A firm can retain its free cash flow, either investing or accumulating it, or pay out its free cash flow through a dividend or share repurchase. The choice between these options is determined by the firm's payout policy.

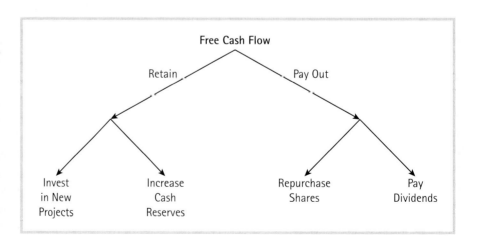

1. Strictly speaking, Figure 17.1 is for an all equity firm. For a levered firm, we would begin with the firm's free cash flow to equity, which we define in Chapter 18 as free cash flow less (after-tax) payments to debt holders.

FIGURE 17.2　　**Important Dates for Microsoft's Special Dividend**

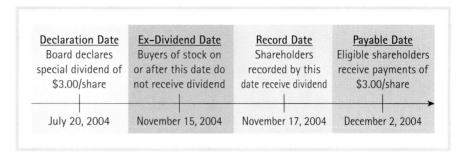

Microsoft declared the dividend on July 20, 2004, payable on December 2 to all shareholders of record on November 17. Because the record date was November 17, the ex-dividend date was two days earlier, or November 15, 2004.

$3.00 dividend in 2004. Figure 17.3 shows the dividends paid by GM from 1983 to 2006. In addition to regular dividends, GM paid special dividends in December 1997 and again in May 1999 (associated with spin-offs of subsidiaries, discussed further in Section 17.7).

Notice that GM split its stock in March 1989 so that each owner of one share received a second share. This kind of transaction is called a 2-for-1 stock split. More generally, in a **stock split** or **stock dividend**, the company issues additional shares rather than cash to

FIGURE 17.3

Dividend History for GM Stock, 1983–2006

Since 1983, GM has paid a regular dividend each quarter. GM paid additional special dividends in December 1997 and May 1999, and had a 2-for-1 stock split in March 1989.

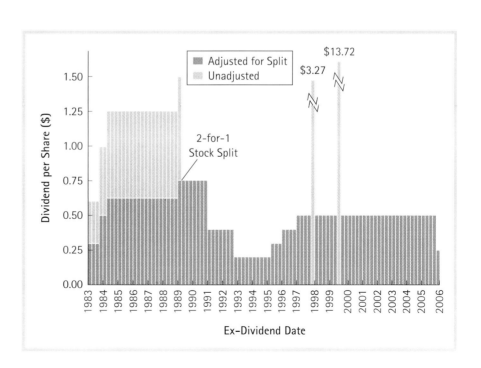

its shareholders. In the case of GM's stock split, the number of shares doubled, but the dividend per share was cut in half (from $1.50 per share to $0.75 per share), so that the total amount GM paid out as a dividend was the same just before and just after the split. (We discuss stock splits and stock dividends further in Section 17.7.) While GM raised its dividends throughout the 1980s, it cut its dividend during the recession in the early 1990s. GM raised its dividends again in the late 1990s, but was forced to cut its dividend again in early 2006 when it encountered financial difficulties.

Dividends are a cash outflow for the firm. From an accounting perspective, dividends generally reduce the firm's current (or accumulated) retained earnings. In some cases, dividends are attributed to other accounting sources, such as paid-in capital or the liquidation of assets. In this case the dividend is known as a **return of capital** or a **liquidating dividend**. While the source of the funds makes little difference to a firm or to investors directly, there is a difference in tax treatment: A return of capital is taxed as a capital gain rather than as a dividend for the investor.[2]

Share Repurchases

An alternative way to pay cash to investors is through a share repurchase or buyback. In this kind of transaction, the firm uses cash to buy shares of its own outstanding stock. These shares are generally held in the corporate treasury, and they can be resold if the company needs to raise money in the future. We now examine three possible transaction types for a share repurchase.

Open Market Repurchase.   An **open market repurchase** is the most common way that firms repurchase shares. A firm announces its intention to buy its own shares in the open market, and then proceeds to do so over time like any other investor. The firm may take a year or more to buy the shares, and it is not obligated to repurchase the full amount it originally stated. Also, the firm must not buy its shares in a way that might appear to manipulate the price. For example, SEC guidelines recommend that the firm not purchase more than 25% of the average daily trading volume in its shares on a single day, nor make purchases at the market open or within 30 minutes of the close of trade.[3]

While open market share repurchases represent about 95% of all repurchase transactions,[4] other methods are available to a firm that wants to buy back its stock. These methods are used when a firm wishes to repurchase a substantial portion of its shares, often as part of a recapitalization.

Tender Offer.   A firm can repurchase shares through a **tender offer** in which it offers to buy shares at a prespecified price during a short time period—generally within 20 days. The price is usually set at a substantial premium (10%–20% is typical) to the current market price. The offer often depends on shareholders tendering a sufficient number of shares. If shareholders do not tender enough shares, the firm may cancel the offer and no buyback occurs.

---

2. There is also a difference in the accounting treatment. A cash dividend reduces the cash and retained earnings shown on the balance sheet, whereas a return of capital reduces paid-in capital. This accounting difference has no direct economic consequence, however.

3. SEC Rule 10b-18, introduced in 1983, defines guidelines for open market share repurchases.

4. G. Grullon and D. Ikenberry, "What Do We Know About Stock Repurchases?" *Journal of Applied Corporate Finance* 13(1) (2000): 31–51.

A related method is the **Dutch auction** share repurchase, in which the firm lists different prices at which it is prepared to buy shares, and shareholders in turn indicate how many shares they are willing to sell at each price. The firm then pays the lowest price at which it can buy back its desired number of shares.

Targeted Repurchase.   A firm may also purchase shares directly from a major shareholder in a **targeted repurchase**. In this case the purchase price is negotiated directly with the seller. A targeted repurchase may occur if a major shareholder desires to sell a large number of shares but the market for the shares is not sufficiently liquid to sustain such a large sale without severely affecting the price. Under these circumstances, the shareholder may be willing to sell shares back to the firm at a discount to the current market price. Alternatively, if a major shareholder is threatening to take over the firm and remove its management, the firm may decide to eliminate the threat by buying out the shareholder—often at a large premium over the current market price. This type of transaction is called **greenmail**.

CONCEPT CHECK **1.** How is a stock's ex-dividend date determined, and what is its significance?

2. What is a Dutch auction share repurchase?

17.2 Comparison of Dividends and Share Repurchases

If a corporation decides to pay cash to shareholders, it can do so through either dividend payments or share repurchases. How do firms choose between these alternatives? In this section, we show that in the perfect capital markets setting of Modigliani and Miller, the method of payment does not matter.

Consider the case of Genron Corporation, a hypothetical firm. Genron has $20 million in excess cash and no debt. The firm expects to generate additional free cash flows of $48 million per year in subsequent years. If Genron's unlevered cost of capital is 12%, then the enterprise value of its ongoing operations is

$$\text{Enterprise Value} = PV(\text{Future FCF}) = \frac{\$48 \text{ million}}{12\%} = \$400 \text{ million}$$

Including the cash, Genron's total market value is $420 million.

Genron's board is meeting to decide how to pay out its $20 million in excess cash to shareholders. Some board members have advocated using the $20 million to pay a $2 cash dividend for each of Genron's 10 million outstanding shares. Others have suggested repurchasing shares instead of paying a dividend. Still others have proposed that Genron raise additional cash and pay an even larger dividend today, in anticipation of the high future free cash flows it expects to receive. Will the amount of the current dividend affect Genron's share price? Which policy would shareholders prefer?

Let's analyze the consequences of each of these three alternative policies and compare them in a setting of perfect capital markets.

Alternative Policy 1: Pay Dividend with Excess Cash

Suppose the board opts for the first alternative and uses all excess cash to pay a dividend. With 10 million shares outstanding, Genron will be able to pay a $2 dividend immediately. Because the firm expects to generate future free cash flows of $48 million per year, it anticipates paying a dividend of $4.80 per share each year thereafter. The board declares the dividend and sets the record date as December 14, so that the ex-dividend date is December 12. Let's compute Genron's share price just before and after the stock goes ex-dividend.

The fair price for the shares is the present value of the expected dividends given Genron's equity cost of capital. Because Genron has no debt, its equity cost of capital equals its unlevered cost of capital of 12%. Just before the ex-dividend date, the stock is said to trade **cum-dividend** ("with the dividend") because anyone who buys the stock will be entitled to the dividend. In this case,

$$P_{cum} = \text{Current Dividend} + PV(\text{Future Dividends}) = 2 + \frac{4.80}{0.12} = 2 + 40 = \$42$$

After the stock goes ex-dividend, new buyers will not receive the current dividend. At this point the share price will reflect only the dividends in subsequent years:

$$P_{ex} = PV(\text{Future Dividends}) = \frac{4.80}{0.12} = \$40$$

The share price will drop on the ex-dividend date, December 12. The amount of the price drop is equal to the amount of the current dividend, \$2. We can also determine this change in the share price using the market value balance sheet (values in millions of dollars):

	December 11 (Cum-Dividend)	December 12 (Ex-Dividend)
Cash	20	0
Other assets	400	400
Total market value	420	400
Shares (millions)	10	10
Share price	**$42**	**$40**

As the market value balance sheet shows, the share price falls when a dividend is paid because the reduction in cash decreases the market value of the firm's assets. Although the stock price falls, holders of Genron stock do not incur a loss overall. Before the dividend, their stock was worth \$42. After the dividend, their stock is worth \$40 and they hold \$2 in cash from the dividend, for a total value of \$42.[5]

The fact that the stock price falls by the amount of the dividend also follows from the assumption that no opportunity for arbitrage exists. If it fell by less than the dividend, an investor could earn a profit by buying the stock just before it goes ex-dividend and selling it just after, as the dividend would more than cover the capital loss on the stock. Similarly, if the stock price fell by more than the dividend, an investor could profit by selling the stock just before it goes ex-dividend and buying it just after. Therefore, no arbitrage implies

In a perfect capital market, when a dividend is paid, the share price drops by the amount of the dividend when the stock begins to trade ex-dividend.

---

5. For simplicity, we have ignored the short delay between the ex-dividend date and the payable date of the dividend. In reality, the shareholders do not receive the dividend immediately, but rather the *promise* to receive it within several weeks. The stock price adjusts by the present value of this promise, which is effectively equal to the amount of the dividend unless interest rates are extremely high.

Alternative Policy 2: Share Repurchase (No Dividend)

Suppose that Genron does not pay a dividend this year, but instead uses the $20 million to repurchase its shares on the open market. How will the repurchase affect the share price?

With an initial share price of $42, Genron will repurchase $20 million ÷ $42 per share = 0.476 million shares, leaving only $10 - 0.476 = 9.524$ million shares outstanding. Once again, we can use Genron's market value balance sheet to analyze this transaction:

	December 11 (Before Repurchase)	December 12 (After Repurchase)
Cash	20	0
Other assets	400	400
Total market value of assets	420	400
Shares (millions)	10	9.524
Share price	**$42**	**$42**

In this case, the market value of Genron's assets falls when the company pays out cash, but the number of shares outstanding also falls. The two changes offset each other, so the share price remains the same.

Genron's Future Dividends.   We can also see why the share price does not fall after the share repurchase by considering the effect on Genron's future dividends. In future years, Genron expects to have $48 million in free cash flow, which can be used to pay a dividend of $48 million ÷ 9.524 million shares = $5.04 per share each year. Thus, with a share repurchase, Genron's share price today is

$$P_{rep} = \frac{5.04}{0.12} = \$42$$

In other words, by not paying a dividend today and repurchasing shares instead, Genron is able to raise its dividends *per share* in the future. The increase in future dividends compensates shareholders for the dividend they give up today. This example illustrates the following general conclusion about share repurchases:

In perfect capital markets, an open market share repurchase has no effect on the stock price, and the stock price is the same as the cum-dividend price if a dividend were paid instead.

Investor Preferences.   Would an investor prefer that Genron issue a dividend or repurchase its stock? Both policies lead to the same *initial* share price of $42. But is there a difference in shareholder value *after* the transaction? Consider an investor who currently holds 2000 shares of Genron stock. Assuming the investor does not trade the stock, the investor's holdings after a dividend or share repurchase are as follows:

Dividend	Repurchase
$40 × 2000 = $80,000 stock	$42 × 2000 = $84,000 stock
$ 2 × 2000 = $ 4000 cash	

In either case, the value of the investor's portfolio is $84,000 immediately after the transaction. The only difference is the distribution between cash and stock holdings. Thus it

Repurchases and the Supply of Shares

There is a misconception that when a firm repurchases its own shares, the price rises due to the decrease in the supply of shares outstanding. This intuition follows naturally from the standard supply and demand analysis taught in microeconomics. Why does that analysis not apply here?

When a firm repurchases its own shares, two things happen. First, the supply of shares is reduced. At the same time, however, the value of the firm's assets declines when it spends its cash to buy the shares. If the firm repurchases its shares at their market price, these two effects offset each other, leaving the share price unchanged.

This result is similar to the dilution fallacy discussed in Chapter 14: When a firm issues shares at their market price, the share price does not fall due to the increase in supply. The increase in supply is offset by the increase in the firm's assets that results from the cash it receives from the issuance.

might seem the investor would prefer one approach or the other based on whether she needs the cash.

But if Genron repurchases shares and the investor wants cash, she can raise cash by selling shares. For example, she can sell $4000 \div $42 per share = 95 shares to raise about $4000 in cash. She will then hold 1905 shares, or 1905 × $42 ≈ $80,000 in stock. Thus, in the case of a share repurchase, by selling shares an investor can create a *homemade dividend.*

Similarly, if Genron pays a dividend and the investor does not want the cash, she can use the $4000 proceeds of the dividend to purchase 100 additional shares at the ex-dividend share price of $40 per share. As a result she will hold 2100 shares, worth 2100 × $40 = $84,000.[6]

We summarize these two cases below:

Dividend + Buy 100 shares	Repurchase + Sell 95 shares
$40 × 2100 = $84,000 stock	$42 × 1905 ≈ $80,000 stock
	$42 × 95 ≈ $ 4000 cash

By selling shares or reinvesting dividends, the investor can create any combination of cash and stock desired. As a result, the investor is indifferent between the various payout methods the firm might employ:

In perfect capital markets, investors are indifferent between the firm distributing funds via dividends or share repurchases. By reinvesting dividends or selling shares, they can replicate either payout method on their own.

Alternative Policy 3: High Dividend (Equity Issue)

Let's look at a third possibility for Genron. Suppose the board wishes to pay an even larger dividend than $2 per share right now. Is that possible and, if so, will the higher dividend make shareholders better off?

Genron plans to pay $48 million in dividends starting next year. Suppose the firm wants to start paying that amount today. Because it has only $20 million in cash today,

---

6. In fact, many firms allow investors to register for a dividend reinvestment program, or *DRIP*, which automatically reinvests any dividends into new shares of the stock.

Genron needs an additional $28 million to pay the larger dividend now. It could raise cash by scaling back its investments. But if the investments have positive NPV, reducing them would lower firm value. An alternative way to raise more cash is to borrow money or sell new shares. Let's consider an equity issue. Given a current share price of $42, Genron could raise $28 million by selling $28 million ÷ $42 per share = 0.67 million shares. Because this equity issue will increase Genron's total number of shares outstanding to 10.67 million, the amount of the dividend per share each year will be

$$\frac{\$48 \text{ million}}{10.67 \text{ million shares}} = \$4.50 \text{ per share}$$

Under this new policy, Genron's cum-dividend share price is

$$P_{cum} = 4.50 + \frac{4.50}{0.12} = 4.50 + 37.50 = \$42$$

As in the previous examples, the initial share value is unchanged by this policy, and increasing the dividend has no benefit to shareholders.

EXAMPLE 17.1

Homemade Dividends

Problem
Suppose Genron does not adopt the third alternative policy, and instead pays a $2 dividend per share today. Show how an investor holding 2000 shares could create a homemade dividend of $4.50 per share × 2000 shares = $9000 per year on her own.

Solution
If Genron pays a $2 dividend, the investor receives $4000 in cash and holds the rest in stock. To receive $9000 in total today, she can raise an additional $5000 by selling 125 shares at $40 per share just after the dividend is paid. In future years, Genron will pay a dividend of $4.80 per share. Because she will own 2000 − 125 = 1875 shares, the investor will receive dividends of 1875 × $4.80 = $9000 per year from then on.

Modigliani–Miller and Dividend Policy Irrelevance

In our analysis we considered three possible dividend policies for the firm: (1) pay out all cash as a dividend, (2) pay no dividend and use the cash instead to repurchase shares, or (3) issue equity to finance a larger dividend. These policies are illustrated in Table 17.1.

TABLE 17.1   **Genron's Dividends per Share Each Year Under the Three Alternative Policies**

	Initial Share Price	Dividend Paid ($ per share)			
		Year 0	Year 1	Year 2	...
Policy 1:	$42.00	2.00	4.80	4.80	...
Policy 2:	$42.00	0	5.04	5.04	...
Policy 3:	$42.00	4.50	4.50	4.50	...

> **COMMON MISTAKE**   **The Bird in the Hand Fallacy**

"A bird in the hand is worth two in the bush."

The **bird in the hand hypothesis** states that firms choosing to pay higher current dividends will enjoy higher stock prices because shareholders prefer current dividends to future ones (with the same present value).

According to this view, alternative policy 3 would lead to the highest share price for Genron.

Modigliani and Miller's response to this view is that with perfect capital markets, shareholders can generate an equivalent homemade dividend at any time by selling shares. Thus the dividend choice of the firm should not matter.*

---

*The bird in the hand hypothesis is proposed in Lintner and Gordon's early studies of dividend policy. See M. J. Gordon, "Optimal Investment and Financing Policy," *Journal of Finance* 18(2) (1963): 264–272, and J. Lintner, "Dividends, Earnings, Leverage, Stock Prices and the Supply of Capital to Corporations," *Review of Economics and Statistics* 44(3) (1962): 243–269.

Table 17.1 shows an important tradeoff: If Genron pays a higher *current* dividend per share, it will pay lower *future* dividends per share. For example, if the firm raises the current dividend by issuing equity, it will have more shares and therefore smaller free cash flows per share to pay dividends in the future. If the firm lowers the current dividend and repurchases its shares, it will have fewer shares in the future, so it will be able to pay a higher dividend per share. The net effect of this tradeoff is to leave the total present value of all future dividends, and hence the current share price, unchanged.

The logic of this section matches that in our discussion of capital structure in Chapter 14. There we explained that in perfect capital markets, buying and selling equity and debt are zero-NPV transactions that do not affect firm value. Moreover, any choice of leverage by a firm could be replicated by investors using homemade leverage. As a result, the firm's choice of capital structure is irrelevant.

Here we have established the same principle for a firm's choice of a dividend. Regardless of the amount of cash the firm has on hand, it can pay a smaller dividend (and use the remaining cash to repurchase shares) or a larger dividend (by selling equity to raise cash). Because buying or selling shares is a zero-NPV transaction, such transactions have no effect on the initial share price. Furthermore, shareholders can create a homemade dividend of any size by buying or selling shares themselves.

Modigliani and Miller developed this idea in another influential paper published in 1961.[7] As with their result on capital structure, it went against the conventional wisdom that dividend policy could change a firm's value and make its shareholders better off even absent market imperfections. We state here their important proposition:

MM Dividend Irrelevance: *In perfect capital markets, holding fixed the investment policy of a firm, the firm's choice of dividend policy is irrelevant and does not affect the initial share price.*

---

7. See M. Modigliani and M. Miller, "Dividend Policy, Growth, and the Valuation of Shares," *Journal of Business* 34(4) (1961): 411–433. See also J. B. Williams, *The Theory of Investment Value* (Cambridge, MA: Harvard University Press, 1938).

Dividend Policy with Perfect Capital Markets

The examples in this section illustrate the idea that by using share repurchases or equity issues a firm can easily alter its dividend payments. Because these transactions do not alter the value of the firm, neither does dividend policy.

This result may at first seem to contradict the idea that the price of a share should equal the present value of its future dividends. As our examples have shown, however, a firm's choice of dividend today affects the dividends it can afford to pay in the future in an offsetting fashion. Thus, while dividends *do* determine share prices, a firm's choice of dividend policy does not.

As Modigliani and Miller make clear, the value of a firm ultimately derives from its underlying free cash flow. A firm's free cash flow determines the level of payouts that it can make to its investors. In a perfect capital market, whether these payouts are made through dividends or share repurchases does not matter. Of course, in reality capital markets are not perfect. As with capital structure, it is the imperfections in capital markets that should determine the firm's payout policy.

CONCEPT CHECK
1. Explain the misconception that when a firm repurchases its own shares, the price rises due to the decrease in the supply of shares outstanding.

2. In a perfect capital market, how important is the firm's decision to pay dividends versus repurchase shares?

17.3 The Tax Disadvantage of Dividends

As with capital structure, taxes are an important market imperfection that influence a firm's decision to pay dividends or repurchase shares.

Taxes on Dividends and Capital Gains

Shareholders typically must pay taxes on the dividends they receive. They must also pay capital gains taxes when they sell their shares. Table 17.2 shows the history of U.S. tax rates applied to dividends and long-term capital gains for investors in the highest tax bracket.

Do taxes affect investors' preferences for dividends versus share repurchases? When a firm pays a dividend, shareholders are taxed according to the dividend tax rate. If the firm repurchases shares instead, and shareholders sell shares to create a homemade dividend, the homemade dividend will be taxed according to the capital gains tax rate. If dividends are taxed at a higher rate than capital gains, which has been true until the most recent change to the tax code, shareholders will prefer share repurchases to dividends.[8] As we saw in Chapter 15, recent changes to the tax code have equalized the tax rates on dividends and capital gains. But because long-term investors can defer the capital gains tax until they sell, there is still a tax advantage for share repurchases over dividends.

The higher tax rate on dividends also makes it undesirable for a firm to raise funds to pay a dividend. Absent taxes and issuance costs, if a firm raises money by issuing shares and then gives that money back to shareholders as a dividend, shareholders are no better

---

8. Not all countries tax dividends at a higher rate than capital gains. In Germany, for example, dividends are taxed at a lower rate than capital gains for most classes of investors.

| TABLE 17.2 | Long-Term Capital Gains Versus Dividend Tax Rates in the United States, 1971–2005 | |

Year	Capital Gains	Dividends
1971–1978	35%	70%
1979–1981	28%	70%
1982–1986	20%	50%
1987	28%	39%
1988–1990	28%	28%
1991–1992	28%	31%
1993–1996	28%	40%
1997–2000	20%	40%
2001–2002	20%	39%
2003–*	15%	15%

*The current tax rates are set to expire in 2008 unless they are extended by Congress. The tax rates shown are for financial assets held for one year. For assets held less than one year, capital gains are taxed at the ordinary income tax rate (currently 35% for the highest bracket); the same is true for dividends if the assets are held for less than 61 days. Because the capital gains tax is not paid until the asset is sold, for assets held for longer than one year the *effective* capital gains tax rate is equal to the present value of the rate shown, when discounted by the after-tax risk-free interest rate for the additional number of years the asset is held.

or worse off—they get back the money they put in. When dividends are taxed at a higher rate than capital gains, however, this transaction hurts shareholders because they will receive less than their initial investment.

EXAMPLE 17.2

Issuing Equity to Pay a Dividend

Problem
Suppose a firm raises $10 million from shareholders and uses this cash to pay them $10 million in dividends. If the dividend is taxed at a 40% rate, and if capital gains are taxed at a 15% rate, how much will shareholders receive after taxes?

Solution
Shareholders will owe 40% of $10 million, or $4 million in dividend taxes. Because the value of the firm will fall when the dividend is paid, shareholders' capital gain on the stock will be $10 million less when they sell, lowering their capital gains taxes by 15% of $10 million or $1.5 million. Thus, in total, shareholders will pay $4 million − $1.5 million = $2.5 million in taxes, and they will receive back only $7.5 million of their $10 million investment.

Optimal Dividend Policy with Taxes

When the tax rate on dividends exceeds the tax rate on capital gains, shareholders will pay lower taxes if a firm uses share repurchases for all payouts rather than dividends. This tax savings will increase the value of a firm that uses share repurchases rather than dividends.

FIGURE 17.4

The Declining Use of Dividends

This figure shows the percentage of U.S. firms each year that made payouts to shareholders. The shaded regions show the firms that used dividends exclusively, repurchases exlusively, or both. Note the trend away from the use of dividends over time, with firms that made payouts showing a greater reliance on share repurchases, together with a sharp decrease in the percentage of firms making payouts of any kind.

Source: Compustat.

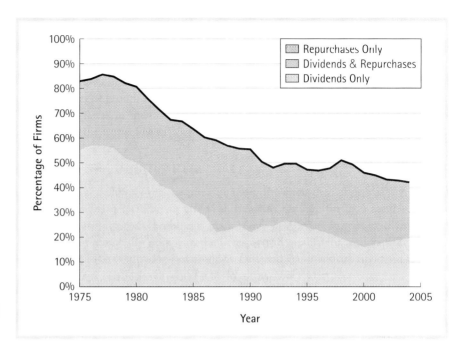

We can also express the tax savings in terms of a firm's equity cost of capital. Firms that use dividends will have to pay a higher pre-tax return to offer their investors the same after-tax return as firms that use share repurchases.[9] As a result, the optimal dividend policy when the dividend tax rate exceeds the capital gain tax rate is to *pay no dividends at all.*

While firms do still pay dividends, substantial evidence shows that many firms have recognized their tax disadvantage. For example, prior to 1980, most firms used dividends exclusively to distribute cash to shareholders (see Figure 17.4). But by 2000, only 16% of firms relied on dividends. At the same time, 30% of all firms (and more than 65% of firms making payouts to shareholders) used share repurchases exclusively or in combination with dividends. The trend away from dividends has reversed slightly, however, since 2000.[10]

We see a more dramatic trend if we consider the relative magnitudes of both forms of corporate payouts. Figure 17.5 shows the relative importance of share repurchases as a proportion of total payouts to shareholders. While dividends accounted for more than 80% of corporate payouts until the early 1980s, the importance of share repurchases grew dramatically in the mid-1980s. Repurchase activity slowed during the 1990–1991 recession,

---

9. For an extension of the CAPM that includes investor taxes, see M. Brennan, "Taxes, Market Valuation and Corporation Financial Policy," *National Tax Journal* 23(4) (1970): 417–427.

10. See G. Grullon and R. Michaely, "Dividends, Share Repurchases, and the Substitution Hypothesis," *Journal of Finance* 57(4) (2002): 1649–1684, and E. Fama and K. French, "Disappearing Dividends: Changing Firm Characteristics or Lower Propensity to Pay?" *Journal of Financial Economics* 60(3) (2001): 3–43. For an examination of the changing trend since 2000, see B. Julio and D. Ikenberry, "Reappearing Dividends," *Journal of Applied Corporate Finance* 16(4) (2004): 89–100.

Changes in the Effective Dividend Tax Rate

Problem

Consider an individual investor in the highest U.S. tax bracket who plans to hold a stock for one year. What was the effective dividend tax rate for this investor in 2002? How did the effective dividend tax rate change in 2003? (Ignore state taxes.)

Solution

From Table 17.2, in 2002 we have $\tau_d = 39\%$ and $\tau_g = 20\%$. Thus

$$\tau_d^* = \frac{0.39 - 0.20}{1 - 0.20} = 23.75\%$$

This indicates a significant tax disadvantage of dividends; each $1 of dividends is worth only $0.7625 in capital gains. However, after the 2003 tax cut, $\tau_d = 15\%$, $\tau_g = 15\%$, and

$$\tau_d^* = \frac{0.15 - 0.15}{1 - 0.15} = 0\%$$

Therefore, the 2003 tax cut eliminated the tax disadvantage of dividends for a one-year investor.

Tax Differences Across Investors

The effective dividend tax rate τ_d^* for an investor depends on the tax rates the investor faces on dividends and capital gains. These rates differ across investors for a variety of reasons.

Income Level. Investors with different levels of income fall into different tax brackets and face different tax rates.

Investment Horizon. Capital gains on stocks held less than one year, and dividends on stocks held for less than 61 days, are taxed at higher ordinary income tax rates. Long-term investors can defer the payment of capital gains taxes (lowering their effective capital gains tax rate even further). Investors who plan to bequeath stocks to their heirs avoid the capital gains tax altogether.

Tax Jurisdiction. U.S. investors are subject to state taxes that differ by state. For example, New Hampshire imposes a 5% tax on income from interest and dividends, but no tax on capital gains. Foreign investors in U.S. stocks are subject to 30% withholding for dividends they receive (unless that rate is reduced by a tax treaty with their home country). There is no similar withholding for capital gains.

Type of Investor or Investment Account. Stocks held by individual investors in a retirement account are not subject to taxes on dividends or capital gains.[15] Similarly, stocks held through pension funds or nonprofit endowment funds are not subject to dividend or capital gains taxes. Corporations that hold stocks are able to exclude 70% of dividends they receive from corporate taxes, but are unable to exclude capital gains.[16]

To illustrate, consider four different investors: (1) a "buy and hold" investor who holds the stock in a taxable account and plans to transfer the stock to her heirs, (2) an investor

---

15. While taxes (or penalties) may be owed when the money is withdrawn from the retirement account, these taxes do not depend on whether the money came from dividends or capital gains.

16. Corporations can exclude 80% if they own more than 20% of the shares of the firm paying the dividend.

who holds the stock in a taxable account but plans to sell it in one year, (3) a pension fund, and (4) a corporation. Under the current maximum U.S. federal tax rates, the effective dividend tax rate for each would be

1. Buy and hold individual investor: $\tau_d = 15\%$, $\tau_g = 0$, and $\tau_d^* = 15\%$
2. One-year individual investor: $\tau_d = 15\%$, $\tau_g = 15\%$, and $\tau_d^* = 0$
3. Pension fund: $\tau_d = 0$, $\tau_g = 0$, and $\tau_d^* = 0$
4. Corporation: Given a corporate tax rate of 35%, $\tau_d = (1 - 70\%) \times 35\% = 10.5\%$, $\tau_g = 35\%$, and $\tau_d^* = -38\%$

As a result of their different tax rates, these investors have varying preferences regarding dividends. Long-term investors are more heavily taxed on dividends, so they would prefer share repurchases to dividend payments. One-year investors, pension funds, and other non-taxed investors have no tax preference for share repurchases over dividends; they would prefer a payout policy that most closely matches their cash needs. For example, a non-taxed investor who desires current income would prefer high dividends so as to avoid the brokerage fees and other transaction costs of selling the stock.

Finally, the negative effective dividend tax rate for corporations implies that corporations enjoy a tax *advantage* associated with dividends. For this reason, a corporation that chooses to invest its cash will prefer to hold stocks with high dividend yields.

Clientele Effects

Table 17.3 summarizes the different preferences across investor groups. These differences in tax preferences create **clientele effects**, in which the dividend policy of a firm is optimized for the tax preference of its investor clientele. Individuals in the highest tax brackets have a preference for stocks that pay no or low dividends, whereas tax-free investors and corporations have a preference for stocks with high dividends. In this case, a firm's dividend policy is optimized for the tax preference of its investor clientele.

TABLE 17.3	Differing Dividend Policy Preferences Across Investor Groups	
Investor Group	**Dividend Policy Preference**	**Proportion of Investors**
Individual investors	Tax disadvantage for dividends Prefer share repurchase	~52%
Institutions, pension funds, retirement accounts	No tax preference Prefer dividend policy that matches income needs	~47%
Corporations	Tax advantage for dividends	~1%

Source: Proportions based on *Federal Reserve Flow of Funds Accounts,* 2003.

Evidence supports the existence of tax clienteles. For example, Franklin Allen and Roni Michaely[17] report that in 1996 individual investors held 54% of all stocks by market value, yet received only 35% of all dividends paid, indicating that individuals tend to hold

---

17. F. Allen and R. Michaely, "Payout Policy," in *Handbook of the Economics of Finance: Corporate Finance Volume* 1A, Chapter 7, Elsevier, Amsterdam, The Netherlands (2003) (ed: G. M. Constantinides, M. Harris, R. M. Stulz).

stocks with low dividend yields. Of course, the fact that high-tax investors receive any dividends at all implies that the clienteles are not perfect—dividend taxes are not the only determinants of investors' portfolios.

Another clientele strategy is a dynamic clientele effect, also called the **dividend-capture theory**.[18] This theory states that absent transaction costs, investors can trade shares at the time of the dividend so that non-taxed investors receive the dividend. That is, non-taxed investors need not hold the high-dividend-paying stocks all the time; it is necessary only that they hold them when the dividend is actually paid.

An implication of this theory is that we should see large volumes of trade in a stock around the ex-dividend day, as high-tax investors sell and low-tax investors buy the stock in anticipation of the dividend, and then reverse those trades just after the ex-dividend date. Consider Figure 17.6, which illustrates the price and volume for the stock of Value Line, Inc., during 2004. On April 23, Value Line announced it would use its accumulated cash to pay a special dividend of $17.50 per share, with an ex-dividend date of May 20.

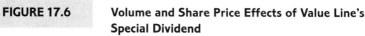

FIGURE 17.6   **Volume and Share Price Effects of Value Line's Special Dividend**

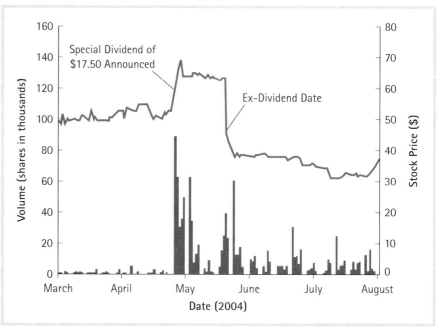

On announcement of the special dividend of $17.50 per share, Value Line's share price rose, as did the volume of trade. The share price dropped by $17.91 on the ex-dividend date, and the volume gradually declined over the following weeks. This pattern of volume is consistent with non-taxed investors buying the stock before the ex-dividend date and selling it afterward. (We consider reasons for the jump in the stock price on the announcement of the dividend in Sections 17.5 and 17.6.)

---

18. This idea is developed by A. Kalay, "The Ex-Dividend Day Behavior Of Stock Prices: A Re-examination of the Clientele Effect," *Journal of Finance* 37(4) (1982): 1059–1070. See also J. Boyd and R. Jagannathan, "Ex-Dividend Price Behavior of Common Stocks," *Review of Financial Studies* 7(4) (1994): 711–741, who discuss the complications that arise with multiple tax clienteles.

Note the substantial increase in the volume of trade around the time of the special dividend. The volume of trade in the month following the special dividend announcement was more than 25 times the volume in the month prior to the announcement. In the three months following the announcement of the special dividend, the cumulative volume exceeded 65% of the total shares available for trade.

While this evidence supports the dividend-capture theory, it is also true that many high-tax investors continue to hold stocks even when dividends are paid. For a small ordinary dividend, the transaction costs and risks of trading the stock probably offset the benefits associated with dividend capture.[19] Large increases in volume, as in the case of Value Line, tend to be associated with large special dividends. Thus, while clientele effects and dividend-capture strategies reduce the relative tax disadvantage of dividends, they do not eliminate it.[20]

CONCEPT CHECK

1. Under what conditions will investors have a tax preference for share repurchases rather than dividends?

2. What does the dividend-capture theory imply about the volume of trade in a stock around the ex-dividend day?

17.5 Payout Versus Retention of Cash

Looking back at Figure 17.1, we have thus far considered only one aspect of a firm's payout policy: the choice between paying dividends and repurchasing shares. But how should a firm decide the amount it should pay out to shareholders and the amount it should retain?

To answer this question, we must first consider what the firm will do with cash that it retains. It can invest the cash in new projects or in financial instruments. We will demonstrate that in the context of perfect capital markets, once a firm has taken all positive-NPV investments, it is indifferent between saving excess cash and paying it out. But once we consider market imperfections, there is a tradeoff: Retaining cash can reduce the costs of raising capital in the future, but it can also increase taxes and agency costs.

Retaining Cash with Perfect Capital Markets

If a firm retains cash, it can use those funds to invest in new projects. If new positive-NPV projects are available, this decision is clearly the correct one. Making positive-NPV investments will create value for the firm's investors, whereas saving the cash or paying it out

19. The risk of the dividend-capture strategy is the risk that the stock price may fluctuate for reasons unrelated to the dividend before the transaction can be completed. See J. Koski and R. Michaely, "Prices, Liquidity, and the Information Content of Trades," *Review of Financial Studies* 13(3) (2000): 659–696, who demonstrate that in some cases the risk can be eliminated by negotiating a purchase and sale simultaneously, but with settlement dates before and after the ex-dividend date. In this case the amount of dividend-related volume is greatly increased.

20. These effects are one reason it is difficult to find evidence that the equity cost of capital increases with dividend yields as one would expect if long-term investors are an important clientele. While evidence was found by R. Litzenberger and K. Ramaswamy ["The Effects of Personal Taxes and Dividends on Capital Asset Prices: Theory and Empirical Evidence," *Journal of Financial Economics* 7(2) (1979): 163–195], this evidence is contradicted by the results of F. Black and M. Scholes ["The Effects of Dividend Yield and Dividend Policy on Common Stock Prices and Returns," *Journal of Financial Economics* 1(1) (1974): 1–22]. A. Kalay and R. Michaely provide an explanation for the differing results of these studies and do not find a significant impact of dividend yields on expected returns ["Dividends and Taxes: A Reexamination," *Financial Management* 29(2) (2000): 55–75].

will not. However, once the firm has already taken all positive-NPV projects, any additional projects it takes on are zero or negative-NPV investments. Taking on negative-NPV investments will reduce shareholder value, as the benefits of such investments do not exceed their costs.

Of course, rather than waste excess cash on negative-NPV projects, a firm can hold the cash in the bank or use it to purchase financial assets. The firm can then pay the money to shareholders at a future time or invest it when positive-NPV investment opportunities become available.

What are the advantages and disadvantages of retaining cash and investing in financial securities? In perfect capital markets, buying and selling securities is a zero-NPV transaction, so it should not affect firm value. Shareholders can make any investment a firm makes on their own if the firm pays out the cash. Thus it should not be surprising that with perfect capital markets, the retention versus payout decision—just like the dividend versus share repurchase decision—is irrelevant.

Delaying Dividends with Perfect Markets

Problem

Barston Mining has $100,000 in excess cash. Barston is considering investing the cash in one-year Treasury bills paying 6% interest, and then using the cash to pay a dividend next year. Alternatively, the firm can pay a dividend immediately and shareholders can invest the cash on their own. In a perfect capital market, which option will shareholders prefer?

Solution

If Barston pays an immediate dividend, the shareholders receive $100,000 today. If Barston retains the cash, at the end of one year the company will be able to pay a dividend of

$$\$100,000 \times (1.06) = \$106,000$$

This payoff is the same as if shareholders had invested the $100,000 in Treasury bills themselves. In other words, the present value of this future dividend is exactly $106,000 \div (1.06)$ = $100,000$. Thus shareholders are indifferent about whether the firm pays the dividend immediately or retains the cash.

As Example 17.4 illustrates, there is no difference for shareholders if the firm pays the cash immediately or retains the cash and pays it out at a future date. This example provides yet another illustration of Modigliani and Miller's fundamental insight regarding financial policy irrelevance in perfect capital markets:

MM Payout Irrelevance: *In perfect capital markets, if a firm invests excess cash flows in financial securities, the firm's choice of payout versus retention is irrelevant and does not affect the initial share price.*

Thus, the decision of whether to retain cash depends on market imperfections, which we turn to next.

Taxes and Cash Retention

Example 17.4 assumed perfect capital markets, and so ignored the effect of taxes. How would our result change with taxes?

Retaining Cash with Corporate Taxes

Problem

Suppose Barston must pay corporate taxes at a 35% rate on the interest it will earn from the one-year Treasury bill paying 6% interest. Would pension fund investors (who do not pay taxes on their investment income) prefer that Barston use its excess cash to pay the $100,000 dividend immediately or retain the cash for one year?

Solution

If Barston pays an immediate dividend, shareholders receive $100,000 today. If Barston retains the cash for one year, it will earn an after-tax return on the Treasury bills of

$$6\% \times (1 - 0.35) = 3.90\%$$

Thus, at the end of the year, Barston will pay a dividend of $100,000 \times (1.039) = $103,900.

This amount is less than the $106,000 the investors would have earned if they had invested the $100,000 in Treasury bills themselves. Because Barston must pay corporate taxes on the interest it earns, there is a tax disadvantage to retaining cash. Pension fund investors will therefore prefer that Barston pays the dividend now.

As Example 17.5 shows, corporate taxes make it costly for a firm to retain excess cash. This effect is the very same effect we identified in Chapter 15 with regard to leverage: When a firm pays interest, it receives a tax deduction for that interest, whereas when a firm receives interest, it owes taxes on the interest. As we discussed in Chapter 14, cash is equivalent to *negative* leverage, so the tax advantage of leverage implies a tax disadvantage to holding cash.

Microsoft's Special Dividend

Problem

In the introduction to this chapter, we described Microsoft's special dividend of $3 per share, or $32 billion, during late 2004. If Microsoft had instead retained that cash permanently, what would the present value of the additional taxes paid be?

Solution

If Microsoft retained the cash, the interest earned on it would be subject to a 35% corporate tax rate. Because the interest payments are risk free, we can discount the tax payments at the risk-free interest rate under the assumption that Microsoft's marginal corporate tax rate will remain constant (or that any changes to it have a beta of zero). Thus, the present value of the tax payments on Microsoft's additional interest income would be

$$\frac{\$32 \text{ billion} \times r_f \times 35\%}{r_f} = \$32 \text{ billion} \times 35\% = \$11.2 \text{ billion}$$

So, on a per share basis, Microsoft's tax savings from paying out the cash rather than retaining it is $3 \times 35\% = $1.05 per share.

Adjusting for Investor Taxes

The decision to pay out versus retain cash may also affect the taxes paid by shareholders. While pension and retirement fund investors are tax exempt, most individual investors must pay taxes on interest, dividends, and capital gains. How do investor taxes affect the tax disadvantage of retaining cash?

We illustrate the tax impact with a simple example. Consider a firm whose only asset is $100 in cash, and suppose all investors face identical tax rates. Let's compare the option of paying out this cash as an immediate dividend of $100 with the option of retaining the $100 permanently and using the interest earned to pay dividends.

Suppose the firm pays out its cash immediately as a dividend and shuts down. Because the ex-dividend price of the firm is zero (it has shut down), using Eq. 17.2 we find that before the dividend is paid the firm has a share price of

$$P_{cum} = P_{ex} + Div_0 \times \left(\frac{1 - \tau_d}{1 - \tau_g} \right) = 0 + 100 \times \left(\frac{1 - \tau_d}{1 - \tau_g} \right) \tag{17.4}$$

This price reflects the fact that the investor will pay tax on the dividend at rate τ_d, but will receive a tax credit (at capital gains tax rate τ_g) for the capital loss when the firm shuts down.

Alternatively, the firm can retain the cash and invest it in Treasury bills, earning interest at rate r_f each year. After paying corporate taxes on this interest at rate τ_c, the firm can pay a perpetual dividend of

$$Div = 100 \times r_f \times (1 - \tau_c)$$

each year and retain the $100 in cash permanently. What price will an investor pay for the firm in this case? The investor's cost of capital is the after-tax return that she could earn by investing in Treasury bills on her own: $r_f \times (1 - \tau_i)$, where τ_i is the investor's tax rate on interest income. Because the investor must pay taxes on the dividends as well, the value of the firm if it retains the $100 is[21]

$$P_{retain} = \frac{Div \times (1 - \tau_d)}{r_f \times (1 - \tau_i)} = \frac{100 \times r_f \times (1 - \tau_c) \times (1 - \tau_d)}{r_f \times (1 - \tau_i)}$$
$$= 100 \times \frac{(1 - \tau_c)(1 - \tau_d)}{(1 - \tau_i)} \tag{17.5}$$

Comparing Eqs. 17.5 and 17.4,

$$P_{retain} = P_{cum} \times \frac{(1 - \tau_c)(1 - \tau_g)}{(1 - \tau_i)} = P_{cum} \times (1 - \tau^*_{retain}) \tag{17.6}$$

where τ^*_{retain} measures the effective tax disadvantage of retaining cash:

$$\tau^*_{retain} = \left[1 - \frac{(1 - \tau_c)(1 - \tau_g)}{(1 - \tau_i)} \right] \tag{17.7}$$

---

21. There is no capital gains tax consequence in this case because the share price will remain the same each year.

Because the dividend tax will be paid whether the firm pays the cash immediately or retains the cash and pays the interest over time, the dividend tax rate does not affect the cost of retaining cash in Eq. 17.7.[22] The intuition for Eq. 17.7 is that when a firm retains cash, it must pay corporate tax on the interest it earns. In addition, the investor will owe capital gains tax on the increased value of the firm. In essence, the interest on retained cash is taxed twice. If the firm paid the cash to its shareholders instead, they could invest it and be taxed only once on the interest that they earn. The cost of retaining cash therefore depends on the combined effect of the corporate and capital gains taxes, compared to the single tax on interest income. Using 2005 tax rates (see Table 15.3), $\tau_c = \tau_i = 35\%$ and $\tau_g = 15\%$, we get an effective tax disadvantage of retained cash of $\tau^*_{retain} = 15\%$. Thus, after adjusting for investor taxes, there remains a substantial tax *disadvantage* for the firm to retaining excess cash.

Issuance and Distress Costs

If there is a tax disadvantage to retaining cash, why do some firms accumulate large cash balances? Generally, they retain cash balances to cover potential future cash shortfalls. For example, if there is a reasonable likelihood that future earnings will be insufficient to fund future positive-NPV investment opportunities, a firm may start accumulating cash to make up the difference. This motivation is especially relevant for firms that may need to fund large-scale research and development projects or large acquisitions.

The advantage of holding cash to cover future potential cash needs is that this strategy allows a firm to avoid the transaction costs of raising new capital (through new debt or equity issues). The direct costs of issuance range from 1% to 3% for debt issues and from 3.5% to 7% for equity issues. There can also be substantial indirect costs of raising capital due to the agency and adverse selection (lemons) costs discussed in Chapter 16. A firm must therefore balance the tax costs of holding cash with the potential benefits of not having to raise external funds in the future. Firms with very volatile earnings may also build up cash reserves to enable them to weather temporary periods of operating losses. By holding sufficient cash, these firms can avoid financial distress and its associated costs.

Agency Costs of Retaining Cash

There is no benefit to shareholders when a firm holds cash above and beyond its future investment or liquidity needs, however. In fact, in addition to the tax cost, there are likely to be agency costs associated with having too much cash in the firm. As discussed in Chapter 16, when firms have excessive cash, managers may use the funds inefficiently by

---

22. Equation 17.7 also holds if the firm uses share repurchases instead of dividends in both cases or uses the same mix of dividends and share repurchases. However, if the firm initially retains cash by cutting back only on share repurchases, and then later uses the cash to pay a mix of dividends and repurchases, then we would replace τ_g in Eq. 17.7 with the average tax rate on dividends and capital gains, $\tau_e = \alpha\tau_d + (1 - \alpha)\tau_g$, where α is the proportion of dividends versus repurchases. In that case, τ^*_{retain} equals the effective tax disadvantage of debt τ^* we derived in Eq. 15.7, where we implicitly assumed that debt was used to fund a share repurchase (or to avoid an equity issue), and that the future interest payments displaced a mix of dividends and share repurchases. Using τ_g here is sometimes referred to as the "new view" or "trapped-equity" view of retained earnings; see, for example, A. J. Auerbach, "Tax Integration and the 'New View' of the Corporate Tax: A 1980s Perspective," *Proceedings of the National Tax Association–Tax Institute of America* (1981): 21–27. Using τ_e corresponds to the "traditional view"; see, for example, J. M. Poterba and L. H. Summers, "Dividend Taxes, Corporate Investment, and 'Q'," *Journal of Public Economics*, 22 (1983): 135–167.

continuing money-losing pet projects, paying excessive executive perks, or over-paying for acquisitions. Leverage is one way to reduce a firm's excess cash; dividends and share repurchases perform a similar role by taking cash out of the firm.

Thus paying out excess cash through dividends or share repurchases can boost the stock price by reducing managers' ability and temptation to waste resources. For example, the roughly $10 increase in Value Line's stock price on the announcement of its special dividend, shown in Figure 17.6, likely corresponds to the perceived tax benefits and reduced agency costs that would result from the transaction.

Cutting Negative-NPV Growth

Problem

Rexton Oil is an all-equity firm with 100 million shares outstanding. Rexton has $150 million in cash and expects future free cash flows of $65 million per year. Management plans to use the cash to expand the firm's operations, which will in turn increase future free cash flows by 12%. If the cost of capital of Rexton's investments is 10%, how would a decision to use the cash for a share repurchase rather than the expansion change the share price?

Solution

If Rexton uses the cash to expand, its future free cash flows will increase by 12% to $65 million × 1.12 = $72.8 million per year. Using the perpetuity formula, its market value will be $72.8 million ÷ 10% = $728 million, or $7.28 per share.

If Rexton does not expand, the value of its future free cash flows will be $65 million ÷ 10% = $650 million. Adding the cash, Rexton's market value is $800 million, or $8.00 per share. If Rexton repurchases shares, there will be no change to the share price: It will repurchase $150 million ÷ $8.00 / share = 18.75 million shares, so it will have assets worth $650 million with 81.25 million shares outstanding, for a share price of $650 million ÷ 81.25 million shares = $8.00 / share.

In this case, cutting investment and growth to fund a share repurchase increases the share price by $0.72 per share. The reason is the expansion has a negative NPV: It costs $150 million, but increases future free cash flows by only $7.8 million, for an NPV of

$$-\$150 \text{ million} + \$7.8 \text{ million} / 10\% = -\$72 \text{ million, or} -\$0.72 \text{ per share}$$

Ultimately, firms should choose to retain cash for the same reasons they would use low leverage[23]—to preserve financial slack for future growth opportunities and to avoid financial distress costs. These needs must be balanced against the tax disadvantage of holding cash and the agency cost of wasteful investment. It is not surprising, then, that high-tech and biotechnology firms, which typically choose to use little debt, also tend to retain and accumulate large amounts of cash. See Table 17.4 for a list of some U.S. firms with large cash balances.

As with capital structure decisions, however, payout policies are generally set by managers whose incentives may differ from those of shareholders. Managers may prefer to retain and maintain control over the firm's cash rather than pay it out. The retained cash can be used to fund investments that are costly for shareholders but have benefits for

---

23. As discussed in Chapter 14, we can view excess cash as negative debt. As a consequence, the trade-offs from holding excess cash are very similar to those involved in the capital structure decision.

TABLE 17.4		Firms with Large Cash Balances	
Ticker	Company	Cash ($ billion)	Percentage of Market Capitalization
MSFT	Microsoft	34.7	12%
PFE	Pfizer	22.2	12%
MRK	Merck	15.6	21%
MOT	Motorola	14.8	25%
INTC	Intel	12.8	11%
HPQ	Hewlett-Packard	12.0	13%

Source: Yahoo! Finance, April 2006.

managers (for instance, pet projects and excessive salaries), or it can simply be held as a means to reduce leverage and the risk of financial distress that could threaten managers' job security. According to the managerial entrenchment theory of payout policy, managers pay out cash only when pressured to do so by the firm's investors.[24]

CONCEPT CHECK

1. Is there an advantage for a firm to retain its cash instead of paying it out to shareholders in perfect capital markets?

2. How do corporate taxes affect the decision of a firm to retain excess cash?

17.6 Signaling with Payout Policy

One market imperfection that we have not yet considered is asymmetric information. When managers have better information than investors regarding the future prospects of the firm, their payout decisions may signal this information. In this section, we look at managers' motivations when setting a firm's payout policy, and we evaluate what these decisions may communicate to investors.

Dividend Smoothing

Firms can change dividends at any time, but in practice they vary the sizes of their dividends relatively infrequently. For example, General Motors (GM) has changed the amount of its regular dividend only seven times over a 20-year period. Yet during that same period, GM's earnings varied widely, as shown in Figure 17.7.

The pattern seen with GM is typical of most firms that pay dividends. Firms adjust dividends relatively infrequently, and dividends are much less volatile than earnings. This practice of maintaining relatively constant dividends is called **dividend smoothing**. Firms also increase dividends much more frequently than they cut them. For example, from 1971

---

24. Recall from Section 16.7 that the managerial entrenchment theory of capital structure argued that managers choose low leverage to avoid the discipline of debt and preserve their job security. Applied to payout policy, the same theory implies that managers will reduce leverage further by choosing to hold too much cash.

FIGURE 17.7

GM's Earnings and Dividends per Share, 1985–2006

Compared to GM's earnings, its dividend payments have remained relatively stable. (Data adjusted for splits, earnings exclude extraordinary items.)
Source: Compustat and CapitalIQ.

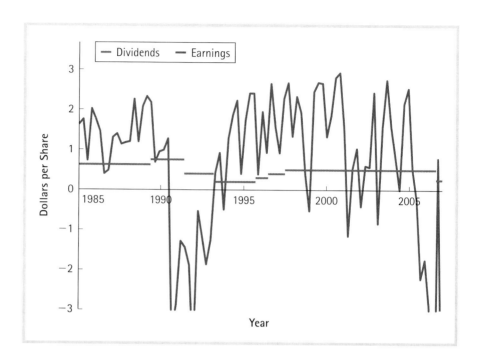

to 2001, only 5.4% of dividend changes were decreases.[25] In a classic survey of corporate executives, John Lintner[26] suggested that these observations resulted from (1) management's belief that investors prefer stable dividends with sustained growth, and (2) management's desire to maintain a long-term target level of dividends as a fraction of earnings. Thus firms raise their dividends only when they perceive a long-term sustainable increase in the expected level of future earnings, and cut them only as a last resort.[27]

How can firms keep dividends smooth as earnings vary? As we have already discussed, firms can maintain almost any level of dividend in the short run by adjusting the number of shares they repurchase or issue and the amount of cash they retain. However, due to the tax and transaction costs of funding a dividend with new equity issues, managers do not wish to commit to a dividend that the firm cannot afford to pay out of regular earnings. For this reason, firms generally set dividends at a level they expect to be able to maintain based on the firm's earnings prospects.

Dividend Signaling

If firms smooth dividends, the firm's dividend choice will contain information regarding management's expectations of future earnings. When a firm increases its dividend, it sends a positive signal to investors that management expects to be able to afford the higher div-

25. F. Allen and R. Michaely, "Payout Policy," in G. Constantinides, M. Harris, and R. Stulz, eds., *Handbook of the Economics of Finance* (2003).

26. J. Lintner, "Distribution of Incomes of Corporations Among Dividends, Retained Earnings and Taxes," *American Economic Review* 46 (1956): 97–113.

27. While perhaps a good description of how firms *do* set their dividends, as we have shown in this chapter there is no clear reason why firms *should* smooth their dividends, nor convincing evidence that investors prefer this practice.

Royal & SunAlliance's Dividend Cut

In some quarters, Julian Hance must have seemed like a heretic. On November 8, the finance director of Royal & SunAlliance, a U.K.-based insurance group with £12.6 billion (€20.2 billion) in annual revenue, did the unthinkable—he announced that he would cut the firm's dividend.

Many observers gasped at the decision. Surely, they argued, cutting the dividend was a sign of weakness. Didn't companies only cut their dividend when profits were falling?

Quite the contrary, countered Hance. With insurance premiums rising around the world, particularly following the World Trade Center tragedy, Royal & SunAlliance believed that its industry offered excellent growth opportunities.

"The outlook for business in 2002 and beyond makes a compelling case for reinvesting capital in the business rather than returning it to shareholders," explains Hance.

The stock market agreed with him, sending Royal & SunAlliance's shares up 5% following its dividend news. "Cutting the dividend is a positive move," observes Matthew Wright, an insurance analyst at Credit Lyonnais. "It shows the company expects future profitability to be good."

Source: Justin Wood, CFO Europe.com, December 2001.

---

idend for the foreseeable future. Conversely, when managers cut the dividend, it may signal that they have given up hope that earnings will rebound in the near term and so need to reduce the dividend to save cash. The idea that dividend changes reflect managers' views about a firm's future earnings prospects is called the **dividend signaling hypothesis**.

Studies of the market's reaction to dividend changes are consistent with this hypothesis. For example, during the period 1967–1993, firms that raised their dividend by 10% or more saw their stock prices rise by 1.34% after the announcement, while those that cut their dividend by 10% or more experienced a price decline of −3.71%.[28] The average size of the stock price reaction increases with the magnitude of the dividend change, and is larger for dividend cuts.[29]

Dividend signaling is similar to the use of leverage as a signal that we discussed in Chapter 16. Increasing debt signals that management believes the firm can afford the future interest payments, in the same way that raising the dividend signals the firm can afford to maintain the dividends in the future. However, while cutting the dividend is costly for managers in terms of their reputation and the reaction of investors, it is by no means as costly as failing to make debt payments. As a consequence, we would expect dividend changes to be a somewhat weaker signal than leverage changes. Indeed, empirical studies have found average stock price increases of more than 10% when firms replace equity with debt, and decreases of 4% to 10% when firms replace debt with equity.[30]

---

28. See G. Grullon, R. Michaely, and B. Swaminathan, "Are Dividend Changes a Sign of Firm Maturity?" *Journal of Business* 75(3) (2002): 387–424. The effects are even larger for dividend initiations (+3.4%) and omissions (−7%), according to studies by R. Michaely, R. Thaler, and K. Womack, "Price Reactions to Dividend Initiations and Omissions: Overreaction or Drift?" *Journal of Finance* 50(2) (1995): 573–608, and similar results by P. Healy and K. Palepu, "Earnings Information Conveyed by Dividend Initiations and Omissions," *Journal of Financial Economics* 21(2) (1988): 149-176.

29. Not all of the evidence is consistent with dividend signaling, however. For example, it has been difficult to document a relationship between dividend changes and realized future earnings [S. Benartzi, R. Michaely and R. Thaler, "Do Changes in Dividends Signal the Future or the Past?" *Journal of Finance* 52(3) (1997): 1007–1034].

30. C. Smith, "Raising Capital: Theory and Evidence," in D. Chew, ed., *The New Corporate Finance* (McGraw-Hill, 1993).

While an increase of a firm's dividend may signal management's optimism regarding its future cash flows, it might also signal a lack of investment opportunities. For example, Microsoft's move to initiate dividends in 2003 was largely seen as a result of its declining growth prospects as opposed to a signal about its increased future profitability.[31] Conversely, a firm might cut its dividend to exploit new positive-NPV investment opportunities. In this case, the dividend decrease might lead to a positive—rather than negative—stock price reaction (see the box on Royal and SunAlliance's dividend cut). In general, we must interpret dividends as a signal in the context of the type of new information managers are likely to have.

Signaling and Share Repurchases

Share repurchases, like dividends, may also signal managers' information to the market. However, several important differences distinguish share repurchases and dividends. First, managers are much less committed to share repurchases than to dividend payments. As we noted earlier, when firms announce authorization for an open market share repurchase, they generally announce the maximum amount they plan to spend on repurchases. The actual amount spent, however, may be far less. Also, it may take several years to complete the share repurchase.[32] Second, unlike with dividends, firms do not smooth their repurchase activity from year to year. As a result, announcing a share repurchase today does not necessarily represent a long-term commitment to repurchase shares. In this regard, share repurchases may be less of a signal than dividends about future earnings of a firm.

A third key difference between dividends and share repurchases is that the cost of a share repurchase depends on the market price of the stock. If managers believe the stock is currently over-valued, a share repurchase will be costly to the firm. That is, buying the stock at its current (over-valued) price is a negative-NPV investment. By contrast, repurchasing shares when managers perceive the stock to be under-valued is a positive-NPV investment. Managers will clearly be more likely to repurchase shares if they believe the stock to be under-valued.

Thus share repurchases may signal that managers believe the firm to be under-valued (or at least not severely over-valued). Share repurchases are a credible signal that the shares are under-priced, because if they are over-priced a share repurchase is costly for current shareholders. If investors believe that managers have better information regarding the firm's prospects and act on behalf of current shareholders, then investors will react favorably to share repurchase announcements.

In a 2004 survey, 87% of CFOs agreed that firms should repurchase shares when their stock price is a good value relative to its true value.[33] Investors also appear to interpret share repurchases as a positive signal. The average market price reaction to the announcement of an open market share repurchase program is about 3% (with the size of the reac-

---

31. See "An End to Growth?" *The Economist* (July 22, 2004): 61.

32. See C. Stephens and M. Weisbach, "Actual Share Reacquisitions in Open-Market Repurchase Programs," *Journal of Finance* 53(1) (1998): 313–333, for an analysis of how firms' actual repurchases compare to their announced plans. For details of how share repurchase programs are implemented, see D. Cook, L. Krigman, and J. Leach, "On the Timing and Execution of Open Market Repurchases," *Review of Financial Studies* 17(2) (2004): 463–498.

33. A. Brav, J. Graham, C. Harvey, and R. Michaely, "Payout Policy in the 21st Century," *Journal of Financial Economics* 77(3) (2005): 483–527.

tion increasing in the portion of shares outstanding sought).[34] The reaction is much larger for fixed-price tender offers (12%) and Dutch auction share repurchases (8%).[35] Recall that these methods of repurchase are generally used for very large repurchases conducted in a very short timeframe and are often part of an overall recapitalization. Also, the shares are repurchased at a premium to the current market price. Thus tender offers and Dutch auction repurchases are even stronger signals than open market repurchases that management views the current share price as under-valued.

Share Repurchases and Market Timing

Problem

Clark Industries has 200 million shares outstanding, a current share price of $30, and no debt. Clark's management believes that the shares are under-priced, and that the true value is $35 per share. Clark plans to pay $600 million in cash to its shareholders by repurchasing shares at the current market price. Suppose that soon after the transaction is completed, new information comes out that causes investors to revise their opinion of the firm and agree with management's assessment of Clark's value. What is Clark's share price after the new information comes out? How would the share price differ if Clark waited until after the new information came out to repurchase the shares?

Solution

Clark's initial market cap is $30/share $\times$ 200 million shares = $6 billion, of which $600 million is cash and $5.4 billion corresponds to other assets. At the current share price, Clark will repurchase $600 million $\div$ $30/share = 20 million shares. The market value balance sheet before and after the transaction is shown below (in millions of dollars):

	Before Repurchase	After Repurchase	After New Information
Cash	600	0	0
Other assets	5,400	5,400	6,400
Total market value of assets	6,000	6,400	5,400
Shares (millions)	200	180	180
Share Price	**$30**	**$30**	**$35.56**

According to management, Clark's initial market capitalization should be $35/share $\times$ 200 million shares = $7 billion, of which $6.4 billion would correspond to other assets. As the market value balance sheet shows, after the new information comes out Clark's share price will rise to $35.56.

If Clark waited for the new information to come out before repurchasing the shares, it would buy shares at a market price of $35 per share. Thus it would repurchase only 17.1 million shares. The share price after the repurchase would be $6.4 billion $\div$ 182.9 shares = $35.

---

34. See D. Ikenberry, J. Lakonishok, and T. Vermaelen, "Market Underreaction to Open Market Share Repurchases," *Journal of Financial Economics* 39(2) (1995): 181–208, and G. Grullon and R. Michaely, "Dividends, Share Repurchases, and the Substitution Hypothesis," *Journal of Finance* 57(4) (2002): 1649–1684.

35. R. Comment and G. Jarrell, "The Relative Signaling Power of Dutch-Auction and Fixed-Price Self-tender Offers and Open-Market Share Repurchases," *Journal of Finance* 46(4) (1991): 1243–1271.

Hence, by repurchasing shares while the stock is under-priced, the ultimate share price will be $0.56 higher, for a total gain of $0.56 × 180 million shares = $100 million. This gain equals the gain from buying 20 million shares at a price that is $5 below their true value. It comes at the expense of shareholders who sold shares for $30/share as part of the repurchase.

As this example shows, the gain from buying shares when the stock is under-priced leads to an increase in the firm's long-run share price. Similarly, buying shares when the stock is over-priced will reduce the long-run share price. The firm may therefore try to time its repurchases appropriately. Anticipating this strategy, shareholders may interpret a share repurchase as a signal that the firm is undervalued.

CONCEPT CHECK

1. What possible signals does a firm give when it cuts its dividend?

2. Would managers be more likely to repurchase shares if they believe the stock is under- or over-valued?

17.7 Stock Dividends, Splits, and Spin-offs

In this chapter, we have focused on a firm's decision to pay cash to its shareholders. But a firm can pay another type of dividend that does not involve cash: a stock dividend. In this case, each shareholder who owns the stock before it goes ex-dividend receives additional shares of stock of the firm itself (a stock split) or of a subsidiary (a spin-off). Here we briefly review these two types of transactions.

Stock Dividends and Splits

If a company declares a 10% stock dividend, each shareholder will receive one new share of stock for every 10 shares already owned. Stock dividends of 50% or higher are generally referred to as stock splits. For example, with a 50% stock dividend, each shareholder will receive one new share for every two shares owned. Because a holder of two shares will end up holding three new shares, this transaction is also called a 3 : 2 ("3-for-2") stock split. Similarly, a 100% stock dividend is equivalent to a 2 : 1 stock split.

With a stock dividend, a firm does not pay out any cash to shareholders. As a result, the total market value of the firm's assets and liabilities, and therefore of its equity, is unchanged. The only thing that is different is the number of shares outstanding. The stock price will therefore fall because the same total equity value is now divided over a larger number of shares.

Let's illustrate a stock dividend for Genron. Suppose Genron paid a 50% stock dividend (a 3 : 2 stock split) rather than a cash dividend. Table 17.5 shows the market value balance sheet and the resulting share price before and after the stock dividend.

A shareholder who owns 100 shares before the dividend has a portfolio worth $42 × 100 = $4200. After the dividend, the shareholder owns 150 shares worth $28, giving a portfolio value of $28 × 150 = $4200. (Note the important difference between a stock split and a share issuance: When the company issues shares, the number of shares increases, but the firm also raises cash to add to its existing assets. If the shares are sold at a fair price, the stock price should not change.)

Unlike cash dividends, stock dividends are not taxed. Thus, from both the firm's and shareholders' perspectives, there is no real consequence to a stock dividend. The number

	TABLE 17.5	**Cum and Ex-Dividend Share Price for Genron with a 50% Stock Dividend ($ million)**	

	December 11 (Cum-Dividend)	December 12 (Ex-Dividend)
Cash	20	20
Other assets	400	400
Total market value of assets	420	420
Shares (millions)	10	15
Share price	$42	$28

of shares is proportionally increased and the price per share is proportionally reduced so that there is no change in value.

Why, then, do companies pay stock dividends or split their stock? The typical motivation for a stock split is to keep the share price in a range thought to be attractive to small investors. Stocks generally trade in lots of 100 shares, and in any case do not trade in units less than one share. As a result, if the share price rises significantly, it might be difficult for small investors to afford one share, let alone 100. Making the stock more attractive to small investors can increase the demand for and the liquidity of the stock, which may in

Berkshire Hathaway's A & B Shares

Many managers split their stock to keep the price affordable for small investors, making it easier for them to buy and sell the stock. Warren Buffett, chairman and chief executive of Berkshire Hathaway, disagrees. As he commented in Berkshire's 1983 annual report: "We are often asked why Berkshire does not split its stock . . . we want [shareholders] who think of themselves as business owners with the intention of staying a long time. And, we want those who keep their eyes focused on business results, not market prices." In its 40-year history, Berkshire Hathaway has never split its stock.

As a result of Berkshire Hathaway's strong performance and the lack of stock splits, the stock price climbed. By 1996, it exceeded $30,000 per share. Because this price was much too expensive for some small investors, several financial intermediaries created unit investment trusts whose only investment was Berkshire shares. (Unit

investment trusts are similar to mutual funds, but their investment portfolio is fixed.) Investors could buy smaller interests in these trusts, effectively owning Berkshire stock with a much lower initial investment.

In response, in February 1996 Buffett announced the creation of a second class of Berkshire Hathaway stock, the Class B shares. Each owner of the original shares (now called Class A shares) was offered the opportunity to convert each A share into 30 B shares. "We're giving shareholders a do-it-yourself split, if they care to do it," Buffett said. Through the B shares, investors could own Berkshire stock with a smaller investment, and they would not have to pay the extra transaction costs required to buy stock through the unit trusts.

In May 2006, the price of one share of Berkshire Hathaway Class A shares was more than $92,000 per share.*

*We should note that Buffet's logic for not splitting the stock is a bit puzzling. Why should letting the stock price rise to a very high level attract a "better" investor clientele compared to splitting the stock and keeping its price in a more typical range? And if an extremely high stock price were advantageous, Buffet could have obtained it much sooner through a reverse split of the stock.

John Connors was Senior Vice President and Chief Financial Officer of Microsoft. He retired in 2005 and is now a partner at Ignition Partners, a Seattle venture capital firm.

QUESTION: *Microsoft declared a dividend for the first time in 2003. What goes into the decision of a company to initiate a dividend?*

ANSWER: Microsoft was in a unique position. The company had never paid a dividend and was facing shareholder pressure to do something with its $60 billion cash buildup. The company considered five key questions in developing its distribution strategy:

1. Can the company sustain payment of a cash dividend in perpetuity and increase the dividend over time? Microsoft was confident it could meet that commitment and raise the dividend in the future.

2. Is a cash dividend a better return to stockholders than a stock buyback program? These are capital structure decisions: Do we want to reduce our shares outstanding? Is our stock attractively priced for a buyback, or do we want to distribute the cash as a dividend? Microsoft had plenty of capacity to issue a dividend *and* continue a buyback program.

3. What is the tax effect of a cash dividend versus a buyback to the corporation and to shareholders? From a tax perspective to shareholders, it was largely a neutral decision in Microsoft's case.

4. What is the psychological impact on investors, and how does it fit the story of the stock for investors? This is a more qualitative factor. A regular ongoing dividend put Microsoft on a path to becoming an attractive investment for income investors.

5. What are the public relations implications of a dividend program? Investors don't look to Microsoft to hold cash but to be a leader in software development and provide equity growth. So they viewed the dividend program favorably.

QUESTION: *How does a company decide whether to increase its dividend, have a special dividend, or repurchase its stock to return capital to investors?*

ANSWER: The decision to increase the dividend is a function of cash flow projections. Are you confident that you have adequate cash flow to sustain this and future increases? Once you increase the dividend, investors expect future increases as well. Some companies establish explicit criteria for dividend increases. In my experience as a CFO, the analytic framework involves a set of relative comparables. What are the dividend payouts and dividend yields of the market in general and of your peer group, and where are we relative to them? We talk to significant investors and consider what is best for increasing shareholder value long-term.

A special dividend is a very efficient form of cash distribution that generally involves a nonrecurring situation, such as the sale of a business division or a cash award from a legal situation. Also, companies without a comprehensive distribution strategy use special dividends to reduce large cash accumulations. For Microsoft, the 2004 special dividend and announcement of the stock dividend and stock buyback program resolved the issue of what to do with all the cash and clarified our direction going forward.

QUESTION: *What other factors go into dividend decisions?*

ANSWER: Powerful finance and accounting tools help us to make better and broader business decisions. But these decisions involve as much psychology and market thinking as math. You have to consider non-quantifiable factors such as the psychology of investors. Not long ago, everyone wanted growth stocks; no one wanted dividend-paying stocks. Now dividend stocks are in vogue. You must also take into account your industry and what the competition is doing. In many tech companies, employee ownership in the form of options programs represents a fairly significant percentage of fully diluted shares. Dividend distributions reduce volatility of stock and hence the value of options.

At the end of the day, you want to be sure that your cash distribution strategy helps your overall story with investors.

turn boost the stock price. On average, announcements of stock splits are associated with a 2% increase in the stock price.[36]

Most firms use splits to keep their share prices from exceeding $100. From 1990 to 2000, Cisco Systems split its stock nine times, so that one share purchased at the IPO split into 288 shares. Had it not split, Cisco's share price at the time of its last split in March 2000 would have been 288 × $72.19, or $20,790.72.

Firms also do not want their stock prices to fall too low. First, a stock price that is very low raises transaction costs for investors. For example, the spread between the bid and ask price for a stock has a minimum size of one tick ($0.01 for the NYSE and Nasdaq exchanges) independent of the stock price. In percentage terms, the tick size is larger for stocks with a low price than for stocks with a high price. Also, exchanges require stocks to maintain a minimum price to remain listed on an exchange (for example, the NYSE and Nasdaq require listed firms to maintain a price of at least $1 per share).

If the price of the stock falls too low, a company can engage in a **reverse split** and reduce the number of shares outstanding. For example, in a 1 : 10 reverse split, every 10 shares of stock are replaced with a single share. As a result, the share price increases tenfold. Reverse splits became necessary for many dot-coms after the Internet bust in 2000. Infospace.com, for instance, split 2 : 1 three times in 1999 through 2000, but was forced to implement a 1 : 10 reverse split in 2002 when its share price dropped below $0.40.

Through a combination of splits and reverse splits, firms can keep their share prices in any range they desire. As Figure 17.8 shows, almost all firms have stock prices below $100 per share, with most firms' prices being between $5 and $60 per share.

Spin-offs

Rather than pay a dividend using cash or shares of its own stock, a firm can also distribute shares of a subsidiary in a transaction referred to as a **spin-off**. Non-cash special dividends are commonly used to spin off assets or a subsidiary as a separate company. For example, after selling 15% of Monsanto Corporation in an IPO in October 2000, Pharmacia Corporation announced in July 2002 that it would spin off its remaining 85% holding of Monsanto Corporation. The spin-off was accomplished through a special dividend in which each Pharmacia shareholder received 0.170593 share of Monsanto per share of Pharmacia owned. After receiving the Monsanto shares, Pharmacia shareholders could trade them separately from the shares of the parent firm.

On the distribution date of August 13, 2002, Monsanto shares traded for an average price of $16.21. Thus the value of the special dividend was

$$0.170593 \text{ Monsanto shares} \times \$16.21 \text{ per share} = \$2.77 \text{ per share}$$

A shareholder who initially owned 100 shares of Pharmacia stock would receive 17 shares of Monsanto stock, plus cash of 0.0593 × $16.21 = $0.96 in place of the fractional shares.

---

36. S. Nayak and N. Prabhala, "Disentangling the Dividend Information in Splits: A Decomposition Using Conditional Event-Study Methods," *Review of Financial Studies* 14(4) (2001): 1083–1116. For evidence that stock splits are successful at attracting individual investors, see R. Dhar, W. Goetzmann, and N. Zhu, "The Impact of Clientele Changes: Evidence from Stock Splits," *Yale ICF Working Paper* no. 03-14 (2004). While splits seem to increase the number of shareholders, evidence of their impact on liquidity is mixed; see, for example, T. Copeland, "Liquidity Changes Following Stock Splits," *Journal of Finance* 34(1) (1979): 115–141, and J. Lakonishok and B. Lev, "Stock Splits and Stock Dividends: Why, Who and When," *Journal of Finance* 42(4) (1987): 913–932.

FIGURE 17.8

Distribution of Stock Prices for NYSE Firms (April 2005)

By using splits and reverse splits, most firms keep their share prices between $5 and $60 to reduce transaction costs for investors.

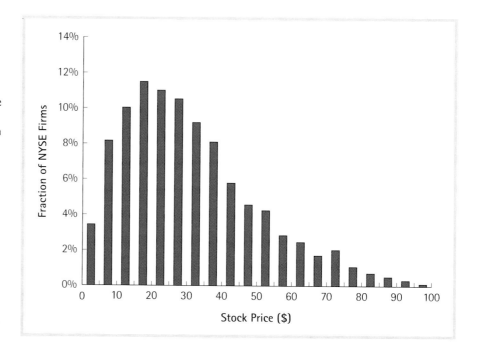

Alternatively, Pharmacia could have sold the shares of Monsanto and distributed the cash to shareholders as a cash dividend. The transaction Pharmacia chose offers two advantages over that strategy: (1) It avoids the transaction costs associated with such a sale, and (2) the special dividend is not taxed as a cash distribution. Instead, Pharmacia shareholders who received Monsanto shares are liable for capital gains tax only at the time they sell the Monsanto shares.[37]

Here we have considered only the methods of distributing the shares of the firm that has been spun off, either by paying a stock dividend or by selling the shares directly and then distributing (or retaining) the cash. The decision of whether to do the spin-off in the first place raises a new question: When is it better for two firms to operate as separate entities, rather than as a single combined firm? The issues that arise in addressing this question are the same as those that arise in the decision to merge two firms, which we discuss further in Chapter 28.

CONCEPT CHECK

1. What is the difference between a stock dividend and a stock split?

2. What is the main purpose of a reverse split?

---

37. The capital gain is computed by allocating a fraction of the cost basis of the Pharmacia shares to the Monsanto shares received. Because Pharmacia was trading at an ex-dividend price of $42.54 on the distribution date, the special dividend amounted to 6.1% = 2.77 / (2.77 + 42.54) of total value. Thus the original cost basis of the Pharmacia stock was divided by allocating 6.1% to the Monsanto shares and the remaining 93.9% to the Pharmacia shares.

Summary

1. When a firm wants to distribute cash to its shareholders, it can pay a cash dividend or it can repurchase shares.
   a. Most companies pay regular, quarterly dividends. Sometimes firms announce one-time, special dividends.
   b. Firms repurchase shares using an open market repurchase, a tender offer, a Dutch auction repurchase, or a targeted repurchase.

2. On the declaration date, firms announce that they will pay dividends to all shareholders of record on the record date. The ex-dividend date is the first day on which the stock trades without the right to an upcoming dividend; it is usually two trading days prior to the record date. Dividend checks are mailed on the payment date.

3. In a stock split or a stock dividend, a company distributes additional shares rather than cash to shareholders.

4. In perfect capital markets, the stock price falls by the amount of the dividend when a dividend is paid. An open market share repurchase has no effect on the stock price, and the stock price is the same as the cum-dividend price if a dividend were paid instead.

5. The Modigliani-Miller dividend irrelevance proposition states that in perfect capital markets, holding fixed the investment policy of a firm, the firm's choice of dividend policy is irrelevant and does not affect the initial share price.

6. In reality, capital markets are not perfect, and market imperfections affect firm dividend policy.

7. Taxes are an important market friction that affects dividend policy.
   a. Considering taxes as the only market imperfection, when the tax rate on dividends exceeds the tax rate on capital gains, the optimal dividend policy is for firms to pay no dividends. Firms should use share repurchases for all payouts.
   b. The effective dividend tax rate, τ_d^*, measures the net tax cost to the investor per dollar of dividend income received.

$$\tau_d^* = \left(\frac{\tau_d - \tau_g}{1 - \tau_g} \right) \tag{17.3}$$

   The effective dividend tax rate varies across investors for several reasons, including income level, investment horizon, tax jurisdiction, and type of investment account.
   c. Different investor taxes create clientele effects, in which the dividend policy of a firm suits the tax preference of its investor clientele.

8. Modigliani-Miller payout policy irrelevance says that, in perfect capital markets, if a firm invests excess cash flows in financial securities, the firm's choice of payout versus retention is irrelevant and does not affect the initial share price.

9. Corporate taxes make it costly for a firm to retain excess cash. Even after adjusting for investor taxes, retaining excess cash brings a substantial tax disadvantage for a firm.

10. Even though there is a tax disadvantage to retaining cash, some firms accumulate cash balances. Cash balances help firms minimize the transaction costs of raising new capital when they have future potential cash needs. However, there is no benefit to shareholders from firms holding cash in excess of future investment needs.

11. In addition to the tax disadvantage of holding cash, agency costs may arise, as managers may be tempted to spend excess cash on inefficient investments and perks. Without pressure from shareholders, managers may choose to horde cash to spend in this way or as a means of reducing a firm's leverage and increasing their job security.

12. Dividends and share repurchases help minimize the agency problem of wasteful spending when a firm has excess cash.

13. Firms typically maintain relatively constant dividends. This practice is called dividend smoothing.

14. The idea that dividend changes reflect managers' views about firms' future earnings prospects is called the dividend signaling hypothesis.

    a. Managers usually increase dividends only when they are confident the firm will be able to afford higher dividends for the foreseeable future.

    b. When managers cut the dividend, it may signal that they have lost hope that earnings will improve.

15. Share repurchases may be used to signal positive information, as repurchases are more attractive if management believes the stock is under-valued at its current price.

16. With a stock dividend, shareholders receive either additional shares of stock of the firm itself (a stock split) or shares of a subsidiary (a spin-off). The stock price generally falls proportionally with the size of the split.

17. A reverse split decreases the number of shares outstanding, and therefore results in a higher share price.

Key Terms

bird in the hand hypothesis *p. 540*
clientele effect *p. 547*
cum-dividend *p. 536*
declaration date *p. 532*
dividend puzzle *p. 544*
dividend signaling hypothesis *p. 557*
dividend smoothing *p. 555*
dividend-capture theory *p. 548*
Dutch auction *p. 535*
effective dividend tax rate *p. 545*
ex-dividend date *p. 532*
greenmail *p. 535*
liquidating dividend *p. 534*

open market repurchase *p. 534*
payable date (distribution date) *p. 532*
payout policy *p. 532*
record date *p. 532*
return of capital *p. 534*
reverse split *p. 563*
special dividend *p. 532*
spin-off *p. 563*
stock dividend *p. 533*
stock split *p. 533*
targeted repurchase *p. 535*
tender offer *p. 534*

Further Reading

Readers interested in delving deeper into the issues covered in this chapter might want to begin with the following comprehensive review of the literature on payout policy: F. Allen and R. Michaely, "Payout Policy," in G. Constantinides, M. Harris, and R. Shulz, eds., *Handbook of the Economics of Finance*, Chapter 7 (Elsevier, 2003).

The literature on payout policy is extensive. It is impossible, given the space requirements, to cover all the relevant further readings here. Nevertheless, readers interested in specific issues might find the following articles interesting:

On the information content of payout policy: K. L. Dewenter and V. A. Warther, "Dividends, Asymmetric Information, and Agency Conflicts: Evidence from a Comparison of the Dividend Policies of Japanese and U.S. Firms," *Journal of Finance* 53(3) (1998): 879–904; E. Dyl and R. Weigand, "The Information Content of Dividend Initiations: Additional Evidence," *Financial Management* 27(3) (1998): 27–35; and G. Grullon and R. Michaely, "The Information Content of Share Repurchase Programs," *Journal of Finance* 59(2) (2004): 651–680.

On the decision corporations make between dividends and share repurchases: L. S. Bagwell and J. B. Shoven, "Cash Distributions to Shareholders," *Journal of Economic Perspectives* 3(3) (1989): 129–140; M. J. Barclay and C.W. Smith, "Corporate Payout Policy: Cash Dividends Versus Open-Market Repurchases," *Journal of Financial Economics* 22(1) (1988): 61–82; A. Dittmar, "Why Do Firms Repurchase Stock?" *Journal of Business* 73(3) (2000): 331–355; G. W. Fenn and N. Liang, "Corporate Payout Policy and Managerial Stock Incentives," *Journal of Financial Economics* 60(1) (2001): 45–72; W. Guay and J. Harford, "The Cash-Flow Permanence and Information Content of Dividend Increases Versus Repurchases," *Journal of Financial Economics* 57(3) (2000): 385–415; M. Jagannathan, C. P. Stephens, and M. Weisbach, "Financial Flexibility and the Choice Between Dividends and Stock Repurchases," *Journal of Financial Economics* 57(3) (2000): 355–384; K. Kahle, "When a Buyback Isn't a Buyback: Open Market Repurchases and Employee Options," *Journal of Financial Economics* 63(2) (2002): 235–261; and M. Rozeff, "How Companies Set Their Dividend Payout Ratios," in Joel M. Stern and Donald H. Chew, eds., *The Revolution in Corporate Finance* (New York: Basil Blackwell, 1986).

On tax clienteles: F. Allen, A. E. Bernardo, and I. Welch, "A Theory of Dividends Based on Tax Clienteles," *Journal of Finance* 55(6) (2000): 2499–2536.

On the timing of share repurchases: P. Brockman and D. Y. Chung, "Managerial Timing and Corporate Liquidity: Evidence from Actual Share Repurchases," *Journal of Financial Economics* 61(3) (2001): 417–448; and D. O. Cook, L. Krigman, and J. C. Leach, "On the Timing and Execution of Open Market Repurchases," *Review of Financial Studies* 17(2) (2004): 463–498.

Problems

All problems in this chapter are available in MyFinanceLab.

Distributions to Shareholders

1. ABC Corporation announced that it will pay a dividend to all shareholders of record as of Monday, April 3, 2006. It takes three business days of a purchase for the new owners of a share of stock to be registered.
   a. When is the last day an investor can purchase ABC stock and still get the dividend payment?
   b. When is the ex-dividend day?

2. Describe the different mechanisms available to a firm to use to repurchase shares.

Comparison of Dividends and Share Repurchases

3. Natsam Corporation has $250 million of excess cash. The firm has no debt and 500 million shares outstanding with a current market price of $15 per share. Natsam's board has decided to pay out this cash as a one-time dividend.

a. What is the ex-dividend price of a share in a perfect capital market?

b. If the board instead decided to use the cash to do a one-time share repurchase, in a perfect capital market what is the price of the shares once the repurchase is complete?

c. In a perfect capital market, which policy (in part a or b) makes investors in the firm better off?

4. Suppose the board of Natsam Corporation decided to do the share repurchase in Problem 3(b), but you, as an investor, would have preferred to receive a dividend payment. How can you leave yourself in the same position as if the board had elected to make the dividend payment instead?

5. Suppose you work for Oracle Corporation, and part of your compensation takes the form of stock options. The value of the stock option is equal to the difference between Oracle's stock price and an exercise price of $10 per share at the time that you exercise the option. As an option holder, would you prefer that Oracle use dividends or share repurchases to pay out cash to shareholders? Explain.

The Tax Disadvantage of Dividends

6. The HNH Corporation will pay a constant dividend of $2 per share, per year, in perpetuity. Assume all investors pay a 20% tax on dividends and that there is no capital gains tax. The cost of capital for investing in HNH stock is 12%.

a. What is the price of a share of HNH stock?

b. Assume that management makes a surprise announcement that HNH will no longer pay dividends but will use the cash to repurchase stock instead. What is the price of a share of HNH stock now?

Dividend Capture and Tax Clienteles

7. What was the effective dividend tax rate for a U.S. investor in the highest tax bracket who planned to hold a stock for one year in 1981? How did the effective dividend tax rate change in 1982 when the Reagan tax cuts took effect? (Ignore state taxes.)

8. The dividend tax cut passed in 2003 lowered the effective dividend tax rate for a U.S. investor in the highest tax bracket to a historic low. During which other periods in the last 35 years was the effective dividend tax rate as low?

9. On Monday, November 15, 2004, TheStreet.Com reported: "An experiment in the efficiency of financial markets will play out Monday following the expiration of a $3,08 dividend privilege for holders of Microsoft." The story went on: "The stock is currently trading ex-dividend both the special $3 payout and Microsoft's regular 8-cent quarterly dividend, meaning a buyer doesn't receive the money if he acquires the shares now." Microsoft stock ultimately opened for trade at $27.34 on the ex-dividend date (November 15), down $2.63 from its previous close.

a. Assuming that this price drop resulted only from the dividend payment (no other information affected the stock price that day), what does this decline in price imply about the effective dividend tax rate for Microsoft?

b. Based on this information, which investors are most likely to be the marginal investors (the ones who determine the price) in Microsoft stock?

   i. Long-term individual investors

   ii. One-year individual investors

   iii. Pension funds

   iv. Corporations

10. At current tax rates, which investors are most likely to hold a stock that has a high dividend yield?

   a. Individual investors

   b. Pension funds

   c. Mutual funds

   d. Corporations

11. A stock that you know is held by long-term individual investors paid a large one-time dividend. You notice that the price drop on the ex-dividend date is about the size of the dividend payment. You find this relationship puzzling given the tax disadvantage of dividends. Explain how the dividend-capture theory might account for this behavior.

Payout Versus Retention of Cash

 12. Assume capital markets are perfect. Kay Industries currently has $100 million invested in short-term Treasury securities paying 7%, and it pays out the interest payments on these securities as a dividend. The board is considering selling the Treasury securities and paying out the proceeds as a one-time dividend payment.

   a. If the board went ahead with this plan, what would happen to the value of Kay stock upon the announcement of a change in policy?

   b. What would happen to the value of Kay stock on the ex-dividend date of the one-time dividend?

   c. Given these price reactions, will this decision benefit investors?

 13. Redo Problem 12 but assume that Kay must pay a corporate tax rate of 35%, and investors pay no taxes.

 14. Redo Problem 12 but assume that investors pay a 15% tax on dividends but no capital gains taxes, and Kay does not pay corporate taxes.

15. Use the data in Table 15.3 to calculate the tax disadvantage of retained cash in

   a. 1998.

   b. 1976.

Signaling with Payout Policy

16. Explain under which conditions an increase in the dividend payment can be interpreted as a signal of

   a. Good news.

   b. Bad news.

17. Why is an announcement of a share repurchase considered a positive signal?

*18. AMC Corporation currently has an enterprise value of $400 million and $100 million in excess cash. The firm has 10 million shares outstanding and no debt. Suppose AMC uses its excess cash to repurchase shares. After the share repurchase, news will come out that will change AMC's enterprise value to either $600 million or $200 million.

   a. What is AMC's share price prior to the share repurchase?

   b. What is AMC's share price after the repurchase if its enterprise value goes up? What is AMC's share price after the repurchase if its enterprise value declines?

   c. Suppose AMC waits until after the news comes out to do the share repurchase. What is AMC's share price after the repurchase if its enterprise value goes up? What is AMC's share price after the repurchase if its enterprise value declines?

d. Suppose AMC management expects good news to come out. Based on your answers to parts (b) and (c), if management desires to maximize AMC's ultimate share price, will they undertake the repurchase before or after the news comes out? When would management undertake the repurchase if they expect bad news to come out?

e. Given your answer to part (d), what effect would you expect an announcement of a share repurchase to have on the stock price? Why?

Stock Dividends, Splits, and Spin-offs

 19. Suppose the stock of Host Hotels & Resorts is currently trading for $20 per share.

a. If Host issued a 20% stock dividend, what will its new share price be?

b. If Host does a 3 : 2 stock split, what will its new share price be?

c. If Host does a 1 : 3 reverse split, what will its new share price be?

20. Explain why most companies choose to pay stock dividends (split their stock).

21. When might it be advantageous to undertake a reverse stock split?

22. After the market close on May 11, 2001, Adaptec, Inc., distributed a dividend of shares of the stock of its software division, Roxio, Inc. Each Adaptec shareholder received 0.1646 share of Roxio stock per share of Adaptec stock owned. At the time, Adaptec stock was trading at a price of $10.55 per share (cum-dividend), and Roxio's share price was $14.23 per share. In a perfect market, what would Adaptec's ex-dividend share price be after this transaction?

Data Case

In your role as a consultant at a wealth management firm, you have been assigned a very powerful client who holds one million shares of Amazon.com purchased on February 28, 2003. In researching Amazon, you discovered that they are holding a large amount of cash, which was surprising since the firm has only relatively recently begun operating at a profit. Additionally, your client is upset that the Amazon stock price has been somewhat stagnant as of late. The client is considering approaching the Board of Directors with a plan for half of the cash the firm has accumulated, but can't decide whether a share repurchase or a special dividend would be best. You have been asked to determine which initiative would generate the greatest amount of money after taxes, assuming that with a share repurchase your client would keep the same proportion of ownership. Because both dividends and capital gains are taxed at the same rate (15%), your client has assumed that there is no difference between the repurchase and the dividend. To confirm, you need to "run the numbers" for each scenario.

1. Go to the Nasdaq homepage (www.nasdaq.com), enter the symbol for Amazon (AMZN), and click "Summary Quote."

   a. Record the current price and the number of shares outstanding.

   b. Click on company financials and then select the balance sheet. Right-click with the cursor in the middle of the balance sheet and select "Export to Microsoft Excel."

2. Using one-half of the most recent cash and cash equivalents reported on the balance sheet (in thousands of dollars), compute the following:

   a. The number of shares that would be repurchased given the current market price.

   b. The dividend per share that could be paid given the total number of shares outstanding.

3. Go to Yahoo! Finance (http://finance.yahoo.com) to obtain the price at which your client purchased the stock on February 28, 2003.

   a. Enter the symbol for Amazon and click "Get Quotes."

   b. Click "Historical Prices," enter the date your client purchased the stock as the start date and the end date, and hit enter. Record the adjusted closing price.

4. Compute the total cash that would be received by your client under the repurchase and the dividend both before taxes and after taxes.

5. The calculation in the last step reflects your client's immediate cash flow and tax liability, but it does not consider the final payoff for the client after any shares not sold in a repurchase are liquidated. To incorporate this feature, you first decide to see what happens if the client sells all remaining shares of stock immediately after the dividend or the repurchase. Assume that the stock price will fall by the amount of the dividend if a dividend is paid. What are the client's total after-tax cash flows (considering both the payout and the capital gain) under the repurchase of the dividend in this case?

6. Under which program would your client be better off before taxes? Which program is better after taxes, assuming the remaining shares are sold immediately after the dividend is paid?

7. Because your client is unlikely to sell all 1 million shares today, at the time of dividend/ repurchase, you decide to consider two longer holding periods: Assume that under both plans the client sells all remaining shares of stock 5 years later, or the client sells 10 years later. Assume that the stock will return 10% per year going forward. Also assume that Amazon will pay no other dividends over the next 10 years.

   a. What would the stock price be after 5 years or 10 years if a dividend is paid now?

   b. What would the stock price be after 5 years or 10 years if Amazon repurchases shares now?

   c. Calculate the total after-tax cash flows at both points in time (when the dividend payment or the share repurchase takes place, and when the rest of the shares are sold) for your client if the remaining shares are sold in 5 years under both initiatives. Compute the difference between the cash flows under both initiatives at each point in time. Repeat assuming the shares are sold in 10 years.

8. Repeat Question 7 assuming the stock will return 20% per year going forward. What do you notice about the difference in the cash flows under the two initiatives when the return is 20% and 10%?

9. Calculate the NPV of the difference in the cash flows under both holding period assumptions for a range of discount rates. Based on your answer to Question 8, what is the correct discount rate to use?

Valuation

Chapter 18

**Capital Budgeting
and Valuation
with Leverage**

Chapter 19

**Valuation and
Financial Modeling:
A Case Study**

The Law of One Price Connection.   In this part of the text we return to the topic of valuation and integrate our understanding of risk, return, and the firm's choice of capital structure. Chapter 18 combines the knowledge of the first five parts of the text and develops the three main methods for capital budgeting with leverage and market imperfections: The weighted average cost of capital (WACC) method, the adjusted present value (APV) method, and the flow-to-equity (FTE) method. While the Law of One Price guarantees that all three methods ultimately lead to the same assessment of value, we will identify conditions that can make one method easiest to apply. Chapter 19 applies Chapter 18's methods of valuation to value a corporation in the context of a leveraged acquisition. Chapter 19 thus serves as a capstone case that illustrates how all the concepts developed to date in the text are used to make complex real-world financial decisions.

18

Capital Budgeting and Valuation with Leverage

notation

FCF_t	free cash flows at date t
r_{wacc}	weighted average cost of capital
r_E, r_D	equity and debt costs of capital
r_D^*	equity-equivalent debt cost of capital
E	market value of equity
D	market value of debt (net of cash)
τ_c	marginal corporate tax rate
D_t	incremental debt of project on date t
V_t^L	value of a levered investment on date t
d	debt-to-value ratio
r_U	unlevered cost of capital
V^U	unlevered value of investment
T^s	value of predetermined tax shields
k	interest coverage ratio
Int_t	interest expense on date t
D^s	debt net of predetermined tax shields
ϕ	permanence of the debt level
τ_e, τ_i	tax rate on equity and interest income
τ^*	effective tax advantage of debt

In mid-2006, General Electric Company had a market capitalization of approximately $350 billion. With debt of close to $370 billion, GE's total enterprise value was $720 billion, making it the most valuable business in the world, with almost twice the value of its closest rival. GE's businesses include power generation and air transportation equipment, health care and medical equipment, consumer appliances, consumer and commercial financing and insurance, as well as entertainment through its affiliate, NBC Universal. With a debt-equity ratio exceeding 50%, leverage is clearly part of GE's business strategy. How should a firm that uses leverage, like GE, incorporate the costs and benefits associated with leverage into its capital budgeting decisions? And how should a firm adjust for the differences in risk, and debt capacity, associated with its different business activities?

We introduced capital budgeting in Chapter 7. There we outlined the following basic procedure: First we estimate the incremental free cash flow generated by the project; then we discount the free cash flow based on the project's cost of capital to determine the NPV. While that basic procedure is correct, in this chapter we discuss complexities that were absent from our earlier analysis, integrating the lessons from Parts IV and V of the text into our capital budgeting framework. In particular, we address how to estimate the appropriate cost of capital for a project and explore how the financing decision of the firm can affect both the cost of capital and the set of cash flows that we ultimately discount.

In this chapter, we introduce the three main methods for capital budgeting with leverage and market imperfections: the weighted average cost of capital (WACC) method, the adjusted present value (APV) method, and the flow-to-equity (FTE) method. While their details differ, when appropriately applied each method produces the same estimate of an investment's (or firm's) value. The choice of method is thus guided by which is the simplest to use in a given setting.

Throughout this chapter, we focus on the intuition and implementation of the main capital budgeting methods. The appendix to the chapter provides additional details about the justification for and assumptions behind some of the results we use in the chapter. It also introduces advanced computational techniques that can be used in Excel to solve for leverage and value simultaneously.

18.1 Overview

We introduce the three main methods of capital budgeting in Sections 18.2 through 18.4. To illustrate these methods and the relationships between them most clearly, we apply each method to a single example in which we have made a number of simplifying assumptions:

1. *The project has average risk.* We assume initially that the market risk of the project is equivalent to the average market risk of the firm's investments. In that case, the project's cost of capital can be assessed based on the risk of the firm.

2. *The firm's debt-equity ratio is constant.* We initially consider a firm that adjusts its leverage continuously to maintain a constant debt-equity ratio in terms of market values. This policy determines the amount of debt the firm will take on when it accepts a new project. It also implies that the risk of the firm's equity and debt, and therefore its weighted average cost of capital, will not fluctuate due to leverage changes.

3. *Corporate taxes are the only imperfection.* We assume initially that at the firm's debt-equity ratio the main effect of leverage on valuation is due to the corporate tax shield. We ignore personal taxes and issuance costs, and we assume that other imperfections (such as financial distress or agency costs) are not significant at the level of debt chosen.

While these assumptions are special, they are also a reasonable approximation for many projects and firms. The first assumption is likely to fit typical projects of firms with investments concentrated in a single industry. In that case, the market risk of both the project and the firm will primarily depend on the sensitivity of the industry to the overall economy. The second assumption, while unlikely to hold exactly, reflects the fact that firms tend to increase their levels of debt as they grow larger; some may even have an explicit target for their debt-equity ratio. Finally, for firms without very high levels of debt, the interest tax shield is likely to be the most important market imperfection affecting the capital budgeting decision. Hence, the third assumption is a reasonable starting point to begin our analysis.

Of course, while these three assumptions may be a reasonable approximation in many situations, there are certainly projects and firms for which they do not apply. The remainder of the chapter therefore relaxes these assumptions and shows how to generalize the methods to more complicated settings. In Section 18.5, we adjust these methods for projects whose risk or debt capacity is substantially different from the rest of the firm. These adjustments are especially important for multidivisional firms, such as GE. In Section 18.6, we consider alternative leverage policies for the firm (rather than maintaining a constant debt-equity ratio) and adapt the APV method to handle such cases. We consider the consequence of other market imperfections, such as issuance, distress, and agency costs, on valuation in Section 18.7. Finally, in Section 18.8, we investigate a number of advanced topics, including periodically adjusted leverage policies and the effect of investor taxes.

CONCEPT CHECK   1. Describe three simplifying assumptions that we make in valuing a project.

2. In what scenario is a project's risk likely to match the risk of the firm overall?

18.2   The Weighted Average Cost of Capital Method

A project's cost of capital depends on its risk. When the market risk of the project is similar to the average market risk of the firm's investments, then its cost of capital is equivalent to the cost of capital for a portfolio of all of the firm's securities; that is, the project's cost of capital is equal to the firm's weighted average cost of capital (WACC). As we showed in Chapter 15, the WACC incorporates the benefit of the interest tax shield by using the firm's *after-tax* cost of capital for debt:

$$r_{wacc} = \frac{E}{E+D} r_E + \frac{D}{E+D} r_D(1 - \tau_c) \tag{18.1}$$

In this formula,

E = market value of equity $\qquad$ r_E = equity cost of capital

D = market value of debt (net of cash) $\qquad$ r_D = debt cost of capital

τ_c = marginal corporate tax rate

For now, we assume that the firm maintains a constant debt-equity ratio and that the WACC calculated in Eq. 18.1 remains constant over time.[1] Because the WACC incorporates the tax savings from debt, we can compute the *levered value* of an investment, which is its value including the benefit of interest tax shields given the firm's leverage policy, by discounting its future free cash flow using the WACC. Specifically, if FCF_t is the expected free cash flow of an investment at the end of year t, then the investment's initial levered value, V_0^L, is[2]

$$V_0^L = \frac{FCF_1}{1 + r_{wacc}} + \frac{FCF_2}{(1 + r_{wacc})^2} + \frac{FCF_3}{(1 + r_{wacc})^3} + \cdots \tag{18.2}$$

The intuition for the WACC method is that the firm's weighted average cost of capital represents the average return the firm must pay to its investors (both debt and equity holders) on an after-tax basis. Thus, to be profitable, a project should generate an expected return of at least the firm's weighted average cost of capital.

Using the WACC to Value a Project

Let's apply the WACC method to value a project. Avco, Inc., is a manufacturer of custom packaging products. Avco is considering introducing a new line of packaging, the RFX series, that will include an embedded radio-frequency identification (RFID) tag, which is a miniature radio antenna and transponder that allows a package to be tracked much more efficiently and with fewer errors than standard bar codes.

---

1. In Section 18.8 we consider the case in which the WACC changes over time due to changes in leverage.

2. See Appendix Section 18A.1 for a formal justification of this result.

Avco engineers expect the technology used in these products to become obsolete after four years. During the next four years, however, the marketing group expects annual sales of $60 million per year for this product line. Manufacturing costs and operating expenses are expected to be $25 million and $9 million, respectively, per year. Developing the product will require upfront R&D and marketing expenses of $6.67 million, together with a $24 million investment in equipment. The equipment will be obsolete in four years and will be depreciated via the straight-line method over that period. Avco bills the majority of its customers in advance, and it expects no net working capital requirements for the project. Avco pays a corporate tax rate of 40%. Using this information, the spreadsheet in Table 18.1 projects the project's expected free cash flow.

TABLE 18.1 SPREADSHEET	Expected Free Cash Flow from Avco's RFX Project

Year	0	1	2	3	4
Incremental Earnings Forecast ($ million)					
1 Sales	—	60.00	60.00	60.00	60.00
2 Cost of Goods Sold	—	(25.00)	(25.00)	(25.00)	(25.00)
3 Gross Profit	—	35.00	35.00	35.00	35.00
4 Operating Expenses	(6.67)	(9.00)	(9.00)	(9.00)	(9.00)
5 Depreciation	—	(6.00)	(6.00)	(6.00)	(6.00)
6 EBIT	(6.67)	20.00	20.00	20.00	20.00
7 Income Tax at 40%	2.67	(8.00)	(8.00)	(8.00)	(8.00)
8 Unlevered Net Income	(4.00)	12.00	12.00	12.00	12.00
Free Cash Flow					
9 Plus: Depreciation	—	6.00	6.00	6.00	6.00
10 Less: Capital Expenditures	(24.00)	—	—	—	—
11 Less: Increases in NWC	—	—	—	—	—
12 Free Cash Flow	(28.00)	18.00	18.00	18.00	18.00

The market risk of the RFX project is expected to be similar to that for the company's other lines of business. Thus we can use Avco's equity and debt to determine the weighted average cost of capital for the new project. Table 18.2 shows Avco's current market value balance sheet and equity and debt costs of capital. Avco has built up $20 million in cash for investment needs, so that its *net* debt is $D = 320 - 20 = \$300$ million. Avco's enterprise value, which is the market value of its non-cash assets, is $E + D = \$600$ million. Avco intends to maintain a similar (net) debt-equity ratio for the foreseeable future, including any financing related to the RFX project.

TABLE 18.2	Avco's Current Market Value Balance Sheet ($ million) and Cost of Capital Without the RFX Project

Assets		**Liabilities**		**Cost of Capital**	
Cash	20	Debt	320	Debt	6%
Existing Assets	600	Equity	300	Equity	10%
Total Assets	620	Total Liabilities and Equity	620		

With this capital structure, Avco's weighted average cost of capital is

$$r_{wacc} = \frac{E}{E+D}r_E + \frac{D}{E+D}r_D(1-\tau_c) = \frac{300}{600}(10.0\%) + \frac{300}{600}(6.0\%)(1-0.40)$$

$$= 6.8\%$$

We can determine the value of the project, including the tax shield from debt, by calculating the present value of its future free cash flows, V_0^L, using the WACC:

$$V_0^L = \frac{18}{1.068} + \frac{18}{1.068^2} + \frac{18}{1.068^3} + \frac{18}{1.068^4} = \$61.25 \text{ million}$$

Because the upfront cost of launching the product line is only $28 million, this project is a good idea—taking the project results in an NPV of $61.25 - 28 = \$33.25$ million for the firm.

Summary of the WACC Method

To summarize, the key steps in the WACC valuation method are as follows:

1. Determine the free cash flow of the investment.
2. Compute the weighted average cost of capital using Eq. 18.1.
3. Compute the value of the investment, including the tax benefit of leverage, by discounting the free cash flow of the investment using the WACC.

In many firms, the corporate treasurer performs the second step, calculating the firm's WACC. This rate can then be used throughout the firm as the companywide cost of capital for new investments *that are of comparable risk to the rest of the firm and that will not alter the firm's debt-equity ratio.* Employing the WACC method in this way is very simple and straightforward. As a result, it is the method that is most commonly used in practice for capital budgeting purposes.

EXAMPLE 18.1

Valuing an Acquisition Using the WACC Method

Problem

Suppose Avco is considering the acquisition of another firm in its industry that specializes in custom packaging. The acquisition is expected to increase Avco's free cash flow by $3.8 million the first year, and this contribution is expected to grow at a rate of 3% per year from then on. Avco has negotiated a purchase price of $80 million. After the transaction, Avco will adjust its capital structure to maintain its current debt-equity ratio. If the acquisition has similar risk to the rest of Avco, what is the value of this deal?

Solution

The free cash flows of the acquisition can be valued as a growing perpetuity. Because its risk matches the risk for the rest of Avco, and because Avco will maintain the same debt-equity ratio going forward, we can discount these cash flows using the WACC of 6.8%. Thus the value of the acquisition is

$$V^L = \frac{3.8}{6.8\% - 3\%} = \$100 \text{ million}$$

Given the purchase price of $80 million, the acquisition has an NPV of $20 million.

Implementing a Constant Debt-Equity Ratio

Thus far we have simply assumed the firm adopted a policy of keeping its debt-equity ratio constant. In fact, an important advantage of the WACC method is that you do not need to know how this leverage policy is implemented to make the capital budgeting decision. Nevertheless, keeping the debt-equity ratio constant has implications for how the firm's total debt will change with new investment. For example, Avco currently has a debt-equity ratio of 300 / 300 = 1 or, equivalently, a debt-to-value ratio $[D/(E + D)]$ of 50%. To maintain this ratio, the firm's new investments must be financed with debt equal to 50% of their market value.

By undertaking the RFX project, Avco adds new assets to the firm with initial market value $V_0^L = \$61.25$ million. Therefore, to maintain its debt-to-value ratio, Avco must add 50% × 61.25 = \$30.625 million in new debt.[3] Avco can add this debt either by reducing cash or by borrowing and increasing debt. Suppose Avco decides to spend its \$20 million in cash and borrow an additional \$10.625 million. Because only \$28 million is required to fund the project, Avco will pay the remaining 30.625 − 28 = \$2.625 million to shareholders through a dividend (or share repurchase). Table 18.3 shows Avco's market value balance sheet with the RFX project in this case.

TABLE 18.3	**Avco's Current Market Value Balance Sheet (\$ million) with the RFX Project**		

Assets		Liabilities	
Cash	—	Debt	330.625
Existing Assets	600.00		
RFX Project	61.25	Equity	330.625
Total Assets	661.25	Total Liabilities and Equity	661.25

This financing plan maintains Avco's 50% debt-to-value ratio. The market value of Avco's equity increases by 330.625 − 300 = \$30.625 million. Adding the dividend of \$2.625 million, the shareholders' total gain is 30.625 + 2.625 = \$33.25 million, which is exactly the NPV we calculated for the RFX project.

In general, we define an investment's **debt capacity**, D_t, as the amount of debt at date t that is required to maintain the firm's target debt-to-value ratio, d. If V_t^L is the project's levered continuation value on date t—that is, the levered value of its free cash flow after date t—then

$$D_t = d \times V_t^L \tag{18.3}$$

We compute the debt capacity for the RFX project in the spreadsheet in Table 18.4. Starting with the project's free cash flow, we compute its levered continuation value at

---

3. We can also evaluate the project's debt as follows: Of the \$28 million upfront cost of the project, 50% (\$14 million) will be financed with debt. In addition, the project generates an NPV of \$33.25 million, which will increase the market value of the firm. To maintain a debt-equity ratio of 1, Avco must add debt of 50% × 33.25 = \$16.625 million at the time when the NPV of the project is anticipated (which could occur before the new investment is made). Thus the total new debt is 14 + 16.625 = \$30.625 million.

each date (line 2) by discounting the future free cash flow at the WACC as in Eq. 18.2. Because the continuation value at each date includes the value of all subsequent cash flows, it is even simpler to compute the value at each date by working backward from period 4, discounting next period's free cash flow and continuation value:

$$V_t^L = \frac{\overbrace{FCF_{t+1} + V_{t+1}^L}^{\text{Value of } FCF \text{ in year } t+2 \text{ and beyond}}}{1 + r_{wacc}} \qquad (18.4)$$

Once we have computed the project's value V_t^L at each date, we apply Eq. 18.3 to compute the project's debt capacity at each date (line 3). As the spreadsheet shows, the project's debt capacity declines each year, and falls to zero by the end of year 4.

TABLE 18.4 SPREADSHEET	**Continuation Value and Debt Capacity of the RFX Project over Time**

	Year	0	1	2	3	4
Project Debt Capacity ($ million)						
1 Free Cash Flow		(28.00)	18.00	18.00	18.00	18.00
2 Levered Value, V^L (at r_{wacc} = 6.8%)		61.25	47.41	32.63	16.85	—
3 Debt Capacity (at d = 50%)		30.62	23.71	16.32	8.43	—

Debt Capacity for an Acquisition

Problem
Suppose Avco proceeds with the acquisition described in Example 18.1. How much debt must Avco use to finance the acquisition and still maintain its debt-to-value ratio? How much of the acquisition cost must be financed with equity?

Solution
From the solution to Example 18.1, the market value of the assets acquired in the acquisition, V^L, is $100 million. Thus, to maintain a 50% debt-to-value ratio, Avco must increase its debt by $50 million. The remaining $30 million of the $80 million acquisition cost will be financed with new equity. In addition to the $30 million in new equity, the value of Avco's existing shares will increase in value by the $20 million NPV of the acquisition, so in total the market value of Avco's equity will rise by $50 million.

CONCEPT CHECK
1. Describe the key steps in the WACC valuation method.
2. What is the intuition of using the WACC method to value a project?

18.3 The Adjusted Present Value Method

The **adjusted present value (APV)**, method is an alternative valuation method in which we determine the levered value V^L of an investment by first calculating its *unlevered value* V^U, which is its value without any leverage, and then adding the value of the interest tax shield and deducting any costs that arise from other market imperfections:

Calculating the Free Cash Flow to Equity

The first step in the FTE method is to determine the project's **free cash flow to equity** (**FCFE**). The FCFE is the free cash flow that remains after adjusting for interest payments, debt issuance, and debt repayment. The spreadsheet shown in Table 18.6 calculates the FCFE for Avco's RFX project.

TABLE 18.6 SPREADSHEET	Expected Free Cash Flows to Equity from Avco's RFX Project					

	Year	0	1	2	3	4
Incremental Earnings Forecast ($ million)						
1 Sales		—	60.00	60.00	60.00	60.00
2 Cost of Goods Sold		—	(25.00)	(25.00)	(25.00)	(25.00)
3 Gross Profit		—	35.00	35.00	35.00	35.00
4 Operating Expenses		(6.67)	(9.00)	(9.00)	(9.00)	(9.00)
5 Depreciation		—	(6.00)	(6.00)	(6.00)	(6.00)
6 EBIT		(6.67)	20.00	20.00	20.00	20.00
7 Interest Expense		—	(1.84)	(1.42)	(0.98)	(0.51)
8 Pretax Income		(6.67)	18.16	18.58	19.02	19.49
9 Income Tax at 40%		2.67	(7.27)	(7.43)	(7.61)	(7.80)
10 Net Income		(4.00)	10.90	11.15	11.41	11.70
Free Cash Flow to Equity						
11 Plus: Depreciation		—	6.00	6.00	6.00	6.00
12 Less: Capital Expenditures		(24.00)	—	—	—	—
13 Less: Increases in NWC		—	—	—	—	—
14 Plus: Net Borrowing		30.62	(6.92)	(7.39)	(7.89)	(8.43)
15 Free Cash Flow to Equity		2.62	9.98	9.76	9.52	9.27

Comparing the FCFE estimates in Table 18.6 with the free cash flow estimates in Table 18.1, we notice two changes. First, we deduct interest expenses (computed in Table 18.5) on line 7, before taxes. As a consequence, we compute the incremental net income of the project on line 10, rather than its *unlevered* net income as we do when computing free cash flows. The second change appears on line 14, where we add the proceeds from the firm's net borrowing activity. These proceeds are positive when the firm issues debt; they are negative when the firm reduces its debt by repaying principal. For the RFX project, Avco issues $30.62 million in debt initially. At date 1, however, the debt capacity of the project falls to $23.71 million (see Table 18.4), so that Avco must repay $30.62 - 23.71 = \$6.91$ million of the debt.[9] In general, given the project's debt capacity D_t,

$$\text{Net Borrowing at Date } t = D_t - D_{t-1} \qquad (18.8)$$

As an alternative to Table 18.6, we can compute a project's FCFE directly from its free cash flow. Because interest payments are deducted before taxes in line 7, we adjust the firm's FCF by their after-tax cost. We then add net borrowing to determine FCFE:

Free Cash Flow to Equity

$$FCFE = FCF - \underbrace{(1 - \tau_c) \times (\text{Interest Payments})}_{\text{After-tax interest expense}} + (\text{Net Borrowing}) \qquad (18.9)$$

---

9. The $0.01 million difference in the spreadsheet is due to rounding.

We illustrate this alternative calculation for Avco's RFX project in Table 18.7. Note that the project's FCFE is lower than its FCF in years 1 through 4 due to the interest and principal payments on the debt. In year 0, however, the proceeds from the loan more than offset the negative free cash flow, so FCFE is positive (and equal to the dividend we calculated in Section 18.2).

TABLE 18.7 SPREADSHEET	Computing FCFE from FCF for Avco's RFX Project

Year	0	1	2	3	4
Free Cash Flow to Equity ($ million)					
1 Free Cash Flow	(28.00)	18.00	18.00	18.00	18.00
2 After-tax Interest Expense	—	(1.10)	(0.85)	(0.59)	(0.30)
3 Net Borrowing	30.62	(6.92)	(7.39)	(7.89)	(8.43)
4 Free Cash Flow to Equity	2.62	9.98	9.76	9.52	9.27

Valuing Equity Cash Flows

The project's free cash flow to equity shows the expected amount of additional cash the firm will have available to pay dividends (or conduct share repurchases) each year. Because these cash flows represent payments to equity holders, they should be discounted at the project's equity cost of capital. Given that the risk and leverage of the RFX project are the same as for Avco overall, we can use Avco's equity cost of capital of $r_E = 10.0\%$ to discount the project's FCFE:

$$NPV(FCFE) = 2.62 + \frac{9.98}{1.10} + \frac{9.76}{1.10^2} + \frac{9.52}{1.10^3} + \frac{9.27}{1.10^4} = \$33.25 \text{ million}$$

The value of the project's FCFE represents the gain to shareholders from the project. It is identical to the NPV we computed using the WACC and APV methods.

Why isn't the project's NPV lower now that we have deducted interest and debt payments from the cash flows? Recall that these costs of debt are offset by cash received when the debt is issued. Looking back at Table 18.6, the cash flows from debt in lines 7 and 14 have an NPV of zero assuming the debt is fairly priced.[10] In the end, the only effect on value comes from a reduction in the tax payments, leaving the same result as with the other methods.

---

10. The interest and principal payments for the RFX project are as follows:

Year	0	1	2	3	4
1 Net Borrowing	30.62	(6.92)	(7.39)	(7.89)	(8.43)
2 Interest Expense	—	(1.84)	(1.42)	(0.98)	(0.51)
3 Cash Flow from Debt	30.62	(8.76)	(8.81)	(8.87)	(8.93)

Because these cash flows have the same risk as the debt, we discount them at the debt cost of capital of 6% to compute their NPV:

$$30.62 + \frac{-8.76}{1.06} + \frac{-8.81}{1.06^2} + \frac{-8.87}{1.06^3} + \frac{-8.93}{1.06^4} = 0.$$

Summary of the Flow-to-Equity Method

The key steps in the flow-to-equity method for valuing a levered investment are as follows:

1. Determine the free cash flow to equity of the investment using Eq. 18.9.
2. Determine the equity cost of capital, r_E.
3. Compute the equity value, E, by discounting the free cash flow to equity using the equity cost of capital.

Applying the FTE method was simplified in our example because the project's risk and leverage matched the firm's, and the firm's equity cost of capital was expected to remain constant. Just as with the WACC, however, this assumption is reasonable only if the firm maintains a constant debt-equity ratio. If the debt-equity ratio changes over time, the risk of equity—and, therefore, its cost of capital—will change as well.

In this setting, the FTE approach has the same disadvantage associated with the APV approach: We need to compute the project's debt capacity to determine interest and net borrowing before we can make the capital budgeting decision. For this reason, in most settings the WACC is easier to apply. The FTE method can offer an advantage when calculating the value of equity for the entire firm, if the firm's capital structure is complex and the market values of other securities in the firm's capital structure are not known. In that case the FTE method allows us to compute the value of equity directly. In contrast, the WACC and APV methods compute the firm's enterprise value, so that a separate valuation of the other components of the firm's capital structure is needed to determine the value of equity. Finally, by emphasizing a project's implication for equity, the FTE method may be viewed as a more transparent method for discussing a project's benefit to shareholders—a managerial concern.

EXAMPLE 18.4

Using the FTE Method to Value an Acquisition

Problem

Consider again Avco's acquisition from Examples 18.1 through 18.3. The acquisition will contribute $3.8 million in free cash flows the first year, growing by 3% per year thereafter. The acquisition cost of $80 million will be financed with $50 million in new debt initially. What is the value of this acquisition using the FTE method?

Solution

Because the acquisition is being financed with $50 million in new debt, the remaining $30 million of the acquisition cost must come from equity:

$$FCFE_0 = -80 + 50 = -\$30 \text{ million}$$

In one year, the interest on the debt will be 6% × 50 = $3 million. Because Avco maintains a constant debt-equity ratio, the debt associated with the acquisition is also expected to grow at a 3% rate: 50 × 1.03 = $51.5 million. Therefore, Avco will borrow an additional 51.5 − 50 = $1.5 million in one year.

$$FCFE_1 = +3.8 - (1 - 0.40) \times 3 + 1.5 = \$3.5 \text{ million}$$

After year 1, FCFE will also grow at a 3% rate. Using the cost of equity $r_E = 10\%$, we compute the NPV:

$$NPV(FCFE) = -30 + 3.5 / (10\% - 3\%) = \$20 \text{ million}$$

This NPV matches the result we obtained with the WACC and APV methods.

What Counts as "Debt"?

Firms often have many types of debt as well as other liabilities, such as leases. Practitioners use different guidelines to determine which to include as debt when computing the WACC. Some use only long-term debt. Others use both long-term and short-term debt, plus lease obligations. Students are often confused by these different approaches and are left wondering: Which liabilities should be included as debt?

In fact, any choice will work if done correctly. We can view the WACC and FTE methods as special cases of a more general approach in which we *value the after-tax cash flows from a set of the firm's assets and liabilities by discounting them at the after-tax weighted average cost of capital of the firm's remaining assets and liabilities.* In the WACC method, the FCF does not include the interest and principal payments on debt, so debt is included in

the calculation of the weighted average cost of capital. In the FTE method, the FCFE incorporates the after-tax cash flows to and from debt holders, so debt is excluded from the weighted average cost of capital (which is simply the equity cost of capital).

Other combinations are also possible. For example, long-term debt can be included in the weighted average cost of capital, and short-term debt can be included as part of the cash flows. Similarly, other assets (such as cash) or liabilities (such as leases) can be included either in the weighted average cost of capital or as part of the cash flow. All such methods, if applied consistently, will lead to an equivalent valuation. Typically, the most convenient choice is the one for which the assumption of a constant debt-to-value ratio is a reasonable approximation.

CONCEPT CHECK   1. Describe the key steps in the flow to equity method for valuing a levered investment.

2. Does the flow to equity method produce the same assessment of the project's value as the WACC and APV methods?

18.5 Project-Based Costs of Capital

Up to this point we have assumed that both the risk and the leverage of the project under consideration matched those characteristics for the firm as a whole. This assumption allowed us, in turn, to assume that the cost of capital for a project matched the cost of capital of the firm.

In the real world, specific projects often differ from the average investment made by the firm. Consider General Electric Company, discussed in the introduction to this chapter. Projects in its health care division are likely to have different market risk than projects in air transportation equipment or at NBC Universal. Projects may also vary in the amount of leverage they will support—for example, acquisitions of real estate or capital equipment are often highly levered, whereas investments in intellectual property are not. In this section, we show how to calculate the cost of capital for the project's cash flows when a project's risk and leverage differ from those for the firm overall.

Estimating the Unlevered Cost of Capital

We begin by explaining how to calculate the unlevered cost of capital of a project with market risk that is very different from the rest of the firm. Suppose Avco launches a new plastics manufacturing division that faces different market risks than its main packaging business. What unlevered cost of capital would be appropriate for this division?

We can estimate r_U for the plastics division by looking at other single-division plastics firms that have similar business risks. For example, suppose two firms are comparable to the plastics division and have the following characteristics:

Firm	Equity Cost of Capital	Debt Cost of Capital	Debt-to-Value Ratio, $D/(E + D)$
Comparable #1	12.0%	6.0%	40%
Comparable #2	10.7%	5.5%	25%

Assuming that both firms maintain a target leverage ratio, we can estimate the unlevered cost of capital for each competitor by using the pretax WACC from Eq. 18.6:

$$\text{Competitor 1: } r_U = 0.60 \times 12.0\% + 0.40 \times 6.0\% = 9.6\%$$

$$\text{Competitor 2: } r_U = 0.75 \times 10.7\% + 0.25 \times 5.5\% = 9.4\%$$

Based on these comparable firms, we estimate an unlevered cost of capital for the plastics division of about 9.5%.[11] With this rate in hand, we can use the APV approach to calculate the value of Avco's investment in plastic manufacturing. To use either the WACC or FTE method, however, we need to estimate the project's equity cost of capital, which will depend on the incremental debt the firm will take on as a result of the project.

Project Leverage and the Equity Cost of Capital

Suppose the firm will fund the project according to a target leverage ratio. This leverage ratio may differ from the firm's overall leverage ratio, as different divisions or types of investments may have different optimal debt capacities. We can rearrange terms in Eq. 18.6 to get the following expression for the equity cost of capital:[12]

$$r_E = r_U + \frac{D}{E}(r_U - r_D) \tag{18.10}$$

Equation 18.10 shows that the project's equity cost of capital depends on its unlevered cost of capital, r_U, and the debt-equity ratio of the incremental financing that will be put in place to support the project. For example, suppose that Avco plans to maintain an equal mix of debt and equity financing as it expands into plastics manufacturing, and it expects its borrowing cost to remain at 6%. Given its 9.5% unlevered cost of capital, the plastics division's equity cost of capital is

$$r_E = 9.5\% + \frac{0.50}{0.50}(9.5\% - 6\%) = 13.0\%$$

Once we have the equity cost of capital, we can use Eq. 18.1 to determine the division's WACC:

$$r_{WACC} = 0.50 \times 13.0\% + 0.50 \times 6.0\% \times (1 - 0.40) = 8.3\%$$

Based on these estimates, Avco should use a WACC of 8.3% for the plastics division, compared to the WACC of 6.8% for the packaging division that we calculated in Section 18.2.

---

11. If we are using the CAPM to estimate expected returns, this procedure is equivalent to unlevering the betas of comparable firms using Eq. 14.9:

$$\beta_U = [E/(E + D)]\,\beta_E + [D/(D + E)]\,\beta_D.$$

12. In a CAPM setting, Eq. 18.10 is equivalent to relevering the beta according to Eq. 14.10.

In fact, we can combine Eqs. 18.1 and 18.10 to obtain a direct formula for the WACC when the firm maintains a target leverage ratio for the project. If d is the project's debt-to-value ratio, $D/(E + D)$, then[13]

Project-Based WACC Formula

$$r_{wacc} = r_U - d\tau_c r_D \tag{18.11}$$

For example, in the case of Avco's plastics division:

$$r_{wacc} = 9.5\% - 0.50 \times 0.40 \times 6\% = 8.3\%$$

EXAMPLE 18.5

Computing Divisional Costs of Capital

Problem

Hasco Corporation is a multinational provider of lumber and milling equipment. Currently, Hasco's equity cost of capital is 12.7%, and its borrowing cost is 6%. Hasco has tradition-ally maintained a 40% debt-to-value ratio. Hasco engineers have developed a GPS-based inventory control tracking system, which the company is considering developing commer-cially as a separate division. Management views the risk of this investment as similar to that of other technology companies' investments, with comparable firms typically having an unlevered cost of capital of 15%. Suppose Hasco plans to finance the new division using 10% debt financing (a constant debt-to-value ratio of 10%) with a borrowing rate of 6%, and its corporate tax rate is 35%. Estimate the unlevered, equity, and weighted average costs of capital for each division.

Solution

For the lumber and milling division, we can use the firm's current equity cost of capital r_E = 12.7% and debt-to-value ratio of 40%. Then

$$r_{wacc} = 0.60 \times 12.7\% + 0.40 \times 6\% \times (1 - 0.35) = 9.2\%$$
$$r_U = 0.60 \times 12.7\% + 0.40 \times 6\% = 10.0\%$$

For the technology division, we estimate its unlevered cost of capital using comparable firms: r_U = 15%. Because Hasco's technology division will support 10% debt financing,

$$r_E = 15\% + \frac{0.10}{0.90}(15\% - 6\%) = 16\%$$
$$r_{wacc} = 15\% - 0.10 \times 0.35 \times 6\% = 14.8\%$$

Note that the cost of capital is quite different across the two divisions.

Determining the Incremental Leverage of a Project

To determine the equity or weighted average cost of capital for a project, we need to know the amount of debt to associate with the project. For capital budgeting purposes, the proj-ect's financing is the *incremental* financing that results if the firm takes on the project.

---

13. We can derive Eq. 18.11 even more simply by comparing the WACC and pretax WACC in Eqs. 18.1 and 18.6. This formula for the WACC was proposed by R. Harris and J. Pringle, "Risk Adjusted Dis-count Rates: Transition from the Average Risk Case," *Journal of Financial Research* 8(3) (1985): 237–244.

COMMON MISTAKE   **Re-levering the WACC**

When computing the WACC using its definition in Eq. 18.1, always remember that the equity and debt costs of capital, r_E and r_D, will change for different choices of the firm's leverage ratio. For example, consider a firm with a debt-to-value ratio of 25%, a debt cost of capital of 6.67%, an equity cost of capital of 12%, and a tax rate of 40%. From Eq. 18.1, its current WACC is

$$r_{wacc} = 0.75(12\%) + 0.25(6.67\%)(1 - 0.40)$$
$$= 10\%$$

Suppose the firm increases its debt-to-value ratio to 50%. It is tempting to conclude that its WACC will fall to

$$0.50(12\%) + 0.50(6.67\%)(1 - 0.40) = 9\%$$

In fact, when the firm increases leverage, its equity and debt cost of capital will rise. To compute the new WACC correctly, we must first determine the firm's unlevered cost of capital from Eq. 18.6:

$$r_U = 0.75(12\%) + 0.25(6.67\%) = 10.67\%$$

If the firm's debt cost of capital rises to 7.34% with the increase in leverage, then from Eq. 18.10 its equity cost of capital will rise as well:

$$r_E = 10.67\% + \frac{0.50}{0.50}(10.67\% - 7.34\%) = 14\%$$

Using Eq. 18.1, with the new equity and debt cost of capital, we can correctly compute the new WACC:

$$r_{wacc} = 0.50(14\%) + 0.50(7.34\%)(1 - 0.40)$$
$$= 9.2\%$$

We can also calculate the new WACC using Eq. 18.11:

$$r_{wacc} = 10.67 - 0.50(0.40)(7.34\%) = 9.2\%$$

Note that if we fail to incorporate the effect of an increase in leverage on the firm's equity and debt costs of capital, we will overestimate the reduction in its WACC.

That is, it is the change in the firm's total debt (net of cash) with the project versus without the project.

The incremental financing of a project need not correspond to the financing that is directly tied to the project. As an example, suppose a project involves buying a new warehouse, and the purchase of the warehouse is financed with a mortgage for 90% of its value. However, if the firm has an overall policy to maintain a 40% debt-to-value ratio, it will reduce debt elsewhere in the firm once the warehouse is purchased in an effort to maintain that ratio. In that case, the appropriate debt-to-value ratio to use when evaluating the warehouse project is 40%, not 90%.

Here are some important concepts to remember when determining the project's incremental financing.

Cash Is Negative Debt.   A firm's leverage should be evaluated based on its debt net of any cash. Thus, if an investment will reduce the firm's cash holdings, it is equivalent to the firm adding leverage. Similarly, if the positive free cash flow from a project will increase the firm's cash holdings, then this growth in cash is equivalent to a reduction in the firm's leverage.

A Fixed Payout Policy Implies 100% Debt Financing.   Consider a firm whose dividend payouts and expenditures on share repurchases are set in advance and will not be affected by a project's free cash flow. In this case, the only source of financing is *debt*— any cash requirement of the project will be funded using the firm's cash or borrowing, and any cash that the project produces will be used to repay debt or increase the firm's cash. As a result, the incremental effect of the project on the firm's financing is to change the level of debt, so this project is 100% debt financed (that is, its debt-to-value ratio $d = 1$). If the firm's payout policy is fixed for the life of a project, the appropriate WACC for the project is $r_U - \tau_c r_D$. This case can be relevant for a highly levered firm that devotes its free cash flow to paying down its debt or for a firm that is hoarding cash.

Optimal Leverage Depends on Project *and* Firm Characteristics.   Projects with safer cash flows can support more debt before they increase the risk of financial distress for the firm. But, as we discussed in Part V of the text, the likelihood of financial distress that a firm can bear depends on the magnitude of the distress, agency, and asymmetric information costs that it may face. These costs are not specific to a project, but rather depend on the characteristics of the entire firm. As a consequence, the optimal leverage for a project will depend on the characteristics of both the project and the firm.

Safe Cash Flows Can Be 100% Debt Financed.   When an investment has risk-free cash flows, a firm can offset these cash flows 100% with debt and leave its overall risk unchanged. If it does so, the appropriate discount rate for safe cash flows is $r_D(1 - \tau_c)$.

EXAMPLE 18.6

Debt Financing at Cisco Systems

Problem

In mid-2005, Cisco Systems held more than $16 billion in cash and securities and no debt. Consider a project with an unlevered cost of capital of $r_U = 12\%$. Suppose Cisco's payout policy is fixed during the life of this project, so that the free cash flow from the project will affect only Cisco's cash balance. If Cisco earns 4% interest on its cash holdings and pays a 35% corporate tax rate, what cost of capital should Cisco use to evaluate the project?

Solution

Because the inflows and outflows of the project change Cisco's cash balance, the project is financed by 100% debt; that is, $d = 1$. The appropriate cost of capital for the project is

$$r_{wacc} = r_U - \tau_c r_D = 12\% - 0.35 \times 4\% = 10.6\%$$

Note that the project is effectively 100% debt financed, even though Cisco itself had no debt.

CONCEPT CHECK

1. How do we estimate a project's unlevered cost of capital when the project's risk is different from that of a firm?

2. What is the incremental debt associated with a project?

18.6 APV with Other Leverage Policies

To this point, we have assumed that the incremental debt of a project is set to maintain a constant debt-equity (or, equivalently, debt-to-value) ratio. While a constant debt-equity ratio is a convenient assumption that simplifies the analysis, not all firms adopt this leverage policy. In this section, we consider two alternative leverage policies: constant interest coverage and predetermined debt levels.

When we relax the assumption of a constant debt-equity ratio, the equity cost of capital and WACC for a project will change over time as the debt-equity ratio changes. As a result, the WACC and FTE method are difficult to implement (see Section 18.8 for further details). The APV method, however, is relatively straightforward to use and is therefore the preferred method with alternative leverage policies.

Constant Interest Coverage Ratio

As discussed in Chapter 15, if a firm is using leverage to shield income from corporate taxes, then it will adjust its debt level so that its interest expenses grow with its earnings. In this case, it is natural to specify the firm's incremental interest payments as a target fraction, k, of the project's free cash flow:[14]

$$\text{Interest Paid in Year } t = k \times FCF_t \qquad (18.12)$$

When the firm keeps its interest payments to a target fraction of its FCF, we say it has a **constant interest coverage ratio**.

To implement the APV approach, we must compute the present value of the tax shield under this policy. Because the tax shield is proportional to the project's free cash flow, it has the same risk as the project's cash flow and so should be discounted at the same rate—that is, the unlevered cost of capital, r_U. But the present value of the project's free cash flow at rate r_U is the unlevered value of the project. Thus

$$PV(\text{Interest Tax Shield}) = PV(\tau_c k \times FCF) = \tau_c k \times PV(FCF)$$

$$= \tau_c k \times V^U \qquad (18.13)$$

That is, with a constant interest coverage policy, the value of the interest tax shield is proportional to the project's unlevered value. Using the APV method, the value of the project with leverage is given by the following formula:

Levered Value with a Constant Interest Coverage Ratio

$$V^L = V^U + PV(\text{Interest Tax Shield}) = V^U + \tau_c k \times V^U$$

$$= (1 + \tau_c k)V^U \qquad (18.14)$$

For example, we calculated the unlevered value of Avco's RFX project as $V^U = \$59.62$ million in Section 18.3. If Avco targets interest to be 20% of its free cash flow, the value with leverage is $V^L = [1 + 0.4 (20\%)] 59.62 = \$64.39$ million. (This result differs from the value of $61.25 million for the project that we calculated in Section 18.3, where we assumed a different leverage policy of a 50% debt-to-value ratio.)

Equation 18.14 provides a simple rule to determine an investment's levered value based on a leverage policy that may be appropriate for many firms.[15] Note also that if the investment's free cash flows are expected to grow at a constant rate, then the assumption of constant interest coverage and a constant debt-equity ratio are equivalent, as in Example 18.7.

---

14. It might be even better to specify interest as a fraction of taxable earnings. Typically, however, taxable earnings and free cash flows are roughly proportional, so the two specifications are very similar. Also, for Eq. 18.12 to hold exactly, the firm must adjust debt continuously throughout the year. We will relax this assumption in Section 18.8 to a setting in which the firm adjusts debt periodically based on its expected level of future free cash flow (see Example 18.10).

15. J. Graham and C. Harvey report that a majority of firms target a credit rating when issuing debt ["The Theory and Practice of Corporate Finance: Evidence from the Field," *Journal of Financial Economics* 60 (2001)]. The interest coverage ratios are important determinants of credit ratings. Firms and rating agencies also consider the *book* debt-equity ratio, which often fluctuates in tandem with a firm's cash flows, rather than with its market value. (For example, book equity increases when the firm invests in physical capital to expand, which generally results in higher cash flows.)

Valuing an Acquisition with Target Interest Coverage

Problem

Consider again Avco's acquisition from Examples 18.1 and 18.2. The acquisition will contribute $3.8 million in free cash flows the first year, growing by 3% per year thereafter. The acquisition cost of $80 million will be financed with $50 million in new debt initially. Compute the value of the acquisition using the APV method assuming Avco will maintain a constant interest coverage ratio for the acquisition.

Solution

Given Avco's unlevered cost of capital of $r_U = 8\%$, the acquisition has an unlevered value of

$$V^U = 3.8 / (8\% - 3\%) = \$76 \text{ million}$$

With $50 million in new debt and a 6% interest rate, the interest expense the first year is 6% $\times$ 50 = $3 million, or $k = \text{Interest}/FCF = 3/3.8 = 78.95\%$. Because Avco will maintain this interest coverage, we can use Eq. 18.14 to compute the levered value:

$$V^L = (1 + \tau_c \, k) \, V^U = [1 + 0.4 \, (78.95\%)] \, 76 = \$100 \text{ million}$$

This value is identical to the value computed using the WACC method in Example 18.1, where we assumed a constant debt-equity ratio.

Predetermined Debt Levels

Rather than set debt according to a target debt-equity ratio or interest coverage level, a firm may adjust its debt according to a fixed schedule that is known in advance. Suppose, for example, that Avco plans to borrow $30.62 million and then will reduce the debt on a fixed schedule to $20 million after one year, to $10 million after two years, and to zero after three years. The RFX project will have no other consequences for Avco's leverage, regardless of its success. How can we value an investment like this one when its future *debt levels*, rather than the *debt-equity ratio*, are known in advance?

Because the debt levels are known, we can immediately compute the interest payments and the corresponding interest tax shield, as shown in Table 18.8.

TABLE 18.8 SPREADSHEET

Interest Payments and Interest Tax Shield Given a Fixed Debt Schedule for Avco's RFX Project

	Year	0	1	2	3	4
Interest Tax Shield ($ million)						
1 Debt Capacity, D_t		30.62	20.00	10.00	—	—
2 Interest Paid (at $r_D = 6\%$)		—	1.84	1.20	0.60	—
3 Interest Tax Shield (at $\tau_c = 40\%$)		—	0.73	0.48	0.24	—

At what rate should we discount this tax shield to determine the present value? In Section 18.3, we used the project's unlevered cost of capital because the amount of debt—and, therefore, the tax shield—fluctuated with the value of the project itself and so had similar risk. However, with a fixed debt schedule, the amount of the debt will not fluctuate. In this case, the tax shield is less risky than the project, so it should be discounted at a lower rate. Indeed, the risk of the tax shield is similar to the risk of the debt payments. We therefore advise the following general rule:[16]

When debt levels are set according to a fixed schedule, we can discount the predetermined interest tax shields using the debt cost of capital, r_D.

In Avco's case, $r_D = 6\%$:

$$PV(\text{Interest Tax Shield}) = \frac{0.73}{1.06} + \frac{0.48}{1.06^2} + \frac{0.24}{1.06^3} = \$1.32 \text{ million}$$

We then combine the value of the tax shield with the unlevered value of the project (which we already computed in Section 18.3) to determine the APV:

$$V^L = V^U + PV(\text{Interest Tax Shield}) = 59.62 + 1.32 = \$60.94 \text{ million}$$

The value of the interest tax shield computed here, $1.32 million, differs from the value of $1.63 million we computed in Section 18.3 based on constant debt-equity ratio. Comparing the firm's debt in the two cases, we see that it is paid off more rapidly in Table 18.8 than in Table 18.4. Also, because the debt-equity ratio for the project changes over time in this example, the project's WACC also changes, making it difficult—though not impossible—to apply the WACC method to this case. We show how to do so, and verify that we get the same result, as part of the advanced topics in Section 18.8.

A particularly simple example of a predetermined debt level occurs when the firm has permanent fixed debt, maintaining the same level of debt forever. We discussed this debt policy in Section 15.2 and showed that if the firm maintains a fixed level of debt, D, the value of the tax shield is $\tau_c \times D$.[17] Hence the value of the levered project in this case is

Levered Value with Permanent Debt

$$V^L = V^U + \tau_c \times D \tag{18.15}$$

A Cautionary Note. When debt levels are predetermined, the firm will not adjust its debt based on fluctuations to its cash flows or value. Therefore, we are no longer in a setting in which the firm maintains a target leverage ratio, so Eqs. 18.6, 18.10, and 18.11 do not apply. For example, if we compute the WACC using Eq. 18.11 and apply it in the case of permanent debt, the value we estimate will *not* be consistent with Eq. 18.15. To obtain the correct result, we need to use a more general version of Eq. 18.11, which we provide in Eq. 18.21 in Section 18.8.

A Comparison of Methods

We have introduced three methods for valuing levered investments: WACC, APV, and FTE. How do we decide which method to use in which circumstances?

When used consistently, each method produces the same valuation for the investment. Thus the choice of method is largely a matter of convenience. As a general rule, the WACC method is the easiest to use when the firm will maintain a fixed debt-to-value

---

16. The risk of the tax shield is not literally equivalent to that of the debt payments, because it is based on only the interest portion of the payments and is subject to the risk of fluctuations in the firm's marginal tax rate. Nevertheless, this assumption is a reasonable approximation absent much more detailed information.

17. Because the interest tax shield is $\tau_c r_D D$ in perpetuity, using the discount rate r_D we get $PV(\text{Interest Tax Shield}) = \tau_c r_D D / r_D = \tau_c D$.

ratio over the life of the investment. For alternative leverage policies, the APV method is usually the most straightforward approach. The FTE method is typically used only in complicated settings for which the values of other securities in the firm's capital structure or the interest tax shield are themselves difficult to determine.

1. What condition must the firm meet to have a constant interest coverage policy?
2. What is the appropriate discount rate for tax shields when the debt schedule is fixed in advance?

18.7 Other Effects of Financing

The WACC, APV, and FTE methods determine the value of an investment incorporating the tax shields associated with leverage. However, as we discussed in Chapter 16, some other potential imperfections are associated with leverage. In this section, we investigate ways to adjust our valuation to account for imperfections such as issuance costs, security mispricing, personal taxes, and financial distress and agency costs.

Issuance and Other Financing Costs

When a firm takes out a loan or raises capital by issuing securities, the banks that provide the loan or underwrite the sale of the securities charge fees. Table 18.9 lists the typical fees for common transactions. The fees associated with the financing of the project are a cost that should be included as part of the project's required investment, reducing the NPV of the project.

TABLE 18.9	Typical Issuance Costs for Different Securities, as a Percentage of Proceeds

Financing Type	Underwriting Fees
Bank loans	< 2%
Corporate bonds	
Investment grade	1–2%
Non-investment grade	2–3%
Equity issues	
Initial public offering	8–9%
Seasoned equity offering	5–6%

Source: Data based on typical underwriting, legal, and accounting fees for $50 million transaction. See, e.g., I. Lee, S. Lochhead, J. Ritter, and Q. Zhao, "The Cost of Raising Capital," *Journal of Financial Research* 19(1) (1996): 59–74.

For example, suppose a project has a levered value of $20 million and requires an initial investment of $15 million. To finance the project, the firm will borrow $10 million and fund the remaining $5 million by reducing dividends. If the bank providing the loan charges fees (after any tax deductions) totaling $200,000, the project NPV is

$$NPV = V^L - (\text{Investment}) - (\text{After Tax Issuance Costs}) = 20 - 15 - 0.2 = \$4.8 \text{ million}$$

Airline Loan Guarantees after September 11, 2001

On September 22, 2001, President George W. Bush signed into law the Air Transportation Safety and System Stabilization Act, which established the Air Transportation Stabilization Board (ATSB). The ATSB was authorized to distribute $5 billion in cash and issue up to $10 billion in federal loan guarantees. The purpose of the loan guarantees was to enable air carriers to obtain credit at a time when it was difficult for them to do so otherwise, so that they could make the investments necessary to maintain a safe, efficient, and viable commercial avia-

tion system in the United States in the aftermath of the September 11 tragedy. U.S. Airways received the largest loan guarantee of $900 million, and America West Airlines received the second largest, for $380 million. These loan guarantees protect creditors in the event of an airline's default, and they therefore enabled the airlines to obtain loans at a lower interest rate than they would without the guarantee. Because of the lower interest rate on the loans, the loans obtained with the help of the federal guarantee had a positive NPV for the airlines.

Security Mispricing

With perfect capital markets, all securities are fairly priced and issuing securities is a zero-NPV transaction. However, as discussed in Chapter 16, sometimes management may believe that the securities they are issuing are priced at less than (or more than) their true value. If so, the NPV of the transaction, which is the difference between the actual money raised and the true value of the securities sold, should be included in the value of the project. For example, if the financing of the project involves an equity issue, and if management believes that the equity will sell at a price that is less than its true value, this mispricing is a cost of the project for the *existing* shareholders.[18] It can be deducted from the project NPV in addition to other issuance costs.

When a firm borrows funds, a mispricing scenario arises if the interest rate charged differs from the rate that is appropriate given the actual risk of the loan. For example, a firm may pay an interest rate that is too high if news that would improve its credit rating has not yet become public. With the WACC method, the cost of the higher interest rate will result in a higher weighted average cost of capital and a lower value for the investment. With the APV method, we must add to the value of the project the NPV of the loan cash flows when evaluated at the "correct" rate that corresponds to their actual risk.[19]

EXAMPLE 18.8

Valuing a Loan

Problem

Gap, Inc., is considering borrowing $100 million to fund an expansion of its stores. Given investors' uncertainty regarding its prospects, Gap will pay a 6% interest rate on this loan. The firm's management knows, however, that the actual risk of the loan is extremely low and that the appropriate rate on the loan is 5%. Suppose the loan is for five years, with all principal being repaid in the fifth year. If Gap's marginal corporate tax rate is 40%, what is the net effect of the loan on the value of the expansion?

---

18. New shareholders, of course, benefit from receiving the shares at a low price.

19. We must also use the correct rate for r_D when levering or unlevering the cost of capital.

Solution

Shown below are the cash flows (in $ millions) and interest tax shields of a fair loan, at a 5% interest rate, and of the above-market rate loan Gap will receive, with a 6% interest rate. For each loan, we compute both the NPV of the loan cash flows and the present value of the interest tax shields, using the correct rate $r_D = 5\%$.

	Year	0	1	2	3	4	5
1	Fair Loan	100.00	(5.00)	(5.00)	(5.00)	(5.00)	(105.00)
2	Interest Tax Shield		2.00	2.00	2.00	2.00	2.00
3	At $r_D = 5\%$:						
4	NPV(Loan Cash Flows)	0.00					
5	PV(Interest Tax Shield)	8.66					
6	Actual Loan	100.00	(6.00)	(6.00)	(6.00)	(6.00)	(106.00)
7	Interest Tax Shield		2.40	2.40	2.40	2.40	2.40
8	At $r_D = 5\%$:						
9	NPV(Loan Cash Flows)	(4.33)					
10	PV(Interest Tax Shield)	10.39					

For the fair loan, note that the NPV of the loan cash flows is zero. Thus the benefit of the loan on the project's value is the present value of the interest tax shield of $8.66 million. For the actual loan, the higher interest rate increases the value of the interest tax shield but implies a negative NPV for the loan cash flows. The combined effect of the loan on the project's value is

$$NPV(\text{Loan Cash Flows}) + PV(\text{Interest Tax Shield}) = -4.33 + 10.39 = \$6.06 \text{ million}$$

While leverage is still valuable due to the tax shields, paying the higher interest rate reduces its benefit to the firm by $8.66 - 6.06 = \$2.60$ million.

Financial Distress and Agency Costs

As discussed in Chapter 16, one consequence of debt financing is the possibility of financial distress and agency costs. Because these costs affect the future free cash flows that will be generated by the project, they can be incorporated directly into the estimates of the project's expected free cash flows. When the debt level—and, therefore, the probability of financial distress—is high, the expected free cash flow will be reduced by the expected costs associated with financial distress and agency problems. Conversely, as discussed in Chapter 16, lower levels of debt may improve management's incentives and increase the firm's free cash flow.

Financial distress and agency costs also have consequences for the cost of capital. For example, financial distress is more likely to occur when economic times are bad. As a result, the costs of distress cause the value of the firm to fall further in a market downturn. Financial distress costs therefore tend to increase the sensitivity of the firm's value to market risk, raising the *unlevered* cost of capital for highly levered firms.

How do we incorporate these effects into the valuation methods described in this chapter? First, we must adjust the free cash flow estimates to include expected distress and agency costs. Second, because these costs also affect the systematic risk of the cash flows, the unlevered cost of capital, r_U, will no longer be independent of the firm's leverage.[20] Let's consider an example.

---

20. Indeed, calling r_U the *unlevered* cost of capital is, in this case, somewhat of a misnomer. It is the appropriate discount rate for the free cash flows ignoring any tax benefits of leverage, but including financial distress and agency consequences of leverage.

Valuing Distress Costs

Problem

Your firm currently has no leverage, and it expects to generate free cash flows of $10 million per year in perpetuity. The firm's current (unlevered) cost of capital is 10%, and its marginal corporate tax rate is 35%. You would like to determine whether adding leverage would increase the firm's value. Simulating the firm's future cash flows, you have estimated the likelihood and cost of financial distress with different levels of permanent debt and have produced the following estimates:

Debt Level, D	0	20	40	60	80
$E(FCF)$	10.0	9.9	9.8	9.5	9.0
r_U	10.0%	10.5%	11.0%	11.8%	13.0%

Based on this information, which level of permanent debt is optimal for the firm?

Solution

Because the debt level is known, the simplest course of action is to apply the APV method. The unlevered value of the firm can be computed as a perpetuity, $V^U = E(FCF) / r_U$. With permanent debt, the value of the tax shield is $\tau_c D$. Adding these together yields the estimate of the firm's levered value:

Debt Level, D	0	20	40	60	80
$V^U - E(FCF) / r_U$	100.0	94.3	89.1	80.5	69.2
$PV(ITS) = \tau_c D$	0.0	7.0	14.0	21.0	28.0
$V^L = V^U + \tau_c D$	100.0	101.3	103.1	101.5	97.2

Of the debt levels shown here, the value of the firm is maximized with $D = \$40$ million. This debt level provides the best tradeoff of tax benefits versus financial distress and agency costs.

An alternative method of incorporating financial distress and agency costs is to first value the project ignoring these costs, and then value the incremental cash flows associated with financial distress and agency problems separately. Because these costs tend to occur only when a firm is in (or near) default, valuing them is best done using the option valuation techniques introduced in Part VII of the text.

CONCEPT CHECK

1. How do we deal with issuance costs and security mispricing costs in our assessment of a project's value?

2. How would financial distress and agency costs affect a firm's use of leverage?

18.8 Advanced Topics in Capital Budgeting

In the previous sections, we have highlighted the most important methods for capital budgeting with leverage and demonstrated their application in common settings. In this section, we consider several more complicated scenarios and show how our tools can be extended to these cases. First, we consider leverage policies in which firms keep debt fixed in the short run, but adjust to a target leverage ratio in the long run. Second, we look at the relationship between a firm's equity and unlevered cost of capital for alternative leverage policies. Third, we implement the WACC and FTE methods when the firm's debt-equity ratio changes over time. We then conclude the section by incorporating the effects of personal taxes.

Periodically Adjusted Debt

To this point, we have considered leverage policies in which debt is either adjusted continuously to a target leverage ratio[21] or set according to a fixed plan that will never change. As Figure 18.1 shows, most real-world firms do not, in fact, appear to adjust debt levels continuously to maintain a target leverage ratio at all times. (See also Figure 15.6 in Chapter 15 for the behavior of aggregate leverage ratios over time.) Instead, most firms allow the debt-equity ratio of the firm to stray from the target and periodically adjust leverage to bring it back into line with the target. We next consider the effect of such a debt policy.

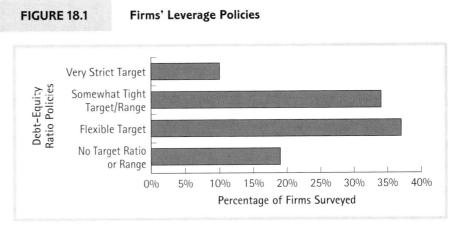

FIGURE 18.1   **Firms' Leverage Policies**

Of 392 CFOs surveyed by Professors J. Graham and C. Harvey, 81% reported having a target debt-equity ratio. However, only 10% of respondents viewed the target as set in stone. Most were willing to let the debt-equity ratio of the firm stray from the target and periodically adjust leverage to bring it back into line.

Source: J. R. Graham and C. Harvey, "The Theory and Practice of Corporate Finance: Evidence from the Field," *Journal of Financial Economics* 60 (2001): 187–243.

Suppose the firm adjusts its leverage every s periods, as shown in Figure 18.2. Then the firm's interest tax shields up to date s are predetermined, so they should be discounted at rate r_D. In contrast, interest tax shields that occur after date s depend on future adjustments the firm will make to its debt, so they are risky. If the firm will adjust the debt according to a target debt-equity ratio or interest coverage level, then the future interest tax shields should be discounted at rate r_D for the periods that they are known, but at rate r_U for all earlier periods when they are still risky.

---

21. While we have simplified our exposition earlier in the chapter by calculating debt and interest payments on an annual basis, the formulas we have used in the case of a constant debt-equity or interest coverage ratio are based on the assumption that debt changes during the year.

FIGURE 18.2   **Discounting the Tax Shield with Periodic Adjustments**

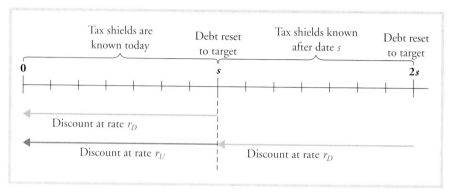

If the debt is reset to a target leverage ratio every *s* periods, then interest tax shields within the first *s* periods are known and should be discounted at rate r_D. Interest tax shields that occur after date *s* are not yet known, so they should be discounted at rate r_D for the periods when they will be known and at rate r_U for earlier periods.

An important special case is when the debt is adjusted annually. In that case, the expected interest expense on date *t*, Int_t, is known as of date $t-1$. Therefore, we discount the interest tax shield at rate r_D for one period, from date *t* to $t-1$ (because it will be known at that time), and then discount it from date $t-1$ to 0 at rate r_U:

$$PV(\tau_c \times Int_t) = \frac{\tau_c \times Int_t}{(1+r_U)^{t-1}(1+r_D)} = \frac{\tau_c \times Int_t}{(1+r_U)^t} \times \left(\frac{1+r_U}{1+r_D}\right) \quad (18.16)$$

Equation 18.16 implies that we can value the tax shield by discounting it at rate r_U as before, and then multiply the result by the factor $(1+r_U)/(1+r_D)$ to account for the fact that the tax shield is known one year in advance.

This same adjustment can be applied to other valuation methods as well. For example, when the debt is adjusted annually rather than continuously to a target debt-to-value ratio *d*, the project-based WACC formula of Eq. 18.11 becomes,[22]

$$r_{WACC} = r_U - d\tau_c r_D \frac{1+r_U}{1+r_D} \quad (18.17)$$

Similarly, when the firm sets debt annually based on its expected future free cash flow, the constant interest coverage model in Eq. 18.14 becomes

$$V^L = \left(1 + \tau_c k \frac{1+r_U}{1+r_D}\right) V^U \quad (18.18)$$

Example 18.10 illustrates these methods in a constant growth setting.

---

22. This formula for the WACC was proposed by J. A. Miles and J. R. Ezzell, "The Weighted Average Cost of Capital, Perfect Capital Markets and Project Life: A Clarification," *Journal of Financial and Quantitative Analysis* 15(3) (1980): 719–730.

EXAMPLE
18.10

Annual Debt Ratio Targeting

Problem

Celmax Corporation expects free cash flows this year of $7.36 million and a future growth rate of 4% per year. The firm currently has $30 million in debt outstanding. This leverage will remain fixed during the year, but at the end of each year Celmax will increase or decrease its debt to maintain a constant debt-equity ratio. Celmax pays 5% interest on its debt, pays a corporate tax rate of 40%, and has an unlevered cost of capital of 12%. Estimate Celmax's value with this leverage policy.

Solution

Using the APV approach, the unlevered value is $V^U = 7.36 / (12\% - 4\%) = \$92.0$ million. In the first year, Celmax will have an interest tax shield of $\tau_c\, r_D\, D = 0.40 \times 5\% \times \$30$ million $= \$0.6$ million. Because Celmax will adjust its debt after one year, the tax shields are expected to grow by 4% per year with the firm. The present value of the interest tax shield is therefore

$$PV(\text{Interest Tax Shield}) = \underbrace{\frac{0.6}{(12\% - 4\%)}}_{\substack{PV \text{ at rate } r_U}} \times \underbrace{\left(\frac{1.12}{1.05}\right)}_{\substack{\text{Debt is set 1 year} \\ \text{in advance}}} = \$8.0 \text{ million}$$

Therefore, $V^L = V^U + PV(\text{Interest Tax Shield}) = 92.0 + 8.0 = \$100.0$ million.

We can also apply the WACC method. From Eq. 18.17, Celmax's WACC is

$$r_{WACC} = r_U - d\tau_c r_D \frac{1 + r_U}{1 + r_D} = 12\% - \frac{30}{100}(0.40)(5\%)\frac{1.12}{1.05}$$

$$= 11.36\%$$

Therefore, $V^L = 7.36 / (11.36\% - 4\%) = \$100$ million.

Finally, the constant interest coverage model can be applied (in this setting with constant growth, a constant debt-equity ratio implies a constant interest coverage ratio). Given interest of 5% × $30 million = $1.50 million this year, from Eq. 18.18

$$V^L = \left(1 + \tau_c k \frac{1 + r_U}{1 + r_D}\right) V^U$$

$$= \left(1 + 0.40 \times \frac{1.50}{7.36} \times \frac{1.12}{1.05}\right) 92.0 = \$100 \text{ million}$$

Leverage and the Cost of Capital

The relationship between leverage and the project's costs of capital in Eqs. 18.6, 18.10, and 18.11 relies on the assumption that the firm maintains a target leverage ratio. That relationship holds because in that case the interest tax shields have the same risk as the firm's cash flows. But when debt is set according to a fixed schedule for some period of time, the interest tax shields for the scheduled debt are known, relatively safe cash flows. These safe cash flows will reduce the effect of leverage on the risk of the firm's equity. To account for this effect, we should deduct the value of these "safe" tax shields from the debt—in the same way that we deduct cash—when evaluating a firm's leverage. That is, if T^s is the present value of the interest tax shields from predetermined debt, the risk of a firm's equity will depend on its *debt net of the predetermined tax shields:*

$$D^s = D - T^s \qquad (18.19)$$

We show in Appendix Section 18A.2 that Eqs. 18.6 and 18.10 continue to apply with D replaced by D^s, so that the more general relationship between the unlevered and equity costs of capital are related as follows:

Leverage and the Cost of Capital with a Fixed Debt Schedule

$$r_U = \frac{E}{E + D^s} r_E + \frac{D^s}{E + D^s} r_D \text{ or, equivalently, } r_E = r_U + \frac{D^s}{E}(r_U - r_D) \qquad (18.20)$$

We can also combine Eq. 18.20 with the definition of the WACC in Eq. 18.1 and generalize the project-based WACC formula in Eq. 18.11:

Project WACC with a Fixed Debt Schedule

$$r_{wacc} = r_U - d\tau_c[r_D + \phi(r_U - r_D)] \qquad (18.21)$$

where $d = D/(D + E)$ is the debt-to-value ratio, and $\phi = T^s/(\tau_c D)$ is a measure of the permanence of the debt level, D. Here are three cases commonly used in practice, which differ according to the frequency with which the debt is assumed to adjust to the growth of the investment:[23]

1. Continuously adjusted debt: $T^s = 0$, $D^s = D$, and $\phi = 0$

2. Annually adjusted debt: $T^s = \dfrac{\tau_c r_D D}{1 + r_D}$, $D^s = D\left(1 - \tau_c \dfrac{r_D}{1 + r_D}\right)$, and $\phi = \dfrac{r_D}{1 + r_D}$

3. Permanent debt: $T^s = \tau_c D$, $D^s = D(1 - \tau_c)$, and $\phi = 1$

Finally, note that unless d and ϕ remain constant over time, the WACC and equity cost of capital must be computed period by period.

EXAMPLE 18.11

APV and WACC with Permanent Debt

Problem
International Paper Company is considering the acquisition of additional forestland in the southeastern United States. The wood harvested from the land will generate free cash flows of $4.5 million per year, with an unlevered cost of capital of 7%. As a result of this acquisition, International Paper will permanently increase its debt by $30 million. If International Paper's tax rate is 35%, what is the value of this acquisition using the APV method? Verify this result using the WACC method.

---

23. Case 1 reduces to the Harris-Pringle formula (see footnote 13), case 2 is the Miles-Ezzell formula (see footnote 22), and case 3 is equivalent to the Modigliani-Miller-Hamada formula with permanent debt. See F. Modigliani and M. Miller, "Corporate Income Taxes and the Cost of Capital: A Correction," *American Economic Review* 53(3) (1963): 433–443; and R. Hamada, "The Effect of a Firm's Capital Structure on the Systematic Risks of Common Stocks," *Journal of Finance* 27(2) (1972): 435–452.

Solution

Using the APV method, the unlevered value of the land is $V^U = FCF/r_U = 4.5/0.07 = 64.29 million. Because the debt is permanent, the value of the tax shield is $\tau_c D = 0.35(30) = 10.50$. Therefore, $V^L = 64.29 + 10.50 = 74.79 million.

To use the WACC method, we apply Eq. 18.21 with $\phi = T^s/(\tau_c D) = 1$ and $d = 30/74.79 = 40.1\%$. Therefore, the WACC for the investment is

$$r_{wacc} = r_U - d\tau_c r_U = 7\% - 0.401 \times 0.35 \times 7\% = 6.017\%$$

and $V^L = 4.5/0.06017 = 74.79 million.

The WACC or FTE Method with Changing Leverage

When a firm does not maintain a constant debt-equity ratio for a project, the APV method is generally the most straightforward method to apply. The WACC and FTE methods become more difficult to use because when the proportion of debt financing changes, the project's equity cost of capital and WACC will not remain constant over time. With a bit of care, however, these methods can still be used (and, of course, will lead to the same result as the APV method).

As an example, the spreadsheet in Table 18.10 computes the equity cost of capital and WACC for the RFX project each year given the fixed debt schedule shown in line 3. The value of the project with leverage using the APV method is computed in line 7 as the total of the unlevered value and the value of the tax shield. With the project's equity value and net debt D^s in hand, we can use Eq. 18.20 to calculate the project's equity cost of capital each year (line 11). Note that the equity cost of capital declines over time as the project's leverage ratio D^s/E declines. By year 3, the debt is fully repaid and the equity cost of capital equals the unlevered cost of capital of 8%.

TABLE 18.10 SPREADSHEET **Adjusted Present Value and Cost of Capital for Avco's RFX Project with a Fixed Debt Schedule**

	Year	0	1	2	3	4
Unlevered Value ($ million)						
1 Free Cash Flow		(28.00)	18.00	18.00	18.00	18.00
2 Unlevered Value, V^U (at $r_u = 8.0\%$)		59.62	46.39	32.10	16.67	—
Interest Tax Shield						
3 Debt Schedule, D_t		30.62	20.00	10.00	—	—
4 Interest Paid (at $r_d = 6\%$)		—	1.84	1.20	0.60	—
5 Interest Tax Shield (at $\tau_c = 40\%$)		—	0.73	0.48	0.24	—
6 Tax Shield Value, T^s (at $r_D = 6.0\%$)		1.32	0.67	0.23	—	—
Adjusted Present Value						
7 Levered Value, $V^L = V^U + T^s$		60.94	47.05	32.33	16.67	—
Effective Leverage and Cost of Capital						
8 Equity, $E = V^L - D$		30.32	27.05	22.33	16.67	—
9 Effective Debt, $D^s = D - T^s$		29.30	19.33	9.77	—	—
10 Effective Debt-Equity Ratio, D^s/E		0.966	0.715	0.438	0.000	
11 Equity Cost of Capital, r_E		9.93%	9.43%	8.88%	8.00%	
12 WACC, r_{wacc}		6.75%	6.95%	7.24%	8.00%	

Given the project's equity cost of capital, we compute its WACC using Eq. 18.1 in line 12. For example, at the beginning of the project,

$$r_{wacc} = \frac{E}{E+D}r_E + \frac{D}{E+D}r_D(1 - \tau_c)$$

$$= \frac{30.32}{60.94}9.93\% + \frac{30.62}{60.94}6\%(1 - 0.40) = 6.75\%$$

Note that as the leverage of the project falls, its WACC rises, until it eventually equals the unlevered cost of capital of 8% when the project debt is fully repaid at year 3.

Once we have computed the WACC or the equity cost of capital, we can value the project using the WACC or FTE method. Because the cost of capital changes over time, we must use a different discount rate each year when applying these methods. For example, using the WACC method, the levered value each year is computed as

$$V_t^L = \frac{FCF_{t+1} + V_{t+1}^L}{1 + r_{wacc}(t)} \qquad (18.22)$$

where $r_{wacc}(t)$ is the project's WACC in year t. This calculation is shown in Table 18.11. Note that the levered value matches the result from the APV method (line 7 in Table 18.10). The same approach can be used when applying the FTE method.[24]

TABLE 18.11 SPREADSHEET	WACC Method for Avco's RFX Project with a Fixed Debt Schedule					

	Year	0	1	2	3	4
WACC Method ($ millions)						
1 Free Cash Flow		(28.00)	18.00	18.00	18.00	18.00
2 WACC, r_{wacc}		6.75%	6.95%	7.24%	8.00%	
3 Levered Value V^L (at r_{wacc})		60.94	47.05	32.33	16.67	—

Personal Taxes

As we discussed in Chapter 15, leverage has tax consequences for both investors and for corporations. For individuals, interest income from debt is generally taxed more heavily than income from equity (capital gains and dividends). So how do personal taxes affect our valuation methods?

If investors are taxed on the income they receive from holding equity or debt, it will raise the return they require to hold those securities. That is, the equity and debt cost of capital in the market *already* reflects the effects of investor taxes. As a result, *the WACC method does not change in the presence of investor taxes*; we can continue to compute the WACC according to Eq. 18.1 and compute the levered value as in Section 18.2.

---

24. You will notice, however, that we used the APV to compute the debt-equity ratio each period, which we needed to calculate r_E and r_{wacc}. If we had not already solved for the APV, we would need to determine the project's value and WACC simultaneously, using the approach described in Appendix Section 18A.3.

The APV approach, however, requires modification in the presence of investor taxes because it requires that we compute the unlevered cost of capital. This computation *is* affected by the presence of investor taxes. Let τ_e be the tax rate investors pay on equity income (dividends) and τ_i be the tax rate investors pay on interest income. Then, given an expected return on debt r_D, define r_D^* as the expected return on equity income that would give investors the same after-tax return:

$$r_D^* \, (1 - \tau_e) = r_D \, (1 - \tau_i)$$

So

$$r_D^* \equiv r_D \, \frac{(1 - \tau_i)}{(1 - \tau_e)} \tag{18.23}$$

Because the unlevered cost of capital is for a hypothetical firm that is all equity, investors' tax rates on income for such a firm are the equity rates, so we must use the rate r_D^* when computing the unlevered cost of capital. Therefore, Eq. 18.20 becomes

Unlevered Cost of Capital with Personal Taxes

$$r_U = \frac{E}{E + D^s} r_E + \frac{D^s}{E + D^s} r_D^* \tag{18.24}$$

Next, we must compute the interest tax shield using the effective tax advantage of debt, τ^*, in place of τ_c. The effective tax rate τ^* incorporates the investors' tax rate on equity income, τ_e, and on interest income, τ_i, and was defined in Chapter 15 as follows:

$$\tau^* = 1 - \frac{(1 - \tau_c)(1 - \tau_e)}{(1 - \tau_i)} \tag{18.25}$$

We then calculate the interest tax shield using tax rate τ^* and interest rate r_D^*:

$$\text{Interest Tax Shield in Year } t = \tau^* \times r_D^* \times D_{t-1} \tag{18.26}$$

Finally we discount the interest tax shields at rate r_U if the firm maintains a target leverage ratio or at rate r_D^* if the debt is set according to a predetermined schedule.[25]

EXAMPLE 18.12

Using the APV Method with Personal Taxes

Problem

Apex Corporation has an equity cost of capital of 14.4% and a debt cost of capital of 6%, and the firm maintains a debt-equity ratio of 1. Apex is considering an expansion that will contribute $4 million in free cash flows the first year, growing by 4% per year thereafter. The expansion will cost $60 million and will be financed with $40 million in new debt initially with a constant debt-equity ratio maintained thereafter. Apex's corporate tax rate is 40%; the tax rate on interest income is 40%; and the tax rate on equity income is 20%. Compute the value of the expansion using the APV method.

---

25. If the debt is permanent, for example, the value of the tax shield is $\tau^* r_D^* D / r_D^* = \tau^* D$, as shown in Chapter 15.

Solution

First, we compute the value without leverage. From Eq. 18.23, the debt cost of capital of 6% is equivalent to an equity rate of

$$r_D^* = r_D \frac{1 - \tau_i}{1 - \tau_e} = 6\% \times \frac{1 - 0.40}{1 - 0.20} = 4.5\%$$

Because Apex maintains a constant debt-equity ratio, $D^s = D$ and Apex's unlevered cost of capital is, using Eqs. 18.23 and 18.24,

$$r_U = \frac{E}{E + D^s} r_E + \frac{D^s}{E + D^s} r_D^* = 0.50 \times 14.4\% + 0.50 \times 4.5\% = 9.45\%$$

Therefore, $V^U = 4 / (9.45\% - 4\%) = \$73.39$ million.

From Eq. 18.25, the effective tax advantage of debt is

$$\tau^* = 1 - \frac{(1 - \tau_c)(1 - \tau_e)}{(1 - \tau_i)} = 1 - \frac{(1 - 0.40)(1 - 0.20)}{(1 - 0.40)} = 20\%$$

Apex will add new debt of $40 million initially, so from Eq. 18.26 the interest tax shield is $20\% \times 4.5\% \times 40 = \$0.36$ million the first year (note that we use r_D^* here). With a growth rate of 4%, the present value of the interest tax shield is

$$PV(\text{Interest Tax Shield}) = 0.36 / (9.45\% - 4\%) = \$6.61 \text{ million}$$

Therefore the value of the expansion with leverage is given by the APV:

$$V^L = V^U + PV(\text{Interest Tax Shield}) = 73.39 + 6.61 = \$80 \text{ million}$$

Given the cost of $60 million, the expansion has an NPV of $20 million.

Let's check this result using the WACC method. Note that the expansion has the same debt-to-value ratio of $40/80 = 50\%$ as the firm overall. Thus its WACC is equal to the firm's WACC:

$$r_{wacc} = \frac{E}{E + D} r_E + \frac{D}{E + D} r_D (1 - \tau_c)$$

$$= 0.50 \times 14.4\% + 0.50 \times 6\% \times (1 - 0.40) = 9\%$$

Therefore, $V^L = 4 / (9\% - 4\%) = \$80$ million, as before.

As the Example 18.12 illustrates, the WACC method is much simpler to apply than the APV method in the case with investor taxes. More significantly, the WACC approach does not require knowledge of investors' tax rates. This fact is important because in practice, estimating the marginal tax rate of the investor can be very difficult.

If the investment's leverage or risk does not match the firm's, then investor tax rates are required even with the WACC method to calculate r_U and re-lever the WACC as in Section 18.5. When the investor's tax rate on interest income exceeds that on equity income, an increase in leverage will lead to a smaller reduction in the WACC (see Problem 25).

CONCEPT CHECK

1. When a firm has pre-determined tax shields, how do we measure its net debt when calculating its unlevered cost of capital?

2. If the firm's debt-equity ratio changes over time, can the WACC method still be applied?

Summary

1. The key steps in the WACC valuation method are as follows:
   a. Determine the unlevered free cash flows of the investment.
   b. Compute the weighted average cost of capital:

$$r_{wacc} = \frac{E}{E+D}r_E + \frac{D}{E+D}r_D(1-\tau_c) \qquad (18.1)$$

   c. Compute the value with leverage, V^L, by discounting the free cash flows of the investment using the WACC.

2. To determine the value of a levered investment using the APV method, proceed as follows:
   a. Determine the investment's value without leverage, V^U, by discounting its free cash flows at the unlevered cost of capital, r_U.
   b. Determine the present value of the interest tax shield.
      i. Given debt D_t on date t, the tax shield on date $t+1$ is $\tau_c r_D D_t$.
      ii. If the debt level varies with the investment's value or free cash flow, use discount rate r_U. If the debt is predetermined, discount the tax shield at rate r_D.
   c. Add the unlevered value V^U to the present value of the interest tax shield to determine the value of the investment with leverage, V^L.

3. The key steps in the flow-to-equity method for valuing a levered investment are as follows:
   a. Determine the free cash flow to equity of the investment:

$$FCFE = FCF - (1-\tau_c) \times (\text{Interest Payments}) + (\text{Net Borrowing}) \qquad (18.9)$$

   b. Compute the equity value, E, by discounting the free cash flow to equity using the equity cost of capital.

4. The unlevered and equity costs of capital are related as follows:

$$r_U = \frac{E}{E+D^s}r_E + \frac{D^s}{E+D^s}r_D \text{ or, equivalently, } r_E = r_U + \frac{D^s}{E}(r_U - r_D)$$

   where
   a. $D^s = D$, the firm's net debt, if the firm maintains a target leverage ratio (see Eqs. 18.6 and 18.10).
   b. If some of the firm's debt is predetermined, then $D^s = D - T^s$, where T^s is the value of predetermined interest tax shields (see Eq. 18.20).

5. If a project's risk is different from that of the firm as a whole, we must estimate its cost of capital separately from the firm's cost of capital. We estimate the project's unlevered cost of capital by looking at the unlevered cost of capital for other firms with similar market risk as the project.

6. If $d = D/(D+E)$ is the debt-to-value ratio of the project,
   a. Its WACC is equal to $r_{wacc} = r_U - d\tau_c r_D$, if the firm maintains a target leverage ratio (see Eq. 18.11).
   b. If some of the tax shields are predetermined, then

$$r_{wacc} = r_U - d\tau_c[r_D + \phi(r_U - r_D)] \qquad (18.21)$$

   where $\phi = T^s/(\tau_c D)$ reflects the permanence of the debt level.

7. When assessing the leverage associated with a project, we must consider its incremental impact on the debt, net of cash balances, of the firm overall and not just the specific financing used for that investment.

8. A firm has a constant interest coverage policy if it sets debt to maintain its interest expenses as a fraction, k, of free cash flow. The levered value of a project with such a leverage policy is $V^L = (1 + \tau_c k) V^U$.

9. If a firm chooses to keep the level of debt at a constant level, D, permanently, then the levered value of a project with such a leverage policy is $V^L = V^U + \tau_c \times D$.

10. In general, the WACC method is the easiest to use when a firm has a target debt-equity ratio that it plans to maintain over the life of the investment. For other leverage policies, the APV method is usually the most straightforward method.

11. Issuance costs and any costs or gains from mispricing of issued securities should be included in the assessment of a project's value.

12. If a firm adjusts its debt annually to a target leverage ratio, the value of the interest tax shield is enhanced by the factor $(1 + r_U) / (1 + r_D)$.

13. Financial distress costs are likely to (1) lower the expected free cash flow of a project and (2) raise its unlevered cost of capital. Taking these effects into account, together with other agency and asymmetric information costs, may limit a firm's use of leverage.

14. The WACC method does not need to be modified to account for investor taxes. For the APV method, we use the interest rate

$$r_D^* \equiv r_D \frac{(1 - \tau_i)}{(1 - \tau_e)} \qquad (18.23)$$

in place of r_D and we replace τ_c with the effective tax rate:

$$\tau^* = 1 - \frac{(1 - \tau_c)(1 - \tau_e)}{(1 - \tau_i)} \qquad (18.25)$$

Key Terms

adjusted present value (APV) *p. 581*

constant interest coverage ratio *p. 594*

debt capacity *p. 580*

flow to equity (FTE) *p. 585*

free cash flow to equity (FCFE) *p. 586*

target leverage ratio *p. 582*

unlevered cost of capital *p. 582*

Further Reading

For a further treatment of the valuation with leverage, see: T. Copeland, T. Koller, and J. Murrin, *Valuation: Measuring and Managing the Value of Companies*, 3rd ed. (New York: McGraw-Hill, 2000); and S. P. Pratt, R. F. Reilly, and R. P. Schweihs, *Valuing a Business: The Analysis and Appraisal of Closely Held Companies*, 4th ed. (New York: McGraw-Hill, 2000).

For a more detailed treatment of the issues discussed in this chapter, the interested reader will find these articles useful: E. R. Arzac and L. R. Glosten, "A Reconsideration of Tax Shield Valuation," *European Financial Management* 11(4) (2005): 453–461; R. S. Harris and J. J. Pringle, "Risk-Adjusted Discount Rates—Extensions from the Average-Risk Case," *Journal of Financial Research* 8(3) (1985): 237–244; I. Inselbag and H. Kaufold, "Two DCF Approaches in Valuing Companies Under Alternative Financing Strategies (and How to Choose Between Them)," *Journal of Applied Corporate Finance* 10(1) (1997): 114–122;

T. A. Luehrman, "Using APV: A Better Tool for Valuing Operations," *Harvard Business Review* 75 (May–June 1997): 145–154; J. A. Miles and J. R. Ezzell, "The Weighted Average Cost of Capital, Perfect Capital Markets, and Project Life: A Clarification," *Journal of Financial and Quantitative Analysis* 15(3) (1980): 719–730; J. A. Miles and J. R. Ezzell, "Reformulation Tax Shield Valuation: A Note," *Journal of Finance* 40(5) (1985): 1485–1492; R. Ruback, "Capital Cash Flows: A Simple Approach to Valuing Risky Cash Flows," *Financial Management* 31(2) (2002): 85–104; and R. A. Taggart, "Consistent Valuation and Cost of Capital Expressions with Corporate and Personal Taxes," *Financial Management* 20(3) (1991): 8–20.

Problems

All problems in this chapter are available in MyFinanceLab. An asterisk (*) indicates problems with a higher level of difficulty.

Overview

1. Explain whether each of the following projects is likely to have risk similar to the average risk of the firm.

    a. The Clorox Company considers launching a new version of Armor All designed to clean and protect notebook computers.

    b. Google, Inc., plans to purchase real estate to expand its headquarters.

    c. Target Corporation decides to expand the number of stores it has in the southeastern United States.

    d. GE decides to open a new Universal Studios theme park in China.

2. Suppose Caterpillar, Inc., has 665 million shares outstanding with a share price of $74.77, and $25 billion in debt. If in three years, Caterpillar has 700 million shares outstanding trading for $83 per share, how much debt will Caterpillar have if it maintains a constant debt-equity ratio?

3. In 2006, Intel Corporation had a market capitalization of $112 billion, debt of $2.2 billion, cash of $9.1 billion, and EBIT of more than $11 billion. If Intel were to increase its debt by $1 billion and use the cash for a share repurchase, which market imperfections would be most relevant for understanding the consequence for Intel's value? Why?

The Weighted Average Cost of Capital Method

4. Suppose Goodyear Tire and Rubber Company is considering divesting one of its manufacturing plants. The plant is expected to generate free cash flows of $1.5 million per year, growing at a rate of 2.5% per year. Goodyear has an equity cost of capital of 8.5%, a debt cost of capital of 7%, a marginal corporate tax rate of 35%, and a debt-equity ratio of 2.6. If the plant has average risk and Goodyear plans to maintain a constant debt-equity ratio, what after-tax amount must it receive for the plant for the divestiture to be profitable?

5. Suppose Lucent Technologies has an equity cost of capital of 10%, market capitalization of $10.8 billion, and an enterprise value of $14.4 billion. Suppose Lucent's debt cost of capital is 6.1% and its marginal tax rate is 35%.

    a. What is Lucent's WACC?

    b. If Lucent maintains a constant debt-equity ratio, what is the value of a project with average risk and the following expected free cash flows?

Year	0	1	2	3
FCF	−100	50	100	70

    c. If Lucent maintains its debt-equity ratio, what is the debt capacity of the project in part (b)?

6. Acort Industries has 10 million shares outstanding and a current share price of $40 per share. It also has long-term debt outstanding. This debt is risk free, is four years away from maturity, has an annual coupon rate of 10%, and has a $100 million face value. The first of the remaining coupon payments will be due in exactly one year. The riskless interest rates for all maturities are constant at 6%. Acort has EBIT of $106 million, which is expected to remain constant each year. New capital expenditures are expected to equal depreciation and equal $13 million per year, while no changes to net working capital are expected in the future. The corporate tax rate is 40%, and Acort is expected to keep its debt-equity ratio constant in the future (by either issuing additional new debt or buying back some debt as time goes on).

   a. Based on this information, estimate Acort's WACC.

   b. What is Acort's equity cost of capital?

The Adjusted Present
Value Method

7. Suppose Goodyear Tire and Rubber Company has an equity cost of capital of 8.5%, a debt cost of capital of 7%, a marginal corporate tax rate of 35%, and a debt-equity ratio of 2.6. Suppose Goodyear maintains a constant debt-equity ratio.

   a. What is Goodyear's WACC?

   b. What is Goodyear's unlevered cost of capital?

   c. Explain, intuitively, why Goodyear's unlevered cost of capital is less than its equity cost of capital and higher than its WACC.

8. You are a consultant who was hired to evaluate a new product line for Markum Enterprises. The upfront investment required to launch the product line is $10 million. The product will generate free cash flow of $750,000 the first year, and this free cash flow is expected to grow at a rate of 4% per year. Markum has an equity cost of capital of 11.3%, a debt cost of capital of 5%, and a tax rate of 35%. Markum maintains a debt-equity ratio of 0.40.

   a. What is the NPV of the new product line (including any tax shields from leverage)?

   b. How much debt will Markum initially take on as a result of launching this product line?

   c. How much of the product line's value is attributable to the present value of interest tax shields?

9. Consider Lucent's project in Problem 5.

   a. What is Lucent's unlevered cost of capital?

   b. What is the unlevered value of the project?

   c. What are the interest tax shields from the project? What is their present value?

   d. Show that the APV of Lucent's project matches the value computed using the WACC method.

The Flow-to-Equity
Method

10. Consider Lucent's project in Problem 5.

   a. What is the free cash flow to equity for this project?

   b. What is its NPV computed using the FTE method? How does it compare with the NPV based on the WACC method?

11. In year 1, AMC will earn $2000 before interest and taxes. The market expects these earnings to grow at a rate of 3% per year. The firm will make no net investments or changes to net working capital. Assume that the corporate tax rate equals 40%. Right now, the firm has $5000 in risk-free debt. It plans to keep a constant ratio of debt to equity every year, so that on average the debt will also grow by 3% per year. Suppose the risk-free rate equals 5%, and the expected return on the market equals 11%. The asset beta for this industry is 1.11.

a. If AMC were an all-equity (unlevered) firm, what would its market value be?

b. Assuming the debt is fairly priced, what is the amount of interest AMC will pay next year? If AMC's debt is expected to grow by 3% per year, at what rate are its interest payments expected to grow?

c. Even though AMC's debt is *riskless* (the firm will not default), the future growth of AMC's debt is uncertain, so the exact amount of the future interest payments is risky. Assuming the future interest payments have the same beta as AMC's assets, what is the present value of AMC's interest tax shield?

d. Using the APV method, what is AMC's total market value, V^L? What is the market value of AMC's equity?

e. What is AMC's WACC? (*Hint:* Work backward from the FCF and V^L.)

f. Using the WACC method, what is the expected return for AMC equity?

g. Show that the following holds for AMC: $\beta_A = \dfrac{E}{D+E}\beta_E + \dfrac{D}{D+E}\beta_D$.

h. Assuming that the proceeds from any increases in debt are paid out to equity holders, what cash flows do the equity holders expect to receive in one year? At what rate are those cash flows expected to grow? Use that information plus your answer to part (f) to derive the market value of equity using the FTE method. How does that compare to your answer in part (d)?

Project-Based Costs
of Capital

12. Prokter and Gramble (PG) has historically maintained a debt-equity ratio of approximately 0.20. Its current stock price is $50 per share, with 2.5 billion shares outstanding. The firm enjoys very stable demand for its products, and consequently it has a low equity beta of 0.50 and can borrow at 4.20%, just 20 basis points over the risk-free rate of 4%. The expected return of the market is 10%, and PG's tax rate is 35%.

a. This year, PG is expected to have free cash flows of $6.0 billion. What constant expected growth rate of free cash flow is consistent with its current stock price?

b. PG believes it can increase debt without any serious risk of distress or other costs. With a higher debt-equity ratio of 0.50, it believes its borrowing costs will rise only slightly to 4.50%. If PG announces that it will raise its debt-equity ratio to 0.5 through a leveraged recap, determine the increase in the stock price that would result from the anticipated tax savings.

13. Amarindo, Inc. (AMR), is a newly public firm with 10 million shares outstanding. You are doing a valuation analysis of AMR. You estimate its free cash flow in the coming year to be $15 million, and you expect the firm's free cash flows to grow by 4% per year in subsequent years. Because the firm has only been listed on the stock exchange for a short time, you do not have an accurate assessment of AMR's equity beta. However, you do have beta data for UAL, another firm in the same industry:

	Equity Beta	Debt Beta	Debt-Equity Ratio
UAL	1.5	0.30	1

AMR has a much lower debt-equity ratio of 0.30, which is expected to remain stable, and its debt is risk free. AMR's corporate tax rate is 40%, the risk-free rate is 5%, and the expected return on the market portfolio is 11%.

a. Estimate AMR's equity cost of capital.

b. Estimate AMR's share price.

EXCEL **14.** Remex (RMX) currently has no debt in its capital structure. The beta of its equity is 1.50. For each year into the indefinite future, Remex's free cash flow is expected to equal $25 million. Remex is considering changing its capital structure by issuing debt and using the proceeds to buy back stock. It will do so in such a way that it will have a 30% debt-equity ratio after the change, and it will maintain this debt-equity ratio forever. Assume that the required (i.e., expected) return on the debt Remex will be issuing is 6.5%. Remex faces a corporate tax rate of 35%. Except for the corporate tax rate of 35%, there are no market imperfections. Assume that the CAPM holds, the risk-free rate of interest is 5%, and the expected return on the market is 11%.

a. Using the information provided, fill in the table below:

	Debt-Equity Ratio	Debt Cost of Capital	Equity Cost of Capital	Weighted Average Cost of Capital
Before change in capital structure	0	N/A		
After change in capital structure	0.30	6.5%		

b. Using the information provided and your calculations in part (a), determine the value of the tax shield acquired by Remex if it changes its capital structure in the way it is considering.

APV with Other
Leverage Policies

15. Tybo Corporation adjusts its debt so that its interest expenses are 20% of its free cash flow. Tybo is considering an expansion that will generate free cash flows of $2.5 million this year and is expected to grow at a rate of 4% per year from then on. Suppose Tybo's marginal corporate tax rate is 40%.

a. If the unlevered cost of capital for this expansion is 10%, what is its unlevered value?

b. What is the levered value of the expansion?

c. If Tybo pays 5% interest on its debt, what amount of debt will it take on initially for the expansion?

d. What is the debt-to-value ratio for this expansion? What is its WACC?

e. What is the levered value of the expansion using the WACC method?

EXCEL **16.** You are on your way to an important budget meeting. In the elevator, you review the project valuation analysis you had your summer associate prepare for one of the projects to be discussed:

	0	1	2	3	4
EBIT		10.0	10.0	10.0	10.0
Interest (5%)		−4.0	−4.0	−3.0	−2.0
Earnings Before Taxes		6.0	6.0	7.0	8.0
Taxes		−2.4	−2.4	−2.8	−3.2
Depreciation		25.0	25.0	25.0	25.0
Cap Ex	−100.0				
Additions to NWC	−20.0				20.0
Net New Debt	80.0	0.0	−20.0	−20.0	−40.0
FCFE	−40.0	28.6	8.6	9.2	9.8
NPV at 11% Equity Cost of Capital	5.9				

Looking over the spreadsheet, you realize that while all of the cash flow estimates are correct, your associate used the flow-to-equity valuation method and discounted the cash flows using the *company's* equity cost of capital of 11%. However, the project's incremental leverage is very different from the company's historical debt-equity ratio of 0.20: For this project, the company will instead borrow $80 million upfront and repay $20 million in year 2, $20 million in year 3, and $40 million in year 4. Thus the *project's* equity cost of capital is likely to be higher than the firm's, not constant over time—invalidating your associate's calculation.

Clearly, the FTE approach is not the best way to analyze this project. Fortunately, you have your calculator with you, and with any luck you can use a better method before the meeting starts.

a. What is the present value of the interest tax shield associated with this project?

b. What are the free cash flows of the project?

c. What is the best estimate of the project's value from the information given?

17. Your firm is considering building a $600 million plant to manufacture HDTV circuitry. You expect operating profits (EBITDA) of $145 million per year for the next ten years. The plant will be depreciated on a straight-line basis over ten years (assuming no salvage value for tax purposes). After ten years, the plant will have a salvage value of $300 million (which, since it will be fully depreciated, is then taxable). The project requires $50 million in working capital at the start, which will be recovered when the project shuts down. The corporate tax rate is 35%. All cash flows occur at the end of the year.

a. If the risk-free rate is 5%, the expected return of the market is 11%, and the asset beta for the consumer electronics industry is 1.67, what is the NPV of the project?

b. Suppose that you can finance $400 million of the cost of the plant using ten-year, 9% coupon bonds sold at par. This amount is incremental new debt associated specifically with this project and will not alter other aspects of the firm's capital structure. What is the value of the project, including the tax shield of the debt?

Other Effects of Financing

EXCEL 18. DFS Corporation is currently an all-equity firm, with assets with a market value of $100 million and 4 million shares outstanding. DFS is considering a leveraged recapitalization to boost its share price. The firm plans to raise a fixed amount of permanent debt (i.e., the outstanding principal will remain constant) and use the proceeds to repurchase shares. DFS pays a 35% corporate tax rate, so one motivation for taking on the debt is to reduce the firm's tax liability. However, the upfront investment banking fees associated with the recapitalization will be 5% of the amount of debt raised. Adding leverage will also create the possibility of future financial distress or agency costs; shown below are DFS's estimates for different levels of debt:

Debt amount ($ million):	0	10	20	30	40	50
Present value of expected distress and agency costs ($ million):	0.0	−0.3	−1.8	−4.3	−7.5	−11.3

a. Based on this information, which level of debt is the best choice for DFS?

b. Estimate the stock price once this transaction is announced.

19. Your firm is considering a $150 million investment to launch a new product line. The project is expected to generate a free cash flow of $20 million per year, and its unlevered cost of capital is 10%. To fund the investment, your firm will take on $100 million in permanent debt.

a. Suppose the marginal corporate tax rate is 35%. Ignoring issuance costs, what is the NPV of the investment?

b. Suppose your firm will pay a 2% underwriting fee when issuing the debt. It will raise the remaining $50 million by issuing equity. In addition to the 5% underwriting fee for the equity issue, you believe that your firm's current share price of $40 is $5 per share less than its true value. What is the NPV of the investment in this case? (Assume all fees are on an after-tax basis.)

20. Consider Avco's RFX project from Section 18.3. Suppose that Avco is receiving government loan guarantees that allow it to borrow at the 6% rate. Without these guarantees, Avco would pay 6.5% on its debt.

   a. What is Avco's unlevered cost of capital given its true debt cost of capital of 6.5%?

   b. What is the unlevered value of the RFX project in this case? What is the present value of the interest tax shield?

   c. What is the NPV of the loan guarantees? (*Hint:* Because the actual loan amounts will fluctuate with the value of the project, discount the expected interest savings at the unlevered cost of capital.)

   d. What is the levered value of the RFX project, including the interest tax shield and the NPV of the loan guarantees?

Advanced Topics in Capital Budgeting

21. Arden Corporation is considering an investment in a new project with an unlevered cost of capital of 9%. Arden's marginal corporate tax rate is 40%, and its debt cost of capital is 5%.

   a. Suppose Arden adjusts its debt continuously to maintain a constant debt-equity ratio of 50%. What is the appropriate WACC for the new project?

   b. Suppose Arden adjusts its debt once per year to maintain a constant debt-equity ratio of 50%. What is the appropriate WACC for the new project now?

   c. Suppose the project has free cash flows of $10 million per year, which are expected to decline by 2% per year. What is the value of the project in parts (a) and (b) now?

22. XL Sports is expected to generate free cash flows of $10.9 million per year. XL has permanent debt of $40 million, a tax rate of 40%, and an unlevered cost of capital of 10%.

   a. What is the value of XL's equity using the APV method?

   b. What is XL's WACC? What is XL's equity value using the WACC method?

   c. If XL's debt cost of capital is 5%, what is XL's equity cost of capital?

   d. What is XL's equity value using the FTE method?

EXCEL *23. Propel Corporation plans to make a $50 million investment, initially funded completely with debt. The free cash flows of the investment and Propel's incremental debt from the project are shown below:

Year	0	1	2	3
Free cash flows	−50	40	20	25
Debt	50	30	15	0

Propel's incremental debt for the project will be paid off according to the predetermined schedule shown. Propel's debt cost of capital is 8%, and its tax rate is 40%. Propel also estimates an unlevered cost of capital for the project of 12%.

   a. Use the WACC method to determine the levered value of the project at each date and its initial NPV.

   b. Calculate the WACC for this project at each date. How does the WACC change over time? Why?

   c. Compute the project's NPV using the WACC method.

d. Compute the equity cost of capital for this project at each date. How does the equity cost of capital change over time? Why?

e. Compute the project's equity value using the FTE method. How does the initial equity value compare with the NPV calculated in parts (a) and (c)?

24. Gartner Systems has no debt and an equity cost of capital of 10%. Gartner's current market capitalization is $100 million, and its free cash flows are expected to grow at 3% per year. Gartner's corporate tax rate is 35%. Investors pay tax rates of 40% on interest income and 20% on equity income.

   a. Suppose Gartner adds $50 million in permanent debt. What will Gartner's levered value be in this case?

   b. Suppose instead Gartner decides to maintain a 50% debt-to-value ratio going forward. If Gartner's debt cost of capital is 6.67%, what will Gartner's levered value be in this case?

EXCEL *25. Revtek, Inc., has an equity cost of capital of 12% and a debt cost of capital of 6%. Revtek maintains a constant debt-equity ratio of 0.5, and its tax rate is 35%.

   a. What is Revtek's WACC given its current debt-equity ratio?

   b. Assuming no personal taxes, how will Revtek's WACC change if it increases its debt-equity ratio to 2?

   c. Now suppose an investor pays tax rates of 40% on interest income and 15% on income from equity. How will Revtek's WACC change if it increases its debt-equity ratio to 2 in this case?

   d. Provide an intuitive explanation for the difference in your answers to parts (b) and (c).

Data Case

Toyota Motor Company is expanding the production of their gas-electric hybrid drive systems and plans to begin production in the United States. To enable the expansion they are contemplating investing $1.5 billion in a new plant with an expected ten-year life. The anticipated free cash flows from the new plant would be $220 million the first year of operation and grow by 10% for each of the next two years and then 5% per year for the remaining seven years. As a newly hired MBA in the capital budgeting division you have been asked to evaluate the new project using the WACC, Adjusted Present Value, and Flow-to-Equity methods. You will compute the appropriate costs of capital and the net present values with each method. Because this is your first major assignment with the firm, they want you to demonstrate that you are capable of handling the different valuation methods. You must seek out the information necessary to value the free cash flows but will be provided some directions to follow. (This is an involved assignment, but at least you don't have to come up with the actual cash flows for the project!)

1. Go to MarketWatch.com (www.marketwatch.com) and get the quote for Toyota (symbol: TM).

   a. Click on "Financials." The income statements for the last four fiscal years will appear. Place the cursor in the middle of the statements and right-click the mouse. Select "Export to Microsoft Excel."

   b. Go back to the Web page and select "Balance Sheets" from the top of the page. Repeat the download procedure for the balance sheets, then copy and paste them into the same worksheet as the income statements.

   c. Click on "Historical Quote" in the left column, and find Toyota's stock price for the last day of the month at the end of each of the past four fiscal years. Record the stock price on each date in your spreadsheet.

2. Create a timeline in Excel with the free cash flows for the ten years of the project.

3. Determine the WACC using Eq. 18.1.

   a. For the cost of debt, r_D:

      i. Go to NasdBondInfo.com (www.nasdbondinfo.com) and click to search by symbol. Enter Toyota's symbol and press enter.

      ii. Find the yield for the Toyota Motor Credit Corp. bond with a maturity of 1/25/2016. Enter the yield on your spreadsheet as an estimate of Toyota's debt cost of capital.

   b. For the cost of equity, r_E:

      i. Get the yield on the ten-year U.S. Treasury Bond from Yahoo! Finance (http://finance.yahoo.com). Scroll down to the Market Summary. Enter that yield as the risk-free rate.

      ii. Find the beta for Toyota from Nasdaq.com. Enter the symbol for Toyota and click on "Summary Quote." The beta for Toyota will be listed there.

      iii. Use a market risk premium of 4.50% to compute r_E using the CAPM.

   c. Determine the values for E and D from Eq. 18.1 for Toyota and the debt-to-value and equity-to-value ratios.

      i. To compute the net debt for Toyota add the long-term debt and the short-term debt and subtract cash and cash equivalents for each year on the balance sheet.

      ii. Multiply the historical stock prices by the "Basic Weighted Shares Outstanding" data in the income statement to compute Toyota's market capitalization at the end of each fiscal year.

      iii. Compute Toyota's enterprise value at the end of each fiscal year by combining the values obtained for its equity market capitalization and its net debt.

      iv. Compute Toyota's debt-to-value ratio at the end of each year by dividing its net debt by its enterprise value. Use the average ratio from the last four years as an estimate for Toyota's target debt-to-value ratio.

   d. Determine Toyota's tax rate by dividing the income tax by earnings before tax for each year. Take the average of the four rates as Toyota's marginal corporate tax rate.

   e. Compute the WACC for Toyota using Eq. 18.1.

4. Compute the NPV of the hybrid engine expansion given the free cash flows you calculated using the WACC method of valuation.

5. Determine the NPV using the Adjusted Present Value Method, and also using the Flow-to-Equity method. In both cases, assume Toyota maintains the target leverage ratio you computed in Question 3(c).

6. Compare the results under the three methods and explain how the resulting NPVs are achieved under each of the three different methods.

CHAPTER 18 APPENDIX

Foundations and Further Details

In this appendix we look at the foundations for the WACC method, and for the relationship between a firm's levered and unlevered costs of capital. We also address how we can solve for a firm's leverage policy and value simultaneously.

18A.1   Deriving the WACC Method

The WACC can be used to value a levered investment, as in Eq. 18.2 on page 577. Consider an investment that is financed by both debt and equity. Because equity holders require an expected return of r_E on their investment and debt holders require a return of r_D, the firm will have to pay investors a total of

$$E(1 + r_E) + D(1 + r_D) \tag{18A.1}$$

next year. What is the value of the investment next year? The project generates free cash flows of FCF_1 at the end of the year. In addition, the interest tax shield of the debt provides a tax savings of $\tau_c \times$ (interest on debt) $\approx \tau_c r_D D$.[26] Finally, if the investment will continue beyond next year, it will have a continuation value of V_1^L. Thus, to satisfy investors, the project cash flows must be such that

$$E(1 + r_E) + D(1 + r_D) = FCF_1 + \tau_c r_D D + V_1^L \tag{18A.2}$$

Because $V_0^L = E + D$, we can write the WACC definition in Eq. 18.1 as

$$r_{wacc} = \frac{E}{V_0^L} r_E + \frac{D}{V_0^L} r_D(1 - \tau_c) \tag{18A.3}$$

If we move the interest tax shield to the left side of Eq. 18A.2, we can use the definition of the WACC to rewrite Eq. 18A.2 as follows:

$$\underbrace{E(1 + r_E) + D[1 + r_D(1 - \tau_c)]}_{V_0^L(1 + r_{wacc})} = FCF_1 + V_1^L \tag{18A.4}$$

---

26. The return on the debt r_D need not come solely from interest payments. If C_t is the coupon paid and D_t is the market value of the debt in period t, then in period t, r_D is defined as

$$r_D = \frac{E[\text{Coupon Payment} + \text{Capital Gain}]}{\text{Current Price}} = \frac{E[C_{t+1} + D_{t+1} - D_t]}{D_t}$$

The return that determines the firm's interest expense is

$$\bar{r}_D = \frac{E[C_{t+1} + \bar{D}_{t+1} - \bar{D}_t]}{D_t}$$

where $\bar{D}_t$ is the value of the debt on date t according to a fixed schedule set by the tax code based on the difference between the bond's initial price and its face value, which is called the bond's *original issue discount* (OID). (If the bond is issued at par and the firm will not default on the next coupon, then $\bar{D}_t = \bar{D}_{t+1}$ and $\bar{r}_D = C_{t+1} / D_t$, which is the bond's *current yield*.) Thus the true after-tax cost of debt is $(r_D - \tau_c \bar{r}_D)$. In practice, the distinction between r_D and $\bar{r}_D$ is often ignored, and the after-tax cost of debt is computed as $r_D(1 - \tau_c)$. Also, the debt's yield to maturity is often used in place of r_D. Because the yield to maturity ignores default risk, it generally overstates r_D and therefore the WACC.

Dividing by $(1 + r_{wacc})$, we can express the value of the investment today as the present value of next period's free cash flows and continuation value:

$$V_0^L = \frac{FCF_1 + V_1^L}{1 + r_{wacc}} \tag{18A.5}$$

In the same way, we can write the value in one year, V_1^L, as the discounted value of the free cash flows and continuation value of the project in year 2. If the WACC is the same next year, then

$$V_0^L = \frac{FCF_1 + V_1^L}{1 + r_{wacc}} = \frac{FCF_1 + \dfrac{FCF_2 + V_2^L}{1 + r_{wacc}}}{1 + r_{wacc}} = \frac{FCF_1}{1 + r_{wacc}} + \frac{FCF_2 + V_2^L}{(1 + r_{wacc})^2} \tag{18A.6}$$

By repeatedly replacing each continuation value, and *assuming the WACC remains constant,* we can derive Eq. 18.2:[27]

$$V_0^L = \frac{FCF_1}{1 + r_{wacc}} + \frac{FCF_2}{(1 + r_{wacc})^2} + \frac{FCF_3}{(1 + r_{wacc})^3} + \cdots \tag{18A.7}$$

That is, *the value of a levered investment is the present value of its future free cash flows using the weighted average cost of capital.*

18A.2 The Levered and Unlevered Cost of Capital

In this appendix, we derive the relationship between the levered and unlevered cost of capital for the firm. Suppose an investor holds a portfolio of all of the equity and debt of the firm. Then the investor will receive the free cash flows of the firm plus the tax savings from the interest tax shield. These are the same cash flows an investor would receive from a portfolio of the unlevered firm (which generates the free cash flows) and a separate "tax shield" security that paid the investor the amount of the tax shield each period. Because these two portfolios generate the same cash flows, by the Law of One Price they have the same market values:

$$V^L = E + D = V^U + T \tag{18A.8}$$

where T is the present value of the interest tax shield. Equation 18A.8 is the basis of the APV method. Because these portfolios have equal cash flows, they must also have identical expected returns, which implies

$$Er_E + Dr_D = V^U r_U + Tr_T \tag{18A.9}$$

where r_T is the expected return associated with the interest tax shields. The relationship between r_E, r_D, and r_U will depend on the expected return r_T, which is determined by the risk of the interest tax shield. Let's consider the two cases discussed in the text.

Target Leverage Ratio

Suppose the firm adjusts its debt continuously to maintain a target debt-to-value ratio, or a target ratio of interest to free cash flow. We show below that in this case, the risk of the interest

---

27. This expansion is the same approach we took in Chapter 9 to derive the discounted dividend formula for the stock price.

tax shield will be equal to that of the firm's free cash flow, so $r_T = r_U$. With this observation, Eq. 18A.9 becomes

$$Er_E + Dr_D = V^U r_U + Tr_U = (V^U + T)r_U$$
$$= (E + D)r_U \qquad (18A.10)$$

Dividing by $(E + D)$ leads to Eq. 18.6 on page 582.

Predetermined Debt Schedule

Suppose some of the firm's debt is set according to a predetermined schedule that is independent of the growth of the firm. Suppose the value of the tax shield from the scheduled debt is T^s, and the remaining value of the tax shield $T - T^s$ is from debt that will be adjusted according to a target leverage ratio. Because the risk of the interest tax shield from the scheduled debt is similar to the risk of the debt itself, Eq. 18A.9 becomes

$$Er_E + Dr_D = V^U r_U + Tr_T = V^U r_U + (T - T^s)r_U + T^s r_D \qquad (18A.11)$$

Subtracting $T^s r_D$ from both sides, and using $D^s = D - T^s$,

$$Er_E + D^s r_D = (V^U + T - T^s)r_U = (V^L - T^s)r_U$$
$$= (E + D^s)r_U \qquad (18A.12)$$

Dividing by $(E + D^s)$ leads to Eq. 18.20 on page 604.

Risk of the Tax Shield with a Target Leverage Ratio

The previous analysis relied on the fact that with a target leverage ratio, it is reasonable to assume that $r_T = r_U$. Why should this be the case?

We define a target leverage ratio as a setting in which the firm adjusts its debt at date t to be a proportion $d(t)$ of the investment's value, or a proportion $k(t)$ of its free cash flow. (The target ratio for either policy need not be constant over time, but can vary according to a predetermined schedule.)

With either policy, the value at date t of the incremental tax shield from the project's free cash flow at date s, FCF_s, is proportional to the value of the cash flow $V_t^L(FCF_s)$, so it should be discounted at the same rate as FCF_s. The assumption $r_T = r_U$ therefore follows as long as at each date the cost of capital associated with the value of each future free cash flow is the same (a standard assumption in capital budgeting).[28]

18A.3 Solving for Leverage and Value Simultaneously

When we use the APV method, we need to know the debt level to compute the interest tax shield and determine the project's value. But if a firm maintains a constant debt-to-value ratio, we need to know the project's value to determine the debt level. How can we apply the APV method in this case?

When a firm maintains a constant leverage ratio, to use the APV method we must solve for the debt level and the project value simultaneously. While complicated to do by hand, it is (fortunately) easy to do in Excel. We begin with the spreadsheet shown in Table 18A.1, which illustrates the standard APV calculation outlined in Section 18.3 of the text. For now, we have just inserted arbitrary values for the project's debt capacity in line 3.

---

28. If the risk of the individual cash flows differs, then r_T will be a weighted average of the unlevered costs of capital of the individual cash flows, with the weights depending on the schedule d or k. See P. DeMarzo, "A Note on Discounting Tax Shields and the Unlevered Cost of Capital," a working paper, 2006.

TABLE 18A.1
SPREADSHEET

Adjusted Present Value for Avco's RFX Project with Arbitrary Debt Levels

	Year	0	1	2	3	4
Unlevered Value ($ million)						
1 Free Cash Flow		(28.00)	18.00	18.00	18.00	18.00
2 Unlevered Value, V^U (at r_u = 8.0%)		59.62	46.39	32.10	16.67	—
Interest Tax Shield						
3 Debt Capacity (arbitrary)		30.00	20.00	10.00	5.00	—
4 Interest Paid (at r_d = 6%)		—	1.80	1.20	0.60	0.30
5 Interest Tax Shield (at τ_c = 40%)		—	0.72	0.48	0.24	0.12
6 Tax Shield Value, T (at r_u = 8.0%)		1.36	0.75	0.33	0.11	—
Adjusted Present Value						
7 Levered Value, $V^L = V^U + T$		60.98	47.13	32.42	16.78	—

Note that the debt capacity specified in line 3 is not consistent with a 50% debt-to-value ratio for the project. For example, given the value of $60.98 million in year 0, the initial debt capacity should be 50% × $60.98 million = $30.49 million in year 0. But if we change each debt capacity in line 3 to a *numerical* value that is 50% of the value in line 7, the interest tax shield and the project's value will change, and we will still not have a 50% debt-to-value ratio.

The solution is to enter in line 3 a *formula* that sets the debt capacity to be 50% of the project's value in line 7 in the same year. Now line 7 depends on line 3, and line 3 depends on line 7, creating a circular reference in the spreadsheet (and you will most likely receive an error message). By changing the calculation option in Excel to calculate the spreadsheet iteratively (Tools > Options menu, Calculation Tab, and check the Iteration box), Excel will keep calculating until the values in line 3 and line 7 of the spreadsheet are consistent, as shown in Table 18A.2.

TABLE 18A.2
SPREADSHEET

Adjusted Present Value for Avco's RFX Project with Debt Levels Solved Iteratively

	Year	0	1	2	3	4
Unlevered Value ($ million)						
1 Free Cash Flow		(28.00)	18.00	18.00	18.00	18.00
2 Unlevered Value, V^U (at r_u = 8.0%)		59.62	46.39	32.10	16.67	—
Interest Tax Shield						
3 Debt Capacity (at d = 50%)		30.62	23.71	16.32	8.43	—
4 Interest Paid (at r_d = 6%)		—	1.84	1.42	0.98	0.51
5 Interest Tax Shield (at τ_c = 40%)		—	0.73	0.57	0.39	0.20
6 Tax Shield Value, T (at r_u = 8.0%)		1.63	1.02	0.54	0.19	—
Adjusted Present Value						
7 Levered Value, $V^L = V^U + T$		61.25	47.41	32.63	16.85	—

The same method can be applied when using the WACC method with known debt levels. In that case, we need to know the project's value to determine the debt-to-value ratio and compute the WACC, and we need to know the WACC to compute the project's value. Again, we can use iteration within Excel to determine simultaneously the project's value and debt-to-value ratio.

Valuation and Financial Modeling: A Case Study

notation

R_s	return on security s
r_f	risk-free rate
α_s	the alpha of security s
β_s	the beta of security s
R_{mkt}	return of the market portfolio
$E[R_{mkt}]$	expected return of the market portfolio
ε_s	the regression error term
β_U	the beta of an unlevered firm
β_E	the beta of the equity of a levered firm
β_D	the beta of the debt of a levered firm
r_U	unlevered cost of capital
V_T^L	continuing value of a project at date T
FCF_t	free cash flow at date t
r_{wacc}	weighted average cost of capital
g	growth rate
V^U	unlevered value
T^s	predetermined tax shield value
r_D	debt cost of capital

The goal of this chapter is to apply the financial tools we have developed thus far to demonstrate how they are used in practice to build a valuation model of a firm. In this chapter, we will value a hypothetical firm, Ideko Corporation. Ideko is a privately held designer and manufacturer of specialty sports eyewear based in Chicago. In mid-2005, its owner and founder, June Wong, has decided to sell the business, after having relinquished management control about four years ago. As a partner in PKK Investments, you are investigating purchasing the company. If a deal can be reached, the acquisition will take place at the end of the current fiscal year. In that event, PKK plans to implement operational and financial improvements at Ideko over the next five years, after which it intends to sell the business.

Ideko has total assets of $87 million and annual sales of $75 million. The firm is also quite profitable, with earnings this year of almost $7 million, for a net profit margin of 9.3%. You believe a deal could be struck to purchase Ideko's equity at the end of this fiscal year for an acquisition price of $150 million, which is almost double Ideko's current book value of equity. Is this price reasonable?

We begin the chapter by estimating Ideko's value using data for comparable firms. We then review PKK's operating strategies for running the business after the acquisition, to identify potential areas for improvements. We build a financial model to project cash flows that reflect these operating improvements. These cash flow forecasts enable us to value Ideko using the APV model introduced in Chapter 18 and estimate the return on PKK's investment. Finally, we explore the sensitivity of the valuation estimates to our main assumptions.

19.1   Valuation Using Comparables

As a result of preliminary conversations with Ideko's founder, you have estimates of Ideko's income and balance sheet information for the current fiscal year shown in Table 19.1. Ideko currently has debt outstanding of $4.5 million, but it also has a substantial cash balance. To obtain your first estimate of Ideko's value, you decide to value Ideko by examining comparable firms.

<table>
<tr><td rowspan="2">**TABLE 19.1**
SPREADSHEET</td><td colspan="2">**Estimated 2005 Income Statement and Balance Sheet Data for Ideko Corporation**</td></tr>
</table>

Income Statement ($ 000)	Year 2005	Balance Sheet ($ 000)	Year 2005
1 Sales	75,000	Assets	
2 Cost of Goods Sold		1 Cash and Equivalents	12,664
3 Raw Materials	(16,000)	2 Accounts Receivable	18,493
4 Direct Labor Costs	(18,000)	3 Inventories	6,165
5 Gross Profit	41,000	4 **Total Current Assets**	37,322
6 Sales and Marketing	(11,250)	5 Property, Plant, and Equipment	49,500
7 Administrative	(13,500)	6 Goodwill	–
8 EBITDA	16,250	7 **Total Assets**	86,822
9 Depreciation	(5,500)	Liabilities and Stockholder's Equity	
10 EBIT	10,750	8 Accounts Payable	4,654
11 Interest Expense (net)	(75)	9 Debt	4,500
12 Pretax Income	10,675	10 **Total Liabilities**	9,154
13 Income Tax	(3,736)	11 Stockholder's Equity	77,668
14 Net Income	6,939	12 **Total Liabilities and Equity**	86,822

A quick way to gauge the reasonableness of the proposed price for Ideko is to compare it to that of other publicly traded firms using the method of comparable firms introduced in Chapter 9. For example, at a price of $150 million, Ideko's price-earnings (P/E) ratio is $150,000 / 6939 = 21.6$, roughly equal to the market average P/E ratio in mid-2005.

It is even more informative to compare Ideko to firms in a similar line of business. Although no firm is exactly comparable to Ideko in terms of its overall product line, three firms with which it has similarities are Oakley, Inc., Luxottica Group, and Nike, Inc. The closest competitor is Oakley, which also designs and manufactures sports eyewear. Luxottica Group is an Italian eyewear maker, but much of its business is prescription eyewear; it also owns and operates a number of retail eyewear chains. Nike is a manufacturer of specialty sportswear products, but it concentrates in footwear. You also decide to compare Ideko to a portfolio of firms in the sporting goods industry.

A comparison of Ideko's proposed valuation to this peer set, as well as to the average firm in the sporting goods industry, appears in Table 19.2. The table not only lists P/E ratios, but also shows each firm's enterprise value (EV) as a multiple of sales and EBITDA (earnings before interest, taxes, depreciation, and amortization). Recall that enterprise value is the total value of equity plus net debt, where net debt is debt less cash and investments in marketable securities that are not required as part of normal operations. Ideko has $4.5 million in debt, and you estimate that it holds $6.5 million of cash in excess of its working capital needs. Thus Ideko's enterprise value at the proposed acquisition price is $150 + 4.5 - 6.5 = \$148$ million.

TABLE 19.2   **Ideko Financial Ratios Comparison, Mid-2005**

Ratio	Ideko (Proposed)	Oakley, Inc.	Luxottica Group	Nike, Inc.	Sporting Goods Industry
P/E	21.6×	24.8×	28.0×	18.2×	20.3×
EV/Sales	2.0×	2.0×	2.7×	1.5×	1.4×
EV/EBITDA	9.1×	11.6×	14.4×	9.3×	11.4×
EBITDA/Sales	21.7%	17.0%	18.5%	15.9%	12.1%

At the proposed price, Ideko's P/E ratio is low relative to those of Oakley and Luxottica, although it is somewhat above the P/E ratios of Nike and the industry overall. The same can be said for Ideko's valuation as a multiple of sales. Thus, based on these two measures, Ideko looks "cheap" relative to Oakley and Luxottica, but is priced at a premium relative to Nike and the average sporting goods firm. The deal stands out, however, when you compare Ideko's enterprise value relative to EBITDA. The acquisition price of just over nine times EBITDA is below that of all of the comparable firms as well as the industry average. Ideko's low EBITDA multiple is a result of its high profit margins: At 16,250 / 75,000 = 21.7%, its EBITDA margin exceeds that of all of the comparables.

While Table 19.2 provides some reassurance that the acquisition price is reasonable compared to other firms in the industry, it by no means establishes that the acquisition is a good investment opportunity. As with any such comparison, the multiples in Table 19.2 vary substantially. Furthermore, they ignore important differences such as the operating efficiency and growth prospects of the firms, and they do not reflect PKK's plans to improve Ideko's operations. To assess whether this investment is attractive requires a careful analysis both of the operational aspects of the firm and of the ultimate cash flows the deal is expected to generate and the return that should be required.

Valuation by Comparables

Problem

What range of acquisition prices for Ideko is implied by the range of multiples for P/E, EV/Sales, and EV/EBITDA in Table 19.2?

Solution

For each multiple, we can find the highest and lowest values across all three firms and the industry portfolio. Applying each multiple to the data for Ideko in Table 19.1 yields the following results:

Multiple	Range		Price ($ million)	
	Low	High	Low	High
P/E	18.2×	28.0×	126.3	194.3
EV/Sales	1.4×	2.7×	107.0	204.5
EV/EBITDA	9.3×	14.4×	153.1	236.0

For example, Nike has the lowest P/E multiple of 18.2. Multiplying this P/E by Ideko's earnings of $6.94 million gives a value of $18.2 \times 6.94 = \$126.3$ million. The highest multiple of enterprise value to sales is 2.7 (Luxottica); at this multiple, Ideko's enterprise value is $2.7 \times 75 = \$202.5$ million. Adding Ideko's excess cash and subtracting its debt implies a purchase price of $202.5 + 6.5 - 4.5 = \$204.5$ million. The above table demonstrates that while comparables provide a useful benchmark, they cannot be relied upon for a precise estimate of value.

<table>
<tr><td>**CONCEPT CHECK**</td><td>1. What is the purpose of the valuation using comparables?</td></tr>
<tr><td></td><td>2. If the valuation using comparables indicates the acquisition price is reasonable compared to other firms in the industry, does it establish that the acquisition is a good investment opportunity?</td></tr>
</table>

19.2 The Business Plan

While comparables provide a useful starting point, whether this acquisition is a successful investment for PKK depends on Ideko's post-acquisition performance. Thus it is necessary to look in detail at Ideko's operations, investments, and capital structure, and to assess its potential for improvements and future growth.

Operational Improvements

On the operational side, you are quite optimistic regarding the company's prospects. The market is expected to grow by 5% per year, and Ideko produces a superior product. Ideko's market share has not grown in recent years because current management has devoted insufficient resources to product development, sales, and marketing. Conversely, Ideko has overspent on administrative costs. Indeed, Table 19.1 reveals that Ideko's current administrative expenses are $13,500 / 75,000 = 18\%$ of sales, a rate that exceeds its expenditures on sales and marketing (15% of sales). This is in stark contrast to its rivals, which spend less on administrative overhead than they do on sales and marketing.

PKK plans to cut administrative costs immediately and redirect resources to new product development, sales, and marketing. By doing so, you believe Ideko can increase its market share from 10% to 15% over the next five years. The increased sales demand can be met in the short run using the existing production lines by increasing overtime and running some weekend shifts. Once the growth in volume exceeds 50%, however, Ideko will need to undertake a major expansion to increase its manufacturing capacity.

The spreadsheet in Table 19.3 shows sales and operating cost assumptions for the next five years based on this plan. In the spreadsheet, numbers in blue represent data that has been entered, whereas numbers in black are calculated based on the data provided. For example, given the current market size of 10 million units and an expected growth rate of 5% per year, the spreadsheet calculates the expected market size in years 1 through 5. Also shown is the expected growth in Ideko's market share.

Note that Ideko's average selling price is expected to increase because of a 2% inflation rate each year. Likewise, manufacturing costs are expected to rise. Raw materials are forecast to increase at a 1% rate and, although you expect some productivity gains, labor costs will rise at a 4% rate due to additional overtime. The table also shows the reallocation of resources from administration to sales and marketing over the five-year period.

		Year	2005	2006	2007	2008	2009	2010
TABLE 19.3 SPREADSHEET	**Ideko Sales and Operating Cost Assumptions**							

		Year	2005	2006	2007	2008	2009	2010
Sales Data	**Growth/Year**							
1 Market Size	(000 units)	5.0%	10,000	10,500	11,025	11,576	12,155	12,763
2 Market Share		1.0%	10.0%	11.0%	12.0%	13.0%	14.0%	15.0%
3 Average Sales Price	($/unit)	2.0%	75.00	76.50	78.03	79.59	81.18	82.81
Cost of Goods Data								
4 Raw Materials	($/unit)	1.0%	16.00	16.16	16.32	16.48	16.65	16.82
5 Direct Labor Costs	($/unit)	4.0%	18.00	18.72	19.47	20.25	21.06	21.90
Operating Expense and Tax Data								
6 Sales and Marketing	(% sales)		15.0%	16.5%	18.0%	19.5%	20.0%	20.0%
7 Administrative	(% sales)		18.0%	15.0%	15.0%	14.0%	13.0%	13.0%
8 Tax Rate			35.0%	35.0%	35.0%	35.0%	35.0%	35.0%

EXAMPLE 19.2

Production Capacity Requirements

Problem

Based on the data in Table 19.3, what production capacity will Ideko require each year? When will an expansion be necessary?

Solution

Production volume each year can be estimated by multiplying the total market size and Ideko's market share in Table 19.3:

	Year	2005	2006	2007	2008	2009	2010
Production Volume (000 units)							
1 Market Size		10,000	10,500	11,025	11,576	12,155	12,763
2 Market Share		10.0%	11.0%	12.0%	13.0%	14.0%	15.0%
3 Production Volume (1 × 2)		1,000	1,155	1,323	1,505	1,702	1,914

Based on this forecast, production volume will exceed its current level by 50% by 2008, necessitating an expansion then.

Capital Expenditures: A Needed Expansion

The spreadsheet in Table 19.4 shows the forecast for Ideko's capital expenditures over the next five years. Based on the estimates for capital expenditures and depreciation, this spreadsheet tracks the book value of Ideko's plant, property, and equipment starting from its level at the beginning of 2005. Note that investment is expected to remain at its current level over the next two years, which is roughly equal to the level of depreciation. Ideko will expand its production during this period by using its existing plant more efficiently. In 2008, however, a major expansion of the plant will be necessary, leading to a large increase in capital expenditures in 2008 and 2009.

The depreciation entries in Table 19.4 are based on the appropriate depreciation schedule for each type of property. Those calculations are quite specific to the nature of the property and are not detailed here. The depreciation shown will be used for tax purposes.[1]

---

1. Firms often maintain separate books for accounting and tax purposes, and they may use different depreciation assumptions for each. Because depreciation affects cash flows through its tax consequences, tax depreciation is more relevant for valuation.

TABLE 19.4 SPREADSHEET	Ideko Capital Expenditure Assumptions					

	Year	2005	2006	2007	2008	2009	2010
Fixed Assets and Capital Investment ($ 000)							
1 Opening Book Value		50,000	49,500	49,050	48,645	61,781	69,102
2 Capital Investment		5,000	5,000	5,000	20,000	15,000	8,000
3 Depreciation		(5,500)	(5,450)	(5,405)	(6,865)	(7,678)	(7,710)
4 Closing Book Value		49,500	49,050	48,645	61,781	69,102	69,392

Working Capital Management

To compensate for its weak sales and marketing efforts, Ideko has sought to retain the loyalty of its retailers in part by maintaining a very lax credit policy. This policy affects Ideko's working capital requirements: For every extra day that customers take to pay, another day's sales revenue is added to accounts receivable (rather than received in cash). From Ideko's current income statement and balance sheet (Table 19.1), we can estimate the number of days of receivables:

$$\text{Accounts Receivable Days} = \frac{\text{Accounts Receivable (\$)}}{\text{Sales Revenue (\$ / yr)}} \times 365 \text{ days / yr}$$

$$= \frac{18,493}{75,000} \times 365 \text{ days} = 90 \text{ days} \qquad (19.1)$$

The standard for the industry is 60 days, and you believe that Ideko can tighten its credit policy to achieve this goal without sacrificing sales.

You also hope to improve Ideko's inventory management. Ideko's balance sheet in Table 19.1 lists inventory of $6.164 million. Of this amount, approximately $2 million corresponds to raw materials, while the rest is finished goods. Given raw material expenditures of $16 million for the year, Ideko currently holds $(2 / 16) \times 365 = 45.6$ days worth of raw material inventory. While maintaining a certain amount of inventory is necessary to avoid production stoppages, you believe that, with tighter controls of the production process, 30 days worth of inventory will be adequate.

Capital Structure Changes: Levering Up

With little debt, excess cash, and substantial earnings, Ideko appears to be significantly underleveraged. You plan to greatly increase the firm's debt, and have obtained bank commitments for loans of $100 million should an agreement be reached. These term loans will have an interest rate of 6.8%, and Ideko will pay interest only during the next five years. The firm will seek additional financing in 2008 and 2009 associated with the expansion of its manufacturing plant, as shown in the spreadsheet in Table 19.5. While Ideko's credit quality should improve over time, the steep slope of the yield curve suggests interest rates may increase, and so on balance you expect Ideko's borrowing rate to remain at 6.8%.

Given Ideko's outstanding debt, its interest expense each year is computed as[2]

$$\text{Interest in Year } t = \text{Interest Rate} \times \text{Ending Balance in Year } (t - 1) \qquad (19.2)$$

The interest on the debt will provide a valuable tax shield to offset Ideko's taxable income.

---

2. Equation 19.2 assumes that changes in debt occur at the end of the year. If debt changes during the year, it is more accurate to compute interest expenses based on the average level of debt during the year.

<table>
<thead>
<tr><th>TABLE 19.5
SPREADSHEET</th><th colspan="7">Ideko's Planned Debt and Interest Payments</th></tr>
</thead>
<tbody>
<tr><td>Year</td><td>2005</td><td>2006</td><td>2007</td><td>2008</td><td>2009</td><td>2010</td></tr>
<tr><td colspan="7">Debt and Interest Table ($ 000)</td></tr>
<tr><td>1 Outstanding Debt</td><td></td><td>100,000</td><td>100,000</td><td>100,000</td><td>115,000</td><td>120,000</td><td>120,000</td></tr>
<tr><td>2 Interest on Term Loan</td><td>6.80%</td><td></td><td>(6,800)</td><td>(6,800)</td><td>(6,800)</td><td>(7,820)</td><td>(8,160)</td></tr>
</tbody>
</table>

In addition to the tax benefit, the loan will allow PKK to limit its investment in Ideko and preserve its capital for other investments and acquisitions. The sources and uses of funds for the acquisition are shown in the Table 19.6 spreadsheet. In addition to the $150 million purchase price for Ideko's equity, $4.5 million will be used to repay Ideko's existing debt. With $5 million in advisory and other fees associated with the transaction, the acquisition will require $159.5 million in total funds. PKK's sources of funds include the new loan of $100 million as well as Ideko's own excess cash (which PKK will have access to). Thus PKK's required equity contribution to the transaction is $159.5 - 100 - 6.5 = \$53$ million.

<table>
<thead>
<tr><th>TABLE 19.6
SPREADSHEET</th><th colspan="4">Sources and Uses of Funds for the Ideko Acquisition</th></tr>
</thead>
<tbody>
<tr><td colspan="5">Acquisition Financing ($ 000)</td></tr>
<tr><td colspan="2">Sources</td><td></td><td colspan="2">Uses</td></tr>
<tr><td>1 New Term Loan</td><td>100,000</td><td></td><td>Purchase Ideko Equity</td><td>150,000</td></tr>
<tr><td>2 Excess Ideko Cash</td><td>6,500</td><td></td><td>Repay Existing Ideko Debt</td><td>4,500</td></tr>
<tr><td>3 PKK Equity Investment</td><td>53,000</td><td></td><td>Advisory and Other Fees</td><td>5,000</td></tr>
<tr><td>4 Total Sources of Funds</td><td>159,500</td><td></td><td>Total Uses of Funds</td><td>159,500</td></tr>
</tbody>
</table>

CONCEPT CHECK

1. What are the different operational improvements PKK plans to make?

2. Why is it necessary to consider these improvements to assess whether the acquisition is attractive?

19.3 Building the Financial Model

The value of any investment opportunity arises from the future cash flows it will generate. To estimate the cash flows resulting from the investment in Ideko, we begin by projecting Ideko's future earnings. We then consider Ideko's working capital and investment needs and estimate its free cash flow. With these data in hand, we can forecast Ideko's balance sheet and statement of cash flows.

Forecasting Earnings

We can forecast Ideko's income statement for the five years following the acquisition based on the operational and capital structure changes proposed. This income statement is often referred to as a **pro forma** income statement, because it is not based on actual data but rather depicts the firm's financials under a given set of hypothetical assumptions. The pro forma income statement translates our expectations regarding the operational improvements PKK can achieve at Ideko into consequences for the firm's earnings.

To build the pro forma income statement, we begin with Ideko's sales. Each year, sales can be calculated from the estimates in Table 19.3 as follows:

$$\text{Sales} = \text{Market Size} \times \text{Market Share} \times \text{Average Sales Price} \qquad (19.3)$$

For example, in 2006, Ideko has projected sales of 10.5 million $\times$ 11% $\times$ 76.5 = $88.358 million. The spreadsheet in Table 19.7 shows Ideko's current (2005) sales as well as projections for five years after the acquisition (2006–2010).

The next items in the income statement detail the cost of goods sold. The raw materials cost can be calculated from sales as

$$\text{Raw Materials} = \text{Market Size} \times \text{Market Share} \times \text{Raw Materials per Unit} \qquad (19.4)$$

In 2006, the cost of raw materials is 10.5 million $\times$ 11% $\times$ 16.16 = $18.665 million. The same method can be applied to determine the direct labor costs. Sales, marketing, and administrative costs can be computed directly as a percentage of sales. For example:

$$\text{Sales and Marketing} = \text{Sales} \times (\text{Sales and Marketing \% of Sales}) \qquad (19.5)$$

Therefore, sales and marketing costs are forecast to be $88.358 million $\times$ 16.5% = $14.579 million in 2006.

TABLE 19.7 SPREADSHEET	Pro Forma Income Statement for Ideko, 2005–2010						
Year	2005	2006	2007	2008	2009	2010
Income Statement ($ 000)							
1 Sales		75,000	88,358	103,234	119,777	138,149	158,526
2 Cost of Goods Sold							
3 Raw Materials		(16,000)	(18,665)	(21,593)	(24,808)	(28,333)	(32,193)
4 Direct Labor Costs		(18,000)	(21,622)	(25,757)	(30,471)	(35,834)	(41,925)
5 Gross Profit		41,000	48,071	55,883	64,498	73,982	84,407
6 Sales and Marketing		(11,250)	(14,579)	(18,582)	(23,356)	(27,630)	(31,705)
7 Administrative		(13,500)	(13,254)	(15,485)	(16,769)	(17,959)	(20,608)
8 EBITDA		16,250	20,238	21,816	24,373	28,393	32,094
9 Depreciation		(5,500)	(5,450)	(5,405)	(6,865)	(7,678)	(7,710)
10 EBIT		10,750	14,788	16,411	17,508	20,715	24,383
11 Interest Expense (net)		(75)	(6,800)	(6,800)	(6,800)	(7,820)	(8,160)
12 Pretax Income		10,675	7,988	9,611	10,708	12,895	16,223
13 Income Tax		(3,736)	(2,796)	(3,364)	(3,748)	(4,513)	(5,678)
14 Net Income		6,939	5,193	6,247	6,960	8,382	10,545

Deducting these operating expenses from Ideko's sales, we can project EBITDA over the next five years as shown in Table 19.7. Subtracting the depreciation expenses we estimated in Table 19.4, we arrive at Ideko's earnings before interest and taxes. We next deduct interest expenses according to the schedule given in Table 19.5.[3] The final expense is the corporate income tax, which we computed using the tax rate in Table 19.3 as

$$\text{Income Tax} = \text{Pretax Income} \times \text{Tax Rate} \qquad (19.6)$$

---

3. This interest expense should be offset by any interest earned on investments. As we discuss later in this chapter, we assume that Ideko does not invest its excess cash balances, but instead pays them out to its owner, PKK. Thus net interest expenses are solely due to Ideko's outstanding debt.

After income taxes, we are left with Ideko's projected pro forma net income as the bottom line in Table 19.7. Based on our projections, net income will rise by 52% from $6.939 million to $10.545 million at the end of five years, though it will drop in the near term due to the large increase in interest expense from the new debt.

Forecasting Income

Problem

By what percentage is Ideko's EBITDA expected to grow over the five-year period? By how much would it grow if Ideko's market share remained at 10%?

Solution

EBITDA will increase from $16.25 million to $32.09 million, or $(32.09 / 16.25) - 1 = 97\%$, over the five years. With a 10% market share rather than a 15% market share, sales will be only $(10\% / 15\%) = 66.7\%$ of the forecast in Table 19.7. Because Ideko's operating expenses are proportional to its sales, its expenses and EBITDA will also be 66.7% of the current estimates. Thus EBITDA will grow to $66.7\% \times 32.09 = \$21.40$ million, which is an increase of only $(21.40 / 16.25) - 1 = 32\%$.

Working Capital Requirements

The spreadsheet in Table 19.8 lists Ideko's current working capital requirements and forecasts the firm's future working capital needs. (See Chapter 26 for a further discussion of working capital requirements and their determinants.) This forecast includes the plans to tighten Ideko's credit policy, speed up customer payments, and reduce Ideko's inventory of raw materials.

TABLE 19.8 SPREADSHEET **Ideko's Working Capital Requirements**

		Year	2005	>2005
Working Capital Days				
Assets	**Based on:**		**Days**	**Days**
1 Accounts Receivable	Sales Revenue		90	60
2 Raw Materials	Raw Materials Costs		45	30
3 Finished Goods	Raw Materials + Labor Costs		45	45
4 Minimum Cash Balance	Sales Revenue		30	30
Liabilities				
5 Wages Payable	Direct Labor + Admin Costs		15	15
6 Other Accounts Payable	Raw Materials + Sales and Marketing		45	45

Based on these working capital requirements, the spreadsheet in Table 19.9 forecasts Ideko's net working capital (NWC) over the next five years. Each line item in the spreadsheet is found by computing the appropriate number of day's worth of the corresponding revenue or expense from the income statement (Table 19.7). For example, accounts receivable in 2006 is calculated as[4]

---

4. If products are highly seasonal, large fluctuations in working capital may occur over the course of the year. When these effects are important, it is best to develop forecasts on a quarterly or monthly basis so that the seasonal effects can be tracked.

$$\text{Accounts Receivable} = \text{Days Required} \times \frac{\text{Annual Sales}}{365 \text{ days / yr}}$$

$$= 60 \text{ days} \times \frac{\$88.358 \text{ million / yr}}{365 \text{ days / yr}} = \$14.525 \text{ million} \quad (19.7)$$

Similarly, Ideko's inventory of finished goods will be $45 \times (18.665 + 21.622) / 365 = \$4.967$ million.

TABLE 19.9 SPREADSHEET	Ideko's Net Working Capital Forecast					

	Year	2005	2006	2007	2008	2009	2010
Working Capital ($ 000)							
Assets							
1 Accounts Receivable		18,493	14,525	16,970	19,689	22,709	26,059
2 Raw Materials		1,973	1,534	1,775	2,039	2,329	2,646
3 Finished Goods		4,192	4,967	5,838	6,815	7,911	9,138
4 Minimum Cash Balance		6,164	7,262	8,485	9,845	11,355	13,030
5 Total Current Assets		30,822	28,288	33,067	38,388	44,304	50,872
Liabilities							
6 Wages Payable		1,294	1,433	1,695	1,941	2,211	2,570
7 Other Accounts Payable		3,360	4,099	4,953	5,938	6,900	7,878
8 Total Current Liabilities		4,654	5,532	6,648	7,879	9,110	10,448
Net Working Capital							
9 Net Working Capital (5 − 8)		26,168	22,756	26,419	30,509	35,194	40,425
10 Increase in Net Working Capital			(3,412)	3,663	4,089	4,685	5,231

Table 19.9 also lists Ideko's minimum cash balance each year. This balance represents the minimum level of cash needed to keep the business running smoothly, allowing for the daily variations in the timing of income and expenses. Firms generally earn little or no interest on these balances, which are held in cash or in a checking or short-term savings accounts. As a consequence, we account for this opportunity cost by including the minimal cash balance as part of the firm's working capital.

We assume that Ideko will earn no interest on this minimal balance. (If it did, this interest would reduce the firm's net interest expense in the income statement.) We also assume that Ideko will pay out as dividends all cash not needed as part of working capital. Therefore, Ideko will hold no excess cash balances or short-term investments above the minimal level reported in Table 19.9. If Ideko were to retain excess funds, these balances would be included as part of its financing strategy (reducing its net debt), and not as part of working capital.[5]

Ideko's net working capital for each year is computed in Table 19.9 as the difference between the forecasted current assets and current liabilities. Increases in net working capital represent a cost to the firm. Note that as a result of the improvements in accounts receivable and inventory management, Ideko will reduce its net working capital by more than $3.4 million in 2006. After this initial savings, working capital needs will increase in conjunction with the growth of the firm.

---

5. Firms often hold excess cash in anticipation of future investment needs or possible cash shortfalls. Because Ideko can rely on PKK to provide needed capital, excess cash reserves are unnecessary.

Forecasting Free Cash Flow

We now have the data needed to forecast Ideko's free cash flows over the next five years. Ideko's earnings are available from the income statement (Table 19.7), as are its depreciation and interest expenses. Capital expenditures are available from Table 19.4, and changes in net working capital can be found in Table 19.9. We combine these items to estimate the free cash flows in the spreadsheet in Table 19.10.

TABLE 19.10 SPREADSHEET	Ideko's Free Cash Flow Forecast						
	Year	2005	2006	2007	2008	2009	2010
Free Cash Flow ($ 000)							
1 Net Income			5,193	6,247	6,960	8,382	10,545
2 Plus: After-Tax Interest Expense			4,420	4,420	4,420	5,083	5,304
3 Unlevered Net Income			9,613	10,667	11,380	13,465	15,849
4 Plus: Depreciation			5,450	5,405	6,865	7,678	7,710
5 Less: Increases in NWC			3,412	(3,663)	(4,089)	(4,685)	(5,231)
6 Less: Capital Expenditures			(5,000)	(5,000)	(20,000)	(15,000)	(8,000)
7 Free Cash Flow of Firm			13,475	7,409	(5,845)	1,458	10,328
8 Plus: Net Borrowing			—	—	15,000	5,000	—
9 Less: After-Tax Interest Expense			(4,420)	(4,420)	(4,420)	(5,083)	(5,304)
10 Free Cash Flow to Equity			9,055	2,989	4,735	1,375	5,024

To compute Ideko's free cash flow, which excludes cash flows associated with leverage, we first adjust net income by adding back the after-tax interest payments associated with the net debt in its capital structure:[6]

$$\text{After-Tax Interest Expense} =$$
$$(1 - \text{Tax Rate}) \times (\text{Interest on Debt} - \text{Interest on Excess Cash}) \quad (19.8)$$

Because Ideko has no excess cash, its after-tax interest expense in 2006 is $(1 - 35\%) \times 6.8 = \$4.42$ million, providing unlevered net income of $5.193 + 4.42 = \$9.613$ million. We could also compute the unlevered net income in Table 19.10 by starting with EBIT and deducting taxes. In 2006, for example, EBIT is forecasted as $14.788 million, which amounts to $14.788 \times (1 - 35\%) = \$9.613$ million after taxes.

To compute Ideko's free cash flow from its unlevered net income, we add back depreciation (which is not a cash expense), and deduct Ideko's increases in net working capital and capital expenditures. The free cash flow on line 7 of Table 19.10 shows the cash the firm will generate for its investors, both debt and equity holders. While Ideko will generate substantial free cash flow over the next five years, the level of free cash flow varies substantially from year to year. It is highest in 2006 (due mostly to the large reduction in working capital) and is forecasted to be negative in 2008 (when the plant expansion will begin).

To determine the free cash flow to equity, we first add Ideko's net borrowing (that is, increases to net debt):

$$\text{Net Borrowing in Year } t = \text{Net Debt in Year } t - \text{Net Debt in Year } (t - 1) \quad (19.9)$$

---

6. If Ideko had some interest income or expenses from working capital, we would *not* include that interest here. We adjust only for interest that is related to the firm's *financing*—that is, interest associated with debt and *excess* cash (cash not included as part of working capital).

Ideko will borrow in 2008 and 2009 as part of its expansion. We then deduct the after-tax interest payments that were added in line 2.

As shown in the last line of Table 19.10, during the next five years Ideko is expected to generate a positive free cash flow to equity, which will be used to pay dividends to PKK. The free cash flow to equity will be highest in 2006; by 2010, PKK will recoup a significant fraction of its initial investment.

EXAMPLE 19.4

Leverage and Free Cash Flow

Problem

Suppose Ideko does not add leverage in 2008 and 2009, but instead keeps its debt fixed at $100 million until 2010. How would this change in its leverage policy affect its expected free cash flow? How would it affect the free cash flow to equity?

Solution

Because free cash flow is based on unlevered net income, it will not be affected by Ideko's leverage policy. Free cash flow to equity will be affected, however. Net borrowing will be zero each year, and the firm's after-tax interest expense will remain at the 2006 level of $4.42 million:

Year	2005	2006	2007	2008	2009	2010
Free Cash Flow ($ 000)						
1 Free Cash Flow of Firm		13,475	7,409	(5,845)	1,458	10,328
2 Plus: Net Borrowing		–	–	–	–	–
3 Less: After-Tax Interest Expense		(4,420)	(4,420)	(4,420)	(4,420)	(4,420)
4 Free Cash Flow to Equity		9,055	2,989	(10,265)	(2,962)	5,908

In this case, Ideko will have a negative free cash flow to equity in 2008 and 2009. That is, without additional borrowing, PKK will have to invest additional capital in the firm to fund the expansion.

The Balance Sheet and Statement of Cash Flows (Optional)

The information we have calculated so far can be used to project Ideko's balance sheet and statement of cash flows through 2010. While these statements are not critical for our valuation, they often prove helpful in providing a more complete picture of how a firm will grow during the forecast period. These statements for Ideko are shown in the spreadsheets in Tables 19.11 and 19.12.

On the balance sheet (Table 19.11), current assets and liabilities come from the net working capital spreadsheet (Table 19.9). The inventory entry on the balance sheet includes both raw materials and finished goods. Property, plant, and equipment information comes from the capital expenditure spreadsheet (Table 19.4), and the debt comes from Table 19.5. The goodwill entry arises from the difference in the acquisition price and Ideko's initial book value of equity in Table 19.1:[7]

$$\text{New Goodwill} = \text{Acquisition Price} - \text{Existing Book Value of Equity} \quad (19.10)$$

---

7. There are a number of potential complications to the goodwill calculation that we ignore here. In particular, transaction fees directly attributable to the acquisition (but not to the debt issue) would generally be included in the purchase price. Also, in some cases a portion of the purchase price can be allocated to intangible assets as opposed to goodwill.

Given the acquisition price of $150 million, the new goodwill is $150 − 77.668 = 72.332 million. The stockholders' equity of $48 million in 2005 arises from PKK's initial equity contribution of $50 million (the $150 million purchase price less $100 million financed with debt) less the $2 million in dividends paid ($6.5 million in excess cash less $4.5 million in debt repaid). The stockholders' equity increases each year through retained earnings (net income less dividends) and new capital contributions. Dividends after 2005 are taken from the free cash flow to equity given in Table 19.10. (If free cash flow to equity were negative in any year, it would appear as a capital contribution in line 14 of the balance sheet.) As a check on the calculations, note that the balance sheet does, indeed, balance: Total assets equal total liabilities and equity.[8]

TABLE 19.11 SPREADSHEET

Pro Forma Balance Sheet for Ideko, 2005–2010

Year	2005	2006	2007	2008	2009	2010
Balance Sheet ($ 000)						
Assets						
1 Cash and Cash Equivalents	6,164	7,262	8,485	9,845	11,355	13,030
2 Accounts Receivable	18,493	14,525	16,970	19,689	22,709	26,059
3 Inventories	6,165	6,501	7,613	8,854	10,240	11,784
4 Total Current Assets	30,822	28,288	33,067	38,388	44,304	50,872
5 Property, Plant, and Equipment	49,500	49,050	48,645	61,781	69,102	69,392
6 Goodwill	72,332	72,332	72,332	72,332	72,332	72,332
7 Total Assets	152,654	149,670	154,044	172,501	185,738	192,597
Liabilities						
8 Accounts Payable	4,654	5,532	6,648	7,879	9,110	10,448
9 Debt	100,000	100,000	100,000	115,000	120,000	120,000
10 Total Liabilities	104,654	105,532	106,648	122,879	129,110	130,448
Stockholder's Equity						
11 Starting Stockholder's Equity		48,000	44,138	47,396	49,621	56,628
12 Net Income		5,193	6,247	6,960	8,382	10,545
13 Dividends	(2,000)	(9,055)	(2,989)	(4,735)	(1,375)	(5,024)
14 Capital Contributions	50,000	—	—	—	—	—
15 Stockholder's Equity	48,000	44,138	47,396	49,621	56,628	62,149
16 Total Liabilities and Equity	152,654	149,670	154,044	172,501	185,738	192,597

Ideko's book value of equity will decline in 2006, as Ideko reduces its working capital and pays out the savings as part of a large dividend. The firm's book value will then rise as it expands. Ideko's book debt-equity ratio will decline from $100,000 / 48,000 = 2.1$ to $120,000 / 62,149 = 1.9$ during the five-year period.

The statement of cash flows in Table 19.12 starts with net income. Cash from operating activities includes depreciation as well as changes to working capital items (other than cash) from Table 19.9. Cash from investing activities includes the capital expenditures in Table 19.4. Cash from financing activities includes net borrowing from Table 19.10,

---

8. In Table 19.11, goodwill is assumed to remain constant. If the transaction were structured as an acquisition of assets (as opposed to stock), the goodwill would be amortizable over 15 years for tax reporting as specified in section 197 of Internal Revenue Code. For financial accounting purposes, goodwill is not amortized but is subject to an impairment test at least once a year as specified in FASB 142, so the amount of goodwill may change over time (though any changes in goodwill due to impairment have no tax accounting consequences).

TABLE 19.12 SPREADSHEET	Pro Forma Statement of Cash Flows for Ideko, 2005–2010

Year	2005	2006	2007	2008	2009	2010
Statement of Cash Flows ($ 000)						
1 Net Income		5,193	6,247	6,960	8,382	10,545
2 Depreciation		5,450	5,405	6,865	7,678	7,710
3 Changes in Working Capital						
4 Accounts Receivable		3,968	(2,445)	(2,719)	(3,020)	(3,350)
5 Inventory		(336)	(1,112)	(1,242)	(1,385)	(1,544)
6 Accounts Payable		878	1,116	1,231	1,231	1,338
7 **Cash from Operating Activities**		15,153	9,211	11,095	12,885	14,699
8 Capital Expenditures		(5,000)	(5,000)	(20,000)	(15,000)	(8,000)
9 Other Investment		—	—	—	—	—
10 **Cash from Investing Activities**		(5,000)	(5,000)	(20,000)	(15,000)	(8,000)
11 Net Borrowing		—	—	15,000	5,000	—
12 Dividends		(9,055)	(2,989)	(4,735)	(1,375)	(5,024)
13 Capital Contributions		—	—	—	—	—
14 **Cash from Financing Activities**		(9,055)	(2,989)	10,265	3,625	(5,024)
15 **Change in Cash** (7 + 10 + 14)		1,098	1,223	1,360	1,510	1,675

and dividends or capital contributions determined by the free cash flow to equity in Table 19.10. As a final check on the calculations, note that the change in cash and cash equivalents on line 15 equals the change in the minimum cash balance shown on the balance sheet (Table 19.11).

CONCEPT CHECK

1. What is a pro forma income statement?

2. How do we calculate the firm's free cash flow, and the free cash flow to equity?

19.4 Estimating the Cost of Capital

To value PKK's investment in Ideko, we need to assess the risk associated with Ideko and estimate an appropriate cost of capital. Because Ideko is a private firm, we cannot use its own past returns to evaluate its risk, but must instead rely on comparable publicly traded firms. In this section, we use data from the comparable firms identified earlier to estimate a cost of capital for Ideko.

Our approach is as follows. First, we use the techniques developed in Part IV of the text to estimate the equity cost of capital for Oakley, Luxottica Group, and Nike. We then estimate the unlevered cost of capital for each firm based on its capital structure. The unlevered cost of capital of the comparable firms are next used to estimate Ideko's unlevered cost of capital. Once we have this estimate, we can use Ideko's capital structure to determine its equity cost of capital or WACC, depending on the valuation method employed.

CAPM-Based Estimation

To determine an appropriate cost of capital, we must first determine the appropriate measure of risk. PKK's investment in Ideko will represent a large fraction of its portfolio. As a consequence, PKK itself is not well diversified. But PKK's investors are primarily pension funds and large institutional investors which are themselves well diversified and which evaluate their performance relative to the market as a benchmark. Thus you decide that estimating market risk using the CAPM approach is justified.

Using the CAPM, we can estimate the equity cost of capital for each comparable firm based on the beta of its equity. As outlined in Chapter 12, the standard approach to estimating an equity beta is to determine the historical sensitivity of the stock's returns to the market's returns by using linear regression to estimate the slope coefficient in the equation:

$$\underbrace{R_s - r_f}_{\substack{\text{Excess return} \\ \text{of stock } s}} = \alpha_s + \beta_s \underbrace{(R_{mkt} - r_f)}_{\substack{\text{Excess return} \\ \text{of market portfolio}}} + \varepsilon_s \qquad (19.11)$$

As a proxy for the market portfolio, we will use a value-weighted portfolio of all NYSE, AMEX, and Nasdaq stocks. With data from 2000 to 2004, we calculate the excess return—the realized return minus the yield on a one-month Treasury security—for each firm and for the market portfolio. We then estimate the equity beta for each firm by regressing its excess return onto the excess return of the market portfolio. We perform the regression for both monthly returns and ten-day returns. The estimated equity betas, together with their 95% confidence intervals, are shown in Table 19.13.

TABLE 19.13   **Equity Betas with Confidence Intervals for Comparable Firms**

	Monthly Returns		Ten-Day Returns	
Firm	**Beta**	**95% C.I.**	**Beta**	**95% C.I.**
Oakley	1.99	1.2 to 2.8	1.37	0.9 to 1.9
Luxottica	0.56	0.0 to 1.1	0.86	0.5 to 1.2
Nike	0.48	−0.1 to 1.0	0.69	0.4 to 1.0

While we would like to assess risk and, therefore, estimate beta based on longer horizon returns (consistent with our investors' investment horizon), the confidence intervals we obtain using monthly data are extremely wide. These confidence intervals narrow somewhat when we use ten-day returns. In any case, the results make clear that a fair amount of uncertainty persists when we estimate the beta for an individual firm.

Unlevering Beta

Given an estimate of each firm's equity beta, we next "unlever" the beta based on the firm's capital structure. Here we use Eq. 14.9 (which is equivalent, in terms of returns, to calculating the pretax WACC as in Eq. 18.6):

$$\beta_U = \left(\frac{\text{Equity Value}}{\text{Enterprise Value}} \right) \beta_E + \left(\frac{\text{Net Debt Value}}{\text{Enterprise Value}} \right) \beta_D \qquad (19.12)$$

Recall that we must use the *net* debt of the firm—that is, we must subtract any cash from the level of debt—so we use the enterprise value of the firm as the sum of debt and equity in the formula.[9] Table 19.14 shows the capital structure for each comparable firm. Oakley has no debt, while Luxottica has about 17% debt in its capital structure. Nike holds cash that exceeds its debt, leading to a negative net debt in its capital structure.

TABLE 19.14		**Capital Structure and Unlevered Beta Estimates for Comparable Firms**			
Firm	$\dfrac{E}{E + D}$	$\dfrac{D}{E + D}$	β_E	β_D	β_U
Oakley	1.00	0.00	1.50	—	1.50
Luxottica	0.83	0.17	0.75	0	0.62
Nike	1.05	−0.05	0.60	0	0.63

Table 19.14 also estimates the unlevered beta of each firm. Here we have used an equity beta for each firm within the range of the results from Table 19.13. Given the low or negative debt levels for each firm, assuming a beta for debt of zero is a reasonable approximation. We then compute an unlevered beta for each firm according to Eq. 19.12.

The range of the unlevered betas for these three firms is large. Both Luxottica and Nike have relatively low betas, presumably reflecting the relative noncyclicality of their core businesses (prescription eyewear for Luxottica and athletic shoes for Nike). Oakley has a much higher unlevered beta, perhaps because the high-end specialty sports eyewear it produces is a discretionary expense for most consumers.

Ideko's Unlevered Cost of Capital

The data from the comparable firms provides guidance to us for estimating Ideko's unlevered cost of capital. Ideko's products are not as high end as Oakley's eyewear, so their sales are unlikely to vary as much with the business cycle as Oakley's sales do. However, Ideko does not have a prescription eyewear division, as Luxottica does. Ideko's products are also fashion items rather than exercise items, so we expect Ideko's cost of capital to be closer to Oakley's than to Nike's or Luxottica's. We therefore use 1.20 as our preliminary estimate for Ideko's unlevered beta, which is somewhat above the average of the comparables in Table 19.14.

We use the security market line of the CAPM to translate this beta into a cost of capital for Ideko. In mid-2005, one-year Treasury rates were approximately 4%; we use this rate for the risk-free interest rate. We also need an estimate of the market risk premium. Since 1960, the average annual return of the value-weighted market portfolio of U.S. stocks has exceeded that of one-year Treasuries by approximately 5%. However, this estimate is a backward-looking number. As we mentioned in Chapter 12, some researchers believe that future stock market excess returns are likely to be lower than this historical average. To be conservative in our valuation of Ideko, we will use 5% as the expected market risk premium.

---

9. Recall from Chapter 18 that Eq. 19.12 assumes that the firm will maintain a target leverage ratio. If the debt is expected to remain fixed for some period, we should also deduct the value of the predetermined tax shields from the firm's net debt.

Based on these choices, our estimate of Ideko's unlevered cost of capital is

$$r_U = r_f + \beta_U(E[R_{mkt}] - r_f) = 4\% + 1.20(5\%)$$
$$= 10\%$$

Of course, as our discussion has made clear, this estimate contains a large amount of uncertainty. Thus we will include sensitivity analysis with regard to the unlevered cost of capital in our analysis.

Estimating the Unlevered Cost of Capital

Problem

Using the monthly equity beta estimates for each firm in Table 19.13, what range of unlevered cost of capital estimates is possible?

Solution

Oakley has the highest equity beta of 1.99, which is also its unlevered beta (it has no debt). With this beta, the unlevered cost of capital would be $r_U = 4\% + 1.99(5\%) = 13.95\%$. At the other extreme, given its capital structure, Luxottica's equity beta of 0.56 implies an unlevered beta of $(0.56)(0.83) = 0.46$. With this beta, the unlevered cost of capital would be $r_U = 4\% + 0.46(5\%) = 6.3\%$.

As with any analysis based on comparables, experience and judgment are necessary to come up with a reasonable estimate of the unlevered cost of capital. In this case, our choice would be guided by industry norms, an assessment of which comparable is closest in terms of market risk, and possibly knowledge of how cyclical Ideko's revenues have been historically.

CONCEPT CHECK

1. How do we estimate a firm's unlevered cost of capital using data from comparable publicly traded firms?

2. What is a standard approach to estimate an equity beta?

19.5 Valuing the Investment

Thus far, we have forecasted the first five years of cash flows from PKK's investment in Ideko, and we have estimated the investment's unlevered cost of capital. In this section, we combine these inputs to estimate the value of the opportunity. The first step is to develop an estimate of Ideko's value at the end of our five-year forecast horizon. To do so, we consider both a multiples approach and a discounted cash flow (DCF) valuation using the WACC method. Given Ideko's free cash flow and continuation value, we then estimate its total enterprise value in 2005 using the APV method. Deducting the value of debt and PKK's initial investment from our estimate of Ideko's enterprise value gives the NPV of the investment opportunity. In addition to NPV, we look at some other common metrics, including IRR and cash multiples.

The Multiples Approach to Continuation Value

Practitioners generally estimate a firm's continuation value (also called the terminal value) at the end of the forecast horizon using a valuation multiple. While forecasting cash flows explicitly is useful in capturing those specific aspects of a company that distinguish the firm from its competitors in the short run, in the long run firms in the same industry typically have similar expected growth rates, profitability, and risk. As a consequence, multiples are likely to be relatively homogeneous across firms. Thus applying a multiple is potentially as reliable as estimating the value based on an explicit forecast of distant cash flows.

Of the different valuation multiples available, the EBITDA multiple is most often used in practice. In most settings, the EBITDA multiple is more reliable than sales or earnings multiples because it accounts for the firm's operating efficiency and is not affected by leverage differences between firms. We estimate the continuation value using an EBITDA multiple as follows:

$$\text{Continuation Enterprise Value at Forecast Horizon} =$$
$$\text{EBITDA at Horizon} \times \text{EBITDA Multiple at Horizon} \quad (19.13)$$

From the income statement in Table 19.7, Ideko's EBITDA in 2010 is forecast to be $32.09 million. If we assume its EBITDA multiple in 2010 is unchanged from the value of 9.1 that we calculated at the time of the original purchase, then Ideko's continuation value in 2010 is $32.09 \times 9.1 = 292.05 million. This calculation is shown in the spreadsheet in Table 19.15. Given Ideko's outstanding debt of $120 million in 2010, this estimate corresponds to an equity value of $172.05 million.

TABLE 19.15 SPREADSHEET	**Continuation Value Estimate for Ideko**

Continuation Value: Multiples Approach ($ 000)		Common Multiples	
1 EBITDA in 2010	32,094	Common Multiples	
2 EBITDA multiple	9.1×	EV/Sales	1.8×
3 Continuation Enterprise Value	292,052	P/E (levered)	16.3×
4 Debt	(120,000)	P/E (unlevered)	18.4×
5 Continuation Equity Value	172,052		

Table 19.15 also shows Ideko's sales and P/E multiples based on this continuation value. The continuation value is 1.8 times Ideko's 2010 sales, and the equity value is 16.3 times Ideko's 2010 earnings. Because the P/E multiple is affected by leverage, we also report Ideko's **unlevered P/E ratio**, which is calculated as its continuing enterprise value divided by its unlevered net income in 2010 (listed in Table 19.10). Ideko would have this P/E ratio if it had no debt in 2010, so this information is useful when comparing Ideko to unlevered firms in the industry.

We can use the various multiples to assess the reasonableness of our estimated continuation value. While the value-to-sales ratio is high compared to the overall sporting goods industry, these multiples are otherwise low relative to the comparables in Table 19.2, and we would consider this estimate of Ideko's continuation value as reasonable (if not relatively conservative).

The Discounted Cash Flow Approach to Continuation Value

One difficulty with relying solely on comparables when forecasting a continuation value is that we are comparing *future* multiples of the firm with *current* multiples of its competitors. In 2010, the multiples of Ideko and the comparables we have chosen may all be very different, especially if the industry is currently experiencing abnormal growth. To guard against such a bias, it is wise to check our estimate of the continuation value based on fundamentals using a discounted cash flow approach.

To estimate a continuation value in year T using discounted cash flows, we assume a constant expected growth rate, g, and a constant debt-equity ratio. As explained in Chapter 18, when the debt-equity ratio is constant, the WACC valuation method is the simplest to apply:

$$\text{Enterprise Value in Year } T = V_T^L = \frac{FCF_{T+1}}{r_{wacc} - g} \qquad (19.14)$$

To estimate free cash flow in year $T + 1$, recall that free cash flow is equal to unlevered net income plus depreciation, less capital expenditures and increases in net working capital (see Table 19.10):

$$FCF_{T+1} = \text{Unlevered Net Income}_{T+1} + \text{Depreciation}_{T+1}$$
$$- \text{Increases in NWC}_{T+1} - \text{Capital Expenditures}_{T+1} \qquad (19.15)$$

Suppose the firm's sales are expected to grow at a nominal rate g. If the firm's operating expenses remain a fixed percentage of sales, then its unlevered net income will also grow at rate g. Similarly, the firm's receivables, payables, and other elements of net working capital will grow at rate g.

What about capital expenditures? The firm will need new capital to offset depreciation; it will also need to add capacity as its production volume grows. Given a sales growth rate g, we may expect that the firm will need to expand its investment in fixed assets at the same rate. In that case,[10]

$$\text{Capital Expenditures}_{T+1} = \text{Depreciation}_{T+1} + g \times \text{Fixed Assets}_T$$

Thus, given a growth rate of g for the firm, we can estimate its free cash flow as

$$FCF_{T+1} = (1 + g) \times \text{Unlevered Net Income}_T - g \times \text{Net Working Capital}_T$$
$$- g \times \text{Fixed Assets}_T \qquad (19.16)$$

Together, Eqs. 19.14 and 19.16 allow us to estimate a firm's continuation value based on its long-run growth rate.

A DCF Estimate of the Continuation Value

Problem
Estimate Ideko's continuation value in 2010 assuming a future expected growth rate of 5%, a future debt-to-value ratio of 40%, and a debt cost of capital of 6.8%.

---

10. Here, fixed assets are measured according to their book value net of accumulated depreciation. This level of capital expenditures is required to maintain the firm's ratio of sales to fixed assets (also called its fixed asset turnover ratio). However, a number of factors could affect the required level of capital expenditures needed to sustain a given growth rate. For example, some amount of revenue growth may be accommodated through productivity gains (or be the result of inflation), rather than an increase in fixed assets. Also, the book value of the firm's fixed assets may misrepresent the cost of adding new assets (one could consider market value instead). Absent knowledge of these details, the approach taken here provides a reasonable estimate.

Solution

In 2010, Ideko's unlevered net income is forecasted to be $15.849 million (Table 19.10), with working capital of $40.425 million (Table 19.9). It has fixed assets of $69.392 million (Table 19.4). From Eq. 19.16, we can estimate Ideko's free cash flow in 2011:

$$FCF_{2011} = (1.05)(15.849) - (5\%)(40.425) - (5\%)(69.392) = \$11.151 \text{ million}$$

This estimate represents nearly an 8% increase over Ideko's 2010 free cash flow of $10.328 million. It exceeds the 5% growth rate of sales due to the decline in the required additions to Ideko's net working capital as its growth rate slows.

With a debt-to-value ratio of 40%, Ideko's WACC can be calculated from Eq. 18.11:

$$r_{wacc} = r_U - d\,\tau_c\,r_D = 10\% - 0.40(0.35)\,6.8\% = 9.05\%$$

Given the estimate of Ideko's free cash flow and WACC, we can estimate Ideko's continuation value in 2010:

$$V_{2010}^L = \frac{11.151}{9.05\% - 5\%} = \$275.33 \text{ million}$$

This continuation value represents a terminal EBITDA multiple of 275.33 / 32.09 − 8.6.

Both the multiples approach and the discounted cash flow approach are useful in deriving a realistic continuation value estimate. Our recommendation is to combine both approaches, as we do in Table 19.16. As shown in the spreadsheet, our projected EBITDA multiple of 9.1 can be justified according the discounted cash flow method with a nominal long-term growth rate of about 5.3%.[11] Given an inflation rate of 2%, this nominal rate represents a real growth rate of about 3.3%. This implied growth rate is another important reality check for our continuation value estimate. If it is much higher than our expectations of long-run growth for the industry as a whole, we should be more skeptical of the estimate being used.

TABLE 19.16 SPREADSHEET	**Discounted Cash Flow Estimate of Continuation Value, with Implied EBITDA Multiple**

Continuation Value: DCF and EBITDA Multiple ($ 000)			
1 Long-Term Growth Rate	5.3%		
2 Target D/(E + D)	40.0%		
3 Projected WACC	9.05%		
Free Cash Flow in 2011			
4 Unlevered Net Income	16,695	Continuation Enterprise Value	292,052
5 Less: Increase in NWC	(2,158)		
6 Less: Increase in Fixed Assets*	(3,705)	Implied EBITDA Multiple	9.1×
7 Free Cash Flow	10,832		

*The increase in fixed assets equals the difference between capital expenditures and depreciation, and so subtracting this amount is equivalent to adding back depreciation and subtracting capital expenditures.

---

11. The exact nominal growth rate needed to match an EBITDA multiple of 9.1 is 5.33897%, which can be found using Solver in Excel.

COMMON MISTAKE   Continuation Values and Long-Run Growth

The continuation value is one of the most important estimates when valuing a firm. A common mistake is to use an overly optimistic continuation value, which will lead to an upward bias in the estimated current value of the firm. Here are several pitfalls to beware of:

Using multiples based on current high growth rates. Continuation value estimates are often based on current valuation multiples of existing firms. But if these firms are currently experiencing high growth that will eventually slow down, their multiples can be expected to decline over time. In this scenario, if we estimate a continuation value based on today's multiples without accounting for this decline as growth slows, the estimate will be biased upward.

Ignoring investment necessary for growth. When using the discounted cash flow method, we cannot assume that $FCF_{T+1} = FCF_T (1 + g)$ if the firm's growth rate has changed between T and $T + 1$. Whenever the growth rate changes, expenditures on working and fixed capital will be affected, and we must take this effect into account as we do in Eq. 19.16.

Using unsustainable long-term growth rates. When using the discounted cash flow method, we must choose a long-term growth rate for the firm. By choosing a high rate, we can make the continuation value estimate extremely high. In the long run, however, firms cannot continue to grow faster than the overall economy. Thus we should be suspicious of long-term growth rates that exceed the expected rate of GDP growth, which has averaged between 3% and 4% in *real* terms (that is, not including inflation) in the United States over the past several decades.

APV Valuation of Ideko Equity

Our estimate of Ideko's continuation value summarizes the value of the firm's free cash flow beyond the forecast horizon. We can combine it with our forecast for free cash flow through 2010 (Table 19.10, line 7) to estimate Ideko's value today. Recall from Chapter 18 that because the debt is paid on a fixed schedule during the forecast period, the APV method is the easiest valuation method to apply.

The steps to estimate Ideko's value using the APV method are shown in the spreadsheet in Table 19.17. First, we compute Ideko's unlevered value V^U, which is the firm's value if we were to operate the company without leverage during the forecast period and sell it for its continuation value at the end of the forecast horizon. Thus the final value in 2010 would be the continuation value we estimated in Table 19.15. The value in earlier periods includes the free cash flows paid by the firm (from Table 19.10) discounted at the unlevered cost of capital r_U that we estimated in Section 19.4:

$$V_{t-1}^U = \frac{FCF_t + V_t^U}{1 + r_U} \tag{19.17}$$

Next, we incorporate Ideko's interest tax shield during the forecast horizon. The interest tax shield equals the tax rate of 35% (Table 19.3) multiplied by Ideko's scheduled interest payments (see Table 19.5). Because the debt levels are predetermined, we compute the value T^s of the tax shield by discounting the tax savings at the debt interest rate, $r_D = 6.80\%$:

$$T_{t-1}^s = \frac{\text{Interest Tax Shield}_t + T_t^s}{1 + r_D} \tag{19.18}$$

Combining the unlevered value and the tax shield value gives the APV, which is Ideko's enterprise value given the planned leverage policy. By deducting debt, we obtain our estimate for the value of Ideko's equity during the forecast period.

TABLE 19.17 SPREADSHEET	APV Estimate of Ideko's Initial Equity Value						
Year		2005	2006	2007	2008	2009	2010
APV Method ($ 000)							
1 Free Cash Flow			13,475	7,409	(5,845)	1,458	10,328
2 Unlevered Value V^u		202,732	209,530	223,075	251,227	274,891	292,052
3 Interest Tax Shield			2,380	2,380	2,380	2,737	2,856
4 Tax Shield Value T^s		10,428	8,757	6,972	5,067	2,674	—
5 APV: $V^L = V^u + T^s$		213,160	218,287	230,047	256,294	277,566	292,052
6 Debt		(100,000)	(100,000)	(100,000)	(115,000)	(120,000)	(120,000)
7 Equity Value		113,160	118,287	130,047	141,294	157,566	172,052

Thus our estimate for Ideko's initial enterprise value is $213 million, with an equity value of $113 million. As PKK's initial cost to acquire Ideko's equity is $53 million (see Table 19.6), based on these estimates the deal looks attractive, with an NPV of $113 million − $53 million = $60 million.

A Reality Check

At this point, it is wise to step back and assess whether our valuation results make sense. Does an initial enterprise value of $213 million for Ideko seem reasonable compared to the values of other firms in the industry?

Here again, multiples are helpful. Let's compute the initial valuation multiples that would be implied by our estimated enterprise value of $213 million and compare them to Ideko's closest competitors as we did in Table 19.2. Table 19.18 provides our results.

Naturally, the valuation multiples based on the estimated enterprise value of $213 million, which would correspond to a purchase price of $215 million given Ideko's existing debt and excess cash, are higher than those based on a purchase price of $150 million. They are now at the top end or somewhat above the range of the values of the other firms that we used for comparison. While these multiples are not unreasonable given the operational improvements that PKK plans to implement, they indicate that our projections may be somewhat optimistic and depend critically on PKK's ability to achieve the operational improvements it plans.

COMMON MISTAKE   **Missing Assets or Liabilities**

When computing the enterprise value of a firm from its free cash flows, remember that we are valuing only those assets and liabilities whose cash flow consequences are included in our projections. Any "missing" assets or liabilities must be added to the APV estimate to determine the value of equity. In this case, we deduct the firm's debt and add any excess cash or other marketable securities that have not been included (for Ideko, excess cash has already been paid out and will remain at zero, so no adjustment is needed). We also adjust for any other assets or liabilities that have not been explicitly considered. For example, if a firm owns vacant land, or if it has patents or other rights whose potential cash flows were not included in the projections, the value of these assets must be accounted for separately. The same is true for liabilities such as stock option grants, potential legal liabilities, leases (if the lease payments were not included in earnings), or underfunded pension liabilities.

TABLE 19.18	**Ideko Financial Ratios Comparison, Mid-2005, Based on Discounted Cash Flow Estimate Versus Proposed Purchase Price**

Ratio	Ideko (Estimated Value)	Ideko (Purchase Price)	Oakley, Inc.	Luxottica Group	Nike, Inc.	Sporting Goods
P/E	31.0×	21.6×	24.8×	28.0×	18.2×	20.3×
EV/Sales	2.8×	2.0×	2.0×	2.7×	1.5×	1.4×
EV/EBITDA	13.1×	9.1×	11.6×	14.4×	9.3×	11.4×

Our estimated initial EBITDA multiple of 13.1 also exceeds the multiple of 9.1 that we assumed for the continuation value. Thus our estimate forecasts a decline in the EBITDA multiple, which is appropriate given our expectation that growth will be higher in the short run. If the multiple did not decline, we should question whether our continuation value is too optimistic.

IRR and Cash Multiples

While the NPV method is the most reliable method when evaluating a transaction like PKK's acquisition of Ideko, real-world practitioners often use IRR and the *cash multiple* (or *multiple of money*) as alternative valuation metrics. We discuss both of these methods in this section.

To compute the IRR, we must compute PKK's cash flows over the life of the transaction. PKK's initial investment in Ideko, from Table 19.6, is $53 million. PKK will then receive cash dividends from Ideko based on the free cash flow to equity reported in Table 19.10. Finally, we assume that PKK will sell its equity share in Ideko at the end of five years, receiving the continuation equity value. We combine these data to determine PKK's cash flows in the spreadsheet in Table 19.19. Given the cash flows, we compute the IRR of the transaction, which is 33.3%.

TABLE 19.19 SPREADSHEET	**IRR and Cash Multiple for PKK's Investment in Ideko**

	Year	2005	2006	2007	2008	2009	2010
IRR and Cash Multiple							
1 Initial Investment		(53,000)					
2 Free Cash Flow to Equity			9,055	2,989	4,735	1,375	5,024
3 Continuation Equity Value							172,052
4 PKK Cash Flows		(53,000)	9,055	2,989	4,735	1,375	177,077
5 IRR		33.3%					
6 Cash Multiple		3.7×					

While an IRR of 33.3% might sound attractive, it is not straightforward to evaluate in this context. To do so, we must compare it to the appropriate cost of capital for PKK's investment. Because PKK holds an equity position in Ideko, we should use Ideko's equity cost of capital. Of course, Ideko's leverage ratio changes over the five-year period, which

INTERVIEW WITH
Joseph L. Rice, III

J oseph L. Rice, III is a founding
partner and Chairman of Clayton,
Dubilier & Rice (CD&R). Since its
formation in 1978, the firm has
invested more than $6 billion in
38 businesses with an aggregate transaction value in excess of $40 billion.

QUESTION: *How has private equity
business changed since you began
in the industry?*

ANSWER: The term "private equity"
is very broad and today can cover virtually every kind
of investing, short of investing in the stock or bond
markets. The buyout business represents a significant
component of the private equity market. Since I started
in 1966, I've seen many changes as the asset class has
matured. In the 1960s and 1970s, the buyout business
had relatively little following. Limited capital availability
kept transactions small, and we relied on unconven-
tional funding sources. The total purchase price of my
first transaction was approximately $3 million, financed
through a secured bank line and from individuals contributing amounts ranging from $25,000 to $50,000.
In contrast, recently we bought Hertz from Ford for
approximately $15 billion.

As the industry has evolved, the attractive returns
generated from buyout investments has attracted
broader interest from both institutions and high net
worth individuals. Buyout firms apply a variety of value
creation models, including financial engineering, multiple arbitrage, and industry sector bets, such as technology or healthcare. Today there is more focus on
generating returns from improving business performance—which has always been CD&R's underlying
investment approach. The character of the businesses
that we buy has also changed. Traditionally, this was an
asset-heavy business, with much of the financing coming
from banks that lent against percentages of inventory
and receivables and the liquidation value of hard assets.
Now it's become more of a cash flow business.

QUESTION: *What makes a company a good buyout
candidate?*

ANSWER: We look to acquire good businesses at fair
prices. Acquiring non-core, underperforming divisions
of large companies and making them more effective has

been a fertile investment area for
CD&R. These divestiture buyouts
tend to be complex and require
experience and patience to execute.
For example, we were in discussions
with Ford management for three
years prior to leading the Hertz division acquisition.

After running a series of projections based on information from
management, we develop a capital
structure designed to insure the
viability of the acquisition candidate.
We are relatively unconcerned with EPS but are
very return conscious, focusing on cash and creating
long-term shareholder value. We must also believe that
we can generate a return on equity that meets our standards and justifies our investors' commitments to us.

We also acquire businesses confronting strategic
issues where our operating expertise can bring value,
such as Kinko's, a great brand franchise that we reorganized and expanded. We prefer service and distribution
businesses to large manufacturers because of the wage
differential between Asia and the United States and
Europe. We also prefer businesses with a diversity of suppliers and customers and where there are multiple levers
under our control to improve operating performance.

QUESTION: *Post acquisition, what is the role of the
private equity firm?*

ANSWER: CD&R brings both a hands-on ownership
style and capital. After closing a transaction, we assess
current management's capability to do the job our
investment case calls for. If necessary, we build and
strengthen the management team. Then we work with
them to determine the appropriate strategy to produce
outstanding results. Finally, we aggressively pursue
productivity, cost reduction, and growth initiatives
to enhance operating and financial performance. At
Kinko's, we restructured 129 separate S-corporations
into one centralized corporation and installed a new
management team. Our key strategic decision was trans-
forming Kinko's from a loose confederation of consumer
and small business-oriented copy shops into a highly
networked company serving major corporations. In the
end, that is what made the company an attractive acquisition for FedEx in 2004.

will change the risk of its equity. Thus there is no single cost of capital to compare to the IRR.[12]

The spreadsheet in Table 19.19 also computes the cash multiple for the transaction. The **cash multiple** (also called the multiple of money or absolute return) is the ratio of the total cash received to the total cash invested. The cash multiple for PKK's investment in Ideko is

$$\text{Cash Multiple} = \frac{\text{Total Cash Received}}{\text{Total Cash Invested}}$$
$$= \frac{9055 + 2989 + 4735 + 1375 + 177,077}{53,000} = 3.7 \quad (19.19)$$

That is, PKK expects to receive a return that is 3.7 times its investment in Ideko. The cash multiple is a common metric used by investors in transactions such as this one. It has an obvious weakness: The cash multiple does not depend on the amount of time it takes to receive the cash, nor does it account for the risk of the investment. It is therefore useful only for comparing deals with similar time horizons and risk.

CONCEPT CHECK

1. What are the main methods of estimating the continuation value of the firm at the end of the forecast horizon?

2. What are the potential pitfalls of analyzing a transaction like this one based on its IRR or cash multiple?

19.6 Sensitivity Analysis

Any financial valuation is only as accurate as the estimates on which it is based. Before concluding our analysis, it is important to assess the uncertainty of our estimates and to determine their potential impact on the value of the deal.

Once we have developed the spreadsheet model for PKK's investment in Ideko, it is straightforward to perform a sensitivity analysis to determine the impact of changes in different parameters on the deal's value. For example, the spreadsheet in Table 19.20 shows the sensitivity of our estimates of the value of PKK's investment to changes in our assumptions regarding the exit EBITDA multiple that PKK obtains when Ideko is sold, as well as Ideko's unlevered cost of capital.

TABLE 19.20 SPREADSHEET — **Sensitivity Analysis for PKK's Investment in Ideko**

Exit EBITDA Multiple		6.0	7.0	8.0	9.1	10.0	11.0
Implied Long-Run Growth Rate		1.60%	3.43%	4.53%	5.34%	5.81%	6.21%
Ideko Enterprise Value	($ million)	151.4	171.3	191.2	213.2	231.1	251.0
PKK Equity Value	($ million)	51.4	71.3	91.2	113.2	131.1	151.0
PKK IRR		14.8%	22.1%	28.0%	33.3%	37.1%	40.8%

Unlevered Cost of Capital		9.0%	10.0%	11.0%	12.0%	13.0%	14.0%
Implied Long-Run Growth Rate		3.86%	5.34%	6.81%	8.29%	9.76%	11.24%
Ideko Enterprise Value	($ million)	222.1	213.2	204.7	196.7	189.1	181.9
PKK Equity Value	($ million)	122.1	113.2	104.7	96.7	89.1	81.9

---

12. See the appendix to this chapter for a calculation of Ideko's annual equity cost of capital.

In our initial analysis, we assumed an exit EBITDA multiple of 9.1. Table 19.20 shows that each 1.0 increase in the multiple represents about $20 million in initial value.[13] PKK will break even on its $53 million investment in Ideko with an exit multiple of slightly more than 6.0. The table also shows, however, that an exit multiple of 6.0 is consistent with a future growth rate for Ideko of less than 2%, which is even less than the expected rate of inflation and probably unrealistically low.

Table 19.20 also illustrates the effect of a change to our assumption about Ideko's unlevered cost of capital. A higher unlevered cost of capital reduces the value of PKK's investment; yet, even with a rate as high as 14%, the equity value exceeds PKK's initial investment. However, if the unlevered cost of capital exceeds 12%, the implied long-term growth rate that justifies the assumed exit EBITDA multiple of 9.1 is probably unrealistically high. Thus, if we believe the unlevered cost of capital falls within this range, we should lower our forecast for the exit EBITDA multiple, which will further reduce the value of PKK's equity. Conversely, if we are confident in our estimate of the exit multiple, this analysis lends further support to our choice for the unlevered cost of capital.

The exercises at the end of this chapter continue the sensitivity analysis by considering different levels of market share growth and changes to working capital management.

CONCEPT CHECK

1. What is the purpose of the sensitivity analysis?

2. Table 19.20 shows the sensitivity analysis for PKK's investment in Ideko. Based on the exit EBITDA multiple, do you recommend the acquisition of Ideko?

Summary

1. Valuation using comparables may be used as a preliminary way to estimate the value of a firm.

2. The value of an investment ultimately depends on the firm's future cash flows. To estimate cash flows, it is first necessary to look at a target firm's operations, investments, and capital structure to assess the potential for improvements and growth.

3. A financial model may be used to project the future cash flows from an investment.
   a. A pro forma income statement projects the firm's earnings under a given set of hypothetical assumptions.
   b. The financial model should also consider future working capital needs and capital expenditures to estimate future free cash flows.
   c. Based on these estimates, we can forecast the balance sheet and statement of cash flows.

4. To value an investment, we need to assess its risk and estimate an appropriate cost of capital. One method for doing so is to use the CAPM.
   a. Use the CAPM to estimate the equity cost of capital for comparable firms, based on their equity betas.
   b. Given an estimate of each comparable firm's equity beta, unlever the beta based on the firm's capital structure.
   c. Use the CAPM and the estimates of unlevered betas for comparable firms to estimate the unlevered cost of capital for the investment.

---

13. In fact, we can calculate this directly as the present value of Ideko's projected EBITDA in 2010: ($32.094 million) / (1.10^5) = $19.928 million.

5. In addition to forecasting cash flows for a few years, we need to estimate the firm's continuation value at the end of the forecast horizon.

    a. One method is to use a valuation multiple based on comparable firms.

    b. To estimate a continuation value in year T using discounted cash flows, it is common practice to assume a constant expected growth rate g and a constant debt-equity ratio:

$$\text{Enterprise Value in Year } T = V_T^L = \frac{FCF_{T+1}}{r_{wacc} - g} \tag{19.14}$$

6. Given the forecasted cash flows and an estimate of the cost of capital, the final step is to combine these inputs to estimate the value of the opportunity. We may use the valuation methods described in Chapter 18 to calculate firm value.

7. While the NPV method is the most reliable approach for evaluating an investment, practitioners often use the IRR and cash multiple as alternative valuation metrics.

    a. We use the cash flows over the lifetime of the investment to calculate the IRR.

    b. The cash multiple for an investment is the ratio of the total cash received to the total cash invested:

$$\text{Cash Multiple} = \frac{\text{Total Cash Received}}{\text{Total Cash Invested}} \tag{19.19}$$

8. Sensitivity analysis is useful for evaluating the uncertainty of estimates used for valuation, and the impact of this uncertainty on the value of the deal.

Key Terms

cash multiple (multiple of money, absolute return) *p. 647*

pro forma *p. 629*

unlevered P/E ratio *p. 640*

Further Reading

These books are a good reference for those readers who want to go into more detail on the issues involved in the valuation and financial modeling of companies and projects: T. Copeland, T. Koller, and J. Murrin, *Valuation: Measuring and Managing the Value of Companies*, 3rd ed. (Hoboken, NJ: John Wiley & Sons, 2000); S. Z. Benninga and O. Sarig, *Corporate Finance: A Valuation Approach* (New York: McGraw-Hill/Irwin, 1996); E. R. Arzac, *Valuation for Mergers, Buyouts and Restructuring* (Hoboken, NJ: John Wiley & Sons, 2004); and S. P. Pratt, R. F. Reilly, and R. P. Schweihs, *Valuing a Business: The Analysis and Appraisal of Closely Held Companies*, 4th ed. (New York: McGraw-Hill, 2000).

Problems

An asterisk (*) indicates problems with a higher level of difficulty.

Valuation Using
Comparables

1. You would like to compare Ideko's profitability to its competitors' profitability using the EBITDA/sales multiple. Given Ideko's current sales of $75 million, use the information in Table 19.2 to compute a range of EBITDA for Ideko assuming it is run as profitably as its competitors.

2. Assume that Ideko's market share will increase by 0.5% per year rather than the 1% used in the chapter. What production capacity will Ideko require each year? When will an expansion become necessary (when production volume will exceed the current level by 50%)?

3. Under the assumption that Ideko market share will increase by 0.5% per year, you determine that the plant will require an expansion in 2010. The cost of this expansion will be $15 million. Assuming the financing of the expansion will be delayed accordingly, calculate the projected interest payments and the amount of the projected interest tax shields (assuming that the interest rates on the term loans remain the same as in the chapter) through 2010.

EXCEL   4. Under the assumption that Ideko's market share will increase by 0.5% per year (and the investment and financing will be adjusted as described in Problem 3), you project the following depreciation:

Year	2005	2006	2007	2008	2009	2010
Fixed Assets and Capital Investment ($ 000)						
2 New Investment	5,000	5,000	5,000	5,000	5,000	20,000
3 Depreciation	(5,500)	(5,450)	(5,405)	(5,365)	(5,328)	(6,795)

Using this information, project net income through 2010 (that is, reproduce Table 19.7 under the new assumptions).

EXCEL   5. Under the assumptions that Ideko's market share will increase by 0.5% per year (implying that the investment, financing, and depreciation will be adjusted as described in Problems 3 and 4) and that the forecasts in Table 19.8 remain the same, calculate Ideko's working capital requirements though 2010 (that is, reproduce Table 19.9 under the new assumptions).

EXCEL   6. Under the assumptions that Ideko's market share will increase by 0.5% per year (implying that the investment, financing, and depreciation will be adjusted as described in Problems 3 and 4) but that the projected improvements in net working capital do not transpire (so the numbers in Table 19.8 remain at their 2005 levels through 2010), calculate Ideko's working capital requirements though 2010 (that is, reproduce Table 19.9 under these assumptions).

EXCEL   7. Forecast Ideko's free cash flow (reproduce Table 19.10), assuming Ideko's market share will increase by 0.5% per year; investment, financing, and depreciation will be adjusted accordingly; and the projected improvements in working capital occur (that is, under the assumptions in Problem 5).

EXCEL   8. Forecast Ideko's free cash flow (reproduce Table 19.10), assuming Ideko's market share will increase by 0.5% per year; investment, financing, and depreciation will be adjusted accordingly; and the projected improvements in working capital do *not* occur (that is, under the assumptions in Problem 6).

EXCEL   *9. Reproduce Ideko's balance sheet and statement of cash flows, assuming Ideko's market share will increase by 0.5% per year; investment, financing, and depreciation will be adjusted accordingly; and the projected improvements in working capital occur (that is, under the assumptions in Problem 5).

EXCEL   *10. Reproduce Ideko's balance sheet and statement of cash flows, assuming Ideko's market share will increase by 0.5% per year; investment, financing, and depreciation will be adjusted accordingly; and the projected improvements in working capital do *not* occur (that is, under the assumptions in Problem 6).

11. Calculate Ideko's unlevered cost of capital when Ideko's unlevered beta is 1.1 rather than 1.2, and all other required estimates are the same as in the chapter.

12. Calculate Ideko's unlevered cost of capital when the market risk premium is 6% rather than 5%, the risk-free rate is 5% rather than 4%, and all other required estimates are the same as in the chapter.

13. Using the information produced in the income statement in Problem 4, use EBITDA as a multiple to estimate the continuation value in 2010, assuming the current value remains unchanged (reproduce Table 19.15). Infer the EV/sales and the unlevered and levered P/E ratios implied by the continuation value you calculated.

14. How does the assumption on future improvements in working capital affect your answer to Problem 13?

15. Approximately what expected future long-run growth rate would provide the same EBITDA multiple in 2010 as Ideko has today (i.e., 9.1)? Assume that the future debt-to-value ratio is held constant at 40%; the debt cost of capital is 6.8%; Ideko's market share will increase by 0.5% per year until 2010; investment, financing, and depreciation will be adjusted accordingly; and the projected improvements in working capital occur (that is, the assumptions in Problem 5).

16. Approximately what expected future long-run growth rate would provide the same EBITDA multiple in 2010 as Ideko has today (i.c., 9.1). Assume that the future debt-to-value ratio is held constant at 40%; the debt cost of capital is 6.8%; Ideko's market share will increase by 0.5% per year; investment, financing, and depreciation will be adjusted accordingly; and the projected improvements in working capital do *not* occur (that is, the assumptions in Problem 6).

17. Using the APV method, estimate the value of Ideko and the NPV of the deal using the continuation value you calculated in Problem 13 and the unlevered cost of capital estimate in Section 19.4. Assume that the debt cost of capital is 6.8%; Ideko's market share will increase by 0.5% per year until 2010; investment, financing, and depreciation will be adjusted accordingly; and the projected improvements in working capital occur (that is, the assumptions in Problem 5).

18. Using the APV method, estimate the value of Ideko and the NPV of the deal using the continuation value you calculated in Problem 13 and the unlevered cost of capital estimate in Section 19.4. Assume that the debt cost of capital is 6.8%; Ideko's market share will increase by 0.5% per year; investment, financing, and depreciation will be adjusted accordingly; and the projected improvements in working capital do *not* occur (that is, the assumptions in Problem 6).

19. Use your answers from Problems 17 and 18 to infer the value today of the projected improvements in working capital under the assumptions that Ideko's market share will increase by 0.5% per year and that investment, financing, and depreciation will be adjusted accordingly.

CHAPTER 19
APPENDIX

notation

r_E equity cost of
capital

Compensating Management

The success of PKK's investment critically depends on its ability to execute the operational improvements laid out in its business plan. PKK has learned from experience that it is much more likely to achieve its goals if the management team responsible for implementing the changes is given a strong incentive to succeed. PKK therefore considers allocating 10% of Ideko's equity to a management incentive plan. This equity stake would be vested over the next five years, and it would provide Ideko's senior executives with a strong financial interest in the success of the venture. What is the cost to PKK of providing this equity stake to the management team? How will this incentive plan affect the NPV of the acquisition?

To determine the value of the acquisition to PKK, we must include the cost of the 10% equity stake granted to management. Because the grant vests after five years, management will not receive any of the dividends paid by Ideko during that time. Instead, management will receive the equity in five years time, at which point we have estimated the value of Ideko's equity to be $172 million (see Table 19.15). Thus the cost of management's stake in 2010 is equal to 10% × $172 million = $17.2 million according to our estimate. We must determine the present value of this amount today.

Because the payment to the managers is an equity claim, to compute its present value we must use an equity cost of capital. We take an FTE valuation approach to estimate the cost of management's share in Ideko, shown in the spreadsheet in Table 19A1.

To compute Ideko's equity cost of capital r_E, we use Eq. 18.20, which applies when the debt levels of the firm follow a known schedule:

$$r_E = r_U + \frac{D - T^s}{E}(r_U - r_D)$$

Using the debt, equity, and tax shield values from the spreadsheet in Table 19.17 to compute the effective leverage ratio $(D - T^s) / E$, we compute r_E each year as shown in the spreadsheet. We then compute the cost of management's equity share by discounting at this rate:

$$\text{Cost of Management's Share}_t = \frac{\text{Cost of Management's Share}_{t+1}}{1 + r_E(t)} \tag{19A.1}$$

Once we have determined the cost of management's equity share, we deduct it from the total value of Ideko's equity (from Table 19.17) to determine the value of PKK's share of Ideko's equity, shown as the last line of the spreadsheet. Given the initial cost of the acquisition to PKK of $53 million, PKK's NPV from the investment, including the cost of management's compensation, is $103.58 million − $53 million = $50.58 million.

TABLE 19A.1
SPREADSHEET

FTE Estimate of the Cost of Management's Share and PKK's Equity Value

	Year	2005	2006	2007	2008	2009	2010
	Management/PKK Share ($ 000)						
1	Management Payoff (10% share)						17,205
2	Effective Leverage $(D - T^s)/E$	0.792	0.771	0.715	0.778	0.745	
3	Equity Cost of Capital r_E	12.53%	12.47%	12.29%	12.49%	12.38%	
4	Cost of Management's Share	(9,576)	(10,777)	(12,120)	(13,610)	(15,309)	(17,205)
5	Ideko Equity Value	113,160	118,287	130,047	141,294	157,566	172,052
6	PKK Equity	103,583	107,511	117,927	127,684	142,256	154,847

VII

Options

Chapter 20
Financial Options

Chapter 21
Option Valuation

Chapter 22
Real Options

The Law of One Price Connection. Having developed the tools to make current investment decisions, we turn to settings in which the firm or an investor has the option to make a future investment decision. Chapter 20 introduces financial options, which give investors the right to buy or sell a security in the future. Financial options are an important tool for corporate financial managers seeking to manage or evaluate risk. Options are an example of a derivative security. In the last 30 years there has been enormous growth in the derivative securities markets in general and options markets in particular. This growth can be traced directly to the discovery of methods for valuing options, which we derive in Chapter 21 using the Law of One Price. An important corporate application of option theory is in the area of real investment decision making. Future investment decisions within the firm are known as real options and Chapter 22 applies real option theory to corporate decision making.

CHAPTER

20

Financial Options

notation

PV present value

Div dividend

C call option price

P put option price

S stock price

K strike price

dis discount from face value

NPV net present value

In this chapter we introduce the financial option, a financial contract between two parties. Since the introduction of publicly traded options on the Chicago Board Options Exchange (CBOE) in 1973, financial options have become one of the most important and actively traded financial assets. Consequently, they have also become important tools for corporate financial managers. For example, many large corporations have operations in different parts of the world, so they face exposure to exchange rate risk and other types of business risk. To control this risk, they use options as part of their corporate risk management practices. In addition, the capitalization of the firm itself—that is, its mix of debt and equity—can be thought of as options on the underlying assets of the firm. As we will see, viewing the firm's capitalization in this way yields important insights into the firm's capital structure as well as the conflicts of interests that arise between equity investors and debt investors.

Before we can discuss the corporate applications of options, we first need to understand what options are and what factors affect their value. In this chapter, we provide an overview of the basic types of financial options, introduce important terminology, and describe the payoffs to various option-based strategies. We next discuss the factors that affect option prices. Finally, we model the equity and debt of the firm as options to gain insight into the conflicts of interest between equity and debt holders, as well as the pricing of risky debt.

20.1 Option Basics

A **financial option** contract gives its owner the right (but not the obligation) to purchase or sell an asset at a fixed price at some future date. Two distinct kinds of option contracts exist: call options and put options. A **call option** gives the owner the right to *buy* the asset; a **put option** gives the owner the right to *sell* the asset. Because an option is a contract between two parties, for every owner of a financial option, there is also an **option writer**, the person who takes the other side of the contract.

The most commonly encountered option contracts are options on shares of stock. A stock option gives the holder the option to buy or sell a share of stock on or before a given date for a given price. For example, a call option on 3M Corporation stock might give the holder the right to purchase a share of 3M for $75 per share at any time up to, for example, January 18, 2008. Similarly, a put option on 3M stock might give the holder the right to sell a share of 3M stock for $50 per share at any time up to, say, June 20, 2008.

Understanding Option Contracts

Practitioners use specific words to describe the details of option contracts. When a holder of an option enforces the agreement and buys or sells a share of stock at the agreed-upon price, he is **exercising** the option. The price at which the holder buys or sells the share of stock when the option is exercised is called the **strike price** or **exercise price**.

There are two kinds of options. **American options**, the most common kind, allow their holders to exercise the option on any date up to and including a final date called the **expiration date**. **European options** allow their holders to exercise the option *only* on the expiration date—holders cannot exercise before the expiration date. The names *American* and *European* have nothing to do with the location where the options are traded: Both types are traded worldwide.

As with other financial assets, options can be bought and sold. Standard stock options are traded on organized exchanges, while more specialized options are sold through dealers. The market price of the option is also called the option premium.

An option contract is a contract between two parties. The option buyer, also called the option holder, holds the right to exercise the option and has a *long* position in the contract. The option seller, also called the option writer, sells (or writes) the option and has a *short* position in the contract. Because the long side has the option to exercise, the short side has an *obligation* to fulfill the contract. For example, suppose you own a call option on Hewlett-Packard stock with an exercise price of $10. Hewlett-Packard stock is currently trading for $25, so you decide to exercise the option. The person holding the short position in the contract is obligated to sell you a share of Hewlett-Packard stock for $10. Your $15 gain—the difference between the price you pay for the share of stock and the price at which you can sell the share in the market—is the short position's loss.

Investors exercise options only when they stand to gain something. Consequently, whenever an option is exercised, the person holding the short position funds the gain. That is, the obligation will be costly. Why, then, do people write options? The answer is that when you sell an option you get paid for it—options always have positive prices. This upfront payment compensates the seller for the risk of loss in the event that the option holder chooses to exercise the option.

Interpreting Stock Option Quotations

Stock options are traded on organized exchanges. The oldest and largest is the Chicago Board Options Exchange (CBOE). By convention, all traded options expire on the Saturday following the third Friday of the month.

TABLE 20.1   **Option Quotes for Amazon.com Stock**

AMZN   48.35 —
Nov 29, 2005 @ 11:35 ET (Data 15 Minutes Delayed)   Bid 48.35   Ask 48.37   Vol 3831766

Calls	Last Sale	Net	Bid	Ask	Vol	Open Int	Puts	Last Sale	Net	Bid	Ask	Vol	Open Int
05 Dec 45.00 (ZQN LI-E)	4.00	pc	3.70	3.90	0	16021	05 Dec 45.00 (ZQN XI-E)	0.30	−0.05	0.30	0.40	30	20788
05 Dec 47.50 (ZQN LW-E)	2.20	−0.25	1.90	2.00	86	18765	05 Dec 47.50 (ZQN XW-E)	0.75	−0.15	0.95	1.05	292	13208
05 Dec 50.00 (ZQN LJ-E)	0.80	—	0.75	0.85	144	9491	05 Dec 50.00 (ZQN XJ-E)	2.30	+0.20	2.30	2.40	177	5318
05 Dec 55.00 (ZQN LK-E)	0.15	pc	0.05	0.10	0	2497	05 Dec 55.00 (ZQN XK-E)	6.10	pc	6.60	6.80	0	895
06 Jan 45.00 (ZQN AI-E)	4.93	pc	4.80	5.00	0	18765	06 Jan 45.00 (ZQN MI-E)	1.20	−0.10	1.20	1.30	8	29717
06 Jan 47.50 (ZQN AW-E)	3.70	+0.10	3.20	3.30	5	8068	06 Jan 47.50 (ZQN MW-E)	1.95	+0.15	2.05	2.15	10	6632
06 Jan 50.00 (ZQN AJ-E)	2.15	+0.15	1.95	2.05	208	27416	06 Jan 50.00 (ZQN MJ-E)	3.30	+0.20	3.30	3.50	162	6668
06 Jan 55.00 (ZQN AK-E)	0.70	+0.10	0.60	0.70	65	8475	06 Jan 55.00 (ZQN MK-E)	6.90	−2.50	7.00	7.10	67	5621

Source: Chicago Board Options Exchange at www.cboe.com.

Table 20.1 shows near-term options on Amazon taken from the CBOE Web site (www.cboe.com) on November 29, 2005. Call options are listed on the left and put options on the right. Each line corresponds to a particular option. The first two digits in the option name refer to the year of expiration. The option name also includes the month of expiration, the strike or exercise price, and the ticker symbol of the individual option (in parentheses). Looking at Table 20.1, the first line of the left column is a call option with an exercise price of $45 that expires on the Saturday following the third Friday of December 2005 (December 17, 2005). The columns to the right of the name display market data for the option. The first of these columns shows the last sale price, followed by the net change from the previous sale price ("pc" indicates that no trade has occurred on this day, so the last sale price is the previous closing price), the current bid and ask prices, and the daily volume. The final column is the **open interest**, the total number of contracts of that particular option that have been written.

Above the table we find information about the stock itself. In this case, Amazon's stock last traded at a price of $48.35 per share. We also see the current bid and ask prices for the stock, as well as the volume of trade.

When the exercise price of an option is equal to the current price of the stock, the option is said to be **at-the-money**. Notice that much of the trading occurs in options that are closest to being at-the-money—that is, calls and puts with exercise prices of either $47.50 or $50. Notice how the December 50 calls have high volume. They last traded for 80¢, midway between the current bid price (75¢) and the ask price (85¢), which indicates that the trade likely occurred recently because the last traded price is a current market price.

Stock option contracts are always written on 100 shares of stock. If, for instance, you decided to purchase one December 47.50 call contract, you would be purchasing an option to buy 100 shares at $47.50 per share. Option prices are quoted on a per-share basis, so the ask price of $2.00 implies that you would pay $100 \times 2 = \$200$ for the contract. Similarly, if you decide to buy a December 45 put contract, you would pay $100 \times 0.40 = \$40$ for the option to sell 100 shares of Amazon stock for $45 per share.

Note from Table 20.1 that for each expiration date, call options with lower strike prices have higher market prices—the right to buy the stock at a lower price is more valuable than the right to buy it for a higher price. Conversely, because the put option gives the holder the right to sell the stock at the strike price, for the same expiration puts with higher strikes are more valuable. On the other hand, holding fixed the strike price, both calls and puts are more expensive for a longer time to expiration. Because these options are American-style options that can be exercised at any time, having the right to buy or sell for a longer period is more valuable.

If the payoff from exercising an option immediately is positive, the option is said to be **in-the-money**. Call options with strike prices below the current stock price are in-the-money, as are put options with strike prices above the current stock price. Conversely, if the payoff from exercising the option immediately is negative, the option is **out-of-the-money**. Call options with strike prices above the current stock price are out-of-the-money, as are put options with strike prices below the current stock price. Of course, a holder would not exercise an out-of-the-money option. Options where the strike price and the stock price are very far apart are referred to as **deep in-the-money** or **deep out-of-the-money**.

EXAMPLE 20.1

Purchasing Options

Problem

It is midday on November 29, 2005, and you have decided to purchase 10 January call contracts on Amazon stock with an exercise price of $50. Because you are buying, you must pay the ask price. How much money will this purchase cost you? Is this option in-the-money or out-of-the-money?

Solution

From Table 20.1, the ask price of this option is $2.05. You are purchasing 10 contracts and each contract is on 100 shares, so the transaction will cost $2.05 \times 10 \times 100 = \$2,050$ (ignoring any commission fees). Because this is call option and the exercise price is above the current stock price ($48.35), the option is currently out-of-the-money.

Options on Other Financial Securities

Although the most commonly traded options are written on stocks, options on other financial assets do exist. Perhaps the most well known are options on stock indexes such as the S&P 100 index, the S&P 500 index, the Dow Jones Industrial index, and the NYSE index. These options have become very popular because they allow investors to protect the value of their investments from adverse market changes. As we will see shortly, a stock index put option can be used to offset the losses on an investor's portfolio in a market downturn. Using an option to reduce risk in this way is called **hedging**. Options also allow investors to **speculate**, or place a bet on the direction in which they believe the market is likely to move. By purchasing a call, for example, investors can bet on a market rise with a much smaller investment than investing in the market index itself.

Options are also traded on Treasury securities. These options allow investors to bet on or hedge interest rate risk. Similarly, options on currencies and commodities allow investors to hedge or speculate on risks in these markets.

CONCEPT CHECK   1. What is the difference between an American option and a European option?

2. Does the holder of an option have to exercise it?

20.2 Option Payoffs at Expiration

From the Law of One Price, the value of any security is determined by the future cash flows an investor receives from owning it. Therefore, before we can assess what an option is worth, we must determine an option's payoff at the time of expiration.

Long Position in an Option Contract

Assume you own an option with a strike price of $20. If, on the expiration date, the stock price is greater than the strike price, say $30, you can make money by exercising the call (by paying $20, the strike price, for the stock) and immediately selling the stock in the open market for $30. The $10 difference is what the option is worth. Consequently, when the stock price on the expiration date exceeds the strike price, the value of the call is the difference between the stock price and the strike price. When the stock price is less than the strike price at expiration, the holder will not exercise the call, so the option is worth nothing. These payoffs are plotted in Figure 20.1.[1]

Thus, if S is the stock price at expiration, K is the exercise price, and C is the value of the call option, the value of the call at expiration is

Call Value at Expiration

$$C = max(S - K, 0) \tag{20.1}$$

where *max* is the maximum of the two quantities in the parentheses. The call's value is the maximum of the difference between the stock price and the strike price, $S - K$, and zero.

FIGURE 20.1

Payoff of a Call Option with a Strike Price of $20 at Expiration

If the stock price is greater than the strike price ($20), the call will be exercised, and the holder's payoff is the difference between the stock price and the strike price. If the stock price is less than the strike price, the call will not be exercised, and so has no value.

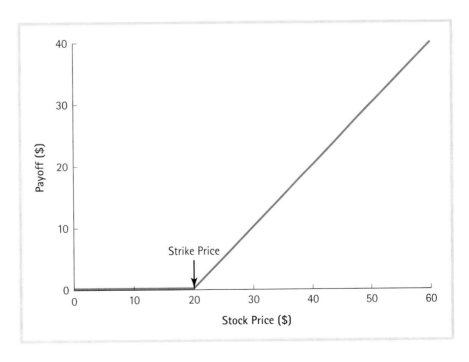

---

1. Payoff diagrams like the ones in this chapter seem to have been introduced by Louis Bachelier in 1900 in his book, *Theorie de la Speculation* (Paris: Villars, 1900). Reprinted in English in P. H. Cootner (ed.), *The Random Character of Stock Market Prices* (Cambridge, MA: M.I.T. Press, 1964).

The holder of a put option will exercise the option if the stock price S is below the strike price K. Because the holder receives K when the stock is worth S, the holder's gain is equal to $K - S$. Thus, the value of a put at expiration is

Put Price at Expiration

$$P = max(K - S, 0) \qquad (20.2)$$

EXAMPLE

20.2

Payoff of a Put Option at Maturity

Problem

You own a put option on Sun Microsystems stock with an exercise price of $20 that expires today. Plot the value of this option as a function of the stock price.

Solution

Let S be the stock price and P be the value of the put option. The value of the option is

$$P = max(20 - S, 0)$$

Plotting this function gives

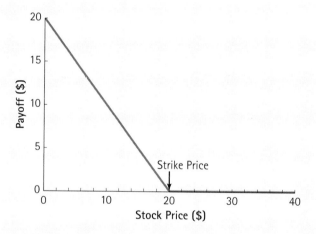

Short Position in an Option Contract

An investor holding a short position in an option has an obligation: This investor takes the opposite side of the contract to the investor who is long. Thus the short position's cash flows are the negative of the long position's cash flows. Because an investor who is long an option can only receive money at expiration—that is, the investor will not exercise an option that is out-of-the-money—a short investor can only pay money.

To demonstrate, assume you have a short position in a call option with an exercise price of $20. If the stock price is greater than the strike price of a call—for example, $25—the holder will exercise the option. You then have the obligation to sell the stock for the strike price of $20. Because you must purchase the stock at the market price of $25, you lose the difference between the two prices, or $5. However, if the stock price is less than the strike price at the expiration date, the holder will not exercise the option, so in this case you lose nothing; you have no obligation. These payoffs are plotted in Figure 20.2.

FIGURE 20.2

Short Position in a Call Option at Expiration

If the stock price is greather than the strike price, the call will be exercised, so a person on the short side of a call will lose the difference between the stock price and the strike price. If the stock price is less than the strike price, the call will not be exercised, and the seller will have no obligation.

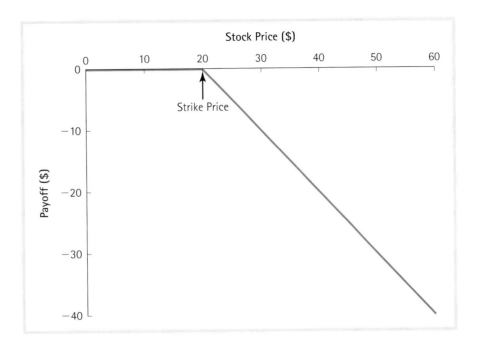

EXAMPLE 20.3

Payoff of a Short Position in a Put Option

Problem

You are short a put option on Sun Microsystems stock with an exercise price of $20 that expires today. What is your payoff at expiration as a function of the stock price?

Solution

If S is the stock price, your cash flows will be

$$-max(20 - S, 0)$$

If the current stock price is $30, then the put will not be exercised and you will owe nothing. If the current stock price is $15, the put will be exercised and you will lose $5. The figure plots your cash flows:

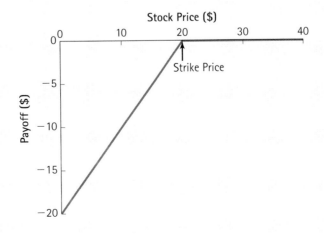

Notice that because the stock price cannot fall below zero, the downside for a short position in a put option is limited to the strike price of the option. A short position in a call, however, has no limit on the downside (see Figure 20.2).

Profits for Holding an Option to Expiration

Although payouts on a long position in an option contract are never negative, the profit from purchasing an option and holding it to expiration could well be negative because the payout at expiration might be less than the initial cost of the option.

To see how this works, let's consider the potential profits from purchasing the 06 January 50.00 call option on Amazon stock quoted in Table 20.1. The option costs $2.05 and expires in 52 days. Assume you choose to finance the purchase by borrowing $2.05 at an interest rate of 3% per year. If the stock price at expiration is S, then the profit is the call payoff minus the amount owed on the loan: $max(S - 50, 0) - 2.05 \times 1.03^{52/365}$, shown as the red curve in Figure 20.3. Once the cost of the position is taken into account, you make a positive profit only if the stock price exceeds $52.06. As we can see from Table 20.1, the further in-the-money the option is, the higher its initial price and so the larger your potential loss. An out-of-the-money option has a smaller initial cost and hence a smaller potential loss, but the probability of a gain is also smaller because the point where profits become positive is higher.

Because a short position in an option is the other side of a long position, the profits from a short position in an option are just the negative of the profits of a long position. For example, a short position in an out-of-the-money call like the 06 January 55 Amazon call in Figure 20.3 produces a small positive profit if Amazon's stock is below $55.70, but leads to losses if the stock price is above $55.70.

FIGURE 20.3

Profit from Holding a Call Option to Expiration

The curves show the profit per share from purchasing the January call options in Table 20.1 on November 29, 2005, financing this purchase by borrowing at 3%, and holding the position until the expiration date.

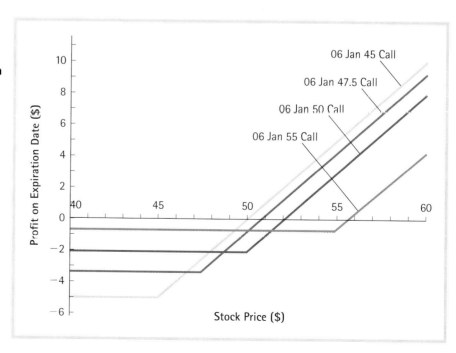

Profit on Holding a Position in a Put Option Until Expiration

Problem
Assume you decided to purchase each of the January put options quoted in Table 20.1 on November 29, 2005, and you financed each position by shorting a two-month bond with a yield of 3%. Plot the profit of each position as a function of the stock price on expiration.

Solution
Suppose S is the stock price on expiration, K is the strike price, and P is the price of each put option on November 29. Then your cash flows on the expiration date will be

$$\max(K - S, 0) - P \times 1.03^{52/365}$$

Plotting is shown below. Note the same tradeoff between the maximum loss and the potential for profit as for the call options.

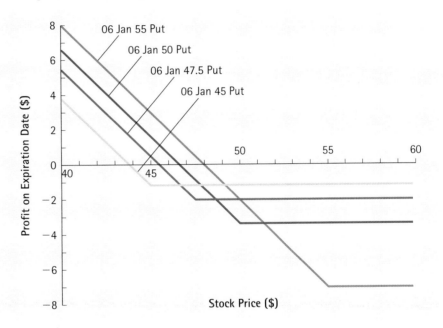

Returns for Holding an Option to Expiration

We can also compare options based on their potential returns. Figure 20.4 shows the return from purchasing one of the January 2006 options in Table 20.1 on November 29, 2005, and holding it until the expiration date. Let's begin by focusing on call options, shown in panel (a). In all cases, the maximum loss is 100%—the option may expire worthless. Notice how the curves change as a function of the strike price—the distribution of returns for out-of-the-money call options are more extreme than those for in-the-money calls. That is, an out-of-the money call option is more likely to have a −100% return, but if the stock goes up sufficiently it will also have a much higher return than an in-the-money call option. Similarly, all call options have more extreme returns than the stock itself (given Amazon's initial price of $48.35, the range of stock prices shown in the plot represent returns from −17% to +24%). As a consequence, the risk of a call option is amplified relative to the risk of the stock, and the amplification is greater for

FIGURE 20.4   **Option Returns from Purchasing an Option and Holding It to Expiration**

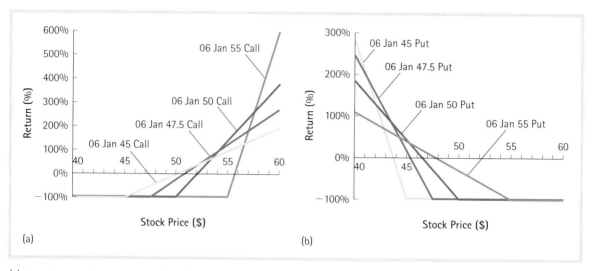

(a) The return on the expiration date from purchasing one of the January call options in Table 20.1 on November 29, 2005, and holding the position until the expiration date; (b) the same return for the January put options in the table.

deeper out-of-the-money calls. Thus, if a stock had a positive beta, call options written on the stock will have even higher betas and expected returns than the stock itself.[2]

Now consider the returns for put options. Look carefully at panel (b) in Figure 20.4. The put position has a higher return in states with *low* stock prices; that is, if the stock has a positive beta, the put has a negative beta. Hence, put options on positive beta stocks have lower expected returns than the underlying stock. The deeper out-of-the-money the put option is, the more negative its beta, and the lower its expected return. As a result, put options are generally not held as an investment, but rather as insurance to hedge other risk in a portfolio.

Combinations of Options

Sometimes investors combine option positions by holding a portfolio of options. In this section, we describe the most common combinations.

Straddle.   What would happen at expiration if you were long both a put option and a call option with the same strike price? Figure 20.5 shows the payout on the expiration date of both options.

By combining a call option (blue line) with a put option (red line), you will receive cash so long as the options do not expire at-the-money. The farther away from the money the options are, the more money you will make (solid line). However, to construct the combination requires purchasing both options, so the profits after deducting this cost are negative for stock prices close to the strike price and positive elsewhere (dashed line). This combination of options is known as a **straddle**. This strategy is sometimes used by

---

2. In Chapter 21, we explain how to calculate the expected return and risk of holding an option. In doing so, we will derive these relations rigorously.

FIGURE 20.5

FIGURE 20.5

Payoff and Profit from a Straddle

A combination of a long position in a put and a call with the same strike price and expiration date provides a positive payoff (solid line) so long as the stock price does not equal the strike price. After deducting the cost of the options, the profit is negative for stock prices close to the strike price and positive elsewhere (dashed line).

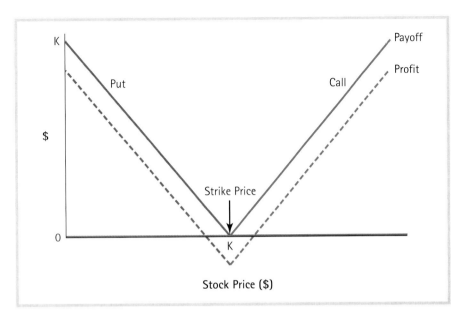

investors who expect the stock to be very volatile and move up or down a large amount, but who do not necessarily have a view on which direction the stock will move. Conversely, investors who expect the stock to end up near the strike price may choose to sell a straddle.

EXAMPLE 20.5

Strangle

Problem

You are long both a call option and a put option on Hewlett-Packard stock with the same expiration date. The exercise price of the call option is $40; the exercise price of the put option is $30. Plot the payoff of the combination at expiration.

Solution

The red line represents the put's payouts and the blue line represents the call's payouts. In this case, you do not receive money if the stock price is between the two strike prices. This option combination is known as a **strangle**.

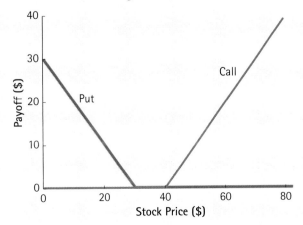

Butterfly Spread

The yellow line represents the payoff from a long position in a $20 call. The red line represents the payoff from a long position in a $40 call. The blue line represents the payoff from a short position in two $30 calls. The black line shows the payoff of the entire combination, called a butterfly spread, at expiration.

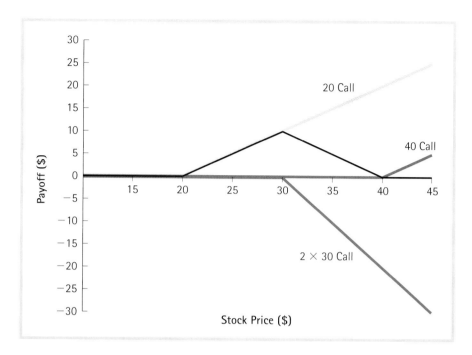

Butterfly Spread.   The combination of options in Figure 20.5 makes money when the stock and strike prices are far apart. It is also possible to construct a combination of options that has the opposite exposure: It pays off when the stock price is close to the strike price.

Suppose you are long two call options with the same expiration date on IBM stock: one with an exercise price of $20 and the other with an exercise price of $40. In addition, suppose you are short two call options on IBM stock, both with an exercise price of $30. Figure 20.6 plots the value of this combination at expiration.

The yellow line in Figure 20.6 represents the payoff at expiration from the long position in the $20 call. The red line represents the payoff from the long position in the $40 call. The blue line represents the payoff from the short position in the two $30 calls. The black line shows the payoff of the entire combination. For stock prices less than $20, all options are out-of-the-money, so the payoff is zero. For stock prices greater than $40, the losses from the short position in the $30 calls exactly offsets the gain from $20 and $40 option, and the value of the entire portfolio of options is zero.[3] Between $20 and $40, however, the payoff is positive. It reaches a maximum at $30. Practitioners call this combination of options a **butterfly spread**.

Because the payoff of the butterfly spread is positive, it must have a positive initial cost. (Otherwise, it would be an arbitrage opportunity.) Therefore, the cost of the $20 and $40 call options must exceed the proceeds from selling two $30 call options.

Portfolio Insurance.   Let's see how we can use combinations of options to insure a stock against a loss. Assume you currently own Amazon stock and you would like to insure the stock against the possibility of a price decline. To do so, you could simply sell the stock, but you would also give up the possibility of making money if the stock price increases.

---

3. To see this, note that $(S - 20) + (S - 40) - 2(S - 30) = 0$.

FIGURE 20.7   **Portfolio Insurance**

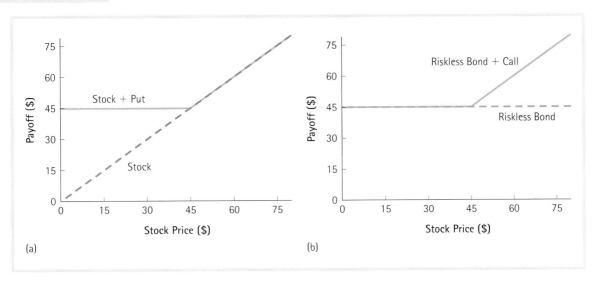

The plots show two different ways to insure against the possibility of the price of Amazon stock falling below $45. The orange line in (a) indicates the value on the expiration date of a position that is long one share of Amazon stock and one European put option with a strike of $45 (the blue dashed line is the payoff of the stock itself). The orange line in (b) shows the value on the expiration date of a position that is long a zero-coupon risk-free bond with a face value of $45 and a European call option on Amazon with a strike price of $45 (the green dashed line is the bond payoff).

How can you insure against a loss without relinquishing the upside? You can purchase a put option, sometimes known as a **protective put**.

For example, suppose you want to insure against the possibility that the price of Amazon stock will drop below $45. You decide to purchase a January 45 European put option. The orange line in Figure 20.7(a) shows the value of the combined position on the expiration date of the option. If Amazon stock is above $45 in January, you keep the stock, but if it is below $45 you exercise your put and sell it for $45. Thus, you get the upside, but are insured against a drop in the price of Amazon's stock.

You can use the same strategy to insure against a loss on an entire portfolio of stocks by using put options on the portfolio of stocks as a whole rather than just a single stock. Consequently, holding stocks and put options in this combination is known as **portfolio insurance**.

Purchasing a put option is not the only way to buy portfolio insurance. You can achieve exactly the same effect by purchasing a bond and a call option. Let's return to the insurance we purchased on Amazon stock. Amazon stock does not pay dividends, so there are no cash flows before the expiration of the option. Thus, instead of holding a share of Amazon stock and a put, you could get the same payoff by purchasing a risk-free zero-coupon bond with a face value of $45 and a European call option with a strike price of $45. In this case, if Amazon is below $45, you receive the payoff from the bond. If Amazon is above $45, you can exercise the call and use the payoff from the bond to buy the stock for the strike price of $45. The orange line in Figure 20.7(b) shows the value of the combined position on the expiration date of the option; it achieves exactly the same payoffs as owning the stock itself and a put option.

1. What is a straddle?

2. Explain how you can use put options to create portfolio insurance. How can you create portfolio insurance using call options?

20.3 Put-Call Parity

Consider the two different ways to construct portfolio insurance illustrated in Figure 20.7: (1) purchase the stock and a put or (2) purchase a bond and a call. Because both positions provide exactly the same payoff, the Law of One Price requires that they must have the same price.

Let's write this concept more formally. Let K be the strike price of the option (the price we want to ensure that the stock will not drop below), C be the call price, P be the put price, and S be the stock price. Then, if both positions have the same price,

$$S + P = PV(K) + C$$

The left side of this equation is the cost of buying the stock and a put (with a strike price of K); the right side is the cost of buying a zero-coupon bond with face value K and a call option (with a strike price of K). Recall that the price of a zero-coupon bond is just the present value of its face value, which we have denoted by $PV(K)$. Rearranging terms gives an expression for the price of a European call option for a non-dividend-paying stock:

$$C = P + S - PV(K) \qquad (20.3)$$

This relationship between the value of the stock, the bond, and call and put options is known as **put-call parity**. It says that the price of a European call equals the price of the stock plus an otherwise identical put minus the price of a bond that matures on the exercise date of the option. In other words, you can think of a call as a combination of a levered position in the stock, $S - PV(K)$, plus insurance against a drop in the stock price, the put P.

Using Put-Call Parity

Problem

You are an options dealer who deals in non-publicly traded options. One of your clients wants to purchase a one-year European call option on HAL Computer Systems stock with a strike price of $20. Another dealer is willing to write a one-year European put option on HAL stock with a strike price of $20, and sell you the put option for a price of $1.50 per share. If HAL pays no dividends and is currently trading for $18 per share, and if the risk-free interest rate is 6%, what is the lowest price you can charge for the option and guarantee yourself a profit?

Solution

Using put-call parity, we can replicate the payoff of the one-year call option with a strike price of $20 by holding the following portfolio: Buy the one-year put option with a strike price of $20 from the dealer, buy the stock, and sell a one-year risk-free zero-coupon bond with a face value of $20. With this combination, we have the following final payoff depending on the final price of HAL stock in one year, S_1:

	Final HAL Stock Price	
	$S_1 < \$20$	$S_1 > \$20$
Buy Put Option	$20 - S_1$	0
Buy Stock	S_1	S_1
Sell Bond	-20	-20
Portfolio	0	$S_1 - 20$
Sell Call Option	0	$-(S_1 - 20)$
Total Payoff	0	0

Note that the final payoff of the portfolio of the three securities matches the payoff of a call option. Therefore, we can sell the call option to our client and have future payoff of zero no matter what happens. Doing so is worthwhile as long as we can sell the call option for more than the cost of the portfolio, which is

$$P + S - PV(K) = \$1.50 + \$18 - \$20/1.06 = \$0.632$$

What happens if the stock pays a dividend? In that case, the two different ways to construct portfolio insurance do not have the same payout because the stock will pay a dividend while the zero-coupon bond will not. Thus the two strategies will cost the same to implement only if we add the present value of future dividends to the combination of the bond and the call:

$$S + P = PV(K) + PV(Div) + C$$

The left side of this equation is the value of the stock and a put; the right side is the value of a zero-coupon bond, a call option, and the future dividends paid by the stock during the life of the options, denoted by Div. Rearranging terms gives the general put-call parity formula:

Put-Call Parity

$$C = P + S - PV(K) - PV(Div) \tag{20.4}$$

In this case, the call is equivalent to having a levered position in the stock without dividends plus insurance against a fall in the stock price.

CONCEPT CHECK

1. Explain put-call parity.

2. If a put option trades at a higher price from the value indicated by the put-call parity equation, what action should you take?

20.4 Factors Affecting Option Prices

Put-call parity gives the price of a European call option in terms of the price of a European put, the underlying stock, and a zero-coupon bond. Therefore, to compute the price of a call using put-call parity, you have to know the price of the put. In Chapter 21, we explain how to calculate the price of a call without knowing the price of the put. Before we get there, let's first investigate the factors that affect option prices.

Strike Price and Stock Price

As we noted earlier for the Amazon option quotes in Table 20.1, the value of an otherwise identical call option is higher if the strike price the holder must pay to buy the stock is lower. Because a put is the right to sell the stock, puts with a lower strike price are less valuable.

For a given strike price, the value of a call option is higher if the current price of the stock is higher, as there is a greater likelihood the option will end up in-the-money. Conversely, put options increase in value as the stock price falls.

Arbitrage Bounds on Option Prices

We have already seen that an option's price cannot be negative. Furthermore, because an American option carries all the same rights and privileges as an otherwise equivalent European option, it cannot be worth less than a European option. If it were, you could make arbitrage profits by selling a European call and using part of the proceeds to buy an otherwise equivalent American call option. Thus *an American option cannot be worth less than its European counterpart.*

The maximum payoff for a put option occurs if the stock becomes worthless (if, say, the company files for bankruptcy). In that case, the put's payoff is equal to the strike price. Because this payoff is the highest possible, *a put option cannot be worth more than its strike price.*

For a call option, the lower the strike price, the more valuable the call option. If the call option had a strike price of zero, the holder would always exercise the option and receive the stock at no cost. This observation gives us an upper bound on the call price: *A call option cannot be worth more than the stock itself.*

The **intrinsic value** of an option is the value it would have if it expired immediately. Therefore, the intrinsic value is the amount by which the option is currently in-the-money, or 0 if the option is out-of-the-money. If an American option is worth less than its intrinsic value, you could make arbitrage profits by purchasing the option and immediately exercising it. Thus *an American option cannot be worth less than its intrinsic value.*

The **time value** of an option is the difference between the current option price and its intrinsic value. Because an American option cannot be worth less than its intrinsic value, it cannot have a negative time value.

Option Prices and the Exercise Date

For American options, the longer the time to the exercise date, the more valuable the option. To see why, let's consider two options: an option with one year until the exercise date and an option with six months until the exercise date. The holder of the one-year option can turn her option into a six-month option by simply exercising it early. That is, the one-year option has all the same rights and privileges as the six-month option, so by the Law of One Price, it cannot be worth less than the six-month option: *An American option with a later exercise date cannot be worth less than an otherwise identical American option with an earlier exercise date.* Usually the right to delay exercising the option is worth something, so the option with the later exercise date will be more valuable.

What about European options? The same argument will not work for European options, because a one-year European option cannot be exercised early at six months. As a consequence, a European option with a later exercise date may potentially trade for less than an otherwise identical option with an earlier exercise date. For example, think about a European call on a stock that pays a liquidating dividend in six months (a liquidating dividend is paid when a corporation chooses to go out of business, sells off all of its assets, and pays out the proceeds as a dividend). A one-year European call option on this stock would be worthless, but a six-month call would be worth something.

Option Prices and Volatility

An important criterion that determines the price of an option is the volatility of the underlying stock. Consider the following simple example.

Option Value and Volatility

Problem

Two European call options with a strike price of $50 are written on two different stocks. Suppose that tomorrow, the *low-volatility* stock will have a price of $50 for certain. The *high-volatility* stock will be worth either $60 or $40, with each price having equal probability. If the exercise date of both options is tomorrow, which option will be worth more today?

Solution

The expected value of *both* stocks tomorrow is $50—the low-volatility stock will be worth this amount for sure, and the high-volatility stock has an expected value of 40\left(\frac{1}{2}\right)$ + 60\left(\frac{1}{2}\right)$ = $50. However, the options have very different values. The option on the low-volatility stock is worth nothing because there is no chance it will expire in-the-money (the low-volatility stock will be worth $50 and the strike price is $50). The option on the high-volatility stock is worth a positive amount because there is a 50% chance that it will be worth $60 − $50 = $10 and a 50% chance that it will be worthless. The value today of a 50% chance of a positive payoff (with no chance of a loss) is positive.

Example 20.7 illustrates an important principle: *The value of an option generally increases with the volatility of the stock.* The intuition for this result is that an increase in volatility increases the likelihood of very high and very low returns for the stock. The holder of a call option benefits from a higher payoff when the stock goes up and the option is in-the-money, but earns the same (zero) payoff no matter how far the stock drops once the option is out-of-the-money. Because of this asymmetry of the option's payoff, an option holder gains from an increase in volatility.

Recall that adding a put option to a portfolio is akin to buying insurance against a decline in value. Insurance is more valuable when there is higher volatility—hence put options on more volatile stocks are also worth more.

CONCEPT CHECK   1. What is the intrinsic value of an option?

2. Can a European option with a later exercise date be worth less than an identical European option with an earlier exercise date?

20.5 Exercising Options Early

One might guess that the ability to exercise the American option early would make an American option more valuable than an equivalent European option. Surprisingly, this is not always the case—sometimes, they have equal value. Let's see why.

Non-Dividend-Paying Stocks

Let's consider first options on a stock that will not pay any dividends prior to the expiration date of the options. In that case, the put-call parity formula for the value of the call option is (see Eq. 20.3):

$$C = P + S - PV(K)$$

We can write the price of the zero-coupon bond as $PV(K) = K - dis(K)$, where $dis(K)$ is the amount of the discount from face value. Substituting this expression into put-call parity gives

$$C = \underbrace{S - K}_{\text{Intrinsic value}} \underbrace{+ \; dis(K) + P}_{\text{Time value}} \qquad (20.5)$$

In this case, both terms that make up the time value of the call option are positive before the expiration date: As long as interest rates remain positive, the discount on a zero-coupon bond before the maturity date is positive, and the put price is also positive, so a European call always has a positive time value. Because an American option is worth at least as much as a European option, it must also have a positive time value before expiration. Hence, *the price of any call option on a non-dividend-paying stock always exceeds its intrinsic value.*

This result implies that it is *never* optimal to exercise a call option on a non-dividend-paying stock early—you are always better off just selling the option. It is straightforward to see why. When you exercise an option, you get its intrinsic value. But as we have just seen, the price of a call option on a non-dividend-paying stock always exceeds its intrinsic value. Thus, if you want to liquidate your position in a call on a non-dividend-paying stock, you will get a higher price if you sell it rather than exercise it. Because it is never optimal to exercise an American call on a non-dividend-paying stock early, the right to exercise the call early is worthless. For this reason, *an American call on a non-dividend-paying stock has the same price as its European counterpart.*

Intuitively, there are two benefits to delaying the exercise of a call option. First, the holder delays paying the strike price, and second, by retaining the right not to exercise, the holder's downside is limited. (These benefits are represented by the discount and put values in Eq. 20.5.)

What about an American put option on a non-dividend-paying stock? Does it ever make sense to exercise it early? The answer is yes, under certain circumstances. To see why, note that we can rearrange the put-call parity relationship as expressed in Eq. 20.5 to get the price of a European put option:

$$P = \underbrace{K - S}_{\text{Intrinsic value}} \underbrace{- \; dis(K) + C}_{\text{Time value}} \qquad (20.6)$$

In this case, the time value of the option includes a negative term, the discount on a bond with face value K. When the put option is sufficiently deep in-the-money, this discount will be large relative to the value of the call, and the time value of a European put option will be negative. In that case, the European put will sell for less than its intrinsic value. However, its American counterpart cannot sell for less than its intrinsic value (because otherwise arbitrage profits would be possible by immediately exercising it), which implies that the American option can be worth more than an otherwise identical European option. Because the only difference between the two options is the right to exercise the option early, this right must be valuable—there must be states in which it is optimal to exercise the American put early.

TABLE 20.2   **Microsoft Option Quotes**

MSFT   27.77 −0.24
Dec 05, 2005 @ 14:14 ET (Data 15 Minutes Delayed)   Bid 27.77   Ask 27.78   Size 706 × 872   Vol 28153894

Calls	Bid	Ask	Open Int	Puts	Bid	Ask	Open Int
06 Jan 12.00 (MQF AM-E)	15.80	15.90	2104	06 Jan 12.00 (MQF MM-E)	0	0.05	59938
06 Jan 14.50 (MQF AN-E)	13.30	13.40	1680	06 Jan 14.50 (MQF MN-E)	0	0.05	28571
06 Jan 17.00 (MQF AO-E)	10.80	10.90	7486	06 Jan 17.00 (MQF MO-E)	0	0.05	44030
06 Jan 19.50 (MQF AP-E)	8.30	8.40	9702	06 Jan 19.50 (MQF MP-E)	0	0.05	55980
06 Jan 22.00 (MSQ AQ-E)	5.80	6.00	70604	06 Jan 22.00 (MSQ MQ-E)	0	0.05	119339
06 Jan 22.50 (MSQ AX-E)	5.30	5.50	7184	06 Jan 22.50 (MSQ MX-E)	0	0.05	26216
06 Jan 24.50 (MSQ AR-E)	3.40	3.50	98595	06 Jan 24.50 (MSQ MR-E)	0	0.05	170096
06 Jan 25.00 (MSQ AJ-E)	2.90	3.00	96467	06 Jan 25.00 (MSQ MJ-E)	0	0.05	44883
06 Jan 27.00 (MSQ AS-E)	1.15	1.20	303164	06 Jan 27.00 (MSQ MS-E)	0.25	0.30	120877
06 Jan 27.50 (MSQ AY-E)	0.85	0.90	124235	06 Jan 27.50 (MSQ MY-E)	0.40	0.50	29864
06 Jan 29.50 (MSQ AT-E)	0.15	0.20	85528	06 Jan 29.50 (MSQ MT-E)	1.75	1.85	28802
06 Jan 30.00 (MSQ AK-E)	0.10	0.15	86016	06 Jan 30.00 (MSQ MK-E)	2.20	2.30	7141
06 Jan 32.00 (MSQ AA-E)	0	0.05	141821	06 Jan 32.00 (MSQ MA-E)	4.20	4.30	14879
06 Jan 32.50 (MSQ AZ-E)	0	0.05	4728	06 Jan 32.50 (MSQ MZ-E)	4.70	4.80	12
06 Jan 34.50 (MSQ AB-E)	0	0.05	24347	06 Jan 34.50 (MSQ MB-E)	6.70	6.80	1042
06 Jan 37.00 (MSQ AC-E)	0	0.05	56712	06 Jan 37.00 (MSQ MC-E)	9.20	9.30	71
06 Jan 42.00 (MSQ AE-E)	0	0.05	17409	06 Jan 42.00 (MSQ ME-E)	14.20	14.30	24
06 Jan 44.50 (MSQ AF-E)	0	0.05	4812	06 Jan 44.50 (MSQ MF-E)	16.70	16.80	119
06 Jan 47.00 (MSQ AG-E)	0	0.05	23629	06 Jan 47.00 (MSQ MG-E)	19.20	19.30	191
06 Jan 52.00 (MQV AH-E)	0	0.05	5437	06 Jan 52.00 (MQV MH-E)	24.20	24.30	53
06 Jan 57.00 (MQV AI-E)	0	0.05	6342	06 Jan 57.00 (MQV MI-E)	29.20	29.30	52
06 Jan 62.00 (MQV AU-E)	0	0.05	917	06 Jan 62.00 (MQV MU-E)	34.20	34.30	197
06 Jan 67.00 (MQV AV-E)	0	0.05	4185	06 Jan 67.00 (MQV MV-E)	39.20	39.30	81

Source: Chicago Board Options Exchange at www.cboe.com.

Let's examine an extreme case to illustrate when it is optimal to exercise an American put early: Suppose the firm goes bankrupt and the stock is worth nothing. In such a case, the value of the put equals its upper bound—the strike price—so its price cannot go any higher. Thus no future appreciation is possible. However, if you exercise the put early, you can get the strike price today and earn interest on the proceeds in the interim. Hence it makes sense to exercise this option early. Although this example is extreme, it illustrates that it is often optimal to exercise deep in-the-money put options early.

Early Exercise of a Put Option on a Non-Dividend-Paying Stock

Problem
Table 20.2 lists the quotes from the CBOE on December 5, 2005, for options on Microsoft stock expiring in January 2006. Microsoft will not pay a dividend during this period. Identify any option for which exercising the option early is better than selling it.

Solution

Because Microsoft pays no dividends during the life of these options (December 2005 to January 2006), it should not be optimal to exercise the call options early. In fact, we can check that the bid price for each call option exceeds that option's intrinsic value, so it would be better to sell the call than to exercise it. For example, the payoff from exercising early a call with a strike of 12 is $27.77 - 12 = \$15.77$, while the option can be sold for $15.80.

On the other hand, the holder of a Microsoft put option with a strike price of $30 or higher is better off exercising—rather than selling—the option. For example, the payoff from buying the stock and exercising the 67 put is $67 - 27.78 = \$39.22$. The option itself can be sold for only $39.20, so the holder is better off by 2¢ by exercising the put rather than selling it. The same is not true of the other put options, however. For example, the holder of the 29.5 put option who exercises it early would net $29.5 - 27.78 = \$1.72$ whereas the put can be sold for $1.75. Thus, early exercise is only optimal for the deep in-the-money put options.[4]

Dividend-Paying Stocks

When stocks pay dividends, the right to exercise an option on them early is generally valuable for both calls and puts. To see why, let's write out the put-call parity relationship for a dividend-paying stock:

$$C = \underbrace{S - K}_{\text{Intrinsic value}} + \underbrace{dis(K) + P - PV(Div)}_{\text{Time value}} \qquad (20.7)$$

If $PV(Div)$ is large enough, the time value of a European call option can be negative, implying that its price could be less than its intrinsic value. Because an American option can never be worth less than its intrinsic value, the price of the American option can exceed the price of a European option.

To understand when it is optimal to exercise the American call option early, note that when a company pays a dividend, investors expect the price of the stock to drop to reflect the cash paid out. This price drop hurts the owner of a call option because the stock price falls, but unlike the owner of the stock, the option holder does not get the dividend as compensation. However, by exercising early and holding the stock, the owner of the call option *can* capture the dividend. Thus the decision to exercise early trades off the benefits of waiting to exercise the call option versus the loss of the dividend. Because a call should only be exercised early to capture the dividend, it will only be optimal to do so just before the stock's ex-dividend date.

Early Exercise of a Call Option on a Dividend-Paying Stock

Problem

General Electric (ticker: GE) stock goes ex-dividend on December 22, 2005 (only equity holders on the previous day are entitled to the dividend). The dividend amount is $0.25. Table 20.3 lists the quotes for GE options on December 21, 2005. From the quotes, identify the options that should be exercised early rather than sold.

---

4. Selling versus exercising may have different tax consequences or transaction costs for some investors, which could also affect this decision.

Solution

The holder of a call option on GE stock with a strike price of $32.50 or less is better off exercising—rather than selling—the option. For example, exercising the 06 January 10 call and immediately selling the stock would net $35.52 - 10 = \$25.52$. The option itself can be sold for \$25.40, so the holder is better off by 12¢ by exercising the call rather than selling it. To understand this result, note that interest rates were about 0.33% per month, so the value of delaying payment of the \$10 strike price until January was worth only \$0.033, and the put option was worth less than \$0.05. Thus, from Eq. 20.7, the benefit of delay was much less than the \$0.25 value of the dividend.[5]

TABLE 20.3	**Option Quotes on GE on December 21, 2005**
	(GE pays $0.25 dividend with ex-dividend date of December 22, 2005)

GE   35.52 −0.02

Dec 21, 2005 @ 11:50 ET (Data 20 Minutes Delayed)   Bid N/A   Ask N/A   Size N/A × N/A   Vol 8103000

Calls	Last Sale	Net	Bid	Ask	Vol	Open Int	Puts	Last Sale	Net	Bid	Ask	Vol	Open Int
06 Jan 10.00 (GE AB-E)	25.50	pc	25.40	25.60	0	738	06 Jan 10.00 (GE MB-E)	0.10	pc	0	0.05	0	12525
06 Jan 15.00 (GE AC-E)	19.00	pc	20.40	20.60	0	234	06 Jan 15.00 (GE MC-E)	0.05	pc	0	0.05	0	30624
06 Jan 20.00 (GE AD-E)	16.10	pc	15.40	15.60	0	1090	06 Jan 20.00 (GE MD-E)	0.05	pc	0	0.05	0	8501
06 Jan 25.00 (GE AE-E)	11.20	pc	10.40	10.60	0	29592	06 Jan 25.00 (GE ME-E)	0.05	pc	0	0.05	0	36948
06 Jan 27.50 (GE AY-E)	8.30	pc	7.90	8.10	0	1922	06 Jan 27.50 (GE MY-E)	0.05	pc	0	0.05	0	19071
06 Jan 30.00 (GE AF-E)	5.50	−0.10	5.40	5.60	10	37746	06 Jan 30.00 (GE MF-E)	0.05	pc	0	0.05	0	139548
06 Jan 32.50 (GE AZ-E)	3.20	+0.10	2.95	3.10	31	13630	06 Jan 32.50 (GE MZ-E)	0.05	pc	0	0.05	0	69047
06 Jan 35.00 (GE AG-E)	0.70	−0.10	0.70	0.75	76	146682	06 Jan 35.00 (GE MG-E)	0.30	−0.05	0.30	0.35	32	140014
06 Jan 37.50 (GE AS-E)	0.10	+0.05	0.05	0.10	20	74867	06 Jan 37.50 (GE MS-E)	2.20	−0.05	2.20	2.30	1	12116
06 Jan 40.00 (GE AH-E)	0.05	—	0	0.05	10	84366	06 Jan 40.00 (GE MH-E)	4.70	pc	4.70	4.80	0	4316
06 Jan 42.50 (GE AV-E)	0.05	pc	0	0.05	0	3559	06 Jan 42.50 (GE MV-E)	6.90	pc	7.20	7.30	0	903
06 Jan 45.00 (GE AI-E)	0.05	pc	0	0.05	0	7554	06 Jan 45.00 (GE MI-E)	9.40	pc	9.70	9.80	0	767
06 Jan 50.00 (GE AJ-E)	0.05	pc	0	0.05	0	17836	06 Jan 50.00 (GE MJ-E)	14.40	pc	14.70	14.80	0	383
06 Jan 55.00 (GE AK-E)	0	pc	0	0.05	0	5	06 Jan 55.00 (GE MK-E)	21.70	pc	19.70	19.80	0	320
06 Jan 60.00 (GE AL-E)	0.05	pc	0	0.05	0	7166	06 Jan 60.00 (GE ML-E)	26.00	pc	24.70	24.80	0	413

Source: Chicago Board Options Exchange at www.cboe.com.

Although most traded options are American, European options trade in a few circumstances. For example, European options written on the S&P 500 index exist. Table 20.4 lists the price of two-year European put options on the S&P 500 index. All the puts with strike prices of $1400 or higher trade for less than their immediate exercise value. To see why, let's write out the put-call parity relation for puts:

$$P = \underbrace{K - S}_{\text{Intrinsic value}} + \underbrace{C - dis(K) + PV(Div)}_{\text{Time value}} \tag{20.8}$$

In this case, the size of the discount on a two-year zero-coupon bond is large (over 4% per year), while the dividend yield of the S&P index is low (less than 2% per year). Also, for options with a high strike price the call has little value. Thus the discount term dominates, giving a negative time value for the deep in-the-money puts.

---

5. We have analyzed the early exercise decision ignoring taxes. Some investors may face higher taxes if they exercise the option early rather than sell or hold it.

TABLE 20.4	**Two-Year Put Options on the S&P 500 Index**

.SPX
Dec 12, 2005 @ 21:08 ET
(Data 15 Minutes Delayed)   1260.43 +1.06

Puts	Bid	Ask	Intrinsic Value
07 Dec 1300. (SZT XW-E)	88.40	91.40	39.57
07 Dec 1350. (SZT XK-E)	107.40	110.40	89.57
07 Dec 1400. (SZT XA-E)	129.90	132.90	139.57
07 Dec 1450. (SZT XS-E)	156.00	159.00	189.57
07 Dec 1500. (SZV XT-E)	185.80	188.80	239.57
07 Dec 1550. (SZV XJ-E)	218.90	221.90	289.57
07 Dec 1600. (SZV XO-E)	255.20	258.20	339.57
07 Dec 1650. (SZV XK-E)	294.00	297.00	389.57

Source: Chicago Board Options Exchange at www.cboe.com.

CONCEPT CHECK

1. Is it ever optimal to exercise an American call on a non-dividend paying stock early?

2. When may it be optimal to exercise an American put option early?

20.6 Options and Corporate Finance

Although we will delay much of the discussion of how corporations use options until after we have explained how to value an option, one very important application does not require understanding how to price options and is therefore worth exploring immediately: interpreting the capital structure of the firm as options on the firm's assets. We begin by explaining why equity can be thought of as an option.

Equity as a Call Option

A share of stock can be thought of as a call option on the assets of the firm with a strike price equal to the value of debt outstanding.[6] To illustrate, consider a single-period world in which at the end of the period the firm is liquidated. If the firm's value does not exceed the value of debt outstanding at the end of the period, the firm must declare bankruptcy and the equity holders receive nothing. Conversely, if the value exceeds the value of debt outstanding, the equity holders get whatever is left once the debt has been repaid. Figure 20.8 illustrates this payoff. Note how the payoff to equity looks exactly the same as the payoff of a call option.

Viewed this way, a share of equity is a call option on the firm's assets. Recall that the price of an option increases with the volatility level of the underlying security. That means

---

6. This insight has been known at least since Black and Scholes wrote their path-breaking option valuation paper. See F. Black and M. Scholes, "The Pricing of Options and Corporate Liabilities," *Journal of Political Economy* 81(3) (1973): 637–654.

FIGURE 20.8

Equity as a Call Option
If the value of the firm's assets exceeds the required debt payment, the equity holders receive the value that remains after the debt is repaid; otherwise, the firm is bankrupt and its equity is worthless. Thus the payoff to equity is equivalent to a call option on the firm's assets with a strike price equal to the required debt payment.

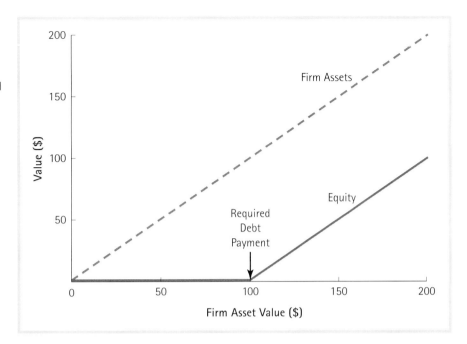

equity holders benefit from high-volatility investments. Because the price of equity is increasing with the volatility of the firm's assets, equity holders benefit from a zero-NPV project that increases the volatility of the firm's assets. Taking on such a project does not change the value of the firm as a whole but, because it increases the value of equity, the value of the debt claims must decrease by the amount the equity has increased. This effect creates a conflict of interest between equity holders and debt holders. Options pricing theory helps us understand why this conflict of interest arises.

The option price is more sensitive to changes in volatility for at-the-money options than it is for in-the-money options. In the context of corporate finance, equity is at-the-money when a firm is close to bankruptcy. In this case, the loss in equity value that results from taking on a negative-NPV investment might be outweighed by the gain in equity value from the increase in volatility. Hence, equity holders have an incentive to take on negative-NPV, high-volatility investments. As we saw in Chapter 16, this kind of debt overhang problem is of concern to debt holders, who bear its cost.

Debt as an Option Portfolio

Debt can also be represented using options. In this case, you can think of the debt holders as owning the firm *and* having sold a call option with a strike price equal to the required debt payment. If the value of the firm exceeds the required debt payment, the call will be exercised; the debt holders will therefore receive the strike price (the required debt payment) and give up the firm. If the value of the firm does not exceed the required debt payment, the call will be worthless, the firm will declare bankruptcy, and the debt holders will be entitled to the firm's assets. Figure 20.9 illustrates this payoff.

There is also another way to view corporate debt: as a portfolio of riskless debt and a short position in a put option on the firm's assets with a strike price equal to the required

Debt as an Option Portfolio

If the value of the firm's assets exceeds the required debt payment, debt holders are fully repaid. Otherwise, the firm is bankrupt and the debt holders receive the value of the assets. Note that the payoff to debt (orange line) can be viewed either as (i) the firm's assets, less the equity call option, or (ii) a risk-free bond, less a put option on the assets with a strike price equal to the required debt payment.

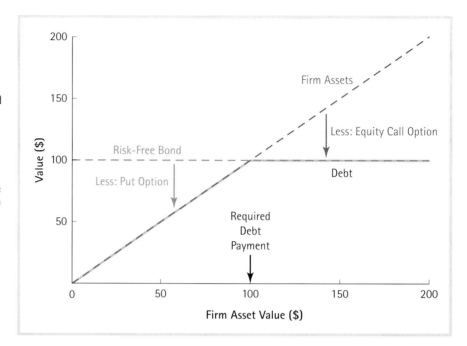

debt payment. When the firm's assets are worth less than the required debt payment, the put is in-the-money; the owner of the put option will therefore exercise the option and receive the difference between the required debt payment and the firm's asset value (see Figure 20.9). This leaves the portfolio holder (debt holder) with just the assets of the firm. If the firm's value is greater than the required debt payment, the put is worthless, leaving the portfolio holder with the required debt payment.

Viewing debt as an option portfolio is useful as it provides insight into how credit spreads for risky debt are determined. Let's illustrate with an example.

Calculating the Yield on New Corporate Debt

Problem

As of December 2005, Google (ticker: GOOG) had no debt. Suppose the firm's managers consider recapitalizing the firm at the start of the new year by issuing zero-coupon debt with a face value of $90 billion due in January of 2008, and using the proceeds to repurchase stock. Suppose Google currently has 300 million shares outstanding trading at $405.85 per share, implying a market value of $121.8 billion. The two-year risk-free rate is 4.5%. Using the option market data in Table 20.5, estimate the credit spread Google will have to pay on the debt.

Solution

Let's suppose for simplicity that Google's current market value of $121.8 billion already reflects any future tax benefits, distress costs, or other side effects of the new debt. Thus, the total value of Google's equity and debt should remain unchanged after the recapitalization.

The $90 billion face value of the debt is equivalent to a claim of $90 billion / (300 million shares) = $300 per share on Google's current assets. Because Google's shareholders will only receive the value of Google in excess of this debt claim, the value of Google's equity after the recap is equivalent to the current value of a call option with a strike price of $300. From the quotes below, such a call option has a value of approximately $158.90 per share (using the average of the bid and ask quotes). Multiplying by Google's total number of shares, we can estimate the total value of Google's equity after the recap as $158.90 × 300 million shares = $47.7 billion.

To estimate the value of the new debt, we can subtract the estimated equity value from Google's total value of $121.8 billion; thus, the estimated debt value is 121.8 − 47.7 = $74.1 billion. Because the debt matures 25 months from the date of the quotes, this value corresponds to a yield to maturity of

$$\left(\frac{90}{74.1} \right)^{12/25} - 1 = 9.8\%$$

Thus, Google's credit spread for the new debt issue would be about 9.8% − 4.5% = 5.3%.

TABLE 20.5	Google Call Option Quotes

| GOOG | | 405.85 −11.85 | |
| Dec 05, 2005 (Closing) | | Vol 10311740 | |

Calls	Bid	Ask	Open Int
08 Jan 300.0 (YVC AT–E)	157.60	160.20	353
08 Jan 310.0 (YVC AB–E)	151.10	153.90	201
08 Jan 320.0 (YVC AD–E)	144.80	147.80	220
08 Jan 330.0 (YVC AF–E)	138.70	141.90	214
08 Jan 340.0 (YVC AH–E)	132.90	136.10	166
08 Jan 350.0 (YVC AJ–E)	127.20	130.40	209
08 Jan 360.0 (YVC AL–E)	121.70	124.90	196
08 Jan 370.0 (YVC AN–E)	116.40	119.50	380
08 Jan 380.0 (YVC AU–E)	111.40	114.40	123
08 Jan 390.0 (YVC AV–E)	106.50	109.50	165
08 Jan 400.0 (YVC AW–E)	102.00	104.60	1131
08 Jan 410.0 (YVC AX–E)	97.30	100.00	214

Source: Chicago Board Options Exchange at www.cboe.com.

The usefulness of options to corporate managers is by no means limited to the applications we discuss in this section. However, to understand the other applications, we need deeper knowledge of what determines the option price. In Chapter 21, we explore how to calculate the price of an option.

CONCEPT CHECK   1. Explain how equity can be viewed as a call option on the firm.

2. Explain how debt can be viewed as an option portfolio.

Summary

1. A call option gives the holder the right (but not the obligation) to purchase an asset at some future date.

2. An option that gives the holder the right to sell an asset at some future date is called a put option.

3. When a holder of an option enforces the agreement and buys or sells the share of stock at the agreed-upon price, the holder is exercising the option.

4. The price at which the holder agrees to buy or sell the share of stock when the option is exercised is called the strike price or exercise price.

5. The last date on which the holder has the right to exercise the option is known as the expiration date.

6. An American option can be exercised on any date up to, and including, the exercise date. A European option can be exercised only on the expiration date.

7. If you would make money by exercising an option immediately, the option is in-the-money. Conversely, if you would lose money by exercising an option immediately, the option is out-of-the-money.

8. The value of a call option at expiration is

$$C = max(S - K, 0) \tag{20.1}$$

9. The value of a put option at expiration is

$$P = max(K - S, 0) \tag{20.2}$$

10. An investor holding a short position in an option has an obligation; he or she takes the opposite side of the contract to the investor who is long.

11. Put-call parity relates the value of the European call to the value of the European put and the stock.

$$C = P + S - PV(K) - PV(Div) \tag{20.4}$$

12. Call options with lower strike prices are more valuable than otherwise identical calls with higher strike prices. Conversely, put options are more valuable with higher strike prices.

13. Call options increase in value, and put options decrease in value, when the stock price rises.

14. Arbitrage bounds for option prices:
    a. An American option cannot be worth less than its European counterpart.
    b. A put option cannot be worth more than its exercise price.
    c. A call option cannot be worth more than the stock itself.
    d. An American option cannot be worth less than its intrinsic value.
    e. An American option with a later exercise date cannot be worth less than an otherwise identical American option with an earlier exercise date.

15. The value of an option generally increases with the volatility of the stock.

16. It is never optimal to exercise an American call option on a non-dividend-paying stock early. Thus, an American call option on a non-dividend-paying stock has the same price as its European counterpart.

17. It can be optimal to exercise a deep in-the-money American put option. It can be optimal to exercise an American call option just before the stock goes ex-dividend.

18. Equity can be viewed as a call option on the firm.

19. The debt holders can be viewed as owning the firm *and* having sold a call option with a strike price equal to the required debt payment. You can also think of corporate debt as a portfolio of riskless debt and a short position in a put option on the firm's cash flow with a strike price equal to the required debt payment.

Key Terms

American options *p. 656*
at-the-money *p. 657*
butterfly spread *p. 666*
call option *p. 656*
deep in-the-money *p. 658*
deep out-of-the-money *p. 658*
European options *p. 656*
exercising (an option) *p. 656*
expiration date *p. 656*
financial option *p. 656*
hedge *p. 658*
in-the-money *p. 658*
intrinsic value *p. 670*

open interest *p. 657*
option writer *p. 656*
out-of-the-money *p. 658*
portfolio insurance *p. 667*
protective put *p. 667*
put option *p. 656*
put-call parity *p. 668*
speculate *p. 658*
straddle *p. 664*
strangle *p. 665*
strike (exercise) price *p. 656*
time value *p. 670*

Further Reading

Readers interested in a deeper discussion of options and other derivative securities will find the following books useful: R. L. McDonald, *Derivative Markets* (Boston: Addison Wesley, 2003); and J. C. Hull, *Options, Futures and Other Derivatives*, 5th ed. (Upper Saddle River, NJ: Prentice Hall, 2005).

Problems

A blue box (■) indicates problems available in MyFinanceLab. An asterisk (*) indicates problems with a higher level of difficulty.

Option Basics

1. Explain what the following financial terms mean:
   a. Option
   b. Expiration date
   c. Strike price
   d. Call
   e. Put

2. What is the difference between a European option and an American option? Are European options available exclusively in Europe and American options available exclusively in America?

3.   Below is an option quote on IBM from the CBOE Web site. Explain what each column means.

| IBM | | | | | | | | | | | | | 92.64 +0.29 | |
| Mar 10, 2005 @ 10:25 ET (Data 20 Minutes Delayed) | | | | | | Bid N/A | Ask N/A | | Size N/A × N/A | | | Vol 491000 | |
Calls	Last Sale	Net	Bid	Ask	Vol	Open Int	Puts	Last Sale	Net	Bid	Ask	Vol	Open Int
05 Mar 85.00 (IBM CQ-E)	9.10	pc	7.60	7.80	0	497	05 Mar 85.00 (IBM OQ-E)	0.10	pc	0	0.05	0	2678
05 Mar 90.00 (IBM CR-E)	2.80	−0.20	2.70	2.85	10	3883	05 Mar 90.00 (IBM OR-E)	0.20	pc	0.05	0.15	0	5998
05 Mar 95.00 (IBM CS-E)	0.10	pc	0.05	0.15	0	19563	05 Mar 95.00 (IBM OS-E)	2.75	pc	2.40	2.50	0	6843
05 Mar 100.0 (IBM CT-E)	0.05	pc	0	0.05	0	4067	05 Mar 100.0 (IBM OT-E)	6.80	pc	7.30	7.50	0	77
05 Apr 85.00 (IBM DQ-E)	8.00	pc	7.90	8.10	0	6049	05 Apr 85.00 (IBM PQ-E)	0.20	pc	0.10	0.25	0	11595
05 Apr 90.00 (IBM DR-E)	3.60	+0.10	3.50	3.70	102	22532	05 Apr 90.00 (IBM PR-E)	0.75	pc	0.65	0.80	0	25586
05 Apr 95.00 (IBM DS-E)	0.75	pc	0.80	0.85	0	25117	05 Apr 95.00 (IBM PS-E)	3.00	pc	2.95	3.10	0	28055
05 Apr 100.0 (IBM DT-E)	0.15	pc	0.10	0.15	0	17512	05 Apr 100.0 (IBM PT-E)	7.70	pc	7.30	7.50	0	2678

Source: Chicago Board Options Exchange at www.cboe.com.

4.   Explain the difference between a long position in a put and a short position in a call.

Option Payoffs at Expiration

EXCEL   5.   You own a call option on Intuit stock with a strike price of $40. The option will expire in exactly three months' time.
   a. If the stock is trading at $55 in three months, what will be the payoff of the call?
   b. If the stock is trading at $35 in three months, what will be the payoff of the call?
   c. Draw a payoff diagram showing the value of the call at expiration as a function of the stock price at expiration.

EXCEL   6.   Assume that you have shorted the call option in Problem 5.
   a. If the stock is trading at $55 in three months, what will you owe?
   b. If the stock is trading at $35 in three months, what will you owe?
   c. Draw a payoff diagram showing the amount you owe at expiration as a function of the stock price at expiration.

EXCEL   7.   You own a put option on Ford stock with a strike price of $10. The option will expire in exactly six months' time.
   a. If the stock is trading at $8 in six months, what will be the payoff of the put?
   b. If the stock is trading at $23 in six months, what will be the payoff of the put?
   c. Draw a payoff diagram showing the value of the put at expiration as a function of the stock price at expiration.

EXCEL   8.   Assume that you have shorted the put option in Problem 7.
   a. If the stock is trading at $8 in three months, what will you owe?
   b. If the stock is trading at $23 in three months, what will you owe?
   c. Draw a payoff diagram showing the amount you owe at expiration as a function of the stock price at expiration.

9.   What position has more downside exposure: a short position in a call or a short position in a put? That is, in the worst case, in which of these two positions would your losses be greater?

10.   You are long both a call and a put on the same share of stock with the same exercise date. The exercise price of the call is $40 and the exercise price of the put is $45. Plot the value of this combination as a function of the stock price on the exercise date.

11. You are long two calls on the same share of stock with the same exercise date. The exercise price of the first call is $40 and the exercise price of the second call is $60. In addition, you are short two otherwise identical calls, both with an exercise price of $50. Plot the value of this combination as a function of the stock price on the exercise date. What is the name of this combination of options?

*12. A forward contract is a contract to purchase an asset at a fixed price on a particular date in the future. Both parties are obligated to fulfill the contract. Explain how to construct a forward contract on a share of stock from a position in options.

13. Explain why an option can be thought of as an insurance contract.

14. You own a share of Costco stock. You are worried that its price will fall and would like to insure yourself against this possibility. How can you purchase insurance against this possibility?

Put-Call Parity

15. Dynamic Energy Systems stock is currently trading for $33 per share. The stock pays no dividends. A one-year European put option on Dynamic with a strike price of $35 is currently trading for $2.10. If the risk-free interest rate is 10% per year, what is the price of a one-year European call option on Dynamic with a strike price of $35?

16. You happen to be checking the newspaper and notice an arbitrage opportunity. The current stock price of Intrawest is $20 per share and the one-year risk-free interest rate is 8%. A one-year put on Intrawest with a strike price of $18 sells for $3.33, while the identical call sells for $7. Explain what you must do to exploit this arbitrage opportunity.

Factors Affecting Option Prices

17. What is the maximum value that a call option and a put option can have?

18. What is the intrinsic value of an option?

19. Why is an American option with a longer time to expiration generally worth more than an otherwise identical option with a shorter time to expiration?

20. Is an increase in a stock's volatility good for the holder of a call option? Is it good for the holder of a put option?

Exercising Options Early

*21. Why is it *never* optimal to exercise an American call option on a non-dividend-paying stock early?

*22. Explain why an American call option on a non-dividend-paying stock always has the same price as its European counterpart.

*23. Under what conditions is it optimal to exercise an American call option early?

*24. Under what conditions is it optimal to exercise an American put option early?

Options and Corporate Finance

25. Explain why equity can be viewed as a call option on a firm.

26. How can debt be viewed as an option on a firm?

*27. Express the position of an equity holder in terms of put options.

28. Express the position of a debt holder in terms of put options.

29. Use the data in Table 20.5 to determine the rate Google would pay on $105 billion in zero-coupon debt due in January 2008. Suppose Google currently has 300 million shares outstanding, implying a market value of $121.8 billion. The current two-year risk-free rate is 4.5%.

Data Case

Your uncle owns 10,000 shares of Wal-Mart stock. He is concerned about the short-term outlook for Wal-Mart's stock due to an impending "major announcement." This announcement has received much attention in the press so he expects the stock price will change significantly in the next month, but is unsure whether it will be a profit or a loss. He hopes the price will increase, but he also doesn't want to suffer if the price were to fall in the short term.

His broker recommended he buy a "protective put" on the stock, but your uncle has never traded options before and is not much of a risk taker. He wants you to devise a plan for him to capitalize if the announcement is positive but still be protected if the news causes the price to drop. You realize that a protective put will protect him from the downside risk, but you think a straddle may offer similar downside protection, while increasing the upside potential. You decide to show him both strategies and the resulting profits and returns he could face from each.

1. Download option quotes on options that expire in approximately one month on Wal-Mart from the Chicago Board Options Exchange (www.cboe.com) into an Excel spreadsheet. If you choose to down load "near-term at-the-money" options you will get a range of options expiring in about a month. You can only get active quotes while the exchange is open; bid or ask prices are not available when it is closed.

2. Determine your uncle's profit and return using the protective put.
   a. Identify the expiring put with an exercise price closest to, but not below, the current stock price. Determine the investment required to protect all 10,000 shares.
   b. Determine the put price at expiration for each stock price at $5 increments from $25 to $65 using Eq. 20.2.
   c. Compute the profit (or loss) on the put for each stock price used in part (b).
   d. Compute the profit on the stock from the current price for each stock price used in part (b).
   e. Compute his overall profit (or loss) of the protective put, that is, combining the put and his stock for each price used in parts (c) and (d).
   f. Compute the overall return of the protective put.

3. Determine your uncle's profit and return using the straddle.
   a. Compute the investment your uncle would have to make to purchase the call and put with the same exercise price and expiration as the put option in Question 2, to cover all 10,000 of his shares.
   b. Determine the value at expiration of the call and the put options at each $5 increment of stock prices from $25 to $65 using Eqs. 20.1 and 20.2.
   c. Determine the profit (or loss) on the options at each stock price used in part (b).
   d. Determine the profit (or loss) on the stock from the current price for each stock price used in part (b).
   e. Compute his overall profit (or loss) of the stock plus straddle, that is, combining the position in both options and his stock for each price used in parts (c) and (d).
   f. Compute the overall return of this position.

4. Was the broker correct that the protective put would prevent your uncle from losing if the announcement caused a large decrease in the stock value? What is your uncle's maximum possible loss using the protective put?

5. What is the maximum possible loss your uncle could experience using the straddle?

6. Which strategy, the protective put or the straddle, provides the maximum upside potential for your uncle? Why does this occur?

Option Valuation

Robert Merton and Myron Scholes were awarded the 1997 Nobel Prize in economics for their 1973 discovery, together with Fischer Black,[1] of a formula to calculate the price of an option: the *Black-Scholes Option Pricing Model.* Although the formula itself represented an enormous contribution to economics, even more important were the techniques that Black, Scholes, and Merton developed to value options. It is not an exaggeration to say that these techniques changed the course of financial economics and gave birth to a new profession: financial engineering.

Prior to the Black-Scholes formula, most economists and practitioners did not anticipate that mathematical formulas could be derived that could accurately price financial securities such as options. Today, however, financial engineers routinely use formulas to price financial securities in much the same way as mechanical engineers use Newton's laws to build bridges. The most important factor contributing to the huge growth in the types of financial securities that are available today are the techniques financial engineers use to price them. All of these techniques can be traced back to the Black-Scholes formula. Today, most large corporations rely on these financial securities to manage risk. Without the Black-Scholes formula, the job of corporate managers would be very different: many corporations would be forced to bear much more risk than they now do.

Why do these formulas work so well? As we will see, they rely primarily on the Law of One Price. That is, they do not depend on knowing unobservable parameters such as investor tastes and beliefs. It is the need, in most applications, to model human preferences that makes economics an inexact science. The great insight that Merton, Black, and Scholes brought to economics is that in the case of options it is not necessary to model preferences. As we will explain in this chapter, their work

---

1. The Black-Scholes formula was derived in a paper jointly written by Fischer Black and Myron Scholes ("The Pricing of Options and Corporate Liabilities," *Journal of Political Economy*, 81, 1973) which relied on earlier work by Robert Merton. Unfortunately, Black died two years before the prize was awarded (Nobel Prizes cannot be awarded posthumously).

demonstrated how to apply the Law of One Price to value a vast new range of financial securities based on the current market prices of stocks and bonds.

With the importance of the Black-Scholes formula kept firmly in mind, our objective in this chapter is to explain the most commonly used techniques (all of which derive from Black and Scholes' insights) for calculating the price of an option: the Binomial Option Pricing Model, the Black-Scholes formula, and risk-neutral probabilities. We apply these techniques to show how to value stock options and quantify their risk and return. We then show how to use the Black-Scholes formula to estimate the beta of risky debt. With this foundation in place, we will be able to cover important applications of option pricing for corporate managers in subsequent chapters.

21.1 The Binomial Option Pricing Model

We begin our study of option pricing with the **Binomial Option Pricing Model**, a technique for pricing options that was derived by John Cox, Stephen Ross, and Mark Rubinstein.[2] This model makes the simplifying assumption that at the end of the next period, the stock price has only two possible values. This assumption allows us to demonstrate the key insight of Black and Scholes—that option payoffs can be replicated exactly by constructing a portfolio out of a risk-free bond and the underlying stock. Furthermore, we will see that the model can be quite realistic if we consider stock price movements over very short time intervals.

A Two-State Single-Period Model

Let's start by calculating the price of a single-period option in a very simple world. We will value the option by first constructing a **replicating portfolio**, a portfolio of other securities that has exactly the same value in one period as the option. Then, because they have the same payoffs, the Law of One Price implies that the current value of the call and the replicating portfolio must be equal.

Consider a European call option that expires in one period and has an exercise price of $50. Assume that the stock price today is equal to $50. We also assume here and throughout the chapter that the stock pays no dividends (unless explicitly indicated). In one period, the stock price will either rise by $10 or fall by $10. The one-period risk-free rate is 6%. We can summarize this information on a **binomial tree**—a timeline with two branches at every date representing the possible events that could happen at those times:

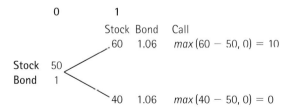

---

2. See J. Cox, S. Ross, and M. Rubinstein, "Option Pricing, A Simplified Approach," *Journal of Financial Economics* 7(3) (1979): 229–263. In a concurrent paper, J. R. Rendleman, and B. J. Bartter ["Two-State Option Pricing," *Journal of Finance* 34(5) (December 1979): 1093–1110] develop the same technique.

The binomial tree contains all the information we currently know: the value of the stock, bond, and call options in each state in one period, as well as the price of the stock and bond today (for simplicity, we assume the bond price today is $1, so in one period it will be worth $1.06). We define the state in which the stock price goes up (to $60) as the *up* state and the state in which the stock price goes down (to $40) as the *down* state.

In order to determine the value of the option using the Law of One Price, we must show that we can replicate its payoffs using a portfolio of the stock and the bond. Let Δ be the number of shares of stock we purchase, and let B be our initial investment in bonds. To create a call option using the stock and the bond, the value of the portfolio consisting of the stock and bond must match the value of the option in every possible state. Thus, in the up state, the value of the portfolio must be $10 (the value of the call in that state):

$$60\Delta + 1.06B = 10 \tag{21.1}$$

In the down state, the value of the portfolio must be zero (the value of the call in that state):

$$40\Delta + 1.06B = 0 \tag{21.2}$$

Equations 21.1 and 21.2 are two simultaneous equations with two unknowns, Δ and B. We'll write down the general formula to solve these equations shortly, but in this case we can check that the solution is

$$\Delta = 0.5$$
$$B = -18.8679$$

A portfolio that is long 0.5 share of stock and short approximately $18.87 worth of bonds (i.e., we have borrowed $18.87 at a 6% interest rate) will have a value in one period that exactly matches the value of the call. Let's verify this explicitly:

$$60 \times 0.5 - 1.06 \times 18.87 = 10$$
$$40 \times 0.5 - 1.06 \times 18.87 = 0$$

Therefore, by the Law of One Price, the price of the call option today must equal the current market value of the replicating portfolio. The value of the portfolio today is the value of 0.5 shares at the current share price of $50, less the amount borrowed:

$$50\Delta + B = 50(0.5) - 18.87 = 6.13 \tag{21.3}$$

Thus the price of the call today is $6.13.[3]

Figure 21.1 illustrates how we can use the stock and the bond to replicate the payoff of the call option in this case. As a function of the future stock price, the payoff of the replicating portfolio is a line with a slope of $\Delta = 0.5$, and an intercept of $1.06\,B = 1.06(-18.87) = -20$. This line is very different from the line showing the payoff of the call option, which is zero below the strike price of $50 and increases 1 : 1 with the stock price above $50. The secret of the binomial model is that, while the option and the replicating portfolio do not have the same payoffs in general, they have the same payoffs given the only two outcomes we have assumed possible for the stock price: $40 and $60.

Note that by using the Law of One Price, we are able to solve for the price of the option *without knowing the probabilities of the states in the binomial tree.* That is, we did not need

---

3. If the call's price were different, there would be an arbitrage opportunity. For example, if the call price were $6.50, we could earn a profit by buying the replicating portfolio for $6.13 and selling the call option for $6.50. Because they have the same future payoff, we have taken no risk, and earn an immediate profit of $6.50 - 6.13 = 0.37 per option sold.

FIGURE 21.1

Replicating an Option in the Binomial Model

The red line shows the payoff of the replicating portfolio and the blue line shows the payoff of the call option, as a function of next period's stock price. While they do not match everywhere, they do match for the two possible outcomes of the stock price next period, $40 and $60.

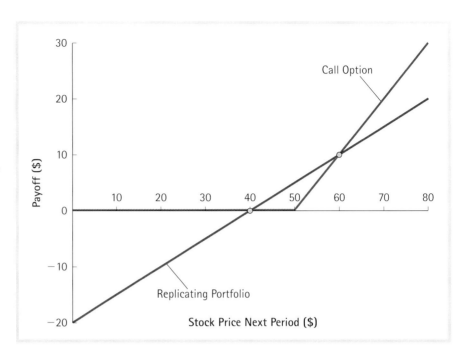

to specify the likelihood that the stock would go up versus down. This remarkable result was a very important discovery because the probabilities of future states are part of investor beliefs, so they are very difficult to estimate. The preceding argument shows that we do not need to know these probabilities to value options. It also means that we do not need to know the expected return of the stock, which will depend on these probabilities.

The Binomial Pricing Formula

Now that we have seen the basic idea, let's consider a more general example. Suppose the current stock price is S, and the stock price will either go up to S_u or down to S_d next period. The risk-free interest rate is r_f. Let's determine the price of an option that has a value of C_u if the stock goes up, and C_d if the stock goes down:

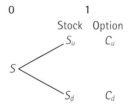

Note that in the depiction of the binomial tree above, for simplicity we did not write down the bond payoff since it earns a return of r_f in either case.

What is the value of the option today? Again, we must determine the number of shares of stock, Δ, and the position in the bond, B, such that the payoff of the replicating portfolio matches the payoff of the option if the stock goes up or down:

$$S_u \Delta + (1 + r_f)B = C_u \quad \text{and} \quad S_d \Delta + (1 + r_f)B = C_d \tag{21.4}$$

Solving these two equations for the two unknowns Δ and B we get the general formula for the replicating formula in the binomial model:

Replicating Portfolio in the Binomial Model

$$\Delta = \frac{C_u - C_d}{S_u - S_d} \quad \text{and} \quad B = \frac{C_d - S_d\Delta}{1 + r_f} \tag{21.5}$$

Note that the formula for Δ in Eq. 21.5 can be interpreted as the sensitivity of the option's value to changes in the stock price. It is equal to the slope of the line showing the payoff of the replicating portfolio in Figure 21.1

Once we know the replicating portfolio, we can calculate the value C of the option today as the cost of this portfolio:

Option Price in the Binomial Model

$$C = S\Delta + B \tag{21.6}$$

Equations 21.5 and 21.6 summarize the binomial option pricing model. Though they are relatively simple, by applying them in different ways we will see that they are quite powerful. For one thing, they do not require that the option we are valuing is a call option—we can use them to value *any* security whose payoff depends on the stock price. For example, we can use them to price a put, as in the next example.

EXAMPLE 21.1

Valuing a Put Option

Problem
Suppose a stock is currently trading for $60, and in one period will either go up by 20% or fall by 10%. If the one-period risk-free rate is 3%, what is the price of a European put option that expires in one period and has an exercise price of $60?

Solution
We begin by constructing a binomial tree:

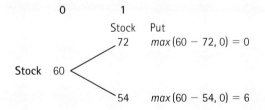

Thus, we can solve for the value of the put by using Eqs. 21.5 and 21.6 with $C_u = 0$ (the value of the put when the stock goes up) and $C_d = 6$ (the value of the put when the stock goes down). Therefore,

$$\Delta = \frac{C_u - C_d}{S_u - S_d} = \frac{0 - 6}{72 - 54} = -0.3333 \quad \text{and} \quad B = \frac{C_d - S_d\Delta}{1 + r_f} = \frac{6 - 54(-0.3333)}{1.03} = 23.30$$

This portfolio is short 0.3333 shares of the stock, and has $23.30 invested in the risk-free bond. Let's check that it replicates the put if the stock goes up or down:

$$72(-0.3333) + 1.03(23.30) = 0 \quad \text{and} \quad 54(-0.3333) + 1.03(23.30) = 6$$

Thus, the value of the put is the initial cost of this portfolio. Using Eq. 21.6:

$$\text{Put value} = C = S\Delta + B$$
$$= 60(-0.3333) + 23.30 = \$3.30$$

You might be skeptical at this point. Showing that we can value call and put options in a simple two-state one-period example is one thing; pricing real-world options is another matter altogether. Yet, as we show in the next section, this simple two-state model is easily generalized.

A Multiperiod Model

The problem with the simple two-state example is that there are many more than two possible outcomes for the stock price in the real world. To make the model more realistic, we must allow for the possibility of many states and periods.

Let's consider a two-period binomial tree for the stock price:

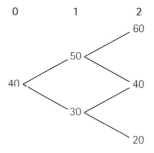

The key property of the binomial model is that in each period, there are only two possible outcomes—the stock either goes up or down. But by adding an additional period, the number of possible stock prices at the end has increased. Let's assume again that the risk-free rate of interest is 6% per period and consider how to price a call option with a strike price of $50 that expires in two periods.

To calculate the value of an option in a multiperiod binomial tree, we start at the end of the tree and work backwards. At time 2, the option expires, so its value is equal to its intrinsic value. In this case, the call will be worth $10 if the stock price goes up to $60, and will be worth zero otherwise.

Next let's determine the value of the option in each possible state at time 1. What is the value of the option if the stock price has gone up to $50 at time 1? In this case, because the option expires next period, the remaining part of the binomial tree is as follows:

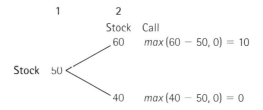

This binomial tree is exactly the same tree that we considered in the one-period model at the start of this section. There we computed the replicating portfolio as having

$\Delta = 0.5$ shares of stock and a bond position of $B = -\$18.87$, for an initial call value of $6.13 (see Eq. 21.3).

What if the stock price has dropped to $30 at time 1? In that case the binomial tree for the next period is

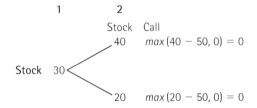

The option is worthless in both states at time 2, so the value of the option in the down state at time 1 must also be zero (and the replicating portfolio is simply $\Delta = 0$ and $B = 0$).

Given the value of the call option in either state at time 1, we can now work backwards and determine the value of the call at time 0. In that case, we can write the binomial tree over the next period as follows:

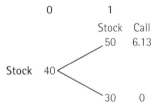

In this case, the call values at the end of the tree (time 1) are not the final payoffs of the option, but are the values of the option one period prior to expiration. Nonetheless, we can use the same binomial formulas to calculate the replicating portfolio at time 0, which is a portfolio whose value will match the value of the option at time 1. From Eq. 21.5:

$$\Delta = \frac{C_u - C_d}{S_u - S_d} = \frac{6.13 - 0}{50 - 30} = 0.3065 \quad \text{and}$$

$$B = \frac{C_d - S_d\Delta}{1 + r_f} = \frac{0 - 30(0.3065)}{1.06} = -8.67$$

From Eq. 21.6, the initial value of the call option is equal to the initial cost of this portfolio:

$$C = S\Delta + B = 40(0.3065) - 8.67 = \$3.59$$

Therefore, the initial value of the call option at time 0 is $3.59.

For this two-period call option, while we can still construct the option out of the stock and the bond, we now need to adjust our replicating portfolio at the end of each period. That is, we start off long 0.3065 shares of stock and borrow $8.67 (for an initial cost of $3.59). If the stock price drops to $30, our shares are worth $30 × 0.3065 = $9.20, and our debt has grown to $8.67 × 1.06 = $9.20. Thus, the net value of the portfolio is worthless (matching the option value), and we can liquidate the portfolio (at no cost). If the stock price rises to $50, the net value of the portfolio rises to $6.13. In that case, the new Δ of the replicating portfolio is 0.5. We therefore buy 0.50 − 0.3065 = 0.1935 more shares of stock and pay for it by borrowing 0.1935 × $50 = $9.67. This re-trading requires no new money; at the end our total debt will be $8.67 × 1.06 + 9.67 = $18.87, which matches the value for *B* we calculated earlier. Therefore, on the expiration date at time 2, the value of the portfolio is $10 if the stock goes up to $60, and is zero otherwise.

The idea that you can replicate the option payoff by dynamically trading in a portfolio of the underlying stock and a risk-free bond was one of the most important contributions of the original Black-Scholes paper. Today, this kind of replication strategy is called a **dynamic trading strategy**.

Using The Binomial Option Pricing Model to Value a Put Option

Problem

Suppose the current price of Narver Network Systems stock is $50 per share. In each of the next two years, the stock price will either increase by 20% or decrease by 10%. The 3% one-year risk-free rate of interest will remain constant. Calculate the price of a two-year European put option on Narver Network Systems stock with a strike price $60.

Solution

Here is the binomial tree for the stock price, together with the final payoffs of the put option:

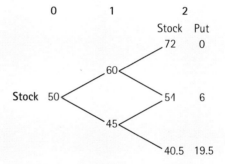

If the stock goes up to $60 at time 1, we are in exactly the same situation as in Example 21.1. Using our result there, we see that if the stock is worth $60 at time 1, the value of the put option is $3.30.

If the stock goes down to $45 at time 1, then at time 2 the put option will be worth either $6 if the stock goes up, or $19.50 if the stock goes down. Using Eq. 21.5:

$$\Delta = \frac{C_u - C_d}{S_u - S_d} = \frac{6 - 19.5}{54 - 40.5} = -1 \text{ and } B = \frac{C_d - S_d\Delta}{1 + r_f} = \frac{19.5 - 40.5(-1)}{1.03} = 58.25$$

This portfolio is short 1 share of the stock, and has $58.25 invested in the risk-free bond. Because the value of the bond will grow to $58.25 × 1.03 = $60 at time 2, the value of the replicating portfolio will be $60 less the final price of the stock, matching the payoff of the put option. Thus, the value of the put is the cost of this portfolio. Using Eq. 21.6:

$$\text{Put value} = C = S\Delta + B = 45(-1) + 58.25 = \$13.25$$

Now consider the value of the put option at time 0. In period 1, we have calculated that the put will be worth $3.30 if the stock goes up to $60, and $13.25 if the stock falls to $45. The binomial tree at time 0 is

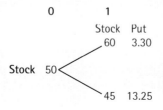

Using Eq. 21.5 and Eq. 21.6, the replicating portfolio and put value at time 0 are

$$\Delta = \frac{C_u - C_d}{S_u - S_d} = \frac{3.30 \quad 13.25}{60 - 45} = -0.6633,$$

$$B = \frac{C_d - S_d\Delta}{1 + r_f} = \frac{13.25 - 45(-0.6633)}{1.03} = -41.84, \quad \text{and}$$

Put value $= C = S\Delta + B = 50(-0.6633) + 41.84 = \$8.68$

Thus, the value of European put option at time 0 is \$8.68.

Making the Model Realistic

Using the methods of the previous section, we can value options given any number of periods in the binomial stock price tree. But of course, to price an option for an actual stock, the binomial tree must be a realistic model of the way the stock is likely to evolve in the future.

While binary up or down movements are not the way stock prices behave on an annual or even daily basis, they are a much more reasonable description of stock prices over very short time periods, such as the time between trades. By decreasing the length of each period, and increasing the number of periods in the stock price tree, we can construct a realistic model for the stock price. Figure 21.2 shows an example of a stock price path in which the stock price moves up or down by 1% each of 900 periods over the year. With many short periods, these stock price paths look very similar to the price charts for real stocks. Practitioners routinely use this method to calculate the prices of options and other

FIGURE 21.2

A Binomial Stock Price Path

The figure depicts a stock price path with 900 periods during the year, and a random stock return of +1% or −1% each period. With a large number of periods, and small movements in the stock price each period, the binomial model is a realistic model of stock price behavior.

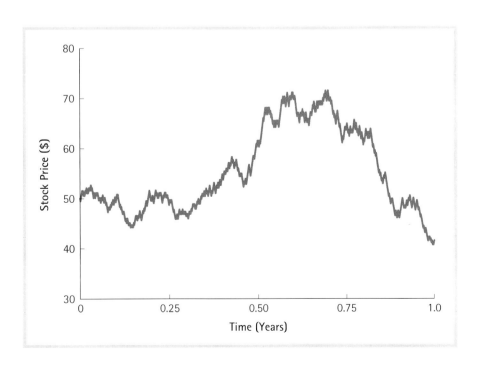

types of derivative securities. With a fast computer, prices can be computed very quickly even with thousands of periods.[4]

As we mentioned earlier, the techniques of the binomial option pricing model are not specific to European call and put options. We can use it to price any security whose payoff depends on the stock price. But for the special case of European call and put options, there is an alternative approach. If we let the length of each period shrink to zero, and the number of periods per year grow to infinity, the results of the binomial option pricing model can be calculated using a single, simple formula: The Black-Scholes formula. We consider it next.

CONCEPT CHECK   1. Why don't we need to know the probabilities of the states in the binominal tree in order to solve for the price of the option?

2. What is a replicating portfolio?

21.2   The Black-Scholes Option Pricing Model

Although Black and Scholes did not originally derive it that way, the **Black-Scholes Option Pricing Model** can be derived from the Binomial Option Pricing Model by making the length of each period, and the movement of the stock price per period, shrink to zero and letting the number of periods grow infinitely large. Rather than derive the formula here, we will state it and focus on its applications.

The Black-Scholes Formula

Before stating the Black-Scholes formula for the price of an option, it is necessary to introduce some terminology. Let S be the current price of the stock, T be the number of years left to expiration, K be the exercise price, and σ be the annual volatility (standard deviation) of the stock's return. Then the value, at time t, of a call option on a stock that does not pay dividends prior to the option's expiration date is given by

**Black-Scholes Price of a Call Option
on a Non-Dividend-Paying Stock**

$$C = S \times N(d_1) - PV(K) \times N(d_2) \tag{21.7}$$

where $N(d)$ is the **cumulative normal distribution**—that is, the probability, as shown in Figure 21.3, that a normally distributed variable is less than d—and

$$d_1 = \frac{\ln[S/PV(K)]}{\sigma\sqrt{T}} + \frac{\sigma\sqrt{T}}{2} \quad \text{and} \quad d_2 = d_1 - \sigma\sqrt{T} \tag{21.8}$$

$PV(K)$ is the present value (price) of a risk-free zero-coupon bond that pays K on the expiration date of the option.

We need only five input parameters to price the call: the stock price, the strike price, the exercise date, the risk-free interest rate (to compute the present value of the strike

---

4. There is a question of how to calibrate the up or down movements each period. A standard approach is to assume the stock's return each period is $\pm \sigma / \sqrt{n}$, where σ is the stock's volatility and n is the number of periods per year.

FIGURE 21.3

Normal Distribution

$N(d)$, the cumulative normal distribution, is the probability that a normally distributed random variable will take on a value less than d. This probability is equal to the area under the normal distribution (bell curve) to the left of the point d—the shaded area in the figure. Because it is a probability, $N(d)$ has a minimum value of 0 and a maximum value of 1. It can be calculated using the function NORMSDIST(d) in Excel.

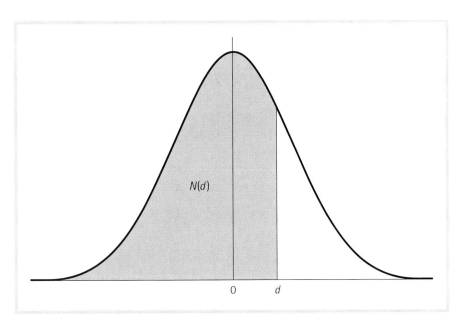

price), and the volatility of the stock. What is equally notable is what we do *not* need. Just as we do not need to know the probabilities in the Binomial Option Pricing Model, we do not need to know the expected return on the stock to calculate the option price in the Black-Scholes Option Pricing Model. The expected return of the stock is difficult to measure with great accuracy as we learned in Part IV of the text; if it were a required input, we could not expect the formula to deliver the option price with much accuracy. Indeed, the only parameter in the Black-Scholes formula that we need to forecast is the stock's volatility. Because a stock's volatility is much easier to measure (and forecast) than its expected return, the Black-Scholes formula can be very precise.

You might wonder how it is possible to compute the value of a security like an option that appears to depend critically on the future stock price without knowing the expected return of the stock. In fact, the expected return of the stock is already incorporated into the current stock price, and the value of the option today depends on the stock price today.

The Black-Scholes formula is derived assuming that the call is a European option. Recall from Chapter 20 that an American call option on a non-dividend-paying stock always has the same price as its European counterpart. Thus the Black-Scholes formula can be used to price American or European call options on non-dividend-paying stocks.

EXAMPLE 21.3

Valuing a Call Option with the Black-Scholes Formula

Problem

Oracle Corporation does not pay dividends. Using the data in Table 21.1, compare the price on December 6, 2005, for the January 2006 American call option on Oracle with a strike price of $12.50 to the price predicted by the Black-Scholes formula. Assume that the volatility of Oracle is 25% per year and that the short-term risk-free rate of interest on December 6, 2005, is 4.38% per year.

Solution

We use $12.585 (the mean between the bid and ask prices) for the per-share price of Oracle stock. Because the January contract expires on the Saturday following the third Friday of January (January 21), there are 45 days left until expiration. The present value of the strike price is $PV(K) = 12.50/(1.0438)^{45/365} = \$12.434$. Calculating d_1 and d_2 from Eq. 21.8 gives

$$d_1 = \frac{\ln[S/PV(K)]}{\sigma\sqrt{T}} + \frac{\sigma\sqrt{T}}{2}$$

$$= \frac{\ln(12.585/12.434)}{0.25\sqrt{\frac{45}{365}}} + \frac{0.25\sqrt{\frac{45}{365}}}{2} = 0.181$$

$$d_2 = d_1 - \sigma\sqrt{T} = 0.181 - 0.25\sqrt{\tfrac{45}{365}} = 0.094$$

Substituting d_1 and d_2 into the Black-Scholes formula given by Eq. 21.7 results in

$$C = S N(d_1) - PV(K)\, N(d_2)$$

$$= 12.585 \times 0.572 - 12.434 \times 0.537$$

$$= \$0.52$$

In Table 21.1 the bid and ask prices for this option are $0.50 and $0.60.

Figure 21.4 plots the value of the call option in Example 21.3 as a function of Oracle's stock price. Notice how the value of the option always lies above its intrinsic value.

European Put Options. We can use the Black-Scholes formula to compute the price of a European put option on a non-dividend-paying stock by using the put-call parity formula we derived in Chapter 20 (see Eq. 20.3). The price of a European put from put-call parity is

$$P = C - S + PV(K)$$

TABLE 21.1   **Oracle Option Quotes**

ORCL   12.58 +0.07

Dec 06, 2005 @ 12:35 ET (Data 15 Minutes Delayed)   Bid 12.58   Ask 12.59   Size 643 × 999   Vol 15062810

Calls	Bid	Ask	Vol	Open Int	Puts	Bid	Ask	Vol	Open Int
06 Jan 11.00 (ORQ AM-E)	1.65	1.75	0	524	06 Jan 11.00 (ORQ MM-E)	0.05	0.10	0	5
06 Jan 12.50 (ORQ AV-E)	0.50	0.60	42	66697	06 Jan 12.50 (ORQ MV-E)	0.35	0.45	60	67775
06 Jan 14.00 (ORQ AP-E)	0.05	0.10	0	1876	06 Jan 14.00 (ORQ MP-E)	1.40	1.50	0	444
06 Jan 15.00 (ORQ AC-E)	0	0.05	0	118175	06 Jan 15.00 (ORQ MC-E)	2.40	2.45	0	49860

Source: Chicago Board Options Exchange at www.cboe.com.

FIGURE 21.4

Black-Scholes Value on December 6, 2005, of the January 2006 12.50 Call on Oracle Stock

The red curve is the Black-Scholes value of the call. The black line is the immediate exercise (intrinsic) value of the call. The value of the call always exceeds its intrinsic value.

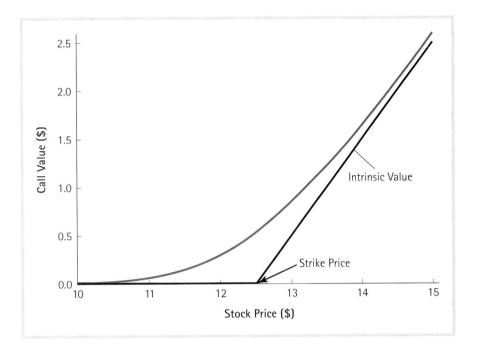

Substituting for C using the Black-Scholes formula gives

Black-Scholes Price of a European Put Option on a Non-Dividend-Paying Stock

$$P = PV(K)[1 - N(d_2)] - S[1 - N(d_1)] \tag{21.9}$$

Valuing a Put Option with the Black-Scholes Formula

Problem

Using the Black-Scholes formula and the data in Table 21.1, compute the price of a January 2006 $14 put option and compare it to the price in the market. Is the Black-Scholes formula the correct way to price these options? Assume that the standard deviation of Oracle is 25% per year and that the short-term risk-free rate of interest (on December 6, 2005) is 4.38% per year.

Solution

The present value of the strike price is $PV(K) = 14 / (1.0438)^{45/365} = \$13.926$. Calculating d_1 and d_2 from Eq. 21.8 gives

$$d_1 = \frac{\ln[S/PV(K)]}{\sigma\sqrt{T}} + \frac{\sigma\sqrt{T}}{2}$$

$$= \frac{\ln(12.585/13.926)}{0.25\sqrt{\frac{45}{365}}} + \frac{0.25\sqrt{\frac{45}{365}}}{2} = -1.110$$

$$d_2 = d_1 - \sigma\sqrt{T} = -1.110 - 0.25\sqrt{\frac{45}{365}} = -1.197$$

Substituting d_1 and d_2 into the Black-Scholes formula for a put option, using Eq. 21.9, gives

$$P = PV(K)[1 - N(d_2)] - S[1 - N(d_1)]$$
$$= 13.926 \times (1 - 0.116) - 12.585 \times (1 - 0.133)$$
$$= \$1.40$$

Given the bid and ask prices of $1.40 and $1.50, respectively, for the option, this estimate of the options value is equal to the bid price. But the Black-Scholes formula for puts is valid only for European options, and the quotes are for American options. Hence, in this case, the Black-Scholes option price is only a lower bound on the actual value of the put (recall that American options cannot be worth less than their European counterparts). In this case the value of the American put is at least its intrinsic value of $14 − 12.59 = \$1.41.

Figure 21.5 plots the value of the put option in Example 21.4 as a function of Oracle's stock price. Notice how the value of the option can lie below its intrinsic value. The Black-Scholes formula prices European puts and, as you will recall from Chapter 20, the time value of deep-in-the-money puts can be negative.

Dividend-Paying Stocks.   The Black-Scholes formula applies to call options on non-dividend-paying stocks. However, we can easily adjust the formula for European options on dividend-paying stocks.

The holder of a European call option does not receive the benefit of any dividends that will be paid prior to the expiration date of the option. Indeed, as we saw in Chapter 17, the stock price tends to drop by the amount of the dividend when the stock goes

FIGURE 21.5

Black-Scholes Value on December 6, 2005, of the January 2006 $14.00 Put on Oracle Stock

The red curve is the Black-Scholes value of the put. The black line is the intrinsic value of the put. When the put is deep in-the-money, the European put's value is less than its intrinsic value.

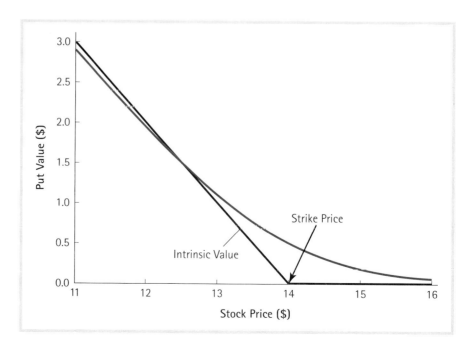

COMMON MISTAKE   **Valuing Employee Stock Options**

In the last 20 years, it has become common practice to compensate executives by granting them **executive stock options (ESOs)**—call options on their company's stock. Until 2005, U.S. accounting standards did not require firms to include stock option grants as part of their compensation expense. Now, however, firms are required to expense these options when calculating their earnings. Regardless of the accounting requirement, both firms and employees would like to know the value of this compensation. While it is tempting to use the Black-Scholes formula to value an ESO, there are several important pitfalls to be aware of when doing so.

To understand the difficulties of using the Black-Scholes formula to value ESOs, it is important to appreciate how they are usually granted. ESOs are typically American-style options with exercise dates up to ten years in the future. However, there is usually a vesting period (often as long as four years) during which the employee does not actually own the option. Instead, he or she owns a right to the option at the end of the vesting period. If the employee leaves the firm during this period, the individual forfeits this right and so does not get the option. Once the vesting period has passed, the employee owns the option but *it is not tradeable*—the only way the employee can liquidate the option is by exercising it. Furthermore, most executives face restrictions in trading their own company stock, so they effectively cannot construct a replicating portfolio. Because of these restrictions, ESOs are not worth the same amount to the employee and the firm.

One obvious difficulty with applying the Black-Scholes formula to such options is that the formula requires an estimate of the volatility of the stock over the life of the option. Forecasting volatility up to ten years in the future is extremely difficult. But even if the stock's volatility were known, the Black-Scholes formula does not account for the following important differences between ESOs and ordinary stock options:

1. *ESOs are dilutive.* When exercised, they increase the number of shares outstanding of the firm.
2. *ESOs may be forfeited.* If the employee leaves the firm, options that are not vested are immediately forfeited.

Options already vested are forfeited if not exercised within three months of the employee's departure.
3. *ESOs may be exercised early.* Once vested, the employee can exercise the options at any time.

Unless the number of options is large relative to the total number of shares outstanding, the first difference is not that important. The second difference is important for employees and firms with high employee turnover.

The third difference is very important for employees and all firms. Employees are risk-averse, but are not permitted to hedge the risk of the option by trading the replicating portfolio. As a consequence, the employee's preferences and beliefs matter in computing the ESO's value: A more risk-averse employee will attach a lower value to the option than a less risk averse employee. Furthermore, the only way an employee can eliminate his or her risk from the option is to exercise it and sell the stock. *Hence most employees choose to exercise early.*[*] In this case, employees are forfeiting the (often substantial) remaining time value of their options in exchange for a reduction in their risk.

Thus the Black-Scholes formula (which assumes no early exercise) overestimates the cost of the option to the firm and its benefit to the employee. Because the firm can hedge its option liabilities, risk is not an issue when evaluating the cost of the option to the firm. Thus, the Black-Scholes formula overstates the cost by not accounting for forfeitures and early exercise. Because the employee cannot sell nor hedge, the risk of the option, the Black-Scholes formula overstates the value of the option to the employee even further by not accounting for the personal cost of bearing risk.

How important are these differences? The answer appears to be *very* important. In a recent paper, Professors Ashish Jain and Ajay Subramanian adjust for these differences and find that for reasonable parameter values, the Black-Scholes formula can overestimate the *cost to the firm* of a vested five-year option by as much as 40%.[†] But the value to the employee can be much lower. Once one considers the personal cost of being under-diversified while holding the option, its value to the employee can be as low as one-third of the cost of the option to the firm.

---

[*]See S. Huddart and M. Lang, "Employee Stock Option Exercises: An Empirical Analysis," *Journal of Accounting and Economics* 21(1) (1996): 5–43.
[†]The Intertemporal Exercise and Valuation of Employee Options," *Accounting Review* 79(3) (2004): 705–743.

ex-dividend. Because the final stock price will be lower, dividends decrease the value of a call option.

Let $PV(Div)$ be the present value of any dividends paid prior to the expiration date of the option. Then a security that is identical to the stock, but did not pay any of the these dividends, would have a current market price of

$$S^x = S - PV(Div) \tag{21.10}$$

The value S^x is the current price of the stock excluding any dividends prior to expiration. *Because a European call option is the right to buy the stock without these dividends, we can evaluate it using the Black-Scholes formula with S^x in place of S.*

A useful special case is when the stock will pay a dividend that is proportional to its stock price at the time the dividend is paid. If q is the stock's (compounded) dividend yield until the expiration date, then[5]

$$S^x = S / (1 + q) \tag{21.11}$$

Valuing a Dividend-Paying European Call Option with the Black-Scholes Formula

Problem

World Wide Plants will pay an annual dividend yield of 5% on its stock. Plot the value of a one-year European call option with a strike price of $20 on World Wide Plants stock as a function of the stock price. Assume that the volatility of World Wide Plants stock is 20% per year and that the one-year risk-free rate of interest is 4%.

Solution

The price of the call is given by the standard Black-Scholes formula, Eq. 21.7, but with the stock price replaced throughout with $S^x = S/(1.05)$. For example, with a stock price of $30, $S^x = 30/(1.05) = 28.57$, $PV(K) = 20/1.04 = 19.23$, and

$$d_1 = \frac{\ln[S^x / PV(K)]}{\sigma\sqrt{T}} + \frac{\sigma\sqrt{T}}{2}$$

$$= \frac{\ln(28.57 / 19.23)}{0.2} + 0.1 = 2.08$$

$$d_2 = d_1 - \sigma\sqrt{T} = 2.08 - 0.2 = 1.88$$

so

$$C(S) = S^x N(d_1) - PV(K)\, N(d_2) = 28.57(0.981) - 19.23(0.970) = 9.37$$

---

5. We can compute this value as follows. Suppose that whenever the dividend is paid, we reinvest it. Then if we buy 1 share today, at expiration we will have $(1 + q)$ shares. So if we buy $1 / (1 + q)$ shares today, at expiration we will own $[1 / (1 + q) \times (1 + q)] = 1$ share. Thus, by the Law of One Price, the value today of 1 share at expiration (and no intervening dividends) is $S / (1 + q)$.

Plotting this function (in red) gives

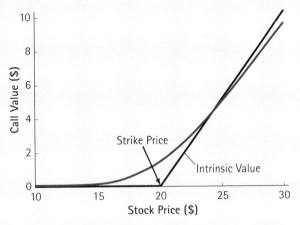

Notice that in this case the call can be worth less than its intrinsic value.

Implied Volatility

Of the five required inputs in the Black-Scholes formula, four are directly observable: S, K, T, and the risk-free interest rate. Only one parameter, σ, the volatility of the stock price, is not observable directly. Practitioners use two strategies to estimate the value of this variable. The first, most straightforward approach is to use historical data. The second approach is to "back out" the volatility using the Black-Scholes formula itself. That is, you can take the option price quoted in the market as an input and solve for the volatility. This estimate of a stock's volatility is known as the **implied volatility**. The implied volatility from one option can be used to estimate the value of other options on the stock with the same expiration date (as well as those with different expiration dates if the stock's volatility is not expected to change over time).

Using Implied Volatility to Value Options

Problem

Use the price of the January 2006 call on Oracle with a strike price of $11 in Table 21.1 to calculate the 45-day implied volatility for Oracle on December 6, 2005. Assume the risk-free rate of interest is 4.38% per year.

Solution

The price of the call is $1.70 (the average between the bid and ask prices), the time to expiration is 45 days, the price of the stock is $12.585 (the average between the bid and ask prices), and $PV(K) = 11/(1.0438)^{45/365} = \$10.942$. Substituting these values into the Black-Scholes formula, Eq. 21.7, gives

$$C = 12.585 N(d_1) - 10.942\, N(d_2)$$

where

$$d_1 = \frac{\ln(12.585\,/\,10.942)}{\sigma\sqrt{\frac{45}{365}}} + \frac{\sigma\sqrt{\frac{45}{365}}}{2} \quad \text{and} \quad d_2 = d_1 - \sigma\sqrt{\frac{45}{365}}$$

We can compute the Black-Scholes option value C for different volatilities using this equation. The option value C increases with σ, and is equal to 1.70 when $\sigma = 30.6\%$. (You can find this value by trial and error or by using Excel's solver tool.) Thus the implied volatility for Oracle stock derived from Oracle's option prices is about 30%. This number is close to the 25% volatility we used in Examples 21.3 and 21.4. If you use 25% as the volatility, the 06 January 11.00 call price is $1.67, so the difference in volatilities is within the bid-ask spread for the option.

The Replicating Portfolio

Although we introduced the concept of the replicating portfolio in the discussion of the Binomial Option Pricing Model, it was actually Black and Scholes who discovered this important insight while deriving their model. To see how the replicating portfolio is constructed in the Black-Scholes Model, recall from the Binomial Option Pricing Model that the price of a call option is given by the price of the replicating portfolio as shown in Eq. 21.6:

$$C = S\Delta + B$$

Comparing this expression to the Black-Scholes formula from Eq. 21.7 gives the amount of stock and bonds in the Black-Scholes replicating portfolio:

Black-Scholes Replicating Portfolio of a Call Option

$$\Delta = N(d_1)$$

$$B = -PV(K)N(d_2) \qquad (21.12)$$

Recall that $N(d)$ is the cumulative normal distribution function; that is, it has a minimum value of 0 and a maximum value of 1. So Δ is between 0 and 1, and B is between $-K$ and 0. The **option delta**, Δ, has a natural interpretation: It is the change in the price of the option given a $1 change in the price of the stock. Because Δ is always less than 1, the change in the call price is always less than the change in the stock price.

EXAMPLE

21.7

Computing the Replicating Portfolio

Problem
PNA Systems pays no dividends and has a current stock price of $10 per share. If its returns have a volatility of 40% and the risk-free rate is 5%, what portfolio would you hold today to replicate a one-year at-the-money call option on the stock?

Solution
We can apply the Black-Scholes formula with $S = 10$, $PV(K) = 10 / 1.05 = 9.524$, and

$$d_1 = \frac{\ln[S/PV(K)]}{\sigma\sqrt{T}} + \frac{\sigma\sqrt{T}}{2} = \frac{\ln(10/9.524)}{40\%} + \frac{40\%}{2} = 0.322$$

$$d_2 = d_1 - \sigma\sqrt{T} = 0.322 - 0.40 = -0.078$$

From Eq. 21.12, the replicating portfolio for the option is

$$\Delta = N(d_1) = N(0.322) = 0.626$$

$$B = -PV(K)N(d_2) = -9.524 \times N(-0.078) = -4.47$$

That is, we should buy 0.626 shares of the PNA stock, and borrow \$4.47, for a total cost of $10(0.626) - 4.47 = \$1.79$, which is the Black-Scholes value of the call option.

Figure 21.6 illustrates the replicating portfolio and call option value, as a function of the stock price, for Example 21.7. Because the red curve and yellow line are tangent (with slope Δ) at the initial stock price, the value of the replicating portfolio will approximate the value of the call option for small changes to the stock price. But as the stock price changes, the replicating portfolio will need to be updated to maintain accuracy. For example, if the stock price increases, the replicating portfolio will correspond to a new, steeper tangent line higher on the red curve. Because a steeper line corresponds to a higher Δ, to replicate the option it is necessary to buy shares as the stock price increases.

This dynamic trading strategy is analogous to the ones we derived earlier for the Binomial Option Pricing Model. In the binomial model, we were able to replicate the payoff of an option because we only needed to match two of its payoffs at any time. The great insight of Black, Scholes, and Merton was that if we can update our portfolio continuously, we can replicate an option on the stock by constantly adjusting our portfolio to remain on a line that is tangent to the value of the option.

Notice that the replicating portfolio of a call option always consists of a long position in the stock and a short position in the bond; in other words, the replicating portfolio is

FIGURE 21.6

Replicating Portfolio for the Call Option in Example 21.7

The replicating portfolio has the same initial value as the call option, and the same initial sensitivity to the stock price (given by Δ). Because the red curve and yellow line are tangent, the value of the replicating portfolio will approximate the value of the call option for small changes to the stock price. But to maintain accuracy, the replicating portfolio must be updated as the stock prices changes.

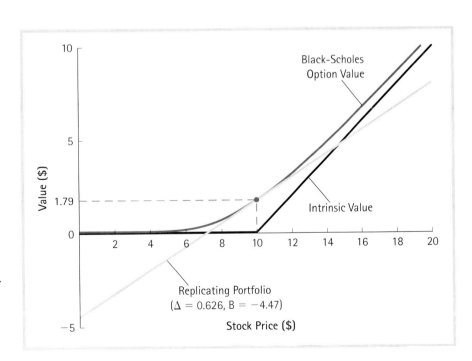

a leveraged position in the stock. Because a leveraged position in a stock is riskier than the stock itself, this implies that call options on a positive beta stock are *more* risky than the underlying stock and therefore have higher returns and higher betas.

We can also derive the replicating portfolio for a put option. Comparing the Black-Scholes price of a put from Eq. 21.9 with Eq. 21.6 gives

Black-Scholes Replicating Portfolio of a Put Option

$$\Delta = -[1 - N(d_1)]$$

$$B = PV(K)[1 - N(d_2)] \tag{21.13}$$

In this case, Δ is between -1 and 0, and B is between 0 and K. Thus the replicating portfolio of a put option always consists of a long position in the bond and a short position in the stock, implying that put options on a positive beta stock will have a negative beta.

CONCEPT CHECK

1. What are the inputs of the Black-Scholes option pricing formula?

2. How do we calculate the implied volatility of a call?

21.3 Risk-Neutral Probabilities

In both the Binomial and Black-Scholes Pricing Models, we do not need to know the probability of each possible future stock price to calculate the option price. But what if we did know these probabilities? In that case we could calculate the price of the option as we have done for other financial assets: We could calculate the expected payoff of the option and discount it at the appropriate cost of capital. The drawback of this approach is that even if we know the probabilities, it is very difficult to estimate the cost of capital for a particular asset, and options are no exception. There is, however, one case in which the cost of capital can be precisely estimated. If all market participants were risk neutral, then *all* financial assets (including options) would have the same cost of capital—the risk-free rate of interest. Let's consider that scenario and see its implications for option prices.

A Risk-Neutral Two-State Model

Imagine a world consisting of only risk-neutral investors, and consider the two-state example in Section 21.1 in the risk-neutral world. Recall that the stock price today is equal to $50. In one period it will either go up by $10 or go down by $10, and the one-period risk-free rate of interest is 6%. Let ρ be the probability that the stock price will increase, which means $(1 - \rho)$ is the probability that it will go down. The value of the stock today must equal the present value of the expected price next period discounted at the risk-free rate:

$$50 = \frac{60\rho + 40(1 - \rho)}{1.06} \tag{21.14}$$

This equation is solved with $\rho = 65\%$. Because we now know the probability of each state, we can price the call by calculating the present value of its expected payoff next period. Recall that the call option had an exercise price of $50, so it will be worth either $10 or nothing at expiration. The present value of the expected payouts is

$$\frac{10(0.65) + 0(1 - 0.65)}{1.06} = 6.13 \tag{21.15}$$

This is precisely the value we calculated in Section 21.1 using the Binomial Option Pricing Model where we did *not* assume that investors were risk neutral. It is not a coincidence. Because no assumption on the risk preferences of investors is necessary to calculate the option price using either the Binomial Model or the Black-Scholes formula, the models must work for any set of preferences, *including* risk-neutral investors.

Implications of the Risk-Neutral World

Let's take a step back and consider the importance of the conclusion that if we use the Binomial Model or Black-Scholes Model to price options, we do not need to make any assumption regarding investor risk preferences, the probability of each state, or the stock's expected return. These models *give the same option price no matter what the actual risk preferences and expected stock returns are.* To understand how these two settings can be consistent with the same prices for securities note that:

- In the real world, investors are risk averse. Thus, the expected return of a typical stock includes a positive risk premium to compensate investors for risk.

- In the hypothetical risk-neutral world, investors do not require compensation for risk. So for the stock price to be the same as in real world, investors must be more pessimistic. Thus, stocks that in reality have expected returns above the risk-free rate, when evaluated using these more pessimistic probabilities have expected returns that equal the risk-free rate.

In other words, the ρ in Eqs. 21.14 and 21.15 is not the actual probability of the stock price increasing. Rather, it represents how the actual probability would have to be adjusted to keep the stock price the same in a risk-neutral world. For this reason, we refer to ρ and $(1 - \rho)$ as **risk-neutral probabilities**. These risk-neutral probabilities are known by other names as well: **state-contingent prices**, **state prices**, or **martingale prices**.

To illustrate, suppose the stock considered above, with a current price of $50, will increase to $60 with a true probability of 75%, or fall to $40 with a true probability of 25%:

This stock's true expected return is therefore

$$\frac{60 \times 0.75 + 40 \times 0.25}{50} - 1 = 10\%$$

Given the risk-free interest rate of 6%, this stock has a 4% risk premium. But as we calculated earlier in Eq. 21.14, the risk-neutral probability that the stock will increase is $\rho = 65\%$, which is less than the true probability. Thus the expected return of the stock in the risk-neutral world is $(60 \times 0.65 + 40 \times 0.35)/50 - 1 = 6\%$ (equal to the risk-free rate). To ensure that all assets in the risk-neutral world have an expected return equal to the risk-free rate, relative to the true probabilities, the risk-neutral probabilities overweight the bad states and underweight the good states.

Risk-Neutral Probabilities and Option Pricing

We can exploit the insight that if the stock price dynamics are the same in the risk-neutral and risk-averse worlds, the option prices must be the same, to develop another technique for pricing options. Consider again the general binomial stock price tree:

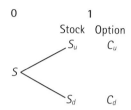

First we can compute the risk-neutral probability that makes the stock's expected return equal to the risk-free interest rate:

$$\frac{\rho S_u + (1 - \rho)S_d}{S} - 1 = r_f$$

Solving this equation for the risk-neutral probability ρ we get

$$\rho = \frac{(1 + r_f)S - S_d}{S_u - S_d} \tag{21.16}$$

We can then compute the value of the option by computing its expected payoff using the risk-neutral probabilities, and discount the expected payoff at the risk-free interest rate.

EXAMPLE 21.8

Option Pricing with Risk-Neutral Probabilities

Problem

Using Narver Network Systems stock from Example 21.2, imagine all investors are risk neutral and calculate the probability of every state in the next two years. Use these probabilities to calculate the price of a two-year call option on Narver Network Systems stock with a strike price $60. Then price a two-year European put option with the same strike price.

Solution

The binomial tree in the three-state example is

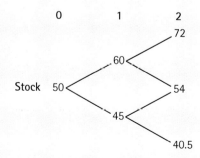

First we use Eq. 21.16 to compute the risk-neutral probability that the stock price will increase. At time 0 we have,

$$\rho = \frac{(1 + r_f)S - S_d}{S_u - S_d} = \frac{(1.03)50 - 45}{60 - 45} = 0.433$$

Because the stock has the same returns (up 20% or down 10%) at each date, we can check that the risk-neutral probability is the same at each date as well.

Consider the call option with a strike price of $60. This call pays $12 if the stock goes up twice, and zero otherwise. The risk-neutral probability that the stock will go up twice is 0.433×0.433, so the call option has an expected payoff of

$$0.433 \times 0.433 \times \$12 = \$2.25$$

We compute the current price of the call option by discounting this expected payoff at the risk-free rate: $C = \$2.25 / 1.03^2 = \$2.12$.

Consider next the European put option with a strike price of $60. The put ends up in the money if the stock goes down twice, if it goes up and then down, or if it goes down and then up. Because the risk-neutral probability of a drop in the stock price is $1 - 0.433 = 0.567$, the expected payoff of the put option is

$$0.567 \times 0.567 \times \$19.5 + 0.433 \times 0.567 \times \$6 + 0.567 \times 0.433 \times \$6 = \$9.21$$

The value of the put today is therefore $P = \$9.21 / 1.03^2 = \$8.68$, which is the price we calculated in Example 21.2.

As the calculation of the put price in Example 21.8 makes clear, by using the probabilities in the risk-neutral world we can price any **derivative security**—that is, any security whose payoff depends solely on the prices of other marketed assets. After we have constructed the tree and calculated the probabilities in the risk-neutral world, we can use them to price the derivative by simply discounting its expected payoff (using the risk-neutral probabilities) at the risk-free rate.

The risk-neutral pricing method is the basis for a common technique for pricing derivative assets called **Monte Carlo simulation**. In this approach, the expected payoff of the derivative security is estimated by calculating its average payoff after simulating many random paths for the underlying stock price. In the randomization, the risk-neutral probabilities are used, and so the average payoff can be discounted at the risk-free rate to estimate the derivative security's value.

CONCEPT CHECK   1. What are risk-neutral probabilities?

2. Does the binominal model or Black-Scholes model assume that investors are risk neutral?

21.4   Risk and Return of an Option

To measure the risk of an option, we must compute the option beta. The simplest way to do so is to compute the beta of the replicating portfolio. Recall that the beta of a portfolio is just the weighted average beta of the constituent securities that make up the portfolio. In this case the portfolio consists of $S \times \Delta$ dollars invested in the stock and B dollars invested in the bond, so the beta of an option is

$$\beta_{option} = \frac{S\Delta}{S\Delta + B}\beta_S + \frac{B}{S\Delta + B}\beta_B$$

where β_S is the stock's beta and β_B is the bond's beta. In this case the bond is riskless, so $\beta_B = 0$. Thus the option beta is

Beta of an Option

$$\beta_{option} = \frac{S\Delta}{S\Delta + B}\beta_S \qquad (21.17)$$

Recall that for a call option, Δ is greater than zero and B is less than zero. Thus, for a call written on a stock with positive beta, the beta of the call always exceeds the beta of the stock. For a put option, Δ is less than zero and B is greater than zero; thus the beta of a put option written on a positive beta stock is always negative. This result should not be surprising. A put option is a hedge, so its price goes up when the stock price goes down.

<table><tr><td>

EXAMPLE

21.9

</td><td>

Beta of an Option

Problem
Calculate the betas of the $12.50 call and $14 put options in Examples 21.3 and 21.4. Assume that the volatility of Oracle stock is 25% per year and its beta is 1.34. The short-term risk-free rate of interest is 4.38% per year.

Solution
The beta of the January $12.50 call option is given by

$$\beta_{Call} = \frac{S\Delta}{S\Delta + B}\beta_{Stock} = \frac{S \times N(d_1)}{C}\beta_{Stock}$$

$$= \frac{12.585 \times 0.572}{0.52} \times 1.34$$

$$= 18.55$$

Similarly, the beta of the January $14 put option is given by

$$\beta_{Put} = \frac{S\Delta}{S\Delta + B}\beta_{Stock} = \frac{-S[1 - N(d_1)]}{P}\beta_{Stock}$$

$$= \frac{-12.585[1 - 0.133]}{1.40} \times 1.34$$

$$= -10.44$$

</td></tr></table>

The expression $S\Delta/(S\Delta + B)$ is the ratio of the amount of money in the stock position in the replicating portfolio to the value of the replicating portfolio (or the option price); it is known as the **leverage ratio**. Figure 21.7 shows how the leverage ratio changes for puts and calls. As the figure shows, the magnitude of the leverage ratio for options can be very large, especially for out-of-the-money options. Thus, calls and puts on a positive beta stock have very large positive and negative betas, respectively. Note also that as the

FIGURE 21.7

Leverage Ratios of Options

The leverage ratio for a call option is always greater than 1, but out-of-the-money calls have higher leverage ratios than in-the-money calls. Put leverage ratios are always negative, and out-the-money puts have more negative leverage ratios than in-the-money puts. Data shown is for one-year options on a stock with a 30% volatility, given a risk-free interest rate of 5%.

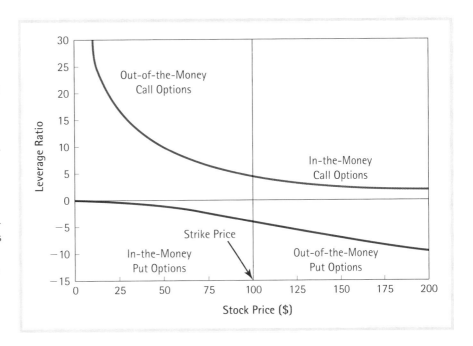

FIGURE 21.8

Security Market Line and Options

The figure shows how the expected return of different options are related.

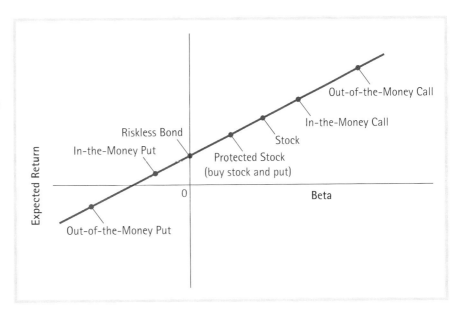

stock price changes, the beta of an option will change, with its magnitude falling as the option goes in-the-money.

Recall that expected returns and beta are linearly related. Hence, out-of-the-money calls have the highest expected returns and out-of-the-money puts have the lowest expected returns. The expected returns of different options are plotted on the security market line in Figure 21.8.

CONCEPT CHECK   **1.** Is the beta of a call greater or smaller than the beta of the underlying stock?

2. What is the leverage ratio of a call?

21.5 Beta of Risky Debt

We close this chapter by developing an important corporate application of option pricing: unlevering the beta of equity and calculating the beta of risky debt.[6] In Chapter 14, we explained how to calculate the beta of equity from the unlevered beta of equity. We showed there that when we make the approximation that the beta of debt is zero, then

$$\beta_E \approx \left(1 + \frac{D}{E}\right)\beta_U \tag{21.18}$$

where β_E is the beta of equity and β_U is the beta of unlevered equity (or the beta of the firm's assets). However, for companies with high debt-to-equity ratios, the approximation that the beta of debt is zero is unrealistic; such corporations have a positive probability of bankruptcy, and this uncertainty usually has systematic components.

To derive an expression for the beta of equity when the beta of debt is not zero, recall from the discussion in Chapter 20 that equity can be viewed as a call option on the firm's assets. If we let A be the value of the firm's assets, E be the value of equity, and D be the value of debt, then because equity is a call option on the assets of the firm, $E = S\Delta + B$ with $A = E + D = S$. Substituting these expressions into Eq. 21.17 gives an expression for the beta of equity that does not assume the beta of debt is zero:

$$\beta_E = \Delta\frac{A}{E}\beta_U = \Delta\left(1 + \frac{D}{E}\right)\beta_U \tag{21.19}$$

where we have used the fact that $A = D + E$. The important difference between this expression and the expression we derived in Chapter 14 (i.e., Eq. 21.18) is that the earlier expression does not contain Δ. When the debt is riskless, the firm's equity is always in-the-money; thus $\Delta = 1$.

We can derive the beta of debt in a similar fashion. Debt, D, is equal to a portfolio consisting of a long position in the assets of the firm and a short position in its equity. The beta of debt is the beta of this portfolio (the weighted average beta):

$$\beta_D = \frac{A}{D}\beta_U - \frac{E}{D}\beta_E$$

Using Eq. 21.19 and simplifying gives an expression for the beta of debt in terms of the beta of assets:

$$\beta_D = (1 - \Delta)\frac{A}{D}\beta_U = (1 - \Delta)\left(1 + \frac{E}{D}\right)\beta_U \tag{21.20}$$

Again, when the debt is riskless, $\Delta = 1$ and $\beta_D = 0$, the assumption we made in Chapter 14.

---

6. The ideas in this section were first developed by R. C. Merton in "On the Pricing of Corporate Debt: The Risk Structure of Interest Rates," *Journal of Finance* 29 (1974): 449–470.

FIGURE 21.9

Beta of Debt and Equity
The blue curve is the beta of equity and the red curve is the beta of debt as a function of the firm's debt-to-equity ratio. The black line is the approximation derived in Chapter 14—the beta of equity when the beta of debt is assumed to be zero. The firm is assumed to hold five-year zero-coupon debt and reinvest all its earnings. (The firm's beta of assets is 1, the risk-free interest rate is 3% per year, and the volatility of assets is 20% per year.)

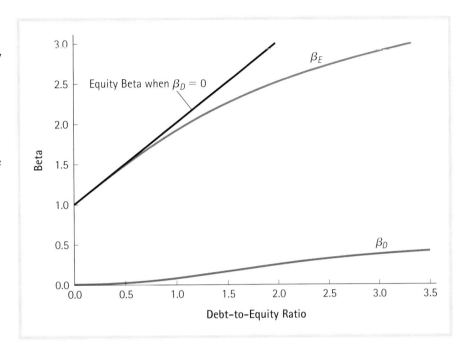

Figure 21.9 plots an example of the beta of debt and equity as a function of the firm's leverage using Eq. 21.12. For simplicity, we have assumed that the firm's beta of assets is 1. For low levels of debt, the approximation we used in Chapter 14—that the beta of debt is zero—works well. In this case, the beta of equity increases linearly with the debt-to-equity ratio.

When the debt-to-equity ratio becomes larger, however, the beta of debt begins to rise above zero and the beta of equity is no longer linear. Note that for very large debt-to-equity ratios, the approximation made in Chapter 14 breaks down. Notice also that the beta of debt can never exceed 1, the beta of the assets.

In most applications, the beta of equity can be estimated. Using the beta of equity, we can calculate the beta of debt and the unlevered beta. For example, to unlever the beta, we can solve Eq. 21.19 for β_U:

$$\beta_U = \frac{\beta_E}{\Delta\left(1 + \dfrac{D}{E}\right)} \qquad (21.21)$$

Computing the Beta of Debt

Problem
You would like to know the beta of debt for BB Industries. The value of BB's outstanding equity is $40 million, and you have estimated its beta to be 1.2. However, you cannot find enough market data to estimate the beta of its debt, so you decide to use the Black-Scholes

formula to find an approximate value for the debt beta. BB has four-year zero-coupon debt outstanding with a face value of $100 million that currently trades for $75 million. BB pays no dividends and reinvests all of its earnings. The four-year risk-free rate of interest is currently 5.13%. What is the beta of BB's debt?

Solution

We can intepret BB's equity as a 4-year call option on the firm's assets with a strike price of $100 million. The present value of the strike price is $100 million/$(1.0513)^4 = \$81.86$ million. The current market value of BB's assets is $40 + 75 = \$115$ million. Therefore, the implied volatility of BB's assets is equal to the implied volatility of a call option whose price is 40 when the stock price is 115 and the present value of the strike price is 81.86. Using trial and error, we find an implied volatility of about 25%. With this volatility, the delta of the call option is

$$\Delta = N(d_1) = N\left(\frac{\ln(115/81.86)}{0.25(2)} + 0.25\right) = 0.824$$

First we use Eq. 21.21 to solve for BB's unlevered beta:

$$\beta_U = \frac{\beta_E}{\Delta\left(1 + \dfrac{D}{E}\right)} = \frac{1.2}{0.824\left(1 + \dfrac{75}{40}\right)} = 0.51$$

We can then use Eq. 21.20 to estimate the beta of BB's debt:

$$\beta_D = (1 - \Delta)\left(1 + \frac{E}{D}\right)\beta_U = (1 - 0.824)\left(1 + \frac{40}{75}\right)0.51 = 0.14$$

CONCEPT CHECK

1. How can we estimate the beta of debt?

2. Can the beta of debt exceed the beta of the firm's assets?

Nobel Prize   The 1997 Nobel Prize in Economics

In a modern market economy, it is essential that firms and households are able to select an appropriate level of risk in their transactions. Markets for options and other so-called derivatives are important in the sense that agents who anticipate future revenues or payments can ensure a profit above a certain level or insure themselves against a loss above a certain level. A prerequisite for efficient management of risk, however, is that such instruments are correctly valued, or priced. A new method to determine the value of derivatives stands out among the foremost contributions to economic sciences over the last 25 years.

This year's laureates, Robert Merton and Myron Scholes, developed this method in close collaboration with Fischer Black, who died in his mid-fifties in 1995. Black, Merton, and Scholes thus laid the foundation for the rapid growth of markets for derivatives in the last ten years. Their method has more general applicability, however, and has created new areas of research—inside as well as outside of financial economics. A similar method may be used to value insurance contracts and guarantees, or the flexibility of physical investment projects.

Quoted from www.nobelprize.org

Summary

1. An option can be valued using a portfolio that replicates the payoffs of the option in different states. The Binomial Option Pricing Model assumes two possible states for the next time period, given today's state.

2. The value of an option is the value of the portfolio that replicates its payoffs. The replicating portfolio will hold the underlying asset and risk-free debt, and will need to be rebalanced over time.

3. The replicating portfolio for the Binomial Option Pricing Model is

$$\Delta = \frac{C_u - C_d}{S_u - S_d} \quad \text{and} \quad B = \frac{C_d - S_d\Delta}{1 + r_f} \tag{21.5}$$

4. Given the replicating portfolio, the value of the option is

$$C = S\Delta + B \tag{21.6}$$

5. The Black-Scholes option pricing formula for the price of a call option on a non-dividend-paying stock is:

$$C = S N(d_1) - PV(K) N(d_2) \tag{21.7}$$

where $N(d)$ is the cumulative normal distribution and

$$d_1 = \frac{\ln[S/PV(K)]}{\sigma\sqrt{T}} + \frac{\sigma\sqrt{T}}{2}$$

$$d_2 = d_1 - \sigma\sqrt{T} \tag{21.8}$$

Only five input parameters are required to price a call: the stock price, the strike price, the exercise date, the risk-free rate, and the volatility of the stock. We do not need to know the expected return on the stock to calculate the option price.

6. The Black-Scholes option pricing formula for the price of a European put option on a non-dividend paying stock is

$$P = PV(K)[1 - N(d_2)] - S[1 - N(d_1)] \tag{21.9}$$

7. We can evaluate a European option on a stock that pays using the Black-Scholes formula with S^x in place of S where

$$S^x = S - PV(Div) \tag{21.10}$$

If the stock pays a (compounded) dividend yield of q prior to the expiration date, then

$$S^x = S/(1 + q) \tag{21.11}$$

8. The Black-Scholes replicating portfolio is
   a. For a call option on a non-dividend paying stock

$$\Delta = N(d_1) \quad \text{and} \quad B = -PV(K)N(d_2) \tag{21.12}$$

   b. For a European put option on a non-dividend paying stock

$$\Delta = -[1 - N(d_1)] \quad \text{and} \quad B = PV(K)[1 - N(d_2)] \tag{21.13}$$

   c. The replicating portfolio must be continuously updated to remain tangent to the option value

9. Risk-neutral probabilities are the probabilities that equate the expected value of the payoffs of an asset discounted by the risk-free rate to the asset's price today. These probabilities can be used to price any other asset for which the payoffs in each state are known.

10. In a binomial tree, the risk-neutral probability ρ that the stock price will increase is given by

$$\rho = \frac{(1 + r_f)S - S_d}{S_u - S_d} \tag{21.16}$$

11. The price of any derivative security can be obtained by discounting the expected cash flows computed using the risk-neutral probabilities at the risk-free rate.

12. The beta of an option can also be calculated by computing the risk of its replicating portfolio. For stocks with positive betas, calls will have larger betas than the underlying stock, while puts will have negative betas.

13. When the beta of debt is nonzero, the Black-Scholes formula can be used to unlever the equity beta of the firm and find the beta of debt.

Key Terms

Binomial Option Pricing Model *p. 686*
binomial tree *p. 686*
Black-Scholes Option Pricing
    Model *p. 694*
cumulative normal distribution *p. 694*
derivative security *p. 707*
dynamic trading strategy *p. 692*
executive stock option (ESO) *p. 699*
implied volatility *p. 701*

leverage ratio *p. 708*
martingale prices *p. 705*
Monte Carlo simulation *p. 707*
option delta *p. 702*
replicating portfolio *p. 686*
risk-neutral probabilities *p. 705*
state prices *p. 705*
state-contingent prices *p. 705*

Further Reading

The seminal article on options was written by Fischer Black and Myron Scholes: "The Pricing of Options and Corporate Liabilities," *Journal of Political Economy* 81(3) (1973): 637–654. It followed an earlier article by Robert Merton, "Theory of Rational Option Pricing," *Bell Journal of Economics and Management Science* 4(1) (1973): 141–183.

Readers interested in a deeper discussion of options and other derivative securities will find the following texts useful: R. L. McDonald, *Derivative Markets* (Boston: Addison Wesley, 2003); J. Hull, *Options, Futures, and Other Derivatives*, 5th ed. (Upper Saddle River, NJ: Prentice Hall, 2005); R. Jarrow and S. Turnbull, *Derivative Securities*, 2nd ed. (Cincinnati, OH: South-Western, 1999); and P. Wilmott, *Paul Wilmott on Quantitative Finance* (Hoboken, NJ: John Wiley & Sons, 2000).

The following articles by Fischer Black contain an interesting account of the development of the Black-Scholes formula as well as some of its limitations: "How We Came Up with the Option Formula," *Journal of Portfolio Management* 15(2) (1989): 4–8; "The Holes in Black-Scholes," *RISK Magazine* 1 (1988): 30–33; and "How to Use the Holes in Black-Scholes," *Journal of Applied Corporate Finance* 1 (Winter 1989): 67–73.

Problems

A blue box (■) indicates problems available in MyFinanceLab. An asterisk (*) indicates problems with a higher level of difficulty.

1. The current price of Estelle Corporation stock is $25. In each of the next two years, this stock price will either go up by 20% or go down by 20%. The stock pays no dividends. The one-year risk-free interest rate is 6% and will remain constant. Using the Binomial Model, calculate the price of a one-year call option on Estelle stock with a strike price of $25.

2. Using the information in Problem 1, use the Binomial Model to calculate the price of a one-year put option on Estelle stock with a strike price of $25.

3. The current price of Natasha Corporation stock is $6. In each of the next two years, this stock price can either go up by $2.50 or go down by $2.00. The stock pays no dividends. The one-year risk-free interest rate is 3% and will remain constant. Using the Binomial Model, calculate the price of a two-year call option on Natasha stock with a strike price of $7.

4. Using the information in Problem 3, use the Binomial Model to calculate the price of a two-year European put option on Natasha stock with a strike price of $7.

5. Suppose the option in Example 21.1 actually sold in the market for $8.00. Describe a trading strategy that yields arbitrage profits.

*6. Suppose the option in Example 21.2 actually sold today for $5.00. You do not know what the option will trade for next period. Describe a trading strategy that will yield arbitrage profits.

7. Rebecca is interested in purchasing a European call on a hot new stock, Up, Inc. The call has a strike price of $100 and expires in 90 days. The current price of Up stock is $120, and the stock has a standard deviation of 40% per year. The risk-free interest rate is 6.18% per year.
   a. Using the Black-Scholes formula, compute the price of the call.
   b. Use put-call parity to compute the price of the put with the same strike and expiration date.

8. Oracle Corporation does not pay dividends. Using the data in Table 21.1, compare the price on December 6, 2005, of the January 2006 call option on Oracle stock with a strike price of $11 to the price predicted by the Black-Scholes formula. Assume that the standard deviation of Oracle is 25% per year and that the short-term risk-free rate of interest is 4.38% per year.

9. Using the market data in Table 20.5 and a risk-free rate of 4.5% per annum, calculate the two-year implied volatility of Google stock in December 2005, using the 310 January 2008 put option.

10. Plot the value of a two-year European put option with a strike price of $20 on World Wide Plants as a function of the stock price. Recall that World Wide Plants has a constant dividend yield of 5% per year and that its volatility is 20% per year. The two-year risk-free rate of interest is 4%. Explain why there is a region where the option trades for less than its intrinsic value.

11. Using the implied volatility you calculated in Problem 9, and the information in that problem, use the Black-Scholes option pricing formula to calculate the value of the 340 January 2008 put option.

12. Using the information in Problem 1, calculate the risk-neutral probabilities. Then use them to price the option.

13. Using the information in Problem 3, calculate the risk-neutral probabilities. Then use them to price the option.

14. Explain the difference between the risk-neutral and actual probabilities. In which states is one higher than the other? Why?

15. Explain why risk-neutral probabilities can be used to price derivative securities in a world where investors are risk averse.

16. Calculate the beta of the 06 January 14.00 call option on Oracle listed in Table 21.1. Assume that the volatility of Oracle is 25% per year and its beta is 1.34. The short-term risk-free rate of interest is 4.38% per year. What is the option's leverage ratio?

17. Calculate the beta of the 06 January 12.50 put option on Oracle listed in Table 21.1. Assume that the volatility of Oracle is 25% per year and its beta is 1.34. The short-term risk-free rate of interest is 4.38% per year. What is the option's leverage ratio?

18. Return to Example 20.10, in which Google was contemplating issuing $90 billion in zero-coupon debt due in two years and using the proceeds to repurchase stock. Google currently has a market value of $122.4 billion and the two-year risk-free rate is 4.5%. Using the market data in Table 20.5 and the implied volatility you calculated in Problem 9, estimate the percentage increase in Google's beta of equity when this debt is issued.

*19. You would like to know the unlevered beta of Schwartz Industries (SI). SI's value of outstanding equity is $400 million, and you have estimated its beta to be 1.2. SI has four-year zero-coupon debt outstanding with a face value of $100 million that currently trades for $75 million. SI pays no dividends and reinvests all of its earnings. The four-year risk-free rate of interest is currently 5.13%. Use the Black-Scholes formula to estimate the unlevered beta of the firm.

CHAPTER 22

Real Options

NPV	net present value
S^x	value of stock excluding dividends
S	stock price
PV	present value
Div	dividend
K	strike price
$\ln$	natural logarithm
T	years until the exercise date of an option
σ	volatility of the return of the underlying asset
C	call option price
$N(d)$	cumulative normal distribution
ρ	risk-neutral probability

The most important application of options in corporate finance is in the capital budgeting decision. Let's use Amgen, a global biotechnology company, as an example. Amgen had 2004 revenues of more than $10.5 billion, and it spent almost 20% of its revenues on research and development. Even though only a very small number of early-stage drug development projects ultimately reach the market, the ones that do can be highly successful. How does Amgen manage its research and development expenses to maximize value?

For Amgen, investing in R&D is like purchasing a call option. When research results on early-stage drug development projects are favorable, Amgen commits additional resources to the next stage of product development. If research results are not promising, Amgen withdraws resources from the project. Amgen, by selectively investing in those technologies that prove to be the most promising, exercises its option to develop a product: The additional investment is equivalent to paying the strike price and getting the underlying asset—in this case, the benefits of further product development. By choosing not to make further investments (thereby mothballing or abandoning the research and development project) Amgen chooses not to exercise its option.

While real investment options, like Amgen's, can be very important in capital budgeting, the effect of such real options on the capital budgeting decision is generally very specific to the particular application. Unlike the material we have covered so far, no standard theory exists that applies across all applications. In light of this fact, in this chapter we show how the general principles we have already developed that govern capital budgeting and option pricing can be applied to evaluate real options in the capital budgeting decision. Using these principles we illustrate, in the context of a few stylized examples, the three most common options that occur in capital budgeting: the option to wait for the optimal time to invest, the option to grow in the future, and the option to abandon a poorly performing project. We then consider an important application: deciding which of two mutually exclusive projects of different lengths is the wisest investment. Finally, we explain rules of thumb that managers often use to account for real options in the capital budgeting decision.

22.1 Real Versus Financial Options

The financial options we have studied in the previous two chapters give their holders the right to buy, or sell, a traded asset such as a stock. Amgen's option to invest in research and development for new products is an example of a different type of option, called a **real option**. A real option is the right to take a particular business decision, such as make a capital investment. A key distinction between a real option and a financial option is that real options, and the underlying assets on which they are based, are often not traded in competitive markets; for example, there is no market for Amgen's R&D in a particular drug.

Despite this distinction, many of the principles that we developed in the last two chapters for financial options also apply to real options. In particular, because real options allow a decision maker to choose the most attractive alternative after new information has been learned, the presence of real options adds value to an investment opportunity. This value can be substantial, especially in environments with a great deal of uncertainty. Thus, to make an investment decision correctly, the value of these options must be included in the decision-making process.

Our approach to capital budgeting thus far has focused on the initial investment decision without explicitly considering future decisions that may need to be made over the life of a project. Rather, we assumed that our forecast of the project's expected future cash flows already incorporated the effect of future decisions that would be made. In this chapter, we take a closer look at how these cash flows, and therefore the NPV of a project, are determined when a firm must react to changing business conditions over the life of a project. To do so, we begin by introducing a new analytical tool called a decision tree.

CONCEPT CHECK   1. What is the difference between a real option and a financial option?

22.2 Decision Tree Analysis

Most investment projects allow for the possibility of reevaluating the decision to invest at a later point in time. Let's illustrate with a simple example. Suppose Megan is financing part of her MBA education by running a small business. She purchases goods on eBay and resells the merchandise at farmers' markets and swap meets. Megan would like to run her business more efficiently, so she decides to use some of the knowledge she has gained in graduate school. Swap meets and farmers' markets typically charge her $500 in advance to set up her small booth. Ignoring the cost of the booth, if she goes to every meet, her average profit on the goods that she sells is $1100 per meet. Let's represent Megan's options with regard to setting up her booth on a **decision tree**, a graphical representation of future decisions and uncertainty resolution.

Figure 22.1 represents Megan's initial decision tree. The box at the node (represented by a square) indicates that Megan must decide which branch to follow. Note that there is an important difference between the decision tree in Figure 22.1 and the binomial trees in Chapter 21. There, the uncertainty was not under the control of the decision maker.

FIGURE 22.1

Megan's Choices
The optimal decision appears in blue.

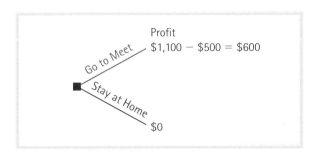

FIGURE 22.2

Effect of the Weather on Megan's Options
The optimal decision appears in blue.

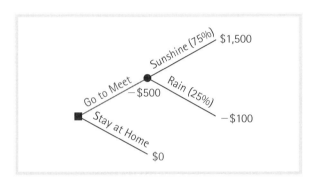

Here, Megan decides how the uncertainty is resolved. Because the NPV of setting up a booth is $1100 − $500 = $600, the optimal decision (shown in blue) would be to set up the booth.

Mapping Uncertainties on a Decision Tree

While going to the swap meet appears to be the optimal decision, Megan is aware that attendance at swap meets and farmer's markets is weather dependent: In good weather her profits are much higher (usually around $1500); in bad weather, which occurs about 25% of the time, business is so slow that she usually drops her prices and, including her setup costs, averages a small loss of about $100. This adds another element of uncertainty for Megan's consideration. Figure 22.2 represents this uncertainty on a decision tree.

Notice that the decision tree now contains two kinds of nodes: **decision nodes** that are marked with square boxes (pay the fee and go to the meet versus do nothing) and **information nodes** in which uncertainty is involved that is out of the control of the decision maker (rain or sunshine) that are marked with circles. Figure 22.2 also indicates the point at which each cash flow is committed. Because the booth fee is paid in advance, the cash flow is incurred before Megan finds out about the weather.

Notice, however, that the decision tree in Figure 22.2 is not a full description of Megan's alternatives. Although the fee for the booth is sunk once Megan finds out about the weather, she is not forced to go to the meet, sit in the booth, and lose the additional $100. That is, it does not make sense for her to commit to go to the swap meet *before* she finds out what the weather is like. Figure 22.3 represents her decision tree when Megan

FIGURE 22.3

Megan's Decision Tree When She Can Observe the Weather Before She Makes the Decision to Go to the Meet
Her optimal decisions are shown in blue.

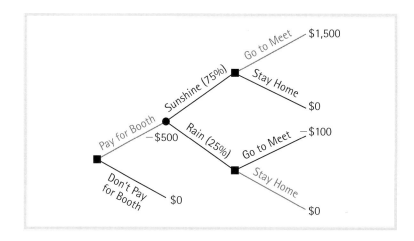

optimally chooses to wait until the day of the meet to decide whether she will go: If it rains, she optimally chooses to stay at home. The $500 loss for the booth is unavoidable, but in bad weather she does not incur the additional $100 loss at the meet.

Real Options

The difference between the decision trees in Figures 22.2 and 22.3 is an example of a real option. Megan has the option to wait until she finds out what the weather is like before she decides whether she should go to the meet. This flexibility has value (she can avoid a further $100 loss). By committing ahead of time, she gives up this value.

How valuable is the real option to Megan? Let's assume for simplicity that Megan is risk neutral about the risk from the weather, and that the time delays are short so that we can ignore discounting. We can compute the value of the real option by comparing her expected profit *without the real option* to wait until the weather is revealed (Figure 22.1 or 22.2) to the value *with the option* to wait (Figure 22.3). If Megan commits to go regardless of the weather, her expected profit is $0.75 \times \$1500 + 0.25 \times (-\$100) = \$1100$, her average profit if she goes to every meet. However, if she goes only when the weather is good, her profit is $0.75 \times \$1500 - \$1125$. The value of the real option is the difference, $\$1125 - \$1100 = \$25$.

Should Megan pay for the booth? Let's assume she has to pay for the booth only the day before the meet, so we can ignore the time value of money. Then the NPV of paying for the booth is $\$1125 - \$500 = \$625$, which is positive. Thus Megan should always pay for the booth.

Many corporate investment decisions contain real options like Megan's. Unfortunately, in most cases these options are investment specific, so it is impossible to present a general theory of real options. Instead, we will concentrate on the three kinds of real options that are most frequently encountered in practice: (1) the option to delay an investment opportunity, (2) the option to grow, and (3) the option to abandon an investment opportunity.

CONCEPT CHECK   1. What makes real options valuable?

2. How do you calculate the value of a real option?

22.3 The Option to Delay an Investment Opportunity

The simple example of Megan's swap meet illustrates how choosing the optimal time to commit to an investment opportunity has value. In this case the decision about when to commit (go to the swap meet) is easy: Once the booth is paid for, there is no cost to waiting to find out about the weather. In the real world, of course, there is often a cost to delaying an investment decision. For example, by choosing to wait for more information you give up any profits the project might generate in the interim. In addition, a competitor could use the delay to develop a competing product. The decision to wait therefore involves a tradeoff between these costs and the benefit of remaining flexible.

Investment as a Call Option

Consider the following investment opportunity. You have negotiated a deal with a major restaurant chain to open one of its restaurants in your hometown. The terms of the contract specify that you must open the restaurant either immediately or in exactly one year. If you do neither, you lose the right to open the restaurant at all. Figure 22.4 shows these choices on a decision tree.

You are wondering how much you should pay for this opportunity. It will cost you $5 million to open the restaurant, whether you open it now or in one year. If you open the restaurant immediately, you expect it to generate $600,000 in free cash flow the first year. While future cash flows will vary with the consumer tastes and the state of the economy, on average these cash flows are expected to grow at a rate of 2% per year. The appropriate cost of capital for this investment is 12%, so that you estimate the value of the restaurant, if it were open today, would be

$$V = \frac{\$600,000}{12\% - 2\%} = \$6 \text{ million} \tag{22.1}$$

You also double check this value using comparables. Suppose there exists a publicly traded firm operating equivalent franchises elsewhere in the state, and this firm provides an essentially perfect comparable for your investment. This firm has an enterprise value equal to 10 times its free cash flow, leading to an equivalent valuation.

FIGURE 22.4

Restaurant Investment Opportunity

The restaurant must be opened either immediately or in exactly one year. If we wait to open the restaurant, our decision can be based on new information about the restaurant's value, which can take on many values.

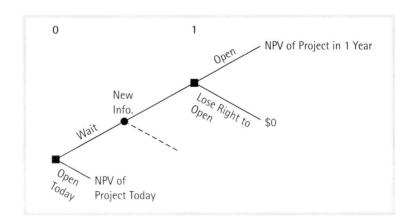

Thus, the NPV of opening the restaurant immediately is $1 million, implying that the contract is worth at least $1 million. But given the flexibility you have to delay opening for one year, should you be willing to pay more? And when should you open the restaurant?

To answer these questions, we need to evaluate the NPV from waiting to open the restaurant. If we wait, then one year from now we will have the choice to invest $5 million to open the restaurant, or lose our right to open it and receive nothing. Thus, at that time, the decision is easy—we will open the restaurant if its value at that time, based on any new information about the economy and consumer tastes and trends, is above $5 million. But because trends in this industry can change quickly, there is a great deal of uncertainty as to what the expected cash flows and the value of the restaurant will be at that time.

We can incorporate this uncertainty into our estimate of the contract's value by recognizing that our payoff if we delay is equivalent to the payoff of a one-year European call option on the restaurant with a strike price of $5 million. Because the final payoff in one year is equivalent to a call option, we can use the techniques of Chapter 21 to value it. Suppose that the risk-free interest rate is 5%. We can estimate the volatility of the value of the restaurant by looking at the return volatility of the publicly traded comparable firm; suppose this volatility is 40%. Finally, if we wait to open the restaurant we will lose out on the $600,000 in free cash flow we would have earned in the first year. In terms of a financial option, this free cash flow is equivalent to a dividend paid by a stock—the holder of a call option does not receive the dividend until the option is exercised. Let's assume for now this cost is the only cost of delay—there are no additional costs in terms of lost growth of the restaurant cash flows, for example.

Table 22.1 shows how we can reinterpret the parameters for the Black-Scholes formula for financial options to evaluate this real option to invest in the restaurant. To apply the Black-Scholes formula, recall from Eq. 21.10 that we must compute the current value of the asset *without* the dividends that will be missed:

$$S^x = S - PV(Div) = \$6 \text{ million} - \frac{\$0.6 \text{ million}}{1.12} = \$5.46 \text{ million}$$

Note that we compute the present value of the lost cash flow using the project's cost of capital of 12%. Next we need to compute the present value of the cost to open the restaurant in one year. Because this cash flow is certain, we discount it at the risk-free rate:

$$PV(K) = \frac{\$5 \text{ million}}{1.05} = \$4.76 \text{ million}$$

TABLE 22.1		Black-Scholes Option Value Parameters for Evaluating a Real Option to Invest	
Financial Option		**Real Option**	**Example**
Stock Price	S	Current Market Value of Asset	$6 million
Strike Price	K	Upfront Investment Required	$5 million
Expiration Date	T	Final Decision Date	1 year
Risk-free Rate	r_f	Risk-free Rate	5%
Volatility of Stock	σ	Volatility of Asset Value	40%
Dividend	Div	FCF Lost from Delay	$0.6 million

Now we can compute the value of the call option to open the restaurant using Eqs. 21.7 and 21.8:

$$d_1 = \frac{\ln[S^x / PV(K)]}{\sigma \sqrt{T}} + \frac{\sigma \sqrt{T}}{2} = \frac{\ln(5.46 / 4.76)}{0.40} + 0.20 = 0.543$$

$$d_2 = d_1 - \sigma \sqrt{T} = 0.543 - 0.40 = 0.143$$

and therefore,

$$C = S^x N(d_1) - PV(K) N(d_2)$$

$$= (\$5.46 \text{ million}) \times (0.706) - (\$4.76 \text{ million}) \times (0.557)$$

$$= \$1.20 \text{ million} \qquad\qquad (22.2)$$

The result in Eq. 22.2 states that the value today from waiting to invest in the restaurant next year, and only opening it if it is profitable to do so, is $1.20 million. This value exceeds the NPV of $1 million from opening the restaurant today. Thus, we are better off waiting to invest, and the value of the contract is $1.20 million.

What is the advantage of waiting in this case? If we wait, we will learn more about the likely success of the business by observing the performance of the comparable firm. Because our investment in the restaurant is not yet committed, we can cancel our plans if the popularity of the restaurant should decline. By opening the restaurant today, we give up this option to "walk away."[1]

Of course, there is a tradeoff—if we wait to invest we give up the profits the restaurant will generate the first year. Whether it is optimal to invest today will depend on the magnitude of these lost profits, compared to the benefit of preserving our right to change our decision. To see this tradeoff, suppose instead that the first-year free cash flow of the restaurant is projected to be $700,000, so that the current value of the restaurant is $7 million (using the 10x multiple of the comparable, or a similar calculation to Eq. 22.1). In this case, the same analysis shows that the value of the call option would be $1.91 million. Because the value of opening the restaurant today is $7 million − 5 million = $2 million, in this case it would not be optimal to wait, and we would open the restaurant immediately.

Figure 22.5 plots the NPV of investing today (red line) and the value of waiting (yellow curve) as a function of today's value of the restaurant. As the figure makes clear, you should invest today (and give up the option to wait) only if the current value of a restaurant exceeds $6.66 million. Thus your optimal investment strategy is to invest today only if the NPV of the investment opportunity exceeds 6.66 − 5 = $1.66 million.

Factors Affecting the Timing of Investment

This example illustrates how the real option to wait affects the capital budgeting decision. When you do not have the option to wait, it is optimal to invest in any positive-NPV project. *When you have the option of deciding when to invest, it is usually optimal to invest only when the NPV is substantially greater than zero.* One way to see why you sometimes

---

1. A second benefit from waiting is that the cost of opening the restaurant is assumed to stay the same ($5 million), so the present value of this cost declines if we wait. This benefit is specific to the example. Depending on the scenario, the cost of investing may rise or fall over time.

FIGURE 22.5

The Decision to Invest in the Restaurant

The red line denotes the NPV of investing today. The yellow curve shows the value today of waiting one year to make the decision (i.e., the value of the call option). The black curve indicates the value of the contract, which gives us the option to invest today, in one year, or not at all. The optimal investment strategy is to invest today only if the value of the operating restaurant exceeds $6.66 million.

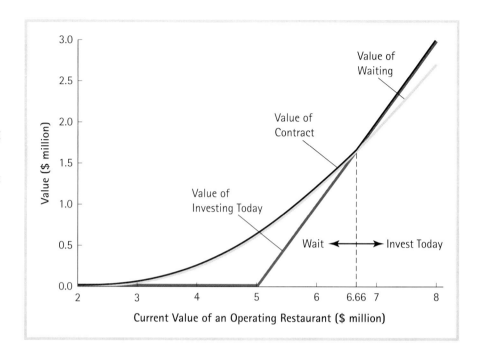

choose not to invest in a positive-NPV project is to think about the decision of when to invest as a choice between two mutually exclusive projects: (1) invest today or (2) wait. As we pointed out in Chapter 6, in this case the optimal course of action is to choose the project with the higher NPV. Hence you invest today only when the NPV of investing today exceeds the value of the option of waiting, which from option pricing theory we know to be always positive.

An interesting aspect of the restaurant investment opportunity is the value of the deal when the ongoing value of a restaurant is less than $5 million. In this case the NPV of opening a restaurant is negative, so without the option to wait the investment opportunity is worthless. But from Figure 22.5 we see that, with the option to wait, the investment opportunity is clearly not worthless. Even if the current value of a restaurant is $4 million (which means the NPV of investing today is −$1 million), the value of the opportunity is still worth about $248,000. That is, you would still be willing to pay up to $248,000 to sign the deal. Thus, given the option to wait, an investment that currently has a negative NPV can have a positive value.

Aside from the current NPV of the investment, what other factors affect the value of an investment and the decision to wait? From Figure 22.5 we can see that factors that increase the value of the call option will increase the benefit of waiting. Recall from our study of financial options in Chapters 20 and 21 that both the volatility and the dividends of the stock affect the value of a call option and the optimal time to exercise the call. These factors have their counterparts for real options:

- *Volatility:* By delaying an investment, we can base our decision on additional information. The option to wait is most valuable when there is a great deal of uncertainty regarding what the value of the investment will be in the future. If there is little uncertainty, the benefit of waiting is diminished.

Why Are There Empty Lots in Built-up Areas of Big Cities?

Have you ever wondered why there are empty lots (for example, a parking lot) right next to a multistory building in a city? After all, if it was optimal for the next-door neighbor to build a multistory building, why would someone choose to leave the lot empty? In many cases, the property taxes exceed the revenue generated by the empty lot, so by putting a revenue-producing building on the lot, the owner could turn a negative cash flow into a positive cash flow. However, by building on the lot, the owner gives up the option to construct a different building in the future. If there is a large amount of uncertainty about the kind of building to put on the lot, and if this uncertainty might be resolved in the future, it might make sense to wait for additional information before breaking ground on a building. The value of waiting might exceed the net present value of building today.*

A similar effect can be seen in the price of agricultural land that is close to big cities. Even though the land might produce the same agricultural revenue as similar land 100 miles away, the price of the land closer to the city is higher because the price reflects the possibility that the city might grow to the point that it becomes economical to put the land to non-agricultural use—that is, subdivide it and build single-family housing. The option to one day use the land in this way is reflected in the current price of the land.

*S. Titman, "Urban Land Prices Under Uncertainty," *American Economic Review* 75 (1985): 505–514, develops this idea.

- *Dividends:* Recall that absent dividends, it is not optimal to exercise a call option early. In the real option context, the dividends correspond to any value from the investment that we give up by waiting. It is always better to wait unless there is a cost to doing so. The greater the cost, the less attractive the option to delay becomes.

EXAMPLE 22.1

Evaluating the Decision to Wait

Problem
Suppose your current estimate of the restaurant's value is $6 million. What would be the value of the restaurant contract if the volatility of the restaurant's value were 25% rather than 40%? Alternatively, suppose the volatility is 40%, but waiting would lead competitors to expand and reduce the future free cash flows of the restaurant by 10%. What is the value of the contract in this case?

Solution
With a lower volatility of 25%, we have

$$d_1 = \frac{\ln[S^x/PV(K)]}{\sigma\sqrt{T}} + \frac{\sigma\sqrt{T}}{2} = \frac{\ln(5.46/4.76)}{0.25} + 0.125 = 0.674$$

$$d_2 = d_1 - \sigma\sqrt{T} = 0.674 - 0.25 = 0.424$$

The value of the call option is

$$C = S^x N(d_1) - PV(K)N(d_2)$$

$$= (\$5.46 \text{ million}) \times (0.750) - (\$4.76 \text{ million}) \times (0.664)$$

$$= \$0.93 \text{ million}$$

Therefore, it is better to invest immediately and get an NPV of $1 million, rather than wait. With the lower volatility, not enough information will be learned over the next year to justify the cost of waiting.

Now let's suppose the volatility is 40%, but waiting leads to increased competition. In this case, we should deduct the loss from increased competition as an additional "dividend" that we forgo by waiting. Thus,

$$S^x = S - PV(\text{First-Year FCF}) - PV(\text{Lost FCF from Competition})$$

$$= \left(\$6 \text{ million} - \frac{\$0.6 \text{ million}}{1.12} \right) \times (1 - 0.10) = \$4.92 \text{ million}$$

Now,

$$d_1 = \frac{\ln[S^x / PV(K)]}{\sigma\sqrt{T}} + \frac{\sigma\sqrt{T}}{2} = \frac{\ln(4.92 / 4.76)}{0.40} + 0.20 = 0.283$$

$$d_2 = d_1 - \sigma\sqrt{T} = 0.283 - 0.40 = -0.117$$

The value of the call option in this case is

$$C = S^x N(d_1) - PV(K)N(d_2)$$

$$= (\$4.92 \text{ million}) \times (0.611) - (\$4.76 \text{ million}) \times (0.453)$$

$$= \$0.85 \text{ million}$$

Again, it would not be optimal to wait. In this case, despite the information to be gained, the costs associated with waiting are too high.

CONCEPT CHECK

1. What is the economic tradeoff between investing immediately or waiting?

2. How does the option to wait affect the capital budgeting decision?

22.4 Growth Options

Imagine that you formed a corporation. Acting on behalf of this corporation, you signed the restaurant contract described in the last section. Assume the current value of an operating restaurant is $4 million, so the NPV of investing today is negative. If the corporation has no other assets, what is the value of the corporation? As we have already seen, even though it does not make sense to invest today, the value of the *contract* is $248,000 because it gives the corporation the option to open the restaurant in a year. Because the corporation owns this contact, it is worth $248,000. Even though the corporation produces no cash flows and owns only a right to invest in a project that has a negative NPV, the corporation is worth a positive amount.

When a firm has a real option to invest in the future, as in the restaurant example, it is known as a **growth option**. Because these options have value, they contribute to the value of any firm that has future possible investment opportunities.

Valuing the Growth Potential of a Firm

Future growth opportunities can be thought of as a collection of real call options on potential projects. Out-of-the-money calls are riskier than in-the-money calls, and because most growth options are likely to be out-of-the-money, the growth component of firm value is likely to be riskier than the ongoing assets of the firm. This observation might explain why young firms (and small firms) have higher returns than older, established firms. It also explains why R&D intensive firms often have high costs of capital even when most of the R&D risk is idiosyncratic.[2]

It is tempting to use the Black-Scholes formula to value future growth options, but often there are good reasons why this formula might not price these options correctly. For example, the Black-Scholes formula values European options, whereas most growth options can be exercised at any time. As we explained in Chapter 21, an alternative to using the Black-Scholes formula is to compute the value of growth options using risk-neutral probabilities. Let's demonstrate how to go about valuing real options in this way by using an example.

StartUp Incorporated is a new company whose only asset is a patent on a new drug. If produced, the drug will generate certain profits of $1 million per year for the life of the patent, which is 17 years (after then, competition will drive profits to zero). It will cost $10 million today to produce the drug. Assume that the yield on a 17-year risk-free annuity is currently 8% per year. What is the value of the patent?

Using the formula for the present value of an annuity, the NPV of investing today in the drug is

$$NPV = \frac{1}{0.08}\left(1 - \frac{1}{1.08^{17}}\right) - 10 = -\$878,362$$

Based on this calculation, it does not make sense to invest in the drug today. But what if interest rates change? Let's assume that interest rates will change in exactly one year. At that time, all risk-free interest rates in the economy will be either 10% per year or 5% per year, and then will remain at that level forever. Clearly, an increase in interest rates will make matters worse. Because interest rates will remain at the new, higher level forever, it will never be optimal to invest. Thus the value of this growth option is zero in that state. However, if rates drop, the NPV of undertaking the investment is

$$NPV = \frac{1}{0.05}\left(1 - \frac{1}{1.05^{16}}\right) - 10 = \$837,770$$

In this case it is optimal to invest. We can put this information on a decision tree, as shown in Figure 22.6.

Recall from Chapter 21 that to find risk-neutral probabilities, we solve for the probabilities that set the value of a financial asset today equal to the present value of its future cash flows. In Chapter 21, we used stock as the financial asset; in this case, we use the 17-year risk-free annuity that pays $1000 per year as the financial asset. The value today of this annuity is

$$S = \frac{1000}{0.08}\left(1 - \frac{1}{1.08^{17}}\right) = \$9122$$

2. Readers interested in a more in-depth discussion of the relation between R&D risk and returns can consult J. B. Berk, R. C. Green, and V. Naik, "The Valuation and Return Dynamics of New Ventures," *Review of Financial Studies* 17 (2004): 1–35.

FIGURE 22.6

Start Up's Decision to Invest in the Drug

If interest rates rise, it does not make sense to invest. If rates fall, it is optimal to develop the drug.

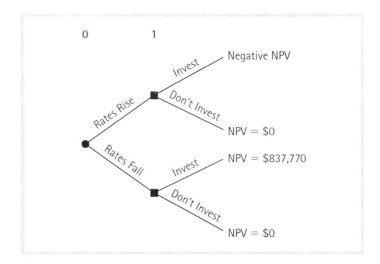

A year from now, the annuity will pay $1000, and it will have 16 years left to maturity. Therefore, including the payment, it will be worth either

$$S_u = 1000 + \frac{1000}{0.1}\left(1 - \frac{1}{1.1^{16}}\right) = \$8824$$

if interest rates go up, or, if interest rates fall,

$$S_d = 1000 + \frac{1000}{0.05}\left(1 - \frac{1}{1.05^{16}}\right) = \$11,838$$

Suppose the current one-year risk-free interest rate is equal to 6%. (Note that this rate is below the current 17-year annuity rate of 8%; Thus, the current yield curve is upward sloping). Recall that the risk-neutral probability of interest rates increasing to 10%, which we denote by ρ, is the probability such that the expected return of the annuity is equal to the risk-free rate of 6%. From Eq. 21.16,

$$\rho = \frac{(1 + r_f)S - S_d}{S_u - S_d} = \frac{1.06 \times 9122 - 11,838}{8824 - 11,838} = 71.95\%$$

The value today of the investment opportunity is the present value of the expected cash flows (using risk-neutral probabilities) discounted at the risk-free rate:

$$PV = \frac{837,770 \times (1 - 0.7195) + 0 \times 0.7195}{1.06} = \$221,693$$

In this example, even though the cash flows of the project are known with certainty, the uncertainty regarding future interest rates creates substantial option value for the firm. The firm's ability to use the patent and grow should interest rates fall is worth close to a quarter of a million dollars.

Staged Investment: The Option to Expand

Future growth options are not only important to firm value, but can also be important in the value of an individual project. By undertaking a project, a firm often gets the opportunity to invest in new projects that firms outside the industry do not have easy access to. For example, a fashion designer might introduce a new line of clothes knowing that if the line proves popular, he has the option to launch a new line of accessories based on those clothes.

Consider an investment opportunity with an option to grow that requires a $10 million investment today. In one year we will find out whether the project, which entails introducing a new product into the business machines market, is successful. The risk-neutral probability that the project will generate $1 million per year in perpetuity is 50%; otherwise, the project will generate nothing. At any time we can double the size of the project on the original terms. Figure 22.7 represents these decisions on a decision tree.

Assume that risk-free rates are constant at 6% per year. If we ignore the option to double the size of the project and we invest today, then the expected cash flows are $1 million $\times$ 0.5 = $500,000 per year. Computing the NPV gives

$$NPV_{\text{without growth option}} = \frac{500,000}{0.06} - 10,000,000 = -\$1.667 \text{ million}$$

Based on this analysis, it appears that it is not optimal to undertake the project today. Of course, that also means we will never find out whether the project is successful.

Consider undertaking the project and exercising the growth option to double the size in a year if the product takes off. The NPV of doubling the size of the project in a year in this state is

$$NPV_{\text{doubling after a year}} = \frac{1,000,000}{0.06} - 10,000,000 = \$6.667 \text{ million}$$

FIGURE 22.7

Staged Investment Opportunity

At any time the size of the project can be doubled on the original terms. It is optimal to make this decision after we find out whether the project is a success. This growth option can make the initial investment worthwhile.

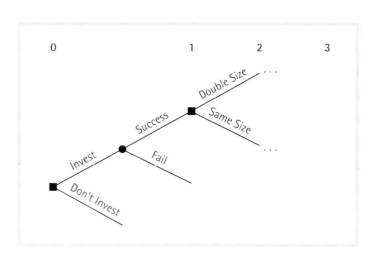

Scott Mathews

Scott Mathews is Associate Technical Fellow with the Computational Finance and Stochastic Modeling team within Boeing's advanced research and development division. He has expertise in "Business Engineering," a technology that features complex financial and investment risk models applying real asset option pricing for new products and strategically significant projects. Mr. Mathews has a number of patents in the field of real options.

QUESTION: *How can real options be used to manage projects?*

ANSWER: High-potential projects typically have substantial uncertain cash flows owing to technology and market uncertainties, and therefore your corporate finance team has to be more active in managing these projects. Essentially they act as internal venture capitalists, seeking high payoffs from risky projects. We use real options to evaluate these types of investment opportunities. With real options, we can answer the questions: Given the technical and market risks of the project, how much should we spend at the early stages? Does each incremental investment increase my return opportunities or decrease risk, and how? What amount of technology and market 'learning' must be accomplished to merit a follow-on investment?

Real options are call options on an opportunity, giving you the right to stop, start or modify a project at some future date. They are contingent, so you can make a strategic, rather than tactical, investment. By investing a small amount at each stage, you can gather enough information to decide what to do next. This limits your losses but still lets you capitalize on opportunities that arise. You don't reject (or approve) the project outright, but make incremental investments in the technology or market to gather sufficient information to determine whether this investment optimizes the company's strategy and produces positive returns over the long term.

QUESTION: *Explain the concepts of "pilot" and "commercial" stages?*

ANSWER: The "pilot" stage refers to the incremental, staged investments we make to move projects through "decision gates," investing a small and appropriate amount to gather information about the technology and the market, while driving down the project risks. At the end of each decision gate the project is re-evaluated. If there is a reasonable weighted probability of a successful outcome, we invest again and continue to the next decision gate. Projects go through several gates, and at each one we focus on reducing uncertainty, until arriving at a decision point of whether to make a large, discretionary, one-time investment (the "strike price") that launches the "piloted" concepts into production—the "commercial" stage—or terminate the project.

QUESTION: *How does staging development create a real option with value?*

ANSWER: Staging development is how we use real options to manage projects. By staging development we are buying knowledge, especially about the project risks and opportunities. As a project moves through gates, projects compete for funding, and we use this knowledge to decide which projects should proceed and which ones should be deferred. The approach brings together the engineering, marketing, and finance disciplines to give a uniform look at risks and investment opportunities. This is one of the huge powers of the technique.

Boeing's ability to solve aviation challenges with a high degree of efficiency is our competitive advantage and allows us to "buy" these options at below their market value through investments (the "premium") in our engineering processes. Buying an option for less provides direct value to shareholders. We can leverage our internal knowledge with a relatively small amount of money and hedge the risks. It's a tricky process, and is not completely financial. It often requires judgment as well.

The risk-neutral probability that this state will occur is 50%, so the expected value of this growth option is $6.667 \times 0.5 = \$3.333$ million. The present value of this amount today is

$$PV_{\text{growth option}} = \frac{3.333}{1.06} = \$3.145 \text{ million}$$

We have this option only if we choose to invest today (otherwise, we never find out how the product performs), so the NPV of undertaking this investment is the NPV we calculated above plus the value of the growth option we obtain by undertaking the project:

$$NPV = NPV_{\text{without growth option}} + PV_{\text{growth option}}$$

$$= -1.667 + 3.145 = \$1.478 \text{ million}$$

Our analysis shows that the NPV of the investment opportunity is positive and the firm should undertake it.

Notice that it is optimal to undertake the investment today only because of the existence of the future expansion option. If we could find out how well the product would sell without actually producing it, then it would not make sense to invest until we found out this information. Because the only way to find out if the product is successful is to make and market it, it is optimal to proceed. In this case the project is viable because we can experiment at a low scale and preserve the option to grow later.

This project is an example of a strategy that many firms use when they undertake big projects. Rather than commit to the entire project initially, a firm experiments by undertaking the project in stages. It implements the project on a smaller scale first; if the small-scale project proves successful, the firm then exercises the option to grow the project.

CONCEPT CHECK

1. Why can a firm with no ongoing projects, and investment opportunities that currently have negative NPVs, still be worth a positive amount?

2. Why is it sometimes optimal to invest in stages?

22.5 Abandonment Options

Implementing a project in stages, as demonstrated in the previous section, presents a third real option. An **abandonment option** is the option to walk away. Abandonment options can add value to a project because a firm can drop a project if it turns out to be unsuccessful.

The Option to Shutdown

To illustrate, assume you are the CFO of a publicly traded nationwide chain of gourmet food stores. Your company is considering opening a new store in the recently renovated Ferry Building in New York. If you do not sign the lease on the store today, someone else will, so you will not have the opportunity to open a store later. There is a clause in the lease that allows you to break the lease at no cost in two years.

Including the lease payments, the new store will cost $10,000 per month to operate. Because the building has just reopened, you do not know what the pedestrian traffic will be. If your customers are mainly limited to morning and evening commuters, you expect to generate $8000 per month in revenue in perpetuity. If, however, the building follows the lead of the Ferry Building in San Francisco and becomes a tourist attraction, you believe that your revenue will be double that amount. You estimate there is a 50% probability that the Ferry Building will become a tourist attraction. The costs to set up the store will be $400,000. Assume that the risk-free interest rate is constant at 7% per year.

The number of tourists visiting the New York Ferry Building represents idiosyncratic uncertainty (recall that this is the kind of uncertainty investors in your company can costlessly diversify away). Hence the appropriate cost of capital is the risk-free rate of 7% per year. Note that

$$1.07^{1/12} = 1.00565$$

This means the monthly discount rate is 0.565%. If you were forced to operate the store under all circumstances, then the expected revenue will be $8000 \times 0.5 + \$16,000 \times 0.5 = \$12,000$. The NPV of the investment is the present value of the revenues minus the costs:

$$NPV = \frac{12,000}{0.00565} - \frac{10,000}{0.00565} - 400,000 = -\$46,018$$

It would not make sense to open the store.

Of course, you do not have to keep operating the store. You have an option to get out of the lease after two years at no cost, and after the store is open it will be immediately obvious whether the Ferry Building is a tourist attraction. In this case, the decision tree looks like Figure 22.8.

If the Ferry Building is a tourist attraction, the NPV of the investment opportunity is

$$NPV = \frac{16,000}{0.00565} - \frac{10,000}{0.00565} - 400,000 = \$661,947$$

If the Ferry Building does not become a tourist attraction, you will close the store after two years. The NPV of the investment opportunity in this state is just the NPV of operating for two years:

$$NPV = \frac{8000}{0.00565}\left(1 - \frac{1}{1.00565^{24}}\right) - \frac{10,000}{0.00565}\left(1 - \frac{1}{1.00565^{24}}\right) - 400,000$$
$$= -\$444,770$$

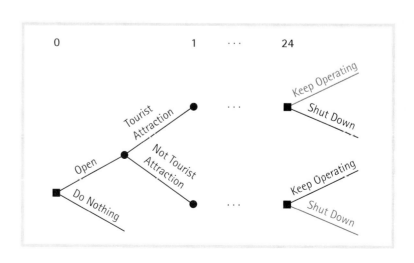

FIGURE 22.8

Decision to Open a Store in the New York Ferry Building

You must decide now whether to sign the lease and open the store, but you have an option to abandon the lease in 24 months (2 years). The profitability of the store depends on whether the Ferry Building becomes a tourist attraction.

There is an equal probability of each state and, because the risk is idiosyncratic, the actual and risk-neutral probabilities are the same. Thus the NPV of opening the store is just the expected value using the actual probabilities:

$$\$661{,}947 \times 0.5 - \$444{,}770 \times 0.5 = \$108{,}589$$

By exercising the option to abandon the venture, you limit your losses and so the NPV of undertaking the investment is positive. The value of the option to abandon is the difference between the NPV with and without the option: $108{,}589 - (-46{,}018) = \$154{,}607$.

Often, the decision to abandon a project entails costs, which may be either positive or negative. For example, you might be able to recoup some salvage value by selling off the plant and equipment. But more often than not, there is an opportunity cost of abandoning a project: If you shut down the project and later decide to start it up again, you have to pay the costs of restarting the project. For example, if you abandon the Ferry Building, your space will likely be leased to someone else, so you probably will not have the option to return later if the outlook improves.

The Option to Prepay

An important abandonment option that most people encounter at some point in their lives is the option to abandon their mortgage. As most homeowners know, mortgage interest rates are higher than comparable risk-free rates like the yield on the 30-year U.S. Treasury bond, as illustrated in Figure 22.9. You might conjecture that mortgage rates are higher than Treasury rates because mortgages are riskier. In fact, this risk is small. Not only are mortgage default rates very low, but mortgage loans are also secured by the houses they are written on. Furthermore, in many cases, mortgage lenders are insured against default

FIGURE 22.9

Historical Interest Rates

The graph shows historical yields on 30-year fixed-rate mortgages (red), the 30-year U.S. government bond (blue), and long-term AAA-rate corporate bonds (yellow). Notice how mortgage rates have generally been higher than both corporate bond rates and Treasury rates.

Source: Adapted from Federal Reserve Board Web site, http://www.federalreserve.gov/releases/h15/data.htm#fn27.

by government agencies such as GNMA. Yet mortgage rates still exceed even the rates on corporate debt (see Figure 22.9).

Mortgage interest rates are higher than Treasury rates because mortgages have an abandonment option that Treasuries do not have: You can **prepay** your mortgage at any time, while the U.S. government can repay its debt only according to the schedule outlined in the bond contract.[3] Consequently, if interest rates drop, a mortgage holder can **refinance**—that is, repay the existing mortgage and take out a new mortgage at a lower rate. From the perspective of the bank that issued the mortgage, this is a no-win situation. If, after the bank issues the mortgage, rates go down, the mortgage holder will repay the mortgage and replace it with a new mortgage at a lower rate. If rates go up after the mortgage is issued, the bank is stuck with a loan that is below market rate. That is, it has written an option.

Of course, banks understand they have written an option, so they demand a higher rate on the loan than the rate they would demand if the mortgage did not have the abandonment option. Determining how much higher is a complicated problem that depends on the current level of interest rates and expected future levels of interest rates. In fact, the pricing of mortgage-backed bonds was one of the first problems early financial engineers tackled. We provide a simple example of how to value the abandonment option and determine the rate to offer on a mortgage in the appendix to this chapter.

Corporate bonds also often contain embedded abandonment options: The issuing firm sometimes has the option to *call* the bond—that is, repay it (usually at face value). These kind of bonds are known as *callable bonds*. Another popular option gives holders of the bond the option to convert the bond into equity. These kinds of bonds are called *convertible bonds*. We will discuss these features of corporate bonds in more detail in Chapter 24 when we cover corporate debt.

As we have already explained, although the types of real options we have discussed thus far occur in most investments, there is no "boilerplate" application that we can present that can be generalized to all cases. Instead, in the next section we will describe an important application that we have not considered so far in this book: how to decide between investing in two mutually exclusive projects of different lengths.

CONCEPT CHECK

1. How can an abandonment option add value to a project?

2. Describe the embedded abandonment options contained in most mortgages and corporate bonds.

22.6 Application: Deciding Between Mutually Exclusive Investments of Different Lengths

Consider the following problem faced by a financial analyst at Canadian Motors. Last year, an engineering firm named Advanced Mechanics was asked to design a new machine that will attach car chassis to bodies. The firm has produced two designs. The cheaper design will cost $10 million to implement and last five years. The more expensive design will cost $17 million and last 10 years. In both cases, the machines are expected to save Canadian Motors $3 million per year. If the cost of capital is 10%, which design should Canadian Motors approve?

---

3. For a few years, 30-year bonds were issued with a call provision; the government could repay the bonds after 25 years if it wanted to.

NPV of Each Design

The NPV of adopting the shorter-lived design is

$$NPV = \frac{3}{0.1}\left(1 - \frac{1}{1.1^5}\right) - 10 = \$1.37 \text{ million}$$

The NPV of the longer-lived design is

$$NPV = \frac{3}{0.1}\left(1 - \frac{1}{1.1^{10}}\right) - 17 = \$1.43 \text{ million}$$

If the analyst simply picked the design with the higher NPV, he would choose the longer-lived design. However, the preceding NPV calculation ignores the difference in these projects' life spans.

NPV if Costs Rise

One reason the longer-lived design has a higher NPV is because its benefits last longer. Whether these additional benefits are worth their additional NPV depends on what happens in the next five years. To illustrate, let's assume that the costs of the machines will rise by 3% per year. After five years, the cost of a new short-lived, cheaper machine will be $10 \times 1.03^5 = \$11.59$ million. At that point, the NPV of replacing the machine with a new one is

$$NPV = \frac{3}{0.1}\left(1 - \frac{1}{1.1^5}\right) - 11.59 = -0.22 \text{ million}$$

It is not optimal to replace the shorter-lived machine with another shorter-lived machine in five years. Instead, Canadian Motors should revert to using existing technology. In this case, the correct decision is to assume that the shorter-lived machine is not replaced and just compare the NPVs of the two designs, implying that the longer-lived design should be implemented.

NPV if Future Costs Are Uncertain

In reality, the future cost of a machine is uncertain. Because of technological advances, machines may become less expensive rather than more expensive (think about the steadily declining prices of computers). Conversely, costs often rise because of inflation. The uncertainty about the cost of the machine in the future gives Canadian Motors an abandonment option: It needs to replace the shorter-lived design only if it is advantageous to do so. To illustrate, assume that the cost of the machine in the shorter-lived design will either increase by 3% or decrease by 3%. Assume that the risk-neutral probability of each state is 50%. What is the optimal decision under these circumstances?

As we have seen, if costs rise, Canadian Motors will not replace the machine, but will use the original technology instead. If costs fall, then the machine will cost $10(1 - 0.03)^5 = \$8.59$ million. At that point, the NPV of replacing the machine is

$$NPV = \frac{3}{0.1}\left(1 - \frac{1}{1.1^5}\right) - 8.59 = \$2.78 \text{ million}$$

FIGURE 22.10

Five-Year Design

If the five-year design is adopted and costs increase, it does not make sense to readopt this design. If costs decrease, the design should be readopted. These optimal decisions are shown in blue.

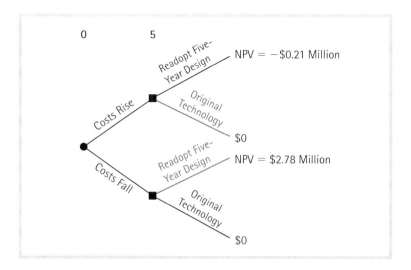

The NPV of adopting the five-year design is therefore the NPV of using the machine for five years plus the NPV of optimally replacing the machine in five years. This situation is depicted in the decision tree in Figure 22.10.

Computing the NPV gives

$$NPV = 1.37 + \frac{0.50 \times 2.78}{1.1^5} = \$2.23 \text{ million}$$

Now, the NPV of adopting the five-year design and *optimally* replacing it in five years exceeds the NPV of adopting the ten-year design, so the five-year design is the superior investment. By committing to a longer-lived project, the firm would give up its real option to react to technological and market changes.

Equivalent Annual Benefit Method

Traditionally, managers have used the **equivalent annual benefit method** to choose between projects of different lives. This approach accounts for the difference in project lengths by calculating the constant payment over the life of the project that is equivalent to receiving the NPV today and then selecting the project with the higher equivalent annual benefit. It ignores the value of any real options because it assumes that the projects will always be replaced at their original terms. Let's see how this method would work for Canadian Motors.

The NPV of the shorter-lived design is $1.37 million. Let x be the equivalent annual benefit. The present value of the equivalent annual benefit each year equals the NPV today. So the equivalent annual benefit of the shorter-lived design is given by

$$1.37 = \frac{x}{0.1}\left(1 - \frac{1}{1.1^5}\right)$$

$$x = \frac{1.37 \times 0.1}{1 - \dfrac{1}{1.1^5}} = \$0.361 \text{ million}$$

Repeating the calculation for the longer-lived design gives

$$1.43 = \frac{x}{0.1}\left(1 - \frac{1}{1.1^{10}}\right)$$

$$x = \frac{1.43 \times 0.1}{1 - \dfrac{1}{1.1^{10}}} = \$0.233 \text{ million}$$

Notice that the longer-lived design has a lower equivalent annual benefit. Based on the equivalent annual benefit method, the analyst should select the shorter-lived design. This is the correct decision if we assume the cost of the machine will not change. But if the future costs (or benefits) are uncertain, we must use a real options approach to determine the correct decision.

CONCEPT CHECK

1. Why is it inappropriate to simply pick the higher NPV project when comparing mutually exclusive investment opportunities of different lengths?

2. What is a major shortcoming of the equivalent annual benefit method?

22.7 Rules of Thumb

One of the major drawbacks of using the concepts introduced in this chapter is that they are difficult to implement. In practice, correctly modeling the sources of uncertainty and the appropriate dynamic decisions usually requires an extensive amount of time and financial expertise. Furthermore, in most cases, the solutions are problem specific, so the time and expertise spent on one problem are not transferable to other problems. Consequently, many firms resort to following rules of thumb.[4] Here we examine two commonly used rules of thumb: the profitability index and hurdle rates.

The Profitability Index Rule

As we explained in Section 22.1, when an investment opportunity can be delayed, it is optimal to invest only when the NPV of the investment project is sufficiently high. In most applications, it is quite difficult to calculate precisely how high the NPV must be to trigger investment. As a result, some firms use the following rule of thumb: Invest whenever the profitability index exceeds a specified level.

Recall from Chapter 6 that in the simple case of a project where the only resource is the upfront investment, the profitability index is

$$\text{Profitability Index} = \frac{\text{NPV}}{\text{Initial Investment}}$$

The **profitability index rule** directs you to invest whenever the profitability index exceeds some predetermined number. When the investment cannot be delayed, the optimal rule is to invest whenever the profitability index is greater than zero. When there is an option to delay, a good rule of thumb is to invest only when the index is at least 1. Often, firms

---

4. See Robert McDonald, "Real Options and Rules of Thumb in Capital Budgeting," in M. J. Brennan and L. Trigeorgis (eds.), *Project Flexibility, Agency, and Competition* (London: Oxford University Press, 2000), for a detailed analysis of the performance of different rules of thumb.

set even higher thresholds because the cost of investing at the wrong time is usually asymmetric. It is often better to wait too long (use a profitability index criterion that is too high) than to invest too soon (use a profitability index criterion that is too low).

The Hurdle Rate Rule

The profitability index rule of thumb raises the bar on the NPV to take into account the option to wait. Rather than invest when the NPV is zero, you wait until the NPV is a multiple of the initial investment. Instead of raising the bar on the NPV, the **hurdle rate rule** raises the discount rate. The hurdle rate rule uses a higher discount rate than the cost of capital to compute the NPV, but then applies the regular NPV rule: Invest whenever the NPV calculated using this higher discount rate is positive. This higher discount rate is known as the **hurdle rate** because if the project can jump this hurdle—that is, have a positive NPV at this higher discount rate—then it should be undertaken.

When the source of uncertainty that creates a motive to wait is interest rate uncertainty, the hurdle rate is relatively easy to calculate. In this case, the rule of thumb is to multiply the cost of capital by the ratio of the **mortgage interest rate**, which is the rate on a risk-free annuity that is prepayable (callable) at any time, to the risk-free riskless rate:

$$\text{Hurdle Rate} = \text{Cost of Capital} \times \frac{\text{Mortgage Rate}}{\text{Risk-Free Rate}} \tag{22.3}$$

We should then invest whenever the NPV of the project is positive using this hurdle rate as the discount rate.

Figure 22.11 shows the historical ratio of 30-year mortgage rates to long-term risk-free rates in the United States. This ratio has generally hovered around 1.2: Mortgage rates have generally been 20% higher than long-term risk-free rates. Thus this rule of thumb implies using a hurdle rate that is approximately 20% greater than the cost of capital.

What do mortgage rates have to do with the optimal time to make an investment? Recall that mortgage rates exceed risk-free rates because mortgages carry an option to

FIGURE 22.11

Historical Ratio of Mortgage Rates to Risk-Free Rates

The graph shows the ratio of the 30-year fixed-rate mortgage yield to the yield on the 30-year U.S. government bond. Historically, mortgage rates have generally been 20% higher than long-term risk-free rates.

Source: Adapted from Federal Reserve Board Web site, http://www.federalreserve.gov/releases/h15/data.htm#fn27.

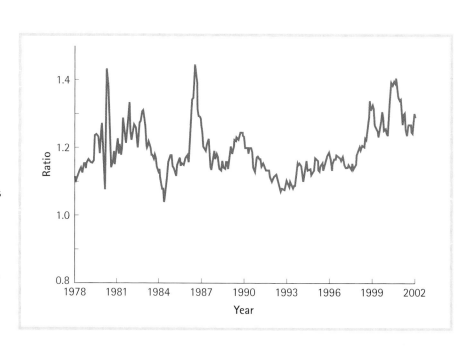

repay the loans early.[5] Let's assume you have a risk-free project that you can delay. It currently has a positive NPV. You intend to borrow the initial investment but you are unsure whether you should wait in the hope that interest rates will fall. If you take out a regular loan and interest rates decrease, you will be stuck paying a higher rate. However, if you take out a mortgage loan and interest rates fall, then you can refinance and take advantage of the lower rates. So, if the project has a positive NPV using the mortgage interest rate as the discount rate, you can have your cake and eat it too: You can immediately get the benefits of the investment by undertaking it and still take advantage of a lower rate if rates fall. Thus it makes sense to invest immediately. The rule of thumb approximately implements this decision rule. Let's see why in the context of an example.

EXAMPLE 22.2

Using the Hurdle Rate Rule for the Option to Delay

Problem

You have the opportunity to invest in a risk-free technology. The investment will require an upfront payment of $1 million and will provide a constant annual cash flow of $96,000 every year in perpetuity. Because the investment is risk free, the cost of capital is the risk-free rate. Assume that all interest rates will either be 10% or 6% in one year with risk-neutral probabilities of 64.375% and 35.625%, respectively. The one-year risk-free interest rate is 7%, and today's rate on a risk-free perpetual bond is 8%. In the appendix to this chapter, we show that under these assumptions the rate of an equivalent perpetual bond that is repayable at any time (the mortgage rate) is 9.6%. Should you invest in the technology today, or wait and see if rates drop and then invest?

Solution

Using the hurdle rate rule of thumb, we multiply the cost of capital by the ratio of the mortgage rate to the risk-free rate. Here the cash flows are risk free, so the cost of capital is the risk-free rate, which implies that the hurdle rate is the mortgage rate. Hence,

$$NPV = \frac{96,000}{0.096} - 1,000,000 = 0$$

The rule of thumb implies that you are indifferent. Let's see if this is correct. The actual cost of capital is 8% (the rate offered on a risk-free perpetuity), so the investment opportunity clearly has a positive NPV:

$$NPV = \frac{96,000}{0.08} - 1,000,000 = \$200,000$$

Let's see what the NPV of waiting is. If we delay the investment, it makes sense to invest only if rates drop because

$$NPV_{\text{rates go up}} = \frac{96,000}{0.1} - 1,000,000 = -\$40,000$$

$$NPV_{\text{rates go down}} = \frac{96,000}{0.06} - 1,000,000 = \$600,000$$

---

5. In fact, mortgage borrowers do not always prepay their mortgages optimally. Borrowers are usually required to pay off their mortgages if they sell their home, and so may prepay even if rates have gone up. Also, not all borrowers refinance when rates drop. As a result, actual mortgage rates are lower than the true mortgage rate that would be charged if the borrower prepaid optimally, and so represent a lower bound for the hurdle rate.

The present value today of the expected NPV using risk-neutral probabilities is therefore

$$\frac{600,000 \times 0.35625}{1.07} = \$199,766 \approx \$200,000$$

The rule of thumb is correct: You really are indifferent between investing today and waiting.[6]

In situations like Example 22.2, when the cash flows are constant and perpetual, and the reason to wait derives solely from interest rate uncertainty, the rule of thumb is always exact.[7] However, when these conditions are not satisfied, the rule of thumb merely approximates the correct decision.

While using a hurdle rate rule for deciding when to invest might be a cost-effective way to make investment decisions, it is important to remember that this rule does not provide an accurate measure of *value*. The value of making an investment is the NPV calculated using the cost of capital as the discount rate, not the hurdle rate. Thus, while the rule of thumb provides the correct time to invest in Example 22.2, the actual value of undertaking the investment is $200,000—the NPV when the correct cost of capital is used as the discount rate.

Applying Hurdle Rates and the Profitability Index Simultaneously

Potentially there could be an advantage to using both rules of thumb simultaneously. For example, when a firm faces the same uncertainty for most of its investment decisions, using a single profitability index criterion for all projects can provide a useful rule of thumb to account for cash flow uncertainty. To account for interest rate uncertainty, the hurdle rate rule can be applied to augment the profitability index. That is, the decision when to invest can be made by first computing the NPV using a hurdle rate that is equal to the cost of capital multiplied by the ratio of the mortgage rate to the risk-free rate, which is the hurdle rate in Eq. 22.3. The profitability index can be calculated using this NPV. If the profitability index exceeds a predetermined criterion, the firm should undertake the project.

CONCEPT CHECK

1. What is the hurdle rate rule?

2. Explain the profitability index rule of thumb.

Summary

1. A real option is an option where the underlying asset is a physical, rather than a financial asset.

2. A decision tree is a graphical way to represent alternative decisions and potential outcomes in an uncertain economy. It contains decision nodes and information nodes.

---

6. The slight difference is due to the fact that the actual mortgage rate is 9.59664% but we rounded it to 9.6% earlier.

7. A proof of this fact can be found in Jonathan B. Berk, "A Simple Approach for Deciding When to Invest," *American Economic Review* 89 (1999): 1319–1326.

3. By waiting before committing to an investment, a firm can obtain more information about the investment's returns. By correctly choosing the time to commit to an investment, it can add value.

4. When you have the option of deciding when to invest, it is usually optimal to invest only when the NPV is substantially greater than zero.

5. Given the option to wait, an investment that currently has a negative NPV can have a positive value.

6. The option to wait is most valuable when there is a great deal of uncertainty regarding what the value of the investment will be in the future.

7. In the real option context, the dividends correspond to any value from the investment that we give up by waiting. Absent dividends, a call option should not be exercised early.

8. By undertaking a project, a firm often gets the opportunity to make investments that it would not have otherwise. The opportunity to invest in projects in the future—that is, the firm's growth options—is worth something today.

9. When firms find themselves involved in a project that is losing money, with little prospect of turning things around in the future, they can exercise their abandonment option and walk away.

10. In choosing between investments of different maturities, a firm must take into account its option to extend the life of the shorter-lived project at the end of its original life.

11. Managers use the equivalent annual benefit method to compare projects of different lengths. It implicitly assumes that the projects can be replaced at their original terms. Using the equivalent annual benefit method might produce different recommendations than when future uncertainty is taken into account.

12. The profitability index rule of thumb calls for investing whenever the profitability index exceeds some predetermined number.

13. The hurdle rate rule of thumb computes the NPV using the hurdle rate, a discount rate higher than the cost of capital, and specifies that the investment should be undertaken only when the NPV computed this way is positive.

Key Terms

abandonment option *p. 731*
decision node *p. 719*
decision tree *p. 718*
equivalent annual benefit method *p. 736*
growth option *p. 726*
hurdle rate *p. 738*
hurdle rate rule *p. 738*

information node *p. 719*
mortgage interest rate *p. 738*
prepay *p. 734*
profitability index rule *p. 737*
real option *p. 718*
refinance *p. 734*

Further Reading

Many people believe that by not explicitly accounting for the real options described in this chapter, managers make costly mistakes. For an in-depth discussion of this issue, see T. E. Copeland, V. Antikarov, and T. Texere, *Real Options: A Practitioner's Guide*, Revised ed. (New York: W. W. Norton & Company, 2003).

These books cover the topics of this chapter in more detail and depth: M. Amran and N. Kulatilaka, *Real Options: Managing Strategic Investments in an Uncertain World* (Boston: Harvard Business School Press, 1999); M. Brennan and L. Trigeorgis, eds., *Flexibility, Natural Resources, and Strategic Options* (Oxford: Oxford University Press, 1998); A. K. Dixit and R. S. Pindyck, *Investment Under Uncertainty* (Princeton, NJ: Princeton University Press, 1994); H. Smit and L. Trigeorgis, *Strategic Investment, Real Options and Games* (Princeton, NJ: Princeton University Press, 2004); and L. Trigeorgis, *Real Options* (Cambridge, MA: MIT Press, 1996).

For a discussion of how well the rules of thumb covered in this chapter perform in practice, see R. McDonald, "Real Options and Rules of Thumb in Capital Budgeting," in M. J. Brennan and L. Trigeorgis (eds.), *Project Flexibility, Agency, and Competition* (London: Oxford University Press, 2000).

For more information on how real options affect the view academics and practitioners have of corporate finance, see T. A. Luehrman, "Strategy as a Portfolio of Real Options," *Harvard Business Review* (September–October 1998): 89–99; S. P. Mason and R. C. Merton, "The Role of Contingent Claims Analysis in Corporate Finance," in E. I. Altman and M. G. Subrahmanyan (eds.), *Recent Advances in Corporate Finance* (Homewood, IL: Richard D. Irwin, 1985); and A. Triantris and A. Borison, "Real Options: State of the Practice," *Journal of Applied Corporate Finance* 14(2) (2001): 8–24.

Problems

A blue box (■) indicates problems available in MyFinanceLab. An asterisk (*) indicates problems with a higher level of difficulty.

Decision Tree Analysis

1. Your company is planning on opening an office in Japan. Profits depend on how fast the economy in Japan recovers from its current recession. There is a 50% chance of recovery this year. You are trying to decide whether to open the office now or in a year. Construct the decision tree that shows the choices you have to open the office either today or one year from now.

EXCEL
2. You are trying to decide whether to make an investment of $500 million in a new technology to produce Everlasting Gobstoppers. There is a 60% chance that the market for these candies will produce profits of $100 million annually, a 20% chance the market will produce profits of $50 million, and a 20% chance that there will be no profits. The size of the market will become clear one year from now. Currently, the cost of capital of the project is 11% per year. There is a 20% chance that the cost of capital will drop to 9% in a year and stay at that level forever, and a 80% chance that it will stay at 11% forever. Movements in the cost of capital are unrelated to the size of the candy market. Construct the decision tree that shows the choices you have to make the investment either today or one year from now.

3. Using the information in Problem 2, rework the problem assuming you find out the size of the Everlasting Gobstopper market one year *after you make the investment.* That is, if you do not make the investment, you do not find out the size of the market. Construct the decision tree that shows the choices you have under these circumstances.

4. Describe the benefits and costs of delaying an investment opportunity.

5. You are a financial analyst at Global Conglomerate and are considering entering the shoe business. You believe that you have a very narrow window for entering this market. Because of Christmas demand, the time is right today and you believe that exactly a year from now would also be a good opportunity. Other than these two opportunities, you do not think another opportunity will exist to break into this business. It will cost you $35 million to enter the

market. Because other shoe manufacturers exist and are public companies, you can construct a perfectly comparable company. Hence you have decided to use the Black-Sholes formula to decide when and if you should enter the shoe business. Your analysis implies that the current value of an operating shoe company is $40 million. However, the flow of customers is uncertain, so the value of the company is volatile—your analysis indicates that the volatility is 25% per year. The company will generate 15% of its current value in free cash flow (cash available to you to spend how you wish) per year. Because this cash is earned each day over the course of the year, a good approximation is that it is paid continuously over the course of the year. If the one-year risk-free rate of interest is 4%:

a. Should Global enter this business and, if so, when?

b. How will the decision change if the current value of a shoe company is $36 million instead of $40 million?

c. Plot the value of your investment opportunity as a function of the current value of a shoe company.

6. It is the beginning of September and you have been offered the following deal to go heli-skiing. If you pick the first week in January and pay for your vacation now, you can get a week of heli-skiing for $2500. However, if you cannot ski because the helicopters cannot fly due to bad weather, there is no snow, or you get sick, you do not get a refund. There is a 40% probability that you will not be able to ski. If you wait until the last minute and go only if you know that the conditions are perfect and you are well, the vacation will cost $4000. You estimate that the pleasure you get from heli-skiing is worth $6000 per week to you (if you had to pay any more than that, you would choose not to go). If your cost of capital is 8% per year, should you book ahead or wait?

EXCEL **7.** A professor in the Computer Science department at United States Institute of Technology has just patented a new search engine technology and would like to sell it to you, an interested venture capitalist. The patent has a 17-year life. The technology will take a year to implement (if you invest today, the first cash flow occurs at the end of the first year) and has an upfront cost of $100 million. You believe this technology will be able to capture 1% of the Internet search market, and currently this market generates profits of $1 billion per year. Over the next five years, the risk-neutral probability that profits will grow at 10% per year is 20% and the risk-neutral probability that profits will grow at 5% per year is 80%. This growth rate will become clear one year from now (after the first year of growth). After five years, profits are expected to decline 2% annually. No profits are expected after the patent runs out. Assume that all risk-free interest rates are constant (regardless of the term) at 10% per year.

a. Calculate the NPV of undertaking the investment today.

b. Calculate the NPV of waiting a year to make the investment decision.

c. What is your optimal investment strategy?

*8. The management of Southern Express Corporation is considering investing 10% of all future earnings in growth. The company has a single growth opportunity that it can take either now or in one period. Although the managers do not know the return on investment with certainty, they know it is equally likely to be either 10% or 14% per year. In one period they will find out which state will occur. Currently the firm pays out all earnings as a dividend of $10 million; if it does not make the investment, dividends are expected to remain at this level forever. If Southern Express undertakes the investment, the new dividend will reflect the realized return on investment and will grow at the realized rate forever. Assuming the opportunity cost of capital is 10.1%, what is the value of the company just before the current dividend is paid (the cum-dividend value)?

*9. What decision should you make in Problem 2 if the one-year cost of capital is 15.44% and the profits last forever?

10. Your R&D division has just synthesized a material that will superconduct electricity at room temperature; you have given the go ahead to try to produce this material commercially. It will take five years to find out whether the material is commercially viable, and you estimate that the probability of success is 25%. Development will cost $10 million per year, paid at the beginning of each year. If development is successful and you decide to produce the material, the factory will be built immediately. It will cost $1 billion to put in place, and will generate profits of $100 million at the end of every year in perpetuity. Assume that the current five-year risk-free interest rate is 10% per year, and the yield on a perpetual risk-free bond will be either 12%, 10%, 8%, or 5% in five years. Assume that the risk-neutral probability of each possible rate is the same. What is the value today of this project?

*11. You are an analyst working for Goldman Sachs, and you are trying to value the growth potential of a large, established company, Big Industries. Big Industries has a thriving R&D division that has consistently turned out successful products. You estimate that, on average, the division launches two projects every three years, so you estimate that there is a 66% chance that a project will be produced every year. Typically, the investment opportunities the R&D division produces require an initial investment of $10 million and yield profits of $1 million per year that grow at one of three possible growth rates in perpetuity: 3%, 0%, and −3%. All three growth rates are equally likely for any given project. These opportunities are always "take it or leave it" opportunities: If they are not undertaken immediately, they disappear forever. Assume that the cost of capital will always remain at 12% per year. What is the present value of all future growth opportunities Big Industries will produce?

*12. Repeat Problem 11, but this time assume that all the probabilities are risk-neutral probabilities, which means the cost of capital is always the risk-free rate and risk-free rates follow the path in Example 22.1: The current interest rate for a risk-free perpetuity is 8%; in one year, there is a 64.375% chance that all risk-free interest rates will be 10% and stay there forever and a 35.625% chance that they will be 6% and stay there forever. The current one-year risk-free rate is 7%.

13. You own a small networking startup. You have just received an offer to buy your firm from a large, publicly traded firm, JCH Systems. Under the terms of the offer, you will receive 1 million shares of JCH. JCH stock currently trades for $25 per share. You can sell the shares of JCH that you will receive in the market at any time. But as part of the offer, JCH also agrees that at any time during the next year, it will buy the shares back from you for $25 per share if you desire. Suppose the current one-year risk-free rate is 6.18%, the volatility of JCH stock is 30%, and JCH does not pay dividends.

a. Is this offer worth more than $25 million? Explain.

b. What is the value of the offer?

14. You own a wholesale plumbing supply store. The store currently generates revenues of $1 million per year. Next year, revenues will either decrease by 10% or increase by 5%, with equal probability, and then stay at that level as long as you operate the store. You own the store outright. Other costs run $900,000 per year. There are no costs to shutting down; in that case you can always sell the store for $500,000. What is the business worth today if the cost of capital is fixed at 10%?

EXCEL ***15.** You own a copper mine. The price of copper is currently $1.50 per pound. The mine produces 1 million pounds of copper per year and costs $2 million per year to operate. It has enough copper to operate for 100 years. Shutting the mine down would entail bringing the land up to EPA standards and is expected to cost $5 million. Reopening the mine once it is shut down would be an impossibility given current environmental standards. The price of copper has an equal (and independent) probability of going up or down by 25% each year for the next two years and then will stay at that level forever. Calculate the NPV of continuing to operate the mine if the cost of capital is fixed at 15%. Is it optimal to abandon the mine or keep it operating?

16. An original silver dollar from the late eighteenth century consists of approximately 24 grams of silver. At a price of 19¢ per gram ($6 per troy ounce), the silver content of the coin is currently worth about $4.50. Assume that these coins are in plentiful supply and are not collector's items, so they have no numismatic value. If the current price of silver is 19¢ per gram, will the price of the coin be greater than, less than, or equal to $4.50? Justify your answer.[7]

Application: Deciding Between Mutually Exclusive Investments of Different Lengths

17. What implicit assumption is made when managers use the equivalent annual benefit method to decide between two projects with different lives that use the same resource?

18. You own a cab company and are evaluating two options to replace your fleet. Either you can take out a five-year lease on the replacement cabs for $500 per month per cab, or you can purchase the cabs outright for $30,000, in which case the cabs will last eight years. You must return the cabs to the leasing company at the end of the lease. The leasing company is responsible for all maintenance costs, but if you purchase the cabs, you will buy a maintenance contract that will cost $100 per month for the life of each cab. Each cab will generate revenues of $1000 per month. Assume the cost of capital is fixed at 12%.

   a. Calculate the NPV per cab of both possibilities: purchasing the cabs or leasing them.

   b. Calculate the equivalent monthly annual benefit of both opportunities.

   c. If you are leasing a cab, you have the opportunity to buy the used cab after five years. Assume that in five years a five-year-old cab will cost either $10,000 or $16,000, with equal likelihood; will have maintenance costs of $500 per month; and will last three more years. Which option should you take?

*19. You own a piece of raw land in an up-and-coming area in Gotham City. The costs to construct a building increase disproportionately with the size of the building. A building of q square feet costs $0.1 \times q^2$ to build. After you construct a building on the lot, it will last forever but you are committed to it: You cannot put another building on the lot. Buildings currently rent at $100 per square foot per month. Rents in this area are expected to increase in five years. There is a 50% chance that they will rise to $200 per square foot per month and stay there forever and a 50% chance that they will stay at $100 per square foot per month forever. The cost of capital is fixed at 12% per year.

   a. Should you construct a building on the lot right away? If so, how large should the building be?

   b. If you choose to delay the decision, how large a building will you construct in each possible state in five years?

---

7. This question appeared on author Jonathan Berk's Ph.D. qualifying examination, which was set by Professor Jonathan Ingersoll.

20. Assume that the project in Example 22.2 pays an annual cash flow of $100,000 (instead of $96,000).

    a. What is the NPV of investing today?

    b. What is the NPV of waiting and investing tomorrow?

    c. Verify that the hurdle rate rule of thumb gives the correct time to invest in this case.

21. Assume that the project in Example 22.2 pays an annual cash flow of $90,000 (instead of $96,000).

    a. What is the NPV of investing today?

    b. What is the NPV of waiting and investing tomorrow?

    c. Verify that the hurdle rate rule of thumb gives the correct time to invest in this case.

Calculating Mortgage Interest Rates

To understand how to value the abandonment option in a mortgage, let's consider the following highly simplified example:

> You are an innovative mortgage banker who has created a new product: an annual-pay, interest-only, perpetual mortgage. You are trying to determine what rate your bank should offer on these mortgages. The mortgages will last forever and require annual interest payments but borrowers will be able to retire the loan at any time by repaying the original principal. The mortgages are guaranteed by the U.S. government, so there is no chance of default. The current one-year risk-free rate of interest is 7%, and the yield on a risk-free, annual-pay, perpetual bond that is *not* repayable is 8%. One year from now, all interest rates will drop to 6% or rise to 10% and then stay at these levels forever. What rate should you offer on the perpetual mortgage loan?

Step 1: Calculate the Risk-Neutral Probability of Each State

To answer this problem, we will need to calculate the risk-neutral probability of each state. We will use the risk-free perpetual bond. If the bank extends a perpetual risk-free loan with a $100 face value today that pays $8 of interest every year (by the Law of One Price, if the loan is priced at $100, the bank interest rate must match the yield on the perpetual bond), after one year this loan will be worth either

$$8 + \frac{8}{0.06} = \$141.33$$

if rates drop to 6% or

$$8 + \frac{8}{0.1} = \$88.00$$

if rates rise to 10%. Because the interest rate offered on this loan is the current market rate, the loan is worth its face value ($100) today. So the value of the loan today is also the expected value the end of the first year using the risk-neutral probabilities, discounted at the one-year risk-free rate:

$$100 = \frac{\rho \times 88 + (1 - \rho) \times 141.33}{1.07}$$

$$\rho = 64.375\%$$

(We can also solve for $\rho = 64.375\%$ using Eq. 21.16.) The risk-neutral probability of rates rising to 10% is, therefore, 64.375%.

Step 2: Build a Decision Tree and Calculate Present Value

Assume the bank originates a $100,000 perpetual mortgage and charges an interest rate of x. At the end of the first year, the bank will receive $100,000 \times x$. If rates go up, because the borrower will then have a below-market mortgage, the borrower will not choose to refinance the mortgage. Therefore, the bank will receive this amount every year forever. However, if rates go down, the borrower will choose to refinance at 6%, so the bank will get the face value of the loan returned at time 1. We put this information on a decision tree, as shown in Figure 22A.1.

If at time 1 interest rates go up, then the value of the loan is the present value of the value of the remaining cash flows plus the interest payment:

$$PV_{up} = \frac{100,000x}{0.1} + 100,000x$$

Optimal Prepayment

If rates drop, the mortgage borrower will repay the principal balance outstanding. If rates rise, the borrower will pay interest on the original schedule (once a year).

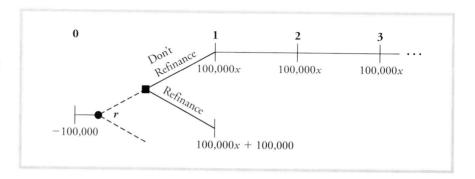

If interest rates go down, then the borrower will refinance by repaying the face amount of the loan to the bank. The value of the loan in that state is the face value of the loan plus the interest owed for one year:

$$PV_{\text{down}} = 100,000 + 100,000x$$

Thus the expected value of this loan under the risk-neutral probabilities at the end of the first year is

$$PV_1 = 0.64375\,PV_{\text{up}} + (1 - 0.64375)\,PV_{\text{down}}$$

$$= \left(\frac{100,000x}{0.1}\right)0.64375 + 100,000 \times 0.35625 + 100,000x$$

Step 3: Solve for the Interest Rate

The present value of this loan today must equal the face value of the loan (what the bank gets in exchange for the cash flows), so

$$100,000 = \frac{PV_1}{1.07} = \frac{(1,000,000x)0.64375 + 100,000 \times 0.35625 + 100,000x}{1.07}$$

Solving for x gives $x = 0.095966$. Thus you will be prepared to offer a rate of about 9.6% on the mortgage, implying a spread of about 1.6% over a comparable loan that does not have the option to repay it early.

PART

VIII

Chapter 23
The Mechanics of Raising Equity Capital

Chapter 24
Debt Financing

Chapter 25
Leasing

Long-Term Financing

The Law of One Price Connection.   How should a firm raise the funds it needs to undertake its investments? In the capital structure part of the text, we discussed the financial manager's choice between the major categories of financing, debt, and equity. In this part of the book, we explain the mechanics of implementing these decisions. Chapter 23 describes the process a company goes through when it raises equity capital. In Chapter 24, we review firms' use of debt markets to raise capital. Chapter 25 introduces an alternative to long-term debt financing, leasing. By presenting leasing as a financing alternative, we apply the Law of One Price to determine that the benefits of leasing must derive from tax differences, incentive effects, or other market imperfections.

The Mechanics of Raising Equity Capital

As we pointed out in Chapter 1, most businesses in the United States are small sole proprietorships and partnerships. That said, as a whole, these firms generate less than 15% of total U.S. sales. One limitation of a sole proprietorship is that it does not allow access to outside equity capital, so the business has relatively little capacity for growth. Another limitation is that the sole proprietor is forced to hold a large fraction of his or her wealth in a single asset—the company—and therefore is likely to be undiversified. By incorporating, businesses can gain access to capital and founders can reduce the risk of their portfolios by selling some of their equity and diversifying. Consequently, even though corporations make up only about 20% of U.S. businesses, they account for 85% of sales in the U.S. economy.

In this chapter, we discuss how companies raise equity capital. To illustrate this concept, we follow the case of a real company, RealNetworks, Inc. (ticker: RNWK). RealNetworks is a leading creator of digital media services and software. Customers use RealNetworks products to find, play, purchase, and manage digital music, videos, and games. RealNetworks was founded in 1993 and incorporated in 1994. Using the example of RealNetworks, we first discuss the alternative ways new companies can raise capital and then examine the impact of these funding alternatives on current and new investors.

23.1 Equity Financing for Private Companies

The initial capital that is required to start a business is usually provided by the entrepreneur herself and her immediate family. Few families, however, have the resources to finance a growing business, so growth almost always requires outside capital. A private company must seek sources that can provide this capital, but it must also understand how the infusion of outside capital will affect the control of the company, particularly when outside investors decide to cash out their investments in the company.

Sources of Funding

When a private company decides to raise outside equity capital, it can seek funding from several potential sources: angel investors, venture capital firms, institutional investors, and corporate investors.

Angel Investors. Individual investors who buy equity in small private firms are called **angel investors**. For many start-ups, the first round of outside private equity financing is often obtained from angels. These investors are frequently friends or acquaintances of the entrepreneur. Because their capital investment is often large relative to the amount of capital already in place at the firm, they typically receive a sizeable equity share in the business in return for their funds. As a result, these investors may have substantial influence in the business decisions of the firm. Angels may also bring expertise to the firm that the entrepreneur lacks.

Although in some cases the capital available from angel investors is sufficient, in most cases firms need more capital than what a few angels can provide. Finding angels is difficult—often it is a function of how well connected the entrepreneur is in the local community. Most entrepreneurs, especially those launching their first start-up company, have few relationships with people with substantial capital to invest. At some point, many firms that require equity capital for growth must turn to the venture capital industry.

Venture Capital Firms. A **venture capital firm** is a limited partnership that specializes in raising money to invest in the private equity of young firms. Table 23.1 lists the ten most active U.S. venture capital firms in 2005, based on the number of deals completed.

Typically, institutional investors, such as pension funds, are the limited partners. The general partners work for the venture capital firm and run the venture capital firm; they are called **venture capitalists**. Venture capital firms offer limited partners a number of advantages over investing directly in start-ups themselves as angel investors. Because these firms invest in many start-ups, limited partners are more diversified. They also benefit from the expertise of the general partners. However, these advantages come at a cost. General partners usually charge substantial fees, taken mainly as a percentage of the positive returns they generate. Most firms charge 20% of any positive return they make, but the successful firms may charge more than 30%. They also generally charge an annual management fee of about 2% of the fund's committed capital.

Venture capital firms can provide substantial capital for young companies. For example, during 2004, venture capital firms invested almost $21 billion in about 2900 venture capital deals, for an average investment of about $7.3 million per deal. In return, venture capitalists often demand a great deal of control. Paul Gompers and Josh Lerner[1] report

---

1. Paul A. Gompers and Josh Lerner, *The Venture Capital Cycle* (Cambridge, MA: MIT Press, 1999).

TABLE 23.1	**Most Active U.S. Venture Capital Firms in 2005 (by number of deals completed)**

Venture Capital Firm	Number of Deals	Number of Companies
Draper Fisher Jurvetson	80	73
New Enterprise Associates	73	66
U.S. Venture Partners	71	64
Venrock Associates	59	48
Sequoia Capital	49	46
Polaris Venture Partners	49	42
Kleiner Perkins Caufield & Byers	48	41
Intel Capital	47	45
Accel Parters	46	40
Morgenthaler Ventures	45	42

Source: M. Sheahan, "Year in Review: Deals," *Venture Capital Journal* (February 2006) 12–18.

that venture capitalists typically control about one-third of the seats on a start-up's board of directors, and often represent the single largest voting block on the board. Although entrepreneurs generally view this control as a necessary cost of obtaining venture capital, it can actually be an important benefit of accepting venture financing. Venture capitalists use their control to protect their investments, so they may therefore perform a key nurturing and monitoring role for the firm.

The importance of the venture capital sector has grown enormously in the last 50 years. As Figure 23.1 shows, growth in the sector increased in the 1990s and peaked at the height of the Internet boom. Although the size of the industry has decreased substantially since then, it remains larger than it was in 1997.

Institutional Investors. Institutional investors such as pension funds, insurance companies, endowments, and foundations manage large quantities of money. They are major investors in many different types of assets, so, not surprisingly, they are also active investors in private companies. Institutional investors may invest directly in private firms, or they may invest indirectly by becoming limited partners in venture capital firms. Institutional interest in private equity has grown dramatically in recent years. For example, *The Wall Street Journal* reported that universities, endowments, and pension funds invested $17.6 billion in venture capital during 2004, up 67% from 2003.

Corporate Investors. Many established corporations purchase equity in younger, private companies. A corporation that invests in private companies is called many different names, including **corporate investor**, **corporate partner**, **strategic partner**, and **strategic investor**. Most of the other types of investors in private firms that we have considered so far are primarily interested in the financial return that they will earn on their investments. Corporate investors, by contrast, might invest for corporate strategic objectives in addition

FIGURE 23.1

Venture Capital Funding in the United States

Panel (a) indicates the total number of venture capital deals by year. Panel (b) shows the total dollar amount of venture capital investment.

Source: Venture Economics.

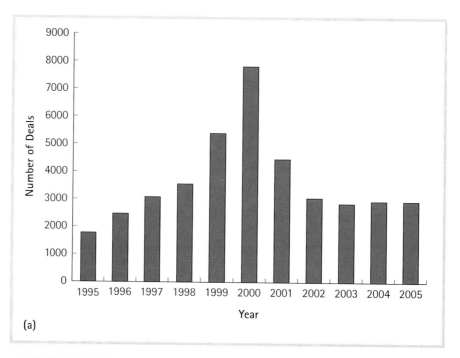

(a)

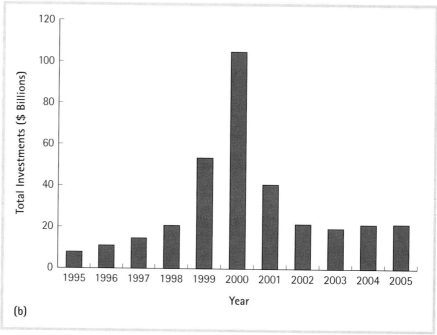

(b)

to the desire for investment returns. For example, in 2001 Microsoft Corporation, as part of a strategic partnership, invested $51 million in Groove Networks, Inc. At the time Microsoft CEO Steve Ballmer said, "We look forward to working with [Groove] to deliver solutions to our customers that further advance our vision of empowering people through great software."

Outside Investors

When a company founder decides to sell equity to outside investors for the first time, it is common practice for private companies to issue preferred stock rather than common stock to raise capital. **Preferred stock** issued by mature companies such as banks usually has a preferential dividend and seniority in any liquidation and sometimes special voting rights. Conversely, the preferred stock issued by young companies typically does not pay regular cash dividends. However, this preferred stock usually gives the owner an option to convert it into common stock on some future date, so it is often called **convertible preferred stock**. In short, it will have all of the future rights and benefits of common stock if things go well. Of course, if the company runs into financial difficulties, the preferred stockholders have a senior claim on the assets of the firm relative to any common stockholders (who are often the employees of the firm).

RealNetworks, which was founded by Robert Glaser in 1993, was initially funded with an investment of approximately $1 million by Glaser. As of April 1995, Glaser's $1 million initial investment in RealNetworks represented 13,713,439 shares of Series A preferred stock, implying an initial purchase price of about $0.07 per share. RealNetworks needed more capital, and management decided to raise this money by selling equity in the form of convertible preferred stock.

The company's first round of outside equity funding was Series B preferred stock. Real-Networks sold 2,686,567 shares of Series B preferred stock at $0.67 per share in April 1995.[2] After this funding round the distribution of ownership was

	Number of Shares	Price per Share ($)	Total Value ($ million)	Percentage Ownership
Series A	13,713,439	0.67	9.2	83.6%
Series B	2,686,567	0.67	1.8	16.4%
	16,400,006		11.0	100.0%

The Series B preferred shares were new shares of stock being sold by RealNetworks. At the price the new shares were sold for, Glaser's shares were worth $9.2 million and represented 83.6% of the outstanding shares. The value of the prior shares outstanding at the price in the funding round ($9.2 million in this example) is called the **pre-money valuation**. The value of the whole firm (old plus new shares) at the funding round price ($11.0 million) is known as the **post-money valuation**.

EXAMPLE 23.1

Funding and Ownership

Problem

You founded your own firm two years ago. You initially contributed $100,000 of your money and, in return received 1,500,000 shares of stock. Since then, you have sold an additional 500,000 shares to angel investors. You are now considering raising even more capital

---

2. The number of shares of RealNetworks preferred stock given here for this and subsequent funding comes from the IPO prospectus (available on EDGAR at http://www.sec.gov/edgar/searchedgar/webusers.htm). For simplicity, we have ignored warrants to purchase additional shares that were also issued and a small amount of employee common stock that existed.

from a venture capitalist. This venture capitalist would invest $6 million and would receive 3,000,000 newly issued shares. What is the post-money valuation? Assuming that this is the venture capitalist's first investment in your company, what percentage of the firm will she end up owning? What percentage will you own? What is the value of your shares?

Solution

After this funding round, there will be a total of 5,000,000 shares outstanding:

Your shares	1,500,000
Angel investors' shares	500,000
Newly issued shares	3,000,000
Total	5,000,000

The venture capitalist would be paying $6,000,000 / 3,000,000 = $2 per share. Therefore, the post-money valuation would be 5,000,000($2) = $10 million. Because she is buying 3,000,000 shares, and there will be 5,000,000 total shares outstanding after the funding round, the venture capitalist will end up owning 3,000,000 / 5,000,000 = 60% of the firm. You will own 1,500,000 / 5,000,000 = 30% of the firm, and the post-money valuation of your shares is 1,500,000($2) = $3,000,000.

Over the next few years, RealNetworks raised three more rounds of outside equity in addition to the Series B funding round:

Series	Date	Number of Shares	Share Price ($)	Capital Raised ($ million)
B	April 1995	2,686,567	0.67	1.8
C	Oct. 1995	2,904,305	1.96	5.7
D	Nov. 1996	2,381,010	7.53	17.9
E	July 1997	3,338,374	8.99	30.0

In each case, investors bought preferred stock in the private company. These investors were very similar to the profile of typical investors in private firms that we described earlier. Angel investors purchased the Series B stock. The investors in Series C and D stock were primarily venture capital funds. Microsoft purchased the Series E stock as a corporate investor.

Exiting an Investment in a Private Company

Over time, the value of a share of RealNetworks' stock and the size of its funding rounds increased. Because investors in Series E were willing to pay $8.99 for a share of preferred stock with equivalent rights in July 1997, the post-money valuation of existing preferred stock was $8.99 per share. Because RealNetworks was still a private company, however, investors could not liquidate their investment by selling their stock in the public stock markets.

An important consideration for investors in private companies is their **exit strategy**— how they will eventually realize the return from their investment. Investors exit in two main ways: through an acquisition or through a public offering. Often large corporations purchase successful start-up companies. In such a case, the acquiring company purchases the outstanding stock of the private company, allowing all investors to cash out. Roughly 85% of venture capital exits from 2001–2005 occurred through mergers or acquisitions.[3]

The alternative way to provide liquidity to its investors is for the company to become a publicly traded company.

CONCEPT CHECK

1. What are the main sources of funding for private companies to raise outside equity capital?

2. What is a venture capital firm?

23.2 The Initial Public Offering

The process of selling stock to the public for the first time is called an **initial public offering (IPO)**. In this section we look at the mechanics of IPOs and discuss some related puzzles.

Advantages and Disadvantages of Going Public

The two advantages of going public are greater liquidity and better access to capital. By going public, companies give their private equity investors the ability to diversify. In addition, public companies typically have access to much larger amounts of capital through the public markets, both in the initial public offering and in subsequent offerings. For example, during 2004, the ten largest equity issues in the world each raised more than $2 billion, as shown in Table 23.2. In RealNetworks' case, its last round of private equity funding raised about $30 million in July 1997. The firm raised $43 million when it went public in November of the same year; less than two years later, it raised an additional $267 million by selling more stock to the public. As a public company, RealNetworks was able to raise substantially more money.

TABLE 23.2	Largest Global Equity Issues, 2004	
Issuer	**Date**	**Amount ($ billion)**
ENEL	Oct. 22	9.5
France Telecom	Sept. 1	6.2
Royal Bank of Scotland	May 5	4.8
Belgacom	March 20	4.4
GE	March 8	3.8
Bayerische Hypo-Vereinsbk	April 6	3.7
Deutsche Telekom	Oct. 11	3.7
Electric Power Dev.	Sept. 27	3.4
Total	Sept. 29	3.2
Genworth Financial	May 24	2.9

Source: Diya Gullapalli, "Underwriting Volume Rises to a Record," *The Wall Street Journal,* January 3, 2005, p. R17.

---

3. The National Venture Capital Association.

The major advantage of undertaking an IPO is also one of the major disadvantages of an IPO: When investors diversify their holdings, the equity holders of the corporation become more widely dispersed. This undermines investors' ability to monitor the company's management and thus represents a loss of control. Furthermore, once a company goes public, it must satisfy all of the requirements of public companies. Several high-profile corporate scandals during the early part of the twenty-first century prompted tougher regulations designed to address corporate abuses. Organizations such as the Securities and Exchange Commission (SEC), the securities exchanges (including the New York Stock Exchange and the Nasdaq), and Congress (through the Sarbanes-Oxley Act of 2002) adopted new standards that focused on more thorough financial disclosure, greater accountability, and more stringent requirements for the board of directors. These standards, in general, were designed to provide better protection for investors. However, compliance with the new standards is costly and time-consuming for public companies.

Types of Offerings

After deciding to go public, managers of the company work with an **underwriter**, an investment banking firm that manages the offering and designs its structure. Choices include the type of shares to be sold and the mechanism the financial advisor will use to sell the stock.

Primary and Secondary Offerings.   At an IPO, a firm offers a large block of shares for sale to the public for the first time. The shares that are sold in the IPO may either be new shares that raise new capital, known as a **primary offering**, or existing shares that are sold by current shareholders (as part of their exit strategy), known as a **secondary offering**.

Best-Efforts, Firm Commitment, and Auction IPOs.   For smaller IPOs, the underwriter commonly accepts the deal on a **best-efforts** basis. In this case, the underwriter does not guarantee that the stock will be sold, but instead tries to sell the stock for the best possible price. Often such deals have an all-or-none clause: either all of the shares are sold in the IPO, or the deal is called off.

More commonly, an underwriter and an issuing firm agree to a **firm commitment** IPO, in which the underwriter guarantees that it will sell all of the stock at the offer price. The underwriter purchases the entire issue (at a slightly lower price than the offer price) and then resells it at the offer price. If the entire issue does not sell out, the underwriter is on the hook: The remaining shares must be sold at a lower price and the underwriter must take the loss. The most notorious loss in the industry happened when the British government privatized British Petroleum. In a highly unusual deal, the company was taken public gradually. The British government sold its final stake in British Petroleum at the time of the October 1987 stock market crash. The offer price was set just before the crash, but the offering occurred after the crash.[4] At the end of the first day's trading, the underwriters were facing a loss of $1.29 billion. The price then fell even further, until the Kuwaiti Investment Office stepped in and started purchasing a large stake in the company.

In recent years, the investment banking firm of W.R. Hambrecht and Company has attempted to change the IPO process by selling new issues directly to the public using an online **auction IPO** mechanism called OpenIPO. Rather than setting the price itself in the

---

4. This deal was exceptional in that the offer price was determined more than a week before the issue date. In the United States, the underwriter usually sets the final offer price within a day of the IPO date.

traditional way, Hambrecht lets the market determine the price of the stock by auctioning off the company.[5] Investors place bids over a set period of time. An auction IPO then sets the highest price such that the number of bids at or above that price equals the number of offered shares. All winning bidders pay this price, even if their bid was higher. The first OpenIPO was the $11.55 million IPO for Ravenswood Winery, completed in 1999.

Auction IPO Pricing

Problem

Fleming Educational Software, Inc., is selling 500,000 shares of stock in an auction IPO. At the end of the bidding period, Fleming's investment bank has received the following bids:

Price ($)	Number of Shares Bid
8.00	25,000
7.75	100,000
7.50	75,000
7.25	150,000
7.00	150,000
6.75	275,000
6.50	125,000

What will the offer price of the shares be?

Solution

First, we compute the total number of shares demanded at or above any given price:

Price ($)	Cumulative Demand
8.00	25,000
7.75	125,000
7.50	200,000
7.25	350,000
7.00	500,000
6.75	775,000
6.50	900,000

For example, the company has received bids for a total of 125,000 shares at $7.75 per share or higher (25,000 + 100,000 = 125,000).

Fleming is offering a total of 500,000 shares. The winning auction price would be $7.00 per share, because investors have placed orders for a total of 500,000 shares at a price of $7.00 or higher. All investors who placed bids of at least this price will be able to buy the stock for $7.00 per share, even if their initial bid was higher.

In this example, the cumulative demand at the winning price exactly equals the supply. If total demand at this price were greater than supply, all auction participants who bid prices higher than the winning price would receive their full bid (at the winning price). Shares would be awarded on a pro rata basis to bidders who bid exactly the winning price.

---

5. You can find details about Hambrecht's auction IPO process at http://www.openipo.com/ind/index .html.

Google's IPO

On April 29, 2004, Google, Inc., announced plans to go public. Breaking with tradition, Google startled Wall Street by declaring its intention to rely heavily on the auction IPO mechanism for distributing its shares. Google had been profitable since 2001, so, according to Google executives, access to capital was not the only motive to go public. The company also wanted to provide employees and private equity investors with liquidity.

One of the major attractions of the auction mechanism was the possibility of allocating shares to more individual investors. Google also hoped to discourage short-term speculation by letting market bidders set the IPO price. After the Internet stock market boom, there were many lawsuits related to the way underwriters allocated shares. Google hoped to avoid the allocation scandals by letting the auction allocate shares.

Investors who wanted to bid opened a brokerage account with one of the deal's underwriters and then placed their bids with the brokerage house. Google and its underwriters identified the highest bid that allowed the company to sell all of the shares being offered. They also had the flexibility to choose to offer shares at a lower price.

On August 18, 2004, Google sold 19.6 million shares at $85 per share. The $1.67 billion raised was easily the largest auction IPO ever. Google stock (ticker: GOOG) opened trading on the Nasdaq market the next day at $100 per share. Although the Google IPO sometimes stumbled along the way, it represents the most significant example of the use of the auction mechanism as an alternative to the traditional IPO mechanism.

Sources: Kevin Delaney and Robin Sidel, "Google IPO Aims to Change the Rules," *The Wall Street Journal*, April 30, 2004, p. C1; Ruth Simon and Elizabeth Weinstein, "Investors Eagerly Anticipate Google's IPO," *The Wall Street Journal*, April 30, 2004, p. C1; Gregory Zuckerman, "Google Shares Prove Big Winners—for a Day," August 20, 2004, p. C1.

Although the auction IPO mechanism seemed to represent an alternative to traditional IPO procedures, it has not been widely adopted either in the United States or abroad. Between 1999 and 2004, Hambrecht completed less than a dozen auction IPOs. However, in 2004 Google went public using the auction mechanism, which generated renewed interest in this alternative. In May 2005, Morningstar raised $140 million in its IPO using a Hambrecht OpenIPO auction.[6]

The Mechanics of an IPO

The traditional IPO process follows a standardized form. In this section, we explore the steps that underwriters go though during an IPO.

Underwriters and the Syndicate.   Many IPOs, especially the larger offerings, are managed by a group of underwriters. The **lead underwriter** is the primary banking firm responsible for managing the deal. The lead underwriter provides most of the advice and arranges for a group of other underwriters, called the **syndicate**, to help market and sell the issue. Table 23.3 shows the lead underwriters who were responsible for the largest number of IPOs in the United States during 2005. As you can see, the major U.S. investment and commercial banks dominate the underwriting business.

Underwriters market the IPO, and they help the company with all the necessary filings. More importantly, they actively participate in determining the offer price. In many

6. Interested readers can find more about auction and traditional IPOs in A. E. Sherman, "Global Trends in IPO Methods: Book Building versus Auctions with Endogenous Entry," *Journal of Financial Economics* 78(3) (2005): 615–649.

TABLE 23.3	International IPO Underwriter Ranking Report for 2005		
Rank	Lead Underwriter	Number of Issues	Total Net Proceeds ($ million)
1	Morgan Stanley	17	6,429
2	Citigroup	21	6,004
3	Goldman Sachs	19	5,281
4	CS First Boston	16	3,149
5	Lehman Brothers	14	2,288
6	Merrill Lynch	14	2,094
7	J.P. Morgan	8	1,502
8	UBS Investment Bank	10	1,496
9	Bear Sterns	5	862
10	Friedman Billings	5	563

Source: IPO Home by Renaissance Capital (rankings are based on data collected by Renaissance Capital from December 21, 2004, to December 21, 2005, for lead underwriters only), http://www.ipohome.com/marketwatch/urankings.asp?list=proceeds&nav=f.

cases, the underwriter will also commit to making a market in the stock after the issue, thereby guaranteeing that the stock will be liquid.

SEC Filings. The SEC requires that companies prepare a **registration statement**, a legal document that provides financial and other information about the company to investors, prior to an IPO. Company managers work closely with the underwriters to prepare this registration statement and submit it to the SEC. Part of the registration statement, called the **preliminary prospectus** or **red herring**, circulates to investors before the stock is offered.

The SEC reviews the registration statement to make sure that the company has disclosed all of the information necessary for investors to decide whether to purchase the stock. Once the company has satisfied the SEC's disclosure requirements, the SEC approves the stock for sale to the general public. The company prepares the final registration statement and **final prospectus** containing all the details of the IPO, including the number of shares offered and the offer price.[7]

To illustrate this process, let's return to RealNetworks. Figure 23.2 shows the cover page for the final prospectus for RealNetworks' IPO. This cover page includes the name of the company, the list of lead underwriters, and summary information about the pricing of the deal. The offering was a primary offering of 3 million shares.

Valuation. Before the offer price is set, the underwriters work closely with the company to come up with a price range that they believe provides a reasonable valuation for the firm using the techniques described in Chapter 9. As we pointed out in that chapter,

---

7. Registration statements may be found at EDGAR, the SEC Web site providing registration information to investors: http://www.sec.gov/edgar/searchedgar/webusers.htm.

FIGURE 23.2

The Cover Page of RealNetworks' IPO Prospectus

The cover page includes the name of the company, a list of lead underwriters, and summary information about the pricing of the deal.

3,000,000 Shares

RealNetworks, Inc.
(formerly "Progressive Networks, Inc.")

Common Stock
(par value $.001 per share)

All of the 3,000,000 shares of Common Stock offered hereby are being sold by RealNetworks, Inc. Prior to the offering, there has been no public market for the Common Stock. For factors considered in determining the initial public offering price, see "Underwriting".

The Common Stock offered hereby involves a high degree of risk. See "Risk Factors" beginning on page 6.

The Common Stock has been approved for quotation on the Nasdaq National Market under the symbol "RNWK," subject to notice of issuance.

THESE SECURITIES HAVE NOT BEEN APPROVED OR DISAPPROVED BY THE SECURITIES AND EXCHANGE COMMISSION OR ANY STATE SECURITIES COMMISSION NOR HAS THE SECURITIES AND EXCHANGE COMMISSION OR ANY STATE SECURITIES COMMISSION PASSED UPON THE ACCURACY OR ADEQUACY OF THIS PROSPECTUS. ANY REPRESENTATION TO THE CONTRARY IS A CRIMINAL OFFENSE.

	Initial Public Offering Price(1)	Underwriting Discount(2)	Proceeds to Company(3)
Per Share	$12.50	$0.875	$11.625
Total(4)	$37,500,000	$2,625,000	$34,875,000

(1) In connection with the offering, the Underwriters have reserved up to 300,000 shares of Common Stock for sale at the initial public offering price to employees and friends of the Company.

(2) The Company has agreed to indemnify the Underwriters against certain liabilities, including liabilities under the Securities Act of 1933, as amended. See "Underwriting".

(3) Before deducting estimated expenses of $950,000 payable by the Company.

(4) The Company has granted the Underwriters an option for 30 days to purchase up to an additional 450,000 shares at the initial public offering price per share, less the underwriting discount, solely to cover over-allotments. If such option is exercised in full, the total initial public offering price, underwriting discount and proceeds to Company will be $43,125,000, $3,018,750 and $40,106,250, respectively. See "Underwriting".

The shares offered hereby are offered severally by the Underwriters, as specified herein, subject to receipt and acceptance by them and subject to their right to reject any order in whole or in part. It is expected that certificates for the shares will be ready for delivery in New York, New York on or about November 26, 1997, against payment therefor in immediately available funds.

Goldman, Sachs & Co.
　　BancAmerica Robertson Stephens
　　　　NationsBanc Montgomery Securities, Inc.

The date of this Prospectus is November 21, 1997.

there are two ways to value a company: estimate the future cash flows and compute the present value, or estimate the value by examining comparable companies. Most underwriters use both techniques. However, when these techniques give substantially different answers, they often rely on comparables based on recent IPOs.

Once an initial price range is established, the underwriters try to determine what the market thinks of the valuation. They begin by arranging a **road show**, in which senior management and the lead underwriters travel around the country (and sometimes around the world) promoting the company and explaining their rationale for the offer price to the underwriters' largest customers—mainly institutional investors such as mutual funds and pension funds.

EXAMPLE 23.3

Valuing an IPO Using Comparables

Problem

Wagner, Inc., is a private company that designs, manufactures, and distributes branded consumer products. During the most recent fiscal year, Wagner had revenues of $325 million and earnings of $15 million. Wagner has filed a registration statement with the SEC for its IPO. Before the stock is offered, Wagner's investment bankers would like to estimate the value of the company using comparable companies. The investment bankers have assembled the following information based on data for other companies in the same industry that have recently gone public. In each case, the ratios are based on the IPO price.

Company	Price/Earnings	Price/Revenues
Ray Products Corp.	18.8×	1.2×
Byce-Frasier, Inc.	19.5×	0.9×
Fashion Industries Group	24.1×	0.8×
Recreation International	22.4×	0.7×
Mean	21.2×	0.9×

After the IPO, Wagner will have 20 million shares outstanding. Estimate the IPO price for Wagner using the price/earnings ratio and the price/revenues ratio.

Solution

If the IPO price of Wagner is based on a price/earnings ratio that is similar to those for recent IPOs, then this ratio will equal the mean of recent deals, or 21.2. Given earnings of $15 million, the total market value of Wagner's stock will be ($15 million)(21.2) = $318 million. With 20 million shares outstanding, the price per share should be $15.90.

Similarly, if Wagner's IPO price implies a price/revenues ratio equal to the recent average of 0.9, then using its revenues of $325 million, the total market value of Wagner will be ($325 million)(0.9) = $292.5 million, or ($292.5 / 20) = $14.63 per share.

Based on these estimates, the underwriters will probably establish an initial price range for Wagner stock of $13 to $17 per share to take on the road show.

At the end of the road show, customers inform the underwriters of their interest by telling the underwriters how many shares they may want to purchase. Although these commitments are nonbinding, the underwriters' customers value their long-term relationships with the underwriters, so they rarely go back on their word. The underwriters then add up the total demand and adjust the price until it is unlikely that the issue will fail. This process for coming up with the offer price based on customers' expressions of interest is called **book building**. Because no offer price is set in an auction IPO, book building is not as important in that venue as it is in traditional IPOs. In a recent paper, Professors Ravi Jagannathan and Ann Sherman examine why auctions have failed to become a popular

IPO method and have been plagued by inaccurate pricing and poor aftermarket performance. They sugguest that, since auctions do not use the book building process which aids in price discovery, investors are discouraged from participating in auctions.[8]

Pricing the Deal and Managing Risk.   In the RealNetworks' IPO, the final offer price was $12.50 per share.[9] Also, the company agreed to pay the underwriters a fee, called a **spread**, of $0.875 per share—exactly 7% of the issue price. Because this was a firm commitment deal, the underwriters bought the stock from RealNetworks for $12.50 − $0.875 = $11.625 per share and then resold it to their customers for $12.50 per share.

Recall that when an underwriter provides a firm commitment, it is potentially exposing itself to the risk that the banking firm might have to sell the shares at less than the offer price and take a loss. However, according to Tim Loughran and Jay Ritter, between 1990 and 1998, just 9% of U.S. IPOs experienced a fall in share price on the first day.[10] For another 16% of firms, the price at the end of the first day was the same as the offer price. Therefore, the vast majority of IPOs experienced a price increase on the first day of trading, indicating that the initial offer price was generally lower than the price that stock market investors were willing to pay.

Underwriters appear to use the information they acquire during the book-building stage to intentionally underprice the IPO, thereby reducing their exposure to losses. Furthermore, once the issue price (or offer price) is set, underwriters may invoke another mechanism to protect themselves against a loss—the **over-allotment allocation**, or **greenshoe provision**.[11] This option allows the underwriter to issue more stock, amounting to 15% of the original offer size, at the IPO offer price. Look at footnote 4 on the front page of the RealNetworks prospectus in Figure 23.2. This footnote is a greenshoe provision.

Let's illustrate how underwriters use the greenshoe provision to protect themselves against a loss and thereby manage risk. The RealNetworks prospectus specified that 3 million shares would be offered at $12.50 per share. In addition, the greenshoe provision allowed for the issue of an additional 450,000 shares at $12.50 per share. Underwriters initially market both the initial allotment and the allotment in the greenshoe provision— in RealNetworks' case, all 3.45 million shares (the $12.50 per share price is set so that all 3.45 million shares are expected to sell)—by short selling the greenshoe allotment. Then, if the issue is a success, the underwriter exercises the greenshoe option, thereby covering its short position. If the issue is not a success, the underwriter covers the short position by repurchasing the greenshoe allotment (450,000 shares in the RealNetworks IPO) in the aftermarket, thereby supporting the price.[12]

Once the IPO process is complete, the company's shares trade publicly on an exchange. The lead underwriter usually makes a market in the stock and assigns an analyst to cover

---

8. "Why Do IPO Auctions Fail?," NBER working paper 12151, March 2006.

9. Stock prices for RealNetworks throughout this chapter have not been adjusted for two subsequent stock splits.

10. "Why Don't Issuers Get Upset About Leaving Money on the Table in IPOs?" *Review of Financial Studies* 15(2) (2002): 413–443.

11. The name derives from the Green Shoe Company, the first issuer to have an over-allotment option in its IPO.

12. Reena Aggarwal, "Stabilization Activities by Underwriters After IPOs," *Journal of Finance* 55(3) (2000): 1075–1103, finds that underwriters initially oversell by an average 10.75% and then cover themselves if necessary using the greenshoe option.

it. By doing so, the underwriter increases the liquidity of the stock in the secondary market. This service is of value to both the issuing company and the underwriter's customers. A liquid market ensures that investors who purchased shares via the IPO are able to easily trade those shares. If the stock is actively traded, the issuer will have continued access to the equity markets in the event that the company decides to issue more shares in a new offering. In most cases, the preexisting shareholders are subject to a 180-day **lockup**; they cannot sell their shares for 180 days after the IPO. Once the lockup period expires, they are free to sell their shares.

IPO Puzzles

Four characteristics of IPOs puzzle financial economists. First, on average, IPOs appear to be underpriced: The price at the end of trading on the first day is often substantially higher than the IPO price. Second, the number of issues is highly cyclical. When times are good, the market is flooded with new issues; when times are bad, the number of issues dries up. Third, the costs of the IPO are very high, and it is unclear why firms willingly incur such high costs. Finally, the long-run performance of a newly public company (three to five years from the date of issue) is poor. That is, on average, a three- to five-year buy and hold strategy appears to be a bad investment.

Underpricing. Generally, underwriters set the issue price so that the average first-day return is positive. For RealNetworks, the underwriters offered the stock at an IPO price of $12.50 per share on November 21, 1997. RealNetworks stock opened trading on the Nasdaq market at a price of $19.375 per share, and it closed at the end of its first trading day at $17.875. Such performance is not atypical. On average, between 1960 and 2003, the price in the U.S. aftermarket was 18.3% higher at the end of the first day of trading.[13] As is evident in Figure 23.3, the one-day average return for IPOs has historically been very large around the world.

Who benefits from the underpricing? We have already explained how the underwriters benefit by controlling their risk. Of course, investors who are able to buy stock from underwriters at the IPO price also gain from the first-day underpricing. Who bears the cost? The pre-IPO shareholders of the issuing firms. In effect, these owners are selling stock in their firm for less than they could get in the aftermarket.

So why do shareholders of issuing firms put up with this underpricing? A naive view is that they have no choice because the relatively small number of underwriters control the market. In fact, this is unlikely to be the explanation. The industry, at least anecdotally, appears to be highly competitive. In addition, new entrants offering cheaper alternatives to the traditional underwriting process, like W.R. Hambrecht, have not been very successful at gaining significant market share.

Given the existence of underpricing, it might appear that investing in new IPOs would be a very lucrative deal. If, on average, the one-day return is 18.3%, and you could invest in a new IPO at the beginning of every working day and sell your shares at the end of the day for 250 business days per year, your cumulative annual return would be $(1.183)^{250} = 176,273,146,575,531,000,000\%$. Why don't all investors do this? Because they can't.

---

13. See Tim Loughran, Jay R. Ritter, and Kristian Rydqvist, "Initial Public Offerings: International Insights," *Pacific-Basin Finance Journal* 2 (2004): 165–199.

FIGURE 23.3

International Comparison of First-Day IPO Returns

The bars show the average initial returns from the offer price to the first closing market price. For China, the bar shows the average initial return on A share IPOs, available only to residents of China. The date in parenthesis indicate the sample period for each country.

Source: Adapted courtesy of Jay Ritter (http://bear.cba.ufl.edu/ritter).

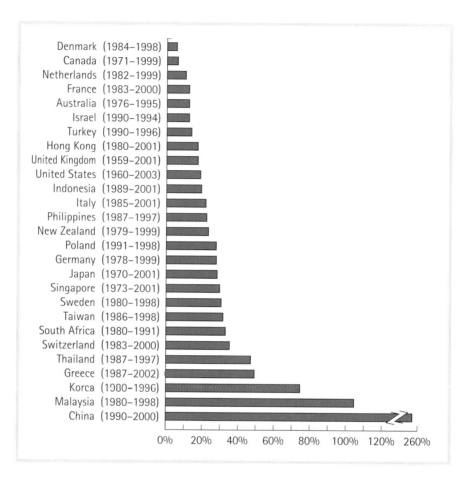

The preceding calculation assumes that each day you can invest the proceeds of the previous day's investment. However, when an IPO goes well, the demand for the stock exceeds the supply. (This is another way of saying that the stock is underpriced.) Thus the allocation of shares for each investor is rationed. Conversely, when an IPO does not go well, demand at the issue price is weak, so all initial orders are filled completely. In this scenario, if you followed the strategy of reinvesting whatever you made on the last IPO in the next one, your orders would be completely filled when the stock price goes down, but you would be rationed when it goes up. This is a form of adverse selection referred to as the **winner's curse**: You "win" (get all the shares you requested) when demand for the shares by others is low, and the IPO is more likely to perform poorly. This effect may be substantial enough so that the strategy of investing in every IPO does not yield above-market returns.[14] Furthermore, this effect implies that it may be necessary for the underwriter to underprice its issues on average in order for less informed investors to be willing to participate in IPOs, as the following example demonstrates.

---

14. This explanation was first proposed by Kevin Rock: "Why New Issues Are Underpriced," *Journal of Financial Economics* 15(2) (1986): 197–212. See also M. Levis, "The Winner's Curse Problem, Interest Costs and the Underpricing of Initial Public Offerings," *Economic Journal* 100(399) (1990): 76–89.

IPO Investors and the Winner's Curse

Problem

Thompson Brothers, a large underwriter, is offering its customers the following opportunity: Thompson will guarantee a piece of every IPO it is involved in. Suppose you are a customer. On each deal you must commit to buying 2000 shares. If the shares are available, you get them. If the deal is oversubscribed, your allocation of shares is rationed in proportion to the oversubscription. Your market research shows that typically 80% of the time Thompson deals are oversubscribed 16 to 1 (there are 16 orders for every 1 order that can be filled). This excess demand would lead to a price increase on the first day of 20%. However, 20% of the time Thompson's deals are not oversubscribed, and while Thompson supports the price in the market (by not exercising the greenshoe provision and instead buying back shares), on average the price tends to decline by 5% on the first day. Based on these statistics, what is the average underpricing of a Thompson IPO? What is your average return as an investor?

Solution

First note that the average first-day return for Thompson Brothers deals is large: $0.8(20\%) + 0.2(-5\%) = 15\%$. If Thompson had one IPO per month, after a year you would earn an annual return of $1.15^{12} - 1 = 435\%$!

In reality, you cannot earn this return. For successful IPOs you will earn a 20% return, but you will only receive $2000/16 = 125$ shares. Assuming an average IPO price of $15 per share, your profit is

$$20\%(125 \text{ shares}) \times \$15/\text{share} = \$375$$

For unsuccessful IPOs you will receive your full allocation of 2000 shares. Because these stocks tend to fall by 5%, your profit is

$$-5\%(2000 \text{ shares}) \times \$15/\text{shares} = -\$1500$$

Because 80% of Thompson's IPOs are successful, your average profit is therefore

$$0.80(\$375) + 0.20(-\$1500) = \$0$$

That is, on average you are just breaking even! As this example shows, even though the average IPO may be profitable, because you receive a higher allocation of the less successful IPOs, your average return may be much lower. Also, if Thompson's average underpricing were less than 15%, uninformed investors would lose money and be unwilling to participate in its IPOs.

Cyclicality

Figure 23.4 shows the number and dollar volume of IPOs by year from 1975 to 2004. As the figure makes clear, the dollar volume of IPOs has grown significantly, reaching a peak in 2000. An even more important feature of the data is that the trends related to volume and number of issues are cyclical. Sometimes, such as in 2000, the volume of IPOs is unprecedented by historical standards; yet, within a year or two, the volume of IPOs may decrease significantly. This cyclicality by itself is not particularly surprising. We would expect there to be a greater need for capital in times with more growth opportunities than in times with fewer growth opportunities. What is surprising is the magnitude of the swings. It is very difficult to believe that the availability of growth opportunities and the

FIGURE 23.4

Cyclicality of Initial Public Offerings in the United States, (1975–2004)

Part (a) shows the number of IPOs by year, Part (b) shows the annual cumulative dollar volume of shares offered. The number and volume of IPOs reached a peak in 2000 and is highly cyclical.

Source: Adapted courtesy of Jay R. Ritter from "Some Factoids About the 2004 IPO Market" (http://bear.cba.ufl.edu/ritter).

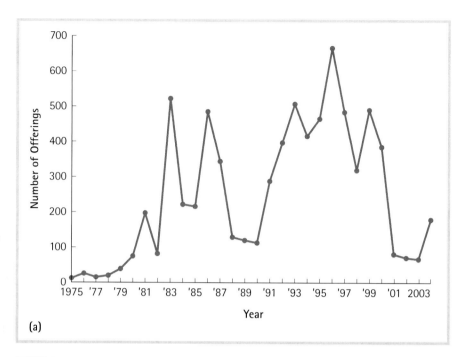

(a)

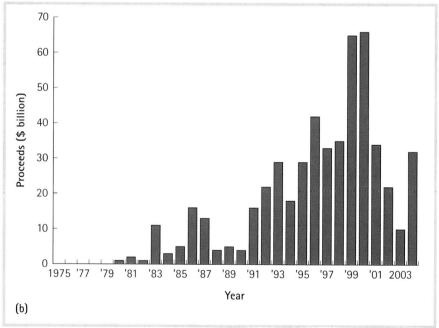

(b)

need for capital changed so drastically between 2000 and 2001 as to cause a decline of 48% in the dollar volume of new issues, as seen in Figure 23.4(b). It appears that the number of IPOs is not solely driven by the demand for capital. Sometimes firms and investors seem to favor IPOs; at other times firms appear to rely on alternative sources of capital and financial economists are not sure why.

FIGURE 23.5

Relative Costs of Issuing Securities

This figure shows the total direct costs (all underwriting, legal, and auditing costs) of issuing securities as a percentage of the amount of money raised. The figure reports results for IPOs, seasoned equity offerings (subsequent equity offerings), convertible bonds, and straight bonds, for issues of different sizes from 1990–1994.

Source: Adapted from I. Lee, S. Lochhead, J. Ritter, and Q. Zhao, "The Costs of Raising Capital," *Journal of Financial Research* 19(1) (1996): 59–74.

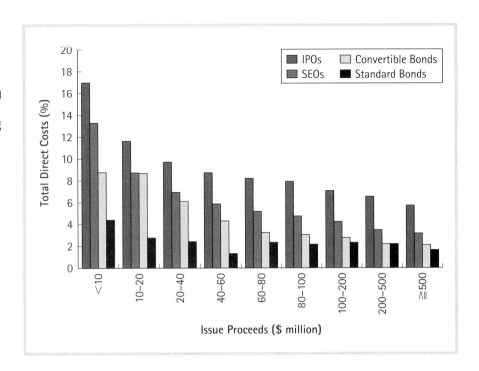

Cost of Issuing an IPO

A typical spread—that is, the discount below the issue price at which the underwriter purchases the shares from the issuing firm—is 7% of the issue price. For an issue size of $50 million, this amounts to $3.5 million. By most standards this fee is large, especially considering the additional cost to the firm associated with underpricing. As Figure 23.5 shows, compared to other security issues, the total cost of issuing stock for the first time is substantially larger than the costs for other securities.

Even more puzzling is the seeming lack of sensitivity of fees to issue size. Although a large issue requires some additional effort, one would not expect the increased effort to be rewarded as lucratively. For example, Hsuan-Chi Chen and Jay Ritter found that almost all issues ranging in size from $20 million to $80 million paid fees of about 7%.[15] It is difficult to understand how a $20 million issue can be profitably done for "only" $1.4 million, while an $80 million issue requires paying fees of $5.6 million.

No researcher has provided a satisfactory answer to this puzzle. Chen and Ritter argue for implicit collusion by the underwriters, but in response to their paper Robert Hansen finds no evidence of any such collusion.[16] He shows that there is low underwriting industry concentration, that there have been significant new entrants in the IPO-underwriting market, and that a 7% spread is less profitable than normal investment banking activities.

One possible explanation is that by attempting to undercut its rivals, an underwriter may risk signaling that it is not the same quality as its higher-priced competitors, making

---

15. Hsuan-Chi Chen and Jay R. Ritter, "The Seven Percent Solution," *Journal of Finance* 55(3) (2000): 1105–1131.

16. Robert S. Hansen, "Do Investment Banks Compete in IPOs?: The Advent of the '7% Plus Contract'," *Journal of Financial Economics* 59(3) (2001): 313–346.

firms less likely to select that underwriter. Craig Dunbar examined this hypothesis.[17] He found that underwriters charging slightly lower fees appear to enjoy a greater market share, but those charging significantly lower fees have smaller market shares. Indeed, in support of the idea that the quality of the underwriter is important, underwriters that charge very high fees gain market share.

Long-Run Underperformance

We know that the shares of IPOs generally perform very well immediately following the public offering. It's perhaps surprising, then, that Jay Ritter found that newly listed firms subsequently appear to perform relatively poorly over the following three to five years after their IPOs.[18] In follow-up studies, Alon Brav, Christopher Geczy, and Paul Gompers found that IPOs between 1975 and 1992 underperformed by an average of 44% relative to the S&P 500 over the subsequent five years.[19] Jay Ritter and Ivo Welch found that IPOs between 1980 and 2001 underperformed the market by an average of 23.4% during the subsequent three years.[20]

As we will see in the next section, underperformance is not unique to an initial public issuance of equity: It is associated with subsequent issuances as well. Recently, researchers have begun to explore the possibility that underperformance might not result from the issue of equity itself, but rather from the conditions that motivated the equity issuance in the first place. We will explain this idea in more detail in the next section after we explain how a public company issues additional equity.

CONCEPT CHECK   1. Explain the mechanics of an auction IPO.

2. List and discuss four characteristics about IPOs that financial economists find puzzling.

23.3 The Seasoned Equity Offering

A firm's need for outside capital rarely ends at the IPO. Usually, profitable growth opportunities occur throughout the life of the firm, and in some cases it is not feasible to finance these opportunities out of retained earnings. Thus, more often than not, firms return to the equity markets and offer new shares for sale, a type of offering called a **seasoned equity offering (SEO)**.

The Mechanics of an SEO

When a firm issues stock using an SEO, it follows many of the same steps as for an IPO. The main difference is that a market price for the stock already exists, so the price-setting process is not necessary.

RealNetworks has conducted several SEOs since its IPO in 1997. On June 17, 1999, the firm offered 4 million shares in an SEO at a price of $58.00 per share. Of these shares,

17. Craig G. Dunbar, "Factors Affecting Investment Banks Initial Public Offering Market Share," *Journal of Financial Economics* 55(1) (2000): 3–41.

18. Jay R. Ritter, "The Long-Run Performance of Initial Public Offerings," *Journal of Finance* 46(1) (1991): 3–27.

19. "Is the Abnormal Return Following Equity Issuances Anomalous?" *Journal of Financial Economics* 56 (2000): 209–249.

20. "A Review of IPO Activity, Pricing, and Allocations," *Journal of Finance* 57(4) (2002): 1795–1828.

3,525,000 were **primary shares**—new shares issued by the company. The remaining 475,000 shares were **secondary shares**—shares sold by existing shareholders, including the company's founder, Robert Glaser, who sold 310,000 of his shares. Most of the rest of RealNetworks' SEOs occurred between 1999 and 2004 and included secondary shares sold by existing shareholders rather than directly by RealNetworks.

Historically, intermediaries would advertise the sale of stock (both IPOs and SEOs) by taking out advertisements in newspapers called **tombstones**. Through these ads, investors would know who to call to buy stock. Today, investors become informed about the impending sale of stock by the news media, via a road show, or through the book-building process, so these tombstones are purely ceremonial. Figure 23.6 shows the tombstone advertisement for one RealNetworks SEO.

Two kinds of seasoned equity offerings exist: a cash offer and a rights offer. In a **cash offer**, the firm offers the new shares to investors at large. In a **rights offer**, the firm offers

FIGURE 23.6

Tombstone Advertisement for a RealNetworks SEO

This tombstone appeared in *The Wall Street Journal* and advertised the underwriters' participation in this RealNetworks SEO.

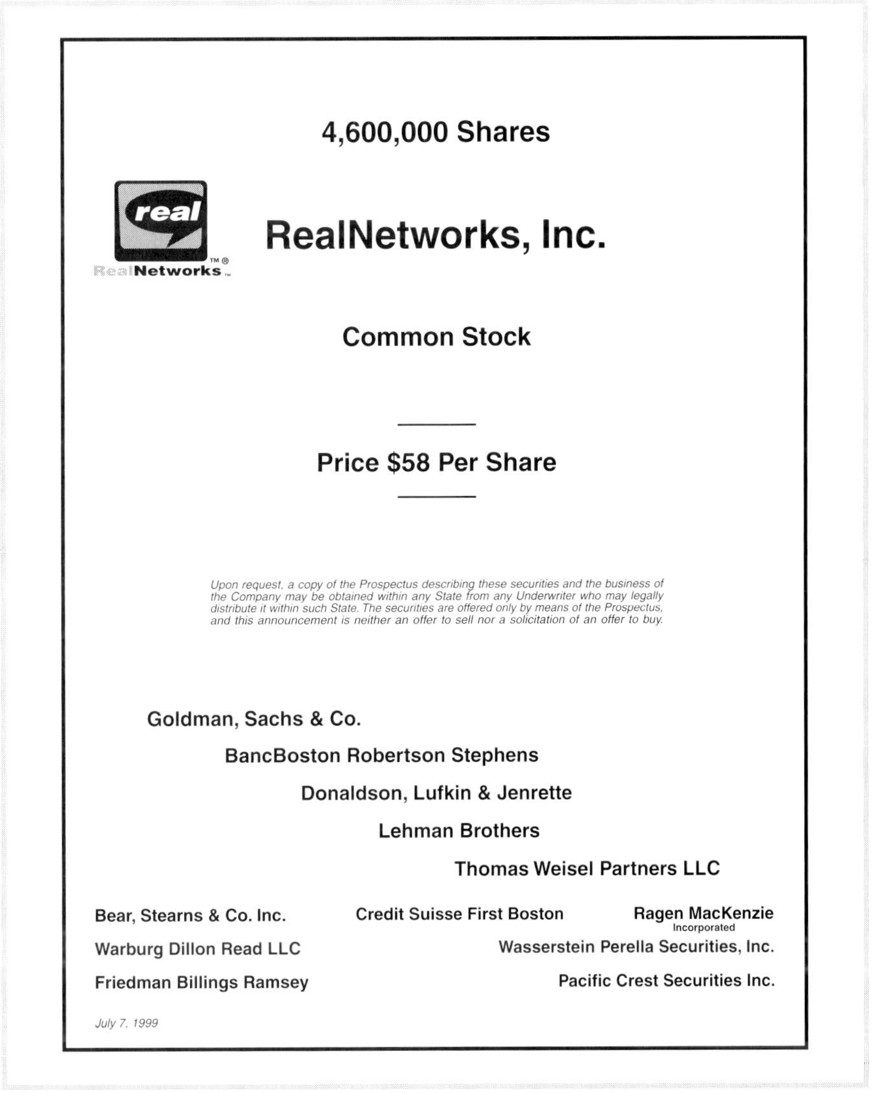

4,600,000 Shares

RealNetworks, Inc.

Common Stock

———

Price $58 Per Share

———

Upon request, a copy of the Prospectus describing these securities and the business of the Company may be obtained within any State from any Underwriter who may legally distribute it within such State. The securities are offered only by means of the Prospectus, and this announcement is neither an offer to sell nor a solicitation of an offer to buy.

Goldman, Sachs & Co.

BancBoston Robertson Stephens

Donaldson, Lufkin & Jenrette

Lehman Brothers

Thomas Weisel Partners LLC

Bear, Stearns & Co. Inc.	Credit Suisse First Boston	Ragen MacKenzie Incorporated
Warburg Dillon Read LLC		Wasserstein Perella Securities, Inc.
Friedman Billings Ramsey		Pacific Crest Securities Inc.

July 7, 1999

the new shares only to existing shareholders. In the United States, most offers are cash offers, but the same is not true internationally. For example, in the United Kingdom, most seasoned offerings of new shares are rights offers.

Rights offers protect existing shareholders from underpricing. To see how, suppose a company holds $100 in cash and has 50 shares outstanding. Each share is worth $2. The company announces a cash offer for 50 shares at $1 per share. Once this offer is complete, the company will have $150 in cash and 100 shares outstanding. The price per share is now $1.50 to reflect the fact that the new shares were sold at a discount. The new shareholders therefore receive a $0.50 windfall at the expense of the old shareholders.

The old shareholders would be protected if, instead of a cash offer, the company did a rights offer. In this case, rather than offer the new shares for general sale, every shareholder would have the right to purchase an additional share for $1 per share. If all shareholders chose to exercise their rights, then after the sale the value of the company would be the same as with a cash offer: It would be worth $150 with 100 shares outstanding and a price of $1.50 per share. In this case, however, the $0.50 windfall accrues to existing shareholders, which exactly offsets the drop in the stock price. Thus, if a firm's management is concerned that its equity may be underpriced in the market, by using a rights offering the firm can continue to issue equity without imposing a loss on its current shareholders.

Raising Money with Rights Offers

Problem
You are the CFO of a company that is currently worth $1 billion. The firm has 100 million shares outstanding, so the shares are trading at $10 per share. You need to raise $200 million and have announced a rights issue. Each existing shareholder is sent one right for every share he or she owns. You have not decided how many rights you will require to purchase a share of new stock. You will require either four rights to purchase one share at a price of $8 per share, or five rights to purchase two new shares at a price of $5 per share. Which approach will raise more money?

Solution
If all shareholders exercise their rights, then in the first case, 25 million new shares will be purchased at a price of $8 per share, raising $200 million. In the second case, 40 million new shares will be purchased at a price of $5 per share, also raising $200 million. If all shareholders exercise their rights, both approaches will raise the same amount of money.

In both cases, the value of the firm after the issue is $1.2 billion. In the first case, there are 125 million shares outstanding, so the price per share after the issue is $9.60. This price exceeds the issue price of $8, so the shareholders will exercise their rights. In the second case, the number of shares outstanding will grow to 140 million, resulting in a post-issue stock price of $1.2 billion for 140 million shares = $8.57 per share (also higher than the issue price). Again, the shareholders will exercise their rights. In both cases, the same amount of money is raised.

Price Reaction

Researchers have found that, on average, the market greets the news of an SEO with a price decline. Often the value destroyed by the price decline can be a significant fraction of the new money raised. This price decline is consistent with the adverse selection we discussed in Chapter 16. Because a company concerned about protecting its existing shareholders will tend to sell only at a price that correctly values or overvalues the firm, investors infer

FIGURE 23.7

Post-SEO Performance

The figure plots the risk-adjusted return (realized alpha using the Fama-French-Carhart factor specification) of a portfolio made up of seasoned equity offerings between 1976 and 1992. The long-run underperformance appears much more pronounced among smaller firms.

Source: Adapted from A. Brav, C. Geczy, and P. Gompers, "Is the Abnormal Return Following Equity Issuances Anomalous," *Journal of Financial Economics* 56 (2000): 209–249, Figure 3.

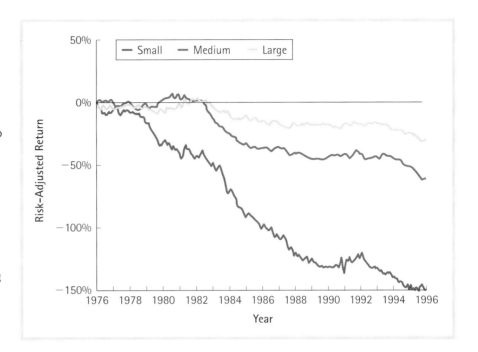

from the decision to sell that the company is likely to be overvalued; hence the price drops with the announcement of the SEO.

Although adverse selection is a plausible explanation for SEO price reaction, some puzzles remain unexplained. First, by offering a rights issue, a company can mitigate the adverse selection. It is not clear, then, at least in the United States, why companies do not initiate more rights issues. Second, as with IPOs, evidence suggests that companies underperform following a seasoned offering (see Figure 23.7). At first glance, this underperformance appears to suggest that the stock price decrease is not large enough, because underperformance implies that the price following the issue was too high.

A possible explanation for SEO subsequent underperformance, put forward by Murray Carlson, Adlai Fisher, and Ron Giammarino, is that this outcome might not have to do with the SEO announcement itself, but rather with the conditions that led the firm to choose a SEO.[21] The decision to raise financing externally usually implies that a firm plans to pursue an investment opportunity. As explained in Chapter 22, when a firm invests, it is exercising its growth options. Growth options are riskier than projects themselves, so upon exercise the firm's beta decreases, which explains the post-SEO lower returns. Researchers have found empirical support for this hypothesis.[22]

---

21. Murray Carlson, Adlai Fisher, and Ronald Giammarino, "Corporate Investment and Asset Price Dynamics: Implications for the Cross-section of Returns," *Journal of Finance* 59(6) (2004): 2577–2603.

22. Alon Brav, Christopher Geczy, and Paul Gompers (referenced in footnote 19); Espen Eckbo, Ronald Masulis, and Oyvind Norli, "Seasoned Public Offerings: Resolution of the New Issues Puzzle," *Journal of Financial Economics* 56(2) (2000): 251–291; Evgeny Lyandres, Le Sun, and Lu Zhang, "Investment-Based Underperformance Following Seasoned Equity Offerings" (July 2005), NBER working paper no. W11459, http://ssrn.com/abstract=755695; and Murray Carlson, Adlai Fisher, and Ronald Giammarino, "SEOs, Real Options, and Risk Dynamics: Empirical Evidence," University of British Columbia working paper (2006).

Costs

Although not as costly as IPOs, as Figure 23.5 shows, seasoned offerings are still expensive. Underwriting fees amount to 5% of the proceeds of the issue and, as with IPOs, the variation across issues of different sizes is relatively small. Furthermore, rights offers have lower costs than cash offers.[23] Given the other advantages of a rights offer, it is a puzzle why the majority of offers in the United States are cash offers. The one advantage of a cash offer is that the underwriter takes on a larger role and, therefore, can credibly certify the issue's quality. If there is a large amount of asymmetric information and a large proportion of existing shareholders are buying the offering anyway, the benefits of certification might overcome the cost difference. Espen Eckbo and Ronald Masulis have found empirical support for this hypothesis.[24]

CONCEPT CHECK

1. What is the difference between a cash offer and a rights offer for a seasoned equity offering?

2. What is the average stock price reaction to an SEO?

Summary

1. Private companies can raise outside equity capital from angel investors, venture capital firms, institutional investors, or corporate investors.

2. When a company founder sells stock to an outsider to raise capital, the founder's ownership share and control over the company are reduced.

3. Equity investors in private companies plan to sell their stock eventually through one of two main exit strategies: an acquisition or a public offering.

4. An initial public offering (IPO) is the first time a company sells its stock to the public.

5. The main advantages of going public are greater liquidity and better access to capital. Disadvantages include regulatory and financial reporting requirements and the undermining of the investors' ability to monitor the company's management.

6. During an IPO, the shares sold may represent either a primary offering (if the shares are being sold to raise new capital) or a secondary offering (if the shares are sold by earlier investors).

7. Stock may be sold during an IPO on a best-efforts basis, as a firm commitment IPO, or using an auction IPO. The firm commitment process is the most common practice in the United States.

8. An underwriter is an investment bank that manages the IPO process and helps the company sell its stock.

   a. The lead underwriter is responsible for managing the IPO.

   b. The lead underwriter forms a group of underwriters, called the syndicate, to help sell the stock.

---

23. In the United Kingdom, Myron Slovin, Marie Sushka, and Kam Wah Lai [*Journal of Financial Economics* 57(2) (2000)] found that the average fee for a cash offer is 6.1% versus 4.6% for an underwritten rights offer.

24. "Adverse Selection and the Rights Offer Paradox," *Journal of Financial Economics* 32 (1992): 293–332.

9. The SEC requires that a company file a registration statement prior to an IPO. The preliminary prospectus is part of the registration statement that circulates to investors before the stock is offered. After the deal is completed, the company files a final prospectus.

10. Underwriters value a company before an IPO using valuation techniques and by book building.

11. Underwriters face risk during an IPO. A greenshoe provision is one way underwriters manage the risk associated with IPOs.

12. Several puzzles are associated with IPOs.

    a. IPOs are underpriced on average.

    b. New issues are highly cyclical.

    c. The transaction costs of an IPO are very high.

    d. Long-run performance after an IPO is poor on average.

13. A seasoned equity offering (SEO) is the sale of stock by a company that is already publicly traded.

14. Two kinds of SEOs exist: a cash offer (when new shares are sold to investors at large) and a rights offer (when new shares are offered only to existing shareholders).

15. The stock price reaction to an SEO is negative on average.

Key Terms

angel investors *p. 752*
auction IPO *p. 758*
best-efforts *p. 758*
book building *p. 763*
cash offer *p. 771*
convertible preferred stock *p. 755*
corporate investor, corporate partner,
    strategic partner, strategic investor
    p. 753
exit strategy *p. 756*
final prospectus *p. 761*
firm commitment *p. 758*
initial public offering (IPO) *p. 757*
lead underwriter *p. 760*
lockup *p. 765*
over-allotment allocation
    (greenshoe provision) *p. 764*
post-money valuation *p. 755*
preferred stock *p. 755*

preliminary prospectus (red herring)
    p. 761
pre-money valuation *p. 755*
primary offering *p. 758*
primary shares *p. 771*
registration statement *p. 761*
rights offer *p. 771*
road show *p. 763*
seasoned equity offering (SEO) *p. 770*
secondary offering *p. 758*
secondary shares *p. 771*
spread *p. 764*
syndicate *p. 760*
tombstone *p. 771*
underwriter *p. 758*
venture capital firm *p. 752*
venture capitalist *p. 752*
winner's curse *p. 766*

Further Reading

We advise a reader who is interested in a more detailed coverage of the topics in this chapter to begin by reading one of the following recent survey articles on security issuance: B. Espen Eckbo, R. W. Masulis, and O. Norli, "Security Offerings: A Survey," Tuck School of Business working paper no. 2005-28 (November 2005). Available at SSRN: http://ssrn.com/abstract=863664; and J. R. Ritter, "Investment Banking and Securities Issuance." In G. M. Constantinides, M. Harris, and R. Stulz (eds.), *Handbook of the Economics of Finance* (Amsterdam: Elsevier Science, 2003).

Readers interested in more detailed coverage of specific topics should consult the following resources:

Venture Capital

P. Gompers, "Venture Capital." In B. Espen Eckbo (ed.), *Handbook of Corporate Finance: Empirical Corporate Finance, Volume A (Handbooks in Finance Series)* (Elsevier/North Holland, 2006); P. Gompers and L. Lerner, "The Venture Capital Revolution," *Journal of Economic Perspectives* 15(2) (2001): 145–168; and S. N. Kaplan and P. Stromberg, "Contract, Characteristics and Actions: Evidence from Venture Capitalist Analysis," *Journal of Finance* 59(5) (2004): 2177–2210.

IPOs

Jay Ritter's Web site (http://bear.cba.ufl.edu/ritter/) contains a wealth of information and links to cutting-edge research on the subject of IPOs. Other references of interest include L. M. Benveniste and W. J. Wilhelm, Jr., "Initial Public Offerings: Going by the Book," *Journal of Applied Corporate Finance* 10(1) (1997): 98–108; F. Cornelli and D. Goldreich, "Bookbuilding and Strategic Allocation," *Journal of Finance* 56(6) (2001): 2337–2369; A. Ljungqvist, "IPO Underpricing." In B. Espen Eckbo (ed.), *Handbook of Corporate Finance: Empirical Corporate Finance, Volume A (Handbooks in Finance Series)* (Elsevier/North Holland, 2006); T. Jenkinson and A. Ljungqvist, *Going Public: The Theory and Evidence on How Companies Raise Equity Finance*, 2nd ed. (Oxford: Oxford University Press, 2001); Michelle Lowry and G. William Schwert, "IPO Market Cycles: Bubbles or Sequential Learning?" *Journal of Finance* 57(3) (2002): 1171–1200; M. Pagano, F. Panetta, and L. Zingales, "Why Do Companies Go Public? An Empirical Analysis," *Journal of Finance* 53(1) (1998): 27–64; L. Pastor and P. Veronesi, "Rational IPO Waves," *Journal of Finance* 60(4) (2005): 1713–1757; and I. Welch, "Seasoned Offerings, Imitation Costs and the Underpricing of Initial Public Offerings," *Journal of Finance* 44(2) (1989): 421–449.

SEOs

A. Brav, C. Geczy, and P. Gompers, "Is the Abnormal Return Following Equity Issuances Anomalous?" *Journal of Financial Economics* 56(2) (2000): 209–249; J. Clarke, C. Dunbar, and K. Kahle, "Long-Run Performance and Insider Trading in Completed and Canceled Seasoned Equity Offerings," *Journal of Financial and Quantitative Analysis* 36(2) (2001): 415–430; and B. Espen Eckbo and R. Masulis, "Seasoned Equity Offerings: A Survey." In R. Jarrow et al. (eds.), *Handbooks in Operations Research and Management Science*, 9th ed. (1995: 1017 1059).

Costs of Raising Equity

Altinkilic and R. S. Hansen, "Are There Economies of Scale in Underwriting Fees? Evidence of Rising External Financing Costs," *Review of Financial Studies* 13(1) (2000): 191–218.

Problems

A blue box (■) indicates problems available in MyFinanceLab.

Equity Financing for Private Companies

1. What are some of the alternative sources from which private companies can raise equity capital?

2. What are the advantages and the disadvantages to a private company of raising money from a corporate investor?

3. Starware Software was founded last year to develop software for gaming applications. The founder initially invested $800,000 and received 8 million shares of stock. Starware now needs to raise a second round of capital, and it has identified a venture capitalist who is interested in investing. This venture capitalist will invest $1 million and wants to own 20% of the company after the investment is completed.

   a. How many shares must the venture capitalist receive to end up with 20% of the company? What is the implied price per share of this funding round?

   b. What will the value of the whole firm be after this investment (the post-money valuation)?

EXCEL 4. Three years ago, you founded your own company. You invested $100,000 of your money and received 5 million shares of Series A preferred stock. Your company has since been through three additional rounds of financing.

Round	Price ($)	Number of Shares
Series B	0.50	1,000,000
Series C	2.00	500,000
Series D	4.00	500,000

   a. What is the pre-money valuation for the Series D funding round?

   b. What is the post-money valuation for the Series D funding round?

   c. Assuming that you own only the Series A preferred stock (and that each share of all series of preferred stock is convertible into one share of common stock), what percentage of the firm do you own after the last funding round?

The Initial Public Offering

5. What are the main advantages and disadvantages of going public?

6. Do underwriters face the most risk from a best-efforts IPO, a firm commitment IPO, or an auction IPO? Why?

7. Roundtree Software is going public using an auction IPO. The firm has received the following bids:

Price ($)	Number of Shares
14.00	100,000
13.80	200,000
13.60	500,000
13.40	1,000,000
13.20	1,200,000
13.00	800,000
12.80	400,000

Assuming Roundtree would like to sell 1.8 million shares in its IPO, what will the winning auction offer price be?

EXCEL 8. Three years ago, you founded Outdoor Recreation, Inc., a retailer specializing in the sale of equipment and clothing for recreational activities such as camping, skiing, and hiking. So far, your company has gone through three funding rounds:

Round	Date	Investor	Shares	Share Price ($)
Series A	Feb. 2002	You	500,000	1.00
Series B	Aug. 2003	Angels	1,000,000	2.00
Series C	Sept. 2004	Venture capital	2,000,000	3.50

It is currently 2007 and you need to raise additional capital to expand your business. You have decided to take your firm public through an IPO. You would like to issue an additional 6.5 million new shares through this IPO. Assuming that your firm successfully completes its IPO, you forecast that 2007 net income will be $7.5 million.

    a. Your investment banker advises you that the prices of other recent IPOs have been set such that the P/E ratios based on 2007 forecasted earnings average 20.0. Assuming that your IPO is set at a price that implies a similar multiple, what will your IPO price per share be?

    b. What percentage of the firm will you own after the IPO?

9. What is IPO underpricing? If you decide to try to buy shares in every IPO, will you necessarily make money from the underpricing?

10. Margoles Publishing recently completed its IPO. The stock was offered at a price of $14.00 per share. On the first day of trading, the stock closed at $19.00 per share. What was the initial return on Margoles? Who benefited from this underpricing? Who lost, and why?

11. IPOs are very cyclical. In some years, there are large numbers of IPOs; in other years, there are very few. Why is this cyclicality a puzzle?

12. Chen Brothers, Inc., sold 4 million shares in its IPO, at a price of $18.50 per share. Management negotiated a fee (the underwriting spread) of 7% on this transaction. What was the dollar cost of this fee?

The Seasoned Equity Offering

13. On January 20, Metropolitan, Inc., sold 8 million shares of stock in an SEO. The current market price of Metropolitan at the time was $42.50 per share. Of the 8 million shares sold, 5 million shares were primary shares being sold by the company, and the remaining 3 million shares were being sold by the venture capital investors. Assume the underwriter charges 5% of the gross proceeds as an underwriting fee.

    a. How much money did Metropolitan raise?

    b. How much money did the venture capitalists receive?

14. What are the advantages to a company of selling stock in an SEO using a cash offer? What are the advantages of a rights offer?

15. MacKenzie Corporation currently has 10 million shares of stock outstanding at a price of $40 per share. The company would like to raise money and has announced a rights issue. Every existing shareholder will be sent one right per share of stock that he or she owns. The company plans to require ten rights to purchase one share at a price of $40 per share. How much money will it raise?

Debt Financing

notation

YTC yield to call on
      a callable bond

YTM yield to maturity
       on a bond

PV present value

In the middle of 2005, Ford Motor Company decided to put one of its sub-sidiaries, Hertz Corporation, up for competitive bid. On September 13, 2005, *The Wall Street Journal* reported that a group of private investors led by Clayton, Dubilier & Rice (CDR), a private equity firm, had reached a deal with Ford to purchase Hertz's outstanding equity for $5.6 billion. In addition, Hertz had $9.1 billion in existing debt that needed to be refinanced as part of the deal. CDR planned to finance the transaction in part by raising over $11 billion in new debt. Using this Hertz deal as an illustrative example, in this chapter we examine how corporations use the debt markets to raise capital.

When companies raise capital by issuing debt, they have several potential sources from which to seek funds. To complete the Hertz purchase, the group led by CDR ended up relying on at least four different kinds of debt: domestic- and foreign-denominated high-yield bonds, bank loans, and asset-backed securities. In addition, each debt issue has its own specific terms, determined at the time of issue. We there-fore begin our exploration of debt financing by explaining the process of issuing debt.

Corporations are not the only entities that use debt financing. Governments, munic-ipalities, and other local entities as well as quasi-government entities (such as state-owned corporations) also use the debt markets to raise capital. Hence the scope of this chapter is necessarily broader than that of the last chapter. Here, we introduce all of the important types of debt that exist—not just corporate debt. Finally, we discuss some of the more advanced features of bonds such as the call provision.

24.1   Corporate Debt

Recall from Chapter 23 our discussion of how private companies become public companies. The deal in which CDR bought Hertz is an example of the opposite transition—a public company becoming private, in this case through a leveraged buyout. In a **leveraged buyout (LBO)**, a group of private investors purchases all the equity of a public corporation.[1] With a total value of $15.2 billion,[2] the leveraged buyout of Hertz was the second largest transaction of its kind at the time of its announcement (the largest LBO at the time was the $31.3 billion takeover of RJR-Nabisco in 1989, surpassed in 2006 by a $33 billion buyout of hospital owner HCA). Taking a public corporation private in this way requires issuing large amounts of corporate debt. Table 24.1 shows the debt that was issued to finance the Hertz LBO. Using these debt issues as an example, let's begin by explaining how corporations issue debt.

TABLE 24.1	New Debt Issued as Part of the Hertz LBO
Type of Debt	**Amount ($ million)**
Public debt	
Junk bond issues	2,668.9
Private debt	
Term loan	1,707.0
Asset-backed revolving line of credit	400.0
Asset-backed "fleet" debt	6,348.0
Total	**$11,123.9**

Public Debt

Corporate bonds are securities issued by corporations. They account for a significant amount of invested capital. At the end of 2005, the value of outstanding U.S. corporate bonds was about $5 trillion.

The Prospectus.   A public bond issue is similar to a stock issue. A prospectus or offering memorandum must be produced that describes the details of the offering (Figure 24.1). In addition, for public offerings, the prospectus must include an **indenture**, a formal contract between the bond issuer and a trust company. The trust company represents the bondholders and makes sure that the terms of the indenture are enforced. In the case of default, the trust company represents the bondholders' interests.

---

1. At the time of the deal, Hertz was a wholly owned subsidiary of Ford Motor Company, which itself is a public company. Prior to Ford's acquisition of Hertz's outstanding shares in 2001, Hertz was publicly traded.

2. The total value includes $5.6 billion in equity, $9.1 billion in debt, and $0.5 billion in fees and expenses. In addition to $11.1 billion in new debt, the transaction was financed using $1.8 billion of Hertz's own cash and securities (including a $1.2 billion obligation from Ford, which was forgiven as part of the payment to Ford). The remaining $2.3 billion in private equity was contributed by Clayton, Dubilier & Rice; The Carlyle Group and Merrill Lynch Global Private Equity.

FIGURE 24.1

Front Cover of the Offering Memorandum of the Hertz Junk Bond Issue

OFFERING MEMORANDUM   CONFIDENTIAL

CCMG Acquisition Corporation
to be merged with and into The Hertz Corporation
$1,800,000,000 8.875% Senior Notes due 2014
$600,000,000 10.5% Senior Subordinated Notes due 2016
€225,000,000 7.875% Senior Notes due 2014

The Company is offering $1,800,000,000 aggregate principal amount of its 8.875% Senior Notes due 2014 (the "Senior Dollar Notes"), $600,000,000 aggregate principal amount of its 10.5% Senior Subordinated Notes due 2016 (the "Senior Subordinated Notes") and, together with the Senior Dollar Notes, the "Dollar Notes"), and €225,000,000 aggregate principal amount of its 7.875% Senior Notes due 2014 (the "Senior Euro Notes"). The Senior Dollar Notes and the Senior Euro Notes are collectively referred to as the "Senior Notes," and the Dollar Notes and the Senior Euro Notes are collectively referred to as the "Notes."

The Senior Notes will mature on January 1, 2014 and the Senior Subordinated Notes will mature on January 1, 2016. Interest on the Notes will accrue from December 21, 2005. We will pay interest on the Notes on January 1 and July 1 of each year, commencing July 1, 2006.

We have the option to redeem all or a portion of the Senior Notes and the Senior Subordinated Notes at any time (1) before January 1, 2010 and January 1, 2011, respectively, at a redemption price equal to 100% of their principal amount plus the applicable make-whole premium set forth in this offering memorandum and (2) on or after January 1, 2010 and January 1, 2011, respectively, at the redemption prices set forth in this offering memorandum. In addition, on or before January 1, 2009, we may, on one or more occasions, apply funds equal to the proceeds from one or more equity offerings to redeem up to 35% of each series of Notes at the redemption prices set forth in this offering memorandum. If we undergo a change of control or sell certain of our assets, we may be required to offer to purchase Notes from holders.

The Senior Notes will be senior unsecured obligations and will rank equally with all of our senior unsecured indebtedness. The Senior Subordinated Notes will be unsecured obligations and subordinated in right of payment to all of our existing and future senior indebtedness. Each of our domestic subsidiaries that guarantees specified bank indebtedness will guarantee the Senior Notes with guarantees that will rank equally with all of the senior unsecured indebtedness of such subsidiaries and the Senior Subordinated Notes with guarantees that will be unsecured and subordinated in right of payment to all existing and future senior indebtedness of such subsidiaries.

We have agreed to make an offer to exchange the Notes for registered, publicly tradable notes that have substantially identical terms as the Notes. The Dollar Notes are expected to be eligible for trading in the Private Offering, Resale and Trading Automated Linkages (PORTAL™) market. This offering memorandum includes additional information on the terms of the Notes, including redemption and repurchase prices, covenants and transfer restrictions.

Investing in the Notes involves a high degree of risk. See "Risk Factors" beginning on page 23.

We have not registered the Notes under the federal securities laws of the United States or the securities laws of any other jurisdiction. The Initial Purchasers named below are offering the Notes only to qualified institutional buyers under Rule 144A and to persons outside the United States under Regulation S. See "Notice to Investors" for additional information about eligible offerees and transfer restrictions.

Price for each series of Notes: 100%

We expect that (i) delivery of the Dollar Notes will be made to investors in book-entry form through the facilities of The Depository Trust Company on or about December 21, 2005 and (ii) delivery of the Senior Euro Notes will be made to investors in book-entry form through the facilities of the Euroclear System and Clearstream Banking, S.A. on or about December 21, 2005.

Joint Book-Running Managers

Deutsche Bank Securities		**Lehman Brothers**
Merrill Lynch & Co.	**Goldman, Sachs & Co.**	**JPMorgan**

Co-Lead Managers

BNP PARIBAS	**RBS Greenwich Capital**	**Calyon**

The date of this offering memorandum is December 15, 2005.

While corporate bonds almost always pay coupons semiannually, a few corporations (for instance, Coca-Cola) have issued zero-coupon bonds. Corporate bonds have historically been issued with a wide range of maturities. Most corporate bonds have maturities of 30 years or less, although in the past there have been original maturities of up to 999 years. In July 1993, for example, Walt Disney Company issued $150 million in bonds with a maturity of 100 years; these bonds soon became known as the "Sleeping Beauty" bonds.

FIGURE 24.2

A Bearer Bond and Its Unclipped Coupons Issued by the Elmira and Williamsport Railroad Company for $500

The face value or principal amount of the bond is denominated in standard increments, most often $1000. The face value does not always correspond to the actual money raised because of underwriting fees and the possibility that the bond might not actually sell for its face value when it is offered for sale initially. If a coupon bond is issued at a discount, it is called an **original issue discount (OID)** bond.

Bearer Bonds and Registered Bonds.   In a public offering, the indenture lays out the terms of the bond issue. Most corporate bonds are coupon bonds, and coupons are paid in one of two ways. Historically, most bonds were **bearer bonds**, like the one pictured in Figure 24.2. Bearer bonds are like currency: Whoever physically holds the bond certificate owns the bond. To receive a coupon payment, the holder of a bearer bond must provide explicit proof of ownership. The holder does so by literally clipping a coupon off the bond certificate and remitting it to the paying agent. Anyone producing such a coupon is entitled to the payment—hence the name "coupon" payment. Besides the obvious hassles associated with clipping coupons and mailing them in, there are serious security concerns with bearer bonds. Losing such a bond certificate is like losing currency.

Consequently, almost all bonds that are issued today are **registered bonds**. The issuer maintains a list of all holders of its bonds. Brokers keep issuers informed of any changes in ownership. On each coupon payment date, the bond issuer consults its list of registered owners and mails each owner a check (or directly deposits the coupon payment into the owner's brokerage account). This system also facilitates tax collection because the government can easily keep track of all interest payments made.

Types of Corporate Debt.   Four types of corporate debt are typically issued: **notes, debentures, mortgage bonds,** and **asset-backed bonds** (Table 24.2). Debentures and notes are **unsecured debt**, which means that in the event of a bankruptcy bondholders

TABLE 24.2   **Types of Corporate Debt**

Secured	Unsecured
Mortgage bonds (secured with property)	Notes (original maturity less than 10 years)
Asset-backed bonds (secured with any asset)	Debentures

have a claim to only the assets of the firm that are not already pledged as collateral on other debt. Notes typically have shorter maturities (less than ten years) than debentures. Asset-backed bonds and mortgage bonds are **secured debt**: Specific assets are pledged as collateral that bondholders have a direct claim to in the event of bankruptcy. Mortgage bonds are secured by real property, whereas asset-backed bonds can be secured by any kind of asset. Although the word "bond" is commonly used to mean any kind of debt security, technically a corporate bond must be secured.

Let's illustrate these concepts by returning to the Hertz LBO. Recall that CDR intended to refinance approximately $9 billion of existing Hertz corporate debt. So, subsequent to the agreement, Hertz made a tender offer—a public announcement of an offer to all existing bondholders to buy back its existing debt. This debt repurchase was financed by issuing several kinds of new debt (both secured and unsecured), all of which were claims on Hertz's corporate assets.

As part of the financing, CDR planned to issue $2.7 billion worth of unsecured debt[3]—in this case, high-yield notes known as junk bonds (bonds rated below investment grade).[4] The high-yield issue was divided into three kinds of debt or **tranches** (Table 24.3), all of which made semiannual coupon payments and were issued at par. The largest tranche was a $1.8 billion face-value note maturing in eight years. It paid a coupon of 8.875%, which at the time represented a 4.45% spread over Treasuries. The rest of the debt financing was made up of asset-backed debt that was sold privately and bank loans.

Seniority.   Recall that debentures and notes are unsecured. Because more than one debenture might be outstanding, the bondholder's priority in claiming assets in the event of default, known as the bond's **seniority**, is important. As a result, most debenture issues contain clauses restricting the company from issuing new debt with equal or higher priority than existing debt.

When a firm conducts a subsequent debenture issue that has lower priority than its outstanding debt, the new debt is known as a **subordinated debenture**. In the event of default, the assets not pledged as collateral for outstanding bonds cannot be used to pay off the holders of subordinated debentures until all more senior debt has been paid off. In Hertz's case, one tranche of the junk bond issue is a note that is subordinated to the other two tranches. In the event of bankruptcy, this note has a lower-priority claim on the firm's assets. Because holders of this tranche are likely to receive less in the event Hertz defaults,

---

3. In the end, the firm issued only $2 billion in debt because fewer existing bondholders tendered their bonds than expected ($1.6 billion of existing debt remained on the balance sheet after the LBO was completed).

4. A description of corporate credit ratings can be found in Chapter 8 (see Table 8.4).

TABLE 24.3   **Hertz's December 2005 Junk Bond Issues**

	Senior Dollar-Denominated Note	Senior Euro-Denominated Note	Subordinated Dollar-Denominated Note
Face value	$1.8 billion	€225 million	$600 million
Maturity	December 1, 2014	December 1, 2014	December 1, 2016
Coupon	8.875%	7.875%	10.5%
Issue price	Par	Par	Par
Yield	8.875%	7.875%	10.5%
Call features	Up to 35% of the outstanding principal callable at 108.875% in the first three years.	Up to 35% of the outstanding principal callable at 107.875% in the first three years.	Up to 35% of the outstanding principal callable at 110.5% in the first three years.
	After four years, fully callable at:	After four years, fully callable at:	After five years, fully callable at
	• 104.438% in 2010	• 103.938% in 2010	• 105.25% in 2011
	• 102.219% in 2011	• 101.969% in 2011	• 103.50% in 2012
	• Par thereafter	• Par thereafter	• 101.75% in 2013
			• Par thereafter
Settlement	December 21, 2005	December 21, 2005	December 21, 2005
Rating **Standard and Poor's**	B	B	B
Moody's	B1	B1	B3
Fitch	BB−	BB−	B+

the yield on this debt is higher than that of the other tranches—10.5% compared to 8.875% for the first tranche.

Bond Markets.   The third tranche of Hertz's junk bond issue is a note that is denominated in euros rather than U.S. dollars—it is an international bond. International bonds are classified into four broadly defined categories. **Domestic bonds** are bonds issued by a local entity and traded in a local market, but purchased by foreigners. They are denominated in the local currency. **Foreign bonds** are bonds issued by a foreign company in a local market and are intended for local investors. They are also denominated in the local currency. Foreign bonds in the United States are known as **Yankee bonds**. In other countries, foreign bonds also have special names. For example, in Japan they are called **Samurai bonds**; in the United Kingdom, they are known as **Bulldogs**.

Eurobonds are international bonds that are not denominated in the local currency of the country in which they are issued. Consequently, there is no connection between the physical location of the market on which they trade and the location of the issuing entity. They can be denominated in any number of currencies that might or might not be connected to the location of the issuer. The trading of these bonds are not subject to any particular nation's regulations. **Global bonds** combine the features of domestic, foreign, and

Eurobonds, and are offered for sale in several different markets simultaneously. The Hertz junk bond issue is an example of a global bond issue: It was simultaneously offered for sale in the United States and Europe.

A bond that makes its payments in a foreign currency contains the risk of holding that currency and, therefore, is priced off the yields of similar bonds in that currency. Hence the euro-denominated note of the Hertz junk bond issue has a different yield from the dollar-denominated note, even though both bonds have the same seniority and maturity. While they have the same default risk, they differ in their exchange rate risk—the risk that the foreign currency will depreciate in value relative to the local currency.

Private Debt

In addition to the junk bond issue, Hertz took out more than $2 billion in bank loans. Bank loans are an example of **private debt**, debt that is not publicly traded. The private debt market is larger than the public debt market. Private debt has the advantage that it avoids the cost of registration but has the disadvantage of being illiquid.

There are two segments of the private debt market: term loans and private placements.

Term Loans. Hertz negotiated a $1.7 billion **term loan**, a bank loan that lasts for a specific term. The term of the Hertz loan was seven years. This particular loan is an example of a **syndicated bank loan**: a single loan that is funded by a group of banks rather than just a single bank. Usually, one member of the syndicate (the lead bank) negotiates the terms of the bank loan. In the Hertz case, Deutsche Bank AG negotiated the loan with CDR and then sold portions of it off to other banks—mostly smaller regional banks that had excess cash but lacked the resources to negotiate a loan of this magnitude by themselves.

Most syndicated loans are rated as investment grade. However, Hertz's term loan is an exception. Term loans such as Hertz's that are associated with LBOs are known as leveraged syndicated loans and are rated as speculative grade; in Hertz's case, Standard and Poor's rated the term loan as BB and Moody's rated it as Ba2.

In addition to the term loan, Dow Jones reported that Hertz negotiated an asset-backed revolving line of credit. A **revolving line of credit** is a credit commitment for a specific time period up to some limit (five years and $1.6 billion in Hertz's case), which a company can use as needed. Hertz's initial draw on the line of credit was $400 million. Because the line of credit is backed by specific assets, it is more secure than the term loan, so Standard and Poor's gave it a BB+ rating.

Private Placements. A **private placement** is a bond issue that does not trade on a public market but rather is sold to a small group of investors. Because a private placement does not need to be registered, it is less costly to issue. Instead of a indenture, often a simple promissory note is sufficient. Privately placed debt also need not conform to the same standards as public debt; as a consequence, it can be tailored to the particular situation.

Returning to the Hertz deal, CDR privately placed an additional $4.2 billion of U.S. asset-backed securities and $2.1 billion of international asset-backed securities. In this case, the assets backing the debt were the fleet of rental cars Hertz owned; hence this debt was termed "Fleet Debt" in the offering memorandum.

In 1990, the U.S. Securities and Exchange Commission (SEC) issued Rule 144A, which significantly increased the liquidity of certain privately placed debt. Private debt issued under this rule can be traded by large financial institutions among themselves. The rule was motivated by a desire to increase the access of foreign corporations to U.S. debt markets. Bonds that are issued under this rule are nominally private debt, but because they are tradeable between financial institutions they are only slightly less liquid than public debt. In fact, the $2.8 billion Hertz junk bond issue in Table 24.3 is actually debt issued under Rule 144A (which explains why the offering document in Figure 24.1 is called a "offering memorandum" rather than a "prospectus," because the latter term is reserved for public offerings). As part of the offering, however, the issuers agreed to publicly register the bonds within 390 days.[5] Because the debt was marketed and sold with the understanding that it would become public debt, we classified that issue as public debt.

CONCEPT CHECK
1. List four types of corporate debt that are typically issued.
2. What are the four categories of international bonds?

24.2 Other Types of Debt

Corporations are not the only entities that use debt. We begin with the largest debt sector, loans to government entities.

Sovereign Debt

Sovereign debt is debt issued by national governments. Recall that bonds issued by the U.S. government are called Treasury securities. It represents the single largest sector of the U.S. bond market. On November 30, 2005, the market value of outstanding Treasury securities was $4.17 trillion. These bonds enable the U.S. government to borrow money so that it can engage in deficit spending (that is, spending more than what is received in tax revenues).

The U.S. Treasury issues four kinds of securities (Table 24.4). Treasury bills are pure discount bonds that have original maturities ranging from a few days to 26 weeks. Currently the Treasury issues bills with original maturities of 4, 13, and 26 weeks. Treasury notes are semi-annual coupon bonds with original maturities of between 1 and 10 years. The Treasury issues notes with maturities of 2, 3, 5, and 10 years at the present time. Treasury bonds are semiannual-paying coupon bonds with maturities longer than 10 years. In the past, the Treasury has issued bonds with maturities of 30 years (often called **long bonds**) and 20 years. Both kinds of bonds still trade in the bond market. Recently, the Treasury resumed sales of Treasury bonds with a 30-year bond that was issued on Feb-

TABLE 24.4	Existing U.S. Treasury Securities	
Treasury Security	**Type**	**Original Maturity**
Bills	Discount	4, 13, and 26 weeks
Notes	Coupon	2, 3, 5, and 10 years
Bonds	Coupon	20 and 30 years
Inflation indexed	Coupon	5, 10, and 20 years

---

5. If Hertz failed to fulfill this commitment, the interest rate on all the outstanding bonds would increase by 0.5%.

ruary 15, 2006; in the future, it plans to sell 30-year bonds four times a year, in February, May, August, and November.

The last type of security that the U.S. Treasury is currently issuing is inflation-indexed bonds called **TIPS** (Treasury Inflation-Protected Securities) with maturities of 5, 10, and 20 years. These bonds are standard coupon bonds with one difference: The outstanding principal is adjusted for inflation. Thus, although the coupon *rate* is fixed, the dollar coupon varies because the semiannual coupon payments are a fixed rate of the inflation-adjusted principal. The final repayment of principal at maturity (but not the interest payments) is protected against deflation. That is, if the final principal amount is less than the original principal amount, the original principal amount is repaid.

EXAMPLE 24.1

Coupon Payments on Inflation-Indexed Bonds

Problem
On January 15, 1998, the U.S. Treasury issued a ten-year inflation-indexed note with a coupon of $3\frac{5}{8}$%. On the date of issue, the consumer price index (CPI) was 161.55484. On January 15, 2004, the CPI had increased to 184.77419. What coupon payment was made on January 15, 2004?

Solution
Between the issue date and January 15, 2004, the CPI appreciated by 184.77419 / 161.55484 = 1.14372. Consequently, the principal amount of the bond increased by this amount; that is, the original face value of $1000 increased to $1143.72. Because the bond pays semiannual coupons, the coupon payment was $1143.72 × 0.03625 / 2 = $20.73.

Treasury securities are initially sold to the public by auction. Two kinds of bids are allowed: competitive bids and noncompetitive bids. Noncompetitive bidders (usually individuals) just submit the amount of bonds they wish to purchase and are guaranteed to have their orders filled at the auction. All competitive bidders submit sealed bids in terms of yields and the amount of bonds they are willing to purchase. The Treasury then accepts the lowest-yield (highest-price) competitive bids up to the amount required to fund the deal. The highest yield accepted is termed the **stop-out yield**. All successful bidders (including the noncompetitive bidders) are awarded this yield. In the case of a Treasury bill offering, the stop-out yield is used to set the price of the bill and all bidders then pay this price. In the case of a Treasury note or Treasury bond offering, this yield determines the coupon of the bond and then all bidders pay the par value for the bond or note.[6] All income from Treasury securities is taxable at the federal level. This income, however, is not taxable at the state or local level.[7]

Zero-coupon Treasury securities with maturities longer than one year also trade in the bond market. They are called **STRIPS** (Separate Trading of Registered Interest and Principal Securities). The Treasury itself does not issue STRIPS. Instead, investors (or, more usually, investment banks) purchase Treasury notes and bonds and then resell each coupon and principal payment separately as a zero-coupon bond.

---

6. Because coupons are specified in eighths, if the winning yield is not divisible by 8, the coupon is set at the rate that produces a price closest to, but not over, par.

7. For more details, see the U.S. Treasury Web site http://www.treasurydirect.gov/.

Agency Securities

Agency securities are issued by agencies of the U.S. government or by U.S. government-sponsored enterprises. The Government National Mortgage Association (GNMA, or "Ginnie Mae") is an example of an agency; the Student Loan Marketing Association ("Sallie Mae") is an example of a government-sponsored enterprise. Although most of these securities are not explicitly backed by the full faith and credit of the U.S. government (Ginnie Mae is an exception because its issues do contain this explicit guarantee), many investors doubt that the government would allow any of its agencies to default; thus they believe that these issues contain an implicit guarantee.

Agency securities are issued in a variety of types and maturities. By far, the largest fraction of the issues consists of mortgage-backed securities. Mortgage-backed securities, such as GNMAs, are **pass-through** securities. That is, each security is backed by an underlying portfolio or **pool** of mortgages. When homeowners in the pool make their mortgage payments, this cash is passed through (minus servicing fees) to the holders of the GNMA. Consequently, the cash flows of mortgage-backed securities mirror the cash flows of home mortgages: They are annuities that pay fixed monthly payments for 30 years. As with all annuities, the principal is not returned at maturity; instead, it is paid back gradually over the life of the bond.

As discussed in Chapter 22, a mortgage borrower always has an option to repay some or all of the mortgage loan early (often because the borrower moves or refinances), and this early repayment of principal is also passed through to owners of mortgage-backed securities. Thus holders of GNMAs face prepayment risk—the risk that the bond will be partially (or wholly) repaid earlier than expected.

Municipal Bonds

Municipal bonds ("munis") are issued by state and local governments. Their distinguishing characteristic is that the income on municipal bonds is not taxable at the federal level. Consequently, municipal bonds are sometimes also referred to as tax-exempt bonds. Some issues are also exempt from state and local taxes.

Most municipal bonds pay semiannual coupons. A single issue will often contain a number of different maturity dates. Such issues are often called **serial bonds** because the bonds are scheduled to mature serially over a number of years. The coupons on municipal bonds can be either *fixed* or *floating*. A fixed-coupon bond has the same coupon over the life of the bond. In a floating-rate issue, the coupon of the bond is adjusted periodically. The reset formula is a spread over a reference rate like the rate on Treasury bills that is established when the bond is first issued. There are also a few zero-coupon municipal bond issues.

Bonds backed by the full faith and credit of a local government are known as **general obligation bonds** and are not as secure as bonds backed by the full faith and credit of the federal government. Sometimes local governments strengthen the commitment further by tying the promise to a particular revenue source, such as a special fee. Because a local government can always use its general revenue to repay such bonds, this commitment is over and above the usual commitment, so these bonds are called **double-barreled**. Not all municipal bonds are backed by the full faith and credit of the local government, however. Instead, the local government can pledge specific revenues generated by projects that were initially financed by the bond issue. These bonds are called **revenue bonds**.

CONCEPT CHECK
1. List four different kinds of securities issued by the U.S. Treasury.

2. What is the distinguishing characteristic of municipal bonds?

24.3 Bond Covenants

Covenants are restrictive clauses in a bond contract that limit the issuer from taking actions that may undercut its ability to repay the bonds. One might guess that such covenants would not be necessary—after all, why would managers voluntarily take actions that increase the firm's default risk? However, recall from Chapter 16 that when a firm is levered, managers may have an incentive to take actions that benefit equity holders at the expense of debt holders.

For example, once bonds are issued, equity holders have an incentive to increase dividends at the expense of debt holders. Think of an extreme case in which a company issues a bond, and then immediately liquidates its assets, pays out the proceeds (including those from the bond issue) in the form of a dividend to equity holders, and declares bankruptcy. In this case, the equity holders receive the value of the firm's assets plus the proceeds from the bond, while bondholders are left with nothing. Consequently, bond agreements often contain covenants that restrict the ability of management to pay dividends. Other covenants may restrict the level of further indebtedness and specify that the issuer must maintain a minimum amount of working capital. If the issuer fails to live up to any covenant, the bond goes into default. Covenants in the Hertz junk bond issue limited Hertz's ability to incur more debt, make dividend payments, redeem stock, make investments, create liens, transfer or sell assets, and merge or consolidate. They also included a requirement to offer to repurchase the bonds at 101% of face value if the corporation experiences a change in control.

Recall that CDR made a tender offer to repurchase all of Hertz's outstanding debt. CDR made this offer because the outstanding debt had a restrictive covenant that made it difficult to complete a merger or takeover of Hertz. Once the group led by CDR owned more that 50% of this debt, the terms of the prospectus gave CDR the ability to unilaterally change any covenant, thus allowing them to proceed with the LBO.

You might expect that equity holders would try to include as few covenants as possible in a bond agreement. In fact, this is not necessarily the case. The stronger the covenants in the bond contract, the less likely the issuer will default on the bond, and so the lower the interest rate investors will require to buy the bond. That is, by including more covenants, issuers can reduce their costs of borrowing. As discussed in Chapter 16, if the covenants are designed to reduce agency costs by restricting management's ability to take negative NPV actions that exploit debt holders, then the reduction in the firm's borrowing cost can more than outweigh the cost of the loss of flexibility associated with covenants.

CONCEPT CHECK

1. What happens if an issuer fails to live up to a bond covenant?

2. Why can bond covenants reduce a firm's borrowing cost?

24.4 Repayment Provisions

A bond issuer repays its bonds by making coupon and principal payments as specified in the bond contract. However, this is not the only way an issuer can repay bonds. For example, the issuer can repurchase a fraction of the outstanding bonds in the market, or it can make a tender offer for the entire issue, as Hertz did on its existing bonds. Another way issuers repay bonds is to exercise a *call* provision that allows the issuer to repurchase the bonds at a predetermined price. Bonds that contain such a provision are known as **callable bonds**.

Call Provisions

Hertz's junk bonds are examples of callable bonds. Table 24.3 lists the call features in each tranche. A call feature allows the issuer of the bond the right (but not the obligation) to retire all outstanding bonds on (or after) a specific date (the **call date**), for the **call price**. The call price is generally set at or above, and expressed as a percentage of, the bond's face value. In Hertz's case, the call dates of the two senior tranches are at the end of the fourth year. For the duration of 2010, the $1.8 billion issue has a call price of 104.438% of the face value of the bond. In the following years, the call price is gradually reduced until in 2012 the bond becomes callable at par. The euro-denominated bond has similar terms at slightly different call prices. The subordinated tranche's call date is a year later and has a different call price structure.

The Hertz bonds are also partially callable in the first three years. Hertz has the option to retire up to 35% of the outstanding principal at the call prices listed in Table 24.3, as long as the funds needed to repurchase the bonds are derived from the proceeds of an equity issuance.

To understand how call provisions affect the price of a bond, we first need to consider when an issuer will exercise its right to call the bond. An issuer can always retire one of its bonds early by repurchasing the bond in the open market. If the call provision offers a cheaper way to retire the bonds, however, the issuer will forgo the option of purchasing the bonds in the open market and call the bonds instead.

Let's examine a more concrete example. Consider a case in which an issuer has issued two bonds that are identical in every respect except that one is callable at par (redeemable at face value) and the other is not callable. This issuer wants to retire one of the two bonds. How does it decide which bond to retire? If bond yields have dropped since the issue date, the non-callable bond will be trading at a premium. Thus, if the issuer wished to retire this bond (by repurchasing it in the open market), it would have to repay more than the outstanding principal. If it chose to call the callable bond instead, the issuer

New York City Calls Its Municipal Bonds

In November 2004, New York City announced plans to call $430 million of its municipal bonds. New York City was an AAA-rated borrower, and these bonds paid relatively high interest rates of 6% to 8%. The city would be refinancing the bonds with new bonds that paid interest rates between 3% and 5%. In total, New York City called 63 individual bond issues with original maturities between 2012 and 2019.

Investors were attracted to the older municipal bonds because of their higher yields. Despite these yields, they did not expect New York City to call these bonds, so the market price for these bonds earlier in the year was 10% to 20% higher than their face value. When New York City announced its plans to call the bonds at prices slightly higher than the face value investors were caught off guard and the market value of the bonds fell accordingly. Investors suffered losses of 15% or more on their AAA-rated investment.

Investors did not expect New York City to call these bonds because it had already refinanced the debt in the early 1990s. According to Internal Revenue Service rules, the city could not refinance again with another tax-exempt issue. However, New York City surprised the market when it decided to refinance the bonds by issuing taxable bonds instead. Although it happens rarely, this example illustrates that investors are sometimes surprised by issuer call strategies.

Source: Aaron Lucchetti, "Municipal-Bond Bans Get a Rude Awakening—Call Feature Can Catch Investors and Money Managers Off Guard," *The Wall Street Journal*, February 8, 2005, p. C1.

would simply pay the outstanding principal. Hence, if yields have dropped, it is cheaper to retire the callable bond. Note that because bond yields have dropped, by exercising the call on the callable bond and then immediately refinancing, the issuer can lower its borrowing costs. Conversely, if yields increased after the issue date, there is no reason to refinance. In addition, both bonds would be trading at a discount. Even if the issuer wished to retire some bonds, it would be better off by repurchasing either bond at less than par in the market than by calling the callable bond for par. Thus when yields have risen, the issuer will not choose to exercise the call on the callable bond.

Let's consider this scenario from the perspective of a bondholder. As we have seen, the issuer will exercise the call option only when the coupon rate of the bond exceeds the prevailing market rate. Therefore, the only time the call is exercised, the bondholder finds herself in the position of looking for an alternative investment when market rates are lower than the bond's coupon rate. That is, the holder of a callable bond faces reinvestment risk precisely when it hurts: when market rates are lower than the coupon rate she is currently receiving. This makes the callable bond relatively less attractive to the bondholder than the identical non-callable bond. Consequently, a callable bond will trade at a lower price (and therefore a higher yield) than an otherwise equivalent non-callable bond.

To understand the relationship between the prices of otherwise identical callable and non-callable bonds, first consider what happens to a bond that is callable at par on only one specific date. Figure 24.3 plots the price of a callable bond and an otherwise identical non-callable bond on the call date as a function of the yield on the non-callable bond. When the yield of the non-callable bond is less than the coupon, the callable bond will be called, so its price is $100. If this yield is greater than the coupon, then the callable bond will not be called, so it has the same price as the non-callable bond. Note that the callable bond price is capped at par: The price can be low when yields are high, but does not rise above the par value when the yield is low.

FIGURE 24.3

Prices of Callable and Non-callable Bonds on the Call Date

This figure shows the prices of a callable bond (gold line) and an otherwise identical non-callable bond (blue line) on the call date as a function of the yield on the non-callable bond. Both bonds have a 5% coupon rate. (The callable bond is assumed to be callable at par on one date only.)

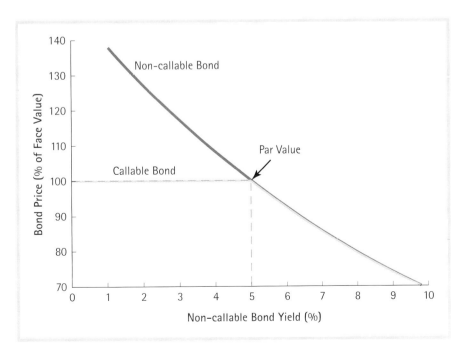

FIGURE 24.4

Prices of Callable and Non-callable Bonds Prior to the Call Date

When non-callable bond yields are high relative to the callable bond coupon, investors anticipate that the likelihood of exercising the call is low and the callable bond price is similar to that of an otherwise identical non-callable bond. When market yields are low relative to the bond coupon, investors anticipate that the bond will likely be called, so its price is close to the price of a non-callable bond that matures on the call date.

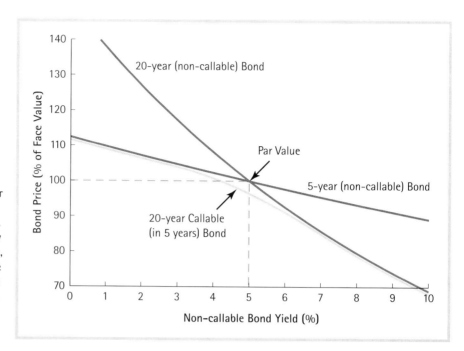

Before the call date, investors anticipate the optimal strategy that the issuer will follow, and the bond price reflects this strategy, as Figure 24.4 illustrates. When market yields are high relative to the bond coupon, investors anticipate that the likelihood of exercising the call is low and the bond price is similar to an otherwise identical non-callable bond. On the other hand, when market yields are low relative to the bond coupon, investors anticipate that the bond will likely be called, so its price is close to the price of a non-callable bond that matures on the call date.

The yield to maturity of a callable bond is calculated as if the bond were not callable. That is, the yield is still defined as the discount rate that sets the present value of the promised payments equal to the current price, *ignoring* the call feature. We can think of the yield of a callable bond as the interest rate the bondholder receives if the bond is not called and repaid in full. Because the price of a callable bond is lower than the price of an otherwise identical non-callable bond, the yield to maturity of a callable bond will be higher than the yield to maturity for its non-callable counterpart. The assumption that underlies the yield calculation of a callable bond—that it will not be called—is not always realistic, so bond traders often quote the yield to call. The **yield to call (YTC)** is the annual yield of a callable bond assuming that the bond is called at the earliest opportunity.

Calculating the Yield to Call

Problem

IBM has just issued a callable (at par) five-year, 8% coupon bond with annual coupon payments. The bond can be called at par in one year or anytime thereafter on a coupon payment date. It has a price of $103 per $100 face value. What is the bond's yield to maturity and yield to call?

Solution

The timeline of the promised payments for this bond (if it is not called) is

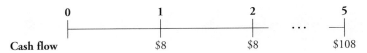

Setting the present value of the payments equal to the current price gives

$$103 = \frac{8}{(YTM)}\left(1 - \frac{1}{(1 + YTM)^5}\right) + \frac{100}{(1 + YTM)^5}$$

Solving for YTM (using the annuity spreadsheet) gives the bond's yield to maturity:

	NPER	RATE	PV	PMT	FV	Excel Formula
Given	5		− 103	8	100	
Solve for Rate		7.26%				=RATE(5,8,−103,100)

The bond has a yield to maturity of 7.26%.

The timeline of the payments if the bond is called at the first available opportunity is

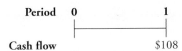

Setting the present value of these payments equal to the current price gives

$$103 = \frac{108}{(1 + YTC)}$$

Solving for YTC gives the yield to call:

$$YTC = \frac{108}{103} - 1 = 4.85\%$$

The annuity spreadsheet can be used to derive the same result:

	NPER	RATE	PV	PMT	FV	Excel Formula
Given	1		− 103	8	100	
Solve for Rate		4.85%				=RATE(1,8,−103,100)

Sinking Funds

Another way bonds are repaid is through a **sinking fund**. Instead of repaying the entire principal balance on the maturity date, the company makes regular payments into a sinking fund administered by a trustee over the life of the bond. These payments are then used to repurchase bonds. In this way, the company can reduce the amount of outstanding debt without affecting the cash flows of the remaining bonds.

How does the trustee decide which bonds to repurchase? If the bonds are trading at below their face value, the company simply repurchases the bonds in the market. But if a bond is trading at above its face value, because the bonds are repurchased at par the decision is made by lottery.

Sinking fund provisions usually specify a minimum rate at which the issuer must contribute to the fund. In some cases, the issuer has the option to accelerate these payments. Because the sinking fund allows the issuer to repurchase the bonds at par, the option to accelerate the payments is another form of call provision.

The manner in which an outstanding balance is paid off using a sinking fund depends on the issue. Some issues specify equal payments over the life of the bond, ultimately retiring the issue on the maturity date of the bond. In other cases, the sinking fund payments are not sufficient to retire the entire issue and the company must make a large payment on the maturity date, known as a **balloon payment**. Often, sinking fund payments start only a few years after the bond issue. Bonds can be issued with both a sinking fund and call provision.

Convertible Provisions

Another way bonds are retired is by converting them into equity. Some corporate bonds have a provision that gives the bondholder an option to convert each bond owned into a fixed number of shares of common stock at a ratio called the **conversion ratio**. Such bonds are called **convertible bonds**. The provision usually gives bondholders the right to convert the bond into stock at any time up to the maturity date for the bond.[8]

To understand how a conversion feature changes the value of a bond, note that this provision gives a call option to the holder of a bond. Thus a convertible bond can be thought of as a regular bond plus a special type of call option called a **warrant**. A warrant is a call option written by the company itself on *new* stock (whereas a regular call option is written on existing stock). That is, when a holder of a warrant exercises it and thereby purchases stock, the company delivers this stock by issuing new stock. In all other respects, a warrant is identical to a call option.[9]

On the maturity date of the bond, the strike price of the embedded warrant in a convertible bond is equal to the face value of the bond divided by the conversion ratio—that is, the **conversion price**. So, on the maturity date of a convertible bond with a $1000 face value and a conversion ratio of 15, if you converted the bond into stock, you would receive 15 shares. If you did not convert, you would receive $1000. Hence by converting you essentially "paid" $1000 for 15 shares, implying a price per share of $1000 / 15 = $66.67. If the price of the stock exceeds $66.67, you would choose to convert; otherwise, you would take the cash. At maturity, you will choose to convert whenever the stock price exceeds the conversion price. As shown in Figure 24.5, the value of the bond is the maximum of its face value ($1000) and the value of 15 shares of stock.

What about prior to the maturity date? If the stock does not pay a dividend, then we know from our discussion of call options in Chapter 20 that it is never optimal to exercise a call early. Hence, the holder of a convertible bond should wait until the maturity date of the bond before deciding whether to convert. The value of the bond prior to

---

8. Some convertible bonds do not allow conversion for a specified amount of time after the issue date.

9. When a regular call is exercised, the loss incurred by the writer of the call accrues to an unknown third party. However, when a warrant is exercised, the loss accrues to the equity holders of the firm (because they are forced to sell new equity at below-market value), which *includes* the holder of the warrant (upon exercise, the warrant holder becomes an equity holder). This dilution effect implies that the gain from exercising a warrant is less than that from a call, so warrants are worth less than calls.

FIGURE 24.5

Convertible Bond Value

At maturity, the value of a convertible bond is the maximum of the value of a $1000 straight bond and 15 shares of stock, and will be converted if the stock is above the conversion price. Prior to maturity, the value of the convertible bond will depend upon the likelihood of conversion, and will be above that of a straight bond or 15 shares of stock.

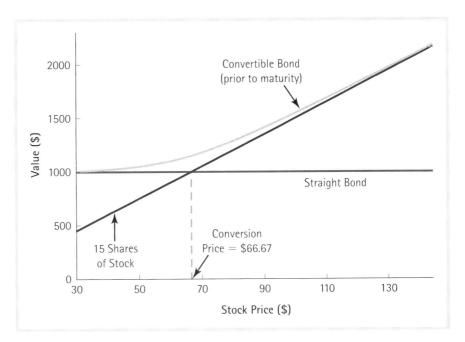

maturity is plotted in Figure 24.5. If the stock price is low so that the embedded warrant is deep out-of-the-money, the conversion provision is not worth much and the bond's value is close to the value of a straight bond—an otherwise identical bond without the conversion provision. When the stock price is high and the embedded warrant is deep in-the-money, then the convertible bond trades close to—but higher than (to reflect the time value of the option)—the value of the bond if converted.

Often companies issue convertible bonds that are callable. With these bonds, if the issuer calls them, the holder can choose to convert rather than let the bonds be called. When the bonds are called, the holder faces exactly the same decision as he would on the maturity date of the bonds: He will choose to convert if the stock price exceeds the conversion price and let the bonds be called otherwise. Thus, by calling the bonds, a company can force bondholders to make their decision to exercise the conversion option earlier than they would otherwise like to. Calling a convertible bond therefore transfers the remaining time value of the conversion option from bondholders to shareholders.

When a corporation issues convertible debt, it is giving the holder an option—a warrant, in this case. As we learned in Chapter 20, options always have a positive value; hence a convertible bond is worth more than an otherwise identical straight bond. Consequently, if both bonds are issued at par, the non-convertible bond must offer a higher interest rate. Many people point to the lower interest rates of convertible bonds and argue that therefore convertible debt is cheaper than straight debt.

As we learned in Chapter 14, in a perfect market the choice of financing cannot affect the value of a firm. Hence the argument that convertible debt is cheaper because it has a lower interest rate is fallacious. Convertible debt carries a lower interest rate because it has an embedded warrant. If the price of a firm were subsequently to rise so that the bond-holders choose to convert, the current shareholders will have to sell an equity stake in their firm for below-market value. The lower interest rate is compensation for the possibility that this event will occur.

1. What is a sinking fund?

2. Do callable bonds have a higher or lower yield than otherwise identical bonds without a call feature? Why?

3. Why does a convertible bond have a lower yield than an otherwise identical bond without the option to convert?

Summary

1. Companies can raise debt using different sources. Typical types of debt are public debt, which trades in a public market, and private debt, which is negotiated directly with a bank or a small group of investors. The securities that companies issue when raising debt are called corporate bonds.

2. For public offerings, the bond agreement takes the form of an indenture, a formal contract between the bond issuer and a trust company. The indenture lays out the terms of the bond issue.

3. Four types of corporate bonds are typically issued: notes, debentures, mortgage bonds, and asset-backed bonds. Notes and debentures are unsecured.

4. Corporate bonds differ in their level of seniority. In case of bankruptcy, senior debt is paid in full first before subordinated debt is paid.

5. International bonds are classified into four broadly defined categories: domestic bonds that trade in foreign markets, foreign bonds that are issued in a local market by foreign entity, Eurobonds that are not denominated in the local currency of the country in which they are issued, and global bonds that trade in several markets simultaneously.

6. Private debt can be in the form of term loans or private placements. A term loan is a bank loan that lasts for a specific term. A private placement is a bond issue that is sold to a small group of investors.

7. Governments, states, and other state-sponsored enterprises issue bonds as well.

8. The U.S. Treasury has issued four different kinds of securities: Treasury bills, Treasury notes, Treasury bonds, and TIPS.

9. Agency securities are issued by agencies of the U.S. government or by U.S. government-sponsored enterprises. The Government National Mortgage Association ("Ginnie Mae") is an example of an agency; the Student Loan Marketing Association ("Sallie Mae") is an example of a government-sponsored enterprise.

10. Holders of Ginnie Mae securities face prepayment risk, which is the risk that they will find that the bond will be partially (or wholly) repaid earlier than expected.

11. Municipal bonds ("munis") are issued by state and local governments. Their distinguishing characteristic is that the income on municipal bonds is not taxable at the federal level.

12. Covenants are restrictive clauses in the bond contract that help investors by limiting the issuer's ability to take actions that will increase the default risk and reduce the value of the bonds.

13. A call provision gives the issuer of the bond the right (but not the obligation) to retire the bond after a specific date (but before maturity).

14. A callable bond will generally trade at a lower price than an otherwise equivalent non-callable bond.

15. The yield to call is the yield of a callable bond assuming that the bond is called at the earliest opportunity.

16. Another way in which a bond is repaid before maturity is by periodically repurchasing part of the debt through a sinking fund.

17. Some corporate bonds, known as convertible bonds, have a provision that allows the holder to convert them into equity.

18. Convertible debt carries a lower interest rate than other comparable non-convertible debt.

Key Terms

agency securities *p. 788*
asset-backed bonds *p. 782*
balloon payment *p. 794*
bearer bonds *p. 782*
Bulldogs *p. 784*
call date *p. 790*
call price *p. 790*
callable bonds *p. 789*
conversion price *p. 794*
conversion ratio *p. 794*
convertible bonds *p. 794*
covenants *p. 789*
debentures *p. 782*
domestic bonds *p. 784*
double-barreled *p. 788*
Eurobonds *p. 784*
foreign bonds *p. 784*
general obligation bonds *p. 788*
global bonds *p. 784*
indenture *p. 780*
leveraged buyout (LBO) *p. 780*
long bonds *p. 786*
mortgage bonds *p. 782*
municipal bonds *p. 788*
notes *p. 782*

original issue discount (OID) *p. 782*
pass-through *p. 788*
pool *p. 788*
private debt *p. 785*
private placement *p. 785*
registered bonds *p. 782*
revenue bonds *p. 788*
revolving line of credit *p. 785*
Samurai bonds *p. 784*
secured debt *p. 783*
seniority *p. 783*
serial bond *p. 788*
sinking fund *p. 793*
sovereign debt *p. 786*
stop-out yield *p. 787*
STRIPS *p. 787*
subordinated debenture *p. 783*
syndicated bank loan *p. 785*
term loan *p. 785*
TIPS *p. 787*
tranches *p. 783*
unsecured debt *p. 782*
warrant *p. 794*
Yankee bonds *p. 784*
yield to call (YTC) *p. 792*

Further Reading

Students interested in a comprehensive summary of the bond market should consult either of the following texts: F. Fabozzi (ed.), *Handbook of Fixed Income Securities*, 6th ed. (McGraw-Hill, 2000); M. Stigum, *The Money Market*, 3rd ed. (McGraw-Hill, 1990).

Readers interested in more depth on subjects covered in this chapter can consult the following sources:

Convertible Debt

R. S. Billingsley and D. M. Smith, "Why Do Firms Issue Convertible Debt?" *Financial Management* 25(2) (1996): 93–99; M. J. Brennan and E. S. Schwartz, "The Case for Convertibles," *Journal of Applied Corporate Finance* 1(1) (1988): 55–64; W. Bühler and C. Koziol, "Valuation of Convertible Bonds with Sequential Conversion," *Schmalenbach Business Review*

54 (October 2002): 302–334; R. Green, "Investment Incentives, Debt and Warrants," *Journal of Financial Economics* 13 (1984), 115–136; C. Hennessy and Y. Tserlukevich, "Taxation, Agency Conflicts and the Choice between Callable and Convertible Debt," University of California, Berkeley, working paper; J. Stein, "Convertible Bonds as Backdoor Equity Financing," *Journal of Financial Economics* 32(1) (1992): 3–21.

Callable Debt

P. Asquith, "Convertible Bonds Are Not Called Late," *Journal of Finance* 50(4) (1995): 1275–1289; M. J. Brennan and E. S. Schwartz, "Saving Bonds, Retractable Bonds, and Callable Bonds," *Journal of Financial Economics* 5(1) (1997): 67–88.

Bond Covenants

C. Smith and J. Warner, "On Financial Contracting: An Analysis of Bond Covenants," *Journal of Financial Economics* 7 (1979): 117–161; M. Bradley and M. R. Roberts, "The Structure and Pricing of Corporate Debt Covenants," SSRN working paper series (2004).

Problems

A blue box (■) indicates problems available in MyFinanceLab.

Corporate Debt

1. Explain some of the differences between a public debt offering and a private debt offering.

2. Why do bonds with lower seniority have higher yields than equivalent bonds with higher seniority?

3. Explain the difference between a secured corporate and an unsecured corporate bond.

4. What is the difference between a foreign bond and a Eurobond?

Other Types of Debt

5. Describe the kinds of securities the U.S. government uses to finance the federal debt.

6. On January 15, 2010, the U.S. Treasury issued a five-year inflation-indexed note with a coupon of 3%. On the date of issue, the consumer price index (CPI) was 250. By January 15, 2015, the CPI had increased to 300. What principal and coupon payment was made on January 15, 2015?

7. On January 15, 2020, the U.S. Treasury issued a ten-year inflation-indexed note with a coupon of 6%. On the date of issue, the CPI was 400. By January 15, 2030, the CPI had decreased to 300. What principal and coupon payment was made on January 15, 2030?

8. Describe what prepayment risk in a GNMA is.

9. What is the distinguishing feature of how municipal bonds are taxed?

Bond Covenants

10. Explain why bond issuers might voluntarily choose to put restrictive covenants into a new bond issue.

Repayment Provisions

 11. General Electric has just issued a callable (at par) ten-year, 6% coupon bond with annual coupon payments. The bond can be called at par in one year or anytime thereafter on a coupon payment date. It has a price of $102. What is the bond's yield to maturity and yield to call?

 12. Boeing Corporation has just issued a callable (at par) three-year, 5% coupon bond with semi-annual coupon payments. The bond can be called at par in two years or anytime thereafter on a coupon payment date. It has a price of $99. What is the bond's yield to maturity and yield to call?

13. Explain why the yield on a convertible bond is lower than the yield on an otherwise identical bond without a conversion feature.

 14. You own a bond with a face value of $10,000 and a conversion ratio of 450. What is the conversion price?

Data Case

You are still employed at The Home Depot. Recall the presentation of Chapter 15's plan to increase leverage to Board of Directors. The idea of changing Home Depot's capital structure stirred some conversations among top executives. The CFO and other top managers in the finance division are all aware that increasing the debt load will have ramifications in the credit markets. Specifically, they realize that the firm's debt rating could change, which will raise the cost of borrowing as well as possibly lower the value of the existing debt. No one is exactly sure what the impact will be, but they all agree that it deserves investigation.

Because you prepared the spreadsheet data, you have been summoned to an executive-level meeting and asked to estimate the impact of increasing the debt of the firm. Use the spreadsheet from Chapter 15's Data Case as a starting point. You are to consider four different scenarios: issuing $1 billion, $10 billion, $20 billion, and $30 billion in new debt. In each case, proceeds from the debt will be used to repurchase stock. The CFO believes that the $1 billion level will not affect the firm's credit rating. However, each larger increase in debt will cause the debt to be downgraded one level. For example, the $10 billion scenario will lower the current debt rating one level, the $20 billion scenario would lower the rating still another level, and so on. Your job is to determine the impact of additional debt on borrowing costs at each debt level. Assume the new debt will be raised by issuing 10-year bonds.

1. Determine the current debt rating for The Home Depot.
   a. Research the current bond rating at NASD BondInfo.com (www.nasdbondinfo.com). Click to search by symbol, and then enter the symbol for Home Depot (HD). (By the way, well done on being savvy enough not to ask the executives for Home Depot's bond rating!)
   b. What is the Moody's bond rating on the Home Depot bond with the maturity closest to ten years from today? What is the yield on this bond?

2. Because lower bond ratings will lead to higher interest costs, you will need to determine those costs. Go to Bonds Online (www.bondsonline.com) and click on "Today's Market." Next, click on "Corporate Bond Spreads." You will see a table of bond spreads prepared by Reuters and the date the table was prepared right below it. These spreads represent the increased yield a bond must pay over the U.S. Treasury of the same maturity. Choose the 10-year spread for Home Depot's current rating and the three ratings below it. The spreads are in basis points; a basis point is 1/100th of a percentage point (thus, 50 basis points is 0.5%). We will adjust these old spreads to estimate the current spread.
   a. Because these spreads are dated, you will need to create new yield spreads for the various ratings. Use the current difference between the Home Depot bond's yield and the 10-year Treasury as the true spread for the rating. Using Excel, compute the spreads for the other ratings, by adding the *difference* in spreads from the table to the new true spread for Home Depot's rating. Finally, determine the yield for each rating by adding the new spread to the yield on the 10-year Treasury bond.
   b. Compute the required yields on 10-year bonds at each of the new debt levels requested.

3. What factors cause the bond rating to fall, and the bond yields to increase, as Home Depot increases its debt levels?

Leasing

notation

L lease payments

PV present value

r_D debt cost of capital

τ_c marginal corporate income tax rate

r_U unlevered cost of capital

r_{wacc} weighted average cost of capital

To implement an investment project, a firm must acquire the necessary property, plant, and equipment. As an alternative to purchasing these assets outright, the firm can lease them. You are probably familiar with leases if you have leased a car or rented an apartment. These consumer rentals are similar to the leases used by businesses: The owner retains title to the asset, and the firm pays for its use of the asset through regular lease payments. When firms lease property, plant, or equipment, the leases generally exceed one year. This chapter focuses on such long-term leases.

If you can purchase an asset, you can probably lease it. Commercial real estate, computers, trucks, copy machines, airplanes, and even power plants are all examples of assets that firms can lease rather than buy. Equipment leasing is a rapidly growing industry, with more than one half of the world's leasing now being done by companies in Europe and Japan. In 2003, more than 30% of the productive assets acquired by U.S. companies were procured through leasing contracts, for a total leasing volume exceeding $200 billion. Eighty percent of U.S. companies lease all or some of their equipment, and more than 25% of the world's jet fleet, by dollar value, is leased.[1] The top aircraft leasing company by fleet size at the start of 2005 was GE Commercial Aviation Services. GE owns approximately 1300 aircraft, the world's largest commercial airplane fleet, and has orders in place for $10 billion in new aircraft.[2] GE leases these commercial aircraft to some 200 airline customers in 60 countries.

As you will learn, leases are not merely an alternative to purchasing; they also function as an important financing method for tangible assets. In fact, long-term leasing is the most common method of equipment financing. How do companies such as GE

---

1. Equipment Leasing Association, *Industry Overview*, 2005.

2. Susan Carey, Kathryn Kranhold, and Melanie Trottman, "GE's Bailouts of Troubled Carriers Divide Airline Industry," *Wall Street Journal*, March 31, 2005, p. B1.

Commercial Aviation Services set the terms for their leases? How do their customers—the commercial airlines—evaluate and negotiate these leases? In this chapter, we first discuss the basic types of leases and provide an overview of the accounting and tax treatment of leases. We next show how to evaluate the lease-versus-buy decision. Firms often cite various benefits to leasing as compared to purchasing property and equipment, and we conclude the chapter with an evaluation of their reasoning.

25.1 The Basics of Leasing

A lease is a contract between two parties: the lessee and the lessor. The **lessee** is liable for periodic payments in exchange for the right to use the asset. The **lessor** is the owner of the asset, who is entitled to the lease payments in exchange for lending the asset.

Most leases involve little or no upfront payment. Instead, the lessee commits to make regular lease (or rental) payments for the term of the contract. At the end of the contract term, the lease specifies who will retain ownership of the asset and at what terms. The lease also specifies any cancellation provisions, the options for renewal and purchase, and the obligations for maintenance and related servicing costs.

Examples of Lease Transactions

Many types of lease transactions are possible based on the relationship between the lessee and the lessor. In a **sales-type lease**, the lessor is the manufacturer (or a primary dealer) of the asset. For example, IBM both manufactures and leases computers. Similarly, Xerox leases its copy machines. Manufacturers generally set the terms of these leases as part of a broader sales and pricing strategy, and they may bundle other services or goods (such as software, maintenance, or product upgrades) as part of the lease.

In a **direct lease**, the lessor is not the manufacturer, but is often an independent company that specializes in purchasing assets and leasing them to customers. For example, Ryder Systems, Inc., owns more than 135,000 commercial trucks, tractors, and trailers, which it leases to small businesses and large enterprises throughout the United States, Canada, and the United Kingdom. In many instances of direct leases, the lessee identifies the equipment it needs first and then finds a leasing company to purchase the asset.

If a firm already owns an asset it would prefer to lease, it can arrange a **sale and lease-back** transaction. In this type of lease, the lessee receives cash from the sale of the asset and then makes lease payments to retain the use of the asset. In 2002, San Francisco Municipal Railway (Muni) used the $35 million in proceeds from the sale and leaseback of 118 of its light-rail vehicles to offset a large operating budget deficit. The purchaser, CIBC World Markets of Canada, received a tax benefit from depreciating the rail cars, something Muni could not do as a public transit agency.

With many leases, the lessor provides the initial capital necessary to purchase the asset, and then receives and retains the lease payments. In a **leveraged lease**, however, the lessor borrows from a bank or other lender to obtain the initial capital for the purchase, using the lease payments to pay interest and principal on the loan. Also, in some circumstances, the lessor is not an independent company but rather a separate business partnership, called a **special-purpose entity (SPE)**, which is created by the lessee for the sole purpose of obtaining the lease. SPEs are commonly used in **synthetic leases**, which are designed to obtain specific accounting and tax treatment (discussed further in Section 25.2).

Lease Payments and Residual Values

Suppose your business needs a new $20,000 electric forklift for its warehouse operations, and you are considering leasing the forklift for four years. In this case, the lessor will purchase the forklift and allow you to use it for four years. At that point, you will return the forklift to the lessor. How much should you expect to pay for the right to use the forklift for the first four years of its life?

The cost of the lease will depend on the asset's **residual value**, which is its market value at the end of the lease. Suppose the residual value of the forklift in four years will be $6000. If lease payments of amount L are made monthly, then the lessor's cash flows from the transaction are as follows (note that lease payments are typically made at the beginning of each payment period):

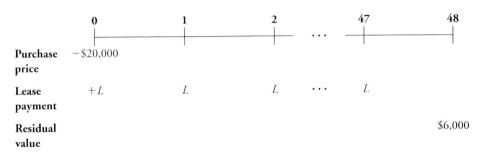

In a perfect capital market (where lessors compete with one another in initiating leases), the lease payment should be set so that the NPV of the transaction is zero and the lessor breaks even:

$$PV(\text{Lease Payments}) = \text{Purchase Price} - PV(\text{Residual Value}) \qquad (25.1)$$

In other words, *in a perfect market, the cost of leasing is equivalent to the cost of purchasing and reselling the asset.*

Thus the amount of the lease payment will depend on the purchase price, the residual value, and the appropriate discount rate for the cash flows.

Lease Terms in a Perfect Market

Problem
Suppose the purchase price of the forklift is $20,000, its residual value in four years is certain to be $6000, and there is no risk that the lessee will default on the lease. If the risk-free interest rate is a 6% APR with monthly compounding, what would be the monthly lease payment for a four-year lease in a perfect capital market?

Solution
Because all cash flows are risk free, we can discount them using the risk-free interest rate of 6% / 12 = 0.5% per month. From Eq. 25.1,

$$PV(\text{Lease Payments}) = \$20,000 - \$6000 / 1.005^{48} = \$15,277.41$$

What monthly lease payment L has this present value? We can interpret the lease payments as an annuity. Because the first lease payment starts today, we can view the lease as an initial payment of L plus a 47-month annuity of L. Thus, using the annuity formula, we need to find L so that

$$15{,}277.41 = L + L \times \frac{1}{0.005}\left(1 - \frac{1}{1.005^{47}}\right) = L \times \left[1 + \frac{1}{0.005}\left(1 - \frac{1}{1.005^{47}}\right)\right]$$

Solving for L, we get

$$L = \frac{15{,}277.41}{1 + \dfrac{1}{0.005}\left(1 - \dfrac{1}{1.005^{47}}\right)} = \$357.01 \text{ per month}$$

Leases Versus Loans

Alternatively, you could obtain a four-year loan for the purchase price and buy the forklift outright. If M is the monthly payment for a fully amortizing loan, the lender's cash flows will be as follows:

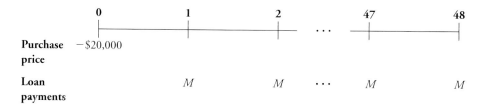

Assuming the loan is fairly priced, the loan payments would be such that

$$PV(\text{Loan Payments}) = \text{Purchase Price} \tag{25.2}$$

Comparing Eq. 25.2 with Eq. 25.1, we see that while with a standard loan we are financing the entire cost of the asset, with a lease we are financing only the cost of the economic depreciation of the asset during the term of the lease. Because we are getting the entire asset when we purchase it with the loan, the loan payments are higher than the lease payments.

EXAMPLE 25.2

Loan Payments in a Perfect Market

Problem
Suppose that you purchase the forklift for $20,000 by borrowing the purchase price using a four-year annuity loan. What would the monthly loan payment be in a perfect capital market where the risk-free interest rate is a 6% APR with monthly compounding, assuming no risk of default? How does this compare with the lease payment of Example 25.1?

Solution
Because all cash flows are risk free, we can discount them using the risk-free interest rate of 6% / 12 = 0.5% per month. Because loan payments are made at the end of each month, using the annuity formula to value the loan payments, Eq. 25.2 becomes

$$\frac{M}{0.005}\left(1 - \frac{1}{1.005^{48}}\right) = 20{,}000$$

Solving for M gives the loan payments:

$$M = \frac{20{,}000}{\frac{1}{0.005}\left(1 - \frac{1}{1.005^{48}}\right)} = \$469.70 \text{ per month}$$

Of course, while the lease payments are lower, with the lease we have the use of the forklift for only four years. With the loan, we own the forklift for its entire life.

The monthly loan payments in Example 25.2 exceed the lease payments in Example 25.1. This difference does not mean the lease is superior to the loan. While the lease payments are lower, with the lease we have use of the forklift for only four years. If we purchase the forklift using the loan, we own it after four years and can sell it for its residual value of $6000. Alternatively, if we lease the forklift and want to keep it after the lease terminates, we can purchase it for its fair market value of $6000. Once we consider the benefit of this residual value by the Law of One Price, the total cost of purchasing with either the loan or the lease is the same. That is, combining Eqs. 25.2 and 25.1,

$$PV(\text{Lease Payments}) + PV(\text{Residual Value}) = PV(\text{Loan Payments}) \qquad (25.3)$$

In other words, *in a perfect market, the cost of leasing and then purchasing the asset is equivalent to the cost of borrowing to purchase the asset.*[3]

End-of-Term Lease Options

In Example 25.5, we assumed that at the end of the lease the forklift would be returned to the lessor, who would then obtain its residual market value of $6000. In reality, other lease terms are possible. In many cases, the lease allows the lessee to obtain ownership of the asset for some price.

- A **fair market value (FMV) lease** gives the lessee the option to purchase the asset at its fair market value at the termination of the lease. (Depending on the asset, determining its fair market value may be complicated. The lease will typically stipulate a procedure for doing so, and it often will require estimates of the fair market value to be provided by an independent third party.) With perfect capital markets, there is no difference between an FMV lease and a lease in which the assets are retained by the lessor, because acquiring the asset at its fair market value is a zero-NPV transaction.

- In a **$1.00 out lease** (also known as a finance lease), ownership of the asset transfers to the lessee at the end of the lease for a nominal cost of $1.00. Thus the lessee will continue to have use of the asset for its entire economic life. The lessee has effectively purchased the asset by making the lease payments. As a result, this type of lease is in many ways equivalent to financing the asset with a standard loan.

---

3. For a theoretical analysis of competitive lease pricing, see Merton Miller and Charles Upton, "Leasing, Buying, and the Cost of Capital Services," *Journal of Finance* 31(3) (1976): 761–786; and Wilbur Lewellen, Michael Long, and John McConnell, "Asset Leasing in Competitive Capital Markets," *Journal of Finance* 31(3) (1976): 787–798.

Calculating Auto Lease Payments

Rather than use the annuity formula to calculate the lease payments, as we did in Example 25.1, in many cases practitioners use the following approximation to calculate the lease payments

$$L = \underbrace{\frac{\text{Purchase Price} - \text{Residual Value}}{\text{Term}}}_{\text{Avg. Depreciation}}$$

$$+ \underbrace{\left(\frac{\text{Purchase Price} + \text{Residual Value}}{2} \right) \times \text{Interest Rate}}_{\text{Financing Cost}}$$

where the purchase price includes any fees charged on the lease (and is net of any down payment), the term is the number of payment periods, and the interest rate is for a payment period. The idea behind this approximation is that the first term is the average depreciation over a payment period and the second term is the interest cost associated with the average value of the asset. The sum is what you have to pay to use the asset over one payment period.

Despite its simplicity, this formula is very accurate for lease terms up to five years and interest rates up to 10%.

Using it to calculate the lease payments in Example 25.1 gives

$$\frac{20,000 - 6000}{48} + \left(\frac{20,000 + 6000}{2} \right) \times 0.005$$

$$= \$356.67$$

which is within $1 of the amount calculated in Example 25.1.

This approximation for the lease payment is used to calculate the payment on automobile leases. In that case the formula is often stated as

$$L = \frac{\text{Purchase Price} - \text{Residual Value}}{\text{Term}}$$

$$+ (\text{Purchase Price} + \text{Residual Value}) \times \text{Money Factor}$$

leaving many first-time car lessees wondering why they have to pay interest on *both* the purchase price and the residual value. In reality, all that has happened is that the factor of 2 is subsumed into the money factor; that is, the money factor is half the interest rate.

- In a **fixed price lease**, the lessee has the option to purchase the asset at the end of the lease for a fixed price that is set upfront in the lease contract. This type of lease is very common for consumer leases (such as for autos). Notice that this kind of lease gives the lessee an option: At the end of the lease, if the market value of the asset exceeds the fixed price, the lessee can buy the asset at below its market value; if the market value of the asset does not exceed the fixed price, however, the leasee can walk away from the lease and purchase the asset for less money elsewhere. Consequently, the lessor will set a higher lease rate to compensate for the value of this option to the lessee.

- In a **fair market value cap lease**, the lessee can purchase the asset at the minimum of its fair market value and a fixed price (the "cap"). The lessee has the same option as in a fixed price lease, although the option in this case is easier to exercise because the lessee does not have to find a similar asset elsewhere to buy when the fixed price exceeds the market value.

Lease Payments and End-of-Lease Options

Problem

Compute the lease payments for the forklift lease of Example 25.1 if the lease is (a) a fair market value lease, (b) a $1.00 out lease, or (c) a fixed price lease that allows the lessee to buy the asset at the end of the lease for $4000.

Solution

With the FMV lease, the lessee can buy the forklift for its fair market value of $6000 at the end of the lease. The lessor obtains a residual value of $6000, either from the forklift itself or from the payment from the lessee. Thus the lease payments will be unchanged from Example 25.1, or $357 per month.

With the $1.00 out lease, the lessor receives essentially no residual value. Thus the lease payments themselves will have to compensate the lessor for the full $20,000 purchase price. The lease payments are therefore

$$L = \frac{20,000}{1 + \frac{1}{0.005}\left(1 - \frac{1}{1.005^{47}}\right)} = \$467.36 \text{ per month}$$

These payments are slightly less than the loan payments of $470 per month calculated in Example 25.1 because the lease payments occur at the beginning—rather than the end—of the month.

With the fixed price lease, because the forklift will be worth $6000 for certain, the lessee will exercise the option to purchase it for $4000. As a result, the lessor will receive only $4000 at the end of the lease. For the lease to have an NPV of zero, the present value of the lease payments must be $20,000 − $4000 / 1.005^{48} = \$16,851.61$. Therefore, the lease payment will be

$$L = \frac{16,851.61}{1 + \frac{1}{0.005}\left(1 - \frac{1}{1.005^{47}}\right)} = \$393.79 \text{ per month}$$

This payment exceeds that of the FMV lease due to the lessee's ability to profit at the end of the lease.

Other Lease Provisions

Leases are privately negotiated contracts and can contain many more provisions than are described here. For example, they may include early cancellation options that allow the lessee to end the lease early (perhaps for a fee). They may contain buyout options that allow the lessee to purchase the asset before the end of the lease term. Clauses may allow the lessee to trade in and upgrade the equipment to a newer model at certain points in the lease. Each lease agreement can be tailored to fit the precise nature of the asset and the needs of the parties at hand.

These features of leases will be priced as part of the lease payment. Terms that give valuable options to the lessee raise the amount of the lease payments, whereas terms that restrict these options will lower them. Absent market imperfections, leases represent another form of zero-NPV financing available to a firm, and the Modigliani-Miller propositions apply: Leases neither increase nor decrease firm value, but serve only to divide the firm's cash flows and risks in different ways.[4]

---

4. For an analysis of options embedded in lease contracts, see John McConnell and James Schallheim, "Valuation of Asset Leasing Contracts," *Journal of Financial Economics* 12(2) (1983): 237–261; and Steven Grenadier, "Valuing Lease Contracts: A Real-Options Approach," *Journal of Financial Economics* 38(3) (1995): 297–331.

CONCEPT CHECK 1. In a perfect capital market, how is the amount of a lease payment determined?

2. What types of lease options would raise the amount of the lease payment?

25.2 Accounting, Tax, and Legal Consequences of Leasing

We have seen that with perfect capital markets, leasing represents yet another zero-NPV financing alternative for a firm. Thus the decision to lease is often driven by real-world market imperfections related to leasing's accounting, tax, and legal treatment.[5] In particular, when a firm leases an asset, a number of important questions arise: Should the firm list the asset on its balance sheet and deduct depreciation expenses? Should the firm list the lease as a liability? Can the lease payments be deducted for tax purposes? In the event of bankruptcy, is the leased asset protected from creditors? As we will see in this section, the answers to these questions depend on how the lease is structured.

Lease Accounting

When publicly traded firms disclose leasing transactions in their financial statements, they must follow the recommendations of the Financial Accounting Standards Board (FASB). For lessees, the FASB distinguishes two types of leases based on the lease terms, and this classification determines the lease's accounting treatment:

- An **operating lease** is viewed as a rental for accounting purposes. In this case, the lessee reports the entire lease payment as an operating expense. The lessee does not deduct a

Operating Leases at Alaska Air Group

Alaska Air Group, Inc., was incorporated in 1985 as a holding company with two main subsidiaries: Alaska Airlines, Inc., and Horizon Air Industries. Alaska Airlines is a major airline with flights throughout the United States. Horizon Air is a regional airline concentrated in the Pacific Northwest. Typical for airlines, Alaska Air Group leases many of its aircraft, as is summarized in the following table:

	Owned	Leased	Total
Alaska Airlines	60	48	108
Horizon Air	3	62	65

Source: Alaska Air Group, Inc., December 2004 10-K.

Alaska Airlines leases almost half of its aircraft, and Horizon leases nearly all of its aircraft. These leases are almost exclusively operating leases. (In many cases, the lessors are trusts established by a third party specifically to purchase, finance, and lease aircraft to Alaska.) In addition, Alaska leases the majority of its airport and terminal facilities.

Because these leases are operating leases, Alaska Air Group reports the entire lease payment as an operating expense. During 2004, Alaska Air reported aircraft rent expense of $187.4 million relative to operating revenues of $2.7 billion. The firm did not deduct a depreciation expense for its leased aircraft, and these aircraft did not show up as an asset on its balance sheet (although Alaska Air does report the value of the aircraft that it owns as assets on its balance sheet). And though the lease obligations are not listed as a liability, if they were they would more than double Alaska Air's reported debt.

---

5. Anyone who has ever considered leasing a car will be familiar with one such imperfection. In most states, lessees do not pay sales tax on the purchase price of the car, only on the lease payments, which usually means lessees can avoid paying a substantial part of the sales tax purchasers must pay.

depreciation expense for the asset and does not report the asset, or the lease payment liability, on its balance sheet. Operating leases are disclosed in the footnotes of the lessee's financial statements.

- A **capital lease** (also called a **finance lease**) is viewed as an acquisition for accounting purposes. The asset acquired is listed on the lessee's balance sheet, and the lessee incurs depreciation expenses for the asset. In addition, the present value of the future lease payments is listed as a liability, and the interest portion of the lease payment is deducted as an interest expense.[6]

The different accounting treatment for each type of lease will affect the firm's balance sheet as well as its debt-equity ratio, as shown in Example 25.4.

EXAMPLE 25.4

Leasing and the Balance Sheet

Problem
Harbord Cruise Lines currently has the following balance sheet (in millions of dollars):

Assets		Liabilities	
Cash	100	Debt	900
Property, Plant, and Equipment	1,500	Equity	700
Total Assets	1,600	**Total Debt plus Equity**	1,600

Harbord is about to add a new fleet of cruise ships. The price of the fleet is $400 million. What will Harbord's balance sheet look like if (a) it purchases the fleet by borrowing the $400 million, (b) it acquires the fleet through a $400 million capital lease, or (c) it acquires the fleet through an operating lease?

Solution
For parts (a) and (b), the balance sheet consequences are the same: The fleet becomes a new asset of the firm, and the $400 million becomes an additional liability.

Assets		Liabilities	
Cash	100	Debt	1300
Property, Plant, and Equipment	1,900	Equity	700
Total Assets	2,000	**Total Debt plus Equity**	2,000

Note that the firm's debt-equity ratio increases in this case (from $900 / 700 = 1.29$ to $1300 / 700 = 1.86$).

If the fleet is acquired through an operating lease, as described in part (c), there is no change in the original balance sheet: The fleet is not listed as an asset, and the lease is not viewed as a liability. Thus the apparent leverage ratio is unchanged.

Because capital leases increase the apparent leverage on the firm's balance sheet, firms sometimes prefer to have a lease categorized as an operating lease to keep it off the balance sheet. In its Statement of Financial Accounting Standards No. 13 (FAS13), the FASB

---

6. The accounting treatment of a capital lease for the lessor will depend on whether it is a sales-type lease, a direct lease, or a leveraged lease (a direct lease in which the lessor obtains more than 60% debt financing to purchase the asset, and the debt is non-recourse in that it is backed solely by the income from the asset).

provides specific criteria that distinguish an operating lease from a capital lease. The lease is treated as a capital lease for the lessee and must be listed on the firm's balance sheet if it satisfies any of the following conditions:

1. Title to the property transfers to the lessee at the end of the lease term.
2. The lease contains an option to purchase the asset at a bargain price that is substantially less than its fair market value.
3. The lease term is 75% or more of the estimated economic life of the asset.
4. The present value of the minimum lease payments at the start of the lease is 90% or more of the asset's fair market value.

These conditions are designed to identify situations in which the lease provides the lessee with use of the asset for a large fraction of its useful life. For example, $1.00 out leases satisfy the second condition and so would be ruled a capital lease for accounting purposes. Firms that prefer to keep a lease off-balance-sheet will often structure lease contracts to avoid these conditions.

EXAMPLE 25.5

Operating Versus Capital Leases

Problem

Consider a seven-year fair market value lease for a $12.5 million Gulfstream Jet with a remaining useful life of ten years. Suppose the monthly lease payments are $175,000 and the appropriate discount rate is a 6% APR with monthly compounding. Would this lease be classified as an operating lease or a capital lease for the lessee? What if the lease contract gave the lessee the option to cancel the contract after five years?

Solution

We compute the present value of the monthly lease payments at the beginning of the lease using the annuity formula with a monthly interest rate of 6% / 12 = 0.5% and $7 \times 12 - 1 = 83$ monthly payments after the initial payment. Thus,

$$PV(\text{Lease Payments}) = 175,000 \times \left[1 + \frac{1}{0.005}\left(1 - \frac{1}{1.005^{83}} \right) \right] = \$12.04 \text{ million}$$

Because the present value of the lease payments is 12.04 / 12.50 = 96.3% of the value of the jet, the lease satisfies condition 4 and so it is a capital lease.

If the lessee can cancel the contract after five years, then the minimum number of lease payments is 60 under the contract. In this case,

$$PV(\text{Lease Payments}) = 175,000 \times \left[1 + \frac{1}{0.005}\left(1 - \frac{1}{1.005^{59}} \right) \right] = \$9.10 \text{ million}$$

This is only 9.10 / 12.5 = 73% of the value of the jet. As no other conditions for a capital lease are satisfied, the lease would be classified as an operating lease.

The Tax Treatment of Leases

The categories used to report leases on the financial statements affect the values of assets on the balance sheet, but they have no direct effect on the cash flows that result from a leasing transaction. The IRS has its own classification rules that determine the tax treatment of a lease. Because the tax treatment does affect the cash flows, these rules are more significant from a financial valuation perspective.

The IRS separates leases into two broad categories: true tax leases and non-tax leases. These categories are roughly equivalent to operating and capital leases, although the defining criteria are not identical.

In a **true tax lease**, the lessor receives the depreciation deductions associated with the ownership of the asset. The lessee can deduct the full amount of the lease payments as an operating expense, and these lease payments are treated as revenue for the lessor.

Although the legal ownership of the asset resides with the lessor, in a **non-tax lease** the lessee receives the depreciation deductions. The lessee can also deduct the interest portion of the lease payments as an interest expense. The interest portion of the lease payment is interest income for the lessor.

IRS Revenue Ruling 55-540 provides the conditions that determine the tax classification of a lease. If the lease satisfies any of these conditions, it is treated as a non-tax lease:

1. The lessee obtains equity in the leased asset.

2. The lessee receives ownership of the asset on completion of all lease payments.

3. The total amount that the lessee is required to pay for a relatively short period of use constitutes an inordinately large proportion of the total value of the asset.

4. The lease payments greatly exceed the current fair rental value of the asset.

5. The property may be acquired at a bargain price in relation to the fair market value of the asset at the time when the option may be exercised.

6. Some portion of the lease payments is specifically designated as interest or its equivalent.[7]

As with the accounting criteria, these rules attempt to identify cases in which a lease is likely to provide the lessee with use of the asset for a large fraction of its useful life. These rules are somewhat vague and are designed to provide the IRS with sufficient latitude to prevent the use of leases solely for tax avoidance.

For example, suppose a $200,000 asset was required to be depreciated by $20,000 per year for ten years for tax purposes. By acquiring the asset through a four-year $1.00 out lease with payments of $50,000 per year, a firm could receive the same $200,000 total deduction at a faster rate if the lease were categorized as a true tax lease.[8] The IRS rules prevent this type of transaction by categorizing such a lease as a non-tax lease (via conditions 3 and 5).

Leases and Bankruptcy

Recall from Chapter 16 that when a firm files for bankruptcy under Chapter 11 of the U.S. bankruptcy code, its assets are protected from seizure by the firm's creditors while existing management is given the opportunity to propose a reorganization plan. Even secured lenders are prevented from taking the assets that serve as collateral for their loans

---

7. IRS Revenue Ruling 55-540, 1955. Additional considerations exist for the tax treatment for the lessor if the lease is a leveraged lease.

8. This transaction would have the opposite tax consequence for the lessor: The lease payments would be taxed as revenues, but the cost of the asset would be depreciated at the slower rate. However, there can be an advantage if the lessor is in a lower tax bracket than the lessee.

Synthetic Leases

Synthetic leases are designed to be treated as an operating lease for accounting purposes and as a non-tax lease for tax purposes. With a synthetic lease, the lessee is able to deduct depreciation and interest expenses for tax purposes, just as if it had borrowed to purchase the asset, but does not need to report the asset or the debt on its balance sheet.

To obtain this accounting and tax treatment, synthetic leases have typically been structured by creating a special-purpose entity that will act as the lessor and obtain financing, acquire the asset, and lease it to the firm. To ensure that the lease qualifies as an operating lease, the lease is structured so that it (1) provides a fixed purchase price at the end of the lease term based on an initial appraised value (and so is not a bargain price), (2) has a term less than 75% of the economic life of the asset (which is renewable under certain conditions), and (3) has minimum lease payments with a present value less than 90% of the fair value of the property. In addition, to avoid balance sheet consolidation, the owner of record of the SPE must make an initial minimum equity investment of 3% that remains at risk during the entire lease term. The

lease can qualify as a non-tax lease by designating some portion of the lease payments as interest.

A major motivation for such leases appears to be that they allow firms to use debt while avoiding the accounting consequences of debt. In particular, by keeping the debt off the balance sheet, the firm's debt-equity ratio is improved, its return on assets is generally raised, and, if the lease payments are less than the interest and depreciation expenses, its reported earnings per share will be higher.

These types of transactions were used and abused by Enron Corporation to boost its earnings and hide its liabilities prior to its downfall. In the wake of the Enron scandal, the FASB has significantly tightened the requirements for SPEs, raising the at-risk equity investment of the SPE to 10% and requiring that ownership truly be independent from the lessor. Investors have also reacted skeptically to such deals, forcing many firms to avoid synthetic leases or unwind structures that were already in place. For example, in 2002, Krispy Kreme Doughnuts Corporation reversed its decision to use a synthetic lease to fund a new $35 million plant after an article critical of the transaction was published in *Forbes* magazine.

---

during this period, which can last from a few months to several years. Instead, bankruptcy law permits the firm to continue to use the assets in an effort to remain a going concern.

The treatment of leased property in bankruptcy will depend on whether the lease is classified as a security interest or a true lease by the bankruptcy judge. If the lease is deemed to be a **security interest**, the firm is assumed to have effective ownership of the asset and the asset is protected against seizure. The lessor is then treated as any other secured creditor and must await the firm's reorganization or ultimate liquidation.

If the lease is classified as a **true lease** in bankruptcy, then the lessor retains ownership rights over the asset. Within 120 days of filing Chapter 11, the bankrupt firm must choose whether to assume or reject the lease. If it assumes the lease, it must settle all pending claims and continue to make all promised lease payments. If it rejects the lease, the asset must be returned to the lessor (with any pending claims of the lessor becoming unsecured claims against the bankrupt firm).

Thus, if a lease contract is characterized as a true lease in bankruptcy, the lessor is in a somewhat superior position than a lender if the firm defaults. By retaining ownership of the asset, the lessor has the right to repossess it if the lease payments are not made, even if the firm seeks bankruptcy protection. While a benefit to the lessor, this right of repossession limits the options for the firm in the event of financial distress.[9]

---

9. For an analysis of the consequences of this treatment of leases for a firm's borrowing capacity, see A. Eisfeldt and A. Rampini, "Leasing, Ability to Repossess, and Debt Capacity," working paper, Northwestern University, 2005.

Whether a transaction is classified as a true lease or a security interest will depend on the facts of each case, but the distinction is very similar to the accounting and tax distinctions made earlier. Operating and true tax leases are generally viewed as true leases by the courts, whereas capital and non-tax leases are more likely to be viewed as a security interest. In particular, leases for which the lessee obtains possession of the asset for its remaining economic life (either within the contract or through an option to renew or purchase at a nominal charge) are generally deemed security interests.[10]

CONCEPT CHECK

1. How is a $1.00 out lease characterized for accounting and tax purposes?

2. Is it possible for a lease to be treated as an operating lease for accounting purposes and as a non-tax lease for tax purposes?

25.3 The Leasing Decision

How should a firm decide whether to buy or lease an asset? Recall that in a perfect market the decision is irrelevant, so the real-world decision depends on market frictions. In this section, we consider one important market friction—taxes—and evaluate the financial consequences of the leasing decision from the perspective of the lessee. We show how to determine whether it is more attractive to lease an asset or to buy it and (potentially) finance the purchase with debt. First we consider a true tax lease, and then we turn to non-tax leases at the end of the section.

Cash Flows for a True Tax Lease

If a firm purchases a piece of equipment, the expense is a capital expenditure. Therefore, the purchase price can be depreciated over time, generating a depreciation tax shield. If the equipment is leased and the lease is a true tax lease, there is no capital expenditure, but the lease payments are an operating expense.

Let's compare the cash flows arising from a true tax lease with those arising from a purchase using an example. Emory Printing needs a new high-speed printing press. It can purchase one for $50,000 in cash. The machine will last five years, and it will be depreciated for tax purposes using straight-line depreciation over that period.[11] This means that Emory can deduct $10,000 per year for depreciation. Given its tax rate of 35%, Emory will therefore save $3500 per year in taxes from the depreciation deduction.

Alternatively, Emory can lease the machine instead of purchasing it. A five-year lease contract will cost $12,500 per year. Emory must make these payments at the beginning of each year. Because the lease is a true tax lease, Emory deducts the lease payments as an operating expense when they are paid. Thus the after-tax cost of each lease payment is $(1 - 35\%) \times 12,500 = \$8125$. The lease contract does not provide for maintenance or servicing of the machine, so these costs are identical whether the machine is leased or purchased.

Table 25.1 shows the free cash flow consequences of buying and leasing. Here we consider only the cash flows that differ as a result of leasing versus buying. We do not need to consider cash flows that would be the same in both situations, such as the sales revenues

---

10. See Article 1 of the Uniform Commercial Code, Section 1-203 at http://www.law.upenn.edu/bll/ulc/ulc.htm#ucc1

11. In practice, a more accelerated depreciation schedule would be used for tax purposes. We use straight-line depreciation here for simplicity.

TABLE 25.1 SPREADSHEET — Cash Flow ($) Consequences from Leasing Versus Buying

Year	0	1	2	3	4	5
Buy						
1 Capital Expenditures	(50,000)	—	—	—	—	—
2 Depreciation Tax Shield at 35%	—	3,500	3,500	3,500	3,500	3,500
3 Free Cash Flow (Buy)	(50,000)	3,500	3,500	3,500	3,500	3,500
Lease						
4 Lease Payments	(12,500)	(12,500)	(12,500)	(12,500)	(12,500)	—
5 Income Tax Savings at 35%	4,375	4,375	4,375	4,375	4,375	—
6 Free Cash Flow (Lease)	(8,125)	(8,125)	(8,125)	(8,125)	(8,125)	—

generated by having the machine and maintenance expenses. We have also assumed the machine has no residual value after five years if it is purchased. If any of these differences existed, we would include them in the cash flows. Recall from Eq. 7.6 of Chapter 7 that free cash flow can be calculated as EBITDA less taxes, capital expenditures and increases in networking capital, plus the depreciation tax shield (i.e., tax rate × depreciation expense). Thus, if Emory buys, the only change to FCF is from capital expenditures and the depreciation tax shield, and if Emory leases, the only change is a reduction in EBITDA, and therefore taxes, from the lease payment.

Note that the cash flows of leasing differ from buying. A purchase requires a large initial outlay followed by a series of depreciation tax credits. In contrast, the cost of a leased machine is more evenly spread over time.

Lease Versus Buy (An Unfair Comparison)

Is it better for Emory to lease or buy the printing press? To begin to answer this question, let's compare the present value of the cash flows in each transaction (or, equivalently, we can compute the NPV of the difference between the cash flows). To compute the present value, we need to determine the cost of capital.

The appropriate cost of capital depends, of course, on the risk of the cash flows. Lease payments are a fixed obligation of the firm. If Emory fails to make the lease payments, it will default on the lease. The lessor will seek the remaining lease payments and, in addition, will take back the printing press. In that sense, a lease is similar to loan secured with the leased asset as collateral. Moreover, as discussed in Section 25.2, in a true lease the lessor is in an even better position than a secured creditor if the firm files for bankruptcy. Thus *the risk of the lease payments is no greater than the risk of secured debt*, so it is reasonable to discount the lease payments at the firm's secured borrowing rate.

The tax savings from the lease payments and from depreciation expenses are also low-risk cash flows, as they are predetermined and will be realized as long as the firm generates positive income.[12] Therefore, a common assumption in practice is to use the firm's borrowing rate for these cash flows as well.

If Emory's borrowing rate is 8%, the cost of buying the machine has present value

$$PV(\text{Buy}) = -50,000 + \frac{3500}{1.08} + \frac{3500}{1.08^2} + \frac{3500}{1.08^3} + \frac{3500}{1.08^4} + \frac{3500}{1.08^5} = -\$36,026$$

---

12. Even if income is negative, these tax benefits may still be obtained through carryback or carryforward provisions that allow the firm to apply these credits against income that was generated in past or future years.

The cost of leasing the machine has present value

$$PV(\text{Lease}) - -8125 \quad \frac{8125}{1.08} \quad \frac{8125}{1.08^2} - \frac{8125}{1.08^3} - \frac{8125}{1.08^4} - -\$35,036$$

Thus leasing is cheaper than buying, with a net savings of $\$36,026 - \$35,036 = \$990$.

The preceding analysis ignores an important point, however. When a firm enters into a lease, it is committing to lease payments that are a fixed future obligation of the firm. If the firm is in financial distress and cannot make the lease payments, the lessor can seize the machine. Moreover, the lease obligations themselves could trigger financial distress. Therefore, when a firm leases an asset, it is effectively adding leverage to its capital structure (whether or not the lease appears on the balance sheet for accounting purposes).

Because leasing is a form of financing, we should compare it to other financing options that Emory may have. Rather than buy the asset outright, Emory could borrow funds to finance the purchase of the machine, thus matching the leverage of the lease. If Emory does borrow, it will also benefit from the interest tax shield provided by leverage. This tax advantage may make borrowing to buy the machine more attractive than leasing. Thus, to evaluate a lease correctly, we should compare it to purchasing the asset using an equivalent amount of leverage. In other words, the appropriate comparison is not lease versus buy, but rather lease versus borrow.

Lease Versus Borrow (The Right Comparison)

To compare leasing to borrowing, we must determine the amount of the loan that leads to the same level of fixed obligations that Emory would have with the lease. We call this loan the **lease-equivalent loan**. That is, the lease-equivalent loan is the loan that is required on the purchase of the asset that leaves the purchaser with the same obligations as the lessee would have.[13]

The Lease-Equivalent Loan. To compute the lease-equivalent loan in Emory's case, we first compute the difference between the cash flows from leasing versus buying, which we refer to as the incremental free cash flow of leasing. As Table 25.2 shows, relative to buying, leasing saves cash upfront but results in lower future cash flows. The incremental free cash flow in years 1 through 5 represents the effective leverage the firm takes on by leasing. Alternatively, Emory could take on this same leverage by purchasing the printing press and taking on a loan with these same after-tax debt payments. How much could Emory borrow by taking on such a loan? Because the future incremental cash flows are

| | | TABLE 25.2 SPREADSHEET | **Incremental Free Cash Flows of Leasing Versus Buying** | | | | | |

Year	0	1	2	3	4	5
Lease vs. Buy ($)						
1 FCF Lease (Line 6, Table 25.1)	(8,125)	(8,125)	(8,125)	(8,125)	(8,125)	—
2 Less: FCF Buy (Line 3, Table 25.1)	50,000	(3,500)	(3,500)	(3,500)	(3,500)	(3,500)
3 Lease–Buy	41,875	(11,625)	(11,625)	(11,625)	(11,625)	(3,500)

13. See Stewart Myers, David Dill, and Alberto Bautista, "Valuation of Financial Lease Contracts," *Journal of Finance* 31(3) (1976): 799–819, for a development of this method.

the after-tax payments Emory will make on the loan, the initial balance on the lease-equivalent loan is the present value of these cash flows using Emory's after-tax cost of debt:

$$\text{Loan Balance} = PV\,[\text{Future FCF of Lease Versus Buy at } r_D(1 - \tau_c)] \quad (25.4)$$

Using Emory's after-tax borrowing cost of 8% $(1 - 35\%) = 5.2\%$, the initial loan balance is

$$\text{Loan Balance} = \frac{11{,}625}{1.052} + \frac{11{,}625}{1.052^2} + \frac{11{,}625}{1.052^3} + \frac{11{,}625}{1.052^4} + \frac{3500}{1.052^5} = \$43{,}747 \quad (25.5)$$

Eq. 25.5 implies that if Emory is willing to take on the future obligations implied by leasing, it could instead buy the printing press and borrow $43,747. This exceeds the savings in year 0 from leasing of $41,875 shown in Table 25.2. Thus, by buying and borrowing using the lease-equivalent loan, Emory saves an additional $43,747 − 41,875 = $1872 initially, and so leasing the machine is unattractive relative to this alternative.

We verify this result explicitly in the spreadsheet in Table 25.3. There we compute the cash flows that result from buying the machine and borrowing using the lease-equivalent loan. Line 1 shows the lease-equivalent loan balance, which we compute at each date by applying Eq. 25.4. Line 2 shows the initial borrowing and principal payments of the loan (computed as the change in the loan balance from the prior year). Line 3 shows the interest due each year (8% of the prior loan balance), and line 4 computes the interest tax shield (35% of the interest amount). Line 5 then totals the after-tax cash flows of the loan, which we combine with the free cash flow from buying the printing press, to compute the total cash flow from buying and borrowing on line 7.

TABLE 25.3 SPREADSHEET

Cash Flows from Buying and Borrowing Using the Lease-Equivalent Loan

	Year	0	1	2	3	4	5
Lease–Equivalent Loan ($)							
1	Loan Balance (PV at 5.2%)	43,747	34,397	24,561	14,213	3,327	—
Buy with Lease Equivalent Loan ($)							
2	Net Borrowing (Repayment)	43,747	(9,350)	(9,836)	(10,348)	(10,886)	(3,327)
3	Interest (at 8%)		(3,500)	(2,752)	(1,965)	(1,137)	(266)
4	Interest Tax Shield at 35%		1,225	963	688	398	93
5	Cash Flows of Loan (After-tax)	43,747	(11,625)	(11,625)	(11,625)	(11,625)	(3,500)
6	FCF Buy	(50,000)	3,500	3,500	3,500	3,500	3,500
7	Cash Flows of Borrow + Buy	(6,253)	(8,125)	(8,125)	(8,125)	(8,125)	—

Comparing the cash flows from buying the printing press and financing it with the lease-equivalent loan (line 7 of Table 25.3) with the cash flows of the lease (e.g., line 1 of Table 25.2), we see that in both cases Emory has a net future obligation of $8125 per year for four years. But while the leverage is the same for the two strategies, the initial cash flow is not. With the lease, Emory will pay $8125 initially; with the loan, Emory will pay the purchase price of the printing press minus the amount borrowed, or $50,000 − $43,747 = $6253. Again we see that borrowing to buy the machine is cheaper than the lease, with a savings of $8125 − $6253 = $1872. For Emory, the lease is not attractive.

If Emory is willing to take on that much leverage, it would be better off doing so by borrowing to purchase the printing press, rather than leasing it.

A Direct Method. Now that we have seen the role of the lease-equivalent loan, we can use the tools of Chapter 18 to directly compare leasing with an equivalent debt-financed purchase. Recall from Chapter 18 that when the cash flows of an investment will be offset completely with leverage, the appropriate weighted average cost of capital is given by $r_U - \tau_c r_D$, where r_U is the unlevered cost of capital for the investment. Because the incremental cash flows from leasing versus borrowing are relatively safe, $r_U = r_D$ and so $r_{wacc} = r_D(1 - \tau_c)$. Thus *we can compare leasing to buying the asset using equivalent leverage by discounting the incremental cash flows of leasing versus buying using the after-tax borrowing rate.*

In Emory's case, discounting the incremental free cash flow in Table 25.2 at Emory's after-tax borrowing cost of $8\% \times (1 - 35\%) = 5.2\%$, we get

$$PV(\text{Lease Versus Borrow}) = 41{,}875 - \frac{11{,}625}{1.052} - \frac{11{,}625}{1.052^2} - \frac{11{,}625}{1.052^3} - \frac{11{,}625}{1.052^4} - \frac{3500}{1.052^5}$$

$$= -\$1872$$

Notice this is precisely the difference we calculated earlier.

The Effective After-Tax Lease Borrowing Rate. We can also compare leasing and buying in terms of an effective after-tax borrowing rate associated with the lease. This is given by the IRR of the incremental lease cash flows in Table 25.2, which we can calculate as 7.0%:

$$41{,}875 - \frac{11{,}625}{1.07} - \frac{11{,}625}{1.07^2} - \frac{11{,}625}{1.07^3} - \frac{11{,}625}{1.07^4} - \frac{3500}{1.07^5} = 0$$

Thus the lease is equivalent to borrowing at an after-tax rate of 7%. This option is not attractive compared to the after-tax rate of only $8\% \times (1 - 35\%) = 5.2\%$ that Emory pays on its debt. Because we are borrowing (positive followed by negative cash flows), a lower IRR is better. But be careful with this approach—as discussed in Chapter 6, if the cash flows alternate signs more than once, the IRR method cannot be relied upon.

Evaluating a True Tax Lease

In sum, when evaluating a true-tax lease, we should compare leasing to a purchase that is financed with equivalent leverage. We suggest the following approach:

1. Compute the *incremental cash flows* for leasing versus buying, as we did in Table 25.2. Include the depreciation tax shield (if buying) and the tax deductibility of the lease payments if leasing.

2. Compute the NPV of leasing versus buying using equivalent leverage by discounting the incremental cash flows at the *after-tax borrowing rate.*

If the NPV computed in step 2 is negative, then leasing is unattractive compared to traditional debt financing. In this case, the firm should not lease, but rather should acquire the asset using an optimal amount of leverage (based on the tradeoffs and techniques discussed in Parts V and VI of the text).

If the NPV computed in step 2 is positive, then leasing does provide an advantage over traditional debt financing and should be considered. Management should recognize, however, that while it may not be listed on the balance sheet, the lease increases the firm's effective leverage by the amount of the lease-equivalent loan.[14]

Evaluating New Lease Terms

Problem

Suppose Emory rejects the lease we analyzed, and the lessor agrees to lower the lease rate to $11,800 per year. Does this change make the lease attractive?

Solution

The incremental cash flows are shown in the following table:

	Year	0	1	2	3	4	5
Buy							
1	Capital Expenditures	(50,000)	—	—	—	—	—
2	Depreciation Tax Shield at 35%	—	3,500	3,500	3,500	3,500	3,500
3	Free Cash Flow (Buy)	(50,000)	3,500	3,500	3,500	3,500	3,500
Lease							
4	Lease Payments	(11,800)	(11,800)	(11,800)	(11,800)	(11,800)	—
5	Income Tax Savings at 35%	4,130	4,130	4,130	4,130	4,130	—
6	Free Cash Flow (Lease)	(7,670)	(7,670)	(7,670)	(7,670)	(7,670)	—
Lease vs. Buy							
7	Lease–Buy	42,330	(11,170)	(11,170)	(11,170)	(11,170)	(3,500)

Using Emory's after-tax borrowing cost of 5.2%, the gain from leasing versus an equivalently leveraged purchase is

$$NPV(\text{Lease Versus Borrow}) = 42,330 - \frac{11,170}{1.052} - \frac{11,170}{1.052^2} - \frac{11,170}{1.052^3} - \frac{11,170}{1.052^4} - \frac{3500}{1.052^5}$$

$$= 42,330 - 42,141$$

$$= \$189$$

Therefore, the lease is attractive at the new terms.

Evaluating a Non-tax Lease

Evaluating a non-tax lease is much more straightforward than evaluating a true tax lease. For a non-tax lease, the lessee still receives the depreciation deductions (as though the asset was purchased). Only the interest portion of the lease payment is deductible, however. Thus, in terms of cash flows, a non-tax lease is directly comparable to a traditional loan. It is therefore attractive if it offers a better interest rate than would be available with a loan. To determine whether it does offer a better rate, we can discount the lease payments at the firm's *pretax* borrowing rate and compare it to the purchase price of the asset.

---

14. If financial distress or other costs of leverage are large, the firm may wish to offset some of this increase in leverage by reducing other debt of the firm.

EXAMPLE
25.7

Comparing a Non-tax Lease with a Standard Loan

Problem

Suppose the lease in Example 25.6 is a non-tax lease. Would it be attractive for Emory in this case?

Solution

Instead of purchasing the machine for $50,000, Emory will pay lease payments of $11,800 per year. That is, Emory is effectively borrowing $50,000 by making payments of $11,800 per year. Given Emory's 8% borrowing rate, payments of $11,800 per year on a standard loan would allow Emory to borrow

$$PV(\text{Lease Payments}) = 11{,}800 + \frac{11{,}800}{1.08} + \frac{11{,}800}{1.08^2} + \frac{11{,}800}{1.08^3} + \frac{11{,}800}{1.08^4} = \$50{,}883$$

That is, by making the same payments on a loan, Emory could raise more than $50,000. Thus the lease is not attractive at these terms if it is a non-tax lease.

For both the true tax lease and the non-tax lease, we have ignored the residual value of the asset, any differences in the maintenance and service arrangements with a lease versus a purchase, and any cancellation or other lease options. If these features are present, they should also be included when comparing leasing versus a debt-financed purchase.

CONCEPT CHECK

1. Why is it inappropriate to compare leasing to buying?

2. What discount rate should be used for the incremental lease cash flows to compare a true tax lease to borrowing?

3. How can we compare a non-tax lease to borrowing?

25.4 Reasons for Leasing

In Section 25.3, we saw how to determine whether a lease is attractive for the potential lessee. A similar, but reverse argument can be used from the standpoint of the lessor. The lessor could compare leasing the equipment to lending the money to the firm so that it can purchase the equipment. Under what circumstances would leasing be profitable for both the lessor and the lessee? If a lease is a good deal for one of the parties, is it a bad deal for the other? Or are there underlying economic sources of value in a lease contract?

Valid Arguments for Leasing

For a lease to be attractive to both the lessee and the lessor, the gains must come from some underlying economic benefits that the leasing arrangement provides. Here we consider some valid reasons for leasing.

Tax Differences. With a true tax lease, the lessee replaces depreciation and interest tax deductions with a deduction for the lease payments. Depending on the timing of the payments, one set of deductions will have a larger present value. A tax gain occurs if the lease shifts the more valuable deductions to the party with the higher tax rate. Generally speaking, if the asset's tax depreciation deductions are more rapid than its lease payments, a true tax lease is advantageous if the lessor is in a higher tax bracket than the lessee. In contrast, if the asset's tax depreciation deductions are slower than its lease payments, there are tax gains from a true tax lease if the lessor is in a lower tax bracket than the lessee.

EXAMPLE
25.8

Exploiting Tax Differences Through Leasing

Problem
Suppose Emory is offered a true tax lease for the printing press at a lease rate of $11,800 per year. Show that this lease is profitable for Emory as well as for a lessor with a 15% tax rate and an 8% borrowing cost.

Solution
We already evaluated the lease with these terms in Example 25.6. There we found that the NPV of leasing versus borrowing was $189 for Emory. Now let's consider the lease from the standpoint of the lessor. The lessor will buy the printing press and then lease it to Emory. The incremental cash flows for the lessor from buying and leasing are as follows:

	Year	0	1	2	3	4	5
Buy							
1	Capital Expenditures	(50,000)	—	—	—	—	—
2	Depreciation Tax Shield at 15%	—	1,500	1,500	1,500	1,500	1,500
3	Free Cash Flow (Buy)	(50,000)	1,500	1,500	1,500	1,500	1,500
Lease							
4	Lease Payments	11,800	11,800	11,800	11,800	11,800	—
5	Income Tax at 15%	(1,770)	(1,770)	(1,770)	(1,770)	(1,770)	—
6	Free Cash Flow (Lease)	10,030	10,030	10,030	10,030	10,030	—
Lessor Free Cash Flow							
7	Buy & Lease	(39,970)	11,530	11,530	11,530	11,530	1,500

Evaluating the cash flows at the after-tax rate of 8% $\times$ (1 − 15%) = 6.8%, we find the NPV = $341 > 0 for the lessor. (Using the after-tax rate for the lessor implies that the lessor will borrow against the future free cash flows of the transaction.) Thus both sides gain from the transaction due to the difference in tax rates. The gain comes from the fact that for Emory, the lease provides more accelerated tax deductions than the company would receive from depreciating the printing press. Because Emory is in a higher tax bracket than the leasing company, shifting the faster tax deductions to Emory is advantageous.

Reduced Resale Costs.   Many assets are time consuming and costly to sell. If a firm only needs to use the asset for a short time, it is probably less costly to lease it than to buy and resell the asset. In this case, the lessor is responsible for finding a new user for the asset, but lessors are often specialized to do so and so face much lower costs. For example, car dealerships are in a better position to sell a used car at the end of a lease than a consumer is. Some of this advantage can be passed along through a lower lease rate. In addition, while owners of assets are likely to resell them only if the assets are "lemons," a short-term lease can commit the user of an asset to return it regardless of its quality. In this way leases can help mitigate the adverse selection problem in the used goods market.[15]

---

15. For evidence of this effect, see Thomas Gilligan, "Lemons and Leases in the Used Business Aircraft Market," *Journal of Political Economy* 112(5) (2004): 1157–1180.

Efficiency Gains from Specialization.   Lessors often have efficiency advantages over lessees in maintaining or operating certain types of assets. For example, a lessor of office copy machines can employ expert technicians and maintain an inventory of spare parts required for maintenance. Some types of leases may even come with an operator, such as a truck with a driver (in fact, the term "operating lease" originated from such leases). By offering assets together with these complementary services, lessors can achieve efficiency gains and offer attractive lease rates. In addition, if the value of the asset depends upon these additional services, then a firm that purchases the asset would be dependent on the service provider, who could then raise the price for services and exploit the firm.[16] By leasing the asset and the services as a bundle, the firm maintains its bargaining power by retaining its flexibility to switch to competing equipment.

Reduced Distress Costs and Increased Debt Capacity.   As noted in Section 25.2, assets leased under a true lease are not afforded bankruptcy protection and can be seized in the event of default. In addition, the lessor may be better able to recover the full economic value of the asset (by releasing it) than a lender would. Because of the higher recovery value in the event of default, a lessor may be able to offer more attractive financing through the lease than an ordinary lender could. Recent studies suggest that this effect is important for small firms and firms that are capital constrained.[17]

Transferring Risk.   At the beginning of a lease, there may be significant uncertainty about the residual value of the leased asset, and whoever owns the asset bears this risk. Leasing allows the party best able to bear the risk to hold it. For example, small firms with a low tolerance for risk may prefer to lease rather than purchase assets.

Improved Incentives.   When the lessor is the manufacturer, a lease in which the lessor bears the risk of the residual value can improve incentives and lower agency costs. Such a lease provides the manufacturer with an incentive to produce a high-quality, durable product that will retain its value over time. In addition, if the manufacturer is a monopolist, leasing the product gives the manufacturer an incentive not to overproduce and lower the product's residual value, as well as an ability to restrict competition from sales of used goods.

Despite these potential benefits, significant agency costs may also be associated with leasing. For leases in which the lessor retains a substantial interest in the asset's residual value, the lessee has less of an incentive to take proper care of an asset that is leased rather than purchased.[18]

---

16. This concern is often referred to as the hold-up problem. The importance of the hold-up problem in determining the optimal ownership of assets was identified by B. Klein, R. G. Crawford, and A. A. Alchian, "Vertical Integration, Appropriable Rents, and the Competitive Contracting Process," *Journal of Law and Economics* 21 (1978): 297–326.

17. See S. Sharpe and H. Nguyen, "Capital Market Imperfections and the Incentive to Lease," *Journal of Financial Economics* 39(2–3) (1995): 271–294; J. Graham, M. Lemmon, and J. Schallheim, "Debt, Leases, Taxes, and the Endogeneity of Corporate Tax Status," *Journal of Finance* 53(1) (1998): 131–162; and A. Eisfeldt and A. Rampini (referenced in footnote 9).

18. As an example, auto manufacturers require individuals who lease their cars to provide proper maintenance. Without such requirements, individuals would be tempted to avoid paying for oil changes and other maintenance near the end of the lease term. Of course, there are other ways lessees may abuse their cars (driving at excessive speeds, for example) that cannot be easily controlled.

Suspect Arguments for Leasing

Some reasons that lessees and lessors cite for preferring leasing to purchasing are difficult to justify economically. While they may be important in some circumstances, they deserve careful scrutiny.

Avoiding Capital Expenditure Controls.   One reason some managers will choose to lease equipment rather than purchase it is to avoid the scrutiny from superiors that often accompanies large capital expenditures. For example, some companies may place limits on the dollar amounts a manager can invest over a certain period; lease payments may fall below these limits, whereas the cost of the purchase would not. By leasing, the manager avoids having to make a special request for funds. This reason for leasing is also apparent in the public sector, where large assets are often leased to avoid asking the government or the public to approve the funds necessary to purchase the assets. However, the lease may cost more than the purchase, wasting stockholder or taxpayer dollars in the long run.

Preserving Capital.   A common argument made in favor of leasing is that it provides "100% financing" because no down payment is required, so the lessee can save cash to use for other needs. Of course, the firm can also borrow to purchase an asset (possibly using the asset as collateral). For most large corporations, the amount of leverage the firm can obtain through a lease is unlikely to exceed the amount of leverage the firm can obtain through a loan. Thus this benefit is likely to exist only for small or highly capital-constrained firms.

Reducing Leverage Through Off-Balance-Sheet Financing.   By carefully avoiding the four criteria that define a capital lease for accounting purposes, a firm can avoid listing the long-term lease as a liability. Because a lease is equivalent to a loan, the firm can increase its actual leverage without increasing the debt-to-equity ratio on its balance sheet. But whether they appear on the balance sheet or not, lease commitments are a liability for the firm. As a result, they will have the same effect on the risk and return characteristics of the firm as other forms of leverage do. Most financial analysts and sophisticated investors understand this fact and consider operating leases (which must be listed in the footnotes of the financial statements) to be additional sources of leverage.

CONCEPT CHECK

1. What are some of the potential gains from leasing if the lessee plans to hold the asset for only a small fraction of its useful life?

2. If a lease is not listed as a liability on the firm's balance sheet, does it mean that a firm that leases rather than borrows is less risky?

Summary

1. A lease is a contract between two parties: the lessee and the lessor. The lessee is liable for periodic payments in exchange for the right to use the asset. The lessor, who is the owner of the asset, is entitled to the lease payments in exchange for lending the asset.

2. Many types of lease transactions are possible depending on the relationship between the lessee and the lessor.

    a. In a sales-type lease, the lessor is the manufacturer or primary dealer of the asset.

    b. In a direct lease, the lessor is an independent company that specializes in purchasing assets and leasing them to customers.

    c. If a firm already owns an asset it would prefer to lease, it can arrange a sale and lease-back transaction.

3. In a perfect market, the cost of leasing is equivalent to the cost of purchasing and reselling the asset. Also, the cost of leasing and then purchasing the asset is equivalent to the cost of borrowing to purchase the asset.

4. In many cases, the lease provides options for the lessee to obtain ownership of the asset at the end of the lease. Some examples include fair market value leases, $1.00 out leases, and fixed price or fair market value cap leases.

5. The FASB recognizes two types of leases based on the lease terms: operating leases and capital leases. Operating leases are viewed as rentals for accounting purposes. Capital leases are viewed as purchases.

6. The IRS separates leases into two broad categories: true tax leases and non-tax leases. With a true tax lease, the lessee deducts lease payments as an operating expense. A non-tax lease is treated as a loan for tax purposes, so the lessee must depreciate the asset and can expense only the interest portion of the lease payments.

7. In a true lease, the asset is not protected in the event that the lessee declares bankruptcy, and the lessor can seize the asset if lease payments are not made. If the lease is deemed a security interest by the bankruptcy court, then the asset is protected and the lessor becomes a secured creditor.

8. To evaluate the leasing decision for a true tax lease, managers should compare the cost of leasing with the cost of financing using an equivalent amount of leverage.

    a. Compute the incremental cash flows for leasing versus buying.

    b. Compute the NPV by discounting the incremental cash flows at the after-tax borrowing rate.

9. The cash flows of a non-tax lease are directly comparable to the cash flows of a traditional loan, so a non-tax lease is attractive only if it offers a better interest rate than a loan.

10. Good reasons for leasing include tax differences, reduced resale costs, efficiency gains from specialization, reduced bankruptcy costs, risk transfer, and improved incentives.

11. Suspect reasons for leasing include avoiding capital expenditure controls, preserving capital, and reducing leverage through off-balance-sheet financing.

Key Terms

$1.00 out lease *p. 805*
capital (finance) lease *p. 809*
direct lease *p. 802*
fair market value cap lease *p. 806*
fair market value (FMV) lease *p. 805*
fixed price lease *p. 806*
lease-equivalent loan *p. 815*
lessee *p. 802*
lessor *p. 802*
leveraged lease *p. 802*

non-tax lease *p. 811*
operating lease *p. 808*
residual value *p. 803*
sale and leaseback *p. 802*
sales-type lease *p. 802*
security interest *p. 812*
special-purpose entity (SPE) *p. 802*
synthetic lease *p. 802*
true lease *p. 812*
true tax lease *p. 811*

Further Reading

The following books analyze leasing in greater depth: P. K. Nevitt and F. J. Fabozzi, *Equipment Leasing*, 4th ed. (New Hope, PA: Frank Fabozzi Associates, 2000); and J. S. Schallheim, *Lease or Buy? Principles for Sound Decision Making*, (Boston: Harvard Business School Press, 1994).

The academic literature on leasing has been active since the 1970s. Interested readers can explore in more depth empirical studies on the use and effects of leasing: J. Ang and P. P. Peterson, "The Leasing Puzzle," *Journal of Finance* 39(4) (1984): 1055–1065; R. G. Bowman, "The Debt Equivalence of Leases: An Empirical Investigation," *Accounting Review* 55(2) (1980): 237–253; T. K. Mukherjee, "A Survey of Corporate Leasing Analysis," *Financial Management* 20(3) (1991): 96–107; and C. W. Smith, Jr. and L. M. Wakeman, "Determinations of Corporate Leasing Policy," *Journal of Finance* 40(3) (1985): 895–908.

Readers interested in exploring the effects of other market frictions on the leasing decision can consult the following sources: I. Hendel and A. Lizzeri, "The Role of Leasing Under Adverse Selection," *Journal of Political Economy* 110(1) (2002): 113–143; J. Schallheim and K. Wells, "Debt and Taxes: A New Measure for Non-debt Tax Shields," Working paper, 2006; and K. V. Sivarama and R. C. Moyer, "Bankruptcy Costs and Financial Leasing Decisions," *Financial Management* 23(2) (1994): 31–42.

An in-depth analysis of lease valuation is beyond the scope of this book. Readers interested in some of the issues that complicate the analysis can consult these sources: S. R. Grenadier, "An Equilibrium Analysis of Real Estate Leases," *Journal of Business* 78(4) (2005): 1173–1214; J. J. McConnell and J. S. Schallheim, "Valuation of Asset Leasing Contracts," *Journal of Financial Economics* 12(2) (1983): 237–261; J. S. Schallheim, R. E. Johnson, R. C. Lease, and J. J. McConnell, "The Determinants of Yields on Financial Leasing Contracts," *Journal of Financial Economics* 19(1) (1987): 45–67; and R. Stanton and N. Wallace, "An Empirical Test of a Contingent Claims Lease Valuation Model," Working paper, Haas School of Business, 2004.

Problems

A blue box (■) indicates problems available in MyFinanceLab. An asterisk (*) indicates problems with a higher level of difficulty.

Basics of Leasing

1. Suppose an H1200 supercomputer has a cost of $200,000 and will have a residual value of $60,000 in five years. The risk-free interest rate is 5% APR with monthly compounding.

   a. What is the risk-free monthly lease rate in a perfect market?

   b. What would be the monthly payment for a $200,000 risk-free loan to purchase the H1200?

2. Suppose the risk-free interest rate is 5% APR with monthly compounding. If a $2 million MRI machine can be leased for seven years for $22,000 per month, what residual value must the lessor recover to break even in a perfect market?

3. Consider a five-year lease for a $400,000 bottling machine, with a residual value of $150,000 at the end of the five years. If the risk-free interest rate is 6% APR with monthly compounding, compute the monthly lease payment in a perfect market for the following leases:

   a. A fair market value lease

   b. A $1.00 out lease

   c. A fixed price lease with an $80,000 final price

4. Acme Distribution currently has the following items on its balance sheet:

Assets		Liabilities	
Cash	20	Debt	70
Property, Plant, and Equipment	175	Equity	125

How will Acme's balance sheet change if it enters into an $80 million capital lease for new warehouses? What will its book debt-equity ratio be? How will Acme's balance sheet and debt-equity ratio change if the lease is an operating lease?

5. Your firm is considering leasing a $50,000 copier. The copier has an estimated economic life of eight years. Suppose the appropriate discount rate is 9% APR with monthly compounding. Classify each lease below as a capital lease or operating lease, and explain why:

   a. A four-year fair market value lease with payments of $1150 per month

   b. A six-year fair market value lease with payments of $790 per month

   c. A five-year fair market value lease with payments of $925 per month

   d. A five-year fair market value lease with payments of $1000 per month and an option to cancel after three years with a $9000 cancellation penalty

6. Craxton Engineering will either purchase or lease a new $756,000 fabricator. If purchased, the fabricator will be depreciated on a straight-line basis over seven years. Craxton can lease the fabricator for $130,000 per year for seven years. Craxton's tax rate is 35%. (Assume the fabricator has no residual value at the end of the seven years.)

   a. What are the free cash flow consequences of buying the fabricator?

   b. What are the free cash flow consequences of leasing the fabricator?

   c. What are the incremental free cash flows of leasing versus buying?

7. Riverton Mining plans to purchase or lease $220,000 worth of excavation equipment. If purchased, the equipment will be depreciated on a straight-line basis over five years, after which it will be worthless. If leased, the annual lease payments will be $55,000 per year for five years. Riverton's borrowing cost is 8%, and its tax rate is 35%.

   a. If Riverton purchases the equipment, what is the amount of the lease-equivalent loan?

   b. Is Riverton better off leasing the equipment or financing the purchase using the lease-equivalent loan?

   c. What is the effective after-tax lease borrowing rate? How does this compare to Riverton's actual after-tax borrowing rate?

8. Suppose Clorox can lease a new computer data processing system for $975,000 per year for five years. Alternatively, it can purchase the system for $4.25 million. Assume Clorox has a borrowing cost of 7% and a tax rate of 35%, and the system will be obsolete at the end of five years.

   a. If Clorox will depreciate the computer equipment on a straight-line basis over the next five years, is it better to lease or finance the purchase of the equipment?

   b. Suppose that if Clorox buys the equipment, it will use accelerated depreciation for tax purposes. Specifically, suppose it can expense 20% of the purchase price immediately and can take depreciation deductions equal to 32%, 19.2%, 11.52%, 11.52%, and 5.76% of the purchase price over the next five years. Compare leasing with purchase in this case.

*9. Suppose Procter and Gamble (P&G) is considering purchasing $15 million in new manufacturing equipment. If it purchases the equipment, it will depreciate it on a straight-line basis over the five years, after which the equipment will be worthless. It will also be responsible for maintenance expenses of $1 million per year. It can also lease the equipment for $4.2 million per year for the five years, in which case the lessor will provide necessary maintenance. Assume P&G's tax rate is 35% and its borrowing cost is 7%.

   a. What is the NPV associated with leasing the equipment versus financing it with the lease-equivalent loan?

   b. What is the break-even lease rate—that is, what lease amount could P&G pay each year and be indifferent between leasing and financing a purchase?

Reasons for Leasing

EXCEL   ***10.** Suppose Netflix is considering the purchase of computer servers and network infrastructure to facilitate its move into video-on-demand services. In total, it will purchase $48 million in new equipment. This equipment will qualify for accelerated depreciation: 20% can be expensed immediately, followed by 32%, 19.2%, 11.52%, 11.52%, and 5.76% over the next five years. However, because of the firm's substantial loss carryforwards, Netflix estimates its marginal tax rate to be 10% over the next five years, so it will get very little tax benefit from the depreciation expenses. Thus Netflix considers leasing the equipment instead. Suppose Netflix and the lessor face the same 8% borrowing rate, but the lessor has a 35% tax rate. For the purpose of this question, assume the equipment is worthless after 5 years, the lease term is 5 years, and the lease qualifies as a true tax lease.

   a. What is the lease rate for which the lessor will break even?

   b. What is the gain to Netflix with this lease rate?

   c. What is the source of the gain in this transaction?

Short-Term Financing

Chapter 26
Working Capital Management

Chapter 27
Short-Term Financial Planning

The Law of One Price Connection. Most of the financial decisions we have studied to date have been long term, that is, decisions that involve cash flows that occur over a period of time longer than one year. In Part IX, we turn to the details of running the financial side of a corporation and focus on short-term financial management. In a perfect capital market, the Law of One Price and the Modigliani-Miller propositions imply that how a firm chooses to manage its short-term financial needs does not affect the value of the firm. In reality, short-term financial policy does matter because of the existence of market frictions. In this part of the book we identify these frictions and explain how firms set their short-term financial policies. In Chapter 26 we discuss how firms manage their working capital requirements, including accounts receivable, accounts payable, and inventory. In Chapter 27, we explain how firms finance their short-term cash needs.

Working Capital Management

In Chapter 2, we defined a firm's net working capital as its current assets minus its current liabilities. Net working capital is the capital required in the short term to run the business. Thus working capital management involves short-term asset accounts such as cash, inventory, and accounts receivable, as well as short-term liability accounts such as accounts payable.

The level of investment in each of these accounts differs from firm to firm and from industry to industry. It also depends on factors such as the type of business and industry standards. Some firms, for example, require heavy inventory investments because of the nature of their business. Consider The Kroger Company, a retail grocery chain, and Hilton Hotels Corporation, the owner and operator of hotels. Inventory amounted to 21% of Kroger's total assets at the start of 2005, whereas Hilton's investment in inventory was less than 2%. A grocery store requires a large investment in inventory, while a hotel chain's profitability is generated primarily from its investment in plant, property, and equipment—that is, its hotels and furnishings.

There are opportunity costs associated with investing in inventories and accounts receivable, and from holding cash. Excess funds invested in these accounts could instead be used to pay down debt or returned to shareholders in the form of a dividend or share repurchase. This chapter focuses on the tools firms use to manage their working capital efficiently and thereby minimize these opportunity costs. We begin by discussing why firms have working capital and how it affects firm value. In a perfectly competitive market, many of the working capital accounts would be irrelevant. Not surprisingly, the existence of these accounts for real firms can be traced to market frictions. We discuss the costs and benefits of trade credit and evaluate the tradeoffs firms make in managing various working capital accounts. Finally, we discuss the cash balance of a firm and provide an overview of the short-term investments in which a firm may choose to invest its cash.

26.1 Overview of Working Capital

Most projects require the firm to invest in net working capital. The main components of net working capital are cash, inventory, receivables, and payables. Working capital includes the cash that is needed to run the firm on a day-to-day basis. It does not include excess cash, which is cash that is not required to run the business and can be invested at a market rate. As we discussed in Chapter 14, excess cash may be viewed as part of the firm's capital structure, offsetting firm debt. In Chapter 7, we discussed how any increases in net working capital represent an investment that reduces the cash that is available to the firm. Therefore, working capital alters a firm's value by affecting its free cash flow. In this section, we examine the components of net working capital and their effects on the firm's value.

The Cash Cycle

The level of working capital reflects the length of time between when cash goes out of a firm at the beginning of the production process and when it comes back in. A company first buys inventory from its suppliers, in the form of either raw materials or finished goods. Even if the inventory is in the form of finished goods, it may sit on the shelf for some time before it is sold. A firm typically buys its inventory on credit, which means that the firm does not have to pay cash immediately at the time of purchase. When the inventory is disposed of, it is often sold on credit. A firm's **cash cycle** is the length of time between when the firm pays cash to purchase its initial inventory and when it receives cash from the sale of the output produced from that inventory. Figure 26.1 illustrates the cash cycle.

Some practitioners measure the cash cycle by calculating the cash conversion cycle. The **cash conversion cycle (CCC)** is defined as

$$CCC = \text{Inventory Days} + \text{Accounts Receivable Days} - \text{Accounts Payable Days}$$

where

$$\text{Inventory Days} = \frac{\text{Inventory}}{\text{Average Daily Cost of Goods Sold}}$$

$$\text{Accounts Receivable Days} = \frac{\text{Accounts Receivable}}{\text{Average Daily Sales}}$$

$$\text{Accounts Payable Days} = \frac{\text{Accounts Payable}}{\text{Average Daily Cost of Goods Sold}}$$

FIGURE 26.1

The Cash and Operating Cycle for a Firm

The cash cycle is the average time between when a firm pays for its inventory and when it receives cash from the sale of its product.

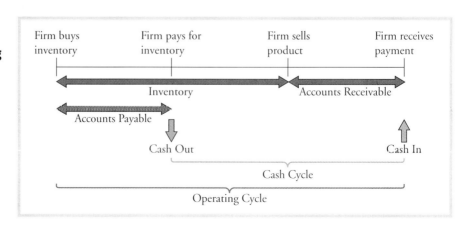

The firm's **operating cycle** is the average length of time between when a firm originally purchases its inventory and when it receives the cash back from selling its product. If the firm pays cash for its inventory, this period is identical to the firm's cash cycle. However, most firms buy their inventory on credit, which reduces the amount of time between the cash investment and the receipt of cash from that investment.

The longer a firm's cash cycle, the more working capital it has, and the more cash it needs to carry to conduct its daily operations. Table 26.1 provides data on the working capital needs for selected firms in a variety of industries.

Because of the characteristics of the different industries, working capital levels vary significantly. For example, a retail grocery store typically sells on a cash-only basis, so you would expect accounts receivable to be a very small percentage of its sales. For Kroger, accounts receivable represent only four days worth of sales.[1] Similar results hold for Southwest Airlines, because many of its customers pay in advance for airline tickets with cash or credit cards. Inventory represents the largest percentage of sales for firms such as Merck and Pulte Homes, which have a long development and sales cycle. Note also the wide variation in the firms' cash conversion cycles; Southwest's cash conversion cycle is negative, reflecting the fact that it receives cash from its customers before having to pay its suppliers.

TABLE 26.1		Working Capital in Various Industries (Fiscal Year End 2005)				
Company	Ticker	Industry	Accounts Receivable Days	Inventory Days	Accounts Payable Days	CCC
Boeing	BA	Aerospace/Defense	24	63	49	38
Hilton	HLT	Lodging	26	29	18	37
Intel	INTC	Semiconductors	37	73	53	57
Kroger	KR	Grocery Stores	4	37	31	10
Mattel	MAT	Toys and Games	54	49	35	68
Merck	MRK	Drug Manufacturers	49	122	35	136
Nordstrom	JWN	Apparel Stores	51	73	39	85
Oracle	ORCL	Application Software	80	0	32	48
Pulte Homes	PHM	Residential Construction	4	260	11	253
Southwest Airlines	LUV	Regional Airlines	9	23	80	−48

Source: www.capitaliq.com.

---

1. When you use your Visa or Mastercard to pay for your groceries, it is a cash sale for the store. The credit card company pays the store cash upon receipt of the credit slip, even if you do not pay your credit card bill on time.

Firm Value and Working Capital

Any reduction in working capital requirements generates a positive free cash flow that the firm can distribute immediately to shareholders. For example, if a firm is able to reduce its required net working capital by $50,000, it will be able to distribute this $50,000 as a dividend to its shareholders immediately.

Costly Working Capital for a Project

Problem

Emerald City Paints would like to construct a new facility that will manufacture paint. In addition to the capital expenditure on the plant, management estimates that the project will require an investment today of $450,000 for net working capital. The firm will recover the investment in net working capital eight years from today, when management anticipates closing the plant. The discount rate for this type of cash flow is 6% per year. What is the present value of the cost of working capital for the paint facility?

Solution

The cash flows for the investment in net working capital are $-$450,000 today and $+$450,000 eight years from today. Putting this on a timeline:

Given a discount rate of 6% per year, the NPV of these cash flows is

$$NPV = -\$450,000 + \frac{\$450,000}{(1 + 0.06)^8} = -\$167,664$$

Although Emerald City Paints receives back all of its investment in working capital, it loses the time value of money on this cash.

Managing working capital efficiently will maximize firm value. We now turn our attention to some specific working capital accounts.

CONCEPT CHECK   1. What is the difference between a firm's cash cycle and operating cycle?

2. How does working capital impact a firm's value?

26.2   Trade Credit

When a firm allows a customer to pay for goods at some date later than the date of purchase, it creates an account receivable for the firm and an account payable for the customer. Accounts receivable represent the credit sales for which a firm has yet to receive payment. The accounts payable balance represents the amount that a firm owes its suppliers for goods that it has received but for which it has not yet paid. The credit that the firm is extending to its customer is known as **trade credit**. A firm would, of course, prefer to be paid in cash at the time of purchase, but a "cash-only" policy may cause it to lose its customers to competition. In this section, we demonstrate how managers can compare the costs and benefits of trade credit to determine optimal credit policies.

Trade Credit Terms

To see how the terms of trade credit are quoted, let's consider some examples. If a supplier offers its customers terms of "net 30," payment is not due until 30 days from the date of the invoice. Essentially, the supplier is letting the customer use its money for an extra 30 days. (Note that "30" is not a magic number; the invoice could specify "net 40," "net 15," or any other number of days as the payment due date.)

Sometimes the selling firm will offer the buying firm a discount if payment is made early. The terms "2/10, net 30" mean that the buying firm will receive a 2% discount if it pays for the goods within 10 days; otherwise, the full amount is due in 30 days. Firms offer discounts to encourage customers to pay early so that the selling firm gets cash from the sale sooner. However, the amount of the discount also represents a cost to the selling firm because it does not receive the full selling price for the product.

Trade Credit and Market Frictions

In a perfectly competitive market, trade credit is just another form of financing. Under the Modigliani-Miller assumptions of perfect capital markets, the amounts of payables and receivables are therefore irrelevant. In reality, product markets are rarely perfectly competitive, so firms can maximize their value by using their trade credit options effectively.

Cost of Trade Credit. Trade credit is, in essence, a loan from the selling firm to its customer. The price discount represents an interest rate. Often, firms offer favorable interest rates on trade credit as a price discount to their customers. Therefore, financial managers should evaluate the terms of trade credit to decide whether to use it.

How do we compute the interest rate on trade credit? Suppose a firm sells a product for $100 but offers its customer terms of 2/10, net 30. The customer doesn't have to pay anything for the first 10 days, so it effectively has a zero-interest loan for this period. If the customer takes advantage of the discount and pays within the 10-day discount period, the customer pays only $98 for the product. The cost of the discount to the selling firm is equal to the discount percentage times the selling price. In this case, it is $0.02 \times \$100$, or $2.00.

Rather than pay within 10 days, the customer has the option to use the $98 for an additional 20 days $(30 - 10 = 20)$. The interest rate for the 20-day term of the loan is $\$2/\$98 = 2.04\%$. With a 365-day year, this rate over 20 days corresponds to an effective annual rate of[2]

$$EAR = (1.0204)^{365/20} - 1 = 44.6\%$$

Thus, by not taking the discount, the firm is effectively paying 2.04% to borrow the money for 20 days, which translates to an effective annual rate of 44.6%! If the firm can obtain a bank loan at a lower interest rate, it would be better off borrowing at the lower rate and using the cash proceeds of the loan to take advantage of the discount offered by the supplier.

---

2. See Eq 5.1 in Chapter 5.

Estimating the Effective Cost of Trade Credit

Problem

Your firm purchases goods from its supplier on terms of 1/15, net 40. What is the effective annual cost to your firm if it chooses not to take advantage of the trade discount offered?

Solution

Because the discount is 1%, for a $100 purchase your firm must pay either $99 in 15 days or $100 in 40 days. Given the difference of 25 days $(40 - 15)$, these terms correspond to an effective annual rate of $(100 / 99)^{365/25} - 1 = 15.8\%$.

Benefits of Trade Credit.   For a number of reasons, trade credit can be an attractive source of funds. First, trade credit is simple and convenient to use, and it therefore has lower transaction costs than alternative sources of funds. For example, no paperwork must be completed, as would be the case for a loan from a bank. Second, it is a flexible source of funds, and can be used as needed. Finally, it is sometimes the only source of funding available to a firm.

Trade Credit Versus Standard Loans.   You might wonder why companies would ever provide trade credit. After all, most companies are not banks, so why are they in the business of making loans? Several reasons explain their willingness to offer trade credit.[3] First, providing financing at below-market rates is an indirect way to lower prices for only certain customers. Consider, for example, an automobile manufacturer. Rather than lower prices on all cars, the financing division may offer specific credit terms that are attractive to customers with bad credit, but unattractive to customers with good credit. In this way, the car manufacturer is able to discount the price only for those customers with bad credit who otherwise might not be able to afford the car.

Second, because a supplier may have an ongoing business relationship with its customer, it may have more information about the credit quality of the customer than a traditional outside lender such as a bank. The supplier may also be able to increase the likelihood of payment by threatening to cut off future supplies if payment is not made. Finally, if the buyer defaults, the supplier may be able to seize the inventory as collateral. This inventory is likely to be more valuable to a company within the industry such as the supplier (which presumably has other customers) than to an outsider.

Managing Float

One factor that contributes to the length of a firm's receivables and payables is the delay between the time a bill is paid and the cash is actually received. This delay, or processing float, will impact a firm's working capital requirements.

---

3. For a detailed discussion of these issues, see B. Biais and C. Gollier, "Trade Credit and Credit Rationing," *Review of Financial Studies* 10(4) (1997): 903–937; and M. A. Petersen and R. G. Rajan, "Trade Credit: Theories and Evidence," *Review of Financial Studies* 10(3) (1997): 661–691.

Collection Float.   **Collection float** is the amount of time it takes for a firm to be able to use funds after a customer has paid for its goods. Firms can reduce their working capital needs by reducing their collection float. Collection float is determined by three factors:

- **Mail float**: How long it takes the firm to receive the check after the customer has mailed it,
- **Processing float**: How long it takes the firm to process the check and deposit it in the bank,
- **Availability float**: How long it takes before the bank gives the firm credit for the funds.

Disbursement Float.   **Disbursement float** is the amount of time it takes before payments to suppliers actually result in a cash outflow for the firm. Like collection float, it is a function of mail time, processing time, and check-clearing time. Although a firm may try to extend its disbursement float in order to lengthen it's payables and reduce its working capital needs, it risks making late payments to suppliers. In such a case, the firm may be charged an additional fee for paying late or may be required to pay before delivery (CBD) or on delivery (COD) for future purchases. In some cases, the supplier may refuse to do business in the future with the delinquent firm.

Electronic Check Processing.   Firms can employ several methods to reduce their collection and disbursement floats. The **Check Clearing for the 21st Century Act (Check 21)**, which became effective on October 28, 2004, eliminated the disbursement float due to the check-clearing process. Under the act, banks can process check information electronically, and the funds are deducted from a firm's checking account on the same day that the firm's supplier deposits the check in its bank in most cases. Unfortunately, even though the funds are taken out of the check writer's account almost immediately under Check 21, the check recipient's account is not credited as quickly. As a result, the act does not serve to reduce collection float.

There are, however, several ways that a firm *can* reduce its collection float. For example, the firm may streamline its in-house check-processing procedures. In addition, with electronic collection, funds are automatically transferred from the customer's bank account to the firm's bank account on the payment date, reducing the collection float to zero. The methods a firm employs to reduce its collection float are not without costs, of course. Therefore, to decide which, if any, to employ, the firm must compare the costs and benefits of systems that allow it to use its cash for a longer period.

CONCEPT CHECK   **1.** What does the term "2/10, net 30" mean?

2. List three factors that determine collection float.

26.3   Receivables Management

So far, we have discussed the costs and benefits of trade credit in general. Next, we look at some issues that arise specifically from the management of a firm's accounts receivable. In particular, we focus on how a firm adopts a policy for offering credit to its customers and how it monitors its accounts receivable on an ongoing basis.

Determining the Credit Policy

Establishing a credit policy involves three steps that we will discuss in turn:

1. Establishing credit standards
2. Establishing credit terms
3. Establishing a collection policy

Establishing Credit Standards.   Management must first decide on its credit standards. Will it extend credit to anyone who applies for it? Or will it be selective and extend credit only to those customers who have very low credit risk? Unless the firm adopts the former policy, it will need to assess the credit risk of each customer before deciding whether to grant credit. Large firms perform this analysis in-house with their own credit departments. Small firms purchase credit reports from credit rating agencies such as Dun & Bradstreet.

The decision of how much credit risk to assume plays a large role in determining how much money a firm ties up in its receivables. While a restrictive policy can result in a lower sales volume, the firm will have a smaller investment in receivables. Conversely, a less selective policy will produce higher sales, but the level of receivables will also rise.

Establishing Credit Terms.   After a firm decides on its credit standards, it must next establish its credit terms. The firm decides on the length of the period before payment must be made (the "net" period) and chooses whether to offer a discount to encourage early payments. If it offers a discount, it must also determine the discount percentage and the discount period. If the firm is relatively small, it will probably follow the lead of other firms in the industry in establishing these terms.

Establishing a Collection Policy.   The last step in the development of a credit policy is to decide on a collection policy. The content of this policy can range from doing nothing if a customer is paying late (generally not a good choice), to sending a polite letter of inquiry, to charging interest on payments extending beyond a specified period, to threatening legal action at the first late payment.

Monitoring Accounts Receivable

After establishing a credit policy, a firm must monitor its accounts receivable to analyze whether its credit policy is working effectively. Two tools that firms use to monitor the accounts receivable are the accounts receivable days (or average collection period) and the aging schedule.

Accounts Receivable Days.   The accounts receivable days is the average number of days that it takes a firm to collect on its sales. A firm can compare this number to the payment policy specified in its credit terms to judge the effectiveness of its credit policy. If the credit terms specify "net 30" and the accounts receivable days outstanding is 50 days, the firm can conclude that its customers are paying 20 days late, on average.

The firm should also look at the trend in the accounts receivable days over time. If the accounts receivable days ratio of a firm has been approximately 35 days for the past few years and it is 43 days this year, the firm may want to reexamine its credit policy. Of course, if the economy is sluggish, the entire industry may be affected. Under these circumstances, the increase might have little to do with the firm itself.

Because accounts receivable days can be calculated from the firm's financial statement, outside investors commonly use this measure to evaluate a firm's credit management policy. A major weakness of the accounts receivable days is that it is merely one number and conceals much useful information. Seasonal sales patterns may cause the number calculated for the accounts receivable days to change depending on when the calculation takes place. The number can also look reasonable even when a substantial percentage of the firm's customers are paying late.

Aging Schedule. An **aging schedule** categorizes accounts by the number of days they have been on the firm's books. It can be prepared using either the number of accounts or the dollar amount of the accounts receivable outstanding. For example, assume that a firm selling on terms of 2/15, net 30, has $530,000 in accounts receivable that has been on the books for 15 or fewer days in 220 accounts. Another $450,000 has been on the books for 16 to 30 days and is made up of 190 accounts, and $350,000 has been on the books for 31 to 45 days and represents 80 accounts. The firm has $200,000 that has been on the books for 46 to 60 days in 60 accounts. Yet another $70,000 has been on the books for more than 60 days and is made up of 20 accounts. Table 26.2 includes aging schedules based on the number of accounts and dollar amounts outstanding.

In this case, if the firm's average daily sales is $65,000, its accounts receivable days is $1,600,000/$65,000 = 25 days. But on closer examination, using the aging schedules in Table 26.2, we can see that 28% of the firm's credit customers (and 39% by dollar amounts) are paying late.

TABLE 26.2   **Aging Schedules**

(a) Number of Accounts

Days Outstanding	Number of Accounts	Percentage of Accounts (%)
1–15	220	38.6
16–30	190	33.3
31–45	80	14.0
46–60	60	10.5
60+	20	3.5
	570	100.0

(b) Dollar Amounts Outstanding

Days Outstanding	Amount Outstanding ($)	Percentage Outstanding (%)
1–15	530,000	33.1
16–30	450,000	28.1
31–45	350,000	21.9
46–60	200,000	12.5
60+	70,000	4.4
	1,600,000	100.0

Aging Schedules

Problem

Financial Training Systems (FTS) bills its accounts on terms of 3/10, net 30. The firm's accounts receivable include $100,000 that has been outstanding for 10 or fewer days, $300,000 outstanding for 11 to 30 days, $100,000 outstanding for 31 to 40 days, $20,000 outstanding for 41 to 50 days, $10,000 outstanding for 51 to 60 days, and $2000 outstanding for more than 60 days. Prepare an aging schedule for FTS.

Solution

With the available information, we can calculate the aging schedule based on dollar amounts outstanding.

Days Outstanding	Amount Outstanding ($)	Percentage Outstanding (%)
1–10	100,000	18.8
11–30	300,000	56.4
31–40	100,000	18.8
41–50	20,000	3.8
51–60	10,000	1.9
60+	2,000	0.3
	532,000	100.0

If the aging schedule gets "bottom-heavy"—that is, if the percentages in the lower half of the schedule begin to increase—the firm will likely need to revisit its credit policy. The aging schedule is also sometimes augmented by analysis of the **payments pattern**, which provides information on the percentage of monthly sales that the firm collects in each month after the sale. By examining past data, a firm may observe that 10% of its sales are usually collected in the month of the sale, 40% in the month following the sale, 25% two months after the sale, 20% three months after the sale, and 5% four months after the sale. Management can compare this normal payments pattern to the current payments pattern. Knowledge of the payments pattern is also useful for forecasting the firm's working capital requirements.

CONCEPT CHECK

1. Describe three steps in establishing a credit policy.

2. What is the difference between accounts receivable days and an aging schedule?

26.4 Payables Management

A firm should choose to borrow using accounts payable only if trade credit is the cheapest source of funding. The cost of the trade credit depends on the credit terms. The higher the discount percentage offered, the greater the cost of forgoing the discount. The cost of forgoing the discount is also higher with a shorter loan period. When a company has a choice between trade credit from two different suppliers, it should take the least-expensive alternative.

In addition, a firm should always pay on the latest day allowed. For example, if the discount period is 10 days and the firm is taking the discount, payment should be made on day 10, not on day 2. If the discount is not taken and the terms are 2/10, net 30, the full payment should be made on day 30, not on day 16. A firm should strive to keep its money working for it as long as possible without developing a bad relationship with its suppliers or engaging in unethical practices. In this section, we examine two techniques that firms use to monitor their accounts payable.

Determining Accounts Payable Days Outstanding

Similar to the situation with its accounts receivable, a firm should monitor its accounts payable to ensure that it is making its payments at an optimal time. One method is to calculate the accounts payable days outstanding and compare it to the credit terms. The accounts payable days outstanding is the accounts payable balance expressed in terms of the number of days of cost of goods sold. If the accounts payable outstanding is 40 days and the terms are 2/10, net 30, the firm can conclude that it generally pays late and may be risking supplier difficulties. Conversely, if the accounts payable days outstanding is 25 days and the firm has not been taking the discount, the firm is paying too early. It could be earning another five days' interest on its money.

Accounts Payable Management

Problem

The Rowd Company has an average accounts payable balance of $250,000. Its average daily cost of goods sold is $14,000, and it receives terms of 2/15, net 40, from its suppliers. Rowd chooses to forgo the discount. Is the firm managing its accounts payable well?

Solution

The firm is not managing its accounts payable well. Rowd's accounts payable days outstanding is $250,000/$14,000 = 17.9 days. If Rowd made payment three days earlier, it could take advantage of the 2% discount. If for some reason it chooses to forgo the discount, it should not be paying the full amount until the fortieth day.

Stretching Accounts Payable

Some firms ignore the payment due period and pay later, in a practice referred to as **stretching the accounts payable**. Given terms of 2/10, net 30, for example, a firm may choose to not pay until 45 days have passed. Doing so reduces the direct cost of trade credit because it lengthens the time that a firm has use of the funds. While the interest rate per period remains the same—$2/$98 = 2.04%—the firm is now using the $98 for 35 days beyond the discount period, rather than 20 days as provided by the trade credit terms.

Cost of Trade Credit with Stretched Accounts Payable

Problem

What is the effective annual cost of credit terms of 1/15, net 40, if the firm stretches the accounts payable to 60 days?

Solution

The interest rate per period is $1/$99 = 1.01%. If the firm delays payment until the sixtieth day, it has use of the funds for 45 days beyond the discount period. There are 365/45 = 8.11 45-day periods in one year. Thus the effective annual cost is $(1.0101)^{8.11} - 1 = 8.49\%$.

Firms may also make a payment on the thirtieth day but pay only the discounted price. Some may pay only the discounted price and pay even later than the thirtieth day. While all of these actions will reduce the effective annual rate associated with the trade credit, the firm may incur costs as a result of these actions. Suppliers may react to a firm whose payments are always late by imposing terms of cash on delivery (COD) or cash before delivery (CBD). The delinquent firm then bears the additional costs associated with these terms and may have to negotiate a bank loan to have the cash available to pay. The supplier may also discontinue business with the delinquent customer, leaving the customer to find another source, which may be more expensive or of lower quality. A poor credit rating might also result, making it difficult for the firm to obtain good terms with any other supplier. Moreover, when a firm explicitly agrees to the terms of the sale, violating these terms constitutes unethical business behavior in most people's minds.

CONCEPT CHECK
1. What do the terms COD and CBD mean?

2. What is the optimal time for a firm to pay its accounts payable?

26.5 Inventory Management

As we discussed earlier, in a perfect markets setting, firms would not need to have accounts payable or receivable. Interest rates on trade credit would be competitive, and firms could use alternative sources of financing. However, unlike trade credit, inventory represents one of the required factors of production. Therefore, even in a perfect markets setting in which the Modigliani-Miller propositions hold, firms still need inventory.

Inventory management receives extensive coverage in a course on operations management. Nevertheless, it is the firm's financial manager who must arrange for the financing necessary to support the firm's inventory policy and who is responsible for ensuring the firm's overall profitability. Therefore, the role of the inventory manager is to balance the costs and benefits associated with inventory. Because excessive inventory uses cash, efficient management of inventory increases firm value.

Benefits of Holding Inventory

A firm needs its inventory to operate for several reasons. First, inventory helps minimize the risk that the firm will not be able to obtain an input it needs for production. If a firm holds too little inventory, **stock-outs**, the situation when a firm runs out of money, may occur, leading to lost sales. Disappointed customers may switch to one of the firm's competitors.

Second, firms may hold inventory because factors such as seasonality in demand mean that customer purchases do not perfectly match the most efficient production cycle. Consider the case of the Sandpoint Toy Company. As is typical for many toy manufacturers, 80% of Sandpoint's annual sales occur between September and December, in anticipation of the holiday gift season. It is more efficient for Sandpoint to manufacture toys at relatively constant levels throughout the year. If Sandpoint produces its toys at a constant rate, its inventory levels will increase to very high levels by August, in anticipation of the increase in sales beginning in September. In contrast, Sandpoint may consider a seasonal manufacturing strategy, producing more toys between September and December when sales are high. Under this strategy, inventory would not accumulate, freeing up cash flow from working capital and reducing the costs of inventory. However, seasonal manufacturing incurs additional costs, such as increased wear and tear on the manufacturing equipment during peak demand and the need to hire and train seasonal workers. Sandpoint must weigh the costs of the inventory buildup under constant production against the benefits of more efficient production. The optimal choice is likely to involve a compromise between the two extremes, so that Sandpoint will carry some inventory.

Costs of Holding Inventory

As suggested by the Sandpoint Toy example, tying up capital in inventory is costly for a firm. We can classify the direct costs associated with inventory into three categories:

- *Acquisition costs* are the costs of the inventory itself over the period being analyzed (usually one year).
- *Order costs* are the total costs of placing an order over the period being analyzed.
- *Carrying costs* include storage costs, insurance, taxes, spoilage, obsolescence, and the opportunity cost of the funds tied up in the inventory.

Minimizing these total costs involves some tradeoffs. For example, if we assume no quantity discounts are available, the lower the level of inventory a firm carries, the lower its carrying cost, but the higher its annual order costs because it needs to place more orders during the year.

In 2003, the apparel chain GAP reduced its investment in inventory significantly by reducing its inventory days outstanding by 24%. This change freed up $344 million for other purposes. GAP invested some of this cash in short-term securities—primarily in U.S. government and agency securities and in bank certificates of deposits with maturities between three months and one year. The firm reported an increase of *$1.2 million* in interest income in fiscal year 2003 compared with fiscal year 2002. It attributed the increase to increases in the average cash balances available for investment.[4]

Some firms seek to reduce their carrying costs as much as possible. With **"just-in-time" (JIT) inventory management**, a firm acquires inventory precisely when needed so that its inventory balance is always zero, or very close to it. This technique requires exceptional coordination with suppliers as well as a predictable demand for the firm's products. In addition, there may be a trickle-down effect when one firm in an industry adopts JIT. For example, in 1999, Toys 'R Us instituted JIT, which caused one of its suppliers, toy manufacturer Hasbro, to make changes in its production schedule.[5]

CONCEPT CHECK
1. What are the direct costs of holding inventory?
2. Describe "just-in-time" inventory management.

26.6 Cash Management

In the Modigliani Miller setting, the level of cash is irrelevant. With perfect capital markets, a firm is able to raise new money instantly at a fair rate, so it can never be short of cash. Similarly, the firm can invest excess cash a fair rate to earn an NPV of zero.

In the real world, of course, markets are not perfect. Liquidity has a cost; for example, holding liquid assets may earn a below-market return, and a firm may face transaction costs if it needs to raise cash quickly. Similarly, recall from Chapter 16 that holding excess cash has a tax disadvantage. In these cases, the optimal strategy for a firm is to hold cash

---

4. GAP 2003 annual report.
5. Hasbro 1999 annual report.

in anticipation of seasonalities in demand for its products and random shocks that affect its business. Risky firms and firms with high-growth opportunities tend to hold a relatively high percentage of assets as cash. Firms with easy access to capital markets (for which the transaction costs of accessing cash are therefore lower) tend to hold less cash.[6] In this section, we examine the firm's motivation for holding cash, tools for managing cash, and the short-term securities in which firms invest.

Motivation for Holding Cash

There are three reasons why a firm holds cash:

- To meet its day-to-day needs
- To compensate for the uncertainty associated with its cash flows
- To satisfy bank requirements

In this section, we examine each of these motivations for holding cash in detail.

Transactions Balance.   Just like you, a firm must hold enough cash to pay its bills. The amount of cash a firm needs to be able to pay its bills is sometimes referred to as a **transactions balance**. The amount of cash a firm needs to satisfy the transactions balance requirement depends on both the average size of the transactions made by the firm and the firm's cash cycle, discussed earlier in the chapter.

Precautionary Balance.   The amount of cash a firm holds to counter the uncertainty surrounding its future cash needs is known as a **precautionary balance**. The size of this balance depends on the degree of uncertainty surrounding a firm's cash flows. The more uncertain future cash flows are, the harder it is for a firm to predict its transactions need, so the larger the precautionary balance must be.

Compensating Balance.   A firm's bank may require it to hold a **compensating balance** in an account at the bank as compensation for services that the bank performs. Compensating balances are typically deposited in accounts that either earn no interest or pay a very low interest rate. This arrangement is similar to a bank offering individuals free checking so long as their balances do not fall below a certain level—say, $1000. Essentially, the customer has $1000 cash that he cannot use unless he is willing to pay a service charge. Similarly, the cash that a firm has tied up to meet a compensating balance requirement is unavailable for other uses.

Alternative Investments

In our discussion of collection and disbursement floats, we assumed that the firm will invest any cash in short-term securities. In fact, the firm may choose from a variety of short-term securities that differ somewhat with regard to their default risk and liquidity risk. The greater the risk, the higher the expected return on the investment. The financial manager must decide how much risk she is willing to accept in return for a higher yield. If her firm expects to need the funds within the next 30 days, the manager will probably avoid the less liquid options. Table 26.3 briefly describes the most frequently used short-term investments; these short-term debt securities are collectively referred to as money market securities.

---

6. See T. Opler, L. Pinkowitz, R. Stulz, and R. Williamson, "The Determinants and Implications of Corporate Cash Holdings," *Journal of Financial Economics* 52(1) (1999): 3–46.

TABLE 26.3   **Money Market Investment Options**

Investment	Description	Maturity	Risk	Liquidity
Treasury Bills	Short-term debt of the U.S. government.	Four weeks, three months (91 days) or six months (182 days) when newly issued.	Default risk free.	Very liquid and marketable.
Certificates of Deposit (CDs)	Short-term debt issued by banks. Minimum denomination of $100,000.	Varying maturities up to one year.	If the issuing bank is insured by the FDIC, any amount up to $100,000 is free of default risk because it is covered by the insurance. Any amount in excess of $100,000 is not insured and is subject to default risk.	Unlike CDs purchased by individuals, these CDs sell on the secondary market, but are less liquid than Treasury bills.
Repurchase Agreements	Essentially a loan arrangement wherein a securities dealer is the "borrower" and the investor is the "lender." The investor buys securities, such as U.S. Treasury bills, from the securities dealer, with an agreement to sell the securities back to the dealer at a later date for a specified higher price.	Very short term, ranging from overnight to approximately three months in duration.	The security serves as collateral for the loan, and therefore the investor is exposed to very little risk. However, the investor needs to consider the creditworthiness of the securities dealer when assessing the risk.	No secondary market for repurchase agreements.
Banker's Acceptances	Drafts written by the borrower and guaranteed by the bank on which the draft is drawn. Typically used in international trade transactions. The borrower is an importer who writes the draft in payment for goods.	Typically one to six months.	Because both the borrower and a bank have guaranteed the draft, there is very little risk.	When the exporter receives the draft, he may hold it until maturity and receive its full value or he may sell the draft at a discount prior to maturity.
Commercial Paper	Short-term, unsecured debt issued by large corporations. The minimum denomination is $25,000, but most commercial paper has a face value of $100,000 or more.	Typically one to six months.	Default risk depends on the credit-worthiness of the issuing corporation.	No active secondary market, but issuer may repurchase commercial paper.
Short-Term Tax Exempts	Short-term debt of state and local governments. These instruments pay interest that is exempt from federal taxation, so their pre-tax yield is lower than that of a similar-risk, fully taxable investment.	Typically one to six months	Default risk depends on the creditworthiness of the issuing government.	Moderate secondary market.

Cash Balances

Corporate liquidity is measured as corporate investments in short-term, marketable securities. In the United States, it rose from $3.6 trillion in 1999 to $5 trillion in 2005, for an increase of almost 40%. According to a 2004 survey of more than 360 companies conducted by Treasury Strategies, Inc., a Chicago consultant, more than half of those firms consider themselves to be net investors, having more short-term investments than short-term debt outstanding.

Why have companies been accumulating more cash? Factors include a shift away from industries such as manufacturing that spend heavily on plant and equipment,

strength in sectors such as financial services that have low capital expenditures and high cash flows, and reluctance by companies to invest heavily after the technology spending spree in the late 1990s. As a result, corporate savings have reached an all-time high.

How are companies investing their cash? A 2004 survey by Treasury Strategies indicated that 36% is invested in money market funds and accounts, 21% is invested in bonds and notes, and the remainder is invested directly in commercial paper, CDs, repurchase agreements, and other investments.

Thus a financial manager who wants to invest the firm's funds in the least risky security will choose to invest in Treasury bills. However, if the financial manager wishes to earn a higher return on the firm's short-term investments, she may opt to invest some or all of the firm's excess cash in a riskier alternative, such as commercial paper.

CONCEPT CHECK

1. List three reasons why a firm holds cash.

2. What tradeoff does a firm face when choosing how to invest its cash?

Summary

1. Working capital management involves managing the firm's short-term assets and short-term liabilities.

2. A firm's cash cycle is the length of time between when the firm pays cash to purchase its initial inventory and when it receives cash from the sale of the output produced from that inventory. The operating cycle is the average length of time between when a firm originally purchases its inventory and when it receives the cash back from selling its product.

3. Trade credit is effectively a loan from the selling firm to its customer. The cost of trade credit depends on the credit terms. The cost of not taking a discount that is offered by a supplier implies an interest rate for the loan.

4. Companies provide trade credit to their customers for two reasons: (a) as an indirect way to lower prices, and (b) because they may have advantages in making loans to their customers relative to other potential sources of credit.

5. A firm should compare the cost of trade credit with the cost of alternative sources of financing in deciding whether to use the trade credit offered.

6. Establishing a credit policy involves three steps: establishing credit standards, establishing credit terms, and establishing a collection policy.

7. The days sales outstanding ratio and aging schedule are two methods used to monitor the effectiveness of a firm's credit policy.

8. Firms should monitor accounts payable to ensure that they are making payments at an optimal time.

9. Firms hold inventory to avoid lost sales due to stock-outs and because of factors such as seasonal demand.

   a. Because excessive inventory uses cash, efficient inventory management increases the firm's free cash flow and thus increases firm value.

   b. The costs of inventory include acquisition costs, order costs, and carrying costs.

10. If a firm's need to hold cash is reduced, the funds can be invested in a number of different short-term securities, including Treasury bills, certificates of deposit, commercial paper, repurchase agreements, banker's acceptances, and short-term tax exempts.

Key Terms

aging schedule *p. 837*
availability float *p. 835*
cash conversion cycle *p. 830*
cash cycle *p. 830*
Check Clearing for the 21st Century Act (Check 21) *p. 835*
collection float *p. 835*
compensating balance *p. 842*
disbursement float *p. 835*
"just-in-time" (JIT) inventory management *p. 841*

mail float *p. 835*
operating cycle *p. 831*
payments pattern *p. 838*
precautionary balance *p. 842*
processing float *p. 835*
stretching the accounts payable *p. 839*
stock-out *p. 840*
trade credit *p. 832*
transactions balance *p. 842*

Further Reading

For more advanced analysis of working capital management, interested students can consult the following textbooks: R. H. Cole and L. Mishler, *Consumer and Business Credit Management*, 11th ed. (New York: McGraw-Hill, 1998); F. J. Fabozzi, S. V. Mann, and M. Choudhry, *The Global Money Markets* (New York: John Wiley, 2002); and T. S. Maness and J. T. Zietlow, *Short-Term Financial Management* (Lawrenceville, NJ: South-Western, 2004).

The following articles address some of the research questions in working capital management.

Cash Management Issues

H. Almeida, M. Campello, and M. S. Weisbach, "The Cash Flow Sensitivity of Cash," *Journal of Finance* 59(4) (2004): 1777–1804; W. Baumol, "The Transactions Demand for Cash: An Inventory Theoretic Approach," *Quarterly Journal of Economics* 66(4) (1952): 545–556; J. A. Gentry, "State of the Art of Short-Run Financial Management," *Financial Management* 17(2) (1988): 41–57; M. Miller and D. Orr, "A Model of the Demand for Money by Firms," *Quarterly Journal of Economics* 80(3) (1966): 413–435; T. Opler, L. Pinkowitz, R. Stulz, and R. Williamson, "The Determinants and Implications of Corporate Cash Holdings," *Journal of Financial Economics* 52(1) (1999): 3–46; C. Payne, "The ABCs of Cash Management," *Journal of Corporate Accounting and Finance* 16(1) (2004): 3–8; L. Pinkowitz and R. Williamson," What Is a Dollar Worth? The Market Value of Cash Holdings," Georgetown University working paper (2004); and L. Pinkowitz and R. Williamson, "Why Do Firms in Countries with Poor Protection of Investor Rights Hold More Cash?" Georgetown University working paper (2004).

Trade Credit

Y. W. Lee and J. D. Stowe, "Product Risk, Asymmetric Information and Trade Credit," *Journal of Financial and Quantitative Analysis* 28(2) (1993): 285–300; M. S. Long, I. B. Malitz, and S. A. Ravid, "Trade Credit, Quality Guarantees, and Product Marketability,"

Financial Management 22(4) (1993): 117–127; S. L. Mian and C. W. Smith, Jr., "Extending Trade Credit and Financing Receivables," *Journal of Applied Corporate Finance* 7(1) (1994): 75–84; S. L. Mian and C. W. Smith, Jr., "Accounts Receivable Management Policy: Theory and Evidence," *Journal of Finance* 47(1) (1992): 169–200; O. K. Ng, J. K. Smith, and R. L. Smith, "Evidence on the Determinants of Credit Terms Used in Interfirm Trade," *Journal of Finance* 54(3) (1999): 1109–1129; F. C. Scherr, "Optimal Trade Credit Limits," *Financial Management* 25(1) (Spring 1996): 71–85; and J. K. Smith, "Trade Credit and Information Asymmetry," *Journal of Finance* 42(4) (1987): 863–872.

Problems

A blue box (■) indicates problems available in MyFinanceLab. An asterisk (*) indicates problems with a higher level of difficulty.

Overview of
Working Capital

1. Answer the following:

   a. What is the difference between a firm's cash cycle and its operating cycle?

   b. How will a firm's cash cycle be affected if a firm increases its inventory, all else equal?

   c. How will a firm's cash cycle be affected if a firm begins to take the discounts offered by its suppliers, all else equal?

2. Does an increase in a firm's cash cycle necessarily mean that a firm is managing its cash poorly?

3. Aberdeen Outboard Motors is contemplating building a new plant. The company anticipates that the plant will require an initial investment of $2 million in net working capital today. The plant will last ten years, at which point the full investment in net working capital will be recovered. Given an annual discount rate of 6%, what is the net present value of this working capital investment?

EXCEL **4.** The Greek Connection had sales of $32 million in 2004, and a cost of goods sold of $20 million. A simplified balance sheet for the firm appears below:

THE GREEK CONNECTION
Balance Sheet
As of December 31, 2004
(thousands of dollars)

Assets		Liabilities and Equity	
Cash	$ 2,000	Accounts payable	$ 1,500
Accounts receivable	3,950	Notes payable	1,000
Inventory	1,300	Accruals	1,220
Total current assets	$ 7,250	Total current liabilities	$ 3,720
Net plant, property		Long-term debt	$ 3,000
and equipment	$ 8,500	Total liabilities	$ 6,720
Total assets	$15,750	Common equity	$ 9,030
		Total liabilities and equity	$15,750

   a. Calculate The Greek Connection's net working capital in 2004.

   b. Calculate the cash conversion cycle of The Greek Connection in 2004.

c. The industry average days sales outstanding ratio is 30 days. What would the cash conversion cycle for The Greek Connection have been in 2004 had it matched the industry average days sales outstanding?

5. Assume the credit terms offered to your firm by your suppliers are 3/5, net 30. Calculate the cost of the trade credit if your firm does not take the discount and pays on day 30.

6. Your supplier offers terms of 1/10, net 45. What is the effective annual cost of trade credit if you choose to forgo the discount and pay on day 45?

7. The Fast Reader Company supplies bulletin board services to numerous hotel chains nationwide. The owner of the firm is investigating the desirability of employing another firm to do her billing and collections. Because the other firm specializes in these services, collection float will be reduced by 20 days. Average daily collections are $1200, and the owner can earn 8% annually on her investments. The other billing firm charges $250 per month for this service. Should the owner employ the other firm?

8. The Saban Corporation is trying to decide whether to switch to a bank that will accommodate electronic funds transfers from Saban's customers. Saban's financial manager believes the new system would decrease its collection float by as much as five days. The new bank would require a compensating balance of $30,000, whereas its present bank has no compensating balance requirement. Saban's average daily collections are $10,000, and it can earn 8% on its short-term investments. Should Saban make the switch? (Assume the compensating balance at the new bank will be deposited in a non-interest-earning account.)

9. What are the three steps involved in establishing a credit policy?

10. The Manana Corporation had sales of $60 million this year. Its accounts receivable balance averaged $2 million. How long, on average, does it take the firm to collect on its sales?

11. The Mighty Power Tool Company has the following accounts on its books:

Customer	Amount Owed ($)	Age (days)
ABC	50,000	35
DEF	35,000	5
GHI	15,000	10
KLM	75,000	22
NOP	42,000	40
QRS	18,000	12
TUV	82,000	53
WXY	36,000	90

The firm extends credit on terms of 1/15, net 30. Develop an aging schedule using 15-day increments through 60 days, and then indicate any accounts that have been outstanding for more than 60 days.

12. What is meant by "stretching the accounts payable"?

 13. Simple Simon's Bakery purchases supplies on terms of 1/10, net 25. If Simple Simon's chooses to take the discount offered, it must obtain a bank loan to meet its short-term financing needs. A local bank has quoted Simple Simon's owner an interest rate of 12% on borrowed funds. Should Simple Simon's enter the loan agreement with the bank and begin taking the discount?

14. Your firm purchases goods from its supplier on terms of 3/15, net 40.

    a. What is the effective annual cost to your firm if it chooses not to take the discount and makes its payment on day 40?

    b. What is the effective annual cost to your firm if it chooses not to take the discount and makes its payment on day 50?

EXCEL ***15.** Use the financial statements supplied below for International Motor Corporation (IMC) to answer the following questions.

    a. Calculate the cash conversion cycle for IMC for both 2003 and 2004. What change has occurred, if any? All else equal, how does this change affect IMC's need for cash?

    b. IMC's suppliers offer terms of net 30. Does it appear that IMC is doing a good job of managing its accounts payable?

INTERNATIONAL MOTOR CORPORATION
Income Statement (in millions)
for the years ending December 31

	2003	2004
Sales	$60,000	$75,000
Cost of goods sold	52,000	61,000
Gross profit	$ 8,000	$ 14,000
Selling and general and administrative expenses	6,000	8,000
Operating profit	$ 2,000	$ 6,000
Interest expense	1,400	1,300
Earnings before tax	$ 600	$ 4,700
Taxes	300	2,350
Earnings after tax	$ 300	$ 2,350

INTERNATIONAL MOTOR CORPORATION
Balance Sheet (in millions)
as of December 31

Assets	2003	2004	Liabilities	2003	2004
Cash	$ 3,080	$ 6,100	Accounts payable	$ 3,600	$ 4,600
Accounts			Notes payable	1,180	1,250
receivable	2,800	6,900	Accruals	5,600	6,211
Inventory	6,200	6,600	Total current		
Total current assets	$12,080	$19,600	liabilities	$10,380	$ 12,061
Net plant, property,			Long-term debt	$ 6,500	$ 7,000
and equipment	$23,087	$20,098	Total liabilities	$16,880	$ 19,061
Total assets	$35,167	$39,698	Equity		
			Common stock	$ 2,735	$ 2,735
			Retained earnings	$15,552	$ 17,902
			Total equity	$18,287	$ 20,637
			Total liabilities and		
			equity	$35,167	$39,698

16. Ohio Valley Homecare Suppliers, Inc. (OVHS), had $20 million in sales in 2004. Its cost of goods sold was $8 million, and its average inventory balance was $2,000,000.

  a. Calculate the days inventory outstanding ratios for OVHS.

  b. The inventory turnover ratio for the industry was five times. By how much would OVHS reduce its investment in inventory if it could improve its inventory turnover ratio to match the industry average?

17. Which of the following short-term securities would you expect to offer the highest before-tax return: Treasury bills, certificates of deposit, short-term tax exempts, or commercial paper? Why?

Data Case

You are the Chief Financial Officer (CFO) of BP. This afternoon you played golf with a member of the company's board of directors. Somewhere during the back nine, the board member enthusiastically described a recent article she had read in a leading management journal. This article noted several companies that had improved their stock price performance through effective working capital management, and the board member was intrigued. She wondered whether BP was managing its working capital effectively and, if not, whether BP could accomplish something similar. How was BP managing its working capital, and how does it compare to its competitors?

Upon returning home, you decide to do a quick preliminary investigation using information freely available on the Internet.

1. Obtain BP's financial statements for the past four years from Nasdaq's Web site (www .nasdaq.com).

   a. Enter the stock symbol (BP) in the box and click on "Summary Quotes."

   b. Next click on "Company Financials" on the left side of the screen.

   c. The income statements will come up first. Place the cursor in the statement and right-click the mouse. Select "Export to Microsoft Excel" from the menu.

   d. Go back to the Web page and click on "Balance Sheets" from the top of the page; repeat the download procedure for the balance sheets.

   e. Copy and paste the balance sheet so that it is on the same worksheet as the income statement.

2. Obtain the industry ratios for comparison from the Reuters Web site (www.reuters.com).

   a. Enter the stock symbol (BP) in the box at the top and click "Go."

   b. Select "Ratios" from the menu on the left side of the page. You will have to register (it's free) or use the username and password supplied by your instructor.

   c. Copy and paste the efficiency ratios onto your spreadsheet where BP's financial statements are located.

3. Compute the cash conversion cycle for BP for each of the last four years.

   a. Compute the Inventory Days using "Cost of Revenue" as cost of goods sold and a 365-day year.

   b. Compute Accounts Receivable Days using a 365-day year.

   c. Compute Accounts Payable Days.

   d. Compute the cash conversion cycle for each year.

4. How has BP's CCC changed over the last few years?

5. Compare BP's inventory and receivables turnover ratios for the most recent year to the industry average.

    a. Compute the inventory turnover ratio as Cost of Revenue / Inventory.

    b. Compute the receivable turnover ratio as Total Revenue / Net Receivables.

    c. How do BP's numbers compare to the industry averages? Do they confirm or refute your answer to Question 4?

6. Determine how BP's free cash flow would change if BP's inventory and accounts receivable balances were adjusted to meet the industry averages.

7. Determine the amount of additional free cash flow that would be available if BP adjusted its Accounts Payable Days to 75 days.

8. Determine the net amount of additional free cash flow and BP's cash conversion cycle if its inventory and receivables turnover ratios were at the industry average and its payable days were 75 days.

9. What are your impressions regarding BP's working capital management based on this preliminary analysis? Discuss any advantages and disadvantages of bringing the cash conversion cycle more in line with the industry averages.

10. You are somewhat concerned about the reliability of financial data from the Internet, and decide to check the data versus BP's SEC filings. To obtain these filings, go to MSN (http://moneycentral.msn.com/home.asp). Type BP into the "Name or Symbol" box and click Go. Once BP comes up, select "SEC Filings" from the vertical menu on the left-hand side. Scroll through the filings to find the latest 20-F, Foreign Annual Reports. Download the PDF version of this report and expand the document bookmarks on the left-hand side. Select Base, then Financial Statements, and then either the Balance Sheet or Income Statement to find the numbers you need. Is there any discrepancy between these numbers and the data you downloaded originally?

Short-Term Financial Planning

notation

EAR effective annual rate

APR annual percentage rate

Mattel, Inc., is a company in the Standard and Poor's 500 index, with year-end 2005 assets of almost $4.4 billion. Mattel designs and manufactures toys throughout the world; its major product lines include the Barbie, Fisher-Price, and American Girl brands. The demand for toys is typically highly seasonal, with demand peaking during the fall in anticipation of December's holiday retailing season. As a result, Mattel's revenues vary dramatically throughout the calendar year. For example, revenues during the fourth quarter of the calendar year are typically more than twice as high as revenues in the first quarter.

Mattel's varying business revenues cause its cash flows to be highly cyclical. The firm generates surplus cash during some months; it has a great demand for capital during other months. These seasonal financing requirements are quite different from its ongoing, long-term demand for permanent capital. How does a company such as Mattel manage its short-term cash needs within each calendar year?

In this chapter, we analyze short-term financial planning. We begin by showing how companies forecast their cash flows to determine their short-term financing needs, and we explore reasons why firms use short-term financing. We next discuss financing policies that guide these financing decisions. Finally, we compare alternative ways a company can finance a shortfall during periods when it is not generating enough cash, including short-term financing with bank loans, commercial paper, and secured financing.

27.1 Forecasting Short-Term Financing Needs

The first step in short-term financial planning is to forecast the company's future cash flows. This exercise has two distinct objectives. First, a company forecasts its cash flows to determine whether it will have surplus cash or a cash deficit for each period. Second, management needs to decide whether that surplus or deficit is temporary or permanent. If it is permanent, it may affect the firm's long-term financial decisions. For example, if a company anticipates an ongoing surplus of cash, it may choose to increase its dividend payout. Deficits resulting from investments in long-term projects are often financed using long-term sources of capital, such as equity or long-term bonds.

In this chapter, we focus specifically on short-term financial planning. With this perspective, we are interested in analyzing the types of cash surpluses or deficits that are temporary and, therefore, short-term in nature. When a company analyzes its short-term financing needs, it typically examines cash flows at quarterly intervals. To illustrate, let's assume that it is currently December 2009 and consider the case of Springfield Snowboards, Inc. Springfield manufactures snowboarding equipment, which it sells primarily to sports retailers. Springfield anticipates that in 2010 its sales will grow by 10% to $20 million and its total net income will be $1,950,000. Assuming that both sales and production will occur uniformly throughout the year, management's forecast of its quarterly net income and statement of cash flows for 2010 is presented in the spreadsheet in Table 27.1 (also shown, in gray, is the income statement from the fourth quarter of 2009).[1]

From this forecast, we see that Springfield is a profitable company. Its quarterly net income is almost $500,000. Springfield's capital expenditures are equal to depreciation, and while Springfield's working capital requirements increase in the first quarter due to the increase in sales, they remain constant thereafter and so have no further cash flow consequence. Based on these projections, Springfield will be able to fund projected sales growth from its operating profit and, in fact, will accumulate excess cash on an ongoing basis. Given similar growth forecasts for next year and beyond, this surplus is likely to be long term. Springfield could reduce the surplus by paying some of it out as a dividend or by repurchasing shares.

Let's now turn to Springfield's potential short-term financing needs. Firms require short-term financing for three reasons: seasonalities, negative cash flow shocks, and positive cash flow shocks.

Seasonalities

For many firms, sales are seasonal. When sales are concentrated during a few months, sources and uses of cash are also likely to be seasonal. Firms in this position may find themselves with a surplus of cash during some months that is sufficient to compensate for a shortfall during other months. However, because of timing differences, such firms often have short-term financing needs.

To illustrate, let's return to the example of Springfield Snowboards. In Table 27.1, management assumed that Springfield's sales occur uniformly throughout the year. In reality, for a snowboard manufacturer, sales are likely to be highly seasonal. Assume that 20% of sales occur during the first quarter, 10% during each of the second and third

---

1. Given the extensive coverage we have provided in Chapters 2 and 19 on how to construct pro forma financial statements, we do not rehash those details here. For simplicity, we have assumed Springfield has no debt, and earns no interest on retained cash.

TABLE 27.1 SPREADSHEET	Projected Financial Statements for Springfield Snowboards, 2010, Assuming Level Sales

	Quarter	2009Q4	2010Q1	2010Q2	2010Q3	2010Q4
Income Statement ($000)						
1	Sales	4,545	5,000	5,000	5,000	5,000
2	Cost of Goods Sold	(2,955)	(3,250)	(3,250)	(3,250)	(3,250)
3	Selling, General and Administrative	(455)	(500)	(500)	(500)	(500)
4	EBITDA	1,136	1,250	1,250	1,250	1,250
5	Depreciation	(455)	(500)	(500)	(500)	(500)
6	EBIT	682	750	750	750	750
7	Taxes	(239)	(263)	(263)	(263)	(263)
8	Net Income	443	488	488	488	488
Statement of Cash Flows						
9	Net Income		488	488	488	488
10	Depreciation		500	500	500	500
11	Changes in Working Capital					
12	Accounts Receivable		(136)	—	—	—
13	Inventory		—	—	—	—
14	Accounts Payable		48	—	—	—
15	**Cash from Operating Activities**		899	988	988	988
16	Capital Expenditures		(500)	(500)	(500)	(500)
17	Other Investment		—	—	—	—
18	**Cash from Investing Activities**		(500)	(500)	(500)	(500)
19	Net Borrowing		—	—	—	—
20	Dividends		—	—	—	—
21	Capital Contributions		—	—	—	—
22	**Cash from Financing Activities**		—	—	—	—
23	**Change in Cash and Equivalents** (15 + 18 + 22)		399	488	488	488

quarters (largely Southern Hemisphere sales), and 60% of sales during the fourth quarter, in anticipation of the (Northern Hemisphere) winter snowboarding season. The spreadsheet in Table 27.2 presents the resulting statement of cash flows. These forecasts continue to assume production occurs uniformly throughout the year.

From Table 27.2, we see that Springfield is still a profitable company, and its annual net income still totals $1,950,000. However, the introduction of seasonal sales creates some dramatic swings in Springfield's short-term cash flows. There are two effects of seasonality on cash flows. First, while cost of goods sold fluctuates proportionally with sales, other costs (such as administrative overhead and depreciation) do not, leading to large changes in the firm's net income by quarter. Second, net working capital changes are more pronounced. In the first quarter, Springfield receives cash by collecting the receivables from last year's high fourth quarter sales. During the second and third quarters, the company's inventory balance increases. Given capacity constraints in its manufacturing equipment, Springfield produces snowboards throughout the year, even though sales during the summer are low. Because production occurs uniformly, accounts payable do not vary over the year. Inventory, however, builds up in anticipation of fourth quarter sales—and increases in inventory use cash. As a consequence, Springfield has negative net cash flows during the second and third quarters, primarily to fund its inventory. By the fourth quarter, high sales recover cash for the company.

**TABLE 27.2
SPREADSHEET**

**Projected Financial Statements for Springfield
Snowboards, 2010, Assuming Seasonal Sales**

	Quarter	2009Q4	2010Q1	2010Q2	2010Q3	2010Q4
Income Statement ($000)						
1	Sales	10,909	4,000	2,000	2,000	12,000
2	Cost of Goods Sold	(7,091)	(2,600)	(1,300)	(1,300)	(7,800)
3	Selling, General and Administrative	(773)	(450)	(350)	(350)	(850)
4	EBITDA	3,045	950	350	350	3,350
5	Depreciation	(455)	(500)	(500)	(500)	(500)
6	EBIT	2,591	450	(150)	(150)	2,850
7	Taxes	(907)	(158)	53	53	(998)
8	Net Income	1,684	293	(98)	(98)	1,853
Statement of Cash Flows						
9	Net Income		293	(98)	(98)	1,853
10	Depreciation		500	500	500	500
11	Changes in Working Capital					
12	Accounts Receivable		2,073	600	—	(3,000)
13	Inventory		(650)	(1,950)	(1,950)	4,550
14	Accounts Payable		48	—	—	—
15	**Cash from Operating Activities**		2,263	(948)	(1,548)	3,903
16	Capital Expenditures		(500)	(500)	(500)	(500)
17	Other Investment		—	—	—	—
18	**Cash from Investing Activities**		(500)	(500)	(500)	(500)
19	Net Borrowing		—	—	—	—
20	Dividends		—	—	—	—
21	Capital Contributions		—	—	—	—
22	**Cash from Financing Activities**		—	—	—	—
23	**Change in Cash and Equivalents** (15 + 18 + 22)		1,763	(1,448)	(2,048)	3,403

Seasonal sales create large short-term cash flow deficits and surpluses. During the second and third quarters, the company will need to find additional short-term sources of cash to fund inventory. During the fourth quarter, Springfield will have a large short-term surplus. Given that its seasonal cash flow needs are likely to recur next year, Springfield may choose to invest this cash in one of the short term investment options discussed in Chapter 26. Management can then use this cash to fund some of its short-term working capital needs during the following year.

Negative Cash Flow Shocks

Occasionally, a company will encounter circumstances in which cash flows are temporarily negative for an unexpected reason. We refer to such a situation as a negative cash flow shock. Like seasonalities, negative cash flow shocks can create short-term financing needs. Returning to the Springfield Snowboards example, assume that during April 2010, management learns that some manufacturing equipment has broken unexpectedly. It will cost an additional $1,000,000 to replace the equipment.[2] To illustrate the effect of this

---

2. For simplicity, assume that the book value of the replaced equipment is zero, so that the equipment change does not have any tax implications. Also, assume that Springfield obtains the replacement equipment quickly, so that any interruption in production is negligible. The general results contained in the discussion still hold if we relax these assumptions, although the calculations are somewhat more complex.

TABLE 27.3 SPREADSHEET

Projected Financial Statements for Springfield Snowboards, 2010, Assuming Level Sales and a Negative Cash Flow Shock

	Quarter	2009Q4	2010Q1	2010Q2	2010Q3	2010Q4
Income Statement ($000)						
1	Sales	4,545	5,000	5,000	5,000	5,000
2	Cost of Goods Sold	(2,955)	(3,250)	(3,250)	(3,250)	(3,250)
3	Selling, General and Administrative	(455)	(500)	(500)	(500)	(500)
4	EBITDA	1,136	1,250	1,250	1,250	1,250
5	Depreciation	(455)	(500)	(500)	(525)	(525)
6	EBIT	682	750	750	725	725
7	Taxes	(239)	(263)	(263)	(254)	(254)
8	Net Income	443	488	488	471	471
Statement of Cash Flows						
9	Net Income			488	488	471	471
10	Depreciation			500	500	525	525
11	Changes in Working Capital						
12	Accounts Receivable			(136)	—	—	—
13	Inventory			—	—	—	—
14	Accounts Payable			48	—	—	—
15	**Cash from Operating Activities**			899	988	996	996
16	Capital Expenditures			(500)	(1,500)	(525)	(525)
17	Other Investment			—	—	—	—
18	**Cash from Investing Activities**			(500)	(1,500)	(525)	(525)
19	Net Borrowing			—	—	—	—
20	Dividends			—	—	—	—
21	Capital Contributions			—	—	—	—
22	**Cash from Financing Activities**			—	—	—	—
23	**Change in Cash and Equivalents** (15 + 18 + 22)			399	(513)	471	471

negative cash flow shock, we return to the base case in which Springfield's sales are level rather than seasonal. (The marginal impact of this negative shock given seasonal sales would be similar.) The spreadsheet in Table 27.3 presents cash flows with level sales and the broken equipment.

In this case, the one-time expenditure of $1 million to replace equipment results in a negative net cash flow of $513,000 during the second quarter of 2010. If its cash reserves are insufficient, Springfield will have to borrow (or arrange for another financing source) to cover the $513,000 shortfall. However, the company continues to generate positive cash flow in subsequent quarters, and by the fourth quarter it will have generated enough in cumulative cash flow to repay any loan. Therefore, this negative cash flow shock has created the need for short-term financing.

Positive Cash Flow Shocks

We next analyze a case in which a positive cash flow shock affects short-term financing needs. Although this surprise is good news, it still creates demand for short-term financing.

During the first quarter of 2010, the director of marketing at Springfield Snowboards announces a deal with a chain of outdoor sporting goods stores located in the Midwest. Springfield will be the exclusive supplier to this customer, leading to an overall sales increase of 20% for the firm. The increased sales will begin in the second quarter. As part

TABLE 27.4 SPREADSHEET	**Projected Financial Statements for Springfield Snowboards, 2010, Assuming Level Sales and a Growth Opportunity**

Quarter	2009Q4	2010Q1	2010Q2	2010Q3	2010Q4
Income Statement ($000)					
1 Sales	4,545	5,000	6,000	6,000	6,000
2 Cost of Goods Sold	(2,955)	(3,250)	(3,900)	(3,900)	(3,900)
3 Selling, General and Administrative	(455)	(1,000)	(600)	(600)	(600)
4 EBITDA	1,136	750	1,500	1,500	1,500
5 Depreciation	(455)	(500)	(525)	(525)	(525)
6 EBIT	682	250	975	975	975
7 Taxes	(239)	(88)	(341)	(341)	(341)
8 Net Income	443	163	634	634	634
Statement of Cash Flows					
9 Net Income		163	634	634	634
10 Depreciation		500	525	525	525
11 Changes in Working Capital					
12 Accounts Receivable		(136)	(300)	—	—
13 Inventory		—	—	—	—
14 Accounts Payable		48	105	—	—
15 **Cash from Operating Activities**		574	964	1,159	1,159
16 Capital Expenditures		(1,500)	(525)	(525)	(525)
17 Other Investment		—	—	—	—
18 **Cash from Investing Activities**		(1,500)	(525)	(525)	(525)
19 Net Borrowing		—	—	—	—
20 Dividends		—	—	—	—
21 Capital Contributions		—	—	—	—
22 **Cash from Financing Activities**		—	—	—	—
23 Change in Cash and Equivalents (15 + 18 + 22)		(926)	439	634	634

of the deal, Springfield has agreed to a one-time expense of $500,000 for marketing in areas where the stores are located. An extra $1 million in capital expenditures is also required during the first quarter to increase production capacity. Likewise, sales growth will affect required working capital.

Managers at Springfield prepared the cash flow forecasts in the spreadsheet in Table 27.4 to reflect this new business. Notice that net income is lower during the first quarter, reflecting the $500,000 increase in marketing expenses. By contrast, net income in subsequent quarters is higher, reflecting the higher sales. Sales increase in each of the first two quarters results in increase in accounts receivable and accounts payable.

Even though the unexpected event in this case—the opportunity to grow more rapidly—is positive, it results in a negative net cash flow during the first quarter, due primarily to the new marketing expenses and capital expenditures. However, because the company will be even more profitable in subsequent quarters, this financing need is temporary.

Now that we have explained how a company determines its short-term needs, let's explore how these needs are financed.

CONCEPT CHECK   1. How do we forecast the firm's future cash requirements?

2. What is the effect of seasonalities on short-term cash flows?

27.2 The Matching Principle

In a perfect capital market, the choice of financing is irrelevant; thus how the firm chooses to finance its short-term cash needs cannot affect value. In reality, important market frictions exist, including transaction costs. For example, one transaction cost is the opportunity cost of holding cash in accounts that pay little or no interest. Firms also face high transaction costs if they need to negotiate a loan on short notice to cover a cash shortfall. Firms can increase their value by adopting a policy that minimizes these kinds of costs. One such policy is known as the matching principle. The **matching principle** states that short-term needs should be financed with short-term debt and long-term needs should be financed with long-term sources of funds.

Permanent Working Capital

Permanent working capital is the amount that a firm must keep invested in its short-term assets to support its continuing operations. Because this investment in working capital is required so long as the firm remains in business, it constitutes a long-term investment. The matching principle indicates that the firm should finance this permanent investment in working capital with long-term sources of funds. Such sources have lower transaction costs than short-term sources of funds, which would have to be replaced more often.

Temporary Working Capital

Another portion of a firm's investment in its accounts receivable and inventory is temporary and results from seasonal fluctuations in the firm's business or unanticipated shocks. This **temporary working capital** is the difference between the actual level of investment in short-term assets and the permanent working capital investment. Because temporary working capital represents a short-term need, the firm should finance this portion of its investment with short-term financing.

To illustrate the distinction between permanent and temporary working capital, we return to the Springfield Snowboards example. Table 27.2 presented cash flow forecasts assuming seasonal sales. In the spreadsheet in Table 27.5, we report the underlying levels of working capital that correspond to these forecasts.

TABLE 27.5 SPREADSHEET	Projected Levels of Working Capital for Springfield Snowboards, 2010, Assuming Seasonal Sales

	Quarter	2009Q4	2010Q1	2010Q2	2010Q3	2010Q4
Net Working Capital Requirements ($000)						
1	Minimum Cash Balance	500	500	500	500	500
2	Accounts Receivable	3,273	1,200	600	600	3,600
3	Inventory	300	950	2,900	4,850	300
4	Accounts Payable	(477)	(525)	(525)	(525)	(525)
5	Net Working Capital	3,595	2,125	3,475	5,425	3,875

In Table 27.5, we see that working capital for Springfield varies from a minimum of $2,125,000 in the first quarter of 2010 to $5,425,000 in the third quarter. The minimum level of working capital, or $2,125,000, can be thought of as the firm's permanent working capital. The difference between this minimum level and the higher levels in subsequent quarters (for example, $5,425,000 - $2,125,000 = $3,300,000 in the third quarter) reflects Springfield's temporary working capital requirements.

Financing Policy Choices

Following the matching principle should, in the long run, help minimize a firm's transaction costs.[3] But what if, instead of using the matching principle, a firm financed its permanent working capital needs with short-term debt? When the short-term debt comes due, the firm will have to negotiate a new loan. This new loan will involve additional transaction costs, and it will carry whatever market interest rate exists at the time. As a result, the firm is also exposed to interest rate risk. Financing part or all of the permanent working capital with short-term debt is known as an **aggressive financing policy**. An ultra-aggressive policy would involve financing even some of the plant, property, and equipment with short-term sources of funds.

When the yield curve is upward sloping, the interest rate on short-term debt is lower than the rate on long-term debt. In that case, short-term debt may appear cheaper than long-term debt. However, we know that with perfect capital markets, Modigliani and Miller's results from Chapter 14 apply: The benefit of the lower rate from short-term debt is offset by the risk that the firm will have to refinance the debt in the future at a higher rate. This risk is borne by the equity holders, and so the firm's equity cost of capital will rise to offset any benefit from the lower borrowing rate.

Why, then, might a firm choose an aggressive financing policy? Such a policy might be beneficial if the market imperfections mentioned in Chapter 16, such as agency costs and asymmetric information, are important. The value of short-term debt is less sensitive to the firm's credit quality than long-term debt; therefore, its value will be less affected by management's actions or information. As a result, short-term debt can have lower agency and lemons costs than long-term debt, and an aggressive financing policy can benefit shareholders. On the other hand, by relying on short-term debt the firm exposes itself to **funding risk**, which is the risk of incurring financial distress costs should the firm not be able to refinance its debt in a timely manner or at a reasonable rate.

Alternatively, a firm could finance its short-term needs with long-term debt, a practice known as a **conservative financing policy**. For example, when following such a policy, a firm would use long-term sources of funds to finance its fixed assets, permanent working capital, and some of its seasonal needs. The firm would use short-term debt very sparingly to meet its peak seasonal needs. To implement such a policy effectively, there will necessarily be periods when excess cash is available—those periods when the firm requires little or no investment in temporary working capital. In an imperfect capital market, this cash will earn a below-market interest rate, thereby reducing the firm's value. It also increases the possibility that managers of the firm will use this excess cash nonproductively—for example, on perquisites for themselves.

Once a firm determines its short-term financing needs, it must choose which instruments it will use for this purpose. In the rest of this chapter, we survey the specific financing options that are available: bank loans, commercial paper, and secured financing.

---

3. Some evidence indicates that most firms appear to follow the matching principle. See W. Beranek, C. Cornwell, and S. Choi, "External Financing, Liquidity, and Capital Expenditures," *Journal of Financial Research* (Summer 1995): 207–222; and M. H. Stohs and D. C. Mauer, "The Determinants of Corporate Debt Maturity Structure," *Journal of Business* 69(3) (1996): 279–312.

1. What is the matching principle?

    2. What is the difference between temporary and permanent working capital?

27.3 Short-Term Financing with Bank Loans

One of the primary sources of short-term financing, especially for small businesses, is the commercial bank. Bank loans are typically initiated with a **promissory note**, which is a written statement that indicates the amount of the loan, the date payment is due, and the interest rate. In this section, we examine three types of bank loans: single, end-of-period payment loans; lines of credit; and bridge loans. In addition, we compare the interest rates and present common stipulations and fees associated with these bank loans.

Single, End-of-Period Payment Loan

The most straightforward type of bank loan is a single, end-of-period-payment loan. Such a loan agreement requires that the firm pay interest on the loan and pay back the principal in one lump sum at the end of the loan. The interest rate may be fixed or variable. With a fixed interest rate, the specific rate that the commercial bank will charge is stipulated at the time the loan is made. With a variable interest rate, the terms of the loan may indicate that the rate will vary with some spread relative to a benchmark rate, such as the yield on one-year Treasury securities or the prime rate. The **prime rate** is the rate banks charge their most creditworthy customers. However, large corporations can often negotiate bank loans at an interest rate that is *below* the prime rate. For example, in its 2004 annual report, Mattel indicated that the weighted average interest rate it paid on average short-term borrowings from domestic institutions was 1.5% in 2004. By comparison, the average prime rate in 2004 was 4.34%.[4] Another common benchmark rate is the **London Inter-Bank Offered Rate**, or **LIBOR**, which is the rate of interest at which banks borrow funds from each other in the London interbank market. It is quoted for maturities of one day to one year for 10 major currencies. As it is a rate paid by banks with the highest credit quality, most firms will borrow at a rate that exceeds LIBOR.

Line of Credit

Another common type of bank loan arrangement is a **line of credit**, in which a bank agrees to lend a firm any amount up to a stated maximum. This flexible agreement allows the firm to draw upon the line of credit whenever it chooses.

Firms frequently use lines of credit to finance seasonal needs.[5] The line of credit may be **uncommitted**, meaning it is an informal agreement that does not legally bind the bank to provide the funds. As long as the borrower's financial condition remains good, the bank is happy to advance additional funds. A **committed line of credit** consists of a written, legally binding agreement that obligates the bank to provide the funds regardless of the

---

4. Mattel 2004 annual report and *Federal Reserve Statistical Release* Web site.

5. Lines of credit may be used for other purposes as well. For example, Gartner, Inc., which provides research and analysis on information technology, announced that it would use both cash on hand and an existing bank line of credit to finance its 2005 acquisition of competitor Meta Group (Craig Schneider, "Dealwatch," *CFO.com*, January 5, 2005).

financial condition of the firm (unless the firm is bankrupt) as long as the firm satisfies any restrictions in the agreement. These arrangements are typically accompanied by a compensating balance requirement (that is, a requirement that the firm maintain a minimum level of deposits with the bank) and restrictions regarding the level of the firm's working capital. The firm pays a commitment fee of $\frac{1}{4}$% to $\frac{1}{2}$% of the unused portion of the line of credit in addition to interest on the amount that the firm borrowed. The line of credit agreement may also stipulate that at some point in time the outstanding balance must be zero. This policy ensures that the firm does not use the short-term financing to finance its long-term obligations.

Banks usually renegotiate the terms of a line of credit on an annual basis. A **revolving line of credit** is a committed line of credit that involves a solid commitment from the bank for a longer period of time, typically two to three years. A revolving line of credit with no fixed maturity is called **evergreen credit**. In its 2004 annual report, Mattel reported that it relied on a $1.3 billion revolving credit facility as the primary source of financing for its seasonal working capital requirements.

Bridge Loan

A **bridge loan** is another type of short-term bank loan that is often used to "bridge the gap" until a firm can arrange for long-term financing. For example, a real estate developer may use a bridge loan to finance the construction of a shopping mall. After the mall is completed, the developer will obtain long-term financing. Other firms use bridge loans to finance plant and equipment until they receive the proceeds from the sale of a long-term debt or an equity issue. After a natural disaster, lenders may provide businesses with short-term loans to serve as bridges until they receive insurance payments or long-term disaster relief.

Bridge loans are often quoted as discount loans with fixed interest rates. With a **discount loan**, the borrower is required to pay the interest at the *beginning* of the loan period. The lender deducts interest from the loan proceeds when the loan is made.

Common Loan Stipulations and Fees

We now turn to common loan stipulations and fees that affect the effective interest rate on a loan. Specifically, we look at loan commitment fees, loan origination fees, and compensating balance requirements.

Commitment Fees. Various loan fees charged by banks affect the effective interest rate that the borrower pays. For example, the commitment fee associated with a committed line of credit increases the effective cost of the loan to the firm. The "fee" can really be considered an interest charge under another name. Suppose that a firm has negotiated a committed line of credit with a stated maximum of $1 million and an interest rate of 10% (EAR) with a bank. The commitment fee is 0.5% (EAR). At the beginning of the year, the firm borrows $800,000. It then repays this loan at the end of the year, leaving $200,000 unused for the rest of the year. The total cost of the loan is

Interest on borrowed funds = 0.10($800,000)	= $80,000
Commitment fee paid on unused portion = 0.005($200,000)	= $ 1,000
Total cost	$81,000

Loan Origination Fee. Another common type of fee is a **loan origination fee**, which a bank charges to cover credit checks and legal fees. The firm pays the fee when the loan is initiated; like a discount loan, it reduces the amount of usable proceeds that the firm receives. Also like the commitment fee, it is effectively an additional interest charge.

To illustrate, assume that Timmons Towel and Diaper Service is offered a $500,000 loan for three months at an APR of 12%. This loan has a loan origination fee of 1%. The loan origination fee is charged on the principal of the loan, so in this case the fee amounts to $0.01 \times \$500,000 = \$5000$, so the actual amount borrowed is $495,000. The interest payment for three months is $\$500,000\left(\frac{0.12}{4}\right) = \$15,000$. Putting these cash flows on a timeline:

Thus the actual three-month interest rate paid is

$$\frac{515,000}{495,000} - 1 = 4.04\%$$

Expressing this rate as an EAR gives $1.0404^4 - 1 = 17.17\%$.

Compensating Balance Requirements. Regardless of the loan structure, the bank may include a compensating balance requirement in the loan agreement that reduces the usable loan proceeds. Recall from Chapter 26 that a compensating balance requirement means that the firm must hold a certain percentage of the principal of the loan in an account at the bank. Assume that, rather than charging a loan origination fee, Timmons Towel and Diaper Service's bank requires that the firm keep an amount equal to 10% of the loan principal in a non-interest-bearing account with the bank as long as the loan remains outstanding. The loan was for $500,000, so this requirement means that Timmons must hold $0.10 \times 500,000 = \$50,000$ in an account at the bank. Thus the firm has only $450,000 of the loan proceeds actually available for use, although it must pay interest on the full loan amount. At the end of the loan period, the firm owes $\$500,000 \times (1 + 0.12/4) = \$515,000$, and so must pay $515,000 - 50,000 = \$465,000$ after using its compensating balance. Putting these cash flows on a timeline:

The actual three-month interest rate paid is

$$\frac{465,000}{450,000} - 1 = 3.33\%$$

Expressing this as an EAR gives $1.0333^4 - 1 = 14.01\%$.

We assumed that Timmons' compensating balance is held in a non-interest-earning account. Sometimes a bank will allow the compensating balance to be held in an account that pays a small amount of interest to offset part of the interest expense of the loan.

Compensating Balance Requirements and the Effective Annual Rate

Problem

Assume that Timmons Towel and Diaper Service's bank pays 1% (APR with quarterly compounding) on its compensating balance accounts. What is the EAR of Timmons' three-month loan?

Solution

The balance held in the compensating balance account will grow to $50,000(1 + 0.01/4) =$ $50,125. Thus the final loan payment will be $500,000 + 15,000 - 50,125 = \$464,875$. Notice that the interest on the compensating balance accounts offsets some of the interest that Timmons pays on the loan. Putting the new cash flows on a timeline:

The actual three-month interest rate paid is

$$\frac{464,875}{450,000} - 1 = 3.31\%$$

Expressing this as an EAR gives $1.0331^4 - 1 = 13.89\%$.

CONCEPT CHECK

1. What is the difference between an uncommitted line of credit and a committed line of credit?

2. Describe common loan stipulations and fees.

27.4   Short-Term Financing with Commercial Paper

Commercial paper is short-term, unsecured debt used by large corporations that is usually a cheaper source of funds than a short-term bank loan. The minimum face value is $25,000, and most commercial paper has a face value of at least $100,000. The interest on commercial paper is typically paid by selling it at an initial discount.

The average maturity of commercial paper is 30 days and the maximum maturity is 270 days. Extending the maturity beyond 270 days triggers a registration requirement with the Securities and Exchange Commission (SEC), which increases issue costs and creates a time delay in the sale of the issue. Commercial paper is referred to as either direct paper or dealer paper. With **direct paper**, the firm sells the security directly to investors. With **dealer paper**, dealers sell the commercial paper to investors in exchange for a spread (or fee) for their services. The spread decreases the proceeds that the issuing firm receives, thereby increasing the effective cost of the paper. Like long-term debt, commercial paper is rated by credit rating agencies.

The Effective Annual Rate of Commercial Paper

Problem

A firm issues three-month commercial paper with a $100,000 face value and receives $98,000. What effective annual rate is the firm paying for its funds?

Solution

Let's put the firm's cash flows on a timeline:

The actual three-month interest rate paid is

$$\frac{100,000}{98,000} - 1 = 2.04\%$$

Expressing this as an EAR gives $1.0204^4 - 1 = 8.42\%$.

CONCEPT CHECK

1. What is commercial paper?

2. What is the maximum maturity of commercial paper?

27.5 Short-Term Financing with Secured Financing

Businesses can also obtain short-term financing by using **secured loans**, which are loans collateralized with short-term assets—most typically the firm's accounts receivables or inventory. Commercial banks, finance companies, and **factors**, which are firms that purchase the receivables of other companies, are the most common sources for secured short-term loans.

Accounts Receivable as Collateral

Firms can use accounts receivable as security for a loan by pledging or factoring.

Pledging of Accounts Receivable. In a **pledging of accounts receivable** agreement, the lender reviews the invoices that represent the credit sales of the borrowing firm and decides which credit accounts it will accept as collateral for the loan, based on its own credit standards. The lender then typically lends the borrower some percentage of the value of the accepted invoices—say, 75%. If the borrowing firm's customers default on their bills, the firm is still responsible to the lender for the money.

Factoring of Accounts Receivable. In a **factoring of accounts receivable** arrangement, the firm sells receivables to the lender (i.e., the factor), and the lender agrees to pay the firm the amount due from its customers at the end of the firm's payment period. For example, if a firm sells its goods on terms of net 30, then the factor will pay the firm the face value of its receivables, less a factor's fee, at the end of 30 days. The firm's customers are usually instructed to make payments directly to the lender. In many cases, the firm can borrow as much as 80% of the face value of its receivables from the factor, thereby receiving its funds in advance. In such a case, the lender will charge interest on the loan in addition to the factor's fee. The lender charges the factor's fee, which may range from $\frac{3}{4}\%$ to $1\frac{1}{2}\%$ of the face value of the accounts receivable, whether or not the firm borrows any of the available funds. Both the interest rate and the factor's fee vary depending on such issues as the size of the borrowing firm and the dollar volume of its receivables. The dollar amounts involved in factoring agreements may be substantial. As of December

A Seventeenth-Century Financing Solution

In recent years, it has become more difficult for small businesses to obtain funding so as to purchase inventory. Several factors have contributed to this trend. First, bigger banks have acquired many small, regional banks that were traditionally important sources of loans to small businesses. Second, large banks have tightened lending requirements for small borrowers. Third, many small businesses rely increasingly on foreign suppliers that demand payment upfront, increasing the immediate demand for capital by small businesses.

Some small businesses have started to rely on a 400-year-old solution: venture merchant financing. This type of financing arrangement began in the seventeenth century, when groups of investors would provide capital for the voyages of Dutch sea captains. The captains would travel the seas, using the capital to purchase exotic merchandise. On their return, the merchant bankers would take about one-third of the captain's profits when the goods were sold as compensation for the financing.

Now consider the Kosher Depot, which sells exotic kosher foods to restaurants and supermarkets in Westbury, New York. It wanted to grow but lacked access to capital to purchase more specialty-foods inventory. Kosher Depot arranged a two-year, $3.3 million venture merchant financing arrangement with Capstone Business Credit. Kosher Depot would prearrange sales and notify Capstone, which would use its capital to buy the goods for Kosher Depot. Capstone would purchase and import the goods, storing them in its own warehouses. The warehouses then filled the orders received by Kosher Depot. For its services, Capstone received about 30% of the profits.

The cost of this arrangement—the 30% margin charged by the venture merchant—may be expensive relative to some of the alternative financing arrangements discussed in this chapter. However, the price may be worthwhile for a small business with no other short-term alternatives.

Source: Marie Leone, "Capital Ideas: A Little Cash'll Do Ya," *CFO.com*, March 3, 2005.

2004, for example, Mattel had sold more than $400 million of its accounts receivable under factoring arrangements.

A factoring arrangement may be **with recourse**, meaning that the lender can seek payment from the borrower should the borrower's customers default on their bills. Alternatively, the financing arrangement may be **without recourse**, in which case the lender bears the risk of bad-debt losses. In this latter case, the factor will pay the firm the amount due regardless of whether the factor receives payment from the firm's customers. If the arrangement is with recourse, the lender may not require that it approve the customers' accounts before sales are made. If the factoring agreement is without recourse, the borrowing firm must receive credit approval for a customer from the factor prior to shipping the goods. If the factor gives its approval, the firm ships the goods and the customer is directed to make payment directly to the lender.

Inventory as Collateral

Inventory can be used as collateral for a loan in one of three ways: as a floating lien, as a trust receipt, or in a warehouse arrangement.

Floating Lien.   In a **floating lien**, **general lien**, or **blanket lien** arrangement, all of the inventory is used to secure the loan. This arrangement is the riskiest setup from the standpoint of the lender because the value of the collateral used to secure the loan dwindles as inventory is sold. When a firm becomes financially distressed, management may be tempted to sell the inventory without making payments on the loan. In such a case, the firm may not have enough funds to replenish its inventory. As a result, the loan may become under-collateralized. To counter this risk, this type of loan bears a higher interest rate than the next two arrangements that we discuss. In addition, lenders will lend a low percentage of the value of the inventory.

Trust Receipt.   With a **trust receipts loan** or **floor planning**, distinguishable inventory items are held in a trust as security for the loan. As these items are sold, the firm remits the proceeds from their sale to the lender in repayment of the loan. The lender will periodically send someone to ensure that the borrower has not sold some of the specified inventory and failed to make a repayment on the loan. Car dealerships often use this type of secured financing arrangement to obtain the funds needed to purchase vehicles from the manufacturer.

Warehouse Arrangement.   In a **warehouse arrangement**, the inventory that serves as collateral for the loan is stored in a warehouse. A warehouse arrangement is the least risky collateral arrangement from the standpoint of the lender. This type of arrangement can be set up in one of two ways.

The first method is to use a **public warehouse**, which is a business that exists for the sole purpose of storing and tracking the inflow and outflow of the inventory. The lender extends a loan to the borrowing firm, based on the value of the inventory stored. When the borrowing firm needs the inventory to sell, it returns to the warehouse and retrieves it upon receiving permission from the lender. This arrangement provides the lender with the tightest control over the inventory. Public warehouses work well for some types of inventory, such as wine and tobacco products, which must age before they are ready to be sold. It is not practical for items that are subject to spoilage or are bulky and, therefore, difficult to transport to and from the warehouse.

The second option, a **field warehouse**, is operated by a third party, but is set up on the borrower's premises in a separate area so that the inventory collateralizing the loan is kept apart from the borrower's main plant. This type of arrangement is convenient for the borrower but gives the lender the added security of having the inventory that serves as collateral controlled by a third party.

Warehouse arrangements are expensive. The business operating the warehouse charges a fee on top of the interest that the borrower must pay the lender for the loan. However, the borrower may also save on the costs of storing the inventory herself. Because the warehouser is a professional at inventory control, there is likely to be little loss due to damaged goods or theft, which in turn lowers insurance costs. Because the control of the inventory remains in the hands of a third party, lenders may be willing to lend a greater percentage of the market value of the inventory than they would under other inventory arrangements.

Calculating the Effective Annual Cost of Warehouse Financing

Problem

The Row Cannery wants to borrow $2 million for one month. Using its inventory as collateral, it can obtain a 12% (APR) loan. The lender requires that a warehouse arrangement be used. The warehouse fee is $10,000, payable at the end of the month. Calculate the effective annual rate of this loan for Row Cannery.

Solution

The monthly interest rate is $12\% / 12 = 1\%$. At the end of the month, Row will owe $\$2,000,000 \times 1.01 = \$2,020,000$ plus the warehouse fee of $\$10,000$. Putting the cash flows on a timeline gives:

The actual one-month interest rate paid is

$$\frac{2,030,000}{2,000,000} - 1 = 1.5\%$$

Expressing this as an EAR gives $1.015^{12} - 1 = 19.6\%$.

The method that a firm adopts when using its inventory to collateralize a loan will affect the ultimate cost of the loan. The blanket lien agreement exposes the lender to the most risk and will, therefore, carry the highest interest rate of the three types of arrangements discussed. While a warehousing arrangement provides the greatest amount of control over the inventory to the lender, resulting in a lower interest rate on the loan itself, the borrowing firm must pay the additional fees charged by the warehouser and accept the inconvenience associated with the loss of control. Although a trust receipts arrangement may offer a lower interest rate than a blanket lien and allows the firm to avoid the high fees associated with a warehouse arrangement, it can be used only with certain types of inventory.

CONCEPT CHECK

1. What is factoring of accounts receivable?

2. What is the difference between a floating lien and a trust receipt?

Summary

1. The first step in short-term financial planning is to forecast future cash flows. The cash flow forecasts allow a company to determine whether it has a cash flow surplus or deficit, and whether the surplus or deficit is short term or long term.

2. Firms need short-term financing to deal with seasonal working capital requirements, negative cash flow shocks, or positive cash flow shocks.

3. The matching principle specifies that short-term needs for funds should be financed with short-term sources of funds, and long-term needs with long-term sources of funds.

4. Bank loans are a primary source of short-term financing, especially for small firms.

   a. The most straightforward type of bank loan is a single, end-of-period payment loan.

   b. Bank lines of credit allow a firm to borrow any amount up to a stated maximum. The line of credit may be uncommitted, which is a nonbinding, informal agreement, or, more typically, may be committed.

   c. A Bridge loan is a short-term bank loan that is used to bridge the gap until the firm can arrange for long-term financing.

5. The number of compounding periods and other loan stipulations, such as commitment fees, loan origination fees, and compensating balance requirements, affect the effective annual rate of a bank loan.

6. Commercial paper is a method of short-term financing that is usually available only to large, well-known firms. It is a low-cost alternative to a short-term bank loan for those firms with access to the commercial paper market.

7. Short-term loans may also be structured as secured loans. The accounts receivable and inventory of a firm typically serve as collateral in short-term secured financing arrangements.

8. Accounts receivable may be either pledged as security for a loan or factored. In a factoring arrangement, the accounts receivable are sold to the lender (or factor), and the firm's customers are usually instructed to make payments directly to the factor.

9. Inventory can be used as collateral for a loan in several ways: a floating lien (also called a general or blanket lien), a trust receipts loan (or floor planning), or a warehouse arrangement. These arrangements vary in the extent to which specific items of inventory are identified as collateral; consequently, they vary in the amount of risk the lender faces.

Key Terms

aggressive financing policy *p. 858*
blanket lien *p. 864*
bridge loan *p. 860*
commercial paper *p. 862*
committed line of credit *p. 859*
conservative financing policy *p. 858*
dealer paper *p. 862*
direct paper *p. 862*
discount loan *p. 860*
evergreen credit *p. 860*
factoring of accounts receivable *p. 863*
factors *p. 863*
field warehouse *p. 865*
floating lien *p. 864*
floor planning *p. 865*
funding risk *p. 858*
general lien *p. 864*
line of credit *p. 859*

loan origination fee *p. 861*
London Inter-Bank Offered Rate
   (LIBOR) *p. 859*
matching principle *p. 857*
permanent working capital *p. 857*
pledging of accounts receivable *p. 863*
prime rate *p. 859*
promissory note *p. 859*
public warehouse *p. 865*
revolving line of credit *p. 860*
secured loans *p. 863*
temporary working capital *p. 857*
trust receipts loan *p. 865*
uncommitted line of credit *p. 859*
warehouse arrangement *p. 865*
with recourse *p. 864*
without recourse *p. 864*

Further Reading

Several textbooks study the topics of short-term financing in great depth. Some books interested readers can look at are listed here: G. W. Gallinger and B. P. Healey, *Liquidity Analysis and Management*, 2nd ed. (Reading, MA: Addison-Wesley, 1991); N. C. Hill and W. L. Sartoris, *Short-Term Financial Management: Text and Cases*, 3rd ed. (Englewood Cliffs, NJ: Prentice-Hall, 1994); J. G. Kallberg and K. Parkinson, *Corporate Liquidity: Management and Measurement* (Burr Ridge, IL: Irwin/McGraw Hill, 1996); F. C. Scherr, *Modern Working Capital Management: Text and Cases* (Englewood Cliffs, NJ: Prentice-Hall, 1989); and K. V. Smith and G. W. Gallinger, *Readings on Short-Term Financial Management*, 3rd ed. (New York: West, 1988).

Problems

A blue box (■) indicates problems available in MyFinanceLab.

Forecasting Short-Term
Financing Needs

1. Which of the following companies are likely to have high short-term financing needs? Why?

   a. a clothing retailer

   b. a professional sports team

   c. an electric utility

   d. a company that operates toll roads

   e. a restaurant chain

2. Sailboats Etc. is a retail company specializing in sailboats and other sailing-related equipment. The following table contains financial forecasts as well as current (month 0) working capital levels. During which months are the firm's seasonal working capital needs the greatest? When does it have surplus cash?

($000)	Month						
	0	1	2	3	4	5	6
Net Income		$10	$12	$15	$25	$30	$18
Depreciation		2	3	3	4	5	4
Capital Expenditures		1	0	0	1	0	0
Levels of Working Capital							
Accounts Receivable	$2	3	4	5	7	10	6
Inventory	3	2	4	5	5	4	2
Accounts Payable	2	2	2	2	2	2	2

The Matching Principle

3. What is the difference between permanent working capital and temporary working capital?

 4. Quarterly working capital levels for your firm for the next year are included in the following table. What are the permanent working capital needs of your company? What are the temporary needs?

($000)	Quarter			
	1	2	3	4
Cash	$100	$100	$100	$100
Accounts Receivable	200	100	100	600
Inventory	200	500	900	50
Accounts Payable	100	100	100	100

5. Why might a company choose to finance permanent working capital with short-term debt?

Short-Term Financing
with Bank Loans

 6. The Hand-to-Mouth Company needs a $10,000 loan for the next 30 days. It is trying to decide which of three alternatives to use:

Alternative A: Forgo the discount on its trade credit agreement that offers terms of 2/10, net 30.

Alternative B: Borrow the money from Bank A, which has offered to lend the firm $10,000 for 30 days at an APR of 12%. The bank will require a (no-interest) compensating balance of 5% of the face value of the loan and will charge a $100 loan origination fee, which means Hand-to-Mouth must borrow even more than the $10,000.

Alternative C: Borrow the money from Bank B, which has offered to lend the firm $10,000 for 30 days at an APR of 15%. The loan has a 1% loan origination fee.

Which alternative is the cheapest source of financing for Hand-to-Mouth?

7. Consider two loans with equal maturity and identical face values: an 8% loan with a 1% loan origination fee and an 8% loan with a 5% (no-interest) compensating balance requirement. Which loan would have the higher effective annual rate? Why?

8. What is the difference between evergreen credit and a revolving line of credit?

9. Which of the following one-year, $1000 bank loans offers the lowest effective annual rate?

   a. a loan with an APR of 6%, compounded monthly

   b. a loan with an APR of 6%, compounded annually, that also has a compensating balance requirement of 10% (on which no interest is paid)

   c. a loan with an APR of 6%, compounded annually, that has a 1% loan origination fee

10. The Needy Corporation borrowed $10,000 from Bank Ease. According to the terms of the loan, Needy must pay the bank $400 in interest every three months for the three-year life of the loan, with the principal to be repaid at the maturity of the loan. What effective annual rate is Needy paying?

Short-Term Financing with Commercial Paper

11. The Treadwater Bank wants to raise $1 million using three-month commercial paper. The net proceeds to the bank will be $985,000. What is the effective annual rate of this financing for Treadwater?

12. Magna Corporation has an issue of commercial paper with a face value of $1,000,000 and a maturity of six months. Magna received net proceeds of $973,710 when it sold the paper. What is the effective annual rate of the paper to Magna?

13. What is the difference between direct paper and dealer paper?

14. The Signet Corporation has issued four-month commercial paper with a $6 million face value. The firm netted $5,870,850 on the sale. What effective annual rate is Signet paying for these funds?

Short-Term Financing with Secured Financing

15. What is the difference between pledging accounts receivable to secure a loan and factoring accounts receivable?

16. The Ohio Valley Steel Corporation has borrowed $5 million for one month at a stated annual rate of 9%, using inventory stored in a field warehouse as collateral. The warehouser charges a $5000 fee, payable at the end of the month. What is the effective annual rate of this loan?

17. Discuss the three different arrangements under which a firm may use inventory to secure a loan.

18. The Rasputin Brewery is considering using a public warehouse loan as part of its short-term financing. The firm will require a loan of $500,000. Interest on the loan will be 10% (APR, annual compounding) to be paid at the end of the year. The warehouse charges 1% of the face value of the loan, payable at the beginning of the year. What is the effective annual rate of this warehousing arrangement?

Special Topics

Chapter 28
**Mergers and
Acquisitions**

Chapter 29
Corporate Governance

Chapter 30
Risk Management

Chapter 31
**International
Corporate Finance**

The Law of One Price Connection. In Part X, the final section of the text, we address special topics in corporate financial management. The Law of One Price continues to provide a unifying framework as we consider these topics. Chapter 28 discusses mergers and acquisitions and Chapter 29 provides an overview of corporate governance. In Chapter 30, we focus on corporations' use of derivatives to manage risk. We use the Law of One Price to evaluate the costs and benefits of risk management. Chapter 31 introduces the issues a firm faces when making a foreign investment and addresses the valuation of foreign projects. We value foreign currency cash flows in the context of internationally integrated capital markets, a condition that we demonstrate with the Law of One Price.

28

Mergers and Acquisitions

notation

EPS	earnings per share
P/E	price-earnings ratio
A	premerger total value of acquirer
T	premerger total value of target
S	value of all synergies
N_A	premerger number of shares of acquirer outstanding
x	number of new shares issued by acquirer to pay for target
P_T	premerger share price of target
P_A	premerger share price of acquirer
N_T	premerger number of shares of target outstanding

On October 28, 2004, Royal Dutch Petroleum Company and Shell Transport and Trading Company announced plans for a merger. Shareholders of Royal Dutch Petroleum would exchange their stock for shares in a new company, Royal Dutch Shell PLC. The new company would then acquire Shell Transport and Trading Company. The deal, valued at about $185 billion, was the largest merger announced during 2004 and one of the largest in history.[1] In fact, 2004 was a strong year for corporate mergers. Fifteen deals were valued at more than $10 billion. Given the potential size of a merger, it is clear that some of the most important decisions financial managers make concern mergers and acquisitions.

Mergers and acquisitions are part of what is often referred to as "the market for corporate control." When one firm acquires another, there is typically a buyer, the **acquirer** or **bidder**, and a seller, the **target** firm. There are two primary mechanisms by which ownership and control of a public corporation can change: Either another corporation or group of individuals can acquire the target firm, or the target firm can merge with another firm. In both cases, the acquiring entity must purchase the stock or existing assets of the target either for cash or for something of equivalent value (such as shares in the acquiring or newly merged corporation). For simplicity, we refer to either mechanism as a **takeover**.

In this chapter, we first provide some historical background about the market for mergers and acquisitions. Next, we discuss some of the reasons why a corporate financial manager may decide to pursue an acquisition. We then review the takeover process. Finally, we address the question of who gets the value that is added when a takeover occurs.

---

1. Prior to the merger, both companies were part of a complicated joint-ownership arrangement. See Chip Cummins, "Shell Shakes Up Corporate Structure," *Wall Street Journal*, October 29, 2004, p. A3. Also see Dennis Berman, "Simmering M&A Sector Reaches a Boil," *Wall Street Journal*, January 3, 2005, p. R10.

28.1 Background and Historical Trends

The global takeover market is highly active, averaging more than $1 trillion per year in transaction value. Table 28.1 lists the ten largest transactions completed during the ten-year period from 1995 through 2005. As the table indicates, takeovers happen between well-known companies, and individual transactions can involve huge sums of money.

The takeover market is also characterized by **merger waves**—peaks of heavy activity followed by quiet troughs of few transactions. Figure 28.1 displays the time series of takeover activity from 1926 to 2005. Merger activity is greater during economic expansions than during contractions and correlates with bull markets. Many of the same technological and economic conditions that lead to bull markets also motivate managers to reshuffle assets through mergers and acquisitions. Thus most likely the same economic activities that drive expansions also drive peaks in merger activity.[2]

Figure 28.1 shows that the periods of the greatest takeover activity occurred in the 1960s, 1980s, and 1990s. Each merger wave was characterized by a typical type of deal. The increase in activity in the 1960s is known as the conglomerate wave because firms typically acquired firms in unrelated businesses. At the time, it was thought that managerial expertise was portable across business lines and that the conglomerate business form offered great financial advantages. This conglomerate fad eventually fell out of favor, and

TABLE 28.1		Ten Largest Merger Transactions, 1995–2005		
Date				
Announced	**Completed**	**Target Name**	**Acquirer Name**	**Value ($ billion)**
Nov. 1999	June 2000	Mannesmann AG	Vodafone AirTouch PLC	203
Oct. 2004	Dec. 2004	Shell Transport and Trading	Royal Dutch Petroleum	185
Jan. 2000	Jan. 2001	Time Warner	America Online, Inc.	182
Nov. 1999	June 2000	Warner-Lambert Co.	Pfizer, Inc.	89
Dec. 1998	Nov. 1999	Mobil Corp.	Exxon Corp.	86
Jan. 2000	Dec. 2000	SmithKline Beecham PLC	Glaxo Wellcome PLC	79
Apr. 1998	Oct. 1998	Citicorp	Travelers Group, Inc.	73
July 2001	Nov. 2002	AT&T Broadband & Internet Services, Inc.	Comcast Corp.	72
July 1998	June 2000	GTE Corp.	Bell Atlantic Corp.	71
May 1998	Oct. 1999	Ameritech Corp.	SBC Communications, Inc.	70

Source: Thomson Financials' SDC M&A Database.

---

2. See J. Harford, "What Drives Merger Waves," *Journal of Financial Economics* 77 (2005): 529–560, for an analysis of why these waves occur.

FIGURE 28.1

Percentage of Public Companies Taken Over Each Quarter, 1926–2005

Mergers appear to occur in distinct waves, with the most recent waves occurring in the 1960s, 1980s, and 1990s.

Source: Jarrad Harford.

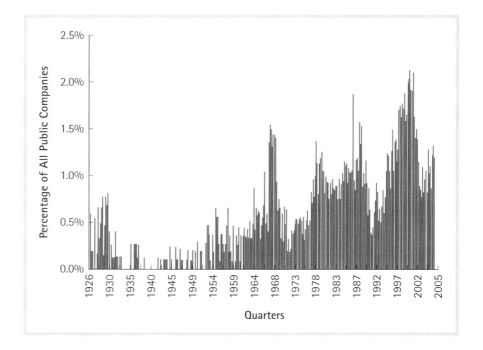

the 1980s were known for hostile, "bust-up" takeovers, in which the acquirer purchased a poorly performing conglomerate and sold off its individual business units for more than the purchase price. The 1990s, in contrast, were known for "strategic" or "global" deals that were more likely to be friendly and to involve companies in related businesses; these mergers often were designed to create strong firms on a scale that would allow them to compete globally. At the end of 2004, takeover activity began to pick up again, starting what many expect to be the next big merger wave, marked by consolidation in many industries such as telecommunications and software.

CONCEPT CHECK   1. What are merger waves?

2. What types of deals were associated with the last three merger waves?

28.2 Market Reaction to a Takeover

In most U.S. states, the law requires that when existing shareholders of a target firm are forced to sell their shares, they receive a fair value for their shares. In most cases, this concept is interpreted as the value exclusive of any value that arises because of the merger itself. For practical purposes, this principle translates into the share price prior to the merger. As a consequence, a bidder is unlikely to acquire a target company for less than its current market value. In practice, most acquirers pay a substantial **acquisition premium**, which is the percentage difference between the acquisition price and the premerger price of the target firm.

Table 28.2 lists the average historical premium and market reaction to a takeover as reported by Gregor Andrade, Mark Mitchell, and Erik Stafford.[3] As the table shows, acquirers pay an average premium of 38% over the premerger price of the target. When a bid is announced, the target shareholders enjoy a gain of 16% on average in their stock price. Although acquirer shareholders see an average *loss* of 1%, this loss is not statistically significantly different from zero. These facts raise three important questions that we answer in this chapter:

1. Why do acquirers pay a premium over the market value for a target company?

2. Although the price of the target company rises on average upon the announcement of the takeover, why does it rise less than the premium offered by the acquirer?

3. Why does the acquirer not experience a price increase?

TABLE 28.2	**Average Acquisition Premium and Stock Price Reactions to Mergers**

Premium Paid over Premerger Price	Announcement Price Reaction	
	Target	Acquirer
38%	16%	−1%

Source: Data based on 4256 deals from 1973 to 1998. G. Andrande, M. Mitchell, and E. Stafford, "New Evidence and Perspectives on Mergers," *Journal of Economic Perspectives* 15(2) (2001): 103–120.

Let's start with the first question—why do acquirers pay a premium over market value? In fact, this question has two parts: (1) Why is the target worth a premium over the current market value? and (2) Even if the target is worth more than its premerger value, why do acquirers pay more than the premerger market price? In the next section, we answer the first part of this question. We delay the discussion of the second part until the end of the chapter, when we fully understand the mechanics of the takeover process.

CONCEPT CHECK

1. On average, what happens to the target share price on the announcement of a takeover?

2. On average, what happens to the acquirer share price on the announcement of a takeover?

---

3. G. Andrade, M. Mitchell, and E. Stafford, "New Evidence and Perspectives on Mergers," *Journal of Economic Perspectives* 15(2) (2001): 103–120. This paper builds on original research done in the 1970s and 1980s documenting that shareholders experience significant gains (between 20% and 30%) upon a successful takeover of their firms. See G. Mandelker, "Risk and Return: The Case of the Merging Firm," *Journal of Financial Economics* 1(4) (1974): 303–335; M. C. Jensen and R. S. Ruback, "The Market for Corporate Control: The Scientific Evidence," *Journal of Financial Economics* 11(1) (1983): 5–50; and M. Bradley, A. Desai, and E. H. Kim, "The Rationale Behind Interfirm Tender Offers: Information or Synergy," *Journal of Financial Economics* 11(1) (1983): 183–206. More recent papers have found combined losses on the order of $240 billion in capitalization at the announcement of takeover bids. This finding appears to be driven by spectacular losses from some large takeovers of public targets, especially in the late 1990s. See T. Loughran and A. Vijh, "Do Long-Term Shareholders Benefit from Corporate Acquisitions?" *Journal of Finance* 52(5) (1997): 1765–1790; and S. Moeller, R. Stulz, and F. Schlinge-mann, "Wealth Destruction on a Massive Scale: A Study of Acquiring Firm Returns in the Recent Merger Wave," *Journal of Finance* 60(2) (2005): 757–782.

28.3 Reasons to Acquire

For most investors an investment in the stock market is a zero-NPV investment. How, then, can an acquirer pay a premium for a target and still satisfy the requirement that the investment is a positive-NPV investment opportunity? The answer is that an acquirer might be able to add economic value, as a result of the acquisition, that an individual investor cannot add.

Large synergies are by far the most common justification that bidders give for the premium they pay for a target. An extreme example is SBC's acquisition of AT&T in 2005 for more than $15 billion. In interviews immediately after the announcement, SBC's Chairman Ed Whitacre was quick to point out that the projected synergies of $15 billion alone could justify the price SBC agreed to pay for AT&T, let alone AT&T's assets.

Such synergies usually fall into two categories: cost reductions and revenue enhancements. Cost-reduction synergies are more common and easier to achieve because they generally translate into layoffs of overlapping employees and elimination of redundant resources. This was the case in the SBC/AT&T acquisition, which forecasted 13,000 layoffs in the first year. Revenue-enhancement synergies, however, are much harder to predict and achieve. For example, Oracle's plan after its 2005 takeover of Peoplesoft was to combine the two product lines so that customers could obtain all of their backoffice software needs from one source. Oracle's hope was that it would be able to steal customers from other vendors such as SAP by offering "one-stop shop" service.

Let's examine in detail the synergies most often cited by acquirers to justify takeovers.

Economies of Scale and Scope

A large company can enjoy **economies of scale**, or savings from producing goods in high volume, that are not available to a small company. Larger firms can also benefit from **economies of scope**, which are savings that come from combining the marketing and distribution of different types of related products (e.g., soft drinks and snack foods). In some cases, these economies are clear. For example, consider the wave of bank mergers that followed the federal government's relaxation of Depression-era banking laws. Today, customers of large banks benefit from other financial services besides traditional services such as loans, checking and savings accounts, and the convenience of branches across the country.

There may also be costs associated with size. Chief among these is that larger firms are more difficult to manage. In a small firm, the CEO is often close to the firm's operations. He or she can keep in touch with the firm's largest customers and most important personnel, thereby keeping abreast of changing market conditions and potential problems. Because they receive information so quickly, small firms are often able to react in a timely way to changes in the economic environment.

Vertical Integration

Vertical integration refers to the merger of two companies in the same industry that make products required at different stages of the production cycle. A company might conclude that it can enhance its product if it has direct control of the inputs required to make the product. Similarly, another company might not be happy with how its products are being distributed, so it might decide to take control of its distribution channels.

The principal benefit of vertical integration is coordination. By putting two companies under central control, management can ensure that both companies work toward a common goal. For example, oil companies are often vertically integrated. They generally own all stages of the production process, from the oil fields, to the refineries, and so on, even down to the gas stations that distribute their primary product—gasoline. Many also have divisions that prospect for new oil.

Vertically integrated companies are large, and as we have already pointed out, large corporations are more difficult to run. Consequently not all successful corporations are vertically integrated. A good example is Microsoft Corporation. Microsoft has chosen to make the operating system that the vast majority of computers use, but not the computers themselves. Rival Apple Computers makes both. Although both companies are successful, Microsoft is more successful than Apple. Some experts have argued that this is due to Microsoft's decision to not integrate vertically.

Expertise

Firms often need expertise in particular areas to compete more efficiently. Faced with this situation, a firm can enter the labor market and attempt to hire personnel with the required skills. However, consider a case in which a new, more efficient technology has been developed to produce a firm's primary output. Hiring experienced workers directly might be very difficult in this scenario. If the firm is unfamiliar with the new technology, it could be difficult for existing managers to identify the talent they need. Even if such people are identified and hired, they must be supervised. In addition, without an in-depth understanding of the production process, effectively managing the process could pose problems.

A more efficient solution may be to purchase the talent as an already functioning unit by acquiring an existing firm. For example, in 2000 Paris-based AXA bought Sanford C. Bernstein, a Wall Street private partnership, to gain expertise and a preexisting client base in the huge U.S. asset management market. Similarly, U.K. builder Amec bought a large stake in Spie Batignolles, a French contractor, to gain local contacts and expertise in the French building industry. Such mergers are common in high-tech industries. Networking firm Cisco Systems is known for its strategy of buying young startup firms that have developed promising new networking technologies.

Monopoly Gains

It is often argued that merging with or acquiring a major rival enables a firm to substantially reduce competition within the industry and thereby increase profits. Society as a whole bears the cost of monopoly strategies, so most countries have antitrust laws that limit such activity.

The extent to which these laws are enforced tends to vary across countries and over time depending on the policy of current leaders. When General Electric (GE) agreed to buy Honeywell in October 2000, the U.S. Justice Department approved the deal with limited conditions. However, the European Commission (EC) determined that putting GE's aircraft leasing division and Honeywell's extensive avionics product line under the same management would lead to unacceptable anticompetitive effects in the avionics market. Despite substantial concessions by GE and top-level political lobbying by U.S. officials, the EC refused to approve the deal, and it was eventually called off. The GE/Honeywell deal was the first time a merger of two U.S. companies that had been approved by U.S. authorities was blocked by European authorities. The EC had no direct jurisdiction over the merger of the companies, but it was in the position to impose crippling restrictions on sales inside the European Union.

Monopoly power could be very valuable, and we would expect that in the absence of strong antitrust laws, companies would merge. However, while all companies in an industry benefit when competition is reduced, only the merging company pays the associated costs (from, for instance, managing a larger corporation). Perhaps this reason, along with existing antitrust regulation, accounts for the lack of convincing evidence that monopoly gains result from the reduction of competition following takeovers. For example, financial researchers have found that the share prices of other firms in the same industry did not significantly increase following the announcement of a merger within the industry.[4]

Efficiency Gains

Another justification acquirers cite for paying a premium for a target is efficiency gains, which are often achieved through an elimination of duplication—for example, as in the SBC/AT&T merger mentioned earlier. Acquirers also often argue that they can run the target organization more efficiently than existing management could.

Although in theory a chief executive of an inefficiently run corporation can be ousted by current shareholders voting to replace the board of directors, very few managers are replaced in this way. Instead, unhappy investors typically sell their stock, so the stock of a corporation with an inept chief executive trades at a discount relative to the price at which it would trade if it had a more capable chief executive. In such a situation, an acquirer could purchase shares at the discounted price to take control of the corporation and replace the chief executive with a more effective one. Once the benefits of the new management team become obvious to investors, the discount for the old management will likely disappear and the acquirer could resell its shares for a profit.

Although identifying poorly performing corporations is relatively easy, fixing them is another matter entirely. As any sports fan knows, replacing a manager of a team with a weak record is no guarantee that the team will start winning more games. Improving the performance of a public company is not a dissimilar problem. Takeovers relying on the improvement of target management are difficult to complete, and post-takeover resistance to change can be great. Thus not all inefficiently run organizations are necessarily more efficient following a takeover.

Operating Losses

When a firm makes a profit, it must pay taxes on the profit. However, when it makes a loss, the government does not rebate taxes. Thus it might appear that a conglomerate has a tax advantage over a single-product firm simply because losses in one division can offset profits in another division. Let's illustrate this scenario with an example.

EXAMPLE 28.1

Taxes for a Merged Corporation

Problem
Consider two firms, Ying Corporation and Yang Corporation. Both corporations will either make $50 million or lose $20 million every year with equal probability. The only difference is that the firms' profits are perfectly negative correlated. That is, any year Yang Corporation

4. See B. E. Eckbo, "Horizontal Mergers, Collusion and Stockholder Wealth," *Journal of Financial Economics* 11(1) (1983): 241–273, and R. Stillman, "Examining Antitrust Policy Toward Horizontal Mergers," *Journal of Financial Economics* 11(1) (1983): 225–240.

earns $50 million, Ying Corporation loses $20 million, and vice versa. Assume that the corporate tax rate is 34%. What are the total expected after-tax profits of both firms when they are two separate firms? What are the expected after-tax profits if the two firms are combined into one corporation called Ying-Yang Corporation, but are run as two independent divisions? (Assume it is not possible to carry back or carry forward losses.)

Solution

Let's start with Ying Corporation. In the profitable state, the firm must pay corporate taxes, so after-tax profits are $50 \times (1 - 0.34) = \$33$ million. No taxes are owed when the firm reports losses, so the expected after-tax profits of Ying Corporation are $33(0.5) - 20(0.5) = \$6.5$ million.

Because Yang Corporation has identical expected profits, its expected profits are also $6.5 million. Thus the expected profit of both companies operated separately is just the sum of the expected profits of each company—$13 million.

The merged corporation, Ying-Yang Corporation, always makes a pretax profit equal to $50 - 20 = \$30$ million. After taxes, expected profits are therefore $\$30 \times (1 - 0.34) = \$19.8$ million. So Ying-Yang Corporation has significantly higher after-tax profits than the combined after-tax profits of Ying Corporation and Yang Corporation.

Although Example 28.1 is an extreme case, it illustrates the benefits of conglomeration. In the United States, however, these benefits are mitigated because the IRS allows companies to carry losses forward up to 20 years. That is, a company can use losses to offset earnings up to 20 years in the future. Furthermore, companies with current-year losses can also use them to offset earnings for the two prior years. These carryback and carryforward provisions essentially deliver the benefits of conglomeration to a small firm with volatile earnings.

To justify a takeover based on operating losses, management would have to argue that the tax savings are over and above what the firm would save using carryback and carryforward provisions. In addition, the IRS will disallow a tax break if it can show that the principal reason for a takeover is tax avoidance, so it is unlikely that the tax advantage could, by itself, be a valid reason to acquire another firm.

Diversification

The benefits of diversification are frequently cited as a reason for a conglomerate merger. The justification for these benefits comes in three forms: direct risk reduction, lower cost of debt or increased debt capacity, and liquidity enhancement. We discuss each in turn.

Risk Reduction.   Like a large portfolio, large firms bear less idiosyncratic risk, so often mergers are justified on the basis that the combined firm is less risky. The problem with this argument is that it ignores the fact that investors can achieve the benefits of diversification themselves by purchasing shares in the two separate firms. Because most stockholders will already be holding a well-diversified portfolio, they get no further benefit from the firm diversifying through acquisition. Moreover, as we have already pointed out, there are costs associated with merging and with running a large diversified firm. Because it may be harder to measure performance accurately in a conglomerate, agency costs may increase and resources may be inefficiently allocated across divisions.[5] As a result, it is cheaper for investors to diversify their own portfolios than to have the corporation do it through acquisition.

---

5. See, e.g., A. M. Goel, V. Nanda, and M. P. Narayanan, "Career Concerns and Resource Allocation in Conglomerates," *Review of Financial Studies* 17(1) (2004): 99–128.

The only class of stockholders who can benefit from the diversification a merger generates are stockholders who do not hold well-diversified portfolios. Some employees, for instance, hold a large fraction of their wealth in shares of the corporation for which they work and are prevented from selling those shares because of stock and option compensation schemes intended as employee motivation. Because these employees are obligated to hold idiosyncratic risk, they benefit when the firm reduces that risk by conglomerating. Consequently, such employees have a self-interested incentive to have their own employer take over other firms. To the extent that these takeovers impose costs, they are not in the interests of most other shareholders.

Debt Capacity and Borrowing Costs.   All else being equal, larger firms, because they are more diversified, have a lower probability of bankruptcy. Consequently, they have a higher debt capacity; in other words, they can increase leverage and thereby lower their costs of capital. This is often voiced as a good reason to engage in diversifying mergers.

We know from the discussion in Chapter 14 that in perfect capital markets, the financial decisions of a firm cannot affect its value. For the preceding argument to be correct, it must therefore rely on some *market imperfection.* The market imperfections cited most often by proponents of this line of reasoning are tax benefits and the costs associated with bankruptcy, such as those we discussed in Chapter 16. By diversifying, a firm may be able to increase its debt and enjoy greater tax savings without incurring significant costs of financial distress. For the increased tax benefits and reduction in bankruptcy costs to justify a merger, the gains must be large enough to offset any disadvantages of running a large firm.

Liquidity.   As we have noted, shareholders of private companies are often under-diversified: They have a disproportionate share of their wealth invested in the private company. Consequently, when an acquirer buys a private target, it provides the target's owners with a way to reduce their risk exposure by cashing out their investment in the private target and reinvesting in a diversified portfolio. This liquidity that the bidder provides to the owners of a private firm can be valuable and often is an important incentive for the target shareholders to agree to the takeover.

Earnings Growth

It is possible to combine two companies with the result that the earnings per share of the merged company exceed the premerger earnings per share of either company, *even when the merger itself creates no economic value.* Let's look at how this can happen.

Mergers and Earnings per Share

Problem

Consider two corporations that both have earnings of $5 per share. The first firm, OldWorld Enterprises, is a mature company with few growth opportunities. It has 1 million shares that are currently outstanding priced at $60 per share. The second company, NewWorld Corporation, is a young company with much more lucrative growth opportunities. Consequently, it has a higher value: Although it has the same number of shares outstanding, its stock price is $100 per share. Assume NewWorld acquires OldWorld using its own stock and the takeover adds no value. In a perfect market, what is the value of NewWorld after the acquisition? At current market prices, how many shares must NewWorld offer to OldWorld's shareholders in exchange for their shares? Finally, what are NewWorld's earnings per share after the acquisition?

Solution

Because the takeover adds no value, the post-takeover value of NewWorld is just the sum of the values of the two separate companies: 100×1 million $+ 60 \times 1$ million $= \$160$ million. To acquire OldWorld, NewWorld must pay $60 million. At its pre-takeover stock price of $100 per share, the deal requires issuing 600,000 shares. As a group, OldWorld's shareholders will then exchange 1 million shares in OldWorld for 600,000 shares in NewWorld, or each shareholder will get 0.6 share in NewWorld for each 1 share in OldWorld. Notice that the price per share of NewWorld stock is the same after the takeover: The new value of NewWorld is $160 million and there are 1.6 million shares outstanding, giving it a stock price of $100 per share.

However, NewWorld's earnings per share have changed. Prior to the takeover, both companies earned $5 / share $\times$ 1 million shares $= \$5$ million. The combined corporation thus earns $10 million. There are 1.6 million shares outstanding after the takeover, so NewWorld's post-takeover earnings per share are

$$EPS = \frac{\$10 \text{ million}}{1.6 \text{ million shares}} = \$6.25 / \text{share}$$

By taking over OldWorld, NewWorld has raised its earnings per share by $1.25.

As Example 28.2 demonstrates, merging a company with little growth potential and a company with high growth potential (and thus low earnings per share) can raise earnings per share. In the past, people have cited this increase as a reason to merge. Of course, a savvy shareholder will see that the merger *adds no economic value*. All that has happened is that the high-growth company, whose value lies in its potential to generate earnings in the future, has purchased a company for which most of the value lies in its current ability to generate earnings. The price-earnings ratio reflects this reality.

EXAMPLE 28.3

Mergers and the Price-Earnings Ratio

Problem

Calculate NewWorld's price-earnings ratio, before and after the takeover described in Example 28.2.

Solution

Before the takeover, NewWorld's price-earnings ratio is

$$P/E = \frac{\$100 / \text{share}}{\$5 / \text{share}} = 20$$

After the takeover, NewWorld's price-earnings ratio is

$$P/E = \frac{\$100 / \text{share}}{\$6.25 / \text{share}} = 16$$

The price-earnings ratio has dropped to reflect the fact that after taking over OldWorld, more of the value of NewWorld comes from earnings from current projects than from its future growth potential.

1. What are the reasons most often cited for a takeover?

2. Explain why diversification benefits and earnings growth are not good justifications for a takeover intended to increase shareholder wealth.

28.4 The Takeover Process

In this section, we explore how the takeover process works. We begin by establishing how a bidder determines the initial offer. We then review the tax and accounting issues specific to a takeover and explain the regulatory approval process. We end by discussing board approval, including defensive strategies that boards implement to discourage takeovers.

Valuation

In Chapter 19, we demonstrated how a bidder values a target company. Recall that we explained, in the context of a single case study, how an acquirer values a target by using two different approaches. The first—and simplest—approach compares the target to other comparable companies. Although this approach is easy to implement, it gives at best a rough estimate of value. Valuing the target using a multiple based on comparable firms does not directly incorporate the operational improvements and other synergistic efficiencies that the acquirer intends to implement. Purchasing a corporation usually constitutes a very large capital investment decision, so it requires a more accurate estimate of value that includes careful analysis of both operational aspects of the firm and the ultimate cash flows the deal will generate. Thus the second approach to valuation requires making a projection of the expected cash flows that will result from the deal and valuing those cash flows.

A key issue for takeovers is quantifying and discounting the value added as a result of the merger. In Chapter 19, the acquirer was expected to implement operational improvements and make adjustments to the target's capital structure, thereby shielding additional income from taxes. As we showed in Section 28.3, a takeover can generate other sources of value. For simplicity, in this section we refer to any additional value created as the *takeover synergies.*

We know that the price paid for a target is equal to the target's pre-bid market capitalization plus the premium paid in the acquisition. If we view the pre-bid market capitalization as the stand-alone value of the target,[6] then from the bidder's perspective, the takeover is a positive-NPV project only if the premium it pays does not exceed the synergies created. Although the premium that is offered is a concrete number, the synergies are not—investors might well be skeptical of the acquirer's estimate of their magnitude. The bidder's stock price reaction to the announcement of the merger is one way to gauge investors' assessments of whether the bidder overpaid or underpaid for the target. As Table 28.2 shows, the average stock price reaction is -1%, and this amount is not statistically significantly different from zero. Thus the market, on average, believes that the premium is approximately equal to the synergies. Nonetheless, there is large variation in the premium across deals. One recent large-scale study of the value effects of mergers

---

6. Rumors about a potential bid for the target will often push its share price up in anticipation of the premium offer. Practitioners refer to the "unaffected" target price, meaning the target's share price before it was affected by rumors of a takeover. This price would be used to compute the stand-alone value of the target.

found that positive reactions to bids are concentrated in smaller bidders. In fact, during the 1990s, 87 large public acquirers announced bids that resulted in $1 billion or more in value reduction at announcement.[7]

The Offer

Once the acquirer has completed the valuation process, it is in the position to make a tender offer—that is, a public announcement of its intention to purchase a large block of shares for a specified price. There is no guarantee that, in fact, the takeover will take place at this price. Often acquirers have to raise the price to consummate the deal.

Not all tender offers are successful. When an acquirer bids for a target, the target firm's board may not accept the bid and recommend that existing shareholders not tender their shares, even when the acquirer offers a significant premium over the pre-offer share price. Even if the target board supports the deal, there is also the possibility that regulators might not approve the takeover. Because of this uncertainty about whether a takeover will succeed, the market price does not rise by the amount of the premium when the takeover is announced.

A bidder can use either of two methods to pay for a target: cash or stock. In a cash transaction, the bidder simply pays for the target, including any premium, in cash. In a stock-swap transaction, the bidder pays for the target by issuing new stock and giving it to the target shareholders; that is, the bidder offers to swap target stock for acquirer stock. The "price" offered is determined by the **exchange ratio**—the number of bidder shares received in exchange for each target share—multiplied by the market price of the acquirer's stock.

A stock-swap merger is a positive-NPV investment for the acquiring shareholders if the share price of the merged firm (the acquirer's share price after the takeover) exceeds the premerger price of the acquiring firm. We can write this condition as follows. Let A be the premerger, or standalone, value of the acquirer, and T be the premerger (standalone) value of the target. Let S be the value of the synergies created by the merger. If the acquirer has N_A shares outstanding before the merger, and issues x new shares to pay for the target, then the acquirer's share price should increase post-acquisition if

$$\frac{A + T + S}{N_A + x} > \frac{A}{N_A} \tag{28.1}$$

The left side of Eq. 28.1 is the share price of the merged firm. The numerator indicates the total value of the merged firm: the standalone value of the acquirer and target plus the value of the synergies created by the merger. The denominator represents the total number of shares outstanding once the merger is complete. The ratio is the postmerger share price. The right side of Eq. 28.1 is the premerger share price of the acquirer, the total premerger value of the acquirer divided by the premerger number of shares outstanding.

Solving Eq. 28.1 for x gives the maximum number of new shares the acquirer can offer and still achieve a positive NPV:

$$x < \left(\frac{T + S}{A}\right) N_A \tag{28.2}$$

---

7. S. Moeller, R. Stulz, and F. Schlingemann, "Wealth Destruction on a Massive Scale: A Study of Acquiring Firm Returns in the Recent Merger Wave," *Journal of Finance* 60(2) (2005): 757–782.

We can express this relationship as an exchange ratio by dividing by the premerger number of target shares outstanding, N_T:

$$\text{Exchange ratio } = \frac{x}{N_T} < \left(\frac{T+S}{A}\right)\frac{N_A}{N_T} \tag{28.3}$$

We can also rewrite Eq. 28.3 in terms of the *premerger* target and acquirer share prices, $P_T = T/N_T$ and $P_A = A/N_A$:

$$\text{Exchange ratio } < \frac{P_T}{P_A}\left(1 + \frac{S}{T}\right) \tag{28.4}$$

EXAMPLE 28.4

Maximum Exchange Ratio in a Stock Takeover

Problem

At the time Sprint announced plans to acquire Nextel, Sprint stock was trading for $25 per share and Nextel stock was trading for $30 per share, implying a premerger value of Nextel of approximately $31 billion. If the projected synergies were $12 billion, what is the maximum exchange ratio Sprint could offer in a stock swap and still generate a positive NPV?

Solution

Using Eq. 28.4,

$$\text{Exchange ratio } < \frac{P_T}{P_A}\left(1 + \frac{S}{T}\right) = \frac{30}{25}\left(1 + \frac{12}{31}\right) = 1.66$$

Merger "Arbitrage"

Once a tender offer is announced, the uncertainty about whether the takeover will succeed adds volatility to the stock price. This uncertainty creates an opportunity for investors to speculate on the outcome of the deal. Traders known as **risk-arbitrageurs**, who believe that they can predict the outcome of a deal, take positions based on their beliefs. While the strategies these traders use are sometimes referred to as arbitrage, they are actually quite risky, so they do not represent a true arbitrage opportunity in the sense we have defined in this book. Let's illustrate the strategy using the 2002 stock-swap merger of Hewlett-Packard (HP) and Compaq.

In September 2001, HP announced that it would purchase Compaq by swapping 0.6325 share of HP stock for each share of Compaq stock. After the announcement, HP traded for $18.87 per share, while the price of Compaq was $11.08 per share. Thus, Compaq's share price after the announcement was $0.8553 below the implied value of HP's offer, $18.87 \times 0.6325 = $11.9353. It follows that if, just after the announcement, a risk-arbitrageur simultaneously purchased 10,000 Compaq shares and short sold 6325 HP shares, he would net $6325 \times $18.87 - 10,000 \times $11.08 = $8553. If the takeover was successfully completed on the original terms, the 10,000 Compaq shares would convert into 6325 HP shares; the risk-arbitrageur could then use those shares to cover the short position in HP and be left with no net exposure. Thus the risk-arbitrageur would pocket the original $8553 as a profit.[8] This potential profit arises from the difference between the

---

8. For simplicity, we are ignoring dividend payments that were made during the period.

target's stock price and the implied offer price, and is referred to as the **merger-arbitrage spread**. However, it is not a true arbitrage opportunity because there is a risk that the deal will not go through. If the takeover did not ultimately succeed, the risk-arbitrageur would eventually have to unwind his position at whatever market prices prevailed. Usually these prices would have moved against him (in particular, the price of Compaq would be likely to decline if the takeover did not occur), so he would face losses on the position.

The HP–Compaq takeover was distinctive in that the uncertainty about the success of the deal stemmed largely from acquirer discomfort with the deal rather than from target shareholder discomfort. Although initially supportive of the merger, the Hewlett family got cold feet. About two months after the deal was announced, Walter Hewlett disclosed his family's opposition to it. On the day of Walter Hewlett's announcement, the price of HP stock rose to $19.81, while Compaq's stock price fell to $8.50, causing the merger-arbitrage spread to widen to $19.81 \times 6325 - \$8.5 \times 10,000 = \$40,298$. We plot the merger-arbitrage spread for the HP-Compaq merger in Figure 28.2. The risk-arbitrage strategy outlined above is effectively a short position on this spread, which pays off if the spread declines. Thus, an arbitrageur who opened the strategy when the deal was announced and closed it after Walter Hewlett announced his opposition would face a loss of $40,298 - \$8553 = \$31,745$.

Although the Hewlett family members were large shareholders of HP, they were not controlling shareholders; they did not have enough shares to block the deal single-handedly. Hence a battle for control of HP ensued between the Hewlett family and CEO Carly Fiorina, the driving force behind the acquisition of Compaq. This conflict was only resolved months later when HP shareholders, by a slim margin, voted in favor of issuing new shares, thereby effectively approving the merger and netting a profit for any risk-arbitrageur who stayed the course. As is clear from Figure 28.2, risk-arbitrageurs who did

FIGURE 28.2

Merger-Arbitrage Spread for the Merger of HP and Compaq

The plot shows the potential profit, given that the merger was ultimately successfully completed, from purchasing 10,000 Compaq shares and short selling 6325 HP shares on the indicated date. A risk-arbitrageur who expects the deal to go through can profit by opening the position when the spread is large, and closing the position after it declines.

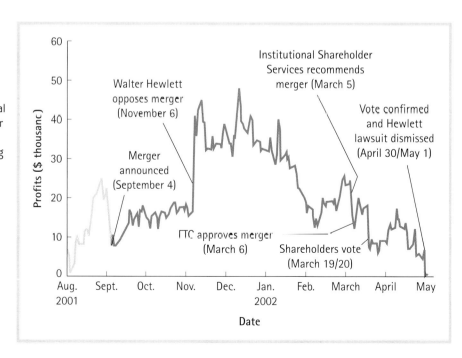

not have the stomach to hold on would have faced large losses at several points during the roller-coaster ride. And while HP CEO Carly Fiorina survived this early challenge to her authority, the performance of HP following the merger vindicated Hewlett's position. HP's board ultimately fired Fiorina in 2005.

Tax and Accounting Issues

Once the terms of trade have been decided, the tax and accounting implications of a merger can be determined. How the acquirer pays for the target affects the taxes of both the target shareholders and the combined firm. Any cash received in full or partial exchange for shares triggers an immediate tax liability for target shareholders. They will have to pay a capital gains tax on the difference between the price paid for their shares in the takeover and the price they paid when they first bought the shares. If the acquirer pays for the takeover entirely by exchanging bidder stock for target stock, then the tax liability is deferred until the target shareholders actually sell their new shares of bidder stock.

If the acquirer purchases the target assets directly (rather than the target stock), then it can **step up** the book value of the target's assets to the purchase price. This higher depreciable basis reduces future taxes through larger depreciation charges. Further, any goodwill created could also be amortized for tax purposes over 15 years. The same treatment applies to a forward cash-out merger, where the target is merged into the acquirer and target shareholders receive cash in exchange for their shares.

Many transactions are carried out as acquisitive reorganizations under the tax code. These structures allow the target shareholders to defer their tax liability on the part of the payment made in acquirer stock but they do not allow the acquirer to step up the book value of the target assets. However, they provide a mechanism for isolating the target's assets and liabilities in a subsidiary of the acquirer. This can be very attractive for an acquirer that does not want to be exposed to the known (or unknown) liabilities of the target.

While the method of payment (cash or stock) affects how the value of the target's assets is recorded for tax purposes, it does not affect the combined firm's financial statements for financial reporting. The combined firm must mark up the value assigned to the target's assets on the financial statements by allocating the purchase price to target assets according to their fair market value. If the purchase price exceeds the fair market value of the target's identifiable assets, then the remainder is recorded as goodwill and is examined annually by the firm's accountants to determine whether its value has decreased. For example, in HP's takeover of Compaq, HP recorded more than $10 billion in goodwill. The footnotes to the statements attributed the goodwill to the value of the Compaq brand name, which is assumed to have an indefinite life.

Even when a merger has a positive NPV, bidding managers are typically very concerned with the effect of the merger on earnings. This is the other side of the earnings-growth argument as a reason to merge. Just as merging two companies can increase earnings without affecting economic value, it can also decrease earnings without affecting economic value. Nevertheless, acquirers are hesitant to commit to a deal that would be dilutive to earnings per share, even if only in the short run.

Board and Shareholder Approval

For a merger to proceed, both the target and the acquiring board of directors must approve the deal and put the question to a vote of the shareholders of the target (and, in some cases, the shareholders of the acquiring firm as well).

In a **friendly takeover**, the target board of directors supports the merger, negotiates with potential acquirers, and agrees on a price that is ultimately put to a shareholder vote. Although it is rare for acquiring boards to oppose a merger, target boards sometimes do not support the deal even when the acquirer offers a large premium. In a **hostile takeover**, the board of directors (together with upper-level management) fights the takeover attempt. To succeed, the acquirer must garner enough shares to take control of the target and replace the board of directors. When a takeover is hostile, the acquirer is often called a **raider**.

If the shareholders of a target company receives a premium over the current market value of their shares, why would a board of directors ever oppose a takeover? There are a number of reasons. The board might legitimately believe that the offer price is too low. In this case, a suitor that is willing to pay more might be found or the original bidder might be convinced to raise its offer. Alternatively, if the offer is for stock-swap, target management may oppose the offer because they feel the acquirer's shares are over-valued, and therefore that the value of the offer is actually less than the standalone value of the target. Finally, managers (and the board) might oppose a takeover because of their own self-interests, especially if the primary motivation for the takeover is efficiency gains. In this case, the acquirer most likely plans to undertake a complete change of leadership of the corporation. Upper-level managers could view opposing the merger as a way of protecting their jobs (and the jobs of their employees). In fact, this concern is perhaps the single biggest reason for the negative associations that hostile takeovers generate. Bear in mind that if substantial efficiency gains are indeed possible, current management is not doing an effective job. A takeover, or threat thereof, might be the only recourse investors have to fix the problem.

In theory, the duty of the target board of directors is to choose the course of action that is in the best interests of the target shareholders. In practice, the courts have given target directors wide latitude under what is called the "business judgment rule" to determine the best course for their companies, including spurning a premium offer if the directors can reasonably argue that more value will eventually be realized for their shareholders by remaining independent.

CONCEPT CHECK

1. What are the steps in the takeover process?

2. What do risk-arbitrageurs do?

28.5 Takeover Defenses

For a hostile takeover to succeed, the acquirer must go around the target board and appeal directly to the target shareholders. This process is known as a **proxy fight**: The acquirer attempts to convince target shareholders to unseat the target board by using their proxy votes to support the acquirers' candidates for election to the target board. Target companies have a number of strategies available to them to stop this process. These strategies can force a bidder to raise its bid or entrench management more securely, depending on the independence of the target board. We begin with the most effective defensive strategy, the poison pill.

Poison Pills

A **poison pill** is a rights offering that gives existing target shareholders the right to buy shares in either the target or the acquirer at a deeply discounted price once certain conditions are met. Because target shareholders can purchase shares at less than the market price, existing shareholders of the acquirer effectively subsidize their purchases. This subsidization makes the takeover so expensive for the acquiring shareholders that they choose to pass on the deal.

The poison pill was invented in 1982 by a takeover lawyer, Martin Lipton, who successfully warded off a takeover attempt of El Paso Electric by General American Oil.[9] Because the original poison pill goes into effect only in the event of a complete takeover (that is, a purchase of 100% of the outstanding shares), one way to circumvent it is to not do a complete takeover. The first time this work-around was used was by Sir James Goldsmith, who took control of Crown Zellerbach by purchasing slightly more than 50% of the outstanding stock. Because he did not purchase the rest, Crown Zellerbach's poison pill was ineffective.

In response to the takeover of Crown Zellerbach, corporate lawyers have perfected the original poison pill. Instead of giving existing shareholders the right to acquire shares in an acquiring company, most poison pills now specify that if a raider acquires more than a trigger amount (typically 20%) of the target shares (but chooses not to execute a complete takeover by purchasing all outstanding shares), existing shareholders—with the exception of the acquirer—have the right to buy more shares in the target at a discounted price.

The name *poison pill* comes from the world of espionage. Once caught, a spy is supposed to take his own life by swallowing a poison pill rather than give up important secrets. Poison pills are very effective in stopping takeovers, but where is the suicide analogy? The answer is that by adopting a poison pill, a company effectively entrenches its management by making it much more difficult for shareholders to replace bad managers, thereby potentially destroying value. Financial research has verified this effect. A firm's stock price typically drops when it adopts a poison pill. Furthermore, once adopted, firms with poison pills have below-average financial performance.[10]

Not surprisingly, companies with poison pills are harder to take over, and when they are taken over, the premium that existing shareholders receive for their stock is higher. That is, because a poison pill increases the cost of a takeover, all else equal, a target company must be in worse shape (there must be a greater opportunity for profit) to justify the expense of waging a takeover battle.

Poison pills also increase the bargaining power of the target firm when negotiating with the acquirer because poison pills make it difficult to complete the takeover without the cooperation of the target board. If used effectively, this bargaining power can allow target shareholders to capture more of the takeover gains by negotiating a higher premium than they would get if no pill existed. Numerous studies on the impact of anti-takeover provisions on takeovers have found that such provisions result in higher premiums accruing to existing shareholders of the target company.[11]

9. For a brief history, see Len Costa, "The Perfect Pill," *Legal Affairs*, (March 2005), http://www.legalaffairs.org.

10. P. H. Malatesta and R. A. Walking, "Poison Pills Securities: Stockholder Wealth, Profitability and Ownership Structure," *Journal of Financial Economics* 20(1) (1988): 347–376; and M. Ryngaert, "The Effects of Poison Pills Securities on Stockholder Wealth," *Journal of Financial Economics* 20(1) (1988): 377–417.

11. Georgeson and Company (1988) study; R. Comment and G. W. Schwert, "Poison or Placebo: Evidence on the Deterrence and Wealth Effects of Modern Antitakeover Measures," *Journal of Financial Economics* 39(1) (1995): 3–43, and N. P. Varaiya, "Determinants of Premiums in Acquisition Transactions," *Managerial and Decision Economics* 8(3) (1987): 175–184; R. Heron and E. Lie, "On the Use of Poison Pills and Defensive Payouts by Takeover Targets," *Journal of Business* 79(4) (2006): 1783–1807.

Staggered Boards

A determined bidder in the face of a poison pill has another option available to it: Get its own slate of directors elected to the target board, which it can submit at the next annual shareholders meeting. If the target shareholders elect those candidates, then the new directors can cancel the poison pill and accept the bidder's offer. To prevent such a coup from happening, about two-thirds of public companies have a **staggered** (or **classified**) **board**. In a typical staggered board, every director serves a three-year term and the terms are staggered so that only one-third of the directors are up for election each year. Thus, even if the bidder's candidates win board seats, it will control only a minority of the target board. A bidder's candidate would have to win a proxy fight two years in a row before the bidder had a majority presence on the target board. The length of time required to execute this maneuver can deter a bidder from making a takeover attempt when the target board is staggered. Most experts consider a poison pill combined with a staggered board to be the most effective defense available to a target company.

White Knights

When a hostile takeover appears to be inevitable, a target company will sometimes look for another, friendlier company to acquire it. This company that comes charging to the target's rescue is known as a **white knight**. The white knight will make a more lucrative offer for the target than the hostile bidder. Incumbent managers of the target maintain control by reaching an agreement with the white knight to retain their positions.

One variant on the white knight defense is the **white squire** defense. In this case, a large investor or firm agrees to purchase a substantial block of shares in the target with special voting rights. This action prevents a hostile raider from acquiring control of the target. The idea is that the white squire itself will not choose to exercise its control rights.

Golden Parachutes

A **golden parachute** is an extremely lucrative severance package that is guaranteed to a firm's senior managers in the event that the firm is taken over and the managers are let go. For example, when Ronald Perelman successfully acquired Revlon Corporation, the firm's former chairman, Michael Bergerac, was reported to have received a golden parachute compensation package worth in excess of $35 million.

Golden parachutes have been criticized because they are seen both as excessive and a misuse of shareholder wealth. In fact, the empirical evidence does not support this view.[12] If anything, it supports the view that an adoption of a golden parachute actually creates value. If a golden parachute exists, management will be more likely to be receptive to being taken over. This means the existence of golden parachutes lessens the likelihood of managerial entrenchment. Researchers have found that stock prices rise on average when companies announce that they plan to implement a golden parachute policy, and that the number of firms bidding against one another for the target and the size of the takeover premium are higher if a golden parachute agreement exists.

Recapitalization

Another defense against a takeover is a recapitalization, in which a company changes its capital structure to make itself less attractive as a target. For example, a company with a lot of cash might choose to pay out a large dividend. Companies without a lot of cash

---

12. M. Narayanan and A. Sundaram, "A Safe Landing? Golden Parachutes and Corporate Behavior," *University of Michigan Business School Working Paper No. 98015* (1998).

might instead choose to issue debt and then use the proceeds to pay a dividend or repurchase stock.

Why does increasing leverage make a firm less attractive as a target? In many cases, a substantial portion of the synergy gains that an acquirer anticipates from a takeover are from tax savings from an increase in leverage as well as other cost reductions. By increasing leverage on its own, the target firm can reap the benefit of the interest tax shields. In addition, the need to generate cash to meet the debt service obligations provides a powerful motivation to managers to run a corporation efficiently. In effect, the restructuring itself can produce efficiency gains, often removing the principal motivation for the takeover in the first place.

Other Defensive Strategies

Corporate managers and defense advisors have devised other mechanisms to forestall a takeover. A corporation's charter can require a supermajority (sometimes as much as 80%) of votes to approve a merger. It can also restrict the voting rights of very large shareholders. Finally, a firm can require that a "fair" price be paid for the company, where the determination of what is "fair" is up to the board of directors or senior management. Beauty is always in the eye of the beholder, so "fair" in this case usually implies an optimistic determination of value.

We might expect the presence of defensive strategies to reduce firm value. However, Gregg Jarrell and Annette Poulsen[13] found that, on average, the public announcement of anti-takeover amendments by 600 firms in the period 1979–1985 had an insignificant effect on the value of announcing firms' shares.

Regulatory Approval

All mergers must be approved by regulators. In the Section 28.2, we discussed monopoly gains from takeovers and the use of antitrust regulations to limit them. In the United States, antitrust enforcement is governed by three main statutes: the Sherman Act, the Clayton Act, and the Hart-Scott-Rodino Act. The Sherman Act of 1890, which was passed in response to the formation of huge oil trusts such as Standard Oil, prohibits mergers that would create a monopoly or undue market control. The Clayton Act, enacted in 1914, strengthened the government's hand by prohibiting companies from acquiring the stock (or, as later amended, the assets) of another company if it would adversely affect competition. Under both the Sherman and Clayton acts, the government had to sue to block a merger. Often by the time a decision was rendered, the merger had taken place and it was difficult to undo it. The Hart-Scott-Rodino (HSR) Act of 1976 put the burden of proof on the merging parties. Under HSR, all mergers above a certain size (the formula for determining whether a transaction qualifies is complicated, but it comes out to approximately $50 million) must be approved by the government before the proposed takeovers occur. The government cannot delay the deal indefinitely, however, because it must respond with approval or a request for additional information within 20 days of receiving notification of the proposed merger.

The European Commission has established a process similar to the HSR process, which requires merging parties to notify the EC, provide additional information if requested about the proposed merger, and wait for approval before proceeding. As discussed in the Honeywell/GE example, even though the EC technically lacks legal authority to block

---

13. G. A. Jarrell and A. B. Poulsen, "Shark Repellents and Stock Prices: The Effects of Antitakeover Amendments Since 1980," *Journal of Financial Economics* 19 (1988): 127–168.

Weyerhaeuser's Hostile Bid for Willamette Industries

In November 2000, Weyerhaeuser, a forest products company based in Federal Way, Washington, announced a hostile bid of $48 per share for its smaller neighbor, Willamette Industries, based in Portland, Oregon. Weyerhaeuser had been pursuing Willamette in private since 1998, when Steve Rogel unexpectedly resigned as CEO of Willamette to become CEO of Weyerhaeuser. Each time Rogel approached his old employer in private, he was rebuffed. The response to the hostile tender offer was no different. Despite the fact that the bid represented a substantial premium to the firm's pre-bid stock price, the Willamette board rejected the offer and urged its shareholders not to tender their shares to Weyerhaeuser.

Willamette's defenses included a staggered board and a poison pill, so Weyerhaeuser made its tender offer conditional on Willamette's board canceling the poison pill. Consequently, Weyerhaeuser initiated a proxy fight at the next annual shareholders' meeting in June 2001. One of the directors up for reelection at that time was Duane McDougall, Willamette's CEO. One month before the

meeting, Weyerhaeuser increased its offer to $50 per share, but Willamette's board still believed that the offer was too low and worried that too many of its long-time employees would face layoffs after the merger. Nonetheless, at the annual meeting, Weyerhaeuser's slate received 1.4% more votes than Willamette's, thereby removing Willamette's CEO from its board.

The loss of the board seats did not change Willamette's position. Willamette unsuccessfully searched for a white knight to generate a bidding contest that would force Weyerhaeuser to up its bid. It also entered into talks to buy Georgia-Pacific's building products division. Such a deal would have increased its size and added enough debt to its balance sheet to render the firm unattractive to Weyerhaeuser.

In the end, Weyerhaeuser increased its offer to $55.50 per share in January 2002, and Willamette finally agreed to a deal and called off its negotiations with Georgia-Pacific. Even without the presence of other bidders, Willamette's board was able to get what it considered to be a fair price from Weyerhaeuser.

a merger of U.S. companies, it can stop a takeover by imposing restrictions on the combined firm's operations and sales in Europe. Although globally, a proposed takeover might have to satisfy antitrust rules in more than 80 jurisdictions, practically the most important jurisdictions besides the home jurisdiction of the firm are Europe and the United States.

CONCEPT CHECK

1. What defensive strategies are available to help target companies resist an unwanted takeover?

2. How can a hostile acquirer get around a poison pill?

28.6 Who Gets the Value Added from a Takeover?

Now that we have explained the takeover process, we can return to the remaining questions we posed at the beginning of this chapter: why the price of the acquiring company does not rise at the announcement of the takeover and why the bidder is forced to pay a premium for the target.

You might imagine that the people who do the work of acquiring the corporation and replacing its management will capture the value created by the merger. Based on the average stock price reaction, it does not appear that the acquiring corporation generally captures this value. Instead, the premium the acquirer pays is approximately equal to the value it adds, which means the *target* shareholders ultimately capture the value added by the acquirer. To see why, we need to understand how market forces react to a takeover announcement.

The Free Rider Problem

Assume you are one of the 1 million shareholders of HighLife Corporation, all of whom own 1 share of stock. HighLife has no debt. Its chief executive is not doing a good job, preferring to spend his time using the company's jets to fly to the corporate condo in Aspen, Colorado, rather than running the company in Chicago. As such, the shares are trading at a substantial discount. They currently have a price of $45 per share, giving HighLife a market value of $45 million. Under a competent manager, the company would be worth $75 million. HighLife's corporate charter specifies that a simple majority is required to make all decisions, so to take control of HighLife a shareholder must purchase half the outstanding shares.

T. Boone Icon decides to fix the situation (and make a profit at the same time) by making a tender offer to buy half the outstanding shares for $60 per share in cash. If fewer than 50% of the shareholders tender their shares, the deal is off.

In principle, this idea could land T. Boone a handsome profit. If 50% of shareholders tender their shares, those shares will cost him $60 × 500,000 = $30 million. Once he has control of the firm, he can replace the managers. When the executive jets and the Aspen condo are sold and the market realizes that the new managers are serious about improving performance, the market value of the firm will rise to $75 million. Hence T. Boone's shares will be worth $75 per share, netting him a profit of $15 × 500,000 = $7.5 million. But will 50% of the shareholders tender their shares?

The offer price of $60 per share exceeds the value of the firm if the takeover does not go through ($45 per share). Hence, the offer is a good deal for shareholders overall. But if all shareholders tender their shares, as an individual shareholder you could do better by not tendering your share. Then if T. Boone takes control, each of your shares will be worth $75 rather than the $60 you would get by tendering. Thus it is wiser to not tender. Of course, if all shareholders think this way no one will tender their shares, and T. Boone's deal will not get off the ground. The only way to persuade shareholders to tender their shares is to offer them at least $75 per share, which removes any profit opportunity for T. Boone. The problem here is that existing shareholders do not have to invest time and effort, but still participate in all the gains from the takeover that T. Boone Icon generates—hence the term "free rider problem." By sharing the gains in this way, T. Boone Icon is forced to give up substantial profits and thus will likely choose not to bother at all.[14]

Toeholds

One way for T. Boone to get around the problem of shareholders' reluctance to tender their shares is to buy the shares secretly in the market. However, SEC rules make it difficult for investors to buy much more than about 10% of a firm in secret.[15] After T. Boone

---

14. A rigorous analysis of the free rider problem in mergers can be found in S. Grossman and O. D. Hart, "Takeover Bids, the Free-Rider Problem, and the Theory of the Corporation," *Bell Journal of Economics* 11(1) (1980): 42–64.

15. The rules actually require that any shareholder who owns more than 5% of a firm publicly disclose this fact, but the time delays in the disclosure process allow investors to accumulate more than 5% of the firm before this information is made public.

acquires such an initial stake in the target, called a **toehold**, he would have to make his intentions public by informing investors of his large stake. To successfully gain control of HighLife, he would have to announce a tender offer to buy an additional 40% of the shares for $75 per share. Once in control, he would be able to sell his stake for $75 per share. Assuming he accumulated the first 10% for $50 per share, his profits in this case will be $25 × 100,000 = $2.5 million. Not bad, but substantially less than the value he is adding.

Why should investors care whether T. Boone's profits are substantially lower than the value he is adding? The answer is that people like T. Boone perform an important service. Because of the threat that such a person might attempt to take over their company and fire them, chief executives are less likely to shirk their duties. Thus the more profitable we make this activity, the less likely we will have to resort to it. If $2.5 million is not enough to justify T. Boone's time and effort, he will not try to acquire HighLife. Current management will remain entrenched and T. Boone will think about acquiring the company only if further erosion in the stock price makes the deal lucrative enough for him.

A number of legal mechanisms exist that allow acquirers to avoid the free rider problem and capture more of the gains from the acquisition. We describe the two most common, the leveraged buyout and the freezeout merger, next.

The Leveraged Buyout

The good news for shareholders is that another significantly lower-cost mechanism allows people like T. Boone Icon to take over companies and fire underperforming managers. Recall from Chapter 24 that this mechanism is called the leveraged buyout (LBO). Let's illustrate how it works by returning to HighLife Corporation.[16]

Assume that T. Boone chooses not to buy any shares secretly in the market, but instead announces a tender offer for half the outstanding shares at a price of $50 per share. However, instead of using his own cash to pay for these shares, he borrows the money and *pledges the shares themselves as collateral on the loan*. Because the only time he will need the money is if the tender offer succeeds, the banks lending the money can be certain that he will have control of the collateral. Even more important, if the tender offer succeeds, because he now has control of the company, the law allows T. Boone to attach the loans directly to the corporation—that is, it is as if the corporation, and not T. Boone Icon, borrowed the money. At the end of this process T. Boone still owns half the shares, but the *corporation* is responsible for repaying the loan. T. Boone has effectively gotten half the shares without paying for them!

You might imagine that no shareholder would be willing to tender her shares under these circumstances. Surprisingly, this conclusion is wrong. If you tender your shares, you will receive $50 for each of them. If you do not tender your shares, but enough other shareholders do, then T. Boone will take control of the company. After he replaces the managers, the enterprise value company will be $75 million. What will your shares be worth if you did not tender them?

For simplicity assume that there are no frictions or taxes. To gain control of the firm, T. Boone borrowed $25 million to purchase half the outstanding shares ($50 × 500,000).

---

16. For a further discussion of this mechanism, see H. M. Mueller and F. Panunzi, "Tender Offers and Leverage," *The Quarterly Journal of Economics* 119 (2004): 1217–1248.

The Leveraged Buyout of RJR-Nabisco by KKR

By the summer of 1988, Ross Johnson, CEO of RJR Nabisco (RJR), was becoming increasingly worried about the poor stock price performance of the conglomerate. Despite a strong earnings record, management had not been able to shake loose of its image as a tobacco company, and the stock price was languishing at $55 per share. In October 1988, Johnson and a small team of RJR's executives, backed by the Wall Street firms of Shearson Lehman Hutton and Salomon Brothers, announced a bid of $75 per share for the company. At this price, the deal would have been valued at $17.6 billion, more than twice as large as the largest LBO completed up to that point. Because this deal involved the current management of the company, it falls into a special category of LBO deals called **management buyouts (MBOs)**.

The announcement focused Wall Street's attention on RJR. Even at this substantial premium, the MBO appeared to be a good deal for Johnson and his team, because soon after the offer went public, it became hotly contested. Foremost among the contenders was the firm of Kohlberg, Kravis, and Roberts (KKR). KKR launched its own bid with a cash offer of $90 per share. A bidding war ensued that saw the offer price ultimately rise to $109 per share, valuing the deal at more than $25 billion. In the end, both Johnson and KKR offered very similar deals although

management's final bid was slightly higher than KKR's. Eventually, RJR's board accepted KKR's bid of $109 per RJR share. The offer price comprised $81 per share in cash, $18 per share in preferred stock, and $10 per share in debenture securities.

From an economic point of view, this outcome is surprising. One would think that given their inside knowledge of the company, management would be in the best position to not only value it, but also run it. Why, then, would an outsider choose to outbid an insider for a company? The answer in RJR's case appeared to point to managers themselves. As the deal proceeded, it became increasingly obvious to investors that executives (and members of the board of directors) enjoyed perks that were unprecedented. For example, Johnson had the personal use of numerous corporate apartments in different cities and literally a fleet of corporate jets that he, the top executives, and members of the corporate board personally used. In their leveraged buyout proposal, they had obtained a 4% equity stake for top executives that was worth almost $1 billion, $52.5 million of golden parachutes, and assurances that the RJR air force (the fleet of corporate jets) and the flamboyant Atlanta headquarters would not be subject to budget cutting.

Because this debt is now attached to HighLife, the total value of HighLife's equity is just the total value of the company, minus the value of debt:

$$\text{Total Value of HighLife Equity} = \$75 \text{ million} - \$25 \text{ million} = \$50 \text{ million}$$

The total number of outstanding shares is the same (remember that T. Boone purchased existing shares), so the price per share is $50 million ÷ 1 million = $50/share. If the tender offer succeeds, you are indifferent: Whether you tender your shares or keep them, each is always worth $50. If you keep your shares and the tender offer fails, the price per share stays at $45. Clearly, it is always in your best interests to tender your shares, so T. Boone's tender offer will succeed. T. Boone also makes substantially more profits than he would if he used a toehold strategy—his profits are the value of his shares upon completion of the takeover: $50 × 500,000 = $25 million.

EXAMPLE 28.5

Leveraged Buyout

Problem

FAT Corporation stock is currently trading at $40 per share. There are 20 million shares outstanding, and the company has no debt. You are a partner in a firm that specializes in leveraged buyouts. Your analysis indicates that the management of this corporation could be improved considerably. If the managers were replaced with more capable ones, you estimate that the value of the company would increase by 50%. You decide to initiate a leveraged buyout and issue a tender offer for at least a controlling interest—50% of the outstanding shares. What is the maximum amount of value you can extract and still complete the deal?

Solution

Currently, the value of the company is 40×20 million = $800 million, and you estimate you can add an additional 50%, or $400 million. If you borrow $400 million and the tender offer succeeds, you will take control of the company and install new management. The total value of the company will increase by 50% to $1.2 billion. You will also attach the debt to the company, so now the company will have $400 million in debt. The value of equity once the deal is done is the total value minus the debt outstanding:

$$\text{Total Equity} = 1200 - 400 = \$800 \text{ million}$$

The value of the equity is the same as the premerger value. You own half the shares, which are worth $400 million, and paid nothing for them, so you have effectively captured all the value you anticipated adding to FAT.

What if you borrowed more than $400 million? Assume you were able to borrow $450 million. The value of equity after the merger would be

$$\text{Total Equity} = 1200 - 450 = \$750 \text{ million}$$

This is lower than the premerger value. Recall, however, that in the United States, existing shareholders must be offered at least the premerger price for their shares. Because existing shareholders anticipate that the share price will be lower once the deal is complete, all shareholders will tender their shares. This implies that you will have to pay $800 million for these shares. To complete the deal you will have to pay $800 - 450 = \$350$ million out of your own pocket. In the end, you will own all the equity, which is worth $750 million. You paid $350 million for it, so your profit is again $400 million. You cannot extract more value than the value you add to the company by taking it over.

The examples we have illustrated are extreme in that the acquirer takes over the target without paying any premium and with no initial investment. In practice, premiums in LBO transactions are often quite substantial—while they can avoid the free-rider problem acquirers must still get board approval to overcome other defenses such as poison pills, as well as outbid other potential acquirers. Also, lender's typically require that the acquirer have a substantial equity stake as protection for the debt holders in case the claimed post-acquisition benefits do not materialize. In the $15.2 billion Hertz LBO (at the same time, the second largest in history), which we described in Chapter 24, the acquirers contributed $2.3 billion in cash out of a total of $5.6 billion that was paid for Hertz's equity.

The Freezeout Merger

Although a leveraged buyout is an effective tool for a group of investors to use to purchase a company, it is less well suited to the case of one company acquiring another. An alternative is the **freezeout merger**: The laws on tender offers allow the acquiring company to freeze existing shareholders out of the gains from merging by forcing non-tendering shareholders to sell their shares for the tender offer price. Let's see how this is accomplished.

An acquiring company makes a tender offer at an amount slightly higher than the current target stock price. If the tender offer succeeds, the acquirer gains control of the target and merges its assets into a new corporation, which is fully owned by the acquirer. In effect, the non-tendering shareholders lose their shares because the target corporation no longer exists. In compensation, non-tendering shareholders get the right to receive the tender offer price for their shares. The bidder, in essence, gets complete ownership of the target for the tender offer price.[17]

Because the value the non-tendering shareholders receive for their shares is equal to the tender price (which is more than the premerger stock price), the law recognizes it as fair value and non-tendering shareholders have no legal recourse. Under these circumstances, existing shareholders will tender their stock, reasoning that there is no benefit to holding out: If the tender offer succeeds, they get the tender price anyway; if they hold out, they risk jeopardizing the deal and forgoing the small gain. Hence the acquirer is able to capture almost all the value added from the merger and, as in a leveraged buyout, is able to effectively eliminate the free rider problem.

The freezeout tender offer has a significant advantage over a leveraged buyout because an acquiring corporation need not make an all-cash offer. Instead of paying the target's shareholders in cash, it can use shares of its own stock to pay for the acquisition. In this case, the bidder offers to exchange each shareholder's stock in the target for stock in the acquiring company. As long as the exchange rate is set so that the value in the acquirer's stock exceeds the premerger market value of the target stock, the non-tendering shareholders will receive fair value for their shares and will have no legal recourse.

Competition

The empirical evidence in Table 28.2 suggests that, despite the availability of both the freezeout merger and the leveraged buyout as acquisition strategies, most of the value added still appears to accrue to the target shareholders. That is, on average acquirers do not have a positive price reaction on the announcement of a takeover. Why do acquirers choose to pay so large a premium that they effectively hand the value they create to the target company's shareholders?

The most likely explanation is the competition that exists in the takeover market. Once an acquirer starts bidding on a target company and it becomes clear that a significant gain exists, other potential acquirers may submit their own bids. The result is effectively an auction in which the target is sold to the highest bidder. Even when a bidding war does not result, most likely it is because rather than participate in a bidding war, an acquirer offered a large enough initial premium to forestall the process. In essence, it must give up most of the value added to the target shareholders.

CONCEPT CHECK

1. What mechanisms allow corporate raiders to get around the free rider problem in takeovers?

2. Based on the empirical evidence, who gets the value added from a takeover? What is the most likely explanation of this fact?

---

17. Y. Amihud, M. Kahan, and R. K. Sundaram, "The Foundations of Freezeout Laws in Takeovers," *Journal of Finance* 59 (2004): 1325–1344, contains a detailed discussion of the mechanics of freezeout mergers.

Summary

1. The global takeover market is active, averaging more than $1 trillion per year in transaction value. The periods of greatest activity have been the 1960s, 1980s, and 1990s. During the 1960s, deals were aimed at building conglomerates. In the 1980s, the trend reversed and conglomerates were split into individual businesses. The 1990s saw a rise in "strategic" or "global" deals designed to create firms that could compete globally.

2. While on average the shareholders of the acquirer firm do not obtain gains, shareholders from the acquired firm typically enjoy gains of 16% on the announcement of a takeover bid.

3. The most common justification given for acquiring a firm is the synergies that can be gained through an acquisition. The most commonly cited sources of synergies are economies of scale and scope, the control provided by vertical integration, gaining monopolistic power, the expertise gained from the acquired company, improvements in operating efficiency, and benefits related to diversification such as increased borrowing capacity and tax savings. Shareholders of a private company that is acquired gain by switching to a more liquid investment.

4. From the bidder's perspective, a takeover is a positive-NPV project only if the premium paid does not exceed the synergies created. The bidder's stock price reaction to the announcement of the merger is one way to gauge investors' assessments of whether the bidder overpaid or underpaid for the target.

5. A tender offer is a public announcement of an intention to purchase a large block of shares for a specified price. Making a tender offer does not guarantee that a deal will take place.

6. Bidders use either of two methods to pay for a target: cash or stock. In a cash transaction, the bidder simply pays for the target in cash. In a stock-swap transaction, the bidder pays for the target by issuing new stock and giving it to the target shareolders. The method used by the bidder to pay for the acquired firm has tax and accounting implications.

7. For a merger to proceed, both the target and the acquiring board of directors must approve the merger and put the question to a vote of the shareholders of the target (and, in some cases, the shareholders of the acquiring firm as well). In a friendly takeover, the target board of directors supports the merger and negotiates with the potential acquirers. If the target board opposes the merger, then the acquirer must go around the target board and appeal directly to the target sharcholders, asking them to elect a new board that will support the merger.

8. A target board of directors can defend itself in several ways to prevent a merger. The most effective defense strategy is the poison pill, which gives target shareholders the right to buy shares in either the target or the acquirer at a deeply discounted price. The purchase is effectively subsidized by the existing shareholders of the acquirer, making the takeover very expensive. Another effective defense strategy is having a staggered board, which prevents a bidder from acquiring control over the board in a short period of time. Other defenses include looking for a friendly bidder (a white knight), making it expensive to replace management, and changing the capital structure of the firm.

9. When a bidder makes an offer for a firm, the target shareholders can benefit by keeping their shares and letting other shareholders sell at a low price. However, because all shareholders have the incentive to keep their shares, no one will sell. This scenario is known as the free rider problem. To overcome this problem, bidders can acquire a toehold in the target, attempt a leveraged buyout, or, in the case when the acquirer is a corporation, offer a freezeout merger.

Key Terms

acquirer (bidder) *p. 873*
acquisition premium *p. 875*
economies of scale *p. 877*
economies of scope *p. 877*
exchange ratio *p. 884*
freezeout merger *p. 896*
friendly takeover *p. 888*
golden parachute *p. 890*
hostile takeover *p. 888*
management buyout (MBO) *p. 895*
merger waves *p. 874*
merger-arbitrage spread *p. 886*

poison pill *p. 888*
proxy fight *p. 888*
raider *p. 888*
risk-arbitrageurs *p. 885*
staggered (classified) board *p. 890*
step up *p. 887*
takeover *p. 873*
target *p. 873*
toehold *p. 894*
vertical integration *p. 877*
white knight *p. 890*
white squire *p. 890*

Further Reading

The literature on mergers and acquisitions is extensive. It is impossible to cover it all in a single chapter, but the following books address the topics of this chapter in more detail: L. Herzel and R. Shepro, *Bidders and Targets: Mergers and Acquisitions in the U.S.* (Cambridge, MA: Basil Blackwell, 1990); S. N. Kaplan (ed.), *Mergers and Productivity* (Chicago: University of Chicago Press, 2000); and J. F. Weston, J. A. Siu, and B. A. Johnson, *Takeovers, Restructuring and Corporate Finance*, 3rd ed. (Upper Saddle River, NJ: Prentice-Hall, 2000).

Problems

A blue box (■) indicates problems available in MyFinanceLab.

Background and Historical Trends

1. What are the two primary mechanisms under which ownership and control of a public corporation can change?

2. Why do you think mergers cluster in time, causing merger waves?

Market Reaction to a Takeover

3. Why do you think shareholders from target companies enjoy an average gain when acquired, while acquiring shareholders on average do not gain anything?

Reasons to Acquire

4. If you are planning an acquisition that is motivated by trying to acquire expertise, you are basically trying to acquire intellectual capital. What concerns would you have in structuring the deal and the postmerger integration that would be different from the concerns you would have when buying physical capital?

5. Do you agree that the European Union should be able to block mergers between two U.S.-based firms? Why or why not?

6. How do the carryforward and carryback provisions of the U.S. tax code affect the benefits of merging to capture operating losses?

7. Diversification is good for shareholders. So why shouldn't managers acquire firms in different industries to diversify a company?

EXCEL   8. Your company has earnings per share of $4. It has 1 million shares outstanding, each of which has a price of $40. You are thinking of buying TargetCo, which has earnings per share of $2, 1 million shares outstanding, and a price per share of $25. You will pay for TargetCo by issuing new shares. There are no expected synergies from the transaction.

  a. If you pay no premium to buy TargetCo, what will your earnings per share be after the merger?

  b. If you pay a 20% premium to buy TargetCo, what will your earnings per share be after the merger?

  c. What explains the change in earnings per share in part (a)? Are your shareholders any better or worse off?

  d. What will your price-earnings ratio be after the merger (if you pay no premium)? How does this compare to your P/E ratio before the merger? How does this compare to TargetCo's premerger P/E ratio?

EXCEL   9. If companies in the same industry as TargetCo (from Problem 8) are trading at multiples of 14 times earnings, what would be one estimate of an appropriate premium for TargetCo?

  10. In 1998, Daimler Benz and Chrysler merged. Using the Internet, assess the postmerger performance of the merged company. Do you think the merger between Daimler Benz and Chrysler has been successful?

The Takeover Process

  11. The NFF Corporation has announced plans to acquire LE Corporation. NFF is trading for $35 per share and LE is trading for $25 per share, implying a premerger value of LE of approximately $4 billion. If the projected synergies are $1 billion, what is the maximum exchange ratio NFF could offer in a stock swap and still generate a positive NPV?

Takeover Defenses

EXCEL 12. BAD Company's stock price is $20, and the firm has 2 million shares outstanding. You believe that if you buy the company and replace its management, its value will increase by 40%. Assume that BAD has a poison pill with a 20% trigger. If it is triggered, all target shareholders—other than the acquirer—will be able to buy one new share in BAD for each share they own at a 50% discount. Assume that the price remains at $20 while you are acquiring your shares. If BAD's management decides to resist your buyout attempt, and you cross the 20% threshold of ownership:

  a. How many new shares will be issued and at what price?

  b. What will happen to your percentage ownership of BAD?

  c. What will happen to the price of your shares of BAD?

  d. Do you lose or gain from triggering the poison pill? If you lose, where does the loss go (who benefits)? If you gain, where does the gain come from (who loses)?

Who Gets the Value Added from a Takeover?

  13. How does a toehold help overcome the free rider problem?

  14. You work for a leveraged buyout firm and are evaluating a potential buyout of UnderWater Company. UnderWater's stock price is $20, and it has 2 million shares outstanding. You believe that if you buy the company and replace its management, its value will increase by 40%. You are planning on doing a leveraged buyout of UnderWater and will offer $25 per share for control of the company.

  a. Assuming you get 50% control, what will happen to the price of non-tendered shares?

a. Assuming you get 50% control, what will happen to the price of non-tendered shares?

b. Given the answer in part (a), will shareholders tender their shares, not tender their shares, or be indifferent?

c. What will your gain from the transaction be?

Data Case

It is the end of July, 2006 and you work as an analyst in a large investment banking firm and specialize in the telecommunications industry. Since the merger of SBC and AT&T, there have been rumors about AT&T's desire to merge with BellSouth. Your challenging assignment is to analyze the potential combination of AT&T and BellSouth. Specifically, you are to determine an appropriate exchange ratio if AT&T were to acquire BellSouth.

After talking with your manager, you decide that the synergies of the merger could reasonably be expected to be a 15% reduction in the combined operating costs of the two firms and you will be able to recover about 10% of the fixed assets of the two companies in cash by efficiently reorganizing the merged company and liquidating redundant assets. Your manager directs you to use a 10% cost of capital for the analysis and to assume the after-tax savings in operating costs would grow at 6% per year. Your manager also expects that for the merger to be appealing to the shareholders of BellSouth, AT&T will have to effectively offer a 10% premium to BellSouth's shareholders. Thus, your manager would also like you to estimate the synergies necessary to justify an exchange rate that would provide the premium to BellSouth's shareholders.

1. Go to Nasdaq's Web site (www.nasdaq.com) to gather financial statements for both companies.

   a. Enter the stock symbols for AT&T (T) and BellSouth (BLS) in separate boxes near the top of the Web page and click on "Summary Quotes."

   b. Collect the current stock price (last sale), number of shares outstanding, and total market value for both stocks and enter the data on a spreadsheet.

   c. Begin with AT&T and select "Company Financials" from the menu to access the income statements for the most recent four years. Place the cursor inside the statements, right-click, and select "Export to Microsoft Excel" from the menu. Copy and paste the downloaded statements to the workbook where you entered the other information. Repeat the download process for the balance sheets and then the entire process for BellSouth.

2. Determine the present value of the reduction in operating expenses.

   a. Compute the total operating expenses for the two firms for the most recent year, but do not include any non-recurring costs in your computation.

   b. Compute the tax rates for each firm for the most recent year as income tax divided by earnings before tax and determine the average of the two rates.

   c. Compute the present value of the after-tax reduction in operating expenses assuming it is a growing perpetuity at the growth rate given by your boss.

3. Determine the free cash flow created by the reduction in the total fixed assets of the two firms as discussed with your boss.

4. Determine the total synergy expected from the merger by combining the values determined in Questions 2 and 3.

5. Use Eq. 28.3 to determine the maximum exchange ratio AT&T should offer to BellSouth shareholders given your synergy estimate from Question 4.

6. Given the current stock prices of AT&T and BellSouth, determine the exchange ratio that would be necessary to provide BellSouth shareholders the equivalent of a 10% premium to BellSouth's current stock price.

7. What total synergy from the merger would be necessary to justify the exchange ratio computed in question 6? (*Hint:* Use the solver or goal-seek function in Excel.)

8. Based on your answer to Question 7 and the assumptions in this case, does the merger look feasible if BellSouth's investors require a 10% offer premium?

9. What other considerations not included in your analysis could be factors in the potential combination of the two firms?

Corporate Governance

The turn of the twenty-first century witnessed scandals and corporate fraud in the United States. The names of once well-respected companies like Enron, WorldCom, Tyco, and Adelphia filled the news. Enron, with stock worth $68 billion at its peak, became almost worthless in a matter of months, wiping out the retirement savings of thousands of employees and other stockholders. The story at WorldCom was similar. The once high-flying stock peaked at a market value of $115 billion after a string of acquisitions that included well-known phone company MCI. In 2002, WorldCom filed the largest bankruptcy ever. After building one of the nation's largest cable companies from scratch, the Rigas family of Adelphia was forced to endure the indignity of watching their own cable system carrying the image of Adelphia's demise into millions of homes.

The common theme among these companies is the accusation of fraud, perpetrated by the manipulation of accounting statements. Shareholders, analysts, and regulators were kept in the dark as the companies' financial situations became ever more precarious, resulting, in the end, in total collapse. How did this happen? Aren't managers supposed to act in the interests of shareholders? Why did auditors go along with the fraud? Where were the boards of directors when all of this was happening?

There is an opportunity cost to bad governance; thus, by replacing bad governance with good governance, it is possible to increase firm *value*—in other words, good governance is a positive-NPV project. Hence we begin by discussing various governance mechanisms that are designed to mitigate the agency conflicts between managers and owners. These agency conflicts cannot be removed completely by a firm's governance mechanisms, so we next discuss regulations that are designed to prohibit managers from taking certain acts that are not in the interests of shareholders. We conclude the chapter with a discussion of corporate governance around the world.

29.1 Corporate Governance and Agency Costs

Any discussion of **corporate governance**—the system of controls, regulations, and incentives designed to prevent fraud—is a story of conflicts of interest and attempts to minimize them. As we saw in Chapter 16, the different stakeholders in a firm all have their own interests. When those interests diverge, we may have agency conflicts. That chapter emphasized the sources of conflicts between bondholders and shareholders. In this chapter, we focus on the conflicts between managers and investors.

The conflict of interest between managers and investors derives from the separation of ownership and control in a corporation. As we pointed out in Chapter 1, the separation of ownership and control is perhaps the most important reason for the success of the corporate organizational form. Because any investor can hold an ownership stake in a corporation, investors are able to diversify and thus costlessly reduce their risk exposures. This is especially true for the managers of a corporation: Because they are not also required to own the firm, their risk exposures are much lower than they would be if ownership and control were not separate.

Once control and ownership are separated, however, a conflict of interest arises between the owners and the people in control of a corporation. The seriousness of this conflict of interest depends on how closely aligned the interests of the managers and shareholders are. Aligning their interests comes at a cost—it increases the risk exposure of the managers. For example, tying managerial compensation to performance aligns managers' incentives with investors' interests, but then managers are exposed to the firm's risk (because the firm might do poorly for reasons unrelated to the manager's performance).

The role of the corporate governance system is to mitigate the conflict of interest that results from the separation of ownership and control without unduly burdening managers with the risk of the firm. The system attempts to align these interests by providing incentives for taking the right action and punishments for taking the wrong action. The incentives come from owning stock in the company and from compensation that is sensitive to performance. Punishment comes when a board fires a manager for poor performance or fraud, or when, upon failure of the board to act, shareholders or raiders launch control contests to replace the board and management. As we will see, these actions interact in complicated ways. For example, as a manager owns more stock in the firm, his incentives become better aligned, but, in addition to the increase in risk the manager must bear, the manager also becomes harder to fire because the block of stock gives him significant voting rights.

Let's now take a closer look at the components of the corporate governance system.

CONCEPT CHECK

1. What is corporate governance?

2. What agency conflict do corporate governance structures address?

29.2 Monitoring by the Board of Directors

At first glance, one might think that there is a simple solution to the conflict of interest problem: monitor the firm's managers closely. The problem with this reasoning is that it ignores the cost of monitoring. When the ownership of a corporation is widely held, no one shareholder has an incentive to bear this cost (because she bears the full cost of monitoring but the benefit is divided among all shareholders). Instead the shareholders as a group elect a board of directors to monitor managers. The directors themselves, however, have the same conflict of interest—monitoring is costly and in many cases directors do not get significantly greater benefits than other shareholders from monitoring the managers closely. Consequently, in most cases, shareholders understand that there are reasonable limits on how much monitoring they can expect from the board of directors.

In principle, the board of directors hires the executive team, sets its compensation, approves major investments and acquisitions, and dismisses executives if necessary. In the United States, the board of directors has a clear fiduciary duty to protect the interests of the owners of the firm—the shareholders. Most other countries give some weight to the interests of other stakeholders in the firm, such as the employees. In Germany, this concept is formalized through a two-tier board structure that gives half of the seats on the upper board—called the supervisory board—to employees.

Types of Directors

Generally, researchers have categorized directors into three groups: inside, gray, and outside (or independent). **Inside directors** are employees, former employees, or family members of employees. **Gray directors** are people who are not as directly connected to the firm as insiders are, but who have existing or potential business relationships with the firm. For example, bankers, lawyers, and consultants who are already retained by the firm, or who would be interested in being retained may sit on a board. Thus their judgment could be compromised by their desire to keep the CEO happy. Finally, all other directors are considered **outside** (or **independent**) **directors** and are the most likely to make decisions solely in the interests of the shareholders.

Board Independence

Researchers have hypothesized that boards with a majority of outside directors are better monitors of managerial effort and actions. One early study showed that a board was more likely to fire the firm's CEO for poor performance if the board had a majority of outside directors.[1] Other studies have found that firms with independent boards make fewer value-destroying acquisitions and are more likely to act in shareholders' interests if targeted in an acquisition.[2]

Despite evidence that board independence matters for major activities such as firing CEOs and making corporate acquisitions, researchers have struggled to find a connection between board structure and firm performance. Although the firm's stock price increases on the announcement of its addition of an independent board member, the increased firm *value* appears to come from the potential for the board to make better decisions on acquisitions and CEO turnover rather than from improvements in the firm's operating performance. Researchers have argued, however, that so many other factors affect firm performance that the effect of a more or less independent board is very difficult to detect.

Another reason why it may be difficult to explicate a relationship between board independence and firm performance is the nature of the role of the independent director. On a board composed of insider, gray, and independent directors, the role of the independent director is really that of a watchdog. But because independent directors' personal wealth

1. M. Weisbach, "Outside Directors and CEO Turnover," *Journal of Financial Economics* 20(1–2) (1988): 431–460.

2. J. Byrd and K. Hickman, "Do Outside Directors Monitor Managers? Evidence from Tender Offer Bids," *Journal of Financial Economics* 32(2) (1992): 195–207; and J. Cotter, A. Shivdasani, and M. Zenner, "Do Independent Directors Enhance Target Shareholder Wealth During Tender Offers?" *Journal of Financial Economics* 43(2) (1997): 195–218. H. Ryan and R. Wiggins show that firms with more outsiders on their boards award directors more equity-based compensation, increasing incentives for the board to monitor. ("Who is in Whose Pocket? Director Compensation, Board Independence, and Barriers to Effective Monitoring," *Journal of Financial Economics* 73 (2204): 497–525.

is likely to be less sensitive to performance than that of insider and gray directors, they have less incentive to closely monitor the firm. Even the most active independent directors spend only one or two days per month on firm business, and many independent directors sit on multiple boards, further dividing their attention.

A board is said to be **captured** when its monitoring duties have been compromised by connections or perceived loyalties to management. Theoretical and empirical research support the notion that the longer a CEO has served, especially when that person is also chairman of the board, the more likely the board is to become captured. Over time, most of the independent directors will have been nominated by the CEO. Even though they have no business ties to the firm, they are still likely to be friends or at least acquaintances of the CEO. The CEO can be expected to stack the board with directors who are less likely to challenge her. When the CEO is also chairman of the board, the nominating letter offering a seat to a new director comes from her. This process merely serves to reinforce the sense that the outside directors owe their positions to the CEO and work for the CEO rather than for the shareholders.

Board Size and Performance

Researchers have found the surprisingly robust result that smaller boards are associated with greater firm value and performance.[3] The likely explanation for this phenomenon comes from the psychology and sociology research, which finds that smaller groups make better decisions than larger groups. Most firms that have just gone public either as young companies or as older firms returning to public status after a leveraged buyout (LBO) choose to start with smaller boards. Boards tend to grow over time as members are added for various reasons. For example, boards are often expanded by one or two seats after an acquisition to accommodate the target CEO and perhaps one other target director.

CONCEPT CHECK
1. What is the difference between gray directors and outside directors?

2. What does it mean for a board to be captured?

29.3 Compensation Policies

In the absence of monitoring, the other way the conflict of interest between managers and owners can be mitigated is by closely aligning their interests through the managers' compensation policy. That is, by tying compensation to performance, the shareholders effectively give the manager an ownership stake in the firm.

Stock and Options

Managers' pay can be linked to the performance of a firm in many ways. The most basic approach is through bonuses based on, for example, earnings growth. During the 1990s, most companies adopted compensation policies that more directly gave managers an ownership stake by including grants of stock or stock options to executives. These grants give managers a direct incentive to increase the stock price to make their stock or options as valuable as possible. Consequently, stock and option grants naturally tie managerial wealth to the wealth of shareholders.

---

3. D. Yermack, "Higher Market Valuation of Companies with Small Boards of Directors," *Journal of Financial Economics* 40(2) (1996): 185–211.

Many studies have examined firms' compensation policies. One of the earlier studies examined the sensitivity of managers' compensation to the performance of their firms.[4] The authors found that for every $1000 increase in firm value, CEO pay changed, on average, by $3.25. Most of this increase came from changes in the value of their stock ownership ($2.00). The rest was driven by options, bonuses, and other compensation changes. The authors of the study argued that this seemed too small a sensitivity to provide managers with the proper incentives to exert extra effort on the behalf of shareholders. Recall, however, that increasing the pay-for-performance sensitivity comes at the cost of burdening managers with risk. As a consequence, the optimal level of sensitivity depends on the managers' level of risk aversion, which is hard to measure.

Pay and Performance Sensitivity

Figure 29.1 shows the dramatic rise in CEO pay during the economic expansion of the 1990s. The median cash pay, consisting of salary and bonuses, rose only moderately. Instead, the factor contributing most to the climb in CEO total compensation was the sharp increase in the value of stock and options granted each year. The median value of options granted rose from less than $200,000 in 1993 to more than $1 million in 2001. Not surprisingly, the substantial use of stock and option grants in the 1990s greatly increased managers' pay-for-performance sensitivity. Consequently, recent estimates put this sensitivity at $25 per $1000 change in wealth.[5] Lately, however, firms have been

FIGURE 29.1

CEO Compensation

This figure shows the median cash pay, stock and option grants, and total pay for CEOs of the 1600 largest public companies (thousands of dollars) over the period 1992 through 2004.

Source: Execucomp.

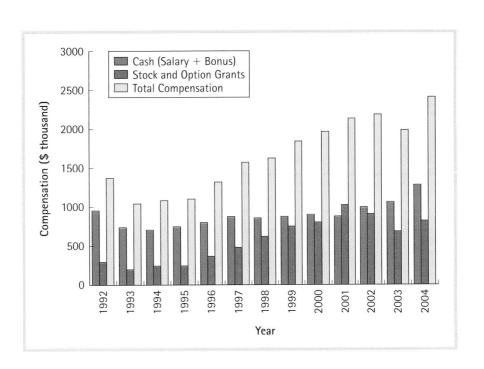

4. M. Jensen and K. Murphy, "Performance Pay and Top-Management Incentives," *Journal of Political Economy* 98(2) (1990): 225–264.
5. B. Hall and J. Liebman, "Are CEOs Really Paid Like Bureaucrats?" *Quarterly Journal of Economics* 103(3) (1998): 653–691.

reducing the fraction of stock and option grants in executive compensation packages (see Figure 29.1), suggesting that that level of sensitivity might have been too high.

Besides increasing managers' risk exposure, increasing the sensitivity of managerial pay and wealth to firm performance has some other negative effects. For example, often options are granted "at the money," meaning that the exercise price is equal to the current stock price. Managers therefore have an incentive to manipulate the release of financial forecasts so that bad news comes out before options are granted (to drive the exercise price down) and good news comes out after options are granted. Studies have found evidence that the practice of timing the release of information to maximize the value of CEO stock options is widespread.[6]

More recently, Erik Lie has found evidence suggesting that many executives have engaged in a more direct form of manipulating their stock option compensation: backdating their option grants.[7] **Backdating** refers to the practice of choosing the grant date of a stock option retroactively, so that the date of the grant would coincide with a date when the stock price was at its low for the quarter or for the year. By backdating the option in this way, the executive receives a stock option that is already in-the-money, with a strike price equal to the lower price on the supposed grant date.

The use of backdating suggests that some executive stock option compensation may not truly have been earned as the result of good *future* performance of the firm. Furthermore, unless it is reported in a timely manner to the IRS and to shareholders, and reflected in the firm's financial statements, backdating is illegal. In mid-2006, SEC and U.S. Justice Department investigations into alleged backdating were ongoing for more than 70 firms. New SEC rules require firms to report option grants within two days of the grant date, which may help prevent further abuses.

CONCEPT CHECK

1. What is the main reason for tying managers' compensation to firm performance?

2. What is the negative effect of increasing the sensitivity of managerial pay to firm performance?

29.4 Managing Agency Conflict

Even with the risk benefits of separating ownership and control, there are still examples of corporations in which the top managers have substantial ownership interests (for example, Microsoft Corporation). One might conjecture that such corporations have suffered less from the conflict of interest between managers and shareholders.

Academic studies have supported the notion that greater managerial ownership is associated with fewer value-reducing actions by managers.[8] But while increasing managerial

---

6. D. Yermack, "Good Timing: CEO Stock Option Awards and Company News Announcements," *Journal of Finance* 52(2) (1997): 449–476. For evidence the option compensation may induce misreporting, see N. Burns and S. Kedia, "The Impact of Performance-Based Compensation on Misreporting," *Journal of Financial Economics* 79 (2006): 35–67.

7. See E. Lie, "On the Timing of CEO Stock Option Awards," *Management Science* 51 (2005): 802–812. Also, R. Heron and E. Lie show that new rules enacted as part of the Sarbanes-Oxley legislation in 2002 that require grants to be reported within two business days have curbed the practice of backdating ("Does Backdating Explain the Stock Price Pattern Around Executive Stock Option Grants?" forthcoming, *Journal of Financial Economics*).

8. See, for example, R. Walkling and M. Long, "Agency Theory, Managerial Welfare, and Takeover Bid Resistance," *Rand Journal of Economics* 15(1) (1984): 54–68.

ownership may reduce perquisite consumption, it also makes managers harder to fire—thus reducing the incentive effect of the threat of dismissal. Thus, the relationship between managerial ownership and firm value is unlikely to be the same for every firm, or even for different executives of the same firm. Shareholders will use all of the tools at their disposal to manage the agency conflict. Thus, if managers have small ownership stakes, shareholders may use compensation policies or a stronger board to create the desired incentives. Harold Demsetz and Kenneth Lehn argue that if you look at a group of firms at any point in time, you should not necessarily see any relationship between ownership and value, unless you are able to control for all of the other, sometimes unobservable, parts of the governance system, including the risk aversion of the manager.[9] More recent studies have supported their position.[10]

Direct Action by Shareholders

If all else fails, the shareholders' last line of defense against expropriation by self-interested managers is direct action. Recall that shareholders elect the board of directors. Typically, these elections look like those in the former Soviet Union—there is only one slate of candidates and you vote "yes" or "no" for the slate as a whole. When shareholders are angry about the management of the company and frustrated by a board unwilling to take action, however, they have a variety of options for expressing that displeasure at their disposal.

Shareholder Voice.   First, any shareholder can submit a resolution that is put to a vote at the annual meeting. A resolution could direct the board to take a specific action, such as discontinue investing in a particular line of business or country, or remove a poison pill. Such resolutions rarely receive majority support, but if large shareholders back them, they can be embarrassing for the board. Some large public pension funds, such as CalPERS (the California Public Employees Retirement System), take an activist role in corporate governance. Typically these funds target firms that are taking actions without considering the concerns of the stockholders; for example, they may privately approach the board of the firm and ask it to reverse its course. The explicit threat at that stage is that if the board fails to comply, the pension fund will put the issue to a shareholder vote. Studies have reported that such activist investors are usually successful in achieving their goals without having to take matters public.[11]

Recently, shareholders have started organizing "no" votes. That is, when they are dissatisfied with a board, they simply refuse to vote to approve the slate of nominees for the board. The most high-profile example of this type of action occurred in 2004 with the Walt Disney Company. Major shareholders were dissatisfied with the recent performance of Disney under long-time CEO and Chairman, Michael Eisner. They began an organized campaign to convince the majority of Disney shareholders to withhold their approval of the reelection of Eisner as director and chairman of the board. When the votes were counted, 45% of Disney's shareholders had voted to withhold approval of Eisner. While

---

9. H. Demsetz and K. Lehn, "The Structure of Corporate Ownership: Causes and Consequences," *Journal of Political Economy* 93(6) (1985): 1155–1177.

10. C. Himmelberg, R. G. Hubbard, and D. Palia, "Understanding the Determinants of Managerial Ownership and the Link Between Ownership and Performance," *Journal of Financial Economics* 53(3) (1999): 353–384; and J. Coles, M. Lemmon, and J. F. Meschke, "Structural Models and Endogeneity in Finance," working paper, Arizona State University, 2004.

11. W. Carleton, J. Nelson, and M. Weisbach, "The Influence of Institutions on Corporate Governance Through Private Negotiations: Evidence from TIAA-CREF," *Journal of Finance* 53(4) (1998): 1335–1362.

Shareholder Activism at Blockbuster

In April 2005, Carl Icahn, owner of about 10% of Blockbuster's shares, publicly blasted the management of the video rental company over the strategic direction of the firm. CEO John Antioco wanted to invest aggressively to pursue new lines of business such as online movie rentals. Icahn disagreed: He wanted Blockbuster to instead cut spending and use its cash to pay bigger dividends. Icahn nominated a slate of alternative directors for the May 2005 annual meeting. The mandate of those directors would be to reduce spending, cut executive bonuses, and increase dividends.

At the meeting, Icahn and the two other directors running on the same slate won the shareholder vote.

Antioco subsequently threatened to quit and collect his $54 million severance package. The board, with Icahn's approval, voted to add another board seat and reappoint Antioco as chairman. Icahn also announced that if Blockbuster's performance did not improve in the next year, he would consider trying to replace more Blockbuster directors in 2006, perhaps eventually gaining majority control.

Sources: Shira Ovide, "Blockbuster Executives Sell Shares," *Wall Street Journal*, June 1, 2005, p. C13; Martin Peers, "Blockbuster Chief Gets Second Chance," *Wall Street Journal*, May 16, 2005, p. A3.

Eisner technically had won reelection, a 45% "no" vote is practically unprecedented in large public companies. The signal was clear, and an embarrassed Eisner and the Disney board decided that Eisner would remain CEO, but relinquish the chairman title. Shortly thereafter, Eisner announced plans to retire completely in 2006.

Shareholder Approval.   In addition to electing the directors of the company, shareholders must approve many major actions taken by the board. For example, target shareholders must approve merger agreements and, in some cases, so must bidder shareholders. Even in cases where bidder shareholders are not required to directly approve a merger, listing requirements on the NYSE, for example, demand that shareholders approve any large issue of new shares, such as might be necessary in a stock-swap merger. Normally, approval is perfunctory, but it cannot be taken for granted. As we saw in Chapter 28, after Hewlett-Packard (HP) CEO Carly Fiorina negotiated the merger of HP and Compaq, the Hewlett family used their board seats and voting block to oppose the deal.

Proxy Contests.   Perhaps the most extreme form of direct action that disgruntled shareholders can take is to hold a proxy contest and introduce a rival slate of directors for election to the board. This action gives shareholders an actual choice between the nominees put forth by management and the current board and a completely different slate of nominees put forth by dissident shareholders. One early study of proxy contests found that the announcement of a contest increased firm stock price by 8% on average, even if the challenge was eventually unsuccessful and the incumbents won reelection.[12]

Management Entrenchment

Given the importance of shareholder action in corporate governance, researchers and large investors alike have become increasingly interested in measuring the balance of power between shareholders and managers in a firm. Over time, the tools that managers can use to entrench themselves have evolved, including antitakeover protections such as

12. P. Dodd and J. Warner, "On Corporate Governance: A Study of Proxy Contests," *Journal of Financial Economics* 11(1) (1983): 401–438.

those discussed in Chapter 28. The Investor Responsibility Research Center (IRRC) has collected information on 24 different characteristics that can entrench, or give more power, to managers vis-à-vis shareholders. These provisions include state antitakeover statutes, poison pills, staggered boards, and restrictions on the ability of shareholders to call special meetings themselves.

Researchers have begun using data from the IRRC as a way to measure how entrenched managers are. One study found that firms with more restrictions on shareholder power performed worse than firms with less restrictions during the 1990s.[13] Other studies have found connections between the degree of entrenchment and the compensation offered to managers, and even to the value of acquisitions made.[14] While the index offered by the IRRC does not capture every aspect of corporate governance, many practitioners are finding it to be a useful summary measure of the degree to which managers are entrenched and less likely to have their actions checked by shareholders.

The Threat of Takeover

Many of the provisions listed in the IRRC index concern protection from takeovers. As we discussed in Chapter 28, one motivation for a takeover can be to replace poorly performing management. When internal governance systems such as ownership, compensation, board oversight, and shareholder activism fail, the one remaining way to remove poorly performing managers is by mounting a hostile takeover. Thus the effectiveness of the corporate governance structure of a firm depends on how well protected its managers are from removal in a hostile takeover.

An active takeover market is part of the system through which the threat of dismissal is maintained. In fact, some research has suggested that an active takeover market complements a board's own vigilance in dismissing incompetent managers. That research found that boards are actually more likely to fire managers for poor performance during active takeover markets than they are during lulls in takeover activity.[15] This finding also has implications internationally because some countries have much more active takeover markets than others. In particular, hostile takeovers are far more common in the United States than in other economies.

CONCEPT CHECK
1. Describe and explain a proxy contest.

2. What is the role of takeovers in corporate governance?

29.5   Regulation

So far we've focused on those parts of the corporate governance system that have evolved over time as economic responses to the need for shareholders to mitigate the conflict of interest between themselves and managers. For example, boards of directors came into

13. P. Gompers, J. Ishii, and A. Metrick, "Corporate Governance and Equity Prices," *Quarterly Journal of Economics* 118(1) (2003): 107–155. The cause of this effect, however, is not clear; see J. Core, W. Guay, and T. Rusticus, "Does Weak Governance Cause Weak Stock Returns? An Examination of Firm Operating Performance and Investors' Expectations," *Journal of Finance* 61(2) (2006): 655–687.

14. G. Garvey, and T. Milbourn, "Asymmetric Benchmarking in Compensation: Executives Are Paid for Good Luck but Not Punished for Bad," *Journal of Financial Economics* (in press); and R. Masulis, C. Wang, and F. Xie, "Corporate Governance and Acquirer Returns," *Journal of Finance,* forthcoming.

15. W. Mikkelson and M. Partch, "The Decline of Takeovers and Disciplinary Managerial Turnover," *Journal of Financial Economics* 44(2) (1997): 205–228.

being long before there was any regulation of the governance of a company, and CEOs have long appointed independent directors to their boards without being required to do so. Nonetheless, from time to time, government has added to existing requirements by passing laws that force minimum standards of governance. The most recent example is the Sarbanes-Oxley Act of 2002 (SOX).

In the wake of the massive failures of large public companies and corporate fraud scandals mentioned in the introduction to this chapter, Congress rushed to enact legislation to fix what it saw as inadequate safeguards against malfeasance by managers of public corporations. The result was the Sarbanes-Oxley Act. Prior to SOX, the largest overhaul of securities markets and introduction of regulation came in response to the stock market crash of 1929 and the Great Depression that followed. The Exchange Acts of 1933 and 1934, among other things, established the Securities and Exchange Commission (SEC) and prohibited trading on private information gained as an insider of a firm.

The Sarbanes-Oxley Act

One of the most critical inputs to the monitoring process is accurate information. If a board of directors has inaccurate information, it cannot do its job. While SOX contains many provisions, the overall intent of the legislation was to improve the accuracy of information given to both boards and to shareholders. SOX attempted to achieve this goal in three ways: (1) by overhauling incentives and independence in the auditing process, (2) by stiffening penalties for providing false information, and (3) by forcing companies to validate their internal financial control processes.

Many of the problems at Enron, WorldCom, and elsewhere were kept hidden from boards and shareholders until it was too late. In the wake of these scandals, many people felt that the accounting statements of these companies, while often remaining true to the letter of GAAP, did not present an accurate picture of the financial health of a company.

Auditing firms are supposed to ensure that a company's financial statements accurately reflect the financial state of the firm. In reality, most auditors have a longstanding relationship with their audit clients; this extended relationship and the auditors' desire to keep the lucrative auditing fees makes auditors less willing to challenge management. More important perhaps, most accounting firms have developed large and extremely profitable consulting divisions. Obviously, if an audit team refuses to accommodate a request by a client's management, that client will be less likely to choose the accounting firm's consulting division for its next consulting contract. SOX addressed this concern by putting strict limits on the amount of non-audit fees (consulting or otherwise) that an accounting firm can earn from the same firm that it audits. It also required that audit partners rotate every five years to limit the likelihood that auditing relationships become too cozy over long periods of time. Finally, SOX called on the SEC to force companies to have audit committees that are dominated by outside directors and required that at least one outside director have a financial background.

SOX also stiffened the criminal penalties for providing false information to shareholders. It required both the CEO and the CFO to personally attest to the accuracy of the financial statements presented to shareholders and to sign a statement to that effect. Penalties for providing false or misleading financial statements were increased under SOX—fines of as much as $5 million and imprisonment of a maximum of 20 years are permitted. Further, CEOs and CFOs must return bonuses or profits from the sale of stock or the exercise of options during any period covered by statements that are later restated.

Finally, Section 404 of SOX requires senior management and the boards of public companies to be comfortable enough with the process through which funds are allocated

Lawrence E. Harris

As Chief Economist of the U.S. Securities and Exchange Commission from 2002 to 2004, Dr. Lawrence E. Harris was the primary advisor to the SEC on all economic issues. He participated extensively in the development of Sarbanes-Oxley (SOX) regulations. Currently Dr. Harris holds the Fred V. Keenan Chair in Finance at the University of Southern California's Marshall School of Business.

QUESTION: *Why is legislation such as Sarbanes-Oxley necessary to protect shareholders?*

ANSWER: Public investors will supply capital to entrepreneurs seeking to fund new business ventures only if they believe it will be used wisely. Regrettably, history has shown that management too often has violated that trust.

The interests of managers and shareholders often conflict. To solve this agency problem, shareholders rely upon information produced by corporate accounting systems. Sarbanes-Oxley mandated accounting and audit standards to improve the quality of corporate financial disclosure.

Opponents of governance regulation believe that shareholders can—and should—take care of themselves. Unfortunately, shareholders often cannot exercise the control necessary to solve agency problems that they could not have anticipated when the firm was first founded. The firm's governance structure, which may have been sensible when the firm was a small company funded primarily by its founders, may no longer be appropriate for a large, widely held corporation operating in the modern economy. Management with little ownership stake may be entrenched, and the directors may be conflicted. When shareholders cannot solve their agency problems, the government must intervene with the lightest possible hand.

QUESTION: *What are the costs and benefits of Sarbanes-Oxley?*

ANSWER: Good corporate disclosure is essential to public finance. SOX improved the quality of disclosure by strengthening accounting and auditing standards. By requiring the CEO and CFO to sign accounts and attest to their accuracy, SOX also put teeth into enforcement if fraud is discovered.

What many people perceive as costs of SOX are really expenditures that weak firms avoided. All well-managed firms must ensure the integrity of their accounting. SOX merely requires that people adopt *existing* best practice. Many companies were already fully compliant with SOX in most essential respects.

Critics claim that SOX made going public more difficult for small firms by increasing the cost of being a public firm. But a public firm *must* have secure control mechanisms to protect shareholders. SOX may decrease the number of firms that go public, but it will also decrease the losses suffered by public investors.

SOX established the Public Corporation Auditing Oversight Board to regulate auditors. Previous efforts at self-regulation failed because accountants would not discipline their peers. Following numerous notable failures, Congress stepped in and created the PCAOB.

QUESTION: *Is SOX a good law?*

ANSWER: Regulators are blamed for failing to regulate when crises occur, but they do not bear the costs of their regulations. This asymmetry often causes them to underestimate the costs of their regulations and thus adopt unnecessary regulations. The problem is greatest when political considerations force Congress to write regulations that would be better written by well-informed specialists in regulatory agencies such as the SEC. Congress wrote SOX in response to the financial accounting crises that greatly offended the public. Although SOX permits the SEC to essentially rewrite any provision that it determines not to be in the public interest, under the circumstances, it could not do so.

SOX is generally good regulation, but it has some notable unintended consequences. The power it gives audit firms over their corporate clients allows them to interpret SOX to their advantage and thereby increase the work necessary to comply with SOX. SOX also imposes unnecessary costs upon mutual funds. Investment companies are subject to SOX because they are public corporations, but they do not face the same accounting problems that operating companies face. In its haste to appease the public, Congress failed to be as discriminating as it could have been.

and controlled, and outcomes monitored throughout the firm, to be willing to attest to their effectiveness and validity. Section 404 has arguably garnered more attention than any other section in SOX because of the potentially enormous burden it places on every firm to validate its entire financial control system. When the SEC estimated the cost of implementing Section 404, its staff economists put the total cost at $1.24 billion. Recent estimates based on surveys by Financial Executives International and the American Electronics Association predict that the actual cost will be between $20 billion and $35 billion.[16] The burden of complying with this provision is greater, as a fraction of revenue, for smaller companies. The surveys cited earlier found that multibillion-dollar companies will pay less than 0.05% of their revenues to comply, whereas small companies with less than $20 million in revenues will pay more than 3% of their revenues to comply.

The Cadbury Commission

It is difficult to determine definitively whether the costs of SOX outweigh its benefits: Even if we could measure the total direct and indirect costs of a law, we could never accurately estimate how much fraud is deterred by that law. One place to turn to for guidance is the experiences of other countries. The following quote from *The Independent*[17] sounds like it was written to describe the motivation behind the Sarbanes-Oxley legislation:

> Prompted by public concern over a string of unexpected collapses of recently audited firms and over big rises in executive pay, exchanges and public officials rode a wave of public outrage to institute corporate governance reforms to strengthen the independence of the board and address the conflicts of interest in the auditing process.

In actuality, this passage was written in 1992, and it described what happened in the United Kingdom in 1991. Following the collapse of some large public companies, the U.K. government commissioned Sir Adrian Cadbury to form a committee to develop a code of best practices in corporate governance. Sir Cadbury, in introducing his recommendations, reportedly said the following:

> The fundamental issue is one of pressure. There is pressure on the company to show the results that the market expects. There is pressure on the auditors who don't want to lose their jobs. The question is whether a structure can emerge out of the dialogue which is robust enough to give the shareholders what they ought to get and what they can rely upon. Internal controls are a part of the legitimate expectations of those who receive accounts.[18]

The problems that the Cadbury Commission identified are the same as those that SOX attempted to address in the United States ten years later. Perhaps not surprisingly, the resulting recommendations were quite similar as well. According to the commission's findings, audit and compensation committees should be made up entirely of independent directors or, at least, have a majority of them. The CEO should not be chairman of the board, and at the very least there should be a lead independent director with similar agenda-setting powers. Auditors should be rotated, and there should be fuller disclosure of non-audit work. Unlike SOX, these recommendations were not backed up by the force

---

16. American Electronics Association, "Sarbanes-Oxley Section 404: The 'Section' of Unintended Consequences and Its Impact on Small Business" (2005).

17. S. Pincombe, "Accountancy and Management: Auditors Look to Pass the Buck as Pressure for Reform Increases," *The Independent* (London), November 12, 1991, p. 21.

18. Ibid.

Martha Stewart and ImClone

The most famous recent insider trading case, which was widely reported in the media, involved Martha Stewart, self-made billionaire and CEO of a media empire built around her name. Stewart sold 3928 shares of ImClone Systems in December 2001, just before the Food and Drug Administration announced that it was rejecting ImClone's application to review a new cancer drug. The SEC investigated, alleging that Stewart sold the shares after receiving a tip from her broker that the ImClone founder and his family had been selling shares.

Even though Stewart was not an employee of ImClone, insider trading laws prohibited her from trading on information gained through a tip, as the origin of the information violated the duty of trust. Nonetheless, in the end, Stewart was charged only with lying to a federal officer and conspiracy to obstruct justice (the investigation of her trades). She was convicted and served five months in prison and an additional five months of home confinement. In addition, she was fined $30,000.

Source: L. A. Times, July 16, 2004.

---

of law. Rather, companies could adopt them or instead explain why they chose not to adopt them in their annual reports. Some researchers have studied firms that adopted the Cadbury recommendations versus those that did not. The results are mixed. While one study found that those firms that separated the position of CEO and chairman performed better, another found no relation between the independence of key board committees and firm performance in the post-Cadbury era.[19]

Insider Trading

One aspect of the conflict of interest between managers and outside shareholders that we have not yet addressed is **insider trading**. Insider trading occurs when a person makes a trade based on privileged information. Managers have access to information that outside investors do not have. By using this information, managers can exploit profitable trading opportunities that are not available to outside investors. If they were allowed to trade on their information, their profits would come at the expense of outside investors and, as a result, outside investors would be less willing to invest in corporations. Insider trading regulation was passed to address this problem.

In the United States, regulation against insider trading traces back to the Great Depression—specifically, to the Exchange Act of 1934. Insiders of a company are defined broadly to include managers, directors, and anyone else who has access to material nonpublic information, including temporary insiders—for example, lawyers working on a merger deal or commercial printers contracted to print the merger agreement documents. Whether information is material has been defined in the courts as referring to whether the information would have been a significant factor in an investor's decision about the value of the security. Some examples include knowledge of an upcoming merger announcement, earnings release, or change in payout policy. The law is especially strict with regard to takeover announcements, prohibiting anyone (whether an insider or not) with nonpublic

---

19. J. Dahya, A. A. Lonie, and D. M. Power, "The Case for Separating the Roles of Chairman and CEO: An Analysis of Stock Market and Accounting Data," *Corporate Governance* 4(2) (1996): 71–77; and N. Vafeas and E. Theodorou, "The Association Between Board Structure and Firm Performance in the UK," *British Accounting Review* 30(4) (1998): 383–407.

information about a pending or ongoing tender offer from trading on that information or revealing it to someone who is likely to trade on it.

The penalties for violating insider trading laws include jail time, fines, and civil penalties. Only the U.S. Justice Department—on its own or at the request of the SEC—can bring charges that carry the possibility of a prison sentence. However, the SEC can bring civil actions if it chooses. In 1984, Congress stiffened the civil penalties for insider trading by passing the Insider Trading Sanctions Act, which allowed for civil penalties of up to three times the gain from insider trading.

CONCEPT CHECK

1. Describe the main requirements of the Sarbanes-Oxley Act of 2002.

2. What is insider trading, and how can it harm investors?

29.6 Corporate Governance Around the World

Most of our discussion in this chapter has focused on corporate governance in the United States. Yet, both the protection of shareholder rights and the basic ownership and control structure of corporations vary across countries. We explore some of those differences here.

Protection of Shareholder Rights

Recent events notwithstanding, investor protection in the United States is generally seen as being among the best in the world. The degree to which investors are protected against expropriation of company funds by managers and even the degree to which their rights are enforced vary widely across countries and legal regimes. In an important study, researchers collected data on aspects of shareholder rights across more than 30 countries.[20] They claimed that the degree of investor protection was largely determined by the legal origin of the country—specifically, whether its legal system was based on British common law (more protection) or French, German, and Scandinavian civil law (less protection). This purported link between legal origin and investor protection has been challenged by other researchers, however, who demonstrate that formal legal protection for investors is a relatively recent development in Great Britain itself.[21] In the late nineteenth and early twentieth centuries, there was essentially no formal legal protection of minority investors.

Controlling Owners and Pyramids

Much of the focus in the United States is on the agency conflict between shareholders, who own the majority of a firm but are a dispersed group, and managers, who own little of the firm and must be monitored. In many other countries, the central conflict is between what are called "controlling shareholders" and "minority shareholders." In Europe, many corporations are run by families that own controlling blocks of shares. For most practical purposes, blocks of shares in excess of 20% are considered to be controlling, as long as no one else has any large concentration of shares. The idea is that if you own 20% and the other 80% is dispersed among many different shareholders, you will have considerable say in the

---

20. R. La Porta, F. Lopez-de-Silanes, A. Shleifer, and R. Vishny, "Law and Finance," *Journal of Political Economy* 106 (1998): 1113–1155.

21. J. Franks, C. Mayer, and S. Rossi, "Ownership: Evolution and Regulation," European Corporate Governance Institute Finance Working Paper (March 25, 2005).

operation of the firm; other shareholders would have to coordinate their activities to try to outvote you—a formidable challenge.

In these firms, there is usually little conflict between the controlling family and the management (it is often made up of family members). Instead, the conflict arises between the minority shareholders (those without the controlling block) and the controlling shareholders. Controlling shareholders can make decisions that benefit them disproportionately relative to the minority shareholders, such as employing family members rather than the most talented managers or establishing contracts favorable to other family-controlled firms.

Dual Class Shares and the Value of Control.   One way for families to gain control over firms even when they do not own more than half the shares is to issue **dual class shares**—a scenario in which companies have more than one class of shares and one class has superior voting rights over the other class. For example, a class B share might have ten votes for every one vote of a class A share. Controlling shareholders—often families—will hold all or most of the shares with superior voting rights and issue the inferior voting class to the public. This approach allows the controlling shareholders to raise capital without diluting their control. Dual class shares are common in Brazil, Canada, Denmark, Finland, Germany, Italy, Korea, Mexico, Norway, Sweden, and Switzerland. In the United States, they are far less common. Some countries, such as Belgium, China, Japan, Singapore, and Spain, outlaw differential voting rights altogether.

Pyramid Structures.   Another way families can control a corporation without owning 50% of the equity is to create a pyramid structure. In a **pyramid structure**, a family first creates a company in which it owns more than 50% of the shares and therefore has a controlling interest. This company then owns a controlling interest—that is, at least 50% of the shares—in another company. Notice that the family controls *both* companies, but *owns* only 25% of the second company. Indeed, if the second company purchased 50% of the shares of a third company, then the family would control all three companies, even though it would own only 12.5% of the third company. The farther you move down the pyramid the less ownership the family has, but it still remains in complete control of all the companies. Although this example is stylized, a variety of pyramid structures based on this idea are quite common outside the United States.

Figure 29.2 details the actual pyramid controlled by the Pesenti family in Italy as of 1995.[22] The Pesenti family effectively controls five companies primarily concentrated in the construction industry—Italmobiliare, Italcementi, Franco Tosi, Cementerie Siciliane, and Cementeri de Sardegna—even though it does not have more than 50% ownership of any one of them. In this case, the family uses a pyramid structure plus shares with special voting rights to control companies even when its ownership share is as little as 7%.

A controlling family has many opportunities to expropriate minority shareholders in a pyramid structure. The source of the problem is that as you move down the pyramid, the difference between the family's control and its cash flow rights increases. Cash flow rights refer simply to the family's direct ownership stake and, therefore, the portion of the cash flows generated by the firm that the family has a right to. Notice that Italcementi gets 74% of the dividends of Cementerie Siciliane; Italmobiliare gets 32% of the dividends of

---

22. P. Volpin, "Governance with Poor Investor Protection: Evidence from Top Executive Turnover in Italy," *Journal of Financial Economics* 64(1) (2002): 61–90.

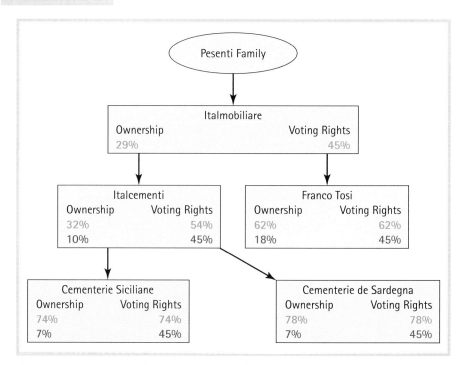

FIGURE 29.2   **Pesenti Family Pyramid, 1995**

Each box contains both ownership and voting rights (which can be different when preferred stock with superior voting rights is used). The first set of numbers (in blue) indicates the rights of the preceding company one step up the pyramid. The second set of numbers (in red) shows the rights of the Pesenti family in that company. For example, Italmobiliare's investment in Italcementi represents 54% of the voting rights but it owns only 32% of the company. The Pesenti family's investment in Italmobiliare plus additional use of preferred shares gives it a 10% ownership of Italcementi but 45% of the voting rights in Italcementi.

Italcementi. Finally, the Pesenti family has rights to 29% of the dividends of Italmobiliare. Thus the family receives only 29% × 32% × 74% = 7% of the dividends of Cementerie Siciliane but still controls it.

A conflict of interest arises because the family has an incentive to try to move profits (and hence dividends) up the pyramid—that is, away from companies in which it has few cash flow rights and toward firms in which it has more cash flow rights. This process is called **tunneling**. An example of how this might occur is if the Pesenti family would have Cementerie Siciliane enter into an agreement to be supplied by Italmobiliare at prices that are extremely favorable to Italmobiliare. Such a move would reduce Cementerie Siciliane's profits and increase Italmobiliare's profits.

Of course, if you are a minority shareholder in one of these subsidiaries, you would rationally anticipate this expropriation and so you would pay less for the shares of firms in which a family has control, especially if it is low in the pyramid. In effect, you would factor in your expected loss from being a minority shareholder rather than a controlling shareholder. Many studies have confirmed this intuition, finding sharp differences between the value of controlling blocks and minority shares.[23] Thus controlling shareholders pay for their control rights because the firm effectively faces a higher cost of equity for outside capital.

The Stakeholder Model

The agency costs and the ways to control them that we have discussed are general to all companies anywhere in the world. However, the United States is somewhat of an exception, in that it focuses solely on maximizing shareholder welfare. Most countries follow what is called the **stakeholder model**, giving explicit consideration to other stakeholders—in particular, rank-and-file employees. As noted earlier, countries such as Germany give employees board representation. Others have mandated works councils, local versions of labor unions that are to be informed and consulted on major corporate decisions. Finally, some countries mandate employee participation in decision making in their constitutions. Table 29.1 summarizes employee standing in the governance of firms in OECD (Organization for Economic Cooperation and Development) countries.

Cross-holdings

While in the United States it is rare for one company's largest shareholder to be another company, it is the norm in many countries such as Germany, Japan, and Korea. In Japan, groups of firms connected through cross-holdings and a common relation to a bank are known as *keiretsu*. Monitoring of each company comes from others in the group holding blocks of its stock and primarily from the main bank of the group, which as a creditor monitors the financial well-being of the group companies closely. In Korea, huge conglomerate groups such as Hyundai, Samsung, LG, and SK comprise companies in widely diversified lines of business and are known as *chaebol*. For example, SK Corporation has subsidiary and group companies in energy, chemicals, pharmaceuticals, and telecommunications. An important difference between the Korean chaebol and the Japanese keiretsu is that in Korea the firms do not share a common relationship with a single bank.

---

23. For estimates based on research on mergers and acquisitions, see P. Hanouna, A. Sarin, and A. Shapiro, "Value of Corporate Control: Some International Evidence," working paper, Marshal School of Business, University of Southern California (2004). Estimates of the value of control have also been done comparing the value of shares with different voting rights. In the United States, see C. Doidge, "U.S. Cross-listings and the Private Benefits of Control: Evidence from Dual Class Shares," *Journal of Financial Economics* 72(3) (2004): 519–553. Italy is a country where the value of control is much larger, Zingales reports a premium of 82% on voting shares, presumably because of lower protection to minority investors. See L. Zingales, "The Value of the Voting Right: A Study of the Milan Stock Exchange Experience," *Review of Financial Studies* 7(1) (1994): 125–148. Other work includes H. Almeida and D. Wolfenzon, "A Theory of Pyramidal Ownership and Family Business Groups," working paper, New York University (2005); L. A. Bebchuk, R. Kraakman, and G. R. Triantis, "Stock Pyramids, Cross-Ownership, and Dual Class Equity," in R. Morck (ed.), *Concentrated Corporate Ownership* (Chicago: University of Chicago Press, 2000): 295–318; M. Bertrand, P. Mehta, and S. Mullainathan, "Ferreting Out Tunneling: An Application to Indian Business Groups," *Quarterly Journal of Economics* 117(1) (2002): 121–148; S. Johnson, R. La Porta, F. Lopez de Silanes, and A. Shleifer, "Tunneling," *American Economic Review* 90(2) (2000): 22–27.

TABLE 29.1	Employee Participation in Corporate Governance in OECD Countries		

Country	Employees Appoint Some Board Members	Works Councils Mandated by Law	Constitutional Reference to Employee Participation in the Management of the Company
Australia	No	No	No
Austria	Yes	Yes	No
Belgium	No	Yes	No
Canada	No	No	No
Czech Republic	Yes	No	No
Denmark	Yes	Yes	No
Finland	No	Yes	No
France	No	Yes	Constitutional right
Germany	Yes	Yes	No
Greece	No	Yes	No
Hungary	No	Yes	No
Ireland	No	No	No
Italy	No	No	Constitutional right
Japan	No	No	No
Korea	No	Yes	No
Mexico	No	No	No
Netherlands	No	Yes	No
New Zealand	No	No	No
Norway	Yes	No	Constitutional right
Poland	No	No	No
Portugal	No	Yes	No
Slovak Republic	No	No	No
Spain	No	Yes	No
Sweden	Yes	No	No
Switzerland	No	No	No
Turkey	No	No	No
United Kingdom	No	No	No
United States	No	No	No

Source: Organization for Economic Cooperation and Development, *Survey of Corporate Governance Developments in OECD Countries* (2004).

CONCEPT CHECK

1. How does shareholder protection vary across countries?

2. How can a minority owner in a business gain a controlling interest?

29.7 The Tradeoff of Corporate Governance

Corporate governance is a system of checks and balances that trades off costs and benefits. As this chapter makes clear, this tradeoff is very complicated. No one structure works for all firms. For example, it would be hard to argue that having Bill Gates as a controlling shareholder of Microsoft was bad for minority investors. For Microsoft, the alignment of incentives that Gate's large stake in Microsoft assured appeared to outweigh the costs of have a such a large shareholder. In other cases, however, this is unlikely to be true.

The costs and benefits of a corporate governance system also depend on cultural norms. Acceptable business practice in one culture is unacceptable in another culture, and thus it is not surprising that there is such wide variation in governance structures across countries.[24]

It is important to keep in mind that good governance is value enhancing and so, in principle, is something investors in the firm should strive for. Because there are many ways to implement good governance, one should expect firms to display—and firms do display—wide variation in their governance structures.

Summary

1. Corporate governance refers to the system of controls, regulations, and incentives designed to prevent fraud from happening.

2. The conflicts between those who control the operations of a firm and those who supply capital to the firm are as old as the corporate organizational structure. Shareholders use a combination of incentives and threats of dismissal to mitigate this conflict.

3. The board of directors hires managers, sets their compensation, and fires them if necessary. Some boards become captured, meaning that they act in the interests of managers rather than shareholders. Boards with strong, outside directors who were nominated before the current CEO took the helm of the firm are the least likely to be captured.

4. Ownership of a company's stock by management can reduce managers' perquisite consumption. However, moderate holdings of shares can have a negative effect by making the managers harder to fire (reducing the threat of dismissal), without fully aligning their interests with those of shareholders.

5. By tying managers' compensation to firm performance, boards can better align managers' interests with shareholders' interests. Care must be taken to make sure managers do not have incentives to try to manipulate the firm's stock price to garner a big compensation payout.

6. If a board fails to act, shareholders are not without recourse. They can propose an alternate slate of directors or vote not to ratify certain actions of the board.

7. A board and management can adopt provisions, such as staggered boards and limitations on special shareholder meetings, that serve to entrench them. These provisions also have the effect of limiting the efficacy of a hostile takeover bid.

---

24. Resources that detail how governance differs across the world include J. Charkham, *Keeping Good Company: A Study of Corporate Governance in Five Countries* (Oxford: Clarendon Press, 1994); J. Franks and C. Mayer, "Corporate Ownership and Control in the U.K., Germany and France," *Journal of Applied Corporate Finance* 9(4) (1997): 30–45; R. La Porta, F. Lopez-de-Silanes, and A. Shleifer, "Corporate Ownership Around the World," *Journal of Finance* 54(4) (1999): 471–517; and D. K. Denis and J. J. McConnell, "International Corporate Governance," *Journal of Financial and Quantitative Analysis* 38(1) (2003): 1–38.

8. Despite the defenses that a determined management can erect, one source of the threat of dismissal comes from a hostile acquirer, which can take over a firm and fire the management, even if the board fails to do so.

9. Regulation is an important piece of the total corporate governance environment. Regulation can be beneficial by reducing asymmetric information between managers and capital providers and thus reducing the overall cost of capital. Regulation also carries with it costs of compliance and enforcement. Good regulation balances these forces to produce a net benefit for society.

10. The most recent overhaul of U.S. governance regulation is the Sarbanes-Oxley Act of 2002. The act was intended to improve shareholder monitoring of managers by increasing the accuracy of their information.

   a. It overhauls incentives and independence in the auditing process.

   b. It stiffens the penalties for providing false information.

   c. It forces companies to validate their internal financial control process.

11. The Exchange Acts of 1933 and 1934 are the basis of insider trading regulation. Over time, the SEC and the courts have developed interpretations of the law that

   a. Prohibit insiders with a fiduciary duty to their shareholders from trading on material nonpublic information in that stock.

   b. Prohibit anyone with nonpublic information about a pending or ongoing tender offer from trading on that information or revealing it to someone who is likely to trade on it.

12. Corporate governance, regulations, and practices vary widely across countries.

   a. Some studies suggest that countries with common-law roots generally provide better shareholder protection than countries with civil-law origin.

   b. Ownership structures in Europe and Asia often involve pyramidal control of a group of companies by a single family. In these situations, the controlling family has many opportunities for expropriation of minority shareholders through tunneling.

   c. Dual class shares with differential voting rights allow a controlling shareholder or family to maintain control of a company or group even if their cash flow rights are relatively small. Dual class shares are common outside the United States.

   d. Most countries give employees some role in governing a firm. Employee involvement usually takes the form of board seats or works councils that are consulted before major decisions.

   e. It is common outside the United States for a company's largest shareholder to be another company. These cross-holdings create incentives for firms to monitor each other.

Key Terms

backdating *p. 908*

captured *p. 906*

corporate governance *p. 904*

dual class shares *p. 917*

gray directors *p. 905*

inside directors *p. 905*

insider trading *p. 915*

outside (independent) directors *p. 905*

pyramid structure *p. 917*

stakeholder model *p. 919*

tunneling *p. 918*

Further Reading

The literature on corporate governance is extensive; we cannot hope to do it justice in this single chapter. Readers interested in delving into this subject more thoroughly can begin by consulting the following surveys: M. Becht, P. Bolton, and A. Roell, "Corporate Governance and Control," in G. Constantinides, M. Harris, and R. Stulz (eds.), *Handbook of the Economics of Finance* (Amsterdam: North-Holland, 2003: 1–109); and A. Shleifer and R. W. Vishny, "A Survey of Corporate Governance," *Journal of Finance* 52(2) (1997): 737–783.

Problems

Corporate Governance and Agency Costs

1. What inherent characteristic of corporations creates the need for a system of checks on manager behavior?

2. What are the advantages and disadvantages of the corporate organizational structure?

Monitoring by the Board of Directors

3. What is the role of the board of directors in corporate governance?

4. How does a board become captured by a CEO?

Compensation Policies

5. What are the advantages and disadvantages of increasing the options granted to CEOs?

Ownership by Management

6. Is it necessarily true that increasing managerial ownership stakes will improve firm performance?

Direct Action by Shareholders

7. How can proxy contests be used to overcome a captured board?

Regulation

8. What is the essential tradeoff faced by government in designing regulation of public firms?

9. Many of the provisions of the Sarbanes-Oxley Act of 2002 were aimed at auditors. How does this affect corporate governance?

10. What are the costs and benefits of prohibiting insider trading?

11. How do the laws on insider trading differ for merger- versus non-merger-related trading?

12. Are the rights of shareholders better protected in the United States or in France?

13. How can a controlling family use a pyramidal control structure to benefit itself at the expense of other shareholders?

Risk Management

notation

r_f	risk-free interest rate
r	current interest rate
r_L	cost of capital for an insured loss
β_L	beta of an insured loss
$r_\$, r_€$	dollar and euro interest rate
S	spot exchange rate
F, F_T	one-year and T-year forward exchange rate
K	option strike price
σ	exchange rate volatility
T	option (or forward) expiration date
$N()$	normal distribution function
C_t	cash flow on date t
P	price of a security
ε	change in interest rate
k	compounding periods per year
A, L, E	market value of assets, liabilities, equity
D_P	duration of security or portfolio P
$\tilde{r}_t$	floating interest rate on date t
δ_t	credit spread on date t
N	notational principal of a swap contract
NPV	net present value

All firms are subject to risk from a variety of sources: changes in consumer tastes and demand for their products, fluctuations in the cost of raw materials, employee turnover, the entry of new competitors, and countless other uncertainties. Entrepreneurs and corporate managers willingly take on these risks in the pursuit of high returns and accept them as part of the cost of doing business. But as with any other cost, firms should manage risk to minimize the effect on the value of the firm.

The primary method of risk management is prevention. For example, firms can avoid or at least reduce many potential risks by increasing safety standards in the workplace, by making prudent investment decisions, and by conducting appropriate due diligence when entering into new relationships. But some risks are too costly to prevent and are inevitable consequences of running a business. As discussed in Part V of the text, the firm shares these business risks with its investors through its capital structure. Some of the risk is passed on to debt holders, who bear the risk that the firm will default. Most of the risk is held by equity holders, who are exposed to the volatility of the stock's realized return. Both types of investors can reduce their risk by holding the firm's securities in a well-diversified portfolio.

Not all risks need to be passed on to the firm's debt and equity holders. Insurance and financial markets allow firms to trade risk and shield their debt and equity holders from some types of risk. For example, after a fire shut down its processing plant in January 2005, Suncor Energy received more than $200 million in settlements from insurance contracts covering both the damage to the plant and the lost business while the plant was being repaired. Much of the loss from the fire was thus borne by Suncor's insurers rather than by its investors. In 2004, Southwest Airlines received $455 million from financial contracts that compensated it for the rise in the cost of jet fuel. At the beginning of 2005, Dell held contracts to protect more than $5 billion worth of projected foreign revenues from fluctuations in exchange rates, and General Electric had contracts to prevent a rise in interest rates from increasing its borrowing costs on more than $24 billion of short-term debt.

In this chapter, we consider the strategies that firms use to manage and reduce the risk borne by their investors. We begin with the most common form of risk management, insurance. After carefully considering the costs and benefits of insurance, we look at the ways firms can use financial markets to offload the risks associated with changes in commodity prices, exchange rate fluctuations, and interest rate movements.

30.1 Insurance

Insurance is the most common method firms use to reduce risk. Many firms purchase **property insurance** to insure their assets against hazards such as fire, storm damage, vandalism, earthquakes, and other natural and environmental risks. Other common types of insurance include:

- **Business liability insurance**, which covers the costs that result if some aspect of the business causes harm to a third party or someone else's property
- **Business interruption insurance**, which protects the firm against the loss of earnings if the business is interrupted due to fire, accident, or some other insured peril
- **Key personnel insurance**, which compensates for the loss or unavoidable absence of crucial employees in the firm

In this section, we illustrate the role of insurance in reducing risk and examine its pricing and potential benefits and costs for a firm.

The Role of Insurance: An Example

To understand the role of insurance in reducing risk, consider an oil refinery with a 1-in-5000, or 0.02%, chance of being destroyed by a fire in the next year. If it is destroyed, the firm estimates that it will lose $150 million in rebuilding costs and lost business. We can summarize the risk from fire with a probability distribution:

Event	Probability	Loss ($ million)
No fire	99.98%	0
Fire	0.02%	150

Given this probability distribution, the firm's expected loss from fire each year is

$$99.98\% \times (\$0) + 0.02\% \times (\$150 \text{ million}) = \$30,000$$

While the expected loss is relatively small, the firm faces a large downside risk if a fire does occur. If the firm could eliminate completely the chance of fire for less than the present value of $30,000 per year, it would do so; such an investment would have a positive NPV. But avoiding *any* chance of a fire is probably not feasible with current technology (or at least would cost far more than $30,000 per year). Consequently, the firm can manage the risk by instead purchasing insurance to compensate its loss of $150 million. In exchange, the firm will pay an annual fee, called an **insurance premium**, to the insurance company. In this way, insurance allows the firm to exchange a random future loss for a certain upfront expense.

Insurance Pricing in a Perfect Market

When a firm buys insurance, it transfers the risk of the loss to an insurance company. The insurance company charges an upfront premium to take on that risk. At what price will the insurance company be willing to bear the risk in a perfect market?

In a perfect market without other frictions, insurance companies should compete until they are just earning a fair return and the NPV from selling insurance is zero. The NPV is zero if the price of insurance equals the present value of the expected payment; in that case, we say the price is **actuarially fair**. If r_L is the appropriate cost of capital given the risk of the loss, we can calculate the actuarially fair premium as follows:[1]

Actuarially Fair Insurance Premium

$$\text{Insurance Premium} = \frac{\Pr(\text{Loss}) \times E[\text{Payment in the Event of Loss}]}{1 + r_L} \qquad (30.1)$$

The cost of capital r_L used in Eq. 30.1 depends on the risk being insured. Consider again the oil refinery. The risk of fire is surely unrelated to the performance of the stock market or the economy. Instead, this risk is specific to this firm and, therefore, diversifiable in a large portfolio. As we discussed in Chapter 10, by pooling together the risks from many policies, insurance companies can create very-low-risk portfolios whose annual claims are relatively predictable. In other words, the risk of fire has a beta of zero, so it will not command a risk premium. In this case, $r_L = r_f$, the risk-free interest rate.

Not all insurable risks have a beta of zero. Some risks, such as hurricanes and earthquakes, create losses of tens of billions of dollars and may be difficult to diversify completely.[2] Other types of losses may be correlated across firms. Increases in the cost of health care or more stringent environmental regulations raise the potential claims from health insurance and liability insurance for all firms. Finally, some risks can have a causal effect on the stock market: The September 11, 2001, terrorist attacks cost insurers $34 billion[3] and also led to a 12% decline in the S&P 500 in the first week of trading following the attacks.

For risks that cannot be fully diversified, the cost of capital r_L will include a risk premium. By its very nature, insurance for nondiversifiable hazards is generally a negative-beta asset (it pays off in bad times); the insurance payment to the firm tends to be *larger* when total losses are high and the market portfolio is low. Thus the risk-adjusted rate r_L for losses is *less than* the risk-free rate r_f, leading to a *higher* insurance premium in Eq. 30.1. While firms that purchase insurance earn a return $r_L < r_f$ on their investment, because of the negative beta of the insurance payoff, it is still a zero-NPV transaction.[4]

---

1. Equation 30.1 assumes insurance premiums are paid at the start of the year, and payments in the event of loss are made at the end of the year. It is straightforward to extend it to alternative timing assumptions.

2. For example, insured losses from hurricanes Katrina, Rita, and Wilma, which pummeled the southeastern United States in 2005, exceeded $40 billion, with total economic losses topping $100 billion. When insuring large risks like these, many insurance companies buy insurance on their own portfolios from *reinsurance companies*. Reinsurance firms pool risks globally from different insurance companies worldwide. For natural disasters, typically one fourth to one third of the insured losses are passed on to reinsurers.

3. Including property, life, and liability insurance, as estimated by the Insurance Information Institute, http://www.iii.org.

4. Not all insurance must have a zero or negative beta; a positive beta is possible if the amount of the insured loss is higher when market returns are also high.

Insurance Pricing and the CAPM

Problem

As the owner of a landmark Chicago skyscraper, you decide to purchase insurance that will pay $1 billion in the event the building is destroyed by terrorists. Suppose the likelihood of such a loss is 0.1%, the risk-free interest rate is 4%, and the expected return of the market is 10%. If the risk has a beta of zero, what is the actuarially fair insurance premium? What is the premium if the beta of terrorism insurance is −2.5?[5]

Solution

The expected loss is 0.1% × $1 billion = $1 million. If the risk has a beta of zero, we compute the insurance premium using the risk-free interest rate: ($1 million)/1.04 = $961,538.

If the beta of the risk is not zero, we can use the CAPM to estimate the appropriate cost of capital. Given a beta for the loss, β_L, of −2.5, and an expected market return, r_{mkt}, of 10%:

$$r_L = r_f + \beta_L \, (r_{mkt} - r_f) = 4\% - 2.5 \, (10\% - 4\%) = -11\%$$

In this case, the actuarially fair premium is ($1 million)/(1 − 0.11) = $1.124 million. Although this premium exceeds the expected loss, it is a fair price given the negative beta of the risk.

The Value of Insurance

In a perfect capital market, insurance will be priced so that it has an NPV of zero for both the insurer and the insured. But if purchasing insurance has an NPV of zero, what benefit does it have for the firm?

Modigliani and Miller have already provided us with the answer to this question: In a perfect capital market, there is no benefit to the firm from any financial transaction, *including insurance*. Insurance is a zero-NPV transaction that has no effect on value. Although insurance allows the firm to divide its risk in a new way (e.g., the risk of fire is held by insurers, rather than by debt and equity holders), the firm's total risk—and, therefore, its value—remains unchanged.

Thus, just like a firm's capital structure, the value of insurance must come from reducing the cost of market imperfections on the firm. Let's consider the potential benefits of insurance with respect to the market imperfections that we considered in Part V of the text.

Bankruptcy and Financial Distress Costs.   When a firm borrows, it increases its chances of experiencing financial distress. In Chapter 16, we saw that financial distress may impose significant direct and indirect costs on the firm, including agency costs such as excessive risk taking and underinvestment. By insuring risks that could lead to distress, the firm can reduce the likelihood that it will incur these costs.

For example, for an airline with a large amount of leverage, the losses associated with an accident involving one of its planes may lead to financial distress. While the actual losses from the incident might be $150 million, the costs from distress might be an additional $40 million. The airline can avoid these distress costs by purchasing insurance that

---

5. Given a market volatility of 18%, a beta of −2.5 is consistent with a market decline of roughly 9% in the event of an attack.

will cover the $150 million loss. In this case, the $150 million paid by the insurer is worth $190 million to the firm.

Issuance Costs.   When a firm experiences losses, it may need to raise cash from outside investors by issuing securities. Issuing securities is an expensive endeavor. In addition to underwriting fees and transaction costs, there are costs from underpricing due to adverse selection as well as potential agency costs due to reduced ownership concentration. Because insurance provides cash to the firm to offset losses, it can reduce the firm's need for external capital and thus reduce issuance costs.

EXAMPLE 30.2

Avoiding Distress and Issuance Costs

Problem
Suppose the risk of an airline accident for a major airline is 1% per year, with a beta of zero. If the risk-free rate is 4%, what is the actuarially fair premium for a policy that pays $150 million in the event of a loss? What is the NPV of purchasing insurance for an airline that would experience $40 million in financial distress costs and $10 million in issuance costs in the event of a loss if it were uninsured?

Solution
The expected loss is 1% × $150 million = $1.50 million, so the actuarially fair premium is $1.50 million/1.04 = $1.44 million.

The total benefit of the insurance to the airline is $150 million plus an additional $50 million in distress and issuance costs that it can avoid if it has insurance. Thus the NPV from purchasing the insurance is

$$NPV = -1.44 + 1\% \times (150 + 50)/1.04 = \$0.48 \text{ million}$$

Tax Rate Fluctuations.   When a firm is subject to graduated income tax rates, insurance can produce a tax savings if the firm is in a higher tax bracket when it pays the premium than the tax bracket it is in when it receives the insurance payment in the event of a loss.

Consider an almond grower with a 10% chance of a weather-related crop failure. If the risk of crop failure has a beta of zero and the risk-free rate is 4%, the actuarially fair premium per $100,000 of insurance is

$$\frac{1}{1.04} \times 10\% \times \$100,000 = \$9615$$

Suppose the grower's current tax rate is 35%. In the event of a crop failure, however, the grower expects to earn much less income and face a lower 15% tax rate. Then the grower's NPV from purchasing insurance is positive:

$$NPV = -\$9615 \times (1 - 0.35) + \underbrace{\frac{1}{1.04} \times 10\% \times \$100,000}_{=\$9615} \times (1 - 0.15)$$

$$= \$1923$$

The benefit arises because the grower is able to shift income from a period in which it has a high tax rate to a period in which it has a low rate. This tax benefit of insurance can be large if the potential losses are significant enough to have a substantial impact on the firm's marginal tax rate.

Debt Capacity.   Firms limit their leverage to avoid financial distress costs. Because insurance reduces the risk of financial distress, it can relax this tradeoff and allow the firm to increase its use of debt financing.[6] In Chapter 16, we found that debt financing provides several important advantages for the firm, including lower corporate tax payments due to the interest tax shield, lower issuance costs, and lower agency costs (through an increase in equity ownership concentration and a reduction in excess cash flow).

Managerial Incentives.   By eliminating the volatility that results from perils outside management's control, insurance turns the firm's earnings and share price into informative indicators of management's performance. The firm can therefore increase its reliance on these measures as part of performance-based compensation schemes, without exposing managers to unnecessary risk. In addition, by lowering the volatility of the stock, insurance can encourage concentrated ownership by an outside director or investor who will monitor the firm and its management.

Risk Assessment.   Insurance companies specialize in assessing risk. In many instances, they may be better informed about the extent of certain risks faced by the firm than the firm's own managers. This knowledge can benefit the firm by improving its investment decisions. Requiring the firm to purchase fire insurance, for example, implies that the firm will consider differences in fire safety, through their effects on the insurance premium, when choosing a warehouse. Otherwise, the managers might overlook such differences. Insurance firms also routinely monitor the firms they insure and can make value-enhancing safety recommendations.

The Costs of Insurance

When insurance premiums are actuarially fair, using insurance to manage the firm's risk can reduce costs and improve investment decisions. But in reality market imperfections exist that can raise the cost of insurance above the actuarially fair price and offset some of these benefits.

Insurance Market Imperfections.   Three main frictions may arise between the firm and its insurer. First, transferring the risk to an insurance company entails administrative and overhead costs. The insurance company must employ sales personnel who seek out clients, underwriters who assess the risks of a given property, appraisers and adjusters who assess the damages in the event of a loss, and lawyers who can resolve potential disputes that arise over the claims. Insurance companies will include these expenses when setting their premiums. In 2004, expenses for the property and casualty insurance industry amounted to approximately 25% of premiums charged.[7]

A second factor that raises the cost of insurance is adverse selection. Just as a manager's desire to sell equity may signal that the manager knows the firm is likely to perform poorly, so a firm's desire to buy insurance may signal that it has above-average risk. If firms

---

6. Indeed, it is not unusual for creditors to require the firm to carry insurance as part of a covenant.

7. Robert Hartwig, "2004 Year End Results," Insurance Information Institute.

have private information about how risky they are, insurance companies must be compensated for this adverse selection with higher premiums.

Agency costs are a third factor that contributes to the price of insurance. Insurance reduces the firm's incentive to avoid risk. For example, after purchasing fire insurance, a firm may decide to cut costs by reducing expenditures on fire prevention. This change in behavior that results from the presence of insurance is referred to as **moral hazard**. The extreme case of moral hazard is insurance fraud, in which insured parties falsify or deliberately cause losses to collect insurance money. Property and casualty insurance companies estimate that moral hazard costs account for more than 11% of premiums.[8]

Addressing Market Imperfections. Insurance companies try to mitigate adverse selection and moral hazard costs in a number of ways. To prevent adverse selection, they screen applicants to assess their risk as accurately as possible. Just as medical examinations are often required for individuals seeking life insurance, plant inspections and reviews of safety procedures are required to obtain large commercial insurance policies. To deter moral hazard, insurance companies routinely investigate losses to look for evidence of fraud or deliberate intent.

Insurance companies also structure their policies in such a way as to reduce these costs. For example, most policies include both a **deductible**, which is the initial amount of the loss that is not covered by insurance, and **policy limits**, which limit the amount of the loss that is covered regardless of the extent of the damage. These provisions mean that the firm continues to bear some of the risk of the loss even after it is insured. In this way, the firm retains an incentive to avoid the loss, reducing moral hazard. Also, because risky firms will prefer lower deductibles and higher limits (because they are more likely to experience a loss), insurers can use the firm's policy choice to help identify its risk and reduce adverse selection.[9]

Adverse Selection and Policy Limits

Problem

Your firm faces a potential $100 million loss that it would like to insure. Because of tax benefits and the avoidance of financial distress and issuance costs, each $1 received in the event of a loss is worth $1.50 to the firm. Two policies are available: One pays $55 million and the other pays $100 million if a loss occurs. The insurance company charges 20% more than the actuarially fair premium to cover administrative expenses. To account for adverse selection, the insurance company estimates a 5% probability of loss for the $55 million policy and a 6% probability of loss for $100 million policy.

Suppose the beta of the risk is zero and the risk-free rate is 5%. Which policy should the firm choose if its risk of loss is 5%? Which should it choose if its risk of loss is 6%?

---

8. Insurance Research Council estimate (2002).

9. Papers on optimal insurance policy design include A. Raviv, "The Design of an Optimal Insurance Policy," *American Economic Review* 69 (1979): 84–96; G. Huberman, D. Mayers, and C. Smith, "Optimal Insurance Policy Indemnity Schedules," *Bell Journal of Economics* 14 (1983): 415–426; and M. Rothschild and J. Stiglitz, "Equilibrium in Competitive Insurance Markets: An Essay on the Economics of Imperfect Information," *Quarterly Journal of Economics* 90 (1976): 629–649.

Solution

The premium charged for each policy is

$$\text{Premium(\$55 million policy)} = \frac{5\% \times \$55 \text{ million}}{1.05} \times 1.20 = \$3.14 \text{ million}$$

$$\text{Premium(\$100 million policy)} = \frac{6\% \times \$100 \text{ million}}{1.05} \times 1.20 = \$6.86 \text{ million}$$

If the risk of a loss is 5%, the NPV of each policy is

$NPV(\$55 \text{ million policy})$

$$= -\$3.14 \text{ million} + \frac{5\% \times \$55 \text{ million}}{1.05} \times 1.50 = \$0.79 \text{ million}$$

$NPV(\$100 \text{ million policy})$

$$= -\$6.86 \text{ million} + \frac{5\% \times \$100 \text{ million}}{1.05} \times 1.50 = \$0.29 \text{ million}$$

Thus, with a 5% risk, the firm should choose the policy with lower coverage. If the risk of a loss is 6%, the policy with higher coverage is superior:

$NPV(\$55 \text{ million policy})$

$$= -\$3.14 \text{ million} + \frac{6\% \times \$55 \text{ million}}{1.05} \times 1.50 = \$1.57 \text{ million}$$

$NPV(\$100 \text{ million policy})$

$$= -\$6.86 \text{ million} + \frac{6\% \times \$100 \text{ million}}{1.05} \times 1.50 = \$1.71 \text{ million}$$

Note that the insurance company's concerns regarding adverse selection are justified: Firms that are riskier will choose the higher-coverage policy.

The Insurance Decision

In a perfect capital market, purchasing insurance does not add value to the firm. It can add value in the presence of market imperfections, but market imperfections are also likely to raise the premiums charged by insurers. For insurance to be attractive, the benefit to the firm must exceed the additional premium charged by the insurer.

For these reasons, insurance is most likely to be attractive to firms that are currently financially healthy, do not need external capital, and are paying high current tax rates. They will benefit most from insuring risks that can lead to cash shortfalls or financial distress, and that insurers can accurately assess and monitor to prevent moral hazard.

Full insurance is unlikely to be attractive for risks about which firms have a great deal of private information or that are subject to severe moral hazard. Also, firms that are already in financial distress have a strong incentive not to purchase insurance—they need cash today and have an incentive to take risk because future losses are likely to be borne by their debt holders.

CONCEPT CHECK   1. How can insurance add value to a firm?

2. Identify the costs of insurance that arise due to market imperfections.

30.2   Commodity Price Risk

Firms use insurance to protect against the unlikely event that their real assets are damaged or destroyed by hazards such as fire, hurricane, accident, or other catastrophes that are outside their normal course of business. At the same time, many risks that firms face arise naturally as part of their business operations. For many firms, changes in the market prices of the raw materials they use and the goods they produce may be the most important source of risk to their profitability. In the airline industry, for example, the second-largest expense after labor is jet fuel. With oil prices tripling between 2000 and 2005, most major carriers have struggled to return to profitability. The industry as a whole lost more than $4 billion as a result of higher fuel prices in 2004, and industry analysts estimate that each $1 increase in the price of oil per barrel equates to a $425 million increase in the industry's annual jet fuel expenses. For an airline, the risk from increases in the price of oil is clearly one of the most important risks that it faces.

In this section, we discuss ways firms can reduce, or *hedge*, their exposure to commodity price movements. Like insurance, hedging involves contracts or transactions that provide the firm with cash flows that offset its losses from price changes.

Hedging with Vertical Integration and Storage

Firms can hedge risk by making real investments in assets with offsetting risk. The most common strategies are vertical integration and storage.

Vertical integration entails the merger of a firm and its supplier (or a firm and its customer). Because an increase in the price of the commodity raises the firm's costs and the supplier's revenues, these firms can offset their risks by merging. For example, a tire manufacturer that is concerned about an increase in the price of rubber could invest in a rubber plantation. As the price of rubber increases, so will the profits of the rubber plantation, offsetting the higher costs of making tires. Similarly, airlines could offset their oil price risk by merging with an oil company.

While vertical integration can reduce risk, it does not always increase value. Recall the key lesson of Modigliani and Miller: Firms add no value by doing something investors can do for themselves. Investors concerned about commodity price risk can diversify by "vertically integrating" their portfolios and buying shares of the firm and its supplier. Because the acquiring firm often pays a substantial premium over the current share price of the firm being acquired, the shareholders of the acquiring firm would generally find it cheaper to diversify on their own. Vertical integration can add value if combining the firms results in important synergies. In many instances, however, diseconomies would be the more likely outcome, as the combined firm would lack a strategic focus (e.g., airlines and oil producers). Finally, vertical integration is not a perfect hedge: A firm's supplier is exposed to many other risks besides commodity prices. By integrating vertically, the firm eliminates one risk but acquires others.

A related strategy is the long-term storage of inventory. An airline concerned about rising fuel costs could purchase a large quantity of fuel today and store the fuel until it is needed. By doing so, the firm locks in its cost for fuel at today's price plus storage costs. But for many commodities, storage costs are much too high for this strategy to be attractive. Such a strategy also requires a substantial cash outlay upfront. If the firm does not have the required cash, it would need to raise external capital—and consequently would suffer issuance and adverse selection costs. Finally, maintaining large amounts of inventory would dramatically increase working capital requirements, a cost for the firm.

Hedging with Long-Term Contracts

An alternative to vertical integration or storage is a long-term supply contract. Firms routinely enter into long-term lease contracts for real estate, fixing the price at which they will obtain office space many years in advance. Similarly, utility companies sign long-term supply contracts with power generators, and steelmakers sign long-term contracts with mining firms for iron ore. Through these contracts, both parties can achieve price stability for their product or input.

A good example is provided by Southwest Airlines. In early 2000, when oil prices were close to $20 per barrel, Chief Financial Officer Gary Kelly developed a strategy to protect the airline from a surge in oil prices. By the time oil prices soared above $30 per barrel later that year and put the airline industry into a financial crisis, Southwest had signed contracts guaranteeing a price for its fuel equivalent to $23 per barrel. The savings from its fuel hedge amounted to almost 50% of Southwest's earnings that year, as shown in Figure 30.1. Kelly went on to become Southwest's CEO, and Southwest has continued this strategy to hedge fuel costs. In 2004, Southwest's earnings of $313 million would have been eliminated had it not been for savings of $455 million from fuel supply contracts.

Of course, like insurance, commodity hedging does not always boost a firm's profits. Had oil prices fallen below $23 per barrel in the fall of 2000, Southwest's hedging policy would have *reduced* the firm's earnings by obligating it to pay $23 per barrel for its oil (and perhaps Kelly might not have gone on to be CEO). Presumably, Southwest felt that it could afford to pay $23 per barrel for oil even if the price fell. While the long-term contracts would have been costly, they would not have led to financial distress. In other words, the long-term contracts stabilized Southwest's earnings at an acceptable level, no matter what happened to oil prices. Figure 30.1 illustrates how hedging stabilizes earnings.

FIGURE 30.1

Commodity Hedging Smoothes Earnings

By locking in its fuel costs through long-term supply contracts, Southwest Airlines has kept its earnings stable in the face of fluctuating fuel prices. With a long-term contract at a price of $23 per barrel, Southwest would gain by buying at this price if oil prices go above $23 per barrel. If oil prices fall below $23 per barrel, Southwest would lose from its commitment to buy at a higher price.

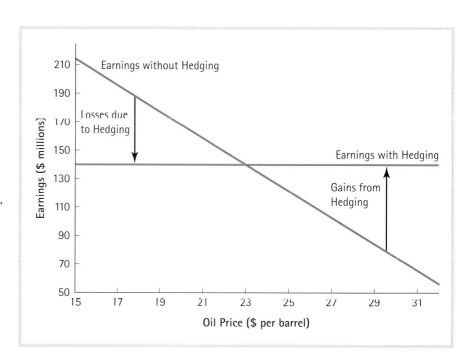

Hedging with Long-Term Contracts

Problem

Consider a chocolate maker that will need 10,000 tons of cocoa beans next year. The current market price of cocoa beans is $1400 per ton. At this price, the firm expects earnings before interest and taxes of $22 million next year. What will the firm's EBIT be if the price of cocoa beans rises to $1950 per ton? What will EBIT be if the price of cocoa beans falls to $1200 per ton? What will EBIT be in each scenario if the firm enters into a supply contract for cocoa beans for a fixed price of $1450 per ton?

Solution

If the price of cocoa beans increases to $1950 per ton, the firm's costs will increase by (1950 − 1400) × 10,000 = $5.5 million. Other things equal, EBIT will decline to $22 million − $5.5 million = $16.5 million. If the price of cocoa beans falls to $1200 per ton, EBIT will rise to $22 million − (1200 − 1400) × 10,000 = $24 million. Alternatively, the firm can avoid this risk by entering into the supply contract that fixes the price in either scenario at $1450 per ton, for an EBIT of $22 million − (1450 − 1400) × 10,000 = $21.5 million.

Often, long-term supply contracts are bilateral contracts negotiated by a buyer and a seller. Such contracts have several potential disadvantages. First, they expose each party to the risk that the other party may default and fail to live up to the terms of the contract. Thus, while they insulate the firms from commodity price risk, they expose them to credit risk. Second, such contracts cannot be entered into anonymously; the buyer and seller know each other's identity. This lack of anonymity may have strategic disadvantages. Finally, the market value of the contract at any point in time may not be easy to determine, making it difficult to track gains and losses, and it may be difficult or even impossible to cancel the contract if necessary.

An alternative strategy that avoids these disadvantages is to hedge with futures contracts. In the next section we investigate this strategy.

Hedging with Futures Contracts

A commodity futures contract is a type of long-term contract designed to avoid the disadvantages cited above. A **futures contract** is an agreement to trade an asset on some future date, at a price that is locked in today. Futures contracts are traded anonymously on an exchange at a publicly observed market price and are generally very liquid. Both the buyer and the seller can get out of the contract at any time by selling it to a third party at the current market price. Finally, through a mechanism we will describe shortly, futures contracts are designed to eliminate credit risk.

Figure 30.2 shows the prices in August 2005 of futures contracts for light, sweet crude oil traded on the New York Mercantile Exchange (NYMEX). Each contract represents a commitment to trade 1000 barrels of oil at the futures price on its delivery date. For example, by trading the June 2008 contract, buyers and sellers agreed in August 2005 to exchange 1000 barrels of oil in June 2008 at a price of $61 per barrel. By doing so, they are able to lock in the price they will pay or receive for oil almost three years in advance.

The futures prices shown in Figure 30.2 are not prices that are paid today. Rather, they are prices *agreed to* today, to be paid in the future. The futures prices are determined in

Futures Prices for Light, Sweet Crude Oil, August 2005

Each point represents the futures price per barrel in August 2005 for the delivery of oil in the month indicated.

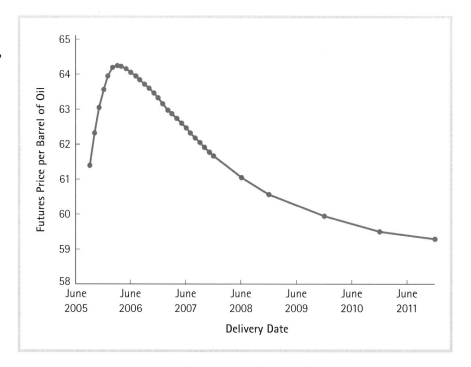

the market based on supply and demand for each delivery date. They depend on expectations of future oil prices, adjusted by an appropriate risk premium.[10]

Eliminating Credit Risk. If a buyer commits to purchase crude oil in June 2008 for $61 per barrel, how can the seller be assured that the buyer will honor that commitment? If the actual price of oil in June 2008 is only $30 per barrel, the buyer will have a strong incentive to renege and default on the contract. Similarly, the seller will have an incentive to default if the actual price of oil is more than $61 in June 2008.

Futures exchanges use two mechanisms to prevent buyers or sellers from defaulting. First, traders are required to post collateral, called **margin**, when buying or selling commodities using futures contracts. This collateral serves as a guarantee that traders will meet

---

10. If we let P_t be the market price of oil at the time of delivery, and F_t be the futures price agreed to today for delivery on date t, then the buyer of a futures contract receives oil worth P_t and pays F_t at delivery, for a net payoff of $P_t - F_t$. The seller's payoff is $F_t - P_t$. We compute the NPV of the contract by discounting the futures price at the risk-free rate (because it is known when we enter the contract) and the expected oil price at a rate r_o that reflects a risk premium for oil. Because competition should drive the NPV to zero, we have

$$0 = \frac{E[P_t]}{(1 + r_o)^t} - \frac{F_t}{(1 + r_f)^t} \quad \text{or} \quad F_t = E[P_t]\frac{(1 + r_f)^t}{(1 + r_o)^t}$$

Also, the futures price cannot exceed cost of storing, or "carrying," oil for the future: $P_0 (1 + r_f)^t + FV(\textit{storage costs})$. Otherwise, buying, storing, and selling oil using futures contracts would offer an arbitrage opportunity. (Because the cheapest way to store oil is to leave it in the ground, the futures price is generally far less than this "cost-of-carry" price. Thus the relationship between the current price, P_0, and the futures price, F_t, will depend on oil producers' ability to shift production across time.)

their obligations. In addition, cash flows are exchanged on a daily basis, rather than waiting until the end of the contract, through a procedure called **marking to market**. That is, gains and losses are computed each day based on the change in the price of the futures contract.

Marking to Market: An Example. Suppose that the price of the June 2008 futures contract varies as shown in Table 30.1 over the 700 remaining trading days between August 2005 and the delivery date in June 2008. A buyer who enters into the contract on date 0 has committed to pay the futures price of $61 per barrel for oil. If the next day the futures price is only $59 per barrel, the buyer has a loss of $2 per barrel on her position. This loss is settled immediately by deducting $2 from the buyer's margin account. If the price rises to $60 per barrel on day 2, the gain of $1 is added to the buyer's margin account. This process continues until the contract delivery date, with the daily gains and losses shown. The buyer's cumulative loss is the sum of these daily amounts and always equals the difference between the original contract price of $61 per barrel and the current contract price.

In June 2008, delivery takes place at the final futures price, which is equal to the actual price of oil at that time.[11] In the example in Table 30.1, the buyer ultimately pays $39 per barrel for oil and has lost $22 per barrel in her margin account. Thus her total cost is $39 + $22 = $61 per barrel, the price for oil she originally committed to. Through this daily marking to market, buyers and sellers pay for any losses as they occur, rather than waiting until the final delivery date. In this way, the firm avoids the risk of default.[12]

In essence, the June 2008 futures contract is the same as a long-term supply contract with a set price of $61 per barrel of oil.[13] But unlike a bilateral contract, the buyer and the seller can close their positions at any time (and accept the cumulative losses or gains

---

TABLE 30.1   **Example of Marking to Market and Daily Settlement for the June 2008 Light, Sweet Crude Oil Futures Contract ($/bbl)**

Trading Day	August 2005 0	1	2	3	4	. . .	698	699	June 2008 700
Futures price	61	59	60	58	57	. . .	36	38	39
Daily marked to market profit/loss		−2	1	−2	−1	. . .	. . .	2	1
Cumulative profit/loss		−2	−1	−3	−4	. . .	−25	−23	−22

---

11. At its delivery date, a futures contract is a contract for immediate delivery. Thus, by the Law of One Price, its price must be the actual price of oil in the market.

12. For this system to work, the buyer's margin account must always have a sufficient balance to cover one day's loss. If a buyer's remaining margin in the account is too low, the exchange will require the buyer to replenish the account in a *margin call*. If the buyer fails to do so, the account will be closed and the buyer's contract will be assigned to a new buyer.

13. Because the daily marked-to-market gains and losses occur over the life of the contract rather than at the end, after we account for interest, the correct future value is actually somewhat higher than $61 per barrel. To account for this effect, which can be sizable for a multiyear contract, practitioners generally reduce the magnitude of their initial position to reflect the interest earned over the life of the contract. This adjustment is called *tailing the hedge*.

Hedging Risk

There are several common mistakes to be avoided when hedging risk:

Account for Natural Hedges. Even though purchases of a commodity may be a firm's largest expense, they may not be a source of risk if the firm can pass along those costs to its customers. For example, gas stations do not need to hedge their cost of oil, because the price of gasoline—and thus their revenues—fluctuate with it. When a firm can pass on cost increases to its customers or revenue decreases to its suppliers, it has a *natural hedge* for these risks. A firm should hedge risks to its profits only after such natural hedges are accounted for, lest it over-hedge and increase risk.

Liquidity Risk. When hedging with futures contracts, the firm stabilizes its earnings by offsetting business losses with gains on the futures contracts and by offsetting business gains with losses on the futures contracts. In the latter scenario, the firm runs the risk of receiving margin calls on its futures positions before it realizes the cash flows from the business gains. To effectively hedge, the

firm must have, or be able to raise, the cash required to meet these margin calls or it may be forced to default on its positions. Hence, when hedging with future contracts the firm is exposed to *liquidity risk*. Such was the case for Metallgesellschaft Refining and Marketing (MGRM), which shut down in 1993 with more than $1 billion in losses in the oil futures market. MGRM had written long-term contracts to supply oil to its customers and hedged its risk that oil prices might rise by buying oil futures. When oil prices subsequently dropped, MGRM faced a cash flow crisis and could not meet the margin calls on its futures positions.

Basis Risk. Futures contracts are available only for a set of standardized commodities, with specific delivery dates and locations. Thus, while a futures contract that promises to deliver crude oil in Oklahoma in June 2006 is a reasonable hedge for the cost of jet fuel in Dallas in July 2006, it will not be a perfect match. *Basis risk* is the risk that arises because the value of the futures contract will not be perfectly correlated with the firm's exposure.

in their margin accounts), and the contract will then be reassigned to a new buyer or seller at its current price. Because of this liquidity and the lack of credit risk, commodity futures contracts are the predominant method by which many firms hedge oil price risk. Similar futures contracts exist for many other commodities, including natural gas, coal, electricity, silver, gold, aluminum, soybeans, corn, wheat, rice, cattle, pork bellies, cocoa, sugar, carbon dioxide emissions, and even frozen orange juice.

Deciding to Hedge Commodity Price Risk

In a perfect market, commodity supply contracts and futures contracts are zero-NPV investments that do not change the value of the firm. But hedging commodity price risk can benefit the firm by reducing the costs of other frictions. Just as with insurance, the potential benefits include reduced financial distress and issuance costs, tax savings, increased debt capacity, and improved managerial incentives and risk assessment. Commodity futures markets, in particular, provide valuable information to commodity producers and users. For example, an oil firm can lock in the future price of oil before it spends millions of dollars on drilling a new well. A farmer unsure of future crop prices can lock in the futures price of wheat when deciding the quantity to plant.

But while hedging commodity price risk has similar potential benefits as buying insurance, it does not have the same costs. In comparison to the market for hazard insurance, the commodity markets are less vulnerable to the problems of adverse selection and moral

Differing Hedging Strategies

In mid-2005, oil prices rose to more than $60 per barrel. As a result of its aggressive hedging policy, Southwest Airlines was paying slightly more than $26 per barrel for 85% of its oil at the time. Many of the major U.S. airlines, however, lacked the cash or creditworthiness necessary to enter into long-term contracts. In 2004, Delta was forced to sell its supply contracts to raise cash so as to avoid defaulting on its debt. United Airlines, which filed for bankruptcy protection in December 2002, had only 30% of its fuel hedged in 2005 at a price of $45 per barrel.*

These differences in strategy are somewhat understandable given the airlines' differing financial positions. Southwest is currently profitable and would like to reduce its risk of becoming financially distressed by hedging its fuel costs. Delta and United are already in financial distress, so hedging would not avoid these costs. And for equity holders, taking a risk by not hedging may be the best strategy—a sudden drop in oil prices would lead to a windfall for equity holders, while losses from further increases would likely be borne by debt holders in default.

*Eric Roston, "Hedging Their Costs," *Time*, June 20, 2005.

---

hazard. Firms generally do not possess better information than outside investors regarding the risk of future commodity price changes, nor can they influence that risk through their actions. Also, futures contracts are very liquid and do not entail large administrative costs.

Trading in these contracts carries other costs, however. First, as Figure 30.1 illustrates, when a firm hedges it will sometimes lose money. These losses will be offset by other gains or savings, but the firm must be sure it can weather the losses until it realizes the offsetting gains. Second, the firm may **speculate** by entering into contracts that do not offset its actual risks. Speculating increases the firm's risk rather than reducing it. When a firm authorizes managers to trade contracts to hedge, it opens the door to the possibility of speculation. The firm must guard against the potential to speculate and add risk to the firm through appropriate governance procedures.

CONCEPT CHECK

1. Discuss risk management strategies that firms use to hedge commodity price risk.

2. What are the potential risks associated with hedging using futures contracts?

30.3 Exchange Rate Risk

Multinational firms face the risk of exchange rate fluctuations. In this section, we consider two strategies that firms use to hedge this risk: currency forward contracts and currency options.

Exchange Rate Fluctuations

Recall from Chapter 3 that an exchange rate is the market rate at which one currency can be exchanged for another currency. Consider the relationship between the U.S. dollar and the euro. At the end of 2004, the value of the euro (€) relative to the dollar peaked at an exchange rate of 0.733 euros per dollar or, equivalently,

$$\frac{1}{€0.733 \, / \, \$} = \$1.364 \text{ per euro}$$

Like most foreign exchange rates, the dollar/euro rate is a **floating rate**, which means it changes constantly depending on the quantity supplied and demanded for each currency in the market. The supply and demand for each currency is driven by three factors:

- *Firms trading goods:* A U.S. dealer exchanges dollars for euros to buy cars from a German automaker.

- *Investors trading securities:* A Japanese investor exchanges yen for dollars to purchase U.S. bonds.

- *The actions of central banks in each country:* The British central bank may exchange pounds for euros to attempt to keep down the value of the pound.

Because the supply and demand for currencies varies with global economic conditions, exchange rates are volatile. Figure 30.3 shows the dollar price of euros from 2000 through mid-2005. Notice that the price of the euro often varies by as much as 10% over periods as short as a few months. From 2002 to 2004, the value of the euro climbed more than 50% relative to the dollar.

Fluctuating exchanges rates cause a problem known as the *importer–exporter dilemma* for firms doing business in international markets. To illustrate, consider the problem faced by Manzini Cyclery, a small U.S. maker of custom bicycles. Manzini needs to import parts from an Italian supplier, Campagnolo. If Campagnolo sets the price of its parts in euros, then Manzini faces the risk that the dollar may fall, making euros, and therefore the parts, more expensive. If Campagnolo sets its prices in dollars, then Campagnolo faces the risk that the dollar may fall and it will receive fewer euros for the parts it sells to the U.S. manufacturer.

FIGURE 30.3

Dollars per Euro ($/€), 2000-2005

Note the dramatic changes in the exchange rate over short periods.

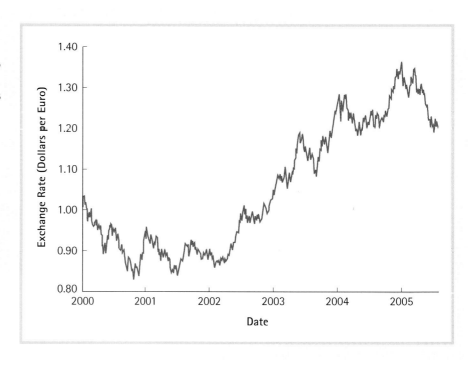

The problem of exchange rate risk is a general problem in any import–export relationship. If neither company will accept the exchange rate risk, the transaction may be difficult or impossible to negotiate. Example 30.5 demonstrates the potential magnitude of the problem.

The Effect of Exchange Rate Risk

Problem
In December 2002, when the exchange rate was $1 per euro, Manzini ordered parts for next year's production from Campagnolo. They agreed to a price of 500,000 euros, to be paid when the parts were delivered in one year's time. One year later, the exchange rate was $1.22 per euro. What was the actual cost in dollars for Manzini when the payment was due? If the price had instead been set at $500,000 (which had equivalent value at the time of the agreement), how many euros would Campagnolo have received?

Solution
With the price set at 500,000 euros, Manzini had to pay ($1.22/euro) × (500,000 euros) = $610,000. This cost is $110,000, or 22% higher than it would have been if the price had been set in dollars.

If the price had been set in dollars, Manzini would have paid $500,000, which would have been worth only $500,000 ÷ ($1.22/euro) = 409,836 euros to Campagnolo, or more than 18% less. Whether the price was set in euros or dollars, one of the parties would have suffered a substantial loss.

Hedging with Forward Contracts

Exchange rate risk naturally arises whenever transacting parties use different currencies: One of the parties will be at risk if exchange rates fluctuate. The most common method firms use to reduce the risk that results from changes in exchange rates is to hedge the transaction using currency forward contracts.

A **currency forward contract** is a contract that sets the exchange rate in advance. It is usually written between a firm and a bank, and it fixes a currency exchange rate for a transaction that will occur at a future date. A currency forward contract specifies (1) an exchange rate, (2) an amount of currency to exchange, and (3) a delivery date on which the exchange will take place. The exchange rate set in the contract is referred to as the **forward exchange rate**, because it applies to an exchange that will occur in the future. By entering into a currency forward contract, a firm can lock in an exchange rate in advance and reduce or eliminate its exposure to fluctuations in a currency's value.

Using a Forward Contract to Lock in an Exchange Rate

Problem
In December 2002, banks were offering one-year currency forward contracts with a forward exchange rate of $0.987/€. Suppose that at that time, Manzini placed the order with Campagnolo with a price of 500,000 euros and simultaneously entered into a forward contract to purchase 500,000 euros at a forward exchange rate of $0.987/€ in December 2003. What payment would Manzini be required to make in December 2003?

Solution

Even though the exchange rate rose to $1.22/€ in December 2003, making the euro more expensive, Manzini would obtain the 500,000 euros using the forward contract at the forward exchange rate of $0.987/€. Thus Manzini must pay

$$500,000 \text{ euros} \times \$0.987/\text{euro} = \$493,500 \text{ in December 2003}$$

Manzini would pay this amount to the bank in exchange for 500,000 euros, which are then paid to Campagnolo.

This forward contract would have been a good deal for Manzini because without the hedge, it would have had to exchange dollars for euros at the prevailing rate of $1.22/€, raising its cost to $610,000. However, the exchange rate could have moved the other way. If the exchange rate had fallen to $0.85/€, the forward contract still commits Manzini to pay $0.987/€. In other words, the forward contract locks in the exchange rate and eliminates the risk—whether the movement of the exchange rate is favorable or unfavorable.

If the forward contract allows the importer to eliminate the risk of a stronger euro, where does the risk go? At least initially, the risk passes to the bank that has written the forward contract. Because the bank agrees to exchange dollars for euros at a fixed rate, it will experience a loss if the euro increases in value. In Example 30.6, the bank receives only $493,500 in the forward contract, but gives up euros that are worth $610,000.

Why is the bank willing to bear this risk? First, the bank is much larger and has more capital than a small importer, so it can bear the risk without being in jeopardy of financial distress. More importantly, in most settings the bank will not even hold the risk. Instead, the bank will find another party willing to trade euros for dollars. By entering into a second forward contract with offsetting risk, the bank can eliminate its risk altogether.

This situation is illustrated in Figure 30.4. A U.S. importer, who must pay for goods with euros, purchases euros from the bank through a forward contract with a forward

FIGURE 30.4

The Use of Currency Forwards to Eliminate Exchange Rate Risk

In this example, the U.S. importer and the U.S. exporter both hedge their exchange rate risk by using currency-forward contracts (shown in blue). By writing offsetting contracts, the bank bears no exchange rate risk and earns a fee from each transaction.

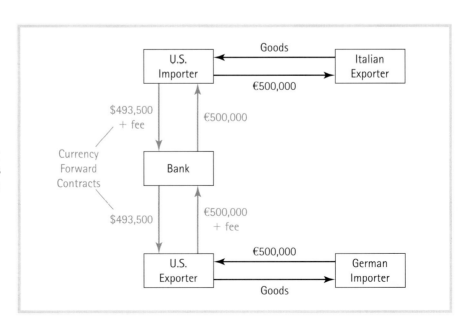

exchange rate of $0.987 per euro. This transaction locks in the importer's cost at $493,500. Similarly, a U.S. exporter, who will receive payment in euros, uses a forward contract to sell the euros to the bank, locking in the exporter's revenue at $493,500. The bank holds both forward contracts—the first to exchange dollars for euros and the second to exchange euros for dollars. The bank bears no exchange rate risk and earns fees from both the exporter and the importer.

Cash-and-Carry and the Pricing of Currency Forwards

An alternative method, the cash-and-carry strategy, also enables a firm to eliminate exchange rate risk. Because this strategy provides the same cash flows as the forward contract, we can use it to determine the forward exchange rate using the Law of One Price. Let's begin by considering the different ways investors can exchange foreign currency in the future for dollars in the future.

The Law of One Price and the Forward Exchange Rate.   Currency forward contracts allow investors to exchange a foreign currency in the future for dollars in the future at the forward exchange rate. We illustrate such an exchange in the **currency timeline** in Figure 30.5, which indicates time horizontally by dates (as in a standard timeline) and currencies vertically (dollars and euros). Thus "dollars in one year" corresponds to the upper-right point in the timeline and "euros in one year" corresponds to the lower-right point in the timeline. To convert cash flows between points, we must convert them at an appropriate rate. The forward exchange rate, indicated by $F\$/€$, tells us the rate at which we can exchange euros for dollars in one year using a forward contract.

Figure 30.5 also illustrates other transactions that we can use to move between dates or currencies in the timeline. We can convert euros to dollars today at the current exchange rate, also referred to as the **spot exchange rate**, $S\$/€$. By borrowing or lending at the dollar interest rate $r_\$$, we can exchange dollars today for dollars in one year. Finally, we can convert euros today for euros in one year at the euro interest rate $r_€$, which is the rate at which banks will borrow or lend on euro-denominated accounts.

| **FIGURE 30.5** | **Currency Timeline Showing Forward Contract and Cash-and-Carry Strategy** |

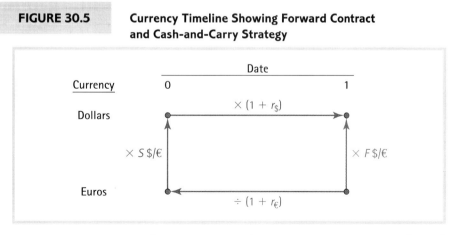

The cash-and-carry strategy (3 transactions in red) replicates the forward contract (in blue) by borrowing in one currency, converting to the other currency at the spot exchange rate, and investing in the new currency.

As Figure 30.5 shows, combining these other transactions provides an alternative way to convert euros to dollars in one year. The **cash-and-carry strategy** consists of the following three simultaneous trades:

1. Borrow euros today using a one-year loan with the interest rate $r_€$.
2. Exchange the euros for dollars today at the spot exchange rate $S \$/€$.
3. Invest the dollars today for one year at the interest rate $r_\$$.

In one year's time, we will owe euros (from the loan in transaction 1) and receive dollars (from the investment in transaction 3). That is, we have converted euros in one year to dollars in one year, just as with the forward contract. This method is called a cash-and-carry strategy because we borrow cash that we then carry (invest) in the future.

Because the forward contract and the cash-and-carry strategy accomplish the same conversion, by the Law of One Price they must do so at the same rate. Combining the rates used in the cash-and-carry strategy leads to the following no-arbitrage formula for the forward exchange rate:

Covered Interest Parity

$$\underbrace{F}_{\frac{\$ \text{ in one year}}{€ \text{ in one year}}} \underbrace{=}_{=} \underbrace{S}_{\frac{\$ \text{ today}}{€ \text{ today}}} \times \underbrace{\frac{1 + r_\$}{1 + r_€}}_{\frac{\$ \text{ in one year}/\$ \text{ today}}{€ \text{ in one year}/€ \text{ today}}} \tag{30.2}$$

Equation 30.2 expresses the forward exchange rate in terms of the spot exchange rate and the interest rates in each currency. Note that on both sides of the equation, the ultimate units are $\$/€$ in one year.

Let's evaluate Eq. 30.2 for an example. In December 2002, the spot exchange rate was $1/euro, while one-year interest rates were 1.66% for dollars and 3.00% for euros. From Eq. 30.2, the no-arbitrage forward exchange rate in December 2002 for an exchange to take place one year later was

$$F = S \times \frac{1 + r_\$}{1 + r_€} = (\$1 / €) \times \frac{1.0166}{1.0300} = \$0.987 / €$$

which is the rate offered by the bank in Example 30.6.

Equation 30.2 is referred to as the **covered interest parity equation**; it states that the difference between the forward and spot exchange rates is related to the interest rate differential between the currencies. When the interest rate differs across countries, investors have an incentive to borrow in the low-interest rate currency and invest in the high-interest rate currency. Of course, there is always the risk that the high-interest rate currency could depreciate while the investment is held. If you try to avoid this risk by locking in the future exchange rate using a forward contract, Eq. 30.2 implies that the forward exchange rate will exactly offset any benefit from the higher interest rate, eliminating any arbitrage opportunity.

EXAMPLE 30.7

Computing the No-Arbitrage Forward Exchange Rate

Problem

In December 2005, the spot exchange rate for the Japanese yen was ¥116/$. At the same time, the one-year interest rate in the United States was 4.85% and the one-year interest rate in Japan was 0.10%. Based on these rates, what forward exchange rate is consistent with no arbitrage?

Solution

We can compute the forward exchange rate using Eq. 30.2. Because the exchange rate is in terms of ¥/$ rather than $/¥, we also need to invert the interest rates in the formula:

$$F = S\frac{1 + r_{¥}}{1 + r_{\$}} = ¥116 / \$ \times \frac{1.0010}{1.0485} = ¥110.7 / \$ \text{ in one year}$$

(A useful rule to remember is that the ratio of interest rates must match the units of the exchange rate. Because the exchange rate is ¥/$, we multiply by the yen interest rate and divide by the dollar interest rate. Of course, we could also solve the problem by converting all the rates to $/¥.) The forward exchange rate is lower than the spot exchange rate, offsetting the higher interest rate on dollar investments.

Advantages of Forward Contracts.   Why do firms use forward contracts rather than the cash-and-carry strategy? First, the forward contract is simpler, requiring one transaction rather than three, so it may have lower transaction fees. Second, many firms are not able to borrow easily in different currencies and may pay a higher interest rate if their credit quality is poor. Generally speaking, cash-and-carry strategies are used primarily by large banks, which can borrow easily and face low transaction costs. Banks use such a strategy to hedge their currency exposures that result from commitments to forward contracts.

EXAMPLE 30.8

Using the Cash-and-Carry Strategy

Problem

In December 2005, a Japanese bank enters into a forward contract with Japanese exporter Shimano, in which Shimano agrees to exchange $100 million for yen in December 2006 at the forward exchange rate of ¥110.7/$. If the current exchange rate is ¥116/$, and one-year interest rates are 4.85% in the United States and 0.10% in Japan, how can the bank hedge its risk if it has no other clients interested in currency forward contracts?

Solution

The forward contract specifies that Shimano will pay $100 million to the bank in exchange for $100 million × ¥110.7/$ = 11.07 billion yen. To hedge its risk, the bank may find another client or clients who would like to exchange yen for dollars. When no such clients can be found, the bank can still hedge its risk using a cash-and-carry strategy:

1. Borrow dollars today at the dollar interest rate of 4.85%. The bank can borrow $100 million/1.0485 = $95.37 million today and repay the loan using the cash received from Shimano.

2. Convert dollars to yen at the spot exchange rate of ¥116/$. The bank can convert the dollars borrowed to $95.37 million × ¥116/$ = ¥11.06 billion.

3. Invest the yen today at the yen interest rate of 0.10%. By depositing the yen for one year, the bank will have 11.06 billion × 1.001 = ¥11.07 billion in one year.

Through this combination of transactions, the bank can lock in its ability to convert dollars to yen at the rate agreed upon in the forward contract with Shimano.

Equation 30.2 easily generalizes to a forward contract longer than one year. Using the same logic, but investing or borrowing for T years rather than one year, the no-arbitrage forward rate for an exchange that will occur T years in the future is

$$F_T = S \times \frac{(1 + r_\$)^T}{(1 + r_€)^T} \qquad (30.3)$$

where the spot and forward rates are in units of $/€, and the interest rates are the current risk-free T-year rates from the yield curve for each currency.

Hedging with Options

Currency options are another method that firms commonly use to manage exchange rate risk. Currency options, like the stock options introduced in Chapter 20, give the holder the right—but not the obligation—to exchange currency at a given exchange rate. Currency forward contracts allow firms to lock in a future exchange rate; currency options allow firms to insure themselves against the exchange rate moving beyond a certain level.

To demonstrate the difference between hedging with forward contracts and hedging with options, let's examine a specific situation. In December 2005, the one-year forward exchange rate was $1.20 per euro. Instead of locking in this exchange rate using a forward contract, a firm that will need euros in one year can buy a call option on the euro, giving it the right to buy euros at a maximum price.[14] Suppose a one-year European call option on the euro with a strike price of $1.20 per euro trades for $0.05 per euro. That is, for a cost of $0.05 per euro, the firm can buy the right—but not the obligation—to purchase euros for $1.20 per euro in one year's time. By doing so, the firm protects itself against a large increase in the value of the euro, but still benefits if the euro declines.

Table 30.2 shows the outcome from hedging with a call option if the actual exchange rate in one year is one of the values listed in the first column. If the spot exchange rate is less than the $1.20 per euro strike price of the option, then the firm will not exercise the option and will convert dollars to euros at the spot exchange rate. If the spot exchange rate is more than $1.20 per euro, the firm will exercise the option and convert dollars to euros at the rate of $1.20 per euro (see the second and third columns). We then add the initial cost of the option (fourth column) to determine the total dollar cost per euro paid by the firm (fifth column).[15]

We plot the data from Table 30.2 in Figure 30.6, where we compare hedging with options to the alternative of hedging with a forward contract or not hedging at all. If the firm does not hedge at all, its cost for euros is simply the spot exchange rate. If the firm hedges with a forward contract, it locks in the cost of euros at the forward exchange rate and the firm's cost is fixed. As Figure 30.6 shows, hedging with options represents a middle ground: The firm puts a *cap* on its potential cost, but will benefit if the euro depreciates in value.

Options Versus Forward Contracts.   Why might a firm choose to hedge with options rather than forward contracts? Many managers want the firm to benefit if the exchange rate moves in their favor, rather than being stuck paying an above-market rate. Firms also

---

14. Currency options can be purchased over the counter from a bank or on an exchange. The Philadelphia stock exchange is one exchange offering currency options.

15. In computing the total cost, we have ignored the small amount of interest that could be earned on the option premium.

| TABLE 30.2 | Cost of Euros ($/€) When Hedging with a Currency Option with a Strike Price of $1.20/€ and an Initial Premium of $0.05/€ | | | |

Dec. 2006 Spot Exchange Rate	Exercise Option?	Exchange Rate Taken	+ Cost of Option	= Total Cost
1.00	No	1.00	0.05	1.05
1.15	No	1.15	0.05	1.20
1.30	Yes	1.20	0.05	1.25
1.45	Yes	1.20	0.05	1.25

FIGURE 30.6

Comparison of Hedging the Exchange Rate Using a Forward Contract, an Option, or No Hedge

The forward hedge locks in an exchange rate and so eliminates all risk. Not hedging leaves the firm fully exposed. Hedging with an option allows the firm to benefit if the exchange rate falls and protects the firm from a very large increase.

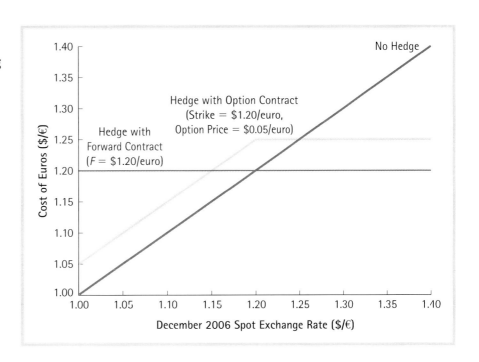

prefer options to forward contracts if the transaction they are hedging might not take place. In this case, a forward could commit them to making an exchange at an unfavorable rate for currency they do not need, whereas an option allows them to walk away from the exchange.

EXAMPLE 30.9

Using Options to Hedge a Conditional Exposure

Problem

ICTV is a U.S. company that develops software for cable television networks. Executives at ICTV have just negotiated a £20 million deal with British cable operator Telewest. ICTV will receive the payment in six months time, after ICTV demonstrates a prototype proving the viability of its technology. If Telewest is not satisfied with the technology, it can cancel the contract at that time and pay nothing. ICTV executives have two major concerns: (1) their engineers may not be able to meet Telewest's technology requirements, and (2) even if the deal succeeds, the British pound may fall, reducing the dollar value of the £20 million payment.

Suppose the current exchange rate is $1.752/£, the six-month forward exchange rate is $1.75/£, and a six-month put option on the British pound with a strike price of $1.75/£ is trading for $0.05/£. Compare ICTV's outcomes if it does not hedge, hedges using a forward contract, or hedges using the put option.

Solution

First, let's plot ICTV's revenue if it chooses not to hedge (the red lines in the plot):

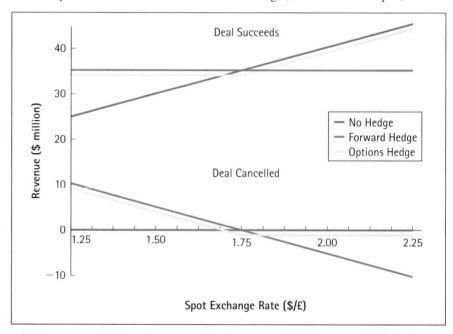

Suppose ICTV does not hedge, and the British pound falls to $1.50/£. Then ICTV's dollar revenue from the deal will be only £20 million × $1.50/£ = $30 million. However, if ICTV hedges the £20 million payment using a forward contract, it will be guaranteed revenue of £20 million × $1.75/£ = $35 million if the deal succeeds (the upper blue line). But if Telewest cancels the deal, ICTV will still be obligated by the forward contract to pay the bank £20 million in exchange for $35 million. If the spot exchange rate rises to $2.00/£, then the £20 million will be worth £20 million × $2.00/£ = $40 million, and ICTV will have a loss of 40 − 35 = $5 million on its forward contract (see the lower blue line).

Thus, if ICTV does not hedge or hedges with a forward contract, there are scenarios that lead to large losses. Now consider hedging with the put option. The upfront cost of the put option is £20 million × $0.05/£ = $1 million, and the results of this hedge are plotted as the yellow curves. For example, if the deal succeeds and the pound falls below $1.75/£, ICTV can exercise the put and receive, net of the cost of the put,

£20 million × $1.75/£ − $1 million = $35 million − $1 million = $34 million

(We have ignored the small amount of interest on the cost of the put over six months.) If Telewest cancels the deal and the spot exchange rate rises, ICTV will lose the $1 million cost of the put. In either case, Telewest has limited its potential losses.

Currency Option Pricing.   In the preceding example, we assumed that ICTV could purchase a currency option at a price of $0.05/£. But how do we determine the price of a currency option? Just as we determined the forward exchange rate by assessing banks' ability to replicate a forward contract using a cash-and-carry strategy, the prices of currency options are determined by identifying banks' ability to replicate them using dynamic trading strategies of the type introduced in Chapter 21 for stock options. In fact, we can apply the same pricing methodologies discussed in Chapter 21, such as the Black-Scholes formula or the binomial model, to currency options. In this case, the underlying asset is the currency, so we use the spot exchange rate in place of the stock price. The foreign interest rate you earn while holding the currency is analogous to the dividend yield for a stock. Recall that to price a European option on a dividend-paying stock, you simply replace the stock price, S, in the Black-Scholes formula with S^x, the current value of the stock excluding any dividends paid during the life of the option. In the case of a currency option, we can interpret the interest earned on the foreign currency as a dividend. For example, if the current spot exchange rate is S dollars per euro and the dollar and euro interest rates are $r_\$$ and $r_€$, respectively, then from Eq. 21.11, $S^x = S/(1 + r_€)^T$, and the price of a European call option on the euro that expires in T years with a strike price of K dollars per euro is[16]

Price of a Call Option on a Currency

$$C = \frac{S}{(1 + r_€)^T} N(d_1) - \frac{K}{(1 + r_\$)^T} N(d_2) \qquad (30.4)$$

where $N()$ is the normal distribution function and d_1 and d_2 are calculated using the fact that $S^x/PV(K) = F_T/K$ where F_T is the forward exchange rate from Eq. 30.3:

$$d_1 = \frac{\ln(F_T/K)}{\sigma\sqrt{T}} + \frac{\sigma\sqrt{T}}{2} \quad \text{and} \quad d_2 = d_1 - \sigma\sqrt{T} \qquad (30.5)$$

We can also use option pricing techniques to estimate the implied volatility of the exchange rate.

EXAMPLE 30.10

Implied Volatility of Exchange Rates

Problem

Suppose the current exchange rate is $1.752/£, the interest rate in the United States is 4.25%, the interest rate in the United Kingdom is 4.5%, and a six-month European call option on the British pound with a strike price of $1.75/£ trades for a price of $0.05/£. Use the Black-Scholes formula to determine the implied volatility of the $/£ exchange rate.

Solution

We can use Eqs. 30.4 and 30.5 to compute the Black-Scholes price of a call option on the British pound. The inputs are S = spot exchange rate = 1.752, K = 1.75, T = 0.5, $r_\$$ = 4.25%, and the U.K. interest rate $r_£$ = 4.5%. The forward exchange rate is $F_{0.5} = 1.752$

---

16. This formula for the price of a currency option was first derived by M. B. Garman and S. W. Kohlhagen, "Foreign-Currency Option Values," *Journal of International Money and Finance* 2 (1983): 231–237.

$\times (1.0425)^{1/2}/(1.045)^{1/2} = 1.75$. With a volatility of 10.3%, we have $d_1 = 0.036$ and $d_2 = -0.036$, with $N(d_1) = 0.514$ and $N(d_2) = 0.486$, and so the Black-Scholes value of the call is \$.048/£. With a volatility of 10.4%, the Black-Scholes value is \$.051/£. Thus the implied volatility of the \$/£ exchange rate is between 10.3% and 10.4% per year.

CONCEPT CHECK

1. How can firms hedge exchange rate risk?

2. Why may a firm prefer to hedge exchange rate risk with options rather than forward contracts?

30.4 Interest Rate Risk

Firms that borrow must pay interest on their debt. An increase in interest rates raises firms' borrowing costs and can reduce their profitability. In addition, many firms have fixed long-term future liabilities, such as capital leases or pension fund liabilities. A decrease in interest rates raises the present value of these liabilities and can lower the value of the firm. Thus, when interest rates are volatile, interest rate risk is a concern for many firms.

In this chapter, we have considered several methods that firms use to manage interest rate risk. Before firms can manage it, however, they must be able to measure it. Thus we begin by discussing the primary tool used to measure interest rate risk, duration. We will then see how firms can use *duration-hedging* to minimize their interest rate risk.

Interest Rate Risk Measurement: Duration

In Chapter 8, we informally introduced the notion of a bond's duration as a measure of its sensitivity to interest rate changes. There we saw that the sensitivity of zero-coupon bonds to interest rates increases with their maturity. For example, for a ten-year, zero-coupon bond, an increase of one percentage point in the yield to maturity from 5% to 6% causes the bond price per \$100 face value to fall from

$$\frac{100}{1.05^{10}} = \$61.39 \quad \text{to} \quad \frac{100}{1.06^{10}} = \$55.84$$

or a price change of $(55.84 - 61.39)/61.39 = -9.0\%$. The price of a five-year bond drops only 4.6% for the same yield change. The interest rate sensitivity of a *single* cash flow is roughly proportional to its maturity. The farther away the cash flow is, the larger the effect of interest rate changes on its present value.

Now consider a bond or portfolio with *multiple* cash flows. How will its value change if interest rates rise? As we saw in Chapter 11, the return of a portfolio is the value-weighted average of the returns of the elements of the portfolio. Because the interest rate sensitivity of a cash flow depends on its maturity, the interest rate sensitivity of a security with multiple cash flows depends on their value-weighted maturity. Thus, we formally define a security's duration as follows:[17]

---

17. This measure is also called the *Macaulay duration*.

Duration of a Security

$$\text{Duration} \equiv \sum_t \frac{PV(C_t)}{P} \times t \tag{30.6}$$

where C_t is the cash flow on date t, $PV(C_t)$ is its present value (evaluated at the bond's yield), and $P = \sum_t PV(C_t)$ is the total present value of the cash flows, which is equal to the bond's current price. Therefore, the duration weights each maturity t by the percentage contribution of its cash flow to the total present value, $PV(C_t)/P$.

EXAMPLE
30.11

The Duration of a Coupon Bond

Problem
What is the duration of a ten-year, zero-coupon bond? What is the duration of a ten-year bond with 10% annual coupons trading at par?

Solution
For a zero-coupon bond, there is only a single cash flow. Thus, in Eq. 30.6, $PV(C_{10}) = P$ and the duration is equal to the bond's maturity of ten years.

For the coupon bond, because the bond trades at par, its yield to maturity equals its 10% coupon rate. Table 30.3 shows the calculation of the duration of the bond using Eq. 30.6.

Note that the duration is shorter than the ten-year maturity of the bond, because the bond pays coupons prior to maturity. Moreover, the higher the coupon rate, the more weight is put on these earlier cash flows, shortening the duration of the bond.

TABLE 30.3   **Computing the Duration of a Coupon Bond**

t (years)	C_t	$PV(C_t)$	$PV(C_t)/P$	$[PV(C_t)/P] \times t$
1	10	9.09	9.09%	0.09
2	10	8.26	8.26%	0.17
3	10	7.51	7.51%	0.23
4	10	6.83	6.83%	0.27
5	10	6.21	6.21%	0.31
6	10	5.64	5.64%	0.34
7	10	5.13	5.13%	0.36
8	10	4.67	4.67%	0.37
9	10	4.24	4.24%	0.38
10	110	42.41	42.41%	4.24
	Bond price = 100.00		100.00%	Duration = 6.76 yrs

Just as the interest rate sensitivity of a single cash flow increases with its maturity, the interest rate sensitivity of a stream of cash flows increases with its duration, as shown by the following result:

Duration and Interest Rate Sensitivity: *If r, the APR used to discount a stream of cash flows, increases to r + ε, where ε is a small change, then the present value of the cash flows changes by approximately*[18]

$$\text{Percent Change in Value} \approx -\text{Duration} \times \frac{\varepsilon}{1 + r/k} \qquad (30.7)$$

where k is the number of compounding periods per year of the APR.

Estimating Interest Rate Sensitivity Using Duration

Problem
Suppose the yield of a ten-year bond with 10% annual coupons increases from 10% to 10.25%. Use duration to estimate the percentage price change. How does it compare to the actual price change?

Solution
In Example 30.11, we found that the duration of the bond is 6.76 years. We can use Eq. 30.7 to estimate the percentage price change:

$$\%\text{Price Change} \approx -6.76 \times \frac{0.25\%}{1.10} = -1.53\%$$

Indeed, calculating the bond's price with a 10.25% yield to maturity, we get

$$10 \times \frac{1}{0.1025}\left(1 - \frac{1}{(1.1025)^{10}}\right) + \frac{100}{(1.1025)^{10}} = \$98.48$$

which represents a 1.52% price drop.

As we see, we can use duration to measure the interest rate sensitivity of a security or a portfolio. We now consider ways firms can hedge this risk.

Duration-Based Hedging

A firm's market capitalization is determined by the difference in the market value of its assets and its liabilities. If changes in interest rates affect these values, they will affect the firm's equity value. We can measure a firm's sensitivity to interest rates by computing the

---

18. The term $\text{Duration}/(1 + r/k)$ is also called the *modified duration*. Thus Eq. 30.7 can also be written as

$$\% \text{ change in value} \approx -(\text{Modified Duration}) \times \varepsilon$$

To see how Eq. 30.7 is derived, note that the approximate price change for a small change in r is equal to the derivative of the price with respect to r:

$$\partial P/\partial r = \sum_t \frac{\partial}{\partial r}\left(\frac{C_t}{(1 + r/k)^{kt}}\right) = \sum_t -\left(\frac{C_t}{(1 + r/k)^{kt+1}}\right)t = -\frac{1}{1 + r/k}\sum_t -PV(C_t)t$$

Equation 30.7 follows by dividing by P to express the price change in percentage terms.

duration of its balance sheet. Moreover, by restructuring the balance sheet to reduce its duration, we can hedge the firm's interest rate risk.

Savings and Loans: An Example. Consider a typical savings and loan (S&L). These institutions hold short-term deposits, in the form of checking and savings accounts, as well as certificates of deposit. They also make long-term loans such as car loans and home mortgages. Most S&Ls face a problem because the duration of the loans they make is generally longer than the duration of their deposits. When the durations of a firm's assets and liabilities are significantly different, the firm has a **duration mismatch**. This mismatch puts the S&L at risk if interest rates change significantly.

As an example, Table 30.4 provides the market-value balance sheet for Acorn Savings and Loan, listing the market value and duration of each asset and liability. What is the combined duration of Acorn's assets and liabilities? The duration of a portfolio of investments is the value-weighted average of the durations of each investment in the portfolio. That is, a portfolio of securities with market values A and B and durations D_A and D_B, respectively, has the following duration:

Duration of a Portfolio

$$D_{A+B} = \frac{A}{A+B}D_A + \frac{B}{A+B}D_B \qquad (30.8)$$

Therefore, the duration of Acorn's assets is

$$D_A = \frac{10}{300} \times 0 + \frac{120}{300} \times 2 + \frac{170}{300} \times 8 = 5.33 \text{ years}$$

Similarly, the duration of Acorn's liabilities is

$$D_L = \frac{120}{285} \times 0 + \frac{90}{285} \times 1 + \frac{75}{285} \times 12 = 3.47 \text{ years}$$

TABLE 30.4	Market-Value Balance Sheet for Acorn Savings and Loan	
	Market Value ($ million)	Duration (years)
Assets		
Cash Reserves	10	0
Auto Loans	120	2
Mortgages	170	8
Total Assets	300	
Liabilities		
Checking and Savings	120	0
Certificates of Deposit	90	1
Long-Term Financing	75	12
Total Liabilities	285	
Owner's Equity	15	
Total Liabilities and Equity	300	

Note the mismatch between Acorn's assets and liabilities. Given their long duration, if interest rates rise, Acorn's assets will fall in value much faster than its liabilities. As a result, the value of equity, which is the difference between assets and liabilities, may drop significantly with a rise in interest rates.

In fact, we can calculate the duration of Acorn's equity by expressing it as a portfolio that is long the assets and short the liabilities:

$$\text{Equity} = \text{Assets} - \text{Liabilities}$$

We can then apply Eq. 30.8 to compute the duration of equity:

Equity Duration

$$D_E = D_{A-L} = \frac{A}{A - L}D_A - \frac{L}{A - L}D_L$$

$$= \frac{300}{15} \times 5.33 - \frac{285}{15} \times 3.47 = 40.67 \text{ years} \qquad (30.9)$$

Therefore, if interest rates rise by 1%, the value of Acorn's equity will fall by about 40%. This decline in the value of equity will occur as a result of the value of Acorn's assets decreasing by approximately 5.33% × 300 = $16 million, while the value of its liabilities decrease by only 3.47% × 285 = $9.9 million. Acorn's market value of equity therefore declines by about 16 − 9.9 = $6.1 million or (6.1/15) = 40.67%.

How can Acorn reduce its sensitivity to interest rates? To fully protect its equity from an overall increase or decrease in the level of interest rates, Acorn needs an equity duration of zero. A portfolio with a zero duration is called a **duration-neutral portfolio** or an **immunized portfolio**, which means that for small interest rate fluctuations, the value of equity should remain unchanged.

To make its equity duration neutral, Acorn must reduce the duration of its assets or increase the duration of its liabilities. The firm can lower the duration of its assets by sell-

The Savings and Loan Crisis

In the late 1970s, many U.S. savings and loans were in exactly the same position as Acorn. The rates offered on deposits by S&Ls were highly regulated by the government, which encouraged these institutions to use their deposits to make long-term home loans at fixed rates to borrowers. As in our Acorn example, these S&Ls were especially vulnerable to a rise in interest rates.

That increase in rates occurred in the early 1980s, with rates rising from less than 9% to more than 15% in less than one year. As a result, many S&Ls quickly became insolvent, with the value of their liabilities being close to or exceeding the value of their assets.

Most firms in this situation would be unable to raise new funds and would quickly default. However, because their deposits were protected by federal deposit insurance, these insolvent S&Ls were able to attract new depositors to pay off old ones and keep their doors open. Many of them embarked on a strategy of making very risky investments in junk bonds and other securities in hopes of a high return that would reestablish their solvency. (Recall the discussion in Chapter 16 regarding the incentives of equity holders to take excessive risk when the firm is near default.) Most of these risky investments also failed, compounding the S&Ls' problems. By the late 1980s, the U.S. government had to shut down more than 50% of the nation's S&Ls and fulfill its deposit insurance obligations by bailing out S&L depositors at a cost of more than $100 billion to taxpayers.

ing some of its mortgages in exchange for cash. We compute the amount to sell from the following formula:[19]

$$\text{Amount to Exchange} = \frac{\text{Change in Portfolio Duration} \times \text{Portfolio Value}}{\text{Change in Asset Duration}} \qquad (30.10)$$

To reduce its risk from interest rate fluctuations, Acorn would like to reduce the duration of its equity from 40.7 to 0. Because the duration of the mortgages will change from 8 to 0 if the S&L sells the mortgages for cash, Eq. 30.10 implies that Acorn must sell $(40.7 - 0) \times 15/(8 - 0) = \$76.3$ million worth of mortgages. If it does so, the duration of its assets will decline to

$$\overbrace{\frac{10 + 76.3}{300}}^{\text{Increased cash balance}} \times 0 + \frac{120}{300} \times 2 + \overbrace{\frac{170 - 76.3}{300}}^{\text{Decreased mortgage holdings}} \times 8 = 3.30 \text{ years}$$

Thus its equity duration will fall to $\frac{300}{15} \times 3.30 - \frac{285}{15} \times 3.47 = 0$, as desired.

Adjusting a portfolio to make its duration neutral is sometimes referred to as **immunizing** the portfolio, a term that indicates it is being protected against interest rate changes. Table 30.5 shows Acorn's market-value balance sheet after immunization. Note that the duration of equity is now zero.

TABLE 30.5	**Market-Value Balance Sheet for Acorn Savings and Loan After Immunization**

	Market Value ($ million)	Duration (years)
Assets		
Cash Reserves	86.3	0
Auto Loans	120	2
Mortgages	93.7	8
Total Assets	300	3.30
Liabilities		
Checking and Savings	120	0
Certificates of Deposit	90	1
Long-Term Financing	75	12
Total Liabilities	285	3.47
Owner's Equity	15	0
Total Liabilities and Equity	300	3.30

---

19. To derive Eq. 30.10, let P be the value of the original portfolio and S be the amount of assets sold, and let D_P and D_S be their respective durations. Let D_B be the duration of the new assets bought. Then new portfolio duration D_P^* is

$$D_P^* = \frac{P}{P}D_P + \frac{S}{P}D_B - \frac{S}{P}D_S$$

Solving for S leads to $S = (D_P - D_P^*)P/(D_S - D_B)$.

A Cautionary Note.   While duration matching is a useful method of interest rate risk management, it has some important limitations. First, the duration of a portfolio depends on the current interest rate. As interest rates change, the market values of the securities and cash flows in the portfolio change as well, which in turn alters the weights used when computing the duration as the value-weighted average maturity. Hence, maintaining a duration-neutral portfolio will require constant adjustment as interest rates change.[20]

The second important limitation is that a duration-neutral portfolio is only protected against interest rate changes that affect *all yields identically*. In other words, it offers protection in the case of parallel up or down movements in the yield curve. If short term interest rates were to rise while long-term rates remained stable, then short-term securities would fall in value relative to long-term securities, despite their shorter duration. Additional methods (beyond the scope of this text) are required to hedge the risk of such changes in the slope of the yield curve.

Swap-Based Hedging

Acorn Savings and Loan was able to reduce its interest rate sensitivity by selling assets. For most firms, selling assets is not an attractive prospect, as those assets are typically necessary to conduct the firms' normal business operations. Interest rate swaps are an alternative means of modifying the firm's interest rate risk exposure without buying or selling assets. An **interest rate swap** is a contract entered into with a bank, much like a forward contract, in which the firm and the bank agree to exchange the coupons from two different types of loans. In this section we describe interest rate swaps and explore how they are used to manage interest rate risk.[21]

In a standard interest rate swap, one party agrees to pay coupons based on a fixed interest rate in exchange for receiving coupons based on the prevailing market interest rate during each coupon period. An interest rate that adjusts to current market conditions is called a *floating rate*. Thus the parties exchange a fixed-rate coupon for a floating-rate coupon, which explains why this swap is also called a "fixed-for-floating interest rate swap."

To demonstrate how an interest swap works, consider a five-year, $100 million interest rate swap with a 7.8% fixed rate. Standard swaps have semiannual coupons, so that the fixed coupon amounts would be $\frac{1}{2}(7.8\% \times \$100$ million$) = \$3.9$ million every six months. The floating-rate coupons are typically based on a six-month market interest rate, such as the six-month Treasury bill rate or the six-month London Interbank Offered Rate (LIBOR).[22] This rate varies over the life of the contract. Each coupon is calculated based on the six-month interest rate that prevailed in the market six months prior to the coupon payment date. Table 30.6 calculates the cash flows of the swap under a hypothetical scenario for LIBOR rates over the life of the swap. For example, at the first coupon date in six months, the fixed coupon is $3.9 million and the floating-rate coupon is $\frac{1}{2}(6.8\% \times \$10$ million$) = \$3.4$ million, for a net payment of $0.5 million from the fixed- to the floating-rate payer.

---

20. Another measure of interest rate sensitivity, *convexity*, provides a measure of the change in duration of a portfolio as interest rates change. See e.g., F. J. Fabozzi, *Duration, Convexity, and Other Bond Risk Measures* (John Wiley & Sons, 1999).

21. Interest rate forward contracts, futures contracts, and options contracts also exist and can be used to manage interest rate risk. Swaps, however, are by far the most common strategy used by corporations.

22. The London Interbank Offered Rate is the rate at which major international banks with offices in London stand ready to accept deposits from one another. It is a common benchmark interest rate for swaps and other financial agreements.

TABLE 30.6   Cash Flows ($ million) for a $100 million
Fixed-for-Floating Interest Rate Swap

Year	Six-Month LIBOR	Fixed Coupon	Floating-Rate Coupon	New Swap Cash Flow: Fixed–Floating
0.0	6.8%			0.0
0.5	7.2%	3.9	3.4	0.5
1.0	8.0%	3.9	3.6	0.3
1.5	7.4%	3.9	4.0	−0.1
2.0	7.8%	3.9	3.7	0.2
2.5	8.6%	3.9	3.9	0.0
3.0	9.0%	3.9	4.3	−0.4
3.5	9.2%	3.9	4.5	−0.6
4.0	8.4%	3.9	4.6	−0.7
4.5	7.6%	3.9	4.2	−0.3
5.0		3.9	3.8	0.1

Each payment of the swap is equal to the difference between the fixed- and floating-rate coupons. Unlike with an ordinary loan, there is no payment of principal. Because the $100 million swap amount is used only to calculate the coupons but is never actually paid, it is referred to as the **notional principal** of the swap. Finally, there is no initial cash flow associated with the swap. That is, the swap contract—like forward and futures contracts—is typically structured as a "zero-cost" security. The fixed rate of the swap contract is set based on current market conditions so that the swap is a fair deal (i.e., has an NPV of zero) for both sides.

Combining Swaps with Standard Loans.   Corporations use interest rate swaps routinely to alter their exposure to interest rate fluctuations. The interest rate a firm pays on its loans can fluctuate for two reasons. First, the risk-free interest rate in the market may change. Second, the firm's credit quality, which determines the spread the firm must pay over the risk-free interest rate, can vary over time. By combining swaps with loans, firms can choose which of these sources of interest rate risk they will tolerate and which they will eliminate. Let's consider a typical example.

Alloy Cutting Corporation (ACC), a manufacturer of machine tools, is in the process of expanding its operations. It needs to borrow $10 million to fund this expansion. Currently, the six-month interest rate (LIBOR) is 4% and the ten-year interest rate is 6%—but these rates are for AA-rated firms. Given ACC's low current credit rating, the bank will charge the firm a spread of 1% above these rates.

ACC's managers are considering whether they should borrow on a short-term basis and then refinance the loan every six months or whether they should borrow using a long-term, ten-year loan. If they borrow for the short term, they worry that if interest rates rise substantially, the higher interest rates they will have to pay when they refinance

TABLE 30.7	Tradeoffs of Long-Term Versus Short-Term Borrowing for ACC	
Strategy	**Pro**	**Con**
Borrow long term at $6\% + 1\% = 7\%$ fixed rate	Lock in current low interest rates at 6%	Lock in current high spread of 1% given low initial credit rating
Borrow short-term at $\tilde{r}_t + \delta_t$	Get benefit of spread δ_t falling below 1% as credit rating improves	Risk of an increase in interest rates $\tilde{r}_t$ above 6%

Note: $\tilde{r}_t$ is the six-month interest rate (LIBOR) on date t. δ_t is the spread ACC must pay based on its credit rating on date t.

the debt could lead to financial distress for ACC. They can avoid this risk if they borrow for the long term and lock in the interest rate for ten years. But long-term borrowing also has a downside. ACC's managers believe that their firm's credit rating will improve over the next few years as the expansion generates additional revenue. If they borrow using a ten-year loan, ACC will be stuck paying a spread based on its current credit quality.

Table 30.7 highlights these tradeoffs. Borrowing long term has the advantage of locking in interest rates, but the disadvantage of not allowing ACC to get the benefit of its improving credit quality. Borrowing short term enables ACC to benefit as its credit quality improves, but it risks an increase in interest rates.

In this situation, ACC can use an interest rate swap to combine the best of both strategies. First, ACC can borrow the $10 million it needs for expansion using a short-term loan that is rolled over every six months. The interest rate on each loan will be $\tilde{r}_t + \delta_t$, where $\tilde{r}_t$ is the new (LIBOR) market rate and δ_t is the spread ACC must pay based on its credit rating at the time. Given ACC's belief that its credit quality will improve over time, δ_t should decline from its current 1% level.

Next, to eliminate the risk of an increase in the interest rate it will pay in the future, $\tilde{r}_t$, ACC can enter into a ten-year interest rate swap in which it agrees to pay a fixed rate of 6% per year in exchange for receiving the floating rate $\tilde{r}_t$.[23] Combining the cash flows from the swap with ACC's short-term borrowing, we can compute ACC's net borrowing cost as follows:

Short-Term Loan Rate	+	Fixed Rate Due on Swap	−	Floating Rate Received from Swap	=	Net Borrowing Cost
$\tilde{r}_t + \delta_t$	+	6%	−	$\tilde{r}_t$	=	$6\% + \delta_t$

That is, ACC will have an initial net borrowing cost of 7% (given its current credit spread of 1%), but this cost will decline in the future as its credit rating improves and the spread δ_t declines. At the same time, this strategy protects ACC from an increase in interest rates.

---

23. The fixed rate on the swap corresponds to the ten-year market rate for a AA-rated borrower. ACC would be able to get this rate on a swap, even though it is not AA-rated, because there is very little credit risk in a swap (because there is no exchange of the $10 million principle associated with a swap contract). As a result, swap rates are relatively independent of the user's credit quality.

Using Interest Rate Swaps

Problem

Bolt Industries is facing increased competition and wants to borrow $10 million in cash to protect against future revenue shortfalls. Currently, long-term AA rates are 10%. Bolt can borrow at 10.5% given its credit rating. The company is expecting interest rates to fall over the next few years, so it would prefer to borrow at short-term rates and refinance after rates drop. However, Bolt's management is afraid that its credit rating may deteriorate as competition intensifies, which may greatly increase the spread the firm must pay on a new loan. How can Bolt benefit from declining interest rates without worrying about changes in its credit rating?

Solution

Bolt can borrow at the long-term rate of 10.5% and then enter into a swap in which it *receives* a fixed rate of 10% and *pays* the short-term rate $\tilde{r}_t$. Its net borrowing cost will then be

Long-Term Loan Rate	+	Floating Rate Due on Swap	−	Fixed Rate Received from Swap	=	Net Borrowing Cost
10.5%	+	$\tilde{r}_t$	−	10%	=	$\tilde{r}_t + 0.5\%$

In this way, Bolt locks in its current credit spread of 0.5% but gets the benefit of lower rates as rates decline.

Using a Swap to Change Duration.   Firms can also use interest rate swaps with duration-hedging strategies. The value of a swap, while initially zero, will fluctuate over time as interest rates change. When interest rates rise, the swap's value will fall for the party receiving the fixed rate; conversely, it will rise for the party paying the fixed rate.

For the party receiving the fixed rate, we can calculate the interest rate sensitivity of a swap by thinking of it as a portfolio that is long a long-term bond and short a short-term bond, each with a face value equal to the notional principal. Thus a ten-year, $10 million interest swap with a 6% fixed rate is equivalent to a portfolio that is long a ten-year, $10 million bond with a 6% coupon rate, and short a six-month, $10 million bond at the current short-term rate. Likewise, the party paying the fixed rate is short the ten-year bond and long a six-month bond.

A swap contract will therefore alter the duration of a portfolio according to the difference in the duration of the corresponding long-term and short-term bonds. We can apply Eq. 30.10 to compute notional principal required to achieve a particular change in duration. Used in this way, swaps are a convenient way to alter the duration of a portfolio without buying or selling assets.

Using a Swap to Immunize a Portfolio

Problem

How can Acorn Savings and Loan use a swap to hedge its interest rate exposure rather than sell its mortgages?

Solution

Acorn needs to reduce the duration of its $15 million in equity from 40.7 to 0. To compute the correct notional amount of the swap, we must first compute the duration of a current ten-year bond. Suppose the duration is 6.76. The duration of a six-month bond is 0.5. Then from Eq. 30.10,

$$N = \frac{40.7 \times 15}{(6.76 - 0.5)} = \$97.5 \text{ million}$$

Acorn should enter into a swap with notional amount of $97.5 million. Because Acorn would like to reduce the duration of its equity, it should enter into a swap of this size in which it *pays* fixed and receives floating, as this swap will increase in value if interest rates rise, immunizing its balance sheet.

CONCEPT CHECK

1. How do we calculate the duration of a portfolio?

2. How do firms manage interest rate risk?

Summary

1. Insurance is a common method firms use to reduce risk. In a perfect market, the price of insurance is actuarially fair. An actuarially fair insurance premium is equal to the present value of the expected loss:

$$\frac{\Pr(\text{Loss}) \times E[\text{Payment in the Event of Loss}]}{1 + r_L} \tag{30.1}$$

2. Insurance for large risks that cannot be well diversified has a negative beta, which raises its cost.

3. The value of insurance comes from its ability to reduce the cost of market imperfections for the firm. Insurance may be beneficial to a firm because of its effects on bankruptcy and financial distress costs, issuance costs, taxes, debt capacity, and risk assessment.

4. The costs of insurance include administrative and overhead costs, adverse selection, and moral hazard.

5. Firms use several risk management strategies to hedge their exposure to commodity price movements.

   a. Firms can make real investments in assets with offsetting risk using techniques such as vertical integration and storage.

   b. Firms can enter into long-term contracts with suppliers or customers to achieve price stability.

   c. Firms can hedge risk by trading commodity futures contracts in financial markets.

6. Firms can manage exchange rate risk in financial markets using currency forward contracts to lock in an exchange rate in advance and currency options contracts to protect against an exchange rate moving beyond a certain level.

7. The cash-and-carry strategy is an alternative strategy that provides the same cash flows as the currency forward contract. By the Law of One Price, we determine the forward exchange rate by the cost-of-carry formula, called the covered interest parity equation. For an exchange that will take place in T years, the corresponding forward exchange rate is:

$$F_T = S \times \frac{(1 + r_\$)^T}{(1 + r_\text{€})^T} \tag{30.3}$$

8. Currency options allow firms to insure themselves against the exchange rate moving beyond a certain level. A firm may choose to use options rather than forward contracts if:

   a. It would like to benefit from favorable exchange rate movements but not be obligated to make an exchange at unfavorable rates.

   b. There is some chance that the transaction it is hedging will not take place.

9. Currency options can be priced using the Black-Scholes formula, with the foreign interest rate as a dividend yield:

$$C = \frac{S}{(1 + r_\text{€})^T} N(d_1) - \frac{K}{(1 + r_\$)^T} N(d_2) \tag{30.4}$$

   where

$$d_1 = \frac{\ln(F_T/K)}{\sigma\sqrt{T}} + \frac{\sigma\sqrt{T}}{2} \quad \text{and} \quad d_2 = d_1 - \sigma\sqrt{T} \tag{30.5}$$

10. Firms face interest rate risk when exchange rates are volatile. The primary tool they use to measure interest rate risk is duration. Duration measures the value-weighted maturity of an asset.

$$\text{Duration} \equiv \sum_t \frac{PV(C_t)}{P} \times t \tag{30.6}$$

11. The interest rate sensitivity of a stream of cash flows increases with its duration. For a small change ε in the interest rate, the change in the present value of a stream of cash flows is given by

$$\text{Percent Change in Value} \approx - \text{Duration} \times \frac{\varepsilon}{1 + r/k} \tag{30.7}$$

   where r is the current interest rate, expressed as an APR with k compounding periods per year.

12. The duration of a portfolio is equal to the value-weighted average duration of each security in the portfolio. The duration of a firm's equity is determined from the duration of its assets and liabilities:

$$D_E = D_{A-L} = \frac{A}{A - L} D_A - \frac{L}{A - L} D_L \tag{30.9}$$

13. Firms manage interest rate risk by buying or selling assets to make their equity duration neutral.

14. Interest rate swaps allow firms to separate the risk of interest rates changes from the risk of fluctuations in the firm's credit quality.

   a. By borrowing long term and entering into an interest rate swap in which the firm receives a fixed coupon and pays a floating-rate coupon, the firm will pay a floating interest rate plus a spread that is fixed based on its initial credit quality.

b. By borrowing short term and entering into an interest rate swap in which the firm receives a floating-rate coupon and pays a fixed coupon, the firm will pay a fixed interest rate plus a spread that will float with its credit quality.

15. Firms use interest rate swaps to modify their interest rate risk exposure without buying or selling assets.

Key Terms

actuarially fair *p. 927*

basis risk *p. 938*

business interruption insurance *p. 926*

business liability insurance *p. 926*

cash-and-carry strategy *p. 944*

covered interest parity equation *p. 944*

currency forward contract *p. 941*

currency timeline *p. 943*

deductible *p. 931*

duration mismatch *p. 953*

duration-neutral portfolio *p. 954*

floating rate *p. 940*

forward exchange rate *p. 941*

futures contract *p. 935*

immunized portfolio *p. 954*

immunizing *p. 955*

insurance premium *p. 926*

interest rate swap *p. 956*

key personnel insurance *p. 926*

liquidity risk *p. 938*

margin *p. 936*

marking to market *p. 937*

moral hazard *p. 931*

natural hedge *p. 938*

notional principal *p. 957*

policy limits *p. 931*

property insurance *p. 926*

speculate *p. 939*

spot exchange rate *p. 943*

vertical integration *p. 933*

Further Reading

For a discussion of the benefits of insurance and risk management for the corporation, see the following article: D. Mayers and C. W. Smith, Jr., "On the Corporate Demand for Insurance," *Journal of Business* 55(2) (1982): 281–296.

Several textbooks specialize in risk management topics: D. M. Chance, *An Introduction to Derivatives and Risk Management* (South-Western College Publishing, 2003); M. Crouhy, D. Galai, and R. Mark, *Risk Management* (McGraw-Hill Professional (2000); C. W. Smith, Jr., C. H. Smithson, and D. S. Wilford, *Managing Financial Risk*, 3rd ed. (New York: McGraw-Hill, 1998); R. M. Stulz, *Risk Management and Derivatives* (Cincinnati, OH: South-Western Publishing, 2002); and S. Sundaresan, *Fixed Income Markets and Their Derivatives*, 2nd ed. (Cincinnati, OH: South-Western College Publishing, 2001).

Other textbooks have an emphasis on international risk management: D. K. Eiteman and A. I. Stonehill, *Multinational Business Finance*, 10th ed. (Reading, MA: Pearson Addison-Wesley, 2003); P. Sercu and R. Uppal, *International Financial Markets and the Firm* (Cincinnati, OH: South-Western College Publishing, 1995); and A. C. Shapiro, *Multinational Financial Management*, 7th ed. (New York: John Wiley & Sons, 2006).

For an in-depth treatment of the use of forwards, futures, and options for risk management, see the following text: R. L. McDonald, *Derivatives Markets*, 2nd ed. (Boston: Addison-Wesley, 2006).

These two articles integrate risk management and the overall strategy of the firm: K. A. Froot, D. Scharfstein, and J. C. Stein, "A Framework for Risk Management," *Harvard Business Review* 72 (November–December 1994): 59–71; and P. Tufano, "How Financial Engineering Can Advance Corporate Strategy," *Harvard Business Review* (January–February 1996).

Interested readers can look deeper into why firms may want to hedge and how to implement a hedging strategy: K. C. Brown and D. J. Smith, "Default Risk and Innovations in the Design of Interest Rate Swaps," *Financial Management* 22(2) (1993): 94–105; P. M. DeMarzo and D. Duffie, "Corporate Incentives for Hedging and Hedge Accounting," *Review of Financial Studies* 8(3) (1995): 743-771; W. Dolde, "The Trajectory of Corporate Financial Risk Management," *Journal of Applied Corporate Finance* 6(3) (1993): 33–41: K. A. Froot, D. S. Scharfstein, and J. C. Stein, "Risk Management: Coordinating Corporate Investment and Financing Policies," *Journal of Finance* 48(5) (1993): 1629–1658; J. R. Graham and C. W. Smith, Jr., "Tax Incentives to Hedge," *Journal of Finance* 54(6) (1999): 2241–2262; M. D. Levi and P. Sercu, "Erroneous and Valid Reasons for Hedging Foreign Exchange Exposure," *Journal of Multinational Financial Management* 1(2) (1991): 25–37; M. P. Ross, "Corporate Hedging: What, Why, and How?" *Working paper* RPF-280, Haas School of Business, University of California at Berkeley (1997); and R. M. Stulz, "Rethinking Risk Management," *Journal of Applied Corporate Finance* 9(3) (1996): 8–24.

Many articles have been written on what firms actually do to manage their risks and on the impact of risk management on stock returns: G. Allayannis and E. Ofek, "Exchange Rate Exposure, Hedging, and the Use of Foreign Currency Derivatives," *Journal of International Money and Finance* 20 (2001): 273–296; H. Berkman and M. E. Bradbury, "Empirical Evidence on the Corporate Use of Derivatives," *Financial Management* 25(2) (1996): 5–13; C. Geczy, B. Minton, and C. Schrand, "Why Firms Use Currency Derivatives," *Journal of Finance* 52(4) (1997): 1323–1354; R. Graham and D. A. Rogers, "Do Firms Hedge in Response to Tax Incentives?" *Journal of Finance* 58(2) (2002): 815–839; W. Guay and S. P. Kothari, "How Much Do Firms Hedge with Derivatives?" *Journal of Financial Economics* 70(3) (2003): 423–461; S. D. Howton and S. Perfect, "Currency and Interest-Rate Derivatives Use in U.S. Firms," *Financial Management* 27(4) (1998): 111–121; J. Koski and J. Pontiff, "How Are Derivatives Used? Evidence from the Mutual Fund Industry," *Journal of Finance* 54(2) (1999): 791–816; S. L. Mian, "Evidence on Corporate Hedging Policy," *Journal of Financial and Quantitative Analysis* 31(3) (1996): 419–439; D. R. Nance, C. W. Smith Jr., and C. W. Smithson, "On the Determinants of Corporate Hedging," *Journal of Finance* 48(1) (1993): 267–284; and P. Tufano, "The Determinants of Stock Price Exposure: Financial Engineering and the Gold Mining Industry," *Journal of Finance* 53(3) (1998): 1014–1052.

Problems

A blue box (■) indicates problems available in MyFinanceLab.

Insurance

1. The William Companies (WMB) owns and operates natural gas pipelines that deliver 12% of the natural gas consumed in the United States. WMB is concerned that a major hurricane could disrupt its Gulfstream pipeline, which runs 691 miles through the Gulf of Mexico. In the event of a disruption the firm anticipates a loss of profits of $65 million. Suppose the likelihood of a disruption is 3% per year, and the beta associated with such a loss is −0.25. If the risk-free interest rate is 5% and the expected return of the market is 10%, what is the actuarially fair insurance premium?

2. Genentech's main facility is located in South San Francisco. Suppose that Genentech would experience a direct loss of $450 million in the event of a major earthquake that disrupted its operations. The chance of such an earthquake is 2% per year, with a beta of −0.5.

    a. If the risk-free interest rate is 5% and the expected return of the market is 10%, what is the actuarially fair insurance premium required to cover Genentech's loss?

    b. Suppose the insurance company raises the premium by an additional 15% over the amount calculated in part (a) to cover its administrative and overhead costs. What amount of financial distress or issuance costs would Genentech have to suffer if it were not insured to justify purchasing the insurance?

3. Your firm imports manufactured goods from China. You are worried that U.S.–China trade negotiations could break down next year, leading to a moratorium on imports. In the event of a moratorium, your firm expects its operating profits to decline substantially and its marginal tax rate to fall from its current level of 40% to 10%.

    An insurance firm has agreed to write a trade insurance policy that will pay $500,000 in the event of an import moratorium. The chance of a moratorium is estimated to be 10%, with a beta of −1.5. Suppose the risk-free interest rate is 5% and the expected return of the market is 10%.

    a. What is the actuarially fair premium for this insurance?

    b. What is the NPV of purchasing this insurance for your firm? What is the source of this gain?

4. Your firm faces a 9% chance of a potential loss of $10 million next year. If your firm implements new policies, it can reduce the chance of this loss to 4%, but these new policies have an upfront cost of $100,000. Suppose the beta of the loss is 0, and the risk-free interest rate is 5%.

    a. If the firm is uninsured, what is the NPV of implementing the new policies?

    b. If the firm is fully insured, what is the NPV of implementing the new policies?

    c. Given your answer to part (b), what is the actuarially fair cost of full insurance?

    d. What is the minimum-size deductible that would leave your firm with an incentive to implement the new policies?

    e. What is the actuarially fair price of an insurance policy with the deductible in part (d)?

Commodity
Price Risk

5. BHP Billiton is the world's largest mining firm. BHP expects to produce 2 billion pounds of copper next year, with a production cost of $0.90 per pound.

    a. What will be BHP's operating profit from copper next year if the price of copper is $1.25, $1.50, or $1.75 per pound, and the firm plans to sell all of its copper next year at the going price?

    b. What will be BHP's operating profit from copper next year if the firm enters into a contract to supply copper to end users at an average price of $1.45 per pound?

    c. What will be BHP's operating profit from copper next year if copper prices are described as in part (a), and the firm enters into supply contracts as in part (b) for only 50% of its total output?

    d. Describe situations for which each of the strategies (a), (b), and (c) might be optimal.

EXCEL **6.** Your utility company will need to buy 100,000 barrels of oil in ten days time, and it is worried about fuel costs. Suppose you go long 100 oil futures contracts, each for 1000 barrels of oil, at the current futures price of $60 per barrel. Suppose futures prices change each day as follows:

a. What is the mark-to-market profit or loss (in dollars) that you will have on each date?

b. What is your total profit or loss after ten days? Have you been protected against a rise in oil prices?

c. What is the largest cumulative loss you will experience over the ten-day period? In what case might this be a problem?

7. Suppose Starbucks consumes 100 million pounds of coffee beans per year. As the price of coffee rises, Starbucks expects to pass along 60% of the cost to its customers through higher prices per cup of coffee. To hedge its profits from fluctuations in coffee prices, Starbucks should lock in the price of how many pounds of coffee beans using supply contracts?

Exchange Rate Risk

EXCEL   **8.** Your start-up company has negotiated a contract to provide a database installation for a manufacturing company in Poland. That firm has agreed to pay you $100,000 in three months time when the installation will occur. However, it insists on paying in Polish zloty (PLN). You don't want to lose the deal (the company is your first client!), but are worried about the exchange rate risk. In particular, you are worried the zloty could depreciate relative to the dollar. You contact Fortis Bank in Poland to see if you can lock in an exchange rate for the zloty in advance.

a. Check out the home page for Fortis Bank (www.fortisbank.com.pl). In the upper left of the page, you can choose "English" from the menu and then "currency exch." There you will be able to find exchange rates for currency forward contracts. Find the rates that applied on March 3, 2006, at 4:15 P.M. What exchange rate could you lock in for the zloty in three months? How many zloty should you demand in the contract to receive $100,000?

b. Given the bank forward rates in part (a), were short-term interest rates higher or lower in Poland than in the United States in March 2006? Explain.

EXCEL   **9.** You are a broker for frozen seafood products for Choyce Products. You just signed a deal with a Belgian distributor. Under the terms of the contract, in one year you will deliver 4000 kilograms of frozen king crab for 100,000 euros. Your cost for obtaining the king crab is $110,000. All cash flows occur in exactly one year.

a. Plot your profits in one year from the contract as a function of the exchange rate in one year, for exchange rates from $0.75/€ to $1.50/€. Label this line "Unhedged Profits."

b. Suppose the one-year forward exchange rate is $1.25/€. Suppose you enter into a forward contract to sell the euros you will receive at this rate. In the figure from part (a), plot your combined profits from the crab contract and the forward contract as a function of the exchange rate in one year. Label this line "Forward Hedge."

c. Suppose that instead of using a forward contract, you consider using options. A one-year call option to buy euros at a strike price of $1.25/€ is trading for $0.10/€. Similarly a one-year put option to sell euros at a strike price of $1.25/€ is trading for $0.10/€. To hedge the risk of your profits, should you buy or sell the call or the put?

d. In the figure from parts (a) and (b), plot your "all in" profits using the option hedge (combined profits of crab contract, option contract, and option price) as a function of the exchange rate in one year. Label this line "Option Hedge." (*Note:* You can ignore the effect of interest on the option price.)

e. Suppose that by the end of the year, a trade war erupts, leading to a European embargo on U.S. food products. As a result, your deal is cancelled, and you don't receive the euros or incur the costs of procuring the crab. However, you still have the profits (or losses) associated with your forward or options contract. In a new figure, plot the profits associated with the forward hedge and the options hedge (labeling each line). When there is a risk of cancellation, which type of hedge has the least downside risk? Explain briefly.

10. Suppose the current exchange rate is $1.80/£, the interest rate in the United States is 5.25%, the interest rate in the United Kingdom is 4.0%, and the volatility of the $/£ exchange rate is 10%. Use the Black-Scholes formula to determine the price of a six-month European call option on the British pound with a strike price of $1.80/£.

Interest Rate Risk

11. Assume each of the following securities has the same yield-to-maturity: a five-year, zero-coupon bond; a nine-year, zero-coupon bond; a five-year annuity; and a nine-year annuity. Rank these securities from lowest to highest duration.

 12. You have been hired as a risk manager for Acorn Savings and Loan. Currently, Acorn's balance sheet is as follows (in millions of dollars):

Assets		Liabilities	
Cash Reserves	50	Checking and Savings	80
Auto Loans	100	Certificates of Deposit	100
Mortgages	150	Long-Term Financing	100
Total Assets	300	Total Liabilities	280
		Owner's Equity	20
		Total Liabilities and Equity	300

When you analyze the duration of loans, find that the duration of the auto loans is two years, while the mortgages have a duration of seven years. Both the cash reserves and the checking and savings accounts have a zero duration. The CDs have a duration of two years and the long-term financing has a ten-year duration.

a. What is the duration of Acorn's equity?

b. Suppose Acorn experiences a rash of mortgage prepayments, reducing the size of the mortgage portfolio from $150 million to $100 million, and increasing cash reserves to $100 million. What is the duration of Acorn's equity now? If interest rates are currently 4% but fall to 3%, estimate the approximate change in the value of Acorn's equity.

c. Suppose that after the prepayments in (b), but before a change in interest rates, Acorn considers managing its risk by selling mortgages and/or buying ten-year Treasury STRIPS. How many should the firm buy or sell to eliminate its current interest rate risk?

EXCEL **13.** The Citrix Fund has invested in a portfolio of government bonds that has a current market value of $34.8 million. The duration of this portfolio of bonds is 13.5 years. The fund has borrowed to purchase these bonds, and the current value of its liabilities (i.e., the current value of the bonds it has issued) is $29.2 million. The duration of these liabilities is 4 years. The equity in the Citrix Fund (or its net worth) is obviously $5.6 million. The market-value balance sheet below summarizes this information:

Assets		Liabilities (Debt) and Equity	
Portfolio of Government Bonds (duration = 13.5)	$44,800,000	Short- and Long-Term Debt (duration = 4.0)	$39,200,000
		Equity	$5,600,000
Total	$44,800,000	Total	$44,800,000

Assume that the current yield curve is flat at 5.5%. You have been hired by the board of directors to evaluate the risk of this fund.

a. Consider the effect of a surprise increase in interest rates, such that the yields rise by 50 basis points (i.e., the yield curve is now flat at 6%). What would happen to the value of the assets in the Citrix Fund? What would happen to the value of the liabilities? What can you conclude about the change in the value of the equity under these conditions?

b. What is the initial duration of the Citrix Fund (i.e., the duration of the equity)?

c. As a result of your analysis, the board of directors fires the current manager of the fund. You are hired and given the objective of minimizing the fund's exposure to interest rate fluctuations. You are instructed to do so by liquidating a portion of the fund's assets and reinvesting the proceeds in short-term Treasury bills and notes with an average duration of two years. How many dollars do you need to liquidate and reinvest to minimize the fund's interest rate sensitivity?

d. Rather than immunizing the fund using the strategy in part (c), you consider using a swap contract. If the duration of a ten-year, fixed-coupon bond is seven years, what is the notational amount of the swap you should enter into? Should you receive or pay the fixed rate portion of the swap?

14. Your firm needs to raise $100 million in funds. You can borrow short term at a spread of 1.00% over LIBOR. Alternatively, you can issue ten-year, fixed-rate bonds at a spread of 2.50% over ten-year Treasuries, which currently yield 7.60%. Current ten-year interest rate swaps are quoted at LIBOR versus the 8.00% fixed rate.

Management believes that the firm is currently "under-rated" and that its credit rating is likely to improve in the next year or two. Nevertheless, the managers are not comfortable with the interest rate risk associated with using short-term debt.

a. Suggest a strategy for borrowing the $100 million. What is your effective borrowing rate?

b. Suppose the firm's credit rating does improve three years later. It can now borrow at a spread of 0.50% over Treasuries, which now yield 9.10% for a seven-year maturity. Also, seven-year interest rate swaps are quoted at LIBOR versus 9.50%. How would you lock in your new credit quality for the next seven years? What is your effective borrowing rate now?

International Corporate Finance

notation

C_{FC} foreign currency cash flow

S spot exchange rate

F forward exchange rate

$r_\$^*$ dollar cost of capital

$r_\$$ dollar risk-free interest rate

r_{FC}^* foreign currency cost of capital

r_{FC} foreign currency risk-free interest rate

r_{wacc} weighted average cost of capital

D market value of debt

E market value of equity

r_E required return on equity

r_D required return on debt

τ_C corporate tax rate

In the 1990s, Starbucks Coffee Company identified Japan as a potentially lucrative new market for its coffee products and decided to invest as much as $10 million in fiscal year 1996 to begin operations there. Because Starbucks realized it needed specialized knowledge of the Japanese market, it established a joint venture with Sazaby, Inc., a Japanese retailer and restaurateur. This venture, called Starbucks Coffee Japan Ltd., intended to open as many as 12 stores in this initial phase. Although stores opened more slowly than expected, the venture had more than 200 stores and sales of ¥29 billion ($252 million) by 2001, and it opened its 500th store in November 2003. To finance this growth, Starbucks Coffee Japan Ltd. used the Japanese capital markets. It held an initial public offering of shares on the Osaka Stock Exchange in October 2001 with a market capitalization of ¥90.88 billion ($756 million), raising ¥18.8 billion ($156 million) in additional capital for expansion. How did Starbucks' managers decide to undertake this investment opportunity? Why did they decide to use the Japanese domestic market to finance it rather than U.S. markets?

This chapter focuses on some of the factors a firm faces when making a foreign investment that it does not face when making a domestic investment. There are three key issues that arise when considering an investment in a foreign project like Starbucks Coffee Japan Ltd.:

- The project will most likely generate foreign currency cash flows, although the firm cares about the home currency value of the project.

- Interest rates and costs of capital will likely be different in the foreign country as a result of the macroeconomic environment.

- The firm will probably face a different tax rate in the foreign country and will be subject to both foreign and domestic tax codes.

As a first step toward evaluating foreign projects, this chapter discusses international capital markets. We begin by examining internationally integrated capital markets, which provide a useful benchmark for comparing different methods of valuing a foreign project. We next explain how to value a foreign project and address the three key issues mentioned previously. We then value foreign currency cash flows using two valuation methodologies and consider the implications of foreign and domestic tax codes. Finally, we explore the implications of internationally segmented capital markets.

31.1 Internationally Integrated Capital Markets

We begin our examination of valuing foreign projects by developing a conceptual benchmark based on the integration of capital markets across currencies and borders. In this framework, capital markets are internationally integrated when the value of a foreign investment does not depend on the currency (home or foreign) we use in the analysis.

Consider a risky foreign asset that is expected to pay the cash flow, C_{FC}, in one period. In a normal market, the price of this asset in a foreign market is the present value of this cash flow using the cost of capital of a local investor:

$$C_{FC} / (1 + r_{FC}^*) \tag{31.1}$$

A U.S. investor who wants to purchase this asset in dollars will have to pay

$$S \times \frac{C_{FC}}{(1 + r_{FC}^*)} \tag{31.2}$$

where S is current spot exchange rate in dollars per foreign currency. Now any U.S. investor who actually purchased this security would have to convert the future cash flow into dollars, so the payoff to such an investor is the dollar cash flow it produces. To value this cash flow, assume that the U.S. investor contracts today to convert the *expected* cash flow in one period at the forward rate, F, quoted as dollars per foreign currency. If we assume that spot exchange rates and the foreign currency cash flows of the security are uncorrelated, then this U.S. investor's expected dollar cash flow is $F \times C_{FC}$.[1] If $r_\$^*$ is the appropriate cost of capital from the standpoint of a U.S. investor, the present value of this expected cash flow is

$$\frac{F \times C_{FC}}{(1 + r_\$^*)} \tag{31.3}$$

By the Law of One Price, this value must be equal to what the U.S. investor paid for the security:

$$S \times \frac{C_{FC}}{(1 + r_{FC}^*)} = \frac{F \times C_{FC}}{(1 + r_\$^*)}$$

---

1. The actual cash flow in foreign currency will be $C_{FC} + \varepsilon$, where ε is the uncertainty in the cash flow and has an expected value of zero. In U.S. dollars, this cash flow is $F \times C_{FC} + S_1 \times \varepsilon$ because the forward contract is only for the amount CF_{FC}; the rest must be converted at the prevailing spot rate in one period, S_1. Taking expectations, $E[S_1 \times \varepsilon] = E[S_1] \times E[\varepsilon] = 0$ because spot rates are uncorrelated with the project cash flows and $E[\varepsilon] = 0$.

Rearranging terms gives

$$F = \frac{(1 + r_\$^*)}{(1 + r_{FC}^*)} S \qquad (31.4)$$

This condition ought to look familiar from Chapter 30, because Eq. 31.4 is simply covered interest parity, here derived for risky cash flows rather than riskless cash flows.

At this point, it is worth taking a step back and considering the assumptions specific to the international context that we needed to derive Eq. 31.4. Recall from Chapter 3 that in a normal market, prices are competitive. In this context, this concept means, among other things, that any investor can exchange either currency in any amount at the spot rate or forward rates and is free to purchase or sell any security in any amount in either country at their current market prices. Under these conditions, which we term **internationally integrated capital markets**, the value of an investment does not depend on the currency we use in the analysis.

Present Values and Internationally Integrated Capital Markets

Problem
You are an American who is trying to calculate the present value of a ¥10 million cash flow that will occur one year in the future. You know that the spot exchange rate is $S = ¥110/\$$ and the one-year forward rate is $F = ¥105.8095/\$$. You also know that the appropriate dollar cost of capital for this cash flow is $r_\$^* = 5\%$ and that the appropriate yen cost of capital for this cash flow is $r^* = 1\%$. What is the present value of the ¥10 million cash flow from the standpoint of a Japanese investor, and what is the dollar equivalent of this amount? What is the present value of the ¥10 million cash flow from the standpoint of a U.S. investor who first converts the ¥10 million into dollars and then applies the dollar discount rate?

Solution
The present value of the yen cash flow is ¥10,000,000/(1.01) = ¥9,900,990, and the dollar equivalent is ¥9,900,990/110 = 90,009. (Note that we adjusted the formula in Eq. 31.2 because the exchange rate is expressed as yen per dollar rather than dollars per yen.) The present value from the standpoint of a U.S. investor who first converts the ¥10 million into dollars using the forward rate and then applies the dollar cost of capital is (¥10,000,000/105.8095)/1.05 = 90,009. (Again, we have adjusted the formula in Eq. 31.3 because the exchange rate is expressed as yen per dollar.) Because the U.S. and Japanese capital markets are internationally integrated, both methods produce the same result.

CONCEPT CHECK

1. What assumptions are needed to have internationally integrated capital markets?

2. What implication does internationally integrated capital markets have for the value of the same asset in different countries?

31.2 Valuation of Foreign Currency Cash Flows

The most obvious difference between a domestic project and a foreign project is that the foreign project will most likely generate cash flows in a foreign currency. If the foreign project is owned by a domestic corporation, managers and shareholders need to determine the home currency value of the foreign currency cash flows.

In an internationally integrated capital market, two equivalent methods are available for calculating the NPV of a foreign project: Either we can calculate the NPV in the foreign country and convert it to the local currency at the spot rate, or we can convert the cash flows of the foreign project into the local currency and then calculate the NPV of these cash flows. The first method is essentially what we have done throughout this book (calculating the NPV of a project in a single currency) with the added step at the end of converting the NPV into the local currency using spot rates. Because this method should be familiar to you at this stage, we will concentrate on the second method.

WACC Valuation Method in Domestic Currency

The second valuation method requires converting the expected dollar value of the foreign currency cash flows and then proceeding to value the project as if it were a domestic project.

Application: Ityesi, Inc.

Ityesi, Inc., a manufacturer of custom packaging products headquartered in the United States, wants to apply the weighted average cost of capital (WACC) technique to value a project in the United Kingdom. Ityesi is considering introducing a new line of packaging in the United Kingdom that will be its first foreign project. The project will be completely self-contained in the United Kingdom, such that all revenues are generated and all costs are incurred there.

Engineers expect the technology used in the new products to be obsolete after four years. The marketing group expects annual sales of £37.5 million per year for this product line. Manufacturing costs and operating expenses are expected to total £15.625 million and £5.625 million per year, respectively. Developing the product will require an upfront investment of £15 million in capital equipment that will be obsolete in four years and an initial marketing expense of £4.167 million. Ityesi pays a corporate tax rate of 40% no matter in which country it manufactures its products. The expected pound free cash flows of the proposed project are projected in the spreadsheet in Table 31.1.

TABLE 31.1 SPREADSHEET	**Expected Foreign Free Cash Flows from Ityesi's U.K. Project**

Year	0	1	2	3	4
Incremental Earnings Forecast (£ million)					
1　Sales	—	37.500	37.500	37.500	37.500
2　Cost of Goods Sold	—	(15.625)	(15.625)	(15.625)	(15.625)
3　Gross Profit	—	21.875	21.875	21.875	21.875
4　Operating Expenses	(4.167)	(5.625)	(5.625)	(5.625)	(5.625)
5　Depreciation	—	(3.750)	(3.750)	(3.750)	(3.750)
6　EBIT	(4.167)	12.500	12.500	12.500	12.500
7　Income tax at 40%	1.667	(5.000)	(5.000)	(5.000)	(5.000)
8　Unlevered Net Income	(2.500)	7.500	7.500	7.500	7.500
Free Cash Flow					
9　Plus: Depreciation	—	3.750	3.750	3.750	3.750
10　Less: Capital Expenditures	(15.000)	—	—	—	—
11　Less: Increases in NWC	—	—	—	—	—
12　Pound Free Cash Flow	(17.500)	11.250	11.250	11.250	11.250

Ityesi's managers have determined that there is no correlation between the uncertainty in these cash flows and the uncertainty in the spot dollar–pound exchange rate. As we explained in the last section, under this condition, the expected value of the future cash flows in dollars is the expected value in pounds multiplied by the forward exchange rate. Obtaining forward rate quotes for as long as four years in the future is difficult, so Ityesi's managers have decided to use the covered interest rate parity formula (Eq. 30.3, in Chapter 30) to compute the forward rates.

Forward Exchange Rates. The current spot exchange rate, S, is \$1.60/£. Suppose that the yield curve in both countries is flat: The risk-free rate on dollars, $r_\$$, is 4%, and the risk-free interest rate on pounds, $r_£$, is 7%. Using the covered interest parity condition for a multiyear forward exchange rate (Eq. 30.3):

$$F_1 = S \times \frac{(1 + r_\$)}{(1 + r_£)} = (\$1.60/£)\frac{(1.04)}{(1.07)} = \$1.5551/£$$

$$F_2 = S \times \frac{(1 + r_\$)^2}{(1 + r_£)^2} = (\$1.60/£)\frac{(1.04)^2}{(1.07)^2} = \$1.5115/£$$

$$F_3 = S \times \frac{(1 + r_\$)^3}{(1 + r_£)^3} = (\$1.60/£)\frac{(1.04)^3}{(1.07)^3} = \$1.4692/£$$

$$F_4 = S \times \frac{(1 + r_\$)^4}{(1 + r_£)^4} = (\$1.60/£)\frac{(1.04)^4}{(1.07)^4} = \$1.4280/£$$

Free Cash Flow Conversion. Using these forward exchange rates, we can now calculate the expected free cash flows in dollars by multiplying the expected cash flows in pounds by the forward exchange rate, as shown in the spreadsheet in Table 31.2.

TABLE 31.2 SPREADSHEET	Expected Dollar Free Cash Flows from Ityesi's U.K. Project				
	0	**1**	**2**	**3**	**4**
Dollar Free Cash Flow ($ million)					
1 Pound FCF (£ million)	(17.500)	11.250	11.250	11.250	11.250
2 Forward Exchange Rate ($/£)	1.600	1.555	1.512	1.469	1.428
3 **Dollar Value of Pound FCF** (1 × 2)	(28.000)	17.495	17.004	16.528	16.065

The Value of Ityesi's Foreign Project with WACC. With the cash flows of the U.K. project now expressed in dollars, we can value the foreign project as if it were a domestic U.S. project. We proceed, as we did in Chapter 18, under the assumption that the market risk of the U.K. project is similar to that of the company as a whole; as a consequence, we can use Ityesi's costs of equity and debt in the United States to calculate the WACC.[2]

---

2. The risk of the foreign project is unlikely to be *exactly* the same as the risk of domestic projects (or the firm as a whole), because the foreign project contains residual exchange rate risk that the domestic projects often do not contain. In Ityesi's case, managers have determined that the additional risk premium for this risk is small, so for practical purposes they have chosen to ignore it and just use the domestic cost of capital.

Ityesi has built up $20 million in cash for investment needs and has debt of $320 million, so its net debt is $D = 320 - 20 = \$300$ million. This amount is equal to the market value of its equity, implying a (net) debt-equity ratio of 1. Ityesi intends to maintain a similar (net) debt-equity ratio for the foreseeable future. The WACC thus assigns equal weights to equity and debt (Table 31.3).

TABLE 31.3	**Ityesi's Current Market Value Balance Sheet ($ million) and Cost of Capital Without the U.K. Project**

Assets		Liabilities		Cost of Capital	
Cash	20	Debt	320	Debt	6%
Existing Assets	600	Equity	300	Equity	10%
	620		620		

With Ityesi's cost of equity at 10% and its cost of debt at 6%, we calculate Ityesi's WACC as follows:

$$r_{wacc} = \frac{E}{E + D} r_E + \frac{D}{E + D} r_D (1 - \tau_C)$$
$$- (0.5)(10.0\%) + (0.5)(6.0\%)(1 - 40\%) = 6.8\%$$

We can now determine the value of the foreign project, including the tax shield from debt, by calculating the present value of the future free cash flows using the WACC:

$$\frac{17.495}{1.068} + \frac{17.004}{1.068^2} + \frac{16.528}{1.068^3} + \frac{16.065}{1.068^4} = \$57.20 \text{ million}$$

Because the upfront cost of launching the product line in dollars is only $28 million, the net present value is $57.20 - 28 = \$29.20$ million. Thus Ityesi should undertake the U.K. project.

Using the Law of One Price as a Robustness Check

To arrive at the NPV of Ityesi's project required making a number of assumptions—for example, that international markets are integrated, and that the exchange rate and the cash flows of the project are uncorrelated. The managers of Ityesi will naturally worry about whether these assumptions are justified. Luckily, there is a way to check the analysis.

Recall that there are two ways to compute the NPV of the foreign project. Ityesi could just have easily computed the foreign NPV by discounting the foreign cash flows at the foreign cost of capital and converting this result to a domestic NPV using the spot rate. Except for the last step, this method requires doing the same calculation we have performed throughout this book—that is, calculate the NPV of a (domestic) project. Determining the NPV requires knowing the cost of capital—in this case, the cost of capital for an investment in the United Kingdom. Recall that to estimate this cost of capital we use return data for publicly traded single-product companies—in this case, U.K. firms. For this method to provide the same answer as the alternative method, the estimate for the foreign cost of capital, $r_£^*$, must satisfy the Law of One Price, which from Eq. 31.4 implies:

$$(1 + r_£^*) = \frac{S}{F}(1 + r_\$^*) \tag{31.5}$$

If it does not, then Ityesi's managers should be concerned that their simplifying assumptions in their analysis are not valid: Market frictions exist so that the market integration assumption is not a good approximation of reality, or perhaps there is a significant correlation between spot exchange rates and cash flows.

We can rewrite Eq. 31.5 as follows. Using the covered interest rate parity relation derived in Chapter 30 (Eq. 30.3), we have

$$\frac{S}{F} = \frac{1 + r_£}{1 + r_\$} \tag{31.6}$$

where $r_£$ and $r_\$$ are the foreign and domestic risk free interest rates, respectively. Combining Eqs. 31.5 and 31.6 and rearranging terms gives the foreign cost of capital in terms of the domestic cost of capital and interest rates:

The Foreign-Denominated Cost of Capital

$$r_£^* = \frac{1 + r_£}{1 + r_\$}(1 + r_\$^*) - 1 \tag{31.7}$$

If the simplifying assumptions Ityesi made in calculating the NPV of its U.K. project are valid, then the cost of capital estimate calculated using Eq. 31.7 will be close to the cost of capital estimate calculated directly using comparable single-product companies in the United Kingdom.

EXAMPLE 31.2

Internationalizing the Cost of Capital

Problem
Use the Law of One Price to infer the pound WACC from Ityesi's dollar WACC. Verify that the NPV of Ityesi's project is the same when its pound free cash flows are discounted at this WACC and converted at the spot rate.

Solution
Using Eq. 31.7 to compute the pound WACC gives

$$r_£^* = \frac{1 + r_£}{1 + r_\$}(1 + r_\$^*) - 1 = \left(\frac{1.07}{1.04}\right)(1.068) - 1 = 0.0988$$

The pound WACC is 9.88%.

We can now use Ityesi's pound WACC to calculate the present value of the pound free cash flows in Table 31.3:

$$\frac{11.25}{1.0988} + \frac{11.25}{1.0988^2} + \frac{11.25}{1.0988^3} + \frac{11.25}{1.0988^4} = £35.75 \text{ million}$$

The NPV in pounds of the investment opportunity is $35.75 - 17.5 = £18.25$ million. Converting this amount to dollars at the spot rate gives £18.25 million $\times$ 1.6\$/£ = \$29.20 million, which is exactly the NPV we calculated before.

CONCEPT CHECK   1. Explain two methods we use to calculate the NPV of a foreign project.

2. When do these two methods give the same NPV of the foreign project?

31.3 Valuation and International Taxation

In this chapter, we assume that Ityesi pays a corporate tax rate of 40% no matter where its earnings are generated. In practice, determining the corporate tax rate on foreign income is complicated because corporate income taxes must be paid to two national governments: the host government (the United Kingdom in this example) and the home government (the United States). If the foreign project is a separately incorporated subsidiary of the parent, the amount of taxes a firm pays generally depends on the amount of profits **repatriated** (brought back to the home country).

Single Foreign Project with Immediate Repatriation of Earnings

We begin by assuming that the firm has a single foreign project and that all foreign profits are repatriated immediately. The general international arrangement prevailing with respect to taxation of corporate profits is that the host country gets the first opportunity to tax income produced within its borders. The home government then gets an opportunity to tax the income from a foreign project to the domestic firm. In particular, the home government must establish a tax policy specifying its treatment of foreign income and foreign taxes paid on that income. In addition, it needs to establish the timing of taxation.

U.S. tax policy requires U.S. corporations to pay taxes on their foreign income at the same rate as profits earned in the United States. However, a full tax credit is given for foreign taxes paid *up to* the amount of the U.S. tax liability. In other words, if the foreign tax rate is less than the U.S. tax rate, the company pays total taxes equal to the U.S. tax rate on its foreign earnings. In this case, all of the company's earnings are taxed at the same rate no matter where they are earned—the working assumption we used for Ityesi.

If the foreign tax rate exceeds the U.S. tax rate, companies must pay this higher rate on foreign earnings. Because the U.S. tax credit exceeds the amount of U.S. taxes owed, no tax is owed in the United States. Note that U.S. tax policy does not allow companies to apply the part of the tax credit that is not used to offset domestic taxes owed, so this extra tax credit is wasted. In this scenario, companies pay a higher tax rate on foreign income and a lower (U.S.) tax rate on income generated in the United States.

Multiple Foreign Projects and Deferral of Earnings Repatriation

Thus far, we have assumed that the firm has only one foreign project and that it repatriates earnings immediately. Neither assumption is realistic. Firms can lower their taxes by pooling multiple foreign projects and deferring the repatriation of earnings. Let's begin by considering the benefits of pooling the income on all foreign projects.

Pooling Multiple Foreign Projects.   Under U.S. tax law, multinational corporations may use any excess tax credits generated in high-tax foreign countries to offset their net U.S. tax liabilities on earnings in low-tax foreign countries. Thus, if the U.S. tax rate exceeds the combined tax rate on all foreign income, it is valid to assume that the firm pays the same tax rate on all income no matter where it is earned. Otherwise, the firm must pay a higher tax rate on its foreign income.

Deferring Repatriation of Earnings. Now consider an opportunity to defer repatriation of foreign profits. This consideration is important because U.S. tax liability is not incurred until the profits are brought back home if the foreign operation is set up as a separately incorporated subsidiary (rather than as a foreign branch). If a company chooses not to repatriate £12.5 million in pre-tax earnings, for example, it effectively reinvests those earnings abroad and defers its U.S. tax liability. When the foreign tax rates exceed the U.S. tax rates, there are no benefits to deferral because in such a case there is no additional U.S. tax liability.

When the foreign tax rate is less than the U.S. tax rate, deferral can provide significant benefits. Deferring repatriation of earnings lowers the overall tax burden in much the same way as deferring capital gains lowers the tax burden imposed by the capital gains tax. Other benefits from deferral arise because the firm effectively gains a real option to repatriate income at times when repatriation might be cheaper. For example, we have already noted that by pooling foreign income, the firm effectively pays the combined tax rate on all foreign income. Because the income generated across countries changes, this combined tax rate will vary from year to year. In years in which it exceeds the U.S. tax rate, the repatriation of additional income does not incur an additional U.S. tax liability, so the earnings can be repatriated tax free.

CONCEPT CHECK
1. What tax rate should we use to value a foreign project?
2. How can a U.S. firm lower its taxes on foreign projects?

31.4 Internationally Segmented Capital Markets

To this point, we have worked under the assumption that international capital markets are integrated. Often, however, this assumption is not appropriate. In some countries, especially in the developing world, all investors do not have equal access to financial securities. In this section, we consider why countries' capital markets might not be integrated—a case called **segmented capital markets**.

Many of the interesting questions in international corporate finance address the issues that result when capital markets are internationally segmented. In this section, we briefly consider the main reasons for segmentation of the capital markets and the implications for international corporate finance.

Differential Access to Markets

In some cases, a country's risk-free securities are internationally integrated but markets for a specific firm's securities are not. Firms may face differential access to markets if there is any kind of asymmetry with respect to information about them. For example, Ityesi may be well known in the United States and enjoy easy access to dollar equity and debt markets there because it regularly provides information to an established community of analysts tracking the firm. It may not be equally well known in the United Kingdom and, therefore, may have difficulty tapping into the pound capital markets because it has no track record there. For this reason, investors in the United Kingdom may require a higher rate of return to persuade them to hold pound stocks and bonds issued by the U.S. firm.

With differential access to national markets, Ityesi would face a higher pound WACC than the pound WACC implied by Eq. 31.7. Ityesi would then view the foreign project as less valuable if it raises capital in the United Kingdom rather than in the United States. In fact, to maximize shareholder value, the firm should raise capital at home; the method of valuing the foreign project as if it were a domestic project would then provide the correct NPV. Differential access to national capital markets is common enough that it provides the best explanation for the existence of **currency swaps**, which are like the interest rate swap contracts we discussed in Chapter 30, but with the holder receiving coupons in one currency and paying coupons denominated in a different currency. Currency swaps generally also have final face value payments, also in different currencies. Using a currency swap, a firm can borrow in the market where it has the best access to capital, and then "swap" the coupon and principal payments to whichever currency it would prefer to make payments in. Thus, swaps allow firms to mitigate their exchange rate risk exposure between assets and liabilities, while still making investments and raising funds in the most attractive locales.

Macro-Level Distortions

Markets for risk-free instruments may also be segmented. Important macroeconomic reasons for segmented capital markets include capital controls and foreign exchange controls that create barriers to international capital flows and thus segment national markets. Many countries regulate or limit capital inflows or outflows, and many do not allow their currencies to be freely converted into dollars, thereby creating capital market segmentation. Similarly, some countries restrict who can hold financial securities.

Political, legal, social, and cultural characteristics that differ across countries may require compensation in the form of a country risk premium. For example, the rate of interest paid on government bonds or other securities in a country with a tradition of weak enforcement of property rights is likely not really a risk-free rate. Instead, interest rates in the country will reflect a risk premium for the possibility of default, so relations such as covered interest rate parity will likely not hold exactly.

EXAMPLE 31.3

Risky Government Bonds

Problem

For June 8, 2006, *The Financial Times* reported a spot ruble–dollar exchange rate of R26.9975/$ and a one-year forward exchange rate of R26.9775/$. At the time, the yield on short term Russian government bonds was about 6%, while the comparable one-year yield on U.S. Treasury securities was 5%. Using the covered interest parity relationship, calculate the implied one-year forward rate. Compare this rate to the actual forward rate, and explain why the two rates differ.

Solution

Using the covered interest parity formula, the implied forward rate is

$$F = S \times \frac{(1 + r_R)}{(1 + r_\$)} = (R26.9975 / \$) \frac{1.06}{1.05} = R27.2546 / \$$$

The implied forward rate is higher than the current spot rate because Russian government bonds have higher yields than U.S. government bonds. The actual forward rate, however, is slightly *lower* than the current spot rate. The difference between the implied forward rate and the actual forward rate likely reflects the default risk in Russian government bonds (the Russian government defaulted on its debt as recently as 1998). A holder of 100,000 rubles seeking a true risk-free investment could convert the rubles to dollars, invest in U.S. Treasuries, and convert the proceeds back to rubles at a rate locked-in with a forward contract. By doing so, the investor would earn

$$\frac{R100,000}{R26.9975 \,/\, \$ \text{ today}} \times \frac{\$1.05 \text{ in 1-yr}}{\$ \text{ today}} \times (R26.9775 \,/\, \$ \text{ in 1-yr}) = R104,922 \text{ in 1-yr}$$

for an effective ruble risk-free rate of 4.922%. The higher rate of 6% on Russian bonds reflects a credit spread of $6\% - 4.922\% = 1.078\%$ to compensate bondholders for default risk.

Implications

A segmented financial market has an important implication for international corporate finance: One country or currency has a higher rate of return than another country or currency, when the two rates are compared in the same currency. If the return difference results from a market friction such as capital controls, corporations can exploit this friction by setting up projects in the high-return country/currency and raising capital in the low-return country/currency. Of course, the extent to which corporations can capitalize on this strategy is naturally limited: If such a strategy was easy to implement, the return difference would quickly disappear as corporations competed to use the strategy. Nevertheless, certain corporations might realize a competitive advantage by implementing such a strategy. For example, as an incentive to invest, a foreign government might strike a deal with a particular corporation that relaxes capital controls for that corporation alone.

EXAMPLE 31.4

Valuing a Foreign Acquisition in a Segmented Market

Problem

Camacho Enterprises is a U.S. company that is considering expanding by acquiring Xtapa, Inc., a firm in Mexico. The acquisition is expected to increase Camacho's free cash flows by 21 million pesos the first year; this amount is then expected to grow at a rate of 8% per year. The price of the investment is 525 million pesos, which is $52.5 million at the current exchange rate of 10 pesos/$. Based on an analysis in the Mexican market, Camacho has determined that the appropriate after-tax peso WACC is 12%. If Camacho has also determined that its after-tax dollar WACC for this expansion is 7.5%, what is the value of the Mexican acquisition? Assume that the Mexican and U.S. markets for risk-free securities are integrated and that the yield curve in both countries is flat. U.S. risk-free interest rates are 6%, and Mexican risk-free interest rates are 9%.

Solution

Let's begin by calculating the NPV of the expansion in pesos and converting the result into dollars at the spot rate. Putting the free cash flows on a timeline:

0	1	2	3
−525 pesos	21 pesos	21 (1.08) pesos	21 (1.08)² pesos

The net present value of these cash flows at the peso WACC is

$$NPV = \frac{21}{0.12 - 0.08} - 525 = 0$$

so the purchase is a zero-NPV transaction. Presumably, Camacho is competing with other Mexican companies for the purchase.

We can also compute the NPV in dollars by converting the expected cash flows into dollars using forward rates. The *N*-year forward rate (Eq. 30.3 in Chapter 30) expressed in pesos/$ is

$$F_N = S \times \frac{(1 + r_p)^N}{(1 + r_\$)^N} = 10 \times \left(\frac{1.09}{1.06}\right)^N = 10 \times 1.0283^N = 10.283 \times 1.0283^{N-1}$$

Thus the dollar expected cash flows are the peso cash flows (from the earlier timeline) converted at the appropriate forward rate (we divide by the forward rate because it is in pesos/$):

$$C_p^N / F_N = \frac{21(1.08)^{N-1}}{10.283 \times 1.0283^{N-1}} = 2.0422 \times 1.0503^{N-1}$$

The dollar expected cash flows are therefore

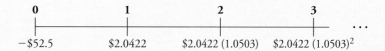

so the dollar cash flows grow at about 5% per year. The NPV of these cash flows is

$$NPV = \frac{2.0422}{0.075 - 0.0503} - 52.5 = \$30.18 \text{ million}$$

Which NPV more accurately represents the benefits of the expansion? The answer depends on the source of the difference. To compute the dollar expected cash flows by converting the peso expected cash flows at the forward rate, we must accept the assumption that spot rates and the project cash flows are uncorrelated. The difference might simply reflect that this assumption failed to hold. Another possibility is that the difference reflects estimation error in the respective WACC estimates.

If Camacho is relatively confident in its assumptions about spot rates and its WACC estimates, a third possibility is that Mexican and U.S. capital markets are not integrated. In this case, Camacho, because of its access to U.S. capital markets, might have a competitive advantage. Perhaps other companies with which it is competing for the purchase of Xtapa are all Mexican firms that do not have access to capital markets outside of Mexico. Hence Camacho can raise capital at a cheaper rate. Of course, this argument also requires that other U.S. companies not be competing for the purchase of Xtapa. Camacho, however, might have special knowledge of Xtapa's markets that other U.S.-based companies lack. This knowledge would give Camacho a competitive advantage in the product market over other U.S. companies and puts it on an equal footing in the product market with other Mexican companies. Because it has a competitive advantage in capital markets over other Mexican companies, the NPV of the purchase is positive for Camacho, but zero for the other bidders for Xtapa.

As Example 31.4 demonstrates, the existence of segmented capital markets makes many decisions in international corporate finance more complicated but potentially more lucrative for a firm that is well positioned to exploit the market segmentation.

CONCEPT CHECK 1. What is the main implication for international corporate finance of a segmented financial market?

2. What are the reasons for segmentation of the capital markets?

31.5 Capital Budgeting with Exchange Risk

The final issue that arises when a firm is considering a foreign project is that the cash flows of the project may be affected by exchange rate risk. The risk is that the cash flows generated by the project will depend upon the future level of the exchange rate. A large part of international corporate finance addresses this foreign exchange risk. This section offers an overview with respect to valuation of foreign currency cash flows.

The working assumptions made thus far in this chapter are that the project's free cash flows are uncorrelated with the spot exchange rates. Such an assumption often makes sense if the firm operates as a local firm in the foreign market—it purchases its inputs and sells its outputs in that market, and price changes of the inputs and outputs are uncorrelated with exchange rates. However, many firms use imported inputs in their production processes or export some of their output to foreign countries. These scenarios alter the nature of a project's foreign exchange risk and, in turn, change the valuation of the foreign currency cash flows.

As an example, let's reconsider what happens if the Ityesi project in the United Kingdom imports some materials from the United States. In this case, the project's pound free cash flows will be correlated with exchange rates. Assuming the cost of the material in the United States remains stable, if the value of a dollar appreciates against the pound, the pound cost of these materials will increase, thereby reducing the pound free cash flows. The reverse is also true: If the dollar depreciates, then the pound free cash flows will increase. Hence, our working assumption that changes in the free cash flows are uncorrelated with changes in the exchange rate is violated, and it is no longer appropriate to calculate the expected dollar free cash flows by converting the expected pound free cash flows at the forward rate.

Whenever a project has cash flows that depend on the values of multiple currencies, the most convenient approach is to separate the cash flows according to the currency they depend on. For example, a fraction of Ityesi's manufacturing costs may be for inputs whose cost fluctuates with the value of the dollar. Specifically, suppose £5.625 million of the costs are denominated in pounds, and an additional $16 million (or £10 million at the current exchange rate of $1.60/£) is for inputs whose price fluctuates with the value of the dollar. In this case, we would calculate Ityesi's pound-denominated free cash flows excluding these dollar-based costs, as shown in Table 31.4.

If the revenues and costs in the spreadsheet in Table 31.4 are not affected by changes in the spot exchange rates, it makes sense to assume that changes in the free cash flows are uncorrelated with changes in the spot exchange rates. Hence we can convert the pound-denominated free cash flows to equivalent dollar amounts using the forward exchange rate, as we did in Section 31.2. Table 31.5 spreadsheet performs this calculation, with the dollar value of the pound-denominated free cash flow shown in line 3.

Next we add the dollar-based cash flows to determine the project's aggregate free cash flow in dollar terms. This calculation is done in lines 4 through 6 of Table 31.5. Note that we deduct Ityesi's dollar-denominated costs, and then add the tax shield associated with these costs. Even if the taxes will be paid in pounds in the U.K., they will fluctuate with the dollar cost of the inputs and so can be viewed as a dollar-denominated cash flow.

TABLE 31.4 SPREADSHEET	Ityesi's Pound Free Cash Flows					
Year	0	1	2	3	4
Incremental Earnings Forecast (£ million)						
1 Sales	—	37.500	37.500	37.500	37.500
2 Cost of Goods Sold	—	(5.625)	(5.625)	(5.625)	(5.625)
3 Gross Profit	—	31.875	31.875	31.875	31.875
4 Operating Expenses	(4.167)	(5.625)	(5.625)	(5.625)	(5.625)
5 Depreciation	—	(3.750)	(3.750)	(3.750)	(3.750)
6 EBIT	(4.167)	22.500	22.500	22.500	22.500
7 Income tax at 40%	1.667	(9.000)	(9.000)	(9.000)	(9.000)
8 Unlevered Net Income	(2.500)	13.500	13.500	13.500	13.500
Free Cash Flow						
9 Plus: Depreciation	—	3.750	3.750	3.750	3.750
10 Less: Capital Expenditures	(15.000)	—	—	—	—
11 Less: Increases in NWC	—	—	—	—	—
12 Pound Free Cash Flow	(17.500)	17.250	17.250	17.250	17.250

Given the dollar-denominated free cash flow in line 6 of Table 31.5, we can now compute the NPV of the investment using Ityesi's dollar WACC:[3]

$$\frac{17.225}{1.068} + \frac{16.473}{1.068^2} + \frac{15.744}{1.068^3} + \frac{15.033}{1.068^4} - 28.000 = \$27.05 \text{ million.}$$

TABLE 31.5 SPREADSHEET	Expected Dollar Free Cash Flows from Ityesi's U.K. Project					
Year	0	1	2	3	4
Dollar Free Cash Flow ($ million)						
1 Pound FCF (£ million)	(17.500)	17.250	17.250	17.250	17.250
2 Forward Exchange Rate ($/£)	1.600	1.555	1.512	1.469	1.428
3 Dollar Value of Pound FCF (1 × 2)	(28.000)	26.825	26.073	25.344	24.633
4 Dollar Costs	—	(16.000)	(16.000)	(16.000)	(16.000)
5 Income tax at 40%	—	6.400	6.400	6.400	6.400
6 Free Cash Flow	(28.000)	17.225	16.473	15.744	15.033

The Ityesi example was simplified because we could easily isolate the cash flows that would vary perfectly with the dollar-pound exchange rate from those that would be uncorrelated with the exchange rate. In practice, determining these sensitivities may be difficult. If historical data is available, the tools of regression can be used to identify the exchange rate risk of project cash flows, in much the same way that we used regression to identify the market risk of security returns in Part IV of the text.

---

3. We again use the domestic WACC to discount the cash flows because we continue to assume that any additional risk premium for the exchange rate risk is small. If this assumption does not hold, then the dollar costs and the dollar value of the expected pound free cash flows would have to be discounted at different rates to reflect the additional exchange rate risk in the pound free cash flows.

In this chapter, we have endeavored to provide an introduction to international capital budgeting. This topic is sufficiently complicated that entire textbooks have been devoted to it. Hence, it is difficult to do this issue justice in a single-chapter treatment. Although we have provided a basic framework for approaching the problem, a reader who is seriously considering undertaking a foreign venture should consult one of the books listed in the Further Readings section at the end of the chapter.

CONCEPT CHECK

1. What conditions cause the cash flows of a foreign project to be affected by exchange rate risk?

2. How do we make adjustments when a project has inputs and outputs in different currencies?

Summary

1. The condition necessary to ensure internationally integrated capital markets is that the value of a foreign investment does not depend on the currency (home or foreign) used in the analysis.

2. Two methods are used to value foreign currency cash flows when markets are internationally integrated and uncertainty in spot exchange rates are uncorrelated with the foreign currency cash flows:

   a. Calculate the foreign currency value of a foreign project as the NPV of the expected foreign currency future cash flows discounted at the foreign cost of capital, and then convert the foreign currency NPV into the home currency using the current spot exchange rate.

   b. Compute the expected value of the foreign currency cash flows in the home currency by multiplying the expected value in the foreign currency by the forward exchange rates, and then compute the NPV of these home currency cash flows using the domestic cost of capital.

3. When markets are internationally integrated and uncertainty in spot exchange rates are uncorrelated with the foreign currency cash flows, the foreign and domestic WACCs are related as follows:

$$r_£^* = \frac{1 + r_£}{1 + r_\$}(1 + r_\$^*) - 1 \tag{31.7}$$

4. A U.S. corporation pays the higher of the foreign or domestic tax rate on its foreign project, so project valuation should use the higher of these two rates as well. The U.S. corporation may be able to reduce its tax liability by undertaking foreign projects in other countries whose earnings can be pooled with those of the new project or by deferring the repatriation of earnings.

5. Capital markets might be internationally segmented. The implication is that one country or currency has a higher cost of capital than another country or currency, when the two are compared in the same currency.

6. When a project has inputs and outputs in different currencies, the foreign-denominated cash flows are likely to be correlated with changes in spot rates. To correctly value such projects, the foreign and domestic cash flows should be valued separately.

Key Terms

currency swaps *p. 978*
internationally integrated capital
    market *p. 971*

repatriated *p. 976*
segmented capital markets *p. 977*

Further Reading

It is difficult to do justice to international corporate finance in a single chapter. However, many excellent textbooks have been written on this topic: R. W. Click and J. D. Coval, *The Theory and Practice of International Financial Management* (Prentice Hall, 2001); M. R. Eaker, F. J. Fabozzi, and D. Grant, *International Corporate Finance* (Fort Worth, TX: the Dryden Press, 1996); D. K. Eiteman and A. I. Stonehill, *Multinational Business Finance*, 10th ed. (Reading, MA: Addison-Wesley, 2003); J. O. Grabbe, *International Financial Markets*, 3rd ed. (Englewood Cliffs, NJ: Prentice-Hall, 1995); M. Levi, *International Finance* (New York: McGraw-Hill, 1996); J. Madura, *International Financial Management* (Mason, OH: South-Western, 2003); P. Sercu and R. Uppal, *International Financial Markets and the Firm* (Cincinnati, OH: South-Western College Publishing, 1995); and A. C. Shapiro, *Multinational Financial Management*, 7th ed. (New York: John Wiley & Sons, 2002).

The effect that international operations have on the value of the firm and its cost of capital is studied in the following articles: V. R. Errunza and L. W. Senbet, "Market Segmentation and the Cost of Capital in International Equity Markets," *Journal of Financial and Quantitative Analysis* 35(4) (2000): 577–600; and R. Stulz, "Globalization, Corporate Finance, and the Cost of Capital," *Journal of Applied Corporate Finance* 12(3) (1999): 8–25.

Problems

A blue box (■) indicates problems available in MyFinanceLab. An asterisk (*) indicates problems with a higher level of difficulty.

**Internationally Integrated
Capital Markets**

1. You are a U.S. investor who is trying to calculate the present value of a €5 million cash inflow that will occur one year in the future. The spot exchange rate is $S = \$1.25/€$ and the forward rate is $F_1 = \$1.215/€$. You estimate that the appropriate dollar discount rate for this cash flow is 4% and the appropriate euro discount rate is 7%.

   a. What is the present value of the €5 million cash inflow computed by first discounting the euro and then converting it into dollars?

   b. What is the present value of the €5 million cash inflow computed by first converting the cash flow into dollars and then discounting?

   c. What can you conclude about whether these markets are internationally integrated, based on your answers to parts (a) and (b)?

2. Mia Caruso Enterprises, a U.S. manufacturer of children's toys, has made a sale in Cyprus and is expecting a C£ 4 million cash inflow in one year. (The currency of Cyprus is the Cypriot pound, C£. Cyprus is a member of the European Union, but has not yet adopted the euro.) The current spot rate is $S = \$1.80/C£$ and the one-year forward rate is $F_1 = \$1.8857/C£$.

   a. What is the present value of Mia Caruso's C£ 4 million inflow computed by first discounting the cash flow at the appropriate Cypriot pound discount rate of 5% and then converting the result into dollars?

b. What is the present value of Mia Caruso's C£ 4 million inflow computed by first converting the cash flow into dollars and then discounting at the appropriate dollar discount rate of 10%?

c. What can you conclude about whether these markets are internationally integrated, based on your answers to parts (a) and (b)?

Valuation of Foreign Currency Cash Flows

 3. Etemadi Amalgamated, a U.S. manufacturing firm, is considering a new project in the euro area. You are in Etemadi's corporate finance department and are responsible for deciding whether to undertake the project. The expected free cash flows, in euros, are shown here:

Year	Free Cash Flow (€ million)
0	−15
1	9
2	10
3	11
4	12

You know that the spot exchange rate is $S = \$1.15/€$. In addition, the risk-free interest rate on dollars is 4% and the risk-free interest rate on euros is 6%.

Assume that these markets are internationally integrated and the uncertainty in the free cash flows is not correlated with uncertainty in the exchange rate. You determine that the dollar WACC for these cash flows is 8.5%. What is the dollar present value of the project? Should Etemadi Amalgamated undertake the project?

EXCEL 4. Etemadi Amalgamated, the U.S. manufacturing company in Problem 3, is still considering a new project in the euro area. All information presented in Problem 3 is still accurate, except the spot rate is now $S = \$0.85/€$, about 26% lower. What is the new present value of the project in dollars? Should Etemadi Amalgamated undertake the project?

5. You work for a U.S. firm, and your boss has asked you to estimate the cost of capital for countries using the euro. You know that $S = \$1.20/€$ and $F_1 = \$1.157/€$. Suppose the dollar WACC for your company is known to be 8%. If these markets are internationally integrated, estimate the euro cost of capital for a project with free cash flows that are uncorrelated with spot exchange rates. Assume the firm pays the same tax rate no matter where the cash flows are earned.

6. Maryland Light, a U.S. light fixtures manufacturer, is considering an investment in Japan. The dollar cost of equity for Maryland Light is 11%. You are in the corporate treasury department, and you need to know the comparable cost of equity in Japanese yen for a project with free cash flows that are uncorrelated with spot exchange rates. The risk-free interest rates on dollars and yen are $r_\$ = 5\%$ and $r_¥ = 1\%$, respectively. Maryland Light is willing to assume that capital markets are internationally integrated. What is the yen cost of equity?

7. The dollar cost of debt for Coval Consulting, a U.S. research firm, is 7.5%. The firm faces a tax rate of 30% on all income, no matter where it is earned. Managers in the firm need to know its yen cost of debt because they are considering launching a new bond issue in Tokyo to raise money for a new investment there. The risk-free interest rates on dollars and yen are $r_\$ = 5\%$ and $r_¥ = 1\%$, respectively. Coval Consulting is willing to assume that capital markets are internationally integrated and that its free cash flows are uncorrelated with the yen–dollar spot rate. What is Coval Consulting's after-tax cost of debt in yen? (*Hint:* Start by finding the after-tax cost of debt in dollars and then find the yen equivalent.)

8. Manzetti Foods, a U.S. food processing and distribution company, is considering an investment in the euro area. You are in Manzetti's corporate finance department and are responsible for deciding whether to undertake the project. The expected free cash flows, in euros, are uncorrelated to the spot exchange rate and are shown here:

Year	Free Cash Flow (€ million)
0	−25
1	12
2	14
3	15
4	15

The new project has similar dollar risk to Manzetti's other projects. The company knows that its overall dollar WACC is 9.5%, so it feels comfortable using this WACC for the project. The risk-free interest rate on dollars is 4.5% and the risk-free interest rate on euros is 7%.

a. Manzetti is willing to assume that capital markets in the United States and the euro area are internationally integrated. What is the company's euro WACC?

b. What is the present value of the project in euros?

Valuation and International Taxation

9. Tailor Johnson, a U.S. maker of fine menswear, has a subsidiary in Ethiopia. This year, the subsidiary reported and repatriated earnings before interest and taxes (EBIT) of 100 million Ethiopian birrs. The current exchange rate is 8 birr/$ or $S_1 = \$0.125/\text{birr}$. The Ethiopian tax rate on this activity is 25%. U.S. tax law requires Tailor Johnson to pay taxes on the Ethiopian earnings at the same rate as profits earned in the United States, which is currently 45%. However, the United States gives a full tax credit for foreign taxes paid up to the amount of the U.S. tax liability. What is Tailor Johnson's U.S. tax liability on its Ethiopian subsidiary?

*10. Tailor Johnson, the menswear company with a subsidiary in Ethiopia described in Problem 9, is considering the tax benefits resulting from deferring repatriation of the earnings from the subsidiary. Under U.S. tax law, the U.S. tax liability is not incurred until the profits are brought back home. Tailor Johnson reasonably expects to defer repatriation for ten years, at which point the birr earnings will be converted into dollars at the prevailing spot rate, S_{10}, and the tax credit for Ethiopian taxes paid will still be converted at the exchange rate $S_1 = \$0.125/\text{birr}$. Tailor Johnson's after-tax cost of debt is 5%.

a. Suppose the exchange rate in ten years is identical to this year's exchange rate, so $S_{10} = \$0.125/\text{birr}$. What is the present value of deferring the U.S. tax liability on Tailor Johnson's Ethiopian earnings for ten years?

b. How will the exchange rate in ten years affect the actual amount of the U.S. tax liability? Write an equation for the U.S. tax liability as a function of the exchange rate S_{10}.

11. Peripatetic Enterprises, a U.S. import–export trading firm, is considering its international tax situation. U.S. tax law requires U.S. corporations to pay taxes on their foreign earnings at the same rate as profits earned in the United States; this rate is currently 45%. However, a full tax credit is given for the foreign taxes paid up to the amount of the U.S. tax liability. Peripatetic has major operations in Poland, where the tax rate is 20%, and in Sweden, where the tax rate is 60%. The profits, which are fully and immediately repatriated, and foreign taxes paid for the current year are shown here:

	Poland	**Sweden**
Earnings before interest and taxes (EBIT)	$80 million	$100 million
Host country taxes paid	$16 million	$60 million
Earnings before interest after taxes	$64 million	$40 million

a. What is the U.S. tax liability on the earnings from the Polish subsidiary assuming the Swedish subsidiary did not exist?

b. What is the U.S. tax liability on the earnings from the Swedish subsidiary assuming the Polish subsidiary did not exist?

c. Under U.S. tax law, Peripatetic is able to pool the earnings from its operations in Poland and Sweden when computing its U.S. tax liability on foreign earnings. Total EBIT is thus $180 million and the total host country taxes paid is $76 million. What is the total U.S. tax liability on foreign earnings? Show how this relates to the answers in parts (a) and (b).

Internationally Segmented Capital Markets

*12. Suppose the interest on Russian government bonds is 7.5%, and the current exchange rate is 28 rubles per dollar. If the forward exchange rate is 28.5 rubles per dollar, and the current U.S. risk-free interest rate is 4.5%, what is the implied credit spread for Russian government bonds?

Capital Budgeting with Exchange Risk

EXCEL *13. Assume that in the original Ityesi example in Table 31.1, all sales actually occur in the United States and are projected to be $60 million per year for four years. Keeping other costs the same, calculate the NPV of the investment opportunity.

Data Case

You are a senior financial analyst with IBM in their capital budgeting division. IBM is considering expanding in Australia due to its positive business atmosphere and cultural similarities to the United States.

The new facility would require an initial investment in fixed assets of $5 billion Australian and an additional capital investment of 3% would be required each year in years 1–4. All capital investments would be depreciated straight line over the 5 years that the facility would operate. First-year revenues from the facility are expected to be $6 billion Australian and grow at 10% per year. Cost of goods sold would be 40% of revenue; the other operating expenses would amount to 12% of revenue. Net working capital requirements would be 11% of sales and would be required the year prior to the actual revenues. All net working capital would be recovered at the end of the fifth year. Assume that the tax rates are the same in the two countries, that the two markets are internationally integrated, and that the cash flow uncertainty of the project is uncorrelated with changes in the exchange rate. Your team manager wants you to determine the NPV of the project in U.S. dollars using a cost of capital of 12%.

1. Go to Nasdaq.com (www.nasdaq.com).

   a. Enter the stock symbol for IBM (IBM) in one of the boxes and click "Summary Quotes."

   b. Click "Company Financials" from the menu on the left. When the income statement appears, place the cursor inside the statement and right-click. Select "Export to Microsoft Excel" from the menu.

2. Obtain exchange rates and comparable interest rates for Australia at Bloomberg's Web site (www.bloomberg.com).

   a. Place the cursor on "Market Data" and click on "Currencies" from the drop-down menu. Export the currency table to Excel and paste it into the same spreadsheet as the IBM income statement.

   b. Go back to the Web page and click on "Rates & Bonds" from the menu on the left. Next click on "Australia" to get the interest rates for Australia. Right-click and export the table to Excel; paste it into the spreadsheet.

   c. Go back to the Web page and click on "U.S." Download the Treasury data and paste it into the spreadsheet.

3. You may have noticed that the one-year and four-year rates are not available at Bloomberg.com for the U.S. Treasury. Go to the U.S. Treasury Web site (www.treas.gov).

   a. To find the one-year rate, type "yield curve" into the search box at the top of the page and select the second link that appears. Be sure it is *not* the link for the "real" rates. Export the yields into Excel on the same spreadsheet as the other data. Add the one-year yield to the other Treasury rates.

   b. To find an estimate of the four-year yield, calculate the average of the three- and five-year yields from the Treasury yield curve.

4. In your Excel spreadsheet, create a new worksheet with a timeline for the project expected cash flows.

   a. Compute the tax rate as the four-year average of IBM's annual income tax divided by annual earnings before tax.

   b. Determine the expected free cash flows of the project.

5. Note that the free cash flows you calculated in Question 4 are in Australian dollars. Use Eq. 30.3 to determine the forward exchange rates for each of the five years of the project. Then use the forward rates to convert the cash flows to U.S. dollars.

6. Compute the NPV of the project in U.S. dollars using the 12% required return given by your team manager.

Glossary

$1.00 out lease   A type of lease, also known as a finance lease, in which ownership of the asset transfers to the lessee at the end of the lease for a nominal cost of $1.00.

10-K   The annual form that U.S. companies use to file their financial statements with the U.S. Securities and Exchange Commission (SEC).

10-Q   The quarterly reporting form that U.S. companies use to file their financial statements with the U.S. Securities and Exchange Commission (SEC).

abandonment option   An option for an investor to cease making investments in a project. Abandonment options can add value to a project because a firm can drop a project if it turns out to be unsuccessful.

absolute return   *See* cash multiple.

accounts payable   The amounts owed to creditors for products or services purchased with credit.

accounts payable days   An expression of a firm's accounts payable in terms of the number of days' worth of cost of goods sold that the accounts payable represents.

accounts receivable   Amounts owed to a firm by customers who have purchased goods or services on credit.

accounts receivable days   An expression of a firm's accounts receivable in terms of the number of days' worth of sales that the accounts receivable represents.

acquirer (or bidder)   A firm that, in a takeover, buys another firm.

acquisition premium   Paid by an acquirer in a takeover, it is the percentage difference between the acquisition price and the premerger price of a target firm.

actuarially fair   When the NPV from selling insurance is zero because the price of insurance equals the present value of the expected payment.

adjusted betas   A beta that has been adjusted toward 1 to account for estimation error.

adjusted present value (APV)   A valuation method to determine the levered value of an investment by first calculating its unlevered value (its value without any leverage) and then adding the value of the interest tax shield and deducting any costs that arise from other market imperfections.

adverse selection   The idea that when the buyers and sellers have different information, the average quality of assets in the market will differ from the average quality overall.

after-tax interest rate   Reflects the amount of interest an investor can keep after taxes have been deducted.

agency costs   Costs that arise when there are conflicts of interest between a firm's stakeholders.

agency securities   Securities issued by agencies of the U.S. government or by U.S. government-sponsored enterprises.

aggressive financing policy   Financing part or all of a firm's permanent working capital with short-term debt.

aging schedule   Categorizes a firm's accounts by the number of days they have been on the firm's books. It can be prepared using either the number of accounts or the dollar amount of the accounts receivable outstanding.

alpha   The difference between a stock's expected return and its required return according to the security market line.

American options   the most common kind of option, they allow their holders to exercise the option on any date up to, and including, the expiration date.

amortization   A charge that captures the change in value of acquired assets. Like depreciation, amortization is not an actual cash expense.

amortizing loan   A loan on which the borrower makes monthly payments that include interest on the loan plus some part of the loan balance.

angel investors   Individual investors who buy equity in small private firms

annual percentage rate (APR)   Indicates the amount of interest earned in one year without the effect of compounding.

annual report   The yearly summary of business sent by U.S. public companies to their shareholders that accompanies or includes the financial statement.

annuity   A stream of equal periodic cash flows over a specified time period. These cash flows can be inflows of returns earned on investments or outflows of funds invested to earn future returns.

annuity spreadsheet   An Excel spreadsheet that can compute any one of the five variables of *NPER, RATE, PV, PMT,* and *FV.* Given any four input variables the spreadsheet computes the fifth.

APR   *See* annual precentage rate.

APT   *See* Arbitrage Pricing Theory.

APV   *See* adjusted present value.

arbitrage   The practice of buying and selling equivalent goods or portfolios to take advantage of a price difference.

arbitrage opportunity   Any situation in which it is possible to make a profit without taking any risk or making any investment.

Arbitrage Pricing Theory (APT)   A model that uses more than one portfolio to capture systematic risk. The portfolios themselves can be thought of as either the risk factor itself or a portfolio of stocks correlated with an unobservable risk factor. Also referred to as a multifactor model.

ask price   The price at which a market maker or specialist is willing to sell a security.

asset-backed bonds   A type of secured corporate debt. Specific assets are pledged as collateral that bondholders have a direct claim to in the event of bankruptcy. Asset-backed bonds can be secured by any kind of asset.

assets   The cash, inventory, property, plant and equipment, and other investments a company has made.

asymmetric information   A situation in which parties have different information. It can arise when, for example, managers have superior information to investors regarding the firm's future cash flows.

at-the-money   Describes options whose exercise prices are equal to the current stock price.

auction IPO   A method for selling new issues directly to the public. Rather than setting a price itself and then allocating shares to buyers, the underwriter in an auction IPO takes bids from investors and then sets the price to clear the market.

auditor   A neutral third party that corporations are required to hire that checks the annual financial statements to ensure they are prepared according to GAAP, and to verify that the information is reliable.

availability float   How long it takes a bank to give a firm credit for customer payments the firm has deposited in the bank.

average annual return   The arithmetic average of an investment's realized returns for each year.

backdating   The practice of choosing the grant date of a stock option retroactively, so that the date of the grant would coincide with a date when the stock price was lower than its price at the time the grant was actually awarded. By backdating the option in this way, the executive receives a stock option that is already in-the-money.

balance sheet   A list of a firm's assets and liabilities that provides a snapshot of the firm's financial position at a given point in time.

basis risk   The risk that the value of a security used to hedge and exposure will not track that exposure perfectly.

balloon payment   A large payment that must be made on the maturity date of a bond.

bearer bond   Similar to currency in that whoever physically holds this bond's certificate owns the bond. To receive a coupon payment, the holder of a bearer bond must provide explicit proof of ownership by literally clipping a coupon off the bond certificate and remitting it to the paying agent.

best-efforts basis   For smaller initial public offerings (IPOs), a situation in which underwriter does not guarantee that the stock will be sold, but instead tries to sell the stock for the best possible price. Often such deals have an all-or-none clause: either all of the shares are sold on the IPO, or the deal is called off.

beta (β)   The expected percent change in the excess return of a security for a 1% change in the excess return of the market (or other benchmark) portfolio.

bid price   The price at which a market maker or specialist is willing to buy a security.

bid-ask spread   The amount by which the ask price exceeds the bid price.

bidder   *See* acquirer.

Binomial Option Pricing Model   A technique for pricing options based on the assumption that each period, the stock's return can take on only two values.

binomial tree   A timeline with two branches at every date representing the possible events that could happen at those times.

bird in the hand hypothesis   The thesis that firms choosing to pay higher current dividends will enjoy higher stock prices because shareholders prefer current dividends to future ones (with the same present value).

Black-Scholes Option Pricing Model   A technique for pricing European-style options when the stock can be traded continuously. It can be derived from the Binomial Option Pricing Model by allowing the length of each period shrink to zero.

blanket lien   *See* floating lien.

board of directors   A group elected by shareholders that has the ultimate decision-making authority in the corporation.

bond   A security sold by governments and corporations to raise money from investors today in exchange for the promised future payment.

bond certificate   States the terms of a bond as well as the amounts and dates of all payments to be made.

book building   A process used by underwriters for coming up with an offer price based on customers' expressions of interest.

book-to-market ratio   The ratio of the book value of equity to the market value of equity.

book value   The acquisition cost of an asset less its accumulated depreciation.

book value of equity   The difference between the book value of a firm's assets and its liabilities; also called stockholders' equity, it represents the net worth of a firm from an accounting perspective.

break-even   The level for which an investment has an NPV of zero.

break-even analysis   A calculation of the value of each parameter for which the NPV of the project is zero.

bridge loan   A type of short-term bank loan that is often used to "bridge the gap" until a firm can arrange for long-term financing.

Bulldogs   A term for foreign bonds in the United Kingdom.

business interruption insurance   A type of insurance that protects a firm against the loss of earnings if the business is interrupted due to fire, accident, or some other insured peril.

business liability insurance   A type of insurance that covers the costs that result if some aspect of a business causes harm to a third party or someone else's property.

butterfly spread   An option portfolio that is long two calls with differing strike prices, and short two calls with a strike price equal to the average strike price of the first two calls.

buying stocks on margin (leverage)   Borrowing money to invest in stocks.

"C" corporations   Corporations that have no restrictions on who owns their shares or the number of shareholders, and therefore cannot qualify for subchapter S treatment and are subject to direct taxation.

callable bonds   Bonds that contain a call provision that allows the issuer to repurchase the bonds at a predetermined price.

call date   The right (but not the obligation) of a bond issuer to retire outstanding bonds on (or after) a specific date.

call option   A financial option that gives its owner the right to buy an asset.

call price   A price specified at the issuance of a bond at which the issuer can redeem the bond.

cannibalization   When sales of a firm's new product displace sales of one of its existing products.

Capital Asset Pricing Model (CAPM)   An equilibrium model of the relationship between risk and return that characterizes a security's expected return based on its beta with the market portfolio.

capital budget   Lists all of the projects that a company plans to undertake during the next period.

capital budgeting   The process of analyzing investment opportunities and deciding which ones to accept.

capital expenditures   Purchases of new property, plant, and equipment.

capital gain   The amount by which the sale price of an asset exceeds its initial purchase price.

capital gain rate   An expression of capital gain as a percentage of the initial price of the asset.

capital (finance) lease   Long-term lease contract that obligates a firm to make regular lease payments in exchange for the use of an asset. Viewed as an acquisition for accounting purposes, the lessee lists the asset on its balance sheet and incurs depreciation expenses. The lessee also lists the present value of the future lease payments as a liability, and deducts the interest portion of the lease payment as an interest expense.

capital market line (CML)   When plotting expected returns versus volatility, the line from the risk-free investment through the efficient portfolio of risky stocks (the portfolio that has the highest possible Sharpe Ratio). In the context of the CAPM, it is the line from the risk-free investment through the market portfolio. It shows the highest possible expected return that can be obtained for any given volatility.

capital structure   The relative proportions of debt, equity, and other securities that a firm has outstanding.

CAPM   *See* Capital Asset Pricing Model.

captured   Describes a board of directors whose monitoring duties have been compromised by connections or perceived loyalties to management.

carryback or carryforward   *See* tax loss carryforwards and carrybacks

cash-and-carry strategy   A strategy used to lock in the future cost of an asset by buying the asset for cash today, and storing (or "carrying") it until a future date.

cash offer   A type of seasoned equity offering (SEO) in which a firm offers the new shares to investors at large.

cash conversion cycle   A measure of the cash cycle calculated as the sum of a firm's inventory days and accounts receivable days, less its accounts payable days.

cash cycle   The length of time between when a firm pays cash to purchase its initial inventory and when it receives cash from the sale of the output produced from that inventory.

cash multiple (multiple of money, absolute return)   The ratio of the total cash received to the total cash invested.

chaebol   Korean term for large conglomerate groups comprised of companies in widely diversified lines of business.

Chapter 11 reorganization   A common form of bankruptcy for large corporations in which all pending collection attempts are automatically suspended, and the firm's existing management is given the opportunity to propose a reorganization plan. While developing the plan, management continues to operate the business as usual. The creditors must vote to accept the plan, and it must be approved by the bankruptcy court. If an acceptable plan is not put forth, the court may ultimately force a Chapter 7 liquidation of the firm.

Chapter 7 liquidation   A provision of the U.S. bankruptcy code in which a trustee is appointed to oversee the liquidation of a firm's assets through an auction. The proceeds from the liquidation are used to pay the firm's creditors, and the firm ceases to exist.

characteristic variable   An observable characteristic of a firm, such as its market price, price-earnings ratio, or book-to-market ratio, that implicitly captures risk factors that affect the firm's future returns.

characteristic variable models   An approach to measuring risk that views firms as a portfolio of different measurable characteristics that together determine the firm's risk and return.

Check Clearing for the 21st Century Act (Check 21)   Eliminates the disbursement float due to the check-clearing process. Under the act, banks can process check information electronically, and, in most cases, the funds are deducted from a firm's checking account on the same day that the firm's supplier deposits the check in its bank.

Check 21   *See* Check Clearing for the 21st Century Act.

chief executive officer or CEO   The person charged with running the corporation by instituting the rules and policies set by the board of directors.

classified board   *See* staggered board.

clean price   A bond's cash price less an adjustment for accrued interest, the amount of the next coupon payment that has already accrued.

clientele effect   When the dividend policy of a firm reflects the tax preference of its investor clientele.

CML   *See* capital market line.

collection float   The amount of time it takes for a firm to be able to use funds after a customer has paid for its goods.

commercial paper   Short-term, unsecured debt issued by large corporations that is usually a cheaper source of funds than a short-term bank loan. Most commercial paper has a face value of at least $100,000. Like long-term debt, commercial paper is rated by credit rating agencies.

committed line of credit   A legally binding agreement that obligates a bank to provide funds to a firm (up to a stated credit limit) as long as the firm satisfies any restrictions in the agreement.

common risk   Perfectly correlated risk.

compensating balance   An amount a firm's bank may require the firm to maintain in an account at the bank as compensation for services the bank may perform.

competitive market   A market in which goods can be bought and sold at the same price.

compounding   Computing the return on an investment over a long horizon by multiplying the return factors associated with each intervening period.

compound interest   The effect of earning "interest on interest."

conservation of value principle   With perfect capital markets, financial transactions neither add nor destroy value, but instead represent a repackaging of risk (and therefore return).

conservative financing policy   When a firm finances its short-term needs with long-term debt.

consol   A bond that promises its owner a fixed cash flow every year, forever.

constant dividend growth model   A model for valuing a stock by viewing its dividends as a constant growth perpetuity.

constant interest coverage ratio   When a firm keeps its interest payments equal to a target fraction of its free cash flows.

continuation value   The current value of all future free cash flow from continuing a project or investment.

continuous compounding   The compounding of interest every instant (an infinite number of times per year).

conversion price   The face value of a convertible bond divided by the number of shares received if the bond is converted.

conversion ratio   The number of shares received upon conversion of a convertible bond, usually stated per $1000 face value.

convertible bonds   Corporate bonds with a provision that gives the bondholder an option to convert each bond owned into a fixed number of shares of common stock.

convertible preferred stock   A preferred stock that gives the owner an option to convert it into common stock on some future date.

corporate bonds   Bonds issued by a corporation.

corporate governance   The system of controls, regulations, and incentives designed to minimize agency costs between managers and investors and prevent corporate fraud.

corporate investor, corporate partner, strategic partner, strategic investor   A corporation that invests in private companies.

corporate partner   *See* corporate investor.

corporation   A legally defined, artificial being, separate from its owners.

correlation   The covariance of the returns divided by the standard deviation of each return; a measure of the common risk shared by stocks that does not depend on their volatility.

cost of capital   The expected return available on securities with equivalent risk and term to a particular investment.

coupon bonds   Bonds that pay regular coupon interest payments up to maturity, when the face value is also paid.

coupon-paying yield curve   A plot of the yield of coupon bonds of different maturities.

coupon rate   Determines the amount of each coupon payment of a bond. The coupon rate, expressed as an APR, is set by the issuer and stated on the bond certificate.

coupons   The promised interest payments of a bond.

covariance   The expected product of the deviation of each return from its mean.

covenants   Restrictive clauses in a bond contract that limit the issuers from undercutting their ability to repay bonds.

covered interest parity equation   States that the difference between the forward and spot exchange rates is related to the interest rate differential between the currencies.

credibility principle   The principle that claims in one's self-interest are credible only if they are supported by actions that would be too costly to take if the claims were untrue.

credit rating   A rating assigned by a rating agency that assesses the likelihood that a borrower will default.

credit risk   The risk of default by the issuer of any bond that is not default free; it is an indication that the bond's cash flows are not known with certainty.

credit spread   The difference between the risk-free interest rate on U.S. Treasury notes and the interest rates on all other loans. The magnitude of the credit spread will depend on investors' assessment of the likelihood that a particular firm will default.

cum dividend   When a stock trades before the ex-dividend date, entitling anyone who buys the stock to the dividend.

cumulative normal distribution   The probability that an outcome from a standard normal distribution will be below a certain value.

currency forward contract   A contract that sets a currency exchange rate, and an amount to exchange, in advance.

currency swaps   A contract in which parties agree to exchange coupon payments and a final face value payment that are in different currencies.

currency timeline   Indicates time horizontally by dates (as in a standard timeline) and currencies vertically (as in dollars and euros).

current assets   Cash or assets that could be converted into cash within one year. This category includes marketable securities, accounts receivable, inventories, and pre-paid expenses such as rent and insurance.

current liabilities   Liabilities that will be satisfied within one year. They include accounts payable, notes payable, short-term debt, current maturities of long-term debt, salary or taxes owed, and deferred or unearned revenue.

current ratio   The ratio of current assets to current liabilities.

data snooping bias   The idea that given enough characteristics, it will always be possible to find some characteristic that by pure chance happens to be correlated with the estimation error of a regression.

dealer paper   Commercial paper that dealers sell to investors in exchange for a spread (or fee) for their services. The spread decreases the proceeds that the issuing firm receives, thereby increasing the effective cost of the paper.

debentures   A type of unsecured corporate debt. Debentures typically have longer maturities (more than ten years) than notes, another type of unsecured corporate debt.

debt capacity   The amount of debt at a particular date that is required to maintain the firm's target debt-to-value ratio.

debt cost of capital   The cost of capital, or expected return, that a firm must pay on its debt.

debt covenants   Conditions of making a loan in which creditors place restrictions on actions that a firm can take.

debt holders   Individuals or institutions who have lent money to a firm.

debt-equity ratio   The ratio of a firm's total amount of short- and long-term debt (including current maturities) to the value of its equity, which may be calculated based on market or book values.

debt-to-value ratio   The fraction of a firm's enterprise value that corresponds to debt.

decision node   A node on a decision tree at which a decision is made, and so corresponds to a real option.

decision tree   A graphical representation of future decisions and uncertainty resolution.

declaration date   The date on which a public company's board of directors authorizes the payment of a dividend.

deductible   A provision of an insurance policy in which an initial amount of loss is not covered by the policy and must be paid by the insured.

deep in-the-money   Describes options that are in-the-money and for which the strike price and the stock price are very far apart.

deep out-of-the-money   Describes options that are out-of-the-money and for which the strike price and the stock price are very far apart.

default   When a firm fails to make the required interest or principal payments on its debt, or violates a debt covenant.

default spread   *See* credit spread.

deferred taxes   An asset or liability that results from the difference between a firm's tax expenses as reported for accounting purposes, and the actual amount paid to the taxing authority.

depreciation   A yearly deduction a firm makes from the value of its fixed assets (other than land) over time according to a depreciation schedule that depends on an asset's life span.

depreciation tax shield   The tax savings that result from the ability to deduct depreciation.

derivative security   A security whose cash flows depend solely on the prices of other marketed assets.

diluted EPS   A firm's disclosure of its potential for dilution from options it has awarded which shows the earnings per share the company would have if the stock options were exercised.

dilution   An increase in the total number of shares that will divide a fixed amount of earnings; often occurs when stock options are exercised or convertible bonds are converted.

dilution fallacy   The idea that issuing shares will, on its own, reduce the value of existing shares.

direct lease   A type of lease in which the lessor is not the manufacturer, but is often an independent company that specializes in purchasing assets and leasing them to customers.

direct paper   Commercial paper that a firms sells directly to investors.

dirty price (invoice price)   A bond's actual cash price.

disbursement float   The amount of time it takes before a firm's payments to its suppliers actually result in a cash outflow for the firm.

discount   The amount by which a cash flow exceeds its present value.

discounted free cash flow model   A method for estimating a firm's enterprise value by discounting its future free cash flow.

discount factor   The value today of a dollar received in the future.

discounting   Finding the equivalent value today of a future cash flow by multiplying by a discount factor, or equivalently, dividing by 1 plus the discount rate.

discount loan   A type of bridge loan in which the borrower is required to pay the interest at the beginning of the loan period. The lender deducts interest from the loan proceeds when the loan is made.

discount rate   The rate used to discount a stream of cash flows; the cost of capital of a stream of cash flows.

distribution date   *See* payable date.

diversifiable risk   *See* firm-specific risk.

diversification   The averaging of independent risks in a large portfolio.

dividend-capture theory   The theory that absent transaction costs, investors can trade shares at the time of the dividend so that non-taxed investors receive the dividend.

dividend-discount model   A model that values shares of a firm according to the present value of the future dividends the firm will pay.

dividend payments   Payments made at the discretion of the corporation to its equity holders.

dividend payout rate   The fraction of a firm's earnings that the firm pays as dividends each year.

dividend puzzle   When firms continue to issue dividends despite their tax disadvantage.

dividend signaling hypothesis The idea that dividend changes reflect managers' views about a firm's future earnings prospects.

dividend smoothing The practice of maintaining relatively constant dividends.

dividend yield The expected annual dividend of a stock divided by its current price. The dividend yield is the percentage return an investor expects to earn from the dividend paid by the stock.

domestic bonds Bonds issued by a local entity and traded in a local market, but purchased by foreigners. They are denominated in the local currency.

double-barreled Describes municipal bonds for which the issuing local or state government has strengthened its promise to pay by committing itself to using general revenue to pay off the bonds.

dual class shares When one class of a firm's shares has superior voting rights over the other class.

duration The sensitivity of a bond's price to changes in interest rates. The value-weighted average maturity of a bond's cash flows.

duration mismatch When the durations of a firm's assets and liabilities are significantly different.

duration-neutral portfolio A portfolio with a zero duration.

Dutch auction A share repurchase method in which the firm lists different prices at which it is prepared to buy shares, and shareholders in turn indicate how many shares they are willing to sell at each price. The firm then pays the lowest price at which it can buy back its desired number of shares.

dynamic trading strategy A replication strategy based on the idea that an option payoff can be replicated by dynamically trading in a portfolio of the underlying stock and a risk-free bond.

EAR *See* effective annual rate.

earnings per share (EPS) A firm's net income divided by the total number of shares outstanding.

EBIT A firm's earnings before interest and taxes are deducted.

EBIT break-even The level of sales for which a project's EBIT is zero.

EBITDA A computation of a firm's earnings before interest, taxes, depreciation, and amortization are deducted.

economic distress A significant decline in the value of a firm's assets, whether or not the firm experiences financial distress due to leverage.

economic profit The difference between revenue and the opportunity cost of all resources consumed in producing that revenue, including the opportunity cost of capital.

Economic Value Added (EVA) The cash flows of project less a capital charge that reflects the opportunity cost of the capital invested, as well as any capital consumed.

economies of scale The savings a large company can enjoy from producing goods in high volume, that are not available to a small company.

economies of scope Savings large companies can realize that come from combining the marketing and distribution of different types of related products.

effective annual rate (EAR) The total amount of interest that will be earned at the end of one year.

effective dividend tax rate The effective dividend tax rate measures the additional tax paid by the investor per dollar of after-tax capital gain income that is instead received as a dividend.

efficient capital market When the cost of capital of an investment depends only on its systematic risk, and not its diversifiable risk.

efficient frontier The set of portfolios that can be formed from a given set of investments with the property that each portfolio has the highest possible expected return that can be attained without increasing its volatility.

efficient markets hypothesis The idea that competition among investors works to eliminate all positive-NPV trading opportunities. It implies that securities will be fairly priced, based on their future cash flows, given all information that is available to investors.

efficient portfolio A portfolio that contains only systematic risk. An efficient portfolio cannot be diversified further; there is no way to reduce the volatility of the portfolio without lowering its expected return. The efficient portfolio is the tangent portfolio, the portfolio with the highest Sharpe ratio in the economy.

empirical distribution A plot showing the frequency of outcomes based on historical data.

enterprise value The total market value of a firm's equity and debt, less the value of its cash and marketable securities. It measures the value of the firm's underlying business.

EPS *See* earnings per share.

equally weighted portfolio A portfolio in which the same dollar amount is invested in each stock.

equal-ownership portfolio A portfolio containing an equal fraction of the total number of shares outstanding of each security in the portfolio. Equivalent to a value-weighted portfolio.

equity The collection of all the outstanding shares of a corporation.

equity cost of capital The expected rate of return available in the market on other investments with equivalent risk to the firm's shares.

equity holder (also shareholder or stockholder) An owner of a share of stock in a corporation.

equivalent annual benefit The annual annuity payment over the life of an investment that has the same NPV as the investment.

equivalent annual benefit method A method of choosing between projects with different lives by selecting the project with the higher equivalent annual benefit. It ignores the value of any real options because it assumes that both projects will be replaced on their original terms.

error term   Represents the deviation from the best-fitting line in a regression. It is zero on average and uncorrelated with any regressors.

ESO   *See* executive stock option.

Eurobonds   International bonds that are not denominated in the local currency of the country in which they are issued.

European options   Options that allow their holders to exercise the option only on the expiration date; holders cannot exercise before the expiration date.

EVA®   *See* Economic Value Added.

EVA investment rule   Accept any investment opportunity in which the present value of all future EVA's is positive.

evergreen credit   A revolving line of credit with no fixed maturity.

excess return   The difference between the average return for an investment and the average return for a risk-free investment.

exchange ratio   In a takeover, the number of bidder shares received in exchange for each target share.

exchange-traded fund   A security that trades directly on an exchange, like a stock, but represents ownership in a portfolio of stocks.

ex-dividend date   A date, two days prior to a dividend's record date, on or after which anyone buying the stock will not be eligible for the dividend.

executive stock option (ESO)   A common practice for compensating executives by granting them call options on their company's stock.

exercise price   *See* strike price.

exercising (an option)   When a holder of an option enforces the agreement and buys or sells a share of stock at the agreed-upon price

exit strategy   An important consideration for investors in private companies, it details how they will eventually realize the return from their investment.

expected (mean) return   A computation for the return of a security based on the average payoff expected.

expiration date   The last date on which an option holder has the right to exercise the option.

face value   The notional amount of a bond used to compute its interest payments. The face value of the bond is generally due at the bond's maturity. Also called par value or principal amount.

factor beta   The sensitivity of the stock's excess return to the excess return of a factor portfolio, as computed in a multifactor regression.

factoring of accounts receivable   An arrangement in which a firm sells receivables to the lender (i.e., the factor), and the lender agrees to pay the firm the amount due from its customers at the end of the firm's payment period.

factor portfolios   Portfolios that can be combined to form an efficient portfolio.

factors   Firms that purchase the receivables of other companies and are the most common sources for secured short-term loans.

fair market value cap lease   A type of lease in which the lessee can purchase the asset at the minimum of its fair market value and a fixed price or "cap".

fair market value (FMV) lease   A type of lease that gives the lessee the option to purchase the asset at its fair market value at the termination of the lease.

Fama-French-Carhart (FFC) factor specification   A multi-factor model of risk and return in which the factor portfolios are the market, small-minus-big, high-minus-low, and PR1YR portfolios identified by Fama, French, and Carhart.

FCFE   *See* free cash flow to equity.

federal funds rate   The overnight loan rate charged by banks with excess reserves at a Federal Reserve bank (called federal funds) to banks that need additional funds to meet reserve requirements. The federal funds rate is influenced by the Federal Reserve's monetary policy, and itself influences other interest rates in the market.

FFC factor specification   *See* Fama-French-Carhart factor specification.

field warehouse   A warehouse arrangement that is operated by a third party, but is set up on the borrower's premises in a separate area. Inventory held in the field warehouse can be used as secure collateral for borrowing.

final prospectus   Part of the final registration statement prepared by a company prior to an IPO that contains all the details of the offering, including the number of shares offered and the offer price.

financial distress   When a firm has difficulty meeting its debt obligations.

financial option   A contract that gives its owner the right (but not the obligation) to purchase or sell an asset at a fixed price at some future date.

financial security   An investment opportunity that trades in a financial market.

financial statements   Firm-issued (usually quarterly and annually) accounting reports with past performance information.

firm commitment   An agreement between an underwriter and an issuing firm in which the underwriter guarantees that it will sell all of the stock at the offer price.

firm-specific, idiosyncratic, unsystematic, unique, or diversifiable risk   Fluctuations of a stock's return that are due to firm-specific news and are independent risks unrelated across stocks.

fixed price lease   A type of lease in which the lessee has the option to purchase the asset at the end of the lease for a fixed price that is set upfront in the lease contract.

floating lien   A financial arrangement in which all of a firm's inventory is used to secure a loan.

floating rate   An interest rate or exchange rate that changes depending on supply and demand in the market.

floor planning   *See* trust receipts loan.

flow to equity (FTE)   A valuation method that calculates the free cash flow available to equity holders taking into account all payments to and from debt holders. The cash flows to equity holders are then discounted using the equity cost of capital.

FMV lease   *See* fair market value lease.

foreign bonds   Bonds issued by a foreign company in a local market and are intended for local investors. They are also denominated in the local currency.

forward contract   An agreement to trade an asset on some future date, at a price that is locked in today.

forward exchange rate   The exchange rate set in a currency forward contract, it applies to an exchange that will occur in the future.

forward earnings   A firm's anticipated earnings over the coming 12 months.

forward P/E   A firm's price-earnings (P/E) ratio calculated using forward earnings.

free cash flow   The incremental effect of a project on a firm's available cash.

free cash flow hypothesis   The view that wasteful spending is more likely to occur when firms have high levels of cash flow in excess of what is needed after making all positive-NPV investments and payments to debt holders.

free cash flow to equity (FCFE)   The free cash flow that remains after adjusting for interest payments, debt issuance, and debt repayment.

freezeout merger   A situation in which the laws on tender offers allow an acquiring company to freeze existing shareholders out of the gains from merging by forcing non-tendering shareholders to sell their shares for the tender offer price.

friendly takeover   When a target's board of directors supports a merger, negotiates with potential acquirers, and agrees on a price that is ultimately put to a shareholder vote.

FTE   *See* flow to equity.

funding risk   The risk of incurring financial distress costs should a firm not be able to refinance its debt in a timely manner or at a reasonable rate.

future value   The value of a cash flow that is moved forward in time.

futures contract   A forward contract that is traded on an exchange.

GAAP   *See* Generally Accepted Accounting Principles.

general lien   *See* floating lien.

Generally Accepted Accounting Principles (GAAP)   A common set of rules and a standard format for public companies to use when they prepare their financial reports.

general obligation bonds   Bonds backed by the full faith and credit of a local government.

global bonds   Bonds that are offered for sale in several different markets simultaneously. Unlike Eurobonds, global bonds can be offered for sale in the same currency as the country of issuance.

golden parachute   An extremely lucrative severance package that is guaranteed to a firm's senior managers in the event that the firm is taken over and the managers are let go.

goodwill   The difference between the price paid for a company and the book value assigned to its assets.

gray directors   Members of a board of directors who are not as directly connected to the firm as insiders are, but who have existing or potential business relationships with the firm.

greenmail   When a firm avoids a threat of takeover and removal of its management by a major shareholder by buying out the shareholder, often at a large premium over the current market price.

greenshoe provision (over-allotment allocation)   *See* over-allotment allocation.

gross profit   The third line of an income statement that represents the difference between a firm's sales revenues and its costs.

growing annuity   A stream of cash flows paid at regular intervals and growing at a constant rate, up to some final date.

growing perpetuity   A stream of cash flows that occurs at regular intervals and grows at a constant rate forever.

growth option   A real option to invest in the future. Because these options have value, they contribute to the value of any firm that has future possible investment opportunities.

growth stocks   Firms with high market-to-book ratios.

hedge   To reduce risk by holding contracts or securities whose payoffs are negatively correlated with some risk exposure.

high-minus-low (HML) portfolio   An annually updated portfolio that is long stocks with high book-to-market ratios and short stocks with low book-to-market ratios.

high-yield bonds   Bonds below investment grade which trade with a high yield to maturity to compensate investors for their high risk of default.

HML portfolio   *See* high-minus-low portfolio.

homemade leverage   When investors use leverage in their own portfolios to adjust the leverage choice made by a firm.

homogeneous expectations   A theoretical situation in which all investors have the same estimates concerning future investment returns.

hostile takeover   A situation in which an individual or organization, sometimes referred to as a corporate raider, purchases a large fraction of a target corporation's stock and in doing so gets enough votes to replace the target's board of directors and its CEO.

hurdle rate   A higher discount rate created by the hurdle rate rule. If a project can jump the hurdle with a positive NPV at this higher discount rate, then it should be undertaken.

hurdle rate rule   Raises the discount rate by using a higher discount rate than the cost of capital to compute the NPV, but then applies the regular NPV rule: Invest whenever the NPV calculated using this higher discount rate is positive.

idiosyncratic risk   *See* firm-specific risk.

immunized portfolio   *See* duration-neutral portfolio.

immunizing   Adjusting a portfolio to make it duration neutral.

implied volatility   The volatility of an asset's return that is consistent with the quoted price of an option on the asset.

income statement   A list of a firm's revenues and expenses over a period of time.

incremental earnings   The amount by which a firm's earnings are expected to change as a result of an investment decision.

incremental IRR investment rule   Applies the IRR rule to the difference between the cash flows of two mutually exclusive alternatives (the *increment* to the cash flows of one investment over the other).

indenture   Included in a prospectus, it is a formal contract between a bond issuer and a trust company. The trust company represents the bondholders and makes sure that the terms of the indenture are enforced. In the case of default, the trust company represents the bondholders' interests.

independent (outside) directors   *See* outside directors.

independent risk   Risks that bear no relation to each other. If risks are independent, then knowing the outcome of one provides no information about the other. Independent risks are always uncorrelated, but the reverse need not be true.

index funds   Mutual funds that invest in stocks in proportion to their representation in a published index, such as the S&P 500 or Wilshire 5000.

inefficient portfolio   Describes a portfolio for which it is possible to find another portfolio that has higher expected return and lower volatility.

information node   A type of node on a decision tree indicating uncertainty that is out of the control of the decision maker.

initial public offering (IPO)   The process of selling stock to the public for the first time.

inside directors   Members of a board of directors who are employees, former employees, or family members of employees.

insider trading   Occurs when a person makes a trade based on privileged information.

insurance premium   The fee a firm pays to an insurance company for the purchase of an insurance policy.

interest coverage ratio   An assessment by lenders of a firm's leverage. Common ratios consider operating income, EBIT, or EBITDA as a multiple of the firm's interest expenses.

interest rate factor   One plus the interest rate, it is the rate of exchange between dollars today and dollars in the future.

interest rate swap   A contract in which two parties agree to exchange the coupons from two different types of loans.

interest tax shield   The reduction in taxes paid due to the tax deductibility of interest payments.

internal rate of return (IRR)   The interest rate that sets the net present value of the cash flows equal to zero.

internal rate of return (IRR) investment rule   A decision rule that accepts any investment opportunity where IRR exceeds the opportunity cost of capital. This rule is only optimal in special circumstances, and often leads to errors if misapplied.

internationally integrated capital markets   When any investor can exchange currencies in any amount at the spot or forward rates and is free to purchase or sell any security in any amount in any country at its current market prices.

in-the-money   Describes an option whose value if immediately exercised would be positive

intrinsic value   The amount by which an option is in-the-money, or zero if the option is out-of-the-money.

inventories   A firm's raw materials as well as its work-in-progress and finished goods.

inventory days   An expression of a firm's inventory in terms of the number of days' worth or cost of goods sold that the inventory represents.

investment-grade bonds   Bonds in the top four categories of creditworthiness with a low risk of default.

invoice price   *See* dirty price.

IPO   *See* initial public offering.

IRR   *See* internal rate of return.

IRR investment rule   *See* internal rate of return investment rule.

JIT inventory management   *See* "just-in-time" inventory management.

junk bonds   Bonds in one of the bottom five categories of creditworthiness (below investment grade) that have a high risk of default.

"just-in-time" (JIT) inventory management   When a firm acquires inventory precisely when needed so that its inventory balance is always zero, or very close to it.

keiretsu   Japanese term for groups of firms connected through cross-holdings and a common relation to a bank.

key personnel insurance   A type of insurance that compensates a firm for the loss or unavoidable absence of crucial employees in the firm.

Law of One Price   In competitive markets, securities or portfolios with the same cash flows must have the same price.

LBO   *See* leveraged buyout.

lead underwriter   The primary banking firm responsible for managing a security issuance.

lease-equivalent loan   A loan that is required on the purchase of an asset that leaves the purchaser with the same net future obligations as a lease would entail.

lemons principle   When a seller has private information about the value of a good, buyers will discount the price they are willing to pay due to adverse selection.

lessee   The party in a lease liable for periodic payments in exchange for the right to use the asset.

lessor   The party in a lease who is entitled to the lease payments in exchange for lending the asset.

leverage   The amout of debt held in a portfolio or issued by a firm. *See also* buying stocks on margin.

leveraged buyout (LBO) When a group of private investors purchases all the equity of a public corporation and finances the purchase primarily with debt.

leveraged lease A lease in which the lessor borrows from a bank or other lender to obtain the initial capital to purchase an asset, using the lease payments to pay interest and principal on the loan.

leverage ratio A measure of leverage obtained by looking at debt as proportion of value, or interest payments as a proportion of cash flows.

leveraged recapitalization When a firm uses borrowed funds to pay a large special dividend or repurchase a significant amount of its outstanding shares.

levered equity Equity in a firm with outstanding debt.

liabilities A firm's obligations to its creditors.

LIBOR *See* London Inter-Bank Offered Rate.

limited liability When an investor's liability is limited to her initial investment.

limited liability company (LLC) A limited partnership without a general partner.

limited partnership A partnership with two kinds of owners, general partners and limited partners.

linear regression The statistical technique that identifies the best-fitting line through a set of points.

line of credit A bank loan arrangement in which a bank agrees to lend a firm any amount up to a stated maximum. This flexible agreement allows the firm to draw upon the line of credit whenever it chooses.

liquid Describes an investment that can easily be turned into cash because it can be sold immediately at a competitive market price.

liquidating dividend A return of capital to shareholders from a business operation that is being terminated.

liquidation Closing down a business and selling off all its assets; often the result of the business declaring bankruptcy.

liquidation value The value of a firm after its assets are sold and liabilities paid.

liquidity risk The risk of being forced to liquidate an investment (at a loss) because the cash is required to satisfy another obligation (most often a margin requirement).

LLC *See* limited liability company.

loan origination fee A bank charge that a borrower must pay to initiate a loan.

lockup A restriction that prevents existing shareholders from selling their shares for some period (usually 180 days) after an IPO.

London Inter-Bank Offered Rate (LIBOR) The rate of interest at which banks borrow funds from each other in the London interbank market. It is quoted for maturities of one day to one year for 10 major currencies.

long bonds Bonds issued by the U.S. Treasury with the longest outstanding maturities (30 years).

long position A positive investment in a security.

long-term debt Any loan or debt obligation with a maturity of more than a year.

MACRS depreciation The most accelerated cost recovery system allowed by the IRS. Based on the recovery period, MACRS depreciation tables assign a fraction of the purchase price that the firm can depreciate each year.

mail float How long it takes a firm to receive a customer's payment check after the customer has mailed it.

management buyout A leveraged buyout in which the buyer is the firm's own management.

management discussion and analysis (MD&A) A preface to the financial statements in which a company's management discusses the recent year (or quarter), providing a background on the company and any significant events that may have occurred.

management entrenchment A situation arising as the result of the separation of ownership and control in which managers may make decisions that benefit themselves at investors' expense.

management entrenchment theory A theory that suggests managers choose a capital structure to avoid the discipline of debt and maintain their own job security.

margin Collateral that investors are required to post when buying or selling securities that could generate losses beyond the initial investment.

marginal corporate tax rate The tax rate a firm will pay on an incremental dollar of pre-tax income.

marketable securities Short-term, low-risk investments that can be easily sold and converted to cash (such as money market investments, like government debt, that mature within a year).

market capitalization The total market value of equity; equals the market price per share times the number of shares.

market index The market value of a broad-based portfolio of securities.

market makers Individuals on the trading floor of a stock exchange who match buyers with sellers.

market portfolio A value-weighted portfolio of all shares of all stocks and securities in the market.

market proxy A portfolio whose return is believed to closely track the true market portfolio.

market risk *See* systematic risk.

market-to-book ratio (price-to-book [PB] ratio) The ratio of a firm's market (equity) capitalization to the book value of its stockholders' equity.

market value balance sheet similar to an accounting balance sheet, with two key distinctions: First, all assets and liabilities of the firm are included, even intangible assets such as reputation, brand name, or human capital that are missing from a standard accounting balance sheet; second, all values are current market values rather than historical costs.

marking to market Computing gains and losses each day based on the change in the market price of a futures contract.

martingale prices *See* risk-neutral probabilites.

matching principle   States that a firm's short-term needs should be financed with short-term debt and long-term needs should be financed with long-term sources of funds.

maturity date   The final repayment date of a bond.

MD&A   *See* management discussion and analysis.

merger-arbitrage spread   In a takeover, the difference between a target stock's price and the implied offer price.

merger waves   Peaks of heavy activity followed by quiet troughs of few transactions in the takeover market.

method of comparables   An estimate of the value of a firm based on the value of other, comparable firms or other investments that are expected to generate very similar cash flows in the future.

momentum strategy   Buying stocks that have had past high returns, and (short) selling stocks that have had past low returns.

Monte Carlo simulation   A common technique for pricing derivative assets in which the expected payoff of the derivative security is estimated by calculating its average payoff after simulating many random paths for the underlying stock price. In the randomization, the risk neutral probabilities are used, and so the average payoff can be discounted at the risk-free rate to estimate the derivative security's value.

moral hazard   When purchasing insurance reduces a firm's incentive to avoid risk.

mortgage bonds   A type of secured corporate debt. Real property is pledged as collateral that bondholders have a direct claim to in the event of bankruptcy.

mortgage interest rate   The rate on a risk-free annuity that is prepayable (callable) at any time; the yield on mortgage-backed bonds such as a GNMA.

multifactor model   A model that uses more than one risk factor to capture risk. Also referred to as Arbitrage Pricing Theory (APT).

multiple of money   *See* cash multiple.

multiple regression   A regression with more than one independent variable.

municipal bonds   Bonds issued by state and local governments. They are not taxable at the federal level (and sometimes at the state and local level as well) and so are sometimes also referred to as tax-exempt bonds.

mutually exclusive projects   Projects that compete with one another; by accepting one, the others cannot be accepted.

net debt   Total debt outstanding minus any cash balances.

net income or earnings   The last or "bottom line" of a firm's income statement that is a measure of the firm's income over a given period of time.

net present value (NPV)   The difference between the present value of a project or investment's benefits and the present value of its costs.

Net Present Value (NPV) Investment Rule   When making an investment decision, take the alternative with the highest NPV. Choosing this alternative is equivalent to receiving its NPV in cash today.

net profit margin   The ratio of net income to revenues, it shows the fraction of each dollar in revenues that is available to equity holders after the firm pays interest and taxes.

net working capital   The difference between a firm's current assets and current liabilities that represents the capital available in the short term to run the business.

95% confidence interval   A confidence interval gives a range of values which is likely to include an unknown parameter. If independent samples are taken repeatedly from the same population, then the true parameter will lie outside the 95% confidence interval 5% of the time. For a normal distribution, the interval corresponds to approximately 2 standard deviations on both sides of the mean.

no-arbitrage price   In a normal market, when the price of a security equals the present value of the cash flows paid by the security.

nominal interest rates   Interest rates quoted by banks and other financial institutions that indicate the rate at which money will grow if invested for a certain period of time.

non-tax lease   A type of lease in which the lessee receives the depreciation deductions for tax purposes, and can also deduct the interest portion of the lease payments as an interest expense. The interest portion of the lease payment is interest income for the lessor.

normal market   A competitive market in which there are no arbitrage opportunities.

notes   A type of unsecured corporate debt. Notes typically are coupon bonds with maturities shorter than 10 years.

notional principal   Used to calculate the coupon payments in an interest rate swap.

NPV   *See* net present value.

NPV Investment Rule   *See* Net Present Value Investment Rule.

NPV Decision Rule   When choosing among investment alternatives, take the alternative with the highest NPV. Choosing this alternative is equivalent to receiving its NPV in cash today.

off-balance sheet transactions   Transactions or arrangements that can have a material impact on a firm's future performance yet do not appear on the balance sheet.

OID (original issue) discount   *See* original issue discount.

on-the-run bonds   The most recently issued treasury security of a particular original maturity.

open interest   The total number of contracts of a particular option that have been written.

open market repurchase   When a firm repurchases shares by buying its shares in the open market.

operating cycle   The average length of time between when a firm originally receives its inventory and when it receives the cash back from selling its product.

operating income   A firm's gross profit less its operating expenses.

operating lease   A type of lease, viewed as a rental for accounting purposes, in which the lessee reports the entire lease payment as an operating expense. The lessee does not deduct a depreciation expense for the asset and does not report the asset, or the lease payment liability, on its balance sheet.

operating margin   The ratio of operating income to revenues, it reveals how much a company has earned from each dollar of sales before interest and taxes are deducted.

opportunity cost   The value a resource could have provided in its best alternative use.

opportunity cost of capital   The best available expected return offered in the market on an investment of comparable risk and term to the cash flow being discounted; the return the investor forgoes on an alternative investment of equivalent riskiness and term when the investor takes on a new investment.

option delta   The change in the price of an option given a $1 change in the price of the stock. The number of shares in the replicating portfolio for the option.

option writer   The seller of an option contract.

original issue discount (OID)   Describes a coupon bond that is issued at a discount

out-of-the-money   Describes an option that if exercised immediately, results in a loss of money.

outside (independent) directors   Any member of a board of directors other than an inside or gray director.

over-allotment allocation (greenshoe provision)   On an IPO, an option that allows the underwriter to issue more stock, usually amounting to 15% of the original offer size, at the IPO offer price.

overhead expenses   Those expenses associated with activities that are not directly attributable to a single business activity but instead affect many different areas of a corporation.

over-investment problem   When a firm faces financial distress, shareholders can gain at the expense of bondholders by taking a negative-NPV project, if it is sufficiently risky.

par   A price at which coupon bonds trade that is equal to their face value.

partnership   A sole proprietorship with more than one owner.

passive portfolio   A portfolio that is not rebalanced in response to price changes.

pass-through security   Describes securities whose payments derive directly from other assets like mortgages.

payable date (distribution date)   A date, generally within a month after the record date, on which a firm mails dividend checks to its registered stockholders.

payback investment rule   The simplest investment rule. Only projects that pay back their initial investment within the payback period are undertaken.

payback period   A specified amount of time used in the payback investment rule. Only investments that pay back their initial investment within this amount of time are undertaken.

payout policy   The way a firm chooses between the alternative ways to pay cash out to equity holders.

P/E   *See* price-earnings ratio.

pecking order hypothesis   The idea that managers will prefer to fund investments by first using retained earnings, then debt and equity only as a last resort.

perfect capital markets   A set of conditions in which investors and firms can trade the same set of securities at competitive market prices with no frictions such as taxes, transaction costs, issuance costs, asymmetric information, or agency costs.

permanent working capital   The amount that a firm must keep invested in its short-term assets to support its continuing operations.

perpetuity   A stream of equal cash flows that occurs at regular intervals and lasts forever.

pledging of accounts receivable   An agreement in which a lender accepts accounts receivable as collateral for a loan. The lender typically lends a percentage of the value of the accepted invoices.

poison pill   A defense against a hostile takeover. It is a rights offering that gives the target shareholders the right to buy shares in either the target or an acquirer at a deeply discounted price.

policy limits   Those provisions of an insurance policy that limit the amount of loss that the policy covers regardless of the extent of the damage.

pool   An underlying portfolio of assets that back a pass-through security.

portfolio insurance   A protective put written on a portfolio rather than a single stock. When the put does not itself trade, it is synthetically created by constructing a replicating portfolio.

portfolio weights   The fraction of the total investment in a portfolio held in each individual investment in the portfolio.

post-money valuation   At the issue of new equity, the value of the whole firm (old plus new shares) at the price the new equity is sold at.

precautionary balance   The amount of cash a firm holds to counter the uncertainty surrounding its future cash needs.

preferred stock   Preferred stock issued by mature companies such as banks usually has a preferential dividend and seniority in any liquidation and sometimes special voting rights. Preferred stock issued by young companies has seniority in any liquidation but typically does not pay cash dividends and contains a right to convert to common stock.

preliminary prospectus (red herring)   Part of the registration statement prepared by a company prior to an IPO that is circulated to investors before the stock is offered.

premium   A price at which coupon bonds trade that is greater than their face value. Also, the price a firm pays to purchase insurance, allowing the firm to exchange a random future loss for a certain upfront expense.

pre-money valuation   At the issuance of new equity, the value of a firm's prior shares outstanding at the price in the funding round.

prepackaged bankruptcy   A method for avoiding many of the legal and other direct costs of bankruptcy in which a firm first develops a reorganization plan with the agreement of its main creditors, and then files Chapter 11 to implement the plan.

prepayment option   An abandonment option that allows a mortgage holder to pay off a mortgage before the end of its scheduled term.

present value (PV)   The value of a cost or benefit computed in terms of cash today.

pretax WACC   The weighted average cost of captial computed using the pretax cost of debt; it can be used to estimate the unlevered cost of captial for a firm that maintains a target leverage ratio.

price-earnings ratio (P/E)   The ratio of the market value of equity to the firm's earnings, or its share price to its earnings per share.

price-to-book (PB) ratio   *See* market-to-book ratio.

price-weighted portfolio   A portfolio that holds an equal number of shares of each stock, independent of their size.

primary offering   New shares available in a public offering that raise new capital.

primary shares   New shares issued by a company in an equity offering.

prime rate   The rate banks charge their most creditworthy customers.

principal or face value   The notational amount used to compute a bond's interest payments; in many cases also the final principal payment on the maturity date of a bond.

principal-agent problem   A problem that arises when employyees in control (the agents) act in their own interest rather than in the interest of the owners (the principals).

PR1YR   *See* prior one-year momentum portfolio.

prior one-year momentum (PR1YR) portfolio   A self-financing portfolio that goes long on the top 30% of stocks with the highest prior year returns, and short on the 30% with the lowest prior year returns, each year.

private company   A company whose shares do not trade on a public market.

private debt   Debt that is not publicly traded.

private placement   A bond issue that is sold to a small group of investors rather to the general public. Because a private placement does not need to be registered, it is less costly to issue.

processing float   How long it takes a firm to process a customer's payment check and deposit it in the bank.

probability distribution   A graph that provides the probability of every possible discrete state.

profitability index   Measures the NPV per unit of resource consumed.

profitability index rule   Recommends investment whenever the profitability index exceeds some predetermined number.

pro forma   Describes a statement that is not based on actual data but rather depicts a firm's financials under a given set of hypothetical assumptions.

project externalities   Indirect effects of a project that may increase or decrease the profits of other business activities of a firm.

promissory note   A written statement that indicates the amount of a loan, the date payment is due, and the interest rate.

property insurance   A type of insurance companies purchase to compensate them for losses to their assets due to fire, storm damage, vandalism, earthquakes, and other natural and environmental risks.

protective put   A long position in a put option held on a stock you already own.

proxy fight   In a hostile takeover, when the acquirer attempts to convince the target's shareholders to unseat the target's board by using their proxy votes to support the acquirers' candidates for election to the target's board.

public companies   Those corporations whose stock is traded on a stock market or exchange, providing shareholders the ability to quickly and easily convert their investments in to cash.

public warehouse   A business that exists for the sole purpose of storing and tracking the inflow and outflow of inventory. If a lender extends a loan to a borrowing firm, based on the value of the inventory, this arrangement provides the lender with the tightest control over the inventory.

pure discount bonds   Zero-coupon bonds.

put option   A financial option that gives its owner the right to sell an asset for a fixed price up to (on a) a fixed date.

put-call parity   The relationship that gives the price of call option in terms of the price of put option plus the price of the underlying stock minus the present value of the strike price and the present value of any dividend payments.

PV   *See* present value.

pyramid structure   A way for an investor to control a corporation without owning 50% of the equity whereby the investor first creates a company in which he has a controlling interest. This company then owns a controlling interest in another company. The investor controls both companies, but may own as little as 25% of the second company.

quick ratio   The ratio of current assets other than inventory to current liabilities.

raider   The acquirer in a hostile takeover.

rational expectations   The idea that investors may have different information regarding expected returns, correlations, and volatilities, but they correctly interpret that information and the information contained in market prices and adjust their estimates of expected returns in a rational way.

real interest rate   The rate of growth of purchasing power after adjusting for inflation.

realized return The return that actually occurs over a particular time period.

real option The right to make a particular business decision, such as a capital investment. A key distinction between real options and financial options is that real options, and the underlying assets on which they are based, are often not traded in competitive markets.

record date When a firm pays a dividend, only shareholders of record on this date receive the dividend.

red herring *See* preliminary prospectus.

refinance Repaying an existing loan and then taking out a new loan at a lower rate.

registered bonds The issuer of this type of bond maintains a list of all holders of its bonds. Coupon and principal payments are made only to people on this list.

registration statement A legal document that provides financial and other information about a company to investors, prior to a security issuance.

regression A statistical technique that estimates a linear relationship between two variables (the dependent and independent variable) by fitting a line that minimizes the squared distance between the data and the line.

repatriated Refers to the profits from a foreign project that a firm brings back to its home country.

replicating portfolio A portfolio consisting of a stock and a risk-free bond that has the same value and payoffs in one period as an option written on the same stock.

required return The expected return of an investment that is necessary to compensate for the risk of undertaking the investment.

residual value An asset's market value at the end of a lease.

retained earnings The difference between a firm's net income and the amount it spends on dividends.

retention rate The fraction of a firm's current earnings that the firm retains.

return The difference between the selling price and purchasing price of an asset plus any cash distributions expressed as a percentage of the buying price.

return of capital When a firm, instead of paying dividends out of current earnings (or accumulated retained earnings), pays dividends from other sources, such as paid-in capital or the liquidation of assets.

return on assets (ROA) The ratio of net income to the total book value of the firm's assets.

return on equity (ROE) The ratio of a firm's net income to the book value of its equity.

revenue bonds Municipal bonds for which the local or state government can pledge as repayment revenues generated by specific projects.

reverse split When the price of a company's stock falls too low and the company reduces the number of outstanding shares.

revolving line of credit A credit commitment for a specific time period, typically two to three years, which a company can use as needed.

rights offer A type of seasoned equity offering (SEO) in which a firm offers the new shares only to existing shareholders.

risk-arbitrageurs Traders who, once a takeover offer is announced, speculate on the outcome of the deal.

risk aversion When investors prefer to have a safe future payment rather than an uncertain one of the same expected amount.

risk-free interest rate The interest rate at which money can be borrowed or lent without risk over a given period.

risk-neutral probabilities The probability of future states that are consistent with current prices of securities assuming all investors are risk neutral. Also known as state-contingent prices, state prices, or martingale prices.

risk premium Represents the additional return that investors expect to earn to compensate them for a security's risk.

ROA *See* return on assets.

road show During an IPO, when a company's senior management and its underwriters travel around the country (and sometimes around the world) promoting the company and explaining their rationale for an offer price to the underwriters' largest customers, mainly institutional investors such as mutual funds and pension funds.

ROE *See* return on equity.

"S" corporations Those corporations that elect subchapter S tax treatment and are allowed, by the U.S. Internal Revenue Tax code, an exemption from double taxation.

sale and lease back Describes a type of lease in which a firm already owns an asset it would prefer to lease. The firm receives cash from the sale of the asset and then makes lease payments to retain the use of the asset.

sales-type lease A type of lease in which the lessor is the manufacturer (or a primary dealer) of the asset.

Samurai bonds A term for foreign bonds in Japan.

scenario analysis An important capital budgeting tool that determines how the NPV varies as a number of the underlying assumptions are changed simultaneously.

seasoned equity offering (SEO) When a public company offers new shares for sale.

secondary offering An equity offering of secondary shares.

secondary shares Shares sold by existing shareholders in an equity offering.

secured debt (loan) A type of corporate loan or debt security in which specific assets are pledged as a firm's collateral.

security interest A classification of a lease in bankruptcy proceedings that assumes a firm has effective ownership of an asset and the asset is protected against seizure.

security market line (SML) The pricing implication of the CAPM, it specifies a linear relation between the risk premium of a security and its beta with the market portfolio.

segmented capital markets Capital markets that are not internationally integrated.

self-financing portfolio   A portfolio that costs nothing to construct.

seniority   A bondholder's priority in claiming assets not already securing other debt.

sensitivity analysis   An important capital budgeting tool that determines how the NPV varies as a single underlying assumption is changed.

SEO   *See* seasoned equity offering.

Separate Trading of Registered Interest and Principal Securities (STRIPS)   *See* STRIPS.

Separation Principle   In a perfect market, the NPV of an investment decision can be evaluated separately from any financial transactions a firm is considering.

serial bonds   A single issue of municipal bonds that are scheduled to mature serially over a period of years.

shareholder (also stockholder or equity holder)   An owner of a share of stock in a corporation.

shareholders' equity, stockholders' equity   An accounting measure of a firm's net worth that represents the difference between the firm's assets and its liabilities.

share repurchase   A situation in which a firm uses cash to buy back its own stock.

Sharpe ratio   The excess return of an asset divided by the volatility of the return of the asset; a measure of the reward per unit risk.

short interest   The number of shares sold short.

short position   A negative amount invested in a stock.

short sale   Selling a security you do not own.

signaling theory of debt   The use of leverage as a way to signal information to investors.

simple interest   Interest earned without the effect of compounding.

single-factor model   A model using an efficient portfolio, capturing all systemic risk alone.

sinking fund   A method for repaying a bond in which a company makes regular payments into a fund administered by a trustee over the life of the bond. These payments are then used to repurchase bonds.

size effect   The observation that small stocks (or stocks with a high book-to-market ratio) have higher returns.

small-minus-big (SMB) portfolio   A portfolio resulting from a trading strategy that each year buys a small market value portfolio and finances that position by selling short a large market value portfolio.

SMB portfolio   *See* small-minus-big portfolio.

SML   *See* security market line.

sole proprietorship   A business owned and run by one person.

sovereign debt   Debt issued by national governments.

SPE   *See* special-purpose entity.

special dividend   A one-time dividend payment a firm makes that is usually much larger than a regular dividend.

specialists   Individuals on the trading floor of the NYSE who match buyers with sellers; also called market makers.

special-purpose entity (SPE)   A separate business partnership created by a lessee for the sole purpose of obtaining a lease.

speculate   When investors use securities to place a bet on the direction in which they believe the market is likely to move.

speculative bonds   Bonds in one of the bottom five categories of creditworthiness that have a high risk of default.

spin-off   When a firm sells a subsidiary by selling shares in the subsidiary alone.

spot exchange rate   The current foreign exchange rate.

spot interest rates   Default-free, zero-coupon yields.

spread   The fee a company pays to its underwriters that is a percentage of the issue price of a share of stock.

staggered (classified) board   In many public companies, a board of directors whose three-year terms are staggered so that only one-third of the directors are up for election each year.

stakeholder model   The explicit consideration most countries (other than the United States) give to other stakeholders besides equity holders, in particular, rank-and-file employees.

standard deviation   A common method used to measure the risk of a probability distribution, it is the square root of the variance, the expected squared deviation from the mean.

standard error   The standard deviation of the estimated value of the mean of the actual distribution around its true value; that is, it is the standard deviation of the average return.

state prices   See risk-neutral probabilities.

state-contingent prices   See risk-neutral probabilities.

statement of cash flows   An accounting statement that shows how a firm has used the cash it earned during a set period.

statement of stockholders' equity   An accounting statement that breaks down the stockholders' equity computed on the balance sheet into the amount that came from issuing new shares versus retained earnings.

step up   Refers to an increase in the book value of a target's assets to the purchase price when an acquirer purchases those assets directly instead of purchasing the target stock.

stock   The ownership or equity of a corporation divided into shares.

stock dividend   *See* stock split.

stockholder (also shareholder or equity holder)   An owner of a share of stock or equity in a corporation.

stockholder's equity   *See* shareholder's equity.

stock exchanges (stock markets)   *See* stock markets.

stock markets (also stock exchanges)   Organized markets on which the shares of many corporations are traded.

stock options   A form of compensation a firm gives to its employees that gives them the right to buy a certain number of shares of stock by a specific date at a specific price.

stock split (stock dividend)   When a company issues a dividend in shares of stock rather than cash to its shareholders.

stop-out yield   The highest yield competitive bid that will fund a particular U.S. Treasury security issue when all successful bidders (including the noncompetitive bidders) are awarded this yield.

straddle   A portfolio that is long a call and a put on the same stock with the same exercise date and the strike price.

straight-line depreciation   A method of depreciation in which an asset's cost is divided equally over its life.

strangle   A portfolio that is long a call and a put with the same exercise date but the strike price of the call exceeds the strike price of the put.

strategic investor   *See* corporate investor.

strategic partner   *See* corporate investor.

stream of cash flows   A series of cash flows lasting several periods.

stretching the accounts payable   When a firm ignores a payment due period and pays later.

strike (exercise) price   The price at which an option holder buys or sells a share of stock when the option is exercised.

STRIPS (Separate Trading of Registered Interest and Principal Securities)   Zero-coupon Treasury securities with maturities longer than one year that trade in the bond market.

subordinated debenture   Debt that, in the event of a default, has a lower priority claim to the firm's assets than other outstanding debt.

sunk cost   Any unrecoverable cost for which a firm is already liable.

syndicate   A group of underwriters who jointly underwrite and distribute a security issuance.

syndicated bank loan   A single loan that is funded by a group of banks rather than just a single bank.

synthetic lease   A lease that commonly uses a special-purpose entity (SPE) and is designed to obtain specific accounting and tax treatment.

systematic, undiversifiable, or market risk   Fluctuations of a stock's return that are due to market-wide news representing common risk.

takeover   Refers to two mechanisms, either a merger or an acquistion, by which ownership and control of a firm can change.

tangent portfolio   A portfolio with the highest Sharpe ratio; the point of tangency to the efficient frontier of a line drawn from the risk-free asset; the market portfolio if the CAPM holds.

target   A firm that is acquired by another in a merger or acquisition.

targeted repurchase   When a firm purchases shares directly from a specific shareholder.

target leverage ratio   When a firm adjusts its debt proportionally to a project's value or its cash flows (where the proportion need not remain constant). A constant market debt-equity ratio is a special case.

tax loss carryforwards and carrybacks   Two features of the U.S. tax code that allow corporations to take losses during a current year and offset them against gains in nearby years. Since 1997, companies can "carry back" losses for two years and "carry forward" losses for 20 years.

temporary working capital   The difference between the actual level of short-term working capital needs and its permanent working capital requirements.

tender offer   A public announcement of an offer to all existing security holders to buy back a specified amount of outstanding securities at a prespecified price over a prespecified period of time.

term   The time remaining until the final repayment date of a bond.

terminal value (*See also* continuation value)   The value of a project's remaining free cash flows beyond the forecast horizon. This amount represents the market value (as of the last forecast period) of the free cash flow from the project at all future dates.

term loan   A bank loan that lasts for a specific term.

term structure   The relationship between the investment term and the interest rate.

timeline   A linear representation of the timing of (potential) cash flows.

time value   The difference between an option's price and its intrinsic value.

time value of money   The difference in value between money today and money in the future; also, the observation that two cash flows at two different points in time have different values.

TIPS (Treasury-Inflation-Protected Securities)   An inflation-indexed bond issued by the U.S. Treasury with maturities of 5, 10, and 20 years. They are standard coupon bonds with one difference: The outstanding principle is adjusted for inflation.

toehold   An initial ownership stake in a firm that a corporate raider can use to initiate a takeover attempt.

tombstone   A newspaper advertisement in which an underwriter advertises a security issuance.

total payout model   A firm's total payouts to equity holders (i.e., all the cash distributed as dividends and stock repurchases) are discounted and then divided by the current number of shares outstanding to determine the share price.

total return   The sum of a stock's dividend yield and its capital gain rate.

trade credit   The difference between receivables and payables that is the net amount of a firm's capital consumed as a result of those credit transactions; the credit that a firm extends to its customers.

tradeoff theory   The firm picks its capital structure by trading off the benefits of the tax shield from debt against the costs of financial distress and agency costs.

trailing earnings   A firm's earnings over the prior 12 months.

trailing P/E   The computation of a firm's P/E using its trailing earnings.

tranches   Different classes of securities that comprise a single bond issuance. All classes of securities are paid from the same cash flow source.

transaction cost   In most markets, an expense such as a broker commission and the bid-ask spread investors must pay in order to trade securities.

transactions balance   The amount of cash a firm needs to be able to pay its bills.

Treasury bills   Zero-coupon bonds, issued by the U.S. government, with a maturity of up to one year.

Treasury bonds   A type of U.S. Treasury coupon securities, currently traded in financial markets, with original maturities of more than ten years.

Treasury Inflation-Protected Securities (TIPS)   *See* TIPS.

Treasury notes   A type of U.S. Treasury coupon securities, currently traded in financial markets, with original maturities from one to ten years.

true lease   A classification of a lease in bankruptcy proceedings in which the lessor retains ownership rights over an asset.

true tax lease   A type of lease in which the lessor receives the depreciation deductions associated with the ownership of the asset. The lessee can deduct the full amount of the lease payments as an operating expense, and these lease payments are treated as revenue for the lessor.

trust receipts loan   A type of loan in which distinguishable inventory items are held in a trust as security for the loan. As these items are sold, the firm remits the proceeds from their sale to the lender in repayment of the loan.

tunneling   A conflict of interest that arises when a shareholder who has a controlling interest in multiple firms moves profits (and hence dividends) away from companies in which he has relatively less cash flow rights toward firms in which he has relatively more cash flow rights.

uncommitted line of credit   A line of credit that does not legally bind a bank to provide the funds a borrower requests.

under-investment problem   A situation in which equity holders choose not to invest in a positive NPV project because the firm is in financial distress and the value of undertaking the investment opportunity will accrue to bondholders rather than themselves.

underwriter   An investment banking firm that manages a security issuance and designs its structure.

undiversifiable risk   *See* systematic risk.

unique risk   *See* firm-specific risk.

unlevered beta   Measures the risk of a firm were it unlevered; beta of the firm's assets; measures the market risk of the firm's business activities, ignoring any additional risk due to leverage.

unlevered cost of capital   The cost of capital of a firm, were it unlevered; for a firm that maintains a target leverage ratio, it can be estimated as the weighted average cost of capital computed without taking into account taxes (pre-tax WACC).

unlevered equity   Equity in a firm with no debt.

unlevered net income   Net income plus after-tax interest expense.

unlevered P/E ratio   The enterprise value of a firm divided by its unlevered net income in a particular year.

unsecured debt   A type of corporate debt that, in the event of a bankruptcy, gives bondholders a claim to only the assets of the firm that are not already pledged as collateral on other debt.

unsystematic risk   *See* firm-specific risk.

valuation multiple   A ratio of a firm's value to some measure of the firm's scale or cash flow.

value additivity   A relationship determined by the Law of One Price, in which the price of an asset that consists of other assets must equal the sum of the prices of the other assets.

value stocks   Firms with low market-to-book ratios.

value-weighted portfolio   A portfolio in which each security is held in proportion to its market capitalization. Also called an equal-ownership portfolio, because it consists of the same fraction of the outstanding shares of each security.

variance   A method to measure the risk of a probability distribution, it is the expected squared deviation from the mean.

venture capital firm   A limited partnership that specializes in raising money to invest in the private equity of young firms.

venture capitalist   One of the general partners who work for and run a venture capital firm.

vertical integration   Refers to the merger of two companies in the same industry that make products required at different stages of the production cycle. Also, the merger of a firm and its supplier or a firm and its customer.

volatility   The standard deviation of a return.

WACC   *See* weighted average coast of capital.

warehouse arrangement   When the inventory that serves as collateral for a loan is stored in a warehouse.

warrant   A call option written by the company itself on new stock. When a holder of a warrant exercises it and thereby purchases stock, the company delivers this stock by issuing new stock.

weighted average cost of capital (WACC)   The average of a firm's equity and after-tax cost of capital, weighted by the fraction of the firm's enterprise value that corresponds to equity and debt, respectively. Discounting free cash flows using the WACC computes their vaule including the interest tax shield.

white knight   A target company's defense against a hostile takeover attempt, in which it looks for another, friendlier company to acquire it.

white squire   A variant of the white knight defense, in which a large, passive investor or firm agrees to purchase a substantial block of shares in a target with special voting rights.

winner's curse   Refers to a situation in competitive bidding when the high bidder, by virtue of being the high bidder, has very likely overestimated the value of the item being bid on.

with recourse A loan or lease in which the lender can claim all the borrower's assets in the event of a default not just explicitly pledged collateral.

without recourse A loan or lease in which the lender's claim on the borrower's assets in the event of a default is limited to only explicitly pledged collateral.

workout A method for avoiding a declaration of bankruptcy in which a firm in financial distress negotiates directly with its creditors to reorganize.

Yankee bonds A term for foreign bonds in the United States.

yield curve A plot of bond yields as a function of the bonds' maturity date.

yield to call (YTC) The yield of a callable bond calculated under the assumption that the bond will be called on the earliest call date.

yield to maturity (YTM) The IRR of an investment in a bond that is held to its maturity date.

YTC *See* yield to call.

YTM *See* yield to maturity.

zero-coupon bond A bond that makes only one payment at maturity.

zero-coupon yield curve A plot of the yield of risk-free zero-coupon bonds (STRIPS) as a function of the bond's maturity date.

Credits

Back cover and p. xxii: Photo of authors overlooking the Financial District, San Francisco, CA: ©2006 Nancy Warner.

p. 395: Nobel Prize: William Sharpe on the CAPM, excerpts from "Revisiting the Capital Asset Pricing Model," Jonathan Burton, *Dow Jones Asset Manager*, May/June 1998, pp. 20–28.

p. 403: Figure 13.1, "Excess Return of Size Portfolios (1926–2005)," Historical return data from Kenneth French's Web site.

p. 404: Figure 13.2, "Excess Return of Book-to-Market Portfolios (1926–2005)," Historical return data from Kenneth French's Web site.

p. 414: Table 13.1: "FFC Portfolio Average Monthly Returns (1926–2005), Historical return data from Kenneth French's Web site.

p. 420: Figure 13.5, "How Firms Calculate the Cost of Capital," reprinted from "The Theory and Practice of Corporate Finance: Evidence from the Field," J. R. Graham and C. R. Harvey, *Journal of Financial Economics* 60 (©2001), pp. 187–243, with permission from Elsevier.

p. 479: Figure 15.7, "Debt-to-Value Ratio $[D/(E + D)]$ for Select Industries," data from Reuters, 2005.

p. 564: Figure 17.8, "Distribution of Stock Prices for NYSE Firms (April 2005)," data from Reuters, April 2005.

p. 757: Table 23.2, "Largest Global Equity Issues, 2004," reprinted from "Underwriting Volume Rises to a Record," Diya Gullapalli, *Wall Street Journal*, January 3, 2005, p. R17.

p. 762: Figure 23.2, "The Cover Page of RealNetworks' IPO Prospectus," courtesy RealNetworks, Inc.

p. 766: Figure 23.3, "International Comparison of First-Day IPO Returns," courtesy Professor Jay Ritter, University of Florida.

p. 768: Figure 23.4, "Cyclicality of Initial Public Offerings in the United States, (1975–2004)," courtesy Professor Jay Ritter, University of Florida.

p. 769: Figure 23.5, "Relative Costs of Issuing Securities," adapted from "The Costs of Raising Capital"; I. Lee, S. Lochhead, J. Ritter, and Q. Zhao; *Journal of Financial Research* 19(1) (1996), 59–74.

p. 771: Figure 23.6, "Tombstone Advertisement for a RealNetworks SEO," courtesy RealNetworks, Inc.

p. 773: Figure 23.7, "Post-SEO Performance," adapted from "Is the Abnormal Return Following Equity Issuances Anomalous?" C. Geczy, and P. Gompers, *Journal of Financial Economics* 56 (©2000), 209–249, with permission from Elsevier.

p. 781: Figure 24.1, "Front Cover of the Offering Memorandum of the Hertz Junk Bond Issue," courtesy Hertz Corporation.

p. 782: Figure 24.2, "A Bearer Bond and Its Unclipped Coupons Issued by the Elmira and Williamsport Railroad Company for $500," couresy Heritage Auctions, Inc. ©1999–2006. www.heritageAuctions.com.

Index

Page numbers in boldface refer to boldface
terms in the text. Figures, tables, examples,
and boxed text are indicated by italicized
f, t, e, and *b.*

A (market value of firm assets), 438, 710, 954
A (premerger total value of acquirer), 884
Abandonment option, **731**–34
    to prepay, 733–34
    to shutdown, 731–33
Accelerated depreciation, 192*e*
    MACRS and 209, 210*t*
Accounting
    leases and, 808–10
    manipulation of, 37–38
    takeover process and, 887
Accounts payable, **23**
    management of, 838–40
Accounts receivable, **22**
    as collateral, 863–64
    monitoring, 836–38
Accounts receivable days, **29**, 836–37
    calculation of, 29, 628
Accrued interest, 215 n.3
Acquirer (bidder), **873**
Acquisition premium, **875**, 876*t*
Acquisitions. *See* Mergers and acquisitions
Actuarially fair, **927**
Actuarially Fair Insurance Premium
        equation, 927
Adelphia Communications, scandal at, 509*b*
Adjusted beta, **389**
Adjusted beta equation, 389
Adjusted present value (APV) method of
        valuation, **581**–85
    with alternative leverage policies, 593–97
    comparison of WACC and FTE methods
        to, 596–97
    example, 585*e*
    Ideko case study of equity value, 643–44
    permanent debt and, 604–5*e*
    with personal taxes, 607–8*e*
    summary of, 584–85
    unlevered value of project and, 582–83
    valuing interest tax shield, 583–84
Adverse selection, **514**
    cost of insurance and, 930, 931–32*e*
    equity issuance and, 514–17
    price reaction to seasoned equity offering
        and, 772, 773
After-tax borrowing lease borrowing rate, 817
After-tax interest equation, 633
After-tax interest rate, **139**–40
    comparing, 140*e*
Agency benefits of leverage, 507–10
Agency conflict, managing, 908–11
    controlling owners and pyramids, 916–19
    direct shareholder actions and, 909–10
    management entrenchment, 910–11
Agency costs, **503**, 599
    of cash retention, 553–55

corporate governance and, 904
    insurance costs and, 931
    of leverage, 503–7
    lowering, by leasing, 821
    tradeoff theory and, 511–12
Agency securities, **788**
Aggarwal, Reena, 764 n.12
Aggressive financing policy, **858**
Aging schedules, **837***t*, 838*e*
Air Alaska Group, Inc., operating leases
        at, 808*b*
Airline companies. *See also names of individual
        airline companies*
    commodity (jet fuel) price risk for, 933,
        934, 939*b*
    equity betas and market debt-equity ratios
        for stocks of, 443–44*e*
    indirect costs of financial distress, 496–97
    loan guarantees for, after September 11,
        2001 terrorist attacks, 598*b*
Air Transportation Safety and System
        Stabilization Act, 598*b*
Air Transportation Stabilization Board
        (ATSB), 598*b*
Akerlof, George, 515*b*
Alchian, Armen A., 821 n.16
Allen, F., 547 n.17, 556 n.25
Almeida, H., 919 n.23
Alpha of stock, **373**–74, 383–84
    implication of positive, 406–9
    Jensen's, 383 n.7
α_i (alpha of security *i*), 382, 383
α_s (alpha of security *s*), 637
α_s (alpha of stock *s*), 409
Alternative investment decision rules, 151–61
Altman, Edward, 496 n.5
Amazon.Com, stock options on, 658, 662–64
    portfolio insurance, 666, 667*f*
    quotes for, 657*t*, 658
American Airlines, 29, 510
American Electronics Association, 914 n.16
American options, **656**
    arbitrage bounds on, 670
    early exercise of, 671–76
    option prices and exercise date, 670–71
American Stock Exchange (AMEX), 13
Amgen company, 459
Amihud, Y., 897 n.17
Amortization, **23**, 27 n.4
    earnings before, 30
Amortizing loan, **130**
Andrade, Gregor, 498, 876
Angel investors, **752**
Anheuser-Busch Companies, 283, 310
    changes in expected returns of, 373–74
Annema, A., 390 n.14
Annual percentage rate (APR), 126 n.1,
        127–29
    continuously compounded, for EAR, 147
    converting, to discount rate, 129*e*
    converting, to EAR, 128

discount rates for continuously
        compounded, 147
    EAR (effective annual rate) for continuously
        compounded, 147
Annual percentage yield (APY), 126 n.1.
        See also Effective annual rate (EAR)
Annual report, **20**
Annuity(ies), **98**–101
    future value of, 101
    growing, 104–6
    mistake of using equation for, when
        discount rates vary, 135*b*
    present value of, 99, 100
    present value of lottery prize, 100*e*
    retirement savings plan, 101*e*
Annuity due, 100 n.6
Annuity spreadsheet, **107**. *See also*
        Spreadsheets
    bond prices, 216, 217
    computing bond price from yield to
        maturity, 217
    computing internal rate of return with, 113*e*
    internal rate of return rule, 153
    notation, 83
    solving for coupon bond yields, 226
    solving for variables other than present
        value or future value, 108–16
    using, 107–8*e*
Antioco, John, 910*b*
Antitrust laws, 878–79, 891–92
Apple Computer, 63*b*, 878
APR. *See* Annual percentage rate (APR)
APV. *See* Adjusted present value (APV)
        method of valuation
APV Formula, 582
Arbitrage, 48, 59–61
    bond, 224–28
    definition, **60**
    homemade leverage and, 434–35*e*
    Law of One Price and, 60–61
    leverage, firm value, and, 432–37
    merger, 885–87
    option prices and, 670
    security prices and no arbitrage, 61–67
    stock index, 66*b*
    with transaction costs, 73–74
    yield rates and bond, 224–28
Arbitrage opportunity, 59, **60**
    call option price as, 687 n.3
    joke about, 60*b*
    Law of One Price and, 60–61
    share repurchase as, 468–69
Arbitrage Pricing Theory (APT), **410**
Arithmetic average of returns, 296*b*
Armin Industry
    impact of financial distress costs for,
        499–500
    leverage and risk of default, 492–93, 494*e*
    value of debt and equity of, with and
        without leverage, 493*t*
Ask price, **13**, 73 n.8

Asquith, Paul, 517 n.37
Asset(s), **21**–23
    current, 21–22
    efficiency gains from specialization in
        ownership of, 821
    financial distress linked to fire sales of, 497
    long-term, 22–23
    missing, in valuation process, 644b
    opportunity cost of idle, 183b
    reducing resale costs of, by leasing, 820
    return on, 30
    valuing, in portfolios, 67e
Asset-backed bonds, **782**, 783t
Asset substitution, 504 n.17
Assumptions, best and worst case, 197t, 198f
Asymmetric information, **512**–20
    capital structure, implications for, 517–20
    equity issuance, implications of, 517
    equity issuance and adverse selection,
        514–17
    leverage as credible signal, 513–14
At-the-money, **657**
Auction IPO, **758**
    Google's, 760b
    pricing of, 759e
Auditing firms, 912
Auditor, **21**
Auerbach, A. J., 553 n.22
Auto lease payments, calculating, 806b
Availability float, **835**
Average annual return, **292**–93
    for small stocks, large stocks,
        corporate bonds, and treasury bills
        (1926–2004), 293t
Average Annual Return of a Security
    equation, 292
Avco, Inc., valuation example, 577–78, 579e

B (risk-free investment in replicating
    portfolio), 687, 702
Bachelier, Louis, 659 n.1
Backdating, **908**
Baker, Malcolm P., 520 n.42
Baker, Nardin, 418
Balance sheet, **21**–27
    analysis of, 25–26
    assets, 21–23
    financial model-building using, 634–36
    leasing and, 809e
    liabilities, 23–24
    market value (see Market value balance
        sheet)
    stockholders' equity, 24–25
Balance sheet analysis, 25–27
    current, and quick ratios, 26–27
    debt-equity ratio, 25–26
    enterprise value, 26
    financial distress, and costs of, 494–98
    market-to-book ratio, 25
    sample, 22t
Balance Sheet Identity equation, 21
Ballmer, Steve, 754
Balloon payment, **794**
Balson, Andrew, on leverage and tax advantage
    of debt, 484b
Banker's acceptances, as short-term investment
    options, 843t

Bank loans, 785–86. *See also* Loan(s)
    short-term financing with, 859–62
Bankruptcy, 11–12, 483–84
    capital structure and, 493
    costs of, 494–96, 881
    default and, in perfect market, 492–93
    firm value and risk of, 494e
    insurance and, 928–29
    leases and, 811–13
    prepackaged, 496
Bankruptcy code, 494–95
Bankruptcy Reform Act of 1978, 495
Banz, Rolf, 403, 404
Bartter, B. J., 686 n.2
Basic risk, 938
Bautista, Alberto, 815 n.13
Bearer bonds, **782**
Bebchuk, L. A., 919 n.23
Benartzi, Shlomo, 408b, 557 n.29
Berenek, W., 858 n.3
Berens, J. L., 481 n.16
Berk, J. B., 315 n.18, 404 n.3, 415 n.16,
    727 n.2, 740 n.7, 745 n.7
Berkshire Hathaway, Class A and Class B
    shares at, 561b
Berman, Dennis, 873 n.1
Bertrand, M., 919 n.23
Best-efforts basis, **758**
"Best fitting line," 382
Beta (β), **308**, 380–83
    adjusted, 389
    for airline company stocks, 443–44e
    estimating, 307–9
    debt, 443 n.5
    estimating from historical returns, 380–82
    expected returns and, 311e
    forecasting, 388–90
    of financial options, 707–10
    levered, and unlevered, 442–44
    market risk and, 368, 369e
    Microsoft Corporation dividend, cash,
        and, 444b
    of portfolio, 372, 442, 443
    required return and, 349–51
    of risky debt, 710–12
    S&P 500 stocks, 309t
    unlevering, 637–38
    using linear regression to estimate, 382–83
Beta β_B (beta of the bond), 708
Beta β_D (beta of debt), 442, 443, 637, 710
Beta β_E (beta of levered equity), 442, 443,
    637, 710
Beta β_s^i (beta of stocks with portfolio i), 411
Beta β_L (beta of insured loss), 928
Beta β_i^{Mkt} (beta of security I with respect
    to the market portfolio), 368, 369, 380
Beta β_{option} (beta of an option), 708
Beta β_i^P (beta or sensitivity of investment I
    to fluctuations of portfolio P), 350
Beta β_s (beta of the stock), 637, 708
Beta β_U (beta of unlevered equity), 442, 443,
    623, 710, 711
Beta of portfolio equations, 372, 442, 443
Beta of Portfolio i with Portfolio P
    equation, 350
Betker, Brian, 496 n.5
Biais, B., 834 n.3

Bid-ask spread, **13**
Bidder (acquirer), **873**
Bid price, **13**, 73 n.8
Binomial Option Pricing Model, **686**–94
    binomial pricing formula, 688–90
    making realistic, 693–94
    multiperiod model, 690–92
    two-state single-period model, 686–88
    valuing put option with, 692–93e
Binomial pricing formula, 688–90
Binomial tree, **686**–87, **690**–91
Bird in the hand hypothesis, **540**
Black, F., 544 n.12, 549 n.20, 676 n.6
Black, Fischer, 383 n.7, 386 n.10, 544 n.12,
    549 n.20, 676 n.6, 685. *See also*
    Black-Scholes Option Pricing Model
Black, Lisa, on bond valuation, 230b
Black-Scholes formula, 694–700
Black-Scholes Option Pricing Model, 685,
    694–704
    Black-Scholes formula and, 694–700
    growth options and, 727
    implied volatility and, 701–2
    option value parameters for evaluating real
        option to invest, 722t
    replicating portfolio and, 702–4
Black-Scholes Price of a Call Option
    on a Non-Dividend Pricing Model
    equation, 694
Black-Scholes Replicating Portfolio of a Call
    Option equation, 702
Black-Scholes Replicating Portfolio of a Put
    Option equation, 704
Blanket lien, **864**–65
Bliss, Robert R., 243 n.5
Blockbuster's company, shareholder activism
    at, 910b
Bloomberg, estimation methods used by, 389t
Blume, M., 389 n.13, 403 n.2
Board of directors, 9, **10**, 904–6
    independence of, 905–6
    size and performance of, 906
    staggered/classified, 890
    takeover process and approval of, 887–88
    types of directors on, 905
Boeing Company, 83, 730
Bogle, John, on index funds and ETF
    funds, 378b
Bolton, Patric, 510 n.29
Bond(s), **61**. *See also* Corporate bond(s);
        Government bond(s)
    asset-backed, 782, 783t
    callable, 734, 789, 792
    cash flows and market prices of risk-free, 68t
    convertible, 28, 734, 794–95
    coupon [*see* Coupon bond(s)]
    coupons (interest payments) on, 212
    covenants, 789
    determining interest rate from prices of, 64
    double-barreled, 788
    duration, 222
    equation for returns on, 64
    general obligation, 788
    high-yield, 231
    historical returns of, 289–97
    interest-rate sensitivity of, 222–23e
    international, 784–85

investment-grade, 231
junk, 231, 783, 784*t*
long, 786–87
maturity date, term, and face value of, 212
mortgage 782, 783*t*
municipal, 788
perpetual, 95, 97*b*
ratings of, 231, 232*t*
repayment provisions for, 789–96
revenue, 788
risky international government, 978–79*e*
serial, 788
speculative, 231
using risk premium to calculate price of, 72*e*
valuation of (*see* Bond valuation)
zero-coupon [*see* Zero-coupon bond(s)]
Bond certificate, **212**
Bond prices, 217–24
    callable, and uncallable bonds, 791*f*, 792*f*
    clean, and dirty, 221*b*
    following coupon payment, 218*t*
    interest rate changes and, 221–24
    risk premium and, 72*e*
    time and, 218–21
    yields and, 224–28
Bond valuation, 211–44
    L. Black on, 230*b*
    corporate bonds, 228–33
    coupon bonds, 214–17, 221*b* [*see also*
        Coupon bond(s)]
    data case, 239–40
    discounts and premiums, 217–18
    dynamic behavior of bond prices, 217–24
    forward interest rates and, 241–44
    problems, 235–39
    summary, 233–34
    terminology, 212
    yield curve and bond arbitrage, 224–28
    zero-coupon bonds, 212–14 [*see also*
        Zero-coupon bond(s)]
Book building, **763**
Book-to-market ratio, **403**
Book value, **22**
Book value of equity, **24**–25
    market value versus, 24*e*
Borrowing
    leasing versus, 815–17
    mergers/acquisitions and cost of, 881
    risk-free saving and, 345–49
    savings rates versus rates of, 384–86
    tradeoffs of long-term and short-term, 958*t*
Boyd, J., 548 n.18
Bradley, M., 876 n.3
Brander, James, 510 n.29
Brav, Alon, 558 n.33, 773 n.22
Break-even, **196**
    EBIT, 197
Break-even analysis, 196–97
Brennan, M., 386 n.9, 543 n.9, 737 n.4
Bridge loan, **860**
Brown, F. E., 315 n.17
Bruner, F., 363 n.1
Bruner, Robert, 391 n.15
Budget, capital, 178. See also Capital
        budgeting
Buffett, Warren, 561*b*
Bulldogs, **784**

Burton, Jonathan, 395 n.
Bush, George W., 475*b*, 598*b*
Business interruption insurance, **926**
Business liability insurance, **926**
Business plan, 626–29
    capital expenditures for needed expansion,
        627, 628*t*
    capital structure changes and levering up,
        628–29
    operational improvements, 626–27
Butterfly spread, **666***f*
Buy, lease versus, 814–15
Buying stocks on margin, **346**–47
Buy-out candidates, valuing. *See* Financial
        modeling, case study of
Byrd, J., 905 n.2

C. See Cash flow (C)
C (call option price), 659, 668, 689, 723
C_n (cash flow at date *n*), 92, 158, 159
C_t (cash flow on date *t*), 951
Cadbury, Adrian, 914
Cadbury Commission, 914–15
Cahart, M., 315 n.19, 413, 415, 415 n.15.
        See also Fama-French-Carhart (FFC)
        factor specification
California Public Employees' Retirement
        System (Calpers), 12
Callable bonds, 734, **789**, 791–92
    calculating yield to call, 792–93*e*
Call date, **790**
Call option, **656**
    on Amazon.com stocks, 657*t*, 658
    Black-Scholes formula and valuing,
        695–96*e*, 697*f*, 698*f*
    Black-Scholes replicating portfolio of,
        702–3*e*
    equity as, 676, 677*f*
    on General Electric stock, 674–75*e*
    investment as, 721–23
    parity with put options, 668–69
    payoff of, 659*f*
    profit from holding, to expiration, 662*f*
    short position in, at expiration, 661*e*
    warrant, 794
Call price, **790**
Call Value at Expiration equation, 659
Campbell, John Y., 243 n.5
Cannibalization, **183**
CapEx. *See* Capital expenditures (CapEx)
Capital
    computing divisional costs of, 591*e*
    cost of (*see* Cost of capital)
    human, 408
    investment, 158–60 (*see also* Capital
        budgeting)
    net working, 23, 187–88
    opportunity cost of, 140–41
    raising equity (*see* Equity capital, mechanics
        of raising)
Capital Asset Pricing Model (CAPM), **312**,
        313, 363–400
    assumptions of, 364–65
    cost of capital estimations based on, 636–37
    data case, 400
    determining beta, 380–83
    determining risk premium, 368–75

estimating cost of capital using, 636–37
    evidence regarding, 392–94
    extending, 383–88
    forecasting beta, 388–90
    identifying efficiency of market portfolio,
        364–68
    identifying market portfolio and use of,
        375–79
    insurance pricing and, 928*e*
    major conclusions of, 374–75
    as most commonly used, 419–21
    in practice, 388–95
    problems, 398–99
    security market line and, 370–72, 390–92
    W. Sharpe on, 395*b*
    summary, 396–97
    with two-stocks, 365–66*e*
Capital budget, 178
Capital budgeting, **178**–210
    advanced topics in, 600–608
    analyzing projects and, 196–99
    data case, 207–8
    determining free cash flow and NPV,
        186–95
    discounted free cash flow model and,
        260–61
    with exchange-rate risk, 981–83
    forecasting earnings, 178–85
    D. Grannis on, 179*b*
    MACRS depreciation and, 192, 209–10
    problems, 201–6
    simplifying assumptions of, applied to
        valuation, 576–77
    summary, 200
    weighted average cost of capital and,
        439–42
Capital budgeting with leverage and market
        imperfections, 575–622
    adjusted present value method of valuation,
        581–85
    advanced topics in capital budgeting and,
        600–608
    APV with other leverage policies, 593–97
    data case, 617–18
    effects of financing, accounting for,
        597–600
    flow-to-equity method of valuation,
        585–88
    overview, 576–77
    problems, 611–17
    project-based costs of capital and, 589–93
    summary, 609–10
    weighted average cost of capital method
        of valuation, 577–81, 619–22
Capital cash flows (CCF), 584 n.6
Capital expenditures (CapEx), **33**
    aggregate sources of funding for,
        U.S. corporations, 519*f*
    earnings forecast and, 180
    equation, 641
    for expansion, business plan and, 627–28
    free cash flow and, 186
Capital gain, **247**
    on stocks, 247
    taxes on, 541, 542*t*
    taxing as income, 193
Capital gain rate, **247**

Capital lease, **23, 809**
  operating lease versus, 810*e*
Capital market(s), **313**
  efficient, 313–15
  internationally integrated, 970–71
  internationally segmented, 977–81
  perfect (*see* Perfect capital markets)
Capital markets line (CML), **366**–67
  choosing CML portfolio, 367*e*, 368*f*
  security market line and, 370–71*f*
Capital structure, 425, **428**
  asymmetric information and, 512–20
  bankruptcy and, 493
  debt and distress and (*see* Financial distress)
  debt and taxes and [*see* Debt and taxes; Leverage; Tax(es)]
  equity issuance and, 517–20
  fallacies of, 445–49
  Law of One Price and, 425, 427
  management entrenchment theory of, 512
  optimal, with taxes, 476–84
  payout policy (*see* Payout policy)
  recapitalization, as takeover defense, 890–91
  review, 520–21
  tradeoff theory and optimal, 501–3
Capital structure in perfect market, 427–57
  capital structure facilities and, 445–49
  data case, 456–57
  equity versus debt financing and, 428–32
  Modigliani-Miller proposition 1 on leverage, arbitrage, and firm value, 432–37
  Modigliani-Miller proposition 2 on leverage, risk, and cost of capital, 437–45
  Modigliani-Miller propositions, influence of, 449–50
  problems, 453–56
  summary, 451–52
CAPM. *See* Capital Asset Pricing Model (CAPM)
Captured board, **906**
Carey, Susan, 801 n.2
Carleton, W., 909 n.11
Carlson, Murray, 773 n.21, 773 n.22
Carlyle Group, 780 n.2
Cash. *See also* Cash flow (C); Cash values
  as current asset, 21–22
  dividends paid with excess, 535–36
  firms with large balances of, 555*t*
  management of, 841–44
  merger/acquisition offers in, 884–85
  Microsoft Corporation dividend, beta, and, 444*b*
  as negative debt, 592
  net debt and, 444–45
  net present value as equivalent to, 56*e*
  retention of, versus payout, 549–55
Cash-and-carry strategy, **944**
  pricing of currency forwards and, 943–46
  using, 945–46*e*
Cash balances, corporate liquidity and, 844*b*
Cash before delivery (CBD), 840
Cash conversion cycle (CCC), **830**
Cash cycle, **830**–31
Cash flow (C)
  comparing and combining values of, 85
  continuously arriving, 147–48
  of coupon bond, 215*e*

for debt and equity of levered firms, 429*t*
  discounting risky, 139*e*
  equation for future value of, 86
  equation for present value of, 88
  financing needs for shocks in, 854–56
  free [*see* Free cash flow (FCF)]
  growing, 101–6
  impact of depreciation on, 34*e*
  of investors, after taxes, 472*f*
  IRR rule and timing of, 164
  of levered and unlevered firms, 463*f*
  moving, back in time, 87–88
  moving, forward in time, 86
  project free cash flow and timing of, 192
  risky, versus risk-free, 68
  short sales and, 340*b*
  solving for, 109–11
  statement of (*see* Statement of cash flows)
  stream of (*see* Stream of cash flows)
  timing of, 164, 165*f*
  for true tax lease, 813–14
  for unlevered equity, 429*t*
  valuation of foreign currency, 971–76
  valuing monthly, 127*e*
  valuing projects with continuous, 148*e*
Cashing out, 505
Cash management, 841–44
  alternative investments, 842, 843*t*
  motivation for holding cash, 842
Cash multiple (multiple of money, absolute return), **647**
  internal rate of return and, 645–47
Cash multiple equation, 647
Cash offer, **771**–72
Cash on delivery (COD), 840
Cash retention
  agency costs of, 553–55
  financial distress costs and, 553
  with perfect capital markets, 549–50
  taxes and, 550–53
Cash values
  calculating, using market prices, 48–50
  calculating, with unavailable competitive market prices, 50
  present value and net present value, 54–59
  using market prices to determine, 48–49, 50*e*
CCC. *See* Cash conversion cycle (CCC)
"C" corporations, **9**
Celmax Corporation, 603*e*
Certain default on bonds, 228–29
Certificates of deposit (CDs), as short-term investment option, 843*t*
Chaebol, 919
Chapter 7 liquidation, **495**
Chapter 11 reorganization, **495**
Characteristic variable model of expected returns, 415–19
  described, **416**
  MSCI Barra model, 416, 417*t*, 418*t*
  returns of portfolios ranked by, 419*f*
Characteristic Variable Model of Stock Returns equation, 417
Charkham, J., 921 n.24
Check Clearing for the 21st Century Act (Check 21), **835**
Chen, Hsuan-Chi, 769 n.15
Chevalier, J., 315 n.18

Chevalier, Judy, 510 n.29
Chew, D., 557 n.30
Chicago Board Options Exchange (CBOE), 655, 656
Chief executive officer (CEO), 9, **10**
  performance of, 11
Choi, S., 858 n.3
Cisco Systems, 149, 563
  cash and beta of, 445*e*
  debt financing at, 593*e*
  estimating beta from historical returns, 380, 381*f*, 382, 383
Clayton, Dubilier & Rice (CDR), 646, 779, 780 n.2, 783
Clayton Act of 1914, 891
Clean price of bonds, 215 n.3, **221***b*
Clements, Jonathan, on portfolio optimization, 354*b*
Clientele effect, **547**
Clientele groups, taxes and investors in, 547–49
CML. *See* Capital markets line (CML)
Coca Cola Company, 324
  two-stock portfolio including Intel Corporation and, 335–44
Coles, J., 909 n.10
Collection float, **835**
Comment, R., 559 n.35, 889 n.11
Commercial paper, short-term financing with, 843*t*, **862**–63
  effective annual rate of, 862–63*e*
Commitment, leverage and, 510
Commitment fees, 860
Committed line of credit, **859**–60
Commodity price risk, 933–39
  deciding to hedge, 938–39
  hedging with future contracts, 935–38
  hedging with long-term contracts, 934–35
  hedging with vertical integration and storage, 933
Common mistakes
  bird in the hand fallacy, 540*b*
  continuation values and long-run growth, 643*b*
  debt versus equity, 441*b*
  discounting one too many times, perpetuities and, 98*b*
  Excel spreadsheet's NPV and IRR functions, 115*b*
  fallacy of long-run diversification, 306*b*
  hedging risk, 938*b*
  investing in own company stock, 408*b*
  mismatched ratios, 30*b*
  missing assets or liabilities, 644*b*
  opportunity cost of idle asset, 183*b*
  re-levering WACC, 592*b*
  share repurchases and supply of shares, 538*b*
  using annuity formula when discount rates vary, 135*b*
  valuing employee stock options, 699*b*
Common risk, **301**
  independent risk versus, 299–302
Compaq, merger with Hewlett Packard, 885, 886*f*, 887
Comparables, valuation using, 624–26
  of IPOs, 763*e*
Compensating balance, **842**
  requirements for, on loans, 861, 862*e*

Compensation, management, 652, 906–8
Competition
   efficient markets and, 268–70
   empirical evidence on capital market,
      313–15
   information, stock prices and, 266–72
   value added in takeovers and, 897
Competitive market, **49**
Compound annual returns, 296*b*
Compounding, **86**, 90–91
   power of, 91*f*
   rule of 72 and, 116*b*
Compound interest, **86**
Concorde effect, 185*b*
Connors, John, on Microsoft dividends, 562*b*
Conservation of value principle, **450**
Conservative financing policy, **858**
Consol, **95**
Consolidated Edison, Inc. (ConEd), valuation
      of, 250*e*
Constant dividend growth, **249**–50, 253
Constant Dividend Growth Model equation,
      249–50
Constantinides, G. M., 547 n.17, 556 n.25
Constant interest coverage ratio, **594**–95
Constitution, U.S., protections for
      corporations under, 3–4, 7
Continuation (terminal) value, **194**
   debt capacity and, 581*t*
   discounted cash flow approach to, 640–42
   discounted cash flow estimate of, 641–42*e*
   mistakes regarding long-run growth
      and, 643*b*
   multiples approach to, 639–40
   with perpetual growth, 194*e*
Continuous compounding, **128**
Continuously Compounded APR for an EAR
      equation, 147
Contracts
   hedging with forward, 941–43
   hedging with future, 935–38
   hedging with long-term, 934, 935*e*
Contracts on financial options, 656
   long position in, 659–60
   short position in, 660–62
Covenants (bond), **789**
Conversion price, **794**
Conversion ratio, **794**
Convertible bonds, 28, 734, **794**
   value of, 795*f*
Convertible preferred stock, **755**
Convexity and interest rate sensitivity,
      956 n.20
Cook, D., 558 n.32
Cooper, M., 415 n.13
Cootner, P. H., 659 n.1
Copeland, T., 563 n.36
Cornwell, C., 858 n.3
Corporate bond(s), **228**–33, 284, 780–85
   average annual returns for
      (1926–2004), 293*t*
   bearer, 782
   L. Black on valuation of, 230*b*
   bond markets, 784–85
   callable, 734, 789, 792
   convertible, 734, 794
   empirical distribution of (1926–2004), 292*f*
   historical interest rates on, 733*f*, 734

prospectus of, 780–82
   ratings, 231, 232*t*
   registered, 782
   seniority of, 783–84
   value of investments in, 284, 285*f*
   volatility of (1926–2004), 294*t*
   volatility versus excess return of
      (1926–2004), 297*t*
   yield curves, 231, 233*f*
   yields, 228–31
Corporate debt, 780–86
   private debt, 785–86
   public debt, 780–85
Corporate governance, 903–23
   agency costs and, 904
   compensation policies, 906–8
   defined, **904**
   L. E. Harris on Sarbanes-Oxley
      regulations, 913*b*
   international, 916–21
   managing agency conflict, 908–11
   monitoring by board of directors, 904–6
   problems, 923
   regulations and, 911–14
   summary, 921–22
   tradeoffs of, 921
Corporate investor, **753**
Corporate management team, 10
Corporate partner, **753**
Corporate raiders, 11
Corporate scandals
   accounting manipulation and reporting
      abuses, 37–38, 912
   excessive perks and, 509*b*
Corporate taxes, 8–9. *See also* Tax(es)
   double taxation and, 475*b*
   weighted average cost of capital with
      and without, 466*t*
Corporation(s), 1, 7–8, 3–17. *See also* Firm(s)
   debt-to-value ratio of U.S.
      (1975–2005), 478*f*
   definition of, **7**
   formation of, 7
   four types of firms including, 4–9
   net external financing and capital
      expenditures by U.S., 477*f*
   ownership of, 7–8
   ownership versus control of, 9–12
   problems, 16–17
   stock markets and, 12–14
   summary, 15
   taxation of, 8–9
   D. Viniar on partnerships and, 6*b*
Corr(R_i,R_j) (correlation between returns
      of *i* and *j*), 327, 328, 329, 330, 370
Correlation, **327**
   computing covariance from, 330*e*
   determining covariance and, 326–30
   efficient portfolio and, 338–39
   historical annual volatilities and, for selected
      stocks, 329*t*
   volatility of portfolio and effects of, 338–39
Cost(s)
   agency (*see* Agency costs)
   of bankruptcy, 494–96
   of capital (*see* Cost of capital)
   comparing, at different points in time, 53*e*
   estimates of, 178

of financial distress, firm value and,
      498–500
   of financial distress, indirect, 496–98
   financing, 597
   of issuing IPOs, 769–70
   of holding inventory, 841
   of insurance, 930–32
   of issuing securities, 769*f*
   opportunity, 140, 141, 182, 183
   of seasoned equity offering, 774
   sensitivity to marketing and support, 198*e*
   sunk, 184, 185*b*
   of trade credit, 833, 834*e*
   transaction [*see* Transaction cost(s)]
   valuing benefits and, 48–51
Costa, Len, 889 n.9
Cost of capital, **141**. *See also* Opportunity
      cost of capital
   CAPM and [*see* Capital Asset Pricing
      Model (CAPM)]
   computing, 312*e*, 355*e*
   efficient portfolio and, 352–55
   equity (*see* Equity cost of capital)
   estimating, 589–90, 636–39
   Fama-French-Carhart (FFC) factor
      specification and calculation of, 413,
      414–15*e*
   internationalizing, 975*e*
   leverage and, 603–5
   levered and unlevered, 620–21
   models for calculating, 420*f*
   project-based, 589–93
   reducing leverage and, 441–42*e*
   risk and, 311–13
   security market line and estimation of,
      390–92
   unlevered, 638–39
   weighted average [*see* Weighted average cost
      of capital (WACC)]
Cost of Capital for Investment *i* equation, 353
Cost of Capital of a Project equation, 311
Cost of Capital of Levered Equity
      equation, 438
Cost of goods sold (COGS), 187
Costs and benefits, valuing, 48–51
   unavailable market prices and, 50
   using market prices to determine cash
      values, 48–50
Cote, J., 911 n.13
Cotter, J., 905
Coupon(s), **212**
Coupon bond(s), **214**–17
   bond prices following coupon
      payment, 218*t*
   cash flows of, 215*e*
   clean and dirty prices for, 221*b*
   computing duration of, 951*t*
   computing price of, from yield to maturity,
      216–17*e*
   determining discount or premium of,
      217, 218*e*
   effect of time on price of, 219, 220*f*
   inflation-indexed, 787*e*
   replicating cash flows of, 224–25
   valuing, using zero-coupon yields, 225–26
   yield to maturity, 215, 216*e*, 226–27
Coupon-paying yield curve, **227**
Coupon Payment equation, 212

Coupon rate, **212**
Cov(R_i,R_j) (covariance between returns
    of *i* and *j*), 327, 328, 329, 372, 380
Covariance, **327**
    computing from correlation, 330*e*
    determining correlation and, 326–30
Covariance between Returns *R_i* and *R_j*
    equation, 327
Covenants, debt maturity and, 506–7
Covered interest parity equation, **944**
Cox, J., 686 n.2
CPN (coupon payment on a bond), 212, 225
"Cram down" reorganization plan, 495 n.3
Crawford, Robert G., 821 n.16
Credibility principle, **513**
Credit
    collection policy for, 836
    evergreen, 860
    line of, 859–60
    revolving line of, 785, 860
    standards for, 836
Creditors
    bankruptcy and, 495–96
    costs of firm's financial distress to, 498
    restrictions (debt covenants) by, 507
Credit policy, determining, 836
Credit rating, debt issuance and targeting,
    594 n.15
Credit risk, **228**
    on bond yields, 228
    eliminating, by hedging with futures
        contracts, 936–37
Credit spread, **138**, **231**
Credit terms, 836
Crown Zellerbach, 889
Cum-dividend, **536**, 539
Cummins, Chip, 873 n.1
Cumulative normal distribution, **694**, 695*f*
Cuny, C. J., 481 n.16
Currency, valuing cash flows of foreign,
    971–76
Currency exchange rates. *See* Exchange rate(s)
Currency forward contract, **941**
Currency forwards, pricing of, 943–46
Currency options, hedging with, 946–50
    of conditional exposure, 947–48*e*
    forward contracts versus, 946–48
    option pricing, 949
Currency swaps, **978**
Currency timeline, **943**
Current assets, 21–22
Current liabilities, **23**
Current ratios, **26**
Customers, financial distress and loss of,
    496–98
Cyclicality of initial public offerings (IPOs),
    in U.S., 767, 768*f*

d (debt-to-value ratio), 580
D (market value of debt), 437, 439, 440, 464,
    501, 502, 511, 577, 596, 710
D_p (duration of security or portfolio *P*),
    955 n.19
D^s (debt net of predetermined tax shields), 604
D_t (incremental debt of project on date *t*), 580
Dahya, J., 915 n.19
Dartmouth College, 3

Dasgupta, S., 510 n.28
Data snooping bias, **404**
Dealer paper, **862**
DeAngelo, H., 481 n.17
Debentures, **782**, 783*t*
    subordinated, 783
Debt. *See also* Debt and taxes; Debt financing;
        Leverage
    agency securities, 788
    APV and WACC methods with permanent,
        604–5*e*
    A. Balson on tax advantage of, 484*b*
    beta of risky, 710, 711–12*e*
    calculating beta of risky, 710–12
    calculating yield on new corporate,
        678–79*e*
    capacity for (*see* Debt capacity)
    cash and net, 444–45
    common mistake regarding equity
        versus, 441*b*
    computing WACC and defining, 589*b*
    corporate, 780–86
    determining actual tax advantage of,
        475–76
    effective tax advantage of, 473*e*, 474*f*
    growth and, 481
    increasing capacity of, by leasing, 821
    interest tax shield with permanent, 463–65
    limits to tax benefits of, 478–80
    loans and [*see* Loan(s)]
    long-term, 23
    market value of, 26 n.3
    municipal bonds, 788
    optimal level of, 502–3*e*, 511–12
    as option portfolio, 677–79
    periodically adjusted, 601–3
    planned, and levering up, 628–29
    predetermined levels of, 595–96
    preference of firms for, 476–78
    private, 785–86
    as signal of strength, 514*e*
    sovereign, 786–88
    ratio of value to (*see* Debt-to-value ratio)
    tradeoff theory and, 512
    systematic risk and risk premiums for
        unlevered equity, levered equity,
        and, 431*t*
Debt and taxes, 459–90
    data case, 490
    interest tax deduction, 460–62
    optimal capital structure with, 476–84
    personal, 471–76
    problems, 486–89
    recapitalizing capture tax shield, 468–71
    summary, 485
    valuing interest tax shield, 462–67
Debt betas, 442–43
Debt capacity, **580**–81
    expected, 583*t*
    insurance and, 930
    mergers/acquisitions and increased, 881
Debt covenants, **507**
Debt-equity ratio, **25**–26
    book, 594 n.15
    equation, 25
    implementation of constant, 580–81
    survey of firms', 601*f*

Debt financing, 779–99
    bond covenants, **789**
    at Cisco Systems, 593*e*
    corporate debt, 780–86
    data case, 799
    with equity, 429–30
    fixed payout policy and, 592–93
    problems, 798–99
    repayment provisions, 789–96
    sovereign debt, 786–88
    summary, 796–97
Debt holders, exploiting, 503–7
Debt levels, predetermined, 595–96
Debt maturity, covenants and, 506–7
Debt overhang, 505 n.18
Debt schedule, predetermined, 621
Debt-to-value ratio, **440**
    for select industries, 479*f*
    of U.S. firms (1975–3005), 477, 478*f*
Decision making. *See* Financial decision
        making; Investment decision rules
Decision node, **719**
Decision tree, **718**–20
    building, 747–48
    mapping uncertainties on, 719–20
    for real options, 720, 728*f*, 732*f*, 736*f*
Declaration date, **532**
Deductible (insurance), **931**
Deep in-the-money, **658**
Deep out-of-the-money, **658**
Default, **492**
    bankruptcy and, in perfect market, 492–94
    certain, 228
    risk of, 229–31
Default spread, **231**
Deferred taxes, **24**
Delaney, Kevin, 760 n.
Delayed investments, internal rate of return
        decision rule and, 153–54
Delphi Automotive Systems, 290 n.1
Dell Inc., 73, 331, 925
Delta ΔNWC (increase in net working capital
        between year *t* and year *t* − 1), 188
Delta Δ (shares of stock in replication of
        portfolio; sensitivity of option price to
        stock price), 687
Delta Δ (credit spread on date *t*), 958
Delta Air Lines, 340*b*, 510, 939*b*
Demand, efficiency of market portfolio
        and supply equaling, 365–66
DeMarzo, P., 387 n.11, 621 n.28
Demsetz, H., 909 n.9
Denis, D. K., 921 n.24
Depreciation, **22**
    accelerated, 192
    free cash flow and, 186
    impact of, on cash flow, 34*e*
    incremental earnings forecast,
        capital expenditures and, 180
    MACRS, 192, 209–10
    straight-line, 180
Depreciation tax shield, **189**
Derivative security, 653, **707**
Desai, A., 876 n.3
Deutsche Bank Securities, 47
D.F. Builders (DFB), 461–62*e*
Dhar, R., 563 n.36

Diluted EPS, **28**
Dilution, **28**, **448**
   fallacy of equity, share issuances and, 448–49
   warrant call option and, 794 n.9
Dimensional Fund Advisors, 412
Direct lease, **802**
Direct paper, **862**
Dirty price, **221**
dis (discount from face value), 672
Disbursement float, **835**
Discount(s), bond, **212**, 217–18
Discounted cash flow, estimate of continuation value and, 641*e*, 642*t*
Discounted free cash flow model, **258**–61
   comparison of, to valuation multiples, 264–65
   connection to capital budgeting, 260
   continuation value and, 640–42
   enterprise valuation and, 258
   implementation of, 258–60
Discounted Free Cash Flow Model equation, 258, 259
Discount factor, **53**
Discounting, **87**–88
   risky cash flows, 139*e*
Discount loan, **860**
Discount rate (*r*), **53**
   adjusting, to different time periods, 126–27
   for continuously compounded APR, 147
   converting APR to, 129*e*
   loans and, 130–31
   mistake of using annuity formula with varying, 135*b*
   NPV plotted as function of, 150, 151*f*, 153, 154*f*
   for present value of cash flow stream using term structure of, 135
   yield curve and, 133–35
Discount rate for security *s* (r_s), 72
Disney. *See* Walt Disney Company
Distress. *See* Financial distress
Distribution date (payable date), **532**
Dittmar, A., 544 n.11
Dittmar, R., 544 n.11
Div (dividend), 674
Div_t (dividends paid in year *t*), 246, 249, 250, 289
Diversification, **301**
   as averaging out of independent risks, 301–2
   fallacy of long-run, 306*b*
   gambling and, 302*e*
   R. Lert on, 314*b*
   mergers/acquisitions and benefits of, 880–81
Diversification in stock portfolios, 303–7
   with equally weighted portfolio of many stocks, 332–34
   fallacy of long-term, 306*b*
   firm-specific versus systematic risk and, 303–5
   with general portfolios, 334–35
   no arbitrage, risk premium, and, 305–7
   risk versus return and efficient portfolio, 341–44
   using different types of stocks, 334*e*

Dividend(s), 7, 532–33
   Black-Scholes formula for stocks paying, 698–701
   changing growth rates, 252–55
   constant growth model, 249–50
   cum, 536
   cutting, for profitable growth, 251–52*e*
   cutting tax rate on, 475*b*
   declining use of, 543*f*
   early exercise of options on stocks paying, 674–76
   effective tax rate on, 545, 546*e*
   equity issuance to pay, 542*e*
   investment and growth versus, 250–52
   liquidating, 534
   Microsoft Corporation cash, beta, and, 444*b*
   Modigliani-Miller on irrelevance of distribution policy toward, 539–40
   optimal policy toward, with taxes, 542–44
   perfect capital markets with policy toward, 541
   promise of, 536 n.5
   real options and, 725
   share repurchases compared to, 535–41
   signaling policy toward, 556–58
   smoothing, 555–56
   special, 532, 533*f*
   taxes on, 541–42, 545–49
Dividend-capture theory, **548**–49
Dividend-discount model, **248**, 249–56
   changing growth rates and, 252–55
   constant dividend growth and, 249–50
   dividends versus investment and growth and, 250–52
   limitations of, 255–56
   J. B. Williams's *Theory of Investment Value* on, 255*b*
Dividend-Discount Model equations, 248–49
Dividend-Discount Model with Constant Long-Term Growth equation, 254
Dividend payment, **7**
Dividend payout rate, **250**
Dividend Payout Rate equations, 250–51
Dividend puzzle, **544**
Dividend reinvestment program (DRIP), 538 n.6
Dividend signaling hypothesis, **557**
Dividend smoothing, **555**–56
Dividend yield, stock, **247**
Dodd, P., 910 n.12
Doherty, Joseph, 496 n.5
Doidge, C., 919 n.23
Dollars
   converting between dollars today and future dollars with risk, 73*f*
   converting between gold, euros, or future dollars, and, 54*e*
   exchange rate fluctuations, 939–41
Domestic bonds, **784**
Double-barreled, **788**
Double taxation, 475*b*
Dow Jones Industrial Average, 66*b*, 377, 658
Dual class shares, **917**
Dunbar, Craig G., 770 n.17
Duration, **222**, **950**–56
   of coupon bond, 951*e*
   hedging based on, 952–56

   interest rate risk measurement and, 950–52
   modified, 952 n.18
   using interest rate swaps to change, 959–60
Duration mismatch, **953**–56
Duration-neutral portfolio, **954**
Duration of a Portfolio equation, 953
Duration of a Security equation, 951
Dutch auction, **535**
Dynamic trading strategy, **692**

E (market value of equity), 437, 439, 440, 465, 466, 468, 577, 582, 710, 954
E[*R*] (expectation of return *R*), 286–87, 325
$E[R_i]$ (expected return of security *i*), 364, 368, 383
Eades, K., 363 n.1
EAR. *See* Effective annual rate (EAR)
EAR for Continuously Compounded APR equation, 147
Earnings, **27**
   calculating free cash flow from, 186–88
   commodity hedging and smoothing of, 934*f*
   forecasting, 178–85
   forecasting, in financial models, 629–31
   incremental (*see* Incremental earnings)
   before interest, taxes, depreciation, and amortization (*see* EBITDA)
   before interest and taxes (*see* EBIT)
   mergers/acquisitions and growth of, 881–82
   per share [*see* Earnings per share (EPS)]
   ratio to price 262–63
   retained, 34
Earnings calculations, 27–28
   earnings before interest and taxes, 27
   gross profit, 27
   operating expenses, 27
   pretax and net income, 28
Earnings per share (EPS), **28**
   equation, 28
   leverage and, 445–46, 447*f*, 448
   mergers and, 881–82*e*
Earthquakes and hurricanes, insurance for, 927
   common versus independent risk in, 299–302
eBay stock, 386
Ebbers, Bernie, 509*b*
EBIT (earnings before interest and taxes), **27**
   break-even, 197
   interest payments as percentage of, 481, 483*f*
EBIT break-even, **197**
EBITDA (earnings before interest, taxes, depreciation, and amortization), **30**
   continuation value using EBITDA multiple, 640, 642
Eckbo, B. E., 879 n.4
Eckbo, Espen, 773 n.22
Economic distress, **493**
Economic profit, **156**, 158. *See also* Economic Value Added (EVA)
Economic Value Added (EVA), **156**–61
   changing investment capital and, 159–60
   constant investment capital and, 158–59
   economic profit and, 156, 158
   equation for EVA when invested capital changes, 159

Economic Value Added (EVA) (continued)
 equation for EVA when invested capital is
  constant, 158
 J. Stern on, 157b
Economies of scale, **877**
Economies of scope, **877**
Economy. *See* U.S. economy
Effective annual rate (EAR), **126**
 commercial paper and, 862–63e
 common loans, 860–61, 862e
 compensating balance requirements
  and, 862e
 for continuously compounded APR, 147
 converting APR to, 128
 cost of trade credit, 833
Effective annual yield (EAY), 126 n.1. *See also*
  Effective annual rate (EAR)
Effective dividend tax rate, **545**
 changes in, 546e
Effective dividend tax rate equation, 545
Effective Tax Advantage of Debt equation, 473
Efficiency
 leasing, and gains in, 821
 mergers/acquisitions and gains in, 879
 notions of, 313
Efficient capital market, **313**
Efficient frontier, **344**
 with differing saving and borrowing rate,
  384–85
Efficient markets, 60 n.6
 competition and, 268–70
Efficient markets hypothesis, **268**, 313–15
 capital market efficiency, 313–15
 no arbitrage versus, 271–72
Efficient portfolio(s), **308**, **349**
 cost of capital and, 349–55
 expected returns and, 351–52
 identifying, 363, 351–52e
 improving returns with, 337–38e
 risk versus return, and choice of, 335–44
Eisfeldt, A., 812 n.9
Eisner, Michael, 12, 909–10
Electronic Business Services (EBS), 427
Ellison, G., 315 n.18
El Paso Corporation, 441–42e
 takeover attempt of, 889
Elton, E., 545 n.14
Empire building by managers, 509
Empirical distribution, **292**
Employee(s)
 expertise of, as reason for takeover, 878
 financial distress and loss of, 497
 stock options for, 482b, 699b
Empty lots in urban areas, 725b
End-of-term lease options, 805–7
Enron Corporation
 bankruptcy costs, 495, 496
 excessive managerial perks at, 509b
 financial reporting abuses by, 37, 912
 use of leases by, 812b
Enterprise value, **26**
 computing, 26e
 discounted free cash flow model and, 258
 equation, 26
Enterprise value multiples, 263
 valuation using, 263–64e
Enterprise value multiples equation, 263
EPS. *See* Earnings per share (EPS)

EPS_t (earnings per share on date t), 262
Epsilon ε (change in interest rate), 952
Epsilon ε_i (error term), 382
Epsilon ε_s (residual risk of stock s), 409, 410
Epsilon ε_s (regression error term), 637
Equally weighted portfolio, **332**
 diversification of, 332–34
Equal-ownership portfolio, **376**
Equations and formulas
 Accounts Receivable Days, 29, 628
 Actuarially Fair Insurance Premium, 927
 Adjusted beta, 389
 Adjusted Present Value, 582
 After-tax interest, 633
 After-Tax Interest Rates, 139
 alpha of stock, 373
 Average Annual Return of a Security, 292
 Balance Sheet Identity, 21
 Beta of an Option, 708
 beta of portfolio, 372, 442, 443
 Beta of Portfolio i with Portfolio P, 350
 binomial pricing formula, 688–90
 Black-Scholes Price of a Call Option on
  a Non-Dividend Pricing Model, 694
 Black-Scholes Replicating Portfolio of
  a Call Option, 702
 Black-Scholes Replicating Portfolio of
  a Put Option, 704
 bond yields from forward rates, 242
 Call Value at Expiration, 659
 capital expenditures, 641
 cash multiple, 647
 Characteristic Variable Model of Stock
  Returns, 417
 Constant Dividend Growth Model, 249–50
 Continuously Compounded APR for
  EAR, 147
 converting ARP to EAR, 128
 Cost of Capital for Investment i, 353
 Cost of Capital of a Project, 311
 Cost of Capital of Levered Equity, 438
 Coupon Payment, 212
 Covariance between Returns R_i and R_j, 327
 Covered Interest Parity, 944
 debt capacity, 580, 581
 Debt-Equity ratio, 25
 Discounted Free Cash Flow Model
  equation, 258, 259
 discount rate for security s (r_s), 72
 Dividend-Discount Model, 248–49
 Dividend-Discount Model with Constant
  Long-Term Growth, 254
 Dividend Payout Rate, 250–51
 Duration of a Portfolio, 953
 EAR for Continuously Compounded
  APR, 147
 Earnings per share, 28
 effective dividend tax rate, 545
 Effective Tax Advantage of Debt, 473
 Enterprise Value, 26
 Enterprise value multiples, 263
 equity beta estimation, 637
 Equity Cost of Capital, 590
 Equity Duration, 954
 Estimate of the Covariance from Historical
  Data, 327
 Estimating a Traded Security's Expected
  Return from Its Beta, 310

EVA in Period n (When Capital
  Depreciates), 159
EVA in Period n (When Capital Lasts
  Forever), 158
exchange ratio, 885
Expected Return, 286, 325, 345
Expected Return of a Security, 351, 364
expected return on risk investment, 69
Face Value of bond, 213
Fama-French-Carhart Factor
  Specification, 413
Foreign-Dominated Cost of Capital, 975
forward interest rates, 241
Free Cash Flow, 189
Free Cash Flow to Equity, 586
Future Value of Annuity, 101e
Future Value of Cash Flow, 86
Future Value of Stream of Cash Flow,
  with Present Value of PV, 93
incremental income tax expense, 181
interest expense on debt, 628
lease payments, 806b
Leverage and the Cost of Capital with
  a Fixed Debt Scheduled, 604
Levered Value with a Constant Interest
  Coverage Ratio, 594
Levered Value with Permanent Debt
  equation, 596
liquidation/salvage value, 193
Loan Payments, 110
market capitalization, 375
Market-To-Book ratio, 25
market value of equity, 436
Multifactor Model of Risk, 411
Multifactor Model of Risk with Self-
  Financing Portfolios, 411
Net Present Value, 54, 164
Net Profit Margin, 29
Net Working Capital, 187
No Arbitrage Price of Security, 63
Operating Margin, 29
Option Price in the Binomial Model, 689
portfolio weight, 324
Present Value of Annuity, 100
Present Value of Cash Flow, 88
Present Value of Cash Flow Stream Using
  Term Structure of Discount Rates, 135
Present Value of Continuously Growing
  Perpetuity, 147
Present Value of Growing Annuity, 104
Present Value of Growing Perpetuity, 103
Present Value of Perpetuity, 96
Present Value of Stream of Cash Flow,
  92–93
Price/Earnings ratio, 30, 262
Price of a Call Option on a Currency, 949
Price of a Coupon Bond, 225
price of stock, 246
Profitability index, 167
Project-Based WACC, 591
Project WACC with a Fixed Debt
  Schedule, 604
Put Price at Expiration, 660
realized return, 289
Replicating Portfolio in the Binomial
  Model, 689
Required Return for Investment i Given
  Current Portfolio P, 350

Retained Earnings, 34
return on bonds, 64
Return on Equity, 30
return on stocks, 247
Risk-Free Interest Rate with Maturity *n*, 214
risk premium, 310
share repurchase and share value, 256
Sharpe ratio, 347
standard deviation, 287, 301
Standard Error of the Estimate of the
    Expected Return, 295
Total Payout Model equation, 257
total value of levered firm, 501
unlevered cost of capital, 639
Unlevered Cost of Capital with a Target
    Leverage Ratio, 582
Unlevered Cost of Capital with Personal
    Taxes equation, 607
unlevered net income, 182
Value Additivity, 66
Value of Interest Tax Shield of Permanent
    Debt, 465
Variance and Standard Deviation of the
    Return Distribution, 287
Variance Estimate Using Realized
    Returns, 293
Variance of an Equally Weighted Portfolio
    of *n* Stocks, 332, 333
Variance of a Two-Stock Portfolio, 330
Volatility of a Portfolio with Arbitrary
    Weights equation, 335
Weighted Average Cost of Capital
    (No Taxes), 439
Weighted Average Cost of Capital with
    Taxes, 465
Yield to Maturity of a Coupon Bond, 215
Yield to Maturity of an *n*-Year Zero-
    Coupon Bond, 213, 214
Equipment Leasing Association, 801 n.1
Equity, **7**. *See also* Stock(s)
    book value of, 24
    as call option, 676–77
    common mistake regarding debt versus, 44*b*
    computing market value of, 436
    effects of leverage on risk and returns to,
        430–32
    fallacy of issuance of, and dilution, 448–49
    financing firms with, 428–29
    financing firms with debt and, 429–30
    issuance of (*see* Equity issuance)
    leverage and equity cost of capital, 437–39
    levered, 429 (*see also* Levered equity)
    market versus book value of, 24*e*, 25, 26
    risk and market value of, 405*e*
    statement of stockholder's equity, 36
    stockholders', 21, 24–25, 36
    unlevered, 429 (see also Unlevered equity)
Equity beta estimation equation, 637
Equity capital, mechanics of raising, 751–78
    initial public offerings for, 757–70
    for private companies, 752–57
    problems, 776–78
    seasoned equity offerings, 770–74
    summary, 774–75
Equity cash flows, valuing, 587
Equity cost of capital (r_E), 246, 248 n.1
    computing, 439*e*
    equation, 590

leverage and, 431–32*e*, 437–39
    project leverage and, 590–91
Equity Duration equation, 954
Equity holder, **7**. *See also* Shareholder(s)
Equity issuance
    adverse selection and, 514–17
    costs of, 597*t*
    insurance and, 929
    largest global (2004), 757*t*
    to pay dividend, 542*e*
    as shareholder distribution, 538–39
Equity markets, adverse selection in, 515–16*e*
Equivalent annual benefit method, **736**–37
Ernst & Young, 35
Error term, **382**
Estimate of the Covariance from Historical
    Data equation, 327
Estimating a Traded Security's Expected
    Return from Its Beta equation, 310
Estimation
    beta, 308–9*e*, 388–90
    of covariance, 327
    of expected return, 307–11
    past and future returns, and error, 294–97
    of risk premium, 310–11
    security market line and cost of capital,
        390–92
    of unlevered cost of capital, 589–90
ETF. *See* Exchange traded fund (ETF)
Eurobonds, **784**, 785
European Commission (EC), 878
    regulatory approval for takeovers and,
        891–92
European options, **656**
    arbitrage bounds on, 670
    binomial option pricing and, 686–87
    Black-Scholes formula for calculating, 695,
        696, 697*e*, 698, 700–701*e*
    currency options, 946, 947*t*
    early exercise of, 671–76
    option prices and exercise date, 670–71
European Union, 20, 878
Euros
    exchange rate fluctuations, 939–41
    international bond issue in, 784–85
EVA. *See* Economic Value Added (EVA)
EVA_n (Economic Value Added at date *n*),
    158, 159
EVA in Period *n* (When Capital Depreciates)
    equation, 159–60
EVA in Period *n* (When Capital Lasts Forever)
    equation, 158
EVA investment rule, **158**
Evergreen credit, **860**
Excel spreadsheet. *See* Microsoft Excel
    spreadsheet
Excess returns, **297**
    of book-to-market portfolio, 403, 404*f*
    historical excess returns of, compared to
        Treasury securities, 391*t*
    of size portfolios (1926–2005), 402, 403*f*
    volatility versus excess return of corporate
        bond (1926–2004), 297*t*
Exchange Act of 1934, 915
Exchange rate(s)
    calculating cash values using market
        prices, 50*e*
    fluctuations of, 939–41

forward, 941–46, 973
    implied volatility of, 949–50*e*
    locking in, using forward contracts,
        941–42*e*
    spot, 943
Exchange rate risk, 939–50
    capital budgeting with, 981–83
    cash-and-carry, and pricing of currency
        forwards, 943–46
    effects of, 941*e*
    fluctuations and, 939–41
    hedging, with forward contracts, 941–43
    hedging, with options, 946–50
Exchange ratio, **884**–85
    maximum, in stock takeover, 885*e*
Exchange-traded fund (ETF), **379**
    J. Bogle on, 378*b*
Ex-dividend date, **532**
Executive stock options (ESO), **699***b*
Exercise date, financial-option prices and,
    670–71
Exercise (strike) price, **656**
Exercising financial options, **656**
    early, 671–76
Exit strategy, **756**–57
Expansion, staged investment and option for,
    729–31. *See also* Growth options
Expectations
    homogeneous, 365
    rational, 386–88
Expected (mean) return, **69**, **286**–87
    accuracy of estimates of, 297*e*
    beta and, 311*e*
    calculating volatility and, 288*e*
    characteristic variable models of, 415–19
    computing stock's, 369*e*
    efficient portfolio and, 351–52
    estimating, 307–11
    of portfolio, 324, 325*e*, 372*e*
    predicting future based on, 294–97
    standard error of estimate of, 295
    volatility and, for multiple stock
        portfolios, 343*f*
    volatility and, for two-stock portfolios,
        336*t*, 33/*f*
Expected (Mean) Return equation, 286,
    325, 345
Expected Return of a Security equation,
    364, 351
Expenditures. *See* Expenses
Expenses
    fixed overhead, 184
    past research and development, 184
Expertise, mergers/acquisitions and
    personnel, 878
Expiration date, **656**
Exxon Mobile, 370
    changes in expected returns of, 373–74
Ezzell, J. R., 602 n.22, 604 n.23

F, F_T (one-year and T-year forward exchange
    rate), 944, 946
f_n (one-year forward rate for year *n*), 241
Fabozzi, F. J., 956 n.20
Face value, **212**
Face Value of bond equation, 213
Factor(s), **863**
Factor betas, **410**

Factoring of accounts receivable, **863**–64
Factor portfolios, **409**–10
Fair market value cap lease, **806**
Fair market value (FMV) lease, **805**
Fama, Eugene, 243 n.5, 392 n.18, 392 n.19, 393 n.20, 402, 413, 543 n.10. *See also* Fama-French-Carhart (FFC) factor specification
Fama-French-Carhart (FFC) factor specification, **413**
  calculating cost of capital using, 413, 414–15*e*
  return of seasoned equity offerings using, 773*f*
Fama-French-Carhart Factor Specification equation, 413
Fan, Joseph, 521 n.43
Fastow, Andrew, 37, 509*b*
FCFE. *See* Free cash flow to equity (FCFE)
FCF*t* (free cash flow in year *t*), 189, 258, 577, 581, 641
Fedak, Marilyn G., on stock valuation, 253*b*
Federal funds rate, **136**
Federal tax rates, U.S., 471, 472*t*
Fees on loans, 860–61
Ferris, Stephen, 496 n.6
FFC. *See* Fama-French-Carhart (FFC) factor specification
Field warehouse, **865**
Final prospectus, **761**
Finance, international. *See* International corporate finance
Finance lease, **809**. *See also* Capital lease
Financial decision making, 47–80. *See also* Investment decision rules
  arbitrage and Law of One Price, 59–61
  arbitrage with transaction costs, 73–74
  interest rates and time value of money, 51–54
  no-arbitrage and security prices, 61–67
  present value and NPV decision rule, 54–59
  price of risk, 67–73
  problems, 76–80
  summary, 75–76
  valuing costs and benefits, 48–51
Financial distress, **491**–529, 599–600
  agency benefits of leverage and motivating managers, 507–10
  agency costs and tradeoff theory, 511–12
  agency costs of leverage, 503–7
  asymmetric information and capital structure, 512–20
  capital structure reviewed, 520–21
  costs of (*see* Financial distress costs)
  default and bankruptcy in perfect market, 492–94
  optimal capital structure and tradeoff theory, 501–3
  problems, 523–29
  summary, 521–22
Financial distress costs
  cash retention and, 553
  determinants of present value of, 501
  firm value and, 498–500
  indirect, 496–98
  insurance and, 928–29
  optimal leverage with taxes and, 502*f*

  optimal leverage with taxes, and agency costs and, 511*f*
  reducing, by leasing, 821
  stock prices and, 500*e*
  valuing, 600*e*
Financial information. *See* Information
Financial market, **61**
Financial modeling, case study of, 623–52
  building, by determining working capital requirements, 631–32
  building, by forecasting earnings, 629–31
  building, by forecasting free cash flow, 633–34
  building, with balance sheet and cash flow statement, 634–36
  business plan and, 626–29
  combining inputs to value investment opportunity, 639–47
  estimating cost of capital, 636–39
  management compensation, 652
  problems, 649–51
  sensitivity analysis, 647–48
  summary, 648–49
  valuation using comparables and, 624–26
Financial option(s), 653, 655–84
  basics of, 656–58
  call (*see* Call option)
  combinations of, 664–67
  as compensation for management, 906–7
  corporate finance through equity and debt, 676–79
  data case, 684
  defined, **656**
  early exercise of, 671–76
  exercising, 656
  factors affecting prices of, 669–71
  hedging with currency, 946–50
  insurance on portfolio of, 666–67
  interpreting stock option quotations, 656–58
  intrinsic value of, 670
  Law of One Price and, 653
  on non-stock securities, 658
  option contracts, 656
  payoffs of, at expiration, 659–68
  problems, 681–83
  purchasing, 658*e*
  put (*see* Put option)
  put-call parity, 668–69
  real options versus, 718 [*see also* Real option(s)]
  stocks, 28, 482*b* (*see also* Stock options)
  summary, 680–81
  time value of, 670
  valuation of (*see* Financial-options valuation)
Financial-option prices, 669–71. *See also* Financial-options valuation
  arbitrage bounds on, 670
  exercise date and, 670–71
  risk neutral probability and, 706–7
  strike price and stock price, 670
  volatility and, 671
Financial-options valuation, 685–716
  beta of risky debt and, 710–12
  binomial option pricing model, 686–94
  Black-Scholes option pricing model, 694–704

  problems, 714–16
  risk and return (computing option beta), 707–10
  risk-neutral probabilities and, 704–7
  summary, 712–13
Financial planning, short-term, 851–69
  forecasting short-term financing needs, 852–56
  matching principle and, 857–59
  problems, 868–69
  short-term financing with bank loans, 859–62
  short-term financing with commercial paper, 862–63
  short-term financing with secured financing, 863–66
  summary, 866–67
Financial ratios. *See* Ratio(s)
Financial statement(s), 19–46
  accounting manipulation and reporting abuses in, 37–38
  balance sheet in, 21–27
  data case, 45–46
  definition of, **20**
  disclosure of financial information in, 20–21
  S. Frieden on, 35*b*
  income statement in, 27–32
  international reporting standards for, 20*b*
  management and discussion analysis in, 36
  notes to, 36
  preparation of, 20–21
  problems, 41–45
  statement of cash flows, 32–34
  statement of stockholder's equity in, 36
  summary, 38–39
  types of, 21
Financing
  bank loans for short-term, 859–62 [*see also* Loan(s)]
  commercial paper for short-term, 862–63
  with debt and equity, 429–30
  effects of leverage on risk and returns to equity and, 430–32
  with equity, 428–29
  forecasting short-term needs for, 852–56
  international (*see* International corporate finance)
  long-term (*see* Debt financing; Equity capital, mechanics of raising; Leasing)
  matching principle and policy choices for, 858
  secured financing for short-term, 863–66
  separating investment and, 65–66*e*
  short-term (*see* Financial planning, short-term; Working capital management)
  venture merchant, 864*b*
Financing activity, statement of cash flows, 33–34
Financing costs, 597
Finetti, Bruno de, 353*b*
Fiorina, Carly, 886–87
Firm(s)
  bankruptcy risk and value of, 494*e*
  cash flows of levered and unlevered, 463*f*
  costs of financial distress and value of, 498–500
  debt-equity ratio policies of, 601*f*

equity financing for private, 752–57
financing with equity and with debt, 428–32
four types of, 4–9
initial public offerings of, 757–70
interest tax shield and value of, 462–63
with large cash balances, 555*t*
leverage, arbitrage, and value of, 432–37
option to shutdown, 731–33
preference of, for debt, 476–77
private (*see* Private companies)
public (*see* Public companies)
season equity offering for, 770–74
stock valuation based on comparable, 261–66
as target of mergers/acquisitions, 873 (*see also* Mergers and acquisitions)
valuing growth potential of, 726–31
venture capital, 752–53
working capital and value of, 832
working capital in select, 831*t*
Firm commitment, **758**
Firm-specific, idiosyncratic, unsystematic, unique, or diversifiable risk, **303**
Firm-specific versus systematic risk in stock portfolios, 303–5
Fisher, Adlai, 773 n.21, 773 n.22
Fixed-coupon bond, 788
Fixed price lease, **806**
Float, managing processing, 834–35
Floating bond, 788
Floating lien, **864**–65
Floating rate (interest rate), **940**, 956, 957*t*
Floor planning, **865**
Flow-to-equity (FTE) method of valuation, **585**–88
calculating free cash flow to equity, 586–87
with changing leverage, 605–6
comparison of APV and WACC methods to, 596–97
debt and, 589*b*
example, 588*e*
summary, 588
valuing equity cash flows, 587
Ford Motor Company, 779, 780 n.1
Foreign bonds, **784**
Foreign-Dominated Cost of Capital equation, 975
Formula. *See* Equations and formula
Forrester, J. R., Jr., 151
Forward contracts
advantages of, 945–46
currency options versus, 946–48
hedging exchange risk with, 941–42
Forward earnings, **262**
Forward exchange rate, **941**
Law of One Price and, 943–45
Forward interest rates (forward rates), **241**–44
computing, 241–42
computing bond yields from, 242
future interest rates and, 242–43
Forward P/E, **262**
Forward rate agreement, **241**
Franks, J., 916 n.21, 921 n.24
Free cash flow (FCF), **186**–95, 258
adding salvage value to, 193*e*
calculating, from earnings, 186–88
calculating directly, 188–89

calculating NPV and, 189–90
equation, 189
to equity, valuation of, 587
expected, 578*t*
factors affecting estimates of project, 191–95
forecasting, and financial modeling, 633–34
leverage and, 634*e*
manufacturing alternatives affecting, 190–91
model of discounted, 258–61
in year *t*, 189
uses of, 532*f* (*see also* Payout policy)
valuing currency cash flow and conversion of, 973
Free cash flow hypothesis, **509**–10
Free cash flow to equity (FCFE), **586**–87
calculation of, adjusted present value method and, 586–87
Free Cash Flow to Equity equation, 586
Free rider problem, 893
Freezeout merger, **896**–97
French, Kenneth, 392 n.18, 393 n.20, 402, 413, 543 n.10. *See also* Fama-French-Carhart (FFC) factor specification
Frieden, Sue, on financial statements, 35*b*
Friend, I., 315 n.17
Friendly takeover, **888**
white knights and, 890
FTE. *See* Flow to equity (FTE) method of valuation
Funding risk, **858**
Futures contract, **935**
hedging with, 935–38
Future value (FV), **86**
of cash flow, 86, 87, 89–90*e*
computing, in Excel spreadsheet, 107
FV. *See* Future value (FV)
FV (face value of bond), 213
FV function (annuity spreadsheet notation for extra final payment), 106
FV_n (future value on date *n*), 86

g (expected dividend growth rate), 249, 251
g (growth rate), 102, 103, 104, 105, 106, 641
g_{FCF} (expected free cash flow growth rate), 259, 262, 263
Galileo, 433*b*
Gambling, diversification and, 302*e*
Gap, Inc., 598–99*e*
Garman, M. B., 949 n.16
Garvey, G., 911 n.14
GE Commercial Aviation Service, 801–2
Geczy, Christopher, 773 n.22
General American Oil company, 889
General Electric (GE) Company, 575, 589, 878, 925
early exercise of call options for, 674–75*e*
option quotes on stocks of, 675*t*
General lien, **864**–65
Generally Accepted Accounting Principles (GAAP), **20**
General Motors Corporation (GM), 25
changes in expected returns of, 373–74
dividend history (1983–2006), 533*f*
earnings and dividends per share (1985–2006), 556*f*

realized returns for, 290*e*, 291
realized returns for (1996–2004), 291*t*
General obligation bonds, **788**
General portfolios, diversification with, 334–35
Geometric series, 96 n.2
Georgeson and Company, 889 n.11
Giammarino, Ronald, 773 n.21, 773 n.22
Gilligan, Thomas, 820 n.15
Gitman, L. J., 151 n.1
Glaser, Robert, 755
Global bonds, **784**
Global Financial Data, 284 n.1
Goedhart, M. H., 390 n.14
Goel, A. M., 880 n.5
Goetzmann, W., 97*b*, 563 n.36
Goff, John, 12 n.
Gold
cash value of, 49
value of, in different markets, 59
Golden parachute, **890**
Goldman Sachs, 6
Goldsmith, James, 889
Gollier, C., 834 n.3
Gompers, P., 911 n.13
Gompers, Paul A., 752, 773 n.22
Goodwill
amortization of, 635 n.8
as asset, **23**
calculation of, 634–35
Google, 25, 387
calculating yield on corporate debt for, 678, 679*t*
initial public offering (IPO) of, 760*b*
Gordon, M. J., 540 n.
Governance. *See* Corporate governance
Government bond(s). *See also* Bond(s); Treasury bonds
consol (perpetual bond), 95
municipal, 788
risky foreign, 978–79*e*
Government National Mortgage Association (GNMA, "Ginnie Mae"), 788
Graham, J., 558 n.33, 594 n.15, 821 n.17
Graham, John, 151, 160*b*, 363 n.1, 392 n.17, 419, 420, 476 n.12, 480 n.15, 481 n.17, 482 n.18
Grannis, Dick, on capital budgeting, 179*b*
Gray directors, **905**
Green, R. C., 315 n.18, 415 n.16, 727 n.2
Green Shoe Company, 764 n.11
Greenmail, **535**
Greenshoe provision (over-allotment allocation), **764**
Grenadier, Steven, 807 n.4
Grinblatt, M., 415 n.14
Groove Networks, Inc., 754
Gross domestic product (GDP), 8
Grossman, S., 893 n.14
Gross profit, **27**
Growing annuity, **104**
present value of, 104
retirement savings with, 105*e*
Growing perpetuity, **102**
endowing, 104*e*
present value of, 103
Growth
changing rates of, 252–55

Growth (continued)
    continuation value and long-run, 643*b*
    continuation value and perpetual, 194*e*
    cutting dividends for profitable, 251–52*e*
    debt and, 481
    profitable, 251–52
    simple model of, 250–51
    unprofitable, 252*e*
    valuing firm's potential for, 726–28
    valuing firms with two different rates of, 254–55*e*
Growth options, **726**–31
    staged investment and option to expand, 729–31
    valuing firm's growth potential, 726–28
Growth stocks, **25**
Gruber, M. J., 315 n.18, 545 n.14
Grullon, G., 534 n.4, 543 n.10, 557 n.28, 559 n.34
Guay, W., 911 n.13
Gutierrez, R., Jr., 415 n.13

Hall, B., 907 n.5
Halley, Edmond, 100 n.5
Hamada, R., 442 n.4, 604 n.23
Hance, Julian, 557*b*
Hanouna, P., 919 n.23
Hansen, Robert S., 769 n.16
Harford, J., 874 n.2
Harris, Dan, 427
Harris, Lawrence E., on Sarbanes-Oxley regulations, 913*b*
Harris, M., 510 n.27, 510 n.28, 547 n.17, 556 n.25
Harris, R., 363 n.1, 591 n.13, 604 n.23
Hart, O. D., 893 n.14
Hart-Scott-Rodino (HSR) Act of 1976, 891
Hartwig, Robert, 930 n.7
Harvey, Campbell, 151, 160*b*, 363 n.1, 392 n.17, 419, 420, 558 n.33, 594 n.15
Haugen, Robert, 418, 498 n.14
Hays, Kristen, 497 n.10
Healy, P., 557 n.28
Heaton, J. B., 509 n.24
Hedging, 658
    of commodity price risk, 938–39
    with currency options, 946–50
    duration-based, 952–56
    with forward contracts, 941–43
    with future contracts, 935–38
    with long-term contracts, 934, 935*e*
    mistakes involving risk, 938*b*
    strategies of, 939*b*
    swap-based, and interest rates, 956–60
    with vertical integration and storage, 933
Hendricks, D. J., 415 n.14
Herman, E. S., 315 n.17
Heron, R., 889 n.11, 908 n.7
Hertz Corporation, 779, 780*t*, 783, 784*t*
Hewlett-Packard (HP), 47
    merger with Compaq, 885, 886*f*, 887
Hickman, K., 905 n.2
Higgins, R., 363 n.1
High-minus-low (HMLM) portfolio, **413**
High-yield bonds, **231**
Hilton Hills Corporation, 829
Himmelberg, C., 909 n.10

Historical returns on stocks and bonds, 289–97
    average annual returns, 292–93
    computing, 289–92
    estimation error, 294–97
    variance and volatility of returns, 293–94
H.J. Heinz, calculating sales by product category, 36–37*e*
HML. *See* High-minus-law (HML) portfolio
Hold-up problem, optimal ownership of assets and, 821 n.16
Homemade leverage, **433**–35
    arbitrage and, 434*e*
HomeNet, capital budgeting example, 178, 180–93, 196–99
Homogeneous expectations, **365**
Honeywell, 878
Horowitz, I., 315 n.17
Hostile takeover, **11**, **888**, 890
Hubbard, R. Glenn, 475*b*, 909 n.10
Huberman, G., 931 n.9
Huddart, S., 699 n.
Human capital, 408
Human resources, profitability index and constraints of, 167–68*e*
Hurdle rate(s), 179*b*, **738**. *See also* Discount rate (*r*)
Hurdle rate rule, **738**–40
    applying, with profitability index rule, 740
    using for option to delay, 739–40*e*
Hurricanes. *See* Earthquakes and hurricanes, insurance for
Husic, F., 403 n.2

i (rate of inflation), 133*f*
I (initial investment), 158
I_n (capital committed to project at date *n*), 159
IBM corporation, 19
    calculating yield to call on bonds from, 792–93*e*
    changes in expected returns of, 373–74
Icahn, Carl, 910*b*
Ideko Corporation, hypothetical valuation of. *See* Financial modeling, case study of
Idle asset, opportunity cost of, 183*b*
Ikenberry, D., 534 n.4, 543 n.10, 559 n.34
ImClone, insider trading case involving, 915*b*
Immunized portfolio, **954**–55
Immunizing portfolios, **955**
    using interest rate swaps for, 959–60*e*
Implied volatility, **701**
Importer-exporter dilemma, 940
Income. *See also* Earnings; Return(s)
    forecasting, 631*e*
    net, 27
    operating, 27
    pretax, and net, 28
    unlevered net, 181, 182
Income statement, 21, **27**–32
    analysis of, 29–30
    earnings calculations, 27–28
    pro forma, 629–31
    sample, 28*t*
Income statement analysis, 29–30
    EBITDA, 30
    investment returns, 30
    leverage ratios, 30

    profitability ratios, 29–30
    valuation ratios, 30–31
    working capital days, 29–30
Incremental earnings, **178**
    forecasting, 180–82, 185*e*
    indirect effects on, 182–84
    real world complexities and, 184
    sunk cost and, 184
Incremental IRR investment rule, **164**–66
    application of, 165
    shortcomings of, 166
The Independent, 914
Independent and identically distributed (IID) returns, 295
Independent (outside) directors, **905**
Independent risk, **301**
    common risk versus, 299–302
Index funds, **379**
    J. Bogle on, 378*b*
Individual preferences, net present value (NPV) and, 57–59
Inefficient portfolio, **337**
Inflation
    rate of (*i*), 133*f*
    real versus nominal interest rates and, 131–32
Inflation-indexed Treasury securities, 786*t*, 787
    coupon payments on, 787*e*
Information
    abuses in reporting of financial, 37–38
    asymmetric, and capital structure, 512–20
    avoiding being outsmarted when lacking access to, 387*e*
    disclosure of financial, 20–21
    insider trading based on privileged, 915–16
    international standards for reporting financial, 20*b*
    rational expectations and investor, 386–88
    Sarbanes-Oxley Act on accuracy of, 912–14
    stock prices, investor competition and, 266–72
Information node, **719**
Ingersoll, Jonathan, 745 n.7
Initial public offering (IPO), **757**–70
    advantages and disadvantages of, 757–58
    auction, 758, 759*e*, 760*b*
    comparison of first-day returns on, 766*f*
    cost of issuing, 769–70
    cyclicality of, 767–68
    Google's, 760*b*
    long-run underperformance, 770
    mechanics of, 760–65
    types of offerings, 758–60
    underpricing puzzle of, 765–67
    valuation of, 761–65
Inside directors, **905**
Insider trading, **915**–16
    Martha Stewart case, 915*b*
Insider Trading Sanctions Act of 1984, 916
Insurance, **926**–32
    common versus independent risk in theft and earthquake, 299–302
    costs of, 930–32
    decisions regarding, 932
    on financial-option portfolios, 666–67
    pricing of, in perfect market, 927–28
    risk management and role of, 926

types of, 926

value of, 928–30

Insurance fraud, 931

Insurance premium, **926**

Intel Corporation, 363

two-stock portfolio including Coca-Cola
and, 335–44

Int_t (interest expense on date *t*), 583

Interest. *See also* Interest rate(s) (*r*)

accrued, 215 n.3

compound, 86

compounding, 90–91

earnings before, 27, 30

as percentage of EBIT for S&P firms, 483*f*

rule of 72, 116*b*

security, 812

short, 340*b*

simple, 127

taxes and, 139 n.7, 140 n.8

tax savings for different levels of, 480*f*

Interest coverage ratio, **30**

Interest expenses

on debt, calculating, 628

incremental earnings forecast and, 180–81

Interest income, 139 n.7

"Interest on interest," 90

Interest rate(s) (*r*), 51–53, 125–48

after-tax, 139–40

annual percentage rates (APR) of, 127–29
[*see also* Annual percentage rates (APR)]

bond prices and changes in, 221–24

on bonds (coupon), 212

comparing short-term, and long-term, 137*e*

for continuously compounded APR, 147

determinants of, 131–38

determining, from bond prices, 64

discount rates for continuously
compounded APR, 147

effective annual, 126

forward rates and future, 242–43

historical, on mortgages and government
bonds, 738*f*

historical, on mortgages, bonds,
and Treasury rates, 733*f*

inflation and, 131–32

mortgage, 738

nominal, 131

quotes and adjustments of, 126–31

problems, 143–46

real, 131–32, 133*f*

recessions in U.S. economy and long-term
versus short-term, 136*f*

risk and, 138–39 (*see also* Interest rate risk)

risk-free, 52, 214, 391 [*see also* Discount
rate (*r*)]

security market line with differing,
385–86

spot, 214

summary, 141–42

term structure of, 133–35

time value of money and, 51–53

Interest rate factor, **52**

Interest rate forward contract, **241**

Interest rate risk, 138–39, 950–60

duration and measurement of, 950–52

duration-based hedging, 952–56

swap-based hedging, 956–60

Interest rate swap, **956**–60

combining with standard loans, 957–59

immunizing portfolio using, 959–60

using, 959*e*

using to change duration, 959–60

Interest tax deduction, 460–62

Interest tax shield, **461**

computing, 461–62*e*

firm value and, 462–63

with permanent debt, 463–65

personal taxes included in, 471–73

recapitalizing to capture, 468–71

valuing, using adjusted present value
method, 583–84

valuing, using WACC, 467*e*

valuing, without risk, 463*e*

valuing, with personal taxes, 474–75

weighted average cost of capital with taxes
and, 465–67

Internal rate of return (IRR), **111**–14

cash multiples and, 645–47

computing, with Excel annuity
spreadsheet, 113*e*

computing directly, 114*e*

Excel spreadsheet function of, 115*b*

IRR rule versus, 156

measuring sensitivity using, 150, 151*f*

multiple, and IRR investment rule,
155–56

nonexistent, and IRR investment rule, 154

Internal rate of return (IRR) investment rule,
152–56

delayed investments and, 153–54

IRR versus, 156

multiple IRRs and, 155–56

nonexistent IRR and, 154

Internal Revenue Service (IRS), ruling
55-540, 811

International Accounting Standards Board, 20*b*

International Accounting Standards
Committee, 20*b*

International bonds, 784–85

International Business Machines (IBM), 19.
See also IBM corporation

International corporate finance, 969–88

capital budgeting with exchange risk,
981–83

data case, 987–88

internationally integrated capital markets,
970–71

internationally segmented capital markets,
977–81

problems, 984–87

summary, 983–84

valuation and international taxation,
976–77

valuation of foreign currency cash flows,
971 76

International corporate governance, 916–21

controlling owners and pyramids, 916–19

cross-holdings, 919

employee participation in, in OECD
countries, 920*t*

protection of shareholder rights, 916

stakeholder model, 919

International Financial Reporting Standards
(IFRS), 20*b*, 35

Internationally integrated capital market,
970, **971**

present values and, 971*e*

Internationally segmented capital markets,
977–81

Interviews

A. Balson, 484*b*

L. Black, 230

J. Bogle, 378

J. Clements, 354

J. Connors, 562

M. Fedak, 253

S. Frieden, 35

D. Grannis, 179

L. Harris, 913*b*

R. Lert, 314

S. Mathews, 730*b*

J. Rice, III, 646

R. Sinquefield, 412

J. M. Stern, 157

D. Viniar, 6

In-the-money, **658**, 662

Intrinsic value, **670**

Inventory(ies), **22**

as collateral, 864–66

long-term storage of, 933

management of, 840–41

Investing

capital market line and optimal, 366–67

on margin, 346–47*e*

optimal, capital market line and, 366–67

in one's own company stock, 408*b*

in risk-free securities, 345, 346*f*

Investment(s). *See also* Investment
opportunities; Project(s)

alternative short-term, 842, 843*t*

as call option, 721–23

delayed, and IRR investment rules, 153–54

decision rules for making [*see* Investment
decision rules)]

dividends versus investment and growth,
250–52

exit strategy for, from private company,
756–57

factors affecting timing of, 723–26

interest rate policy and, 132–33

liquid, 12

net present value of, 94–95*e* [*see also* Net
present value (NPV)]

over-investment, 503–4

reduction of wasteful, 508–10

required return on new, 350–51*e*

return [*see* Return(s)]

risky, 67–73 (*see also* Risk; Risk and return)

separating financing and, 65–66*e*

staged, and option to expand, 729–31

under-investment, 504–5

valuation of (*see* Valuation)

Investment activity, statement of cash flows, 33

Investment capital

EVA and changes in, 159–60

EVA and constant, 158–59

Investment decision rules, 149–74

data case, 173–74

economic profit (EVA) as, 156–61

internal rate of return rule as alternative,
152–56

Investment decision rules (continued)
  mutually exclusive investment opportunities and, 161–66
  net present value and stand-alone projects, 150–51
  payback rule as alternative, 151–52
  persistence of alternatives to NPV, 160b
  problems, 170–73
  project selection with resource constraints, 166–68
  summary, 168–69
Investment-grade bonds, **231**
Investment opportunities. *See also* Project(s)
  alternative rules for evaluating, 151–61
  deciding between mutually exclusive, of different lengths, 734–37
  key issues in foreign, 969–70
  mutually exclusive, 161–66
  NPV and stand-alone, 150–51
  option to delay, 721–26
  with resource constraints, 166–68
  valuing, 639–47 (*see also* Capital budgeting)
Investment returns, 30. *See also* Return(s)
Investor(s). *See also* Shareholder(s)
  angel, 752
  cash flows and stock values for multiyear, 248–49
  cash flows and stock values for one-year, 236
  cash flows of, after taxes, 472f
  clientele groups of, and payout policy, 547–49
  competition based on information about stock and consequences for, 271
  corporate/strategic, 753–54
  information for (*see* Information)
  institutional, 753
  outside, for private companies, 755–56
  preference of, for dividends versus share repurchase, 537–38
  signaling, 513–14, 555–60
  tax differences across, 546–47
  taxes on, and clientele groups of, 547–49
  taxes on, and payout versus cash retention policy, 552–53
Investor Responsibilty Research Center (IRRC), 911
Invoice price (dirty price) of bonds, **221**b
IPO. *See* Initial public offering (IPO)
IRR. *See* Internal rate of return (IRR)
IRR function, Excel, 115b
IRR rule. *See* Internal rate of return investment rule
Ishii, J., 911 n.13
Israel, R., 510 n.28
Issuance. *See* Equity issuance
Ityesi, Inc., valuing foreign currency cash flow, 972–76

Jagannathan, Ravi, 392 n.18, 394 n.21, 408 n.8, 548 n.18, 763
Japan, corporate cross-holdings in, 919
Jarrell, G., 559 n.35
Jarrell, G. A., 891 n.13
Jegadeesh, Narishiman, 406
Jensen, Michael, 383 n.7, 504 n.17, 508 n.22, 509 n.25, 876 n.3, 907 n.4
Jet Sky Airlines (JSA), 448–49
Johnsson, Julie, 495 n.4

Johnson, S., 919 n.23
Johnson, Shane, 506 n.19
Julio, B., 543 n.10
Junk bonds, **231**, 783, 784t
Jurgens, Rick, 497 n.9
"Just-in-time" (JIT) inventory management, **841**

k (compounding periods per year), 952
k (interest coverage ratio), 594
k (number of compounding periods per year), 128
K (option strike price), 949
K (strike price), 659, 668, 694, 701
Kahan, M., 897 n.17
Kaly, A., 548 n.18, 549 n.20
Kaplan, S., 584 n.6
Kaplan, Steven, 498, 584 n.6
Keiretsu, 919
Kellogg company, 178
Kelly, Gary, 934
Kenneth Cole Productions, 245
  stock valuation example, 259–60e, 260–61e, 266f
Key personnel insurance, **926**
Kim, E. H., 876 n.3
Klein, Benjamin, 821 n.16
Kmart Corporation, 497
Kohlberg, Kravis, and Roberts (KKR), leveraged buyout of RJR-Nabisco by, 895b
Kohlhagen, S. W., 949 n.16
Korajczyk, Robert, 517 n.39
Korea, corporate cross-holdings in, 919
Korea First Bank, 97b
Korwar, Ashok, 517 n.37
Koski, J., 545 n.14, 549 n.19
Kozlowski, Dennis, 509b
Kraakman, R., 919
Kranhold, Kathryn, 801 n.2
Krigman, L., 558 n.32
Kroger, John R., 37 n.7
The Kroger Company, 829
Kruse, Timothy, 497 n.11

L (lease payments), 803
L (market value of liabilities), 954
Lai, Kam Wah, 774 n.23
Lakonishok, J., 559 n.34, 563 n.36
Lang, M. H., 482, 699 n.
La Porta, R., 916 n.20, 919 n.23, 921 n.24
Large portfolios
  returns of, 297–98
  tradeoff between risk and return in (1926–2004), 298f
  volatility of, 332–35
Large stocks. *See also* Standard and Poor's 500
  average annual returns for (1926–2004), 293t
  empirical distribution of (1926–2004), 292f
  realized returns for (1996–2004), 291t
  value of investments (1925–2005), 285f
  volatility of (1926–2004), 294t
  volatility versus excess return of (1926–2004), 297t
Laundromat investment opportunity, example of, 161, 162f, 163f, 164, 165f
Lawless, Robert, 496 n.6

Law of One Price, **60**–61, 69, 96 n.3, 871
  capital structure and, 425, 427, 459
  computing net present value of foreign projects and, 974–76
  currency forward exchange rate and, 943–45
  financial options, 653
  forward interest rates and, 241
  long-term financing and, 749
  Modigliani-Miller propositions and, 432, 434
  no-arbitrage argument, and risk premium, 305–6
  option valuation, 685, 686–87
  in perfect capital market, 459
  risk and return, 281
  short-term financing and, 827
  valuation and, 245, 246, 573
LBO. *See* Leveraged buyout (LBO)
Leach, J., 558 n.32
Lead underwriter, **760**
Leary, Mark, 518 n.41
Lease(s)
  bankruptcy and, 811–13
  calculating payments of, 806b
  capital, 809, 810e
  direct, 802
  end-of-lease options, 806–7e
  evaluating new terms of, 818e
  fair-market value, 805
  fair-market value cap, 806
  finance, 809
  fixed-price, 806
  leveraged, 802
  loans versus, 804–5
  non-tax, 811, 818–19
  $1 out, 805
  operating, 808–9, 810e
  payments and residual values of, 803–4
  sales-type, 802
  synthetic, 802, 812b
  tax treatment of, 810–11
  terms of, in perfect market, 803–4e
  true-tax, 811, 813–14, 818–19
Lease, R. C., 496 n.7
Lease-equivalent loan, **815**–17
Leasing, 801–26
  accounting, tax, and legal consequences of, 808–13
  balance sheet and, 809e
  basics of, 802–8
  deciding to purchase or, 813–19
  exploiting tax differences through, 820e
  payment calculation, 806b
  problems, 824–26
  summary, 822–83
  valid and invalid reasons for, 819–22
Lee, I., 597 n.
Lehn, K., 909 n.9
Lehn, Kenneth, 909
Leland, Hayne, 515 n.34
Lemmon, M., 821 n.17, 909 n.10
Lemons principle, **514**–15
Lerner, Josh, 752
Lert, Randall P., on portfolio diversification and risk-return tradeoff, 314b
Lessee, **803**
Lessor, **802**

Lev, B., 563 n.36
Leverage, **25**, **346**. *See also* Debt;
    Debt and taxes
    agency benefits of, 507–10
    agency costs of, 503–7
    arbitrage, firm value, and, 432–37
    A. Balson on, 484*b*
    borrowing and buying stocks on margin,
        346–47
    commitment and, 510
    cost of capital and, 603–5
    as credible signal, 513–14
    earnings per share and, 445–46, 447*f*, 448
    effects of, on risk and returns to equity,
        430–32
    equity cost of capital and, 431–32*e*,
        437–39, 590–91
    fallacy of earnings per share and, 445–48
    free cash flow and, 634*e*
    homemade, 433–35
    interest tax shield and (*see* Interest tax
        shield)
    levered betas, 442–44
    levered equity, 429
    low level of, in U.S. firms, 481–84
    optimal, with taxes, financial distress,
        and agency costs, 511*f*
    optimal, with taxes and financial distress
        costs, 501, 502*f*, 503
    reducing cost of capital and, 441–42*e*
    risk of default and, 492–93
    solving simultaneously for value and,
        621–22
    tax rates and international, 483*t*
    tax savings with different amounts of, 479*t*
    weighted average cost of capital and,
        with perfect capital markets, 440*f*
Leverage and the Cost of Capital with a Fixed
        Debt Scheduled equation, 604
Leveraged buyout (LBO), **780**, 894–96
    calculating value gained from, 895–96*e*
    of RJR-Nabisco by Kohlberg, Kravis,
        and Roberts (KKR), 895*b*
Leveraged lease, **802**
Leveraged recapitalization, **436,** 437t
Leverage ratio(s), 30
    of options, **708**, 709*f*
    targeted, 582, 620–21
Levered betas, 442–44
    unlevering, 637–38
Levered cost of capital, 620–21
Levered equity, **429**, 430
    homemade leverage and replication
        of, 433*t*
    systematic risk and risk premiums for debt,
        unlevered equity, and, 431*t*
Levered portfolio, 346
Levered value of investment, 577
Levered Value with a Constant Interest
        Coverage Ratio equation, 594
Levered Value with Permanent Debt
        equation, 596
Levis, M., 766 n.14
Levitron Industries (LVI), 445–48
Lewellen, Wilbur, 805 n.3
Lewis, Tracy, 510 n.29
Liabilities, **21**, 23–24
    current, 23

long-term, 23–24
    missing, valuation process and, 644*b*
Lie, Erik, 889 n.11, 908
Liebman, J., 907 n.5
Limited liability, **5**
Limited liability company (LLC), **7**
Limited partnership, **5**
Linear regression, **382**
    identifying best-fitting line to identify beta
        from historical returns, 382–83
Line of credit, **859**–60
Linksys Group, 149
Lintner, J., 363, 540 n., 556 n.26
Lintner, L., 312 n.15
Lipton, Martin, 889
Liquid, **12**
Liquidating dividend, **534**
Liquidation, **11**
    financial distress and delayed, 498
Liquidation value, **25**, 192–93
Liquidity of corporations, 12, 842
    cash balances and, 844*b*
    mergers/acquisitions and, 881
Liquidity risk, 938
Liquid market, 269 n.9
Litzenberger, R., 549 n.20
Loan(s)
    bridge, 860
    combining interest rate swaps with
        standard, 957–59
    common stipulations and fees for, 860–61
    comparing non-tax lease with
        standard, 819*e*
    computing balance, 130–31*e*
    computing payments of, 109, 110*e*,
        111, 130
    discount, 860
    discount rates and, 130–31
    guaranteed, for airline companies, 598*b*
    lease-equivalent, 815–17
    lease versus, 804–5
    leveraged buyouts and, 894–96
    payments for, in perfect market, 804–5*e*
    private debt and bank, 785–86
    short-term financing with, 859–62
    single, end-of-period payment of, 859
    solving for loan payments, 109, 110*e*, 111
    syndicated bank, 785
    term, 785
    trade credit versus, 834
    trust receipts, 865
    valuing, 598–99*e*
Loan origination fee, **861**
Lochhead, S., 597 n.
Lockup, **765**
London Inter-Bank Offered Rate (LIBOR),
        859, 956
London Stock Exchange (LSE), 13
Long, Michael, 805 n.3, 908 n.8
Long bonds, **786**
Long position, **339**
    in option contracts, 659–60
Long-run diversification, fallacy of, 306*b*
Long-run growth, continuation values
        and, 643*b*
Long-term assets, 22–23
Long-term contracts, hedging with, 934–35
Long-term debt, **23**

Long-term liabilities, 23–24
Lonie, A. A., 915 n.19
Lopez de Silanes, F., 916 n.20, 919 n.23,
        921 n.24
LoPucki, Lynn, 496 n.5
Lottery prize annuity, present value of, 100*e*
Loughran, Tim, 765 n.13, 876 n.3
Lucas, Deborah, 517
Lucchetti, Aaron, 790*b*
Lyandres, Evgeny, 773 n.22

Macaulay duration, 950 n.17
MacBeth, James, 392 n.19
McConnell, J. J., 496 n.7, 805 n.3, 807 n.4,
        921 n.24
McDonald, Robert, 517, 737 n.4
McDonald's Corporation, 367–68*e*
McDougall, Duane, 892*b*
McGrattan, Ellen, 392 n.18
MACRS (Modified Accelerated Cost Recovery
        System), depreciation using, **192**,
        209, 210*t*
Majluf, Nicholas, 516 n.36
Malatesta, P. H., 889 n.10
Malmendier, Ulrike, 509 n.24
Management. *See also* Manager(s)
    compensation of, 652, 906–8
    conflicts between shareholders and, 908–11
    entrenchment of (*see* Management
        entrenchment)
    golden parachutes for, 890
Management buyout (MBO), 895
Management discussion and analysis
        (MD&A), **36**
Management entrenchment, **507**, 910–11
    poison pills and, 889
Management entrenchment theory, **512**
Manager(s). *See also* Management
    agency benefits of leverage and effects on
        motivation of, 507–10
    compensating, 652, 906–8
    competition based on information about
        stock and implications for corporate, 271
    excessive perks for, scandal and, 509*b*
    insurance and incentives for, 930
    reduction of wasteful investment by,
        508–10
Mandelker, G., 876 n.3
Manufacturing alternatives, evaluating,
        190–91
Marcum, B., 415 n.13
Margin, **936**
Marginal corporate tax rate (τ_c), **181**, 189
Margin call, 937 n.12
Margin investing, 346–47*e*
Market(s). *See also* Capital market(s)
    efficient, 60 n.6
    internationally integrated capital, 970–71
    internationally segmented capital, 977–81
    risk as relative to overall, 70–72
Marketable securities, **21**
Market capitalization, **24**, **375**
Market capitalization equation, 375
Market frictions
    trade credit and, 833–34
    transaction costs as [*see* Transaction cost(s)]
Market indexes, 284, **377**–79

Marketing costs, sensitivity to, 198*e*
Market makers, **13**
Market portfolio, **308**, **364**
　determining risk premium for, 368–75
　with different saving and borrowing rates, 385*f*, 386
　efficiency of, 364–68, 402–6
　financial information and inefficient, 388
　identifying, 375–79
　security market line and, 385–86
Market prices. *See also* Price(s)
　determining cash values using, 48–50
　risk, return, and, 72–73
Market proxy, **379**
　accuracy of, 394
　forecasting beta and, 388–89
　portfolio error, 407
Market reaction to takeovers, 875–76
Market timing, **520**
　share repurchases and, 559–60*e*
Market-to-book ratio (price-to-book[PB] ratio), **25**
Market value balance sheet, **435**–36, 470–71, 578*t*, 580*t*, 953*t*, 955*t*, 974*t*
Market value of equity equation, 436
Marking to market, **937**–38
Markowitz, Henry, 323
　as Nobel prize winner, 353*b*
　on portfolio optimization, 301 n.11, 353*b*
Marshall, Alfred, 156
Marshall, John, Supreme Court opinion by, 3, 4 n.1
Martingale prices, **705**
Masulis, Ronald, 481 n.17, 517 n.37, 773 n.22, 911 n.14
Matching principle, **857**–59
Mathews, Scott, on real options, 730*b*
Mattel, Inc., 851
Maturity date, **212**
Mauer, D. C., 858 n.3
Mayer, C., 916 n.21, 921 n.24
Mayers, D., 931 n.9
Maytag Corporation, 47
Mean reversion, 306*b*
Meckling, William, 504 n.17, 508 n.22
Mehta, P., 919 n.23
Merger-arbitrage spread, **886**
Mergers and acquisitions, 873–902
　background and historical trends, 874–75
　data case, 901–2
　evaluating value of potential, 883–84 (*see also* Capital budgeting with leverage and market imperfections)
　market reaction to takeovers, 875–76
　problems, 899–901
　reasons to acquire, 877–83
　summary, 898
　takeover defenses, 888–92
　takeover process, 883–88
　ten largest transactions (1995–2005), 874*t*
　value added from takeover, 892–97
Merger waves, **874**, 875*f*
Merrill Lynch Global Private Equity, 780 n.2
Merton, Robert, 410, 685, 710 n.6. *See also* Black-Scholes Option Pricing Model
Meschke, J. F., 909 n.10

Method of comparables, **262**
　comparison with discounted cash flow methods, 264–65
　limitations of multiples, 264, 265*t*
　valuation multiples, 262–64
Metrick, A., 911 n.13
Michaely, R., 543 n.10, 547 n.17, 549 n.19, 549 n.20, 556 n.25, 557 n.28, 557 n.29, 558 n.33, 559 n.34
Microsoft Corporation, 8, 331, 878, 908
　J. Connors on dividends paid by, 531, 562*b*
　as corporate investor, 754
　dividend, cash, and beta of, 444*b*
　dividends paid by, 531, 533*f*, 551*e*
　early exercise of put option on stocks of, 673–74*e*
　stock option quotes on, 673*t*
　stock repurchases made by, 531
Microsoft Excel spreadsheet, 106–8. *See also* Annuity spreadsheet; Spreadsheets
　computing future value in, 107*e*
　computing internal rate of return in, 113*e*
　computing variance, covariance, and correlation in, 330*b*
　functions, 106
　IRR function, 196
　mistakes involving NPV and IRR functions of, 115*e*
　NPV function, 189–90
Mikkelson, Wayne, 517 n.37, 911 n.15
Milbourn, T., 911 n.14
Miles, J. A., 602 n.22, 604 n.23
Miller, Merton, 429, 460, 471 n.10, 540 n., 604 n.23, 805 n.3
　as Nobel prize winner, 450*b*
　propositions of (*see* Modigliani-Miller (MM) propositions)
Mitchell, Mark, 876
MM. *See* Modigliani-Miller (MM) propositions
Modeling. *See* Financial modeling, case study of
Modigliani, Franco, 429, 460, 540 n.7, 604 n.23
　as Nobel prize winner, 450*b*
　propositions of (*see* Modigliani-Miller (MM) propositions)
Modigliani-Miller (MM) propositions, 491, 498, 520, 841, 928, 933
　earnings per share and, 447–48*e*
　influence of, 449–50
　on irrelevance of dividend policies, 539–40, 550
　Law of One Price and, 432
　leases and, 807
　pizza analogy and, 464*b*
　proposition I on leverage, arbitrage, and firm value, 432–37, 493
　proposition II on leverage, risk, and cost of capital, 437–45
　real world conditions and, 433*b*
Moeller, S., 876 n.3, 884 n.7
Momentum strategy, **406**
Money, time value of. See Time value of money
Monopoly gains, mergers/acquisitions and potential, 878–79, 891
Monsanto Corporation, 563, 564

Monte Carlo simulation, **707**
Montie, Jeff, 178
Moody's bond ratings, 231, 232*t*
Moral hazard, **931**
Morck, Randall, 508 n.22, 919 n.23
Morellec, Erwan, 512 n.30
Morgan Stanley Capital International World Index, 284 n.1
Mortgage(s)
　agency securities and, 788
　option to prepay, 733–34, 788
　pool, 788
　refinancing, 734
Mortgage bonds, **782**, 783*t*
Mortgage interest rate, **738**
　calculating, 747–48
　historical, 734*f*, 738*f*
Mossin, Jan, 363
MSCI Barra model, 416
　firm characteristics used by, 417*t*
　weights and return estimates, 418*t*
Mueller, H. M., 894 n.16
Mullainathan, S., 919 n.23
Mullins, David, 517 n.37
Multifactor models, **410**. *See also* Capital Asset Pricing Model (CAPM); Characteristic variable model of expected returns; Multifactor model of risk
Multifactor models of risk, 401, 409–15
　building multifactor model, 411
　calculating cost of capital using Fama-French Carhart factor specification, 413–15
　selecting portfolios, 411–13
　using factor portfolios, 409–10
Multifactor Model of Risk equation, 411
Multifactor Model of Risk with Self-Financing Portfolios equation, 411
Multiple regression, **409**
Multiples, cash, 645–47
Multiples, continuation value and, 639–40
Multiples, stock valuation using, 262–64
　limitations of, 264, 265*t*
Multiple securities
　computing WACC with, 442
　valuing equity with, 436*e*
Multiple stock portfolios, 341–44
　efficient frontier with, 344*f*
　volatility and expected return for, 343*f*
Municipal bonds, **788**
　calls on New York City, 790*b*
Murphy, K., 907 n.4
Mutually exclusive projects, **161**
　differences in scale, 161–64
　incremental IRR investment rule and, 164–66
　timing of cash flows and, 164, 165*f*
*MV*ᵢ (total market capitalization of security *i*), 375
Myers, S. C., 582 n.4
Myers, Stewart, 505 n.18, 516 n.36, 518, 815 n.13

N (date of last cash flow in stream of cash flows), 91, 92
N (notational principal of a swap contract), 960

n (number of periods), 214. *See also* Time periods
  solving for, 114–16
N (terminal date or forecast horizon), 249
N_T (premerger number of shares of target outstanding), 885
N_i (number of shares outstanding of security *i*), 375
$N(d)$ (normal distribution), 694, 949
Naik, V., 415 n.15, 727 n.2
Narayanan, M. P., 880 n.5, 890 n.12
NASDAQ, 13, 14*f*, 563, 758
  SOES bandits in, 63*b*
National Venture Capital Association, 757 n.3
Natural hedge, 938
Navistar International, 459
Nayak, S., 563 n.36
NBC Universal, 575, 589
Negative cash flow shocks, financing needs for, 854–55
Neiman Marcus, 29
Nelson, J., 909 n.11
Net debt, cash and, **444**–45
Net income or earnings, **27**, 28
Net present value (NPV), 48, **54**–55, 677
  cutting growth of negative, cash retention and, 554*e*
  equation, 54, 164
  Excel spreadsheet function of, 115*b*
  of foreign projects, 974–75
  free cash flow and, 189–90
  as function of discount rate, 150, 151*f*
  growth potential and calculation of, 727, 729, 731
  individual preferences and, 57–59
  mergers/acquisitions and positive-, 877
  mutually exclusive investments of different lengths and, 734–37
  NPV Decision Rule and, 55–57
  of stream of cash flows, 94–95
  timing of cash flows and, 164, 165*f*
  timing of investments and, 723, 724*f*
  of trading securities, 64–65
Net present value (NPV) investment rule, **149**
  discounted free cash flow model and, 260
  multiple IRRs and, 155, 156*f*
  persistence of rules other than, 160*b*
  stand-alone projects and, 150–51
Net profit margin, **29**
Net working capital (NWC), **23**, 187–88
  changing sales and needs for, 188*e*
  increase of, in year *t*, 188
  management of (*see* Working capital management)
  overview of, 830–32
New York City, municipal bonds, 790*b*
New York Stock Exchange (NYSE), 13, 14*f*, 563, 758
  Composite Index, 389, 658
  stock price distribution for firms on, 564*f*
Nguyen, H., 821
95% confidence interval, **295**
No arbitrage
  efficient markets hypothesis versus, 271–72
  forward exchange rate, 944–45*e*
  portfolio diversification, risk premium, and, 305–7

No arbitrage, security prices and, 61–67
  determining interest rate from bond prices, 64
  determining no-arbitrage price, 62–63
  NPV of trading securities, 64–65
  valuing portfolios, 66–67
  valuing securities, 61–62
No arbitrage price, **62**–63, 469–70
  calculating range of, 74*e*
  computing, 63*e*
  equation, 63
  of risky security, 69–70
Nobel Prize winners
  G. Akerlof, M. Spence, and J. Stiglitz, 515*b*
  H. Markowitz and J. Tobin, 353*b*
  R. Merton and M. Scholes, 685
  F. Modigliani and M. Miller, 450*b*
  W. Sharpe, 395*b*
No default bonds, 228
Nominal interest rate, **131**–32
Non-callable bonds, 791, 792
Non-cash items, free cash flow and, 191–92
Non-dividend paying stocks, early exercise of options on, 672–74
Non-tax lease, **811**
  comparing, with standard loan, 819*e*
  evaluating, 818–19
Nontradable wealth, 407–9
Norli, Oyvind, 773 n.22
Normal market, **60**
Notes (corporate debt), **782**, 783*t*
Notes in financial statements, 36
Notional principal, **957**
Novaes, Walter, 512 n.30
NPER function (annuity spreadsheet notation for number of periods or dates of last cash flow), 106
NPV. *See* Net present value (NPV)
NPV Decision Rule, **55**–57
  accepting/rejecting projects and, 55–56
  choosing among projects and, 56–57
NPV function, Excel, 115*b*
NPV investment rule, **149**. *See also* Net present value (NPV) investment rule (NPV)
NWC (net working capital in year *t*), 188

Off-balance sheet transactions, **36**
Oil, commodity futures contracts for, 935, 936*f*, 939*b*
Olstein, Robert, 38 n.9
$1.00 out lease, **805**
On-the-run bond, **227**
Open interest, **657**
OpenIPO, 758–59
Open market repurchase, **534**
Operating activity, statement of cash flows, 32–33
Operating cycle, **831**
Operating expenses, 27
Operating income, **27**
Operating lease, **808**–10
  at Alaska Air Group, 808*b*
  capital leases versus, 810*e*
Operating losses, mergers/acquisitions and, 879–80

Operating margin, **29**
  equation, 29
Operational improvements, business plan and, 626–27
Opler, Timothy, 497 n.8, 842 n.6
Opportunity cost, **182**
  of capital, 140, **141**
  of idle assets, 183*b*
  of using existing asset, 182 n.3
Optimal capital structure
  with taxes, 476–84
  tradeoff theory and, 501–3
Optimal portfolio, 323–61
  data case, 361
  efficient portfolio, cost of capital and, 349–55
  efficient portfolio, risk versus return and, 335–44
  example of identifying choice of, 348–49*e*
  expected returns, 324–25
  large portfolio volatility, 332–35
  H. Markowitz and J. Tobin on, 353*b*
  problems, 358–60
  risk-free saving and borrowing, 345–49
  summary, 355–57
  two-stock portfolio volatility, 325–32
Option(s). *See* Financial options; Financial-options valuation; Real option(s)
Option delta, **702**
Option Price in the Binomial Model equation, 689
Option writer, **656**
Oracle Corporation, valuing call option with Black-Scholes formula for, 695–96*e*, 697*f*, 698*f*
Organization for Economic Co-operation and Development (OECD), 9
  employee participation in corporate governance in countries of, 920*t*
Original issue discount (OID), **782**
Outliers, beta estimates and, 389, 390*f*
Out-of-the-money, **658**, 662
Outside (independent) directors, **905**
Over-allotment allocation (greenshoe provision), **764**
Overhead expenses, **184**
Over-investment problem, 503, **504**
Ovide, Shira, 910 n.
Ownership. *See also* Shareholder(s)
  concentration of, 507–8
  controlling, and pyramids, 916–19

P (initial loan principal, initial deposit, or initial investment), 99
P (put option price), 660, 668, 696, 697
P_A (premerger share price of acquirer), 885
P_{cum} (cum-dividend stock price), 536, 539, 545
P_{ex} (ex-dividend stock price), 536, 545
P_i (price per share of security *i*), 375
P_r (probability of return *R*), 286
P_{rep} (stock price with share repurchase), 537
P_{retain} (stock price if excess cash is retained), 552
P_T (premerger share price of target), 885
P_t (stock price at end of year *t*), 246, 247
Pacific Gas and Electric Corporation, 497

Palacios-Huerta, Ingacio, 408 n.8
Palacios, Miguel, 408 n.7
Palepu, K., 557 n.28
Palia, D., 909 n.10
Panunzi, F., 894 n.16
Par, **217**
Partch, Megan, 517 n.37, 911 n.15
Partnerships, **5**–7
Passive portfolio, **376**
Pass-through, **788**
Patel, J., 415 n.14
Pay, management performance and, 907–8
Payable date (distribution date), **532**
Payables management, 838–40
Payback investment rule, **151**–52
    using, 152*e*
Payback period, **152**
Payment loan, single, end-of-period, 859
Payments pattern, aging schedules and, **838**
Payoffs of financial options at expiration, 659–68
    combinations of options, 664–67
    long position in option contracts, 659–60
    profits for holding options to expiration, 662–63
    of put option at maturity, 660*e*
    returns for holding options to expiration, 663–64
    short position in option contracts, 660, 661*e*, 662
    from straddle, 665*f*
Payout policy, 531–71
    data case, 570–71
    defined, **532**
    distributions to shareholders, 532–35
    dividend capture and tax clienteles, 545–49
    dividends and share repurchases, 535–41
    fixed, debt financing and, 592–93
    payout versus cash retention, 549–55
    problems, 567–70
    signaling, 555–60
    stock dividends, splits, and spin-offs, 560–64
    summary, 565–66
    tax disadvantage of dividends, 541–44
Pecking order hypothesis, **518**
Peers, Martin, 910 n.
P/E (price/earnings) ratio equation, 30.
    See also Price-earnings (P/E) ratio
Perfect capital markets, 427, **432**. *See also*
    Capital structure in perfect market
    assumptions of, 460
    cash retention with, 549–50
    default and bankruptcy in, 492–94
    delaying dividends with, 550*e*
    dividend policy with, 541
    insurance pricing in, 927–28
    investor payout preferences in, 538
    Law of One Price and, 459
    lease payments in, 803–4*e*
    loan payments in, 804–5*e*
    pizza analogy, Modigliani-Miller
        propositions, and, 450*b*, 464*b*
    stock repurchase in, 537
    weighted average cost of capital
        and leverage with, 440*f*

Performance
    compensation and manager, 906–8
    post-SEO, 773*f*
    size of board of directors and, 906
Period. *See* Time periods
Periodically adjusted debt, 601–3
Permanent working capital, 857
Perotti, E. C., 510 n.28
Perpetual bond, 95, 97*b*
Perpetuity(ies), **95**–98
    common mistakes in determining value
        of, 98*b*
    endowing, 97*e*
    growing, 102–4
    historical examples of, 97*b*
    present value of, 95–96
    present value of continuously growing, 147
    present value of growing, 103
Personal taxes, 471–76
    capital budgeting and, 606–8
    determining actual tax advantage of debt
        and, 474–76
    in interest tax shield, 471–73
    valuing interest tax shield with, 474–75
Peterson, M. A., 834 n.3
Pharmacia Corporation, 563, 564
Phi (ϕ) (permanence of the debt level), 604
Pincombe, S., 914 n.17
Pizza analogy, MM propositions, perfect
    capital markets and, 450*b*, 464*b*
Pledging of accounts receivable, **863**
PMT function (annuity spreadsheet notation
    for cash flow), 106
Poison pill, **888**–89
Policy
    compensation, 652, 906–8
    investment and interest rate, 132–33
    payout, 531–71
Policy limits, **931**
Pool (mortgage), **788**
Portfolio(s), 323–61
    beta of, 372
    calculating returns of, 324–25*e*
    data case, 361
    diversification in stock (*see* Diversification
        in stock portfolios)
    duration-neutral, 954–55
    efficient, 308, 349 [*see also* Efficient
        portfolio(s)]
    equally weighted, 332–34
    equal-ownership, 376
    expected return of, 324–25
    factor, 409–10
    general, diversification with, 334–35
    high-minus-low (HML), 413
    immunized, 954–55
    inefficient, 337
    insurance on financial options, 666–67
    large (*see* Large portfolios)
    levered, 346–47
    market, 308, 364–68
    multiple (*see* Multiple stock portfolios)
    passive, 376
    price-weighted, 377
    prior one-year momentum (PR1YR), 413
    problems, 358–60
    replicating, 686–88, 702–4

returns on large, 297–98
risk-free saving and borrowing and, 345–49
selecting, for multifactor risk model,
    411–13
small-minus-big (SMB), 413
summary, 355–57
tangent, 347–49
two-stock, 325–32, 335–38
valuation of, 66–67
value-weighted, 375–77
volatility, 304–5*e*
volatility of large, 332–35
volatility of two-stock, 325–32
Portfolio insurance, **667**
Portfolio weight, **324**
Portfolio weight equation, 324
Positive cash flow shocks, financing needs for,
    855–56
Post-money valuation, **755**
    funding and ownership and, 755–56*e*
Poterba, James, 476 n.11, 553 n.22
Poulsen, A. B., 891 n.13
Power, D. M., 915 n.19
Prabhala, N., 563 n.36
Precautionary balance, **842**
Predetermined debt levels, 595–96
Predetermined debt schedule, 621
Preferences
    calculating value dependent on, 51*e*
    net present value and individual, 57–59
Preferred stock, **755**
Preliminary prospectus (red herring), **761**
Premium(s), bond, **217**–18
Pre-money valuation, **755**
Prepackaged bankruptcy, **496**
Prepay (mortgage), 733, **734**
Present value (PV), **54**–59. *See also* Net present
    value (NPV)
    adjusted (*see* Adjusted present value (APV)
        method of valuation)
    calculating, 747–48
    of cash flow, 88*e*
    of cash flow stream, 92–93*e*
    computing, using term structure of interest
        rate, 135*e*
    of continuously growing perpetuity, 147–48
    of growing annuity, 104
    of growing perpetuity, 102–4
    internationally integrated capital markets
        and, 971*e*
    of perpetuity, 95–96
    value of investment opportunity, 728
Present Value of Continuously Growing
    Perpetuity equation, 147
Pretax income, 28
Price(s)
    bid, and ask, 13, 73 n.8
    bond (*see* Bond prices)
    competitive, 73
    of currency forwards, 943–46
    of currency options, 949
    determining cash values using market,
        48–50
    factors affecting, on financial options,
        669–71
    financial option (*see* Financial-option prices)
    of initial public offerings (IPOs), 764–65

of insurance, in perfect market, 927–28
no-arbitrage, 62–63
product adoption and changes in, 185*e*
risk, return, and market, 72–73
risk security and no-arbitrage, 69–70
seasoned equity offering and reaction of, 772–73
security, 61–67
underpricing IPOs, 765–67
Price-earnings ratio (P/E), **30**
mergers and, 882*e*
unlevered, 640
valuation multiples and, 262–63
Price-earnings ratio equation, 262
Price of a Call Option on a Currency equation, 949
Price of a Coupon Bond equation, 225
Price risk management liabilities, 37 n.8
Price-to-book [PB] ratio (market-to-book ratio), **25**
Price-weighted portfolio, **377**
Pricing currency options, 949
Pricing initial public offerings (IPOs), 764–65
auction IPOs, 759*e*
underpricing, 765–67
Pricing strategies, scenario analysis of, 199*t*
Primary offering, IPOs, **758**
Primary shares, **771**
Prime rate, **859**
Principal-agent problem, **10**–11
Pringle, J., 591 n.13
Prior one-year momentum (PR1YR) portfolio, **413**
Private companies, **13**
bank loans and debt of, 785–86
equity financing for, 752–57
Private debt, **785**–86
Private information, stock prices and, 269, 270*e*
Private placement, **785**–86
Probability distribution for returns, **286**, 287*f*
variance and standard deviation, 287–89
Processing float, **835**
Product(s), sales by category of, 36–37
Production capacity requirements, 627*e*
Profit(s). *See also* Earnings; Return(s)
gross, 27
for holding options to expiration, 662–63
repatriated, 976–97
from straddle, 665*f*
Profitability index, **167**–68
equation, 167
with human resource constraints, 167–68*e*
shortcomings of, 168
Profitability index rule, **737**–38
applying with hurdle rates and, 740
Profitability ratios, 29
computing, 31*e*
Profitable growth, 251–52
Pro forma
balance sheet, 635*t*, 636*t*, 852 n.1
income statement, **629**–31, 852 n.1
Project(s). *See also* Investment opportunities
analysis of, 196–99
comparing, using net present value, 55–57, 58*f*, 59
cost of capital based on, 589–93

cost of working capital for, 832*e*
foreign (*see* International corporate finance)
net present value rule and stand-alone, 150–51
selection of, with resource constraints, 166–68
valuing, with continuous cash flows, 148*e*
Project-Based WACC formula, 591
Project externalities, **182**–84
Project WACC with a Fixed Debt Schedule equation, 604
Promissory note, **859**
Property, reasons for empty urban lots, 725*b*
Property insurance, **926**
Prospectus, IPO, 761, 762*f*
Protective put, **667**
Proxy contests, 910
Proxy error, 407
Proxy fight, **888**
Public companies, **12**
corporate bonds and debt, 780–85
initial public offerings (IPOs) for, 757–70
merger waves (1926–2005), 875*f*
seasoned equity offerings (SEO), 770–74
Public information, stock prices and, 268–69
Public warehouse, **865**
Pulvino, Todd, 497
Purchase, lease versus, 814–15
Pure discount bond, **212**. *See also* Zero-coupon bond(s)
Put-call parity, **668**–69, 672, 674, 675
Put option, **656**
on Amazon.com stocks, 657*t*, 658
Black-Scholes replication portfolio of, 704
on Microsoft stocks, 673–74*e*
parity with call options, 668–69
payoff of, at maturity, 660*e*
payoff of short position, in put option, 661*e*
profits on holding position in, until expiration, 663*e*
protective, 667
valuing European, with Black-Scholes formula, 696–98
valuing, with binomial pricing formula, 689–90*e*, 692–93*e*
Put Price at Expiration equation, 660
PV. See Present value (PV)
PV function (present value), 106
PV_n (present value on date *n*), 99
Pyle, David, 515 n.34
Pyramid structure, corporate governance and, **917**–19

q (dividend yield), 700
QUALCOMM Incorporated, 179*b*
Quick ratio, **26**

$\bar{R}$ (average return), 292, 293 n.6
r (cost of capital of an investment opportunity), 311
r (discount rate). *See* Discount rate (*r*)
r (interest rate). *See* Interest rate(s) (*r*)
r_A (expected return/cost of capital of firm assets), 439
R_D (return on debt), 438
r_D (expected return/debt cost of capital), 438, 465, 466, 481, 577, 596, 601, 619, 817

r_D^* (equity-equivalent debt cost of capital), 607
r_E (expected return/cost of capital of unlevered equity), 438, 439, 577, 590
r_E (equity cost of capital), 465, 466
R_E (return on levered equity), 438
r_E *See* Equity cost of capital (r_E)
r_f (risk-free interest), **52**, 345, 364, 409, 464, 537, 688
R_i (required return; return of security *i*), 324, 350, 353, 364
r_L (cost of capital for an insured loss), 927
R_{mkt} (return of the market portfolio), 637
r_n (interest rate or discount rate for n-year term), 134–35, 214
R_P (return of portfolio *P*), 324
r_r (real interest rate), 132, 133*f*
r_s (discount rate for security *s*), 72
r_s (return on security), 637
R_s (return of stocks), 409, 417
R_t (realized or total return of a security from date *t* − 1 to *t*), 290
$\bar{r}_t$ (floating interest rate on date *t*), 958
r_U (return on cost of capital), 639
r_U (unlevered cost of capital), 817
R_U (return on unlevered equity), 438
R_U (unlevered cost of capital), 582, 594, 599 n.20, 621
r_{wacc} (weighted average cost of capital), 259, 439, 465, 466, 577, 591, 602, 604, 606, 619, 641, 817
R_{xP} (return of portfolio with fraction *x* invested in portfolio *P* and (1 − *x*) invested in the risk-free security), 345
$r_\$$ (dollar interest rate), 943
$r_€$ (euro interest rate), 943
Raider, **888**
Rajan, R. G., 834 n.3
Ramaswamy, K., 549
Rampini, A., 812 n.9
RATE function (annuity spreadsheet notation for interest rate), 106
Ratio(s)
book-to-market, 403
comparison of financial, valuations and, 644, 645*t*
computing profitability and valuation, 31*e*
conversion, bond-stock, 794
current, 26
debt-equity, 25–26
leverage, 30
leverage, of options, 708, 709*f*
market-to-book, 25
mismatched, 30*b*
price-earnings (*see* Price-earnings (P/E ratio)
profitability, 29, 31
quick, 26
valuation, 30–31
Rational expectations, **387**
Raviv, A., 496 n.6, 510 n.27, 510 n.28, 931 n.9
Real interest rate, **131**–32
Realized return, **289**–90
for S&P 500, GM, and Treasury bills, 291*t*
Realized return equation, 289
RealNetworks, Inc., raising equity capital for, 751, 755, 756, 757, 761, 762*f*, 764, 765, 770, 771*f*

Real option(s), 717–48
    abandonment options, 731–34
    abandonment options in mortgage
        (calculating interest rates), 747–48
    deciding between mutually exclusive
        investments of different lengths, 734–37
    decision tree analysis for, 718–20
    defined, **718**
    delaying/choosing optimal time for
        investment opportunities, 721–26
    financial options versus, 718
    growth options, 726–31
    S. Mathews on, 730*b*
    problems, 742–46
    rules of thumb on, 737–40
    summary, 740–41
Recapitalization
    to capture tax shield, 468–71
    leveraged, 436, 437*t*
    market value balance sheet and, 470*t*, 471
    as takeover defense, 890–91
Receivables
    financial distress and loss of, 497
    management of, 835–38
Recessions, short-term versus long-term
        interest rates and economic, 136*f*
Record date, **532**
Red herring (preliminary prospectus), **761**
Refinance, **734**
Registered bonds, **782**
Registration statement, **761**
Regulation, 911–16
    antitrust, 878–79
    approval for takeovers following, 891–92
    Cadbury Commission, 914–15
    on insider trading, 915–16
    Sarbanes-Oxley Act and, 20*b*, 35, 38,
        513 n.31, 758, 912, 913*b*, 914
Reinsurance companies, 927 n.2
Rendleman, R. J., 686 n.2
Reorganization plans, Chapter 11, 495 n.3
Repatriated profits, **976**–77
Repayment provisions, bonds, 789–96
    calculating yield to call, 792–93*e*
    call provisions, 790–92
    convertible provisions, 794–95
    sinking funds, 793–94
Replicating portfolio, **686**–88
    Black-Scholes formula and, 702–4
Replicating Portfolio in the Binomial Model
        equation, 689
Repurchase agreements, as short-term
        investment options, 843*t*
Required return, **350**
    beta and, 349–51
    Sharpe ratio and, for different
        investments, 352t
Required Return for Investment *i* Given
        Current Portfolio *P* equation, 350
Research and development expenses, 184
Research and development-intensive firms,
        optimal level of debt and, 511–12
Residual value of leases, **803**–4
Resource constraints
    evaluation of projects with, 166–67
    profitability index and, 167–68
Retained earnings, **34**
Retention rate, **251**

Retirement savings plan
    annuity, 101*e*
    growing annuity, 105*e*
Return(s), 30, **64**. *See also* Risk and return
    arithmetic average, versus compound
        annual, 296*b*
    beta and required, 349–51
    beta estimations from historical, 380–82
    on bonds, 64 [*see also* Yield to maturity
        (YTM)]
    calculating portfolio, 324–25*e*
    direct estimation of, 382*b*
    efficiency of market portfolio and past, 406
    empirical distribution of, 292
    on equity with and without leverage, 430*t*
    excess (*see* Excess returns)
    expected, 69 (*see also* Expected (mean)
        return)
    historical, for stocks and bonds, 289–97
    for holding financial options to expiration,
        663, 664*f*
    improving, in efficient portfolios, 337–38*e*
    of individual stocks, 298, 299*f*
    internal rate of, 111–14 ([*ee also* Internal
        rate of return (IRR)]
    on large portfolios, 297–99
    percentage of, versus dollar impact on value,
        163–64
    positive-alpha portfolio and past, 406
    probability distributions of, 286, 287*f*, 289*f*
    relationship to risk (*see* Risk and return)
    required, 349–51
    risk, market prices, and, 72–73 (*see* Risk;
        Risk and return)
    from short sales, 339*e*
    on stocks, 247, 289–99
    total, 290
    for unleveraged equity, 429*t*
    using past, to predict future returns, 294–97
    variance and volatility of, 293–94
Return of capital, **534**
Return on assets (ROA), **30**
Return on equity (ROE), **30**
Reuters, estimation methods used by, 389*t*
Revenue bonds, **788**
Revenue estimates, 178
Reverse split, **563**
Revolving line of credit, **785**, **860**
Rho *ρ* (risk-neutral probability), 704, 705,
        706, 728
Rice, Joseph L. III, on private equity
        businesses, 646*b*
Rigas, John and Timothy, 509*b*
Rights offer, **771**
    raising money with, 772*e*
Risk. *See also* Risk and return
    beta and market, 368–69
    common, versus independent, 299–302
    cost of capital and, 311–13
    credit (*see* Credit risk)
    of defaults on bonds, 229–31
    of financial options, 707–10
    hedging commodity price, 938–39
    insurance and assessment of, 930
    interest rates and, 138–39
    management of (*see* Risk management)
    market value of equity and, 405*e*
    measuring systematic, 308–10

mergers/acquisitions and reduction of,
        880–81
    mistakes in hedging, 938*b*
    multifactor models of, 409–15
    as relative to overall market, 70–72
    return, market prices, and, 72–73
    risk premiums and, 70, 72*t* (*See also* Risk
        premium)
    systematic (*see* Systematic risk)
    taxes and, 138–40
    transferring, by leasing, 821
    in two-stock portfolio, 326
    valuing interest tax shield without, 463*e*
    volatility and independent, 334*e*
Risk, multifactor models of, 409–15
    building multifactor model, 411
    calculating cost of capital using Fama-
        French-Carhart factor specification,
        413–15
    selecting portfolios, 411–13
    using factor portfolios, 409–10
Risk, price of, 67–73. *See also* Risk and return
    case flows and, 68
    no-arbitrage price of risky securities,
        69–70
    relative to overall market, 70–72
    risk, return, and market prices, 72–73
    risk aversion and risk premium, 68–69
Risk and return, 283–322
    capital market efficiency and, 313–15
    common measures of, 286–89
    common versus independent risk and,
        299–302
    data case, 321–22
    diversifiable versus systematic, 306, 307*e*
    diversification of stock portfolios and,
        303–7
    effects of leverage on, 430–32
    efficient portfolio and, 335–44
    estimating expected return, 307–11
    of financial options, 707–10
    first look at, 284–85
    historical returns of stocks and bonds,
        and, 289–97
    historical tradeoff between, 297–99
    R. Lert on portfolio diversification
        and, 314*b*
    models of risk (*see* Capital Asset Pricing
        Model; Systematic risk, alternative
        models of)
    optimal portfolio choice [*see* Optimal
        portfolio; Portfolio(s)]
    problems, 318–21
    returns, arithmetic average versus
        compound annual, 296*b*
    risk and cost of capital, 311–13
    summary, 315–17
Risk arbitrageurs, **885**–87
Risk aversion, **68**–69
Risk-free interest rate (r_f), **52**
    zero-coupon bonds and, 214
Risk-Free Interest Rate with Maturity *n*
        equation, 214
Risk-free saving and borrowing, 345–49
    borrowing and buying stocks on margin,
        346–47
    identifying tangent portfolios, 347–49
    investing in risk-free securities, 345, 346*f*

Risk management, 925–67
  commodity price risk, 933–39
  exchange rate risk, 939–50
  insurance, 926 32
  interest rate risk, 950–60
  in IPOs, 764–65
  problems, 963–67
  summary, 960–62
Risk-neutral probabilities (financial option valuation), 704–7
  calculating, 747
  defined, **705**
  implications of, 705
  option pricing and, 706–7
  risk-neutral two-state model, 704–5
Risk premium, **69**
  CAPM model and determination of, 368–75
  dependence of, on risk, 70
  determining, using security market line, 391–92
  estimating, 310–11
  negative, 70–71*e*
  portfolio diversification, no arbitrage and, 305–7
  risk and, for different securities, 72*t*
  systematic risk and, for debt, unlevered equity, and levered equity, 431*t*
Risk premium equation, 310
Risk tolerance, 354*b*
Risky debt, calculating beta of, 710–12
Ritter, Jay R., 597 n., 765 n.13, 769 n.15, 770 n.19
RJR-Nabisco, leveraged buyout of, by Kohlberg, Kravis, and Roberts (KKR), 895*b*
Road show, **763**
Roberts, Michael, 518 n.41
Rock, Kevin, 766 n.14
Rogel, Steve, 892*b*
Roll, Richard, 394 n.21, 407 n.5, 407 n.6, 509 n.24
Ross, Stephen, 305 n.13, 407 n.5, 410, 514 n.32, 686
Rossi, S., 916 n.21
Rosten, Eric, 939 n.
Rothschild, M., 931 n.9
Rouwenhorst, Geert, 97*b*
Roy, Andrew, 353*b*
Royal & SunAlliance, dividend cut at, 557*b*
Royal Dutch Petroleum Company, merger with Shell Transport and Trading Company, 873
Ruback, R. S., 584 n.6, 876 n.3
Rubinstein, Mark, 386 n.10, 442 n.4, 686
Rule of 72, 116*b*
Russell Investment Group, 314
Rusticus, T., 911 n.13
Rydqvist, Kristian, 765 n.
Ryngaert, M., 889 n.10

S (spot exchange rate), 943
S (stock price), 659, 668, 688, 694, 701, 727
S (value of all synergies), 884
S_x (value of stock excluding dividends), 700, 722
Safeway Inc., 460–61

Sale(s)
  calculating, by product category, 36–37*e*
  net working capital requirements with changing, 188*e*
Sale and leaseback, **802**
Sales-type lease, **802**
Salvage value, 192–93. *See also* Liquidation value
  adding, to free cash flow, 193*e*
Samurai bonds, **784**
Sarbanes-Oxley Act (SOX), 20*b*, 35, 38, 513 n.31, 758, 912–14, 908 n.7
  L. Harris on, 913*b*
Sarig, O. H., 510 n.28
Sarin, A., 919 n.23
Saving
  borrowing rates versus rates of, 382–86
  risk-free borrowing and, 345–49
Savings and loan institutions
  crisis in (1970s), 954*b*
  duration mismatch in, 952–56
Savings plan, solving for number of periods in, 116*e*
Sazaby, Inc., joint venture with Starbucks Coffee, 969
Scale, differences in investment opportunity, 161–64
  changes in scale, 163
  identical scale, 161–62
  percentage return versus dollar impact on value and, 163–64
Scandals. *See* Corporate scandals
Scenario analysis, **198**
  of alternative pricing strategies, 199*t*
Schallheim, James, 807 n.4, 821 n.17
Scharfstein, David, 510 n.29
Scherbina, Anna, 392 n.18
Schlingemann, F., 876 n.3, 884 n.7
Schneider, Craig, 859 n.5
Scholes, Myron, 383 n.7, 471 n.10, 676 n.6, 685. *See also* Black-Scholes Option Pricing Model
Schwert, G. W., 889 n.11
"S" corporations, **9**
SD(*R*) (standard deviation of return R), 287, 327, 329, 330, 333
$SD(R_i)$ (standard deviation (volatility) of the return of security *i*), 380
Seasonalities, short-term financing needs and, 852–54
Seasoned equity offering (SEO), 770–74
  costs, 774
  mechanics of, 770–72
  price reaction, 772–73
Secondary offerings, IPOs, **758**
Secondary shares, **771**
Secured debt, **783**
Secured loans, **863**–66
  accounts receivable as collateral, 863–64
  inventory as collateral, 864–66
Securities and Exchange Commission (SEC), U.S., 20, 513, 758
  filing IPO registration statement with, 761, 762*f*
  Rule 144A, 785–86
Security(ies), **61**. *See also* Bond(s); Stock(s)
  agency (U.S. government), 788

  computing weight average cost of capital with multiple, 442
  derivative, 653, 707
  investing in risk-free, 345, 346*f*
  marketable, 21
  mispricing of, 598
  net present value (NPV) of, 64–65
  no-arbitrage price of risky, 69–70
  options on non-stock, 658
  pass-through, 788
  relative costs of issuing, 769*f*
  Treasury, 786t, 787
  valuing, 61–62
Security interest, **812**
Security market line (SML), **370**–72
  alpha of stocks and, 373–74
  capital market line and, 370–71*f*
  deviations from, 374*f*
  with differing interest rates, 385–86
  empirical, versus CAPM-predicted, 393*f*
  estimating cost of capital from, 390–92
Security prices, 61–67
  determining no-arbitrage price, 62–63
  security value, 61–62
Segmented capital markets, **977**–81
  differential access to, 977–78
  macro-level distortions in, 978–79
  risky government bonds and, 978–79*e*
  valuing foreign acquisition in, 979–80*e*
Self-financing portfolio, **411**
Senber, Lemma, 498 n.14
Sengupta, K., 510 n.28
Senority, **783**
Sensitivity
  estimating interest rate, using duration, 952*e*
  interest rate, of bonds, 222–23*e*
  to marketing and support costs, 198*e*
  measuring, with IRR, 150, 151*f*
Sensitivity analysis, **197**–98
  financial valuation, 647–48
  stock valuation, 260–61*e*
  using IRR, 150, 151*f*
SEO. *See* Seasoned equity offering (SEO)
Separation Principle, **65**
  applied to investment and financing, 65–66*e*
  Modigliani-Miller propositions and, 432
  project evaluation and, 181 n.2
Scrial bonds, **788**
Shackelford, D. A., 482
Shapiro, A., 919 n.23
Share(s). *See also* Stock(s)
  Berkshire Hathaway's A and B class, 561*b*
  dividends on [*see* Dividend(s)]
  dual class, 917
  earnings per [*see* Earnings per share (EPS)]
  price of, and mergers/acquisitions, 875, 8/6t
  of seasoned equity offerings, 771
  stock repurchases and supply of, 538*b*
Shareholder(s), **7**. *See also* Investor(s)
  activism by, 12*b*, 909, 910*b*
  cashing out by, 505
  changing composition of payouts to, 544*f* (*see also* Payout policy)
  conflict between controlling, and minority, 916–19

Shareholder(s). *See also* Investor(s) (continued)
  defenses of, against takeovers, 888–92
  dividend distributions to, 532–34
  dividends distributions to, compared
    to share repurchases, 535–41
  flow-to-equity method of valuation and,
    585–88
  managing conflicts between managers and,
    908–11
  protection of rights of, 916
  share repurchases from, 534–35
  takeover process and approval of, 887–88
  tax considerations of dividend distributions
    to, 541–49
  value added from takeovers and benefits for,
    892–97
Shareholder initiatives, 12*b*
Share repurchase, **256**–57, 534–35
  alternative repurchase prices, 469–70*e*
  dividends compared to, 535–41
  market timing and, 559–60*e*
  open market, 534
  recapitalizing to capture tax shield and,
    468–69
  share price equation, 256
  signaling and, 558–60
  targeted, 535
  tender offer, 534–35, 884–85
  valuation with, 257*e*
Sharpe, S., 821 n.17
Sharpe, William F., 312 n.15, 347 n.8,
    363 n.1. *See also* Sharpe ratio
  Capital Asset Pricing Model and, 363–64
  as Nobel prize winner, 395*b*
Sharpe ratio, **347**, 350
  required return and, for different
    investments, 352*t*
Sheahan, M., 753 n.
Shell Transport and Trading Company,
    merger with Royal Dutch Petroleum
    Company, 873
Sherman, Ann, 760 n.6, 763
Sherman Act of 1890, 891
Sherwin, Henry, 100 n.5
Shiller, Robert J., 243 n.5
Shivdasani, A., 905 n.2, 916 n.20
Shleifer, Andrei, 508 n.22, 919 n.23,
    921 n.24
Sholes, M., 549 n.20
Short interest, **340**
Short position, **339**
  in option contract, 660–62
Short sales, **62**, **339**–41
  mechanics of, 340*b*
  returns from, 339*e*
  two-stock portfolio and, 342*f*
  volatility with, 341*e*
Short term financing. *See* Financial planning,
    short-term; Working capital
    management)
Shutdown, option to, 731–33
Sidel, Robin, 760 n.
Siegel, Jeremy, 392 n.18
Sigma σ (volatility of stock's return), 694,
    701, 722
Signal, leverage as credible, 513–14

Signaling, payout policy as method of, 555–60
  dividends and, 556–58
  dividend smoothing and, 555–56
  share repurchases and, 558–60
Signaling theory of debt, **514**
Simon, Ruth, 760 n.
Simple interest, **127**
Single-factor model, **410**
Sinking fund, **793**–94
Sinquefield, Rex A., on risk models, 412*b*
Sirri, E. R., 315 n.18
Size effect, **402**–5
Skiadas, C., 387 n.11
Slovin, Myron, 774 n.23
Small-minus-big (SMB) portfolio, **413**
Small Order Execution System (SOES)
  "bandits" in, 63*b*
Small stocks, 284
  average annual returns for
    (1926–2004), 293*t*
  empirical distribution of
    (1926–2004), 292*f*
  size effect and returns of, 402–5
  value of investments in (1925–2005), 285*f*
  volatility of (1926–2004), 294*t*
  volatility versus excess return of
    (1926–2004), 297*t*
SMB. *See* Small-minus-big (SMB) portfolio
Smith, C. W., 507 n.20, 557 n.30, 931 n.9
SML. *See* Security market line (SML)
Sole proprietorships, **4**–5
Southwest Airlines, 29, 925, 934, 939*b*
Sovereign debt, **786**–88
Special dividend, **532**, 533*f*
Specialists, **13**
Special-purpose entity (SPE), **802**
Speculate, **658**, **939**
Speculative bonds, **231**
Spence, Michael, 515*b*
Spier, K. E., 510 n.28
Spin-off, **563**, 563–64
Spot exchange rate, **943**
Spot interest rates, **214**
Spread, **764**
Spreadsheets. *See also* Annuity spreadsheet;
    Microsoft Excel spreadsheet
  accelerated depreciation calculation, 192
  adjusted present value, with arbitrary debt
    levels, 622*t*
  adjusted present value, with debt levels
    solved iteratively, 622*t*
  adjusted present value and cost of capital,
    with fixed debt schedule, 605*t*
  APV estimate of initial equity value, 644*t*
  capital expenditure assumptions, 628*t*
  computing free cash flow to equity from
    free cash flow, 587*t*
  continuation value and debt capacity, 581*t*
  continuation value estimate, 640*t*
  discounted cash flow estimate of
    continuation value, with implied
    EBITDA multiple, 642*t*
  expected debt capacity, interest payments,
    and interest tax shield, 583*t*
  expected dollar free cash flows, 973*t*
  expected foreign free cash flows, 972*t*

  expected free cash flow, 578*t*
  expected free cash flows to equity, 586*t*
  free cash flow calculation, 186, 193
  free cash flow forecasts, 633*t*
  free cash flows, pound and dollar, 982*t*
  flow to equity (FTE) estimate of
    management costs, 652*t*
  income statement and balance sheet
    data, 624*t*
  incremental earnings forecast calculation,
    180, 183, 185
  interest payments and interest tax
    shield, 595*t*
  IRR and cash multiple for investment, 645*t*
  IRR calculation, 196
  leasing versus buying, 814*t*, 815*t*, 816*t*
  net present value (NPV) calculation, 190,
    191, 193
  net working capital forecast, 632*t*
  planned debt and interest payments, 629*t*
  pro forma balance sheet, 635*t*
  pro forma income statement, 630*t*
  pro forma statement of cash flows, 636*t*
  projected financial statements, financing
    needs and, 853*t*, 854*t*, 855*t*, 856*t*
  project levels of working capital, financing
    needs and, 857*t*
  sales and operating cost assumptions, 627*t*
  sensitivity analysis for investment, 647*t*
  solving problems using, 106–8
  sources and uses of funds, 629*t*
  WACC method, with fixed debt
    schedule, 606*t*
  working capital requirements calculation,
    187, 188, 631*t*
Springfield Snowboards, Inc., 852
  projected financial statements, 853*t*, 854*t*,
    855*t*, 856*t*
  projected levels of working capital, 857*t*
Stafford, Erik, 876
Staggered (classified) board, **890**
Stakeholder model, **919**
Standard and Poor's bond ratings, 231, 232*t*
Standard and Poor's 500, 66*b*, 284, 379, 658.
    See also Large stocks
  betas with respect to stocks of, 309*t*
  historical excess returns of, compared to
    Treasury securities, 391*t*
  two-year put options on index of, 675, 676*t*
Standard deviation, **287**–89
  Sharpe portfolio and, 347 n.9
Standard deviation equation, 287, 301
Standard error, **295**–96
Standard Error of the Estimate of the Expected
    Return equation, 295
Starbucks Coffee Company, joint venture with
    Japanese company, 969
State-contingent prices, **705**
Statement of cash flows, 21, **32**–34
  financial model-building and, 634–36
  financing activity, 33–34
  investment activity, 33
  operating activity, 32–33
  sample, 33*t*
Statement of stockholders' equity, 21, **36**
State prices, **705**

Stefek, Dan, 417 n.17
Stephens, C., 558 n.32
Step up, **887**
Stern, Joel M., on EVA tool, 157*b*, 158
Stewart, Bennett, 157*b*
Stewart, Martha, insider trading case, 915*b*
Stiglitz, Joseph, 515*b*, 931 n.9
Stillman, R., 879 n.4
Stock(s), 7. *See also* Equity; Share(s)
   alpha, 373–74
   buying on margin, 346–47
   as compensation for management, 906–7
   convertible preferred, 755
   dividends [*see* Dividend(s)]
   growth, 25
   historical returns of, 289–97
   indices for common (*see* Dow Jones
      Industrial Average; Standard and
      Poor's 500)
   investing in one's own company, 408*b*
   large (*see* Large stocks; Standard and
      Poor's 500)
   merger/acquisition offers in, 884–85
   ownership of corporate, 8
   portfolio of [*see* Portfolio(s)]
   preferred, 755
   price (*see* Stock prices)
   returns of individual, 298–99
   share repurchases (*see* Share repurchases)
   small (*see* Small stocks)
   value, 25 (*see also* Stock valuation)
Stock dividends, **533**. *See also* Dividend(s)
   splits and, 560–63
Stock exchanges. *See* Stock markets
Stockholder, 7. *See also* Shareholder(s)
Stockholders' equity, **21**, 24–25
   statement of, 36
Stock index arbitrage, 66*b*
Stock markets, **12**–14
   common indexes, 377–79
   largest, 13, 14*f*
   Nasdaq, 13 (*see also* NASDAQ)
   NYSE, 13 [*see also* New York Stock
      Exchange (NYSE)]
   relative weights of international, by market
      capitalization, 394*f*
Stock options, **28**. *See also* Financial
      option(s)
   on dividend paying stocks, 674–76
   employee, 482*b*, 699*b*
   executive, 699*b*
   interpreting quotations on, 656–58
   on non-dividend paying stocks, 672–74
Stock portfolios. *See* Diversification in stock
   portfolios; Portfolio(s)
Stock prices
   binomial pricing formula and,
      688–90, 693*f*
   distribution of, for firms on NY Stock
      Exchange, 564*f*
   dividend-discount model (*see* Dividend-
      discount model)
   dividend yields, capital gains and total
      returns, 247
   equity issuance and, 517
   financial distress costs and, 500*e*

information, investor competition and,
      266–72
   private information and, 270*e*
   public information and, 269*e*
   reaction of, to mergers/acquisitions,
      875, 876*t*
   strike price and, 670
Stock splits, **533**, 560–63
Stock valuation, 245–80
   data case, 279–80
   dividend-discount model, 249–56
   equity issuance and, 517, 518*f*
   M. Fedak on, 253*b*
   information, competition and stock prices,
      266–72
   Law of One Price and, 245, 246
   problems, 275–79
   stock prices, returns, and investment
      horizon, 246–49
   summary, 272–74
   total payout and free cash flow valuation
      models, 256–61
   valuation based on comparable firms,
      261–66
   valuation techniques, summary, 265, 266*f*
Stohs, M. H., 858 n.3
Stop-out yield, **787**
Straddle, **664**–65
   payoff and profit from, 665*f*
Straight-line depreciation, **180**
Strangle, **665***e*
Strategic investor, **753**
Strategic partner, **753**
Stream of cash flows, 84
   back in time, 87–88
   comparing and combining cash flow
      values, 85
   forward in time, 86
   future value of, with present value
      of PV, 93
   net present value of, 94–95
   present value of, 92–93*e*
   solving for additional variables, 108–16
   timelines showing, 84–85
   valuation of, present and future, 91–94
Stretching the accounts payable, **839**–40
Strike (exercise) price, **656**, 658, 659
   stock price and, 670
STRIPS, **787**
Student Loan Marketing Association
      ("Sallie Mae"), 788
Stulz, R., 842 n.6, 876 n.3
Stulz, R. M., 547 n.17, 556 n.25
Subordinated debenture, **783**
Sullivan, M., 482
Summers, L. H., 553 n.22
Suncor Energy, 925
Sundaram, A., 890 n.12
Sundaram, R. K., 897 n.17
Sundgren, S., 496 n.6
Sunk cost, **184**
Sunk cost fallacy, 185*b*
Sun Le, 773 n.22
Sun Microsystems, payoff of put options
      at maturity for, 660*e*
Suppliers, financial distress and loss of, 497

Supply, efficiency of market portfolio and
      demand equaling, 365–66
Support costs, sensitivity to, 198*e*
Supreme Court, U.S., decision establishing
      corporate property rights (1819), 3–4
Suska, Marie, 774 n.23
Swaminathan, B., 557 n.28
Swartz, Mark, 509*b*
Swiss Air, 497
Syndicate, **760**
Syndicated bank loan, **785**
Synergies of mergers and acquisitions,
      877–83
Synthetic lease, **802**, 812*b*
Systematic, undiversifiable, or market risk, **303**
Systematic risk
   diversifiable versus systematic, 307*e*
   measuring, 308–10
   risk premium and, 306
   risk premiums and, for debt, unlevered
      equity, and levered equity, 431*t*
   versus firm-specific risk in stock portfolios,
      303–5
Systematic risk, alternative models of, 401–24
   characteristic variable models of expected
      returns, 415–19
   efficiency of market portfolio and, 402–6
   implications of positive alphas, 406–9
   methods used in practice, 419–21
   multifactor models of risk, 409–15
   problems, 423–24
   summary, 421–22

T (option or forward expiration date),
      946, 949
T (premerger total value of target), 884
T (years until exercise date of option),
      694, 701
T^s (value of predetermined tax shields),
      604, 621
"Tailing the hedge," 937 n.13
Takeover(s), **873**. *See also* Mergers and
      acquisitions
   agency conflict and threat of, 911
   case study of hostile bid for Willamette
      Industries, 892*b*
   defenses against (*see* Takeover defenses)
   hostile, 888, 892*b*
   friendly, 888
   market reactions to, 875–76
   process of (*see* Takeover process)
   recipients of value added from, 892–97
Takeover defenses, 888–92
   golden parachutes, 890
   other defensive strategies, 891
   poison pills, 888–89
   recapitalization, 890–91
   regulatory approval, 891–92
   staggered boards, 890
   white knights, 890
Takeover process, 883–88
   board and shareholder approval, 887–88
   merger "arbitrage," 885–87
   offers, 884–85
   tax and accounting issues, 887
   valuation, 883–84

Tangent portfolio
   with different saving and borrowing
      rates, 384*f*
   identifying, **347**–49
Target, **873**
Targeted repurchase, **535**
Target leverage ratio, **582**, 620–21
   risk of tax shield with, 621
Tashjian, E., 496 n.7
Tate, Geoffrey, 509 n.24
Tau τ (tax rate), 139, 140
Tau τ_c (corporate tax rate), 181, 189, 258,
      464, 472, 473, 474, 476, 552, 577,
      596, 817
Tau τ_d (dividend tax rate), 545
Tau τ_e (marginal personal tax rate on income
      from equity), 472, 473, 475, 607
Tau τ_i (marginal personal tax rate on income
      from debt), 472, 473
Tau τ_i (tax rate on interest income), 552, 607
Tau τ^* (effective tax advantage of debt), 473,
      474, 476, 501, 607
Tau τ_d^* (effective dividend tax rate), 545, 546
Tau τ_{ex}^* (effective tax advantage on interest in
      excess of EBIT), 480
Tau τ_{retain}^* (effective tax rate on retained cash),
      552, 553
Tax(es), 459–90
   on capital gains, 541–42
   cash retention and, 550–53
   corporations and, 8–9
   cutting rate of dividend, 475*b*
   deferred, 24
   differences in, across investors groups,
      546–49
   on dividends, 541–42, 545–49
   earnings before, 27, 30
   interest and, 139 n.7, 140 n.8
   interest tax deduction, 460–62
   leases and, 810–11, 819–20
   limits to tax benefits of debt, 478–80
   for merged corporation, 879–80*e*
   optimal capital structure with, 476–84
   optimal leverage with financial distress,
      agency costs, and, 511*f*
   optimal leverage with financial distress costs
      and, 502*f*
   personal (*see* Personal taxes)
   rate of [*see* Tax rate (τ)]
   recapitalizing capture tax shield, 468–71
   repatriated earnings and, 976–77
   risk and, 138–40
   short-term exemptions from, 843*t*
   takeover process and, 887
   valuing interest tax shield, 462–67
   weighted cost of capital with, 465–67
Taxation
   of corporate earnings, 8*e*, 475*b*
   double, 475*b*
   of losses for projects in profitable
      companies, 181*e*
   of S corporations, 9*e*
Tax benefit
   of debt, 473*e*, 474*f*, 475–76, 478–80
   recapitalizing to capture tax shield
      and, 468

Tax loss carryforwards and carrybacks, **195**
   carryforwards calculation, 195*e*
Tax rate (τ), 139, 140
   on dividends, 542*t*, 545–46
   fluctuations in, and insurance, 929–30
   international leverage and (1990), 483*t*
   rate of marginal corporate, 181, 182
Tax shield, 481. *See also* Interest tax shield
   risk of, with target leverage ratio, 621
Taymuree, John, 417 n.17
Teachers Insurance and Annuity
      Association, 230*b*
Temporary working capital, **857**–58
Tender offer, **534**–35, **884**–85
10-K form, **20**
10-Q form, **20**
Term, bond, **212**
Terminal (continuation) value, **194**. *See also*
      Continuation (terminal) value
Term loan, **785**
Term structure of interest rates, **133**–35
   computing present values using, 135*e*
   of risk-free U.S. interest rates, 134*f*
Terrorist attacks of September 11, 2006,
      insurance costs of, 927
Thaler, R., 557 n.28, 557 n.29
Theft insurance policies, common versus
      independent risk in, 299–302
Theodorou, E., 915 n.19
Theory of Investment Value (J. B. Williams),
      255*b*, 432 n.2, 449
Thorburn, K., 496 n.6
3M Corporation, 656
Time
   bond prices and, 218–21
   forecasting beta and, 388
Timeline, 83, **84**–85
   constructing, 85*e*
   currency, 943*f*
   three rules on comparing stream of cash
      flows on, 85–90
Time periods
   adjusting discount rate to different, 126–27
   binomial option pricing model for
      multiperiods, 686–88
   binomial option pricing model for
      two-state, single, 686–88
   calculating, in savings plan, 116*e*
   solving for number of, 114–16
Time value, **670**
Time value of money, **51**–53, 83–124
   data case, 123–24
   definition of, **86**
   perpetuities, annuities, and other special
      cases, 95–118
   power of compounding, 90–91
   problems, 119–23
   spreadsheets used to solve problems of,
      106–8
   stream of cash flow, net present value of,
      94–95
   stream of cash flow, solving for additional
      variables, 108–16
   stream of cash flow, timelines of, 84–85
   stream of cash flow, valuation of, 91–94
   summary, 117–18
   three rules relevant to, 85–90

Timing
   of cash flow, 164, 165*f*, 192
   of investment, 723–26
   market, 520, 559–60*e*
TIPS (Treasury Inflation-Protected
      Securities), **787**
Titman, Sheridan, 406, 415 n.14, 497 n.8,
      521 n.43, 725 n.
Tobin, James
   H. Markowitz, 353*b*
   on portfolio optimization, 353*b*
Toehold, 893, **894**
Tokyo Stock Exchange (TSE), 13
Tombstone advertisement, 771*f*
Tools. *See* Interest rate(s); Investment decision
      rules; Time value of money
Total payout model, 585 n.8
   share repurchases and, **256**–57
Total Payout Model equation, 257
Total return, **247**, **290**
Trade credit, **187**, **832**–35
   benefits of, 834
   cost of, 833, 834*e*
   cost of, with stretched accounts
      payable, 839*e*
   market frictions and, 833–34
   standard loans versus, 834
   terms, 833
Tradeoffs in corporate governance, 921
Tradeoff theory, **501**–3
   agency costs and, 511–12
   determinants of present value of financial
      distress costs and, 501
   optimal leverage and, 501–3
Trailing earnings, **262**
Trailing P/E, **262**
Tranches, **783**, 784*t*
Transation(s)
   off-balance sheet, 36
Transactions balance, **842**
Transaction cost(s), **13**, **73**–74
   arbitrage with, 73–74
   matching principle and, 857–59
Treasury bills, **212**, 284, 391, 786*t*
   average annual returns for
      (1926–2004), 293*t*
   empirical distribution of
      (1926–2004), 292*f*
   historical excess returns of S&P 500
      compared to, 391*t*
   realized returns for (1996–2004), 291*t*
   as short-term investment option, 843*t*
   value of investments in (1925–2005), 285*f*
   volatility of (1926–2004), 294*t*
   volatility versus excess return of
      (1926–2004), 297*t*
Treasury bonds, **215**, 786*t*
   L. Black on valuation of, 230*b*
   historical excess returns of S&P 500
      compared to, 391*t*
   yield curves, 227
Treasury notes, **215**, 786*t*
Treasury securities, 786*t*, 787
Treynor, Jack, 363
Triantis, G. R., 919 n.23
Trigeorgis, L., 737 n.4
Trottman, Melanie, 801 n.2

True lease, **812**
True-tax lease, **811**
  cash flow for, 813–14
  evaluating, 817–18
Trust receipts loan, **865**
Tufano, P., 315 n.18
Tunneling, **918**
Twite, Garry, 521 n.43
Two-stock portfolio
  computing covariance and correlation, 328*t*
  efficient portfolios with two stocks, 335–38
  returns on, 326*t*
Two-stock portfolio, volatility of, 325–32
  computing variance and volatility, 330–32
  determining covariance and correlation, 326–30
  risk and, 326
Tyco Corporation, scandal at, 509*f*

U (market value of unlevered equity), 437–38
Uncertainties, mapping on decision tree, 719–20
Uncommitted line of credit, **859**
Under-investment problem, 504, **505**
Underleverage, 628–29
Underperformance, IPOs and long-run, 770
Underpricing, IPOs and existence of, 765–66
Underwriter(s), **758**, 760–61
  lead, 760
  ranking of, 761*t*
United Airlines (UAL Corporation), 939*b*
  bankruptcy of, 491, 495
United Kingdom (UK), 914
U.S. economy
  interest rates, and inflation rates in (1955–2005), 133*f*
  yield curve and, 136–38
Unlevered beta, **443**, 638*t*
Unlevered cost of capital, **582**–83, 620–21
  estimating, 589–90, 638, 639*e*
  financial distress and, 599
  personal taxes and, 606–8
Unlevered Cost of Capital with a Target Leverage Ratio equation, 582
Unlevered Cost of Capital with Personal Taxes equation, 607
Unlevered equity, **429**, 430
  replicating, by holding debt and equity, 434*t*
  systematic risk and risk premiums for debt, levered equity, and, 431*t*
Unlevered net income, **181**
  incremental earnings forecast and, 182
Unlevered P/E ratio, **640**
Unlevered value of project, 582–83
Unprofitable growth, 252*e*
Unsecured debt, **782**
Upton, Charles, 805 n.3
Urošević, Branko, 508 n.23

V_T^L (continuing value of project at date *T*), 641
V_t^L (value of levered investment on date *t*), 462, 467, 468, 501, 502, 511, 580, 581, 582, 602, 606, 621

V_t (enterprise value on date *t*), 245
V^U (value of the unlevered firm), 462, 467, 468, 501, 511, 581, 583
Vafeas, N., 915 n.19
Valuation. *See also* Value(s)
  of bonds (*see* Bond valuation)
  capital budgeting and (*see* Capital budgeting; Capital budgeting with leverage and market imperfections)
  case study modeling and (*see* Financial modeling, case study of)
  of costs and benefits, 48–51
  of executive stock options, 699*b*
  of financial options (*see* Financial-option prices)
  of foreign acquisition in segmented market, 979–80*e*
  of foreign currency cash flows, 971–76
  of initial public offerings (IPOs), 761–64
  of interest tax shield, 462–67
  of investment opportunities (*see* Capital budgeting)
  Law of One Prince and, 245, 246, 583
  of options (*see* Call option; Put option)
  of portfolio, 66–67
  post-money, 755–56
  pre-money, and post-money, 755
  of securities, 61–62
  of stream of cash flows, 91–94
  of stocks (*see* Stock valuation)
  using comparables for, 624–26
Valuation multiples, **262**–64
Valuation ratios, 30–31
  computing, 31*e*
  mismatched, 30*b*
Valuation triad, 267*f*
Value(s). *See also* Valuation
  bankruptcy risk and firm, 494*e*
  comparing and combining, on timelines, 85
  competitive market prices and determination of, 49–50*e*
  continuation (*see* Continuation (terminal) value)
  costs of financial distress and firm's, 498–500
  for debt and equity of levered firms, 429*t*
  dependence of, on preferences, 51*e*
  dollar impact on, versus percentage return, 163–64
  enterprise, 26
  of financial distress costs, 501
  future [*see* Future value (FV)]
  interest tax shield and firm, 462–63
  of leverage, and agency costs, 505–6
  leverage, arbitrage, and firm, 432–37
  net present [*see* Net present value (NPV)]
  present (*see* Present value (PV))
  ratio of debt to [*see* Debt-to-value ratio]
  solving simultaneously for leverage and, 621–22
  time value of money (*see* Time value of money)
Value added from takeovers, 892–97
  competition and, 897
  free rider problem, 893
  freezeout merger, 896–97

  leveraged buyouts, 894–96
  toeholds, 893–94
Value Additivity, **66**–67, 99 n.4
  equation, 66
  stock index arbitrage and, 66*b*
Value of the Interest Tax Shield of Permanent Debt equation, 465
Value-weighted portfolios, **375**–77
  computing, 376*e*
  maintaining, 377*e*
Value Line, Inc.
  estimation methods used by, 389*t*
  value and share price effects of special dividend from, 548*f*
Value stocks, **25**
Vanguard Group, 378*b*
Var(R) (variance of return R), 287, 293, 330, 331, 332, 333
Varaiya, N. P., 889 n.11
Variance, **287**–89
  computing portfolio, 330–32
  of equally weighted portfolio of many stocks, 332–33
  of returns, 293–94
Variance and Standard Deviation of the Return Distribution equation, 287
Variance Estimate Using Realized Returns equation, 293
Variance of an Equally Weighted Portfolio of *n* Stocks equation, 332, 333
Variance of a Two-Stock Portfolio equation, 330
Venture capital firms, **752**, 753*t*
  funding by, in U.S., 754*f*
Venture capitalists, **752**
Venture merchant financing, 864*b*
Vermaelen, T., 559 n.34
Vertical integration, **877**–78
  hedging with, **933**
Vickers, D., 315 n.17
Vijh, A., 876 n.3
Viniar, David, on partnerships versus corporations, 6
Vishny, R., 916 n.20
Vishny, Robert W., 508 n.22, 916 n.20
Volatility, **288**
  Black-Scholes option pricing model and implied, 701–2
  calculating, 304–5*e*
  calculating expected return and, 288*e*
  computing historical, 294*e*
  expected return and, for multiple stock portfolio, 343*f*
  expected return and, for two-stock portfolios, 336*t*, 337*f*
  financial-option prices and, 671*e*
  historical annual correlations and, for selected stocks, 329*t*
  implied, of exchange rates, 949–50*e*
  implied, valuing options and, 701–2
  of large portfolio, 332–35
  real options and investment, 724
  of returns, 293, 294*t*
  when risks are independent, 334
  of two-stock portfolio, 325–32
  of Type S and I stocks, 304*f*

Volatility of a Portfolio with Arbitrary
    Weights equation, 335
Volpin, P., 917 n.22
Voting rights of shareholders, 12*b*

w_s^i (standardized weight of the ith
    characteristic for form s), 417
WACC. *See* Weighted average cost of capital
Walk away, decision to. *See* Abandonment
    option
Walking, R. A., 889 n.10, 908 n.8
Wal-Mart Stores, 29
    computing profitability and valuation ratios
      for, 31*e*
    data case on financial options, 684
Walt Disney Company, 12*b*, 324
    shareholder actions at, 909–10
Wang, C., 911 n.14
Wang, Zhenu, 394 n.22, 408 n.8
Warehouse arrangement, inventory as collateral
    and, **865**
    calculating effective annual cost of, 865–66*e*
Warner, J., 910 n.12
Warner, J. B., 507 n.20
Warner, Jerold, 496 n.5, 507 n.21
Warrant (call option), **794**
Watts, Ross, 507 n.21
Wealth, non-tradable, 407–9
Weighted average cost of capital (WACC),
    259, 439
    capital budgeting and, 439–42
    with changing leverage, 605–6
    computing, with multiple securities, 442
    leverage and, with perfect capital
      markets, 440*f*
    method of valuation using (*see* Weighted
      average cost of capital method of
      valuation)
    permanent debt and, 604–5*e*
    project-based, 591
    with taxes, 465–67
    valuing interest tax shield using, 467*e*
Weighted Average Cost of Capital (No Taxes)
    equation, 439
Weighted average cost of capital method
    of valuation, 577–81, 641
    application of, 577–79
    comparison of APV and FTE methods to,
      596–97
    debt and, 589*b*
    deriving, 619–20
    formula for, 577
    implementing constant debt-equity ratio,
      580–81
    re-levering WACC, mistakes of, 592*b*
    summary of, 579
    valuing foreign currency cash flows by,
      972–74

Weighted Average Cost of Capital with Taxes
    equation, 465
Weinstein, Elizabeth, 760 n.
Weisbach, M., 558 n.32, 905 n.1, 909 n.11
Weiss, Lawrence, 496 n.5, 498
Welch, Ivo, 392 n.17
Wermers, R., 313 n.16
Weyerhaeuser, hostile bid for Willamette
    Industries by, 892*b*
Whirlpool Corporation, 47
White knight, **890**
White squire, **890**
Willamette Industries, Weyerhaeuser's hostile
    bid for, 892*b*
Williams, John Burr, 432 n.2, 449, 540 n.7
    dividend-discount model and *Theory of*
      Investment Value by 255*b*
Williamson, R., 842 n.6
Wilshire 500 index, 379, 389
Winner's curse, **766**
    IPO investors and, 767*e*
Without recourse, factoring arrangement, **864**
With recourse, factoring arrangement, **864**
Wolfenzon, D., 919 n.23
Womack, K., 557 n.
Wood, Justin, 557 n.
Working capital. *See also* Net working capital
    (NWC)
    firm value and, 832
    management of (*see* Working capital
      management)
    overview of, 830–32
    permanent, 857
    requirements for, and financial modeling,
      631–32
    temporary, 857–58
    in various industries (2005), 831*t*
Working capital days, 29–30
Working capital management, 829–50
    business plan and, 628
    cash cycle and, 830–31
    cash management, 841–44
    data case, 849–50
    firm value and, 832
    inventory management, 840–41
    payables management, 838–40
    problems, 846–49
    receivables management, 835–38
    summary, 844–45
    trade credit, 832–35
Workout, **496**
World Bank Indicators, 8 n.3
WorldCom
    bankruptcy costs, 495
    excessive managerial perks at, 509*b*
    financial reporting abuses by, 38, 912
World Portfolio, 284
    value of investments in (1925–2005), 285*f*

W. R. Hambrecht and Company, 758–59
Wright, Matthew, 557*b*
Wruck, Karen, 498, 507 n.21
Wurgler, Jeffrey A., 520 n.42

x (number of new shares issued by acquirer to
    pay for target), 884
x_i (fraction invested in security i), 324
x_i (portfolio weight of investment in i), 409
Xie, F., 911 n.14

Yahoo!, 310, 311
Yankee bonds, **784**
Yermack, D., 906 n.3, 908 n.6
Yield curve, **133**–35
    bond arbitrage and, 224–28
    corporate bonds, 231, 233*f*
    discount rates and, 133–35
    Treasury bonds, 227
    U.S. economy and, 136–38
Yield to call (YTC), callable bonds, **792**
Yield to maturity (YTM), **213**
    bond price fluctuations over time and, 223*f*
    for callable and non-callable bonds, 792
    corporate bonds, 228–31
    on coupon bonds, 215, 216*e*, 217, 226–27
    forward interest rates and, 242
    on zero-coupon bonds, 213, 214
Yield to Maturity of a Coupon Bond
    equation, 215
Yield to Maturity of an n-Year Zero-Coupon
    Bond equation, 213, 214
YTM_n (yield o maturity on a zero-coupon
    bond with n periods to maturity),
    213, 214

Zechner, J., 512 n.30
Zeckhauser, R., 415 n.14
Zenner, M., 905 n.2
Zero-coupon bond(s), **212**, 212–14
    effect of time on, 220*f*
    risk-free interest rates and, 214
    Treasury securities, 787
    valuing coupon bond using yields of,
      225–26
    yield to maturity, 213, 214*e*
    yields and prices for, 225*t*
Zero-coupon yield curve, **214**
Zhang, Lu, 773 n.22
Zhao, Q., 597 n.
Zhu, N., 563 n.36
Zingales, Luigi, 512 n.30, 919 n.23
Zuckerman, Gregory, 760 n.
Zwiebel, Jeffrey, 512 n.30

KEY EQUATIONS

EQ. #	EQ. TITLE	PAGE	EQ. #	EQ. TITLE	PAGE
(2.1)	The Balance Sheet Identity	21	(6.4)	Profitability Index	167
(3.1)	Net Present Value	54	(7.5)	Free Cash Flow	189
(3.3)	No Arbitrage Price of a Security	63	(8.1)	Coupon Payment	212
(3.5)	Value Additivity	66	(8.3)	Yield to Maturity of an n-Year Zero-Coupon Bond	214
(4.1)	Future Value of a Cash Flow	86	(8.4)	Risk-Free Interest Rate with Maturity n	214
(4.2)	Present Value of a Cash Flow	88	(8.5)	Yield to Maturity of a Coupon Bond	215
(4.3)	Present Value of a Cash Flow Stream	92	(8.6)	Price of a Coupon Bond	225
(4.4)	Future Value of a Cash Flow Stream with a Present Value of PV	93	(9.2)	Total Return	247
(4.5)	Present Value of a Perpetuity	96	(9.4)	Dividend-Discount Model	248
(4.7)	Present Value of an Annuity	100	(9.6)	Constant Dividend Growth Model	249
(4.8)	Future Value of an Annuity	101	(9.14)	Dividend-Discount Model with Constant Long-Term Growth	254
(4.9)	Present Value of a Growing Perpetuity	103	(9.16)	Total Payout Model	257
(4.10)	Present Value of a Growing Annuity	104	(9.19)	Discounted Free Cash Flow Model	258
(4.12)	Loan Payment	110	(10.1)	Expected (Mean) Return	286
(5.3)	Converting an APR to an EAR	128	(10.2)	Variance and Standard Deviation of the Return Distribution	287
(5.5)	The Real Interest Rate	132	(10.6)	Average Annual Return of a Security	292
(5.7)	Present Value of a Cash Flow Stream Using a Term Structure of Discount Rates	135	(10.7)	Variance Estimate Using Realized Returns	293
(5.8)	After-Tax Interest Rate	139	(10.8)	Standard Error of the Estimate of the Expected Return	295
(5A.1)	The EAR for a Continuously Compounded APR	147	(10.10)	Estimating a Traded Security's Expected Return from Its Beta	310
(5A.2)	The Continuously Compounded APR for an EAR	147	(10.11)	Cost of Capital of a Project	311
(5A.3)	Present Value of a Continuously Growing Perpetuity	147	(11.4)	Covariance between Returns R_i and R_j	327
(6.1)	EVA in Period n (When Capital Lasts Forever)	158	(11.5)	Estimate of the Covariance from Historical Data	327
(6.2)	EVA in Period n (When Capital Depreciates)	159			

KEY EQUATIONS

EQ. #	EQ. TITLE	PAGE	EQ. #	EQ. TITLE	PAGE
(11.8)	The Variance of a Two-Stock Portfolio	330	(18.15)	Levered Value with Permanent Debt	596
(11.12)	Variance of an Equally Weighted Portfolio of n Stocks	333	(18.20)	Leverage and the Cost of Capital with a Fixed Debt Schedule	604
(11.13)	Volatility of a Portfolio with Arbitrary Weights	335	(18.21)	Project WACC with a Fixed Debt Schedule	604
(11.19)	Beta of Portfolio i with Portfolio P	350	(18.24)	Unlevered Cost of Capital with Personal Taxes	607
(11.20)	Required Return for Investment i Given Current Portfolio P	350	(20.1)	Call Value at Expiration	659
(11.21)	Expected Return of a Security	351	(20.2)	Put Price at Expiration	660
(11.22)	Cost of Capital for Investment i	353	(20.4)	Put-Call Parity	669
(13.8)	Multifactor Model of Risk	411	(21.5)	Replicating Portfolio in the Binomial Model	689
(13.9)	Multifactor Model of Risk with Self-Financing Portfolios	411	(21.6)	Option Price in the Binomial Model	689
(13.10)	Fama-French-Carhart Factor Specification	413	(21.7)	Black-Scholes Price of a Call Option on a Non-Dividend-Paying Stock	694
(13.11)	The Characteristic Variable Model of Stock Returns	417	(21.9)	Black-Scholes Price of a European Put Option on a Non-Dividend-Paying Stock	697
(14.5)	Cost of Capital of Levered Equity	438	(21.12)	Black-Scholes Replicating Portfolio of a Call Option	702
(14.7)	Weighted Average Cost of Capital (No Taxes)	439	(21.13)	Black-Scholes Replicating Portfolio of a Put Option	704
(15.4)	Value of the Interest Tax Shield of Permanent Debt	465	(21.17)	Beta of an Option	708
(15.5)	Weighted Average Cost of Capital with Taxes	465	(30.1)	Actuarially Fair Insurance Premium	927
(15.7)	Effective Tax Advantage of Debt	473	(30.2)	Covered Interest Parity	944
(18.5)	The APV Formula	582	(30.4)	Price of a Call Option on a Currency	949
(18.6)	Unlevered Cost of Capital with a Target Leverage Ratio	582	(30.6)	Duration of a Security	951
(18.9)	Free Cash Flow to Equity	586	(30.8)	Duration of a Portfolio	953
(18.11)	Project-Based WACC Formula	591	(30.9)	Equity Duration	954
(18.14)	Levered Value with a Constant Interest Coverage Ratio	594	(31.7)	The Foreign-Denominated Cost of Capital	975